THE WORLD OF INFORMATION Europe REVIEW

1997
Tenth edition

Publisher's note

Every possible effort has been made to ensure that the information contained in this book is accurate at the time of going to press and the publishers cannot accept responsibility for any errors or omissions, however caused.

First published in 1985

2 Market Street
Saffron Walden
Essex CB10 1HZ, UK
Tel: +44 (0)1799 521150
Fax: +44 (0)1799 524805
e-mail: waldenpub@easynet.co.uk

Published by:
Walden Publishing Ltd

ISBN 0 904439-92-5
ISSN 0269 3844

Printed in Great Britain by
Unwin Brothers Ltd, Woking

The Economic and Business Report

THERE ARE
110 MILLION KILLERS AT LARGE
IN THE WORLD.

THEY OFTEN LIE IN WAIT
FOR YEARS.

THEY ATTACK MAINLY CIVILIANS.

THEY KILL OR MAIM
AT ANY TIME.

THEY PICK ON MEN, WOMEN
AND CHILDREN ALIKE.

THEY'RE CALLED LANDMINES.

HELP US GET RID OF THEM.

INTERNATIONAL COMMITTEE OF THE RED CROSS (ICRC)

LANDMINES MUST BE STOPPED

Contents

Currencies

	Currency Unit	Units per US Dollar				Units per £ Sterling
		January 1993	January 1994	January 1995	January 1996	November 1996
Albania	Lek	109.86	109.81	43.33	93.85	170.97
Andorra	French Franc	5.47	5.90	5.37	4.93	8.56
	Spanish Peseta	114.52	142.93	133.77	121.01	212.54
Armenia	Dram	0.56	**228.00	403.57(o)	402.00	707.80(o)
Austria	Schilling	11.41	12.19	10.91	10.11	17.77
Azerbaijan	Manat	0.56	†182.50	‡4,395.00	4,440.00	7,111.26(o)
Belarus	Belarus Rouble	0.78	††24,000.00	11,194.50(o)	11,500.00(o)	38,481.50(o)
	(introduced Aug 1994; sole legal tender from Oct 1994)					
Belgium	Belgian Franc	33.33	36.15	32.06	29.54	52.07
Bosnia-Herzegovina	Bosnian Dinar	749.02	n.a.	n.a.	n.a.	149.85
Bulgaria	Lev	23.64	26.80	66.42	72.02	527.04
Croatia	Kuna	867.15	6,575.13	5.68	5.37	8.99
	(replaced Dinar May 1994)					
Cyprus	Cyprus Pound	0.48	0.52	0.48	0.46	0.77
Czech Republic	Czech Koruna	28.90	29.96	28.14	26.62	44.73
Denmark	Danish Krone	6.23	6.79	6.12	5.56	9.70
Estonia	Kroon	12.84	13.86	12.48	11.57	20.21
Finland	Markka	5.40	5.79	4.76	4.35	7.63
France	French Franc	5.46	5.90	5.37	4.93	8.56
Georgia	Coupon	0.56	††250,000.00	‡‡3.5m	n.a.	1.28
	(replaced Rouble Apr 1993) (Lari replaced Coupon 2 Oct 1995)					
Germany	Deutsche Mark	1.61	1.74	1.55	1.44	2.53
Gibraltar	Gibraltar Pound	0.65	0.68	0.64	0.64	1.00
Greece	Drachma	216.46	249.35	241.92	236.20	398.46
Greenland	Danish Krone	6.23	6.79	6.12	5.56	9.70
The Holy See	Italian Lira	1,490.48	1,712.00	1,629.45	1,579.75	2,522.60
Hungary	Forint	83.90	100.75	113.22	136.46	261.46
Iceland	Icelandic Krona	63.23	72.42	69.03	65.59	110.81
Ireland	Punt	0.61	0.71	0.65	0.62	1.00
Italy	Italian Lira	1,490.48	1,712.00	1,629.45	1,579.75	2,522.60
Latvia	Lat	0.56	0.60	0.55	0.54	0.91
Liechtenstein	Swiss Franc	1.48	1.49	1.31	1.16	2.13
Lithuania	Lit	0.56	3.89	4.02	4.00	6.73
Luxembourg	Luxembourg Franc	33.33	38.15	32.06	29.54	52.07
Former Yugoslav Republic of Macedonia	Macedonian Denar	202.17	§42.12	‡39.30	39.30	67.14
Malta	Maltese Lira	0.39	0.39	0.37	0.35	0.60
Moldova	Moldovan Leu	0.65	4.00 (a)	‡4.53	4.53	7.86
Monaco	French Franc	5.46	5.90	8.04	4.93	8.56
The Netherlands	Guilder	1.81	1.94	1.74	1.61	2.83
Norway	Norwegian Krone	6.82	7.52	6.80	6.34	10.65
Poland*	Zloty	15,815.00	21,344.00	2.44	2.48	4.73
Portugal	Escudo	146.00	176.70	160.29	149.58	255.22
Romania	Romanian Leu	470.00	1,296.87	1,792.08	2,660.00	5,997.50
Russia	Rouble	0.56 (o)	0.59 (o)	0.67 (o)	0.64 (o)	9,244.64 (m)
San Marino	San Marino Lira	1,490.48	1,712.00	1,629.45	1,579.75	2,522.60
Slovakia	Slovak Koruna	28.90	33.22	31.41	29.62	51.70
Slovenia	Slovene Tolar	98.83	131.78	128.92	129.88	227.90
Spain	Peseta	114.52	142.93	133.77	121.02	212.54
Sweden	Swedish Krone	7.23	8.34	7.52	6.61	11.13
Switzerland	Swiss Franc	1.48	1.49	1.30	1.16	2.13
Turkey	Turkish Lira	8,662.08	14,921.50	40,273.70	59,250.00	168,526.90
Ukraine	Hryvna	0.11	30,947.60	104,837.00	179,900.00	2.97
	(Hryvna replaced Karbovanets Sep 1996)					
United Kingdom	UK Pound	0.65	0.68	0.64	0.64	1.00
Federal Republic of Yugoslavia (Serbia, Montenegro)	Dinar	749.02	§1.00	n.a.	4.77	8.40
	(New Yugoslav Dinar replaced Old Dinar Jan 1994)					

*Poland sliced four zeroes off its currency 1 Jan 1995 **Mar 1994 †May 1994 ††Jun 1994 ‡Sep 1995 ‡‡Jul 1995
§End-Sep 1994 (a) Average rate Jan-Sep 1994 (o) Official rate (m) Market rate

Key indicators 1995

	Population (millions)	Area ('000 sq km)	GDP per capita (US$)	Inflation (annual) (%)	GDP real growth (%)	Balance of trade (US$m)
Albania	3.40	27.4	600	10.0	6.0	-400
Andorra	0.07	0.5	15,000 (e, n)	–	–	–
Armenia	3.76	30.0	700	210.0	5.0	-414
Austria	8.04	83.9	28,980	2.2	1.8	-8,100
Azerbaijan	7.80	86.6	54 (1)	84.6	-6.5	-120
Belarus	10.30	208.0	900	250.0	-10.0	–400
Belgium	10.10	30.5	26,280	1.5	1.9	8,800
Bosnia-Herzegovina	3.50	51.1	524	10.0 (e)	–	–
Bulgaria	8.91	111.0	1,400	68.0	2.8	400
Croatia	4.50	56.5	3,300	3.5	4.0	-1,300
Cyprus	0.74	9.3	10,250 (n, 1)	2.6	5.0 (n, 1)	-1,800 (1)
Czech Republic	10.30	78.9	4,300	8.9	4.8	-3,400.
Denmark	5.20	43.1	28,082 (1)	2.1	2.6	5,600
Estonia	1.63	45.1	2,340 (e)	28.9	5.0 (e)	-795
Finland	5.11	338.1	18,900 (1)	1.0	4.2	9,600
France	58.30	544.0	26,200	2.1	2.2	20,900
Georgia	4.40	70.0	200	250.0	-5.0	-13,700
Germany	81.80	357.0	25,100 (1)	1.8	1.9	61,500
Gibraltar	0.03	0.0	15,000 (e, n)	–	–	–
Greece	10.65	132.0	9,300 (1)	8.4	1.5	-16,000
Greenland	0.06	2,175.6	17,000 (n, 1)	–	–	–
Hungary	10.23	93.0	3,882	28.2	1.5	-2,500 (e)
Iceland	0.27	103.1	23,037 (1)	1.6	3.0	200
Ireland	3.58	70.3	17,000	2.4 (1)	7.5	10,900
Italy	57.31	301.3	17,800 (1)	5.7	3.4	25,500
Latvia	2.53	64.6	1,176 (1)	23.3	0.4	-580
Liechtenstein	0.03	0.2	33,000 (e, n)	1.8	–	–
Lithuania	3.72	65.2	1,078 (e)	35.7	2.5	-200 (e)
Luxembourg	0.41	2.6	39,961	1.9	3.7	6,400
Former Yugoslav Republic of Macedonia	1.90	25.7	700	6.0	-4.0	-300
Malta	0.37	0.3	8,136 (1)	5.4 (1)	4.8 (1)	-560 (1)
Moldova	4.40	34.0	390	25.0	-3.0	-10
Monaco	0.03	0.0	25,000 (e, n)	–	–	–
The Netherlands	15.40	41.5	21,300 (1)	2.0	2.1	19,281
Norway	4.36	324.0	25,268 (1)	2.4	3.3	8,300 (1)
Poland	38.60	312.7	3,050	21.6	6.5	-2,600
Portugal	9.90	92.1	10,769	4.1	1.9	-10,300
Romania	23.20	237.5	1,250 (e)	35.0	5.0 (e)	-1,200
Russia	149.50	1,050.0	2,393	150.0	-4.0	14,700
San Marino	0.02	0.1	30,000 (e, n)	5.4	–	–
Slovakia	5.40	49.0	3,244	10.6	6.4	59
Slovenia	1.99	20.2	9,100	9.0	4.8	-800
Spain	39.20	504.8	12,335 (1)	4.4	2.9	-17,700
Sweden	8.85	449.0	22,300 (1)	2.7	3.5	15,973
Switzerland	7.20	41.3	42,518	1.8	1.1	1,000
Turkey	62.30	775.5	2,733	64.9	7.1	-8,960
Ukraine	51.44	603.0	600	380.0	-11.8	400
United Kingdom	58.40	244.1	16,304	2.9	2.4	-18,385
Federal Republic of Yugoslavia (Serbia, Montenegro)	10.00	102.1	1,550	79.0	6.0	-1,000

(e) estimate (n) GNP (1) 1994

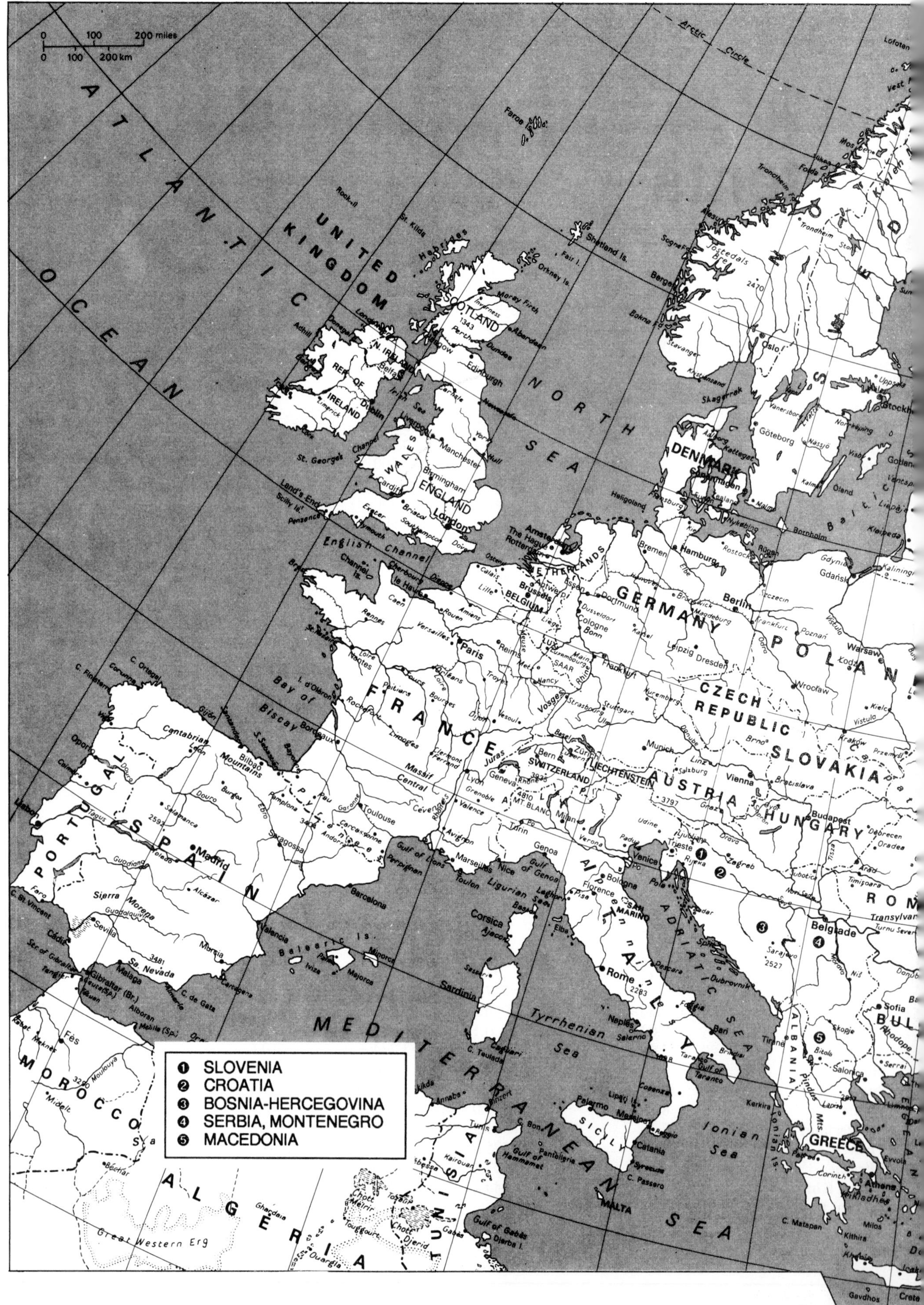

1 SLOVENIA
2 CROATIA
3 BOSNIA-HERCEGOVINA
4 SERBIA, MONTENEGRO
5 MACEDONIA

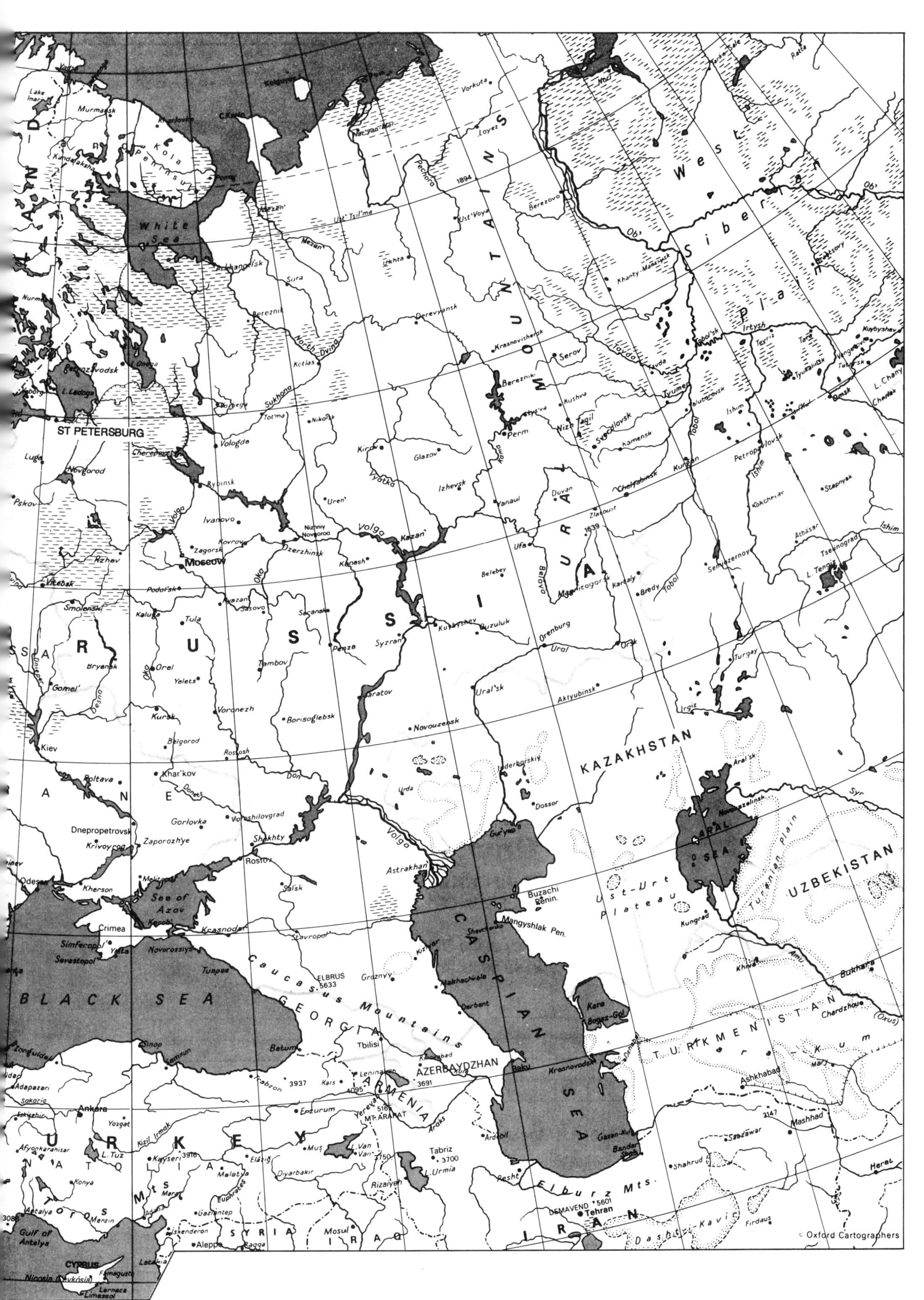

Lake Inari
Murmansk
Kola Peninsula
Kandalaksha
White Sea
Kolguyev I.
Vorkuta
Nar'yan-Mar
Loyez
Pechora
1894
Mezen'
Ust' Tsil'ma
Ust' Voya
Berezovo
Ob'
West Siberian Plain
Mezen'
Ukhta
Arkhangel'sk
Sura
Khanty-Mansiysk
Bratsovy
Bereznik
Derevyansk
North Dvina
Kotlas
Krasnovishersk
Serov
Tavda
Tobol'sk
Irtysh
Tevriz
Tara
Kuybyshev
Petrozavodsk
L. Onega
L. Ladoga
Sukhona
Tot'ma
Nikol'sk
Berezniki
Kushva
Tyumen
Yalutorovsk
Ishim
Omsk
L. Chany
ST PETERSBURG
Vologda
Cherepovets
Perm
Nizh Tagil
Sverdlovsk
Kamensk
Tobol
Petropavlovsk
Luga
Novgorod
Kirov
Glazov
Vyatka
Izhevsk
Kama
Chelyabinsk
Kurgan
Ishim
Rybinsk
Pskov
Uren'
Yanaul
Duvan
Kokchetav
Stepnyak
Volga
Ivanovo
Nizhniy Novgorod
Kazan'
Zlatoust
1639
Ishim
Kovrov
Zagorsk
Dzerzhinsk
Ufa
Atbasar
Tselinograd
Rzhev
Moscow
Kanash
Belebey
Semiozernoye
L. Tengiz
Vitebsk
Podol'sk
Oka
Belaya
Magnitogorsk
Kartaly
Bredy
Tobol
Smolensk
Ryazan
Sasovo
Kaluga
Tula
Saransk
Kuybyshev
Buzuluk
URAL MOUNTAINS
R U S S I A
Penza
Syzran
Orenburg
Ural
Orsk
Turgay
Bryansk
Orel
Tambov
Yelets
Gomel'
Saratov
Ural'sk
Aktyubinsk
Irgiz
Desna
Kursk
Voronezh
Borisoglebsk
Novouzensk
Kiev
Belgorod
Rossosh
KAZAKHSTAN
Inderborskiy
Aral'sk
Kharkov
Don
Poltava
Donets
Urda
Dossor
Novokazalinsk
Syr
Gorlovka
Voroshilovgrad
Dnepropetrovsk
Zaporozh'ye
Krivoy Rog
Shakhty
Volga
Gur'yev
ARAL SEA
Rostov
Odessa
Kherson
Melitopol'
Astrakhan'
Sal'sk
Sea of Azov
Kerch
Buzachi Penin.
Ust-Urt Plateau
Turanian plain
UZBEKISTAN
Crimea
Krasnodar
Stavropol'
Mangyshlak Pen.
Kungrad
Simferopol'
Yalta
Sevastopol
Novorossiysk
Tuapse
Shevchenko
Kizlyar
CASPIAN SEA
ELBRUS
5633
Groznyy
Makhachkala
Khiva
Amu
Bukhara
Caucasus Mountains
BLACK SEA
Derbent
Kara Bogaz-Gol
Chardzhou
(Oxus)
GEORGIA
TURKMENISTAN
Kara Kum
Zonguldak
Sinop
Samsun
Batum
Tbilisi
Kirovabad
Baku
Krasnovodsk
Mary
Adapazari
Trabzon
3937
Kars
Leninakan
3691
AZERBAYDZHAN
Kura
Ashkhabad
Sakaria
Ankara
Erzurum
Yerevan
ARMENIA
4095
5165
MT ARARAT
Araks
Mashhad
Eskişehir
Yozgat
Kizil Irmak
TURKEY
Ardebil
Gasan-Kuli
3147
Sabzawar
Afyonkarahisar
L. Tuz
Kayseri
3916
Muş
L. Van
Van
Tabriz
3700
Bandar Shah
Shahrud
Herat
ANATOLIA
Elaziğ
Diyarbakir
L. Urmia
Rizaiyeh
Resht
Elburz Mts.
Konya
Malatya
Maraş
Euphrates
DEMAVEND
5601
Tehran
TAURUS Mts
Antalya
Adana
Gaziantep
Mersin
IRAN
Dasht-i-Kavir
Firdaus
Gulf of Antalya
Iskenderon
SYRIA
Mosul
IRAQ
Aleppo
Raqqa
CYPRUS
Latakia
Nicosia (Levkosia)
Famagusta
Larnaca
Limassol
© Oxford Cartographers

Contributors

Dan Bindman is a British freelance journalist. He has written for *The Guardian* and other newspapers in the UK and has degrees from British universities in politics, international journalism and American studies.

William Chislett, a former *Financial Times* correspondent, is the author of the *Central Hispano Handbook on Spain* published in January 1996 and planned as a yearly book.

Anthony Griffin is a UK-based journalist specialising in the emerging markets. He regularly contributes articles to many British and international publications.

Michael Griffin is a London-based writer/photographer/broadcaster specialising in economic and development issues. He is a contributor to the *Financial Times*, *The Guardian* and a senior writer with the Food and Agriculture Organisation.

Howard Hill is editor of *The Europe Review*.

Bob Jiggins is a UK-based lecturer and freelance writer, specialising in the political and economic affairs of the former Eastern bloc, particularly with respect to communications. He is also an Honorary Visiting Research Fellow in the Research Unit in South-east European Studies at the University of Bradford.

Marko Milivojevic is a freelance writer and consultant on politic-economic affairs in central and eastern Europe and the former Soviet Union. He is also an Honorary Visiting Research Fellow at the Research Unit in South-east European Studies, University of Bradford. In 1993 he published *Yugoslavia in Transition* co-edited with John Allcock and John Horton.

Principal statistical sources used: EBRD, FAO, IMF, OECD, UNDP, World Bank.

World of Information

Publisher Anthony Axon
Managing Editor Rennie Campbell
Database Co-ordinator Marianne Keating
Subscription Manager Shaunagh Cowell

Editorial office
2 Market Street
Saffron Walden, Essex CB10 1HZ, U K
Tel: +44 (0)1799 521150
Fax: +44 (0)1799 524805
e-mail: waldenpub@easynet.co.uk

Subscription office
Tel: +44 (0)1403 782644

Advertising sales office
XL Communications Ltd
4/F Crusader House
145-157 St John Street
London EC1V 4QJ
Tel: +44 (0)171 490 7997
Fax: +44 (0)171 490 7272

Albania

Marko Milivojevic

Five years after the chaotic fall of Albania's infamous communist regime in 1991, its future political and economic prospects remained surrounded by uncertainty. Increased political polarisation and instability are likely following the intensely controversial May 1996 elections. Although popular support for President Sali Berisha and the Partia Demokratike Shqiperise (Democratic Party) (PDS) seemed to decline in 1995, before reviving nearer election time, most impartial observers agree that the elections did not properly represent the will of the electorate.

Politics

Had the May 1996 parliamentary elections been free and fair it is unlikely that the PDS would have been re-elected to undisputed power, despite having all the in-built advantages accruing to the ruling party in Albania. If the elections had been fair the PDS may at best have won a lower parliamentary representation, with the possibility of creating a new coalition government. At worst, they would have been defeated outright. The PDS's efforts at election rigging and other abuses committed in light of the May 1996 elections seem to have paid handsomely.

Popular support for the opposition Partia Socialiste e Shqiperise (PSS) (Socialist Party of Albania) began to gel in October 1994 when Berisha suffered a major political defeat – his proposal for a highly unitary constitution based on extensive presidential powers was rejected by the Albanian electorate in a nationwide referendum. Other negative political factors such as official corruption and endless feuding in the ruling party also worked in the PSS's favour.

In 1995 and into 1996 Berisha and the PDS mounted an all-out political offensive to stay in power as long as possible, encouraged by the growing dissent within the PSS itself, and feuding within other opposition parties. The PDS's strategy before and after the 1996 election to vilify and criminalise the PSS was highly controversial, both domestically and abroad, with the government-controlled media playing a key role in this strategy.

Preparing for election

With a working majority in parliament since first coming to power in 1992, Berisha and the PDS have been able to push through legislation aimed at perpetuating its effective monopoly of political power. In September 1995, parliament passed a so-called 'Genocide Law' to prevent selected former communist party members from standing for public office, thereby disqualifying many PSS leaders from contesting the 1996 election. Quickly upheld by the PDS-controlled Constitutional Court after appeals by the PSS and the Social Democratic Party (SDP), this law effectively criminalised the entire PSS. Earlier, in a related development, the PSS was weakened by the arrest of its leader, Fatos Nano, for alleged corruption when he was Albanian premier during the early 1990s. A related so-called 'Law on Dossiers' was passed in November 1995. Under its provisions, a PDS-appointed vetting committee used old secret police files dating back to the communist period to disqualify certain individuals from holding public office in Albania. Material from these files was used by the PDS to vilify the PSS and other opposition leaders.

Albania's secret police, the SHIK, has effectively become an instrument to serve the needs of the ruling party. This has resulted in growing politically motivated violence in Albania, including a number of unexplained murders, bombings

KEY FACTS — Albania

Official title: Republic of Albania

Head of state: President Dr Sali Berisha (since 9 Apr 1992)

Head of government: Prime Minister Aleksander Meksi (PDS) (since 10 Apr 1992)

Ruling party: Partia Demokratike Shqiperise (Democratic Party) (PDS) election 26 May 1996; further elections, date unknown)

Capital: Tirana

Official Languages: Albanian (sub-divided into Gheg and Tosk dialects)

Currency: Lek (L) = 100 qintars

Exchange rate: Lek 102.20 per US$ (Dec 1996)

Area: 27,398 sq km

Population: 3.4m (1995)

GDP per capita: US$600 (1995)

GDP real growth: 6% (1995)

GNP per capita: US$850 (1994)

GNP real growth: 7% (1994)

Unemployment: 15% (officially recorded end-1995)

Inflation: 10% (1995)

Trade balance: -US$400m (1995)

Foreign debt: US$900m (1995)

Aid flows: US$400m (1994)*

* estimated figure

KEY INDICATORS — Albania

	Unit	1991	1992	1993	1994	1995
Population	m	3.30	3.36	3.40	3.37	3.37
Gross domestic product (GDP)	US$bn	0.6	0.8	1.1	1.6	1.8
GDP per capita	US$	200	250	350	500	600
GDP real growth	%	-27.0	-10.0	-11.0	7.4	6.0
Inflation	%	36	226	85	15	10
Industrial output	%	-25	-15	-10	-2	-8
Agricultural output	%	-15	-10	15	10	11
Agricultural production	1979-81=100	92.17	109.34	110.48	119.80	135.36
Exports	US$m	82	82	112	141	200
Imports	US$m	314	540	583	600	600
Balance of trade	US$m	-232	-458	-471	-459	-400
Current account	US$m	-213	-101	-70	-150	-180
Hard currency reserves	US$m	–	–	400	420	**420
Foreign debt	US$m	450	600	650	750	900
Exchange rate	L per US$	14.6	75.1	102.1	95.0	101.0

** incl gold bullion holdings

and officially-approved public disorders. Opposition rallies and other activities in Tirana became particularly targeted and have been banned under legislation dating back to the communist period. In December 1995 the PDS amended Albania's existing electoral law in favour of itself, mainly by reducing the number of parliamentary seats allocated via proportional representation.

Regional relations

The text of the 1995 Dayton peace accords in the former Yugoslavia omitted any mention of Albania's principal regional foreign policy problem – the disputed status of its large diaspora in the Serbian province of Kosovo and the western areas of the Former Yugoslav Republic of Macedonia (FYROM). Albanian pressure on the west and the US in particular to help resolve the problem of refugees proved largely ineffectual, particularly concerning the proposed recreation of a so-called 'Greater Albania' in the southern Balkans.

The Serbo-Albanian conflict over Kosovo is now unlikely to drag Albania into any wider southern Balkan conflict and there is a steady normalisation of relations with Greece, which entered into a long-delayed Friendship and Co-operation Treaty with Albania in March 1996. Among other things, this will enable Albania to seek closer integration with the European Union (EU), beginning with possible associate membership of Europe's premier grouping in 1997. Full Albanian membership of the EU, however, is only a viable proposition in the longer-term. Full Albanian membership of Nato also remains highly improbable under any circumstances.

The alleged electoral improprieties relating to the May 1996 elections have been a growing concern to many of Albania's allies, of which the US in particular has taken public exception. Although the EU and other key western institutions remain for the most part strongly committed to economically supporting Albania, this may be threatened in the longer-term by some of the policies of the present government, especially its handling of the election. However, some EU governments have shown tolerance of Albania's present government, going so far as to endorse publicly its reelection.

Economic performance

Up by 11 per cent in 1993 and 7.4 per cent in 1994, Albanian GDP increased by a lower, but still respectable, 6 per cent in 1995. In 1995, officially declared GDP and GDP per capita was US$1.8 billion and US$600 respectively. Despite these improvements, Albania still remained by far the poorest country in Europe in 1995, when total output of goods and services was only 74 per cent of its level in 1990. But the large size of the unofficial or black economy meant that actual GDP and GDP per capita were almost certainly far higher than that suggested by official figures in 1995. The key supplement to local incomes is the hard currency repatriated by *émigrés*, particularly the 300,000-plus Albanian citizens working in Greece. Estimated at anywhere between US$300 million and US$500 million in 1995 alone, these hard currency remittances accounted for nearly a third of officially declared GDP. Overall, the entirely cash-based and hence officially unrecorded black economy may have accounted for up to 40 per cent of officially declared GDP in 1995.

Based on agriculture-food processing and services, the private-sector was economically dominant at around 70 per cent of GDP in 1995. One positive result of this has been a fall in officially recorded unemployment from 18 per cent of the employed workforce at the end of 1994 to 15 per cent at the end of 1995, although these figures do not give a true indication of actual joblessness and under-employment.

The dominant component of GDP as recently as 1990, industry's share of GDP was no more than 25 per cent in 1995, when overall industrial output declined by a further 8 per cent. Reviving traditional capital goods industries is probably impossible at the present time. In the longer-term mining and oil are the keys to Albania's future industrial development.

Privatisation

Initially largely confined to the decollectivisation of agricultural farmlands and the disposal of most other real estate and services previously owned by the state, large-scale privatisation entered a decisive stage in 1995, when voucher-based ownership transformation of the remaining state industrial sector began only 10 months after being introduced by the government in 1994. Since October 1995, by which time vouchers had been distributed to one million Albanian citizens over the age of 18, the National Agency for Privatisation (NAP) has held two auction rounds, with a third planned by mid-1996. Initially involving around 70 state industrial enterprises nominally valued at around L2 billion by the NAP, this ongoing ownership privatisation has been relatively effective and popular, not least because it has been largely insider-orientated to date.

The government plans to establish privatisation investment funds in 1996/97, which have already been legislated for in parliament. Part of a wider reform of the country's undeveloped financial system, this policy also saw the creation of the Tirana Stock Exchange in May 1996. Politically, the PDS government sees continued large-scale privatisation as the best way to increase its popularity. However, privatisation has been marred by widespread official corruption in recent years.

Large-scale privatisation of the state industrial sector remains somewhat problematical, however. The main problem is that much of it is technically insolvent and largely unreconstructed. According to the opposition, the entire exercise is politically motivated and is aimed at both boosting the PDS domestically and fooling its foreign creditors. To back up these charges, opposition critics of the government's large-scale privatisation programme have pointed out that the PDS-controlled NAP has typically disposed of shares at hefty discounts to its supporters.

It is not clear how newly privatised enterprises might be adequately reconstructed and recapitalised in the future. The absence of proper auditing and bankruptcy procedures also make it difficult to determine which enterprises are viable and which are not. On a sectoral basis, the biggest loss-makers are in capital goods, while food-processing, light manufacturing and construction have greater economic potential.

Still largely unreconstructed and burdened by high indebtedness, mining and extractive companies like Albchrome and Albpetrol also have relatively good prospects in the longer-term, but only after they have been radically reformed. For these two companies, it is also unclear as to whether the government will ever cede effective control of strategic assets.

Foreign investment in privatisation

Externally, the large-scale privatisation programme in Albania is now a key litmus test of local economic reform. Whether or not it succeeds in reviving the local industrial sector almost certainly depends on how much foreign capital is made available for new investment in local enterprises. From 1996, foreign aid financing for such purposes was expected to increase substantially.

Foreign direct investment (FDI) by private-sector foreign investors, however, is not expected to increase unless a proper politico-legal framework for such foreign investment is created. So far, the little FDI in Albania has been mainly confined to the mining and oil-gas sectors. At the end of 1995, total FDI in Albania was just US$200 million. In the longer-term, Albania has considerable potential for increased FDI, particularly in agriculture-food processing, light manufacturing and services led by tourism. So far, little of this potential has been realised, thereby creating further doubts about Albania's future economic development.

Agriculture's role

Much of the economic growth since 1993 has been generated by agriculture and food processing, which accounted for a record 55 per cent of GDP in 1995, compared to around 35 per cent of GDP in 1990. Difficulties lie ahead if, as suspected, the growth in agricultural output has reached its peak. In 1995, agricultural output increased by 11 per cent, after a 10 per cent increase in 1994 and 15 per cent in 1993. A key structural problem is that newly privatised farmlands are constantly being sub-divided, so further reducing already-low productivity levels. An exodus of the rural poor to Tirana and other cities has been a consequence, putting pressure on resources there. Structurally, more intensive economic development in agriculture and food-processing presupposes increased investment, but this remains low because of continued confusion over land tenure and lack of new credits for private farmers.

Resources

Although only a fraction of what it was in 1990 (1.2 million tonnes), chrome ore output by Albchrome increased by 12 per cent to around 300,000 tonnes in 1995. In the energy sector, onshore Albpetrol oil output continues to decline. Down from 2 million tonnes per annum at the end of the 1980s to around 500,000 tonnes in 1995, this drop is mainly because of under-investment in existing production and processing capacity. In the longer-term, this may change, especially if new offshore oil-gas fields in the Adriatic prove to be substantial.

Despite growing FDI in this sector of the economy, no commercially recoverable oil has so far been found. Other than oil and chromium production, Albania's industrial sector has little to offer to foreign investors. Accounting for around 20 per cent of officially recorded GDP in 1995, but probably double that, largely privately owned services have better growth potential, particularly as regards hydro-electric power generation exports, tourism, construction, transport, telecommunications and retail and wholesale trade. Even so, FDI has been virtually non-existent in these sectors, mainly because of the political, legal and economic uncertainties in Albania.

Financial stabilisation

Further to the terms of a 1993 three-year International Monetary Fund (IMF) Enhanced Structural Adjustment Facility (ESAF) worth US$84 million, macroeconomic stabilisation continued to make good progress in 1995, when year-end inflation fell to 10 per cent, compared to 15 per cent in 1994 and 85 per cent in 1993. The 1996 state budget (agreed in December 1995) envisages a 13.5 per cent rise in expenditures to L99.3 billion (about US$1 billion) and a 14.5 per cent increase in revenue to L62.3 billion (US$620 million).

As a proportion of projected GDP, the resultant budget deficit will be around 7 per cent in 1996, compared to a deficit of 5 per cent in 1995. Although expansionary, this budget is not expected to be inflationary, mainly because its projected deficit will be mainly financed by foreign aid, increased National Bank of Albania (NBA) borrowing abroad and a greater reliance on Treasury bonds.

Foreign economic aid in kind, grants and credits continues to be of vital importance for Albania, worth a total of US$2.2 billion between 1991 and early 1996. Amounting to around US$400 million (around 25 per cent of GDP in 1995), this aid is now shifting away from emergency food and other deliveries, and general balance of payments financing, towards funding for infrastructure development. As the largest single foreign aid provider to date, the EU is expected to provide most of these new resources, beginning with a three-year (1996-99) Phare allocation of Ecu212 million (US$273 million) for local infrastructure development. Over the same period, a further US$1.3 billion of foreign aid will also be made available from G-24 governments, the IMF and the World Bank.

Based on a restrictive NBA monetary-credit policy and non-inflationary fiscal instruments mainly based on foreign aid and borrowing, Albania's declining inflation rate means that it has now created the conditions for high and non-inflationary economic growth in the future. Related to this is the stability of its exchange rate, for which the NBA has successfully maintained a parity of around L100 per US$1 since 1993. Although, monetary stability has resulted, this parity may have to be revalued downwards in due course in order to boost exports and curb high import growth.

Albania's exchange rate policy – a managed float leading to eventual external convertibility on the current account – brings significantly lower hard currency reserves. At the end of 1995, these remained precarious at around US$420 million, including NBA gold bullion holdings. The major problems are a still limited ability to borrow money outside the context of tightly monitored official foreign aid agreements. FDI and foreign tourism service income also remains very low in Albania. Economically and hence politically, Albania's room for manoeuvre on domestic economic policy is extremely limited.

Domestically, savings and hence new investments remain low, mainly because of the continued absence of any sort of financial system. Albania is largely a cash-based society in which there is little popular confidence in the integrity of state commercial banks. Consequently the government and the NBA have largely been unable to augment local hard currency reserves by tapping into substantial *émigré* hard currency remittances, most of which are immediately used on current consumption and not on productive investment in the local economy. Structurally, the absence of proper and effective financial intermediaries can only impede Albania's economic development.

Money lending and changing is primarily a function of the informal economy, parts of which are controlled by the underworld, and real government control over local financial and other transfers is often purely nominal. The government and the NBA are now aiming to change this state of affairs through better regulation of a commercial banking system that will also be privatised in due course – a process that is expected to begin with the privatisation of the Rural Commercial Bank of Albania.

Foreign trade imbalance

Accounting for a record 30 per cent of GDP in 1995, Albania's imports were over three times its exports – US$680 million compared to US$205 million. Although an improvement over 1994, when imports of US$601 million exceeded exports (US$141 million) by a factor of four, this large foreign trade imbalance remains a major structural weakness of the Albanian economy. On a more positive note, exports grew by 45 per cent in 1995, against import growth of 13 per cent.

Albania's foreign trade is now increasingly orientated towards the EU, and in 1995 Italy accounted for 50 per cent of the country's exports and 35 per cent of its imports. Following the normalisation of relations with Greece, Greco-Albanian trade is expected to grow substantially in the future. Greece accounted for 25 per cent of Albania's imports, but only 10 per cent of its exports in 1995. In the communist period most of Albania's foreign trade was in non-EU markets, of which the then-Yugoslavia was the most important.

In 1994/95, export growth was mainly due to higher chrome ore and chromium output. In 1995, metals, minerals and fuels accounted for 55 per cent of total exports. Future export growth is now dependent on higher chrome ore production. Since 1993, foodstuffs and electricity have also become more important export categories. Machinery and equipment were the single largest import categories at a combined 30 per cent of total imports in 1995. During the 1990s, imports of consumer goods and foodstuffs have also become ever more important. Unofficially, actual imports of such goods are almost certainly higher than official figures suggest. Although, mainly sourced in Greece, unofficial cross-border smuggling for both imports and exports is also substantial with Kosovo, Montenegro and FYROM.

Albania's current account deficit increased to US$180 million in 1995, compared to US$150 million in 1994, as the trade deficit deteriorated to US$475 million. Foreign aid in 1995 was slightly less than the country's trade deficit in that year. In the longer-term, foreign aid will almost certainly decline, making future export growth imperative. In addition, *émigré* hard currency remittances will also have to make a greater contribution to the country's official balance of payments, but this will only happen when confidence is restored in local commercial banks. Unofficially,

COUNTRY PROFILE — ALBANIA

Historical profile

Local name 'eagles country' reflects remote, mountainous nature. 1912 independence declared after four centuries of Turkish rule. 1914-20 occupied by Italy. 1925 republic declared. 1928 former president became King Zog I. 1939 occupied first by Italy then by Germany. 1944 the communist-led National Liberation Front (established with Yugoslav help) took power. 1945 Enver Hoxha elected leader. 1946 King Zog deposed. Proclamation of Socialist Peoples' Republic of Albania. 1948 Communist Party renamed Albanian Party of Labour (PLA). Fears of Yugoslav expansionism encouraged closer ties with the USSR, but relations were soured in the 1960s when Albania supported Beijing in the Sino-Soviet dispute on ideology; Albania withdrew from CMEA and the Warsaw Pact. 1976 disenchanted by improvement in US-Chinese relations, Albania declared itself an independent Peoples' Socialist Republic and reaffirmed its policy of self-reliance. 1985 death of Hoxha, ruler for 41 years despite several coup attempts (one in 1974 Chinese-backed). Ramiz Alia replaced Hoxha as first secretary of the PLA. 1991 in June democratically-elected all-Socialist government was forced to resign. Caretaker government then formed. 1992 in March the Democratic Party won the elections. President Ramiz Alia resigned in April and Dr Sali Berisha was elected president – Albania's first non-communist president.

Political system

Albania was renamed the Republic of Albania under an interim constitution adopted on 29 April 1991. Political authority is held by the unicameral People's Assembly, whose 140 members are directly elected for a four-year term and which elects the president of the republic and the Council of Ministers.

Political parties

The (communist) Party of Labour (PLA) was the sole legal political party until December 1990, when the government bowed to popular protest and authorised the formation of opposition parties. Party in government: Partia Demokratike Shqiperise (Democratic Party) (PDS). Other major parties: Partia Socialdemokratike e Shqiperise (Social Democratic Party) (PSDS); Partia Republikana Shqiperise (Republican Party) (PRS); Socialist Party of Albania (PSS) – previously known as the Party of Labour (PLA); Human Rights Union (EAD) – originally the Greek Albanian organisation Democratic Union of the Greek Minority, Omonia); six PDS deputies formed Democratic Alliance in November 1992.

Population

Albanians make up 97 per cent, with the minorities dominated by Greeks, at around 2 per cent of the total. Others include Macedonian, Montenegrin, Vlach and Gypsy groups. Religion: Muslim (70%), Orthodox (20%), Roman Catholic (10%).

Main cities/towns

Tirana (population 300,000 in 1995), Durrës (Durrazzo) (124,900), Elbasan (101,300), Vlora (88,000), Shkodra (Scutari) (81,000), Fier (74,000), Berati (71,000), Korca (50,000).

Language

The Albanian language is divided into two dialects – Gheg, north of the river Shkumbinit, and Tosk in the south. Since 1945, the official language has been based on Tosk.

Media

Press: State news agency, ATA (Albanian Telegraphic Agency). Newspapers all officially controlled.
Dailies: Most influential – *Zeri i Popullit* (organ of the PLA) and *Bashkimi* (organ of the Democratic Front).
Weeklies: Mostly controlled by local party/committees.
Business: Bimonthly foreign trade magazine published by the Albanian Chamber of Commerce *Tregtia e Jashtme Popullore.*
Radio: Approximately 200,000 receivers in use, served by one national and seven regional stations. Wire relay service covers whole country. Radio Tirana broadcasts in several European languages.
Television: Approximately 10,000 receivers in use served by stations at Tirana, Kukes, Berat, Pogradec. Greek and Austrian programmes are broadcast. Italian TV is relayed in censored form.

Domestic economy

Abandoning a centrally planned economy, Albania embarked upon reform in 1991. However, the country was in the throes of an economic crisis deeper than that facing virtually any other reforming socialist country. Albania ranks as one of the poorest countries in Europe. Low levels of productivity and capital investment combined with shortages of skilled labour have been major constraints on growth. In 1995 Albania had one of the highest growth rates in the region (6 per cent). Privatisation is progressing well. Biggest asset is wealth of natural resources.

Employment

About 41 per cent of the workforce is female.

External trade

Foreign trade has been liberalised, however, licences must be obtained for the import and export of certain goods. Principal trading partners: former Yugoslavia (trade turnover around US$50m) and Greece (trade turnover around US$70m). Other trading partners include Bulgaria, China, former Czechoslovakia, France, Germany, Hungary, Italy, Poland and Romania. The EU signed 10-year trade and co-operation accord with Albania on 11 May 1992 and in December 1992 the EFTA countries signed a declaration on co-operation with Albania. Albania lifted sanctions against the Yugoslav federation in December 1995.
Exports: Exports totalled US$200m in 1995. Major exports include chrome, copper wire, ferro-nickel ore, bitumen, oil, hydroelectricity.
Imports: Imports totalled US$600m in 1995. Imports include chemicals, machinery, textiles, vehicles, lubricants and various consumer goods. Import licences are not required for food and consumer goods.

however, such hard currency resources have been widely used for undocumented or smuggled imports, notably from Greece and Italy. Including the large black economy, the private-sector may have accounted for around 60 per cent of Albania's foreign trade by 1995.

Foreign debt and payments

Kept artificially low for political reasons during the communist period, Albania's foreign debt has doubled during the 1990s, reaching US$900 million by the end of 1995. The US$2.2 billion worth of foreign aid provided since 1991 has not greatly increased the country's foreign debt, given that most of it was in kind or in the form of grants. New credits at this time were provided on a soft-loan basis, with concessionary interest rates and repayment schedules typically extending over 10 to 15 years, but these are effectively foreign subsidies that will likely decline in the future. Even before this decline begins, Albania will have to substantially increase normal foreign borrowings for balance of payments financing, building up local hard currency reserves and local infrastructure development. The problem is that such foreign borrowing will almost certainly remain officially sourced for some years to come.

Albania formally rescheduled nearly half its foreign debt (US$500 million) with the London Club (LC) of commercial bank creditors in May 1995. The NBA converted most of these outstanding liabilities into 30-year Brady-type government bonds. Prior to this agreement, Albanian LC debt was traded in secondary markets at 20 US cents to the US$. Agreement was also reached with the Paris Club of creditors in 1994 to reschedule about US$60 million of Albania's debt. Earlier in the 1990s, the NBA had run-up large losses on disastrous currency speculation in the Euromarkets. Combined with other negative factors, this gave Albania a very poor image in international financial markets. Following its recent agreement with the LC, this is now changing for the better, although Albanian access to the Euromarkets remains limited.

Future prospects

Relative to its own disastrous communist past, if not the rest of eastern Europe, Albania has made relatively good progress as regards at least its socio-economic transformation in recent years. Although still highly dependent on foreign aid and *émigré* hard currency remittances – as opposed to exports, normal foreign borrowing and increased FDI – Albanian economic growth since 1993 has been respectable. Other developments include declining inflation, exchange rate stability and structural reform based on privatisation that is increasingly irreversible.

Post-communist political transformation in Albania, however, is more problematical and full of potential dangers. Here the major problem is the determination of Berisha and the PDS to retain indefinite power no matter what the consequences for Albania domestically and internationally. Regionally, considerable political uncertainty and insecurity remain over the large ethnic Albanian diaspora in Kosovo, FYROM and, to a lesser extent, Greece.

COUNTRY PROFILE — ALBANIA

Agriculture

The sector is mainstay of the economy, accounting for 35 per cent of the country's GNP in 1994 and employing 60 per cent of the workforce. Some 460 co-operatives produced around 75 per cent of the output. Emphasis on production of cereals. Despite rapid mechanisation and extensive irrigation programme, sector remained underdeveloped. Major crops include sugar-beet, cotton, grains, beans and sunflower seeds. Also livestock sector. By mid-1992 nearly 75 per cent of the arable land had been distributed to individuals, but transportation, distribution, and marketing constraints continued to hamper agricultural output. In March 1993 it was announced that under a four-year US$36m plan, Albania would inject badly needed money into the rural economy. Agricultural output increased by 13 per cent in 1995.

Industry

Predominantly small-scale with bias towards engineering, chemicals, metals, construction materials, food processing and other agro-allied industries. The sector employed 10 per cent of workforce and accounted for 20 per cent of GNP in 1994. Lack of raw materials and outdated technology. Albania is attempting to attract foreign investment into its chromium industry which, until 1990, accounted for about 5 per cent of world production. Chromium is processed in two ferrochrome factories in Bureli and in Elbasan. They process an average of 100,000 tonnes of chromium ore a year into some 30,000 tonnes of ferrochrome. In 1995 another three factories are being built, bringing processed chromium to some 250,000 tonnes of ferrochrome a year; a further two factories are expected to produce about 100,000 tonnes of ferrochrome a year.

Tourism

The tourism sector in Albania is said to offer great potential for development. However, the existing infrastructure needs to be improved. About 57,000 foreigners visited Albania during the first nine months of 1995, an increase of 27.8 per cent over same period of 1994. Investment totalled US$150m in 1995.

Mining

The sector contributed 20 per cent to GNP in 1994 and employed 15 per cent of the workforce. World's third-largest producer and second largest exporter of chromium. Chromite reserves estimated to be about 26m tonnes, found mainly around Burgize. Extensive reserves of copper, iron, zinc and nickel; smaller reserves of uranium, titanium-magnetite, gold and silver. In 1995 another two chromium mines, whose annual output will be approximately 200,000 tonnes, are being developed. Of the 930,000 tonnes of ferro-nickel ore mined on average every year, 40 per cent are exported.

Hydrocarbons

Crude oil is major source of primary energy. Oil production largely from two small fields at Patos and Morinza. Refining capacity 1.5m tonnes per annum. Major gas fields at Diviak and Bubuline. Oil and gas are produced onshore. There are estimated to be about 350m barrels of oil offshore.

Energy

Hydroelectricity developed, with surplus exported. A hydropower station due to be constructed at Bushat, in the northern Shkodra district during 1996, and DM170m will be spent on modernising electricity network, with the aim of increasing electricity exports.

Stock exchange

Stock exchange launched May 1996.

Legal system

Justice administered under the constitution by the Supreme Court, and by district, village and county courts.

Membership of international organisations

CCC, Council of Europe, CSCE, FAO, IAEA, IDA, IFC, IMF, ITU, MIGA, OIC, Partnership for Peace, UN, UNESCO, UPU, WFTU, WHO, WMO, World Bank.

BUSINESS GUIDE

Time

GMT +1 hr (GMT +2 hrs summer).

Climate

Mediterranean; average annual temperature 16°C. Warmest in south-west, coldest in north-east.

Entry requirements

Visa: Visas are issued at the border to EU (except for Greek), US and Canadian passport holders. Other nationalities should confirm requirements before arrival. Visas available from Albanian embassies in Paris, Rome, Belgrade and Stockholm.

Air access

From Athens, Bucharest, Budapest, Ioannina, Ljubljana Paris, Rome, Zurich.
National airline: Albanian Airlines is owned by Amsterdam-based Aviation World MAK (AWM) (bought for US$1m January 1995 after going bankrupt in July 1994); resumed scheduled flights in October 1995. It gave five per cent of equity to the Albanian state company Albtransport.
Other airlines: Ada, Adria, Alitalia, Austrian, Balkan Air, Croatian, Hemus, Lufthansa, Malev, Olympic, Swissair.
Tax: International departures US$10, excluding transit passengers and infants under two years.
International airport: Rinas (TIA), 29 km from Tirana.

Surface access

Border crossing with Greece at Kakavia and Kristalopigi, and with Yugoslavia at Han-i-Hotit, Vrbnica and Cafasan. Rail link with Yugoslavia completed in 1985, carrying freight only, but closed in 1989.
Main port: Durres. At present this is the only working port. It is too shallow to allow container ships to dock.

Hotels

All bookings handled by Albturist, except for business visitors who should make arrangements through business contacts.

Car hire

It is advisable to hire local car and driver through travel agencies.

City transport

Taxis: Taxi service available only in Tirana.
Buses: Flat-fare bus service in Tirana.

National transport

Air: No regular internal air service.
Road: Network of about 21,000 km (3,000 km paved); mountain roads often impassable. Considered to be the worst roads in Europe (less than half can carry cars).
Buses: National bus network.
Rail: Unelectrified rail network of about 750 km.
Water: Ferry service connects Durres and Vlora with Trieste, Ancona, Brindisi, Bari (Italy) and Rijeka and Pula (Croatia).

Public holidays

1 Jan (New Year's Day), 1 May (May Day), 28 Nov (Independence Day), 29 Nov (Liberation Day), 25 Dec (Christmas Day).

Telecommunications

Telephone and telefax: Dialling code for Albania, IDD access code + 355 followed by area code (52 for Durres, 42 for Tirana), followed by subscriber's number. New telephone exhange in Tirana; by end-September 1996 additional 42,000 telephone numbers available.
Telex: Country code for telex: 604 AB.

Banking

With the help of the IMF, reform of the banking system has begun and a two-tier banking system has been established. The State Bank has been transformed into the Central Bank for Albania and has the power to authorise new banks including those with foreign capital. The EBRD is also involved in development and privatisation of the banking system.
Central bank: Central Bank of Albania.
Other banks: See 'Business Directory, Banking'.

Business information

Wholly foreign-owned enterprises permitted. Permits are needed for companies with foreign participation in the following sectors: minerals, oil and gas, the postal service, electricity, forestry and transport. Joint ventures are granted a reduced tax rate. Corporate income tax rates range from 15 per cent to 40 per cent depending on the industry.

Representation in capital

Bulgaria, China, Cuba, Egypt, France, Germany, Greece, Guyana, Hungary, Italy, Korea DPR, Poland, Romania, Russia, Turkey, United Kingdom, United States of America, Vietnam.

BUSINESS DIRECTORY

Hotels

Tirana (area code 42)
Dajti (tel: 423-3326).

Europapark (tel: 423-5035).

International (tel: 423-4185).

Car hire

Tirana
Hertz: Tirana Airport (tel: 42-918; tx: 39-509); Br Asim Vokshi 125 (tel: 423-5009; fax: 423-5018).

Academic/research institutes

University of Tiranë.

Chambers of Commerce

Chamber of Commerce, Konferenca e Pezës Street 6, Tirana (tel: 32-435/154/934, 27-997; fax: 27-997).

Banking

Central Bank of Albania, Sheshi Skënderbej 1, Tirana (tel: 32-435, 32-154; tx: 2153, 2133).

Albanian State Agricultural Bank, Tirana (tel: 27-738).

Albanian State Bank for Foreign Relations, Tirana.

Dardania Bank, Rruga e Durresit, ish Shkolla e partise (tel: 42-566; fax: 42-566).

Iliria Bank, St Vaso Pasha, Tirana.

Travel information

Albtransport – State Organisation for Air Transport, Kongresii Permetit Street 202, Tirana (tel: 3026; tx: 2124 AERIN AB); also at Rinas Airport, Tirana (tel: 3107; tx: 2445 AJTRAN AB).

Albturist – State Tourist Organisation, Deshmore e Kombit, Boulevard 6, Tirana (tel: 3860, 4853; tx: 2148 HODAJT AB).

Other useful addresses

Agroeksport – State Trade Organisation for the Export of Agricultural and Food Products, 4 Shkurti Street 6, Tirana (tel: 25-227, 25-229, 23-128; tx: 2137 AGREKS AB).

Albanian Telecom, Myslim Shyri 42, Tirina (tel: 32-047; fax: 33-323).

Albanian Telegraphic Agency (ATA), Boulevard Marcel Cachin 23, Tirana (tel: 4412; tx: 2142).

Albimpeks – State Trading Organisation for the Import of Materials, Rue 4, Shurti Street 6, Tirana (tel: 2711, 6123, 4540, 4051, 5490, 7353, 7358; tx: 2112 EXIMP AB).

Albkontrol – Organisation for Inspection of Exported and Imported Goods, Rruga Skënderbeu 15, Durrës (tel: 22-354; fax: 22-791).

Artimpex – State Organisation for Export, 4 Shkurti Street 6, Tirana.

Bureau for the Registration of Patents & Trade Marks, Konferenca e Pezes Street 6, Tirana.

Centroco-op – Central Union of Consumers' Cooperative for Export and Import, Rue Mujo Ulquinaku 2, Tirana (tel: 3228).

Committee of Environmental Protection, Ministry of Health and Environmental Protection, Bulevari Bajran Curri, Tirana (tel: 42-682; 35-229; fax: 35-229).

Department of Economic Development and Foreign Aid Co-ordination, Tirana (tel: 28-467; fax: 28-363).

Drejtkursig – Savings and Insurance Offices of Albania (Head Office), Tirana (tel: 3206).

Drejtoria e Statistikës, Tirana.

Foreign Investment Promotion Centre, Ekspozita Shqiperia Sot (Protokolli), Blvd Jeanne d'Arc, Tirana (tel: 27-626; fax: 28-439, 42-133).

Industrialeksport – 4 Shkurti Street 6, Tirana (tel: 4550; tx: 2127 MAKIMP AB).

Institute of Statistics, Tirana (tel: 22-411; fax: 28-300).

Kinostudio – 'Shquiperia e Rue', Cinematographic Studios 'New Albania', Rue Aleksander Moisiu 76, Tirana (tel: 3338, 2747).

Makinaimport – State Trade Organisation for the Import of Machinery, 4 Shkurti Street 6, Tirana (tel: 25-220, 25-221; tx: 2128 MAKIMP AB).

Mineralimpex – State Organisation for Export of Minerals, 4 Shkurti Street 6, Tirana (tel: 25-832, 23-848; tx: 2123, 2116 MIMPEX AB).

Ministry of Agriculture and Food, Blvd Deshmoret e Kombit Tirana (tel: 28-318, 32-675; fax: 23-806, 27-924).

Ministry of Energy and Mineral Resources (tel: 32-833; fax: 34-052).

Ministry of Finance and Economy, Dëshmoret e Kombit, Tirana (tel: 28-405; fax: 28-494).

Ministry of Foreign Affairs, Tirana (tel: 34-797; fax: 32-793/4).

Ministry of Health and Environment, Ministria e Shendetesise, Tirana (tel and fax: 34-615).

Ministry of Industry, Transport and Trade, Sheshi Skenderbey, Tirana (tel: 25-353, 32-289; fax: 27-773, 616-835).

Ministry of Tourism, Blvd Deshmoret e Kombit, Tirana (tel: 28-123); fax: 27-922).

Ministry of Transport and Telecommunications, Sheshi Skenderbey, Tirana (tel: 25-353; tel/fax: 27-773/616/835).

National Agency for Privatisation (tel/fax: 27-937).

National Committee of Energy, Deshmoret e Kombit, Tirana (tel/fax: 28-475).

Ndermarria E Librit – State Organisation for the Book Trade, Konferenca e Pezes Street, Tirana (tel: 3323).

President's Office, Tirana (tel: 28-491; fax: 33-761).

Prime Minister's Office, Tirana (tel: 34-816; fax: 34-818).

Transshqip – State Organisation for the Transport of Goods in Foreign Trade, 4 Shkurti Street 6, Tirana (tel: 23-076, 24-659; tx: 2131, 2132 TRANSH AB).

Andorra

Anthony Griffin

The opening verse of Andorra's national anthem: 'El Gran Carlemany, mon pare' ('Great Charlemagne, my father') gives an indication of the principality's sense of history. Today, Andorra's economic policy continues to walk the line between opportunity and respectability, between historical anachronism and twentieth century trading state. Tourism is a vital part of this small Catalan-speaking nation straddling the French and Spanish borders accounting for about 80 per cent of GDP and much of the overwhelming pollution that affects Andorra la Vella in the summer months, as cars, coaches and trucks all squeeze into the narrow streets. The principal motivation for visiting Andorra is duty-free shopping, particularly for electronic goods, designer clothing and ski-wear and equipment. Other income is derived from the sale of electric power to Catalonia, postage stamps, livestock and tobacco. Financial services are also on the increase, but Andorra has a long way to go if it is to rival Europe's better known offshore centres. The principality's 12 million visitors also come to enjoy the Catalan cooking, hiking in the north, and skiing at resorts such as Pas de la Casa/Grau Roig, Soldeu-El Tarter and Ordino-Arcalis. A customs union with the European Union (EU) was set up in 1991 and, in 1993, the co-principality's Andorran citizens voted to have power devolved to them after centuries of it resting in France and Spain. Andorrans are in a minority in their own state - about 80 per cent of the population are immigrants, mostly from Spain. Only native Andorrans can participate in elections.

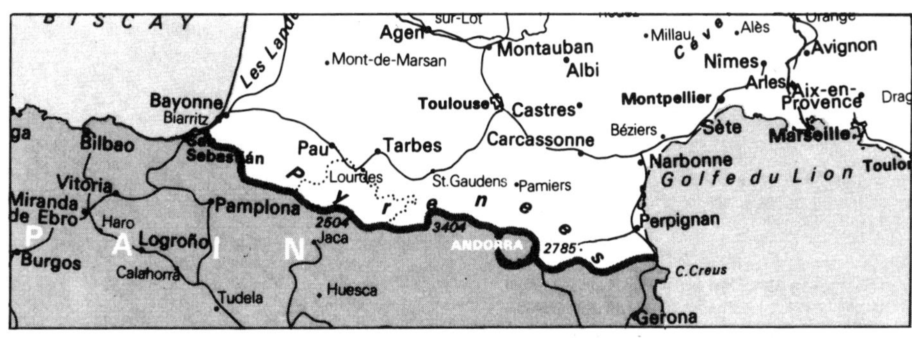

KEY FACTS — Andorra

Official title: Principat d'Andorra (Principality of Andorra)

Head of state: Co-Princes: Bishop of Seu d'Urgel and President of France

Head of government: President of Executive Council Marc Forné Molné (UL)

Ruling party: Unió Liberal (Liberal Union) (UL)

Capital: Andorra la Vella

Official Languages: Catalan

Currency: French Franc (Ff) and Spanish Peseta (Pta)

Exchange rate: Ff5.25 per US$; Pta1130.85 per US$ (Dec 1996)

Area: 468 sq km

Population: 65,780 (1995)

GNP per capita: US$15,000 (1995)*

Visitor numbers: 13m (1995)*

* estimated figure

Politics

Andorra has been a parliamentary democracy since 1993. Under Andorra's 14 March 1993 constitution, the 28-member Consell General de las Valls (General Council of the Valleys), the country's elected parliament, became the focus of political life in Andorra; political parties and trade unions were no longer outlawed. The Spanish and French co-princes (the French President and the Bishop of the small Spanish town of Seu d'Urgel) are still the constitutional heads of state but these positions became largely ceremonial after 1993. They are represented locally by officials called veguers.

New government

Much of the credit for Andorra's constitutional reforms can be given to Oscar Ribas Reig, Andorra's political leader for a dozen years starting in 1982. Although Ribas was able to win the support of the electorate in the first general election held under the constitution (December 1993), his Agrupment Nacional Democratica-led government fell less than a year later in November 1994. Ribas' undoing was a vote of non-confidence over the 1995 budget; five deputies of the New Democracy party withdrew their support for this measure and the government collapsed.

Marc Forne of the Liberal Union (UL), a centre-right party, was able to form a government consisting of the UL, the Liberal Group, the National Andorran Coalition and the Canillo-La Massana Grouping. Forne was made president of the executive council (head of government) on 21 December 1994.

Economy

As a popular tourist destination, with its year-round resorts, Andorra attracts some 12 million visitors each year. Until the 1970s Andorra was one of the few states in the world that used to close its frontiers completely at night: good for the local hotel and restaurant trade. Although such anachronisms no longer exist, Andorra still has no currency of its own – both the French franc and the Spanish peseta are used – and whilst emitting its own stamps, it lacks an independent postal service (the French and Spanish run two separate postal systems). In 1991 Andorra ended 900 years of fiscal isolation by joining the EU's customs union and thereby adopted the common external tariff, adhering to the common trade policy that provides for the free movement of goods within the Union. Exceptions were granted for agricultural produce and the duty-free transit of goods imported from EU countries. The country has a very small agriculture sector due to the shortage of arable land.

Banking in Andorra has been famous for its high level of service, secrecy and discretion, but financial service providers are facing increasing external pressure – particularly from the EU – to bring more transparency to their activities. The banking sector has been targeted by the government for growth and a more open banking system should help enhance the country's reputation as a prime offshore financial centre while satisfying EU and international banking watchdogs. A number of the Principality's main banks are owned by major Spanish banks such as the Banco de Bilbao. Fears that Andorra could become a money laundering haven for the international drug trade have proved misplaced, possibly because of the general tightening of banking regulations. The principality's banking community is, in effect Spanish – or more precisley Catalan. The overlap between Andorran and Barcelona business circles is significant and creates a powerful business grouping.

COUNTRY PROFILE — ANDORRA

Historical profile

One of the world's tiniest countries, with one of the smallest populations, Andorra is also one of the oldest nations in Europe, established by Charlemagne as a buffer state against Spanish muslims.
1278 Co-principality established between France (originally a nominee of the king, then the emperor and latterly the president himself) and Spain (in the person of the Bishop of Seu d'Urgel).
1981 Constitutional reforms (see Political system) part of continuing attempt to clarify exact constitutional status and liberate elected body from power of feudal co-princes.
1983 Introduction of income tax following storm damage and general recession.
1985 Universal suffrage for Andorrans, continuing gradual extension of franchise (until 1970 only third-generation Andorran males aged over 25 had the vote).
1986 Co-princes met to discuss status of co-principality in relation to EC, following Spain's accession to Community.
1991 Joined EU Customs Union.
1993 Democratic constitution and full sovereignty. First elections held in December, won by Agrupament Nacional Democratic (National Democratic Grouping).
1994 Coalition government led by Unión Liberal.

Political system

Principat d'Andorra (Principality of Andorra) is also known by its local short form *Andorra Digraph.* Co-principality under joint sovereignty of president of France and Spanish bishop of Seo de Urgel, who are represented locally by officials called *veguers.* Day-to-day government by an elected head of government and the 28-member *Consell General de las Valls* (four representatives from each of seven *parroquies* (parishes)). Andorra's first written constitution was adopted 14 March 1993 after a referendum. The constitution allows Andorra to hold full sovereignty, to be able to form and join trades unions and political parties, and to have an independent judiciary. It can also decide its own foreign policy and join international organisations. The co-principality held its first democratic parliamentary elections 12 December 1993.

Political parties

Unió Liberal (Liberal Union) (UL) is the party in government. Other major parties include Agrupacio Nacional Democratica (National Democratic Grouping) (AND); Coalisió Nacional Andorana (National Andorran Coalition (CNA); Nova Democratica (New Democracy (ND); Iniciativa Democratica Nacional (National Democratic Initiative (IDN).

Population

Of Andorra's total population, only about 30 per cent are natives with the right to vote. The rest include Spaniards (61%), French (6%), Portuguese, English, Australians, Moroccans and others. Population growth rate 2.72 per cent; birth rate 12.92 births/1,000 population; death rate 7.25 deaths/1,000 population; life expectancy 78.52 years male; 75.65 years female (1995 estimates). Main religion: Roman Catholicism.

Main city

Andorra la Vella, estimated population 22,210.

Language

Catalan (official), French.

Media

Press: Several local weeklies and newspapers including *Poble Andorra, Correu Andorra, Informacions, Diari d'Andorra* and *Diari Informacions.*
Broadcasting: There are two radio stations. One state-owned (Radio Andorra) and one privately owned (Radio Valira). Around six TV stations and several radio stations can be received from France and Spain.

Domestic economy

Economic activity based on small-scale agriculture, commerce and tourism.

Employment

Large immigrant workforce, mainly Spanish. Tourism and allied industries major employer.

External trade

In 1991 Andorra joined the European Community Customs Union. Major entrepôt for numerous European goods owing to favourable excise duties.
Exports: Main exports include electricity, tobacco products, furniture. Main destinations: France and Spain.
Imports: Reliance on imports of foodstuffs, raw materials, manufactures and consumer goods from Spain and France.

Agriculture

Agricultural production is limited by a scarcity of arable land, and most food has to be imported. Traditional small-scale farming. Principal crops tobacco and potatoes; rye, wheat, barley, oats and some other vegetables also grown. Also animal husbandry and forestry. The principal livestock activity is sheep raising. Land use: 2 per cent permanent crops, 56 per cent forest and woodland, 20 per cent irrigated land.

Industry

Small manufacturing sector primarily servicing tourism, but also including cigarettes, cigars and furniture.

Tourism

Tourism is the mainstay of Andorra's economy, accounting for about 80 per cent of GDP. The number of visitors, attracted by Andorra's duty-free status and by its ski-ing resorts, has increased from 2.5m in 1970 to approximately 13m per annum.

Environment

Current issues are deforestation and overgrazing of mountain meadows contributing to soil erosion. Natural hazards – snowslides, avalanches.

Mining

Natural resources of iron ore and lead.

Energy

Near self-sufficiency in hydroelectricity. Remainder comes from France and Spain. Electricity capacity 35,000 kW; production 140m kW.

Legal system

Based on French and Spanish civil codes. Supreme Court of Andorra at Perpignan (France) for civil cases, the Ecclesiastical Court of the bishop of Seo de Urgel (Spain) for civil cases, (*Tribunal des Cortes* (Tribunal of the Courts) for criminal cases.

Membership of international organisations

Council of Europe, ECE, IFRCS (associate), INTERPOL, IOC, ITU, UN, UNESCO.

BUSINESS GUIDE

Time

GMT +1 hr (GMT +2 hrs from late Mar to late Sep).

Climate

Warm summers and moderately cold winters; temperatures range from 0-30°C.

Entry requirements

For nationals of France and Spain, only an identity card is required; others require a passport. There are no health requirements.
Currency: No currency restrictions. French and Spanish currencies in use.

BUSINESS GUIDE

Air access

Nearest international aiports are Barcelona (Spain), 200 km, and Toulouse (France), 180 km from Andorra.

Surface access

From Spain
Rail: Barcelona to Puigcerda, then by bus to La Seu d'Urgel and Andorra. Madrid to Lleida (Lérida), then bus to La Seu d'Urgel and Andorra.
Road: Barcelona-Andorra via Puigcerda and La Seu d'Urgel; Barcelona-Andorra via Igualada, Calaf, Ponts and La Seu d'Urgel.
From France
Rail: Trains to Ax-les-Thermes, L'Hospitalet or La Tour de Carol (Toulouse-Perpignan lines), then bus to Andorra.
Road From L'Hospitalet or La Tour de Carol to Pas de la Casa, on the Andorran frontier, then Port d'Envalira.

Hotels

Around 250 hotels, most with modern facilities.

National transport

Road: There are 186 km of roads of which 162 km are paved.
Buses: Constant minibus services link all the villages.

Public holidays

Fixed dates: 1 Jan (New Year's Day), 8 Sep (Mare de Deu de Meritxell), 25 Dec (Christmas).
Variable dates: Easter.

Working hours

Banking: (Mon-Fri) 0900–1300, 1500–1700; (Sat) 0900–1200.

Telecommunications

Telephone and telefax: Automatic service connects every part of country. Approximately 430 phones per thousand inhabitants. International dialling code: 376 followed by customer's number (no area code required). Public telephones take Spanish pesetas (French francs in Pas de la Casa) or an Andorran *teltarja* which operates on the same principle as telephone cards. *Teletarges* (plural) worth 50 and 100 units can be purchased at post offices, tobacconists and tourist offices.
Telex: Modern telex service. Country code: 590 AND.
Telegram: Service available main hotels and Spanish and French post offices in Andorra la Vella.

Postal service

Service operated by Spanish and French in capital. Andorran stamps used for international correspondence. Postal service within Andorra free.

Banking

The banking sector with its 'tax haven' status, contributes substantially to the economy. Seven commercial banks with some 34 branches. See 'Business Directory, Banking'. French and Spanish currencies in use. Strict secrecy laws in force.

BUSINESS DIRECTORY

Hotels

Andorra la Vella
Andorra Center, Doctor Nequi 12 (tel: 24-999; fax: 28-329).

Andorra Palace, Prat de la Creu (tel: 21-072; fax: 29-018).

Andorra Park, Roureda Guillemó (tel: 20-979; fax: 28-329).

Avet d'Or, Av Meritxell 31 (tel: 20-558).

Bellavista, Av Meritxell 26 (tel: 21-288; tx: 305 AND).

Bellpi, Av Santa Coloma 30 (tel: 20-651).

Cassany, Av Meritxell 28 (tel: 20-636).

Celler d'En Toni, Verge del Pilar 4 (tel: 21-252).

Cerqueda (Santa Coloma), c/ Mn Lluis Pujol (tel: 20-235).

Consul, Plaça Rebés 5 (tel: 20-196).

Conxita, Av Dr Mitjavila 26 (tel: 21-298).

Cornella, Av Meritxell 61 (tel: 21-480; tx: 341).

Costa, Av Meritxell 44, 3 (tel: 21-439).

Davos, c/ Esteve Dolsa s/n (tel: 60-615).

Eden Roc, Av Dr Mitjavila 1 (tel: 21-000; fax: 60-319).

El Racó d'En Joan, c/ de la Vall 20 (tel: 20-811).

El Roure, Av Dr Mitjavila 24 (tel: 25-483).

Enclar, Roureda de Sansa 18 (tel: 20-310).

Festa Brava, c/ La Llacuna 7 (tel: 20-741).

Freixanet, c/ la Creu Grossa s/n (tel: 20-549).

Galàxia, Av Meritxell 7 (tel: 26-975).

Garcia, Av Princep Benlloch 51 (tel: 20-968).

Garden (Santa Coloma), Av d'Enclar 93 (tel: 21-751).

Hostal Calones, Antic c/ Major 8 (tel: 21-312).

Hostal del Sol, Plaça Guillemó 3 (tel: 23-701).

Hotel de l'Isard, Av Meritxell 36 (tel: 20-092; tx: 377 AND).

Indalo, Av Dr Mitjavila 27 (tel: 21-871).

Internacional, Mossén Tremosa 2 (tel: 21-422; tx: 269).

Jaime I, Roureda de Sansa 2 (tel: 20-061; tx: 203).

L'Arribada, Av Princep Benlloch 67 (tel: 20-867).

La Pedrera, Av Dr Mitjavila 6 (tel: 20-014).

Les Arcades, Plaça Vuillermó 5 (tel: 21-355).

Les Fonts, c/ de l'Agüeta 7 (tel: 21-393).

Mercure Andorra, Av Meritxell 58 (tel: 20-773; fax: 29-018).

Montserrat, Av Meritxell 68 (tel: 20-083).

Nevada, c/ M Cinto Verdaguer 1 (tel: 24-361).

Normandia, Av Princep Benlloch 49 (tel: 20-125).

Parador Santa Coloma (Santa Coloma), Av d'Enclar 104 (tel: 21-804).

Pensió La Rosa, Antic c/ Major 16 bis (tel: 21-810).

Principat, Av Princep Benlloch 57 (tel: 20-219).

Pyrenees, 20 Av Princep Benlloch 20 (tel: 20-508; tx: 421 AND).

Reata (Santa Coloma), Av d'Enclar 78 (tel: 22-040).

Residència Albert, Av Dr Mitjavila 16 (tel: 26-975).

Residència Benazet, c/ La Llacuna 19 (tel: 20-698).

Residència Charvi, Av Meritxell 86 (tel: 22-156).

Residència Envalira, c/ Sant Salvador 3 (tel: 20-689).

Residència Marticella, Av Meritxell 124 (tel: 21-415).

Residència Monicel, Av Santa Coloma 26 (tel: 20-633).

Residència Paris, Av Meritxell 43 (tel: 20-843).

Restaurant Andorrà, Av Princep Benlloch 24 (tel: 20-997).

Restaurant Lleida, Av Meritxell 70 (tel: 20-312).

Sant Jordi, Av Princep Benlloch 45 (tel: 20-865).

Sasplugas, Av Bisbe Princep Iglesias s/n (tel: 20-311).

Serola, c/ Tobira, s/n (tel: 20-647).

Torres, c/ Anna M. Janer 3 (tel: 20-371).

Valmar, Av Meritxell 75 (tel: 21-667).

Viena, c/ de la Vall (tel: 29-233; fax: 29-906).

Y Sem Bé, Av Santa Coloma 20 (tel: 20-846).

Car hire

Andorra la Vella
Europcar: Carrer de la Roda (tel: 686-8986; fax: 686-9596).

Hertz: Casa Perez Sa, Pyrenees, 9 Ave Moritxell, located on the 3rd floor (tel: 9738-20414 Ext 196; tx: 205).

Banking

Banc Agricol i Comercial d'Andorra, Mossen Cinto 6, Andorra la Vella (tel: 21-333; tx: 201).

Banca Cassany SA, Avinguda Meritxell 39-41, Andorra la Vella.

Banc Internacional, Avinguda Meritxell 32, Andorra la Vella (tel: 20-037; tx: 206 AND).

Banca Mora SA, Placa Coprinceps 2, Les Escaldes (tel: 20-607; tx: 222).

Banca Reig, Avinguda Meritxell, Andorra la Vella (tel: 22-618).

Credit Andorra, Avinguda Princep Benlloch 19, Andorra la Vella (tel: 20-326; tx: 200 CREDIAND).

La Caixa, Pl Rebés, Andorra la Vella (tel: 20-015; tx: 261).

Principal newspapers

Correu Andorra, Av. Meritxell 114, 4-2, Andorra la Vella (tel: 22-500; fax: 22-938).

Diari d'Andorra, C/Bra. Riberaygua 39, 4rt, Edif. Alexandre, Andorra la Vella (tel: 63-700; fax: 63-800).

Diari Informacions, Avinguda Meritxell 101, 1er Andorra la Vella (tel: 63-197; fax: 63-193).

Informacions, c/ de l'unio 2, Andorra la Vella (tel: 21-134, 20-073; fax: 60-839).

Poble Andorra, Carretera de la Comella, Andorra la Vella (tel: 22-506; fax: 26-696).

Travel information

Caseta d'Informació i Turisme (tourism kiosk opposite Restaurant Marti\01), Andorra la Vella (tel: 27-117).

Sindicat d'Iniciativa Oficina de Turisme (national tourist office at the top of Carrer Doctor Vilanova between Plaça del Poble and Plaça Rebés), Andorra la Vella (tel: 20-214).

Other useful addresses

French Post Office, C/Bonaventura Armengol, Andorra la Vella (tel: 20-408).

Ministry of Finance, Andorra la Vella.

Ministry of Commerce, Industry and Agriculture, Andorra la Vella.

Ministry of Tourism and Sport, Andorra la Vella.

Pas de la Casa Customs, Franco-Andorran frontier (tel: 55-120).

Police (tel: 21-222).

Sant Julia de Loria Customs, Spanish-Andorran frontier (tel: 41-090).

Servei de Telecomunicacions d'Andorra STA, Avinguda Meritxell 110 (tel: 21-021).

Sindicat d'Iniciativa de les Valls d'Andorra, c/Dr Vilanova, Andorra la Vella (tel: 20-214).

Spanish Post Office, c/o Joan Maragall, Andorra la Vella (tel: 20-257).

Armenia

Marko Milivojevic

Economic reforms continued to make good progress in 1995 and 1996. Higher growth was mainly fuelled by rising domestic demand and investment, including substantially increased foreign capital inflows. President Levon Ter-Petrosian won the September 1996 presidential elections, but only after a strong challenge from Vazgen Manukyan who blamed vote-rigging for his defeat. Regionally, the Armenian-Azeri conflict over Nagorno-Karabakh and other disputed territories in Azerbaijan continues to blight Armenia's prospects.

Politics

Re-elected to power in July 1995, when a new constitution based on an executive presidency was also approved, the Armenian Pan-National Movement (HHSh) government now presides over an authoritarian de facto one-party state. Although banned in controversial circumstances in December 1994, the main opposition Dashnaktsyutyun or Dashnak Party (Armenian Revolutionary Front) party continues to exercise considerable influence in the political sphere. However, it was another opposition grouping, the four party National Alliance, whose candidate, Vaxgen Manukyan, caused the greatest surprise. Manukyan won 41.29 per cent of the vote in the September 1996 presidential election compared to 51.75 per cent for Ter-Petrosian. Widespread protests and demonstrations followed the election as Manukyan and his supporters claimed, with some justification, that the election had been fixed.

The demonstrations in Yerevan turned violent after rumours spread that Manukyan had been arrested. Several opposition leaders were detained and accused of plotting a coup, while the president ordered tanks and troops onto the streets of the capital. Ter-Petrosian undoubtedly underestimated the extent of popular dissatisfaction at his radical economic reform programme, as voters blamed this rather than the conflict with Azerbaijan and the break-up of the USSR for declining living standards.

In a belated attempt to appease the opposition, Ter-Petrosian forced the resignation of his prime minister, Hrant Bagratian, in November 1996, blaming him for the economic hardships and his own poor performance in the election. The new prime minister, Armen Sarkisyan, was formerly Armenia's ambassador to the UK, and is a diplomat rather than an economist. Even so, it is likely that Bagratian's reform programme will be continued.

Under the terms of the constitution approved in July 1995, Armenia's system of government is being extensively reformed. In September 1995 this began with changes to local government, where Armenia's existing 37 regions were replaced by nine provinces and one separate administrative territory, Yerevan. Known as the nine-plus-one plan, this centralised power still further to the advantage of the HHSh government. The HHSh is widely suspected of corrupt collusion with the old communist elite and underworld, particularly with regard to their dominance of the local economy. On the other hand, the government claims that it is the Dashnaks who are criminals and even terrorists.

Dashnak party

The banning of the Dashnak Party in the July 1995 parliamentary elections inevitably caused difficulties for Armenia internationally, and with the European Union (EU) and the Organisation for Security and Co-operation in Europe (OSCE) in particular. The Supreme Court stipulated that the initial six month ban on the Dashnak Party be lifted in July 1995. This was ignored by the HHSh government, which imposed a further one-year Dashnak ban in August 1995.

The significance of the well-organised and funded Dashnak Party is that they are the main representatives of the large and powerful Armenian diaspora, which is of critical importance, notably in North America. So far, the Armenian lobby in the USA has generally persuaded Washington to tilt towards Armenia in the Transcaucasus, but this may change in due course.

International relations

Armenia's alliance with Russia in the Commonwealth of Independent States (CIS) continues to have the effect of reinforcing Armenian intransigence towards Azerbaijan. For its part, Russia is content to indefinitely perpetuate the status quo in Transcaucasia, and will not allow a final settlement of the Armenian-Azeri conflict until Azerbaijan capitulates to all of its demands.

Now openly supported by the USA, which dominates the Azerbaijan International Oil Consortium (AIOC), Azerbaijan is unwilling to allow the deployment of OSCE-mandated Russian troops on any part of its territory or to tolerate an effective veto by Russia over oil development and export plans now increasingly orientated towards Turkey and the west.

Following the signing of a key deal between Azerbaijan and the AIOC in October 1995, Washington's pro-Armenian policy is being modified to the advantage of Baku. According to Washington, there is a short window of opportunity for a negotiated settlement before the Azeris seek to change the status quo through force of arms.

Within Azerbaijan, the political pressures for such a scenario are growing, although it remains unclear how the country can hope to prevail over Armenia on the battle field. Supported by Russia and now Iran, Armenia retains the military advantage in the conflict and, as long as it does, it will not compromise on territorial issues.

The Turkish-Azeri economic blockade of Armenia continues without respite. The negotiations mediated by the OSCE on this conflict remain dead locked, with neither side willing to make the compromises required. Having won the whole of Nagorno-Karabakh plus 20 per cent of Azerbaijan proper by 1994, Armenia is unwilling to cede any territory, particularly the strategic Lachin corridor.

Economy

Following the first economic growth of the post-Soviet period in 1994, when GDP increased by 5.4 per cent, total output of goods and services in Armenia increased by a further 6.9 per cent in 1995. In 1996, GDP growth is projected at about 6.5 per cent.

Earlier in the 1990s, the Azeri economic blockade, payments problems and the absence of macro-economic stabilisation and reform resulted in a catastrophic economic collapse – and all this after Armenia had been devastated by a major earthquake in 1988. In 1994, the ceasefire in Nagorno-Karabakh and the end of the civil war in neighbouring Georgia meant that energy supplies from Russia improved slightly. In November 1995 the Medzamor nuclear reactor also came on line for the first time since 1989.

Recent increases in GDP, however, remain relatively insignificant given the low foundation they are based on. At around US$200 in 1995, GDP per capita is still low, although actual average incomes could have been double this due to large *émigré* hard currency remittances and a black economy that may have accounted for as much as 50 per cent of officially declared GDP in 1995.

Including the black economy, actual GDP may have been in the region of US$1 billion, compared to an official figure of US$700 million in 1995. Previously accounting for 46 per cent of GDP, but probably no more than 25 per cent by 1995, industrial output grew by 6.4 per cent in 1994 and 2.4 per cent in 1995, with the fastest growth recorded in light manufacturing and food-processing.

KEY FACTS

Official title: Republic of Armenia

Head of state: President Levon Ter-Petrosian (since Oct 1991; re-elected 22 Sep 1996 with 51.75% of vote)

Head of government: Prime Minister Armen Sarkisyan (from 4 Nov 1996)

Ruling party: Armenian Pan-National Movement (APNM) (since the Jul 1995 parliamentary elections the APNM has dominated a so-called Republican Bloc, which is also supported by the Shamiram Women's Party)

Capital: Yerevan

Official Languages: Armenian

Currency: Dram (D) = Luma 100 (introduced 22 Nov 1993)

Exchange rate: D421.02 per US$ (Dec 1996)

Area: 29,800 sq km

Population: 3.76m (1995)

GDP per capita: US$700 (1995)

GDP real growth: 5% (1995)

GNP per capita: US$900 (1994)

GNP real growth: -2% (1994)

Labour force: 1.5m (1994)

Unemployment 8.4% (Jan 1996)

Inflation: 210% (1995)

Trade balance: -US$413.6m (1995)

Foreign debt: US$1.5bn (1995)

KEY INDICATORS — Armenia

	Unit	1991	1992	1993	1994	1995
Population	m	3.36	3.49	3.50	3.65	3.76
Gross national product (GNP)	US$bn	3.6	3.0	2.8	3.0	–
GNP per capita	US$	1,630	950	910	900	–
GNP real growth	%	-11.4	-52.0	-28.0	-2.0	–
Inflation	%	174.1	729.0	6,446.0	5,062.0	210.0
Employment	'000	–	1,578	1,543	1,500	1,465
Unemployment	%	–	3.4	5.2	6.4	6.6
Unemployment	'000	–	–	86.9	105.4	105.5
Industrial production	1990=100	–	47.8	42.9	45.9	47.0
Manufacturing	1990=100	92.9	47.8	42.6	–	–
Mining	1990=100	87.7	32.0	22.1	–	–
Cement	'000 tonnes	1,507	385	198	128	228
Retail sales volume	1990=100	–	20.3	11.9	7.5	9.5
Exports	US$m	–	–	–	215.5	247.5
Imports	US$m	–	–	–	393.8	661.1
Balance of trade	US$m	–	–	–	-178.3	-413.6
Exchange rate	D per US$	–	–	**75	406	402

** Dram introduced Nov 1993

The major economic challenges for Armenia are in the still largely-unreformed state industrial sector, where output of capital goods continues to decline. In 1995, its precarious finances were further undermined by increases in energy prices, which have also been imposed on domestic consumers under International Monetary Fund (IMF) pressure.

Following the beginnings of long-delayed large-scale privatisation in 1995, major changes were expected in the state industrial sector in 1996, making higher unemployment inevitable in at least the short-term. Because of the rapid development of private sector services, officially-recorded unemployment was only 6.6 per cent at the end of 1996. All new job creation and new investment is now in the private-sector, which accounted for about 50 per cent of GDP by mid-1996.

Agriculture

Accounting for around 45 per cent of GDP in 1995, the largely privately-owned agricultural sector continues to act as a motor for economic growth. In 1995, agricultural output increased by 10 per cent, with particularly high growth recorded in viniculture. Food-processing is also a high growth sector with good prospects. Externally, Armenian foodstuff exports are reviving, notably to Russia, although Armenia remains a net importer of basic agricultural products such as wheat.

Services

Including the black economy (mainly extensive cross-border smuggling) privately-owned services continue to experience high growth. Accounting for around 40 per cent of GDP in 1995, services of all types are expected to become economically central in Armenia within the next few years.

Initially dominated by retail and wholesale trade, Armenian services are expected to grow particularly fast in the transport, telecommunications and construction sectors. Improved overseas funding has led to the beginnings of infrastructure development. Emigré hard currency remittances are also funding the rebuilding of local housing stock damaged in the 1988 earthquake. In the longer-term, Armenia has considerable potential as a regional transportation hub, particularly in relation to trans-shipments between Russia, Turkey and Iran. Financial services are also another high growth area.

Reform

Macro-economic stabilisation achieved its greatest successes in 1995, success that was rewarded with a US$148 million Enhanced Structural Adjustment Facility (ESAF) by the IMF in February 1996. Hyper-inflation at the end of 1994 (1,885 per cent) was reduced to 32 per cent by the end of 1995. The introduction of a new national currency, the dram (D) in November 1993 was accompanied by a stand-by agreement with the IMF. Based on restrictive monetary-credit and fiscal policies by the government and the Central Bank of Armenia (CBA), Armenia's continued macro-economic stabilisation was expected to result in year-end inflation of around 19 per cent in 1996.

Overseen by the then prime minister Hrant Bagratian (an *émigré* technocrat), Armenia's economic reforms were given a further boost in July 1995 when a cabinet reshuffle placed the liberal economics minister, Anren Egiazarian, into the key chairmanship of the parliamentary economic committee. Announced in September 1995, the government's economic development programme for the rest of the 1990s reconfirmed a continued commitment to more radical economic reform.

In 1994 and 1995, around two-thirds of the government's budget outlays were financed by foreign credits. In addition, Armenia continued to receive substantial international humanitarian aid, mainly in the form of foodstuffs, medicines and other essential goods.

Equivalent to a massive 48.2 per cent of GDP in 1993 and 16.1 per cent of GDP in 1994, the government budget deficit fell to

COUNTRY PROFILE — ARMENIA

Historical profile

Democratic revolution in 1990. Independence from Russia declared 23 September 1991. In 1994 the war with Azerbaijan over Nagorno-Karabakh (the Armenian-populated enclave in Azerbaijan) settled into an uneasy stalemate, with local Armenians in control of the disputed enclave and large swathes of Azeri territory between Karabakh and Armenia occupied by Armenian forces. A ceasefire between Azerbaijan and Armenia has generally been honoured.

Political system

The 190-seat National Assembly is the supreme legislative body. The president has been directly elected since October 1991 and a new constitution was approved by referendum in July 1995. Multiparty republic. Constitutional Court formed in February 1996. Armenia is divided into various provincial divisions *marz.*

Political parties

Coalition government: Republican Bloc, the major party being Pan Armenian National Movement (HHSh). Other major parties: Dashnaktsutyun (Armenian Revolutionary Front) (ARF); National Alliance; Shamiram Women's Party; Communist Party.

Population

Armenians (96%), Kurds (1.8%), Russians (1.2%) Azerbaijanis (2%), others (1%). Annual population growth rate 0.4 per cent (1994). Approximately 32 per cent rural and 68 per cent urban. Adult literacy 98.8 per cent. Average life expectancy 71.2 years. Religions: Armenian Orthodox (94%), other (6%).

Main cities/towns

Yerevan, capital (estimated population 1.2m in 1994), Gyumri, Kirovakan.

Language

Armenian (official), Russian (2 per cent).

Media

Broadcasting: Ashtarak is a popular cable television station.

Domestic economy

For years, Armenia depended on cheap, subsidised oil, gas and raw materials from the former Soviet republics and relied on Soviet consumers to buy its exports. The ceasefire in Nagorno-Karabakh and the stabilisation of the situation in Georgia has allowed the import of oil and gas to resume. The economy started to recover in the first nine months of 1995. The World Bank approved a US$12m rehabilitation loan in November 1995. IDA credits worth US$63.8m were approved in March 1996, to help the government implement a reform programme to stabilise the economy, generate growth and improve living conditions.

External trade

Armenia is a landlocked country and is dependent on trade through its four neighbours, Azerbaijan, Georgia, Turkey and Iran, but its main trade partner is still Russia. Traditionally, Armenia's rail and road links to Turkey only handled limited trade while there are no major land connections to Iran. The war over Nagorno-Karabakh cut off Armenia's primary rail and road routes linking it through Azerbaijan to the rest of the former Soviet economy. Armenia's only remaining trade route was also cut off by turmoil in Georgia. The partial resolution of both these conflicts in 1994 has allowed trade to improve. The government has eliminated export taxes and import restrictions.
Exports: Exports totalled almost US$200m in 1995.
Imports: Imports totalled about US$516m in 1995. The government reduced the rate of customs duty on imports in early-1996: imports of essential goods, including fuel, foodstuffs, equipment and raw materials are exempt from customs duty, while duty on other goods is levied at a unified rate of 10 per cent.

Agriculture

This sector is less important than the industrial sector due to mountainous terrain and lack of arable land. It contributed 45 per cent to GNP in 1994 and employed 22 per cent of the workforce. In 1991 Armenia was the first former Soviet republic to privatise agricultural land. By the end of 1993, some 87 per cent of land had been privatised, and by early-1994, the ownership of land could also be transferred through sale. Major producer of grapes, citrus fruit, vegetables, dairy products and some cotton; also sheep breeding. Armenia's 1995 wheat grain harvest reached 273,000 tonnes, up 35,000 tonnes from that of 1994.

Industry

The economy relies heavily on the industrial sector. The industrial sector accounted for 31 per cent of GNP in 1994 and employed 42 per cent of the working population. Mainly based on

8.7 per cent of GDP in 1995, mainly due to higher foreign borrowings, improved tax collection and real cuts in public expenditures. The ending of various production and other subsidies has caused considerable dissension in Armenia, where energy had often been supplied at below cost price or even gratis. Although still excessive in relation to GDP and government spending as a whole, national defence expenditures are falling in real terms, mainly because of the ceasefire with Azerbaijan in 1994. The 1996 budget deficit is expected to be 7.7 per cent of projected GDP. Lower inflation means that in 1996 real wages and welfare benefits are expected to rise for the first time since 1990.

Dram

Now one of the more stable CIS currencies, the dram appreciated against the US$ in 1995. Caused by lower inflation and expanding hard currency reserves, this positive trend is expected to continue in 1996/97. Against the Russian rouble, the dram is also appreciating, making imports from Russia cheaper. On the negative side, a stronger dram has inhibited improved export performance, notably in Russia.

Domestically, exchange rate stability and lower inflation has increased the attractiveness of dram-denominated assets, so boosting CBA and commercial bank hard currency reserves. Relative to GDP, foreign credits and *émigré* hard currency remittances are now very high. In 1995, this led to some concern that increased foreign capital inflows could adversely impact upon local money supply and hence inflation in the longer-term.

The CBA is now committed to improved regulation of the booming financial services sector, where corruption is still strong. As in other CIS republics, the amount of hard currency saved in the form of cash is thought to be substantial, where such resources almost certainly exceed money deposited by savers in local commercial banks.

Privatisation and investment

Preceded by radical land reform and the small-scale privatisation of services in the early 1990s, large-scale ownership transformation of the state industrial sector began in earnest in 1994. Delayed by endless political wrangling, such privatisation has so far mainly benefited the old Armenian élite and their 'associates'. Expected eventually to involve up to 5,000 medium-to-large-sized enterprises, large-scale privatisation was given a major boost when the HHSh government was re-elected in July 1995. With a new mandate, the government approved the privatisation of an initial 246 large enterprises in the industrial sector in September 1995, the same time as its economic development programme for 1996-2000 was announced.

Armenia had promised the IMF and the World Bank that 900 enterprises would be privatised in 1995. In the event, only 75 were disposed of. Progress picked up in 1996 however, and by August 626 medium and large enterprises had been sold off, the majority through public subscription. Politically, one of the main reasons for the nine-plus-one local government plan was to curb opposition to transparent and proper privatisation at the municipal level. Other than such political opposition, the other major problem is a poor legal framework. Expected to be improved, these legislative changes will also be accompanied by new laws for bankruptcy and auditing standards.

There has been relatively little restructuring of the Armenian state industrial sector and much-needed recapitalisation is lacking because of the insider nature of privatisation. Many companies are technically insolvent or highly indebted. As in other former Soviet republics, the largest loss-makers are in capital goods and primary production.

The enterprises with the best prospects are in food-processing, light manufacturing and construction materials. Based on vouchers already distributed to the public, the privatisation programme has led to a tight

COUNTRY PROFILE — ARMENIA

Industry (contd): the extraction and processing of natural resources, particularly ores and chemicals. Other industries are mechanical engineering, electronic generators, textiles, synthetic rubber, wine and cognac, mineral water and food processing. Privatisation legislation introduced in February 1991. Armenia still feels the effects of the 1988 earthquake which destroyed enterprises, workplaces and buildings that accounted for 40 per cent of the country's manufacturing. According to the Armenian Statistics Department, only 93 businesses were in operation within the Industry Ministry during the first quarter of 1993. Large-scale privatisation began in 1994. Foreign investment encouraged and some success achieved from emigrés. In 1996 the Kanaz aluminium smelter is being upgraded, a new copper smelter in Alaverdi in north-west Armenia is being designed, Armenia is looking for investment in two new copper smelters, and construction of a gold refinery in Yerevan is planned.

Mining

The sector accounted for 2 per cent of GNP in 1994 and employed 3 per cent of the workforce. Large deposits of copper, zinc, aluminium and other metals, including gold. In 1995 the mining and metallurgical industry posted overall output up 66 per cent on 1994.

Energy

Reliant on imported energy from Russia, Turkmenistan and Iran; Armenia is being connected to the Iranian power grid in 1996. Due to a severe energy shortage, the nuclear power station at Medzamor, which was put into operation in 1979 and halted in spring 1989 for safety reasons, was restarted in 1996.

Stock exchange

There is a commodity exchange in Yerevan but it is only trading on a minimal level.

Membership of international organisations

CIS, CSCE, EU Special Guest Status (from 26 January 1996), IAEA, IDA, IMF, NACC, NAM (observer), UN, World Bank.

BUSINESS GUIDE

Time

GMT +3 hrs.

Climate

The average winter temperature in Yerevan is -4 degrees C, while summer averages 25 degrees C. Annual rainfall in Yerevan averages 33 cm but is much higher in mountain regions.

Entry requirements

Passport: Required by all.
Visa: Nationals of all CIS countries, Bulgaria, China, Hungary, Laos, Mongolia, North Korea, Poland, Romania, Slovenia, Serbia-Montenegro (Federal Republic of Yugoslavia) do not require visas.
Customs: Small amount of personal goods duty-free. On arrival declare all foreign currency and valuable items such as jewellery, cameras, computers and musical instruments.

Health precautions

Mandatory: Vaccination certificates are required for cholera or yellow fever if travelling from an infected area.
Advisable: Water precautions recommended (water purification tablets may be useful). It is advisable to be 'in date' for the following immunisations: polio (within 10 years), tetanus (within 10 years), typhoid fever, cholera (within six months), hepatitis 'A' (moderate risk only). There has been a significant increase in the number of cases of diphtheria. While the low dose, adult booster is unavailable, travellers are advised to be boosted with a reduced dose (0.1ml) of the paediatric single antigen vaccine. If never immunised, use three dose course of the vaccine. Any medicines required by the traveller should be taken by the visitor, and it could be wise to have precautionary antibiotics if going outside major urban centres. A travel kit including a disposable syringe is a reasonable precaution.

Air access

National airline: Armenian Airlines.
Other airlines: Aeroflot.

Surface access

Road: A 192-metre road bridge over the Araks river, linking Armenia with Iran, was opened in Armenia in January 1996. The cost totalled US$2.46m, of which Iran contributed about US$1m.
Rail: Two single track rail lines pass through Azerbaijan to Russia. These have been subject to disruptions due to blockade. Armenia lacks established rail links.

concentration of share ownership, mainly because many Armenians have been forced to sell their vouchers for much needed cash rather than invest in privatised companies.

Secondary share trading has been beset by scandals involving so-called privatisation investment funds often controlled by local organised crime rings. Tighter official regulation of their activities is expected in 1996/97.

Considerable hard currency resources are thought to be in private hands in Armenia. Once used to finance basic consumption, more of this money may be productively invested in local enterprises in the future. Externally, political and economic uncertainties have precluded higher foreign direct investment (FDI). At the end of 1995, total FDI was only US$22 million.

The large-scale privatisations planned for 1996/97 may lead to increased FDI, principally by *émigré* investors in the first instance. Among other things, the government plans direct sales of newly privatised assets to foreign investors. Partly financed by the World Bank and the European Bank for Reconstruction and Development (EBRD), a recently created Private Investment Finance Corporation (PIFCO) is also to be used to encourage *émigré*-sourced FDI. Another recent initiative, the Armenia Business Forum, aims to increase FDI from the EU, where Armenia has particularly close relations with France. In September 1995, the Armenian parliament approved a number of key economic agreements with the US, including a bilateral investment guarantee treaty. North America is now expected to be the main source of FDI in the future.

A particular priority for the government in 1996 was telecommunications. Within the CIS, Armenia's close relations with Russia have already resulted in increased Russian FDI, notably in the form of debt-for-equity swaps in the country's energy sector. Regionally, another rising economic player is Iran.

External trade

With increasing output and improved payments Armenia's foreign trade recorded an improvement in 1995. Totalling US$874 million, Armenia's foreign trade turnover exceeded officially recorded GDP. Excluding unrecorded cross-border trade, which is thought to be substantial, total exports in 1995 were US$255 million, compared to US$209 million in 1994. Highly orientated towards the CIS, where Russia alone received over 80 per cent of Armenia's exports in 1995, the republic's exports are mainly foodstuffs, raw materials, intermediate products and consumer goods. Capital goods exports, on the other hand, continue to decline. Structurally, Armenia's reliance on relatively lower added value exports and bilateral barter are the two major weaknesses of its foreign trade. Exports to non-CIS markets remain relatively insignificant, mainly because of Armenia's isolation and an internationally uncompetitive industrial sector.

Armenia's trade with Iran is growing. Under different political circumstances, Turkey could become a major trading partner of Armenia and its gateway to the EU. Political factors will also determine whether or not there is a revival of once significant Armenian-Azeri trade in the future.

In 1995, imports increased substantially, mainly because of improved payments and better transport links with Russia; total imports were US$619 million, compared to US$401 million in 1994. Significantly, Armenia's imports were broadly divided between CIS and non-CIS suppliers, of which the EU was the most important.

The government now aims to diversify its energy supplies, notably from Iran. Local energy use efficiency is also to be improved. Another growing trend is higher imports of consumer goods, mainly from Turkey. Imports of capital goods from non-CIS suppliers are also rising. But because imports substantially exceed exports, a record trade deficit of US$364 million was recorded in 1995, compared to US$192 million in 1994; this deficit is set to increase in the future.

BUSINESS DIRECTORY — ARMENIA

Public holidays

1 Jan (New Year's Day), 6 Jan (Orthodox Christmas), 7 Apr (Women's Day), 24 Apr (Day of Remembrance of the Victims of the Genocide), 9 May (Victory and Peace Day), 28 May (Declaration of First Republic, 1918), 5 Jul (Constitution Day), 21 Sep (Independence Day), 7 Dec (Day of Remembrance of the Victims of the Earthquake, 1988).

Working hours

Business: (Mon–Fri) 0900–1800 (appointments best between 0900–1000).
Shops: (Mon) 0800–1900, (Tue–Sat) 0800–2100.

Telecommunications

Telephone and telefax: Since 27 May 1995 Armenia has had direct telephone links via satellite with more than 50 countries worldwide, replacing the previous routeing via Moscow. There were 587,000 main telephone lines in operation in 1994, 15.6 main lines per 100 inhabitants. Dialling code for Armenia, IDD access code + 374 (formerly 7 885), followed by area code (8852 for Yerevan), followed by subscriber's number.

Banking

Many of the country's older banks need new regulations while newer ones have no experience in commercial banking. Many banks are insolvent and make too many risky loans.
Central bank: Central Bank of the Republic of Armenia.
Other banks: See 'Business Directory, Banking'.

Business information

The government has set up a commission to sell off some 10,000 smaller enterprises, 700 larger firms and 4,000 unfinished construction sites. It hoped to privatise all small-scale enterprises and about 25 per cent of the large manufacturing concerns by end-1995.

BUSINESS DIRECTORY

Hotels

Yerevan (area code 8852)
Ani, 19 Sayat-Nova Avenue (tel: 523-961; fax: 151-514).

Armenia, 1 Vramshapouh Arkai Street (tel: 525-383; fax: 151-802).

Bass, 3 Aygedzor Street (tel: 221-353).

Dvin, 40 Paronian Street (tel: 536-343; fax: 151-528).

Hrazdan, 72 Pionerakan Street (tel: 535-332/302; fax: 537-095).

Chambers of commerce

Chamber of Commerce and Industry of the Republic of Armenia, ul Alaverdyana 39, 375010 Yerevan (tel: 565-438; fax: 565-071).

Banking

Ardshinbank of the Republic of Armenia, 3 Deghatan St, Yerevan (tel: 560-611; fax: 151-155).

Armagrobank, 7a Movses Khorenacu Street, 375015 Yerevan (tel: 534-341; fax: 390-712/6).

Armeconombank, 32 G Nzdehi Street, 375026 Yerevan (tel: 562-705, 531-115; fax: 151-149).

Armimex Bank, 2 Nalbandian Street, 375010 Yerevan (tel: 589-927, 567-183; fax: 151-786, 151-815).

Credit, 2/8 Vramshapouh Arkay Street, 375010 Yerevan (tel: 589-065; fax: 580-083).

Erebuni, 13 Khagakh-Don Street, 375097 Yerevan (tel and fax: 577-256).

Haykap, 22 Sarian Street, 375002 Yerevan (tel: 532-080; fax: 390-703/3).

Mellat, 1 P Byusandy, Yerevan (tel: 581-354; fax: 151-811).

Midland Armenia Bank, 1 Vramghapouh Arkai Street, Yerevan (tel: 563-229, 151-717; fax: 151-886).

National Bank of the Republic of Armenia (central bank), 6 Nalbandian Street, 375010 Yerevan (tel: 583-841; fax: 583-882).

Prometeus, 19 Kochari Street, 375012 Yerevan (tel: 273-000; fax: 274-818).

Travel information

Armenian Airlines, Zvarnots Airport, 375042 Yerevan-42 (tel: 773-313).

Other useful addresses

Armenian Foreign Trade Organisation, V/O Armentorg, Dom Pravitelstva, Ploschad Lenina, 375010 Yerevan.

Armenian State Foreign Economic and Trade Association, Str 25 Hr Kochar, 375012 Yerevan (tel: 224-310; fax: 220-034).

The large trade deficit in 1995 resulted in a record current account deficit of US$183 million, compared to US$15 million in 1994. Foreign capital inflows of all types are growing rapidly, and since 1994 Armenia's capital account has benefited from around US$500 million worth of foreign loans. *Emigré* hard currency remittances are thought to have exceeded this figure over the last two years. FDI, however, remains relatively low, as does other service income.

The present political difficulties with Azerbaijan means that Armenia does not figure in the pipeline building plans of the AIOC, although it is the shortest direct route between the Azeri oilfields and Turkey. Another longer-term possibility is tourism, including visiting émigrés. In this context, the Armenian diaspora is over twice the size of the present population of Armenia.

Foreign debt

Mainly provided by the IMF, the World Bank and other foreign multilateral and bilateral creditors, Armenia's foreign borrowings have become substantial in recent years. In 1995, total foreign debt reached US$1.5 billion, compared to US$1 billion in 1994. New foreign borrowings are expected to remain significant in the future. Given that foreign debt already exceeds GDP, this could lead to debt servicing problems for Armenia in due course, although much of this borrowing has been on highly concessionary terms. In relation to Russia, Armenia has also benefited from large inter-state rouble credits and energy supply debt reschedulings in recent years. Domestically, one result of this has been growing hard currency reserves, which were around US$500 million at the end of 1995, compared to around US$250 million at the end of 1994.

Most of the hard currency currently circulating in Armenia remains in the form of cash, mainly because of doubts about local commercial banks and widespread tax evasion. Government policy is to seek to harness these resources through better CBA regulation of local commercial banks and, related to this, the elimination of organised crime influences in financial services.

Despite having the IMF's seal of approval, Armenia has so far been unable to obtain significant western commercial bank funding. This may change in the longer-term. One positive development in this area was the opening of the Midland-Armenian Bank in 1996. In the longer-term, the government plans to privatise a number of local commercial banks, probably beginning with Armagrobank in 1996 or 1997; the PIFCO is expected to play a major role. The EBRD is also reported to be interested in acquiring equity stakes in domestic commercial banks and other financial institutions in the future.

Outlook

Having survived a robust challenge in the September 1996 presidential election, where he proved vulnerable to opposition attacks over the state of the economy and its domination by a shadowy alliance of the old communist elite and underworld structures, Levon Ter-Petrosian is now in a position to consolidate his political dominance in Armenia more or less indefinitely.

The Armenian-Azeri conflict over the status of Nagorno-Karabakh and associated territories in Azerbaijan could once again flare into open warfare in the near future. The only external factor that could induce a major change of policy towards Azerbaijan in Armenia would be the withdrawal of western financial support. However, this seems very unlikely given the power of the Armenian lobby and the country's role as a model economic reformer. The success of Armenia's economic reform programme is a positive development achieved in very difficult circumstances. Whether or not this continues will largely be determined by external factors. The continuation of foreign financial support is thus of vital economic importance.

BUSINESS DIRECTORY — ARMENIA

Useful addresses (contd):

British Embassy, Armenia Hotel, 1 Vramshapouh Arka Str, 375010 Yerevan (tel: 234-1211; fax: 215-1807).

Committee of Privatisation and Management of State Property, Ul Budakhian 1, 375014 Yerevan (tel: 280-120).

Ministry of Agriculture and Food Supplies, 1 Government House, Republican Square, 375010 Yerevan (tel: 524-641; fax: 151-086, 151-583).

Ministry of Communications, 22 Sarian Street, 375002 Yerevan (tel: 526-632; fax: 151-446, 151-151).

Ministry of Culture, Youth and Sports, 5 Toumanian Street, 375010 Yerevan (tel: 528-869, 561-920; fax: 523-930, 523-922, 526-869).

Ministry of Defence, Proshian Settlement, 60 G. Shaush Road, Yerevan (tel: 357-822; fax: 526-560).

Ministry of Ecology and Natural Resources, 35 Moskovian Street, 375012 Yerevan (tel: 530-741; fax: 534-902).

Ministry of Economy, 1 Government House, Republican Square, 375010 Yerevan (tel: 527-342; fax: 151-069).

Ministry of Education and Science, 13 Movses Khorenatsi Street, 375010 Yerevan (tel: 526-602; fax: 151-150).

Ministry of Energy, 1 Government House, Republican Square, 375010 Yerevan (tel: 521-964; fax: 151-036).

Ministry of Finance, 1 Melik-Adamian Street, 375010 Yerevan (tel: 527-082; fax: 151-154).

Ministry of Foreign Affairs, 2 Government House, 1 Republican Square, 375010 Yerevan (tel: 523-531; fax: 151-042).

Ministry of Health, 8 Tumanian Street, 375001 Yerevan (tel: 582-413; fax: 151-097).

Ministry of Industry, 4 Y Kochar Street, 375033 Yerevan (tel: 226-500, 221-309; fax: 151-058).

Ministry for Inter-Governmental Matters (tel: 520-321).

Ministry of Justice, 8 Parliament Street, 375010 Yerevan (tel: 582-157).

Ministry of Local Government Affairs (tel: 525-274).

Ministry of Social Affairs, 18 Issahakian Street, 375025 Yerevan (tel: 565-321; fax: 151-920).

Ministry of Trade, Services and Tourism, 69 Terian Street, 375008 Yerevan (tel: 562-591, 538-321; fax: 151-675, 151-081).

Ministry of Transport, 10 Zakiyan Street, 375015 Yerevan (tel: 563-391; fax: 525-268).

Ministry of Urban Planning and Construction, 1 Government House, Republican Square, Yerevan (tel: 525-274; fax: 151-036).

Prime Minister's Office, 1 Government House, Republican Square, 375101 Yerevan (tel: 520-360; fax: 151-035).

Secretariat of the Council of Ministers (tel: 520-933, 522-482).

State Commission for Statistics and Data (tel: 524-213).

State Commission for Tax Inspection (tel: 538-101, 538-073).

State TV and Radio, 5 Alex Manoogian, 375025 Yerevan (tel: 555-033).

Austria

Bob Jiggins

For Austria, a new member of the European Union (EU), due in October 1996 to conduct the first elections for the European Parliament, some considerable economic changes lie ahead. The traditional neutral status of the country is likewise under pressure, with the agreement to allow NATO troops and equipment to transit en route for Bosnia-Herzegovina. Politically, the recent general election confirmed the desire of the electorate for stability rather than radical change.

Election

A crisis between the ruling Social Democratic Party (SPÖ) and the rightist People's Party (ÖVP) regarding the 1996 budget triggered the general election of 17 December 1995. Although the result was expected to be close, it was also widely predicted that the ÖVP would win.

Instead, the electorate decided to remain with stability and thus opted for the more leftward inclined SPÖ. Both these main parties increased their share of the vote at the expense of the extreme right-wing and nationalist party, the Freedom Alliance. Of the 183 members of parliament, 71 are from the SPÖ, 53 are from the ÖVP, 40 from the Freedom Party (FPÖ), 10 from the Liberal Forum (LF), and 9 Greens.

Although the SPÖ was ultimately successful, polling prior to the election indicated that most voters were undecided, with others frequently changing their voting intentions. This trend towards greater fluidity within Austrian politics started in 1994, when decades of the ÖVP-SPÖ consensus resulted in the terrain being dominated by three medium parties and two smaller ones.

KEY FACTS — *Austria*

Official title: Republik Österreich (Republic of Austria)

Head of state: Federal President Dr Thomas Klestil

Head of government: Federal Chancellor Viktor Klima (Sozialdemokratische Partei (Social Democratic Party) (SPÖ))

Ruling party: Coalition of Sozialdemokratische Partei (Social Democratic Party) (SPÖ) and conservative ÖsterreichischeVolkspartei (People's Party) (ÖVP)

Capital: Vienna

Official Languages: German

Currency: Austrian Schilling (S) = 100 Groschen

Exchange rate: S10.94 per US$ (Dec 1996)

Area: 83,855 sq km

Population: 8.04m (1995)

GDP per capita: US$28,980 (1995)

GDP real growth: 0.3% (4th qtr 1996, not seasonally adjusted)

GNP per capita: US$24,950 (1994)

Unemployment: 7% (Apr 1996)

Inflation: 2.1% (12 months to Oct 1996, consumer prices, not seasonally adjusted)

Trade balance: -US$8.1bn (12 months to Dec 1995, not seasonally adjusted)

Visitor numbers: 117.1m (1995, overnight bookings)

Neutrality fades

Austria has for many years been proud of its neutrality but recent developments indicate, as in Switzerland, that this may be set to change. Early in 1996 the US ambassador, Swanee Hunt, informed the Austrian government of the existence of covert Central Intelligence Agency (CIA) weapons dumps left behind when US troops departed in 1955. The official line is that the dumps were merely forgotten, but the suspicion is that this was part of an attempt to bring Austria firmly into the NATO, and hence US, orbit. Like similar discoveries in Italy it has kindled a debate over US influence during the Cold War, and hence the real extent of national sovereignty.

Other events are more mundane. With membership of the EU Austria now sends 21 MEPs to the European Parliament in Strasbourg, but these have been selected; direct elections were scheduled for October 1996. There is now increased pressure to participate in the Western European Union (WEU) and perhaps in NATO. These changes are being proposed from groups within the rightist ÖVP and are opposed by the more leftwing SPÖ, which remembers the way in which the right used the armed forces against the socialists in 1934. Another proposal – this time from the Austrian left in the shape of the SPÖ's interior minister, Caspar Einem – is for the army to be abolished and replaced with a strengthened police force and a small armed force to participate in international detachments. Although this has sparked an intense debate in Austria, and provoked further friction between the coalition partners, it is beyond dispute that military expenditure has decreased since the end of the Cold War. The army has already been reduced from 200,000 to 120,000 personnel, and the share of GDP spent on the military is currently 0.9 per cent; this is the second lowest in Europe.

Budget

Budgeting for the deficit was responsible for the December 1995 general election – the deadlock between the coalition partners was unbreakable. Both the SPÖ and the ÖVP wish to see the deficit reduced to below 3 per cent of GDP in 1997, as this is the target for entry into European Monetary Union (EMU). The budgets for both 1996 and 1997 are being negotiated together; the deficits are targeted at 3.7 per cent and 2.7 per cent respectively, down from 5.5 per cent in 1995. Cuts in public expenditure will be made and taxes will be increased to save some US$9.9 billion over the two years. Consequently, growth should not rise much in the short term, perhaps by only 1.4 per cent in 1996, with a slight increase to 1.9 per cent in 1997.

The deficit reduction package will be effected by spreading the load across cuts in expenditure (66 per cent) and increased taxes (33 per cent). The tax increases will be mainly targeted at groups with above average income, as appropriate to the socially minded nature of the SPÖ. Increased taxes on business, with the exception of so-called 'green' energy taxes for environmental purposes, will be avoided.

Most public expenditure cuts are to be targeted at subsidies to public sector enterprises, a reduction in the number of civil servants, and a restructuring of the state's contribution to pension funds.

Unemployment, which was 8.7 per cent in the first quarter of 1996, could rise still further – the public-sector has traditionally been used as a buffer to keep Austria's unemployment rate low. Some 70 per cent of graduates traditionally find employment within this sector, and hence there are now substantial rises in graduate unemployment and a general lowering of starting wages to be expected.

Growth

Annual economic growth in 1995 reached 1.8 per cent according to government statistics, with the largest growth coming in the first and second quarters of the year (2.7 per cent and 3.0 per cent respectively). In the third quarter, growth fell sharply to 1.4 per cent and again in the fourth quarter to 0.3 per cent.

The sharp drop can be partially explained by cuts in public expenditure, and growth in this area has been falling steadily from year-on-year figures of 2.7 per cent at the beginning of 1994, to 1.2 per cent in the third quarter of 1995. The slow-down in the construction industry and in tourism are also to blame. Industrial production rose by an average of 5 per cent in 1995 compared with the previous year.

Inflation

The inflation rate in 1995 was 2.2 per cent, the lowest since 1988, and fell further to 1.7 per cent in the first quarter of 1996. The Austrian Chamber of Commerce said that prices would have been up by 3 per cent in 1995 if the country had not joined the EU.

Consumer prices were just 1.5 per cent higher in February 1996 than in the same period in 1995. This was the lowest rate since 1987 and is largely as a result of entry into the EU and the slowdown in growth. The EU average is a higher 3.1 per cent. EU membership has meant some substantial changes in government policy, in particular the phasing out of agricultural subsidies in the form of price controls. Prices tended to rise in sectors other than manufacturing. Services averaged an

KEY INDICATORS

	Unit	1991	1992	1993	1994	1995
Population	m	7.81	7.91	7.99	8.03	8.04
Gross domestic product (GDP)	US$bn	162.0	186.2	181.2	195.6	–
GDP per capita	US$	20,740	23,270	22,790	24,700	28,980
GDP real growth	%	3.0	1.5	-0.5	2.6	1.8
Inflation	%	3.3	4.0	2.6	3.0	2.2
Unemployment	%	3.7	4.0	4.8	4.4	6.8
Wages (monthly earnings)	1990=100	105.2	110.3	116.1	120.7	–
Consumer prices	1990=100	103.3	107.5	111.4	114.7	117.3
Share prices	1990=100	85.2	66.9	65.5	74.9	64.9
Agricultural production	1979-81=100	113.03	109.67	111.25	111.86	109.57
Industrial production	1990=100	101.5	100.4	98.4	102.4	–
Coal production	m toe	0.7	0.6	0.6	0.5	0.4
Exports (FOB)	S bn	479.03	487.56	467.66	511.89	–
Imports (CIF)	S bn	591.90	593.92	565.56	629.42	–
Balance of trade	US$m	-8,597	-8,841	-7,825	-8,900	-8,700
Current account	US$m	-61	-631	-762	-2,452	–
Total reserves minus gold	US$m	10,332	12,383	14,610	16,822	18,730
Foreign exchange	US$m	9,655	11,506	13,866	16,088	17,867
Discount rate	%	8.00	8.00	5.25	4.50	3.00
Exchange rate	S per US$	11.68	10.99	11.63	11.42	10.09

annual rise of 3.7 per cent in 1995, and housing and fuel prices were particularly changeable. Housing costs for the final quarter of 1995 were calculated to have risen by some 8 per cent and energy prices by 5.8 per cent, of which only a small proportion can be explained by the increase in tax. The increase in energy prices looks set to continue well into the third quarter of 1996.

External trade

EU membership has required changes to the way in which Austria calculates its trade, and consequently there is little data of an official nature to evaluate. At the time of writing the Austrian government had not released trade data for 1995, and thus the following information comes from other sources. According to the Chamber of Commerce, whose figures give a good guide, both import and export growth have been slowing in the second half of 1995. Compared with year earlier figures, export growth slowed from 13.6 per cent in the first half of 1995 to 6.7 per cent in the second. Import growth similarly fell, albeit more abruptly, over the same period from 11.6 per cent to 0.7 per cent. In absolute terms exports increased by S51 billion from 1994 to S564 billion in 1995, and imports similarly increased by S38 billion to S667 billion. This would leave a slightly decreased trade deficit of S103 billion in 1995. Other sources broadly confirm this trend with the Austrian Institute for Economic Research (WIFO) reporting export and import growths in 1995 of 9.2 per cent and 7.5 per cent respectively. Data from the central bank corroborates this, as export and import payments decreased markedly in the final months of 1995. There are two probable reasons for the notable decline in import growth: the first is a direct result of EU accession with citizens making more 'suitcase trade' purchases within other EU countries, especially Germany; the second, a slowdown in investment in the final half of 1995. The latest figures for January 1996 suggest that exports have now increased substantially (by some 23 per cent) over the previous year leaving a balance of payments surplus of S6.5 billion.

Investment and privatisation

Austria's entry into the EU in January 1995 has prompted a major influx of investment – some US$5 billion to date. A large part of this has been directed into the western province of Vorarlberg where, since the positive referendum on EU membership, 85 foreign firms have set up business. They have contributed to a regional growth rate of 13 per cent in the third quarter of 1995. Much of the investment has been by Austrian subsidiaries of foreign firms, and as such does not appear in the foreign direct investment (FDI) statistics. Typical of this is Opel Austria, a subsidiary of the US General Motors, which is investing S7.5 billion in production near Vienna over the next two years. Other firms committed to major investment, albeit of a lower order, include BMW-Austria, Siemens-Austria and Hoffmann-La Roche.

Various privatisations and takeovers have also taken place, with South Korea's Daewoo in particular now placed for a major assault on the European market for diesel engines by the purchase of 65 per

COUNTRY PROFILE — AUSTRIA

Historical profile

For centuries the Austrian (later Austro–Hungarian) Empire covered most of central Europe.
1918 Defeat in First World War; independence and declaration of first Austrian Republic. Three-quarters of Empire's territory ceded to neighbouring states.
1920–21 Many deaths from starvation in hyperinflation.
1938 *Anschluss* (link-up) with Germany on invasion by Hitler.
1945–55 Defeat in Second World War; Austria divided into four zones of occupation by the USA, Great Britain, France and USSR. Conservative People's Party and Socialist Party in coalition government.
1955 Independence; declaration of second Austrian Republic.
1966 People's Party in power after 20 years of coalition.
1970–87 Socialist Party in power, until 1983 alone, and then in coalition with the liberal Freedom Party.
1986 Presidential election won by former foreign minister and UN secretary general, Dr Kurt Waldheim (independent but with People's Party backing). Controversy surrounded allegations of his implication in Nazi atrocities in the Balkans (1942–45), culminating in his listing as an undesirable alien by the US Department of Justice.
1987 Following an inconclusive election, formation of Socialist Party/People's Party coalition.

Political system

Federal democratic republic with nine *Länder* (states), each with its own state legislature and government. Bicameral parliament consisting of the *Nationalrat*, whose 183 constituent members are elected every four years by proportional representation, and the *Bundesrat*, containing 63 members elected for various terms by the state legislatures and reflecting party political strengths there. Executive power rests with the head of the federal government, who is the chancellor and usually the leader of the largest party in the *Nationalrat*. The president is elected by popular vote every six years. The one-year-old governing coalition collapsed on 12 October 1995 over the 1996 budget. In the general election held on 17 December 1995, the official results gave the Social Democratic Party 71 deputies in the 183-seat parliament, as against 65 won in the last election in October 1994. The conservative People's Party took 53 seats and the right-wing Freedom Party 40. The Greens won nine seats and the Liberal Forum 10.

Political parties

Coalition government of Sozialdemokratische Partei (Social Democratic Party) (SPÖ) and Österreichische Volkspartei (People's Party) (ÖVP). Other major parties: Freiheitliche Partei Österreichs (Freedom Party of Austria) (FPÖ); die Grüne Alternative (Green Alternative) (GA); Vereinte Grüne Österreichs (United Greens) (VGÖ); Liberales Forum (Liberal Forum) (LF).

Population

Around 93 per cent are of Austrian nationality. Life expectancy 76 years; birth rate per 11.6 per thousand; death rate 11.2 per thousand (1995). Minorities: Slovenes, Croats, Hungarians and Czechs. Religion: Roman Catholic (75 per cent); Protestant (5 per cent).

Main cities/towns

Vienna (population 1.8m in 1994), Graz, Linz, Salzburg, Innsbruck, Klagenfurt, Villach, Wels, St Poelten, Dornbirn.

Language

The official language is German. About 94 per cent of the Austrian nationals speak German; heavy dialect is in daily use. Linguistic minorities of Slovenes, Croats, Hungarians and Czechs.

Media

Dailies: National dailies include *Kronen Zeitung, Kurier, Die Presse, Der Standard* and *Wiener Zeitung* (government newspaper), all published in Vienna but read throughout the country. Quality regional papers also exist, e.g. *Salzburger Nachrichten*.
Weeklies: Weekend editions of newspapers tend to be bigger than dailies and contain a large amount of advertising. Several weekly illustrated magazines and technical and trade magazines published.
Business: Major business/political magazines include *Profil* (weekly), *Wirtschaftwoche-Austria* (weekly), *Gewinn* (weekly) and *Trend* (monthly). German magazines are also widely read. The only English business magazine published is *Europe Business & Economy* (bi-monthly).
Broadcasting: With satellite broadcasting and the trend to deregulation, state-run corporations control of radio and TV likely to diminish. Private radio stations began operating 1990.
Radio: Approximately 2.7m receivers in use. There are three national programmes, 10 local programmes and an overseas service. In Vienna, Radio Blue Danube broadcasts in English, French and Spanish; and Austrian National Radio (ORF) puts out a news summary in English each morning at 0805 and in French at 0810.
Television: There are two channels broadcast for an average of 12–15 hours per day. Videotext on a limited scale. Skychannel, Superchannel and cable increasingly available.
Advertising: Adspend per head US$170 a year (1995). Covers all media. TV advertising is popular but restricted facilities and high demand means space must be booked several months in advance. Newspapers (especially weekend editions) and magazines are also popular. Poster sites are available under the auspices of the Municipal Authorities. Advertising in cinemas and by direct mail is also widely used. Information can be obtained from Osterreichischer Werberat in Vienna (tel: 50-105/0). Main media for adverts: newspapers, TV and magazines. Major categories advertised: retail, services and food.

Domestic economy

Gradual shift of economic base since 1950s from agriculture to heavy industry and services. The pace of change has led to growth in cent of the shares in Steyr-Daimler Puch. The Steyr group is currently making a loss and is a subsidiary of the state owned bank Creditanstalt Bankverein. The bank is scheduled for privatisation and the sale of the engineering group should enhance its attractiveness and eventual profitability. Delays have however occurred due to scandals involving Daewoo in its South Korea home, and the reluctance of Creditanstalt Bankverein to relax its insistence on a degree of employment protection.

Austria has recently embarked on a privatisation programme, and large parts of the former state-owned Austrian Industries Group have been split and sold off. Most of these have turned deficits into respectable profits, in particular the steel firm Boehler-Uddeholm which reported a 600 per cent increase in profits in the first three quarters of 1995, and VA-Stahl which announced a 400 per cent increase over the same period.

Elsewhere, the proposed new Brenner tunnel appears to be running into difficulties. This 240 km long tunnel linking Germany and Italy is proving however to be expensive costing perhaps as much as S280 billion. The EU reportedly offered some S30 billion towards the construction and S800 million for planning, but this is effectively a very small drop in an extremely large ocean as far as Austria is concerned. A final decision is, however, some years off. The European Investment Bank (EIB) has granted a loan of S9.6 billion towards rail development in Austria, to which must be added another S12 billion provided by the government.

Within the field of communications, the bidding process which commenced in 1995 for the cellular mobile phone network has ended. This is the first private network to be established in Austria (the postal service already has one in operation) and the contract has been won by Ö-call, one of the five bidding consortia. Ö-call is comprised of Siemens; De-Te Mobil; BAWAG; Kronenzeitung; the Bundesländerverischerung; EA-Generali; and the Bayerische Landesbank. This opening up of the cellular network is to be followed by the gradual abolition of the PTT monopoly in providing land-based data and voice networks. EU regulations are such that liberalisation must be complete by 1998.

Outlook

The outlook for Austria in the medium and long term looks good, although the impact of the austerity policies are expected to have an impact on growth and unemployment. GDP will increase perhaps at around 1.4 per cent in 1996 rising to 1.9 per cent in 1997, while unemployment will probably remain in the region of 6.6 per cent in 1996, and slightly higher the following year. The tax increases on certain items are expected to keep inflation at around the 2 per cent mark or so for most of 1997. Politically, entry into a wider Europe in the form of the EU is expected to keep the debate over the Western European Union (WEU) and NATO alive, with the right arguing for the abandonment of neutrality. This is the issue which will form the major fault line between the two main parties, the SPÖ and the ÖVP, and in the years ahead could well make for a stormy relationship.

COUNTRY PROFILE — AUSTRIA

Domestic economy (contd): industrial output, high living standards and moderate levels of unemployment. Large public sector with government investment in industry now being partly privatised. Economy also characterised by heavy dependence on tourism and trade with Germany. Broad consensus among trades unions, business and government on commitment towards full employment and sustained economic growth. Government economic policy directed towards reducing the budget deficit and debt burden and keeping inflation down. The sharp decline in the German economy affected Austria, yet in 1993, the country's economic performance already fulfilled almost all the criteria for economic and monetary union.

Employment

Wage increases moderated in line with inflation which, with strong productivity gains, have led to a gradual decline in unit labour costs. Industrial relations are very good, with no major disputes. About 40 per cent of the workforce is female.

External trade

Regular trade deficit owing to growth in import demand for both consumer and capital goods. However, income from tourism and net capital inflows largely offset trade deficit. In January 1995 Austria became member of EU.

Exports: Major exports include machinery and transport equipment, chemicals (chiefly plastics and pharmaceuticals) and manufactured goods. Main destinations: Germany (38.1% of 1994 total), Italy (8.1%), Switzerland (6.4%), USA (3.5%), Japan 1.6%), other EU countries (16.7%), eastern Europe (13.6%), other countries (9.5%), other EFTA countries (2.5%).

Imports: Major imports are mineral fuels, chemicals, machinery, foodstuffs and consumer durables.

Main sources: Germany (40% of 1994 total), Italy (8.8%), USA (4.4%), Japan (4.3%), Switzerland (4.1%), other EU countries (17.1%), other countries (10%), eastern Europe (8%), other EFTA countries (2.8%).

Agriculture

Contributed 3 per cent to GDP in 1994 and employed 6.9 per cent of the labour force. About 18.2 per cent of land is crop land, 24.1 per cent permanent pasture land, and 39 per cent forests and woodland. Dominated by small scale farming (50 per cent of farms cover less than 10ha), although trend is towards larger, more mechanised units leading to increased productivity. Farming is concentrated in Upper Austria, the northern part of Lower Austria, Burgenland and Styria. Principal products are milk, beef, veal, pork, sugar-beet, maize, barley, wheat and wine, but government is encouraging diversification to oilseeds, herbs, spices, hops and fast-growing timber. Although output fluctuates, the country remains almost 90 per cent self-sufficient. Forestry remains a major source of income within agriculture.

Industry

Contributed 35.3 per cent to GDP in 1994 and employed 33.8 per cent of the labour force. Nationalised companies administered by holding company, Austrian Industries, account for 17 per cent total industrial output and produce about 18 per cent of exports. In 1987, however, the government initiated a series of reorganisations and privatisations, aimed at reducing inefficiency and bureaucracy. Traditional industries such as steel and textiles have been declining in recent years, and government industrial policy is to switch from these to newer industries such as electronics, chemicals and vehicles. Austria's only smelter closed at the end of 1992. In 1993 the paper export industry was in crisis due to worldwide overcapacity, and Hallein-Papier, the largest industrial company in Salzburg, was forced into liquidation. The annual change in industrial production was 4.7 per cent in 1995.

Mining

The mining sector accounted for 0.7 per cent of GDP in 1994 and employed 1 per cent of the workforce. Deposits of various minerals, notably magnesite (world's largest producer), iron, lead and zinc ores, salt, graphite, coal and gypsum. Commercial exploitation restricted by very small number of viable deposits and geological difficulties.

Hydrocarbons

Coal production 0.5m tonnes oil equivalent (1994), down by 16.7 per cent on 1993 output.

Energy

Despite successful energy conservation programme and increase in local oil and gas production, still heavy dependence on energy imports, especially gas from the former USSR. Domestic oil and gas reserves are expected to be depleted by early 1990s. Environmentalist opposition has caused the only nuclear power station (at Zwentendorf) to be dismantled, unused. Hydroelectric power is the mainstay of Austria's electricity supply, accounting for 70 per cent of total production. Austria is the leading European nation in terms of solar energy utilisation.

Stock exchange

The Vienna Stock Exchange, one of the smallest in Western Europe, launched an all-electronic trading system in June 1996.

Legal system

Civil law system with Roman law origins. Constitution adopted 1920 – repromulgated 1945.

Membership of international organisations

AG (observer), CERN, Council of Europe, CSCE, EEA, ESA, EU (from 1 Jan 1995), IAEA, IDA, IFC, IMF, NAM (guest), OECD, World Bank, WTO.

BUSINESS GUIDE

Time

GMT +1 (GMT +2 from late Mar to late Sep).

BUSINESS GUIDE — AUSTRIA

Climate

Moderate central European. Wide variations in temperature with altitude, from -4°C (Jan) to 25°C (Jul). Winters are cold with considerable snowfall, but summers can be very warm. Wettest months are May to August. Snow Dec–Mar, warm and sunny May–Oct.

Entry requirements

Visa: Holders of British and Irish passports do not require a visa to enter Austria. Visas are required by nationals of some Commonwealth countries. For changing planes at the airport, nationals of the following countries require visas: Afghanistan, Bangladesh, Ghana, Iraq, Iran, Liberia, Libya, Nigeria, Pakistan, Somalia, Sri Lanka and Zaïre.
Health: Vaccination certificates required if travelling from infected areas. Recommended immunisations: tetanus and inoculation against tick-bites when visiting countryside in summer.
Currency: Exchange controls have been abolished.
Customs: Personal baggage and items for personal use not dutiable.

Air access:

Regular flights operated by most international airlines.
National airlines: Austrian Airlines, also Lauda Air and Tyrolean Airways.
Main international airport: Schwechat (VIE) 18 km south-east of Vienna.
International airports: Graz (GRZ), 12 km from city, Salzburg (SZG), 4 km west of city, Innsbruck (INN), Klagenfurt (KLU), 4 km north of city, Linz (LNZ), 15 km from city.

Surface access

Good rail and road links with all surrounding countries. Motorists should check advisability of routes, especially in winter, with OAMTC or ARBO (Austrian automobile clubs).

Hotels

Generally of a high standard with a large selection available in most cities. Classified from five stars to one star. Rates vary according to category but are generally cheaper outside the capital.

Restaurants

Wide choice in Vienna. Service charge of 10.5–15 per cent included in bills. Customary to leave 5 per cent tip as well.

Credit cards

Eurocard, Mastercard and Visa are accepted, and less widely, American Express and Diners Club.

Car hire

Self-drive and chauffeur-driven services available at railway stations, airports and in major cities. Rates per day vary with size of car, plus additional charge per kilometre, and fuel is extra. Also available on weekly basis at cheaper rates. VAT at 20 per cent (32 per cent if rental over 21 days) must be paid but insurance is optional. Speed limit 100 kph on most roads, 130 kph on motorways, in built-up areas 50 kph, unless otherwise stipulated.

City transport

Good public transport network covering all of Vienna. Frequent bus, tram, city railway and metro services. It is advisable to purchase tickets in advance at official salespoints or at a tobacconist (*Trafik*). Block tickets are available for four rides, each to include any transfers within capital's system. Three-day Vienna Card is available from tourist information centres for unlimited travel as well as discounts on a range of key tourist destinations and goods. The Kuring Ring circle tram is a good way to see many of the public buildings and parks.
Taxis: Widely available from stands or via radio/telephone services. Fares are metered but expensive and in some areas zone charges or set charges for standard trips apply, e.g. from Vienna Airport to the city an additional amount is added to the fare to cover the return journey. Tip about 10 per cent.

National transport

Air: Austrian Air Services, Tyrolean Airways and Rheintalflug operate regular flights between Vienna and Graz, Linz, Klagenfurt, Innsbruck and Salzburg. Also between Innsbruck and Graz and Linz; and Linz and Salzburg.
Road: Over 200,000 km of roads including some 1,400 km of motorways and around 35,000 km of main roads.
Rail: State-owned network of almost 6,000 km, most of which is electrified. Also about 20 private railways covering a total 660 km. Frequent intercity service from Vienna to Salzburg, Innsbruck, Graz and Klagenfurt.
Water: 350 km of navigable waterways. Passenger service between Vienna and the Black Sea and on upper Danube. Austrian Federal Railways operate passenger services on all the larger lakes.

Public holidays

Fixed dates: 1 Jan (New Year's Day), 6 Jan (Epiphany), 1 May (Labour Day), 15 Aug (Assumption Day), 26 Oct (National Day), 1 Nov (All Saints' Day), 8 Dec (Immaculate Conception), 25 Dec (Christmas Day), 26 Dec (St Stephen's Day). Each province has a holiday on the day of its patron saint.
Variable dates: Easter, Ascension, Whitsun and Corpus Christi.

Working hours

Government and business: (Mon–Fri) 0800–1230, 1300–1730 (many offices/companies do not work Fridays pm).
Banking: (Mon, Tue, Wed and Fri) 0800–1230 and 1330–1500; (Thu) 0800–1230 and 1330–1730. Banks are closed on Saturdays and Sundays. The exchange counters at airports and main railway stations are usually open from the first to the last plane or train, i.e. from 0800–2200 seven days a week.
Shops: (Mon–Fri) 0800–1830; many shops close for two hours at midday. (Sat) 0800–1300; first Saturday of the month 0800–1700. A law was approved 4 December 1996 to allow shops to remain open until 1930 on weekdays and until 1700 on Saturdays, starting January 1997.

Social customs

Appointments must be made in advance and punctuality is important; the usual form of address is *Herr* or *Frau*, followed by family or surname; handshaking is universal in business and private meetings, both when arriving and leaving. Business is usually conducted in German. For restaurant meetings, dress formally, as for business meetings. Exchange pleasantries for a few minutes before getting down to business. When visiting private homes, it is usual to take flowers or confectionery for the host or hostess. Traditional Austrian food includes *Wienerschnitzel, goulash, knoedel* (dumplings), and *sachertorte* (gateau); lunch is the main meal of the day.

Business language and interpreting/translation

Available through the Interpreters' Institute of Vienna University. Commercial firms can usually find someone to interpret without too much difficulty. The language spoken in Austria is German, but English is widely spoken.

Telecommunications

Telephone and telefax: International dialling code: 43 followed by 1 for Vienna, 512 for Innsbruck, 662 for Salzburg. Reduced rates for calls outside working hours. For IDD access from Austria dial 00.
Telex: Widespread availability. Country code 47 A.
Telegram: Available at any post office.

Postal service

No deliveries on Sat, and only larger post offices open on Sat mornings (0800–1200 hours), with the exception of main station offices in main cities which are open 24 hours a day, seven days a week. Stamps can be purchased at tobacconists and newsagents as well as post offices.

Banking

The largest bank since October 1991 is the Bank Austria followed by Creditanstalt-Bankverein. Both are currently state-controlled, although there are plans for privatisation, and have large industrial holdings of their own and, as financiers to industry, exert wide influence on Austrian business. Full services also provided by savings banks and co-operative banks, whose role is proportionately much greater than that of similar institutions in the English-speaking world. See also 'Business Directory, Banking'.

Trade fairs

Most important is Vienna International Fair held every spring and autumn. Several others including biennial industrial fair held in Graz, Young International Fashion Fair every Mar and Sep in Salzburg, annual timber fair in Klagenfurt, tourism and catering in Innsbruck, textiles in Dornbirn, and many others covering a wide range of industries.

BUSINESS GUIDE

Electricity supply

220 V AC.

Representation in capital

Afghanistan, Algeria, Albania, Argentina, Australia, Belgium, Bolivia, Brazil, Bulgaria, Canada, Chile, China, Colombia, Côte d'Ivoire, Cuba, Denmark, Ecuador, Egypt, Finland, France, Germany, Greece, Guatemala, The Holy See, Hungary, India, Indonesia, Iran, Iraq, Ireland, Israel, Italy, Japan, Korea DPR, Republic of Korea, Kuwait, Lebanon, Libya, Luxembourg, Malaysia, Mexico, Morocco, Netherlands, New Zealand, Nicaragua, Nigeria, Norway, Oman, Pakistan, Panama, Peru, Philippines, Poland, Portugal, Qatar, Romania, Russia, Saudi Arabia, Senegal, South Africa, Spain, Sweden, Switzerland, Thailand, Tunisia, Turkey, UAE, UK, Uruguay, USA, Venezuela, Zaïre.

BUSINESS DIRECTORY

Hotels

Vienna (area code 1)
Ambassador, Neuer Markt 6, A-1010 (tel: 51-466; fax: 513-2999).

Beethoven, Millockergasse 6, A-1060 (tel: 587-4482(0); fax: 587-442).

Bellevue, Althanstrasse 5, A-1091 (tel: 345-631(0); fax: 3456-31801).

Bristol, Karntner Ring 1, A-1015 (tel: 515-160).

Clima City, Theresianumgasse 21a, A-1040 (tel: 505-1696; fax: 650-9604).

Clima Johann Strauss, Favoritenstrasse 12, A-1040 (tel: 505-7624, 657-624; fax: 505-7628).

Clima Villenhotel, Nussberggasse 2C, A-1190 (tel: 371-516; fax: 371-392).

Clima Villenhotel, Nussberggasse 2C, A-1190 (tel: 371-516; fax: 371-392).Cottage, Hasenauerstrasse 12, A-1190 (tel: 312-571/2; fax: 312-571).

Hilton, Am Stadtpark, A-1030 (tel: 717-000; fax: 713-0691).

Holiday Inn, Triester Strasse 72, 1100 (tel: 60-530; fax: 6053-0580).

Hotel am Schubertring, Schubertring 11, A-1010 (tel: 717-020).

Im Palais Schwarzenberg, Schwarzenbergplatz 9, A-1030 (tel: 784-515; fax: 784-714).

Imperial, 1 Kaerntner Ring 16, A-1010 (tel: 50-110/0; fax: 5011-0410).

Inter-Continental, Johannesgasse 28, A-1037 (tel: 71-122; fax: 713-4489).

Kaiserhof, Frankenberggasse 10, A-1040 (tel: 505-1701; fax: 505-8875).

König von Ungarn, Schulerstrasse 10, A-1010 (tel: 51-584; fax: 51-5848).

Marriott, Parkring 12a, A-1010 (tel: 51-518/0; fax: 51-518/6736).

Pullman Belvedere, Am Heumarkt 35-37, A-1030 (tel: 752-535/0; fax: 7525-35844).

Rosen Burgenland, Wilhelm Exner-Gasse 4, A-1090 (tel: 439-122).

Rosen International, Buchfeldgasse 8, A-1080 (tel: 435-291).

Royal, Singerstrasse 3, A-1010 (tel: 51-568; fax: 513-9698).

SAS Palais, Parkring 14, A-1010 (tel: 515-170; fax: 512-2216).

Sacher, Philharmonikerstrasse 4, A-1015 (tel: 51-456; fax: 51-457/8/10).

Savoy, Lindengasse 12, A-1070 (tel: 934-646).

Car hire

Vienna
Budget: Schwechat Airport, 1300 (tel: 7111-02711; fax: 714-7238); Hilton Hotel, Land Str, Haupstr 2A, Amstadtpark, 1030 (tel: 714-6565; fax: 714-7238).

Europcar: Erdbergstrasse 202/1 Ebene Park And Ride U3, 1010 (tel: 799-6176; fax: 505-4129).

Hertz: Kaerntner Ring 17 (tel: 512-8677; fax: 512-5034); Schwechat Airport (tel: 7111-02661; fax: 71111-05395); Simmeringer Haupstrasse 2-4 (tel: 7954-2661; fax: 7135-801601).

Chambers of commerce

Austrian Chamber of Commerce (Wirtschaftskammer Österreich), Wiedner Haupstrasse 63, A-1045, Vienna (tel: 501-050; fax: 5020-6255, 5020-6240).

Banking

Österreichische Nationalbank (central bank), A-1090 Vienna, Otto Wagner-Platz 3 (tel: 40-420/0; tx: 114-778).

BAWAG Bank f. Arbeit und Wirtschaft, Seitzergasse 2 - 4, A-1010 Vienna (tel: 534-530; fax: 5345-32930).

Creditanstalt-Bankverein, Schottengasse 6 - 8, A-1011 Vienna (tel: 531-310; fax: 3133-37566).

Die Erste Österreichische, Spar-Kasse Bank, Graben 21, A1010 Vienna (tel: 531-000; fax: 5310-0625),

Girocredit Bank AG d. Sparkassen, Schubertring 5 - 7, A-1010 Vienna (tel: 711-940; fax: 713-7032).

Österreichische Postsparkasse, Georg Coch-Platz 2, A1020 Vienna (tel: 514-000; fax: 5140-01700).

Österreichische Volksbanken AG, Peregringasse 3, A-1090 Vienna (tel: 313-400; fax: 3134-03683).

Raiffeisen Zentralbank, Österreich AG, Am Stadtpark 9, A-1030 Vienna (tel: 717-070).

Z-Länderbank Bank Austria AG, Am Hof 2, A-1010 Vienna (tel: 531-240; fax: 5312-4155).

Principal newspapers

Amtsblatt der Stadt Wien, Litfass-strasse 6, A-1031 Vienna (tel: 79-597; fax: 79-89200).

Der Standard, Herrengasse 1, A-1014 Vienna (tel: 53-170; fax: 53170-249).

Die Presse, Parkring 12A, A-1010 Vienna (tel: 51-4140; fax: 5141-4400).

Kurier, Lindengasse 48-52, A-1072 Vienna (tel: 52-100; 5210-02263).

Neue Kronenzeitung, Muthgasse 2, A-1190 Vienna, (tel: 36-010; fax: 368-385).

Neue Tiroler Tageszeitung, Etzelstrasse 30, A-6021 Innsbruck (tel: 53-540; fax: 57-524).

Salto, Kalsersrasse 67/1/DG, A-1070 Vienna (tel: 52-166; fax: 521-66207).

Wiener Zeitung, Rennweg 12a, A-1037 Vienna (tel; 97-890; fax: 797-88433).

Wirtschaftsblatt, Davidg. 79/1/4, A-1100 Vienna (tel: 601-170; fax: 602-0858).

Travel information

Austrian Airlines (Österreichische Luftverkehrs), PO Box 50, Fontanastrasse 1, Vienna A-1010 (tel: 683-5110; fax: 685-505).

Lauda Air Luftfahrt, World Trade Centre, PO Box 56, Vienna-Schwechat A-1300 (tel: 7007-2081; fax: 7007-2091).

OAMTC (Österreichischer Automobil-Motorrad und Touring Club), A-1010 Vienna, Schubertring 1-3 (tel: 711-990; tx: 133-907).

Österreich Werbung (Austrian National Tourist Office), A-1040 Vienna, Margarethenstr. 1 (tel: 587-2000; fax: 588-6620).

Tyrolean Airways (Tiroler Luftfahrt), Postfach 58, Innsbruck A-6026 (tel: 2222; fax: 293-490).

Other useful addresses

Austria Business Agency, Opernring 3, A-1010 Vienna (tel: 588-580; fax: 586-8659).

Austria Presse-Agentur (APA) (Cooperative Agency of the Austrian Newspapers and Broadcasting Co), A-1199 Vienna, Gunoldstrasse 14 (tel: 36-050; tx: 114-721).

Federal Chancellor's Office, Ballhausplatz 2, 1014 Vienna (tel: 53115-2432; fax: 53115-2880).

Federal Ministry for Agriculture & Forestry, Stubenring 1, 1011 Vienna (tel: 71100-0; fax: 71379-93).

Federal Ministry for Defence, Dampfschiffstr. 2, 1020 Vienna (tel: 51595-2020; fax: 51595-2126).

Federal Ministry for Economic Affairs, Stubenring 1, 1011 Vienna (tel: 71100-5130; fax: 71379-95).

Federal Ministry for Education, Minoritenplatz 5, 1014 Vienna (tel: 53120-4904; fax: 53120-4906).

Federal Ministry for Environment, Radetzkystr. 2, 1030 Vienna (tel: 71158-4607; fax: 71388-90).

Federal Ministry for Finance, Himmelpfortg. 8, 1015 Vienna (tel: 51433-1447; fax: 51278-69).

Federal Ministry for Foreign Affairs, Ballhausplatz 2, 1014 Vienna (tel: 53115-3416; fax: 53185-213).

Federal Ministry for Health, Radetzkystr. 2, 1031 Vienna (tel: 71172-4619; fax: 71172-4830).

Federal Ministry for the Interior, Herrengasse 7, 1010 Vienna (tel: 53126-2234; 53126-2240).

Federal Ministry for Justice, Museumstr. 7, 1070 Vienna (tel: 52152-0; fax: 52152-727).

Federal Ministry for Labour and Social Affairs, Stubenring 1, 1011 Vienna (tel: 71100-6155; fax: 71100-6469).

Federal Ministry for Science, Research, Arts, Public Services and Transport, Minoritenplatz 5, 1014 Vienna (tel: 53120-5150; fax: 53377-97).

Federal Ministry for Women's Issues, Ballhausplatz 1, 1014 Vienna (tel: 53115-2414; fax: 53115-2869).

Interpreters' Institute of Vienna University (tel: 347-649 ext. 298).

Österreichischer Rundfunk, (Austrian Radio), Argentinierstrasse 30a, 1040 Vienna, (tel: 501-010; fax: 5010-18250).

Österreichisches Statistisches Zentralamt (Central Statistical Office), Hintere Zollamtstrasse 2b, A-1030 Vienna (tel: 711-280; fax: 7112-87728).

Vereinigung Österreichischer Industrieller (Association of Austrian Industrialists), A-1030 Vienna, Schwarzenbergplatz 4 (tel: 711-350; tx: 131-717).

Wiener Börse (Vienna Stock Exchange), A-1011 Vienna, Wipplingerstrasse 34 (tel: 53-499; tx: 132-447).

Zentralstelle Aussenhandel u. Zoll (Ministry of Economic Affairs), Export/Import Licensing Office, A-1030 Vienna, Landstrasser Hauptstrasse 55-57 (tel: 711-02).

Azerbaijan

Bob Jiggins

In the eventful November 1995 parliamentary elections, allegations of harassment of political opponents and violation of democratic procedures were voiced. Russian pressure in foreign relations and encouragement of the opposition parties has placed Azerbaijan's government under increased strain, although the prospects for the economy seem to be on the up, albeit from an extremely low base.

Electoral manipulation

The November 1995 parliamentary elections featured alleged manipulations of the electoral process by the president, Geidar Aliyev. The immediate run-up to the poll was marked by the arrest of a number of opposition leaders, assumed to be no more than a heavy-handed attempt to intimidate their respective parties.

Immediately prior to the elections a former foreign minister, Tofig Gasimov, was arrested on charges of involvement in an attempted coup against the President in March 1995. The coup was precipitated by the actions of President Aliyev in disbanding a police unit under the control of the deputy interior minister, Rovshan Dzhavadov. The coup involved troops led by the deputy interior minister, and resulted in a number deaths, including that of Dzhavadov himself.

Gasimov's connection to the coup was by virtue of being head of the Centre for Strategic International Studies, which was implicated. Evidence for this came allegedly from records obtained by a police raid on the centre, although as Mr Gasimov had planned to contest the next elections for the Musavet party, it has been suggested that his arrest had more to do with removing a potential troublemaker from the political scene.

Gasimov may be the most prominent politician to be arrested on charges of anti-government activity, but he was not the only one. Other arrests involved political opponents of the President, lending weight to charges that the government was becoming increasingly authoritarian.

Shortly after Gasimov's arrest Aga Ahundov, a deputy in the parliament, was also arrested on charges of maintaining a weapons dump near Baku for use in deposing the government. Also implicated in this (on evidence provided by Mr Ahundov) was the chairman of the Labour Party, Sabutai Hajiyev. Mr Hajiyev subsequently admitted in questioning by the security forces that the Labour Party had merely been established to serve as a front organisation for the former president, Ayaz Mutalibov, who is now resident in Moscow. He further implicated the Social Democratic Party as being allied with Mr Mutalibov. The extent to which these allegations are true is open to much doubt, although it was certainly true that Moscow has been involved in manipulating domestic discontent and opposition forces to its own advantage.

KEY FACTS — *Azerbaijan*

Official title: Republic of Azerbaijan

Head of state: President Geidar Aliyev (since 18 Jun 1993; President Aliyev won 97 per cent of the vote in the 12 Nov 1995 election)

Head of government: Prime Minister Fuad Guliyev (from Nov 1995)

Ruling party: New Azerbaijan Party (YAP) (won 70 per cent of the vote in Nov 1995 elections; in run-off elections 4 Feb 1996 for 15 seats, YAP gained 12 seats, Azerbaijan Popular Front one, Muslim Democratic Party (Musarat) one; complaints of vote rigging)

Capital: Baku

Official Languages: Azeri (Turkic)

Currency: Manat (M) = 100 gopik

Exchange rate: M4,230 per US$ (Dec 1996)

Area: 86,600 sq km

Population: 7.8m (1995)

GDP per capita: US$54 (1994)

GDP real growth: -6.5% (1995)

GNP per capita: US$680 (1994)

GNP real growth: -22% (1994)

Labour force: 2.7m (1994)

Unemployment: 24.5% (1995)

Inflation: 84.6% (1995)

Oil reserves: 1.2bn barrels (1995)

Trade balance: -US$120.3m (1995)

It is obvious, though, that these events are electorally advantageous for President Aliyev, and have been used as such. Both the two previous coups, in March 1995 and October 1994, had been used by the President as evidence that Russia was conspiring against the Azeri nation. Mr Gasimov was imprisoned for 15 years in February 1996 and another 25 people have likewise been given sentences of between 10 and 15 years for their part in anti-government activities.

Standards lacking

The November 1995 elections were largely held at the insistence of various international organisations, including western governments. Concern had been expressed at intergovernmental level as to the fairness in the run-up to these elections, and the Azeri government had appeared to have acknowledged this. Consequently, various measures were apparently taken by the government to ensure that at least a modicum of western democratic norms were being observed, including the reinstatement of several political parties and a partial withdrawal of press censorship.

The November elections resulted in some seats polling less than 50 per cent for the victor, and thus were rescheduled for a run-off in February of 1996. Of these last 15 seats, 12 were won by representatives of New Azerbaijan, the party of President Aliyev. Overall the elections have resulted, as expected, in an overwhelming victory for the President and his party.

Ultimately though, the elections were described by the Organisation for Security and Co-operation in Europe (OSCE) as not 'in accordance with international standards'. This was a polite way of referring to such events as multiple voting, the presence of armed police in polling stations and the theft of ballot boxes.

In September 1995 several parties that had been banned were re-instated. These included the Popular Front of Azerbaijan; the Communist Party; and the Social Democratic Party, which has since been charged with illegal anti-government extra-parliamentary activities. Some parties have however not been so favoured, including the Islamic Party.

Similarly, censorship of the press has been partially lifted, with the government now apparently only continuing censorship of military matters by the security forces, rather than the all pervading censorship hitherto applied. Having noted this, however, October 1995 saw the imprisonment of five journalists from the newspaper Cheshme for publishing an article that allegedly insulted the President – these sentences were for between three and five years, although they have now been pardoned.

KEY INDICATORS

	Unit	1991	1992	1993	1994	1995
Population	m	7.22	7.15	7.35	7.50	7.80
Gross national product (GNP)	US$bn	6.8	6.0	6.0	5.0	–
GNP per capita	US$	960	950	800	680	–
GNP real growth	%	-0.4	-28.2	-14.4	-22.0	–
GDP real growth	%	–	–	-13.3	-21.9	-6.5
Employment	'000	2,901	2,743	2,710	2,587	2,600
Unemployment	%	–	0.24	0.48	0.83	0.99
Inflation	%	101.8	1,063.0	1,113.0	1,664.0	84.6
Industrial production	1990=100	104.8	80.0	74.4	57.55	45.2
Manufacturing	1990=100	104.7	78.0	72.6	54.3	–
Mining	1990=100	93.5	87.8	79.0	70.1	–
Mineral fertiliser	m tonnes	188.0	81.2	32.3	5.0	1.7
Crude steel	'000 tonnes	564.0	411.0	236.0	40.1	10.7
Cement	'000 tonnes	923	823	622	467	192
Crude petroleum output	m tonnes	26.6	25.8	23.0	20.3	20.5
Natural gas output	bn cu metres	8.0	7.4	6.3	6.0	6.2
Imports	US$m	–	–	721	778	668
Exports	US$m	–	–	716	637	547
Balance of trade	US$m	–	–	–	-141.1	-120.3
Exchange rate	M per US$	–	–	–	4,182	4,440

New legislature

The new legislative body, which replaces the un-elected and virtually powerless Milli Mejlis, is a unicameral body of 125 seats. Of these, 25 are elected from the party list and 100 from single member constituencies. These 125 seats are further divided by region, so that 26 are elected from the capital Baku, and the remaining 99 from all other areas outside the capital.

As approximately half the population live in Baku, it follows that those living outside the capital possess a greater influence over the final outcome – and it has also been noted by western observers that the opposition has greatest influence in Baku, rather than the regions. Thus, the distribution of seats appears to be deliberately biased in favour of the government.

Furthermore, the requirements for obtaining the necessary number of signatures (2,000 in the case of the single-member constituencies and 50,000 for the party list) to qualify for electoral participation, require details which are frequently difficult to obtain and verify. Thus of the 18 parties which claimed to have collected enough signatures by the qualifying date (17 October 1996), only 8 were approved by the Central Election Commission to participate in the election. Azerbaijan's oldest party, Musavat (Equality), founded in 1912, was banned and the Islamic and Communist parties failed to obtain the necessary nominations.

Oil-field salvation?

The main reason why western governments (as well as others) are so interested in Azerbaijan and the establishment of democratic norms, is the potentially large oil wealth of the country, derived from its position on the Caspian Sea. The export of oil has persistently remained a problem, with a number of routes for an overland pipeline being considered.

SOCAR, the state-owned oil company, has been developing the Azeri field in conjunction with an international consortium led by British Petroleum (BP) and Norway's Statoil. Debate has centred, however, on the precise route for export – although it has now been chosen for the early products of the field. The plan is to route the pipeline through both Russia and Georgia, rather than solely through Russia. This concerned a number of western powers, especially the USA, as the latter option might give Russia too great an influence over the Azeri supply.

A recent development has been the granting of a US$1.7 billion contract to develop the Karabakh oil and gas field. The consortium is headed by the Russian giant Lukoil, and includes Agip of Italy and the American Pennzoil. SOCAR is taking a small 7.5 per cent.

Aid depends on privatisation

In September 1995 the World Bank credited Azerbaijan with US$32 million, and a second credit of US$32 million is expected in 1997. This first payment is seen as a reward for continued economic reform started earlier in 1995, as monetary and fiscal policies have all been tightened. Subsequent payments are, however, very much conditional on further progress towards privatisation.

The International Monetary Fund (IMF) likewise has approved a standby credit of US$132 million to support the 1995/96 economic reform programme. In July 1995 the government passed legislation that enabled the privatisation of much of the country's industry through a voucher scheme, although little has been done so far in terms of the necessary restructuring preparation of enterprises.

Disputes in the Caspian

One of Azerbaijan's most valuable exports is caviar, and it produces some ten per cent of the total world production. It's worth to the economy is estimated at perhaps US$1 million each year. There are however other countries involved in the trade from around the Caspian Sea, which accounts for 90 per cent of the world production. It is for these reasons that the carving up of the Caspian, and its oil rights, is causing much dispute between Azerbaijan, and especially Russia. Azerbaijan wants an exclusive 40km limit, whilst Russia wants 10km.

Little policing of the Caspian takes place, and there is much illegal fishing and smuggling. Furthermore, there is evidence that the area is being over-fished, and is already under threat from pollution and the hydro-electric plants on the Kura, Azerbaijan's river. The development of the Caspian oil fields potentially further threatens the industry, and it was to be expected that volume will fall further, with consequent price rises. This is already occurring, with western prices rising by 50 per cent between 1994 and 1995.

Nagorny-Karabakh

The conflict with the Russian-backed Armenian separatists in Nagorno-Karabakh seems to be on the back-burner for a while. A ceasefire has been in effect since 1995, although sporadic skirmishes still take place, which led to polling in the Khankhend constituency being postponed in the recent election.

The conflict, which the Azeri forces have largely lost, has resulted in substantial loss of life and the loss of 20 per cent of Azerbaijan's territory to the separatists. Peace talks are continuing, although Armenia withdrew from these in September 1995 on the pretext that Azeri agents were responsible for the bombing of a vital pipeline carrying Armenian oil through Georgia.

The talks have since restarted, with various meetings in the latter half of 1995 and early 1996 in Moscow, Finland, Bonn and The Hague. These have been held under the auspices of the Minsk group of the OSCE, and are so far floundering on three main issues: troop withdrawals and refugees; the security of the Karabakh population; and the status of the Lachin corridor connecting the enclave with Armenia.

It is possible that with electoral victory and forthcoming benefits of an oil economy, President Aliyev may be tempted to restart the conflict in a bid to recover territory and prestige. Such a renewed conflict could spell disaster for Azerbaijan, although given the west's interest in protecting what is possibly the last great oil boom, it is unlikely that the country would be regarded as expendable.

COUNTRY PROFILE — AZERBAIJAN

Historical profile

Following recent Armenian successes in the conflict over Nagorno-Karabakh, a peace settlement was negotiated between Armenia and Azerbaijan. However, this settlement was not accepted by the people of Nagorno-Karabakh and it is unclear whether the conflict will continue. In September 1993 Geidar Aliyev, head of state of Azerbaijan, offered talks with Armenian leaders.

Political system

Azerbaijan, formerly under USSR administration for a period of 71 years, announced its independence on 30 August 1991. Albulfaz Elchibey, the leader of the People's Front, was elected to presidency in June 1992. There is a National Assembly (60-70 elected representatives), a Cabinet of Ministers and a prime minister. President Elchibey fled the capital in June 1993 and ex-communist Geidar Aliyev returned to power. Referendum on new constitution and first parliamentary elections 12 and 26 November 1995. The New Azerbaijan Party (YAP), closely aligned to the president, secured 70 per cent of the vote and the president won 97 per cent.

Political parties

The New Azerbaijan Party was formed in 1995 and is openly supported by President Aliyev; Popular Front Party. The ban on the Communist Party was lifted in September 1995.

Population

Population growth rate 1.32% (1995 estimate). Life expectancy: 71.09 years (1995 estimate). Ethnic makeup: Azeri (90%), Dagestani Peoples (3.2%), Russian (2.5%), Armenian (2.3%), other (2%) (1995 estimates). Almost all Armenians live in the separatist Nagorno-Karabakh region. Religions: Shi'ite Muslim (93.4%), Russian Orthodox (2.5%), Armenian Orthodox (2.3%), other (1.8%) (1995 estimates).

Main cities/towns

Baku (capital, estimated population 1.8m in 1994), Gyandzha, Mingechaur, Sheki, Stepanakert, Lakataly, Geokchay, Sumgait, Kuba, Ali Bayramli, Lenktran, Binkechevin, Tazlab, Haftalan and Shusha.

Language

Azeri (89%), Russian (3%), Armenian (2%), others (6%) (1995 estimates).

Media

Media state-controlled, subservient to the president.
Press: There are 151 newspapers including 141 in Azerbaijani, and 64 periodicals including 55 in Azerbaijani. Handful of opposition newspapers that are aligned with, and in some cases funded by, opposition parties, virtually unobtainable outside Baku. One independent Russian-language weekly newspaper *Zerkalo*. Circulation of all newspapers very small (maximum 14,300).
Broadcasting: Radio Baku broadcasts in Azerbaijani, Russian, Arabic, Persian and Turkish and Baku Television broadcasts programmes in Azerbaijani and Russian. One independent TV station ANS-TV.

Domestic economy

Azerbaijan's economic performance was the worst among the CIS states in the first nine months of 1995 when it fell by 17.4 per cent.

Employment

There are large numbers of unemployed and underemployed workers who are not included in the 0.9 per cent December 1994 unemployment rate, which includes officially registered unemployed.

External trade

Russia and Ukraine take the largest share in Azerbaijan's foreign trade. Azerbaijan and Moldova signed a trade and economic co-operation agreement in September 1995. Under the terms of the accord, Azerbaijan is to export mainly oil, oil products and oil equipment in exchange for vegetables, grain, flour and consumer goods. Under a separate protocol, Moldova is to supply Azerbaijan with 200,000 tonnes of grain and 50,000 tonnes of flour in exchange for oil products.
Exports: Exports totalled US$553m in 1995. Exports and re-exports include: refined petroleum products, cotton fibre, machinery for metallurgy, cement, plastics, tyres, trucks, lighting equipment and aluminium products.
Imports: Imports totalled US$725m in 1995. Imports include: cement, chemical fertilisers, plastics, rolled products, coal, tyres, sewing machinery, agricultural machinery, rolling machines, tractors, passenger cars, machinery for metallurgy, trucks, lighting equipment, machinery and equipment for services sector.

Agriculture

Agriculture accounted for 31 per cent of GNP in 1994 and employed 34 per cent of the labour force. Adversely affected by periodic drought but a wide range of crops is grown, notably cotton, tobacco, grapes, grain, tea, vegetables and citrus fruits. Grain is the leading agricultural product, followed by raw cotton. Vegetables, particularly early varieties, fruits, walnuts and hazelnuts are also promising crops. Fishing is important.

Industry

Industry accounted for 33 per cent of GNP in 1994 and employed 20 per cent of the labour force. The industrial sector is poorly developed and hindered by an underdeveloped infrastructure. Primary resource availability has enabled the development of a petro-chemicals industry as well as other manufacturing industries such as iron and steel production, mechanical engineering, clothing and

COUNTRY PROFILE

Industry (contd): foodstuffs. Salyan on the Kura River is the centre for processing and canning of fish. Cotton and wool fabrics, shoes, processing and canning of meat, vegetables and fruit are also among the light industry products. Industrial production growth rate -25 per cent in 1994.

Mining

The mining sector accounted for 7 per cent of GNP in 1994 and employed 4 per cent of the workforce. The republic has abundant mineral resources, including iron, lead, zinc and copper ores, cobalt, bauxite, matrium sulphate, marl, limestone, marble, lake and rock salts, and some small amounts of gold and silver.

Hydrocarbons

High-quality crude oil is tapped in the eastern part of the republic, both on- and off-shore, and unofficial estimates indicate significant oil reserves and small deposits of natural gas. Proven natural gas reserves 4.3 trillion cu feet (end-1995); gas production 5.5m tonnes oil equivalent in 1995, up 3.1 per cent on 1994 output. Oil reserves totalled 1.2bn barrels (end-1995). Oil production 185,000 barrels per day (bpd) in 1995, down 4.2 per cent on 1994 output. Radical modernisation is necessary to develop this sector. Nearly 2,000 wells are inoperative for lack of funds for repair work. Azerbaijan has two refineries with a total capacity of 406,000 bpd and a capacity utilisation of about 80 per cent. In 1992 BP (UK) and Statoil (Norway) signed an agreement with the Azeri government to develop the Dostlug (formerly Kaverochkin) field in the Caspian Sea at present estimated at more than 1bn barrels, and to explore the Shak Deniz (formerly Shakhovo More) area, together with Kaspmorneftegaz and Azerineft (local oil and gas producers). In March 1993 Turkey and Azerbaijan agreed to build a US$1.4bn pipeline from the Baku oilfields to the Turkish Mediterranean to take Azerbaijani crude to western markets. This, however, is being disputed by Russia. Azerbaijan's oil output in 1994 was 195,000 bpd 8.6 per cent less than the 1993 figure. Coal is mined. Ramco, the Scotland-based energy company, signed an alliance agreement in July 1996 with Schlumberger, the Franco-American oil service company, to manage the proposed development of the Muradhanli onshore oil field, 130 km south-west of Baku, which is estimated to contain more than 1m barrels of light, low sulphur oil.

Membership of international organisations

CIS, CSCE, Economic Co-operation Organisation (ECO), IMF, MIGA, NACC, OIC, Partnership for Peace, World Bank.

BUSINESS GUIDE

Time

GMT +3 hrs.

Climate

Extremes of temperature. Visitors can see nine of the world's thirteen climatic zones, from Alpine meadows to the subtropics. The climate in Baku is dry and subtropical, of a Mediterranean type. Spring begins in March. The long summers are dry and hot, beginning in May, and lasting until the middle of September. Winters are often without snow or frost, and with a few sunny days. The average rainfall is between 110 and 250 mm, and falls mainly in the early spring and late autumn. The average annual temperature is 14.5 degrees C, and the average daily temperature of the hottest period in July and August reaches 26 degrees C. In autumn, the days are warm, dry and balmy. The winters in Baku are mild, with an average temperature in January of 3-5 degrees C.

Entry requirements

Visa: Visas are required and can be obtained from the Azerbaijan Embassy, or by applying direct to the consular Department of the Ministry of Foreign Affairs of Azerbaijan in Baku. Visitors are recommended to obtain a visa prior to their arrival. Travellers with a valid Georgian visa are permitted to enter Azerbaijan for five days, but after that, are required to obtain an Azeri visa. The applicant is required to complete an application form, and provide two photographs, a letter of invitation by a sponsor written in Russian or Azeri and a valid passport. Visas can be obtained in Baku by surrendering passport at Baku Airport for processing and collecting visa and passport from the Ministry of Foreign Affairs the following working day. Validity for a single-entry visa is from three days to three months (obtainable within three working days for a basic fee, or within 24-48 hours for a higher fee), while a multiple-entry visa is valid for one year (obtainable in no less than five working days at a high charge, no express service). A re-entry visa can be obtained by foreigners who complete application forms and present their passports as they leave Azerbaijan, and this will give them permission to re-enter Azerbaijan provided they return within one month. To obtain a tourist visa, visitors must have a letter of invitation from an individual in Azerbaijan. If they have no previous contacts in the country, they are recommended to contact Azerbaijan Airlines, which can provide a letter of invitation from a tourist company working with the airline.
Currency: Foreign currency must be declared on arrival. The local currency, the manat, cannot be imported or exported. All transactions are in cash, either the manat, or US dollars (bills must be in good condition otherwise they will not be accepted). There is no difficulty in exchanging US dollars, UK pounds or Deutsche Marks at hotels, banks and even shops containing currency exchange points.
Customs: On arrival declare all foreign currency and valuable items such as jewellery, cameras, computers etc.

Health precautions

Advisable: Water precautions recommended: water purification tablets may be useful or drink bottled water. It is advisable to be 'in date' for the following immunisations: polio (within 10 years), tetanus (within 10 years), typhoid fever, cholera (within six months), hepatitis 'A' (moderate risk only). There has been a significant increase in the number of cases of diphtheria. While the low dose, adult booster is unavailable, travellers are advised to be boosted with a reduced dose (0.1ml) of the paediatric single antigen vaccine. If never immunised, use three dose course of the vaccine. Anti-malarial precautions advisable. Any medicines required by the traveller should be taken by the visitor, and it could be wise to have precautionary antibiotics if going outside major urban centres. A travel kit including a disposable syringe is a reasonable precaution.

Representation overseas

Ankara, Beijing, Bonn, Brussels, Cairo, Geneva, Istanbul, London, Moscow, New York, Paris, Riyadh, Tehran, Washington.

Air access

National airline: Azal (Azerbaijan Hava Yollari) (Azerbaijan Airlines).
Other airlines: Aeroflot, Belavia, Donavia, Iran Air, PIA, Sibavia Airlines, Transaero, Turkish Airlines.

Hotels

Hotel space in Baku is very limited. Payment for the full stay is required in advance upon arrival at the hotel in cash (in US dollar bills which should be in good condition).

Credit cards

Credit card facilities are non-existent.

Car hire

Available in Baku.

City transport

Taxis: Volga taxis with sign on top. Agree a price beforehand. Taxis are cheap but drivers are unlikely to speak English. As the cost of a trip can vary widely, it is better to use hotel taxis or pre-arrange a car with driver. Taxi services (tel: 621-256).
Metro: There is a metro in Baku.

Public holidays

Fixed dates: 1 Jan (New Year's Day), 20 Jan (Sorrow Day), 8 Mar (International Women's Day), 28 May (Republic Day), 9 Oct (Armed Forces Day), 18 Oct (State Independence Day), 17 Nov (Day of National Revival), 31 Dec (Solidarity day of Azeris throughout the world).
Variable dates: Ramazan Bayrami (Fast of Ramadan), Kurban Bayrami (Feast of the Sacrifice), Novuz (Spring Holiday).

Telecommunications

Azerbaijan operates an enhanced total access cellular system (an analogue system); no plans to introduce a global system for mobile communications.
Telephone and telefax: Dialling code for Azerbaijan, IDD access code + 994 followed by area code (12 for Baku). Mobile telephones are frequently used. International telephone and facsimile services exist at all major hotels. Calls placed outside regular business hours must be booked. Public telephones require tokens which can be purchased at subway stations.
For IDD access from Azerbaijan dial 8-10; international operator 007; national and former Soviet Union calls 07; for direct dialling cities of Azerbaijan dial first 8, and then the city code.

Banking

The International Bank of Azerbaijan and Halkbank, Turkey, are correspondent banks. Accounts have been opened at Halkbank for all the export-import and banking procedures to be carried out between Azerbaijan and other countries of the world.
Central bank: The Azerbaijan Central Republican Bank, established February 1992.
Other banks: The National Bank of Azerbaijan handles the foreign trade transactions. See also 'Business Directory, Banking'.

Business information

In March 1992 the law of foreign investments was published which allowed foreign investors to contribute in joint ventures, create enterprises owned completely by themselves, buy real estate and securities and participate in the privatisation of the state and municipal enterprises. Joint ventures, with more than 30 per cent foreign capital, are exempt from corporate income tax for a period of three years from the start of operation, and pay 25 per cent in subsequent years. Establishments with more than 30 per cent foreign capital may export goods manufactured to any foreign country without licence. No licence or customs duty required for goods to be brought in as investment capital for the company or as needs of personnel. Privatisation of small enterprises began 1993-94. Large plants and factories will be privatised in the second stage.

Representation in capital

Australia, Austria, Belgium, Canada, China, Denmark, Egypt, France, Germany, Ghana, Greece, India, Iran, Iraq, Israel, Italy, Japan, Kazakhstan, Mexico, Netherlands, Norway, Pakistan, Russia, Saudi Arabia, Slovak Republic, South Africa, South Korea, Spain, Sudan, Sweden, Switzerland, Turkey, UAE, UK, USA, Zambia.

Hotels

Baku (area code 12)
Absheron, Azadlyg Square 674, 370010 (tel: 987-209, 987-384).

Anba, 1 Mehti Hussein Street, 370148 (tel: 929-301, 989-111).

Azerbaijan, Azadlyg Avenue 1, 370000 (tel: 989-004, 989-006).

Baki, 9 Fikrat Amirov Street, 370075 (tel: 988-206/200).

Hyatt Regency, 1 Bakikhanov Street, 370022 (tel: 981-234).

Intourist, Neftchilar Ave 63, 370004 (tel: 926-306, 924-073, 944-456).

Janub, 31 Azerbaijan Ave, 370000 (tel: 931-416, 938-400).

Republic, managed by the Office of the President, 15 Istiglaliyyat Street, 370001 (tel: 925-475, 926-403).

Tayara, Bina Airport, 370109 (tel: 243-864).

Useful telephone numbers

Fire: 01.
Police: 02.
Ambulance: 03.
Gas: 04.
Enquiries: 001.
General information: 009, 933-544.
Taxi services: 621-256.

Chambers of commerce

Azerbaijan Chamber of Commerce, ul Kommunisticheskaya 31–33, 370601 Baku (tel: 398-503; 994-8922, 928-259; tx: 142211).

Baku Board of Commerce, 112 Samad Vurghun Street, 370022 (tel: 956-336, 956-848).

Banking

Azerbaijan Central Republican Bank (central bank), Ul Fizuli 71, 370010 Baku (tel: 930-561).

Azakbank (joint stock bank), 25 Khagani Str, 370070 Baku (tel: 983-109, 932-491, 936-535; fax: 932-085).

AzEcoBank (joint stock bank), 11/39 Mustafa Subhi Street, Baku 370001 (tel: 927-656; fax: 980-407; e-mail: ecob@ecob.crack.azerbaijan.su).

Azerbaijan Agricultural Industrial Bank (joint stock commercial bank), 125 Gadirli Street, Baku 370006 (tel: 389-923; fax: 389-115).

Azerbaijan Commercial Savings Bank, 71 Fizuli Street, Baku 370010 (tel: 930-561; fax: 939-489).

Azerbaijan Industrial Investment Bank (joint stock commercial bank), Ul Fizuli 71, 370010 Baku (tel: 931-701/5, 987-946; fax: 931-266; 931-705).

Azerbaijan National Bank, 19 Bulbul Ave, Baku 370070 (tel: 987-167; fax: 937-374).

Azerdemiryolbank (private commercial bank), 31 Garabagh Street, Baku 370008 (tel: 987-936, 671-220, 675-321; fax: 987-936).

International Bank of the Azerbaijan Republic, 3 Zeynalabdin Taghiyev Street, Baku 370005 (tel: 989-122; fax: 934-091).

Promtekhbank (joint stock commercial bank), 69 Fizuli Street, Baku 370014 (tel: 957-874; fax: 958-360; e-mail: bank@devi.baku.az).

Rabitabank (joint stock commercial bank) (services to the communications industry), Buniat Sardarov Street, Baku 370001 (tel: 925-761; fax: 981-844).

Tajbank (commercial investment bank), 185 Azadlyg Ave, Baku 370087 (tel: 691-464; fax: 691-474).

Travel information

Airlines information office (tel: 937-121).

Azal (Azerbaijan Hava Yollari) (Azerbaijan Airlines), Prospect Azadlig 11, Baku 370000 (tel: 934-434; fax: 985-237, 651-120).

Azertur Travel Agency of the State Council for Foreign Tourism (tours, hotel reservations, translation and interpreting services), 1 Azadlyg Ave, Baku 370000 (tel: 933-481; fax: 933-481).

Baku Metro, 33 Azerbaijan Avenue, Baku 370002 (tel: 961-013).

Bina airport general enquiries (tel: 257-900, 242-018).

Central bus station (tel: 388-581 (information).

Marine passenger terminal (tel: 930-868).

Railway station (tel: 982-039, 995-480).

Train tickets (tel: 931-698, 931-702, 931-807, 931-946).

Other useful addresses

Assa-Irada (international independent information agency), 2nd Floor, 85 Salatyn Askarova Street, Baku 370002 (tel: 949-373; fax: 958-537).

Azerbaijan News Service, Block 504, 1128 Street, Baku 370073 (building of the Institute of Zoology) (tel: 929-221/3; fax: 989-498).

Azerbintorg Foreign Trade Association, 14 Boyuk Gala Str, 370004 Baku (tel: 920-481, 926-492, 924-545; fax: 923-818).

Azerinform (Azerbaijan Information Agency), Baku.

Baku General Customs Board, 62 Neftchilar Ave, Baku 370601 (tel: 939-588).

Baku Statistics Office, 10 Tabriz Street, Baku 370008 (tel: 669-327, 672-265).

Baku Telegraph Office, 41 Azerbaijan Avenue, Baku 370000 (tel: 936-142).

Baku Television, M. Husein St 1, Baku.

Board of Azerbaijan Railways, 230 Dilara Aliyeva Street, Baku 370010 (tel: 984-467).

Caspian Shipping Company, 5 Rasulzade Street, Baku 370005 (tel: 922-058; fax: 935-339).

Central Post Office, 36 Uzeyir Hajibeyov Street, Baku 370000 (tel: 985-251).

EU Co-ordinating Unit in Azerbaijan, Government House, 8th Floor, Room 851, Baku 370016 (tel: 936-018; fax; 937-638).

Ministry of Agriculture and Food, 4 Shykhali Gurbanov Street, Baku 370079 (tel: 945-355; fax: 945-390).

Ministry of Communications, 33 Azerbaijan Ave, Baku 370139 (tel: 930-004; fax: 984-285).

Ministry of Culture, Government House, Baku 370016 (tel: 934-398; fax: 935-605).

Ministry of Defence, 3 Azizbeyov Ave, Baku 370601 (tel: 394-362; fax: 382-296).

Ministry of Economics, Government House, Baku 370016 (tel: 936-920; fax: 932-025).

Ministry of Education, Government House, Baku 370016 (tel: 937-266; fax: 984-207).

Ministry of Finance, Sameda Vurguna Ul 6, Baku 370601 (tel: 933-012; fax: 937-691).

Ministry of Foreign Affairs, Gandjlar Meydani 3, Baku 370005 (tel: 923-401; fax: 651-038).

Ministry of Foreign Economic Relations, 23 Niyazi Street, Baku 370066 (tel: 929-457; fax: 980-011).

Ministry of Grain Products, 13 Yusifzade Street, Baku 370033 (tel: 667-451; fax: 939-023).

Ministry of Information and Press, 12 Ahmad Javad Street, Baku 370000 (tel: 926-747; fax: 925-811).

Ministry of Internal Affairs, 7 Husu Hajiyev Street, Baku 370005 (tel: 982-285; fax: 923-471).

Ministry of Justice, 13 Bulbul Avenue, Baku 370601 (tel: 984-941; fax: 938-3670).

Ministry of Material resources, 83-23 Alaskar Alakbarov Street, Baku 370141 (tel: 394-296; fax: 399-176).

Ministry of National Security, 2 Parliament Ave, Baku 370-602 (tel: 950-491; fax: 936-296).

Ministry of Public Health, 4 Kichik Sahil Street, Baku 370-005 (tel: 932-977; fax: 988-559).

Ministry of Social Welfare, Government House, Baku 370016 (tel: 930-543; fax: 939-472).

Ministry of Trade, Government House, Baku 370016 (tel: 936-463; fax: 987-431).

Ministry of Youth and Sports, 98a Fatali Khan Khoisky Stret, Baku 370110 (tel: 981-426; fax: 643-650).

Office of the President of the Azerbaijan Republic, 19 Istiglaliyyat Street, Baku 370066 (tel: 983-113).

Radio Baku, M. Husein St 1, 370011 Baku.

State Committee for Statistics, 24 Inshaatchylar Ave, Baku 370136 (tel: 381-171; fax: 380-577).

State Customs Committee, 2 Inshaatchilar Ave, Baku 370073 (tel: 927-545).

State Oil Company of the Azerbaijan Republic (SOCAR), 73 Neftchilar Ave, Baku 370004 (tel: 920-685; fax: 923-204).

UK Embassy, 2 Izmir Street, Baku 370065 (tel: 924-813; fax: 985-558).

UN Representative, 3 Istiglaliyyat Street, Baku 370001 (tel: 989-888; fax; 983-235).

US Embassy, 83 Azadlyg Ave, Baku 370007 (tel: 980-335; fax: 983-755).

Belarus

Marko Milivojevic

Following new parliamentary elections in July 1994 and an associated referendum on closer ties with Russia in May 1995, President Aleksander Lukashenko continued to move towards ever closer political and economic union with Russia. Never more than nominal, Belarus' statehood and independence may eventually disappear altogether. Meanwhile, the post-Soviet economic decline continued unabated in 1995 and 1996.

Politics

President Lukashenko's conflict with parliament came to a head in November 1996 when he held a referendum to changing the constitution and so increase his own powers at the expense of parliament's. With total control of the media and the security forces – as well as widespread popular support – it was no surprise that he received the backing of 70.5 per cent of those who voted, to enable him to rule with virtually no reference to parliament.

The referendum was the culmination of several months of an increasingly bitter feud between Lukashenko and a parliament which was fighting for its very survival. The referendum called for the president's term in office to be extended from five to seven years, parliament to be reduced in size and divided into two chambers of presidential appointees, the majority of constitutional court judges to be presidential appointees, as well as giving the president the power to dissolve parliament.

An alternative referendum held by parliament which proposed to abolish the position of president failed to achieve any substantial support. Parliamentary Speaker Syamen Sharetsky led the protests against Lukashenko, but the opposition could not gain enough support form within parliament to impeach the president. Despite these protests and condemnation from the European Union (EU), the Organisation for Security and Co-operation in Europe (OSCE) and the USA, Lukashenko has succeeded in reducing parliament's role to that of a figurehead while establishing a de facto presidential dictatorship reminiscent of the Soviet era.

President Lukashenko's unconditional espousal of a full union with Russia increased the conflict between him and parliament, which finally became quorate following new parliamentary elections for previously unfulfilled seats in November-December 1995.

During a prolonged period in 1994/95 when Belarus' parliament did not have a working quorum, Lukashenko threatened to abolish it altogether. Although dominated by leftwing and pro-Russian parties supportive of union with Russia, parliament remains unwilling to be wholly subordinate to Lukashenko's presidential administration.

Despite being numerically insignificant, Belarus' largely nationalist opposition may gain a more important political role as the implications of full union with Russia become clearer. Externally, the other key variable is the west; Belarus faces the prospect of increased international isolation as it moves ever closer to Russia in all spheres, not to mention Lukashenko's undisguised moves towards totalitarian rule.

Union with Russia

Always at the centre of politics in Belarus in the post-Soviet period, the issue of closer union with Russia entered a possibly decisive stage in 1995/96. Most recently mandated to seek ever-closer ties with Russia in a nationwide referendum in May 1995, President Lukashenko began this move back to Russia in the economic sphere through a new customs union later the same year. Although initially agreed as long ago as April 1994, the actual signing of this customs union was endlessly delayed, mainly because of Russian doubts about its high economic costs.

KEY FACTS — Belarus

Official title: Republic of Belarus

Head of state: President Aleksander Lukashenka (landslide victory in 1994 elections)

Head of government: Prime Minister Sergei Ling (from 18 Nov 1996)

Ruling party: Reformist government: Party of Communists of Belarus (CPB) (42 seats in the 1995 elections) and the Agrarian Party (33 seats)

Capital: Minsk

Official Languages: Belarussian for all official documents; Russian widely spoken

Currency: Belarus Rouble (R) (an interim currency was introduced on 26 Jul 1993; it was redenominated by a factor of 10 on 20 Aug 1994)

Exchange rate: R22,750 per US$ (Dec 1996)

Area: 208,000 sq km

Population: 10.3m (1995)

GDP per capita: US$900 (1995)

GDP real growth: -10% (1995)

GNP per capita: US$2,500 (1994)

GNP real growth: 5-7% (1995)*

Labour force: 4.8m (1994)

Unemployment: 2.5% (1995); (real unemployment figures estimated at 20%)

Inflation: 250% (1995)

Trade balance: -US$400m (1995)

Foreign debt: US$3bn (1995)

* estimated figure

Belarus' customs union and later union treaty with Russia in April 1996 only came into being because of developments in its eastern neighbour over the last year or so. Faced with critically important presidential elections in June 1996, Russian President Boris Yeltsin seized the political initiative from his communist opponents by agreeing a full union with Belarus. This was done in the context of the April 1996 agreement providing for a grouping of pro-Russian Commonwealth of Independent States (CIS) states, known as the Commonwealth of Sovereign States (SSR). The communist-dominated Russian Duma effectively forced Yeltsin to do this when, in the previous month, it voted down the laws that formally disposed of the former Soviet Union in 1991. Consequently, Russian politics will largely determine whether the recent union between Belarus and Russia becomes real or remains a dead letter.

A communist victory in the June 1996 Russian presidential elections would certainly have made this union real and irreversible. However, with Yeltsin's re-election Russia's future policy towards Belarus remained uncertain. It is significant that the customs union and union treaty between Belarus and Russia were purposefully vague, with few binding commitments coming from the Russian side, indicating continued Russian ambivalence about the entire exercise.

The second largest party in parliament, the Agrarians, now seem to be moving away from the pro-Russian Communist Party of Belarus (CPB) in favour of a more centrist position supportive of at least nominal statehood and independence for Belarus. This development was given added significance when the Agrarian leader, Syamen Sharetsky, was elected to the key chairmanship of the Supreme Soviet or parliament in late 1995. One result of this was that parliament was not entirely dominated by the CPB in 1996.

In a related series of developments in December 1995, the Constitutional Court proved more resilient than expected by blocking Lukashenko's attempts to create one-man rule in Belarus. Combined with other ongoing political trends, this may mean that Lukashenko's personal dictatorship may prove to be a temporary phenomenon in the longer-term, with everything now in effect dependent on developments in Russia.

KEY INDICATORS — Belarus

	Unit	1991	1992	1993	1994	1995
Population	m	10.30	10.30	10.30	10.30	10.30
Gross domestic product (GDP)	US$bn	–	9.5	11.0	10.0	9.0
GDP per capita	US$	–	950	1,100	1,000	900
GDP real growth	%	-1	-9	-11	-22	-10
Inflation	%	84	1,000	1,100	2,220	250
Employment	'000	5,020	4,887	4,824	4,696	4,600
Unemployment	%	–	0.22	1.13	1.85	2.50
Agricultural output	%	-2	-5	-9	-15	-10
Industrial production	%	-1-8	-8	-11	-27	-10.8
Manufacturing	1990=100	99.1	89.9	83.4	68.4	–
Mining	1990=100	92.1	80.8	68.1	78.3	–
Mineral fertiliser	m tonnes	5.2	4.1	2.6	3.0	3.4
Crude steel	'000 tonnes	1,123	1,105	946	873	741
Cement	'000 tonnes	2,042	2,065	1,907	1,488	1,236
Natural gas output	m cu metres	293.6	291.8	291.3	294.0	265.7
Crude petroleum output	'000 tonnes	2,060	2,000	2,004	2,000	1,932
Imports	US$bn	3.4	2.4	3.1	3.6	3.5
Exports	US$bn	3.3	2.8	2.8	3.1	3.1
Balance of trade	US$m	-100	400	-300	-500	-400
Current account	US$m	-200	100	-300	-550	-400
Hard currency reserves	US$m	100	200	400	900	500
Foreign debt	US$bn	–	–	1.0	2.0	3.0
Exchange rate	R per US$	–	–	–	10,600	11,500

Economy

With total output of goods and services no more than 40 per cent of their 1990 level in 1995, Belarus continues to experience serious economic decline. In 1995, GDP decreased by 10 per cent. Although this was an improvement of sorts over 1994, when GDP declined by a record 22 per cent, the trend is still downward, with no stabilisation of output expected much before 1997 or even 1998. Nominal GDP and GDP per capita in 1995 were US$9 billion and US$900 respectively.

The major causes of continued economic decline are energy shortages, an industrial sector unable to compete in Russian markets and the lack of any economic reform. As in 1994, the absence of restructuring in the industrial sector resulted in a low unemployment rate of 2.5 per cent in 1995. Unlike Russia, Belarus does not have a significant private sector. Mainly concentrated in services, this accounted for around 15 per cent of GDP in mid-1996. Black market economic activities, however, are increasing in importance, particularly as regards cross-border trade between the European Union (EU) and Russia through Belarus', which has abandoned all duties for such trans-shipped goods – a change of policy that is one of the major unspoken reasons why Russia is interested in Belarus at the present time.

Once accounting for around 50 per cent of GDP, but probably no more than 35 per cent of GDP by 1995, industrial output declined by a further 10.8 per cent in 1995, compared to a fall of 27 per cent in 1994. Out of a total of 1,664 major industrial enterprises in the state sector, two-thirds registered falls in output in 1995, with a particularly severe decline taking place in metal-working, light manufacturing and building materials. Primary production particularly of energy and steel is also declining still further in Belarus.

In 1995, output increased only in base chemicals, paper and pulp, and other wood products. In November 1995, most of the country's major industrial enterprises were loss-makers or in a state of technical insolvency. At that time, total enterprise losses for 1995 alone were R2.2 trillion, or 2.3 per cent of GDP. As in Ukraine, the inability of enterprises to pay their energy bills is a major problem, along with wage arrears. Externally, energy supply debts to Russia totalled US$562 million by the end of 1995. Although an improvement over 1994, when such debts to Russia totalled US$1 billion, these unpaid debts and the issue of energy supplies explained Belarus' drift back to Russia in 1996. In 1994, Belarus rescheduled US$400 million worth of its energy debt to Russia, which finally resolved this problem to the advantage of Belarus in February 1996.

Agriculture

Accounting for around 25 per cent of GDP in 1995, agriculture-food processing remains of considerable economic importance for Belarus. Because of ongoing energy shortages, however, agricultural output continued to decline in 1995, with output falling by 10 per cent after a 15 per cent fall in 1994. Within the agricultural sector, only timber output and processing is increasing.

Once significant foodstuff exports have been badly damaged by the extensive contamination caused by the 1986 Chernobyl disaster in Ukraine. The complete absence of land reform in Belarus has also prevented the revival of its agricultural sector.

Services and construction

Although economically dominant at around 40 per cent of GDP in 1995, services have not realised their full potential because of the slowness of even small-scale privatisation in Belarus to date. Uniquely in the region, Belarus' housing stock still largely remains in the state sector. At the end of 1995, only around a third of this stock, or 50,000 flats, had been sold to tenants. One result of this is low demand for construction services and materials. Retail and wholesale trade continue to experience high growth, particularly trans-shipment of goods from the EU and Poland to nearby Russia.

Financial stabilisation

Supported by an Interntional Monetary Fund (IMF) US$100 million Systemic Transformational Facility (STF) agreed in January 1995, long-delayed macro-economic stabilisation by the government and the National Bank of Belarus (NBB) finally began in that year. Based on a restrictive NBB monetary-credit policy under its then Governor Stanislav Bogdankevich, this resulted in a sharp fall in inflation to 250 per cent year-end in 1995, compared to 2,500 per cent year-end in 1994. In 1993/94, full hyper-inflation had threatened a complete economic collapse in Belarus. Significantly, this change of policy was as much brought about by Russian pressure as by the IMF. Only with lower inflation can Belarus hope to introduce a new national currency, the taler, or enter into monetary union with Russia.

Lukashenko and Bogdankevich parted company in 1994/95 over monetary policy, with the President then favouring monetary union with Russia and the NBB Governor supporting the option of the taler, a feud that culminated in the sacking of Bogdankevich in late 1995. This move was one of the reasons why the IMF stopped all financial support to Belarus in January 1996. In mid-1995, when the IMF approved a further US$300 million worth of new loans for Belarus, Bogdankevich had seemed to be on the rise.

COUNTRY PROFILE — BELARUS

Political system

Known as Belorussia until 18 September 1991; declared independence from the former Soviet Union on 24 August 1991. A presidential constitution was passed on 1 March 1994. This vested legislative power in a 260-member Supreme Council, which replaced the former 360-member Supreme Soviet, and is elected for five-year term by universal adult suffrage. The head of state is the president, who is directly elected for a five-year term. A Council of Ministers led by a Chair (Prime Minister) is responsible to the Supreme Council. Differences have emerged over the distribution of powers between the president and the Supreme Council. Multi-party republic. Aleksander Lukashenko elected president in July 1994. Only 119 out of 260 deputies were elected in the May 1995 parliamentary elections due to a low voter turnout. Run-off elections were held 10 December 1995, in which 198 of 260 seats were filled, 24 more than required for a quorum. The Communists and their Agrarian allies hold a total of about 80 seats.

Political parties

Major parties include Party of Communists of Belorussia; Agrarian Party; United Civic Party; Party of People's Accord; Party of All-Belorussian Unity and Accord; Belorussian Social Democratic Gramada; Belorussian Patriotic Movement; Belorussian Party of the Greens; Republican Party of Labour and Justice.

Population

Belarus (79.5 per cent), Russian (12 per cent), Polish (4%), Ukrainian (2.5%).

Main cities/towns

Minsk (population 1.8m in 1994), Gomel (500,000), Brest (250,000). Minsk is the headquarters for the Commonwealth of Independent States (CIS).

Media

President Lukashenko closed opposition newspapers in 1995 and allowed parties only limited access to television and radio.

Press: Almost 800 different publications are registered, although the number of papers actually printed is lower. All the major national newspapers with large circulations – some of them heavily subsidised – are still owned by the state and under the influence of the government and the president. The biggest and most influential daily *Narodnaya Gazeta*, founded by the parliament, used to be an impartial and balanced paper, but presidential interference with its leadership creates doubts about its independent editorial stance. *Belorusskya Dolovaya Gazeta* (opposition newspaper) is printed by the Lietuvos Rytas Publishing House and *Belorusskya Gazeta* (Minsk political and economic weekly) are both printed in Vilnius, Lithuania, in order to avoid government restrictions.

Broadcasting: The head of the state-owned radio and television is appointed by the president. There are few private radio stations. The obstacle to growth of private radio and television is the country's slow economic development and tiny advertising market.

Domestic economy

Until the break-up, Belarus boasted the former Soviet Union's highest living standards. In 1992 GDP fell by 4.6 per cent but lack of monetary control, declining oil supplies from Russia and a breakdown in the inter-state payments system have contributed to a 13 per cent decline in GDP between January and October 1993. On 7 September 1993 Belarus signed a currency union treaty with Russia and three central Asian republics. On 24 September it joined an economic union pact with nine republics. Under both arrangements, the government in Minsk would leave monetary, tax, trade and bank policy to Moscow. Debts to Russia total around R340bn for oil and R100bn for natural gas. Prices are being liberalised. There are serious environmental problems. Mass privatisation resumed 15 March 1995 after a suspension imposed in July 1994. Agreement in March 1996 on union with Russia.

External trade

Since July 1991 companies have been entitled to allocate some production to barter trade for which a permit is required.

Apart from the obvious lack of central bank independence, the IMF was also concerned about fiscal policy and the country's exchange rate regime. In the fiscal sphere, the 1995 government budget deficit equalled 3.2 per cent of GDP, double its level in 1994 (1.5 per cent), when Belarus' public finances began to improve for the first time in the post-Soviet period. Set in late 1995, the 1996 government budget deficit will almost certainly exceed its 1995 level. According to the IMF, its revenue and expenditure projections are completely unrealistic and in breach of earlier government commitments to the Fund.

Foreign exchange

The exchange rate has remained unchanged since the beginning of 1995. The IMF has argued that the Belarus rouble should be devalued to below R15,200 per US$1. Similar demands have also been made by local exporters and, even more importantly, Russia, which will not consider monetary union with Belarus at anywhere near the present Belarus rouble – Russian rouble parity.

Another major negative effect of Lukashenko's insistence that the exchange rate should remain within a band of between R11,300 and R13,100 per US$ has been severe pressure on NBB hard currency reserves in 1995/96. During the first half of 1995 alone, NBB support of the Belarus rouble cost in excess of US$100 million, with even higher intervention outlays during the third quarter of the year.

With declining NBB hard currency reserves, the government and the central bank had to delay the introduction of the taler. The government and the NBB had earlier intimated that it would be introduced when monthly inflation reached no more than 7 per cent. Although theoretically possible sometime in 1997, the Belarus rouble is unlikely to ever be replaced by the taler, not least because Lukashenko favours full monetary union with Russia and hence the exclusive use of the Russian rouble.

Another cause of the conflict with the IMF was a government decision in December 1995 to impose further restrictions on hard currency trading on the Belarus Interbank Currency Exchange. Already highly restricted, the exchange was placed under the control of the government in mid-1996, making it accountable to the NBB, which was in turn subordinated to the president from parliament. President Lukashenko also turned on the country's commercial banks in August 1996, blaming them for Belarus' economic ills. A presidential decree limited banks' foreign exchange transactions, capped salaries and forced all commercial banks to re-register with the government by 1 Janurary 1997. Lukashenko plans to create a banking sector fully controlled and answerable to the central authorities. The former NBB governor Stanislav Bogdankevich warned that Belarus' 40 commercial banks face closure or nationalisation, including the five largest in which the state has only a minority holding.

The purpose of this policy seemed to be to reduce domestic demand for hard currency so as to maintain the present Belarus rouble – US$ exchange rate. However, in practice all it has done is to drive hard currency trading into unofficial channels, thereby depriving commercial banks (and hence the NBB) of hard currency reserves. In 1995, it was estimated that only 60 per cent of the Belarus roubles in circulation were deposited in local banks.

Belarus has become an increasingly cash-based economy, particularly as regards privately held hard currency. By the end of 1995, such resources reportedly exceeded US$2 billion, including capital illegally exported by local enterprises and individuals. Official hard currency reserves, on the other hand, are declining, and may have been no more than US$500 million at the end of 1995.

Privatisation

Contrary to earlier government promises to the IMF, all types of privatisation were once again endlessly delayed for political reasons in 1995. Belarus has yet to complete even small-scale privatisation, including the disposal of state housing stock to tenants. Designed to involve 375 enterprises at the time of its launch in 1994, large-scale privatisation had only affected less than half that number of companies by the end of 1995.

Begun in July 1994, the distribution of privatisation vouchers for ownership transformation in these companies made very slow progress during 1995. By July 1995, only 40 per cent of those entitled

COUNTRY PROFILE — BELARUS

External trade (contd): On 18 September 1991 the government announced an export levy of 20 per cent on all Belarus products sold outside the republic. (At the last count only 6.5 per cent of exports went outside the former Soviet Union.) Seventy per cent of external trade with CIS.
Exports: Exports totalled US$3.1bn in 1995.
Imports: Imports totalled US$3.5bn in 1995.

Agriculture

The sector accounted for 24 per cent of GNP in 1994 and employed 19 per cent of the working population. Farmland is heavily contaminated by the Chernobyl nuclear disaster of 1986. The main crops are flax, sugar-beet, potatoes and other vegetables. Intensive poultry farming is practiced and dairy farming is increasing. There is a sizeable timber industry.

Industry

Industry accounted for 25 per cent of GNP in 1994 and employed 30 per cent of the workforce. Belarus had a heavily militarised industrial base before the dissolution of the Soviet Union. Output at military plants was halved in 1992 but conversion to civilian products lacks money and ideas. Main industry is micro-electronics and computers centred in and around Minsk. Large chemical and machine-building capabilities. Belarus is poor in natural resources and raw materials have to be imported. More than 80 per cent of Belarus industrial output was exported to the former Soviet republics and it is 100 per cent dependent on Russial energy supplies to run the manufacturing industry, which is its main source of revenue.

Hydrocarbons

Only small amounts of oil and gas.

Energy

Belarus possesses a good supply of peat.

Legal system

Relatively good legislative framework.

Membership of international organisations

CIS, Council of Europe (guest), CSCE, EBRD, IAEA, ICSID, IFC, IMF, MIGA, NACC, MIGA, OSCE, UN, World Bank.

BUSINESS GUIDE

Time

GMT +2 hrs (GMT +3 hrs from late Mar to late Sep).

Climate

Temperature in January 4-9 degrees C; August 14-22 degrees C.

Entry requirements

Visa: Visas are required for holders of passports from the following countries: USA, Canada, UK, Germany, France, Italy, Austria, Switzerland, Sweden, Norway and Finland.
Customs: Small amount of personal goods duty-free. On arrival declare all foreign currency and valuable items such as jewellery, cameras, computers and musical instruments.

Health precautions

Mandatory: Vaccination certificates are required for cholera or yellow fever if travelling from an infected area.
Advisable: Water precautions recommended (water purification tablets may be useful). It is advisable to be 'in date' for the following immunisations: polio (within 10 years), tetanus (within 10 years), typhoid fever, cholera (within six months), hepatitis 'A' (moderate risk only). There has been a significant increase in the number of cases of diphtheria. While the low dose, adult booster is unavailable, travellers are advised to be boosted with a reduced dose (0.1ml) of the paediatric single antigen vaccine. If never immunised, use three dose course of the vaccine. Any medicines required by the traveller should be taken by the visitor, and it could be wise to have precautionary antibiotics if going outside major urban centres. A travel kit including a disposable syringe is a reasonable precaution.

to privatisation vouchers had actually received them. Another deadline for voucher issuance in December 1995 passed with full voucher issuance still incomplete. Furthermore, only a third of those people who had received their vouchers by July 1995 had actually bothered to use them.

Other than popular apathy towards the entire exercise, the main obstacle is the low value of the privatisation vouchers. Nominally priced at R35,000 (US$3), they have typically traded for US$0.15 or less. Voucher trading is also poorly developed, where a functioning stock exchange has yet to be established. The little large-scale privatisation that has taken place to date has been entirely insider-orientated.

Parliamentary opposition to privatisation remains intense and government policy in this area is inconsistent and ineffective. In certain key sectors, such as financial services, government policy has been for tighter state controls. In other and mainly industrial sectors, government decrees have argued for the creation of large economic groups and the tightening of centralised controls over many companies. Covering both state and semi-privatised enterprises, this policy aims to recreate the conglomerates of the Soviet era. However, this will inevitably eliminate what little competition that now exists in Belarus, further impeding the privatisation of local companies.

To the government, the only acceptable foreign economic participation in these groupings is Russian participation. In 1995, one such deal was the takeover of Naftan, which controls the large Novopolotsk oil refinery, by two Russian oil companies, Lukoil and Yukas. Further such debt-for-equity deals are expected in 1996, but only with Russian interests. Although not explicitly disallowed, western foreign direct investment (FDI) in Belarus' flawed privatisation programme is, in practice, highly unlikely.

Foreign investment

So far, western foreign direct investment FDI in Belarus remains very low, at around US$100 million by the end of 1995. Continued political and economic uncertainty in Belarus means this is unlikely to change in the foreseeable future. Furthermore, there is considerable government ambivalence bordering on outright hostility towards the notion of increased FDI from the west in Belarus.

Under different circumstances, however, western FDI could grow substantially, particularly as regards agriculture-food processing, timber products, light manufacturing and services. Regionally, Belarus has considerable potential, located as it is between the EU, Poland and Russia, and the Baltic States and central Europe. In 1995, such considerations motivated Ford to enter into a joint venture for the manufacture of commercial vehicles for local sale and export to the rest of the CIS. Of the little FDI that has entered Belarus, most has been from Germany and Italy in the EU.

External trade

Equal to just over two-thirds of GDP, the total foreign trade turnover of Belarus was around US$6.6 billion in 1995, of which 70 per cent was with the former Soviet Union. In 1995, foreign trade with Russia alone accounted for over 60 per cent of the total. At over 80 per cent of total imports, Russian oil and gas remain of central economic importance. Accounting for only 15 per cent of exports and imports in 1995, foreign trade with the EU remains insignificant.

Previously dominated by higher added value manufactured goods, exports have more recently shifted towards lower value base chemicals, timber products and semi-processed goods. Imports, on the other hand, are mainly higher value energy resources. The fact that such imports from Russia have mainly been supplied at below cost, on extended credit or even gratis, explains the economic survival of Belarus in recent years.

Belarus' major foreign trade challenges are presented by its stagnating exports and over-dependence on barter trade with other CIS republics, particularly Russia. In 1994 and 1995, exports remained constant at US$3.1 billion per annum. Plagued by energy supply and payment problems, Belarus' industrial sector has also been unable to compete in the rapidly changing Russian market. This poor export performance has been further reinforced by the over-valued Belarus rouble. In the EU, Belarus' main exports are timber and other raw materials, plus some base chemicals.

BUSINESS GUIDE — BELARUS

Representation overseas

Consulates: Beijing, Bonn, Geneva, Paris, Tel Aviv, Vienna, Washington, Warsaw.
Representatives: Amsterdam, Berne, London, Rome.

Air access

National airline: Belavia Belorussian Association of Civil Aviation (Belarussian Airlines) (state-owned).
Other airlines: Austrian Airlines, Estonian Airlines, LOT, Lufthansa, Swissair, Transaero.
International airport: Minsk, 3.2 km west of the city.

Hotels

There are no western-standard hotels in Belarus. Intourist operates a number of hotels that can be booked from the west but visitors report bad conditions.

City transport

The public transport system in Minsk is excellent, with a bus line in almost every street. The metro system has been expanded with an east-west line.

National transport

International train tickets and reservations can be made at Francyska Skaryny Prospekt No 18, Minsk.

Public holidays

Fixed dates: 1 Jan (New Year), 7 Jan (Christmas), 8 Mar (Women's Day), 1 May (May Day), 9 May (Victory Day), 27 Aug (Independence Day), 2 Nov (Remembrance Day), 25 Dec (Christmas).
Variable dates: Easter, Orthodox Easter, Radounitsa (ninth day after Orthodox Easter Monday).

Working hours

Business: (Mon–Fri) 0900–1800 (appointments best between 0900–1000).
Shops: (Mon) 0800–1900, (Tue–Sat) 0800–2100.

Telecommunications

Telephone and telefax: Dialling code for Belarus: IDD access code + 375 followed by area code (0172 for Minsk, 01622 for Brest), followed by subscriber's number. It is usually necessary to make calls via the operator.

Banking

The National Bank of Belarus and the Commercial Bank for Foreign Economic Activity were established in 1991. In November 1991 all Belarus enterprises were instructed to transfer their hard currency funds from the Russian Vnesheconombank to the republic's foreign economic bank. Two-tier banking system has begun and guidelines have been established for bank joint ventures, wholly foreign-owned banks and representative offices.
Central bank: National Bank of Belarus.
Other banks: See 'Business Directory, Banking'.

BUSINESS DIRECTORY

Hotels

Minsk
Belarus, 15 Storozhevskaya (tel: 292-610).

Druzhba, 3 Tolbukhin St (tel: 662-481).

Minsk, 11 Leninsky Prosp.

Planeta, 31 Masherov Prosp , 220122 (tel: 267-853).

Yubileynaya, 19 Masherov Prosp, 220122 (tel: 269-023, 269-024).

Car hire

Minsk
Europcar: 11 Masherov Avenue, 220004 (tel: 269-062; fax: 238-716).

Chambers of commerce

Chamber of Commerce and Industry of the Republic of Belarus, Department of Foreign Economic Co-operation, 14 Masherova Ave, Minsk 220035 (tel: 269-169; fax: 269-936, 269-860); Department of International Relations (tel: 269-187, 269-172).

Payments problems in relation to both Russia and the EU have seriously impeded import growth. In 1995, imports were US$3.5 billion, compared to US$3.6 billion in 1994. In 1996, improved oil and gas supplies from Russia may revive imports.

Higher imports and stagnating exports imply greater trade deficits in the future. In 1995, the trade deficit was US$400 million; it may reach US$500 million in 1996. Previously financed by increased foreign borrowings in the west, it is unclear how these growing trade deficits will be financed without a *rapprochement* with the IMF in 1996 or 1997.

On the current account, Belarus registered a deficit of US$400 million in 1995, compared to a US$550 million deficit in 1994. As in 1994, the main reasons for this were lower than expected new foreign borrowings, the continued lack of significant FDI and low service earnings.

The current account deficit would have then been far worse but for Russian forbearance on Belarus' energy supply debts. In return, Belarus earns very little from the transit of Russian gas over its territory. In the longer-term, this may change when major new Russian gas export pipelines over its territory are built by around 2000. Regionally, Belarus also has considerable potential for other trans-shipment, but this will not be fully realised until its transportation infrastructure is much improved. If current political and economic trends continue, Belarus' foreign trade and balance of payments are likely to remain precarious for many years to come.

Foreign debt

Up from US$2 billion in 1994 to US$3 billion in 1995, Belarus' foreign debt continues to increase. As in 1994, around half of this debt was for past Russian oil and gas supplies. Mainly repayable via debt for equity swaps and the waiving of transit fees for Russian gas trans-shipped over Belarus to Poland and the EU, most of these outstanding energy debt liabilities were cancelled by Russia in February 1996. Improved Russian oil and gas supplies in 1996, however, mean this problem will remain. As a result, Russia could gain effective control over the most valuable components of the local economy. This is now a matter of some controversy in Belarus as it is in nearby Ukraine.

Beyond Russia, however, Belarus' foreign debt position remains uncertain after its difficulties with the IMF in 1995/96. Although a total of US$400 million was agreed by the IMF in 1995, less than half this figure had been actually disbursed as of January 1996.

Other western official funding is also tied to these IMF credits. New foreign borrowings from the west were therefore less than expected in 1995/96. In 1993/94, a US$98 million IMF loan enabled Belarus to substantially increase its foreign borrowings from the west for the first time since independence. The main result of that in 1995/96 was a rapid fall in local hard currency reserves, a negative trend that is unlikely to change until Belarus' relations with the IMF and the other multilateral institutions improve.

Outlook

Despite ever closer political and economic relations with Russia in 1995/96, doubts remain as to whether a full union between the two countries will ever take place. Closer relations with Russia imply worsening relations with the west, where Belarus has major difficulties with the IMF and other official creditors. At worst, Belarus could end up with both an unsatisfactory union with Russia and international isolation.

The future course of events in Belarus is also highly uncertain, especially if the proposed union with Russia does not materialise, or, if it does, its expected benefits are less than expected. Whatever happens in relation to Russia and the West, political instability and social unrest can only worsen in the future. The greatest potential danger is Lukashenko's continued attempts to create a full dictatorship in Belarus, where resistance to his one-man rule is growing.

Continued doubts about the desirability and possible consequences of union with Russia could give Belarus' hitherto marginal nationalist opposition a new lease of life in 1996 or 1997. In this regard, the main political danger for Lukashenko is the fact that his opponents now include a number of influential figures, notably former NBB Governor Bogdankevich and former Supreme Soviet Chairman Stanislav Shushkevich.

BUSINESS DIRECTORY — BELARUS

Banking

National Bank of Belarus (central bank), 20 F Skorina Avenue Minsk 220008 (tel: 270-946; fax: 271-801); Foreign Operations Department (tel: 276-658).

Belagroprom Bank, 44 Kropotkina Street, Minsk 220002 (tel: 503-958).

Bel Vnesh Econom Bank (Belarus Bank for Foreign Economic Affairs), 10 Zaslavskaya Street, Minsk 220004 (tel: 269-757, 267-022; fax: 269-759).

Commercial Bank for Reconstruction and Development (Belbusinessbank), 6a Partizansky Ave, 220033 Minsk (tel: 298-147, 768-942; fax: 298-147, 768-504).

Principal newspapers

Belorussia, 4th Zagorodnyi Pereulok 56A, Minsk 220073 (tel: 519-481).

Belorusskaya Delovaya Gazeta, Plochad Svobody 17-518, Minsk 220061 (tel: 267-877, 238-588; fax: 269-678).

Belorusski Predprinimatel, Prospekt Fransiska Skorina 77, Komnata 332, Minsk 220041 (398-732, 398-734).

Ekanamicheskaja Gazeta, PR-T Masherava 23, Minsk 220048 (tel: 269-353, 236-362).

Express-Kontakt, Ulitsa Botanitjeskaja 15, Minsk (377-336; fax: 233-291).

Financy, Magic, Ulitsa Kalinina 7-26, Minsk 220012 (tel: 669-561).

Litteratura Mastatjtva, Belorus Ministry of Culture, GSP, Ulitsa Sacharova 19, Minsk 220041 (tel: 332-461, 332-164).

Minskaja Pravda, County Council of Minsk, Prospekt Fransiska Skorina 79, Minsk 220600 (tel: 322-032, 325-001).

Narodnaya Gazeta, Dom pravityelstva, Komnata 369, Minsk 220010 (tel: 296-044, 646-268, 662-658; fax: 273-763).

Respublika, Ulitsa Sovjetskaja 9, Minsk 220010 (tel: 296-573).

Sovetskaya Belorussiya, Ulitsa B. Hmelnhikova 10A, Minsk 220013 (tel: 682-552, 682-563; fax: 321-451).

Vetjerni Minsk, Prospekt Fransiska Skorini 44, Minsk 220805 (tel: 330-054, 339-223).

Znamija lonosti, Dom Petjati, Prospekt Fransiska Skorina 79, Minsk 220041 (tel: 328-131, 682-684; fax: 325-569).

Zvjazda, Prospekt Fransiska Skorina 77, Minsk 220041 (tel: 325-105, 682-919).

7 Dnei, Belta, Ulitsa Kirova 26, Minsk 220600 (tel: 293-042, 275-858; fax: 271-346).

Travel information

Belavia Belorussian Association of Civil Aviation (Belarussian Airlines), Minsk Aerodromnaya, Str 4, Minsk 220065 (tel: 255-902, 250-836; fax: 251-566, 250-629).

Belintourist Office, Minsk.

Other useful addresses

Belarusintorg Foreign Trade Organisation, Ulitsa Kollektornaya 10, 220048 Minsk (tel: 207-812, 209-756, 208-188; fax: 209-470, 204-763).

Ministry of Agriculture, Dom Pravitelstva, Minsk (tel: 271-377, 271-352, 205-492).

Ministry of Finance, Dom Pravitelstva, 220010 Minsk (tel: 296-949).

Ministry of Foreign Affairs, Leninski Prospekt 8, 220795 Minsk (tel: 272-922; fax: 274-521).

Ministry of Information, Prospekt Mashirova 11, Minsk (tel: 237-574).

News Agency (tel: 293-040).

State Committee for Foreign Economic Affairs, Lenina Ul. D.14, Minsk (tel: 241-758, 296-084).

State Committee for Economic Planning, Dom Pravitelstva, Minsk (tel: 296-944).

Belgium

Dan Bindman

When Belgium's parliament granted the government of Jean-Luc Dehaene sweeping powers in July 1996 to force the economy into line with the European Union's Maastricht criteria on monetary union, it opened the door to major legislation to bring down the country's budget deficit and reform the social security system. This move came against a background of widespread social malaise and unrest following relevations of extensive paedophile rings. These were accompanied by accusations of high level governmental and judicial participation and involvement in cover-up operations. Renewed tensions between the country's Dutch and French language groups also flared despite the new 'healing' constitution being in force for over a year.

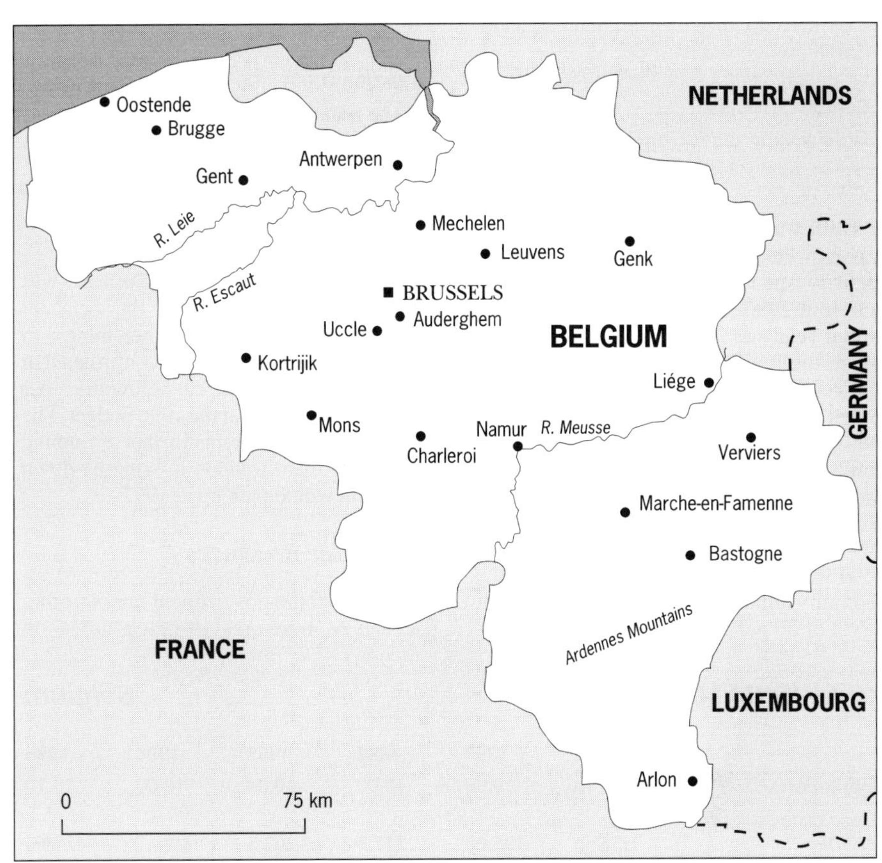

Preparing for 1999

Prime Minister Dehaene is at the head of a four-party centre left coalition. Between them, the four ruling Flemish and Francophone Socialist and Christian Democrat parties held 81 of the 150 seats. Before winning an extension of his power in mid-1996 Mr Dehaene had suffered a personal blow when he lost the chairman of his governing Christian Democrat Party (CVP), Johan Van Hecke. Mr Van Hecke resigned after two and a half years in the job ostensibly for personal reasons, possibly connected with his impending divorce. He had been expected to be re-elected unopposed one week later at a party congress.

The July 1996 victory of the centre-left Dehaene government in securing permission to rule by decree until August 1997 was largely an acknowledgement by the country's political leaders that drastic measures were needed if Belgium was to achieve its desire to participate in the first wave of European currency union in January 1999. The parliament approved the law on the budget and economic and monetary union by 81 votes to 53.

An indication of the depth of Belgium's conviction that it would be among the first countries to join a single currency came in early 1996, when Deputy Prime Minister Elio Di Rupo called on the nation's banks to merge or risk being taken over by foreign banking groups after monetary union.

He argued that competition would become stronger and Belgian banks would lose the protection afforded them by the Belgian franc. Soon afterwards Générale de Banque, the country's largest bank, said it was sticking with its 'stand-alone' philosophy. It announced simultaneously an 8.1 per cent increase in net profit in 1995 to US$451.7 million.

Budget

The 1997 budget was expected to contain revenue-raising measures and spending cuts worth some US$2.6 billion, a little over US$1 billion less than those in the 1996 budget. The principle means of bringing down the budget deficit, which

KEY FACTS — Belgium

Official title: Royaume de Belgique (French), Koninkrijk België (Dutch), Königreich Belgien (German) (The Kingdom of Belgium)

Head of state: King Albert II of Liège

Head of government: Prime Minister Jean-Luc Dehaene (CVP)

Ruling party: Centre-left coalition: Flemish Christian Democrats (CVP), Flemish Socialists (SP), French-speaking Christian Democrats (PSC), French-speaking Socialists (PS)

Capital: Brussels

Official Languages: Dutch and French

Currency: Belgian franc (Bf) = 100 centimes

Exchange rate: Bf32.00 per US$ (Dec 1996)

Area: 30,518 sq km

Population: 10.1m (1995)

GDP per capita: US$26,280 (1995)

GDP real growth: 1.5% (2nd qtr 1996)

Unemployment: 12.8% (Jun 1996) (not seasonally adjusted)

Inflation: 1.5% (1995) (consumer prices)

Trade balance: US$12.1bn (12 months to Jul 1996)

in 1995 was estimated to be 4.5 per cent was expected to be savage cuts in social security spending. The forecast for the deficit in 1996 made after the first quarter of that year was 3.5 per cent, considerably above the maximum deficit of 3 per cent allowed by the Maastricht treaty for economies able to join currency union. Gross public debt, according to the Maastricht definition, was reported by the National Bank to stand at 133.5 per cent of gross domestic product (GDP) at the end of 1995, down from 135.1 per cent in 1994. The downward trend was encouraging, but the economy remained far from the Maastricht target of 60 per cent debt to GDP ratio.

Social security reform

Armed with his new powers, Dehaene was expected to legislate to reform the social security system and, among other things, to impose wage controls. But he confirmed that the deficit would not be cut below the 3 per cent target contained in the 1996 budget. The government was optimistic that economic growth, the main weapon in bringing down the deficit, would pick up in 1997.

Anti-crime measures

In June 1996 the government announced a package of measures to crack down on organised crime. Justice Minister Stefaan De Clercq said the move followed a study into the scale of Belgium's organised crime problem. Rules on telephone tapping by police would be relaxed and the authorities would be given powers to monitor mobile telephone, telex and fax communications. More lenient sentences would be granted to criminals who co-operate with the police and a witness protection programme would be created. The onus would be placed on suspects to prove they obtained goods legally and the law would be widened to include people who were accessories to organised crime.

This crime crackdown came just weeks after the Belgian parliament approved by 129 votes to 13 a measure to erase the country's death penalty law from the statute books. The last execution took place in 1950 and the abolition of capital punishment was in accordance with the widely-held belief in Belgium that it is worthless as a deterrent to crime. It would be replaced by a life sentence of up to 30 years, although this would be limited to a maximum of 14 years in practice.

KEY INDICATORS — Belgium

	Unit	1991	1992	1993	1994	1995
Population	m	9.98	10.00	10.04	10.08	10.10
Gross domestic product (GDP)	US$bn	196.00	217.7	207.5	226.7	268.0
GDP per capita	US$	19,500	21,770	20,690	22,500	26,280
GDP real growth	%	1.9	0.8	-1.2	2.3	1.9
Inflation	%	3.2	2.4	2.8	2.4	1.5
Consumer prices	1990=100	103.2	105.7	108.6	111.2	112.8
Unemployment	%	7.1	7.9	9.8	12.6	*12.1
Agricultural production**	1979-81=100	130.12	139.30	144.53	137.74	137.89
Industrial share prices	1990=100	97	95	99	114	107
Industrial production	1990=100	98.0	97.9	93.0	94.7	–
Exports (FOB) (goods)**	US$m	107,990	116,841	106,302	122,879	157,900
Imports (FOB) (goods)**	US$m	105,991	113,141	100,522	115,949	149,100
Balance of trade**	US$m	1,999	3,700	5,780	6,930	8,800
Current account**	US$m	4,746	6,650	11,237	13,021	15,100
Total reserves minus gold	US$m	12,180	13,801	11,415	13,876	16,177
Foreign exchange	US$m	11,068	12,825	10,474	12,884	14,680
Discount rate	%	8.50	7.75	5.25	4.50	3.00
Deposit rate	%	6.25	6.25	7.11	4.86	4.04
Exchange Rate	Bf per US$	34.15	32.15	34.60	33.46	29.48

* estimated figure **Belgium/Luxembourg Economic Union

Economy

According to the National Bank, Belgium's GDP increased by only 1.9 per cent in 1995, compared with 2.3 per cent in 1994 and compared with average growth across the 15 European Union countries in 1995 of 2.5 per cent. The Organisation for Economic Co-operation and Development in Europe (OECD) estimated in June 1996 that the economy would grow by just 1.1 per cent, just 0.1 per cent higher than an estimate made by the European Union a month earlier.

The 1995 figure masked the fact that the economy had actually contracted during the year, resulting from a slowdown that affected Belgium's main trading partners. The slowdown occurred in the second and third quarters, with respectively an annualised decline in GDP of 1.1 per cent and 1.6 per cent. National Bank figures showed a 1.8 per cent GDP growth in the fourth quarter compared with the third quarter and a 1 per cent growth from the last quarter of 1995 to the first quarter of 1996. Responsibility for the poor performance in 1995 was laid at the door of waning industrial activity, although an improvement occurred in the final months of the year.

Industrial production excluding building ended 4 per cent up in 1995 compared with the previous year, but this figure ignored a drastic fall of just over 19 per cent in the number of building permits in 1995, the first annual drop since 1991. The volume of exports declined by about 5 per cent in the second quarter of 1995 and barely improved in the rest of the year. While import growth also slowed in the second quarter, their volume increased by over 1 per cent, thus detracting from general growth.

Significantly, domestic demand remained relatively steady throughout 1995. Private consumption in the last three quarters and the first quarter of 1996 rose by an average of about 1.8 per cent. After a jittery start in early 1995, over the last three quarters of the year business investment grew by an average of 9.5 per cent. However, the first quarter of 1996 showed a disappointing shortfall, with a decline of 6.7 per cent.

Inflation

Consumer price inflation on an annualised basis hovered around the 2 per cent mark in early 1996. Largely due to higher excise duties on petrol and a rise in the highest value added tax rate on 1 January by 0.5 per cent, bringing it to 21 per cent, inflation increased from just 1.5 per cent in December 1995 to 2 per cent in the following month. An increase in oil prices and a strengthened US dollar contributed to the worsening prices situation. At the end of Nov 1996, year on year inflation stood at 2.4 per cent, compared with 1.3 per cent for the full year 1995.

Employment

At the end of 1995 the number of unemployed job-seekers stabilised, although it was still close to 3 per cent higher than at the same point in 1994. It rose to 3.5 per cent higher year on year in January 1996. However, in the first half of 1996 matters improved slightly. In January, there were 610,000 job seekers and by the end of June there were 585,000 after six months of steady decline. The June 1996 figure was 10,000 down on the corresponding month in 1995.

According to the National Bank, in May 1996 the Belgium's harmonised rate of employment stood at 9.8 per cent of the civilian workforce, compared with 10.8 per cent for the 15 European Union countries.

For those in work, it was forecast that 1996 would see unit wage costs in the business sector increase by 2 per cent, an increase of some 0.4 per cent on 1995. In April 1996 Prime Minister Dehaene agreed a contract for the future, involving a deal in which accepting a mechanism to restrain wage growth and index it with neighbouring countries would be repaid with job creation measures. There would also be a phased reduction in the social costs which burdened employers. Not everyone was happy with the pact, however. Soon afterwards the FGTB union, one of the country's largest, complained that it had not included guarantees on job creation schemes.

One development which was expected to assist job creation was a massive US$2.18 billion investment over 10 years in the Belgian state railway company (NMBS-SNCB), announced in February 1996. All but 10 per cent of the sum would go into new rolling stock, with the residue spent on the modernisation of current rolling stock. The company hoped that the investment, together with a restructuring plan, would make it profitable again by the year 2005.

Greener Belgium

Rail fares formed a key part of a government campaign to reduce pollution, launched in mid-1996, two weeks before Mr Dehaene called for strengthened international co-operation on environmental protection at the congress of the International Confederation of Free Trade Unions. The Belgian anti-pollution measures formed part of a 15-point campaign against the worst atmospheric ozone levels in Europe. They included cutting summer peak railway fares by 25 per cent, involving a government subsidy to NMBS-SNCB, of some US$5 million. Enhanced roadside checks on speeding motorists were also pledged and the acceleration of a programme to close coal-fired power stations was being actively considered.

COUNTRY PROFILE — BELGIUM

Historical profile

Known as 'the cockpit of Europe', its geographical position made Belgium for centuries a battleground for France, Spain and Austria. Despite European powers' pledge of neutrality and independence, invaded by Germany in 1914 and 1940. Interwar years saw rapid industrialisation, developing colonial wealth, forging of links leading to Benelux customs union, and emergence of divisive French/Dutch language and cultural problem. Its peacetime position advantageous for trade and industry, Belgium has become one of Europe's most heavily industrialised countries, and houses the headquarters of NATO and the EU (of which it is a founder member). From the 1970s there has been a succession of unstable coalition governments.
1981 Wilfried Martens became prime minister.
1992 Luc Dehaene, the former Flemish Christian Democrat, was appointed prime minister.
1993 In July King Baudouin I died and was succeeded by his brother, Albert.

Political system

Constitutional and hereditary monarchy, consisting of nine provinces. Legislative power vested in monarch and bicameral parliament (Senate and Chamber). As of May 1995, Senate has 71 members, and Chamber of Representatives has 150 members (deputies). Both chambers can propose and veto legislation, though the political make-up of the government is determined by the composition of the Chamber of Representatives. The existence of three communities (French, Flemish and German-speaking) and of three regions (the Walloon, Flemish and Brussels regions) is constitutionally recognised and various powers have been devolved to their councils (parliaments) and executives (governments). The shift towards federalism has resulted in directly elected regional parliaments. Federal government retains powers of taxation, monetary policy, defence and law and order. Next election by May 1999.

Political parties:

Coalition government: Christelijke Volkspartij (Christian People's Party) (CVP) (Flemish); Parti Social Chrétien (Christian Socialist Party (PS) (Walloon); Socialistische Party (Socialist Party) (SP) (Flemish); Parti Socialist (Socialist Party (PS) (Walloon). Other major parties include Vlaamse Liberalen en Demokraten (Flemish Liberals and Democrats (VLD); Parti Réformateur Libéral (Liberal Reform Party (PRL) (Walloon).

Main cities/towns

Brussels, capital (population 1.8m in 1994), Antwerp, Ghent, Charleroi, Bruges, Liège and Mons.

Language

Dutch or Flemish spoken in north (Flanders), French spoken in south (Wallonia) (both official); small German-speaking minority in east. English also spoken.

Media

Dailies: Over 30 dailies in both French and Dutch, including *Le Soir, La Libre Belgique, De Standaard, Het Laatste Nieuws/de Nieuwe Gazet.*
Weeklies: Weekly publications include *Knack* (Wed, Flemish) and *Le Vif/L'Express* (Fri).
Business: Principal business papers/magazines: *L'Echo* (daily, Tue – Fri), *De Financieel Ekonomische Tijd* (daily, Tue – Fri), *Belgian Business and Industrie Magazine* (monthly), *Trends/Tendances* (weekly, Thur).
Broadcasting: Over 3m TVs and 4.5m radios in use. 'Radio-Télévision Belge de la Communauté Française' (RTBF) broadcasts in French, and 'Belgische Radio en Televisie' (BRT) in Dutch. There are two commercial TV stations: RTBF (French language) and VTM (Dutch) and BRT with no advertising. Several foreign broadcasts received, either direct or via cable. Cable TV covers most of the country.
Advertising: Complicated by language problems. Information available from Ministry of Economic Affairs. Key categories: department stores, shops, automotives and banking.

Domestic economy:

Characterised by broad industrial base with heavy dependence on external trade. Economic growth picked up after the introduction of tight fiscal/monetary policies in 1982, including the 1982 devaluation of the Belgian franc, and wage and price controls. In 1992 the government gave the reduction of the budget deficit and government debt the highest priority. Economy slumped severely in 1992 and 1993 but started to recover by 1994. High unemployment rate in 1995 (14.7 per cent – second highest in EU).

Employment:

Steady decline in employment in traditional industrial and construction sectors, and an increase in service sector. Unemployment rate stabilised owing to employment support measures, rise in service sector vacancies and more work-sharing. Real wages continue to lag behind inflation due to wage increase restrictions and price control. Workforce highly skilled and highly unionised. About 33 per cent of the workforce are female.

External trade

Regular trade deficit reversed from 1983 onwards owing to strong growth in exports. Many companies export more than 80 per cent of their production. Major world exporter of carpets, diamonds, iron and steel, copper products, glass, chemicals and motor vehicles. Around 70 per cent of imports consist of producer goods, of which metal products and petroleum predominate.
Exports: Main destinations: EU, Germany, France, Netherlands.
Imports: Main sources: EU, Germany, Netherlands, France.

Agriculture

The agriculture sector accounted for 2 per cent of GDP in 1994 and employed 2.6 per cent of the workforce. Although small-scale, cultivation is intensive, especially in Flanders. Self-sufficient in sugar, eggs, butter and meat, and exporter of vegetables and horticultural produce. The amount of land under cultivation is falling. Fishing less important, only for domestic market.

Industry

The large-scale, export-based industrial sector contributed 29.7 per cent to GDP in 1994 and employed 28 per cent of the labour force. Main activities include metal working (leading EU producer of non-ferrous metals), cement, chemicals, food processing, diamond cutting, textiles, glass and motor vehicle assembly. Rationalisation of traditional industries together with upturn in export demand has led to growth in industrial production after period of rapid decline.

Mining

The mining sector accounted for 0.3 per cent of GDP in 1994 and employed 0.4 per cent of the workforce. Only coal, clay and sand are mined on any substantial scale.

Hydrocarbons

Coal production from the Kempische Steenkoolmijnen in Limburg has steadily fallen due to declining demand for coke from industry and rapid change-over to nuclear fuel.

Energy

Around 80 per cent of requirements met by imports. Highest energy consumption per head in EU but since introduction of conservation programme in 1982, dependence on imported gas and oil has fallen. Nuclear power accounts for 60 per cent of electricity output.

Membership of international organisations

ADB, AG (observer), BENELUX, BLEU, BOAD, CCC, CERN, Council of Europe, CSCE, DAC, EEA, ECE, ECOSOC, EIB, EMS, ESA, ESRO, EU, European Space Agency, FAO, Food Aid Convention, G-10, IAEA, ICAC, ICAO, ICES, ICO, IDA, IDB, IEA, IFAD, IFC, ILO, IMF, IMO, INTELSAT, Interpol, International Lead and Zinc Study Group, IOOC, IPU, ITC, ITU, MIGA, NACC, NATO, OAS (observer), OECD, UN, UNESCO, UNIDO, UPU, WEU, WHO, WIPO, WMO, World Bank, WSG, WTO.

BUSINESS GUIDE

Time

GMT +1 hr (GMT +2 hrs from late Mar to late Sep).

Climate

Temperate, with warm weather from May–Sep. Summer temperature averages around 18°C, winter around 1°C. Hottest month Jul, coldest Jan. Rain throughout the year, wettest months Oct–Nov.

Entry requirements

Visas not required by nationals of USA, Japan and most western European countries for period of up to three months.
Currency: No restrictions on foreign or local currency movements.
Customs: Personal effects and goods (up to the value of BF25,000 for non-European residents and BF7,500 for European residents) duty free.

Air access:

Frequent first-class and economy flights linking Brussels with over 90 international cities.
National airline: Sabena Belgian World Airlines. The merger of Swissair, Switzerland's national airline, with Sabena was approved in July 1995. Under the deal Swissair acquires a 49.5 per cent stake in Sabena which will remain in Belgian control.
Tax: Adult departure tax Brussels BF510; Antwerp BF250 (Jan 1996), excluding transit passengers.
Main international airport: Brussels (BRU), 13 km north-east of city centre (Zaventem).
International airports: Antwerp (ANR), 3 km from city, Ostend (OST), Liège (LGG), 8 km from city.

Surface access:

Good road and rail access with the main centres of the Netherlands, France, Germany and Luxembourg. Also daily crossings by boat or jetfoil from Ostend or Zeebrugge to UK.
Main ports: Antwerp, Ghent, Zeebrugge, Ostend, Brussels, Liège.

Hotels

Advisable to book hotel or pension in advance either direct or through Belgium Tourist Reservations. All tariffs must be displayed by law. Service charge usually included. Tipping 10 per cent. Major credit cards accepted.

Car hire

Available at airports and in most main towns. Speed limits: urban roads 60 kph, main roads 90 kph. Maximum speed on motorways 120 kph, minimum speed 70 kph. Drive on the right. Wearing of seat belts compulsory. Usually prohibited for children under 12 to sit in front seats.

City transport

A 24-hour tourist ticket valid on all Brussels subway, tram and bus lines is on sale at the Information and Tourist Welcome Office, 63 rue du Marche-aux-Herbes, 1 Grasmarkt, and at the Tourist Information Bureau located in the City Hall (Hôtel de Ville), Grand-Place, Grohe Markt.
Taxis: Readily available. Standardised fare system, which includes service charge. Chauffeur-driven cars cheaper on long runs.
Buses: Regular flat fare tram and bus service.
Metro: Networks in Brussels and Antwerp. Société des Transports Intercommunaud Bruxellois (tel: 515-2000).
Rail: Special airport shuttle service operates from Brussels Central Station and North Station. Train (first and second class) departs every hour.

National transport

Air: Limited internal service.
Road: Extensive road network. Toll-free motorways serve all main towns with the exception of those in the Ardennes. Comprehensive coach service, particularly to rural areas, operated by Société Nationale des Chemins de Fer Belges (SNCB) and Société Nationale des Chemins de Fer Vicinaux (SNCV).
Rail: Belgium said to have densest railway network in world. Service operated by Société Nationale des Chemins de Fer Belges (SNCB). First- and second-class service serves all main towns. Combined tickets allowing for stop-overs in main towns offer best value. Express trains (TEE) ensure rapid connections with French, Dutch and German cities. Over half railway electrified.
Water: Over 1,500 km inland waterways, 50 km per 1,000 sq km. Service operated by Administration des Voies Hydrauliques. Inland canals connect with major French, Dutch and German ports.

Public holidays

Fixed dates: 1 Jan (New Year's Day), 1 May (Labour Day), 21 Jul (Independence Day), 15 Aug (Assumption), 1 Nov (All Saints' Day), 11 Nov (Armistice Day), 25 Dec (Christmas). Fixed-date holidays that fall on a Sun. are observed on the following Mon.
Variable dates: Easter Monday, Ascension Day, Whit Monday. (Also: 11 Jul – Dutch-Speaking Community Day and 27 Sep – French-Speaking Community Day.)

Working hours

Business: (Mon–Fri) 0830–1630.
Government: (Mon–Fri) 0900–1700.
Banking: (Mon–Fri) 0900–1200 and 1400–1600.
Shops: There are large variations in opening hours; typically 0900–1900.

Social customs:

Attention to language sensibility is a must. Two culturally distinct halves – Dutch-speaking Flanders in north, French-speaking Wallonia in south. Brussels speaks mainly French. Polite to be punctual and to shake hands on arrival and departure.

Business language and interpreting/translation

Available from embassies, tourist offices, chambers of commerce and many commercial agencies. German only spoken by a minority. English is widely understood.

Telecommunications

Telephone and telefax: Local and international direct dialling (00). Public telephones take five or 20 cent coins. Telecards available from post offices, railway stations and tobacconists. International dialling code: 32 followed by 2 for Brussels. For 'telefax' transmission of documents dial 1214 or 1314 for conference calls. For IDD access from Belgium dial 00. Directory enquiries: 1380 (local to Brussels); 1329 (within another Belgian zone); 1324 (international).
Telex: Available in most major hotels. Country code 46 B.
Telegram: Service available from telegraph offices (open 24 hrs/day) and by telephone.

Postal service

Post offices open 0930–1200 and 1400–1600 (Mon–Fri), longer in main towns. Mail can be sent Poste Restante to main post offices – passport required when collecting.

Banking:

Divided into three main groups – commercial banks, public credit institutions and private savings banks. Some 85 commercial banks, of which largest are Générale de Banque, Banque Bruxelles Lambert and Kredietbank. Banque Nationale de Belgique is responsible for implementing monetary and credit controls and since major reforms in 1990 it can intervene in money markets and can conduct open market operations, while the Institut Belgo–Luxembourgeois du Change maintains control over foreign exchange transactions. In April 1993 Belgium enacted a law guaranteeing the independence of its central bank and preventing the Treasury from borrowing from the Bank. The law was passed as part of Belgium's efforts to meet the conditions for economic and monetary union.
Central bank: Banque Nationale de Belgique.
Other banks: See 'Business Directory, Banking'.

Trade fairs

Several international exhibitions, of which Brussels International Trade Fair and

COUNTRY PROFILE

Trade fairs (contd): International Fair of Flanders in Ghent are most important. Information available from Ministry of Economic Affairs Exhibitions Office. Belgium ranks second in Europe for the number of international conventions.

Electricity supply

220 V AC.

Representation in capital

Algeria, Angola, Argentina, Australia, Austria, Bangladesh, Barbados, Benin, Bolivia, Botswana, Brazil, Bulgaria, Burkina Faso, Burundi, Cameroon, Canada, Central African Republic, Chad, Chile, China, Colombia, Comoros, Congo, Costa Rica, Côte d'Ivoire, Cuba, Cyprus, Denmark, Dominica, Ecuador, Egypt, Ethiopia, Fiji, Finland, France, Gabon, The Gambia, Germany, Ghana, Greece, Grenada, Guatemala, Guinea, Guinea Bissau, Guyana, Haiti, The Holy See, Honduras, Hungary, Iceland, India, Indonesia, Iran, Iraq, Ireland, Israel, Italy, Jamaica, Japan, Jordan, Kenya, Republic of Korea, Kuwait, Lebanon, Lesotho, Liberia, Libya, Luxembourg, Madagascar, Malawi, Malaysia, Mali, Malta, Mauritania, Mauritius, Mexico, Monaco, Morocco, Mozambique, Netherlands, New Zealand, Nicaragua, Niger, Nigeria, Norway, Pakistan, Panama, Papua New Guinea, Paraguay, Peru, Philippines, Poland, Portugal, Qatar, Romania, Russia, Rwanda, San Marino, São Tomé and Príncipe, Saudi Arabia, Senegal, Sierra Leone, Singapore, Somalia, South Africa, Spain, Sri Lanka, Sudan, Suriname, Swaziland, Sweden, Switzerland, Syria, Tanzania, Thailand, Togo, Trinidad and Tobago, Tunisia, Turkey, Uganda, United Arab Emirates, UK, USA, Venezuela, Western Samoa, Zaïre, Zambia, Zimbabwe.

BUSINESS DIRECTORY

Hotels

Brussels

Archimède, 22/24 rue Archimède, B-1040 (tel: 231-0909; fax: 230-3371).

Bedford, 135 rue du Midi, B-1000 (tel: 512-7840; fax: 514-1759).

Belson, 805 Chaussée de Louvain, 1140 (tel: 735-0000; fax: 735-6043).

Europa, 107 rue de la Loi, B-1040 (tel: 230-1333; fax: 230-3682).

Grand Scheers, 132 Boulevard Adolphe Max, B-1000 (tel: 217-7760; fax: 217-5750).

Hilton, 38 Boulevard de Waterloo, B-1000 (tel: 513-8877; fax: 513-7233).

Jolly Hotel du Grand Sablon, Place du Grand Sablon, B-1000 (tel: 512-8800).

Mayfair, 381/383 Avenue Louise, B-1050 (tel: 649-9800; fax: 640-1764).

Métropole, 31 Place de Brouckère, B-1000 (tel: 217-2300; fax: 218-0220).

Palace, rue Gineste 3, B-1210 (tel: 217-6200; fax: 218-7651).

Park Yser, Avenue de l'Yser 21, B-1040 (tel: 735-7400).

President Nord, 107 Boulevard Adolphe Max, B-1000 (tel: 219-0060; fax: 218-1269).

Queen Anne, 110 Boulevard Emile Jacqmain, B-1000 (tel: 217-1600; fax: 521-3516).

Ramada, Chaussée de Charleroi 38, B-1060 (tel: 539-3000; fax: 538-9014).

Royal Windsor, 5 rue Duquesnoy, B-1000 (tel: 511-4215; fax: 511-6004).

Scandic Crown, 250 rue Royale, B-1210 (tel: 217-1234; fax: 217-8444).

Sheraton, 3 Place Rogier, B-1210 (tel: 219-3400; fax: 218-6618).

Stephanie, Avenue Louise 91-93, B-1050 (tel: 539-0240; fax: 538-0307).

Car hire

Brussels

Budget: Ave Louise 327B, 1050 (tel: 646-5130; fax: 646-2721).

Europcar: international reservations, rue St Denis 117, 1190 (tel: 348-9212; fax: 344-1213); 235 Avenue Louise (tel: 640-9400).

Hertz: Boulevard Lemonnier 8 (tel: 513-2886; fax: 513-509).

Taxis:

Brussels

ATR (tel: 647-2222).

Autolux (tel: 512-3123).

Brussels Transport Company (513-6200).

Taxis Vert (tel: 349-4949).

Chambers of commerce

Antwerp Chamber of Commerce, Markgravestraat 12, B-2000 Antwerp (tel: 232-2219; fax: 233-6442).

Association des Chambres de Commerce et d'Industrie de Wallonie, Place Ryckmans 28, 5000 Namur (tel: 741-898; fax: 741-899).

Bruges–Kamer voor Handel en Nijverheid voor het Noorden van Westvlaanderen, Ezelstraat 25, B-8000 Brugge (tel: 333-696; tx: 81-282).

Brussels Chamber of Commerce, Avenue Louise 500, B-1050 Brussels (tel: 648-5002; fax: 640-9328).

Charleroi–Chambre de Commerce et d'Industrie de Charleroi, 1A Boulevard Général Michel, B-6000 Charleroi (tel: 321-160; tx: 51-624).

Ghent–Kamer van Koophandel & Nijverheid van het Gewest Ghent, Building Lieven Bauwens, 41 Martelaarslaan, B-9000 Ghent (tel: 253-307; tx: 11-871).

Liège: Chambre de Commerce et d'Industrie de Liège, Palais des Congres, Esplanade de l'Europe 2, 4020 Liege (tel: 43-9292; fax: 43-9267).

Nationale Federatie der Kamers Voor Handel en Nijverheid Van Belgie, Kunstlaan 1-2, B10, 1040 Brussel (tel: 217-3671; fax: 217-4634).

Namur–Chambre de Commerce et d'Industrie de Namur, Résidence Paola, Avenue G. Bovesse 117, B-5100 Jambes-lez-Namur (tel: 304-937).

Oostende–Kamer voor Handel en Nijverheid van Oostende, Langestraat 69, B-8400 Oostende (tel: 501-936; tx: 82-057).

Tournai–Chambre de Commerce et d'Industrie du Tournaisis, 9B Placette aux Oignons, B-7500 Tournai (tel: 221-121).

Banking

Banque Nationale de Belgique (central bank), Boulevard de Berlaimont 14, 1000 Brussels (tel: 221-2111; fax: 221-3100).

Aslk Bank N.V., Wolvengracht 48, 1000 Brussels (tel: 213-7147; fax: 213-9134).

Association Belge des Banques/Belgische Vereniging des Banken, 36 rue Ravenstein, Box 5, B-1000 Brussels (represents privately owned banks (tel: 512-5868).

Association des Caisses d'Epargne Priveés (private savings banks), 34–35 Place de Jamblinne de Meux, B-1040 Brussels (tel: 736-9920; tx: 63-186).

Bacob Banque, Rue de Tréves 25, 1040 Brussels (tel: 237-8211).

Bank Van Koophandel Van Brussel, Rue Royale 144 Koningstraat, 1000 Brussels (tel: 220-2111).

Banque Bruxelles Lambert S.A., Avenue Marnixlaan 24, 1050 Brussels (tel: 547-2111; tx: 21-421).

Banque Degroof, Rue de l'Industrie 44, Nijverheidsstraat 44, 1040 Brussels (tel: 287-9111).

Banque Paribas Belgique, WTC – Tour 1, Avenue Emile Jacqmain 162, B-1210 Brussels (tel: 219-3010).

Banque Sud Belge, Rue du Trone 60, 1050 Brussels (tel: 504-1511).

Belgolaise S.A., Cantersteen 1, 1000 Brussels (tel: 518-7211; fax: 518-7515).

Caisse Générale d'Epargne et de Retraite/Algemeene Spaar-en Lijfrentekas (state-owned), rue Fosse aux Loups 48, B-1000 Brussels (tel: 213-6111 ; tx: 26-860).

Caisse Privèe Banque S.A., Place Champ de Mars 2, 1050 Brussels (tel: 518-9211).

CC-Banque Belgique, Rue Fossé-aux-Loups 32, Wolvengracht 32, 1000 Brussels (tel: 221-3211).

Crèdit Communal Gemeentekrediet, Bd Pachécolaan 44, 1000 Brussels (tel: 222-1111).

Crèdit General S.A. De Banque, Grand-Place 5, 1000 Brussels (tel: 5160-1211).

Famibanque, Rue du Trone 60, 1050 Brussels (tel: 504-5111).

Générale de Banque S.A., Montagne du Parc 3, 1000 Brussels (tel: 516-2111; tx: 21-283).

Groep Landbouwkredyet, Jozeff II, straat 56, 1050 Brussels (tel:287-7111),

Groupe Crèdit Agricole, Rue Joseph II 56, 1050 Bruzzels (287-7111).

BUSINESS DIRECTORY — BELGIUM

Banking (contd):

IPPA, Bd du Souverain 23, Vorstlaan 23, 1170 Brussels (tel: 676-1211).

Kredietbank, Arenbergstraat 7, B-1000 Brussels (tel: 517-4111; tx: 21-207).

Metropolitan Bank Bd Du Souverain 191-197, 1160 Brussels).

N.M.K.N., Sterrenkundelaan 14, Avenue de l'Astronomic 14, 1030 Brussels (tel: 214-1211).

Nationale Kas Voor Beroepskrediet, Boulevard Waterloolaan 16, 1000 Brussels (513-6480; fax: 514-3155).

Postcheque, Service Commercial, Division 6.2.5.3., 1160 Brussels (tel: 219-4800).

Principal newspapers

Antwerpse Post, De Vlijt NV, Katwilgweg 2, B-2050 Antwerp (tel: 219-3815; fax: 219-6368).

Brugsch Handelsblad, Roularta NV, Eekhoutstraat 4, B-8000 Bruges (tel: 330-661; fax: 334-633).

De Financieel Economische Tijd, utigeversbedrijf Tijd, Posthoflei 3, B-2600, Antwerp (tel: 286-0211; fax: 286-0210).

De Morgen, De Persgroep Hoste NV, Brusselsesteenweg 347, B-1730 Brussels.

La Côte Libre, Agefi Belgique SA, Rue de Birmingham 131, B-1070, Brussels (tel: 526-5606; fax: 526-5526).

La Dernière Heure/Les Sports, Compagnie Nouvelle de Communications SA, Boulevard E. Jacqmain 127, B-1000 Brussels (tel: 218-3028; fax: 211-2870).

La Libre Belgique/Gazette de Liège, Boulevard E. Jacqmain 127, B-1000 Brussels (tel: 231-933; fax: 224-126).

La Nouvelle Gazette, Regie Rossel, Place de Louvain 21, B-1000 Brussels.

Le Courrier de la Bourse et de la Banque, Agèfi Belgique SA, Rue de Birmingham 131, B-1070 Brussels (tel: 526-5606; fax: 526-5526).

Le Soir, Rossel & Cie SA, Rue Rouale 112, B-1000 Brussels (tel: 217-7750; fax: 217-9816).

Wall Street Journal Europe, Blve Brand Whitlock 87, B-1200 Brussels (tel: 741-1211; fax: 732-1102).

Travel information

Brussels Airport (tel: 720-2415).

Bureau D'Information et D'Accueil Touristiques Belgique, Rue du Marche-aux-Herbes 63, 1000 Brussels (tel: 504-0390; fax: 504-0270).

O.P.T. – Office de Promotion du Tourisme de la Communautè Francaise Wallonie – Bruxelles, Rue du Marchè-aux-Herbes 61, 1000 Brussels (tel: 504-0200, 504-0390; fax: 513-6950).

Sabena Belgian World Airlines (Société Anonyme Belge d'Exploitation de la Navigation Aérienne), 2 Avenue E Mounierlaan, Brussels, B-1200 (tel: 723-4301; fax: 723-4699).

Tourist and Information Bureau, Brussels (TIB), Hôtel de Ville, Grand Place, Grohe Markt, B-1000 Brussels (tel: 513-8940; fax: 514-4538).

Verkehrsamt Der Ostkantone, Mühlenbachstrasse 2, 4780 St-Vith (tel: 227-664; fax: 226-539).

Vlaams Commissariaat-Generaal Voor Toerisme, Rue du Marchè-aux-Herbes 61, 1000 Brussels (tel: 504-0300; fax: 513-8803).

Other useful addresses

Association of Belgian Contractors (ADEBOM), Avenue Grand-champ 148, B-1150 Brussels (tel: 771-6108; tx: 21-449).

Belgian Association of International Trading Houses (ABNEI), Israelietenstraat 7, B-2000 Antwerp (tel: 232-7547; tx: 31-588).

Belgian Foreign Trade Office (BFTO), World Trade Centre, Tower 1, Bld. E. Jacqmain 162, Box 36, 1210 Brussels (tel: 206-3511; fax: 203-1812).

Brussels Business Federation (VEB-UEB), rue Botanique 75, B-1030 Brussels (tel: 219-3223).

Brussels Regional Development Agency, rue Gabrielle Petit 6, 1210 Brussels (tel: 422-5111; fax: 422-5112).

Chambres des Agences-Conseils en Publicité (CACP), 28 Avenue du Barbeau, B-1160 Brussels (tel: 672-2387).

Cobac Assurance-Crèances, rue Montoyerstraat 15, 1040 Brussels (tel: 289-4444; fax: 289-4489).

Commission de la Bourse de Bruxelles (Stock Exchange), Palais de la Bourse, rue H Maus 2, Brussels (tel: 511-3406).

Committee of Belgian Consulting Firms, (BUROBEL), Avenue Louise 430, B-1050 Brussels (tel: 648-1055; tx: 21-591 Cebi b).

Ducroire (Office National Du Ducroire), Square de Meeus 40, 1040 Brussels (tel: 509-4211; fax: 513-5059).

Fédération des Entreprises de Begique (FEB-VBO Belgium Business Federation), 4 rue Ravenstein, B-1000 Brussels (tel: 515-0811; tx: 26-756 febb).

Federation of the Metalworking, Mechanical and Electro-technical Engineering and Plastics Processing Industries (Fabrimetal), 21 rue des Drapiers, B-1050 Brussels (tel: 510-2311).

Flemish Economic Association (VEV), Brouwersvliet 15, Box 7, B-2000 Antwerp (tel: 231-1660; tx: 72-893 vev b).

INBEL (Belgian Institute for Information and Documentation), Avenue des Arts 3, B-1040 Brussels (tel: 217-1111).

Institut National de Statistique, 44 rue de Louvain, Brussels B-1000 (tel: 548-6211; fax: 548-6367).

International Press Centre, 1 Boulevard Charlemagne, B-1041 Brussels (tel: 238-0811).

Ministry of Agriculture and Small and Medium-Sized Enterprises, Rue Marie-Thére\0-2se 1, 1040 Brussels (tel: 211-0611; fax: 219-6130).

Ministry of the Budget, Place Quetelet 7, 1030 Brussels (tel: 219-0119; fax: 219-0914).

Ministry for the Civil Service, Residence Palace, 155 Rue de la Loi, 1040 Brussels (tel: 233-0511; fax: 233-0590).

Ministry of Defence, Rue Lambermont 8, 1000 Brussels (tel: 550-2811; fax: 550-2809).

Ministry of Economic Affairs, Square de Mee ûs 23, 1040 Brussels (tel: 506-5111; fax: 514-4683).

Ministry of Economic Affairs - Service for Foreign Investors, Square de Mee ûs 3, 1040 Brussels (tel: 506-5414; fax: 514-0389).

Ministry of Employment in charge of Equal Opportunities Policy between Men and Women, Rue Belliard 51-53, 1040 Brussels (tel: 233-5111; fax: 230-1067).

Ministry of Finance, 12 rue de la Loi, 1000 Brussels (tel: 238-8111; fax: 233-8003).

Ministry of Foreign Affairs, Rue des Quatre-Bras 2, 1000 Brussels (tel: 516-8211; fax: 511-6385).

Ministry of Foreign Trade, 2 rue des Quatre-Bras, 1000 Brussels (tel: 516-8311; fax: 512-7221).

Ministry of Interior Affairs, rue des Colonies 56, 1000 Brussels (tel: 227-0700; fax: 219-7930).

Ministry of Justice, Boulevard de Waterloo 115, 1000 Brussels (tel: 542-7911; fax: 538-0767).

Ministry of Pensions and Public Health, Batiment Amazone, Avenue Bischoffsheim 33, 1000 Brussels (tel: 220-2011; fax: 220-2067).

Ministry of the Region of Brussels - Capital Foreign Investments Department, rue du Champ de Mars 25, 1050 Brussels (tel: 513-9700; 511-5255).

Ministry for Scientific Policy, 66 Rue de la Loi, 1040 Brussels (tel: 238-2811; fax: 230-3862).

Ministry of Social Affairs, 66 Rue de la Loi, 1040 Brussels (tel: 238-2811; fax: 230-3895).

Ministry of Telecommunications, Rue de la Loi 65, 1040 Brussels (tel: 237-6711; fax: 230-1824).

Ministry of Transport, Rue de la Loi 65, 1040 Brussels (tel: 237-6711; fax: 230-1824).

National Credit Insurance Office (OND-NDD), Square de Mee ûs 40, B-1000 Brussels (tel: 512-3800; tx: 21-147 OFNADUC B).

Prime Minister's Office, Rue de la Loi 16, B-1000 Brussels (tel: 501-0211; fax: 512-6953).

State Secretariat for Development Cooperation, Place du Petit Sablon 8, 1000 Brussels (tel: 515-1665; fax: 515-5021).

State Secretariat for Security, Social Integration and Environment, Avenue Galilee 5 (10eme etage), 1030 Brussels (tel: 210-1911; fax: 217-3328).

Union of Walloon Enterprises (UWE), rue Capitaine sbosnia 42, B-1050 Brussels (tel: 513-4534).

Bosnia-Herzegovina

Marko Milivojevic

This former Yugoslav republic now seems to be at peace for the first time since April 1992. After over four years of civil war and accompanying intense international pressure, a changing balance of power in the region and mutual exhaustion finally forced the parties to the Bosnian conflict to accept a so-called 'General Framework for Peace in Bosnia-Herzegovina' at Dayton, Ohio in November 1995.

Dayton accords

Preceded by months of intensive diplomacy and signed by the Bosnian, Croatian and Serbian Presidents, the US-sponsored Dayton peace accords reaffirmed earlier local ceasefire agreements, and nominally improved the chances of Bosnia's survival as a viable state based on confederal principles. The accords also provided the mechanisms, at least on paper, of its future political and socio-economic reconstruction and provided the mandate for the 12-month deployment of a 60,000-strong Implementation Force (Ifor under NATO command, with the US providing the largest single troop contingent (20,000). The UNPROFOR (UN Protection Force) II, first deployed in Bosnia in 1992, was formally wound up by the UN Security Council.

If successfully implemented, the Dayton agreement could conceivably end the Bosnian conflict, although many problems and potential dangers remain. If the accords collapse, then the Bosnian conflict will continue, with its most likely final outcome being the irreversible partition of Bosnia-Herzegovina between Croatia and Serbia to the disadvantage of the Bosnian Muslims, thereby planting the seeds of more conflict and instability in the region in the long-term.

Post-Dayton politics

The Dayton peace accords are a political compromise, or the least worst deal that could have been realistically agreed upon by all concerned at the time it was negotiated. The agreement is nominally based on a sovereign and internationally recognised Republic of Bosnia-Herzegovina with weak central powers and confederally divided into two theoretically equal entities – the Croat-Muslim Federation and the Republika Srpska (RS) – themselves implicitly confederally bound to Croatia and Serbia respectively. Capable of multiple interpretation and already being criticised locally and internationally, the basic political principles of the Dayton peace accords are in fact unsatisfactory for all the parties to the Bosnian conflict.

According to the Bosnian Muslim-dominated Sarajevo government and some of its international supporters, these political principles at best effectively rule out the possibility of a viable Bosnian state and, at worst, legitimise its final partition into ethnic cantons or statelets controlled by neighbouring powers intent on its demise. Among the Bosnian Serbs and Croats, on the other hand, the view is that too much power was entrusted to the Sarajevo government, thereby threatening their respective secessionist plans for full union with Serbia and Croatia. This basic political contradiction led to the Bosnian civil war in the first place in 1992.

Under the terms of the Dayton peace accords, Bosnia is to be politically reintegrated, based on new constitutional and other structures, although it is not yet clear how this might be done in practice. Constitutionally, it is proposed that the Republic of Bosnia-Herzegovina have its own constitution and assembly two-thirds elected from the Federation and one-third from the RS, each of which will also have their own assemblies.

Parliamentary elections held in September 1996 resulted in victories for the three main nationalist parties, the Bosnian-Muslim Party of Democratic Action (SDA), the Serbian Democratic Party (SDS) and the

KEY FACTS — Bosnia-Herzegovina

Official title: Republic of Bosnia-Herzegovina (since the Washington Treaty of March 1994); since the signing of the 'General Framework for Peace in Bosnia-Herzegovina' at Dayton, Ohio in Nov 1995, the two constituent entities of the Republic of Bosnia-Herzegovina are the Croat-Muslim Federation of Bosnia-Herzegovina and the Republika Srpska (Bosnian Serb Republic)

Head of state: Chairman of the three-man Presidency Council of the Republic of Bosnia-Herzegovina Alija Izetbegovic (leader of the Party of Democratic Action (SDA)); won the first post-war presidential election 19 Sep 1996.

Head of government: Prime Minister of the Republic of Bosnia-Herzegovina and the Federation of Bosnia-Herzegovina Hasan Muratovic (SDA) (from 30 Jan 1996); Prime Minister of the Republika Srpska Gojko Klickovic (SDS) (not internationally recognised as such since his appointment and the removal from office of Rajko Kasagic in May 1996)

Ruling party: Party of Democratic Action (SDA) (Republic of Bosnia-Herzegovina and Federation of Bosnia-Herzegovina); Croatian Democratic Union of Bosnia-Herzegovina (HDZ) (Republic of Bosnia-Herzegovina and Federation of Bosnia-Herzegovina); Serbian Democratic Party (SDS) (Republika Srpska)

Capital: Sarajevo (Republic of Bosnia-Herzegovina and Federation of Bosnia-Herzegovina); Pale (Republika Srpska) (not internationally recognised as such)

Official Languages: Bosniak (Serbo-Croat)

Currency: Bosnian Dinar (D); the Yugoslav Dinar and the Croatian Kuna also circulate widely locally

Exchange rate: D155.37 per US$ (31 Dec 1996)

Area: 51,129 sq km

Population: 3.5m (1995)

GDP per capita: US$524 (1995)

GDP real growth: 35% (1996)*

Unemployment: 50% (1996)*

Inflation: 10% (1995)*

Foreign debt: US$2.5bn (1995) (excluding 10 per cent share of US$4.6bn unallocated former Yugoslav foreign debt)

Aid flows: US$30m (Dec 1995, from UK)

* estimated figure

Croatian Democratic Union (HDZ). Although supervised by the Organisation for Co-operation and Security in Europe (OSCE) there were widespread irregularities and intimidation by all sides. The Dayton agreement had called for the free movement of formally internally displaced persons back to their original places of residence and voting at the time of the last parliamentary and presidential elections in Bosnia in 1990. After over four years of civil war, during which over 100,000 people have been killed and thirty times that number internally and externally displaced by large-scale ethnic cleansing, completely free and fair elections were never likely. While international organisations admitted the vote was far from perfect, the results were validated.

Although the Dayton peace accords proposed the free movement of persons and hence the reversal of the effects of ethnic cleansing, no mechanisms exist to bring this about in practice. In 1994, the Croat-Muslim Federation also provided similar provisions for the free movement of persons, but none have been implemented to date, mainly because, for essentially political reasons, neither side wants it to happen. The result of this has been the continued politico-ethnic division of the Federation. More recently, in 1995–96, territorial exchanges between the Federation and the RS resulted in more ethnic divisions, notably in and around Sarajevo.

At the governmental level, the proposed constitutional arrangements set out in the Dayton peace accords imply major changes, with more power going to the Federation at the expense of the existing republican government in Sarajevo. This is the exact opposite of what presently exists.

KEY INDICATORS — Bosnia-Herzegovina

	Unit	1991	1992	1993	1994	1995
Population	m	–	–	–	4.5	3.5
Exports	US$m	–	–	–	164	295
Imports	US$m	–	–	–	889	759
Aid as % of total imports	%	–	–	–	55.6	26.7
Gross debt as % of GDP	%	–	–	–	–	130

In the RS all real power is vested at Pale and, more recently, Banja Luka. Under the terms of the Dayton agreement, the RS will have to share power with a Federation that in practice it does not recognise.

It was the Bosnian Serbs that decided, in 1992, to abandon existing constitutional politics allegedly hostile to their interests in favour of civil war. To further complicate matters, the political divisions that may yet destroy the Federation are mirrored in equally bitter in-fighting in the RS, where the Serbian government is now attempting to complete a shift of power from Karadzic's Pale stronghold to Banja Luka, a city that gained the most from the recent peace deal in Bosnia and where some SDS leaders are prepared to co-operate with its local implementation.

Growing political extremism

Having collectively led Bosnia-Herzegovina into the disaster of civil war during the 1990s, the various political and military leaders of its three constituent peoples are now expected to end the Bosnian conflict through bitterly contested constitutional arrangements that satisfy none of them. These began with the parliamentary and presidential elections of September 1996.

Under the terms of the Dayton peace accords, a viable Bosnian state can only be based on multi-ethnic politics and the necessary compromises that go with it. In practice, over four years of civil war, endless ethnic cleansing, mass murder and deep-rooted hatreds have created an entirely new demographic and socio-political situation in which the ruling nationalist parties of a deeply divided Bosnia are now more extreme and intolerant in their views than ever. Once the strongest supporter of a multi-ethnic and secular Bosnia, the Bosnian Muslim-dominated Sarajevo government has gradually become more extreme on the national question, following a decisive shift in power to the clerical wing of the SDA by 1994–95. This is a development that has turned President Alija Izetbegovic into little more than a figure-head for external consumption in the SDA, where the key figure is its Vice-President, Ejup Ganic. Another powerful figure in the SDA is the Bosnian Army (BA) Commander, General Rasim Delic. A pro-Islamic and ultra-nationalist faction now dominates the SDA and hence the Sarajevo government.

The decline of the moderate and secular wing of the SDA in Sarajevo has also resulted in the enforced resignation of the one-time Prime Minister of the Republic of Bosnia-Herzegovina and the Federation, Haris Silajdzic, who also strongly objected to the implied partition of Bosnia at Dayton. Within government-controlled Bosnia, only Tuzla is not ruled by SDA and BA hardliners.

In a related series of developments, the nominally separate government of the Croat-Muslim Federation was weakened by endless divisions during 1995, culminating in the post-Dayton resignation of its first Croat President, Kresimir Zubak. Focused on local Croat opposition to the Dayton accords, this seemed to indicate that Zubak remained in the grip of the ultra-nationalist 'Herzegovina Lobby' in western Herzegovina, where the continued existence of the so-called Croatian Union of Herzeg-Bosna (CUHB) raised major doubts about the actual commitment of the HDZ government in Croatia to the survival of the Croat-Muslim Federation. Significantly, the HDZ has particularly strong support in the CUHB, where it is also the only party. During the October 1995 parliamentary elections in Croatia, the CUHB basically enabled the HDZ to retain power in Zagreb. A basic political fact that gives the Croatian President Franjo Tudjman little reason to ever curb the excesses of the Bosnian Croats in Bosnia.

Itself always led by political extremists, the ruling SDS in the RS is completely opposed to any revival of a multi-ethnic Bosnia in any form. Under the terms of the Dayton peace accords, no indicted war criminals can hold public office in Bosnia and as such can no longer represent the RS internationally. In this context the leader of the Bosnian Serbs, Radovan Karadzic, was finally forced to resign as president of the RS in July 1996 following pressure from President Slobodan Milosevic of Serbia who was threatened with the return of sanctions if Karadzic, charged with war crimes by the UN, remained in power. Although prohibited from holding an official post in the RS or participating in the September 1996 elections, Karadzic remains a powerful force behind the scenes. The equally hardline Biljana Plavsic took over as president of the RS pending the September elections. Although the influence of Karadzic and the BSA Commander general Ratko Mladic, another indicted war criminal, has slightly lessened this is unlikely to lead to the revival of multi-ethnic politics among the hardline Bosnian Serbs. In this context, some of the worst ethnic cleansing of the entire Bosnian conflict has been in the Banja Luka area. More recently, the post-Dayton transfer of a number of RS suburbs to Sarajevo government control was also accompanied by a forcible mass exodus of local Serbs at the behest of the SDS authorities in nearby Pale.

Economic collapse

Although Bosnia-Herzegovina accounted for around 20 per cent of the territory and population of former Yugoslavia, its share

Reconciliation or war?

In September 1996, elections were held for a three man Bosnian presidency (one Moslem, one Serb and one Croat) and for a two chamber parliament in accordance with the Dayton peace accords of November 1995. Turnout was expected to be in the region of 60 to 70 per cent; final figures showed that in some areas, even after years of war and population displacement a remarkable 111 per cent of the population succeeded in voting. Despite these and other discrepancies the election was validated by the international community and Alija Izetbegovic became the head of the three-man presidency for an initial two-year term.

Election result for three man presidency

Bosnian-Muslim:	
Alija Izetbegovic (SDA)	731,024
Haris Silajdzic (Party for Bosnia and Herzegovina) (SBiH)	123,784
Croat:	
Kresimir Zubak (HDZ)	329,891
Ivo Kosmic	38,261
Republika Srpska:	
Momcilo Krajisnik (SDS	690,130
Mladen Ivanic (Alliance for Peace and Progress)	305,803

(Open Media Research Institute)

With the election process complete the three victorious nationalist parties formed an uneasy coalition, led by a collective presidency comprising one Moslem, one Serb and one Croat. Irreconcilable differences remained, however. The Serbs wanted to remain part of Yugoslavia, the Croats wanted to become part of Croatia and the Muslims strove for independence.

That was the situation in 1990, after Bosnia's first 'free and fair elections'; within 18 months a bitter civil war was being fought, peace only arriving with the Dayton Accords.

But has anything changed since 1990? Certainly, each side has become more radical, tens of thousands are dead and a Nato led force of 60,000 has enforced peace. Some things never change, however: the Serbs and Croats still want union with their respective big brothers, and the Muslims cling to the idea of sovereignty. During the ceasefire each side has rearmed and retrained with increasingly sophisticated weaponry supplied by their friends abroad. This includes the USA, the driving force behind the peace efforts, which has granted the Bosnian Army US$100 million of military aid – presumably in order to make the next fight a more even one, and certainly an easier option than using Ifor troops to reduce the capacity for war in the region.

On the surface the elections passed peacefully and smoothly, but they were always likely to due to the heavily armed presence of Ifor and, more importantly, the need for each side to gain international legitimacy and validate the consequences of the war. Few of the pre-conditions for elections – freedom of movement, the media and of association – demanded by the Dayton accords were met. Robert Frowick, head of the Sarajevo office of the Organisation for Security and Co-operation in Europe was reduced to claiming that at least 'no-one was shot'. The International Crisis Group's (ICG) (an independent monitoring agency) conclusions on the election were damming. 'Repatriation and reintegration of refugees had not begun; indicted war criminals continued to exert influence behind the scenes; and freedom of movement and expression remained severely restricted,' and 'Under such handicaps, the elections were bound to confirm the effective division of the country on ethnic lines.' The ICG concluded that 'it would be wholly irresponsible to certify the elections as valid or as free, fair and democratic.'

However, to declare the elections invalid would have been to admit that the aims of the Dayton accords were unrealistic – an unacceptable proposal for those behind the Dayton accord. Yet the ratification of the results effectively endorsed the consequences of the war, permitting three nationalist leaderships to consolidate and legitimise their hold in separate territories. Two members of Bosnia's new three man presidency, Momcilo Krajisnik and Kresimir Zubak, have the stated aim of dismembering Bosnia and joining Serbia and Croatia respectively, and with moderate and liberal candidates fairing worse than in 1990, all three sides are likely to use their new found authority to continue the policies of the last five years.

Javier Solona, Nato General Secretary, has said that Dayton could 'amount to little more than the most expensive ceasefire in history if efforts to achieve national reconciliation and reconstruction do not succeed'. After the September 1996 elections the prospects for reconciliation and long-term peace are little more encouraging than after the 1990 election.

of its economic output was relatively low and insignificant. In 1990, the last year of comparative economic normality locally, Bosnia accounted for 12.7 per cent of Yugoslav GDP, with a GDP per capita of around US$1,600, well below the Yugoslav average of US$2,500. Accounting for around 25 per cent of local GDP in 1990, Bosnian agricultural output was only 15 per cent of the Yugoslav total. Bosnia was thus a major importer of foodstuffs in 1990. Accounting for 12.5 per cent of total Yugoslav industrial output in 1990, manufacturing and mining generated around 40 per cent of Bosnia's GDP in that year. Based on immense hydro-electric potential, local power generation capacity met 25 per cent of Yugoslavia's electricity requirements in 1990. Heavily dependent on the Yugoslav market and fiscal transfers from the federal government in Belgrade, Bosnia only accounted for 13 per cent of Yugoslavia's foreign trade in 1990. At around US$2.5 billion in 1990, Bosnia's allocated foreign debt was relatively insignificant at only 15 per cent of the Yugoslav total in that year.

Relatively economically under-developed during the Yugoslav period and seriously weakened by the demise of the former Yugoslav federation and the Yugoslav economic area by 1991, Bosnia experienced a total economic collapse after it descended into civil war and de facto partition in 1992. Over the next four years of war, Bosnia's economy shrank to no more than 25-30 per cent of its pre-war size. Over the same period, GDP per capita declined to Third World levels – about US$500 in 1995. Concentrated in RS territories, agricultural output by 1995 was no more than 20 per cent of its level in 1990. The result of this have been endemic food shortages throughout Bosnia during the 1990s. By 1994–95, around 3 million people out of a pre-war population of 4.5 million were thus directly dependent on foreign food aid for their physical survival. Mainly provided by the UNHCR, the delivery of this food aid was the primary responsibility of UNPROFOR and then Ifor. Largely confined to war-related cottage industries in Sarajevo and other cities by 1995, industrial output in that year was no more than 10 per cent of its level in 1990.

Damaged infrastructure

Apart from the serious economic losses caused by massive population displacement, including the enforced emigration of over one million persons since 1992, territorial partition devoid of all economic logic and the loss of foreign markets and credits, Bosnia has experienced devastating damage to its infrastructure, industrial and other productive capacity, and housing stock over the last four years. Taken together, these cumulative economic losses have been estimated to be in the region of US$40-50 billion. Other estimates put these wartime economic losses at over US$100 billion. Assuming that the Dayton peace accords hold in 1997, then it could take Bosnia at least 20-25 years to fully recover from this socio-economic catastrophe. Economically, the essential preconditions for this are territorial and political reintegration, free movement of persons and capital, common monetary instruments, greater co-operation with the rest of the former Yugoslavia and, above all else, massive infusions of capital and other economic assistance from abroad.

As things stand, the only real economic activity and growth is in private-sector or black market services, notably in Sarajevo and other major cities. Politically, one of the main reasons why local ruling parties want to continue wartime conditions or economic abnormality is that black market activities have proved very lucrative for the politicians and criminals that profit the most from them. Based on current trends, most future economic growth in Bosnia will be concentrated in its urban areas led by Sarajevo.

Economic reconstruction

An integral component of the Dayton peace accords, the proposed economic reconstruction of Bosnia began in 1996, but will only continue if the current peace holds. To be carried out in tandem with the political aspects of these peace accords, economic reconstruction may give local political and military leaders strong material incentives to co-operate in this process of reintegration, although this is by no means guaranteed. During earlier phases of the Bosnian conflict, foreign economic assistance such as UNHCR food aid was generally misused to prolong rather than end the war. Similar misuse of foreign economic aid is almost certain. Here the major problem is widespread official corruption and criminality at all levels of government, where the war also created powerful mafia-like structures. Widespread corruption has also been a major problem among certain UNPROFOR units in recent years.

According to the World Bank, the main co-ordinating agency for the provision of external assistance to Bosnia, minimum economic reconstruction costs are around US$5 billion, with US$3 billion of this sum for the Croat-Muslim Federation and the remainder, in theory at least, for the RS. As regards the latter, no foreign funding will be provided until its present political and military leaders are removed from office and sent to the Hague for trial as alleged war criminals.

In the first instance, infrastructure rehabilitation will take priority, particularly electricity generation/distribution, gas supplies, water and sanitation, transport and telecommunications. In the longer-term, foreign development aid will also have to be found for the rehabilitation of industrial and other productive capacity, and the rebuilding of destroyed housing stock. Given its political and economic importance, Sarajevo is expected to be the main destination of foreign reconstruction credits and grants in the future. A number of other Federation cities will have to be completely rebuilt, beginning with Mostar in Herzegovina. Tuzla and Banja Luka, on the other hand, are relatively undamaged structurally.

Regional benefits

Regionally, the proposed economic reconstruction of Bosnia is expected to mainly benefit Croatia, which controls all maritime, road and rail routes to the Croat-Muslim Federation. To the east, Serbia may play a similar role in relation to the equally land-locked RS. In this context, the UN economic sanctions against Serbia and Montenegro, which were suspended in December 1995 after the signing of the Dayton peace accords, were abolished in October 1996.

Post-Dayton, the main problem is who will provide the money for the economic reconstruction of Bosnia and under what terms. As of March 1996, the EU had offered Ecu1 billion in grant aid over four years. The World Bank has indicated it is prepared to provide large interest-free loans in the future. Large loans or grants may also be forthcoming from the Islamic world, but only for the Croat-Muslim Federation. Other key players in the Bosnian crisis, however, have so far been less generous on this key question and the foremost among these is the US. Politics aside, there are also a number of other problems that could further complicate the inflow of foreign capital into Bosnia, particularly the country's foreign debt, which has been in de facto default throughout the 1990s. Of the US$2.5 billion involved, US$1 billion is owed to western commercial banks, with the remainder repayable to Paris Club governmental creditors and the World Bank, which is owed a total of US$430 million. Under World Bank rules, this will have to be repaid before the Bank can lend any new money to Bosnia. In practice, much of this allocated Bosnian foreign debt will have to be rescheduled. A complete debt write-off by foreign creditors is highly unlikely, especially as regards the London Club of commercial bank creditors, which also wants Bosnia to assume responsibility for 10 per cent of US$4.6 billion of unallocated former Yugoslav foreign debt.

Economic reform

Earlier over-shadowed by the war and its various domestic and international ramifications, questions of economic development and reform are expected to become more important in conditions of peace. These policy questions are now of particular concern to the World Bank and the International Monetary Fund (IMF), where future economic development is now perceived in terms of both immediate economic reconstruction and systemic reform. Because of the war, such reform was generally avoided in Bosnia. As part of an inflationary Yugoslav economy, the whole of Bosnia experienced chronic hyper-inflation throughout most of the early 1990s.

More recently, the Sarajevo government in particular embarked upon macro-economic stabilisation, mainly to stabilise the recently introduced Bosnian Dinar. As a result, inflation in those areas where the Bosnian Dinar is used fell to around 10 per cent year-end in 1995. In the CUHB and the RS, where the Kuna and the Yugoslav Dinar are used, inflation has also been reduced in recent years. On a more negative note, the existence of three separate and mutually non-convertible national currencies in Bosnia cannot but further complicate its proposed economic reintegration and reconstruction.

Although probably only conceivable in the longer-term, structural reform of the local economy is long overdue. Here the main problem is a political one. So far, the war has been used to justify increased state controls over the economy throughout Bosnia and nearly always to the advantage of its ruling parties and their mafia allies. In conditions of peace, privatisation of declining state sectors is as unavoidable in Bosnia as it is in the rest of the former Yugoslavia.

The war created large and often highly dynamic private-sectors or black economies throughout the region and, if stripped of mafia influences, these could form the basis of a legitimate private-sector in the future. Another positive trend in conditions of peace could be increased émigré hard currency remittances from the large Bosnian diaspora abroad. Despite or even because of the war, considerable quantities of hard currency are thought to be in private hands in Bosnia.

During the 1990s, Bosnia benefited from the large hard currency transfers generated by UNPROFOR and then IFOR, particularly in Sarajevo. Externally, the very high operating costs of UNPROFOR and the UNHCR in Bosnia since 1992 led to numerous funding disputes within the Bosnia Contact Group (BCG), the UN, the EU and NATO, where the one-year deployment of IFOR is expected to exceed the US$5 billion-plus already spent by the international community on Bosnia over the last four years. Clearly politically unsustainable in anything but the short-term, such high costs help explain why the US government in particular is determined to ensure that its present miliary commitments in Bosnia will not become indefinite ones. The international community is anxious that the economic reconstruction of Bosnia should proceed in conditions of peace so as to enable it to economically support itself as quickly as possible.

Future prospects

Although many major problems and potential dangers remain as to the durability and realism of the peace accords signed in November 1995, Bosnia's political and economic prospects are marginally better after Dayton than at any time since the conflict began. If these peace accords do hold, Bosnia's political and economic reconstruction can begin. If not, the Bosnian conflict can only resume. The major problems are the uncertainties surrounding the Croat-Muslim Federation and longer-term Bosnian Serb intentions. The possibility of a major arms race in the region is also worrying. In the event of another war in the region, its likely final outcome would be an irreversible Serbo-Croat partition of Bosnia at the expense of its Bosnian Muslim population. This is a possible endgame that would inevitably sow the seeds of yet more conflict and instability in the region in the future.

COUNTRY PROFILE — BOSNIA-HERZEGOVINA

Historical profile

In March 1992 Bosnia-Herzegovina declared independence from Yugoslavia as a result of a referendum in which the Croat and Muslim populations were overwhelmingly in support of independence while the Serbian section of the population boycotted the referendum. Independence was recognised by the EU but almost immediately a brutal civil war broke out between the three ethnic groups; the Republic's population was 44 per cent Muslim, 31 per cent Serb and 17 per cent Croat. Since that time Bosnia has been recognised by most of the world community and has been accepted as a member by the UN.

Political system

A Muslim-Croat federation, to operate parallel to the existing executive institutions, was formally created at the inaugural session of the Federation's Constituent Assembly on 30 May 1994, following the Washington agreement of 1 March 1994. The Assembly of the Republic of Bosnia-Herzegovina assumed a dual capacity as the Federation's interim legislature on 23 June 1994. A new government, jointly of the Republic of Bosnia-Herzegovina and of the new Bosnian Federation incorporating several Croats and led by Haris Silajdzic, met for the first time on 29 June 1994. A peace accord signed in Paris in December 1995 provided for the division of Bosnia into two parts (a Serb Republic and a Muslim-Croat Federation), joined by a loose political structure. Elections held 19 September 1996, won by Alija Izetbegovic (leader of Muslim community) with 729,034 votes; executive powers limited for the period of transition to the new constitution and institutions laid down for Bosnia in the Dayton peace plan; fresh elections Sep 1998); President Momcilo Krajisnik (Serb) (690,373 votes); President Kresimir Zubak (Croat)

Population

Muslims (39%), Serbs (32%) and Croats (18%).

Religion: Islam, Serbian Eastern Orthodoxy, Roman Catholicism.

Main city:

Sarajevo (estimated population 400,000 in 1994).

Agriculture

The sector accounts for 8 per cent of GNP.

Industry

The mining and industrial sectors account for 55 per cent of GNP.

Banking

Bosnia has a tiered banking structure with the National Bank of Bosnia having responsibility for the money supply, the liquidity of financial institutions and foreign currency transactions and reserves.

COUNTRY PROFILE

BOSNIA-HERZEGOVINA

Legal system

Civil law system of former Yugoslavia.

Membership of international organisations

Council of Europe, CSCE, IMF (from December 1995), NAM (guest), OIC (observer), UN, World Bank (from April 1996).

BUSINESS GUIDE

Time

GMT +1 hr (GMT +2 hrs from late Mar to late Sep).

Air access

International airport: Sarajevo (SJJ), 12 km from city. No commercial flights at the moment (mid-1995).

Surface access

Serbia and Bosnia agreed to restore transport links July 1996.

City transport

Taxis: Good service operating in all main cities. All taxis are metered, but there is no basic charge. A 10 per cent tip is usual.
Buses and trams: Most city centres are served by trams, and the suburbs by buses. The service is generally cheap and regular.

Public holidays

Fixed dates: 27 Jul.

Working hours

Business: (Mon–Fri) 0800–1530.
Government: (Mon–Fri) 0730–1530, except (Wed) 0730–1730.
Banking: (Mon–Fri) 0730–1900.
Shops: (Mon–Fri) 0800–1200 and 1700–2000, (Sat) 0800–1500, but many shops open throughout day.

Business language and interpreting/translation

No regular nationwide interpreter service, but a translation service can usually be arranged through hotels, tourist offices or local enterprises.

Telecommunications

Telephone and telefax: Dialling code for Bosnia: IDD access code + 387 followed by area code (71 for Sarajevo), followed by subscriber's number. Serbia and Bosnia agreed to restore telephone links July 1996.
Telex: Service available in most large hotels and at main post offices. Messages can be handed in at telegram counters. Country code 62YU.

Electricity supply

220 V AC.

BUSINESS DIRECTORY

Car hire

Sarajevo

Hertz: Hotel Holiday Inn (tel: 213-983; Butimir Airport (tel: 543-363; tx: 39509).

Chambers of Commerce

Chamber of Economy of Bosnia-Herzegovina, Mis. Irbina, 71000 Sarajevo (tel: 211-777).

Banking

Privredna Banka Sarajevo, Obala Vojvode Ṣtepe 19, 71000 Sarajevo (tel: 213-144; tx: 41-280).

National Bank of Bosnia-Herzegovina, Marsala Tita 25, 71999 Sarajeva (tel: 33-326).

Principal newspapers

Vecernje Novine, Pavla Goranina 13, Sarajevo (tel: 071-518-497; telex: 41732).

Other useful addresses

Directorate for Reconstruction and Development, Saravejo (tel: 650-563).

Elektrodistribucija (Power Distribution Company), Sarajevo (tel: 472-462).

Embassy of the Republic of Bosnia-Herzegovina to the UK, 320 Regent Street, London W1, UK (tel: (0)171-255-3758; fax: 255-3760).

Gras (Public Transport Company), Sarajevo (tel: 664-624).

Institute for City Development Planning, Saravejo (tel: 664-638).

Institute for City Construction, Saravejo (tel: 663-901).

Institute for Information and Statistics, Saravejo (tel: 664-450).

Ministry of External Trade and International Communication, 9 Musala St, 71000 Sarajevo (tel: 664-831; fax: 655-060).

PTT (Post/Telegraph/Telephone), Sarajevo (tel: 664-813).

Sarajevo City Council, Reisa Dz Causevica Street No 3, Sarajevo (tel: 664-773; fax: 648-016).

Sarajevogas (Gas Company), Sarajevo (tel: 467-713).

Sarajevostan (Housing Company), Saravejo (tel: 663-522).

Bulgaria

Marko Milivojevic

Peter Stoyanov, supported by the opposition Union of Democratic Forces (UDF), easily defeated the candidate of the ruling Bulgarian Socialist Party (BSP), Ivan Marazov, in the October 1996 presidential election. The decline of the BSP, which began in 1995 with a poor performance in the local elections, increased pace during 1996 as the party's split between Soviet-style traditionalists and social democratic reformers grew, leading to confused policy making and widespread popular dissatisfaction. The BSP's internal conflict came to a head in December 1996 with the resignation of Prime Minister Zhan Videnov. On the economic front, Bulgaria's high inflation rate (310 per cent in 1996 according to government figures) and the related rapid collapse of the lev in May 1996 have dealt major blows to the country's stabilisation hopes.

UDF on upswing

Although it did not have the parliamentary numbers to topple the BSP government, the anti-communist opposition UDF felt its political prospects improving, following growing splits in the ruling party and confusion in all areas of policy-making during 1995. In May 1996, the opposition was given another major boost when economic conditions began to deteriorate alarmingly. By the beginning of 1997 the drastic decline in living standards and wages, combined with food and energy shortages, led to mass demonstrations demanding the resignation of the BSP government and early elections. Tens of thousands took to the streets in generally peaceful protests and a general strike was called by the Confederation of Labour. Both outgoing President Zhelyu Zhelev and President-elect Peter Stoyanov called for early parliamentary elections, while refusing to give the BSP a mandate to form a new government following the resignation of Prime Minister Videnov in December 1996.

In its second year of power, the BSP's policy confusions had a number of adverse consequences, notably the lack of progress on the economic reform front. Endlessly delayed for essentially political reasons, large-scale privatisation and related restructuring of the crisis-ridden state industrial and financial sectors looks unlikely to be completed before the end of the 1990s, if then. Although the opposition is in favour of economic reform, the political turmoil at the end of 1996 and early 1997 is likely to slow progress in implementing the measures required, at least until some form of stability returns.

Mandated to form a government after winning the parliamentary elections of December 1994, the BSP gained a smaller and declining share of the popular vote in the local elections held in October and November 1995, before an even worse electoral performance in the 1996 presidential elections. The UDF vote, on the other hand, did

KEY FACTS — Bulgaria

Official title: Republic of Bulgaria

Head of state: President Peter Stoyanov (Union of Democratic Forces) (UDF)

Head of government: Zhan Videnov resigned as Prime Minister Dec 1996. Nikolai Dobrev given mandate by President to form government 28 Jan 1997; failure will lead to a caretaker government being appointed and new parliamentary elections in May 1997

Ruling party: Coalition: Bulgarian Socialist Party (BSP); Bulgarian Agrarian National Union (BZNS-NP); Ecoglasnost Political Movement

Capital: Sofia

Official Languages: Bulgarian

Currency: Lev = 100 stotinki

Exchange rate: Lev400 per US$ (Dec 1996)

Area: 110,994 sq km

Population: 8.91m (1995)

GDP per capita: US$1,400 (1995)

GDP real growth: 2.8% (1995)

GNP per capita: US$1,100 (1994)

GNP real growth: 2% (1995)*

Unemployment: 10.8% (1995)

Inflation: 310% (1996)

Trade balance: US$400m (1995)

Foreign debt: US$12.5bn (1995)

* estimated figure

KEY INDICATORS — Bulgaria

	Unit	1991	1992	1993	1994	1995
Population	m	8.98	8.96	8.90	8.91	8.91
Gross domestic product (GDP)	USbn	7.5	8.6	10.4	10.0	12.9
GDP per capita	US$	2,000	1,500	1,450	1,100	1,400
GDP real growth	%	-11.7	-7.3	-2.4	1.4	2.8
Inflation	%	254.0	79.4	72.9	97.0	68.0
Unemployment	%	11.1	13.2	16.3	12.8	10.8
Agricultural production	1979-81=100	87.58	87.42	69.94	67.64	57.42
Industrial output	%	-25	-9	-10.9	4.5	5.6
Coal	'000 tonnes	29,656	31,423	30,183	29,782	31,901
Crude steel	'000 tonnes	1,615	1,552	1,941	2,491	2,725
Cement	'000 tonnes	2,687	2,090	2,006	1,910	2,070
Agricultural output	%	-35	-8	-1	2.4	2.5
Exports	US$bn	3.7	4.0	3.7	4.2	5.0
Imports	US$bn	3.8	4.2	4.6	4.0	4.6
Balance of trade	US$m	-100	-200	-900	200	400
Current account	US$m	-900	-400	-1,200	300	-600
Hard currency reserves	US$bn	1.0	1.4	1.2	1.6	1.4
Exchange rate (annual average)	Lev per US$	18.4	23.2	27.6	54.2	67.2

not decline in the way that many observers had predicted, with the party reconfirming its political dominance in Sofia and other major cities.

In the lead up to the 1995 local elections the BSP was inflicted with in-fighting, corruption, confused economic policy making and a foreign policy in relation to Russia that is full of potential dangers for its own political position and that of Bulgaria more generally. It was also suffering from a marked sense of political drift and opportunism that the opposition hoped would lead to the fall of the BSP government long before the next parliamentary elections in 1998. Another possibly significant factor was the claimant to the Bulgarian throne, King Simeon II, who returned to his country just as its political and economic crisis was entering a decisive stage in May of that year.

In the interim, President Zhelev and the UDF continued attacking the BSP, notably through no-confidence motions in parliament. These motions, including one in November 1996, failed to topple the BSP but they did force the resignations of the Agriculture and Trade Ministers in January 1996.

Videnov's major political challenge was not the opposition, Zhelev or King Simeon, but his own divided party, where the old communists dominate the Bulgarian economy and its political life. Powerful and often accused of being corrupt, BSP hardliners are ambivalent about Videnov's social-democratic and reformist posturings on a wide range of key policy issues, notably large-scale privatisation. Even so, having survived the immediate aftermath of the presidential election, Videnov surprised his opponents by resigning in December 1996. Whether or not this signals the end for the BSP government remains to be seen, but the possibility of parliamentary elections being called early increased the longer the demonstrations continued.

The long-delayed and overdue privatisation policy did not really begin to take shape until 1995, when enabling legislation was finally passed for a voucher-based privatisation programme due to be implemented in 1996/97. Designed to widen the scope of ownership transformation and hence increase the flagging popularity of the BSP, this new approach to local privatisation was earlier opposed by hardliners and criminal elements on the grounds that it could threaten their own economic interests. Extensive wild privatisation in Bulgaria remains a dilemma. BSP hardliners have also objected to continued macroeconomic stabilisation, particularly regarding the proposed phasing-out of state subsidies for industry and agriculture, higher energy prices and other International Monetary Fund (IMF) demands.

Sticking to the targets agreed with the IMF, and hence obtaining new foreign loans, could further widen the divisions in the BSP. In 1996, the presidential elections implied more, rather than less, fiscal expansionism. However, the economic crisis of May 1996 gave the BSP government little room for manoeuvre and the implicit anti-westernism of the BSP still presented major obstacles for Bulgaria.

Focusing on recent and ongoing difficulties with the European Union (EU), the IMF and the west more generally, the anti-western voices in the government insist that Bulgaria's future political and economic interests would be better served through a revival of the old Bulgarian alliance with Russia, possibly as part of a wider 'orthodox' Slav grouping in the Balkans. In April 1996, this issue was the cause of a major domestic political row when the Russian President, Boris Yeltsin, suggested that Bulgaria may want to join a new Commonwealth of Sovereign States (SSR) in due course. Such an idea is an anathema to the centre-right opposition in Bulgaria, where the UDF in particular sees its future in the west and not the east.

EU membership hopes

Significantly, the BSP government has been strangely silent on the SSR issue, which strongly suggests that it now has an hidden agenda in relation to Russia. This sensitive issue can only further polarise Bulgaria and lessen its chances of ever becoming a full member of the EU.

Formally approved by the Bulgarian parliament in December 1995, a government proposal to officially apply for full membership of the EU is expected to be implemented sometime in 1996. But many doubts remain as to when such an application will be acted upon in Brussels. Bulgaria is often praised by the EU Association Council for its economic reforms and positive role in the Balkan region in recent years but is unlikely to be granted full EU membership until well past 2000. The relevant pre-accession strategy negotiations will likely take place only after the conclusion of the forthcoming EU Inter-governmental conference in 1997.

Bulgaria, like nearby Romania, is a second echelon potential member for the EU, where the emphasis now is very much on the Visegrad Group countries in Central Europe and the Baltic states, and not the Balkans. This attitude towards Bulgaria by the EU has recently resulted in worsening relations between the two sides, notably over visas, trade quotas, the country's nuclear power programme and an alleged pro-Russian bias in the foreign policy of its current government. Full Bulgarian membership of the EU is far from assured, even in the longer-term and Bulgarian membership of NATO is even less likely.

Economic performance

After four years of consecutive economic decline, Bulgarian GDP increased by 1.4

per cent in 1994 and 2.8 per cent in 1995, when GDP and GDP per capita were US$12.9 billion and US$1,400 respectively. In 1996, forecast GDP growth of around 3 per cent is possible, but only if the external ramifications of the economic crisis of May 1996 are successfully resolved.

Because of the large size of the unofficial or black economy, which may have accounted for over 30 per cent of officially recorded GDP in 1995, actual economic activity and income in Bulgaria is almost certainly larger than that suggested by official figures. Structurally, most recent economic growth has been sourced in the private-sector, which accounted for 45 per cent of output in agriculture-food processing, 75 per cent of turnover in retail and wholesale trade and 70 per cent of the services provided by local construction companies in 1995. Overall, and including the large black economy, the private-sector may have accounted for over 40 per cent of actual GDP in 1995.

Financial concerns

Down from 97 per cent in 1994 to 68 per cent year-end in 1995, inflation continued to fall in the first few months of 1996. However, a monthly rate of 23.3 per cent was recorded in July, which led the Bulgarian National Statistical Institute to warn that the country could be heading for hyper-inflation. Following the rapidly depreciating lev in May 1996, inflation will almost certainly be higher than expected, due mainly to more expensive imports. The IMF and World Bank are now also demanding full energy price liberalisation in Bulgaria.

Continued macro-economic stabilisation remains contentious in Bulgaria. Based on a restrictive monetary-credit policy by the National Bank of Bulgaria (NBB), its anti-inflationary priorities have often clashed with the political requirements of the BSP. Fiscal expansionism and poor revenue collection in 1995/96 were the trademarks of the BSP government. As expected, the 1995 government budget deficit considerably exceeded the target set out in its enabling budget law. At 6 per cent of officially recorded GDP in 1995, this budget deficit was one of the main reasons for Bulgaria's difficulties with the IMF. Passed by the Bulgarian parliament in February 1996, the 1996 government budget law envisages a deficit equal to 5 per cent of projected GDP, but this will almost certainly not be met, mainly due to rising state sector wages and welfare benefits, and probable declines in tax revenues if future economic growth is less than expected.

The lev

Having earlier stabilised against the US$ and the German DM in 1994/95, a period of declining inflation and an improved balance of payments in Bulgaria, the lev (L) began to sharply depreciate externally towards the end of 1995. The reasons for this were mainly higher demand for hard currency from local importers, growing doubts about the integrity of the country's commercial banking system and the political uncertainties surrounding the BSP government and its confused economic policies. Another major uncertainty was the future intentions of the IMF towards Bulgaria.

In February 1996 the NBB raised its key bank base rate 8 percentage points to 42 per cent in a failed effort to stem the downward pressure on the lev. Later, in May 1996, local interest rates were increased from 67 per cent to a record 102 per cent, thereby completely reversing the interest rate cuts of 1995. In April 1995, when lev stability seemed assured,

COUNTRY PROFILE — BULGARIA

Historical profile

1908 Independence and establishment of monarchy after five centuries of Turkish rule. Territorial ambition led to participation and defeat in twentieth-century wars, including Second World War as an ally of Nazi Germany.
1944 Fatherland Front, left-wing alliance, seized power with the help of USSR.
1946 Republic proclaimed. All opposition parties abolished. Political trials and executions on the Stalinist model until 1953. Rehabilitation commenced from 1956.
1954-89 Todor Zhivkov held key leadership posts in Communist Party.
1980s Government alleged to be attempting forcibly to assimilate its 10 per cent ethnic Turkish population.
1986-89 Despite his calls for structural and administrative reforms aimed at increasing scope for initiative and the acceleration of scientific and technological progress, Zhivkov took a cautious approach to perestroika and glasnost.
1989 Zhivkov replaced by Peter Mladenov as chairman of the Communist Party. Unlike much of the rest of eastern Europe, the communist *ancien régime* in Bulgaria was only transformed and not overthrown in November 1989, when a palace revolution removed the veteran leader of the Bulgarian Communist party (BCP), Todor Zhivkov, from power. In June 1990, renamed the Bulgarian Socialist Party (BSP), won the first multi-party elections in Bulgaria since the interwar period. However, the BSP failed to secure the two-thirds majority required in the unicameral parliament to initiate major constitutional changes.
November 1990, growing political chaos in the fragmented legislature and increased strike activity outside it led to the fall of the first BSP government. An interim government was confirmed in December 1990, under the leadership of Dimitur Popov, and had the responsibility of creating a new constitution (promulgated in July 1991). In October 1991 parliamentary elections, the BSP was voted out of power for the first time, although it remained a significant political force with 106 of the 240 seats. The UDF won 110 seats, which enabled it to form a new government with the support of the 24 MPs of the ethnic Turk Movement for Rights and Freedoms (NRF). A successful no-confidence vote in the parliament initiated by the MRF and supported by the BSP forced Prime Minister Blaga Dimitrova from power in December 1992. Lyuben Berov was then appointed prime minister – backed by the MRF, most BSP and a faction of the UDF (this faction was later to become the New Union for Democracy (NUD)). The Berov cabinet was comprised mostly of non-party technocrats.

Political system

Until 1989 political power was in the hands of the Communist Party. The first free multi-party parliamentary elections were held in June 1990. New democratic constitution passed July 1991, defining Bulgaria as a republic with a parliamentary form of government, and first non-communist head of state was elected. Legislative functions are carried out by the National Assembly consisting of 240 deputies elected for a maximum five-year term by universal adult suffrage. The head of state is the president of the republic elected by parliament.

Political parties

Coalition government: Bulgarian Socialist Party (BSP) (formerly the Communist Party); Bulgarian Agrarian National Union (BZNS-NP); Ecoglasnost Political Movement. Other major parties: Union of Democratic Forces (UDF-SDS); Movement for Rights and Freedoms (MRF); Bulgarian Business Bloc; Democratic Alternative for the Republic; Party of Democratic Changes.

Population

Minority ethnic group: Turkish (9.7% of population).

Main cities/towns

Sofia (capital, population 1.2m in 1994), Plovdiv (364,000), Varna (306,000).

Media

Dailies: Over 30 dailies, including *25 Hours, Trud, Night Trud, Duma, Standard* and *Demo Krazia*. The only English-language daily is *Daily News*.
Weeklies: Main weeklies include *Yellow Trud* and *168 Hours*.
Business: Business publications in main European languages include *Bulgarian Foreign Trade* (bi-monthly), *Economic News of Bulgaria* (published by the Bulgarian Chamber of Commerce and Industry, monthly), *Sofia News* and *Bulgaria Today*. *Bulgarian Economic Review* fortnightly English-language edition of *Pari*, financial and business news daily. There is a monthly foreign trade magazine *Vanshna Targoviya* and *The Insider* is a monthly political and economic digest published by Eltex. Numerous scientific and technical journals. A business weekly *Cash* was launched on 10 March 1993.
Radio: Four home service radio programmes and several local stations. Foreign service broadcasts several hours each week.

Television: Bulgarian Television broadcasts around 118 hours each week.

Employment

Industry is the major employer (38 per cent of workforce), followed by agriculture (16 per cent). Real wages and labour productivity have increased steadily. About 47 per cent of the workforce is female.

External trade

The Bulgarian economy is still export-oriented, though with certain reductions. A complete liberalisation of the trade regime took place in 1991. Bulgaria has suffered from the effects of

the NBB had cut its base rate from 77 per cent to 34 per cent. In practice, whether the NBB can stabilise the free-fall of the lev will ultimately depend on whether the IMF provides new loans. Continued lev depreciation implies higher consumer and other price growth and increased exports.

Borrowing shapes policy

The proposed multi-year IMF stand-by agreement and related three-year World Bank Financial and Enterprise Structural Adjustment Credit (FESAC) have shaped domestic economic policy. New foreign borrowing plays a key role in this equation. Higher foreign debt servicing costs, of US$1.25 billion and US$1.6 billion in 1996 and 1997 respectively, and the drastic fall in NBB hard currency reserves following its major interventions to support the lev in 1995/96, mean that high-conditionality deals with the IMF and the World Bank are inevitable in the future.

These agreements are certain to insist on tougher macro-economic stabilisation and more radical economic reform, beginning with the worsening position of the country's commercial banks and their highly indebted clients in the state industrial sector. The World Bank's FESAC is expected to play a major role.

Still poorly regulated, largely undercapitalised and often technically insolvent, Bulgaria's commercial banks continue to make large losses. Affecting both state and private-sector banks, losses totalled L35 billion at the end of 1995, when state sector industrial enterprise indebtedness and defacto insolvency also reached record levels. Basically caused by undisciplined lending and borrowing based on political criteria, this financial crisis has recently led to large NBB refinancing operations, thereby boosting off-budget outlays and hence fuelling local inflation. This has led to opposition charges of extensive collusion between the BSP government and the country's top commercial banks, many of which were declared insolvent in mid-1996.

Crisis of May 1996

Bulgaria's chronic financial weaknesses were the main cause of the economic crisis of May 1996. Assuming that the IMF and the World Bank agree to resume new lending to Bulgaria, this endemic financial disorder will have to be corrected. Politically, this promises to be very difficult, particularly the reduction of enterprise indebtedness, bankruptcy procedures and financial sector rehabilitation.

Although the government earlier talked of formally liquidating an initial 70 enterprises out of a total of 1,700 in an Industry Ministry rehabilitation programme announced in 1995, not a single company has so far been wound-up in Bulgaria. After May 1996, however, this can no longer be avoided, even if this means significantly higher unemployment and all that this entails for the BSP government politically.

Industrial growth

A particularly significant trend in 1995 was the rapid growth – 50 per cent-plus – of private-sector industrial output. In 1995, this output officially accounted for 12 per cent of the total, compared to 8 per cent in 1994. Its actual share of total industrial output was almost certainly higher, or anywhere between 15 per cent and 20 per cent.

In 1995, all new job creation was in the private-sector. One result of that was a fall in unemployment to 10.7 per cent of the employed workforce at the end of 1995. New investment, which increased by 3 per cent in 1995 (over 1994), is also largely

COUNTRY PROFILE — BULGARIA

External trade (contd): the UN trade embargo against neighbouring Serbia and the government is negotiating for compensation with a number of countries in western Europe. Bulgaria has over 114 trading partners. About 60 per cent of trade is exchanged with the CIS, and 78 per cent with neighbouring countries (former members of CMEA) and with Russia in particular. The proportion of trade with the OECD countries is increasing rapidly, while that with the developing countries is decreasing.
Exports: Exports totalled US$5bn in 1995. Significant exports are hoisting and handling equipment, electro-technical equipment, chemical products, ferrous metals, clothes and underwear and food products.
Imports: Imports totalled US$4.6bn in 1995. Imports include mining, metallurgical and petroleum equipment, raw materials, perfumes and cosmetics, vitamins and public utility goods.

Agriculture

The agriculture sector accounted for 16 per cent of GNP in 1994 and employed 16 per cent of the workforce. Land for agricultural use covers 6.16m ha. Principal crops are wheat, maize, barley, sugar-beet, sunflowers, grapes and tobacco. Also important is dairy and poultry farming. Long-term development of agriculture based on further concentration and specialisation, mechanisation, improved irrigation, increased grain production and expansion of dairy sector. Forests cover 29 per cent of Bulgaria's land area and forest products make a substantial contribution to the national economy.

Industry

The industrial sector accounted for 31 per cent of GNP in 1994 and employed 38 per cent of the workforce. Production has fallen continuously since 1991 with many state companies shutting down or operating only part-time. Rapid development of electrical and electronic engineering, biotechnological and chemical industries, machine-building, textiles, processed foods, consumer durables, beverages and tobacco products. There is a sizeable wine industry.

Tourism

Tourism could play a key part in Bulgaria's economic regeneration. In summer to the Black Sea resorts, in winter for skiing. Cultural and sporting tourism also have large potential. Over Lev1m was earned in 1994 from international hunting tourism in Shoumen where there are nine game farms.

Mining

The mining sector accounted for 2 per cent of GNP in 1994 and employed 2 per cent of the workforce. Bulgaria has some deposits of iron, manganese and chromium, and large reserves of zinc, lead and copper. Apart from zinc, lead and copper, the non-ferrous ores contain some gold, silver and other precious metals. Large deposits of copper ore discovered in the Sredna Gora mountains. There are deposits of marl, limestone, granite, sandstone and clay, and plenty of stone which can be used in the building industry. The Chala gold deposit discovered early-1995 in the area of Haskovski Mineralni Bani is one of Bulgaria's richest. The average gold content is higher than that in Madjarovo where it exceeds 3 grammes per tonne.

Hydrocarbons

Ambitious programme for the development of coal reserves under way. Deposits of coal are estimated at 4.2bn tonnes but most of them are of a low calorific value. Coal production 4.9m tonnes oil equivalent (toe) in 1994, down 2 per cent on 1993 output. Known oil and natural gas deposits are of small amounts and at considerable depth. Exploration for oil and gas concentrated in the north of the country and in the Black Sea. Bulgaria has three oil refineries with a total capacity of 300,000 bpd, consumption needs being about 220,000 bpd.

Energy

Nuclear power is main source of energy. A US$93m World Bank loan was allocated in March 1993 to help the government improve the country's electrical power system to eliminate losses and to ensure that electricity reaches consumers more efficiently. Early-1995 Russia increased its annual supply of natural gas to Bulgaria from 5,000 to 8,000m cubic metres. Bulgaria will close its controversial Soviet-made number one reactor at the Kozloduy plant by May 1996.

Legal system

Based on socialist civil law system. A basic reform is expected.

Membership of international organisations

CCC, Council of Europe, (CSCE), EU, FAO, IAEA, ICAO, IFC, ILO, IMF, IMO, International Grain Council, International Lead and Zinc Study Group, International Medical Organisation, International Organisation of Journalists, International Radio and Television Organisation, IPU, ITC, ITU, MIGA, NACC, NAM (guest), Partnerships for Peace, UNESCO, UPU, WEU (Associate partner), WFTU, WHO, WIPO, WMO, World Bank, WTO.

BUSINESS GUIDE

Time

GMT + 2 hrs (GMT + 3 hrs from late Mar to late Sep).

Climate

Summer hot and dry, Apr-Sep average temperature 23 degrees C. Cold winters, average temperature -1 degrees C, with heavy snow.

sourced in the private-sector. Investment and unemployment in the state industrial sector, on the other hand, continues to decline.

Accounting for around 30 per cent of GDP and employment in 1995, industrial output increased by 4.6 per cent year-end, mainly because of growth in private-sector industrial companies. State sector industrial growth in 1995 was only 1.4 per cent. As in 1994, the pattern of industrial output growth was most uneven in 1995, with certain sectors performing far better than others. Based on export growth, output of base chemicals and ferrous metallurgy was particularly high in 1995 at 16 per cent and 9 per cent respectively. Other high growth industrial sectors orientated towards exports in 1995 included textiles, machine-building and electrical goods. Another high growth area is light manufacturing and consumer goods. Increasingly privately-owned, such industries have relatively good future prospects.

Excepting power generation, which increased by 10 per cent in 1995 compared with 1994, more traditional and largely state-owned capital goods industries continued to decline in 1995. Bulgaria remains heavily dependent on imported oil and gas but 1995 was a particularly good year in the energy and petrochemical sectors, mainly because of improved trade with Russia. Despite EU calls for its closure, Bulgaria continues to operate the Russian-built and serviced Kozluduy nuclear power plant, which generates 40 per cent of the country's electricity output.

Accounting for around 15 per cent of GDP, 10 per cent of employment and 20 per cent of exports in 1995, agriculture-food processing remains of considerable economic importance in Bulgaria. Seriously disrupted by still unresolved disputes over land ownership, agricultural output none the less increased by a further 2.5 per cent in 1995, as against 2.4 per cent in 1994.

Now mainly privately sourced, Bulgarian agriculture has considerable potential, particularly with relation to the revival of foodstuff exports to Russia. Land privatisation is not yet complete and this delay is again basically political given the importance of the rural areas to the BSP.

Economically central by 1995 – collectively accounting for a record 55 per cent of GDP – privately-owned services of all types also have high growth potential. The main growth areas include retail and wholesale trade, construction, transport, telecommunications and, in the longer-term, tourism. Financial services are also growing rapidly in Bulgaria.

Regionally, the suspension of the UN economic sanctions against Serbia and the lifting of the Greek economic blockade against the Former Yugoslav Republic of Macedonia (FYROM) are expected to boost local transport, construction and other services in 1996/97. Bulgarian trade with its former Yugoslav neighbours is also expected to grow rapidly in the future. Earlier in the 1990s, Bulgaria played a major regional sanctions-busting role in relation to Serbia, particularly as regards the supply of oil via FYROM.

Privatisation and investment

Of major concern to the IMF and the World Bank externally, the slowness and confusion that continues to surround the government's proposed large-scale privatisation of the state industrial sector is Bulgaria's major economic weakness in the longer-term. During most of the

BUSINESS GUIDE — BULGARIA

Clothing

Mediumweight for most of year, heavy overcoat in winter.

Entry requirements

Visa: Visas are required for holders of passports from the following countries: Canada, Finland, France, Germany, Italy, Norway, Sweden, Switzerland, and the UK. Visas can be purchased on entry but cost US$68 plus a US$20 'border tax'.
Currency: Traveller's cheques can be changed at official bureaux. It is a serious offence under Bulgarian law to exchange money anywhere except at an officially authorised exchange office. An exchange receipt must always be obtained and kept for Customs inspection on departure. It is illegal to take Leva out of Bulgaria.
Customs: Small quantities of spirits, wines and beverages duty-free. Valuable personal effects should be declared verbally to Customs on entry. No restrictions on goods bought for foreign exchange in duty free shops at ports of entry.

Air access

Main international airlines operate flights to Sofia. Flight frequencies from some western cities are low. Travellers from Scandinavia, the UK and the Netherlands may find it more convenient to fly to Vienna or Zurich and take connecting flights.
National airline: Balkan-Bulgarian Airlines.
Other airlines: Aeroflot, Air Algérie, Air France, Air Koryo, Air Moldova, Air Ukraine, Austrian, Alitalia, British Airways, Cyprus Airways, Czech Airlines (CSA), El Al, Hemus Air, Iberia, Lufthansa, LOT, Malev, Olympic, Tarom, Sabena, Swissair.
Main international airports: Sofia (SOF) (Vrajdebna airport – development plans commissioned in March 1993, target date for completion 1997), 12 km from city centre; Varna (VAR), 9 km from city, Bourgas (BOJ), 13 km from city.

Surface access

Frontier exit/entry points - Serbia-Montenegro (by rail: Dragoman; by road: Kalotina, Zlatarevo, Gjueshevo, Vrashkachuka); Turkey (by road/rail: Svilengrad; by road: Capitan Andreevo); Romania (by road/rail: Rousse, Kardam; by road: Durankulak; by river ferry: Kalafat-Vidin); Greece (by road/rail: Koulata).
Main ports: Varna, Bourgas.

Hotels

Deluxe, first- and second-class ratings system. Hotels for visitors run by Interhotels-Balkantourist, Orbita and Cooptourist. Advisable to book in advance. Some hotels provide guests with special coupons which can be used in other restaurants and cafés. Main international credit cards accepted.

Credit cards

Main international credit cards accepted in some larger hotels and stores, especially in Sofia and on the Black Sea coast, and in some restaurants in larger cities.

Car hire

Service available from Balkantourist, large hotels and at airport. International driving licence not necessary. Most car hire accounts transacted in hard currency. Drivers normally given special petrol coupons, which can be used throughout the country. Speed limits: out of town 80 kph and 120 kph on motorways, in town 60 kph. Drinking and driving strictly prohibited.

City transport

Efficient and cheap tram and bus service. Bus number 84 which travels into the city, stops at the airport departure building every half hour.
Taxis: Available and cheap. Official taxis have meters. A 5-10 per cent tip in local currency is usual. Telephone number (Sofia) 597-108.

National transport

Air: Balkan-Bulgarian Airlines operate eight domestic lines connecting Sofia with all main towns. Shuttle service to Varna and Bourgas. Fares are generally inexpensive.
Road: Good road network.
Rail: Approximately 4,500 km of track connecting all main towns. First-class travel recommended. Necessary to make reservations. In 1993 the Bulgarian State Railways (BDZ) announced plans to privatise all operations which are not central to its main activities. In May 1995 the World Bank and the European Bank for Reconstruction and Development agreed to lend US$95m and US$45m, respectively, for rehabilitation of the Bulgarian railways.

Public holidays

Fixed dates: 1 Jan (New Year's Day), 3 Mar (National Holiday -Liberation from Turkey), 1 May (Labour Day), 24 May (Culture Day), 25 Dec (Christmas).
Variable dates: Orthodox Easter.

Working hours

Government and business: (Mon-Fri) 0830 (0900)–1730 (1800).
Banking: (Mon-Fri) 0800–1200, 1300–1700, also Sat 0800–1100.
Shops: (Mon-Sat) 0800–1300, 1600–1900.

Social customs

A nod of the head means 'No', a shake of the head means 'Yes'.

Business language and interpreting/translation

Business languages: English, German, French and Russian. Service provided free of charge by foreign trading organisations (must be arranged in advance). Also available on paying basis from main hotels and Balkantourist as well as from the World Trade Centre (INTERPRED). Cyrillic alphabet used.

1990s, the absence of proper or transparent privatisation of the state industrial sector afforded endless opportunities for unofficial or criminal management-initiated ownership transformation. Among other things, this has involved vast asset stripping and decapitalisation to the advantage of de facto criminals – practices that have been particularly blatant and widespread under the current BSP government. This, and the government's earlier opposition to voucher-based privatisation, has discredited the entire exercise among a jaded public. Proper voucher-based privatisation may be the only thing that can save the BSP in the longer-term and would certainly win points with the IMF and the World Bank.

The amendments to the 1992 Privatisation Law (PL) of December 1995 provide for voucher-based privatisation for the first time in Bulgaria. The first step is the proposed disposal of around 40 per cent of the equity in around 1,000 enterprises – significantly less than the 1,300 originally proposed in 1995. In addition, the proposed creation of privatisation investment funds may prove to be problematical given their relatively strict capitalisation requirements. Beginning in January 1996, the registration of voucher holders is expected to be very slow, mainly due to popular apathy and the incompetence of the Privatisation Agency (PA) to date.

The PA has been weakened by endless feuding with the Minister for Economic Development Gechev who has often charged its management with deliberate obstruction of its remit. Significantly, Bulgarian privatisation to date has made the best progress at the municipal level of government, where the opposition is often in charge. In 1995, total assets privatised at the local level of government exceeded L19 billion, three times the level of 1994, when the PL was amended to enable this to happen.

PA privatisation at the national level is the sole responsibility of BSP nominees and they are often opposed to it in practice. As in 1994, the full legal registration of newly privatised or decollectivised land was once again endlessly delayed because of BSP hardliner opposition in rural areas.

As expected, the government's initial emphasis on revenue-driven privatisation resulted in very little revenue for the PA in 1994/95. In 1995, the revenue target was L21 billion, but only L17 billion was raised from the disposal of 70 enterprises. So far, there has been very little foreign investor interest in Bulgarian privatisation. At a cumulative total of around US$800 million at the end of 1995, foreign direct investment (FDI) in Bulgaria is relatively low and unlikely to increase substantially until enterprise privatisation and restructuring is more advanced than it is now.

Foreign investors have accused Bulgaria of following inconsistent government policy, particularly regarding taxation. In certain economic sectors, however, FDI has been substantial. An example of this is brewing, where Belgian Interbrew controlled 25 per cent of local beer output by the end of 1995. Other high potential areas for increased FDI include agriculture-food processing, services and consumer goods led by textiles. Energy and petro-chemicals are also of increased interest to foreign investors, including a number from Russia. FDI in other industries is less successful. In 1996, the Varna-based UK-Bulgarian joint venture, Rodcar, was liquidated by its British partner because of poor local sales and excessive excise duties.

Foreign trade doubts

Accounting for around two-thirds of GDP

BUSINESS GUIDE — BULGARIA

Telecommunications

Telephone and telefax: Direct dialling to main European cities. Public telephones operated by a 5 stotinki piece. Credit card facilities also available. For inland calls dial 0121, international calls 0123 and general enquiries 144. IDD access code to Bulgaria: 359 followed by 2 for Sofia. To dial the UK from Bulgaria access code is 0044; for USA dial 001. A new international telephone exchange went into operation in Sofia in June 1995. The exchange has 6,700 lines and a capacity for 1.2m calls.
Telex: Available from most major hotels and central post office (open 24 hours). In many cases international telex cards are not accepted. Payment is usually in hard currency. Country code 67 BG.
Telegram: Available from any post office.

Postal service

Mail for overseas destinations should be clearly marked 'airmail'.

Banking

The National Bank of Bulgaria Act was passed in June 1991 creating a two-tier system in which an independent central bank supervises and regulates commercial banks and has exclusive rights over the issue of currency. There are approximately 72 commercial banks.
Central bank: Bulgarska Narodna Banka (Bulgarian National Bank).
Commercial banks: There are approximately 72 commercial banks.
Other banks: Mineralbank close in May 1996. Eight banks were declared bankrupt in October 1996: state-owned Balkanbank and Stopanska banka and six private banks – TS, Biznes, Slavyani, Mollov, Yambol and Dobrudzha banks

Trade fairs

Annual Plovdiv International Fairs in spring (consumer goods and related equipment) and autumn (technical goods). Annual exhibitions in Sofia in spring (usually with a technical theme).

Electricity supply

220-240 V AC/50 HZ.

BUSINESS DIRECTORY

Hotels

Sofia (area code 2)
Balkan, St Nedelya Square (tel: 876-541).

Bulgaria, 4 Tzar Osvoboditel Boulevard, 1000 Sofia (tel: 802-233; fax: 883-091).

Cosmos-Pliska, 87 Tsarigradski Shosse (tel: 71-281).

Grand, Narodno Sobranie Square (opposite National Assembly) (tel: 878-821).

Hemus, 31 Cherny Vruh Boulevard (tel: 51-631).

Hrankov Souhodol (tel: 202-874, 875-001).

Intercontinental (formerly Vitosha) 100 James Bourchier Boulevard, 1407 (tel: 621-186; fax: 681-225).

Lulin, Serdika Street 8 (tel: 884-341).

Moskva Park, 25 Nezabravka Street, 1113 (5 mins from city centre) (tel: 71-261; tx: 22-411).

Novotel Europa, 131 Knyaginya Maria Louisa/Georgi Dimitrov Boulevard, 1202 (tel: 31-261).

Pliska, 87 Lenin Boulevard, BG 1130 (tel: 71-281, 705-197).

Preslav, Triadiza Street 3 (tel: 876-586).

Rodina, Russki Pametnik Sq 4/8 General Totleben Boulevard (tel: 51-631; fax: 543-225).

Serdika, Levski Sq 1/2 J Sakuzov Boulevard (tel: 443-411).

Sheraton Hotel Balkan, 5 Sveta Nedelya Square, 1000 (tel: 876-541; fax: 871-038).

Slavia, Sofiyski Geroy Street 2 (tel: 525-551).

Slavyanska Besseda, 127 Rabovski Street (tel: 880-441).

Varna (area code 52)
Grand, Sveti Konstantin 9006 (tel: 961-491; fax: 861-920).

Useful telephone numbers

Operator: 121 inland, 123 international.
Directory enquiries: 144 (corporate lines); 145 (private lines).

Fire brigade: 160.

Ambulance: 150.

Police: 166.

Traffic police: 165.

Road service: 146.

Taxi: 142.

Car hire

Sofia
Europcar: 8 Positano Street, 1000 (tel: 860-864; fax: 883-593.

Hertz: reservations office (tel: 808-494; fax: 885-729).

Varna
Europcar: Varna airport (tel: 435-054); Grand Hotel, St Konstantin And Elena Resort (tel: 861-207).

Hertz: Varna airport (tel: 456-805; tx: 24-218); Grand Hotel, St Konstantin (tel: 861-955).

Chambers of commerce

Bulgarian Chamber of Commerce and Industry (BCCI), 11a Suborna Street, 1040 Sofia (tel: 872-631; fax: 873-209).

in 1995, total foreign trade turnover nearly reached its 1990 level in that year, and was expected to do so for the first time in the 1990s in 1996. Exports, at US$5 billion in 1995, continued to grow faster than imports at US$4.6 billion compared with 1994's figures of US$4.2 billion and US$4 billion respectively. Largely caused by the depreciation of the lev and growing trade with Russia in 1995/96, this trend was expected to continue in 1996/97. In 1995, the EU accounted for only a third of Bulgaria's foreign trade, and Organisation for Economic Co-operation and Development (OECD) countries accounted for 45 per cent. As a result of Bulgaria's continued difficulties in EU markets, central and eastern European countries led by Russia continue to account for a significant proportion of its foreign trade, particularly as regards exports to, and imports from, the former Soviet Union. Including Russia, these countries accounted for 35 per cent of Bulgaria's foreign trade in 1995.

The structure of Bulgaria's foreign trade is worsening, with exports increasingly dominated by lower value foodstuffs, raw materials, intermediate goods and consumer items such as textiles. Previously mainly exported to the former Soviet Union, higher value capital goods accounted for only 12 per cent of exports by value by 1995. Sales of such largely uncompetitive goods in EU markets have proved impossible in recent years. Concomitantly, Bulgaria's imports have been increasingly dominated by higher value raw materials, such as oil and gas from Russia previously supplied on concessionary terms or gratis, and manufactured goods from the EU. Unless this situation is rectified, Bulgaria is having to export more in order to import less.

In the short-term, however, the improved export performance and curbed import growth of 1995 resulted in a higher trade surplus of US$400 million in that year, compared to one of US$200 million in 1994. Assuming higher economic growth in the future, imports will have to increase, although the depreciating lev will curb this tendency in 1996 at least.

On the current account, relatively high and increasing foreign debt servicing charges, lower than expected new foreign borrowings, service income and FDI, and precarious local hard currency reserves resulted in an increased deficit of US$600 million in 1995, compared to US$300 million in 1994. Although ultimately dependent on the extent of new foreign borrowings, Bulgaria's current account deficits will almost certainly continue upwards in the future. Other possible sources of service income remain limited. In 1995, tourism earned only US$200 million. Despite earlier government hopes to the contrary, new FDI in 1995 only reached US$100 million, only half its annual level in 1994. Domestically, improved government and NBB access to privately-held hard currency is conditional on a more radical rehabilitation and reform of the country's crisis-ridden commercial banking sector and properly implemented privatisation of the state industrial sector. Here, current trends are anything but favourable, which means that Bulgaria will remain a largely cash-based economy with no proper financial intermediaries between savers and borrowers.

Foreign debt and payments

At US$12.5 billion at the end of 1995, Bulgaria's foreign debt remains the highest in the region relative to GDP, GDP per capita and exports. In 1995, foreign debt servicing charges amounted to US$400 million, of which 77 per cent went to Lon-

BUSINESS DIRECTORY — BULGARIA

Banking

Bulgarska Narodna Banka (Bulgarian National Bank), 1 Alexander Battenberg Square, 1000 Sofia (tel: 886-354, 891-574; fax: 880-558); external department (tel: 886-354; fax: 880-558).

Agricultural Credit Bank, 55 Hristo Botev Blvd., 1606 Sofia (tel: 876-321, 803-524; fax: 510-745).

Biochim Bank, 1 Ivan Vazov Street, 1040 Sofia (tel: 554-604; fax: 541-378).

BulBank (Bulgarian Foreign Trade Bank), 7 Sveta Nedelya Sq, 1000 Sofia (tel: 8491; fax: 884-636, 885-370).

Economic Bank, 8 Slavianska Street, 1000 Sofia (tel: 870-741, 876-321; fax: 872-954, 885-526).

Electronica Bank, 6 Vitosha Boulevard, 1000 Sofia (tel: 878-541; fax: 885-467).

Expressbank, 5 Shipka Street, 9000 Varna (tel: 223-073, 233-778; fax: 231-964).

First Private Bank, 2A Saborna Street, 1000 Sofia (tel: 872-047, 465-312; fax: 655-024).

Hebrosbank, 37 Vazrazhdane Blvd., 4018 Plovdiv (tel: 231-876, 562-320; fax: 223-964, 835-223).

International Bank for Investments and Development, 10 Graf Ignatiev Street, 1000 Sofia (tel: 888-81; 801-685).

State Savings Bank, 19 Moskovska Street, 1000 Sofia (tel: 881-041; fax: 541-355).

United Bulgarian Bank, 70 Maria Louisa Blvd., 1040 Sofia (tel: 318-051, 318-192; fax: 334-168).

Travel information

Balkantourist, 1 Vitosha Boulevard, 1040 Sofia (tel: 43-331; fax: 800-134).

Balkan-Bulgarian Airlines, Sofia Airport, 1540 Sofia (tel: 881-800; tx: 23-097 BALCAN BG).

Central Railway Station, Maria Luisa Boulevard, Sofia (tel: 31-111).

Committee for Tourism, 1 Sveta Nedelya Square, 1000 Sofia (tel: 879-664; fax: 882-066).

Rila International Travel Offices, 5 Gurko Street, Sofia (tel: 870-777).

Sofia Airport (tel: 451-113 (international services); 722-414 (domestic services).

Tourist Publicity Centre, 4 Triaditsa Street, 1000 Sofia (tel: 835-906; tx: 22-127).

Vrajdebna Airport (723-696).

Other useful addresses

Agency for Economic Co-ordination and Development, 1 Vassil Levsky Street, 1000 Sofia (tel: 543-386, fax: 833-323).

Agency for Privatisation, 29 Aksakov St, 1000 Sofia (tel: 873-188; fax: 882-938, 885-395).

Bulgarian Academy of Sciences, 1 7-mi Noemvri Street, 1000 Sofia (tel: 841-41; fax: 803-023).

Bulgarian Industrial Association (BISA), 14 Alabin Street, 1000 Sofia (tel: 879-611, 872-960; fax: 872-604).

Bulgarian National Television, 29 San Stefano Str, 1504 Sofia (tel: 446-329; fax: 662-388).

Bulgarian News Agency (BTA), 49 Tzarigradsko Chaussee Blvd, 1024 Sofia (tel: 877-363, 877-739; fax: 802-488).

Bulgarian Telegraph Agency, Trakija Boulevard 49, Sofia (tel: 8461; tx: 22-586).

Bulgarreklama (advertising agency), 42 Parchevich Street, Sofia 1040 (tel: 85-151).

Central Co-operative Union, 99 Rakovski Street, 1000 Sofia (tel: 84-41; fax: 878-157).

Central Post Office, 4 Gurko Street, Sofia.

don Club (LC) commercial banks. Relative to exports, this gave a fairly high debt service ratio of 8 per cent in 1995. In 1996 and 1997, debt servicing charges will triple and quadruple respectively. Under the terms of the June 1994, US$8.16 billion debt rescheduling agreement with the LC, debt servicing outlays will increase throughout the 1990s and well past 2000.

With local hard currency reserves down from US$1.4 billion at the end of 1995 to below US$800 million by May 1996, Bulgaria will not be able to service its foreign debt unless it obtains significant new foreign loans from the IMF and the World Bank later that year. The only other option would be for Bulgaria to collateralise its limited gold reserves to help meet its external liabilities in 1996 and 1997.

Under the terms of Bulgaria's most recent stand-by agreement with the IMF, in April 1994, a total of US$421 million worth of Fund and World Bank credits was provided for 1994/95. In September 1995, the IMF suspended all funding commitments pending more intensive macro-economic stabilisation and economic reform locally. In particular, the Fund then demanded a credible rehabilitation programme for the country's commercial banks from the BSP government. At the same time, the World Bank's FESAC was suspended for the same reason. In a related development, the World Bank delayed the disbursement of a US$93 million loan for the country's energy sector until local energy prices were fully liberalised. Inevitably, these difficulties with the IMF and the World Bank made all new foreign borrowing for Bulgaria increasingly difficult. For 1996, the IMF may be willing to provide up to US$800 million in new loans, with substantial amounts also coming from the World Bank and other official creditors, but only if Bulgaria agrees to more radical economic reform in the future.

Outlook

Even more than was the case in 1994/95, Bulgaria's economic and political prospects in 1996/97 will ultimately be decided by external factors, notably the attitudes and commitments of the IMF, World Bank and other official foreign creditors. Economically, everything is dependent on new funding deals with the IMF and the World Bank. Assuming that such new funding is forthcoming, then the worst effects of the country's economic crisis may be overcome, putting Bulgaria back on the course of the economic revival that began in 1994 and became more intensive in 1995. Failure to come to terms with the IMF and World Bank, on the other hand, can only mean serious economic troubles for Bulgaria in 1997, complicated by the ambivalence of the BSP government over radical economic reform. Economically and politically, 1997 will be decisive for Bulgaria on this basic question.

Bulgaria's obvious economic weaknesses were worsened by confused policy-making in 1995 and 1996. Political stability and effective policy-making remained far from assured at the beginning of 1997, as the BSP's grip on power weakened by the day.

Externally, a number of issues also threaten to further polarise local politics. Foremost among these is Russia and, related to this, growing disillusionment with the EU and the west in certain quarters in Bulgaria. Already a relatively marginal country for the west, Bulgaria could become increasingly isolated in the future, especially if the current quandary with the IMF is not resolved and the BSP government decides to move closer to Russia. Although unlikely in at least the short-term, such a scenario cannot be definitively ruled out in due course.

BUSINESS DIRECTORY — BULGARIA

Other useful addresses (contd):

Committee for Energy, 8 Triaditsa Street, 1000 Sofia (tel: 861-91; fax: 876-279).

Committee for Forests, 17 Antim I Street, 1000 Sofia (tel: 861-71; fax: 873-235).

Committee for Geology and Mineral Resources, 22 Maria Louisa Blvd., 1000 Sofia (tel: 832-767; fax: 833-976).

Committee for Posts and Telecommunications, 6 Gourko Street, 1000 Sofia (tel: 889-646, 871-837; fax: 814-512, 800-044).

Committee for Television, 29 San Stefano Street, 1504 Sofia (tel: 43-481).

Committee for Standardisation and Metrology, 21 6-ti Septemvri Street, 1000 Sofia (tel: 85-91; fax: 801-402).

Council of Ministers, 1 Dondoukov Blvd., 1000 Sofia (tel: 8501; fax: 884-252).

EU Energy Centre (Thermie), 51 James Boucher Blvd, 1407 Sofia (tel: 681-461; fax: 681-461).

Foreign Aid Agency, 1 Vrabcha Street, 1000 Sofia (tel: 881-951; fax: 885-039).

Foreign Investment Agency, 3 St. Sofia Street, 1000 Sofia (tel: 873-483; fax: 885-517).

Intercommerce (import, export, re-export and transit operations, compensation deals and foreign trade transactions), 21 Aksakov Str, 1000 Sofia (tel: 879-364; fax: 873-753).

International Fair – Plovdiv, G. Dimitrov Boulevard 37 (tel: 553-191, 26-139; tx: 44-432).

International Road Transport (SO MAT), Gorublyane, 1738 Sofia (tel: 712-121, 758-015; fax: 758-015).

Interpred World Trade Center (representation of foreign companies), 36 Dragan Tzankov Boulevard, 1040 Sofia (tel: 7146-4646; fax: 700-006, 706-401).

Law Offices for Foreign Legal Matters (tel: 877-782).

Medical Industry Association, Bademova Gora Street 20-a, Sofia 1404 (tel: 592-111; tx: 23-098).

Ministry of Agriculture, 55 Hristo Botev Boulevard, 1000 Sofia (tel: 85-31; fax: 800-655).

Ministry of Culture, 17 Al. Stamboliiski Blvd., 1000 Sofia (tel: 861-11; fax: 877-339).

Ministry of Defence, 3 Vassil Levsky Street, 1000 Sofia (tel: 546-001; fax: 525-257).

Ministry of Economic Development, 1 Vasil Levski Street, 1000 Sofia (tel: 860-980; fax: 860-980).

Ministry of Education and Science, 18 Al. Stamboliiski Blvd., 1000 Sofia (tel: 84-81; fax: 831-339).

Ministry of Environment, 67 Gladstone Street, 1000 Sofia (tel: 876-151; fax: 521-634).

Ministry of Finance, 102 Rakovski Street, 1000 Sofia (tel: 869-355, 829-222; fax: 801-148); external department (tel: 869-223; fax: 876-008).

Ministry of Foreign Affairs, 2 Al Zhendov Street, 1000 Sofia (tel: 71-431; fax: 885-536).

Ministry of Health, 5 Sveta Nedelya Square, 1000 Sofia (tel: 86-31; fax: 875-040).

Ministry of Industry and Trade, 8 Slavianska Street, 1046 Sofia (tel: 891-915; fax: 871-914); Enterprise Restructuring and Privatisation (tel: 883-220 Ext 421, 870-741 Ext 420).

Ministry of Internal Affairs, 30 Gen. Gourko Street, 1000 Sofia (tel: 878-011; fax: 885-440).

Ministry of Justice, 1 Slavianska Street, 1000 Sofia (tel: 86-01; fax: 867-3226).

Ministry of Labour and Social Care, 2 Triaditsa Street, 1000 Sofia (tel: 86-01; fax: 867-2502).

Ministry of Territorial Development and Construction, 17-19 Sv. Kiril i Metodii Street, 1202 Sofia (tel: 838-41; fax: 872-517).

Ministry of Tourism, 9 Vassil Levski Street, 1000 Sofia (tel: 843-4397, 870-=593; fax: 885-094, 870-593).

Ministry of Trade, 12 Al Batenberg Street, 1000 Sofia (tel: 882-011; fax: 803-968).

Ministry of Transport, 9 Vassil Levski Street, 1000 Sofia (tel: 870-593, 843-4397, 881-203, 872-862; fax: 981-2132, 885-094; 870-593).

National Committee of Energy, Triadiza St 8, 1040 Sofia (tel: 980-1245, 878-981, 665-140; fax: 9801-2444).

National Statistics Institute of Bulgaria, International Relations Division, 2 P Volov Str, 1504 Sofia (tel: 465-147; fax: 463-168).

Patent Office, 52 Dr G M Dimitrov, 1113 Sofia (tel: 712-91; fax: 708-325).

Scientific Institute for International Co-operation and Foreign Economic Activities, 3A 165 Street, Zh K Izgreva, 1113 Sofia (tel: 708-336; fax: 705-154, 700-131).

Sofia Press Agency, 29 Slavianska Street, 1000 Sofia (tel: 885-831; fax: 883-455).

Sofia Customs Office, 1 Aksakov Street, 1000 Sofia (tel: 800-402; fax: 884-909).

State Insurance Institute, 3 Benkovski Street, 1000 Sofia (tel: 879-341; fax: 871-429).

Union for Private Economic Enterprise, 2a Suborna Street, 1000 Sofia (tel: 659-371; fax: 659-411).

Interpreter and translation services

Bulgarian Translators' Union, 16 Graf Ignatiev Street, 1000 Sofia (tel: 661-602, 662-564; fax: 510-845, 661-233).

Croatia

Marko Milivojevic

Peace seems to have come to Croatia after nearly five years of war and chronic political instability. If the domestic political situation stays under control, and if nearby Bosnia-Herzegovina does not get out of hand, then the peace could very well be a lasting one. Whether the existing government survives the peace in Croatia will be ultimately decided by economic factors over the next year or so. Here overall trends are generally positive, with the successful macro-economic stabilisation of 1994 sustained into 1995, when at least the beginnings of a genuine economic recovery also took place.

Politics

Croatian President Franjo Tudjman's military victories over the Krajina Serbs did not have the effects intended in the new parliamentary elections held in October 1995. Clearly brought forward for political purposes and deigned to favour the ruling Croatian Democratic Union (HDZ), these elections failed to secure the two-thirds parliamentary majority required to amend the country's Constitution. The HDZ had hoped to secure such an outcome, which would have allowed it to further strengthen Tudjman's presidential powers.

After the voting, the HDZ only gained the same proportion of the popular vote as it secured in the 1992 parliamentary elections (45 per cent). Compared to the 1992 elections, its number of parliamentary seats in October 1995 actually fell to 75, as opposed to 85 earlier. Had the recent Croatian parliamentary elections been entirely free and fair, the HDZ would have almost certainly lost them.

The October 1995 elections seemed to indicate that the political hegemony of the HDZ was over as Croatia moved from war to issues of peace. A political set-back for the ruling party that may turn into a rout for Tudjman should he decide to contest the country's next presidential elections in 1997.

Confronted with a significant protest vote in the October 1995 parliamentary elections, President Tudjman and the HDZ now have a number of major obstacles in the domestic political arena. Although still politically dominant, the HDZ and Tudjman face a newly reinvigorated opposition, notably in Zagreb, which is no longer a fiefdom of the ruling party in Croatia. Other key areas of the country are also strongly anti-HDZ.

Significantly, the ruling party's strongest supporters are in marginal rural areas and Croat-controlled Bosnia-Herzegovina. Equally significantly, the Croatian opposition is particularly strong in the economically central cities. It is now more centre-left than in the past. Taken together, these new factors in Croatian politics could lead to increased political conflict and instability, especially if Tudjman and the HDZ persist in going for authoritarian solutions to Croatia's problems. This is a trend that is now well established and likely to get worse in the future. The continued dominance of the nationalist 'Herzegovina Lobby' in government is another source of potential conflict and has major international implications for Croatia.

Economic performance

Following the slight economic recovery of 1994, GDP increased by 4 per cent year-end in 1995, when total output of goods and services reached US$16 billion, with a GDP per capita of around US$3,300 in the same year. In 1996, GDP is expected to grow by at least 6 per cent, but only if Croatia remains at peace and begins to restructure its economy seriously. By 1997, Croatian GDP

KEY FACTS — *Croatia*

Official title: Republic of Croatia

Head of state: President Franjo Tudjman (HDZ) (since August 1992)

Head of government: Prime Minister Zlatko Matesa (from Nov 1995)

Ruling party: Croatian Democratic Union (HDZ) (re-elected 29 Oct 1995)

Capital: Zagreb

Official Languages: Croatian

Currency: Croatian Kuna (K) = 100 Lipas (replaced Croatian Dinar (CD) 30 May 1994)

Exchange rate: K5.54 per US$ (Dec 1996)

Area: 56,538 sq km

Population: 4.5m (1995)

GDP per capita: US$3,300 (1995)

GDP real growth: 4% (1995)

GNP per capita: US$2,600 (1994)

GNP real growth: 0.8% (1995)*

Unemployment: 20% (1995)

Inflation: 3.5% (1995)

Trade balance: -US$1.3bn (1995)

Foreign debt: US$3.5bn (1995) (excluding 28.5 per cent share of US$4.6bn unallocated former Yugoslav foreign debt)

Visitor numbers: 1.29m (1994)

* estimated figure

may reach its level of 1990 (US$17.6 billion) – the last year of comparative economic normality in former Yugoslavia. Although not spectacular, recent GDP growth in Croatia indicates that the local economy has been stabilised. On the negative side, real living standards remain relatively low, especially when compared to those of nearby Slovenia.

At the end of 1995, local unemployment also remained high at around 20 per cent of the employed workforce. Once large-scale privatisation of the state industrial sector commences, this is expected to increase still further. In the vital short-term, there are now growing doubts about the sustainability of the recent economic recovery in Croatia, given that most of it was externally sourced, notably through an import boom in 1995.

Accounting for around 30 per cent of GDP and employment in 1994/95, industrial output increased by 5 per cent in 1995 over 1994. However, most of this growth took place during the first half of 1995. During the last two quarters of 1995, many industrial sectors experienced sharply reduced growth, notably in Dalmatia. Structurally, the major causes of this trend are limited domestic demand, energy shortages, declining export competitiveness and stagnant new investment. As a result, industrial output in 1995 was still only 60 per cent of its level in 1990.

By sector, state capital goods industries continue to experience chronic decline. In 199/95, most industrial output growth was in light manufacturing led by textiles, pharmaceuticals and other consumer goods. Accounting for 12.7 per cent of GDP in 1994/95, agriculture-food processing continues to grow slightly, mainly because of incomplete land reform and the occupation of eastern Slavonia by rebel Serbs. Only with the return of eastern Slavonia will Croatian agriculture be able to realise its full potential. Eastern Slavonia is also of critical importance for the country's oil-gas sector, where output in 1995 was below half its level in 1990. One result of this, in 1995, was that the country's largest enterprise, INA, recorded the worst losses in its history.

Accounting for around 40 per cent of GDP in 1994/95, services of all types are now economically central in Croatia. In 1995, tourism services income reportedly exceeded US$1 billion, with even higher growth expected in 1996, although Croatia is unlikely to ever regain the US$3 billion per annum it was earning from foreign tourism in 1990. Emigré hard currency remittances are also rising.

The import boom of 1995 gave a major impetus to wholesale and retail services in Croatia. In 1996/97, the booming construction services sector is expected to be given another major boost from Croatian participation in the proposed economic reconstruction of nearby Bosnia. Major infrastructure development is also now underway in Croatia. Structurally, virtually all services are now in the growing private-sector in Croatia. Including the large black economy, this may have accounted for around 40 per cent of GDP in 1995.

The development of a viable, transparent private-sector has been impeded by government policy, particularly with regard to punitive levels of nominal taxation, over-regulation and lack of access to sources of credit from state commercial banks. Another major difficulty is widespread official corruption in Croatia. Pending large-scale privatisation of the country's

KEY INDICATORS — Croatia

	Unit	1991	1992	1993	1994	1995
Population	m	4.76	4.77	4.60	4.50	4.50
Gross domestic product (GDP)	US$bn	14.2	12.7	14.1	15.0	16.7
GDP per capita	US$	2,800	2,500	2,800	3,000	3,300
Consumer prices	1990=100	224	1,647	26,127	54,122	56,332
GDP real growth	%	-20.9	-9.7	-3.7	0.8	4.0
Inflation	%	123.0	665.0	1,517.0	98.0	3.5
Unemployment	%	14.1	17.8	16.9	18.3	20.0
Agricultural output	%	-15.0	-11.0	-4.0	3.0	3.0
Industrial output	%	-29.0	-15.0	-6.1	5.0	5.0
Industrial production	1990=100	71	61	57	56	56
Total employment	1990=100	86	75	71	70	67
Exports	US$bn	**3.2	4.5	3.9	4.2	4.9
Imports	US$bn	**3.8	4.4	4.2	4.7	6.2
Balance of trade	US$bn	**-0.6	-0.1	-0.7	-1.0	-1.3
Foreign debt	US$bn	2.7	2.6	2.6	3.0	+3.5
Current account	US$m	**-589	-329	105	101	-200
Total reserves minus gold	US$m	–	166.8	613.5	1,409.5	2,037.8
Foreign exchange	US$m	–	166.8	612.4	1,405.0	1,897.5
Discount rate	%	–	1,889.39	34.49	8.50	8.50
Deposit rate	%	–	17.35	18.84	6.51	5.00
Lending rate	%	–	21.92	22.95	22.93	20.24
Exchange rate (annual average)	Kuna per US$	–	–	3.577	5.996	5.230

**incl former Yugoslavia   +excl former Yugoslav debt

industrial sector and more radical land reform in the agricultural sector, the state remains economically dominant in Croatia for essentially political reasons.

Financial stabilisation

After over two years of successful macroeconomic stabilisation, the government and the National Bank of Croatia (NBC) have created the right conditions for non-inflationary economic growth in the future. Year-end inflation in 1995 was only 3.5 per cent, compared to 98 per cent in 1994. Because of higher defence expenditures in 1995, the government budget deficit went slightly into deficit in that year (0.5 per cent of GDP). In 1994, the government budget was broadly in balance.

The deficit in 1995 was financed in non-inflationary ways, notably through higher foreign borrowings and a greater use of Treasury paper. Greater fiscal expansionism has thus not resulted in higher inflation in Croatia. This may change in the longer-term, especially if real wages in the state sector continue to increase for socio-political reasons unrelated to economic productivity. In 1996/97, a peace dividend is expected through lower defence expenditures, thereby allowing greater state financing of infrastructure and other economic development. Overall, however, government spending and revenues continue to account for a very high proportion of GDP – 60 per cent in 1995. One result of that is excessive taxation in Croatia.

First introduced in May 1994, the Kuna (K) is now one of the most stable national currencies in former Yugoslavia. In 1995, when inflation fell sharply in Croatia, the Kuna appreciated in real terms against both the German DM and the US$. At its current parity of K3.7 to DM1, the Croatian national currency is clearly over-valued. Among other things, this has created major difficulties for local exporters, while helping to fuel the import boom of 1995. Despite growing calls for a formal devaluation of the Kuna and a less restrictive monetary-credit policy by the NBC, the government has opted to continue with the tough macroeconomic stabilisation policies originally agreed with the International Monetary Fund (IMF) in 1993/94.

Low inflation and exchange rate stability has made the internally convertible Kuna more attractive to domestic savers in recent years. One result of that has been record levels of savings in Kuna-denominated assets in 1995. Combined with higher foreign borrowings and growing service income, this has meant record NBC and other commercial bank hard currency reserves in 1995 – totalling US$3 billion at the end of 1995 compared to US$1.4 billion at the end of 1994.

In the real economy, ongoing macroeconomic stabilisation in Croatia has had adverse consequences, notably depressed demand. The real cost of investment capital thus remains very high in Croatia. Stimulation of domestic demand without risking the country's low rate of inflation will be the major challenge for the government and the NBC in 1996/97. Assuming lower defence expenditures in the future, this may be done by shifting public spending away from current consumption towards reconstruction and investment, notably through the recently established Croatian Credit Bank for Reconstruction (CCBR).

The HDZ government formed in October 1995 has also called for more borrowed foreign capital to be channelled into local enterprises by state commercial banks. There may be troubles with this – notably the chronic illiquidity of state sector industrial enterprises. Many of these organisations are now technically insolvent and few are able to service their current liabilities to state commercial banks, let alone accept responsibility for new loans repayable in hard currency. The illiquidity of the country's state sector commercial banks also present challenges to the economy but financial rehabilitation finally began in 1995 after endless politically motivated delays.

Privatisation

Large-scale privatisation of the state industrial sector has never been a major priority for the HDZ government, mostly for political reasons. During the 1990s, the HDZ government has actually increased state controls over the economy, justifying this policy because of the war with the Serbs. However, critics have alleged that the increased state controls were put in place

Croatia, the region and the international community

First and foremost, the signing of the Dayton, Ohio peace accords by the Bosnian, Serbian and Croatian Presidents in November 1995 indicates that the Yugoslav wars of the 1990s may be coming to an end. In the case of Croatia, a concomitant and related series of agreements with nearby Serbia provided for the gradual re-establishment of full Croatian government control over eastern Slavonia, the last remaining Serb-controlled enclave in the country.

Earlier, during the spring and summer of 1995, Croatia's successful military seizure of the so-called Serbian Republic of Krajina and related Croatian victories over the Bosnian Serbs in nearby Bosnia created an entirely new balance of power in former Yugoslavia. A weakening of the Serb position in the region that ultimately led to the Dayton, Ohio peace accords.

Any Croatian government attempt to seize forcibly eastern Slavonia could well risk another war with Serbia. In Bosnia, Croatia's declining support for the Croat-Muslim Federation could also lead to another war with the Bosnian Muslims. Politically, Croatia's recent and ongoing rapprochement with Serbia is now increasing the likelihood of a full Serbo-Croat partition of Bosnia at the expense of the Bosnian Muslims.

The relatively good international position that Croatia attained in 1994/95 is not yet fully assured. Among various members of the European Union (EU), the somewhat unsatisfactory nature of the October 1995 elections and subsequent events in Croatia have elicited strong public criticisms of Tudjman and the HDZ government. Following the extensive human rights violations in the former Krajina in 1995/96, there are also major doubts about Croatia's democratic credentials in this sensitive area of public policy internationally. One result of that, in May 1996, was a Council of Europe decision to make Croatia's membership of that European body conditional.

Another potential danger with major international implications is Tudjman's Bosnian policy, or the persistent undermining of the US-sponsored Croat-Muslim Federation in Bosnia, which the Croatian President seems intent on carving-up with Milosevic. As well as risking another disastrous war with the Bosnian Muslims, this policy could also lead to major problems with the US, Croatia's main foreign ally in 1994/95. Similar international problems could also arise in the event of another war with Serbia over eastern Slavonia.

Economically, another around of international isolation for Croatia would be disastrous, given that its need for foreign capital for its future development has never been as acute as it is now. Although ultimately dependent on political factors, the outlook on this score is positive, particularly concerning new foreign borrowing, increased direct foreign investment and the central role that Croatia is expected to play in the economic reconstruction of nearby Bosnia.

merely to let corrupt HDZ loyalists indulge in wild privatisation, or the theft of state property, in Croatia.

In 1995, increased IMF pressure resulted in at least the beginnings of large-scale privatisation, although this has often been purely nominal. On paper, 2,800 enterprises have been slated for privatisation, of which 1,145 had been nominally disposed of by the end of 1995. A further 900 enterprises had only been partly privatised by this time. In practice, much of this ownership transformation has been very insider-orientated, with managers and employees also given long periods of time to pay for their shares. Outside share-holdings in newly privatised Croatian enterprises remain insignificant, as does the newly created Zagreb Stock Exchange.

Large and often critically important areas of the Croatian economy have been placed outside the remit of the government's privatisation programme. Here the HDZ government has announced a separate rehabilitation plan for seven commercial banks and 30 industrial and other enterprises, including the all-important INA energy conglomerate. Accounting for 70 per cent of the total debts of Croatia's enterprises, some of these companies may be privatised in due course, mainly through debt for equity swaps with institutional creditors and investors. This will increase commercial bank control and, hence, state control.

Upon appropriate restructuring, some of Croatia's strategic companies may be viable, including INA and the country's shipyards. Others may have to be liquidated, but little progress has so far been made on bankruptcy procedures. In the state commercial banking sector, the Agency for the Rehabilitation of Banks (ARB) was allocated K4 billion in the 1995 government budget for half the cost of writing-off 50 per cent of non-performing loans held by local banks. Given that 75 per cent of commercial bank assets were non-performing at the end of 1995, these ARB recapitalisation resources may have to be significantly increased in the future, possibly through higher foreign borrowings. In practice, commercial bank and enterprise rehabilitation has only just begun in Croatia, where large-scale privatisation is also not expected to be completed until well into 1996 or 1997.

Foreign investment

The wars of the 1990s and the difficulties of local privatisation have largely inhibited foreign direct investment (FDI) in Croatia. This could begin to change in 1996. In this context, a major priority for the government is increased FDI, beginning with a number of carefully-prepared privatisations open to foreign investors. Foremost among these is the proposed sale of 25 per cent of the equity of JANAF, the company that controls the Adria Pipeline from Rijeka to the Hungarian border, to an Austro-Hungarian consortium for US$131 million in 1996.

Another important share offering in 1996 is for DM150 million worth of shares in Pliva, the country's top and highly profitable pharmaceuticals company. This international share offer has attracted considerable foreign investor interest, not least because the European Bank for Reconstruction and Development (EBRD) has recently decided to provide Pliva with an initial US$20 million loan. This is the first EBRD loan of its kind to a Croatian company and is to be followed by a US$43 million (DM60 million) convertible debt investment in 1996, when the EBRD will hold an 11 per cent stake in Pliva. Following the success of the Pliva share offer internationally, FDI could substantially increase in Croatia in 1996 from the relatively low base of around US$500 million at the end of 1995.

Foreign trade

Croatia's terms of foreign trade and balance of payments sharply deteriorated in 1995. Imports continued to grow faster than exports, notably in relation to the EU, which was responsible for nearly 60 per cent of Croatia's foreign trade in 1995. At US$6.2 billion, imports in 1995 were US$1 billion higher than in 1994, mainly because of a favourable exchange rate and the

COUNTRY PROFILE — CROATIA

Historical profile

Following a declaration by Slovenia of secession from the Federal Republic of Yugoslavia, Croatia held its own free elections in April\May 1990. The Croatian Democratic Union (HDZ) won 205 of the 365 seats in the Sabor (the Zagreb parliament). The government was led by Franjo Tudjman, who was re-elected as president in August 1992. Independence from Yugoslavia declared 25 June 1991. Recognised as an independent state by the EU on 15 January 1992. By January 1993 the Republic of Croatia was recognised by 98 countries. On 14 December 1995 Croatian President Franjo Tudjman, Bosnian President Alija Izetbegovic and President of the Federation of Bosnia-Herzegovina Kresimir Zubak signed an agreement on the establishment of the Joint Council for Co-operation between Croatia and the Republic and Federation of Bosnia-Herzegovina.

Political system

The bicameral legislature, the *Sabor* (Assembly), consists of a 136-seat Chamber of Deputies and a 63-seat Chamber of Districts, each elected for a four-year term. The supreme head of the republic is the president, who is elected for a term of five years. The president appoints the prime minister and, on the proposal of the prime minister, other members of the government. These appointments are subject to confirmation by the Chamber of Deputies. The government was established on 3 August 1991 by agreement of eight parliamentary parties. The Supreme Court is the highest court in the Republic charged with the duty to ensure uniform application of laws and equality of citizens. In parliamentary elections 29 October 1995 Franco Tudjman's ruling nationalist Croatian Democratic Union (HDZ) won with 45 per cent of the vote and over 70 of the 127 seats in parliament.

Political parties

The ruling party is the Croatian Democratic Union (HDZ). Other major parties include Croatian Social Liberal Party (HSLS); Social Democratic Party of Change (SDP); Croatian National Party (HNS); Croatian Party of the Rights (HSP); Croatian Peasant Party (HSS); Serbian National Party (SNS).

Population

Minority ethnic group: Serb (12.2% of population).

Main cities/towns

Zagreb (population 930,000 in 1994), Split (206,612), Rijeka (205,000), Osijek (164,000), Dubrovnik, Zadar, Vinkovci, Pakrac, Vukovar, Karlovac, Pula.

Language:

The principal language is Croatian but German and English are commonly used as second languages. Croatian is written using the Latin alphabet.

Media

Dailies: Vecernji List (Zagreb), *Slobodna Dalmacija* (Split), *Novi List* (Rijeka), *Glas Slavojije* (Osijek).
Weeklies: Globus and ST (Zagreb), *Nedjeljna Dalmacija* (Split).
Business: Privredni Vjesnik (weekly) and *Informator.*

Domestic economy

Since gaining independence, the costs of transforming the economy and the war caused growing inflation. The Croatian government, together with the National Bank of Croatia, prepared a macro-economic programme to decelerate the rate of inflation, initiate a debt programme for companies and to check public expenditure. The government promised to create an institutional base for a market economy. Economic stabilisation plan introduced in autumn of 1993. In 1994 prices and exchange rate were stable and industrial production and tourism picked up. In 1995 the government is undertaking a range of actions aimed at increasing the overall efficiency of the economy and restructuring the less efficient businesses.

External trade

Exports: Exports totalled US$4.9bn in 1995. Main exports: textiles (typically 14% of total), petroleum products (8%), ships (7%), chemicals (7%), leather footwear (6%), processed food (6%), electrical appliances (6%), timber and wood (4%). Main destinations: Italy (23.7% of 1995 total), Germany (21.5%), Slovenia (13.1%), Austria (4.3%).
Imports: Imports totalled US$6.2bn in 1995. Main imports: petroleum products (typically 13% of total), textiles (7%), processed food (6%), electrical appliances (4%), chemicals (3%), leather footwear (3%).

greater availability of hard currency.

At US$4.9 billion in 1995, exports rose by only 20 per cent over their level in 1994 (US$4.2 billion). The main reasons for this were an over-valued exchange rate and declining export competitiveness, notably in European Union (EU) markets. This resulted in a record US$1.3 billion trade deficit in 1995, compared to one of US$1 billion in 1994. As in 1994, most of this growing trade deficit was with the EU and nearby Slovenia. Based on recent trends, a larger trade deficit is expected in 1996, when exports and imports are set to reach US$5.4 billion and US$8.4 billion respectively. Structurally, the only way that this worsening trade deficit can be reduced is through improved export performance, possibly through a competitive devaluation of the Kuna. In the longer-term, higher export growth is conditional on a more radical restructuring of the Croatian industrial sector.

In the short-term, the HDZ government has also recently intimated that import tariffs may be raised in 1996 to stem the alarming surge in imports that took place in 1995. Externally, the problem with this proposed protectionism is that it could conflict with Croatia's desire to secure associate membership of the EU as soon as possible, So far, this has only been granted to Slovenia in former Yugoslavia. Another problem is that such import tariffs are contrary to the rules of the new World Trade Organisation that Croatia also aspires to join in due course. In terms of the domestic economy and local politics, however, protectionist tariffs may be unavoidable in 1996, particularly as regards foodstuffs and consumer goods. Recent import growth has so far resulted in large losses for many Croatian producers. A basic lack of competitiveness that can only be improved by radical economic reform, particularly as regards higher added value manufacturing. During the 1990s, exports of goods from such higher added value sectors declined drastically, whereas those of lower value base chemicals, textiles and pharmaceuticals have increased.

On the current account balance, the trade deficits of 1994/95 were financed by higher service income, growing *émigré* remittances and increased foreign borrowing. In 1995, the current account deficit was thus a relatively manageable US$200 million, compared to a small surplus of US$100 million in 1994. The problem here is that Croatia may find it more difficult to finance higher trade deficits in the future, especially if service income and *émigré* remittances growth is lower than expected. Based on current projections, the 1996 trade deficit will be around US$3 billion, or more than double its level of 1995. Externally, such growing trade deficits also imply far higher new foreign borrowing than has taken place to date. In the longer-term, this could lead to foreign debt servicing problems.

Growing foreign debt

As in 1994, Croatia was able to increase its new foreign borrowings in 1995, when the country's foreign debt reached US$3.5 billion, compared to US$3 billion at the end of 1994. A US$500 million foreign borrowing requirement for 1995 was mainly provided by official multilateral and governmental creditors. In 1994, the IMF provided Croatia with an initial stand-by loan of US$103 million. In 1995, negotiations began for a new multi-year US$250 million IMF loan. Although local macroeconomic indicators remain well within the targets earlier agreed with the IMF, the slow pace of structural reform in Croatia is a negative factor.

In March 1995, US$1.5 billion of Croatian foreign debt was formally rescheduled by its Paris Club creditors and the US$261 million due to Paris Club governmental creditors in 1995 was paid on time. A final and formal rescheduling of the US$1.2 billion owed to London Club (LC) commercial bank creditors is expected sometime in 1996.

Earlier in the 1990s, foreign commercial banks were wary of lending money to Croatia, but in March 1996 a landmark deal was struck for a DM50 million Euroloan to the government-owned and guaranteed CCBR. Arranged by a syndicate of mainly Austrian and German banks, this loan set an important precedent for Croatia, which

COUNTRY PROFILE — CROATIA

External trade (contd):
Main sources: Germany (20.1%) of 1995 total), Italy (18.2%), Slovenia (10.7%), Austria (7.7%).

Agriculture

Agriculture in Croatia is considerably advanced and contributed 14 per cent to GNP in 1994, employing 13 per cent of the workforce. Of a total of 3.2m ha of arable land, 63 per cent is cultivated and the rest is pasture land. Four-fifths of the cultivated land is privately owned. Crop production is especially well developed, covering the needs for cereals, while cattle breeding accounts for almost 50 per cent of agriculture-generated GDP. Croatia also has a well developed fishing and fish processing industry and rapidly developing marine-culture production. Of a total of 2.4m ha of forests and woodland areas, 81 per cent is socially owned and the rest is in private hands. Croatia has a well developed wood processing industry with 40,000 employees and an annual export in this area of US$442m.

Industry

The mining and industrial sectors together contributed 51 per cent to GNP in 1994 and employed 35 per cent of the working population. Manufacturing sector dominated by the food industry, textiles, chemicals, machine building, metal processing, shipbuilding and the production of electrical engines. Ship-building represents a major branch of Croatia's export industry. Those self-managed enterprises which were not sold by end of June 1992 were taken into state ownership and restructured by the Croation Development Fund for sale to private or foreign investors. Approximately 30 per cent of Croatia's total industrial capacity was destroyed by the war. Most affected were the leather industry, the shoe and textile industries, and metalworks and machinery production.

Tourism

Tourism is one of the most important elements in rebuilding Croatia's economy. Under normal circumstances the industry employs about 190,000 people and accounts for almost one-third of Croatia's total foreign exchange earnings. In 1994 there were 20m overnight stays compared with 52.5m in 1990. There are approximately 190,000 beds in hotels and apartments, together with an equal number of beds in private accommodation.

Hydrocarbons

Oil fields located in Slavonia. Production was disrupted by fighting in 1991-92. Croatia was former Yugoslavia's biggest oil producer.

Energy

Approximately 30 per cent of Croatian electricity generation capacity was destroyed in the war. A nuclear power station is planned to replace this capacity.

Stock exchange

Zagreb has a small stock exchange. Computerised stock exchange of the Croatian Chamber of Commerce was inaugurated in Osijek.

Legal system

Croatia has introduced numerous laws, governing the financial and economic sector, designed to confirm with the EU system.

Membership of international organisations

Alps (Adriatic Working Community), Commission Internationale pour l'Exploration Scientifique de la Mer Méditerranée (CIESM), Co-operation in the Field of Science and Technology in Europe (COST), Council of Europe (from April 1996), CSCE, EBRD, ECE, HABITAT, IAEA, ICAO, IDA, IFC, ILO, IMF, IMO, ITU, Central European Initiative (MEI), MIGA, NAM (observer), UN, UNCTAD, UNDP, UNEP, UNFPA, UNICEF, UNHCR, International Railways Union (UIC), UNIDO, UNITAR, UN Special Fund, UNU, WFC, WFP, WHO, World Bank.

BUSINESS GUIDE

Time

GMT + 1 hr (GMT + 2 hrs from late Mar to late Sep).

Climate

Continental climate ranging from –10–C to 30–C. Average temperature: 0 degrees C in January to 20 degrees C in July.

Entry requirements

Visa: Visas are required for the holders of US and Canadian passports.
Currency: Traveller's cheques can be changed at official bureaux.

had hitherto been regarded less favourably than Slovenia in the Euromarkets. The reason for this was its generally poor foreign debt servicing record during the 1990s. More recently, in 1994/95, this had improved. In 1996, Croatia was seeking an investment-grade country credit rating from the main international credit agencies, which had so far only given such a rating to Slovenia in former Yugoslavia.

Another major problem that existed between Croatia and its LC creditors throughout the 1990s was its disputed share of unallocated former Yugoslav foreign debt, which stood at US$4.6 billion at the end of 1995. Earlier contested by Croatia, its share is now to be 28.5 per cent, or around US$1.3 billion, following an agreement with the LC in May 1996. Partly motivated by an earlier and related Slovene government deal with the LC, this agreement gave Croatia a total foreign debt of US$4.8 billion in 1996.

Although Croatia will be able to increase its foreign borrowings in the Euromarkets, the recent Croatian and Slovenian government debt deals with the LC have been implicitly called into question by the central bank of rump Yugoslavia (Serbia and Montenegro), which had earlier claimed that it was the sole legal successor of the former Yugoslav federation and as such responsible for all its outstanding liabilities and assets externally. This contested claim is strongly rejected by both Slovenia and Croatia.

The still-frozen former Yugoslav financial assets abroad totalled around US$2 billion at the end of 1995. Slovenia, Croatia and other former Yugoslav republics are now demanding that they be equitably distributed. This position is supported by the international community, but is still being contested by the rump Yugoslavia.

Future prospects

Assuming Croatia does remain at peace, its future political and economic prospects are now relatively good. However, a number of problems and potential dangers remain. Externally, by far the most serious of these pertain to nearby Bosnia, where the worst possible scenario would be the collapse of the Croat-Muslim Federation, another war with the Bosnian Muslims and a return to international isolation for Croatia. A scenario that cannot as yet be ruled out definitively. The danger of another war with Serbia also persists. Internationally, Croatia's future policies in former Yugoslavia will largely determine whether its ongoing rehabilitation will be completed, notably in the all-important economic sphere. Considerations that may prove to be a decisive constraint on Croatia's Bosnian policy in particular.

Domestically, the maintenance of peace is also central to Croatia's future socio-economic and political development. As things stand, a real peace dividend is possible in 1996. Following on from successful macro-economic stabilisation, a less restrictive monetary-credit policy may be viable in order to stimulate domestic demand. This, and a related devaluation of the Kuna, may be unavoidable in due course. Combined with an improved external environment, this may enable Croatia to go for sustainable and high economic growth, including rising living standards for most of its population. No doubt, Tudjman and the HDZ are hoping for such a scenario in order to strengthen their flagging political positions in the longer-term future. The next major test of Croatian public opinion will be the presidential election in 1997 and this is a review that Tudjman and the HDZ may not be able to pass.

The greatest potential danger domestically is that Tudjman and the HDZ may persist with authoritarian solutions to Croatia's problems, thereby virtually guaranteeing worsening political conflict and instability. Serious social unrest also cannot be ruled out.

Croatia's already questionable democratic credentials and poor human rights record have come between it and the international community, most notably in the EU. As long as this remains so, Croatia's international rehabilitation will stay conditional and by no means irreversible.

BUSINESS GUIDE — CROATIA

Representation overseas

Canberra.

Air access

National airline: Croatia Airlines.
Other airlines: Aeroflot, Air France, Austrian Airlines, Avia Express, Czech Airlines (CSA), Interimpex-Avioimpex, LOT, Lufthansa, SAS, Swissair.
Tax: International departures US$8; domestic departures US$5 (Jan 1996).
International airports: Zagreb (ZAG), (Pleso airport) 17 km from city; Split (SPU), 25 km from city; Rijeka (RJK), 25 km from city, on the island of Krk; Pula (PUY), 6 km from city; Zadar (ZAD), 12 km from city; Dubrovnik (DBV), 16 km from city; Osijek (OSI), 14 km from city, Losinj (LSJ), 10 km from city – in summer only.

Surface access

Main ports: Rijeka, Split and Ploce.

Credit cards

Credit cards, apart from Visa, are widely accepted. Holders of Mastercard and Cirrus cards can withdraw cash from Zagrebacka Banka ITMs.

City transport

Taxis: Good service operating in all main cities. All taxis are metered with basic charge. A 10 per cent tip is usual.
Buses and trams: Trams in Zagreb and Osijek only; buses in other cities and towns. Services are generally cheap and regular. Buses available from airport to Zagreb.

National transport

Road: Out of a total of 29,000 km of roads, 20,000 km are bituminous-surfaced. During 1995 work began on completion of the Rijeka–Zagreb–Hungary highway. Other priority roads are the Zagreb–Macelj section of the European highway from Nürnberg through Graz and Sentilj to Zagreb. The Zagreb–Belgrade motorway reopened 7 May 1996.
Rail: The Croatian Railways and Koncar – Electric Locomotives Company – have signed two letters of intent for the period between 1992 and 2000 to cover the repair of trains and locomotives and production of equipment and vehicles. Of 2,400 km of railroads, 822 km are electrified.
Water: Ferry services connect Rijeka and Pula with Durres and Vlora (Albania).

Public holidays

Fixed dates: 1 Jan (New Year's Day), 6 Jan (Epiphany), 1 May (Labour Day), 30 May (Statehood Day), 22 Jun (Day of the Antifascist Struggle), 15 Aug (Assumption Day), 1 Nov (All Saints' Day), 25 Dec (Christmas Day), 26 Dec (St Etienne's Day).
Variable dates: Easter Monday.

Working hours

Business: (Mon–Fri) 0800–1600.
Government: (Mon–Fri) 0800–1800.
Banking: (Mon–Fri) 0730–1900.
Shops: (Mon–Fri) 0800–1200 and 1700–2000, (Sat) 0800–1430, but many shops open throughout day.

Business language and interpreting/translation

No regular nationwide interpreter service, but a translation service can usually be arranged through hotels, tourist offices or local enterprises.

Telecommunications

Croatian telecommunications are well developed.
Telephone and telefax: Dialling code for Croatia: IDD access code + 385 followed by area code (1 for Zagreb, 21 for Split, 51 for Rijeka), followed by subscriber's number. N.B. International calls from hotels are very expensive.
Telex: Service available in most large hotels and at main post offices. Messages can be handed in at telegram counters.

Banking

Central bank and a two-tier banking system established. New legislation permits foreign investment in banks. There are 52 commercial banks operating in accordance with the Law on Banks and Savings Institutions, October 1993.
Central bank: National Bank of Croatia.
Other banks: See 'Business Directory, Banking'.

Business information

Wholly foreign-owned companies can be established in most sectors of the economy and are subject to a lower corporate tax rate of 20 per cent.

Electricity supply

220 V AC, 50 Hz.

Representation in capital

Austria, Czech Republic, France, Germany,

BUSINESS GUIDE

Representation in capital (contd): The Holy See, Hungary, Italy, Slovak Republic, Slovenia, Sweden, Switzerland, UK, USA.

BUSINESS DIRECTORY

Hotels

Zagreb (area code 1)
Astoria, Petrinjska 75, 41000 (tel: 430-444; fax: 434-956).

Austrotel Palace, Strossmayerov trg 10 (tel: 275-611; fax: 434-956).

Central, Branimorova 3 (tel: 425-777; fax: 420-547).

Dubrovnik, 1 Gajeva Str, 41000 (tel: 455-155).

Esplanade, Mihanoviceva 1, 41000 (tel: 456-6666).

Holiday, Ljubljanska Av BB, 41090 (tel: 157-999).

Inter-Continental, Krsnjavoga 1, 41000 (tel: 455-3411; fax: 444-431).

International, 24 Miramarska Str, 41000 (tel: 611-511).

Jadran, 41000 (tel: 414-600).

Laguna, Kranjceviceva 29, 41000 (tel: 333-533).

Sheraton, Kneza Borne No 2, 10000 (opened 1996) (tel: 455-3535; fax: 455-3035).

Car hire

Zagreb
Europcar: reservations (tel: 272-993); Varsavska 13 (tel:271-469).

Hertz: reservations (tel: 331-760; fax: 331-347).

Chambers of Commerce

Hrvatska Gospodarska Komora (Croatian Chamber of Commerce), Rooseveltov trg 2, Zagreb (tel: 561-555; fax: 448-618).

Banking

Croatian National Bank (central bank), Trg Burze 3, Zagreb (tel: 464-566; fax: 450-598).

Commercial Bank Zagreb, Frankopanska 11, Zagreb (tel: 430-091; fax: 425-063).

Croatia Bank, Gajeva 2a, Zagreb (tel: 272-201; fax: 276-406).

Croatian Bank for Development and Export, Savska c. 41, Zagreb (tel: 536-717; fax: 534-894).

Croatian Bank for Reconstruction and Development, Gajeva 30a, Zagreb (tel: 469-111).

Privredna Banka, Rackoga 6, 41000 Zagreb; PO Box 1032, 41001 Zagreb (commercial, savings) (tel: 410-822; fax: 447-234).

Raffeisenbank Austria, Petrinjska 59, Zagreb (tel: 456-6466; fax: 448-626).

Rijecka Banka, Jadranski trg 3a, PO Box 300, 51000 Rijeka (tel: 208-211; fax: 330-525, 331-880).

Samoborska Banka, Tomislavov tr 8, 41430 Samobor (tel: 782-530; fax: 781-523).

Zagrebacka Banka, International Division, Savska 60, 10000 Zagreb (tel: 518-895; fax: 515-092).

Principal newspapers

Nedjeljna Dalmacija, Splitskog Odreda 4, Split 58000 (tel: 513-888; telex: 26124).

Slobodna Dalmacija, Splitskog Odreda 4, Split 58000 (tel: 513-888; telex: 26124).

Sportske novosti, Lj Gerovac br 1,Zagreb 41000.

Vecernji List, Avenija Bratstva i Jedinstva 4, Zagreb 41000 (tel: 515-555; telex: 21121).

Vjesnik, Avenija Bratstva i Jedinstva 6, Zagreb 41000 (tel: 515-555; telex: 21121).

Travel information

Croatia Airlines, Savska 4A, 41000 Zagreb (tel: 616-0066; fax: 530-475).

Czechoslovak Airlines (tel: 434-355, 431-253).

Hrvatska turisticka zajednica (Croatian Tourist Board), Gundulic\01eva 3, 41000 Zagreb (tel: 424-637, 431-015; fax: 428-674).

Tourist Community of Zagreb, Kaptol 5, 41000 Zagreb (tel: 426-411; fax: 272-628).

Tourist Information Centre, Trg bana Jelacic\01a 11, 41000 Zagreb (tel: 278-855; fax: 274-083).

Other useful addresses

Agency for Restructuring and Development, Strossmayerov trg 9, Zagreb (tel: 435-159, 277-044, 277-941; fax: 430-155).

Amex Representative Office, Atlas Travel Agency, Zrinjevac 17, 41000 Zagreb (tel: 274-118).

Astra International Trade Organisation, U1 Rade Koncara 5, Zagreb (tel: 334-911, 334-466; fax: 330-004).

Croatian Fund for Development, Savska c. 41, Zagreb (tel: 510-109, 519-732; fax: 517-837).

Croatian Privatisation Fund, Gajeva 30a, 41000 Zagreb (tel: 469-168, 469-111; fax: 469-136).

Croatian Radio-Television, Dezmanova 10, Zagreb.

Croatian Railways (HZ-Hrvatske Zeljeznice), Mihanoviceva 12, Zagreb (fax: 457-7597).

Croatian Roads (Hrvatske ceste), Voncinina 3, 10 000 Zagreb (tel: 414-482; fax: 441-856).

Economic Development Corporations – see Ministry of Development and Reconstruction.

Ferimport Trade Organisation, ilica 1, Zagreb (tel: 423-338, 456-111; fax: 425-301).

Government of the Republic of Croatia, Trg svetog Marka 2, Zagreb (tel: 569-222; fax: 432-041).

Hrvatska Radio-Televizija, Prisavlje 3, 10000 Zagreb (tel: 616-3490, 616-3095; fax: 616-3095).

Institute for Planning, Analysis and Prognosis, Strossmayerov trg 9, Zagreb (tel: 433-765; fax: 424-070, 430-155).

Interpublic (advertising agency), Meduliceva 2, Box 315, 4100 Zagreb (tel: 423-222; tx: 21-662).

Ministry of Administration, Republike Austrije 16, Zagreb (tel: 182-111).

Ministry of Agriculture and Forestry, Avenija Vukovar 78, Zagreb (tel: 613-3444; fax: 442-070).

Ministry of Culture, Tg Burze 6, Zagreb (tel: 456-9000; fax: 410-487).

Ministry of Defence, Trg Kralja Petra, Kresimira 4, Zagreb (tel: 456-7111).

Ministry of Development and Reconstruction, Nazorova 1, Zagreb (tel: 184-500, 454-983; fax: 184-550).

Ministry of Economic Affairs, Ulica grada Vukovara 78, Zagreb (tel: 639-444).

Ministry of Education and Sports, Trg Burze 6, Zagreb (tel: 456-9000; fax: 456-9087).

Ministry of Finance, Katanciceva 5, Zagreb (tel: 455-1555; fax: 432-789).

Ministry of Foreign Affairs, Trg N S Zrinskog 7, Zagreb (tel: 456-9964; fax: 456-9977).

Ministry of Health, Barun Trenka 6, Zagreb (tel: 431-068; fax: 431-067).

Ministry of the Interior, Savska 39, Zagreb (tel: 612-2129).

Ministry of Justice, Savska 41, Zagreb (tel: 535-935; fax: 536-321).

Ministry of Labour and Social Welfare, Prisavlje 14, Zagreb (tel: 611-3337; fax: 611-3593).

Ministry of Maritime Affairs, Transportation and Communication, Prisavlje 14, Zagreb (tel: 611-2017; fax: 611-0691).

Ministry of Privatisation and State Property Management, Gajeva 30a, Zagreb (tel: 456-9103, 469-111; fax: 456-9133).

Ministry of Science and Technology, Strossmayerov trg 4, Zagreb (tel: 459-4444; fax: 429-543).

Ministry of Tourism, Avenija Vukovar 78, Zagreb (tel: 613-3477; fax: 611-3216).

Ministry for Trade and Industry, Avenija Vukovar 78, Zagreb (tel: 613-3444; fax: 611-4210).

Ministry of Urban Planning, Construction and Housing, Republike Austrije 20, Zagreb (tel: 182-142).

State Institute for Macroeconomic Analysis and Forecasting, Strossmayerov trg 9, Zagreb (tel: 428-516).

State Institute for Statistics, Ilica 3, Zagreb (tel: 424-422).

State Patent Office, Ulica grada Vukovara 78, Zagreb (tel: 536-657).

Zagrebacki Velesajem (Zagreb International Fair), Dubrovacka Avenija 2, Zagreb (tel: 623-111; fax: 520-6430).

Zagreb Stock Exchange, Ksaver 208, 41000 Zagreb (tel: 428-455; fax: 420-293).

Cyprus

Michael Griffin

Elections on 26 May 1996 gave the centre-right coalition headed by President Glafcos Clerides a further five years in which to realise the two objectives which will secure his place in history: the negotiation of a federal solution to the partition of this deeply divided and highly militarised island and its entry into the European Union (EU). The two issues are indissolubly linked and Cyprus is both a flashpoint and a political football in the regional cold war between Greece and Turkey. Both the EU and the US regard a political solution on the island as the main priority in the region after the settlement of the Bosnian question. The signing of a Customs Union agreement with Turkey has removed one important obstacle to bringing Greek and Turkish Cypriots to the negotiating table but friction between Athens and Ankara nearly erupted into open war in January 1996, further frustrating peace efforts on the island.

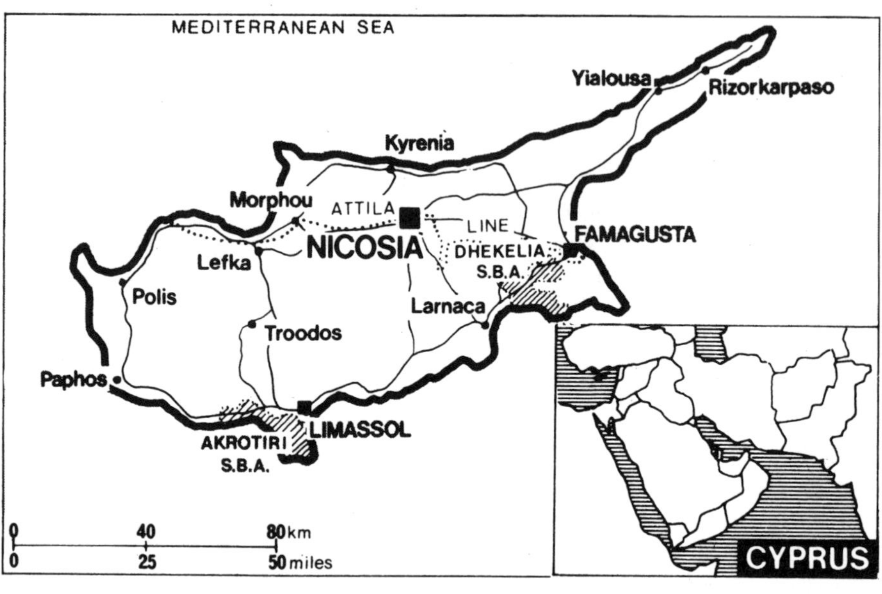

Politics

The May 1996 parliamentary elections produced no great surprises. Though early polls had sensed a growing disenchantment with the ruling Democratic Rally (DISY), whose leadership harks back to the enosis struggle, it saw only a slight fall in share to 33.5 per cent of the vote. Its coalition partner, the Democratic Party (DEKO) fared worse but together they still mustered over 50 per cent of the 56 seats being contested. The Communist Progressive Party of the Working People (AKEL) made a strong showing with 33 per cent. In June 1996 Spyros Kyprianou, leader of DEKO, was elected president of the House of Representatives. Kyprianou is a former president of Cyprus.

There were also elections in the breakaway enclave of the Turkish Republic of Northern Cyprus (TRNC). The coalition between the Democratic Party (DP) and the Republican Turkish Party (CTP), elected in April 1995, collapsed in November of that year when President Rauf Denktash, the godfather of local power-broking, vetoed several of its cabinet appointments. Fresh elections on 15 December 1995 produced a similar nationalist-conservative coalition between the DP and the National Unity Party with a mandate to push through President Denktash's programme of streamlining administration, weeding out corruption and liberalising an economy which has only one legal export market – the Turkish mainland. Though the TRNC's fractious politicians have tended to ape Ankara's views on the Cypriot question, in February 1996 the CTP's new leader, Mehmet Ali Talat, publicly repudiated Denktash's insistence on separate sovereignty for the TRNC. His call for reunification according to the federal model endorsed by UN's Resolution 939 suggested that some Turkish Cypriot leaders, at least, were being converted to the middle ground.

Although efforts to speed up the process of reconciliation produced little of substance in 1995, there are indications that a breakthrough in the 22-year-old schism is at hand. The urgent need to move forward was underscored in early 1996 when Greece and Turkey, the 'guarantors' of the rival Cypriot communities' security, nearly went to war over territorial claims in the eastern Aegean. A special meeting of the UN Security Council on 17 April 1996 voted to back another US initiative to pressure Ankara into renouncing its territorial claim on Cyprus' northern enclave, which currently contains some 30-35,000 Turkish troops. The Turkish demand for separate sovereignty for the TRNC, echoed by Denktash, remains the principal stumbling block to negotiations but local issues, such as the fate of 1,619 Greek Cypriots missing since the 1974 invasion and the recognition of Greek Cypriot property rights in the enclave play a significant part.

EU membership drive

Rather than pour oil on the troubled waters, the question of Cyprus' future membership of the EU has acted more as an irritant. Nicosia is to commence negotiating its admission after the Inter-governmental Conference in 1997, with accession due by 1999. A fast-track process of integration, including the harmonisation of taxation and legal codes, is already underway and the 1996 Cypriot budget contains nearly C£1 billion (US$2.38 billion) for restructuring and investing in transport and communications.

EU membership would bring benefits to both halves of the island, particularly the depressed north where inflation ran at 80 per cent in 1995 and unemployment stood at 17 per cent. But the north's President Denktash has long denounced the EU accession process as the main barrier to the peace process, vetoing any talk of entry until Turkey, which it relies upon for defence, also becomes a member.

The EU has made it clear that there can be no third-party veto of Cyprus' entry, but it is anxious to avoid making the TRNC's anomalous status any more of a vexed issue than it already is. In signing a broad customs agreement with Turkey in October 1995, Brussels may have hoped that it might win concessions from Ankara over the Cyprus question. But on 27 December 1995, the 'Ankara Declaration' reiterated Turkish support for the TRNC, stressing that its new relationship with the EU would not weaken commercial ties with the enclave. Even under the customs union, however, TRNC exports are banned from the single market.

Economy

Cyprus is ahead of its economic targets for accession under the Maastricht guidelines. Inflation was down to 2.6 per cent in 1995, the lowest level since 1987 and well below the EU average. The public deficit fell to 1.3 per cent of GDP, compared to an EU average of 4.7 per cent and the 5 per cent growth rate was impressive, if slightly below the performance of 1994. In October 1995, the IMF gave its approval to the state of the Cypriot economy, but other analysts have taken a bleaker view, pointing out that last year's growth was generated more by consumer spending – particularly on cars and construction – than by exports. Pre-election calculations, moreover, led to the government approving a high-spending budget of C£1.2 billion (US$2.9 billion) for 1996, with a 63.1 per cent increase in the fiscal deficit. Total government debt now represents 85 per cent of GDP, as against the 60 per cent required under Maastricht.

KEY FACTS

Official title: The Republic of Cyprus
Head of state: President Glafcos Clerides
Ruling party: Centre-right coalition comprising the Democratic Rally (DISY) (retained majority in the 26 May 1996 elections) and the Democratic Party (DEKO)
Capital: Lefkosia (Nicosia); Greek spellings in use from 16 Feb 1995
Official Languages: Greek and Turkish
Currency: Cyprus Pound (C£) = 100 cents
Exchange rate: C£0.47 per US$ (Dec 1996)

Area: 9,251 sq km
Population: 740,000 (1995)
GNP per capita: US$10,250 (1994)
GNP real growth: 5% (1994)
Unemployment: 2.7% (1994)
Inflation: 2.6% (1995)
Trade balance: -US$1.8bn (1994)
Foreign debt: US$1.06bn (1994)*
Visitor numbers: 2m (1995)

* estimated figure

Agriculture had an excellent year, with output up by 15.1 per cent due to the weather, but Cyprus' manufacturing sector, accounting for nearly 75 per cent of merchandise exports, is generally in decline. Exports of furniture, textiles and footwear all fell in 1995, due to the low level of technology, low productivity and high costs. The trade deficit grew by 20.3 per cent to C£1.03 billion ($2.3 billion) in the first 11 months of 1995. The government has pledged to lift restrictions on capital movement and to liberalise interest rates in a bid to fund modernisation with finance from the international market. The largest increases were registered in the production of chemicals and plastics (10.3 per cent) and paper products and printing (7.6 per cent).

Tourism

A major problem facing exporters is the rate of the Cypriot pound, which rose by 5 per cent against the UK's pound sterling and 8 per cent against the US dollar in 1995. This has had a major impact on the island's premier industry, tourism, which faced increased competition with Spain, Portugal and Turkey where devaluations occurred.

According to the Cyprus Tourism Office, some 2.1 million tourists are expected in 1996, generating an estimated US$1.6 billion. This is one third of national income and provides one fifth of all jobs. But arrivals in the first nine months of 1995 rose by only 4 per cent, compared to 12.1 per cent in 1994 and the UK market, accounting for 36 per cent of the total, actually fell by 60,000 visitors. Healthy increases were registered from Germany (44.6 per cent), France (25.4 per cent) and the Benelux states (31.9 per-cent) but there is a widespread feeling in the industry that tourism may have peaked.

The European Investment Bank approved a loan in June 1996 for the upgrading of Cyprus' air traffic control system. The loan is worth C£17 million. A new control centre will be built in Lefkosia and new landing systems will be installed at Pafos and Larnaka under this development programme. The upgrading will help enable full integration of Cyprus' air traffic control system with the EU's system.

Diversification

In an attempt to diversify away from tourism, the government is trying to promote the island as a centre of financial services, particularly for investors from the former Soviet bloc. By the end of 1995, a total of 23,000 foreign companies had registered in

May 1996, House of Representatives election results

	Number of votes	Per cent	Change on 1991	Seats
ADISOK	5,311	1.44	-0.96	0
AKEL	121,958	33.00	2.37	19
DEKO	60,726	16.43	-3.12	10
Free Democrats	13,623	3.69	**	2
Ecologists	3,710	1.00	**	0
New Horizons	6,317	1.71	**	0
EDEK	30,033	8.13	-2.76	5
Democratic Rally/Liberial Party	127,380	34.47	-1.34	20
Independents	463	0.13	0.06	0

KEY INDICATORS — Cyprus

	Unit	1991	1992	1993	1994	1995
Population	'000	706.9	718.0	730.0	735.0	740.0
Gross national product (GNP)	US$bn	6.34	6.74	7.00	7.60	–
GNP per capita	US$*	8,800	9,600	9,700	10,250	–
GNP real growth	%	1.5	7.0	1.3	5.0	–
Inflation	%	5.0	6.5	4.9	4.7	2.6
Consumer prices	1990=100	105	112	117	123	126
Unemployment	%	2.5	1.8	2.4	2.7	–
Agricultural production	1979-81=100	76.74	112.69	137.39	116.02	122.86
Industrial production	1990=100	100.7	104.5	97.8	101.2	102.8
Mining	1990=100	98.1	100.1	122.4	132.3	121.9
Exports	C£m	441.79	443.72	431.40	475.47	–
Imports (CIF)	C£m	1,215.83	1,490.76	1,260.05	1,481.66	–
Balance of trade	US$m	-1,488.1	-2,086.8	-1,650.0	-1,800.0	–
Current account	US$m	-461.0	-671.1	88.5	43.7	–
Total reserves minus gold	US$m	1,390.2	1,027.9	1,096.7	1,464.5	1,116.9
Foreign exchange	US$m	1,364.5	992.8	1,061.6	1,427.2	1,079.0
Discount rate	%	6.50	6.50	6.50	6.50	–
Deposit rate	%	5.75	5.75	5.75	5.75	–
Lending rate	%	9.00	9.00	9.00	8.83	–
Exchange rate	US$ per C£	2.16	2.22	2.01	2.03	2.21

Cyprus and offshore investment amounted to some C£161 million. Re-exports, at C£251.2 million, accounted for over 55 per cent of Cypriot trade for the first time, with the main destinations in Bulgaria, Russia, Greece and Romania.

On 29 March 1996, the Cyprus Stock Exchange formally opened for business with an initial share listing for around 40 public companies; it had been transformed from an over-the-counter market. However, by mid-year 1996 local investors became wary due to the prospect of lower tourism revenue and the credit squeeze and this caused share prices to drop by some 20 per cent from their peak in February 1996. But the situation may ease now that the central bank gave the okay to a higher level of foreign ownership of listed companies – 49 per cent. As well, certain requirements that deterred foreign investors, such as the necessity for central bank approval for each market transaction, have been relaxed.

The developing offshore sector dovetails neatly with another of the island's specialties – the shipping industry. With 23.4 million tonnes, Cyprus has the fourth largest registry in the world and the industry contributed C£42 million in government revenue in 1995.

COUNTRY PROFILE — CYPRUS

Political system

Presidential republic with legislative power vested in unicameral House of Representatives, consisting of 80 members elected by universal suffrage for a five-year term – 56 members of the House are Greek Cypriots, elected by the Greek Cypriot community of the island, and 24 members are Turkish Cypriots, elected by the Turkish Cypriot community (at present the Turkish Cypriot members do not take up their seats). The May 1996 election took place on the basis of strict proportional representation. Centre-right coalition comprising the Democratic Rally (DISY) retained majority by winning 34.48% of the votes in the 26 May 1996 elections and the Democratic Party (DIKO) (10.4%). (The Communist Progressive Party of the Working People (AKEL) won 33.03 per cent.)

Main cities/towns

On 16 February 1995 the municipal council voted unanimously to change the capital city's name to Lefkosia, Nicosia's Greek name, the change being the result of a campaign to standardise place-names according to their Greek pronunciation. Lefkosia (Nicosia) (population 178,000 in 1994); Limassol, Larnaka (Larnaca), Pafos (Paphos), Paralimni. In Turkish-occupied sector: Varosha (Famagusta), Kyrenia, Morphou.

Media

Press: In the government-controlled area there are nine dailies (eight in Greek, one in English) and eight weeklies (seven in Greek, one in English). There are also 22 periodicals, several of which are business publications (general topics and current affairs) and some are in English. An official publication on Cyprus affairs is the *Cyprus Bulletin* published by the Press and Information Office in seven languages every fortnight. In the Turkish-occupied area there are six daily papers in circulation, five weeklies and three periodicals.
Broadcasting: Until 1990, all radio and TV programmes were broadcast by Cyprus Broadcasting Corporation (CyBC) a government-controlled commercial station. Programmes broadcast in Greek, Turkish and English. Some radio programmes in Arabic and Armenian. In July 1990 a new law was approved by parliament which provided for the operation of a greater number of broadcasting corporations given that they satisfied certain criteria. Under this new law, several broadcasting corporations were given licence to transmit radio programmes.

Domestic economy

Considerable levels of economic growth since late 1970s, based on increased earnings from manufactured and agricultural exports and on a rapid expansion of earnings from tourism and other services. The New Development Plan (1989–93) aims at fast growth – 5 per cent per annum – under conditions of stability, and places emphasis on technological upgrading, modernisation and improvement of the competitiveness of the Cyprus economy. Economy remains export-oriented with exports of goods comprising mainly manufactured products and, to a lesser extent, agricultural products.

External trade

Widening trade deficit offset by earnings from tourism and capital inflows, largely comprising foreign loans and direct investments. Imports rose over 1987–92 owing to increased domestic consumption and higher demand from tourism. Agreement on full customs union with the EC came into effect in January 1988, while an application for full EC membership was submitted in July 1990. The EU agreed in 1995 to open membership negotiations with Cyprus six months after the end of the inter-governmental conference, probably in early-1998.
Exports: Major agricultural exports include potatoes, fresh vegetables, citrus fruits, fruit juices and wine. Industrial exports include cigarettes, clothing, footwear, paper products, cement, chemicals and toiletries. The European Community is the major export market (typically 41% of total) followed by Middle East (32%).
Imports: Principal imports are inputs for manufacturing, oil, machinery and transport equipment. Main sources: UK (typically 11% of total), Japan (11%), Italy (10%), Germany (9%). Syria is the major source of oil, providing 2% of total Cypriot imports.

Agriculture

The sector contributed 7 per cent to GNP in 1994 and employed 14 per cent of the labour force. It is a significant earner of foreign exchange. Major crops are potatoes, grapes, citrus fruits and barley. Large-scale water development programme culminated in Southern Conveyor Project conveying surplus water from the south-western part of the island to the central and eastern areas in effort to broaden and boost agricultural production, as well as to increase the water supply of the receiver areas.

Industry

The sector contributed 31 per cent to GNP in 1994 and employed about 25 per cent of the working population. Major growth industries, which are mainly export-based, include cement, footwear and clothing. Diversification and foreign investment are being encouraged.

Tourism

Most rapidly expanding sector of the economy. Largest single earner of foreign exchange. In 1995 there were 2m tourists.

COUNTRY PROFILE

Mining

The commercially mined minerals include copper concentrates. Quarry materials include marble, bentonite, umber, sienna, ochra and limonite. Production of most of these falling but exploration programme is taking place with UN assistance. Efforts to revive output constrained by the high level of production costs in relation to export-selling price.

Energy

Almost total dependence on fuel imports, principally oil for electricity generation. Successful energy conservation programme under way involving exploitation of solar energy.

Legal system

Based on common law with civil law modifications.

Membership of international organisations

AALCC, Customs Co-operation Council (CCC), Commonwealth, Council of Europe, CSCE, ECE, FAO, G-77, IAEA, IBRD, ICAO, ICO, IDA, IFAD, IFC, ILC, ILO, IMF, IMO, INTELSAT, INTERPOL, ITC, ITU, MIGA, Non-Aligned Movement, UN, UNCITRAL, UNCTAD, UNDC, UNESCO, UNIDO, UPU, WFC, WFTU, WHO, WIPO, WMO, WTO. Customs Union Agreement with the EU has been in force since January 1988 and an application for full EU membership was submitted in July 1990.

BUSINESS GUIDE

Time

GMT + 2 hrs (GMT + 3 hrs from late Mar to late Sep).

Climate

Mediterranean. Summers long and dry, changeable winters with occasional rain. Temperatures range from 1–27 degrees C (in mountains). 5–40 degrees C (inland) and from 9–35 degrees C (on the coast). Hottest months Jul and Aug, coldest Jan and Feb.

Entry requirements

Visa: Visa not required by nationals of most European countries, Russia, the USA, Canada, Australia and Japan. N.B. Legal entry only by Larnaka and Pafos airports and ports of Pafos, Larnaka and Limassol. Entry to the occupied area either via the Turkish mainland or through the ports and airports of the occupied area is considered illegal by the Government of the Republic of Cyprus.
Health: Tap water is safe to drink, but fruit, especially soft fruit, should be washed. No vaccination is required for any international traveller.
Currency: Only C£50 in Cyprus currency notes may be taken into or out of the country. There is no limit on foreign currency imports, although amounts in excess of the equivalent of US$1,000 should be declared at customs on forms DNR. Amounts so declared may be re-exported on departure.
Customs: Personal items duty-free. Unauthorised export of antiquities is prohibited. Permission of Cyprus Museum is required.

Air access

National airline: Cyprus Airways.
Other airlines: Aeroflot, Air 2000, Air Zimbabwe, Alitalia, Austrian Airlines, Balkan, British Airways, Czech Airlines, Donavia, Egyptair, El Al, Finnair, Gulf Air, Iran Air, JAT, KLM, Kuwait Airways, Lithuanian Airlines, LOT, LTU International Airways, Lufthansa, MALEV, MEA, Olympic Airways, Royal Jordanian, Swiss Air, Syrian Arab Airlines, TAROM, Yemenia.
Main international airport: Larnaka (LCA), 6 km south of town.
International airports: Pafos (PFO), 13 km east of town (76 km from Limassol). Lefkosia international airport has been closed to traffic since 1974.

Surface access:

By ship from Greece, Syria, Israel, Italy, Lebanon and Egypt.
Main ports: Limassol and Larnaka. Also port at Vasilikos serving industrial complexes in the area. The island's main port at Famagusta has been under Turkish occupation since 1974.

Hotels

Over 400 hotels (one to five stars) and hotel apartments (A to C class) plus several other types of tourist accommodation as well as a large number of restaurants and tavernas. Visitors should book well in advance especially during peak holiday season (Apr-Oct). Cyprus Tourism Organisation (CTO) operates rating system, both for hotels and any other licensed tourist accommodation. Tipping is not obligatory. A 10 per cent service charge and a 3 per cent CTO tax are included in the bill.

Restaurants

A wide variety with many specialities available. A 10 per cent service charge and a 3 per cent tax are normally added to bills. Price lists are required to be displayed.

Credit cards

American Express, Diners', Eurocard, Visa, Carte Blanche, Mastercard and Access are all accepted at hotels.

Car hire

Available in all parts of the island. Rates vary depending on size of car, and are also subject to seasonal variation. Prestige service is also available, but at higher prices. Cheap rates for hire periods of more than one week. Visitors should book cars well in advance Jun–Sep. National or international driving licence required. Driving is on the left.

City transport

Taxis: Efficient service throughout the island by metered taxis. The transurban service-taxis are shared taxis connecting all main towns (only during daytime). Prices are regulated. Between 2300 and 0600 an additional 15 per cent is charged. Tipping is standard practice.
Rail: No trains in Cyprus.

National transport

Buses: Efficient 'intra-cud' (inter-city) bus service available. All buses run from central bus depots connecting towns and villages. Rural bus operation is limited to once or twice a day. Urban buses operate frequently during daytime and in certain tourist areas during summer their routes are extended till midnight.

Public holidays

Fixed dates: Government offices
1 Jan (New Year's Day), 25 Mar (Greek Independence Day), 1 May (May Day), 1 Oct (Cyprus Independence Day).
Greek Orthodox
6 Jan (Epiphany), 28 Oct (Ohi Day), 25 Dec (Christmas Day), 26 Dec (Boxing Day).
Turkish
29 Oct (Turkish Republic Day), 19 May, 23 Apr, 30 Aug.
Armenian Catholic and Protestant
6 Jan (Epiphany, Catholics), 25 & 26 Dec (Christmas).
August is traditionally the month when summer holidays are taken.
Variable dates: Greek Orthodox
Green Monday, Good Friday, Holy Saturday, Easter Monday.
Turkish
Birthday of the Prophet, two days Ramazan Bayram, three days Qurban Bayram.
Armenian Catholic and Protestant
Good Friday, Easter.

Working hours

Business: (Mon–Fri) (winter) 0800–1300 and 1430–1730, (summer) 0730–1300 and 1600–1830; (Wed and Sat) half-day all the year round.
Government: (Mon–Fri) 0730–1430; (Thu) 1500–1800.
Banking: (Mon–Fri) 0815–1230 and (specially for tourists) 1530–1730.
Shops: (Mon–Fri) (winter) 0800–1300 and 1430–1730, (summer) 0730–1300 and 1600–1830; (Wed and Sat) half-day.

Social customs

The custom of handshaking is practised. It is considered impolite to refuse drinks offered at a first meeting. Cypriots customarily offer fruit preserves to guests. Between 1300 and 1600 hours is siesta time in summer (May-Sep). Avoid shorts and wear suitable clothing when visiting churches and monasteries.

Telecommunications

Telephone and telefax: Service is automatic and direct dialling is available to over 184 countries. International dialling code: 357, followed by area code (2 for Lefkosia, 4 for Larnaka, 5 for Limassol, 6 for Pafos. As an exception to the above, the following area codes should be preceded by 905 instead of 357: 3 for Famagusta, 7 for Kyrenia, 74 for Morphou.
Telex: Available in major hotels. Country code 605 CY.

Advertising

No code of advertising but CBC operates its own code of practice which restricts cigarette and tobacco advertising. Information can be obtained from the Cyprus Advertising Agents Association at the Cyprus Chamber of Commerce and Industry.

Trade fairs

The Cyprus International Trade (State) Fair held for two weeks every summer (end May – mid-Jun) as well as other specialised fairs. Information from Cyprus State Fairs Authority.

Electricity supply

240 V AC. Socket outlets and sockets of flat 3-pin type are used.

Representation in capital

Australia, Austria, Belgium, Brazil, Bulgaria, Canada, China, Cuba, Egypt, Finland, France, Germany, Greece, The Holy See, Hungary, Iceland, India, Iran, Ireland, Israel, Italy, Jordan, Lebanon, Libya, Nicaragua, Norway, Panama, PLO, Poland, Romania, Russia, Spain, Sweden, Switzerland, Syria, UK, USA, Yemen.

BUSINESS DIRECTORY

Hotels

Larnaka (formerly Larnaca) (area code 4)
Golden Bay (on beach), Larnaka–Dhekelia Road, PO Box 741 (tel: 623-444; fax: 623-451).

Lordos Beach, Larnaka–Dhekelia Road, PO Box 542 (tel: 657-444; fax: 623-847).

Palm Beach (on the beach), Larnaka–Dhekelia Road, PO Box 394 (tel: 657-500; fax: 620-788).

Princess Beach Sunotel, Larnaka–Dhekelia Road, PO Box 858 (tel: 635-500; fax: 635-508).

Sandy Beach, Larnaka–Dhekelia Road, PO Box 857 (tel: 624-333; fax: 656-900).

Sun Hall, Athens Avenue, PO Box 300 (tel: 653-341; fax: 652-717).

Hotels (contd):

Limassol (area code 5)
Amathus Beach (on the beach), Amathus Avenue, PO Box 513 (tel: 321-152; fax: 329-343).

Apollonia Beach, Potamos Yermasoyias, PO Box 594 (tel: 323-351; fax: 321-683).

Churchill, 28th October Avenue, PO Box 1626 (tel: 324-444; fax: 323-494).

Elias Beach (on the beach), Ancient Amathus District, PO Box 4300 (tel: 325-000; fax: 320-880).

Le Meridien, Amathus, PO Box 6560 (tel: 320-660; fax: 329-222).

Poseidonia Beach Sunotel (on the beach), Amathus, PO Box 1206 (tel: 321-000; fax: 327-040).

Sheraton (on the beach), Amathus, PO Box 1064 (tel: 321-100; fax: 324-394).

Lefkosia (formerly Nicosia) (area code 2)
Asty, 12 Prince Charles Street, Ayios Dometios, PO Box 4502 (tel: 473-021; fax: 476-344).

Averof, 19 Averof Street, PO Box 4225 (tel: 463-447; fax: 463-411).

Churchill, 1 Achaeans Street, PO Box 4145 (tel: 448-858; fax: 445-506).

Cleopatra, 8 Florina Street, PO Box 1397 (tel: 445-254; fax: 452-618).

Europa, 16 Alceos Street, Engomi, PO Box 5029 (tel: 454-537; fax: 474-417).

Excelsior, 4 Photiou Stravrou Pitta Street (tel: 368-585; fax: 476-740).

Hilton, Archbishop Makarios Avenue, PO Box 2023 (tel: 464-040; fax: 453-191).

Kennedy, 70 Regaena Street, PO Box 1212 (tel: 475-131; fax: 473-337).

Ledra, Grivas Dhigenis Avenue, Engomi, PO Box 1390 (tel: 352-086; fax: 351-918).

Philoxenia, Eylenja Avenue, Eylenja, PO Box 5466 (tel: 499-700; fax: 498-038).

Useful telephone numbers

Ambulance (tel: 199).

Fire (tel: 1991).

Police (tel: 199).

Car hire

Lefkosia (formerly Nicosia)
Budget: central reservations (tel: 462-042; fax: 266-002); 2 Pindou Street (tel: 462-650; fax: 366-002).

Hertz: reservations (tel: 477-411; fax: 461-428); 45B Griva Digeni Ave (tel & fax: 477-783); 14 Michael Giorgalla St (tel: 477-422; fax: 461-428).

Larnaka (formerly Larnaca)
Budget: airport, Petsas Desk (tel: 643-350).

Europcar: airport (tel: 515-157); Dekelia Road, Shop 5, JGL Constructions Building (tel: 645-590).

Hertz: 3 Archbishop Kyprianos Avenue (tel & fax: 655-145); airport (tel: 643-388; tx: 2611).

Limassol
Budget: Georghiou A Ave, Sea-Breeze Court (tel: 323-672).

Europcar: Georgiou A Street, Belmar Complex, Yermasoyia (tel: 322-050); 38-40 Omonia Ave (tel: 371-141).

Hertz: Anna Court G3, Lefkosia–Limassol Road (tel & fax: 323-758).

Pafos (formerly Paphos)
Budget: Green Court, St Paul's Avenue (tel: 235-522); airport, Petsas Desk, arrivals hall (tel: 249-023).

Europcar: Poseidonos Ave, Natalia Centre (tel: 241-850, 236-944); airport (tel: 515-513, 515-157).

Hertz: 54A St Paul's Avenue (tel: 233-985).

Chambers of commerce

Cyprus Chamber of Commerce and Industry, 38 Grivas Dhigenis Ave. and 3 Deligeorgis Street, Chamber Building, PO Box 1455, Lefkosia (tel: 449-500, 462-312; fax: 449-048, 458-603).

Cyprus British Chamber of Commerce and Industry, 211 Regent Street, London, W1R 8DA (tel: 734-4791/2, 437-3831; fax: 494-0491).

Famagusta Chamber of Commerce and Industry, 339 Ayiou Andreou Street, Andrea Chamber Bldg., PO Box 3124, Limassol (tel: 370-165, 370-167; fax: 370-291).

Larnaka Chamber of Commerce and Industry, 12 12 Gregoriou Afxentiou Str., Skourou Bldg., 4th Floor, PO Box 287, Larnaka (tel: 655-051; fax: 628-281).

Lefkosia Chamber of Commerce and Industry, 38 Grivas Dhigenis Ave. and 3 Deligioris Str., Chamber Building, PO Box 1455, Lefkosia (tel: 449-500; fax: 367-433).

Limassol Chamber of Commerce and Industry, PO Box 347, 25 Spyrou Araouzou Street, Verengaria Building, PO Box 347, Limassol (tel: 362-556; fax: 371-655).

Pafos Chamber of Commerce and Industry, 32 Grivas Dhigenis Avenue, Demetra Court, 2nd Floor, Flat 22, Pafos (tel:235-115; fax: 244-602).

Banking

Central Bank of Cyprus, 80 Kennedy Avenue, Lefkosia (tel: 379-800; fax: 378-153).

Arab Bank Ltd, 28 Santaroza Ave, Lefkosia (tel: 457-111; fax: 457-890). Branches in Limassol, Larnaka, Pafos, Aya Nappa.

Bank of Cyprus Ltd, Box 1472, 86-90 Phaneromeni Street, Lefkosia (tel: 464-064; fax: 464-340).

Barclays Bank Plc, Eleftheria Square, PO Box 1022, Lefkosia (tel: 463-002; fax: 453-499). Branches in Limassol, Pafos and Larnaka.

Central Bank of Cyprus, PO Box 5529, 36 Metochiou Str., Lefkosia (tel: 445-281; fax: 472-012).

Commercial Bank of Greece S.A., 4 Ionos Street and 1 Iona Nicolaou Street, Lefkosia (tel: 473-671; fax: 473-923).

Co-operative Central Bank Ltd, Gregorius Afxentiou Street, Lefkosia (tel: 442-921; fax: 443-088).

Cyprus Development Bank, PO Box 1415, Alpha House, 50 Archbishop Makarios III Avenue, Lefkosia (tel: 457-575; fax: 464-322).

Cyprus Investment and Securities Corporation, 60 Digenis Akritas Avenue, PO Box 597, Lefkosia (tel: 451-535; fax: 445-481).

Cyprus Popular Bank Ltd, PO Box 2032, 39 Archbishop Makarios III Avenue, Lefkosia (tel: 450-000; fax: 449-169).

Hellenic Bank Ltd, PO Box 4747, 92 Digenis Akritas Avenue/Cretes Str., Lefkosia (tel: 360-000; fax: 454-074).

Lombard Natwest Bank Ltd, PO Box 1661, Corner of Chilon and Gladstone Str., Stylianos Lenas Square, Lombard House, Lefkosia (tel: 474-333; fax: 457-870).

National Bank of Greece, PO Box 1191, 36 Archbishop Makarios III Avenue, Lefkosia (tel: 442-211; fax: 447-089).

Principal newspapers

Alithia, 5 Pindaros & Androklis Street, PO Box 1695, Lefkosia (tel: 463-040; fax: 463-945).

Cyprus Mail, 24 Vassilios Voulgaroctonos Street, PO Box 1144, Lefkosia (tel: 462-074; fax: 366-385).

Haravghi, 6 Akamas Street, PO Box 1556, Lefkosia (tel: 476-356; fax: 365-154).

Philelephtheros, 36 Vyronos Avenue, PO Box 1094, Lefkosia (tel: 463-922; fax: 366-121).

Simerini, 31 Archangelos Avenue, PO Box 1836, Strovolos, Lefkosia (tel: 353-532; fax: 352-298).

Travel information

Cyprus Airways, PO Box 1903, 21 Alkeou Street, Lefkosia (tel: 443-054, 461-800; fax: 443-167, 360-075).

Cyprus Hotel Association, PO Box 4772, Lefkosia (tel: 445-251; fax: 365-460).

Cyprus Tourism Organisation (main office, for postal enquiries only), 19 Limassol Ave, PO Box 4535, Lefkosia (tel: 315-715; fax: 313-022); (for personal and telephone enquiries only, open every morning except Sundays, and on Monday and Thursday afternoons) Laiki Yitonia, East of Eleftheria Sq, Lefkosia (tel: 444-264); (24-hour service) Larnaka International Airport (tel: 654-389).

Other useful addresses

Central Post Office, Eleftheria Square, Lefkosia (tel: 303-219).

Cyprus Broadcasting Corporation, PO Box 4824, Lefkosia (tel: 422-231; fax: 314-050).

Cyprus Employers and Industrialists Federation, 30 Grivas Dhigenis Avenue, PO Box 1657, Lefkosia (tel: 445-102; fax: 459-459).

Cyprus News Agency, 97 Ay Omoloyitae Avenue, Lefkosia (tel: 458-413; fax: 442-613).

Cyprus State Fairs Authority, Makedonitissa, Lefkosia (tel: 352-918).

Cyprus Telecommunications Authority, PO Box 4929 (tel: 313-111).

Department of Customs & Excise, Customs Headquarters, 29 Katsonis Street, Ay. Omoloyitae, Lefkosia (tel: 305-404; fax: 355-050).

Department of Statistics and Research, Ministry of Finance, 13 Lord Byron Avenue, PC 162, Lefkosia (tel: 303-208; fax: 456-712).

Ministry of Agriculture, Natural Resources and Environment, Loukis Akritas Avenue, Lefkosia (tel: 302-171; fax: 445-156).

Ministry of Commerce, Industry and Tourism, 2 A. Araouzos Street, Lefkosia (tel: 303-441, 303-456; fax: 366-120).

Ministry of Communication and Works, Dem. Severis Avenue, Lefkosia (tel: 302-161; fax: 465-462, 360-578).

Ministry of Defence, 4 Emmanuel Roides Street, Lefkosia (tel: 303-187, 303-189; fax: 366-225).

Ministry of Education and Culture, Gr. Afxentiou Street, Lefkosia (tel: 303-331; fax: 445-021).

Ministry of Finance, Ex Secretariat Compound, Lefkosia (tel: 302-779; fax: 366-080).

Ministry of Foreign Affairs, Dem. Severis Avenue, Government House No. 18-19, Lefkosia (tel: 302-387; fax: 451-881, 365-778, 369-554).

Ministry of Health, Lefkosia (tel: 303-243; fax: 303-498).

Ministry of Interior, Dem. Severis Avenue, Ex Secretariat Offices, Lefkosia (tel: 302-238; fax: 453-465, 366-709, 348-486).

Ministry of Justice and Public Order, 12 Helioupoleos, Lefkosia (tel: 302-355; fax: 461-427).

Ministry of Labour and Social Insurance, Byron Avenue, Lefkosia (tel: 303-147, 445-977).

Press and Information Office, Apellis Street, Ay Omoloyitae, Lefkosia (tel: 302-640; fax: 302-720 or 366-123).

Czech Republic

Marko Milivojevic

The first former communist country to be admitted into the Organisation for Economic Co-operation and Development (OECD) in November 1995, the Czech Republic continues to enjoy by far the best political and economic prospects in Central-Eastern Europe. The May 1996 parliamentary elections have created some political uncertainty, if not instability, in the Czech Republic, where the ruling three-party coalition government led by Vaclav Klaus' Civic Democratic Party (ODS) failed to secure a working parliamentary majority. However, Klaus was able to get the Social Democratic Party's (CSSD) blessing to form a minority government in June 1996.

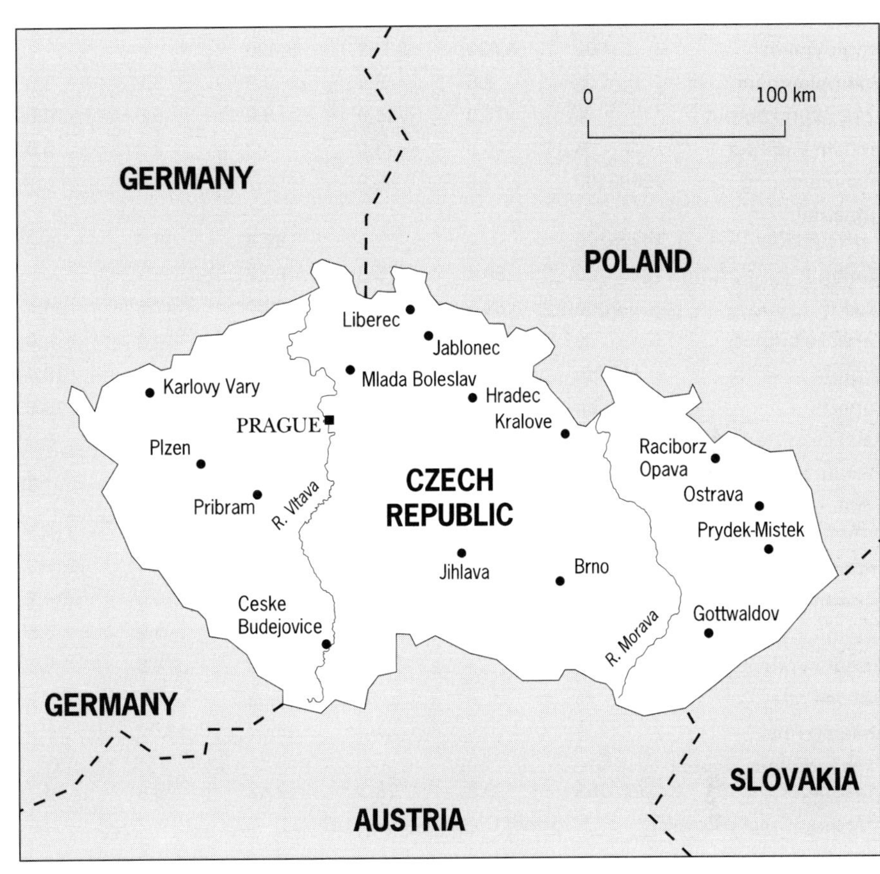

Elections

The main opposition grouping, the CSSD gained a very credible 26.4 per cent of the vote in May 1996, compared to the 29.6 per cent scored by the ODS. The ODS-led coalition failed to gain a working parliamentary majority in the elections, winning only 99 of 200 parliamentary seats, six fewer than in the previous election and two MPs short of a majority. The Civic Democratic Alliance (ODA) won 6.4 per cent of the vote (0.5 per cent higher than 1992) and the Christian Democratic Union-People's Party (KDU-CSL) won 8.1 per cent (1.8 per cent higher than 1992). The hardline Communist Party of Bohemia and Moravia won 10.3 per cent of the vote (3.8 per cent less than in 1992) and the ultra-nationalist Republican Party won 8 per cent of the vote (2 per cent less than in 1992).

Although often politically inconsistent and divided, the centre-left opposition prevented Klaus and the ODS from completing their political consolidation of 1995. Klaus stayed on as prime minister after the President asked him to form a minority government on 6 June 1996; after horse-trading, the CSSD gave the okay to Klaus. The CSSD was never likely to be able to form a government because of its refusal to enter into a coalition with the unreformed Communist Party of Bohemia and Moravia. Any sort of deal between the CSSD and the Republicans was even more improbable.

The results of the May 1996 parliamentary elections have also shattered the myth

KEY FACTS — *Czech Republic*

Official title: Czech Republic

Head of state: President Vaclav Havel (election 1 Jun 1996)

Head of government: Prime Minister Vaclav Klaus (ODS) (re-appointed 2 Jul 1996)

Ruling party: Three-party conservative coalition government led by Civic Democratic Party (ODS) and including the Christian Democrats (KDU) and the Civic Democratic Alliance (ODA) (from Jul 1996)

Capital: Prague

Official Languages: Czech

Currency: Czech koruna (Kc) introduced 6 February 1993

Exchange rate: Kc27.36 per US$ (Dec 1996)

Area: 78,864 sq km

Population: 10.3m (1995)

GDP per capita: US$4,300 (1995)

GDP real growth: 4.3% (1st qtr 1996)

GNP per capita: US$2,800 (1994)

GNP real growth: 4.3% (1995)*

Labour force: 3.4m (1994)

Unemployment: 3.1% (Jan 1996)

Inflation: 9.4% (Jul 1996)

Trade balance: -US$4.6bn (12 months to Jun 1996)

Foreign debt: US$14.7bn (1995)

Visitor numbers: 17m (1994)

* estimated figure

KEY INDICATORS ***Czech Republic***

	Unit	1991	1992	1993	1994	1995
Population	m	10.3	10.3	10.3	10.3	10.3
Gross domestic product (GDP)	US$bn	24.2	27.9	31.0	36.0	45.5
GDP per capita	US$	2,400	2,700	3,100	3,500	4,300
GDP real growth	%	-14.2	-7.1	-0.9	2.6	4.8
Inflation	%	56.7	11.1	20.0	10.0	8.9
Consumer prices	1990=100	–	–	210.4	231.6	252.6
Employment	'000	4,430	3,752	3,420	–	–
Unemployment	%	2.8	3.1	3.0	3.2	3.0
Agricultural output	%	-15.0	-11.0	-8.0	-5.5	0.0
Industrial output	%	-25.0	-8.0	-5.3	2.3	9.0
Manufacturing	1990=100	73.6	62.9	56.7	–	–
Industrial production	1990=100	–	–	68.4	69.8	76.2
Mining	1990=100	86.4	75.3	69.7	–	–
Coal	mtoe	33.5	30.7	29.7	27.6	26.4
Services output	%	2.0	5.0	7.0	10.0	9.0
Exports	US$bn	**8.3	**11.4	13.0	14.1	16.4
Imports	US$bn	**8.8	**13.2	13.3	15.0	19.8
Balance of trade	US$bn	**-0.5	**-1.8	-0.4	-0.4	-3.4
Current account	US$bn	**0.3	**-0.2	6.8	-0.8	-1.3
Total reserves minus gold	US$m	–	–	3,789	6,145	13,843
Foreign exchange	US$m	–	–	3,781	6,145	13,843
Foreign debt	US$bn	**7.2	**6.8	8.7	10.1	14.7
Foreign investment	US$bn	**0.9	**1.4	2.4	3.2	5.5
Discount rate	%	–	–	8.0	8.5	9.5
Deposit rate	%	–	–	7.03	7.07	–
Lending rate	%	–	–	14.07	13.12	–
Exchange rate (annual average)	Kc per US$	***29.5	***28.3	29.2	28.8	26.3

**former Czechoslovakia ***former Czechoslovak Koruna

that the CDP is the natural party of government in the Czech Republic. Although a largely ceremonial office under the Czech constitution, the presidency held by Vaclav Havel moved centre stage in Czech politics, where the key challenge for 1996 was the formation of a new government.

Having earlier improved relations with his two junior coalition partners, Klaus will find it harder to keep it together in the changed political circumstances of 1996. In November 1995, the CDP merged with the Christian Democratic Party (KDS). The small but influential KDU-CSL, which is very close to the Roman Catholic Church, was previously an ally of the ODS, but this may begin to change in 1996. This is even more true of the ODA.

Foreign relations

On the key issue of European Union (EU) membership, for which negotiations will begin in earnest after its Inter-Governmental Conference in 1997, the Czech Republic is now the best placed to be granted admission by around 2000, along with Poland and Hungary of the Visegrad Group. A formal application for full EU membership was presented by the Czech Republic in January 1995.

Although already highly economically integrated with the EU, the Czech Republic now faces a number of problems on the road to full membership of Europe's premier grouping. As an associate member of the EU, the country has yet to harmonise fully its domestic legislation with European law. Another and potentially more serious problem is perceived Czech high-handedness towards the EU, where relations with Germany also remain problematical over various issues dating back to the Second World War. The Czech election campaign of 1995/96 resulted in vitriolic anti-German sentiments by many local politicians, including Klaus. Combined with other negative factors, this could seriously and needlessly complicate what should otherwise be a relatively trouble-free move towards full EU membership by around 2000.

Following its unilateral termination of the special clearing account for foreign trade with Slovakia in October 1995, the Czech Republic showed that it was less interested than ever in its former Czechoslovak partner.

Economic performance

Following on from earlier successful macro-economic stabilisation and radical structural reform of its economy, the Czech Republic achieved high and non-inflationary economic growth in 1995, when GDP increased by a record 4.8 per cent, compared to 2.6 per cent in 1994. In 1996, GDP is expected to grow by a further 4 per cent in real terms.

In 1995, Czech GDP and GDP per capita reached US$45.5 billion and US$4,300 respectively. In relation to the EU, this economic performance gave the Czech Republic a higher standard of living than all of its poorest members in southern Europe. Within the Visegrad Group, Czech GDP per capita is by far the highest.

In 1995, unemployment was only 3 per cent compared to 4 per cent in 1994. In practice, the Czech Republic now has full employment. Politically, not even the ODS-led government has been willing to allow high unemployment, even at the cost of over-manning in many industrial sectors.

Down from 10 per cent in 1994 to 8.9 per cent in 1995, inflation is expected to continue falling for the remainder of the 1990s. In 1995, the main causes of this were continued macro-economic stabilisation, lower food prices and an exchange rate that made imports relatively cheap. Higher economic productivity was seen in 1995 and hence reduced wage-push inflation. Assuming that this continues into 1996, further increases in real wages will be compensated for by higher economic productivity. Economic productivity is still relatively low by advanced EU standards, if not those of central Europe.

Industry

Significantly, small-to-medium-sized company development has been particularly successful, thereby creating an industrial sector similar in structure to that in Germany. Industrial sector restructuring has also made relatively good progress, although a more radical approach to overmanning may be required in due course.

Accounting for 35 per cent of GDP, industrial output grew twice as fast as GDP in 1995, mainly because of increased domestic demand. In 1995, industrial output increased by 9 per cent, compared to 2.3 per cent in 1994. This is a highly significant economic development which seemed to indicate that local industrial firms were switching from foreign to domestic markets.

In many industrial sectors, local producers could not keep pace with rising domestic demand in 1995. Skoda, 70 per cent owned by Germany's Volkswagen, produced a record 209,500 cars in 1995, of which 65,000 were sold on the domestic market (in 1994, 173,600 cars were produced). According to various estimates, demand for Skoda cars alone was twice the number produced for the local market in 1995.

Agriculture and services

Economically marginal at 5 per cent of GDP in 1995, agricultural output basically stabilised in that year, thereby partly reversing earlier declines in this sector of the Czech economy.

Accounting for a record 60 per cent of GDP in 1995, services continued to register very high growth, particularly as regards retail and wholesale trade, construction, transport and telecommunications. Financial services are now also a high growth sector. Some service sectors, such as tourism, which earned over US$2 billion in 1995, may now be peaking. Overall, output of services increased by 9 per cent in 1995, compared to 10 per cent in 1994.

On the employment front, the mainly privately-owned service sector is now the source of most new job creation in the Czech Republic. As a result, job losses in more traditional industrial sectors have been off-set by more new jobs in services and more modern industrial sectors.

Budget

Accounting for 0.9 per cent of GDP in 1994, the government budget deficit disappeared altogether in 1995, when expenditures and revenues were broadly in balance. This trend is expected to continue in 1996, although expenditures are then set to rise faster than revenues, or 15 per cent over 12 per cent year-end. In 1996, public spending is expected to account for 36.5 per cent of projected GDP, compared to 36.4 per cent in 1995.

Foreign exchange

The CDP-led government and the Czech National Bank (CNB) have also become more amenable to the idea of a devaluation of the koruna in due course, mainly because of the record trade and current account deficits of 1995. As things stood at the end of 1995, when the annual average Kc per US$ parity was 26.31, the CNB's fixed-against the DM (65 per cent) and US$ (35 per cent) since May 1993-exchange rate clearly favoured imports over exports. Since its introduction in 1993, the strong koruna has been slowly appreciating against both the US$ and the DM, thereby implicitly damaging Czech export performance.

COUNTRY PROFILE — CZECH REPUBLIC

Historical profile
The Czech Republic and Slovakia previously formed a federation, Czechoslovakia. However, on 1 January 1993 it divided into two independent countries, the Czech Republic (comprising the regions of Bohemia and Moravia) and the Slovak Republic.

Political system
The head of state is the president who is elected for a five-year term. The legislature is made up of a 200-seat Chamber of Deputies (lower house), elected for a four-year term, and an 81-member Senate (upper house), elected in 1996 under a two-round majoritarian system in 81 single-member constituencies, to be renewed partially every two years with one-third of the seats coming up for election; senators serve a six-year term.

Political parties
From July 1996 there is a three-party conservative coalition government led by Civic Democratic Party (ODS) and including the Christian Democrats (KDU) and the Civic Democratic Alliance (ODA). The coalition government, with 99 of parliament's 200 seats, needs the support of the main opposition party Social Democrats (CSSD).

Population
The chief minorities are Slovaks (3% of the population), Poles (0.6%), Germans (0.5%) and Silesians, Romanies (gypsies) and Hungarians.

Main cities/towns
Prague, capital city, (population 1.22m in 1994, Brno (main city of Moravia) (393,000), Ostrava (Moravia) (332,000), Plzen (Pilsen) (179,000).

Language
Czech is the official language spoken in Bohemia and Moravia. The Czech and Slovak languages are mutually comprehensible. Under the previous regime Russian was the second language but is not widely spoken. A large proportion of the population, particularly those engaged in industry and foreign trade, speaks German. English is not so widely known but knowledge of it is increasing, especially among the younger generation. In academic and cultural circles, especially among the older generation and in the ministries, a knowledge of French is usual, but this is declining.

Media
Press: The Bohemian Daily Standard, Prognosis and the Czech Business Journal, have all gone out of business, leaving the *Prague Post* and the *Prague Business Journal* as the principal English language weeklies. Despite the rapid development of television, the press has done its best to keep pace by adopting new technology and producing high-quality, colour newspapers.
Dailies: The main daily newspapers are *Mlada Fronta Dnes, Blesk, Rude Pravo, ZN Noviny, Lidove Noviny, Prace, Svobodne Slovo, Expres* and *Sport.*
Weeklies: Weekly magazines include: *Blesk Magazin, Kvety, Reflex, Mlady Svet.* The Prague Business Journal is a weekly English-language publication.
Radio: There has been significant growth in the number of private radio stations.
Television: Channel CT1 has 100 per cent coverage and attracts large audiences. The first private TV licence was awarded to Central European Television 21, for CT2- the second largest former state channel with national coverage. Channel CT3 has 60 per cent coverage and Channel Premiera covers Prague, Central Bohemia. On 4 February 1994 NOVA, the first nationwide commercial TV station, was launched and has an overwhelming market share of both viewers and advertising. Kabel Net Brno started operations 10 July 1995, offering 16 television channels. About 99 per cent of Czech homes own television sets (1995).
Advertising: Channel CT1 has restrictions on advertising, with only 1 per cent of airtime available for commercial sale. Channel CT2 to increase commercial airtime after privatisation. Channel CT3 has one per cent and Premiera unlimited, commercial airtime. There has been a growth in airtime for advertisers on private radio stations. End-1994 the Czech Republic became the first central European market to set up a self-regulatory advertising standards body, modelled on the UK's Advertising Standards Authority. In 1994 television and print each accounted for 42 per cent of the total media spend. Czech ad budgets very low; adspend per head US$18 a year (1995).

Domestic economy
Privatisation programme began in 1992. In April 1994, the second stage of privatisation began. Most of the 770 medium-to-large-sized companies were privatised by early-1995. A new foreign exchange act took effect from 1 October 1995. It introduces partial liberalisation for capital account and full convertibility for current account transactions in the Czech koruna and it should clear the way for Czech membership of the Organisation for Economic Co-operation and Development which is expected by December 1995. The new act lifts a Kc100,000 limit on the amount of foreign currency Czech citizens can buy and allows for the purchase of real estate abroad. It also enables companies to accept credit from non-resident banks and eases

In order to allow Czech membership of the OECD in November 1995, the CNB made the koruna fully externally convertible for all current account transactions. In the longer-term, this will probably lead to the abandonment of a fixed exchange rate in favour of a managed float and full external convertibility on the capital account. In the interim, the CNB allowed a slight depreciation of the koruna during the first quarter of 1996 to a new parity of Kc27.1 per US$ in March 1996. This trend is expected to continue throughout 1996, thereby, it is hoped, improving export performance and curbing high import growth.

The ability of the CNB to manage an unfixed exchange rate has never been better. At the end of 1995, total hard currency reserves were over US$17 billion, compared to just under US$10 billion a year earlier. Here the main positive trends have been increased savings in koruna-denominated assets in local banks, higher foreign capital inflows of all types, increasing foreign direct investment (FDI) and buoyant service income growth, notably from tourism.

Even more so than was the case in 1994, capital inflows from abroad represented the greatest single threat to local money supply and inflation in 1995. Equal to over 10 per cent of GDP, these foreign capital inflows have had to be curbed by the CNB, mainly by a slight downward movement of its discount rates in 1995. With the recent external convertibility of the koruna, these problems were expected to persist throughout 1996.

Bank privatisation

Following the completion of the second stage of the government's mass and voucher-based privatisation programme in 1995, the third and final component of ownership transformation in the Czech Republic was expected to begin sometime in 1996 or 1997. Around 700 medium-to-large-sized companies from the state industrial sector, worth US$5 billion, had been successfully disposed of by the end of 1995.

Likely to prove politically controversial, the next privatisation stage will focus on the restructuring and privatisation of the country's commercial banking system, where the state still exercises *de facto* control over many newly privatised industrial and other enterprises. Czech commercial banks are also the owners of the country's privatisation investment funds and hence the major players on the Prague Stock Exchange (PSE).

The country's top four commercial banks, which together account for 75 per cent of all local deposits, are largely unreconstructed, with strong monopolistic tendencies. Formally discussed by the CNB, the National Property Fund (NPF) and the Finance Ministry in November 1995, commercial bank restructuring and privatisation is likely to prove extremely difficult in practice. External koruna convertibility and possible EU entry by 2000 demands a far more efficient and competitive commercial banking system than the one that exists at present.

At the end of 1995, the three key issues were: how to encourage bank consolidation; the timing and modalities of bank privatisation; and, whether foreign investors should be allowed to participate in local bank privatisation. So far, bank consolidation has yet to take place. Assuming that it does, privatisation of NPF holdings in the country's top commercial banks is likely to take at least five years, given that the equity involved – over US$1.1 billion at the end of 1995 – could overwhelm the PSE.

Other privatisation

There is still considerable scope for further large-scale privatisation in other sectors of the Czech economy. These include a number of large public utilities. In August 1995, the NPF thus announced it was to dispose of 53 strategic assets in due course, but none were likely to be actually privatised much before 1997. Some may remain in the state sector indefinitely.

COUNTRY PROFILE — CZECH REPUBLIC

Domestic econom (contd): restrictions on direct investment.

Employment
The calibre of the workforce is high; a large percentage is well-educated, and skilled labour is available. The private sector accounts for most of the job creation. Average monthly wages in industry grew by 17 per cent in 1995, and by 14.8 per cent in construction. About 45 per cent of the workforce is female.

External trade
The Czech Republic has a widening trade deficit. There have been substantial imports of capital equipment by Czech industry to modernise production facilities and improve the quality of exports, which have competed on price rather than quality. The investment should help to close the gap between growth of imports and exports.
Exports: Exports totalled US$16.4bn in 1995. Main destinations include EU (55.1% of 1995 total), eastern Europe and former Soviet Union (16.9%), Slovakia (16.2%, developing countries (6.6%), EFTA counyries (1.8%).
Imports: Imports totalled US$19.8bn in 1995. Main sources EU (56.4% of 1995 total), eastern Europe and former Soviet Union (15.7%), Slovakia (13.1%, developing countries (6%), EFTA counyries (2.5%).

Agriculture
The agriculture sector accounted for 6 per cent of GNP in 1994 and employed 11 per cent of the workforce. This is still the most heavily subsidised sector of the economy and is relatively labour intensive. The most common forms are the agricultural co-operative and the state farm. Cultivation of private plots is minimal, accounting for approximately 4 per cent of agricultural land and output. The main crops are sugar beet, wheat, maize and potatoes. In May 1991 the Federal Assembly passed a law on land restitution, under which all agricultural land taken by the state after February 1948 is to be returned to its original owners or if such a return is not possible, for the owners to be compensated. The take up for private ownership seems low although many collective farms are being broken up into smaller units.

Industry
The industrial sector accounted for 35 per cent of GDP in 1994 and employed 45 per cent of the workforce. Industrial output in 1995 grew by 9.2 per cent over 1994. Construction increased by 8.5 per cent in 1995 over 1994.

Hydrocarbons
The mining and hydrocarbons sector accounted for 5 per cent of GNP in 1994 and employed 4 per cent of the workforce. Coal is mined on a large scale, particularly in northern Bohemia. Reserves could last more than 40 years at current production rates. Most is low quality brown coal (lignite) which causes pollution. Oil and natural gas resources are very limited, providing only 1 per cent and less than 5 per cent, respectively, of the country's requirements.

Energy
Most of the electrical capacity comes from thermal sources, the rest comes from hydroelectric and nuclear stations. Emphasis is placed on the commissioning of new nuclear power stations and the upgrading of Chernobyl-style reactors.

Stock exchange
The Prague Stock Exchange (PSE) opened 6 April 1993.

Legal system
The state adopted all federal laws (except those which would be unconstitutional). The Supreme Court ensures uniform interpretation of the law and hears appeals from the regional courts. District courts deal with criminal, civil, family, and labour relations law cases. Regional courts deal with first hearings as well as appeals from the district level.

Membership of international organisations
Bank for International Settlements, CEFTA, Council of Europe, CERN, CSCE, EBRD, EU (associate member), IAEA, IDA, IFC, IMF, MIGA, NACC, OECD (from Dec 1995), Partnership for Peace, WEU (associate partner), World Bank, WTO. EFTA protocol entered into force (except for Austria, which still applies CSFR Agreement) 19 April 1993.

BUSINESS GUIDE

Time
GMT + 1 hr (GMT + 2 hrs from late Mar to late Sep).

Climate
A continental climate (warm summers and cold winters). Maximum temperatures are 32 degrees C to 35 degrees C; July is the hottest month (average 29.9 degrees C). Minimum temperatures are -12 degrees C to -20 degrees C. January is the coldest month (average -8 degrees C). Long-term average rainfall is approximately 490 mm.

Entry requirements
Visa: Not required for nationals of the USA, EU,

So far, only one large public utility has been partly privatised. Accounting for nearly half the new foreign direct investment (FDI) in 1995, this was the sale of 27 per cent of the SPT Telecom monopoly to Telecom Netherlands and the Swiss PT for US$1.4 billion. Following the May 1996 elections, the further sale of shares in SPT Telecom and other major utilities has been placed on indefinite hold for essentially political reasons.

Politically, such large sales of utilities remain far more controversial in the Czech Republic than in other Visegrad Group countries, and Hungary in particular. Although it has been a considerable success to date, the Skoda-Volkswagen company has also been criticised on the grounds that it gives too much power to German economic interests.

Foreign trade

Imports continued to substantially exceed exports in 1995; imports increased by 30 per cent (over 1994), compared to export growth of 10 per cent. The result was a record trade deficit of US$3.4 billion in 1995, based on exports of US$16.4 billion and imports of US$19.8 billion. In 1994 exports were US$14.3 billion and imports US$14.7 billion, with a trade deficit of US$400 million.

The higher economic growth of 1995 and the over-valued koruna were responsible for this import boom, a trend that is expected to continue.

Although export growth in 1995 was three times higher than in 1994 (3 per cent over 1993), it could not keep pace with imports, mainly because of an unfavourable exchange rate for exporters, higher than expected production costs locally and a drift towards lower added value goods in the export trade of the Czech Republic in recent years.

The Czech trade deficit in 1995 was particularly large in relation to the EU, which accounted for 55 per cent of the country's foreign trade in that year. Only in relation to the Central European Free Trade Association (CEFTA) did the Czech Republic register a trade surplus. Czech trade with Slovakia, however, remained in deficit in 1995.

On the current account, the small surpluses registered in 1993 and 1994 were turned into a record US$1.3 billion deficit in 1995. Based on a projected trade deficit of US$4 billion year-end in 1996, the current account deficit is now expected to reach US$2.3 billion in that year.

The rapid growth of both FDI and new foreign borrowing in 1995 resulted in a record surplus of over US$6 billion on the country's capital account. One major consequence of this surplus was record hard currency reserves of US$17 billion year-end in 1995, of which the CNB held around two-thirds at the end of that year. In 1995, the Czech Republic was thus able to finance its growing trade and current account deficits.

Foreign debt

Up from US$10.3 billion at the end of 1994 to US$14.7 billion at the end of 1995, the foreign debt of the Czech Republic increased by nearly 50 per cent in that year alone. Earlier relatively year-on-year, new foreign borrowings have been substantially increased to augment CNB hard currency reserves, finance the country's balance of payments and fund local infrastructure development.

The fundamental economic strength and political stability of the Czech Republic has meant that it has had little difficulty in increasing its new foreign borrowings. In 1996, new foreign borrowings are expected to be in the region of US$3 billion, which will give a total foreign debt of around US$17.7 billion at the end of the year.

In the short-term, foreign debt servicing is not expected to be a major problem, but it could become one in the longer-term. Following its membership of the OECD and 'A' country risk or investment grade status in late 1995, the Czech Republic will find

BUSINESS GUIDE — CZECH REPUBLIC

Entry requirements (contd): EFTA countries for visits up to three months. No visa is needed for UK citizens visiting for periods of up to six months. Visitors required to register with the immigration services for stays over 30 days. People staying in hotels are automatically registered with the authorities. Holders of Canadian passports need to obtain a visa. Visas are free for Australian citizens and are valid for three months.
Health: No vaccination certificates required.
Currency: Traveller's cheques can be exchanged at the main money exchange bureaux.

Weights and measures

Metric system. In addition, the following measures are used: quintal or metric hundredweight = 100 kg. Food is usually purchased by the decagram and kilogram.

Air access

Czech Airlines flies to capital cities in western Europe. Regular shuttles fly from Prague to Bratislava and Kosice in Slovakia.
National airlines: Czech Airlines (CSA); Air Ostrava.
Other airlines: Air Algérie, Delta, Eurowings, Iberia, KLM, Lufthansa, Malev, Sabena, SAS, Syrian Arab Airlines, Tarom, Topair.
International airport: Ruzyne Airport, 15 km from Prague.

Hotels

Prague does not have enough hotels to cope with the influx of visitors from the west. Business travellers are advised to book rooms well in advance. A 10 per cent tip is usual.

Credit cards

Credit cards are accepted by the major hotels and stores, especially in Prague.

Car hire

Best advice: do not drive in city centre. If you park illegally, car wheels can be clamped and fines from Kc300 to Kc1,000 are charged (July 1995). There is a 'zero limit' on drink driving. A 400Kc toll is due for motorway driving.

City transport

Prague's metro and tram systems are very efficient. Consider buying a tourist pass (*turisticka sitova jizdenka*) valid for one to five days, which allows unlimited rides on metros, trams and buses. N.B. There is a Kc200 fine if you are caught riding without a ticket (July 1995). Information on city transport (tel: 229-2520).
Taxis: A ride should cost Kc12 per kilometre (July 1995) but sometimes meters are rigged. Calling ahead to reserve a taxi is best. Fares can be negotiated. Best to avoid the cabs at taxi stands on Wenceslas Square, near Charles Bridge and in the Castle area. Flagging down a Skoda taxi in a less-congested area probably better. A taxi from the airport into the centre should cost around Kc350 but prices up to Kc500 are charged by unethical cabbies (July 1995).
Buses: Reliable flat-fare service. In Prague tickets can be bought in advance from tabak shops and other shops displaying sign *Predprodej Jizdenek*. Bus tickets cost Kc6 (July 1995). On the buses, insert your ticket into the top of machines attached to the poles, then pull the handle towards you. Do not punch a pass; simply keep it with you. City buses mostly serve the outskirts of town. City bus 119 leaves daily every five to seven minutes (peak times) or about every 15 minutes (off-peak) from Dejvicka metro station to the airport and back. From the metro, follow the exit signs for Ruzyne Airport. An ordinary city transport ticket or pass is required before boarding. CSA Czech Airlines bus runs to airport every 30 minutes from its stop just off Revolucni near the river. It also stops at Dejvicka metro station. A ticket from Revolucni to the airport costs Kc30 (July 1995). Look for the sign that says 'Ruzyne'. Bus information (tel: 221-445).
Metro: Three flat fare lines operate in Prague (lines A, B and C) which intersect at three main stations. Service runs from 0500 - 2400. Tickets cost Kc6 (July 1995) for each individual ride completed within one hour; transfers on the metro do not require additional tickets. Buy single-ride tickets at news-stands, 'DP' shops in the metro stations, or from the yellow ticket machines inside metro stations. Some booths at the top of metro escalators also sell tickets. Punch your ticket in the machines at the top of the subway escalators. *Vystup* means exit, and *prestup* means connection.
Trams: Trams cover all major streets and intersect with metro lines. When reading a tram schedule, the stop that is underlined is where you are standing. All stops below the line are where the tram is heading. On the trams, insert your ticket into the top of machines attached to the poles. Do not punch a pass; simply keep it with you. After midnight, night trams run approximately every 40 minutes; they are marked by white numbers on blue signs at every tram stop. Tram 91, the 'historic tram', stops at most of the city's top sights, except for the castle. These trams run Saturdays, Sundays and holidays and make their stops about once an hour during the summer. Tickets are Kc10 for adults, Kc5 for children (July 1995).

it even easier to raise money internationally. The structure of Czech foreign debt will thus improve in the future. In 1995, CNB curbs on short-term portfolio capital inflows from abroad were first introduced, thereby lessening reliance on them by local commercial banks and other financial institutions.

Following its termination of the special clearing account for foreign trade with Slovakia in October 1995, the CNB paid 70 per cent of its outstanding debt to that country, Ecu98.9 million (US$176 million), to the Slovak central bank, with the remaining Ecu32.5 million to be paid in the form of goods in 1996. Itself a major creditor to various countries for foreign trade dating back to the communist period, the Czech Republic is now moving to settle some of these outstanding liabilities, notably those owed by Russia. Involving a total inter-governmental debt of around US$200 million, this problem had inhibited the revival of Czech-Russian foreign trade. In 1996, a final settlement of this problem was expected to involve various pay-back methods, including debt-for-equity swaps by Czech investors in newly privatised Russian enterprises. Debts owed to the Czech Republic by various Middle Eastern countries led by Iraq are unlikely to be repaid in at least the foreseeable future.

Foreign investment

According to the government's foreign investment agency, CzechInvest, total FDI at the end of 1995 reached US$5.5 billion, a US$2.3 billion increase from the end of 1994. Although US$1.4 billion of this FDI was from one deal (the sale of 27 per cent of SPT Telecom) the remainder represented nearly US$1 billion of growing foreign investment in the Czech Republic.

In addition, portfolio investments on the PSE and elsewhere almost certainly matched non-SPT Telecom FDI inflows during 1995. As in 1994, most new FDI in 1995 was from Germany (30 per cent of the total), followed by Switzerland, the US and the Netherlands. By sector, most FDI in 1995 was in telecommunications. Focused on an earlier US$1 billion deal between Skoda and Volkswagen, additional FDI is expected in automotive products in 1996. Other sectors of growing interest to foreign investors include electrical goods, energy, consumer goods, services and construction.

In November 1995, Shell, Agip and Conoco agreed to pay US$173 million for the Czech Refinery Company. Another growing foreign investor in the Czech energy sector has been Slovakia's Slovnaft. In 1995, Czech outward FDI became significant, particularly in Slovakia and the rest of the Visegrad Group and was concentrated in automotive products and consumer goods. Already operating in Poland, Skoda-Volkswagen plans to begin manufacturing cars in Russia for the first time by 1997. Czech FDI in Germany and Austria is also increasing.

Outlook

The Czech Republic continues to have by far the best future prospects in central-eastern Europe. Full EU membership is likely by around 2000 and full membership of NATO is also increasingly probable in due course, although this could take longer than expected due to Russian objections and Czech wariness of closer political co-operation with the rest of the Visegrad Group on this and other issues.

At home, however, the parliamentary elections have created more uncertainty about future political developments in the Czech Republic. Other than the ultimate political outcome of the elections, a number of other problems have to be resolved, notably those pertaining to industrial policy, the exchange rate, financial system reform and the country's balance of payments. Although likely to prove difficult, none are insurmountable. In practice, the Czech Republic is now well on the way to successfully completing its political and economic transformation of the 1990s by around 2000.

BUSINESS GUIDE — CZECH REPUBLIC

National transport

Air: CSA Czech Airlines operates extensive domestic network. Regular daily flights from Prague to Brno, Bratislava, Ostrava, Presov, Holesov, Kosice Piestany, Bystrica, Karlovy Vary and Poprad.
Road: Several major highways linking Prague with main towns (usually marked with an E).
Buses: Buses generally quicker and more comfortable than trains. To buy tickets, go to Florenc Bus Station (tel: 2421-1060); metro Florenc. Cedok travel agency also has information. Cebus (tel: 2481-1676), near Florenc metro station, travels to Brno, Karlovy Vary and other Czech cities.
Rail: Prague connected to all major towns. Seats should be booked in advance on main routes; tickets available from CEDOK travel agency, Na Prikope 18, Prague 1 (tel: 2419-7111) or railway ticket offices. There are two major train stations that serve foreign destinations, Hlavni nadrazi and Nadrazi Hole-sovice. In July 1996 Czech Railways reduced the number of services in the country by 140. This has made it difficult to get to some remote and smaller places.

Public holidays

Fixed dates: 1 Jan (New Year's Day), 1 May (May Day), 8 May (Liberation Day), 5 Jul (Slav Missionaries, St Cyril and St Methodius, Day), 6 Jul (Martyrdom of Jan Hus Day), 28 Oct (National Day), 24-26 Dec (Christmas holiday).
Variable dates: Easter Monday.

Working hours

Business: (Mon-Fri) 0800–1600.

Social customs

Shaking hands is customary when meeting people and on parting. When drinks are served, it is customary to wait for everyone to be served and then wish each person *Na zdravi*. When eating, it is usual to wait for everyone to be served before eating and to wish everyone *bon appetit* or *dobrou chut* just before eating. The terms *Pan* (Mr), *Pani* (Mrs) and *Slecna* (Miss) are used. *Slecna* is used for single women under 30 only; single women over 30 will usually be addressed as *Pani.*

Business language and interpreting/translation

Can be supplied on request. Most Czechs speak some German.

Telecommunications

Telephone and telefax: Direct dialling available from major towns. International dialling code: 420 (from 1 March 1997) followed by area code (2 for Prague, 5 for Brno). N.B. Prague telephone numbers changed in third quarter of 1993. When making an inter-city call from within the Czech Republic, omit the country code 42 and prefix the city code with a zero. Only 40 per cent of households own telephones and there are lengthy waiting lists to get lines installed for both domestic and business use; many mobile phones therefore in use in business (1995).
Telex: Available in most major hotels. Country code: 66C.
Postal services: Most mail travels by air at no extra cost. 24-hour service: Jindrisska 14, Prague 1 (tel: 264-193).

Banking

A two-tier banking system has been introduced. In January 1993 there were five banks with state participation and 19 newly established private banks. There were also nine banks with foreign participation and numerous subsidiaries and branches of foreign banks.
Central bank: Czech National Bank (CNB) was established on 1 January 1993.
Other banks: See 'Business Directory, Banking'.

Trade fairs

For information regarding trade fairs in Prague, contact Prague Trade Fairs (tel: 220-922; fax: 263-060). For information regarding trade fairs in Brno, contact Brno Trade Fairs and Exhibitions Ltd, Prague Office, Washingtonova 9, 112 49 Prague (tel: 220-922; fax: 263-060).

Electricity supply

Domestic: 220 V, 50 cycles AC is almost universal, but there are still a very few areas in Prague where 120 V is supplied. Most of the better hotels have standard international two-pin plugs. Where these are not fitted, standard Czechoslovak sockets are used; ordinary plugs will not fit, as they have an arrangement of two sockets and a grounding pin. Lamp fittings are screw-type. Industrial: 360 V, 50 cycles.

Representation in capital

Afghanistan, Albania, Algeria, Argentina, Austria, Belgium, Bolivia, Brazil, Bulgaria, Canada, China PR, Colombia, Costa Rica, Cuba, Denmark, Ecuador, Egypt, Finland, France, Germany, Ghana, Greece, Hungary, India, Indonesia, Iran, Iraq, Israel, Japan, Kampuchea, Korea DPR, Lebanon, Libya, Mexico, Mongolia, Morocco, Myanmar, Netherlands, Nicaragua, Nigeria, Norway, Peru, Poland, Portugal, Romania, Spain, Sudan, Sweden, Switzerland, Syria, Tunisia, Turkey, UK, Uruguay, USA, Venezuela, Vietnam, Yemen.

BUSINESS DIRECTORY

Hotels

Prague
Diplomat, Europská 15, 16000 (tel: 331-4111; fax: 341-731).

Forum (tel: 419-0111).

Hilton (formerly Atrium), Pobrezni 1, 18000 (tel: 248-411).

Inter-Continental, Namesti Curieovych 5, 11000 (tel: 231-1812, 280-0111; fax: 231-0500).

Interhotel Alcron, Stepanska 40, 11123 (off Wenceslas Square) (tel: 235-9216; tx: 121-814).

Interhotel Ambassador, Vaclavske Namesti 5, 11000 (tel: 214-3111; tx: 122-237).

Interhotel Esplanade, Washingtonova 19, 11000 (tel: 226-056/9; fax: 265-897).

Interhotel Flora, Vinohradska 121, 13000 (tel: 274-241; tx: 122-238).

Interhotel Jalta, Vaclavske Namesti 45, 11000 (on Wenceslas Square) (tel: 265-541/9; fax: 265-347, 226-390).

Interhotel Olympik, Invalidovna, 18000 (tel: 828-541, 684-5501, 819-111; fax: 683-6412).

Interhotel Olympik II – Garni, Invalidovna u Sluncove 186–76 (tel: 828-541/7; tx: 011-236).
Interhotel Panorama, Milevska 7, 14000 (tel: 416-111; fax: 426-263).

International, Koulova 1, 16000 (tel: 331-9891; tx: 121-055).

Karl-Inn, Saldova 54, 18600 (tel: 2481-1718; fax: 2481-2681).

Konopiste Motel, Benesov u Prahy, 25601 (tel: 2053).

Meteor Plaza (tel: 235-8533).

Palace, Panská 12, 11000 (tel: 236-0008; fax: 235-9373).

Parkhotel, Veletrzni 20, 17000 (tel: 3807-1111; fax: 382-010).

Useful telephone numbers

Directory enquiries: 120 (Prague telephone numbers).

International enquiries: 0135.

Telegram service: 127.

Ambulance service: 155.

Breakdown assistance: 777-521.

Car repair service (24-hour service): (tel: 733-351/3).

Emergency calls: 158.

Emergency Medical Aid (24-hour service – doctors speak English and German): 298-341, 290-651.

Lost property office; 235-8887.

Police: 2121-1111.

Traffic accidents: 154, 23664, 2121-3747.

Car hire

Prague
Budget: central reservations (tel: 3330-7737; fax: 316-6727); airport (tel & fax: 316-5214).

Europcar: reservations (tel: 2481-1290, 2481-05150; Parizska Street 28, 11000 (fax: 2481-0039).

Hertz: reservations (tel: 290-122; fax: 297-836); Ruzyne airport (tel: 312-0717; tx: 123-162).

Taxis

Prague
AAA: (tel: 3399, 342-410, 322-444, 312-2112).

Milkrolux: (tel: 350-320, 355-192).

Profi: (tel: 6104-5555, 6104-5550).

Chambers of commerce

District Economic Chamber Brno - mesto, Vystaviste 1, 660 91 Brno (tel: 4115-9538; fax: 4115-3055).

District Economic Chamber Ostrava, Nadraznf 66, Hotelovy dum Jindrich, 701 00 Ostrava 1 (tel: 626-4431, 624-4427; fax: 611-4055).

District Economic Chamber Plzen - City, Safarikovy sady 5, 301 15 Plzen (tel: 722-0642, 722-0672; fax: 723-5586).

District Economic Chamber Prague - East, PO Box 34, 251 01 Ricany (tel: 284; fax: 2847).

Hospodarska komora CR (Economic Chamber of the Czech Republic), Argentinska 38, 170 05 Prague 7 (tel: 6679-4111; fax: 804-894). Foreign relations division (tel: 875-344, 6679-4838; fax: 804-894). Information division (tel: 6671-1112, 6679-4883; fax: 6671-0805).

Regional Chamber of the Capital of Prague, Cs. armady 23, 160 00 Prague 6 (tel: 333-9111; fax: 329-112).

Banking

Ceska narodni banka (Czech National Bank), Na prikope 28, 110 03 Prague 1 (tel: 2441-1111; fax: 235-4141).

ABN AMRO Bank N.V. Amsterdam, pobocka Praha, Revolucni 1, 110 15 Prague 1 (tel: 2481-5141; fax: 2481-5100, 2481-5139).

Agrobanka Praha a.s., Hybernska 18, 110 00 Prague 1 (tel: 691-0783, 2444-1111; fax: 2444-6199, 2444-1500).

AR stavebni sporitelna a.s., Neklanova 38, 140 00 Prague 4 (tel: 290-303; 296-174).

Bank Austria (CR) a.s., Revolucni 15, 110 15 Prague 1 (tel: 2489-2111; fax: 280-6680).

Bankovni asociace (Banking Association), Vodickova ulice 30, 110 00 Prague 1 (tel: 2422-5926; fax: 2422-5957).

Bankovni dum Skala a.s., Seifertova 9, 130 00 Prague 3 (tel: 627-8319; fax: 275-502).

Bayerische Vereinsbank AG Munchen, pobocka Praha, Italska 24, 121 49 Prague 2 (tel: 251-642; fax: 235-0013).

BNP - Dresdner Bank a.s., Opletalova 25, 111 21 Prague 1 (tel: 261-570; fax: 263-008).

Ceska banka a.s., Palackeho 1, 110 00 Prague 1 (tel: 268-914; fax: 268-914).

Ceska exportni banka a.s. (Czech Export Bank), Nabrezi kpt. Jarose 1000, 170 32 Prague 7 (tel: 370-153; fax: 374-488).

Ceska Sporitelna a.s. (Czech Savings Bank), Na Prikope 29, 113 98 Prague 1 (tel: 2422-9268; fax: 2421-3455).

Ceskomoravska stavebni, Ruzova 15, 110 00 Prague 1 (tel: 2407-2024; fax: 2407-2225).

Ceskomoravska zarucni a rozvojova banks a.s., Jeruzalemska 4, 115 20 Prague 1 (tel: 2423-0734; fax: 260-621).

Ceskoslovenska Obchodni Banka a.s., Na Prikope 14, 115 20 Prague 1 (tel: 233-1111; fax: 232-7562).

Citibank a.s., Evropska 178, 116 40 Prague 6 (tel: 333-4111; fax: 316-4796).

Commerzbank AG Frankfurt/Main, pobocka Praha, Masarykovo nabrezi 30, 110 00 Prague 1 (tel: 2491-5077, 2491-5329; fax: 296-282, 2491-5850).

Credit Lyonnais Bank a.s., Jilska 16, 110 00 Prague 1 (tel: 2421-8120; fax: 261-348).

Creditanstalt a.s. Praha, Siroka 5, 110 01 Prague 1 (tel: 2481-1474; fax: 2481-2185).

Czech National Bank, Na Prikope 28, 11003 Prague 1 (tel: 2441-1111, 2391-1111; fax: 2421-7865); external department (tel/fax: 2391-3501).

Deutsche Bank AG, pobocka Praha, Jungmannova 34, 110 00 Prague 1 (tel: 2421-2857; fax: 2422-5727).

Evropabanka a.s., Strosmayerovo nam 1, 170 01 Prague 7 (tel: 6671-2134, 805-248/50; fax: 879-642).

GiroCredit banka Praha a.s., Vaclavske nam 56, PO Box 749, 111 21 Prague 1 (tel: 2403-3333; fax: 265-886).

Hypo-Bank CZ a.s., Stepanska 27, 110 00 Prague 1 (tel: 2421-8580; fax: 2422-1524).

IC Banka a.s., International Business Centre, Pobrezni 3, 186 00 Prague 8 (tel: 232-6508, 232-6551; fax: 232-6549).

Interbanka a.s. Praha, Vaclavske nam. 40, 110 00 Prague 1 (tel: 2440-6111; fax: 265-658).

Internationale Nederlanden Bank N.V. Pobocka Praha, Pobrezni 3, 186 00 Prague 8 (tel: 232-0000; fax: 232-0026).

Investicni a Postovni banka a.s., Senovazne namesti 32, 114 03 Prague 1 (tel: 2407-1111; fax: 2424-4035).

Ivnesticni Banka a Postovni Banka, Senovazne namesti 32, Prague 1 (tel: 2407-1111).

Komercni Banka a.s., Na Prikop 33, 114 07 Prague 1 (tel: 2402-1111; fax: 2424-3020).

Konsolidacni banka Praha s.p.u., nabr. kpt. Jarose 1000, 170 32 Prague 7 (tel: 389-1111; fax: 387-244).

Podnikatelska banka a.s., Rohacova 79, 130 79 Prague 3 (tel: 6121-6089; fax: 6121-6085).

Pragobanka a.s., Vinohradska 230, 100 00 Prague 10 (tel: 772-145; fax: 774-564).

Raiffeisenbank a.s. Praha, Vodickova 38, 110 00 Prague 1 (tel: 2423-1270; fax: 2423-1278).

Banking (contd):
Realitbanka a.s., Antala Staska 32, 146 20 Prague 4 (tel: 6104-5439; fax: 692-1831).

Royal banka CS a.s., Krocinova 1, 110 00 Prague 1 (tel: 2422-8582; fax: 2422-4833).

Societe Generale Banka Komercni banka (SGKB) a.s., Pobrezni 3, PO Box 74, 186 00 Prague 8 (tel: 232-3204; fax: 232-3513).

Vseobecna uverova banka a.s. Bratislava, Celetna 31, 110 00 Prague 1 (tel: 235-7260; fax: 232-8796).

Wustenrot - stavebni sporitelna s.a., Jugoslavska 29, 120 00 Prague 2 (tel: 2400-7200; fax: 2400-7204).

Zivnostenka Banka a.s., Na Prikope 20, 113 80 Prague 1 (tel: 2412-1111; fax: 2412-5555).

Travel information

Air Ostrava, Ostrava International Airport, Mostov CZ 74251 (tel: 58-250; fax: 58-206).

Autoturist (services for foreign visitors), Jecna 40, Prague 2-Nove Mesto (tel: 290-956); (accident and towing services) Malesice, Limuzska 566/12a, Prague 10 (tel: 154, 773-455).

Bohemia Tour, Zlatnicka 7, Prague 1-Stare Mesto (tel: 232-3877).

CBT Travel Avency, Prague (tel: 2422-4646, 2422-4110; fax: 2422-4724).

Cedok (travel and hotel corporation), Na Prikope 18, 111 35 Prague 1-Nove Mesto (tel: 2419-7111; tx: 121-109); (accommodation services for foreign visitors) Panska 5, Prague 1-Nove Mesto (tel: 225-657, 227-004).

Central Automotoclub CSFR, Opletalova 29, 11395 Prague 1 (tel: 223-544).

Ceskoslovenske Statni Drahy (state railways), Na prikope 31, 11005 Prague 1 (tel: 236-3238, 236-8315).

CKM (services for foreign visitors), Jindrisska 28, Prague 2 (tel: 268-532).

Czech Airlines (CSA), Airport Praha, Ruzyne 16008 (tel: 481-5108, 2480-6111; fax: 481-5183, 316-2774).

Pragotour (accommodation, hotel and tourist services), Stare Mesto, U Obecniho domu 2, Prague 1 (tel: 231-7281, 231-7234).

Railway stations

Hlavni nadrazi (the main station; serves most foreign destinations and many Czech cities and towns) general information (tel: 2461-1111; international tickets (tel: 2461-5108); reservations (tel: 2421-7654).
Nadrazi Holesovice (Holesovice station; serves foreign destinations including Berlin, Vienna, Warsaw and Budapest) (tel: 2461-5865/6/7).

REKREA (services for foreign visitors), Josefov, Parizska 28, Prague 1 (tel: 232-1152, 232-0533).

Sport-Turist (services for foreign visitors), Narodni 33, Prague 1-Staré Mesto (tel: 263-351; fax: 235-8274).

Other useful addresses

Asociace investicnich fondu (Association of Investment Companies and Funds), Tynska 21, 110 00 Prague 1 (tel: 2481-0063; fax: 2481-0063).

Asociace obchodnich spolecnosti a podnikatelu CR (Association of Trading Companies and Businessmen), Skretova 6, 120 59 Prague 2 (tel: 2421-5371/81; fax: 2423-0570).

Asociace prazskych realitnich spolecnosti (Association of Prague Real Property Bureaus), Jugoslavska 23, 120 00 Prague 2 (tel: 253-829, 250-004; fax: 259-594).

Association of Czech Entrepreneurs, Skretova 6, 12059 Prague 2 (tel & fax: 2423-0580).

Board of Legislation and Public Administration, Vladislavova 4, PO Box 596, 117 15 Prague 1 (tel: 2419-1111; fax: 2421-5060).

Centrum vnejsich ekonomickych vztahu (Centre For Foreign Economic Relation), Politickych veznu 20, PO Box 791, 111 21 Prague 1 (tel: 2422-1586, 2406-2421; fax: 2422-1575).

Cesky statisticky urad (Czeck Statistical Office), Sokolovska 142, 180 00 Prague 8 (tel: 6604-2414; fax: 684-0729).

Confederation of Industry of the Czech Republic, Mikulandska 7, 11361 Prague 7 (tel: 2499-5679; fax: 297-896).

CzechInvest (Czech Agency for Foreign Investment), Politickych Veznu 20, 112 49 Prague 1 (tel: 2422-1540; fax: 2422-1804).

Czech Centre, 95 Great Portland Street, London W1N 5RA (tel: 0171-436 8200; fax: 0171-436 8300).

Czech Radio, Pankrac, Runczikova Street, Prague 4 (tel: 273-889).

Czech Statistics Office, International Statistics Division, Sokolovska 142, 18604 Prague 8 (tel: 6604-2422; fax: 822-490).

Esces (Free Zone), Tiskarska 563/6, 100 00 Prague 10 (tel: 701-278; fax: 704-785).

EU Energy Sector (Thermie), Soukenicka 23, 11000 Prague 1 (tel: 231-5615; fax: 231-5635).

Exportni garancni a pojistovaci spolecnost a.s. (Export Guarantee and Insurance Company), Nabrezi kpt., Jarose 1000, 170 32 Prague 7 (tel: 370-153; fax: 374-488).

Fond narodniho majetku (National Property Fund), Rasinovo nabrezi 42, 120 00 Prague 2 (tel: 2491-1111; fax: 206-618).

Ministry for the Administration of National Property And Its Privatisation, Lazarska 7, 111 21 Prague 1 (tel: 2419-1111; fax: 2421-5984).

Ministry of Agriculture, Tesnov 17, 117 05 Prague 1 (tel: 2181-2111; fax: 2481-0478).

Ministry of Culture, Valdstejnske nam 4, 118 11 Prague 1 (tel: 513-1111; fax: 2451-0897).

Ministry of Defence, Tychonova 1, 161 00 Prague 6 (tel: 2020-1111; fax: 311-4121).

Ministry of Economy, Starometske Nam 6, 110 00 Prague 1 (tel: 2489-7111; fax: 2489-7333).

Ministry for Economic Competition, Jostova 8, 601 56 Brno (tel: 4216-1111; fax: 4221-0023).

Ministry of Economy, Czech Telecommunications Office (CTO), Klimentska 27, 12502 Prague 1 (tel: 2491-0346; fax; 2491-2556).

Ministry of Education, Youth and Sport, Karmelitska 5, 7-8, 118 12 Prague 1 (tel: 519-3111; fax: 519-3790).

Ministry of the Environment, Vrsovicka 65, 100 10 Prague 10 (tel: 6712-1111; fax: 6731-0308).

Ministry of Finance, Letenska 15, 118 10 Prague 1 (tel: 2454-1111; fax: 2454-2788).

Ministry of Foreign Affairs, Loretanske nam 5, 118 00 Prague 1 (tel: 2418-1111; fax: 2431-0017).

Ministry of Health, Palackeho nam 4, 128 01 Prague 2 (tel: 2497-1111; fax: 290-092).

Ministry of the Interior, Nad Stolou 3, 170 34 Prague 7 (tel: 3351-1111; fax: 378-216).

Ministry of Justice, Vysehradska 16, 128 10 Prague 2 (tel: 2491-5140; fax: 291-720).

Ministry of Labour and Social Affairs, Na poricnim pravu 1, 128 00 Prague 2 (tel: 2490-2111; fax: 2422-4640).

Ministry of Privatisation PARP, Lazarska 7, 11121 Prague 1 (tel: 2419-1111; fax: 2419-1680, 2421-5984); external department (tel: 2455-2758; fax: 540-208).

Ministry of State Control, Za invalidovnou 144, 18000 Prague 8 (tel: 814-1111).

Ministry of Trade and Industry, Na Frantisku 32, 110 15 Prague 1 (tel: 2485-1111; fax: 2481-1089).

Ministry of Transport, Nabr L. Svobody 12, 110 05 Prague 1 (tel: 2303-1111; fax: 2481-0596).

Nejvyssi soud CR (Czech Supreme Court), Buresova 20, 657 37 Brno (tel: 4132-1237; fax: 4121-3493).

NIS (National Information Centre of the Czech Republic), Havelkova 22, 130 00 Prague 3 (tel: 2421-5808/15, 2422-2026/9; fax: 2322-1484, 2422-3177).

Prazska informacni sluzba (Prague Information Service), Senovazne namesti 23, 110 00 Prague 1 (tel: 544-444; fax: 2421-1989).

Presidium of the Government of the Czech Republic, Nabr. Eduarda Benese 4, 110 00 Prague 1 (tel: 2400-2111; fax: 2481-0231).

Sdruzeni soukromych zemedelcu Cech, Moravy a Slezska (Association of Private Farmers of Bohemia, Moravia and Silesia), Tesnov 17, 117 05 Prague 1 (tel: 2491-3606; fax: 2491-0162).

Svaz prumyslu a dopravy CR (Confederation of Industry of the Czech Republic), Mikulandska 7, 113 61 Prague 1 (tel: 2491-5253; fax: 297-876).

UNIDO (Federation of Czech Industries), Mikulandska 7, 113 61 Prague 1 (tel: 2491-5679; fax: 2491-5253).

Ustavni soud CR (Czech Constitutional Court), Jostova 8, 660 83 Brno 2 (tel: 4216-1111; fax: 758-825).

Denmark

Dan Bindman

After a year of steady, if unspectacular, economic performance, the Danish government found itself facing a paradox in 1996. It had an economy worthy of membership of a European common currency but lacked the political mandate to make a commitment to join. In short, some Danes began to regret the opt out of European monetary union negotiated at the Edinburgh summit in 1992 after the Maastricht treaty was rejected in a referendum. The compromise deal was ratified by the Danish people in a further referendum in May 1993. Yet another referendum would be necessary to override the decision. Although a price has been paid in continuing high unemployment levels, anti-inflationary policies have resulted in a stability which poses a stark contrast with the fiscal crisis of the 1980s.

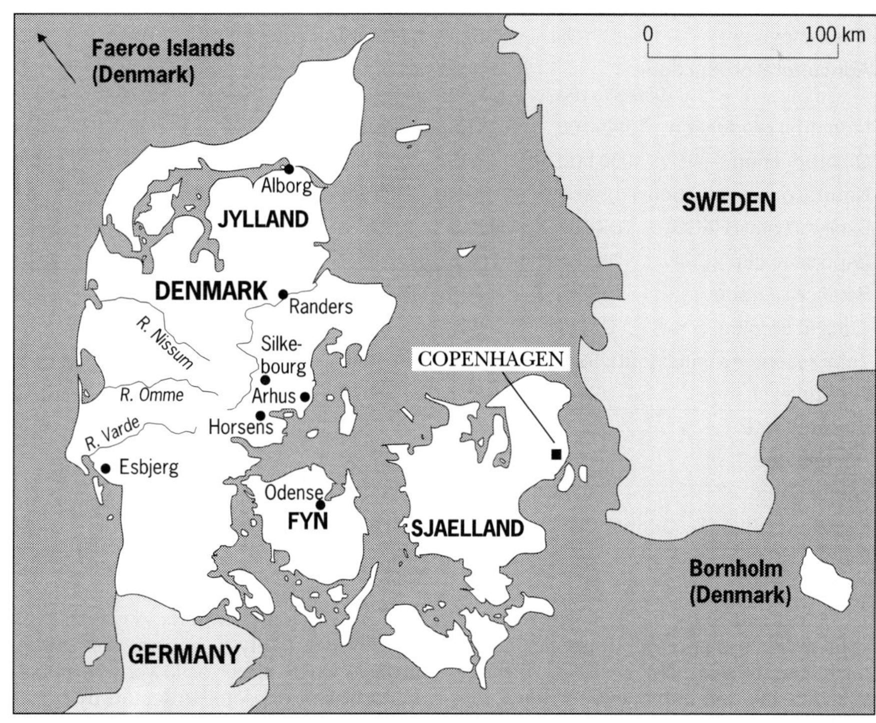

Cross-party policies

Economic stability has been achieved by a cross-party political agreement on the policies which have allowed the government to exercise such tight control on public finances. This grip on fiscal policy was continued in the 1997 budget, presented to parliament in August 1996. Although the opposition Liberal Party leader Uffe Ellemann-Jensen called for deeper cuts in welfare spending, the centre-left coalition government of Poul Nyrup Rasmussen, Denmark's Social Democratic prime minister, enjoyed broad support. However, this backing faltered in November 1995 when the government reached an agreement on its 1996 budget with the opposition Conservative party, leaving the Liberals as sole dissenters.

Economy

Notwithstanding the macroeconomic health of the economy – after two years in which the gross domestic product grew by 4.4 per cent (in 1994) and 2.6 per cent (in 1995) – predictions for growth in 1996 became progressively less optimistic as the year went on. Danske Bank, Denmark's largest bank, lowered its 1996 GDP growth forecast from 1.25 per cent in March 1996 to 0.75 per cent in June 1996. Still, it remained optimistic that signs of a turnaround would emerge in indicators for the second quarter of 1996. The bank's GDP growth forecast for 1997 remained constant at 2.3 per cent.

The nature of the growth in 1995 was partly to blame for the slide in the following year. In 1995 growth was boosted greatly by stockbuilding as production expanded while sales fell and companies restored their ratio of stocks to sales to pre-1993 levels, after which there had been significant destocking. Indeed, stockbuilding was estimated to account for a full 1.3 per cent of growth in 1995. This was not expected to continue in 1996. If re-stocking ceased altogether, it was predicted that this would bring GDP growth to a halt.

Private consumption in the first quarter of

KEY FACTS — Denmark

Official title: The Kingdom of Denmark

Head of state: Queen Margrethe II

Head of government: Prime Minister Poul Nyrup Rasmussen (Social Democrat)

Ruling party: Two-party coalition government: Socialdemokratiet (SD) (Social Democrats); Radikale Venstre (RV) (Social Liberals). (Centrum Demokraterne (CD) (Centre Democrats) withdrew from coalition Dec 1996)

Capital: Copenhagen

Official Languages: Danish

Currency: Danish Krone (DKr) = 100 ore

Exchange rate: DKr5.95 per US$ (Dec 1996)

Area: 43,080 sq km

Population: 5.2m (1995)

GDP per capita: US$28,082 (1994)

GDP real growth: 2.6% (1995)

Unemployment: 8.8% (May 1996)

Inflation: 2.1% (1995) (consumer prices)

Oil reserves: 1bn barrels (1995)

Trade balance: US$5.7bn (12 months to Apr 1996)

KEY INDICATORS **Denmark**

	Unit	1991	1992	1993	1994	1995
Population	m	5.15	5.17	5.18	5.19	5.20
Gross domestic product (GDP)	US$bn	131.0	143.1	135.4	147.4	–
GDP per capita	US$	25,440	27,625	26,130	28,082	–
GDP real growth	%	1.0	1.1	0.2	4.4	2.6
Inflation	%	2.4	2.1	1.3	2.0	2.1
Consumer prices	1990=100	102.4	104.5	105.9	108.0	110.2
Unemployment	%	10.3	11.0	12.1	12.2	10.2
Agricultural production	1979-81=100	135.59	120.47	132.59	132.28	140.75
Industrial production	1990=100	101.8	103.7	101.3	–	–
Oil production	'000 bpd	145	160	170	190	190
Natural gas production	m toe	3.4	3.5	3.9	4.2	4.5
Exports (value) (FOB)	DKr bn	229.8	247.3	241.1	262.4	274.1
Imports (value) (CIF)	DKr bn	206.8	212.1	197.9	220.7	241.6
Balance of trade	US$m	4,748	7,204	8,044	6,000	5,600
Current account	US$m	1,983	4,268	4,711	2,659	–
Total reserves minus gold	US$m	7,404	11,044	10,301	9,056	11,016
Foreign exchange	US$m	6,807	10,477	9,7911	8,444	10,262
Discount rate	%	9.50	9.50	6.25	5.00	4.25
Deposit rate	%	7.20	7.50	6.50	3.80	–
Lending rate	%	11.40	11.60	10.50	8.30	–
Exchange rate	DKr per US$	6.39	6.04	6.48	6.36	5.60

1996 was helped by rising property prices, with cash house prices at 10 per cent above their rate at same point in 1995. A corresponding increase in property taxes was expected to dampen this trend. Consumer confidence remained high into 1996, with real wages forecast to rise by 1.25 per cent through the year and slightly less in 1997. Car sales were also strong in early 1996, as they had been in the previous two years, although much of this was believed to have been financed by borrowing in the previous year.

External trade

Exports were estimated to have contributed just 0.4 per cent to GDP growth in 1995, while imports were estimated to have subtracted from it by 2 per cent. Final domestic demand was thought to have added 2.9 per cent. Although Danish trade figures were considered unreliable, it appeared that exports of industrial goods were affected badly in 1995 by the strengthening of the krone. Exports were expected to deteriorate in 1996 although hopes were high that they would pick up in 1997.

Industrial exports were worst hit and farm exports were also depressed as a result of consumer fears of the 'mad cow disease' which originated in the United Kingdom. In the longer term, though, this trend was expected to be compensated for by a growth in pork exports. A good harvest in 1995 was likely to improve net exports in 1996 by its effect of lowering imports. Imports were expected to decline by 1.5 per cent in 1996, but grow by an even greater volume in 1997. The falling trend in the current account surplus over the previous two years, from some 1.8 per cent of GDP in 1994 to 0.8 per cent in 1995 was expected to stabilise at about 0.5 per cent in 1996 and 1997.

The decline in GDP growth in 1996 had the effect of lowering earlier forecasts of the general government deficit to 2.1 per cent of GDP in 1996 and 1.8 per cent in 1997. Technical changes, including a shift of the Social Pension Fund's assets from mortgage to government bonds was expected to result in a reduction of the public debt to GDP ratio from 72.1 per cent of GDP in 1995 to 71.8 per cent in 1997.

Unemployment

High unemployment has persistently dogged the government, although in March 1996 it had fallen to 9.1 per cent of the workforce, seasonally adjusted, from 10.6 per cent a year earlier. In January 1994 the rate stood at 12 per cent. However, Denmark's unusual labour situation has tended to understate the problem significantly. Several schemes have a distorting effect, including one which enables workers to take a sabbatical from their jobs of between 6 months and a year, while receiving no less than 80 per cent of the maximum unemployment benefit.

This scheme has proved immensely popular and is estimated by the Organisation for Economic Co-operation and Development (OECD) to result in the removal of some 2.5 per cent of the workforce from the labour market at any one time. At the end of 1995 this produced the curious situation that unemployment and employment were simultaneously falling. In an effort to compensate for this programme and others – which amount to job training schemes – the government has developed an assessment of unemployment which excludes all such activities. Under this method, in the third quarter of 1995 the total stood at 18.9 per cent of the workforce, a rate which is still believed to be an understatement.

Social security

The OECD has estimated that in 1993 some 57 per cent of the adult population were in receipt of some form of social security. Also, according to the OECD, unemployment benefit replacement rates – that is pre-tax benefits as a percentage of previous earnings before tax – have been by far the world's highest in the 1990s, standing at more than 60 per cent. The Danish state sector accounts for about a third of all employment, second only in magnitude to Sweden. Although most employed Danes appear willing to pay extremely high taxes, the country's high level of state provision predictably has led to calls on the government to reduce welfare spending on the ground that it is unsustainable.

Banking

After emerging smaller but fitter from the Nordic wave of banking crises of the early 1990s, the Danish banking sector demonstrated robust good health in 1995 with its highest earnings for a decade. While Danske Bank yielded a 27.8 per cent return on equity and its nearest rival Unidanmark yielded 20.6 per cent, the much smaller, newly-formed BG Bank topped them both with a 32.5 per cent yield.

The banks benefited especially from changes in the financial services industry, expanding their own services into mortgage credit and insurance. The expansion exploited major upheavals in the insurance market, including that in which the country's two largest insurers, Baltica and Hafnia, collapsed and had to be rescued. The two bigger banks have also followed the example of their Nordic competitors, by setting up branches elsewhere in the region.

Energy

Denmark's impressive current account surpluses since 1990 have been in large measure due to an improving energy balance, with strong growth in energy output expected to continue in 1996 and 1997. In the field of 'green' energy, the ecologically-minded government has subsidised the output of privately-owned wind turbines. It has also considered ordering large power utilities to install turbines, as well as liberalising the terms for private investment in windmill market. Energy minister Svend Auken has pressed for a tripling of the power produced by windmills by 2005, although this would still only amount to an increase to about 2 per cent of total power consumption and to 6 to 7 per cent of electricity consumption.

In early 1996, turbines capable of producing some 550 megawatts were installed. The turbine construction industry, which directly provides about 1,700 jobs – indeed more than three times that figure when associated employees are taken into account – exported more than 80 per cent of its total sales in the first nine months of 1995. This success represented a complete recovery from the disastrous decline in the industry caused by the abolition a decade ago of tax breaks for investment in windmills by the state of California. However, Danes have shown little enthusiasm for windmills, which are widely viewed as being too noisy and to be lacking in aesthetic appeal.

Telecommunications

Liberalisation has also been promoted by the government in the telecommunications sector, in proposed legislation which would allow competition across the board. The bill would operate in two stages, the first enabling competition in all types of service, including telephone lines. Companies would later be able to install cable-based systems. A rule which limits to two the number of licensed television corporations allowed to transmit signals across local government boundaries would be scrapped. One outcome would be that the part-privatised state-controlled monopoly Tele Danmark would be free to provide radio and television services via cable and satellite, alongside any competitors that might emerge.

Outlook

The strong krone, interest rates of under 5 per cent, inflation running at about 2 per cent and a budget deficit below the 3 per cent required by Maastricht, should limit the damage of possible exclusion from membership of the single currency club.

COUNTRY PROFILE — DENMARK

Historical profile

Ancient kingdom sited on archipelago (outlying territories Greenland and Faroe Islands) which has served historically as a bridge between continental Europe and the Scandinavian peninsula. 1945 End of German occupation. Denmark recognised independence of Iceland.
1948 Faroe Islands: self-government within the kingdom.
1949 Founder member of NATO.
1953 Revision of constitution to allow for female succession to throne, abolition of upper house and introduction of proportional representation.
1971-82 Centre-left and minority governments (eight or nine parties are commonly represented in the *Folketing*) all facing economic problems and electoral dissatisfaction with EU membership.
1972 Queen Margrethe ascended the throne – the first female ruler for 600 years.
1973 EU membership.
1979 Greenland: home rule.
Since 1982 Conservative-led minority government has survived numerous defeats in *Folketing* on NATO's nuclear defence strategy.
1986 Following defeat of proposed EU reforms in *Folketing*, continued membership approved by referendum. Reforms subsequently approved in *Folketing*.
1993 Denmark became holder of the European Community presidency for six months. In January the country was thrown into political crisis when Poul Schlüter, prime minister since 1982, announced his resignation after a judicial enquiry criticised him for misinforming parliament in 1989 over the Tamil visa scandal. A four-party coalition government was formed by Mr Poul Nyrup Rasmussen. In May Denmark voted in favour of the Maastricht treaty on European union (56.8 per cent support).

Political system

Constitutional monarch, with legislative power jointly vested in the monarch (who has no personal authority) and the unicameral parliament *Folketing* (179 members elected under a system of proportional representation for a four-year term). Executive power exercised by the monarch through a cabinet led by the prime minister, who is responsible to the *Folketing*.

Political parties

Two-party coalition government: Socialdemokratiet (SD) (Social Democrats); Radikale Venstre (RV) (Social Liberals). (Centrum Demokraterne (CD) (Centre Democrats) withdrew from coalition Dec 1996). Other major parties: Konservative Fokeparti (KF) (Conservative People's Party; Venstre (V) (Liberal Party); Socialistisk Fokeparti (SF) (Socialist People's Party. On 6 October 1995 the right-wing anti-tax Progress Party split; the Danish People's Party (Dansk Folkeparti) was formed.

Main cities/towns

Copenhagen (population 1.34m in 1994), Aarhus, Odense, Esbjerg, Aalborg.

Media

Press: There are nearly 400 newspapers available in Denmark, reaching 85.6 per cent of all adults. Readership levels are high and Sunday circulations are particularly strong. Most publications privately owned and tend to have fairly strong political leanings.
Dailies: Most popular include *Ekstra Bladet, Politiken, Jyllands-Posten, Berlingske Tidende.*
Weeklies: Most popular include *Familie Journalen*, Billed-Bladet, Hjemmet and *Alt for Damerne.*
Business: There are two business dailies: *Erhvervs-Bladet* and *Børsen.* Most popular business magazines include *Børsens Nyhedsmagasin* (fortnightly) and *Penge & Privaton\18konomi* (monthly).
Broadcasting: Approximately 2m TV licences (which include radio) in use. Programmes broadcast by Radio Denmark. Country's first national advertising-financed television station, TV2, introduced October 1988. German and Swedish programmes can also be received in south of country. over 1m households are cabled. Non-commercial teletext and commercial videotext services are available. Radio Denmark's Programme 3 broadcasts news in English at 0810 on weekdays, and in German (at 0815) and French (at 0820) only May to August.
Advertising: Most widely used media are the press and cinemas. Direct mail also popular. TV2 is Denmark's advertising-financed television station. There is no advertising on radio, and poster sites are heavily regulated.

Domestic economy

Balanced economy with well-developed, export-based manufacturing sector. Also important agricultural sector. Upturn in economic performance from 1982 owing to deflationary policies combined with expansion of exports. This was followed by a period of severe balance of payments problems, a decline in GDP and rising unemployment.

Employment

Around 6 per cent of labour force employed in agriculture, forestry and fishing, 27 per cent in industry and nearly 70 per cent in services. About 45 per cent of the workforce are female.

External trade

Recent current account surpluses, from steady export growth. External position weakened by heavy debt burden. Principal export commodities include meat and meat products, dairy produce, fish, chemicals, basic manufactures, machinery and ships. Major imports are intermediate goods, fuels and lubricants and consumer goods. Around 45 per cent of trade turnover is with other EU countries, primarily Germany, France and Netherlands. Other significant trading partners are Sweden, Norway and USA.

Agriculture

Contributed 4.5 per cent to GDP in 1994 and about 19 per cent of exports, and employed 5.6 per cent of the labour force. Organised into local co-operatives which are united in national federations. Intensive farming concentrated on livestock production, mainly pigmeat, beef, veal, poultry and dairy produce. Also world's third largest fish exporter. In 1987 new legislation was introduced to tackle the urgent problem of nitrate pollution, caused largely by animal slurry. It is now an offence to have non-green fields in winter. Denmark has large world market shares in dairy products such as pigmeat, dairy products, seeds, mink pelts, fish products. A research report for the Ministry of Agriculture in January 1993 concluded that over a 20-year period the country should be able to double the value of production by agriculture and horticulture, the food processing industries and the agro-industrial sector as a whole.

Industry

Highly developed and diversified sector, which is almost wholly under private ownership and contributed 26.5 per cent to GDP in 1994 and employed 26.5 per cent of the labour force. Small manufacturing firms predominate, though 1989 saw a flood of mergers including that between Novo and Nordisk Gentofte forming one of the largest insulin producers in the world. Production, which has increased

COUNTRY PROFILE DENMARK

Industry (contd): rapidly in recent years, is heavily based on imported raw materials, components and semi-manufactures. Main industries include food processing, chemicals, metal production, engineering, shipbuilding, paper, textiles, electronics and furniture.

Mining

The mining sector accounted for 1 per cent of GDP in 1994 and employed 1 per cent of the workforce. Few indigenous minerals except for salt, sulphur, chalk and clay. Large quantities of two of the world's rarest metals, niobium and tantalum, exist in Greenland.

Hydrocarbons

Proven oil reserves 1bn barrels (end-1995). Oil production 190,000 barrels per day (bpd) in 1995, up 0.6 per cent on 1994 output. Proven reserves of natural gas 4 trillion cu feet (end-1995); gas production 4.5m tonnes oil equivalent in 1995, up 8.4 per cent on 1994 figure.

Energy

Emphasis on energy conservation and conversion of power stations from imported coal to locally produced gas.

Main companies

Danske Bank, Unibank, FDB, AP Moeller, EAC, MD Foods and the Lauritzen Group.

Stock exchange

Copenhagen Stock Exchange agreed with the stock exchanges of Sweden, Norway and Finland in June 1993, to establish Nordquote, a common Nordic securities trading system.

Legal system

Civil law system. Constitution adopted 1953.

Membership of international organisations

ADB, AG (observer), BIS, CCC, CERN, Council of Baltic Sea States, Council of Europe, CSCE, DAC, EEA, EMS, ESA, EU, FAO, IAEA, ICAC, ICAO, ICES, ICO, IDA, IDB, IEA, IFAD, IFC, IHO, ILO, IMF, IMO, International Grain Council, International Lead and Zinc Study Group, INTELSAT, Interpol, IPU, ISO, ITC, ITU, MIGA, NACC, NATO, Nordic Council, OECD, UN, UNESCO, UPU, WEU (observer status), WHO, WIPO, WMO, World Bank, WSG, WTO.

BUSINESS GUIDE

Time

GMT + 1 hr (GMT + 2 hrs from late Mar to late Sep).

Climate

Temperate: temperatures range from 22 degrees C to -7 degrees C. Some rain throughout the year.
Clothing: Medium weight throughout the year, warm clothing for winter months.

Entry requirements

Visas required for visitors from Eastern Europe, Arab countries and South Africa; most others need only passports.
Health: Vaccination certificates not usually required. EU nationals covered for medical treatment.
Currency: No restrictions on amount of foreign currency taken in or out of country, or on amount of Danish currency taken in.
Customs: Personal effects duty-free, plus duty-free allowance.

Air access

Regular flights by most major international airlines.
National airline: Scandinavian Airline System (SAS) – jointly owned with Sweden and Norway.
Main international airport: Copenhagen (CPH) at Kastrup, 10 km south-east of capital.
International airports: Aalborg (AAL), 6 km north-west of city, Aarhus (Tirstrup) (AAR), 44 km north-east of city, Billund (BLL), 2 km east of city, Esbjerg (EBJ), 8 km from city. Maersk Air fly between Gatwick and the Faroe Islands via Billund in Denmark.

Surface access

Frequent ferry services from UK, Germany, Poland, Sweden and Norway. Road and rail access from several European countries via Germany.
Main ports: Copenhagen, Aarhus, Hirtshals, Frederikshavn and Esbjerg.

Hotels

No official rating system. Bills include 15 per cent service charge. All usual credit cards accepted. Advisable to book accommodation in Copenhagen in advance especially during summer.

Restaurants:

All bills include 15 per cent service charge and 22 per cent VAT.

Foreign exchange information

Trade policy: Generally no limitations on imports.

Car hire

Available throughout the country at main Danish State Railway (DSB) stations and all airports. Can be booked in advance through stations, international car hire firms and travel agents. Valid driving licence required, which must be carried when driving. Most firms stipulate a minimum age of between 20–25. Speed limits 50 kph in built-up areas, 80 kph out of town and 100 kph on motorways. Even for minor speed limit offences, drivers are liable to pay heavy fines on the spot. If payment cannot be made, the car may be detained.

City transport

Taxis: Good service in all major towns. Can be hailed in the street, by telephone or at ranks, and display green 'Fri' sign when available. Fare includes a tip.
Buses: Frequent efficient services in main cities. Flat-rate fares usual.

National transport

Air: Daily flights operate between Copenhagen and Odense, Billund, Esbjerg, Karup, Skrydstrup, Stauning, Sonderborg, Thisted, Aalborg and Aarhus.
Road: About 70,000 km of roads including 593 km of motorway.
Buses: Good bus service in Copenhagen including night buses until 0230. Country bus network operates where there are no railways.
Rail: Approximately 2,500 km of railways operated by DSB and a few private companies, providing a very efficient service linked to the ferry services.
Water: Frequent ferry services connecting islands of Zealand, Funen and Lolland and Jutland peninsula, operated by DSB. Also over 400 km of inland waterways.

Public holidays

Fixed dates: 1 Jan (New Year's Day), 5 Jun (Constitution Day), 25 Dec (Christmas Day), 26 Dec (Boxing Day).
Variable dates: Maundy Thursday, Good Friday, Easter Monday, General Prayer Day, Ascension Day, Whit Monday.

Working hours

Business: (Mon-Fri) 0800–1600 or 0830–1630.
Government: (Mon-Fri) generally 0900–1700.
Banking: (Mon-Fri) 0930–1600 (Thu 1800).
Shops: (Mon-Fri) 0800–1700 or 0900–1730, (Sat) close at 1300 or 1400.

Telecommunications

Telephone and telefax: Efficient automatic service. International dialling code: 45. There are no area codes. For IDD access from Denmark dial 009. Directory enquiries: in Denmark 118; overseas 113.
Telex: Available 24 hours a day at the Central Telegraph Office in Copenhagen. Can also be dictated over the phone on 'Fonotelex' by dialling 0022. Country code 55DK.
Telegram: Can be sent from any post office or by telephone.

Postal service

Post offices open 0900–1700 Mon-Fri plus Sat mornings. Post Office at Copenhagen Central Station opens late Mon-Fri, Sat 0900–1600, and from 1000–1700 on Sun.

Banking

Commercial banking network comprises over 70 regional and local banks, largest of which are Danske Bank and Unibank. Danmarks Nationalbank is the central bank and the monetary authority. Also over 130 savings banks.
Other banks: See 'Business Directory, Banking'.

Trade fairs

Several specialised international fairs covering most products held throughout the year. Most, such as Scandinavian Fashion Fair, Scandinavian Furniture, the Fisheries Fair, and the Chem Tech International Fair, are held at the Bella Centre in Copenhagen. Other major venues are at Herning and Aalborg.

BUSINESS GUIDE

Electricity supply

220/380 V AC.

Representation in capital

Argentina, Australia, Austria, Belgium, Brazil, Bulgaria, Burkina, Canada, Chile, China, Colombia, Costa Rica, Côte d'Ivoire, Cuba, Egypt, Finland, France, Germany, Ghana, Greece, The Holy See, Hungary, Iceland, India, Indonesia, Iran, Ireland, Israel, Italy, Japan, Korea DPR, Republic of Korea, Lesotho, Libya, Mexico, Morocco, Netherlands, Norway, Pakistan, Poland, Portugal, Romania, Russia, Saudi Arabia, Spain, Sweden, Switzerland, Thailand, Turkey, Uganda, UK, Uruguay, USA, Venezuela.

BUSINESS DIRECTORY

Hotels

Copenhagen
Copenhagen Admiral, Toldbodgade 24, DK-1253 (tel: 3311-8282; fax: 3332-3607, 3332-5542).

Grand, Vesterbrogade 9, DK-1620 (tel: 3331-3600; fax: 3131-3350).

Hotel d'Angleterre, Kongens Nytorv 34, DK-1050 (tel: 3312-0095; fax: 3312-1118).

Kong Frederick, V Voldgade 25-27, DK-1552 (tel: 3312-5902; fax: 3393-5901).

Park, 3 Jarmers Plads, DK-1551 (tel: 3313-3000; fax: 3314-3033).

Plaza Sheraton, Bernstorffsgade 4, DK-1577 (tel: 3314-9262; fax: 3393-9362).

SAS Globetrotter, Engvej 171, DK-2300 (tel: 3155-1433; fax: 3155-8145).

SAS Royal, Hammerichsgade 1, DK-1611 (tel: 3314-1412; fax: 3314-1421).

Sara Dan, Kastruplundgade 15, DK-2770 (tel: 3151-1400; fax: 3151-3701).

Savoy, Vesterbrogade 34, DK-1620 (tel: 3131-4073; fax: 3131-3137).

Scandinavia, Amager Boulevard 70, DK-2300 (tel: 3311-2324; fax: 3357-0193).

Sheraton, 6 Vester Søgade, DK-1601 (tel: 3314-3535; fax: 3332-1223).

Useful telephone numbers

Fire, police, ambulance 112.

Emergency dental treatment 3138-0251.

24-hour chemist 3314-8266.

Car hire

Copenhagen
Budget: central reservations (tel: 3391-3900; fax: 3313-3269).

Europcar: Gyldenlovesgade 17 (tel: 3311-6200); international airport (tel: 3250-3090).

Hertz: Ved Vesterport 3 (tel: 3312-7700; fax: 3315-4955); international airport (tel: 3250-9300; fax: 3252-2216).

Chambers of commerce

Danish Chamber of Commerce, Borsen, DK-1217 Copenhagen K (tel: 3395-0500; fax: 3332-5216).

Banking

Danmarks Nationalbank (central bank), Havnegade 5, DK-1093 Copenhagen (tel: 3314-1411; fax: 3314-5902).

Bikuben, Silkegade 8, DK-1113 Copenhagen K (tel: 3312-0133; fax: 3315-1133).

Bikuben Securities, 30 Finsbury Square, London EC2A 1NR (tel: 628-5522; fax: 256-5445).

Den Danske Bank AS (commercial bank), Holmens Kanal 2-12, DK-1092 Copenhagen K (tel: 3344-0000; fax: 3118-5873).

Den Danske Bank, 75 King William Street, London EC4N 7DT (tel: 410-4949, fax: 283-9526).

Finansradetr (bankers' association), Bankernes Hus, Amaliegade 7, DK-1256 Copenhagen (tel: 3312-0200; fax: 3393-0260).

Girobank, Girostoget 1, DK-2630 Tastrup (tel: 4371-4470; fax: 4358-4470).

Jyske Bank (Bank of Jutland), Vestergade 8-16, DK-8600 Silkeborg (tel: 8922-2222; fax: 8922-2499).

Jyske Bank, Jutland House, 119/120 Chancery Lane, London WC2A 1HU (tel: 831-2778; fax: 405-2257).

Sparekassen Nordjylland, Karlskogavej 4, DK-9000 Aalborg (tel: 9818-7311).

Sydbank, Peberlyk 4, DK-6200 Aabenraa (tel: 7463-1111; fax: 7463-1320).

Unibank AS, Kongens Nytorv 8, DK-1786 Copenhagen K (tel: 3333-3333; fax: 3395-5769).

Unibank plc., 107 Cheapside, London EC2V 6DA (tel: 726-6000; fax: 726-4638).

Principal newspapers

Berlingske Tidende, Pilestraede 34, 1147 Copenhagen K (tel: 3315-7575).

Børsen, Møntergade 19, 1116 Copenhagen K (tel: 3332-0102).

B.T., Kr Bernikowsgade 6, 1147 Copenhagen K (tel: 3314-1234).

Ekstrabladet, Rådhuspladsen 37, 1585 Copenhagen V (tel: 3311-8511).

Erhvervs-Bladet, Vesterbrogade 12, 1620 Copenhagen V (tel: 3352-4001).

Jyllands-Posten, Morgenanvisen, Grøndalsvej 8260 Viby J (tel: 146677).

Politiken, Politikens Hus, Rødhuspladen 37, 1585 Copenhagen V (tel: 3311-8511).

Travel information

Copenhagen Airport, Kastrup, Amager (tel: 3154-1701; fax: 3151-1133).

Copenhagen Airtaxi, Copenhagen Airport Roskilde, DK-4000 Roskilde (tel: 391-114; tx: 43-234).

Danish State Railways – train timetables (tel: 3314-1702); reservations (tel: 3314-8800).

Danmarks Turistrad (tourist board), Vesterbrogade 6 D, 1620 Cogenhagen V (tel: 3311-1415; fax: 3393-1416).

Forened Danske Motorejere (FDM) (the Danish motoring organisation), Blegdamsvej 124, DK-2100 Copenhagen Ø (tel: 3338-2112).

Scandinavian Airlines System (SAS), Frosundaviks Alle 1, Stockholm S-16187, Sweden (tel: (46-8)7970-000; fax: (46-8)858-741).

Other useful addresses

The Central Telegraph Office, Købmagergade 37, DK-1150 Copenhagen K (tel: 3312-0903).

Copenhagen Stock Exchange, Nikolaj Plads 6, DK-1067 Copenhagen K (tel: 3393-3366).

Danish Convention Bureau, 27 Skindergade, 1159 Copenhagen K (tel: 3332-8601; fax: 3332-8803).

Dansk Arbejdsgiverforening (employers' confederation), Vester Voldgade 113, DK-1503 Copenhagen V (tel: 3393-4000; fax: 3312-2976).

Danmarks Agentforening (association of commercial agents of Denmark), Børsen, DK-1217 Copenhagen K (tel: 3314-4941).

Danmarks Statistik, Sejrøgade 11, DK-2100 Copenhagen O (tel: 3917-3917; fax: 3118-4801).

Det Okonomiske Rad (economic council), Kampmannsgade, DK-1604 Copenhagen V (tel: 3313-5128).

Grosserer Societetet, Børsen (royal exchange), DK-1217 Copenhagen (tel: 3391-2323; tx: 19-520).

Industriraadet (Confederation of Danish Industries), H. C. Andersen's Boulevard 18, DK-1790 Copenhagen V (tel: 3377-3377; fax: 3377-3410).

Ministry of Agriculture and Fisheries, Slotsholmsgade 10, 1216 Copenhagen K (tel: 3392-3301; fax: 3314-5042).

Ministry of Business and Industry (including Communications and Tourism), Slotsholmsgade 10-12, 1216 Copenhagen K (tel: 3392-3350; fax: 3312-3778).

Ministry for Culture, Nybrogade 2, 1203 Copenhagen K (tel: 3392-3370; fax: 3391-3388).

Ministry of Defence, Holmens Kanal 42, 1060 Copenhagen K (tel: 3392-3320; fax: 3332-0655).

Ministry of Ecclesiastical Affairs, Frederiksholms Kanal 21, 1220 Copenhagen K (tel: 3392-3390; fax: 3392-3913).

Ministry of Economic Affairs, Slotsholmsgade 12, 1216 Copenhagen K (tel: 3392-3222).

Ministry for Economics, Ved Stranden 8, 1061 Copenhagen K (tel: 3392-3322; fax: 3393-6020).

Ministry for Education, Fredriksholms Kanal 21-25, 1220 Copenhagen K (tel: 3392-5000; fax: 3392-5547).

Ministry of Employment, Holmens Kanal 20, 1060 Copenhagen K (tel: 3392-5900; fax: 3312-1378).

Ministry for the Environment and Energy, Hojbro Plads 4, 1200 Copenhagen K (tel: 3392-7600; fax: 3332-2227).

Ministry of Finance, Christiansborg Slotsplads 1, 1218 Copenhagen K (tel: 3392-3333; fax: 3332-8030).

Ministry of Foreign Affairs, 2 Asiatisk Plads, 1448 Copenhagen K (tel: 3392-0000; fax: 3154-0533).

Ministry for Health, Herluf Trolles Gade 11, 1052 Copenhagen K (tel: 3392-3360; fax: 3393-1563).

Ministry of Housing, Slotsholmgade 12, 1216 Copenhagen K (tel: 3392-6100; fax: 3392-6104).

Ministry for the Interior, Christiansborg Slotsplads 1, 1218 Copenhagen K (tel: 3392-3380; fax: 3311-1239).

Ministry of Justice, Slotsholmsgade 10, 1216 Copenhagen K (tel: 3392-3340; fax: 3393-3510).

Ministry of Research, Bredgade 43, 1260 Copenhagen K (tel: 3392-9700; fax: 3332-3501).

Ministry for Social Affairs, Slotsholmsgade 6, 1216 Copenhagen K (tel: 3392-9300; fax: 3393-2518).

Ministry of State, Christiansborg, Prins Jorgens Gard 11, 1218 Copenhagen K (tel: 3392-3300; fax: 3311-1665).

Ministry for Taxation, Slotsholmsgade 12, 1216 Copenhagen K (tel: 3392-3392; fax: 3332-2227).

Ministry for Transport, Fredriksholms Kanal 27, 1220 Copenhagen K (tel: 3392-3355; fax: 3312-3893).

Parliament, Christiansborg, 1240 Copenhagen K (tel: 3337-5500; fax: 3332-8536).

Regional Development Organisation, Kongens Nytorv 6, 4, sal DK-1050 Copenhagen K (tel: 3333-0300; fax: 3333-7333).

Ritzaus Bureau 1/S (news agency), Mikkel Bryggersgade 3, DK-1460 Copenhagen K.

Teknisk Forlag AS (technical press-publishing house), Skelbaekgade 4, DK-1717 Copenhagen V.

Greenland and Faroe Islands

Anthony Griffin

Denmark comprises not only the 43,080 sq km of the metropolitan area but also the 1,399 sq km of the Faroe Islands and the 2.1 million sq km of Greenland, the world's biggest island. Both territories have home rule legislatures, but defence, foreign policy and the currency are administered by the metropolitan government. Greenland and the Faroes send two representatives each to the Danish Folketing (Parliament).

Greenland was a colony, closed to outsiders, until 1953, when it became an integral part of the Kingdom of Denmark and a programme for the rapid development of the island was inaugurated. In 1979 the Greenlanders obtained a form of home-rule government and have now taken over almost the entire responsibility for local admionmistration. As part of the Kingdom of Denmark, Greenland belongs to NATO (and is host to several key NATO installations), but opted out of European Union (EU) membership with effect from January 1st 1985. Greenland does have an agreement with the EU allowing fishing in Greenland waters for a restricted number of EU vessels in return for access to EU markets for Greenland's fish and fish products, of which shrimps are the most important.While Greenland still struggles economically, the Faroe Islands are hopeful that they will become a significant oil producing territory.

Faroes

After several years the booming economy of the 1980s, stimulated by large investments by the former home-rule government, the first half of the 1990s has seen the virtual devastation of the Faroese economy, which in 1986 had boasted Europe's highest per-capita income, (around US$16,500). The collapse of the fishing industry, (the Faroes' only viable export industry produced a total of 275,741 tonnes in 1995), due to lower fishing stocks and falling prices, has left both government and fishermen with large debts and limited prospects. Unemployment is running at 25 per cent.

However, oil could be lurking in the region between the UK's Shetland Islands and the Faroe Islands and could mean a huge boom for the local economy. Talks are being held between the UK and the Faroe Islands administration to discuss which country is entitled to control, and benefit from, the oil activities in the region. The speculation is that reserves of up to 600 million barrels can be found in the region at the north-west limit of UK territorial waters.

The position of the Danish government on all of this is that the Faroes can keep any revenues that it gets from oil. With this in mind, the local government is preparing a tax regime. But no drilling can be done in the disputed zone until the two governments settle their differences over ownership. This is a particularly difficult situation because the disputed zone is thought to have the greatest possibility of oil wealth. There is a possibility that the issue will have to go to the International Court of Justice. The Faroe Islands have announced that its first oil licensing round will be held in 1997.

Best known internationally as a mention in the shipping weather forecast or for the killing of pilot whales, the Faroes have enjoyed home-rule since 1949. The Faroes do not generally receive much international attention other than in World Cup football matches or, sadly in 1996, with the crash of a Royal Danish Air Force transport aircraft on its approach to the Faroe Islands airport. Among the victims of the crash was Admiral Hans Joergen Garde, Chief of Staff of the Danish Armed Forces.

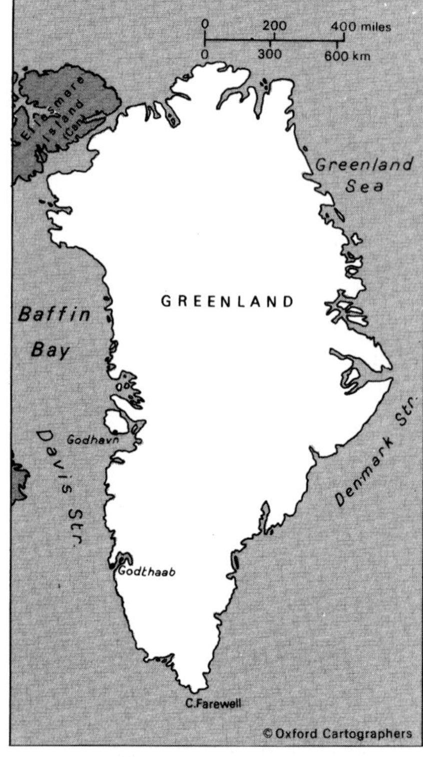

The islands are not part of the European Union, although metroplitan Denmark is, but they do enjoy a free trade arrangement with the EU. The Faroes are also a part of NATO, as is Denmark, but declared themselves a nuclear-free zone in 1983. The islands' reduced financial circumstances have lessened enthusiasm for independence from Denmark. In 1994 the ratio of government debt to GDP rose to a worrying 175 per cent. The metropolitan government was obliged to bail out the Faroes with DKr1 billion of subsidies and with loans amounting to a further DKr three billion. The bail-out produced tensions in the relationship with Denmark; these were later aggravated by the crisis affecting the Faroes' Foroya Banken. Denmark's Den Danske Bank swapped its shares in the Foroya Bank for a stake in the islands' only other bank, Sjovinnbankin. It later emerged that the Foroya Bank had run up huge losses, which

KEY FACTS — Greenland

Official title: Greenland

Head of government: Prime Minister Lars Emil Johansen (Siumut)

Ruling party: Coalition of Siumut (Forward) Party and centre-right Atassut (Community)

Capital: Nuuk (Godthaab)

Official Languages: Greenlandic, Danish

Currency: Danish Krone (DKr) = 100 ore

Exchange rate: DKr5.95 per US$ (Dec 1996)

Area: 2,175,600 sq km

Population: 55,400 (1995)

GNP per capita: US$17,000 (1994)

Visitor numbers: 14,000 (1995)*
* estimated figure

the Faroe Islands' government alone was obliged to underwrite. Faroese suspicions that the Den Danske Bank had prior knowledge of the Foroya's problems did little to improve relations. Against all the odds, in 1994 the government produced a balanced budget of DKr 2,600 million.

In 1995 16 tourist ships called at Thorshaven AND there are hopes that this figure could double. At the start of 1996 some 26 ships had already said that they would be stopping at the port. Tax free sales in 1995 amounted to US$540,000 compared with US$270,000 in 1994.

Perhaps mindful of what the Rob Roy and Braveheart films did for the Scottish tourism industry, the tourism office of the Faroe Islands is hoping that a new US$6 million movie called Barbara, based on a book by the same name, will raise interest in the remote islands as a holiday destination in 1997. Danish director Nils Malmeros is behind the camera for this adaptation of a story by the Faroese author Jorgen Frans Jakobson.

KEY FACTS — Faroe Islands

Official title: Faroe Islands

Head of government: Prime Minister Edmund Joensen

Ruling party: Coalition of Union Party (UP), right-wing People's Party and Social Democrats (SD)

Capital: Torshavn

Official Languages: Faroese, Danish

Currency: Faroese Krone (FKr) (same value as Danish Krone)

Exchange rate: FKr5.95 per US$ (Dec 1996)

Area: 1,399 sq km

Population: 47,300 (1995)

GNP per capita: US$12,000 (1994)

GNP real growth: 10% (1994)

Unemployment: 25% (1995)

Foreign debt: US$1m (1994)

Greenland

Greenland's Santa of the Year award for 1995 was South African President Nelson Mandela. Premier Lars Emil Johansen gave Mandela his prize – US$100,000 – at an awards presentation in South Africa. The Santa Claus of Greenland Foundation is behind the awards which seek to recognise those who struggle to improve the welfare of children around the world.

Greenland has a total population of about 55,000, some 6,000 of which are expatriate Danes. The Greenlanders are a mixed Eskimo-Caucasian race, speaking Greenlandic, with Danish as their second language and the language of administration and government. Most of the population live in the year-round, open-water ports on the west coast, where fishing and fisheries constitute the main industry. In the settlements in East Greenland and Thule in the far north, hunting and fishing are the main activities.

Iron ore, coal, uranium, lead and zinc are among the known mineral deposits in Greenland. Exploration for hydrocarbons off the West coast was abandoned in the 1970s when drilling revealed the wrong type of geological structures. Greenland's underground resources are administered jointly by a Danish-Greenland commission on which both parties have a veto right.

The mining industry appears to be recovering from the setback of the closure of the Black Angel zinc mine. Mineral exploration is now being actively encouraged and the government has reformed its mining regulations and tax policies to stimulate investment. An oil liquids discovery on the Nussuaq Peninsula in the Western Part of Greenland is encouraging more drilling. The Platinova company, in which the Greenland government has a minority stake, is drilling for zinc in the northern tip of Greenland at Peary Land. The discovery of large zinc and cobalt deposits in Canada's Eastern Labrador has also stimulated interest in Greenland, with over 11,000 sq km already staked out in the search for similar deposits.

Some 14,000 tourists arrived in Greenland in 1995 and there were hopes that 1996 would see 16,000 arrivals. Norlandair of Iceland now operates scheduled flights to Greenland; in the summer months they are at the rate of two flights per week.

Elections

The March 1995 General Election resulted in an increased vote for the Forward Party (Siumut), which won 12 seats and 38.5 per cent of the vote. The Siumut had been the major party in the pre-election ruling coalition. Siumut's former coalition partners, the left-wing Innuit Brotherhood (Innuit Ataqatigiit) (IA) won 20.3 per cent of the vote and six seats, but were replaced in the ruling coalition by the centre-right Community Party (Atassut) which had won 29.7 per cent of the vote and 10 seats, following a disagreement between the IA and the Simiut over independence. The IA had called for full independence.

COUNTRY PROFILE — GREENLAND

Historical profile

A Danish possession since the eighteenth century.
1939-45 During the German occupation of Denmark in the Second World War, Greenland came under the protection of the USA.
1949 Faroe Islands granted home rule.
1953 Greenland ceased to be a colony, closed to trade with outsiders, and became part of Denmark.
1979 Home rule for Greenland.
1985 Greenland opted out of EC membership, but is part of NATO.

Political system

Overseas part of Kingdom of Denmark, electing two members to Danish parliament which maintains responsibility for constitutional, foreign and defence matters. Internal affairs under legislative control of *Landsting* (parliament) which has 27 members elected by proportional representation. Strength of parties in *Landsting* determines composition of five-member *Landsstyre* (government) which exercises executive power, and is headed by the premier.

Political parties

The 5 March 1995 general election produced an increased share of the vote for the Siumut (Forward) Party, the major party in the ruling coalition. Siumut's former coalition partner, the left-wing Inuit Ataqatigiit (Inuit Brotherhood) (IA) was replaced by the centre-right Atassut (Community), following a disagreement over independence.

Main city

Nuuk/Godthaab (population 12,800 in 1994).

Language

The official languages and Greenlandic and Danish; an Inuit (Eskimo) language is also spoken.

Media

Dailies: No daily newspapers.
Weeklies: Grønlandsposten/Atuagagdliutit (two languages) and *Sermitsiak.*
Periodicals: Grønland is a general interest periodical, published ten times a year.
Broadcasting: Greenland Radio (KNR) broadcasts in Greenlandic and Danish to entire country via INUKSAT. TV programmes (mostly Danish in origin) transmitted by KNR-TV, which also produces some programmes of its own. Each local community has one or more private TV stations which are allocated a 15-minute broadcast daily on KNR-TV (30 minutes on Sunday). Approximately 22,000 radios and 10,000 TVs in use.
Advertising: Most widely used media are the press and cinemas. Direct mail also popular. There is no advertising on radio, and poster sites are heavily regulated.

Domestic economy

Small economy centred on fishing and livestock farming. Heavy dependence on subsidies from Denmark, largely in the form of block grants. The public sector employs almost two-thirds of all wage earners. Tax-free sales for 1995 in the Faroe Islands were twice what they were in 1994, going from around US$270,000 to approximately US$540,000.

COUNTRY PROFILE

GREENLAND

External trade

Exports: Exports consist mainly of fish and fish products, zinc and chrome ores, lead and skins. Major markets include Denmark, Japan, Germany, Netherlands, Norway, Sweden and the USA. Greenland has an agreement with the EU allowing EU vessels to fish in Greenland waters in exchange for access to EU markets for Greenland fish products.
Imports: Imports, which include foodstuffs, fuels, chemicals, machinery and transport equipment, consumer goods and capital goods, mainly come via Denmark.

Agriculture

Largely confined to sheep farming in the south. Also small-scale reindeer farming. Production of lamb and reindeer meat is mainly for domestic consumption. Arable areas mainly produce hay. Fishing, sealing and hunting is mainstay of economy. Principal products include cod, shrimp, salmon and seal. There have been heavy losses in the fishing industry and the seas have been over-fished.

Industry

Mainly fish processing and packaging. Also some tanning and leatherworking in the south.

Tourism

Dog-sledge safari holidays in West Greenland are being offered in 1996. There was an estimated total of 14,000 visitors to Greenland in 1995 compared to 10,000 in 1994. Total foreign exchange earnings were US$90m in 1995.

Mining

Known reserves of zinc, coal, uranium, iron ore, and possibly oil. Mineral exploration is actively encouraged and the government has reformed its mining regulations and tax policies. An oil liquids discovery was made on the Nuusuaq Peninsula, in the western part of the country. The Black Angel zinc mine closed in 1990. However, Platinova, in which the government has a small minority stake, is drilling for zinc in the northern tip of Greenland at Peary Land. Over 11,000 sq km have been staked out in Greenland to search for mineral deposits similar to those found in Voisey Bay, Canada, across the Labrador Sea from Greenland.

Energy

Almost total energy dependence on Denmark though there is a water power station under construction near Nuuk.

Legal system

As for Denmark.

Membership of international organisations

As for Denmark, except EU.

BUSINESS GUIDE

Time

GMT -3 hrs (-2 hrs summer). Exceptions: Scoresbysund GMT -1 hr (GMT summer); East Greenland, Mesters Vig GMT (GMT summer); Qaanaaq & Thule GMT -4 hrs (GMT -4 hrs summer).

Climate

Arctic; temperatures at Nuuk/Godthaab vary between about -12°C and 11°C.

Entry requirements

As for Denmark except that diplomats need a visa.

Air access

Regular flights from Copenhagen to Kangerlussuaq/Sondre Stromfjord (SFJ) and, during summer, Narsarísuaq (UAK) operated by Grönlandsfly. Also weekly connection between Reykjavík (Iceland) and Nuuk/Godthaab, operated by Grønlandsfly. The Icelandic airline Norlandair began operating scheduled flights to Greenland end-1995.
National airline: Grønlandsfly A/S.
International airports: Nuuk/Godthab, Greenland; Vagar Airport in the Faroes had a 10 per cent gain in air traffic in 1995 compared to 1994.

Surface access

Main port: Nuuk/Godthaab; ports (and heliports) at all towns, as well as helistops at some settlements.

National transport

Grønlandsfly operates daily flights Kangerlussuaq–Nuuk–Narsarísuaq, and twice a week to East Greenland. Other towns are linked by helicopter. Greenland Trade operate two passenger liners on the west coast. Also other smaller vessels in other areas.

Public holidays

Fixed dates: 1 Jan (New Year's Day), 1 May, 21 Jun, 3 Jul, 24, 25, 26 and 31 Dec.
Variable dates: Maundy Thursday, Good Friday, Easter Monday, 'Store Bededag', Ascension Day/General Prayer Day and Whit Monday.

Working hours

Business: (Mon-Fri) 0800–1600 or 0830–1630.
Government: (Mon-Fri) generally 0900–1700.
Banking: (Mon-Fri) 0930–1600 (Thu 1800).
Shops: (Mon-Fri) 0800–1700 or 0900–1730, (Sat) close at 1300 or 1400.

Telecommunications

Administered by Greenland Telecom. All towns and communities linked by telephone and telex facilities through radio link in west Greenland and INUKSAT satellite.
Telephone and telefax: Direct dialling to Denmark and other countries. International dialling code: 299. There are no area codes. Exit code: 009.
Telex: Telex country code 503 GD.

Banking

Grønlandsbanken A/S and NUNA – Bank A/S. Monetary policy and administration headed by Danmarks Nationalbank.

BUSINESS DIRECTORY

Hotels

Nuuk
Grønland and Hans Egede, PO Box 68, 3900 (tel: 24-222; fax: 244-870).

Chambers of commerce

There is no chamber in Greenland. Commercial information may be obtained from:

KNI (Greenland Trade Department), Strandgade 100, Postboks 100, DK-1004, Copenhagen K, Denmark.

Banking

Danmarks Nationalbank (central bank), Havnegad 5, DK-1093 Copenhaven (tel: (45)3314-1411; fax: (45)3314-5902).

Principal newspapers

Grønland, PO Box 145, 3900 Godthab (tel: 22-611).

Grønlandsposten/Atuagagdliutit, PO Box 39, 3900 Godthab (tel: 347-070; tx: 15-805).

Sermitsiaq, PO Box 150, Godthab (tel: 21-902; fax: 22-499).

Travel information

Grønlands Rejsebureau (Greenland travel bureau), 12 Gammel Mnt, PO Box 130, DK-1004 Copenhaven K, Denmark (tel: (45)3313-1011; fax: (45)3313-8592).

Greenland Tourism Internet address (http://www.greenland-guide.dk/).

Grønlandsfly (Greenlandair), Nuuk Airport, PO Box 1012, Nuuk DK 3900 (tel: 28-888; fax: 27-288).

Other useful addresses

All in Denmark except for Godthaab/Nuuk.

Atuakkiorfik (Greenland Publishing House), PO Box 840, DK-3900 Godthaab/Nuuk (tel: 22-122; fax: 22-500).

Commission for Scientific Research in Greenland/

Danish Polar Center, 3 Hansergade, DK1123, Copenhagen K (tel: (45)3315-8666; fax: (45)3313-4976).

Danish High Commissioner for Greenland, PO Box 1030, 3900 Godthab (tel: 21-001).

Greenland Radio, PO Box 1007, 3900 Godthab (tel: 21-172; fax: 24-703).

Grønlands Hjemmestyre, PO Box 1015, 3900 Godthab (tel: 23-000; tx: 90-613 grlhjs).

Greenland Home Rule Government Denmark Office, Sjaeleboderne 2, 1122 Copenhagen K (tel: (45)3313-4224; fax: (45)3332-2024).

Greenland Trade Shipping Department, Grønlandshavnen, DK-9220 Aalborg Ost (tel: (45)9815-7677; tx: 69-688).

Prime Minister's Office, Greenland Department, 3 Hausergade, DK-1128 Copenhagen K (tel: (45)3393-2200; tx: 27-125).

Internet sites

Greenland Tourism (http://www.greenland-guide.dk/).

Estonia

Bob Jiggins

Estonia has maintained its reputation as the most successful Baltic state in terms of the transition to a market economy. True, there have been a number of recent setbacks, but the country remains broadly on course. A bugging/security scandal, disquiet over strong currency rates and persistently high inflation have combined to create an air of political uncertainty. This finally came to a head in October 1995 with the collapse of the governing coalition led by Prime Minister Tiit Vahi. A new coalition has been formed and, broadly speaking, policy continues much as before.

Estonia's 'Watergate'

The most notable recent event has been the resignation of the government over a surveillance scandal. Although tapping of telephones and other such surveillance methods are still in widespread use throughout the former Soviet bloc, Estonia claimed to have distanced itself from former Soviet practices, and thus the affair created a public scandal.

The government's resignation was precipitated by the discovery that the Deputy Prime Minister and head of the Centrist Party, Edgar Savisaar, had made covert tapes of the discussions between the leaders of the parties in the coalition negotiations. The tapes were found after a police raid on the offices of a private security firm with which Mr Savisaar had close connections. Savisaar was finally sacked by Prime Minister Vahi when he refused to resign, resulting in Savisaar removing his party from the government and the end of any effective majority.

Vahi resigned as prime minister, to be requested by President Lennart Meri to form a new government. The new coalition of the Coalition Party and Rural Union (KMU) (this time with the Reform Party) was approved by parliament on October 1995. Additionally, other events have sought to test the Vahi government over the past year, including a no-confidence motion in the economics minister Liina Tonisson. Although the motion was defeated, the accusations made of the minister over a slow-down in privatisation and pro-Russian sympathies in the buy-up of a strategic chemical firm struck home.

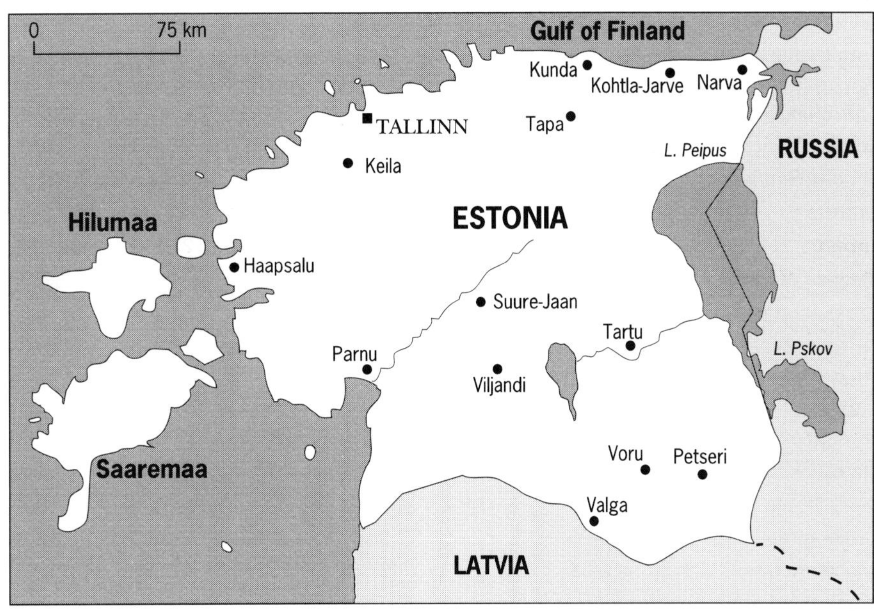

Presidential election

Lennart Meri was re-elected president in September 1996, but only after five attempts. Three rounds of voting in the Riigikogu proved inconclusive with neither Meri nor his main challenger Arnold Ruutel achieving the required two-thirds majority. The election was then sent to an electoral college comprising the 101 members of the Riigikogu and 273 local government representatives. Meri achieved the necessary simple majority at the second attempt after three candidates were eliminated in the first round. The position of president is purely symbolic, but many members of parliament refused to support Meri, claiming that he had interfered with the parliamentary process. He remains popular among Estonians, however.

Military matters

Estonia has applied for NATO membership and this has taken on a greater degree of

KEY FACTS — *Estonia*

Official title: Republic of Estonia

Head of state: President Lennart Meri (since 21 Oct 1992; re-elected Sep 1996)

Head of government: Prime Minister Tiit Vähi (KMU) (from Mar 1995)

Ruling party: Coalition comprising Coalition Party (K) and Rural Union and Union of Families and Pensioners (MU) (together forming KMU) and the Arengupartie (AP) (Progressive Party) (from Nov 1995)

Capital: Tallinn

Official Languages: Estonian

Currency: Kroon (EEK)

Exchange rate: EEK12.43 per US$ (Dec 1996)

Area: 45,100 sq km

Population: 1.63m (1995)

GDP per capita: US$2,340 (1995)*

GDP real growth: 5% (1995)*

GNP real growth: 7% (1995)*

Unemployment: 2.3% (May 1996)

Inflation: 28.8% (Jan 1996, annual) (consumer prices)

Trade balance: -US$795m (1995)

Foreign debt: US$343m (1995)*

* estimated figure

KEY INDICATORS *Estonia*

	Unit	1991	1992	1993	1994	1995
Population	m	1.59	1.54	1.52	1.58	1.63
Gross national product (GNP)	US$bn	4.80	4.00	4.00	4.86	–
GNP per capita	US$	3,100	2,500	2,500	3,200	–
GNP real growth	%	-1.0.0	-19.3	-3.5	5.0	*7.0
Inflation	%	283.0	969.0	36.0	47.6	28.9
Consumer prices	1990=100	8.5	100.0	189.8	280.3	361.3
Unemployment	%	–	0.9	2.1	1.8	1.7
Employment	'000	–	–	669.9	661.7	651.9
Industrial production	1993=100	–	–	100.0	97.8	102.4
Cement	'000 tonnes	905	483	355	402	418
Mineral fertiliser	'000 tonnes	180.5	60.0	14.0	37.8	56.5
Exports	EEKm	–	–	10,642	16,724	21,277
Imports	EEKm	–	–	11,848	21,243	29,110
Balance of trade	EEKm	–	–	-1,206	-4,519	-7,933
Gross foreign debt	EEKm	–	–	1,540.6	2,200.7	3,078.3
Current account	US$m	–	36.1	23.3	-170.8	*-146
Total reserves minus gold	US$m	–	170.18	386.12	443.35	579.91
Foreign exchange	US$m	–	159.56	329.04	441.76	579.61
Interbank rate	%	–	–	–	5.7	4.9
Deposit rate	%	–	–	–	11.5	8.7
Lending rate	%	–	30.5	27.3	23.1	16.0
Exchange rate	EEK per US$	–	12.06	13.24	12.99	11.47

* estimated figure

urgency following the remarks by the Russian deputy foreign minister, Sergei Krylov, that membership by the Baltic states of the defence pact would be regarded as a threat to Russian security. As far as the west is concerned, however, the extension of NATO membership eastward, especially without Russia, is not considered a practical policy. Instead, west European ministers have suggested that former Soviet bloc countries rely on the eventual membership of the European Union (EU) and NATO's Partnership for Peace programme as their best guarantees of security.

Other military matters continue to cause Estonia embarrassment, particularly the level of corruption (partly involving the illicit sale of arms) within the officer corps, and the eventual dismissal of the Commander-in-Chief of the military General Aleksander Einseln, after a series of highly public arguments with the defence minister Andrus Oovel.

Russian relations

The border dispute with Russia, in which Estonia argued that according to the 1920 Treaty of Tartu certain lands should be returned, has been resolved. Estonia has effectively given-up any hope of achieving its goal in the face of fierce Russian claims that the treaty is now little more than a historical document and, as such, irrelevant to the present day.

The Russian troop withdrawal treaty has finally been ratified and the last Russian contingent left the Paldiski submarine base in September 1995. However, they left behind a considerable nuclear waste problem. Difficult foreign relations remain with Russian claims that Russians living in Estonia are discriminated against. This assertion has been strengthened by Estonia's new language law, which requires all citizenship applications to be accompanied by a examination pass in Estonian. As many areas of public life are being increasingly closed off to non-citizens, fluency in the language is now an essential requirement.

Economy

Most economic indicators continue to point to a modest recovery from the slump of 1993. Increased imports, particularly capital goods but also consumer products, plus a substantial rise in exports, combined with a steady fall in unemployment, all indicate that Estonia is steadily recovering from the initial effects of its independence from the USSR. The inflation rate remains problematical although this has fallen from a 47.6 per cent rate in 1994 to 28.9 per cent in 1995 and is forecast to fall to 15 per cent in 1996.

Most authorities agree that GDP grew in 1995, but there is a degree of dispute as to the actual figure, ranging from 3 per cent (Estonian finance ministry) through to 7 per cent. In 1995 the Estonian Department of Statistics managed to contradict the finance ministry by suggesting that the economy was really in recession. Although the latter agency has not yet committed itself it is expected again to contradict the finance ministry, albeit less flamboyantly.

These disagreements serve to indicate that interpreting statistics from many east European states requires a certain degree of caution. Whatever the precise reality, it is certain that the economy is in a recovery phase, although perhaps not as buoyant as could be hoped. This is largely due to the poor performances of industry and of the agricultural sector.

Regional disparities still plague Estonia. Tallinn has become a meritorious boomtown, especially in the provision of services, but it would be wrong to extrapolate this rosy situation to the rest of the country. Many rural areas (especially in the south-east) remain in deep recession.

Inflation

Estonia's biggest economic problem is high, albeit falling, inflation. Average annual figures show a decline and the explanation for the failure to meet government targets can largely be explained by two factors. These are: substantial price rises in energy, housing and transport, and a shift in taxation away from income towards consumption as has occurred in western Europe. Over the course of 1995 price rises have been estimated at just over 46 per cent. It is expected that pricing policy in these areas will be liberalised, although further rises on this scale are unlikely. Inflation is thus expected to fall to an estimated 15 per cent in 1996.

Industry

The industrial sector performed poorly in the first half of 1995, leading to an estimated annual growth figure of 2 per cent, compared with the 7 per cent of 1994. The finance ministry estimates that production only increased by 1.5 per cent year-on-year from January to October 1995, although the Department of Statistics consistently maintains its tradition of pessimism by estimating a fall of 5.9 per cent in the first half of the year. This fall is not mirrored across every industrial sector, though, with rises in production observed in timber production (27 per cent) and metal products (10.9 per cent), compared with the drastic decline of the electrical machinery sector (26.9 per cent). Overall industrial production is however expected to rise to 3 per cent in 1996.

Agriculture

Commensurate with this is a decline in the fortunes of agriculture. This is now almost a historic trend, with the sector contributing less and less to GDP as time goes by, due largely to the traditional export markets of the former USSR having effectively closed their doors to livestock products; protectionist measures in Russia include a crippling 50 per cent import tariff.

From January to September 1995 milk production fell by 6.5 per cent year-on-year and grain by 10 per cent. In general, agriculture in Estonia suffers from having too many small farms (exacerbated by legal wrangles over land ownership) and the governments' commitment to an open market free trade policy.

External trade

Imports continue to grow as a consequence of recovery, although exports are still lagging. The trade deficit is expected to grow as it has done since August 1995 and now stands at US$67 million. This has, however, not proved to be a difficulty because tourism and transport especially are increasing; along with other services, these factors are enough to cope with the trade deficit.

In terms of the pattern of trade, Finland has replaced Russia as the biggest trading partner, which now accounts for 20.9 per cent of exports and 35.7 per cent of imports. Estonia has joined the European Free Trade Association (EFTA) which it hopes will be a prelude to full EU membership. Estonia has long been recognised as one of the most open countries in the former Soviet bloc. Although tariffs have been raised slightly for imported foodstuffs it is expected that these will in time be removed.

Privatisation

As a result of liberalisation Estonia possesses the lead among the Baltic states in terms of foreign investment. Privatisation is continuing, with the sell-offs favouring foreign buy-outs rather than mass public subscription through a voucher scheme. Some sales have been achieved via a voucher scheme, notably the Tallinn Department Store and the Saku Brewery. A major sale, of the chocolate manufacturer Kalev, involved only one buyer, Tallinvest (part of the Bank of Tallinn), which purchased 45 per cent of the shares.

Outlook

Most of the difficult economic reforms that were required for transition have been implemented and the economy is showing signs of a recovery. Consequently, the new coalition government faces little pressure for radical change and is accordingly able to concentrate on other issues, particularly preparation for NATO and EU membership.

In matters of the economy, recovery will continue, albeit modestly, and most commentators are predicting growth in the region of 3.5 per cent in 1996 and 5 per cent in 1997. Inflation will continue to rise as consumer demand picks up, although many price rises have already gone through; unemployment is already the lowest in the Baltic region and is expected to fall further. The country's future is not yet secured, but compared with many other former eastern bloc states, Estonia is well on course.

COUNTRY PROFILE — ESTONIA

Historical profile

1721–1917 Baltic province of Russia.
1918–1940 Independent republic.
1940–1988 Constituent republic of USSR.
1988 Declared sovereignty.
1989 Economic autonomy granted.
1990 Independence from the USSR declared in November.
1991 Independence reaffirmed in August.
1992 Joined IMF in May.

Political system

Constitution adopted 3 July 1992, establishing a parliamentary republic with a 101-member *Riigikogu* (parliament). Only Estonian citizens were allowed to vote in the post-independence elections on 20 September 1992, leaving the 38.5 per cent non-Estonian population largely disenfranchised. The president nominates the prime minister who then forms a government. The cabinet consists of the prime minister and ministers and is the executive arm of the state. Members of the government need not have any political party affiliation.

Political parties

Coalition Party (K) and Rural Union and Union of Families and Pensioners (MU) (together forming KMU) and the Arengupartie (AP) (Progressive Party) form the coalition government. The Reform Party–Liberals left the government in Nov 1996. Other major parties include Estonian Centre Party; Fatherland Alliance; Moderates Bloc; Our Home is Estonia Bloc; Republican Conservative People's Party.

Population

Estonian (61.5%), Russian (30.3%), Ukrainian (3.1%) and Belorussian (1.8%), Finnish (1.1%). Religion: majority Christian (Lutheran); also Russian Orthodox and Catholic. The non-Estonian population is concentrated in the heavy manufacturing areas of the north-east, where the regional centre of Narva is over 95 per cent non-Estonian, and in the capital Tallinn, where Estonians and non-Estonians are split roughly 50-50.

Main cities/towns

Tallinn (population 442,900 1 Jan 1994), Tartu (115,400), Narva (82,300), Kohtla-Järve (76,800), Pärnu (54,200), Sillamäe (20,700), Rakvere (20,100), Viljandi, Voru.

Language

Estonian belongs to the Baltic–Finnic group of the Finno-Ugric languages; the Latin alphabet is used. English is widely spoken and has replaced Russian as the primary business language.

Media

No censorship of the media (Article 45 of the Estonian Constitution).
Press: Daily newspaper: *Postimees* (Tartu); weekly: *The Baltic Independent* (Tallinn, in English) and *Eesti Ekspress. Aripäev* is published by Dagens Industri of Sweden. All major newspapers are privatised. There is a wide range of weeklies and 312 periodicals. The Estonian Newspapers' Association includes 45 newspapers. In addition, there are other newspapers which are not part of the Association. Since June 1995 *Estonian Daily* is published by the owners of former dailies *Hommkikuleht, Pahlevet* and *Rehva Haal* under the aegis of the Estonian Daily Press company.
Broadcasting: The state-owned TV and radio has been transformed into two public service companies, regulated by a new broadcasting law and governed by a General Council, appointed by parliament. The two public service companies have been members of the European Broadcasting Union (EBU) since 1993.
Radio: Radio Estonia broadcasts in eight languages including English – Mon and Thu, Finnish, Swedish, Esperanto. An independent radio station, Radio Kuku, started broadcasting in Tallinn in March 1992. Several local commercial radio stations broadcast all over Estonia. In 1995 there were 25 radio stations operating in Estonia.
Television: National TV broadcasts in Estonian and Russian. Three main private commercial TV channels, and some smaller ones, operate on two networks. Private TV channel, TV3, started broadcasting January 1996.

Domestic economy

Estonia has carried out profound free market refoms since the collapse of the Soviet Union and most state-owned companies are now in private hands. Unemployment is not a particular problem but significant regional variations exist. Inflation reached 47.6 per cent in 1994 but had declined to 19 per cent by the beginning of 1996.

Employment

About 49 per cent of the workforce is female.

External trade

Estonia entered into a 10-year trade and co-operation agreement with the EU which came into force on 1 March 1993. Exports to the west have quadrupled since 1991. In June 1993 Estonia's trade with the former Soviet Union was 28 per cent (including 15 per cent with Russia). Other trading partners: Finland, Sweden, Germany and Latvia. Estonia applied for membership of the EU on 4 December 1995.
Exports: Main destination: Russia (23.1 % of 1994 total). Main exports are textiles (13.7 per cent of 1994 total), timber, shipping, food, furniture, fertilisers, road-building material (granite) and milk products.

Agriculture

The sector employed 18 per cent of the working population and accounted for 13 per cent of GNP in 1994. It accounts for about one fifth of Estonia's total output. Limited food production including cattle-breeding. Some fishing and

Agriculture (contd): timber which is exported to other republics. The main products are milk and dairy products, eggs, meat, fish, cereals, potatoes, vegetables. Forest area 1.8m ha, 40 per cent of total land.

Industry

Industry accounted for 26 per cent of GNP in 1994 and employed 30 per cent of the workforce. It accounts for about one half of Estonia's total output. The main industries are textiles, furniture, electrical and electronic equipment, light machine-making (primarily for the textile and food-processing industries), processed foods and chemicals.

Mining

The mining and hydrocardons sector accounted for 5 per cent of GNP in 1994 and employed 3 per cent of the workforce. Oil shale is strip-mined.

Hydrocarbons

An agreement was signed in 1991 between state-owned Eesti Kutus and Neste Ltd of Finland for a joint Estonian-Finnish shareholding company, Estonial Transoil, to build an oil terminal at Tallin New Port with a handling capacity of at least 2m tonnes of oil per year.

Energy

Large reserves of oil-shale are used to produce energy.

Legal system

Town and county courts where cases are heard by a judge and assistant judges elected by popular vote; judges in the Supreme Court are elected by the Supreme Council.

Membership of international organisations

BC, Conference for Security and Co-operation in Europe (CSCE), CSCE, Council of Baltic Sea States, Council of Europe, IAEA, IMF, NACC, Partnership for Peace, UN, WEU (associate partner), World Bank. Applied for membership of the EU on 4 December 1995. Estonia concluded a free trade agreement with EFTA Dec 1995.

BUSINESS GUIDE

Time

GMT + 2 (summer GMT + 3).

Climate

Mildest areas along the Baltic coast. Summer is short and often very sunny (average 15 degrees C); sunshine may be nine hours a day, though it can be rainy. Winters cold, with slush, ice and repeated light coverings of snow (average –4 degrees C). Spring and autumn are very short. Mean annual air temperature 1.7 to –6.6 degrees C in February – 16.3 degrees C in July.

Clothing

Light jacket or pullover, plus umbrella, for summer. Dress in layers for winter. Fur-lined boots capable of walking through deep slush are vital. Evening wear is unostentatious but chic.

Entry requirements

Visa: No visa required for UK citizens; British subjects may stay in Estonia for three months as visitors; thereafter they will require a work permit, which is said to take a couple of days. Business visitors whose passports would expire within three months of leaving Britain are advised to get a new one before leaving. Other foreign nationals can obtain visa from embassy or from customs checkpoints at Tallinn International Airport and at Tallinn passenger port. N.B. Original passport (no copies) and one passport-sized photograph required. Invitation from an individual or an organisation in Estonia preferable although not essential.
Customs: Small amount of personal goods duty-free. On arrival declare all foreign currency and valuable items such as jewellery, cameras, computers and musical instruments.

Health precautions

Mandatory: Vaccination certificates are required for cholera or yellow fever if travelling from an infected area.
Advisable: Water precautions recommended (water purification tablets may be useful). It is advisable to be 'in date' for the following immunisations: polio (within 10 years), tetanus (within 10 years), typhoid fever, hepatitis 'A' (moderate risk only). There has been a significant increase in the number of cases of diphtheria. While the low dose, adult booster is unavailable, travellers are advised to be boosted with a reduced dose (0.1ml) of the paediatric single antigen vaccine. If never immunised, use three dose course of the vaccine. Any medicines required by the traveller should be taken by the visitor, and it could be wise to have precautionary antibiotics if going outside major urban centres. A travel kit including a disposable syringe is a reasonable precaution. Take mosquito lotion if travelling outside the towns.

Representation overseas

Bonn, Brussels, Copenhagen, Helsinki, London, Moscow, New York, Paris, Riga, Stockholm, Toronto, Vilnius.

Air access

Direct flights from Tallinn to London are planned for late-1995.
National airline: Estonian Air.
Other airlines: Aeroflot, Baltic International Airlines, Finnair, Hamburg Airlines, LOT, Lufthansa, SAS.

Surface access

Main ports: Muuga (Tallinn) is the most modern port, maximum draught of 18 metres; maximum tonnage for bulk vessels 30,000 tonnes (coal), 150,000 tonnes (grain) and 25,000 tonnes (liquid bulk). Other ports of Tallinn, Kopli and Roomassaare handle mainly cargo, deep-sea fishing vessels and tourism. Once a week ro-ro ferry line to Rostock, Germany, via Helsinki from Stockholm. The number of passengers using Estonian ports grew by 60 per cent in the first quarter of 1996 compared to the same period in 1995. The amount of goods passing through Estonian ports grew by 10 per cent in the first quarter of 1996 compared to the same period in 1995. The port of Pärnu opened a new quay in July 1996, designed for the loading of peat.
Water access: The Estline ferry service runs between Stockholm, Sweden, and Tallinn, Estonia.
Road: Construction of the Estonian section of Via Baltica is planned. The Via Baltica will connect with the E4 in both Helsinki and central Europe. Road network 14,771 km, of which 1,190 km were paved main roads. The Estonian Road Administration is the responsible body. N.B. Foreign cars are flagged down at borders to monitor the documents, in an attempt to block the flow of stolen foreign cars. Check insurance before travelling and do not buy cheap insurance at the frontier.
Rail: The total length of the railway lines of the state-owned Eeesti Raudtee (Estonian Railways) is 1,127 km including 132 km of electrified rails. International lines from Tallinn go to Moscow, St Petersburg, Minsk and other cities of the CIS, and the Baltic Express services Riga and Kaunas, extending to Warsaw and Berlin.

Hotels

It is advisable to book a hotel before travelling. There is a severe shortage of hotel rooms in Tallinn. For the peak period of June and July, the Estonian Tourist Board suggests the traveller books in January. Bills must be paid in Estonian kroons if credit cards are not accepted.

Currency

The kroon is the only legal currency. Visa automated-teller machine for kroons. Traveller's cheques and banker's drafts should not be used without checking whether the banks on which they are drawn have correspondent relations with an Estonian bank, otherwise there could be delays. There are money changing booths at railway and bus stations, at airports and seaports, at banks and in the major shops catering for tourists. Clean US dollar bills and Deutsche Marks can be changed everywhere, and sterling in most places. Unofficial money changing is illegal.

Credit cards

Most major hotels and restaurants and a few shops accept American Expresss, Visa, Eurocard and Diners' Club.

Car hire

Never drink and drive – no level of alcohol is permitted. Speed limit is 50 km per hour in built-up areas, and 90 km in the country. Leaded petrol is easy to find and unleaded exists too. In towns there are parking permits, fines and wheel clamps. Driving is on the right.

City transport

Taxis: Good taxi service from Tallinn International Airport to city centre.
Buses: The number 22 bus waiting outside Tallinn International Airport takes 10 minutes into the centre and the Old Town.

BUSINESS GUIDE

National transport

Road: Roads are good but icy and usually ungritted in winter.
Buses: An extensive bus network links every area of the country. Buses are generally faster and always more frequent than trains but sometimes need advance booking.
Rail: Tallinn–Tartu express.

Public holidays

Fixed dates: 1 Jan (New Year's Day), 24 Feb (Independence Day), 1 May (May Day), 23 Jun (Victory Day, anniversary of the Battle of Vonnu), 24 Jun (St John's Day, Midsummer), 25 Dec (Christmas Day), 26 Dec (Boxing Day).
Variable dates: Good Friday.

Working hours

Business: (Mon–Fri) 0900–1800 (appointments best between 0900–1000). Lunch around 1300. Some offices stop work at 1630.
Banking: (Mon–Fri) 0900–1300.
Shops: (Mon) 0800–1900, (Tue–Sat) 0800–2100.

Telecommunications

Telephone and telefax: Dialling code for Estonia: IDD access code + 372 followed by area code (2 for Tallinn; 7 for Tartu), followed by subscriber's number. There are approximately 378,000 main telephone lines in operation, 25 main lines per 100 inhabitants.

Banking

The commercial banking sector is licensed by the central bank set up in December 1989. Foreign-owned banks are permitted to operate.
Central bank: Eesti Pank (Bank of Estonia).
Other banks: See 'Business Directory, Banking'. Bank Baltija went into liquidation in April 1996.

Business information

Joint venture and 100 per cent foreign-owned companies are permitted. There are a number of tax holidays and reduced corporate tax rates for companies with some level of foreign participation.

Representation in capital

Canada, China, Denmark, Finland, France, Germany, Italy, Latvia, Lithuania, Norway, Russia, Sweden, UK, USA.

BUSINESS DIRECTORY

Hotels

Tallinn (area code 2)
Emu (tel: 521-611).

Kungla (tel: 427-040).

Lemmo, Söpruse pst. 182, EE0029 (tel: 520-034).

Noobel (tel: 683-713).

Olümpia, Liivalaia 33 (tel: 605-566, 602-600).

Palace, Vabaduse Väljak 3 (tel: 444-765; fax: 443-098).

Peoleo (15-minute drive out of town on Pärnu road - no public transport links) (tel: 556-566).

Pirita (20-minute bus ride on coast road) (tel: 238-598).

Stroomi (10-minute bus ride from town) (tel: 495-219).

Tallinn (tel: 604-340).

Viru, Viru Väljak 4 (tel: 652-093, 449-314).

Tartu (area code 34)
Taru (tel: 73-700).

Useful telephone numbers

Fire brigade: 01.

Police: 02.

Ambulance: 03.

Gas: 04.

N.B. Numbers 01 – 04 cannot be dialled form mobile telephones. 112 should be dialled instead.

Car hire

Tallinn
Europcar: reservations (tel: 441-637, 449-196); Magdaleena 3 (tel: 650-2559, 650-2561; fax: 650-2560); airport (tel: 638-8031).

Hertz: reservations (tel: 638-8923; fax: 638-8953); international airport (tel & fax: 638-8923).

Ideal Ltd: Tallinn Airport (International Department) (tel: 212-735, 219-222; fax: 212-735).

Refit Ltd: Magasini 20 (tel: 661-046; 682-607; fax: 448-524).

Chambers of commerce

Chamber of Commerce and Industry of the Estonian Republic, Zoom-Kooli 17, EE0001 Tallinn (tel: 444-929, 443-859; fax: 443-656).

Banking

Eesti Pank (Bank of Estonia) (central bank), 1 Suur-Ameerika Street, 13 EE0100 Tallinn (tel: 310-911; fax: 310-836); Pst 13, EE0100 Tallinn (tel: 631-0911; fax: 631-0954); Information Department (310-951, 310-953; fax: 310-954). Balti Uehispank, Tonismaegi 16, EE0106 Tallinn (tel: 682-233; fax; 444-778).

Bank of Tallinn, Vabaduse Väljak 10 (tel: 449-983).

Eesti Innovatsioonipank, Kentmanni 13, EE0100 Tallinn (tel: 441-264; fax: 441-537).

Eesti Pangaliit (Estonian Association of Banks), Parnu mnt 19, EE0100 Tallinn (fax: 455-401).

Eesti Uhispank, Parnu mnt. 6 EE0001 Tallinn (tel: 313-686; fax: 313-685).

Estonian Commercial Bank of Industry, Suur-Karja 7, EE0001 Tallinn (tel: 442-410; fax: 440-495).

Estonian Provincial Bank, Estonian pst 11, EE0105 Tallinn (tel: 441-797).

Estonian Savings Bank, Kinga 1, EE0100 Tallinn (tel: 302-600; fax: 302-602).

Evea Pank (commercial bank of Estonian Small Business Association), Narva Mnt 40, EE0106 Tallinn (tel: 422-122; fax: 421-435).

Hansabank, Liivalaia 12, EE0100 Tallinn (tel: 310-311; fax; 310-410).

North Estonian Bank, Parnu mnt. 12 EE0100 Tallinn (tel: 403-500; fax: 403-501).

Pohia-Eesti Aktsiapank, Narva Mnt 7, EE0001 Tallinn (tel: 422-136; fax: 445-023).

Tartu Kommertspank (commercial bank), Munga 18, EE2400 Tartu (tel: 33-197; fax: 33-593, 32-707).

Union Bank of Finland Tallinn Branch, Harju str. 6 EE0001 Tallinn (tel: 314-040; fax: 314-153).

Principal newspapers

Aripäev, Raua 1A, EE0010 Tallinn (tel: 431-201; fax: 426=700).

The Baltic Independent (formerly The Estonian Independent), PO Box 100, Pärnu mnt. 67a, EE0090 Tallinn (tel: 683=074; fax: 441-483).

Eesti Ekspress, Kentmanni 20, EE0001 Tallinn (tel: 666-864, 666-219).

Päevaleht, Pärnu Mnt 67A, EE0090 Tallinn (tel: 681-235; fax: 442-762).

Postimees, Gildi 1, Box 63, EE2400 Tartu (fax: 33-348).

Travel information

Baltic Tours, Vene 23B, EE0003 Tallinn (tel: 446-331; fax: 440-760).

Estonian Air, Vabaduse, Valjak 10, Tallinn (tel: 446-383, 440-295; fax: 631-2740, 425-045).

Estonian Tourist Board, Ministry of Economy, Pikk Str 71, 0001 Tallinn (tel: 601-700; fax: 602-743); 2-4 Kiriku Str, EE0100 Tallin (tel: 450-486, 450-941; fax: 450-540).

The Estonian Association of Travel Agents, Pikk 71, EE0101 Tallinn (tel: 601-705; fax: 425-594).

Finest Hotel Group, Pärnu Mnt 22, EE0001 Tallinn (tel: 451-510; fax: 446-029).

Other useful addresses

Baltic Trade Company (commercial service organising exhibitions, seminars, joint ventures), Ravl Str 27, EE0007 Tallinn (tel: 455-089; fax: 445-768).

Confederation of Estonian Industry, Gonsiori 29 EE0100 Tallinn (tel: 422-235; fax: 424-962).

Energy Sector, Ministry of Economy, Kiriku 6, EE0100 Tallinn (tel: 443-425, 442-902; fax: 444-740).

Estonian Privatisation Agency/PHARE Privatisation-Baltic Framework Agreem. Ravala 6, EE0105 Tallin (tel: 6305653, 454-490; fax: 630-5699, 455-904).

Estonian Investment Agency (EIA), Rävala str. 6 (room 602B), EE0105 Tallinn (tel: 410-166; fax: 410-312).

Estonian Oil Shale State Company (Eesti Polevkivi), 10 Jaama Str, EE2045 Johvi (tel: (33)26-667; fax: (33)26-654).

Estonian Shipping Co Ltd., 3/5 Estonian Blvd., Tallinn (tel: 640-9500; fax: 640-9595).

Estonian State Energy Department, 29 Gonsiori Street EE0104 Tallinn (tel: 421-579; fax: 425-468, 421-908); external department (tel: 421-480).

Estonian Trade Council, Kiriku Str 2/4, EE0100 Tallinn (tel: 444-703; fax: 444-615).

Loksa Shipyard, EE3020, Tallinn 2 (tel: 575-241; fax: 639-1230).

Ministry of Agriculture, Lai Str 39/41, EE0100 Tallinn (tel: 441-166; fax: 440-601).

Ministry of Economy, Harju 11, EE0001 Tallinn (tel: 442-273, 441-506; fax: 446-860).

Ministry of Education, 9/11 Tonismagi St, EE0100 Tallinn (tel: 628-2334; fax: 628-2300).

Ministry of Finance, Suur-Ameerika Street 1, EE0100 Tallinn (tel: 683-602/616/579; fax: 682-097, 317-810).

Ministry of Foreign Economic Relations, Suur Amerika 1, EE0103 Tallinn (tel: 683-445; fax; 680-097).

Ministry of Industry and Energy, M Lomonosov Str 29, EE0104 Tallinn (tel: 423-550).

Ministry of Transport and Communications, Viru Street 9, EEO100 Tallinn (tel: 446-070, 397-630; fax: 449-206, 397-606; Foreign Relations Department (tel: 639-7630; fax: 639-7606).

Ookean State Stock Corporation (Estonian Fishing Company), Paljassaare Str 28, EE0025 Tallinn (tel: 471-421, 497-212; fax: 498-190).

State Statistical Office of Estonia, Endla 15, EE01100 Tallinn (tel: 452-812, 625-9245; fax: 453-923).

Finland

Howard Hill

As a new European Union (EU) member, Finland is pushing hard for membership of the EU's Economic and Monetary Union (EMU) which should be easier to achieve now that the country's economy is well on the way to recovery. GDP growth in 1995 was a healthy 4.2 per cent (4.4 per cent in 1994) but the outlook for 1996 by the third quarter of that year was for growth of 2 per cent. The very dark spot in this picture remains the high level of unemployment. At 18 per cent in July 1996, joblessness is still unacceptably high and, as a result, the government's fiscal policy is expected to remain tight. The high real interest rates continue to restrict capital expenditure.

Politics

Finland's government, the outcome of the March 1995 elections, consists of a five-party broad-based coalition – from right to left – which has 145 of the 200 seats in parliament. It is led by the Social Democratic Party (SSDP) of Paavo Lipponen and includes the Conservatives, the Swedish People's Party (SFP), the Greens and the former communist Left Alliance. The pragmatic Lipponen became prime minister in April 1995, and had gained the assurances of all coalition members that they would support the welfare and spending cuts he planned to implement. The inclusion of the Greens and Left Alliance was clear evidence of the consensus approach of the government – the Social Democrats and their allies did not actually need them to form a government. The Centre Party (KESK), which headed the previous coalition government, is the main opposition party.

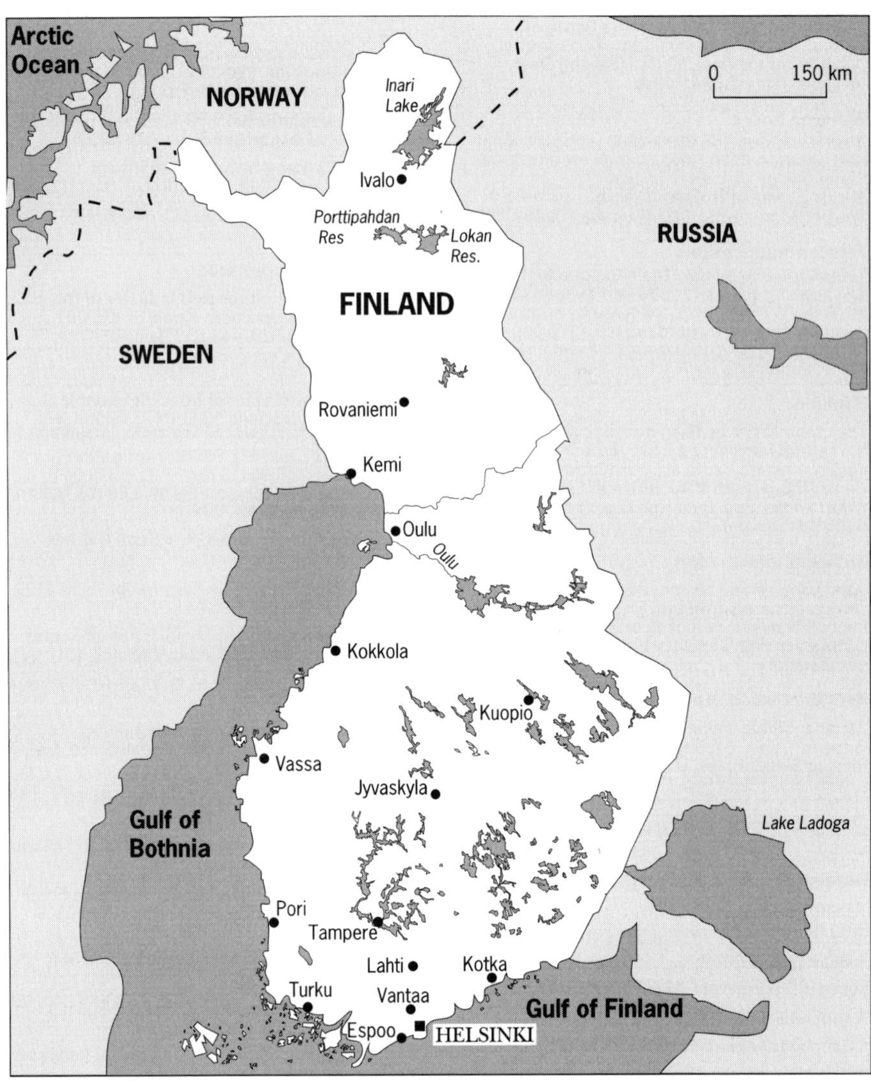

In January 1996 Iiro Viinanen announced that he would be giving up his post as finance minister to become chief executive of the Pohjola insurance group. Viinanen, who came to his finance ministry post in 1991, steered the country through severe economic turbulence although his legacy, aside from bringing back decent growth figures, looks like being Finland's high unemployment level.

Welfare entitlement rules were made more restrictive in 1996 – benefit periods shortened and the rules on eligibility narrowed. The government has brought in these changes to add flexibility to the country's labour market. The strong barriers to lower paid employment, as erected and maintained by the powerful trade unions, still remain.

Prime Minister Lipponen criticised the current expansion plans of NATO in September 1996. Finland is neutral and believes that allowing the Baltic states of Latvia, Lithuania and Estonia to join NATO could destabilise the region. The Finnish government feels that the Baltics' independence would be compromised if they were to join NATO; Russia is against their membership, a major complicating factor. Finland, along with Sweden, wants to foster regional stability through widespread economic and administrative co-operation rather than through military alliances. In June 1996 Finland, along with fellow EU neutrals Austria, Ireland, and Sweden, said that they wished to incorporate peacekeeping, armed humanitarian aid and crisis management in a revision of the Maastricht treaty.

Road to EMU

The government is anxious to be a founder-member of the single European currency in 1997 and this position was made crystal-clear by Prime Minister Lipponen in August 1996. In response to the announcement of the government's intentions regarding EMU, the maarka weakened at a time when other European currencies were strengthening. The markka has been floating since 1992.

Finland's 1997 budget announced in September 1996 was created with EMU membership in mind. In June 1996, an amendment to monetary legislation, enabling Finland to join the Exchange Rate Mechanism (ERM), was adopted. The markka was linked to the ERM in October 1996 at a central parity of FM304 per DM.

The Finnish position *vis-à-vis* Maastricht will be enhanced by the fact that the 1997 budget, due to be ratified in December 1996, will allow Finland to meet all of the Treaty's key EMU qualifying conditions aside from the level of public debt. The level of public debt is to be 61.6 per cent of GDP under the budget, outside the 60 per cent Maastricht target. Budget spending will be reduced by 5 per cent in real terms in 1997. Since 1992 the government has removed the equivalent of 8 per cent of annual GDP from the budget through spending cuts. By the third quarter of 1996, the country was still on track to meet all the Maastricht treaty requirements in 1997.

The 1997 budget proposals show that the budget is to balance for the first time since 1990. Income taxes are to be reduced by FM5.5 billion, with the lost revenue being made up by privatisations and higher energy taxes.

Revenues from taxes on alcohol, at US$1.6 billion, amount to almost 5 per cent of the total tax revenue. The cost of alcoholic drinks in Finland is among the world's highest, due to high taxes and the fact that the state has a monopoly of the sale of alcohol. Cost, combined with the relaxation of duty-free limits after the country joined the EU, are behind the sharp growth of 'booze tourism' which the government claims costs it FM1 billion in lost taxes. In February 1996 the government announced that it was keen to have the duty free limits on imports from Russia and the Baltic states rolled back. The limits were 15 litres of beer

KEY FACTS

Official title: Suomen Tasavalta (Republic of Finland)

Head of state: President Martti Ahtisaari (SSDP)

Head of government: Prime Minister Paavo Lipponen (SSDP)

Ruling party: Five-party coalition comprising: Suomen Sosialidemokraattinen Puolue (SSDP) (Social Democratic Party); Kansallinen Kokoomus (KOK) (National Coalition Party) (conservatives); Vasemmistoliitto (Left-wing Alliance); Svenska Folkpartiet (SFP) (Swedish People's Party) and the Vihrea Liitto (VL) (Green Alliance)

Capital: Helsinki

Official Languages: Finnish and Swedish

Currency: Markka or Finnmark (FM) = 100 penniä

Exchange rate: FM4.64 per US$ (Dec 1996)

Area: 338,144 sq km

Population: 5.11m (1995)

GDP per capita: US$18,900 (1994)

GDP real growth: 2.1% (Aug 1996); 4.2% (1995)

Labour force: 2.5m (1995)

Unemployment: 18% (Jul 1996)

Inflation: 0.6% (first half 1996) (consumer prices)

Trade balance: US$9.6bn (1995)

Foreign debt: US$118bn (1995)

KEY INDICATORS — Finland

	Unit	1991	1992	1993	1994	1995
Population	m	5.03	5.04	5.07	5.09	5.11
Gross domestic product (GDP)	FMbn	480.87	476.78	482.40	509.92	545.73
GDP per capita	US$	25,800	22,780	16,165	18,900	–
GDP real growth	%	-6.4	-3.5	-2.0	4.4	4.2
Inflation	%	4.3	2.9	2.2	1.1	1.0
Consumer prices	1990=100	104.1	106.8	109.1	110.3	111.3
Unemployment	%	7.7	12.7	18.2	18.4	17.2
Agricultural production	1979-81=100	110.06	100.36	106.74	106.93	106.72
Industrial share prices	1990=100	73.1	68.9	116.3	179.5	199.0
Industrial production	1990=100	90.3	92.3	97.4	107.6	–
Exports (goods & services)	FIMbn	109.29	128.27	159.44	182.53	206.57
Imports (goods & services)	FIMbn	112.42	121.88	133.45	150.04	164.00
Balance of trade	US$m	2,321	3,952	6,392	6,400	9,600
Current account	US$m	-6,696	-4,945	-1,123	1,274	5,476
Tourism receipts	US$bn	1.19	1.33	1.21	1.30	–
Total reserves minus gold	US$m	7,608.7	5,213.4	5,410.8	10,662.0	10,038.3
Foreign exchange	US$m	7,108.0	4,774.3	4,993.0	10,050.6	9,293.4
Discount rate	%	8.50	9.50	5.50	5.25	4.88
Deposit rate	%	7.50	7.50	4.75	3.27	3.19
Lending rate	%	11.80	12.14	9.92	7.91	7.75
Exchange rate	FM per US$	4.04	4.48	5.71	5.22	4.34

after a short trip to a non-EU country; until March 1995 a short trip was defined as 20 hours, but the European Commission successfully pressured for a removal of this limit. The limit on spirits is 1 litre per short stay. Each year over 2 million Finns take the ferry to Estonia for cheap shopping and alcohol and many go across the border to Russia for beer and spirits.

Economy

GDP growth in 1996 is expected to fall from 1995's 4.2 per cent growth rate. In the first six months of 1996 the rate was 1.5 per cent, leading to expectations that GDP growth would end the year somewhere between two and three per cent. Private consumption was the main economic growth force in the first half of 1996. Industrial output fell from 11.9 per cent in 1994 to 6.7 per cent in 1995.

Consumer price inflation was steady at one per cent in 1995 (1.1 per cent in 1994) and at 0.6 per cent in the first half of 1996. The low inflation rate was widely attributed to weak demand, low interest rates and continued low food prices.

Total exports were FM207 billion in 1995, an increase of 8.3 per cent over the previous year. Imports, at FM164 billion, grew by a lower 6.3 per cent. Consequently, the balance of trade surplus was FM48 billion in 1995 and this figure is predicted to increase with the renewed emphasis on export growth over consumption.

Employment

Finland has a serious unemployment problem, but the rate could fall with continued implementation of the structural adjustments. However, new hiring has been discouraged by both the high taxation of labour and the relatively high real interest rates (which have typically resulted in the postponement of expansion and development plans).

Prime Minister Lipponen has made employment expansion a top priority and his efforts in this area have started to pay off – the unemployment rate went from 18.4 per cent in 1994 to 17.2 per cent in 1995. Lipponen's goal of cutting the rate in half by the end of his four-year term is widely considered to be an almost impossible task, with a reduction to the still high level of 12 per cent more likely. Some employment law reforms have been proposed which might have the effect of further reducing the jobless numbers: the daily allowance rules might be tightened to reduce benefits and the contributions that employers pay.

Banking

The banking sector is not yet free of trouble, although the signs look encouraging for future sustained growth after the debacle of the early 1990s. The mood at Finland's premier bank group, Merita, is growing more upbeat – it registered fewer loan losses in 1996 and has benefited from the fall in money market interest rates.

Merita was formed in 1995 by the merger of the two largest Finnish banks, Kansallis-Osake-Pankki (KOP) and Unitas. Neither of these banks had posted a profit in the five years before the merger and the outlook was gloomy, based on the number of non-performing loans on their books. According to Merita, the combined operating profits of all Finnish banks was some FM1.5 billion in the first half of 1996.

Privatisation

The government's US$221 million privatisation programme started to pick up steam in September 1996 with the announcement that it would list shares in the Kemira chemicals group. The offering is expected to bring in some US$155 million. Kemira also announced that it was to raise funds for capital investment by issuing up to US$8

COUNTRY PROFILE — FINLAND

Historical profile

1809 Finland, a Swedish province since the fourteenth century, taken by Russia. Population suffered greatly in Tusso-Swedish wars over the centuries. 1905 Strike demanding rights and liberties. Parliamentary government and universal suffrage established (first country to give votes to women). 1917 Collapse of Russian Empire. Finnish declaration of independence followed by brief civil war. 1919 Establishment of Republic, which survived the Soviet Government's attempts to regain control. In the following 70 years more than 60 governments, mainly minority coalitions, held power. 1939 Southern Karelia ceded to the USSR after the 'Winter War', 15 weeks of bitter conflict. 1941 Finland entered Second World War on the side of Nazi Germany in an attempt to recover its territory. 1945 Following German defeat, punitive reparations and the cession of Southern Karelia and its only Arctic port, Petsamo, forced on Finland by the USSR. 1948 Finno-Soviet Pact of Friendship. 1956-81 Powers of strong executive presidency, allowed for in constitution, further enhanced by President Urho Kekkonen. He was followed by President Mauno Koivisto. 1987 Historic coalition government. Conservatives in coalition for the first time in 21 years, with the first conservative prime minister (Harri Holkeri) since 1946. Centre Party out after 50 years in government. The Finnish Christian Union (SKL) party, which opposed EU membership, withdrew from coalition in June 1994 after Finland completed negotiations on joining EU. Finnish membership in EU approved by referendum in October 1994 and by legislature in the following month.

Political system

Constitution adopted 1919. Legislative power held by unicameral parliament and the president. *Eduskunta* (parliament) consists of 200 members elected by system of proportional representation for four years. President elected for six-year term, by popular vote alone. Second round of voting if no candidate receives majority votes. President appoints a cabinet headed by a prime minister, which is responsible to *Eduskunta*, for general administration of country.

Political parties

Five-party coalition comprising: Suomen Sosialidemokraattinen Puolue (Social Democratic Party) (SSDP); Kansallinen Kokoomus (National Coalition Party) (KOK) (conservatives); Vasemmistoliitto (Left-wing Alliance) (VL); Svenska Folkpartiet (Swedish People's Party) (SFP) and the Vihrea Liitto (Green Alliance) (VL). Other major parties include Keskustapuole (Centre Party (KESK); Suomen Kristillinen Liitto (Finnish Christian Union) (SKL); Suomen Maaseudun Puolue (Finnish Rural Party) (SMP); Liberaalinen Kansanpuolue (Liberal People's Party (LKP).

Main cities/towns

Helsinki (population 940,000 in 1994), Espoo, Kuopio, Lahti, Oulu, Tampere, Turku, Vaasa and Vantaa.

Media

Television continues to steal share from newspapers as part of a recessionary trend. The press tends to be regional and influenced by political parties.
Dailies: Over 100 dailies, of which 12 are published in Swedish. Most popular are *Helsingin Sanomat* (Helsinki), *Ilta-Sanomat* (Helsinki), *Aamulehti* (Tampere) and *Turun Sanomat* (Turku) *Kaleva* (Oulu).
Weeklies: Most popular is *Helsingin Sanomat.*
Business: Several covering most aspects of trade and industry, including *Tekniikka & Talous* (weekly), *Kauppalehti* (daily), *Fakta* (monthly), *Finnish Business Report* (monthly), and *Talouselämä* (weekly).
Periodicals: Most popular are general interest magazines, such as *Apu*, *Valitut Palat* (Reader's Digest, monthly) and *Seura*, illustrated news magazines, such as *Suomen Kuvalehti*, and women's magazines such as *Eeva*, Anna, *Me Naiset* and *Kotiliesi.*
Broadcasting: Under general control of Finnish Broadcasting Company 'Oy Yleisradio Ab', which is state-controlled. There is also a wide range of private commercial stations in operation.
Radio: Over 5m radios in use. Four domestic programmes transmitted plus a foreign service broadcasting to Europe, Africa, Middle East and Far East. Private local radio started in 1985.
Television: Over 2m TVs in use, of which over 350,000 also receive cable TV. Finnish broadcasting Company transmits on three channels, two of which carry some programmes produced by the commercial TV company MTV Oy. Channel Three is commercially operated, with advertising. There are over 170 cable stations, the biggest being Helsinki Televisio (HTV). Several satellite channels and about 200 private cable networks are available.

Advertising

Key categories include automotive, food, entertainment, transport and banking. All usual media are available to advertisers. Advertisements can be placed on TV through the commercial TV companies MTV Oy and Kolmostelevisio or via cable TV. Press advertisers are advised to consider whether their target audience is Finnish or Swedish-speaking. Radio advertising is limited to private local stations. Cinema films and posters are widely used.

Domestic economy

Finland is a small market-oriented economy with dependence on foreign trade. Its main economic force is manufacturing. Since the late million new shares. The goal now is to reduce the state's share to 55 per cent of the enlarged capital. The state owned virtually all of Kemira until 1994, when its holding was reduced to 72.3 per cent. Kemira has been groomed for privatisation ever since it began a restructuring programme in 1991; a third of its workforce has been made redundant under the restructuring. There was speculation that the sale would take place by the end of 1996.

Industry

The pulp and paper industry has been on a roller-coaster ride since 1988 due to huge price fluctuations rarely, if ever, seen before. The price rises were especially severe in 1995 and the early part of 1996 but a build-up of inventories since then has caused prices to plummet. Looking at the overall world price trend for pulp in the past 25 years, the 1990s have been a particularly unstable time – caused in large part by new competition provided by Latin American and Asian producers. In response to this situation, a new bourse was launched in Helsinki in September 1996 for pulp derivatives. It is hoped that the new exchange will give some stability to the pulp and paper market. However, the bourse has attracted its critics who point to the failure of a similar scheme in both Canada and Sweden.

Finland is the world's second largest forestry sector exporter after Canada. The pulp and paper lobby, a group with considerable influence in Finland, is against EMU and ERM participation if Sweden does not join as well – the industry fears that Swedish exporters could gain an unfair advantage if the Swedish currency, the krona, was devalued; Finland would not have the same devaluation opportunity if the markka was tied into the ERM/EMU. As of mid-1996 there was a good chance that Sweden would decide to forsake both the ERM and EMU.

The newly-deregulated power industry in the Nordic countries is undergoing a rapid consolidation. The giant Finnish power producer, Imatran Voima (IVO), has 12.5 per cent of the Nordic power market. The company's profits were US$234 million in 1995. In March 1996 IVO bought a 34 per cent share in Gullspangs Kraft of Sweden for US$461 million; the seller was Aga, the industrial gas group. In April 1996 IVO announced a strategic alliance with Stockholm Energi, the number three power supplier in Sweden.

Telecommunications and media

The telecommunications sector is being liberalised. The licensing system and price regulation will be all but done away with and operators' rights to lease lines has been made more clear.

In June 1996 a 75 per cent holding in Telivo, the Finnish telecommunications company, was bought by Telida, Sweden's state-owned telecommunications operator. The seller was the Finnish energy group Imatran Voima (IVO), the country's largest energy producer; it is 96 per cent state- owned. Telivo was founded in 1992 by IVO. Telida will now have a 10 per cent share of the market for international calls and a 4 per cent share for long-distance calls.

In October 1996 the contest to win the license for a fourth national television channel was won by the Ruutunelonen consortium headed by Sanomat, the country's largest newspaper group. The new channel, which is only the second commerical station in the country, is to come on air in August 1997; the license is for a five year duration. Television advertising in Finland is worth FM1 billion and accounts for about 20 per cent of all money spent on advertising. Estimates show that the new television channel will generate some M130 million worth of advertising.

COUNTRY PROFILE — FINLAND

Domestic economy (contd): 1960s the economy expanded at a faster pace than the other western OECD countries despite a relative scarcity of energy resources and raw materials. After fast growth in the 1970s and 1980s the labour supply began to slow, producing labour market tightness and inflationary pay settlements. As a result both competitiveness and export market share were lost. Finland needed complete major structural adjustments after the collapse of the Soviet Union, which amounted to a tenth of Finland's total export market, and the huge drop in the world prices for timber and paper. After a severe recession in 1991, the domestic markets deepened further. The markka was devalued in November 1991 and again in autumn 1992. Since 1992 Finland resolutely embarked on a policy course based on export-led growth and aimed at shifting resources from the domestic sector to the foreign sector of the economy. In the autumn of 1992 Finland abandoned fixed exchange rates. An amendment to constitutional law was passed in 1992 which enabled laws providing for cuts in central government spending to be passed by a simple majority in parliament. Among other measures taken in 1992 to enhance economic efficiency and the public sector's fiscal position, were the introduction of new competition legislation and reform of the state-aid system for local government. Capital taxation was reformed and restrictions on foreign ownership of Finnish shares was lifted with effect from the beginning of 1993. VAT introduced from the beginning of 1994.

Employment

Continuing high levels of unemployment. Finland's jobless rate reached 17.4 per cent in April 1996. A total of 444,100 people were without jobs in April, about 7,500 less than in March, and 15,200 lower than in April 1995. About 47 per cent of the workforce is female.

External trade

From the beginning of 1992 Finland concentrated on a policy based on export-led growth. Despite the collapse of former Soviet trade and the international recession, exports have done very well. In January 1995 Finland became member of EU.

Exports: Main exports are forestry products, metal and engineering products, chemicals, basic metals, other industries and textiles and clothing. Main destinations: EU, EFTA, Germany, Sweden, UK.

Imports: Main imports are raw materials and components, consumer goods, investment goods, crude oil and fuels. Main sources: EU, EFTA, Germany, Sweden, UK.

Agriculture

Farming and forestry contributed 6 per cent to GDP in 1994 and employed 8.6 per cent of the workforce. Forestry is main supplier to local chemical, pulp and paper industries. Although farm holdings are small (average size 13 ha of arable land plus 37 ha of forestry) and productivity remains low, Finland is 85 per cent self-supporting in food grains, dairy products and root crops. Finnish agriculture is among the most protected of OECD countries with net producer subsidies equal to 70 per cent of the value of farm output compared with an average of 40 per cent for the OECD.

Industry

Highly developed export-based sector centred largely on the forest products industry, contributing 31 per cent to GDP in 1994 and employing 27 per cent of the labour force. Expansion of the metal and engineering industries (machines, transport vehicles and electro-technical products), chemicals, plastics, and less on textiles and clothing. Also important are food processing, rubber and shipbuilding to a lesser degree. State-owned companies account for less than 16 per cent of total industrial output. Since 1992 Finland pursued an industrial policy based on diversification, restructuring and improvements in export price competitiveness. Industrial output rose 2.9 per cent in May 1996 from May 1995. In May 1996 capacity utilisation in the forestry sector dropped to 87 per cent, down 10 per cent from the year before, reflecting the slowdown in the pulp and paper market; in the manufacturing industry, capacity utilisation was 84.5 per cent, down 3 per cent; there was a 3 per cent drop in the metal and engineering industry capacity utilisation, to 88 per cent.

Mining

The sector accounts for only 0.3 per cent of GDP. Around a dozen ore mines producing mainly chromium, mercury, zinc, silver, copper and nickel. Deposits are small. Prospecting is being intensified to curb imports; refining technology is a major focus of development work. Outokumpu, the mining and metals group has modernised the production facilities at its Harjavalta plant through an investment programme worth FM1.8bn. The programme includes the copper smelter and nickel production line located at Harjavalta and the copper refinery located at Pori, both towns in western Finland.

Energy

Domestic energy resources - mainly hydro and to a much lesser extent peat and waste wood - make up 30 per cent of total consumption. No indigenous oil, natural gas or coal. Owing to its high proportion of energy-intensive industry, long distances between population centres and geographic situation with a cold climate, Finland's per capita energy consumption is one of the highest among International Energy Agency (IEA) countries. Expansion of nuclear power has reduced dependence on imported

COUNTRY PROFILE — FINLAND

Energy (contd): coal and oil. The paper and pulp industry is actively promoting the commissioning of a fifth nuclear plant. Industry was heavily reliant on imports of oil, gas and electricity from the former USSR.

Stock exchange

The Finnish stock exchange agreed with the stock exchanges of Sweden, Denmark and Norway in June 1993, to establish Nordquote, a common Nordic securities trading system.

Legal system

Civil law system based on Swedish law.

Membership of international organisations

ADB, AG (observer), CCC, CERN, Council of Baltic Sea States, Council of Europe, CSCE, DAC, EEA, ESA (associate), EU (from 1 January 1995), FAO, IAEA, ICAC, ICAO, ICES, ICO, IDA, IDB, IEA, IFAD, IFC, IHO, ILO, International Lead and Zinc Study Group, IMF, IMO, International Grain Council, INTERPOL, IPU, ITU, MIGA, NAM (guest), Nordic Council, OECD, Partnerships for Peace, UN, UNESCO, UPU, WHO, WIPO, WMO, World Bank, WSG, WTO.

BUSINESS GUIDE

Time

GMT + 2 (GMT + 3 from late Mar to late Sep).

Climate

Temperate, with warm summers and cold winters. Summer temperatures average around 17 degrees C, winter around -1 degree C although can reach as low as -30 degrees C in February. Heavy snow from December-April.

Clothing

Lightweight in summer. Medium weight and heavy topcoat in winter – fur hat recommended.

Entry requirements

Visa: Visas not required for nationals of most European countries, and of several other countries.
Customs: Personal effects duty free, plus duty-free allowance.

Health precautions

Mandatory: Polio and tetanus vaccinations.

Air access

Regular daily flights by most major international airlines.
National airline: Finnair.
Main international airport: Helsinki-Vantaa (HEL), 19 km north of capital.
International airports: Jyväskylä (JYV), 21 km from city; Kemi (KEM), 6 km from city; Kokkola (KOK), 22 km from city; Oulu (OUL), 15 km south-west of city; Rovaniemi (RRVN), 10 km from city; Tampere (TMP), 15 km from city; Turku (TKU), 7 km from city; Vaasa (VAA), 12 km from city.

Surface access

Daily ferry services from Sweden, twice weekly from Germany and Poland. Reservations should be made in advance as these tend to be heavily booked, especially during summer and weekends.
Main ports: Helsinki, Kotka, Hamina, Mariehamn, Vaasa, Turku, Pori, Sköldvik, Rauma and Oulu.

Hotels

In Helsinki and surrounding area, classified into five price categories. Generally of a high standard. Rates vary depending on location, facilities and season. Accommodation should be booked well in advance especially during summer. If accommodation is unobtainable, a place may be found through 'Hotellikeskus' (accommodation clearing-house) at the Central Railway Station in Helsinki. All major international credit cards are accepted.

Currency

The markka is related to a trade-weighted basket of currencies.

Foreign exchange information

Account restrictions: Some account restrictions for payment between Finland and countries with currencies (rouble) that are not freely convertible. Certain foreign exchange controls were lifted on 1 July 1990. These allow non-residents to take unlimited amounts of money outside the country without having to get permission from the Bank of Finland.

Car hire

Available in most major towns. Rates include oil, maintenance and insurance. Minimum age limit (usually between 19-23) and at least one year's driving experience required. Speed limits, 50 kph in built-up areas, 80-100 kph on normal roads and 120 kph on motorways. Wearing of seat belts is compulsory. N.B. The use of headlights is at all times obligatory.

City transport

Taxis: Available from ranks, by telephone or can be hailed in the street. Identifiable by 'Taksi' sign on roof. Extra charges at night and weekends. Tipping is not expected.
Buses: Good services throughout country. Flat fare in Helsinki; also 10-journey ticket obtainable.
Trams: Service in Helsinki.

National transport

Air: One of the densest internal networks in Europe. Finnair provides connections between Helsinki and Ivalo, Joensuu, Jyväskylä, Kajaani, Kemi, Kittilä, Kokkola, Kuopio, Kuusamo, Lappeenranta, Mariehamn, Mikkeli, Oulu, Pietarsaari, Pori, Rovaniemi, Savonlinna, Tampere, Turku, Vaasa and Varkaus.
Road: Finland's 77,000-km network of public roads includes 11,494 km of high-grade national highway and 29,703 km of secondary routes, but only 215 km of motorways.
Buses: Efficient coach services cover the entire country, and are main form of transport in Lapland.
Rail: Network of around 6,000 km (including 1,500 km electrified), operated by state railway company 'Valtionrautatiet'. Relatively inexpensive and there are several passes available allowing travel over a set period. Seat reservation is obligatory on special express trains.
Water: Important method of transport, owing to large number of lakes (187,888), which cover 31,500 sq km.

Public holidays

Fixed dates: 1 Jan (New Year's Day), 1 May (May Day), 6 Dec (Independence Day), 24-25 Dec (Christmas), 26 Dec (Boxing Day).
Variable dates: Epiphany, Good Friday, Easter Monday, Ascension Day, Whit Monday, Midsummer and All Saints' Day.

Working hours

Government and business: (Mon-Fri) 0800–1600, close 1515 during summer.
Banking: (Mon-Fri) 0915–1615.
Shops: (Mon-Fri) 0900–1700 or later, (Sat) 0900–1600, close 1400 during summer.

Social customs

When invited into a Finnish home for the first time it is usual to give flowers. 'Skol' is customary - guests do not drink until their health is proposed by their host. Punctuality is important. Business meetings are sometimes held in saunas.

Business language and interpreting/translation

Available through tourist offices or through classified section of telephone directory under *Käänöstoimistoja ja kielenkääntäjiä.*

Telecommunications

Telephone and telefax: Direct dialling to most towns and most European countries. International dialling code: 358 followed by 9 for Helsinki. Changes from October 1996: 13 new area codes and the pan-European 00 has been adopted.
For IDD access from Finland dial 990.
Telex: Service available to most parts of the world. Public facility at Central Post Office in Helsinki. Country code 57 FF.
Telegram: Can be sent from post offices or hotel desks.
Postal services: Stamps available from post offices, book/paper shops, kiosks, stations and hotels. Mail may be sent 'Poste Restante', c/o Main Post Office in Helsinki (or other city).

Banking

System headed by Suomen Pankki (Bank of Finland), which is responsible for monetary policy and foreign credit. Union Bank of Finland Ltd and Kansallis-Osake-Pankki merged in June 1995, under new name of Merita Bank. The severe Finnish recession, the high level of real interest rates, credit losses and non-performing loans caused a crisis in the financial sector. Skopbank, the central bank for Finland's savings banks, needed support from the government guarantee fund in 1991-93 to help it over the country's banking crisis. Restructuring of the troubled banking system began in November 1992.
Other banks: See 'Business Directory, Banking'.

BUSINESS GUIDE

Trade fairs

Most important are Helsinki International Fair (consumer goods) and Helsinki International Technical Fair, which are held alternately every autumn at Helsinki International Fair Centre, at Pasila, about 6 km from the capital. All exhibitions held at the Centre are organised by Finnish Fair Corporation, 'Osuuskunta Suomen Messut'.

Electricity supply

220 V AC.

Representation in capital

Argentina, Austria, Belgium, Brazil, Bulgaria, Canada, China, Colombia, Cuba, Denmark, Egypt, France, Germany, Greece, The Holy See, Hungary, India, Indonesia, Iran, Iraq, Israel, Italy, Japan, Korea DPR, Republic of Korea, Mexico, Netherlands, Norway, Peru, Poland, Portugal, Romania, Russia, South Africa, Spain, Sweden, Switzerland, Turkey, UK, USA, Venezuela.

BUSINESS DIRECTORY

Hotels

Helsinki
Aurora, Helsinginkatu 50 (tel: 717-400; fax: 714-240).

Helsinki, Hallituskatu 12 (tel: 171-401; fax: 176-014).

Hesperia, Mannerheimintie 50 (tel: 43-101; fax: 431-0995).

Inter-Continental, Mannerheimintie 46-48 (tel: 40-551; fax: 405-5255).

Kalastajatorppa, Kalastajatorpantie 1 (tel: 45-811; fax: 458-1668).

Klaus Kurki, Bulevardi 2-4 (tel: 618-911 fax: 608-538).

Marski, Mannerheimintie 10 (tel: 68-061; fax: 642-377).

Olympia, Läntinen Brahenkatu 2 (tel: 750-801; fax: 750-801/205).

Palace, Eteläranta 10 (tel: 134-561; fax: 654-786).

Ramada Presidentti, Eteläinen Rautatiekatu 4 (tel: 6911; fax: 694-7886).

Rantasipi Airport (4km airport), Takamäantie 4, 01510 Vantaa, PO Box 53 (tel: 87-051; fax: 822-846).

Seurahuone, Kaivokatu 12 (tel: 170-441; fax: 664-170).

Strand Inter-Continental, John Stenbergin ranta 4 (tel: 39-351; fax: 761-362).

Tapiola Garden (in Espoo), Tapiontori (tel: 461-711; fax: 462-332).

Torni, Yrjönkatu 26 (tel: 131-131; fax: 131-1361).

Vaakuna, Asema-aukio 2 (tel: 131-181; fax: 1311-8234).

Car hire

Helsinki
Avis: (tel: 441-155).

Budget: reservations (tel: 685-3322; fax: 685-3350).

Europcar: (tel: 758-3700; fax: 755-203).

Hertz: (tel: 7001-9000; fax: 622-1118).

Helsinki-Vantaa Airport
Avis: (tel: 822-833).

Budget: (tel: 870-1606; fax: 870-1604).

Hertz: (tel: 7001-9006; fax: 9082-75350).

Chambers of commerce

Central Chamber of Commerce, Fabianinkatu 14B,00100 Helsinki 10 (tel: 650-133; fax: 650-303).

Banking

Suomen Pankki (The Bank of Finland) (central bank), Snellmaninaukio, POB 160, 00171 Helsinki (tel: 1831; fax: 174-872).

Merita Bank, Aleksanterinkatu 30, 00100 Helsinki 10 (tel: 1651; fax: 165-2648). N.B. Merita Bank replaces Kansallis-Osake-Pankki and Union Bank of Finland Ltd.

Osuuspankkien Keskuspankki Oy (Central Union of the Co-operative Banks), Arkadiankatu 23, 00100 Helsinki 10 (tel: 4041; tx: 124-714).

Pankkien Neuvottelukunta (Joint Delegation of the Finnish Banks), Eteläranta 10, 00130 Helsinki (tel: 629-712).

Postipankki (State-owned), Unioninkatu 20, 00007 Helsinki 7 (tel: 164-3932; tx: 123-816).

Siltapankki Oy (formerly STS-Bank), PO Box 52, SF-00531 Helsinki (tel: 73-181; fax: 7318-2540, 7318-2480).

Suomen Pankkiyhdistys.r.y. (Bankers' Association), Kansakoulukatu 1A, PO Box 1007, 00101 Helsinki (tel: 694-8422).

Suomen Säästöpankkiliitto (Savings Bank Association), Pohjoisesplanadi 35A, 00101 Helsinki 10 (tel: 13-341; tx: 125-768).

Principal newspapers

Helsingin Sanomat, Ludviginkatu 6-8, PO Box 975 (tel: 1221; tx: 124-897).

Ilta-Sanomat, Korkeavuorenkatu 34, PO Box 375, 00101 Helsinki (tel: 1221; tx: 124-897).

Uusi Suomi, PO Box 139, 00101 Helsinki (tel: 53-031; tx: 124-898).

Travel information

Finland Travel Bureau Ltd, Mail Department, PB319, 00101 Helsinki 10 (poste restante service).

Finnair, Tietotie 11A, Helsinki-Vantaa Airport (tel: 81-881; fax: 818-4401).

Finnish Tourist Board, T\03öol\03onkatu 11, PB 625, SF-00100 Helsinki (tel: 403-011; fax: 448-841); tourist information: Unioninkatu 26, 00130 Helsinki (tel: 4030-1300; fax: 4030-1333).

Other useful addresses

Confederation of Finnish Industries, Eteläranta 10, SF 00130, Helsinki 13 (tel: 661-665).

Council of State, Aleksanterinkatu 3 D, 00170 Helsinki (tel: 1601; fax: 160-2163).

FINNIDA (Finnish International Development Agency), c/o Ministry for Foreign Affairs, Merikasarmi, Laivastokatu 22, 00160 Helsinki (tel: 134-151; fax: 629-840).

Finnish Foreign Trade Association, Arkadiankatu 2, PO Box 908, 001001 Helsinki (tel: 69-591; fax: 694-0028).

Helsinki Stock Exchange, Fabianinkatu 14, 00100 Helsinki 10 (tel: 624-161; tx: 123-460).

Invest In Finland, Aleksanterinkatu 17, 00100 Helsinki (tel: 696-9125; fax: 6969-2530).

Liiketyönantajain (Confederation of Commerce Employers), Eteläranta 10, 00130 Helsinki 13 (tel: 19-281; tx: 122-167).

Main Post Office, Mannerheimintie 11, 00100 Helsinki 10.

Meilahti Hospital Haartmanink 3, Helsinki (tel: 4711).

Ministry of Agriculture and Forestry, Hallituskatu 3 A, 00170 Helsinki (tel: 1601; fax: 160-3300).

Ministry of Defence, Et. Makasiinikatu 8 A, 001030 Helsinki (tel: 16-161; fax: 653-254).

Ministry of Education, Meritullinkatu 10, 00170 Helsinki (tel: 134-171; fax: 135-9335).

Ministry of the Environment, Ratakatu 3, 00120 Helsinki (tel: 19-911; fax: 199-1499).

Ministry of Finance, Aleksanterinkatu 3, 00170 Helsinki (tel: 1601; fax: 160-4755).

Ministry for Foreign Affairs, Merikasarmi, Laivastokatu 22, 00160 Helsinki (tel: 134-151; fax: 629-840).

Ministry of the Interior, Kirkkokatu 12, 00170 Helsinki (tel: 1601; fax: 160-2927).

Ministry of Justice, Eteläesplanadi 10, 00130 Helsinki (tel: 18-251; fax: 182-5430).

Ministry of Labour, Eteläesplanadi 4, 00130 Helsinki (tel: 18-561; fax: 185-6427).

Ministry of Social Affairs and Health, Snellmaninkatu 4-6, 00170 Helsinki (tel: 1601; fax: 160-5763).

Ministry of Trade and Industry, Aleksanterinkatu 4, 00170 Helsinki (tel: 1601; fax: 160-3666).

Ministry of Transport and Communications, Eteläesplanadi 16, 00130 Helsinki (tel: 17-361; fax: 173-6340).

Nesté (largest industrial corporation), Keilaniemi, 02150 Espoo, Helsinki (tel: 4501; tx: 124-641).

Oy Suomen Tietotoimisto (news agency), Lönnrotinkatu 5, 00120 Helsinki 12 (tel: 646-224; tx: 124-534).

Statistics Finland, työpajakatu 13, Helsinki (tel: 17-341; fax: 1734-2279).

Suomen Työnantajain Keskusliitto (Finish Employers' Confederation) Eleläranta 10, Helsinki 13 (tel: 17-281; tx: 124-635).

Tullihallitus (Board of Customs), Erottajankatu 2, 00120 Helsinki (tel: 6141).

Ulkomaankaupan Agenttiliitto (Finnish Foreign Trade Agents' Federation Mannerheimintie 42A 00260 Helsinki 26 (tel: 446-768).

France

Bob Jiggins

Late 1995 and early 1996 resembled something of a maelstrom with the social and political unrest of October-November 1995, the disenchantment of the electorate with Jacques Chirac and scandal involving Alain Juppé. For a while it looked as if France, for the first time since the events of 1968, was on the verge of massive upheaval and the potential demise of the Fifth Republic. Paradoxically it took the death of one of France's most distinguished and long-lived politicians, François Mitterrand, to unite the country and remind it of the secure equilibrium that the Fifth Republic has enjoyed since its creation by De Gaulle.

KEY FACTS — ***France***

Official title: The French Republic
Head of state: President Jacques Chirac (RPR)
Head of government: Prime Minister Alain Juppé (RPR)
Ruling party: Coalition comprising Rassemblement pour la République (Rally for the Republic) (RPR); Union pour la Démocratie Française) (UDF)
Capital: Paris
Official Languages: French
Currency: French franc (Ff) = 100 centimes
Exchange rate: Ff5.25 per US$ (1996)

Area: 543,965 sq km
Population: 58.3m (Jan 1996)
GDP per capita: US$26,200 (1995)
GDP real growth: 2.2% (1995)
Labour force: 26m (1996)*
Unemployment: 12.5% (Aug 1996)
Inflation: 2.2% (Jun 1996) (consumer prices)
Trade balance: US$19.8bn (12 months to Apr 1996)
Visitor numbers: 60.64m (1994)

* estimated figure

Politics

For the most part promises made by Jacques Chirac on the campaign trail have not been kept; together with the austerity programme, this was one cause of the widespread social unrest in the winter of 1995. The strikes which broke out on 24 November 1995 were caused by a number of factors, and involved much the same groups as in 1968, namely public sector workers and students. The ostensible cause of the protests was the deficit reduction package of the Juppé government, although other factors at play included the genuine grievances of railway workers and students. The 1996 draft budget and the new social security measures of November 1995 (discussed below) were thus the background on to which other issues were superimposed.

One reason for the unrest has to be the autocratic style of Juppé, whose timing of key measures and public pronouncements appeared to hold a certain regal disregard for the practicalities of politics in a modern democracy. It is true that French presidents have been able to do this without much damage but the population partly expects this from its heads of state, and Juppé has none of the stature of a de Gaulle or a Mitterrand. Both the lack of consultation with the trade unions over the social security reform package and the back-door manner in which the legislation was passed through the assembly serve as indications of his lofty approach to radical measures. Juppé's handling of the crisis once it commenced was insensitive and only served to exacerbate the situation.

Of the organisations involved in the protests, the Force Ouvrière (FO) trade union had perhaps the largest role and the most unanticipated one. The FO is the most moderate of French trade unions and has an extremely high visibility within the government administration. As this is the sector specifically targeted for expenditure reductions, and FO leader Marc Blondel tacitly afforded support to Chirac's election campaign, it would appear that there is a personal element to the FO's role in the crisis. Among the membership too there was a feeling after the elections that the FO had been sold down the river.

The involvement of the student movement was no less vocal, although less surprising, given the fact that students in France have historically been at the forefront in demanding radical change. Student overcrowding, of what is already a mass higher education system, and the high youth unemployment rate (well above the European Union (EU) average) are issues yet to be addressed by the government. There is some evidence, however, that youth unemployment is slowly reducing as a result of the job creation measures of 1995.

Preparing for EMU

One of the main tasks facing the Chirac administration, and one which contributed to the social unrest, is the necessary reduction in both the size of government and it's expenditure in readiness for full Economic and Monetary Union (EMU). This has involved several new measures, including the creation of a new government on 7 November 1995. Juppé wished to create a leaner government in order to push through better the radical changes required – this new

To order your copy, turn to page 119.

government consists of 32 ministers, compared with the 42 in the previous administration. The most important change is the creation of a new ministry of social affairs which has responsibility not only for health and social security, but also for labour and staffing matters. This is a clear recognition by both Chirac and Juppé of the need for one voice in social security reform.

The Mitterrand inheritance

François Mitterrand, one of the longest serving politicians in France, died on 8 January 1996. Mitterrand was a complex figure who as president of the Fifth Republic from 1981-1995 encountered controversy over his role as both an official of the Vichy regime and a resistance leader. Nevertheless, Mitterrand's record is one of stability and continuity and his loss to the French nation was duly mourned in formal and spontaneous informal gatherings. His record as the longest serving president of the Fifth Republic demonstrated its stability with the two periods of cohabitation, despite his opposition to the demise of the Fourth Republic and its replacement by de Gaulle.

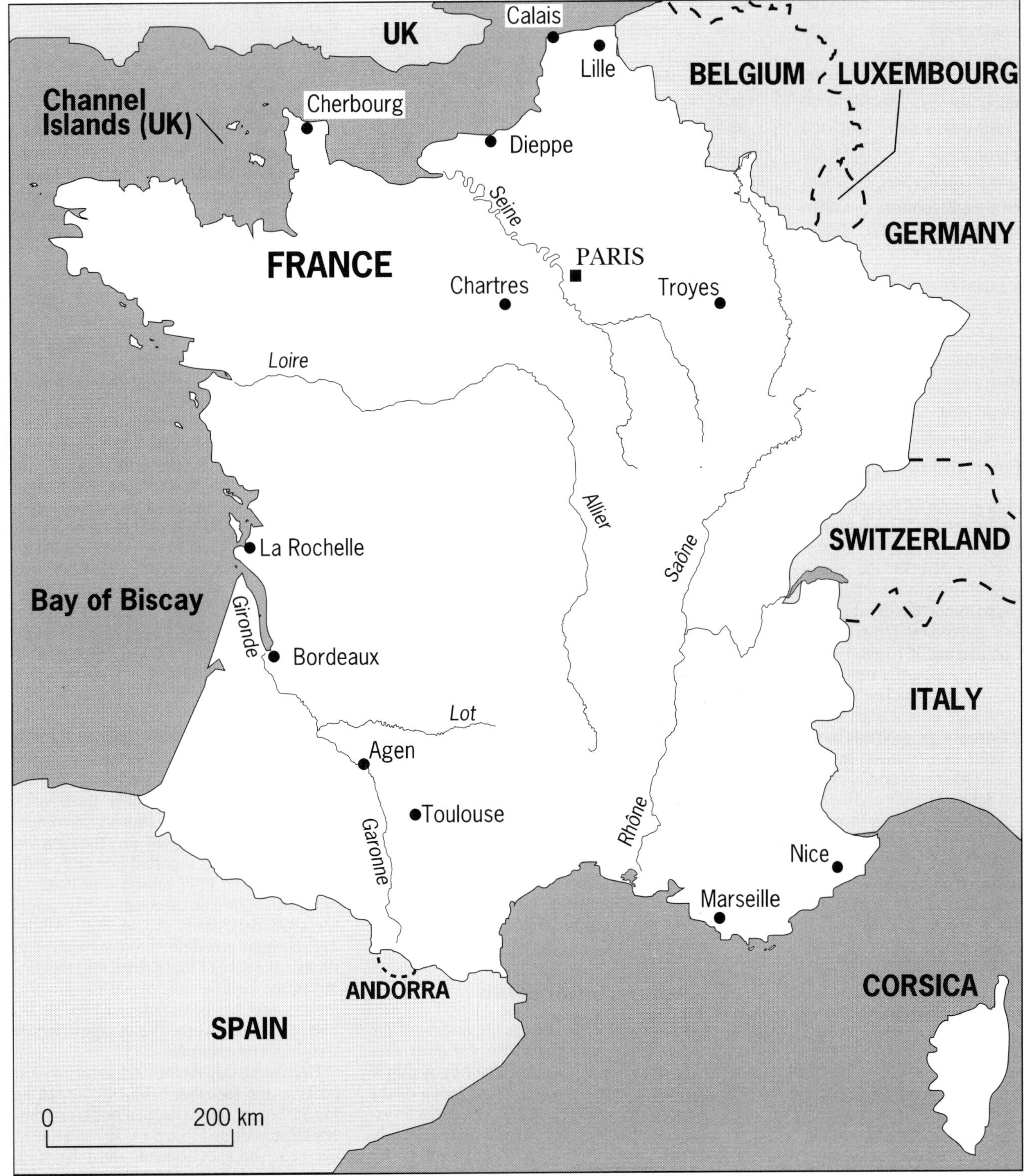

KEY INDICATORS — France

	Unit	1991	1992	1993	1994	1995
Population	m	57.05	57.37	57.66	58.00	58.30
Gross domestic product (GDP)	US$bn	1,192.0	1,346.4	1,254.4	1,318.9	–
GDP per capita	US$	21,030	23,540	21,740	22,800	26,200
GDP real growth	%	1.1	1.8	-0.9	2.9	2.2
Inflation	%	3.2	2.4	2.1	1.7	2.1
Consumer prices	1990=100	103.2	105.7	107.9	109.7	111.6
Unemployment	%	9.4	10.3	11.7	12.3	11.5
Agricultural production	1979-81=100	105.68	112.27	104.24	100.34	101.91
Labour costs	1979-81=100	104.4	108.4	111.7	115.0	116.0
Industrial production	1990=100	99.9	98.9	95.2	99.2	–
Coal production	m toe	7.4	6.9	6,3	5.5	5.1
Exports (FOB) (goods)	US$m	209,172	227,442	199,043	224,000	–
Imports (FOB) (goods)	US$m	218,886	225,071	191,532	215,892	–
Balance of trade	US$m	-10,175	1,755	6,997	19,500	20,900
Current account	US$m	-6,522	3,892	8,9841	8,088	17,479
Total reserves minus gold	US$m	31,284	27,028	22,649	26,257	26,853
Foreign exchange	US$m	28,292	24,384	20,008	23,520	23,142
Deposit rate	%	4.50	4.50	4.50	4.56	4.50
Lending rate	%	10.22	10.00	8.90	7.89	8.12
Exchange rate	Ff per US$	5.64	5.29	5.66	5.55	4.99

Defence and foreign policy

The integration of France with the rest of Europe continues with both the moves towards full EMU and the greater participation within NATO and involvement in Bosnia-Herzegovina. France has long defended its nuclear capability, the *force de frappe*, and although there is still no question of placing it formally under NATO control there is now a move towards more discussion over nuclear matters. Furthermore, France now wishes to participate in NATO meetings, probably as a result of its successful involvement in the Yugoslav conflict. Other substantial changes are due within defence policy and the military, with less reliance being placed on nuclear forces, the end of conscription and the rationalisation of the army. These changes should save around Ff100 billion over the five year period ending in 2001 and should secure a highly mobile and professional force equipped for service almost anywhere in the world.

Economic reform

Chirac has progressively withdrawn the vague promises made in the election campaign, causing some disillusion and friction in the country. The most exacting changes that need to be made are in the social security and taxation system; Juppé announced just after the formation of the new government that the priorities included the reduction of welfare expenditure. He pointed especially to the need to reform social security and taxation and also of urban revitalisation.

The movement towards EMU requires that the general government deficit be reduced to 3 per cent of GDP by 1997. Despite the doubt of Chirac's previous commitment towards EMU, he has recently emphasised this as a priority citing the main factor as the stability resulting from a single currency. It can be expected therefore that the government will make vigorous efforts towards this goal with the overall deficit reduced to the 3 per cent demanded by Maastricht. Interestingly in the light of previous commitments towards employment creation, Chirac now considers that large deficits are associated with high unemployment and thus any meaningful attack on this will have to wait until the deficit is reduced.

Social security reforms

One key aspect of this is the reform of the *Union nationale pour l'emploi dans l'industrie et le commerce* (Unedic) by Juppé – and it is this which caused much of the unrest in November 1995. The French system is now 50 years old and its administration needs to be reformed. The responsibility for its financing and management rests not with the state, but with employers and the trade unions; thus, control is largely out of the hands of the assembly. Juppé wishes to bring the financing of the system under the control of the assembly, so that decisions regarding income and expenditure will be made within the general government budget. This is necessary as the cumulative debt which the system has built up has periodically needed to be written off and action is now needed to ensure that this situation does not arise again.

The deficit for 1995 is estimated at Ff61 billion and while the original objective had been to reduce this to zero by 1997 Juppé now envisages a deficit of Ff17 billion in 1996 (down from the original Ff30 billion) and a surplus the following year. This debt is be repaid by means of a special levy, the social debt repayment tax (*Remboursement de la Dette Sociale [RDS]*), at 0.5 per cent on all incomes including pensions and unemployment benefit. This is estimated to be enough to repay the cumulative debt of Ff250 billion generated since 1992. Indications so far in 1996 though are that the deficit for the year will still be high and exceeding Ff40 billion.

Other measures include the reform of health care, the most expensive element of the whole welfare system. Contributions made by certain sections of the population (the retired, for example) who have previously received a lower rate are to face an increase in their health care insurance from 1.4 per cent to 3.8 per cent of income over the next two years. Added to this must be the general effort to reduce costs of both hospital and ambulatory care where the rise in expenditure will be contained within a 2.1 per cent target. Restrictions in drug costs will also be tackled by relying more on generic medicines.

Privatisation

The privatisation programme, originally started by the Balladur government, did not fare well in 1995 with only three sales taking place. When the Juppé government was formed the original privatisation receipt estimates, as reported last year, were downgraded to Ff47 billion – in itself an optimistic figure. In the event, total receipts for 1995 only amounted to Ff20 billion. This is, approximately, the sum required to finance the debt of those firms still remaining in the state sector; hence the government's debt has been reduced by little or, indeed, nothing since the inauguration of last year's programme.

The overall targets for 1995 and 1996 still point to the fact that Ff62 billion can be raised, but for this to happen both Assurances Générales de France (AGF) and the 51 per cent stake in Renault must be sold, raising perhaps Ff25-30 billion. This would be a good start although further sales need to take place if the targets are to be met.

Unfortunately for the government, those firms which have been transferred into the private sector have not seen their share values hold up well, especially the aluminium group, Pechiney, which was the third sale of 1995. This sale netted a mere Ff4.3 billion and the whole offer was only taken up because of over-subscription by private investors. Institutional investors were considerably more taciturn in their enthusiasm, largely because a number of stock-brokers apprised their clients that the offer price of Fr187 per share was not justified. Trading of the shares at the end of the first day fell by 6 per cent. It would seem therefore that any further sales will be received with a lack of enthusiasm – and this the government will have to address.

Unrest affects growth

The 1996 edition of the *Europe Review* reported that the French economy was in the process of slow recovery from recession, which would have helped with the conditions for EMU entry. Figures now available, however, indicate that the economy has stagnated for the final three quarters of 1995, with increases on previous periods showing growth rates of 0.1 per cent, 0.1 per cent and -0.4 per cent successively until the end of the year – worse than government projections. The fall in the fourth quarter of 1995 is generally considered to be due to the effect of the widespread strike action in November and December of the year, where both foreign trade and consumer demand fell.

Overall growth in 1995 amounted to 2.2 per cent – somewhat below the estimate of 2.9 per cent. In 1996 there has been some recovery in consumer demand which fell in the final quarter of 1995 by 0.2 per cent. Manufactured items increased by 4.9 per cent in the first quarter of 1996 compared with a drop of 1.8 per cent in the previous one, and retail sales similarly increased by 4.6 per cent over the earlier drop of 5.4 per cent. The most substantial change has been in the sale of new cars, which increased by 26.2 per cent. This is due to several factors, including the lagging effects of the reintroduction of the *prime à la casse*. This subsidy encourages the sale of new and therefore, presumably, more efficient and environmentally friendly cars by means of a special subsidy. Under the previous system, which supposedly ceased in 1995, the effective discount has been increased for larger cars from Fr5,000 to Fr7,000 and the applicable age of the traded vehicle reduced from 10 to 8 years.

Unemployment trends

In June 1995 Juppé announced a series of measures aimed at creating 700,000 jobs which appear to have had some, occasionally perverse, effects. This target was at the time regarded as being on the optimistic side and such caution has now been justified, as unemployment has in fact steadily risen from a trough of 11.4 per cent in August 1995 to 11.8 per cent in February 1996. The components which together make up the total figure are also interesting. The employment creation measures of June 1995 were targeted at both youth and long-term unemployment and it appears that at least among the former category there has been some effect, with a drop of 0.3 per cent in February 1996 from 24.2 per cent in December 1995. Disquietingly, however, the number of people unemployed aged over 50 rose from 8.3 per cent to 8.7 per cent over the same period.

There is some evidence that firms have been shedding older, more expensive workers in favour of younger workers, who are subsidised and hence cheaper. Furthermore, it appears that a considerable number of firms which were to expand anyway have now been able to do this 'on the cheap' using the subsidies provided by the taxpayer. For those remaining in work, 1995 has seen slight increases in real wages of approximately 0.5 per cent over the year. In 1996 the indications are that employers are willing to give some 2-3 per cent in money wage rises, partly to offset the new RDS levy.

These rises are however in the private sector. Public sector pay is now much

COUNTRY PROFILE — FRANCE

Historical profile

1939–45 Despite victory in the First World War, France had barely recovered before Hitler's invasion of Poland led to its entry, with Britain, into the Second World War. Within months an armistice followed the German invasion. 'Free France' resistance movement led by General Charles de Gaulle.
1944–46 Following the Liberation of Paris, government led by de Gaulle, who then retired from public life.
1946 Referendum established the Fourth Republic. Until 1958 a succession of 26 different governments, due largely to discontent over high prices and taxes.
1946–54 War in Indonesia leading to independence of Laos, Cambodia and Vietnam.
1958 De Gaulle returned to power with a right wing government and brought in a new constitution instituting the Fifth Republic, allowing for powerful presidency reinforced by direct appeals to the electorate in referendums.
1958–62 Bitterly contested Algerian War in which de Gaulle suppressed a revolt of French army officers and granted Algerian independence.
1961 Founder member of EU. Opposition to Britain's entry.
1966 France withdrew from integrated military structure of NATO though remaining a member of the alliance.
1968 Discontent with low wages, lack of social reform, policies on education, and information led to revolt by students and workers. General strike settled by generous wage rises; student revolt collapsed.
1969 De Gaulle resigned on rejection by referendum of his programme for strengthening the regional government. Succeeded by Georges Pompidou until 1974; by Valéry Giscard d'Estaing until 1981.
1981 François Mitterrand became president on Giscard's electoral defeat, governing with the first left wing cabinet for 23 years.
1986 New system of proportional representation in general election led to unprecedented situation of Socialist president (Mitterrand) 'cohabiting' with right-wing cabinet.
1995 Jacques Chirac succeeded François Mitterrand as president.
1996 Death of François Mitterrand.

Political system

Republic with bicameral parliament consisting of the Senate (upper house) (321 members one-third of its seats being renewed every three years in indirect elections) and the National Assembly (lower house) (577 members including 17 overseas representatives elected for five years on a constituency by constituency basis). System of government based on the Constitution of the Fifth Republic. The president, elected every seven years, appoints the prime minister and other members of the government. Since 1982 much administrative and financial power traditionally held by the state has been devolved to the 22 regions and 96 departments of metropolitan France. Next National Assembly election by March 1998. Next presidential election by April 2002.

Political parties

Coalition comprising neo-gaullist Rassemblement pour la République (Rally for the Republic) (RPR); centre-right Union pour la Démocratie Française (Union for French Democracy) (UDF). Other major parties: Parti Socialiste (Socialist Party) (PS); Parti Communiste Français (Communist Party of France (PCF).

Main cities/towns

Paris (population 9.5m in 1994), Marseille, Nice, Bordeaux, Dijon, Lyon (1.3m), Nantes, Rouen, Saint-Etienne (450,000), Toulouse, Strasbourg, Le Havre, Lille, Grenoble (400,000), Toulon, Valenciennes, Lens, Nancy, Tours, Clermont-Ferrand.

Media

Press: Large number of daily, weekly and monthly newspapers and magazines. Some regional newspapers have a larger readership than national titles. Press information available from Agence France Presse and various directories such as L'Annuaire de la Presse and Tarif Media.
Dailies: The top daily newspapers are *Ouest-France, Le Progrès, Le Parisien, Figaro, Centre Franc, Sud Ouest, Voix du Nord, L'Equipe* and *Le Monde*.
Weeklies: Progrès Dimanche, Sud-Ouest Dimanche and Journal du Dimanche.
Business: Large number covering all aspects of business including *Les Echos* (daily), *La Tribune de l'Expansion* (daily), *L'Express* (weekly), *La Vie Française* (weekly), *Le Nouvel Economiste* (weekly), *Capital* (monthly), and *L'Expansion* (bi-monthly).
Broadcasting: All French broadcasting overseen by independent regulatory commission, the CSA. Actual broadcasting done by Télédiffusion de France.
Radio: Almost 58m receivers in use.

restricted, with government employees subjected to a pay-freeze which could spark further unrest, although this group's secure annual incremental increases within agreed pay-scales. Much, however, of these rises could well be eaten up with inflation which has been steadily rising since the 1.6 per cent year-on-year change of the second quarter of 1995 to 2.1 per cent for the first quarter of 1996. Figures for March 1996 show an even greater increase of 2.3 per cent.

Foreign Trade

The strikes of winter 1995 have had their effect on trade, with both imports and exports falling in the final quarter by 2.5 per cent and 0.2 per cent respectively, although exports of vehicles and food products registered increases over the previous quarter. This reduction in imports coupled with only a smaller decrease in exports has contributed to a record trade surplus of Ff8.54 billion – considerably higher than the Ff6.81 billion of the previous year.

In terms of regional breakdowns, what is noteworthy is the decreasing importance of the EU market (excluding Germany) for exports. The rate of growth has fallen consistently since the third quarter of 1994, so that the rest of the EU accounted for 63.4 per cent of exports in 1995. Exporters have seemingly discovered the attractions of both Asia and eastern Europe.

Trade with Asia has been targeted recently, with Chirac indicating that he would like to see a three-fold increase in French exports. Although, in overall terms, exports to the region only accounted for 6.2 per cent in 1995, there has been a phenomenal and progressive year-on-year increase measured from the 12.8 per cent in 1993 to 28.5 per cent two years later. Eastern Europe also registered increases in exports in 1995 of 23 per cent, compared with the decline of 0.5 per cent in 1993 and the slight increase of 0.6 per cent in 1994 – although the region still only accounts for a low figure in 1995 – 2.6 per cent of the total.

Banking

The troubled banking giant, Crédit Lyonnais, has recovered slightly from its tribulations to make a slight profit of Ff13 million in 1995. The total losses which the bank sustained amounted to Ff21 billion between the years of 1992 and 1994. The government came to the bank's rescue in a deal which the European Commission was originally averse to, yet subsequently accepted. It appears that further action will be required if the bank is to be salvaged. The attention, though, on Crédit Lyonnais, cloaks wider problems within the banking sector, which has seen the aggregate income of every bank decline for the first time since 1945. The worst performer was Banque Paribas which suffered losses of Ff4 billion, although others did badly too including Banque Nationale de Paris (BNP) and Société Générale. Standard and Poor at the end of 1995 have accordingly re-rated the top 15 banks from the AA grade they achieved in 1991 to A. Their conclusion is that France is over-banked and restructuring is needed if bankruptcy is to be avoided, although other measures including rigidity in the labour market and under-pricing of services need also to be addressed.

Outlook

The months ahead will be testing times for France as growth will remain dilatory, unemployment and urban dereliction rise and the problems of educational overcrowding and drop-out rates increase. In respect of foreign policy, nuclear testing has now ceased and the test sites in the south Pacific have closed – thus largely removing the controversy and both the international and domestic embarrassment from this area. Chirac appears to be recovering from his period of unpopularity, in no small measure due to his response to Mitterrand's death, and this new covenant with the population may well help the country's progress towards renewal and development.

COUNTRY PROFILE — FRANCE

Media (contd): Programmes produced by state-owned Radio France and local private stations. Commercial stations operating outside France, such as Radio Luxembourg, Radio Monte Carlo, Sud Radio and Europe No 1, also received.
Television: About 25m receivers in use. There are 6 channels. Antenne 2 and FR3 will remain state-owned, while Télévision Française 1, Canal Plus, La Cinq and M6 are privately owned. Canal Plus is a pay TV channel and has more than 1m subscribers. The state-owned channels accept advertising, but only between programmes. Cable TV has 1.1m households subscribing, but satellite dish ownership is only approximately 100,000.
Advertising: Numerous advertising agencies operating throughout the country. Television advertising is strictly controlled, by Régie Française de Publicité, and is costly. Limited advertising on radio. All other media widely used – newspapers and magazines dominate. Key categories include food, leisure, entertainment, services, retailing, furniture and transport.

Domestic economy

Mixed economy with large agricultural, industrial and service sectors. High level of growth during 1970s halted by onset of world recession. Current economic policy essentially deflationary, aimed at reducing external debt, trade deficit and public expenditure. Major industrial restructuring and modernisation programme complete, with emphasis on production for the home market and expansion of new export capacity. Privatisation of nationalised companies got under way in 1987 but was slowed down by international stock market crisis in October 1987. The Socialist government which took power in early 1988, promised neither to continue privatisation nor to re-nationalise. Decree allowing private shareholders to take up to 49 per cent of public companies under certain conditions. France then went into recession in 1991. The government's ambitious privatisation programme got under way on 20 September 1993. In 1996 the government is attempting to straighten out the country's public finances by reforming France's welfare system, partially privatising telecommunications and trimming the defence industry. Over 17,000 French businesses failed in the second quarter of 1996, more than in any quarter since 1993.

Employment

Minimum wages are revised periodically to keep pace with inflation, while the government may decide on an extra boost. A five-year plan to create jobs was unveiled by the government in August 1993. According to the employment survey of March 1994, there was a working population of 25,136,598, including 13,898,272 men and 11,238,326 women. Unemployment rate 11.9 per cent in June 1996.

External trade

Main trading partners are Argentina, USA, Austria, Brazil, Canada, South Korea, Egypt, Finland, Ghana, Japan, Uruguay, Philipppines, Poland and Singapore. Manufacturing is the mainstay of France's impressive trade performance.
Exports: Exports totalled US$285.2bn in 1995. Main destinations: Germany (17.7% of 1995 total), Italy (9.6%), UK (9.3%), Belgium/Luxembourg (8.5%), Spain (7.3%), USA (5.9%). Major exports include metals, chemicals, industrial equipment, consumer goods and agricultural products.
Imports: Imports totalled US$273.1bn in 1995. Main sources: Germany (18.5% of 1995 total), Italy (10%), Belgium/Luxembourg (9%), UK (8%), USA (7.8%), Spain (6.5%). Principal imports are oil, machinery and equipment, chemicals, iron and steel and foodstuffs.

Agriculture

Major European food producer, with self-sufficiency in dairy produce, and substantial exporter of livestock produce, wine, fruit and vegetables, contributing 4.6 per cent to GDP and employing 6.1 per cent of the labour force. Since 1993 despite steady increase in production and exports, sector has been developing in an unbalanced manner owing to higher feed prices and price distortion under EU's Common Agricultural Policy. Co-operatives account for between 30–50 per cent of agricultural output. Forestry is France's richest natural resource with an annual revenue of about Ff8bn.

Industry

Broad industrial base incorporating large, capital-intensive, state-owned sector and small and medium-sized manufacturing enterprises, contributing about 28 per cent to GDP in 1994 and employing about 27 per cent of the labour force. Industrial policy aimed at reconquest of the domestic market, promotion of 'new technology' sector and internationalisation of state-owned companies. Leading sectors

COUNTRY PROFILE

Industry (contd): include agri-foodstuffs, telecommunications, aerospace, motor industry, metallurgy, chemicals, parachemicals and pharmaceuticals, textiles and clothing. As at June 1996, the manufacturing sector has produced a surplus of Ff10bn or more in each of the last seven quarters, and is the backbone of France's trade surplus success. Among companies with annual sales of above Ff100m, the sectors which registered the worst deterioration in the first half of 1996 were building and public works (up 16 per cent from the first six months of 1995), and industry.

Mining

Significant producer of iron ore, bauxite, potash and coal. Société Le Nickel extracts in New Caledonia, and is world's third largest nickel producer. Also seventh largest uranium producer in the world. In effort to reduce dependence on imported minerals, exploration for lead, zinc, barium and tungsten has been stepped up. Mining sector contributed 1 per cent to GDP in 1994 and employed 0.8 per cent of the workforce.

Hydrocarbons

Coal reserves 139m tonnes (end-1995). Coal production 5.1m tonnes oil equivalent (1995), down 7.3 per cent on 1994 output.

Energy

In the mid-1970s, France faced a problem in power generation. Domestic coal supplies were limited, the best hydroelectricity sites had already been exploited, and there were no domestic gas fields. Some 70 per cent of French electricity is generated by nuclear power stations, one of the highest rates in the world. France exports electricity as the industry has a surplus.

Main companies

Renault, Peugeot, Elf Aquitaine, EDF, CGE, Total CFP, Générale des Eaux, France Télécom, Usinor-Sacilor, Carrefour

Stock exchange

Trading in wheat futures was begun by the *Matif,* the French financial futures market, in the *Bourse de Commerce* in July 1996. Under French law, such trades only became legal in June 1996 when the French parliament approved the lifting of the ban which dated from 1936.

Membership of international organisations

Agency for Cultural & Technical Co-operation, ADB, AG (observer), BDEAC, BIS, BOAD, CERN, Commission for Navigation of the Rhine, Council of Europe, CSCE, DAC, EEA, ESA, EU and its institutions, EIB, EMA, EMS, ESA, ESCAP, European Space Agency, FAO, Francophone, FZ, G-5, G-7, IADB, IAEA, IATP, ICAC, ICAO, ICC, ICES, ICO, IDA, IEA, IFC, IFAD, IHO, ILO, IMO, IMF, INTELSAT, Intergovernmental Maritime Consultative Organisation, International Grain Council, Interpol, International Lead & Zinc Study Group, IOC, IPU, IRC, ISO, ITC, ITU, MIGA, NACC, NATO, NEA, OECD, SPC, UN, UNESCO, UNIDO, UN Security Council (permanent member), UPU, WEU, WHO, WFTU, WIPO, WMO, World Bank, WSG, WTO.

BUSINESS GUIDE

Time

GMT + 1 hr (GMT + 2 hrs from late Mar to late Sep).

Climate

Temperate throughout most of the country. Mediterranean in the south-east. Jul and Aug are the hottest (av. 21-28 degrees C); Jan and Feb are coldest (av. 2-12 degrees C). Driest month is Mar, wettest Aug.

Entry requirements

Visa: Visa not required for nationals of USA, Canada, Japan, South Korea, Singapore, New Zealand, EU and most west European countries for stays up to three months.
Health: Vaccination certificates not usually required. EU nationals covered for medical treatment.
Currency: No limit or amount of French or foreign currency that may be taken in.
Customs: Personal effects duty-free. EU allowances.

Air access

National airline: Air France.
Main international airport: Orly (PAR-ORY), 14 km south of Paris, Charles-de-Gaulle (PAR-CDG), 23 km north-east of Paris.
International airports: Bordeaux (BOD), 12 km from city, Lille (LIL), 15 km from city, Lyon (LYS), 24 km east of Lyon, Marseille (MRS), 24 km north of city, Nice (NCE), 6 km west of Nice, Toulouse (TLS), 10 km from city, Biarritz (BIQ), Nantes (NTE), Perpignan (PGF) and Strasbourg (SXB).

Surface access

Good rail, road and sea connections with all surrounding countries.
Main ports: Marseille (Europe's third largest port), Boulogne, Nice, Calais, Dieppe, Dunkirk, Cherbourg, Le Havre, Rouen.

Hotels

Classified into de luxe and one- to four-star. Reservations (either direct or through centralised booking offices) should be made in advance during holiday season. Single rooms are rare and rates are usually quoted for a double room. All major credit cards accepted. Tip usually 12-15 per cent of bill if no service charge added.

Restaurants

Very wide variety and numerous. It is advisable to book in advance, particularly for Sunday lunch. Tip 12-15 per cent if no service charge included.

Currency

The French franc floats in relation to all other currencies, but is stabilised within the European Monetary System against other EMS currencies.

Foreign exchange information

Account restrictions: No restrictions on non-resident accounts held by foreign companies.
Trade policy: Few restrictions on imports from WTO, OECD and EU member countries. Products from non-member countries may not be imported unless they are a general exception, or import licences or prior authorisation are obtained.

Car hire

All major international hire companies have offices in Paris and other main towns. Drive on the right; *priorité à droite* applies in some built-up areas – cars coming out of side turning on the right have priority. Speed limits: 130 kph on toll motorways, 110 kph on dual carriageways, 90 kph on other roads and 60 kph in towns. Note that these limits are reduced on wet roads. Wearing of seat belts compulsory in front seats.

City transport

Taxis: Only available from ranks (*stations de taxi*). Tipping usually 10-15 per cent.
Buses: In Paris same tickets may be used on buses and métro; a *carnet* of 10 tickets is cheaper. Extensive flat fare service.
Metro: Comprehensive network in Paris and Lyon. Flat fare. N.B. Same tickets may be used on both buses and metro. Lille has two lines; Toulouse has one line 10 km long linking the university and the south-west of the city with the centre and railway station.

National transport

Air: Major cities are linked by Air France and Air Inter. Frequent internal air services to many regional airports are operated by Air Inter the national domestic airline, Air-Alpes, Air Alsace, Air Vendée, Air Littoral, Rousseau Aviation and Touraine Air Transport. Certain services operate only during summer.
Road: Densest road network in the world, longest in the EU. 806,000 km of roads, including 7,100 km of motorways, most of which are toll roads (*autoroutes à péage).*
Buses: Good local bus services. Also some long-distance coach services operated by Société Nationale des Chemins de Fer Français (SNCF).
Rail: SNCF operates nationwide network to over 6,000 destinations. 33,769 km of track of which one-third electrified. There is a TGV high-speed line linking Paris to western France and a TGV link to south-west. France holds the world speed record (515 km/h) with the high-speed TGV train which operates on a special 1,860 km track (4,400 km planned for 2015). Annual capacity 58bn passengers/km (second in world) and 45.9bn tonnes of freight/km (third in world). SNCF is the most heavily indebted and subsidised (Ff38bn a year) company in France.
Water: Extensive inland navigable waterways.

Public holidays

Fixed dates: 1 Jan (New Year's Day), 1 May (Labour Day), 8 May (Victory Day), 14 July (National Day), 15 August (Assumption), 1 Nov (All Saints' Day), 11 Nov (Armistice Day) and 25 Dec (Christmas Day).
Variable dates: Easter Monday, Ascension Day, Whit Monday.

Working hours

Business: (Mon–Fr) 0900–1200 and 1400–1800.
Government: (Mon–Fri) 0830–1800 (staggered nine-hour day with two-hour lunch break).
Banking: (Mon–Fri) 0900–1200 and 1400–1600. Some banks close on Mondays and all close early on the day before a bank holiday.
Shops: (Mon–Sat) variable hours.

Social customs

Handshaking is usual on meeting or parting with personal acquaintances. Many people take their holidays in August.

Business language and interpreting/translation

Business managers generally prefer to speak French. Translation expensive. Details available from chamber of commerce and consular offices.

Telecommunications

Telephone and telefax: New numbering system from 18 October 1996. Subscribers now have a nine figure number, and there are only two regions – Paris and the provinces. Public telephones are operated by coins or telephone card. Dialling code for France: IDD access code +331 for Paris City and Greater Paris. For the rest of the country: IDD access code +33 followed by nine-digit number. For IDD access from France dial 00.
Telex: Facilities available in central post offices of most major towns, and two public telex offices in Paris. Country code 42F.

Postal service

Letters can be sent for collection c/o Poste Restante, Poste Centrale in the town to be visited.

BUSINESS GUIDE

FRANCE

Banking

System divided into commercial banks and finance companies, co-operative institutions and specialised credit institutions. Ceilings on increases in bank credit have been abolished and the Bank of France regulates the money market only by changing interest rates and through open-market operations. Bank reforms approved in June 1993 allow the Bank of France to become an independent central bank in keeping with the terms of the Maastricht treaty. *Other banks:* See 'Business Directory, Banking'.

Trade fairs

Over 50 major international exhibitions held every year, mostly in Paris. Information on exhibitions and other promotional events from the Conference and Incentive Department of the French National Tourist Office.
Contract and Hotel Furniture Show, Feb; International Agricultural Machinery Exhibition, Paris, Mar; Second Euro-Arab Book Fair, Paris, May.

Electricity supply

220 V AC.

Representation in capital

Afghanistan, Albania, Algeria, Angola, Argentina, Australia, Austria, Bahrain, Bangladesh, Belgium, Benin, Bolivia, Brazil, Bulgaria, Burkina Faso, Burundi, Cameroon, Canada, Central African Republic, Chad, Chile, China, Colombia, Comoros, Congo, Costa Rica, Côte d'Ivoire, Cuba, Cyprus, Denmark, Dijoubti, Dominican Republic, Ecuador, Egypt, El Salvador, Equatorial Guinea, Ethiopia, Finland, Gabon, Germany, Ghana, Greece, Guatemala, Guinea, Haiti, The Holy See, Honduras, Hungary, Iceland, India, Indonesia, Iran, Ireland, Italy, Japan, Jordan, Kenya, Republic of Korea, Kuwait, Laos, Lebanon, Liberia, Libya, Luxembourg, Madagascar, Malaysia, Mali, Malta, Mauritania, Mauritius, Mexico, Monaco, Mongolia, Morocco, Mozambique, Myanmar, Nepal, Netherlands, New Zealand, Nicaragua, Niger, Nigeria, Norway, Oman, Pakistan, Panama, Paraguay, Peru, Philippines, Poland, Portugal, Qatar, Romania, Russia, Rwanda, San Marino, Saudi Arabia, Senegal, Seychelles, Singapore, Somalia, South Africa, Spain, Sri Lanka, Sudan, Sweden, Switzerland, Syria, Tanzania, Thailand, Togo, Tunisia, Turkey, Uganda, United Arab Emirates, UK, Uruguay, USA, Venezuela, Vietnam, Republic of Yemen, Zaïre, Zambia, Zimbabwe.

BUSINESS DIRECTORY

Hotels

Paris (area code 1)
Ambassador Concorde, 16 Boulevard Haussmann (tel: 4246-9263; fax: 4022-0874).

Baudin (near Gare du Nord), 10 Rue Pierre Semand (tel: 4281-3711).

Burgundy, 8 Rue Duphot (tel: 4260-3412; fax: 4703-9520).

Campaville Gare du Nord, 26 Rue de l'Aqueduc (tel: 4239-2626).

Elysées Bassano, 24 Rue de Bassano (tel: 4720-4903).

Excelsior Opéra (near opera), 5 Rue Lafayette (tel: 4874-9930; fax: 4874-2193).

Hilton, 18 Avenue de Suffren (tel: 4273-9200; fax: 4783-6266).

Holiday Inn, 10 Place de la République (tel: 4355-4434; fax: 4700-3234).

Inter-Continental, 3 Rue de Castiglione (tel: 4260-3780; fax: 4261-1403).

Keppler (near Arc de Triomphe), 12 Rue Keppler (tel: 4720-6505; fax: 4723-0229).

L'Horset Astor, 11 Rue d'Astorg (tel: 4266-5656; fax: 4265-1837).

La Pérouse, 40 Rue la Pérouse (tel: 4500-8347).

Le Bristol République, 112 Faubourg St Honoré (tel: 4266-9145; fax: 4266-6868).

Le Colbert (near Notre Dame), 7 Rue de l'Hôtel Colbert (tel: 4325-8565; fax: 4325-8019).

Le Grand Inter-Continental, 2 rue Scribe (tel: 4268-1213; fax: 4007-3232).

London Palace, 32 Boulevard des Italiens (tel: 4824-5464; fax: 4800-0883).

Mercure Paris Etoile, 27 Avenue des Ternes (tel: 4766-4918; fax: 4763-7791).

Meridién Paris Etoile, 81 Boulevard Gouvion St Cyr (tel: 4758-1230; fax: 4757-6070).

Ritz, 15 Place Vendôme (tel: 4260-3830; fax: 4286-0091).

Saxe Résidence, 9 Villa de Saxe (tel: 4783-9828; fax: 4782-8547).

Car hire

Paris
Avis: Charles de Gaulle Airport (tel: 4862-3434).

Budget: (tel: 4686-6565; fax: 4686-2217).

Hertz: (tel: 3938-3838; fax: 4788-8357).

Chambers of commerce

Assemblées des Chambres Francaises de Commerce et d'Industrie (ACFCI) (Chambers of Commerce and Industry), 45 avenue d'léna, 75116 Paris (tel:4069-3700; fax: 4720-6128).

Assemblée Permanente des Chambres d'Agriculture (APCA) (Chambers of Agriculture), 9 avenue George-V, 75008 Paris (tel: 4723-5540; fax: 4723-8497).

Chambre de Commerce et d'Industrie de Bordeaux, 12 Place de la Bourse, 33076 Bordeaux.

Chambre de Commerce et d'Industrie de Boulogne, Quai Gambetta, 62204 Boulogne-sur-Mer.

Chambre de Commerce et d'Industrie de Grenoble, 6 Boulevard Gambetta, 38028 Grenoble.

Chambre de Commerce et d'Industrie de Lyon, Palais du Commerce, 20 Rue de la Bourse, 69289 Lyon.

Chambre de Commerce et d'Industrie de Marseille, Palais de la Bourse, 13222 Marseille.

Chambre de Commerce et d'Industrie de Nice, 20 Boulevard Carabaçel 06007 Nice.

Chambre de Commerce et d'Industrie d'Orléans et du Loiret, 23 Place du Martroi, 45044 Orléans.

Chambre de Commerce et d'Industrie Paris, 27 Avenue Friedland, 75008 Paris (tel: 4289-7000; fax: 4289-7868).

Chambre de Commerce et d'Industrie de Rouen, 34 Rue Bouquet, 76000 Rouen (tel: 3598-4728).

Chambre de Commerce et d'Industrie de Toulouse, 2 Rue d'Alsace-Lorraine, 31002 Toulouse.

International Chamber of Commerce, 38 Cours Albert-1er, Paris (tel: 4261-8597).

Banking

Banque de France (central bank), 39 rue Croix des Petits Champs, 75001 Paris (tel: 4292-4292 fax: 4292-3911).

Association Française de Banques, 18 Rue la Fayette, 75009 Paris (tel: 4246-9259).

Banque Française du Commerce Extérieur (BFCE), 21 boulevard Haussmann, 75009 Paris (tel: 4800-4800; fax: 4800-3970).

Banque Indosuez, 96 boulevard Haussmann, 75008 Paris (tel: 4420-2020; fax: 4420-1522).

Banque Nationale de Paris SA, 16 boulevard des Italiens, 75009 Paris (tel: 4014-4546; fax: 4014-5599).

Banque Paribas, 3 rue d'Antin, 75078 Paris Cedex 02 (tel: 4298-1234; fax: 4298-0433).

Caisse Centrale des banques populaires, 10-12 avenue Winston Churchill, 94677 Charenton Le Pont Cedex (tel: 4039-0000; fax: 4039-3940).

Caisse d'Epargne, 19 rue du Louvre, 75001 Paris (tel: 4041-3031; fax: 4233-4518).

Compagnie Bancaire, 5 avenue Kléber, 75798 Paris Cedex 16 (tel: 4525-2525; fax: 4501-7805).

Compagnie Financière de Crédit Industriel et Commercial (CIC Group), Rue de la Victoire 66, 75009 Paris (tel: 4280-8080).

Crédit Agricole, Boulevard Pasteur 91-93, 75015 Paris (tel: 4323-5202).

Crédit Commercial de France (CCF), 103 avenue des Champs-Elysées, 75008 Paris (tel: 4070-7040; fax: 4070-7353).

Crédit Foncier de France, SA, 19 rue des Capucines, 75001 Paris (tel: 4244-8000; fax: 4244-7822).

Crédit local de France, 7-11 quai André Citroen, 75015 Paris (tel: 4392-7777; fax: 4592-7672).

Crédit Lyonnais SA, Boulevard des Italiens 19, 75002 Paris (tel: 4295-7000).

Crédit Mutuel, 88 rue Cardinet, 75017 Paris (tel: 4401-1010; fax: 4401-1227).

Société Générale, Boulevard Haussmann 29, 75009 Paris (tel: 4298-2000).

BUSINESS DIRECTORY

Banking (contd):
Union Europeenne de CIC (CIC Group), 4 rue Gaillon, 75107 Paris Cedex 02 (tel: 4266-7000; fax: 4266-7878).

Principal newspapers

Agence Economique et Financiére (AGEFI) (economy and the stock exchange), 48 rue Notre-Dame-des-Victoires, 75002 Paris (tel: 4488-4646, 4286-1200; fax: 4488-4712, 4015-9962).

Aujourd'hui, 25 avenue Michelet, 93408 Saint-Ouen Cedex (tel: 4010-3030; fax: 4012-9090).

France Soir, 37 rue du Louvre, 75081 Paris Cedex 02 (tel: 4482-8700; fax: 4482-8845).

Info-Matin, 1 place Hubert-Beuve-Méry, 94851 Ivry Cedex (tel: 4960-3640; fax: 4658-5849).

International Herald Tribune (English), 181 Ave Charles de Gaulle, 92521 Neuilly (tel: 4143-9300, fax: 4143-9212).

Investir, 16 rue de la Banque, 75002 Paris (tel: 4296-1451; fax: 4020-0671).

La Croix - L'Evénement, 3-5 rue Bayard, 75393 Paris Cedex 08 (tel: 4435-6060; fax: 4435-6001, 4435-6718).

La Tribune Desfossés (economy and finance), 42-46 rue Notre-Dame-des-Victoires, 75080 Paris Cedex 02 (tel: 4482-1616, 4013-1313; fax: 4482-1716, 4013-1329).

Le Figaro, 37 rue du Louvre, 75002 Paris (tel: 4221-6200; fax: 4221-6405, 4075-2002).

Le Journal Officiel de la République Francaise, 26 rue Desaix, 75727 Paris Cedex 15 (tel: 4058-7500; fax: 4058-7780).

Le Monde, 15 rue Falguiére, 75501 Paris Cedex 15 (tel: 4065-2525; fax: 4065-2599).

Le Parisien Libéré, 25 avenue Michelet, 93408 Saint-Ouen Cedex (tel: 4010-5353; fax: 4012-9090).

Le Quotidien de Paris, 3 rue de l'Atlas, 75019 Paris (tel: 4803-8787; fax: 4803-8796).

Les Echos (economy), 46 rue de la Boétie, 75381 Paris Cedex 08 (tel: 4953-6565; fax: 4561-4892, 4225-6514).

L'Humanité, 32 rue Jean-Jaurés, 93528 Saint-Denis Cedex (tel: 4922-7272; fax: 4922-7300).

Libération, 11 rue Béranger, 75154 Paris Cedex 03 (tel: 4276-1789; fax: 4272-9493).

Travel information

Air France, 45 rue de Paris, Roissy Charles de Gaulle, Paris 95747 (tel: 4156-7800; tx: 200-666).

Direction du Tourisme, 17 Rue de l'Ingénieur Robert Keller, 75740 Paris.

Other useful addresses

Agence France Presse (news agency), 11-15 Place de la Bourse, 75002 Paris (tel: 4041-4646; fax: 4041-4632).

ANIT (public information service), 8 Avenue de l'Opéra, 75001 Paris (tel: 4260-3738).

La Bourse de Paris (Stock Exchange), 39 rue Cambon, 75001 Paris (tel: 4927-7000; fax: 4289-7868).

Bureau international des Expositions (International Exhibition Bureau), 56 avenue Victor-Hugo, 75116 Paris (tel: 4500-3863; fax: 4500-9615).

Caisse Centrale de Co-opération Economique (CCCE), 233 Boulevard Saint-Germain, Paris (tel: 4550-3220).

Centre Française du Commerce Extérieur, 10 Avenue d'léna, 75116 Paris (tel: 4505-3000).

DATAR (government investment agency), 1 Avenue Charles Floquet, 75007 Paris (tel: 4065-1234).

Direction Générale des Impôt, Centre des Non-Résidents, 9 Rue d'Uzés, 75094 Paris.

Institut National de la Statistique et des Etudes Economiques (INSEE), 18 Boulevard Adolphe Pinard, 75675 Paris Cedex 14 (tel: 4117-5050; fax: 4117-6666).

Invest in France Network/DATAR, 1 Avenue Charles Floquet, 75343 Paris Cedex 07 (tel: 4065-1006; fax: 4065-1240).

Ministry of Agriculture, Fisheries and Food, 78 Rue de Varenne, 75700 Paris (tel: 4955-4955; fax: 4955-4039).

Ministry of Capital Works, Housing, Transport and Tourism, 246 bd. Saint-Germain, 75700 Paris (tel: 4081-2122; fax: 4081-3099).

Ministry of the Civil Service, Administrative Reform and Decentralisation, 72 rue de Varenne, 75700 Paris (tel: 4275-8000; fax: 4275-7242).

Ministry of Culture, 3 rue de Valois, 75001 Paris (tel: 4015-8000; fax: 4261-3577).

Ministry of Defence, 14 rue Saint-Dominique, 75700 Paris (tel: 4219-3011; fax: 4551-1428).

Ministry for the Economy and Finance, 139 rue de Bercy, 75572 Paris Cedex 12 (tel: 4004-0404; fax: 5318-9701).

Ministry of the Environment, 20 avenue de Segur, 75302 Paris 07 SP (tel: 4219-2021; fax: 4219-1120).

Ministry of Foreign Affairs, 37 quai d'Orsay, 75700 Paris (tel: 4317-5353; fax: 4551-6012).

Ministry of Industry the Post Office and Telecommunications, 101 Rue de Grenelle, 75700 Paris 9 (tel: 4319-3636; fax: 4319-3052).

Ministry of the Interior, Place Beauvau, 75800 Paris (tel: 4927-4927; fax: 4268-1524).

Ministry of Justice, 13 place Vendome, 75042 Paris (tel: 4477-6060; fax: 4477-6000).

Ministry of Labour and Social Affairs, 127 rue de Grenelle, 75700 Paris (tel: 4438-3838; fax: 4056-6710).

Ministry of National Education, Higher Education and Research, 110 rue de Grenelle, 75700 Paris (tel: 4955-1010; fax: 4955-2511).

Ministry for Relations with Parliament, 69 rue de Varenne, 75700 Paris (tel: 4275-8000; fax: 4081-7300).

Ministry of Small and Medium Sized Enterprises, Trade and Artisan Activities, 80 rue de Lille, 75700 Paris (tel: 4319-2424; fax: 4319-3767).

Ministry of Town and Country Planning, Urban Affairs and Integration, 35 rue Saint-Dominique, 75700 Paris (tel: 4275-8000; fax: 4275-7755).

Prime Minister's Office, 57 Rue de Varenne, 75700 Paris (tel: 4275-8000; fax: 4544-1572).

Service de la Répression des Fraudes et du Contrôle de la Qualité, 44 Boulevard de Grenelle, 75732 Paris.

Georgia

Marko Milivojevic

President Eduard Shevardnadze and his ruling Union of Georgian Citizens (UGC) government easily formally elected to power for the first time in elections held in November 1995. In August 1995 a failed assassination attempt against the life of Shevardnadze by persons unknown prompted a government crack-down on para-military forces and some political opponents of the Georgian president. Other than the weaknesses of a divided opposition, the main factor behind the government's electoral victory in November 1995 was an improving economy. The government's continued macro-economic stabilisation programme, with International Monetary Fund (IMF) assistance, has been generally successful to date. The long-delayed introduction of a new national currency, the Lari (L), finally took place in October 1995.

Politics

Repeatedly postponed by the anarchy in Georgia during most of the 1990s, the November 1995 presidential elections were decisively won by Shevardnadze, who received over 70 per cent of the popular vote. At the same time, the UGC won a plurality of the vote in new parliamentary elections.

In 1994, Shevardnadze's controversial and enforced rapprochement with the Russian-dominated Commonwealth of Independent States (CIS) had led to speculation that his political position might be weakened. Similar controversy arose in 1995 when Shevardnadze offered autonomy to Abkhazia, South Ossetia and other separatist regions, an offer that was furiously denounced by the opposition.

Endless bickering and the espousal of unrealistic policy positions among the opposition parties clearly aided Shevardnadze and the UGC. Even more significantly, a government crack-down against the opposition after August 1995 also strengthened the position of the President, particularly in relation to the unruly Mkhedrioni (horsemen) paramilitary forces led by Saba Ioseliani, a former ally of the Georgian President, but more recently a bitter and dangerous enemy. Widely blamed for the failed assassination attempt against Shevardnadze in August 1995, Ioseliani is no longer a serious political threat to the Georgian President. Shevardnadze's elimination of the Mkhedrioni, although politically helpful, has further weakened Georgia's military capabilities. This lessens the likelihood of any future moves against Abkhazia and South Ossetia.

New constitution

Despite the convincing victories of November 1995, Shevardnadze and the UGC government may prove to be less powerful then they seem. The main reason for this is the country's new democratic constitution. Finally promulgated in August 1995 after endless delays, this gives considerable powers to the Georgian parliament, a unicameral body known as the Republican Council (RC). Almost uniquely in the CIS, presidential power in Georgia is now subjected to major parliamentary constraints. The opposition parties also scored better in the recent parliamentary elections than in the poll for the presidency.

Among other things, this could make it more difficult for the government to pass contentious legislation and other measures through parliament in the future. Amending the constitution will also be very difficult, if not impossible during the current term of the RC. Before the November 1995 elections, Shevardnadze had argued for a bicameral RC, with an upper house representing the country's regions as part of a loose federation designed to break the political stalemate over the Abkhazian and South Ossetian problems. In the event, these radical political proposals were not incorporated into the August 1995 constitution. Instead, they were left over until after the November 1995 elections, which in any event did not take place in either Abkhazia or South Ossetia – regions that continue to maintain that they are independent from Georgia.

Domestic unrest

Two years after a Russian-enforced ceasefire in Abkhazia in May 1994, Georgia has experienced a peace of sorts, although it remains highly precarious and uncertain. The UN-mediated negotiations over the status of Abkhazia failed to make any progress in 1995, mainly because of strong Russian support for Abkhazian separatism in the Duma and elsewhere in Russia.

Any future resolution of the Abkhazian problem is now basically dependent on developments in Russia. However, present trends are not favourable for such a settlement. Other than the requirements of domestic Russian politics, the main factor in this context is the recent decision of the Azerbaijan International Oil Consortium (AIOC) to route only a part of future Azeri oil exports through Georgia and Russia. Strongly supported by the US and Turkey, which is expected to take most Azeri oil exports in the future, the October 1995 AIOC decision is a favourable development for Georgia, but may yet be aborted by Russia so as to leave all future Azeri oil exports from the region in Russian hands.

Any perceived procrastination on the Abkhazian problem is likely to destabilise Georgia. In addition, Russia has other options in Georgia, notably in South Ossetia. South Ossetia remains as adamant as Abkhazia in its separatist aspirations, refusing to accept any sort of autonomy or federal status in Georgia. President Shevardnadze may again have to use military means to reunify his divided country. The local pressures to do this are intense.

The dangers inherent in such a policy, however, are considerable. Defeated in Abkhazia in 1993, Georgia now lacks any credible military forces to retake its rebel provinces. Further, another round of civil war in Georgia would risk an open conflict with Russia, which retains substantial military forces in this former Soviet republic. Accepted under the terms of the September 1995 'stationing og military forces agreement', the Russian military presence severely limits what the Georgian government can realistically attempt in relation to both Abkhazia and South Ossetia.

Russia

Shevardnadze and the UGC government also face major difficulties in parliament over other contentious policy issues, notably those pertaining to economic reform. Although now divided into a United Georgia Communist party (UGCP) and a so-called Movement for Peace, the still-strong communist movement wields considerable influence, notably through the old communist aristocracy, of which Shevardnadze was once a prominent member. This local communist movement is well-connected in Russia.

Communist and trade union pressure on the government has already had marked results, particularly Shevardnadze's pre-election promise in September 1995 to increase wages by 50 per cent in 1996, although it remains unclear how this might be financed in practice. The UGCP in particular favours ever closer economic ties with Russia, notably in the form of proposed new customs and monetary unions in the CIS in 1996/97. Following the introduction of the Lari with IMF financial support in October 1995, the government opposes such proposals, but may find it difficult to resist for wider political and economic reasons in the future.

Following the signing of the AIOC oil pipeline agreement in October 1995, Russia may now decide to further tighten its grip over Georgia. Having effectively forced a reluctant Georgia into the CIS in 1993, Russia thereafter demanded and received other major concessions from the Georgian government, notably the permanent stationing of Russian troops and military bases locally. The September 1995 military agreements between Georgia and Russia were accompanied by a number of key economic agreements. The next step will almost certainly be greater Russian pressure on Georgia in the economic sphere, which remains heavily dependent on Russian trade and energy supplies in particular.

Georgia could thus be forced into the recently created Commonwealth of Sovereign States (SSR) in the CIS, where Armenia is already a member of this new grouping. Regionally, Georgia has also recently moved closer to Russia's only non-CIS ally in the region, Iran. Also involving Armenia, this system of alliances could well embroil Georgia in a wider anti-Azeri and anti-Turkish struggle in Trancaucasia. In 1995, however, Georgia managed to also move closer to Turkey, mainly because of the AIOC oil pipeline agreement.

USA and IMF

Largely ignored by the west during most of

KEY FACTS

Official title: Republic of Georgia

Head of state: President Eduard Shevardnadze (Citizens' Union) (won landslide victory in Nov 1995 presidential election)

Head of government: President Eduard Shevardnadze (Citizens' Union); the State Minister is Nicolai Lekishvili

Ruling party: Union of Georgian Citizens (UGC) (since Nov 1995 presidential and parliamentary elections)

Capital: Tbilisi

Official Languages: Georgian

Currency: Lari replaced Georgian Coupon (GC) 2 Oct 1995

Exchange rate: Lari 1.26 per US$ (Dec 1996)

Area: 69,700 sq km

Population: 4.4m (1995)

GDP per capita: US$200 (1995)

GDP real growth: -5% (1995); -35% (1994)

GNP per capita: US$500 (1994)

GNP real growth: -10% (1994)

Unemployment: 90% (1995)

Inflation: 250% (1995); 3,620% (1994)

Trade balance: -US$92.1m (1st four months 1996); -US$13.7m (1995)

Foreign debt: US$1bn (1995)

* estimated figure

KEY INDICATORS — Georgia

	Unit	1991	1992	1993	1994	1995
Population	m	5.48	5.49	5.46	4.40	4.40
Gross national product (GNP)	US$bn	8.9	5.0	4.0	2.7	–
GNP per capita	US$	1,600	800	730	500	–
GNP real growth	%	-20.6	-40.0	-39.0	-10.0	–
GDP real growth	%	–	–	–	-35	-5
Inflation	%	79	913	11,600	3,620	250.0
Unemployment rate	%	0.0	1.0	5.4	–	9.0
Balance of trade	US$m	–	–	–	*-20.0	-13.7
Exchange rate	GC per US$	–	–	200,000	1.28	**1.25

* estimated figure **Lari replaced GC 2 Oct 1995

the 1990s, Georgia became more important to the USA in 1995, mainly because of the AIOC oil pipeline deal. US support of Georgian participation in the AIOC may have been partly motivated by a desire to help keep Shevardnadze in power in Georgia. In a possibly related development, IMF credits were provided to Georgia for the first time ever in mid-1995. Although conditional on the implementation of economic reform, such IMF support means that Georgia will be able to obtain even-larger foreign loans in 1996. Among other things, this foreign financial support enabled the National Bank of Georgia (NBG) to introduce the Lari in October 1995.

Western financial support may enable Georgia to resist Russian pressure for full Georgian participation in proposed new customs and monetary unions. Another possible positive outcome of the IMF's seal of approval could be higher foreign direct investment (FDI) in due course, notably in the country's energy sector. But all is not entirely mellifluous – the IMF and the World Bank remain concerned about the relatively slow pace of structural reform. Large-scale privatisation of the state industrial sector only really began in 1995.

Economy

Although still dire in 1995, when GDP was only 17 per cent of its level in 1990, Georgia's economic performance began to improve slightly in the post-Soviet period in that year. Down by 30 per cent in 1994, GDP declined by only 5 per cent in 1995, mainly because of rising domestic demand, improved foreign trade and higher new foreign abroad. In 1995, when IMF-supported macro-economic stabilisation finally began, inflation fell to 250 per cent year-end, compared to around 3,600 per cent in 1994.

In 1996, GDP is expected to grow by around 10 per cent. Local living standards remain very low. Based on GDP of around US$900 million in 1995, GDP per capita dropped to US$200. However, the actual GDP and GDP per capita figures were almost certainly higher than official figures suggested, mainly because of the country's large black economy and extensive cross-border smuggling in the region.

In practice, most real economic activity in Georgia is in or closely connected with the black economy, which may have accounted for nearly 60 per cent of officially recorded GDP in 1995. Emigré hard currency and rouble remittances are also very significant, where the population fell from 5.5 million in 1992 to around 4.4 million in 1994.

Of the million or so people who left the country during the 1990s, most are thought to be in Russia. Since 1992, around 250,000 people have also been internally displaced by civil wars in Georgia, where their upkeep remains dependent on international food and other humanitarian aid, notably in and around Tbilisi. Real unemployment and hidden joblessness remains very high, mainly due to the de facto collapse of the Georgian industrial sector.

Formerly accounting for 35 per cent of GDP, but probably no more than 20 per cent, industrial output fell by a further 15 per cent in 1995, mainly because of continued energy supply shortages. The major problem is Georgia's outstanding energy supply debts to Russia and Turkmenistan. In September 1995 the Russian government agreed to help rehabilitate Georgia's energy sector.

External trade

Almost completely wrecked by the political and economic chaos of the 1990s, Georgia's foreign trade began to revive for the first time in the post-Soviet period in 1995. Following the partial re-opening of the main railway line to Russia in Abkhazia in 1994–95, Russian-Georgian trade is improving. Other than Russia, Georgia's only outlet to the outside world is through Turkey.

Devastated by Georgian reluctance to join the CIS, payment problems and the chaos in Abkhazia, this positive foreign trade trend could lead to a stabilisation of industrial output in 1996. In 1995, increased new foreign borrowings improved Georgia's payments position. Including cross-border smuggling, total Georgian exports in 1995 were around US$500 million, compared to around US$400 million in 1994. Even more significantly, far more of what was pledged for delivery abroad was actually delivered in 1995. Prior to 1994, however, little of what was pledged for foreign sale actually arrived because of the Abkhazian problem.

Georgia's improved payments position in 1995 led to a rapid growth of imports. Total imports in 1995 were US$800 million, compared to US$600 million in 1994. Further rapid import growth is expected in the future. Relative to officially declared GDP, total foreign trade turnover of US$1.3 billion was very high. The country's trade deficit increased from US$200 million in 1994 to US$300 million in 1995.

Georgia's main foreign trade problem is its high dependence on Russia, particularly the import of oil and gas. Export dependency on Russia also remains very high. Excepting Turkey, non-CIS exports and imports remained limited in 1995, mainly because of Georgia's isolation from the EU. In 1995, total *émigré* remittances in roubles and US$ may have exceeded the country's export earnings, with most of this money coming from Russia.

On the current account, higher new foreign borrowings in 1995 resulted in a lower deficit of US$400 million in that year. In 1994, when Georgia was not able to borrow large sums of money in the west, the country's current account deficit was US$500 million. Once covered by inter-state rouble credits from Russia, more recent Georgian current account deficits have been mainly financed by western loans. Russian rouble credits to Georgia have been sharply reduced in recent years for essentially political reasons. Following new economic co-operation agreements with Russia in September 1995, Russian credits were due to be increased in 1996. Significantly, Russia continues to support Abkhazia economically and, to a lesser extent, South Ossetia.

Agriculture

Also devastated by the civil wars and fuel shortages of the 1990s, agricultural output finally began to stabilise in 1995, with positive knock-on effects in the important food-processing and wine-making sectors. Accounting for around 45 per cent of GDP in 1995, compared to around 25 per cent in 1990, Georgian agriculture has considerable potential to act as a motor for local economic growth. Its full realisation, however, remains dependent on a stabilisation of the situation in western Georgia, which has traditionally been an area of food surpluses for the food deficient east. Georgia thus remains dependent on international food aid to feed its urban population, notably in and around Tbilisi.

Commented upon by a visiting World Bank mission in August 1995, a particular difficulty is the lack of a proper legal regime for land reform and urban real estate. This has inhibited increased FDI in agriculture-food processing. Georgia was particularly strong in viniculture in the Soviet period.

Services

Accounting for around 55 per cent of GDP in 1995, mainly privately-owned services are the fastest component of the Georgian economy. Focused on large-scale cross-border smuggling with Russia, this remains largely in the unofficial or untaxed economy. A very powerful local underworld operates and it is well connected in Russia.

In the longer-term, the government hopes to boost service income from higher oil pipeline transit fees, but this will only be possible if the AIOC does in fact build new oil export pipelines over Georgian territory from Azerbaijan in the future.

Currency

Blighted by the highest hyper-inflation in the CIS and the completely worthless interim Georgian currency coupon (GCC), Georgia's economy was only partly stabilised in 1995. Externally supported by an IMF stand-by loan of US$157 million in June 1995, the NBG was able to introduce the long-delayed lari (L) at an initial exchange rate of GCC1 million per L1 over a two-week period in September-October 1995. The virtually worthless GCC had traded against the US$ at a parity of around GCC1.3 million per US$ with only slight fluctuations since March 1995.

In relation to the Russian rouble, the GCC had also partly stabilised during the course of 1995, mainly because of declining inflation in Georgia. In September-October 1995, the NBG also exchanged locally held roubles for lari, which then became sole legal tender in Georgia. In practice, however, transactions have continued in both roubles and US$, mainly because of doubts about the lari.

Based on a controlled float pegged to the US$ by the NBG, the L1.3 per US$ exchange rate set in September 1995 has since been maintained, mainly because of active central bank interventions in support of the new national currency. This trend is expected to continue in 1996/97, when year-end inflation is projected to be around 20 per cent.

Budget and spending

In the fiscal sphere, the government budget deficit fell from 17 per cent of GDP in 1994 to 7 per cent of GDP in 1995, mainly because of real spending cuts and increased foreign borrowings. Government expenditures continue significantly to exceed revenues, mainly because of widespread tax evasion. Cross-border smuggling is another major cause of low government revenues.

The IMF and the World Bank are demanding radical tax reform, but this may be very difficult to implement in practice. Government outlays remain dominated by defence expenditures and essential foodstuff and other subsidies. Government spending accounted for a high 60 per cent of officially recorded GDP in 1995.

Banking

Pending a radical overhaul of the country's financial system, Georgia continues to lack a properly regulated and transparent commercial banking sector. Beginning in 1995, the NBG sought to improve its ineffective regulation of local commercial banks, mainly by increasing minimum capitalisation levels. As a result, a number of smaller commercial banks have been stripped of their banking licences. The government has also sought to curb underworld black market currency exchange, illegal capital flight and criminal money-laundering. Also surrounded by scandals, privatisation investment funds are another reported underworld stronghold in Georgia.

The recent introduction of a partly convertible and stable lari may induce greater saving in local banks in due course. Mainly generated by cross-border smuggling and *émigré* remittances, private holdings of both roubles and US$ are thought to be substantial in Georgia's largely cash-based economy. Following on from increased new foreign borrowings in 1995, local hard currency reserves reached a record US$300 million by the end of 1995.

Privatisation

Although still lagging behind macro-economic stabilisation, more radical structural reform of the Georgian economy finally commenced under IMF pressure in 1995. Endlessly delayed by the political chaos in Georgia, voucher-based privatisation began in March 1995.

A mixture of government incompetence, parliamentary opposition and popular apathy has meant that voucher distribution has been very slow to date and unlikely to be completed until late 1996 at the earliest. Secondary trading in vouchers, however, has grown rapidly, doubling the market price of the assets so traded from US$5 million to US$10 million in 1995 alone. According to the government's critics, this proved that assets slated for privatisation have been seriously under-valued.

Most Georgian citizens have immediately sold their vouchers for cash, so creating highly concentrated share ownership, notably by the new privatisation investment funds. Within newly privatised enterprises, the main disposal options have been insider-orientated. The absence of open ownership transformation had resulted in extensive wild privatisation or the open theft of state property by insiders and their underworld

COUNTRY PROFILE GEORGIA

Historical profile

Independence from Russia declared 9 April 1991. Subsequent to its independence, the republic declined to join the CIS. Election of Zviad Gamsakhurdia as the first president in July 1990. Racialist policies caused problems. Overthrown in January 1992. Government left in the hands of Eduard Schevardnadze. Parliamentary elections were held in October 1992 at which Schevardnadze was elected Chairman of the Council. Political struggles ensued in the south Ossetia region of northern Georgia, with war in Abkhazia, in the north-west of the country, which is blocking the main trade route from Russia. On 18 November 1992 Georgia and Azerbaijan formally established diplomatic relations.

Political system

New constitution adopted end-August 1995. This provided for a presidential republic with federal elements, although the breakaway Abkhaz parliament had rejected the proposed status of autonomous republic within Georgia on 22 August 1995. Under the constitution the president is directly elected for five years, can serve no more than two terms, and nominates and heads the Council of Ministers (cabinet). The unicameral parliament is elected for four years and comprises 150 deputies elected by a system of proportional representation and 86 deputies elected by the first past the post system. The head of state holds supreme executive power together with the cabinet of ministers. In the 5 November 1995 presidential and parliamentary elections Eduard Shevardnadze retained the presidency which he has held since a coup in 1992, with 74.3 per cent of the vote, and his party, the Citizens' Union, also came out well ahead, with 23.5 per cent of votes on the party list.

Political parties

Citizen's Union of Georgia is the party in government. Other major parties include All Georgian Union of Revival; Round Table-Free Georgia Bloc; National Democratic Party; National Independence Party; Georgian Popular Front; Democratic Party.

Population

Georgia is a densely populated republic. Georgian (70%), Armenian (8%), Russian (6%), Azerbaijani (6%). Inter-communal strife exists between the Christian Georgians and the Ossetian and Abkhazian ethnic muslim minorities. One million Georgians have emigrated since independence in 1991. Living standards in Georgia, once among the richest of the former Soviet republics, have plummeted after several years of ethnic and civil strife and economic collapse and are now among the lowest in the CIS.

Main cities/towns

Tbilisi (population 1.5m in 1994), Kutaisi (235,000).

Domestic economy

Georgia was one of the earliest republics to adopt market reforms, notably on prices and foreign investment, however, political problems have slowed progress, and the ability to attract foreign investment and introduce further liberal reforms is governed by moves to stabilise the political situation. The European Bank for Reconstruction and Development (EBRD) approved the strategy for the bank's operations in Georgia in December 1992. Although the government had opted for a programme for economic development, the economy is collapsing as conflict stops supplies.

External trade

In February 1993 agreements were signed by Georgia and Iran for co-operation in natural gas, transportation and commerce. Georgia had few goods to export in 1994, and of the US$400m worth of industrial and agricultural exports officially promised to Russia for 1994, only US$50m worth of goods was actually delivered. Imports were also radically reduced in 1994 to US$70-US$80m. Turkey became Georgia's main trade partner in 1995, accounting for 26 per cent of Georgia's foreign trade. Russia's share of Georgia's foreign trade dropped from 17 per cent in 1994 to 10 per cent in 1995.

Agriculture

Georgia is a major agricultural producer. The sector contributed 43 per cent to GNP in 1994

allies. As a result of all this, there is still widespread popular ambivalence about the entire exercise in Georgia.

Pre-privatisation structural reform of the state industrial sector has also been very limited. Here the major problems are high enterprise indebtedness, insolvency and asset valuation. Many Georgian industrial enterprises may have to be closed, notably in the capital goods sectors.

Sectorally, the enterprises with the best prospects are in food-processing, light manufacturing and services. However, even here a number of problems remain, notably incomplete land reform in the agricultural sector.

The economy as a whole suffers from a chronic shortage of new investment capital. During the civil wars of the 1990s, Georgia's infrastructure was seriously damaged and will not easily be rehabilitated with major capital inflows from abroad. On the FDI front, Georgia has considerable potential, notably in its energy sector. Most FDI to date has thus been directed at recently discovered oil and gas reserves, which are believed to be significant. Western FDI, however, remains very limited at around US$20 million at the end of 1995. Hard currency service income is also likely to remain low until the AIOC builds new oil export pipelines across Georgia. In order to facilitate increased FDI in the future, the government passed new foreign investment legislation in August 1995. Highly liberal, this mainly involves generous tax holidays and other exemptions for foreign investors. Other laws of interest to foreign investors are either inadequate or non-existent.

Foreign debt

Following its first IMF loan in June 1995, Georgia was able to increase its new foreign borrowings substantially for the first time in the 1990s. Apart from the IMF, the World Bank and the European Bank for Reconstruction and Development (EBRD) are major creditors of Georgia externally. Turkey has also recently agreed to provide US$150 million of Turkish Eximbank credits, plus an indefinite postponement of the repayment of US$50 million in debt arrears.

With new foreign borrowings of around US$400 million in 1995, Georgia's total foreign debt in that year reached around US$1 billion, compared to US$600 million in 1994. In 1996, Georgia's foreign debt may reach US$500 million by year-end, with most of this new borrowing again largely officially sourced. So far, Georgia has been unable to obtain new loans from western commercial banks, although a number of mainly Greek banks may be prepared to provide new money in 1996/97.

Even in the short-term, Georgia could face difficulties in servicing its growing foreign debt, mainly because of its still relatively poor export performance. With Russia, Georgia may be willing to enter into debt for equity swaps in local enterprises undergoing privatisation in 1996/97, although this issue remains politically sensitive locally. Georgia has yet to formally reschedule its large energy supply debts to Russia and Turkmenistan.

Outlook

Having experienced a catastrophic decline during most of the 1990s, Georgia has been able to improve its political and economic prospects in 1994 and 1995, mainly through a rapprochement with Russia. However, many problems and uncertainties remain, notably over the ultimate status of Abkhazia where the main factor is Russia. Whether or not Russia decides to allow the peaceful reunification with Georgia is also now dependent on future events in Azerbaijan. The US-sponsored AIOC will play a key role in this.

Shevardnadze and the UGC government are politically stronger than before but could still be tripped up. Parliamentary power could impede effective government in Georgia and the risk of further politically motivated violence remains high. Russian influences also remain strong and politically divisive.

Although generally successful to date, local economic reform is not yet irreversible. Externally, western financial support will remain conditional on the advancement of such economic reform. The full economic revival of Georgia is dependent on a final and peaceful resolution of its various political challenges. Above all else, Georgia's political and economic future will largely be determined by external factors over which it has little or no control.

COUNTRY PROFILE — GEORGIA

Agriculture (contd): and employed 27 per cent of the working population. Its warm climate favoured the growing of a range of sub-tropical crops in the coastal region, exporting much of the produce to the northern former constituent republics in return for much-needed supplies of manufactured goods. Crops include tea, grapes, tobacco and fruit. The EBRD's plans for Georgia's agricultural sector place emphasis on the production of small and medium-sized farm equipment and of modern animal feed. They will also focus on food processing and packaging, with the aim of upgrading and expanding existing facilities to improve production efficiency and to increase exports. The bank will also focus on food distribution and marketing and provide assistance for improved physical infrastructure, such as the building of producers' markets in rural areas, wholesale markets in urban areas and related storage facilities.

Industry

The industrial sector accounted for 27 per cent of GNP in 1994 and employed 28 per cent of the working population. Light industrial activities include food-processing and drinks production, metallurgy, shipbuilding, car production, consumer durables, garment-making and oil-processing. Other industries include mining, chemicals, heavy engineering and steel-making. Levels of self-sufficiency in the manufacturing sector are low, and export manufacturing potential is limited. Industrial growth over the first 11 months of 1995 was 115 per cent in comparison with the same period in 1994.

Mining

Major mineral deposits, notably manganese, copper and lead. Small quantities of iron ore are extracted.

Hydrocarbons

There are major coal deposits and some oil. Georgia has only one refinery at the port of Batumi on the Black Sea, with a capacity of 106,000 bpd. With ethnic strife in the country and lack of market for its products, the percentage utilisation declined and stayed at only 40 per cent, the internal consumption being about 40,000 bpd. Georgia's refinery is fed by Azerbaijani crude and by spot cargoes, mainly Libyan and Iraqi crude. Commercial exploitation of a natural gas deposit found in Tbilisi began in January 1996, initial yield expected to be 300 cu metres a day, enough for industrial enterprises during the winter period. From May 1996 when extraction is expected to increase, some gas will be supplied to household consumers in Tbilisi.

Energy

Hydroelectric power is available. Georgia buys natural gas from Turkmenistan (to whom Georgia owes US$450m), Russia and other countries of the CIS. There are plenty of coal deposits but these were not mined under former Soviet rule, because oil and gas were so cheap elsewhere. The EBRD's plans for the energy sector include technical co-operation that will promote commercialisation, structural reform, economic pricing, least cost planning, energy efficiency, and efficient and reliable connections with the energy systems of the region. The bank will also focus on the development of greater energy independence, in particular through rehabilitating and observing domestic hydro resources, and the promotion of efficient and environmentally benign facilities for refining, transporting and storing petroleum and gas products. The Kavkasioni high-voltage power line link with Russia was put back in operation early-December 1995. In January 1996 President Shevardnadze ordered the creation of a state energy corporation to unite Cruzenergo, Cruzneft, Cruznefteprodukty, Gruzgas and Gruzugol.

Banking

In September 1992 the Georgian government planned the legislative basis for the creation of a free banking zone. The rules for preserving bank secrecy would be no less stringent than those in Switzerland. Georgian experts believed that foreign and joint banks should be exempt from taxation on profits for a certain period. The EBRD's plans for the financial sector include supporting the development of a sound legislative, institutional and regulatory framework; creating an advisory group to provide advice on dealing with the state banks' non-performing assets; training; assessing the feasibility of a development bank as a channel

COUNTRY PROFILE

Banking(contd): for small and medium-sized enterprise financing; and reviewing the operations of Georgia's Export/Import Bank to better serve the needs of the export sector.

Stock exchange

Small commodity exchange only.

Membership of international organisations

BSECP, CIS, CSCE, IMF, OSCE, Partnership for Peace, World Bank.

BUSINESS GUIDE

Time

GMT + 3 HRS.

Entry requirements

Customs: Small amount of personal goods duty-free. On arrival declare all foreign currency and valuable items such as jewellery, cameras, computers and musical instruments.

Health precautions

Mandatory: Vaccination certificates are required for cholera or yellow fever if travelling from an infected area.
Advisable: Water precautions recommended (water purification tablets may be useful). It is advisable to be 'in date' for the following immunisations: polio (within 10 years), tetanus (within 10 years), typhoid fever, cholera (within six months), hepatitis 'A' (moderate risk only). There has been a significant increase in the number of cases of diphtheria. While the low dose, adult booster is unavailable, travellers are advised to be boosted with a reduced dose (0.1ml) of the paediatric single antigen vaccine. If never immunised, use three dose course of the vaccine. Any medicines required by the traveller should be taken by the visitor, and it could be wise to have precautionary antibiotics if going outside major urban centres. A travel kit including a disposable syringe is a reasonable precaution.

Air access

As of September 1995, no direct air access to Tblisi from any major EU city. The only international airline with regular flights to Tblisi from Moscow is Russia's Moscow Airways.
National airline: Georgian Airways (Orbi) is a joint venture airline between Orbi Airline and the German airline, Germania. As at June 1996 no further details available.
Other airlines: Donavia.

Surface access

Main port: Batumi – deals mainly with oil exports.
Overland access: There are daily buses from Istanbul (Turkey) to Batumi and Tbilisi. The buses leave Istanbul around 2000 hours and get to the border at Sarp the following night. N.B. The exchange shops do not change Turkish lira.
Road: Difficult terrain and weather conditions restrict road links.
Rail: A major new rail line is under construction between Tbilisi and Orzhonikidze. Trains unreliable.

National transport

The EBRD's plans for the transport sector include improving the maintenance of existing rail, road, port and airport systems; promoting the commercialisation and privatisation of the transport industries; developing Georgian links with the Euro-Asian corridor; encouraging better co-ordination between the Georgian transport systems and those of the other states in the region; and providing technical co-operation for policy development, structural reform, economic analysis, project specification and preparation, and economic and environmental assessment.
Rail: Trains are very unreliable.

Public holidays

Fixed dates: 1 Jan (New Year), 7 Jan (Orthodox Christmas), 1 May (May Day), 26 May (Independence Day), 25 Dec (Christmas).
Variable dates: Easter.

Working hours

Business: (Mon–Fri) 0900–1800 (appointments best between 0900–1000).
Shops: (Mon) 0800 – 1900, (Tue–Sat) 0800 – 2100.

Telecommunications

Telephone and telefax: Dialling code for Georgia: IDD access code + 995 followed by area code (32 for Tbilisi), followed by subscriber's number. There were 9.64 main lines per 100 inhabitants in 1994.

Banking

Central bank: National Bank of Georgia.
Other banks: See 'Business Directory, Banking'.

BUSINESS DIRECTORY

Hotels

Tbilisi
Matekhi Palace, Issani, 380003 (tel: 744-556).

Muza, 27 Kostava St (tel: 933-265, 998-816).

Chambers of commerce

Chamber of Commerce and Industry of Georgia, 11 Chavchavadze Avenue, Prospekt 1, 380079 Tbilisi (tel: 222-554, 230-045, 220-709; fax: 235-760).

Banking

National Bank of Georgia (central bank), Leonidze Ul 3/5, 380027 Tbilisi (tel: 996-505, 998-069; fax: 982-196, 999-885).

Export-Import Bank of Georgia (Eximbank), 5 Chorokhi Str, 380002 Tbilisi (tel: 999-394).

Travel information

Donavia (Donskie Avialinii), Sholokova Prospect 272, Rostov-on-Don 344009, Russia (tel: (7-8632)123-361; fax: (7-8632)520-567).

Georgian Airlines (Orbi), 112 Rustaveli Prospect, Tbilisi.

Other useful addresses

Caucasian Commodity Exchange, Tbilisi (tel: 380-946).

Georgian Oil State Department, Kostava Str 65, 380015 Tbilisi (tel: 361-642; fax: 985-017).

Gruzimpex (Foreign Trade Organisation), 12 Georgiashvili Street, 380008 Tbilisi (tel: 997-090; fax: 997-313).

Gruzinform (State Information Agency), Tbilisi (tel: 933-340, 932-441).

Ministry of Agriculture and Food Industry, Kostava 41, Tbilisi 380023 (tel: 996-261; fax: 985-778, 995-778).

Ministry of Communications, Prospekt Rustaveli 12, Tbilisi 380004 (tel: 999-424).

Ministry of Finance, 170 Barnovi, Tbilisi 380062 (tel: 292-077; fax: 292-368).

Ministry of Foreign Economic Relations, Kazbegi Ul 12, Tbilisi 380060 (tel: 225-186).

Ministry of Health, Dzhorbenadze, Ul K Gamsakurdia 28, Tbilisi 380060 (tel: 387-071).

Ministry of Industry, Ul K Gamsakurdia 28, Tbilisi 380060 (tel: 384-779, 998-643, 934-201, 385-028).

Ministry of Trade, Pr Chavchavadze 64, Tbilisi 380062 (tel: 293-061).

Office of the President, 29 Rustaveli Avenue, Tbilisi 380004 (tel: 933-208, 931-561, 999-292).

Press and Mass Media Committee, Ul Mardjanisthvili 5, Tbilisi (tel: 969-188).

The Press Secretariat of the Head of State of the Republic of Georgia, 29 Rustaveli Avenue, Tbilisi (tel: 969-5181).

Prime Minister's Office, Government House, Ul Ingorokva, Tbilisi 380034 (tel: 221-729, 984-464; fax: 932-727).

State Television and Radio, Ul. Kostava 68, Tbilisi (tel: 362-460).

Germany

Michael Griffin

Five years after the reunification of 1990, Germany faced a drastic reassessment of its economic and social priorities, brought on by the burgeoning cost of reintegrating the east and an economic slowdown that, by 1996, threatened to evolve into a fully-blown recession and bring serious labour union unrest. Germany's consensual approach to the division of power, both politically and in terms of its industrial relations framework, largely failed in 1996 to deliver the stiff measures needed if Europe's economic giant is to regain its competitiveness and staunch the outward flow of jobs and investment.

KEY FACTS — Germany

Official title: The Federal Republic of Germany

Head of state: President Dr Roman Herzog

Head of government: Chancellor Dr Helmut Kohl (Christian Democrat)

Ruling party: Coalition of the Christian Democratic Union (CDU), the Christian Social Union (CSU) and the Free Democratic Party (FDP)

Capital: Berlin; seat of government is Bonn

Official Languages: German

Currency: Deutsche Mark (DM) = 100 pfennig

Exchange rate: DM1.55 per US$ (Dec 1996)

Area: 357,041 sq km

Population: 81.80m (1995)

GDP per capita: US$25,100 (1994)

GDP real growth: 1.9% (1995)

GNP per capita: US$25,580 (1994)

GNP real growth: 2.4% (1994)

Unemployment: 10.3% (Jun 1996, (seasonally adjusted)

Inflation: 1.7% (Mar 1996, year-on-year) (consumer prices)

Trade balance: US$63.7bn (12 months to Mar 1996)

Visitor numbers: 14.5m (1994)

Politics

After 16 years in office, Dr Helmut Kohl is now the country's longest-serving chancellor and, by rights, should have had the leisure to contemplate the stamp he will leave on the history of Germany and the integrated Europe which has been his central foreign policy objective. Instead, he has embarked upon the uphill task of reinventing a new Germany for the 21st century, trimmed of its excess spending and much of its social safety net. Whether Mr Kohl has the stomach for such a bruising battle so late in the fight is already cause for speculation.

The federal elections in October 1994 produced a narrow win for the governing coalition of Kohl's Christian Democrats (CDU), the Bavaria-based Christian Socialists (CSU), under Finance Minister Dr Theodor Waigel, and the Free Democrats (FDP), whose leader until May 1996, Klaus Kinkel, is the current foreign minister. Kohl's majority in the Bundestag, however, fell from 134 seats to just 10. Because there are no by-elections under the German system, the coalition was reasonably assured of an unbroken run of power until the next ballot in November 1998. The weak link in the chain was the possible withdrawal of the centrist FDP which, in 1982, pulled out of another coalition with the Socialist Democratic Party (SDP), setting in train the elections which first brought Kohl to power.

The SDP, weakened by internal divisions for much of 1995, nevertheless narrowly defeated the CDU in 1994 to scoop 36.4 per cent of the vote, laying the foundations for a possibly winning alliance in 1998 with either – or both – the environmentalists or the ex-communist Party of Democratic Socialism (PDS), the east's third largest political group. The government's programme of work until 1997, when it had hoped to present an economy attuned to the criteria for economic and monetary union, demands a far-reaching overhaul of Germany's labour law and benefits system, which can but play into the hands of the opposition. The chancellor, moreover, has said he will not stand in 1998, raising the prospect that the CDU-led government will have lost its most experienced vote-winner at a time when it needs all its electoral muscle to make sure the reform programme does not falter before it has fully run its course.

The FDP has held the balance of power in the Bundestag for over 20 years, ensuring that, whichever of the main blocks ultimately captured Bonn, it was forced to take on board some elements of its smaller partner's liberal agenda. But the FDP has been in steep decline since 1992, when former foreign minister Hans-Dieter Genscher resigned as leader. Its votes poached away by the younger and more dynamic Bundnis 90/Greens alliance, it has lost in 11 state elections in two years and failed to win any seats in the last European parliamentary elections. With the FDP's share of the vote halved to just 6.9 per cent in 1994, doubts were expressed about its ability to survive.

Since early 1995 the FDP has seen a major revival, which has also helped the coalition of which it is a crucial part. In mid-1995, Klaus Kinkel resigned as the FDP leader, to be replaced in June 1995 by Wolfgang Gerhardt, whose first job was to prepare for the March 1996 elections in

To order your copy, turn to page 119

Baden-Württemberg, Rheinland-Pfalz and Schleswig-Holstein, three of the four Länder, or federal states, where the party still has a government presence. Campaigning on the issues of lower taxation and the enfranchisement of Germany's 6 million resident foreigners, its share of the vote almost doubled in Baden-Württemberg to 9.6 per cent and reached 8.9 per cent in Rheinland-Pfalz. In two of the three Länder, the FDP's gains were clearly the SPD's losses, in spite of the replacement in November 1995 of the SPD's lacklustre leader Rudolf Scharping by the more left-wing Oskar Lafontaine. The results in all three

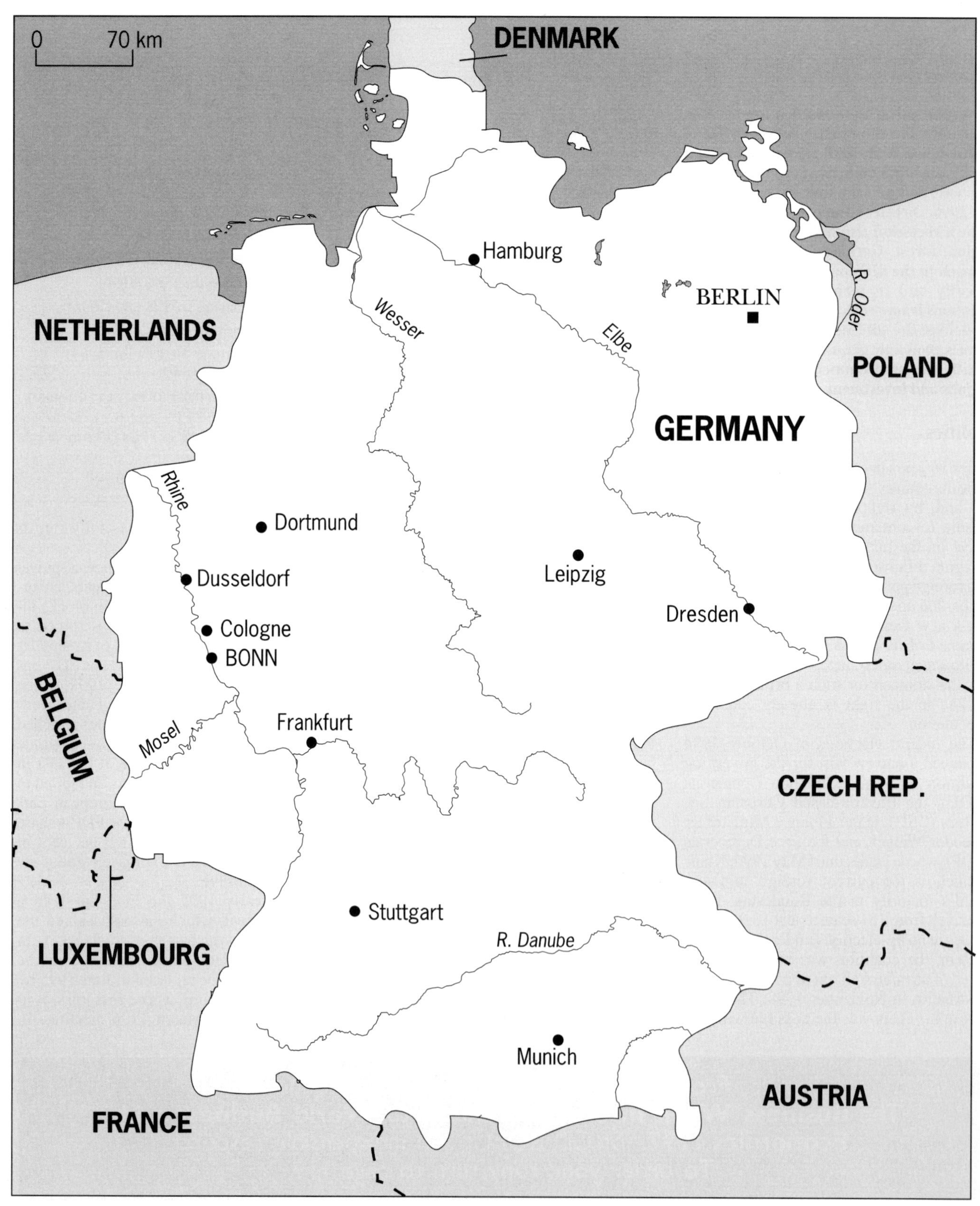

elections, moreover, were taken as a partial vote of confidence for the government's thinly-detailed 'Action Programme for Investment and Jobs', unveiled at the end of January.

SDP

The SDP is still in a position to make life difficult for the government even before the next elections. Under Germany's federal system, financial bills passing through the Bundestag have to be ratified by the Bundesrat, which houses the representatives of the 16 Länder and is dominated by the Socialists. Although short of the two-thirds majority required for an outright veto, it has sufficient votes to delay or dilute government proposals by referring them back for arbitration by members from both houses. Much of the legislation reluctantly outlined by the government in 1996, but yet to pass through the Bundesrat, will hit Länder budgets extremely hard.

Economy

In early 1995, the German economy seemed to have found its second wind after the recession of 1993 and there was confidence that it could achieve the Maastricht debt and deficit objectives by 1997. GDP growth of 2.6 per cent was recorded during the first half of the year; the public sector deficit was down to 2.6 per cent of GDP; and gross debt was 50.2 per cent of GDP. By the middle of 1995, the combination of an 11.7 per cent appreciation of the Deutsche Mark against the dollar, a 4 per cent increase in labour costs and a downswing in the global economy had thrown these calculations awry.

Exports continued to expand but all other key economic indicators were in sharp retreat – except for the German worker's earnings and the jobless rate, both of which climbed relentlessly. In May 1996, the economics ministry revised its growth rate for the year down to 0.75 per cent – half of its October 1995 forecast – as news emerged that industrial production had slumped by 2.8 per cent in one month alone.

In October 1995, Finance Minister Waigel predicted a shortfall of DM35 billion (US$24 billion) in tax revenues for 1995, giving this as the main reason why Germany would exceed its public sector deficit target for 1995. Compared with 1994, the public deficit rose by 42 per cent in the course of the year to DM124 billion (US$87 billion), or 3.6 per cent of GDP. This is an alarming figure for a government that, only a few months earlier, had widely boasted of the need for sound public finances.

Bonn subsequently forecast a 1996 deficit of DM125-135 billion, or 3.5 per cent of GDP, although the Bundesbank later said that this was far too optimistic a projection, suggesting instead 4 per cent, with a return to within the Maastricht guidelines unlikely before 1998. In May 1996, Bonn reported that tax revenues would continue to fall in 1996 to DM807.1 billion (US$520 billion), DM21.7 billion below target, and again in 1997. Meanwhile, the Bundesbank warned that Germany's fiscal shortfalls threatened to upset the capital markets by drawing up too large a slice of available funds.

KEY INDICATORS

	Unit	1991	1992	1993	1994	1995
Population	m	79.98	80.59	80.90	81.20	81.80
Gross domestic product (GDP)	US$bn	1,843.6	1,982.0	2,038.0	2,042.0	–
GDP per capita	US$	22,730	24,440	25,100	25,100	–
GDP real growth	%	3.7	1.5	-1.2	2.9	1.9
Inflation	%	3.5	4.0	4.1	3.5	1.8
Consumer prices	1990=100	103.5	107.6	112.0	115.4	117.4
Unemployment	%	5.1	7.6	8.9	9.6	9.4
Agricultural production	1979-81=100	115.66	107.63	108.38	103.74	102.94
Industrial production	1990=100	103.2	101.3	94.5	97.5	96.9
Natural gas production	m toe	13.2	13.4	13.4	14.0	14.5
Coal production	m toe	102.2	92.5	83.4	76.8	74.6
Exports	DMbn	665.8	658.5	628.4	690.64	727.59
Imports (CIF)	DMbn	643.90	628.20	576.50	617.35	634.28
Balance of trade	US$bn	23.23	32.76	44.54	50.80	61.50
Current account	US$bn	-18.73	-26.37	-15.21	-23.88	–
Total reserves minus gold	US$m	63,001	90,967	77,640	77,363	85,005
Foreign exchange	US$m	57,517	85,887	72,727	72,219	77,794
Discount rate	%	8.0	8.3	5.8	4.5	3.0
Deposit rate	%	7.62	8.01	6.27	4.47	3.85
Lending rate	%	12.46	13.59	12.85	11.48	10.94
Exchange rate	DM per US$	1.65	1.56	1.65	1.62	1.4

Worrying figures

The additional burden of harmonising the east with the rest of Germany restricts Bonn's fiscal manoeuvring space, particularly during the current downturn. Although output began to revive in 1993, increasing by 20 per cent in 1994 and a further 16 per cent in the first half of 1995, flagging consumer demand and rising unemployment have set back a recovery which is now largely supported by injections of federal cash. From 1992-96, transfers of public funds from the west of the country totalled DM854 billion (US$562 billion), of which the authorities expect to receive DM214 billion back in the form of taxes. In May 1996, economics minister Gunter Rexrodt asked the EU to prolong its US$17 billion structural aid fund to the new Länder beyond the proposed 1999 cutoff date, warning that restructuring would last well into the next century and that any termination would generate social problems and lead to the re-transfer of existing new industries back to the west.

The statistic which caused Germans the most alarm was unemployment which, at the end of February 1996, stood at 4.27 million, 443,500 up on the previous year and 111,500 more than in December 1995. The situation in the east was worse, with 17.5 per cent of the labour force out of work, up from 14.8 per cent in 1994. In the west, the rate was 9.6 per cent, but the number of workers on short time rose from 158,000 to 403,400, mainly in the construction industry. If those on short time and in government training schemes are also included, the total number of unemployed in Germany would be 6 million, a rate not equalled since the war.

Costly labour

Since 1991, German industry has shed an estimated 1.13 million jobs and direct investment abroad has soared, doubling to DM52 billion in 1995, confirming that many had been exported to eastern Europe where labour is more flexible and less expensive. Pay in Germany grew by 4 percent in 1995 and a further 5 per cent increase is predicted for 1996, resulting in average hourly costs per worker of DM44, compared to DM22 in the UK. Even in the east, where productivity continues to languish, wages are now 94 per cent of the western level. But the chief reason for Germany's high production costs is less the level of wages than the cost of social security which, borne equally by employer and employee, accounts for over 40 per cent of the total pay packet.

Social security

Germany's social insurance system, founded over a century ago, is in danger of collapsing under its own weight as the number of workers per pensioner declines from three in the 1960s to two in the 1990s and to parity some time after the millennium. Inseparably linked to the country's history of industrial harmony, the *sozialstaat* guarantees workers sickness benefit at full salary for six weeks, a four-week, state-paid spa holiday every three years and even care for the pets that are left at home. The strain on the system has shown in steadily rising contributions, particularly after coverage was extended to east German workers in 1990. Combined with Germany's strict job protection laws, the expense associated with the *sozialstaat* has deterred employers from creating jobs which they find difficult to shed when orders dry up.

Similar rigidities apply in many areas of German economic life, notably its shopping hours. The issue of extending shops' licenses beyond the traditional 6.30 pm weekday deadline came to the fore in 1994 but was shelved for fear of alienating the HBV retail, banking and insurance union in the run-up to the federal elections. Research in 1995 suggested that longer opening hours could add 50,000, mostly part-time jobs to the market and boost retail turnover by 2-3 per cent over as many years. The defence by the unions of such hard-won, if outmoded practises is widely viewed as the most significant obstacle to deregulating a market in order to release its locked-up growth potential.

New economic accords

To combat the haemorrhage of work, Klaus Zwickel, chairman of the IG Metall engineering union, proposed in autumn 1995 an 'Alliance for Jobs', a gesture typical of the 'consensual' style of industrial relations which subsequent events suggested may be heading for extinction. In exchange for commitments from the government not to tamper with benefits and from companies to create 300,000 jobs and postpone redundancies, he proposed a period of voluntary wage restraint within the limits of inflation. It was a gallant, if unreal overture, given the gravity of Germany's economic situation. In October 1995, however, Chancellor Kohl asked Mr Rexrodt to hammer out a more detailed programme for inclusion in

COUNTRY PROFILE — GERMANY

Historical profile

1918 Weakened and defeated in the First World War, Germany was called on to make massive reparations. Instability of economy and of democratic government paved way for the rise of National Socialism under Hitler.
1945 Allied occupation of impoverished Germany followed defeat in Second World War. Treaty of Potsdam provided that Germany be worked as one unit for industrial and trading purposes but western zones (administered by France, UK and the USA) were run on democratic lines, while a communist political and economic system was created in Soviet zone (most of the country east of the River Elbe). West Berlin remained as an 'island' in Soviet zone.
1948 Berlin airlift of vital supplies by USA and UK when Soviets cut all communications from West Berlin.
1949 Federal Republic of Germany established in western zone, and German Democratic Republic in the east, under Socialist Unity Party (SED), following failure of negotiations to establish a unified administration. Continuing FRG aim of reunification cut it off from eastern Europe.
1953 Severe food shortages and policy of 'sovietisation' in GDR led to uprisings and strikes, suppressed by Soviet troops.
1949–66 Dr Konrad Adenauer until 1963, then Dr Ludwig Erhard, successive Christian Democratic Union/Christian Social Union chancellors of FRG, fostered the 'German economic miracle' of economic dynamism and affluence. Identification with the West confirmed in membership of NATO (1955) and founding membership of EC (1957).
1957 Bundestag declared Berlin the capital of Germany. Bonn became the seat of government until reunification.
1960–73 Walter Ulbricht GDR head of state.
1961 GDR constructed Berlin Wall between eastern and western sectors to stem flow of refugees to West Berlin.
1969–74 FRG Chancellorship of Willy Brandt, heading coalition of Social Democratic Party and Free Democratic Party. Implementation of *Ostpolitik*, new policy towards GDR and Eastern Europe.
1976–89 Under Erich Honecker GDR one of the most stable and conservative members of Warsaw Pact/CMEA. In late 1980s Honecker resisted calls for democratisation on the Gorbachev pattern.
1974–82 Helmut Schmidt became FRG chancellor on fall of Brandt in security scandal. Disputes over deteriorating economic situation, nuclear power and defence policy led to coalition instability and withdrawal of FDP.
1982 In FRG Dr Helmut Kohl, CDU leader heading CDU/CSU and FDP coalition, formed government. Won general elections in 1983, 1987, 1990 and 1994.
1989–90 Resignation of Honecker, democratisation of GDR, dismantling of Berlin Wall and moves towards market economy. Reunification of two Germanies 3 October 1990 after currency union in July 1990.

Political system

Parliamentary democracy with power shared by a federal government based in Bonn and 16 *Länder* (regional states), each with its own constitution, parliament and government. Under the 1949 *Grundgesetz* (constitution) federal legislative power is vested in a directly elected *Bundestag* (federal diet), the lower house of parliament, directly elected for a four-year term; the *Bundesrat* (federal council), the upper house of parliament, comprising 68 members of the governments of the 16 *länder*, the *Bundespräsident* (federal president), elected for a five-year term by the *Bundesversammlung* (federal assembly), comprising the members of the *Bundestag* and an equal number of delegates nominated by the *Länder* parliaments; and the *Bundesregierung* (federal government), consisting of the *Bundeskanzler* (federal chancellor), elected by the *Bundestag* on the proposal of the federal president and his or her ministers.

Main cities/towns

Berlin (population 3.5m in 1996, capital), Düsseldorf (capital, North Rhine-Westphalia), Munich (1.3m, Bavaria), Stuttgart (Baden-Württemburg), Hanover (Lower Saxony), Wiesbaden (Hesse), Dresden (Saxony), Mainz (Rhineland-Palatinate), Magdeburg (Saxony-Anhalt), Erfurt (Thuringia), Potsdam (Brandenburg), Kiel (Schleswig-Holstein), Schwerin (Mecklenburg-Western Pomerania), Hamburg (Hamburg), Saarbrücken (Saarland). Other cities include Cologne (1m), Bremen (0.67m, Bremen), Bonn (292,000, seat of government and parliament), Essen, Frankfurt am Main (617,000), Dortmund, Leipzig, Duisburg.

Language

An agreement signed in Vienna, Austria, on 1 July 1996 will eliminate oddities and contradictions from German spelling and will be put into effect in a transitional period from 1 August 1998 to 31 July 2005.

Media

Press: West German press groups sought to extend their interests to eastern Germany by buying up and revamping newspapers formerly linked with the ousted Communist regime or by launching new newspapers. But the east proved a difficult battleground as circulation of some papers rose and fell sharply as editors tried to create publications more in tune with the temperament and interests of east Germans. Germany's highest circulation paper, *Bild*, part of the Springer group, faced competition in the east from a start-up, *Super Illu*, launched there by the Burda publishing house. Gruner and Jahr also launched a big effort to build up the *Berliner Kurier*. The Treuhand (the body set up to supervise the sale of former East German state-owned enterprises) allocated a batch of east German regional papers widely among applicants, though the outcome was complicated by a bid by the Social Democratic Party to assert historical rights to at least a minority interest in some of them. *Die Zeit* the weekly newspaper, was sold in April 1996 to the privately owned Holtzbrinck publishing group.
Dailies: Germany's top dailies include *Bild Zeitung* (circulation February 1995, 4.5m), *ACN Group* (1.6m), *WAZ* (1.2m), *Zeitungsgruppe Thüringen* (532,000), *Freie Presse* (493,000), *Sächsische Zeitung* (420,000), *Mitteldeutsche Zeitung* (417,000) and *Rheinische Post* (399,000). Top regionals include *Die Zeit* (470,000), and *Süddeutsche Zeitung* (406,000).
Weeklies: Most influential weeklies include *Bild am Sonntag* (circulation February 1995, 2.7m) and *Welt am Sonntag* (401,000).
Business: Numerous other trade and business publications, many which have expanded into east Germany.
Broadcasting: Private radio and TV have become more firmly established in western Germany in recent years in competition with the publicly controlled stations and networks. A similar system is operating in eastern Germany.
Radio: The English and 10 other European radio services that used to be transmitted by Deutschlandfunk were taken over by the Cologne-based world radio service Deutsche

the January 1996 annual economic report. Zwickel's proposals, modified by suggestions from the Federation of German Industries (BDI), were adopted on 30 January 1996 as part of a government policy to create at least 2 million jobs by 2000, of which 350,000 would be located in the east.

The 50-point 'Action Programme for Investment and Jobs' focused upon increasing the incentives for work by reducing the costs of employing labour. Among other proposals, it pledged support for new businesses through better access to venture capital, a three-stage reduction in income tax, starting in 1998, a reduction in the cost of social security contributions from 41 to below 40 per cent and a 2 per cent cut in the 'solidarity surcharge' on income and corporation taxes which helps fund the restructuring of the east.

Employers were never particularly enamoured with the 'Alliance for Jobs', although individual companies did reach specific compromises with their own labour forces. In Stuttgart, Mercedes agreed to forego redundancies until 2000, in exchange for the introduction of a third shift and the abolition of that most notorious of German working practises, the five-minute, hourly break. VW and Opel had reached similar deals in 1995, guaranteeing jobs in exchange for increased flexibility.

The government's 1997 budget was approved in July 1996. As expected, spending cuts are to be made with the aim of bringing public sector deficit under the 3 per cent mark – necessary for joining the single European currency. Total spending is to be DM440.2 billion, which is a drop of 2.5 per cent compared with the previous year. Ministries most affected by the budget cuts are defence, labour, transport, and economics.

Discord

Between widespread employer indifference and the bad news pouring from the economic ministries, the 50-point plan quietly died the death. Waigel let it be known in the second quarter of 1995 that he was seeking DM50 billion in further cuts and a two-year wage freeze to ease the fiscal situation, while the BDI insisted on a 20 per cent reduction in the rate of sickness benefit. The public sector union, OTV, threatened to go out on strike if a recently-tabled 4.5 per cent wage demand was not met, putting it on a collision course with the government. On 22 April 1996, the finance ministry confessed its cuts would total DM75 billion, trimmed equally from the federal, state and social insurance budgets, with a further DM35 billion to follow in 1997. Three days later, the coalition finally unveiled a package of 30 cost-cutting measures, which confirmed the worst fears of the unions but failed to go far enough to impress economic analysts.

In addition to the wage freeze, reductions in sick pay, DM12 billion worth of pension cuts and unprecedented erosions in job security, Waigel also pledged a series of tax reforms aimed at reducing the

COUNTRY PROFILE — GERMANY

Media (contd): Welle in July 1993. *English for Europe* is broadcast seven nights a week on medium wave 236.4 m, 1269 kHz, from 20156 to 2100. *Deutsche – warum nicht?*, the language course for English-speakers, goes out from 2000 to 2015 Wednesdays and Saturdays.
Television: Among the private channels, RTL and SAT 1 dominate but there are other new private channels such as Vox, RTL2, NTV, Tele 5 and Deutscher Fernsehfunk (east). State channels are ARD and ZDF.
Advertising: TV, newspapers and consumer magazines are all major outlets in Germany's rich advertising market.

Domestic economy

Starkly divided between strong, technologically advanced and highly competitive western Germany and less developed formerly communist economy of the east, now in throes of free market restructuring. Task of building up and modernising the east initially spurred western economy. Investment strong and consumer spending relatively high, especially in the west, although the economic slow-down experienced since 1993/94 has made both investors and consumers more cautious. Eastern Germany has been undergoing transformation to free-market economy. Privatisation has brought much-needed job cuts, investment in new equipment and introduction of more efficient productive processes. The system is being transformed from one made up of giant industrial concerns into one driven by small and medium-sized firms. The Treuhand has supervised the sales of state-owned enterprises, many going to companies in western Germany.

Employment

Shortage of skilled workers in western Germany initially relieved by influx from east, where unemployment has grown since reunification. Overmanned and uncompetitive enterprises in eastern Germany are shedding many workers. Wages in east being raised in stages to level of those in west and will reach parity by 1996. Trend to shorter hours in Germany accompanied by efforts to operate more flexible working time in factories and other businesses. The fact that official unemployment in the east is 'only' 15 per cent, despite the collapse of most of the region's industry and agriculture, owes much to the generously subsidised early retirement, job creation, maintenance and training schemes. The seasonally adjusted pan-German unemployment rate in September 1996 was 10.4 per cent; in west Germany the rate was 9.3 per cent; in east Germany 15.3 per cent.
Despite the nations's fitful economic recovery, by November 1996 there was a 50,000 jump in the seasonally adjusted total of registered unemployed to 4.1m. This is attributed to the fact that, due to high costs, German industry is shedding labour and investing abroad.

External trade

One of the world's leading exporters accounting for a large proportion of world's merchandise exports. But imports have been growing because of extra demand for capital equipment and consumer goods in eastern Germany. Western Germany's industrial sector has been transformed technologically to remain competitive in world markets, where it generally has a reputation for quality and reliable delivery. Tighter controls have been introduced on exports which might have military uses. As one of world's main trading nations, Germany favours open markets. In international negotiations it is normally a strong advocate of trade liberalisation. Well over half of all German foreign trade is with EU countries.
Exports: Exports totalled DM727.59bn in 1995. Main exports to EU countries include aircraft and motor vehicles, electrical engineering products, heavy machinery, precision and optical instruments and office equipment. Main destinations: France (12% of 1994 total), UK (8%), USA (7.9%), Italy (7.6%), Netherlands (7.5%), Belgium-Luxembourg (6.7%), EU (57.7%).
Imports: Imports totalled DM634.28bn in 1995. About one fifth of imports are foodstuffs. Main sources: France (11% of 1994 total), Italy (8.4%), Netherlands (8.2%), USA (7.3%), UK (6.2%), Belgium-Luxembourg (6.1%), EU (55.4%).

Agriculture

The agriculture sector accounted for 2.5 per cent of GDP in 1994 and employed 3 per cent of the workforce. In western Germany, the number of farms continues to fall as EU pressure to cut prices and surplus production squeezes farm incomes. The number has already fallen more than 50 per cent since 1950. The average farm is smaller than in Britain and France: many are small-scale and part-time family farms. But work, especially on larger farms, is efficient and highly mechanised. In eastern Germany, restructuring continues, with attempts to replace large-scale co-operatives with smaller, privately owned farms. Many have left over-manned co-operatives. German farm output is predominantly wheat, barley, sugar beet, fruit and grapes for wine production, pig meat and dairy products. Eastern Germany is a large grain-producer and self-sufficient in meat, milk and eggs.

Industry

The industrial sector accounted for 36.5 per cent of GDP in 1994 and employed 36.1 per cent of the workforce. Leading European producer of motor vehicles and accessories (which has gained significantly from unification), industrial plant, machine tools, electrical goods, scientific instruments, chemicals, pharmaceuticals and consumer goods. Traditional industries (steel, shipbuilding) have contracted because of foreign competition and weaker demand. Strenuous efforts are being made to modernise industry in western Germany through use of electronics and more flexible production techniques, and to restructure industry in eastern Germany which has remained uncompetitive in terms of price and quality. Worst affected areas are steel, electronics, engineering and chemicals. High production costs in eastern Germany are preventing the region's companies from competing with their western counterparts and are contributing to a high rate of insolvencies. The high costs are the result of unrealistically high wages in eastern Germany despite productivity levels lagging behind the western *Länder*, or states, by as much as 70 per cent in some sectors. Insolvencies were most marked in construction, the main growth sector in eastern Germany.

Mining

The mining sector accounted for 1 per cent of GDP in 1994 and employed 1 per cent of the workforce. Relatively few natural resources other than large supplies of black and brown coal, so largely dependent on imports. Pressure to cut high-cost black coal output and jobs in Ruhr and Saar basins as part of drive for reduced government subsidies and more competition in energy markets. In eastern Germany, brown coal production is likely to be scaled back as supplies are used more efficiently in power stations and as efforts are made to curb pollution.

individual tax burden and creating incentives for small business. These were announced on 22 May 1996, following a wave of public sector strikes in defence of the threatened benefits. In the Bundesrat, the SDP responded by taking up the cudgels on behalf of its Länder, saying that state and local authorities stood to lose over DM40 billion from reductions in direct federal funding and Waigel's proposed cuts to personal and inheritance taxes.

Amid accusations that the historic partnership between government, employer and union had broken down and that the coalition had turned its back on the welfare state, pragmatists queried how much of the Chancellor's get-tough agenda would actually survive its passage through the legislature intact.

Trade balance

In spite of the strong Deutsche Mark and competition of lower-cost producers, the merchandise surplus increased strongly in 1995, with exports growing by 5.3 per cent to US$520.5 billion, as against a 3.1 per cent fall in imports to US$446.8 billion, caused by the weakness of domestic demand.

Export demand fell back towards the end of the year but a backlog of orders built up in 1994 sustained output for much of the year. The outlook for the trade balance will be influenced by the Deutsche Mark/US dollar exchange rate, projected to fall from US$1.43 in 1995 to US$1.55 in 1996 and US$1.65 in 1997. If the German currency does not give up ground, however, demand and output will continue to suffer in 1996 and the trend for German companies to develop facilities abroad will continue to leech jobs, adding to the government's fiscal dilemma.

Revival possible

There are a number of factors which may support a revival of growth towards the end of 1996, notably Germany's 1.5 per cent inflation rate, a tax-induced increase of 0.5 per cent in disposable household income and the Bundesbank's relaxation of interest rates. Germany's central bank cut its discount rates by 50 points on three separate occasions in 1995.

EMU

With the economy in contraction and the prospect receding of Germany meeting its Maastricht benchmarks by 1997, Economic and Monetary Union (EMU) and high unemployment have become synonymous in the minds of a population already nervous at the loss of the Deutsche Mark. In spite of the damage caused to industry by the recent appreciation of the currency, as many as two thirds of voters are firmly opposed to monetary union and many smaller enterprises have come to share their fears. The benefits of

COUNTRY PROFILE — GERMANY

Hydrocarbons
Coal reserves 67.3bn tonnes (end-1995). Coal production 74.6m tonnes oil equivalent (1995), down 2.9 per cent on 1994 output. Natural gas reserves 11.3 trillion cu feet (end-1995). Natural gas production totalled 14.5m tonnes oil equivalent in 1995, up 3.2 per cent on 1994 output.

Energy
With virtually all oil and most natural gas imported, western Germany is highly conscious of need for energy savings. Nuclear reactors provide nearly 40 per cent of western Germany's electricity. East Germany's nuclear reactors accounted for 10 per cent of its electricity until closed for safety reasons in 1990. Brown coal provides over 80 per cent of east Germany's electricity but predominance expected to decline. An investment programme totalling DM46bn will enable the energy sector in eastern Germany to be upgraded to give the region a total annual capacity of 12,300 MW.

Leading industrial companies
Daimler-Benz, Volkswagen, Siemens, Veba, BASF, Hoechst, RWE, Bayer, Thyssen, Bosch.

Legal system
Civil law system. Federal constitutional court reviews legislative acts.

Membership of international organisations
ADB, AG (observer), Alps-Adriatic Working Community, BDEAC, BOAD, CCC, CERN, Council of Baltic Sea States, Council of Europe, CSCE, DAC, EEA, EIB, EMS, ESA, EU, Eureka, FAO, G-5, G-7, G-10, IAEA, ICAC, ICAO, ICC, ICES, ICO, IDA, IDB, IFAD, IEA, IFC, IHO, ILO, IMF, IMO, INTELSAT, International Grain Council, International Lead and Zinc Study Group, INTERPOL, IPU, ITC, ITU, KSVA, KZSE, MIGA, NACC, NAM (guest), NATO, OAS (observer), OECD, UN, UNESCO, UNIDO, UN Security Council (1995-96), UPU, WEU, WHO, WIPO, WMO, World Bank, WSG, WTO.

BUSINESS GUIDE

Time
GMT + 1 hr (GMT + 2 hrs from late Mar to late Sep).

Climate
Temperate; warm summers, fairly cold winters. Warmest month Jul. Rain throughout year.
Clothing: Medium weight for winter, lightweight for summer.

Entry requirements
Visa not required for nationals of European countries and several others.
Health: Vaccination certificates not usually required, unless arriving from infected area. EU nationals covered for medical treatment.
Currency: No restrictions on the movement of local or foreign currency. Imports of money for investment subject to German regulations.
Customs: Personal effects duty-free.

Air access
Regular flights by all major international airlines.
National airline: Lufthansa German Airlines.
International airports: Berlin-Tegel (BER) and Berlin-Schönefeld (SXF), Cologne-Bonn (CGN) 20 km north of Bonn and 14 km south-east of Cologne, Düsseldorf (DUS) 8 km north of city, Frankfurt (FRA) 10 km south-west of city, Hamburg (HAM) 13 km north of city, Hanover (HAJ) 11 km from city, Munich (MUC) 11 km north-east of city, Stuttgart (STR) 14 km south of city, Leipzig (LEJ) and Dresden (DRS).
It was announced in June 1996 that Schönefeld airport is to be re-vamped to become Berlin's main gateway. The single runway will be extended and a second runway built and a new terminal will be constructed next to the existing railway station. The improvements will increase the airport's capacity from around 5m to 23m travellers a year.

Surface access
Good rail, road and sea connections with all surrounding countries.
Main ports: Bremen, Bremerhaven, Hamburg, Kiel, Rostock, Stralsund, Wilhelmshaven and Wismar.

Hotels
No offical rating system. 10–15 per cent service charge. Advisable to book in advance, especially when trade fairs are being held. All major credit cards accepted.

Restaurants
Wide range of types and prices. Do not wait to be seated by waiter; sit at empty table and signal to waiter or waitress. French and English spoken widely in restaurants. Bill usually includes service charge and VAT. Extra tip optional.

Currency
Deutsche Mark floats against all foreign currencies, but is included in European Monetary System float. No multiple exchange rates in Germany.

Foreign exchange information
Account restrictions: No restrictions on deposits of non-residents.
Trade policy: Few import restrictions. No import duties on goods from EU states. Licences only required for military equipment, drugs and agricultural products.

Car hire
Widely available. Special weekend rates available. Speed limits: built up areas 50kph, normal roads 100kph, autobahns 'recommended' top speed of 130 kph. Information from automobile clubs such as Allgemeiner Deutscher Automobil Club eV (ADAC), Automobil Club von Deutschland eV (AvD) and Deutscher Touring Automobil Club eV. Wearing of seat belts compulsory.

City transport
Buses, trams, metro and electric railway services in many towns. Good taxi service in all main cities.

National transport
Air: Frequent services linking Berlin, Hanover, Cologne/Bonn, Düsseldorf, Frankfurt, Hamburg, Bremen, Munich, Nuremberg and Stuttgart. Early morning flights provide direct links between many of these centres.
Road: Good nationwide coach services operated by the German Federal Railways and others.
Rail: Deutsche Bahn (DB) runs reliable Intercity Express and Sprinter services, with high-speed trains between major cities. First and second class. Advisable to book in advance. Eastern Germany's rail system now fully integrated with the west, under the DB umbrella. Faster east–west links being introduced. DB is one of the world's most highly regarded rail systems.
Water: Seaports on the Baltic and North Sea coasts linked to inland waterways and railways. Navigable inland waterways used extensively.

a single currency have been hotly debated in Germany and, while large multinationals and financial institutions expect to be clear winners, companies with less cross-border exposure dread the complexity and the cost of the switch-over.

If the timetable is not met before 1998, the wisdom of EMU and Bonn's entire commitment to the EU are likely to emerge as key issues during the election campaign. This would almost certainly not have happened had the German economy approached the final hurdle at full throttle and Bonn will have to launch a major effort to sell monetary integration to its citizenry.

EU expansion

Important modifications to Germany's policy on the enlargement of the EU were seen in 1995. With the capital scheduled to move to Berlin between 1998 and 2000, the whole balance of Germany is steadily moving east. This tendency is underlined by the outward flow of investment capital, particularly to the Czech Republic and Poland.

Securing the country's eastern flank, notably with Poland, has always been a paramount strand in Chancellor Kohl's foreign policy. During a state visit to Warsaw, he reiterated his pledge that Poland would be an EU member state by 2000. But the expansion of EU membership to the Visegrad countries had always presumed that some form of associate membership would be extended to less economically-sound applicants, such as Slovakia, Croatia and the Baltic Republics.

On 13 December 1995, Bonn overturned that assumption when it urged the EU to limit expansion to the Czech Republic, Hungary and Poland, with the negotiations to commence six months after the 1996 Intergovernmental Conference, matching pledges already made to Cyprus and Malta. The cost to the Common Agricultural Policy was cited as one reason for delaying the admission of other members, but another was certainly the growth of Russian nationalism which might be offended by the admission of its former Baltic vassals.

Security

Moscow is deeply suspicious of the EU's plans for eastward expansion, particularly in the realm of defence, while Germany is eager to speed up the co-ordination of a pan-European security organisation to protect its eastern sphere of influence.

But the whole issue of EU defence is mired by national interest and paranoia, as evidenced by the sharp differences between members over the handling of the Bosnian war. Germany, for its part, has been prevented from possessing nuclear weapons since 1954 – a restriction which

BUSINESS GUIDE — GERMANY

Public holidays

Fixed dates: 1 Jan (New Year's Day), 1 May (Labour Day), 3 Oct (Day of Unity), 25–26 Dec (Christmas). Many businesses, especially in manufacturing industry,close down for a month Jul–Aug.
Variable dates: Good Friday, Easter Monday, Ascension Day, Whit Monday, Day of Prayer and Repentance. Other festivals such as Epiphany, Corpus Christi, Ascension of the Virgin Mary and All Saints' Day are celebrated in some regions.

Working hours

Business: (Mon–Fri) usually 0800–1730.
Government: (Mon–Fri) usually 0800–1700 (close 1500 in Bonn on Fri).
Banking: (Mon–Fri) various hours between 0830 and 1530 (most open until 1800 on Thu).
Shops: (Mon–Fri) 0900–2000;
(Sat) 0900–1600/1800. (Shop hours were extended in 1996.)

Social customs

Shake hands with host. No longer important to address people by their title, though academic titles 'Herr/Frau Doktor' and 'Herr/Frau Professor' should always be used. However, people in small towns more title conscious than those in cities. Do not try to pay bill if invited to a restaurant during business hours. If dining at a German's home it is considered impolite to arrive late; gift of flowers a social 'must'; do not drink until the host has his or her glass.

Telecommunications

Deutsche Telekom is the state-owned monopolist. Deutsche Bundespost is expanding the telephone networks in eastern Germany and connecting, via digital exchange equipment, new subscribers in Dresden, Gera, Halle, Leipzig, Magdeburg and Rostock. Deutsche Bahn's telecoms network, DBKom, is the leading competitor to Deutsche Telekom. DBKom has started converting the network into a faster, digital one which can offer interactive services. As at July 1996, it has laid 4,000 km of fibre-optic cable, and plans to lay 14,000 km by the end of 1998.
Telephone and telefax: International dialling code: 49 followed by area code (30 for Berlin, 228 for Bonn, 351 for Dresden, 69 for Frankfurt/Main, 341 for Leipzig) followed by subscriber's number. Cheaper rate for long-distance calls between 1800 and 0800. For IDD access from Germany dial 00. Efforts being made to provide more telephone links with eastern Germany.
Telex: Widely available in hotels, at fairs and exhibitions. Country code 41D.

Postal service

Air mail outside Europe pays variable surcharges according to weight and distance. Stamps available from hotels, slot machines and post offices. Use of post code (Postleitzahl) obligatory. N.B. On 1 July 1993 all postal codes in Germany changed from four to five-digit codes as a result of rationalistion following German reunification. Residents of the UK can obtain the necessary information by dialling 0800-96-00-74; residents of other countries can dial (49)228-817-350, or (49)228-817-353. The fax number is (49)228-817-366.

Banking

Sophisticated system underpinning country's economic strength. Three main categories: central bank (Bundesbank) basically concerned with monetary stability; multi-purpose banks, including commercial, co-operative and (publicly owned) regional Landesbanks and savings banks; and specialist banks, including mortgage banks and instalment credit houses. Many banks have important shareholdings in industrial companies and bankers sit on the supervisory boards of many companies. Biggest national banks are: Deutsche Bank, Dresdner, Commerzbank, Bayerische Hypotheken und Wechsel Bank, Bayerische Vereinsbank. There are more than 4,000 banks, making the German banking sector highly fragmented. In July 1996 Deutsche Bank (Germany's largest bank) bought a 5.21 per cent stake (US$329m) in Bayerische Vereinsbank.
Central bank: Deutsche Bundesbank.
Other banks: See 'Business Directory, Banking'.

Trade fairs

Host to several of the world's most important international trade fairs, especially in such fields as textiles, foodstuffs, machinery, printing, books, toys, hardware and household goods. Information on events published by Ausstellungs-und Messe-Ausschuss der Deutschen Wirtschaft, in Cologne, which lists in its calendar about 140 fairs and exhibitions of supraregional or international significance. The major fair cities are Berlin, Cologne, Düsseldorf, Essen, Frankfurt, Hamburg, Hanover, Leipzig, Munich, Nuremberg and Stuttgart.
Frankfurt International Spring Fair (Jan–Feb); Hanover International Trade Fair (Apr); Frankfurt International Book Fair (Oct).

Electricity supply

220–250 V AC.

Representation in capital

Afghanistan, Albania, Algeria, Angola, Argentina, Australia, Austria, Bangladesh, Belgium, Benin, Bolivia, Brazil, Bulgaria, Burkina Faso, Burundi, Cameroon, Canada, Central African Republic, Chad, Chile, China, Colombia, Congo, Costa Rica, Côte d'Ivoire, Cuba, Cyprus, Denmark, Dominican Republic, Ecuador, Egypt, El Salvador, Ethiopia, Finland, France, Gabon, Ghana, Greece, Guatemala, Guinea, Haiti, The Holy See, Honduras, Hungary, Iceland, India, Indonesia, Iran, Iraq, Ireland, Israel, Italy, Jamaica, Japan, Jordan, Kenya, Republic of Korea, Kuwait, Lebanon, Lesotho, Liberia, Libya, Luxembourg, Madagascar, Malawi, Malaysia, Mali, Malta, Mauritania, Mexico, Monaco, Morocco, Myanmar, Nepal, Netherlands, New Zealand, Nicaragua, Niger, Nigeria, Norway, Oman, Pakistan, Panama, Papua New Guinea, Paraguay, Peru, Philippines, Poland, Portugal, Qatar, Romania, Russia, Rwanda, Saudi Arabia, Senegal, Singapore, Somalia, South Africa, Spain, Sri Lanka, Sudan, Sweden, Switzerland, Syria, Tanzania, Thailand, Togo, Tunisia, Turkey, Uganda, United Arab Emirates, UK, Uruguay, USA, Venezuela, Vietnam, Yemen, Zaïre, Zambia, Zimbabwe.

BUSINESS DIRECTORY

Hotels

Berlin (area code 30)
Ambassador, Bayreuther Strasse 42–43 (tel: 219-020; fax: 2190-2380).

Berlin, Kurfurstenstrasse 62 (tel: 269-29)

Bristol Kempinski, Kurfurstendamm 27 (tel: 884-340; fax: 883-6075).

Inter-Continental, Budapester Strasse 2 (tel: 26-020; fax: 2602-80760).

Bonn (area code 228)
Bergischer Hof, Münsterplatz 23 (tel: 633-441/42).

Germans largely endorse – but most Germans simultaneously believe that the country must embrace a more pro-active role abroad. The Bundestag's decision on 7 June 1995 to send Tornado bombers to support UNPROFOR in Bosnia – Germany's first military intervention overseas since 1945 – met with popular approval, largely because of the humanitarian factors involved. But events of more crucial significance to Germany's security tactics had begun to unwind one month earlier.

The election of Jacques Chirac as President of France on 17 May 1995 pushed the Franco-German axis into sharp focus and the two leaders held a mini-summit only two days later. Although both committed to deepening European integration at an economic and monetary level, a major difference persists over majority voting, an issue of crucial significance to EU foreign policy and security. The two countries are already involved in military procurement and a Franco-German military brigade, the embryo of a pan-European army, has existed in Strasbourg for several years. But 1995 witnessed momentous strides towards the creation of Franco-German force de frappe.

France's resumption of nuclear tests on 7 September 1995 ignited a diplomatic storm in the South Pacific and earned a blanket condemnation from nine EU members, although Germany and the United Kingdom abstained. Prime Minister Alain Juppé subsequently suggested that France might share its nuclear umbrella with Germany, a proposal that was greeted with equal amounts of interest or vilification by the CDU, on the one hand, and the SDP and Greens on the other. The CDU meanwhile declared that it could not see an EU defence policy, without there being some nuclear element.

Less than one week after the first of France's nuclear tests, Bonn spelled out its programme for the integration of the 10-member Western European Union (WEU) into the 15-member EU as the basis of a future European defence force. Under the proposals, WEU responsibilities would be split, with the humanitarian and peacekeeping roles falling under EU jurisdiction and separate mutual defence agreements under the command of the nations they affect. The WEU general secretary, Werner Hoyer, proposed a compromise over joint decision-making, with majority voting on general foreign policy issues and a national veto over the deployment of troops.

As 1996 passed the halfway mark, French and German military leaders were due to meet in Dijon to further harmonise their security arrangements. Among the proposals to be discussed were a joint division of responsibility, with the 340,000-strong Bundeswehr being maintained in its current size for European defence and the newly-professionalised French army reserved for interventions outside EU borders.

BUSINESS DIRECTORY — GERMANY

Hotels (contd)
Bristol, Poppelsdorfer Allee/Prinz Albert Strasse (tel: 26-980; fax: 269-8222).

Continental, Am Hauptbahnhof 1 (tel: 635-360/63-535).

Etap, Königshof, Adenauerallee 9–11 (tel: 26-010; tx: 886-565).

Hotel am Tulpenfeld, Heussallee 2–10 (tel: 219-081; tx: 088-6328).

Steigenberger, Am Bundeskanzlerplatz (tel: 20-191; tx: 886-363).

Sternhotel, Markt 8 (tel: 72-670; fax: 726-7125).

Bremen (area code 421)
Crest, August-Bebel-Allee 4 (tel: 23-870; tx: 244-560).

Park, Im Burgerpark (tel: 34-080; fax: 340-8602).

Plaza, Hillmannplatz 20 (tel: 17-670; tx: 246-868).

Cologne (Köln) (area code 221)
Ambassador, Barbarossaplatz 4a (tel: 235-181; tx: 888-1780).

Dom, Domkloster 2a (tel: 20-240; fax: 202-4260).

Excelsior Ernst, Domplatz (tel: 2701; fax: 135-150).

Inter-Continental, Helenen Strasse 14 (tel: 2280; fax: 228-1301).

Dortmund (area code 231)
Drees, Hohe Strasse 107 (tel: 12-290; fax: 129-9555).

Novotel Dortmund-West, Brennaborstrasse 2 (tel: 65-485; fax: 650-944).

Parkhotel Witterkindshof, Westfalendamm 270 (tel: 596-081; tx: 822-216).

Westfallen, Strobelallee 41 (tel: 120-4230; tx: 822-413).

Düsseldorf (area code 211)
Breidenbacher Hof, Heinrich-Heine-Allee 36 (tel: 13-030; fax: 130-3830).

Hilton, 20 Georg-Glock-Strasse (tel: 43-770; fax: 437-7650).

Holiday Inn, Konigsallee Graf Adolf Platz (tel: 38-730; fax: 387-3390).

Inter-Continental, Karl Arnold Platz 5 (tel: 45-530; fax: 455-3110).

Nikko, Immermannstrasse 41 (tel: 8340; fax: 161-216).

Ramada, Am Seestern 16 (tel: 591-047; fax: 593-569).

Essen (area code 201)
Bredeney, Theodor-Althoff=Strasse 5 (tel: 7690; fax: 769-3143).

Sheraton, Huyssenallee 55 (tel: 20-951; fax: 231-173).

Frankfurt (Main) (area code 69)
Arabella, Lyoner Strasse 44–48 (tel: 66-330; fax: 663-3666).

Continental, Baseler Strasse 56 (tel: 230-341; fax: 232-914).

Frankfurt Marriott, Hamburger Allee 2–10 (tel: 79-550; fax: 7955-2432).

Hessicher Hof, Friedrich-Ebert-Anlage 40 (tel: 75-400; fax: 754-0924).

Inter-Continental, Wilhelm-Leuschner-Strasse 43 (tel: 26-050; fax: 252-467).

Sheraton, Frankfurt Airport (tel: 69-770; fax: 6977-2209).

Hamburg (area code 40)
Atlantic Kempinski, An der Alster 72–79 (tel: 28-880; fax: 247-129).

Hamburg Marriott, ABC Strasse 52 (tel: 35-050; fax: 3505-1777).

Holiday Inn, Graumannsweg 10 (tel: 228-060; fax: 220-8704).

Inter-Continental, Fontenay 10 (tel: 414-150; fax: 4141-5186).

Plaza, Marseiller Strasse 2 (tel: 35-020; fax: 3502-3333).

Ramada Renaissance, Grosse Bleichen (tel: 349-180; fax: 3491-8431).

Vier Jahreszeiten, Neuer Jungfernstieg 9–14 (tel: 34-940; fax: 349-4602).

Munich (München) (area code 89)
Hilton, Am Tucherkpark 7 (tel: 48-040; fax: 4804-4804).

Holiday Inn, Leopoldstrasse 200 (tel: 381-790; fax: 3817-9888).

Königshof, Karlsplatz 25 (tel: 551-360; fax: 5513-6113).

Sheraton, Arabellastrasse 6 (tel: 92-640; fax: 916-877).

Vier Jahreszeiten Kempinski, Mazimilianstrasse 17 (tel: 230-390; fax: 2303-9693).

Westpark, Garmischer Strasse 2 (tel: 51-960; fax: 519-6649).

Stuttgart (area code 711)
International, Plieninger Strasse 100 (tel: 72-021; fax: 720-2210).

Schlossgarten, Schillerstrasse 23 (tel: 20-260; fax: 202-6888).

Steinberger Graf Zeppelin, Arnulf-Klett-Platz 7 (tel: 299-881; fax: 292-141).

Car hire

Avis: reservations office: (tel: 06171-681-800).
Budget: central reservations headquarters, Munich (tel: (89)666-950; fax: (89)6141-4490).

Europcar: reservations office, Tangstedter Landstrasse 81, 22415 Hamburg (tel: (40)5201-8211; fax: (40)5201-8613).

Hertz: reservations office, Eschborn (tel: (6196)933-900; fax: (6196)937-116).

Chambers of commerce
Berlin – Industrie- und Handelskammern zu Berlin, D-1000 Berlin 12, Hardenbergstrasse 16–18 (tel: 31-801; fax: 318-0278).

Bonn – Industrie- und Handelskammern zu Bonn, D-5300 Bonn, Bonner Talweg 17 (tel: 22-840; tx: 886-9306).

Cologne – Industrie- und Handelskammern zu Köln, D-5000 Cologne 1, Unter Sachsenhausen 10-26 (tel: 16-400; tx: 888-1400).

Düsseldorf – Industrie- und Handelskammern zu Düsseldorf, D-4000 Düsseldorf 1, Ernst–Schneider–Platz 1 (tel: 35-571; tx: 852-815).

Frankfurt – Industrie- und Handelskammern zu Frankfurt/Main, D-6000 Frankfurt/Main 1, Börsenplatz (tel: 21-970; tx: 411-255).

Hanover – Industrie- und Handelskammern zu Hanover–Hildesheim, D-3000 Hanover 1, Schiffgraben 49 (tel: 31-070; tx: 922-769).

Munich – Industrie- und Handelskammern zu München und Oberbayern, D-8000 Munich 2, Max-Joseph-Strasse 2 (tel: 5116; tx: 523-678).

BUSINESS DIRECTORY

Chambers of Commerce (contd):
Münster – Industrie- und Handelskammern zu Münster, D-4400 Münster, Sentmaringer Weg 61 (tel: 7071; tx: 892-817).

Nuremberg – Industrie- und Handelskammern zu Nürnberg, 106, Hauptmarkt 25–27 (tel: 13-350; tx: 622-114).

Stuttgart – Industrie- und Handelskammern Mittlerer Neckar, Sitz Stuttgart, D-7000 Stuttgart 1, Jaegerstrasse 30 (tel: 20-050; tx: 722-031).

Deutscher Industrie- und Handelstag (DIHT) (Federation of German Chambers of Commerce), Adenauerallee 148, D-53113 Bonn (tel: 1040; fax: 104-158).

DIHT - Büro Berlin, An der Kolonnade 10, 10117 Berlin (tel: 238-5647/48; fax: 238-5646).

DIHT - Kammervereinigungen (11) Arbeitsgemeinschaft der Industrie- und Handelskammern in Baden-Württemberg, Jägerstr 30, 70174 Stuttgart (tel: 20-050; fax: 200-5354).

Arbeitsgemeinschaft der Bayerischen Industrie- und Handelskammern, Max-Joseph-Str 2, 80333 München (tel: 51-160; fax: 511-6306).

Banking
Deutsche Bundesbank, Wilhelm-Epstein-Str 14, 60431 Frankfurt aM (tel: 95-661; fax: 1071).

Landeszentralbank in Baden-Württemberg, Marstallstr 3, 70173 Stuttgart (tel: 9440; fax: 944-1903).

Landeszentralbank im Freistaat Bayern, Ludwigstr 13, 80539 München (tel: 28-895/3200; fax: 2889-3598/3890).

Landeszentralbank in Berlin und Brandenburg, Leibnizstr 9-10, 10625 Berlin (tel: 23-870; fax: 652-500).

Landeszentralbank in der Freien Hansestadt Bremen, in Niedersachsen und Sachsen-Anhalt, Georgsplatz 5, 30159 Hannover (tel: 30-330; fax: 303-3500).

Landeszentralbank in der Freien und Hansestadt Hamburg, in Mecklenburg-Vorpommern und in Schleswig-Holstein, Ost-West-Str 73, 20459 Hamburg (tel: 37-070; fax: 3707-3345).

Landeszentralbank in Hessen, Taunusanlage 5, 60329 Frankfurt aM (tel: 23-880; fax: 2388-2130).

Landeszentralbank in Nordrhein-Westfalen, Berliner Allee 14, 40212 Düsseldorf (tel: 8740; fax: 874-2424).

Landeszentralbank in Rheinland-Pflaz und im Saarland, Hegelstr 65, 55122 Mainz (tel: 313-770; fax: 320-989).

Landeszentralbank in den Freistaaten Sachsen und Thüringen, Petersstr 43, 04109 Leipzig (tel: 217-1500; fax: 217-1599).

Principal newspapers
Börsenzeitung und Handelsblatt, 4000 Düsseldorf 1, Kasernenstr 67, Postfach 1102 (tel: 83-880; tx: 1722-1391).

Der Spiegel, 2000 Hamburg 11, Brandstwiete 191 Ost-West Strasse, Postfach 110420 (tx; 216-2477).

Die Welt, 5300 Bonn Godesberger Allee 9 (tel: 3041; tx: 885-714).

Die Zeit, 2000 Hamburg 1, Postfach 106820, Speersort 1, Pressehaus (tel: 32-800; tx: 886-433).

Frankfurter Allgemeine Zeitung, 600 Frankfurt/Main, Hellerhof Strasse 2–4, Postfach 100808 (tel; 75-910; tx: 41-223).

Stern, Gruner und Jahr AG, 2000 Hamburg 36, Postfach 302040 (tel: 41-181; tx: 219-5213).

Süddeutsche Zeitung, 8000 Munich 2, Sendlingerstr 80, Postfach 202220 (tel: 21-830; tx: 523-426).

Wirtschaftswoche, 4000 Düsseldorf 1, Kasernenstr 67, Postfach 3734 (tel: 83-880).

Travel information
Allgemeiner Deutscher Automobil Club (ADAC) eV, Am Westpark 8, D-8000 Munich 70 (tel: 7676/0).

Automobil Club von Deutschland (AvD) eV, Lyoner Strasse 16, D-6000 Frankfurt/Main 71 (tel: 6606/0).

Corps Touristique, Vereinigung ausländischer Vertreter für Fremdenverkehr und Eisenbahnen in Deutschland, Düsseldorfer Str 15-17, 60329 Frankfurt aM (tel: 252-033; fax: 236-000).

Deutsche Zentrale für Tourismus eV (tourist board), Beethovenstrasse 69, 60325 Frankfurt aM (tel: 75-720; fax: 751-903).

Deutscher Touring Automobil Club eV, Amalienburgstrasse 23, D-8000 Munich 60 (tel: 811-1048).

Lufthansa German Airlines, Von Gablenz Strasse 2-6, Cologne D-50679 (tel: 8260; fax: 826-3818; 696-3002).

Other useful addresses
Arbeitskreis Deutscher Marktforschungsinstitut (ADM) (association of German market research institutes), Burgschmiedstrasse 2, D-8500 Nuremberg (tel: 3951).

Arbeitsgemeinschaft der Deutschen Exporteurvereine (federation of German exporters), Gotenstrasse 21, D-2000 Hamburg 1 (tel: 280-1337).

Aussenhandelsvereinigung des Deutschen Einzelhandels (AVE) (foreign trade association of the German retail trade), Weyerstrasse 2, D-5000 Cologne 1 (tel: 217-617).

Ausstellungs- und Messe-Ausschuss der Deutschen Wirtschaft, Lindenstrasse 8, D-5000 Cologne 1.

Berlin Economic Development Corporation (BEDC), Budapester Strasse 1, D-1000 Berlin 30 (tel: 2636/1; tx: 184-467).

Bund Deutscher Unternehmensberater (BDU) (association of German business consultants), Gotenstrasse 161, D-5300 Bonn (tel: 379-001).

Bund Deutscher Verkaufsförderer und Verkaufstrainer (BDVT) (association of German sales promoters and sales trainers), Mühlenfeld 69, D-4005 Meerbusch 2 (tel: 4121).

Bundesamt für gewerbliche Wirtschaft (federal office for trade and industry), Frankfurter Strasse 29-31, D-6236 Eschborn 1 (tel: 4041).

Bundesanstalt für Arbeit (federal labour office), Feuerbachstrasse 42, D-6000 Frankfurt/Main (tel: 71-111).

Bundeskanzleramt (federal chancellery), Adenauerallee 139-141, PO Box 120535, D-53113 Bonn (tel: 561; fax: 562-357).

Bundesministerium für Arbeit und Sozialordnung (ministry of labour and social affairs), Rochustrasse 1, PO Box 140280, D-53123 Bonn (tel: 5271; fax: 527-2965).

Bundesministerium für Bildung, Forschung und Technologie (ministry for education, research and technology), Heinemannstrasse 2, PO Box 200240, D-53175 Bonn (tel: 590; fax: 593-601).

Bundesministerium für Ernährung, Landwirtschaft und Forsten (ministry of food, agriculture and forestry), Rochusstrasse 1, PO Box 140270, D-53123 Bonn (tel: 5291; fax: 529-4262).

Bundesministerium für Familie Senioren, Frauen und Jugend (ministry for families, senior citizens, women and youth), Godesberger Allee 140, D-53175 Bonn (tel: 3060; fax: 306-2259).

Bundesministerium der Finanzen (ministry of finance), Graurheindorfer Strasse 108, PO Box 1308, D-53117 Bonn (tel: 6820; fax: 682-4420).

Bundesministerium für Gesundheit (ministry of health), Deutschherrenstr 87, D-53177 Bonn (tel: 9300; fax: 930-4978).

Bundesministerium der Justiz (ministry of justice), Heinemannstrasse 6, PO Box 200365, D-53175 Bonn (tel: 581; fax: 584-525).

Bundesministerium für Post und Telekommunikation (ministry of posts and telecommunications), Heinrich-von-Stephan-Strasse 1, D-53175 Bonn (tel: 140; fax: 148-872).

Bundesministerium für Raumordnung, Bauwesen und Städtebau (ministry for regional planning, building and urban development), Deichmanns Aue 31-37, D-53179 Bonn (tel: 3370; fax: 337-3060).

Bundesministerium für Umwelt, Naturschutz und Reaktorsicherheit (ministry for the environment, nature conservation and nuclear safety), Kennedyallee 5, PO Box 120629, D-53175 Bonn (tel: 3050; fax: 305-3225).

Bundesministerium für Verkehr (ministry of transport), Kennedyallee 72, PO Box 200100, D-53175 Bonn (tel: 3000/01; fax: 300-3428/29).

Bundesministerium der Verteidigung (ministry of defence), Hardthöhe, PO Box 1328, D-53125 Bonn (tel: 121; fax: 125-357/58).

Bundesministerium für Wirtschaft (ministry of economics), Villemomblerstrasse 76, PO Box 140260, D-53123 Bonn (tel: 6151; fax: 615-4436).

Bundesministerium für wirtschaftliche Zusammenarbeit (ministry for economic co-operation), Friedrich-Ebert-Allee 114-116, PO Box 120322, D-53113 Bonn (tel: 5350; fax: 535-202).

Bundesstelle für Aussenhandelsinformation (BfA) (German foreign trade information office), Blaubach 13, D-5000 Cologne (tel: 20-571).

Bundesverband des Deutschen Gross- und Aussenhandels (federation of German wholesale and foreign trade), Kaiser-Friedrich-Strasse 13, D-5300 Bonn 1 (tel: 26-004/0).

Bundesverband der Deutschen Industrie (BDI) (federation of German industries), Gustav-Heinemann-Ufer 84–88, D-5000 Cologne 51 (tel: 3708/0).

Bundesverband der Dolmetscher und Ubersetzer (interpreters), Rüdigerstr 79a, D-5300 Bonn 2 (tel: 345-000).

Bundersverband deutscher Markt- und Sozialforscher (BVM) (association of German market researchers), Schlossstrasse 4, D-6050 Offenbach (tel: 805-9266).

Bundesvereinigung der Deutschen Arbeitgeberverbände (BDA) (federation of German employers' associations), Gustav-Heinemann-Ufer 72, D-5000 Cologne 51 (tel: 37-950).

Bundesvereinigung der Fachverbände des Deutschen Handwerks (federation of German crafts), Johanniter-Strasse 1, D-5300 Bonn (tel: 5451).

Bundesvereinigung Deutscher Einkaufsverbände (BEV) (federation of German purchasing associations), Neumarkt 14, D-5000 Cologne (tel: 219-456).

Centre for Economic Promotion, Landesgewerbeamt Baden-Württemberg (contact: Dr Reuss), Postfach 831, D-7000 Stuttgart 1 (tel: 123-2222; tx: 723-931).

Centralvereinigung Deutscher Handelsvertreter- und Handelsmakler-Verbände (CDH) (federation of German trade agents and brokers' associations), Geleniusstrasse 1, D-5000 Cologne 41 (tel: 514-043).

Deutsche Presse-Agentur GmbH (dpa) (news agency), D-2000 Hamburg 13, Mittelweg 38.

Deutsche Public Relations Gesellschaft (DPRG) (German society for public relations), Flandrische Strasse 4, D-5000 Cologne 1 (tel: 212-499).

Other useful addresses (contd):
Deutscher Gewerkschaftsbund (DGB) (federation of German trades unions), Hans-Böckler-Strasse 39, D-4000 Düsseldorf 30 (tel: 43-010).

Deutscher Kommunikationsverband (BDW) (association of German advertising consultants), Adenauerallee 209, D-5300 Bonn (tel: 211-047).

Deutsches Institut für Wirtschaftsforschung (DIW) (economic research institute), Königin-Luise-Strasse 5, D-1000 Berlin (tel: 829-910).

Deutsches Kongressbüro (German convention bureau), Münchener Str 48, 60329 Frankfurt aM (tel: 236-655; fax: 236-663).
Economic Development and Investment Promotion Agencies

Baden-Württemberg
Gesellschaft für internationale wirtschaftliche, Zusammenarbeit Baden-Württemberg mbH-GWZ-, PO Box 101751, D-70015 Stuttgart (tel: 227-870; fax: 227-8722).

Bayern (Bavaria)
Bayerisches Staatsministerium für Wirtschaft und Verkehr, Referat für Wirtschaftsförderung, Standortwerbung und Ansiedlungsberatung, Prinzregentenstrasse 28, D-80525 München (tel: 2162-2642; fax: 2162-2760).

Berlin
Wirtschaftsförderung Berlin GmbH, Hallerstrasse 6, D-10587 Berlin (tel: 399-800; fax: 3998-0239).

Brandenburg
Wirtschaftsförderung Brandenburg GmbH, Am Lehnitzsee, D-14476 Potsdam-Neufahrland (tel: 96-750; fax: 967-5100).

Bremen
Bremen Business International, Birkenstrasse 15, D-28195 Bremen (tel: 174-660; fax: 174-6622).

Wirtschaftsförderungs-GesellschaftWeser-Jade mbH, PO Box 100225, D-28002 Bremen (tel: 320-111; fax: 325-422).

Hamburg
HWF, Hamburgische Gesellschaft für Wirtschaftsförderung mbH, Hamburger Strasse 11, D-22083 Hamburg (tel: 227-0190; fax: 2270-1929).

Hessen
Wirtschaftsförderung Hessen, Investitionsbank AG, Hessische Landesentwicklungs-und Treuhandgessellschaft-HLT-, PO Box 3107, D-65021 Wiesbaden (tel: 7740; fax: 774-265).

Mecklenburg-Vorpommern (Mecklenburg-Western Pomerania)
Gesellschaft für Wirtschaftsförderung Mecklenburg-Vorpommern mbH, Schlossgartenallee 15, D-19061 Schwerin (tel: 592-250; fax: 592-2512).

Niedersachsen (Lower Saxony)
Investment Promotion Agency Niedersachsen, Hamburger Allee 4, D-30161 Hannover (tel: 343-466; fax: 361-5909).

Nordrhein-Westfalen (North Rhine Westphalia)
Gesellschaft für Wirtschaftsförderung, Nordrhein-Westfalen mbH, PO Box 200309, D-40101 Düsseldorf (tel: 130-000; fax: 130-0054).

Rheinland-Pfalz (Rhineland-Palatinate)
Rheinland-Pfälzische Gesellschaft für Wirtschaftsförderung mbH-RPW-, Erthalstrasse 1, D-55118 Mainz (tel: 632-066/67; fax: 670-725).

Saarland
Gesellschaft für Wirtschaftsförderung Saar mbH, Bismarckstrasse 39-41, D-66121 Saarbrücken (tel: 948-550; fax: 948-5511).

Sachsen (Saxony)
Wirtschaftsförderung Sachsen GmbH, PO Box 100532, D-01075 Dresden (tel: 596-2782; fax: 3199-1099).

Sachsen-Anhalt (Saxony-Anhalt)
Wirtschaftsförderungsgesellschaft für das Land Sachsen-Anhalt mbH, Wilhelm-Höpfner-Ring 4, D-39116 Magdeburg (tel: 568-990; fax: 568-9999).

Schleswig-Holstein
Wirtschaftsförderungsgesellschaft Schleswig-Holstein mbH, Lorentzendamm 43, D-24103 Kiel (tel: 51-446; fax: 555-178).

Thüringen (Thuringia)
Thüringer Landes-WirtschaftsförderungsgesellschaftmbH-TLW-, Tschaikowskistrasse 11, D-99096 Erfurt (tel: 42-920; fax: 429-2202).

Foreign Investor Information Center, Federal Ministry of Economics, Berlin Office, PO Box, D-10109 Berlin (tel: 399-85100/101; fax: 399-85235).

Gesellschaft für Konsum-, Markt- und Absatzforschung (GfK) (market research institute), Burgschmietstrasse 2, D-8500 Nuremberg (tel: 3951).

Hauptgemeinschaft des Deutschen Einzenhandels (HDE) (central association of German retail trade), Sachsenring 89, D-5000 Cologne 1 (tel: 322-091).

Ifo-Institut für Wirtschaftforschung (economic research institute), Poschinger Strasse 5, D-8000 Munich (tel: 92-241).

Infratest (market research institute), Landsberger Strasse 338, D-8000 Munich (tel: 56-001).

Institut der Deutschen Wirtschaft (economic research institute), Gustav-Heinemann-Ufer 84, D-5300 Bonn (tel: 37-041).

Institut für Wirtschaftforschung (HWWA) (economic research institute), Neuer Jungfernstieg 21, D-2000 Hamburg 36 (tel: 35-621).

Kontakstelle zur Einfuhr aus Entwicklungsländern (central office for imports from developing countries), Kaiser-Friedrich-Strasse 13, D-5300 Bonn (tel: 218-051).

Ko-operationsbüro der rationalisierungs-Kuratoriums (German industrial standardisation board), Düsseldorfer Strasse 40, D-6236 Eschborn (tel: 4951).

Ministry of Defence, Hardthohe, PO Box 1328, D-53125 Bonn (tel: 228-121; fax: 228-125-357, 228-125-358).

Ministry of Economic Co-operation, Friedrich-Ebert-Allee 114-116, PO Box 120322, D-53113 Bonn (tel: 228-5350; fax: 228-535-202).

Ministry of Economics, Villemomblerstrasse 76, PO Box 140260, D-53123 Bonn (tel: 228-6151; fax: 228-615-4436).

Ministry of Finance, Graurheindorfer Strasse 108, PO Box 1308, D-53117 Bonn (tel: 228-6820; fax: 228-682-4420).

Ministry of Food, Agriculture and Forestry, Rochusstrasse 1, PO Box 140270, D-53123 Bonn (tel: 228-5291; fax: 228-529-4262).

Ministry of Foreign affairs, Adenauerallee 99-103, D-53113 Bonn, PO Box 1148, D-53001 Bonn (tel: 228-170; fax: 228-173-402).

Ministry of the Interior, Graurheindorfer Strasse 198, PO Box 170290, D-53117 Bonn (tel: 228-6811; fax: 228-681-4665).

Ministry of Justice, Heinemannstrasse 6, PO Box 200365, D-53175 Bonn (tel: 228-581; fax: 228-584-525).

Ministry of Labour and Social Affairs, Rochustrasse 1, PO Box 140280, D-53123 Bonn (tel: 228-5271; fax: 228-527-2965).

Ministry of Posts and Telecommunications, Heinrich-von-Stephan-Strasse 1, D-53175 Bonn (tel: 228-140; fax: 228-148-872).

Ministry of Press and Information, Welckerstrasse 11, PO Box 2160, D-53113 Bonn (tel: 228-2080; fax: 228-208-2555).

Ministry of Transport, Kennedyallee 72, PO Box 200100, D-53175 Bonn (tel: 228-3000-01; fax: 228-300-3428, 228-300-3429).

Statisches Bundesamt (StBa) (federal statistical office), Postfach 5528, Gustav-Stresemann-Ring 11, D-65189 Wiesbaden (tel: 751; fax: 724-000).

Treuhandanstalt, Leipziger Strasse 5–7, 0-1080 Berlin (tel: West Berlin 31-540 or East Berlin 2320).

Verband beratender Ingenieure (VBI) (association of consulting engineers), Zweigstrasse 37, D-4300 Essen (tel: 792-044).

Verband der Fertigwarenimporteure (VFI) (association of finished goods importers), Gotenstrasse 21, D-2000 Hamburg (tel: 280-1337).

Verband unabhängig beratender Ingenieurfirmen (association of independent consulting engineers), Winston-Churchill-Strasse 1, D-5300 Bonn (tel: 217-064).

Verlag W. Kohlhammer (publisher of federal statistics), Philip-Reis-Strasse 3, D-6500 Mainz 42 (tel: 59-094).

Verlag moderne Industrie (publisher of 'Who's Who in Marketing and Communications'), Justus-von-Liebig-Strasse 1, D-8910 Landsberg (tel: 1251).

Zentralausschuss der Deutschen Werbewirtschaft (ZAW) (central committee of the German advertising industry), Villichgasse 17, D-5300 Bonn (tel: 351-025).

Gibraltar

Howard Hill

The Gibraltar Social Democrats (GSD) were elected in May 1996 after a decisive victory at the polls. Populist Joe Bossano, head of the Gibraltar Socialist Labour party (GSLP) and leader of the Gibraltar government for eight years, had to move over for GSD leader Peter Caruana. The change will mean Gibraltar will be much more pro-business under barrister Caruana than under former trade unionist Bossano. Relations with both London and Madrid could also improve.

KEY FACTS — Gibraltar

Official title: The City of Gibraltar

Head of state: Queen Elizabeth II

Head of government: Chief Minister Peter Caruana (leader of GSD) (from May 1996)

Ruling party: Gibraltar Social Democrats (GSD) (from May 1996)

Capital: Gibraltar

Official Languages: English

Currency: Gibraltar Pound (G£) = 100 pence (sterling)

Exchange rate: G£0.60 per US$ (Dec 1996)

Area: 5.8 sq km

Population: 30,000 (1995)

GNP per capita: US$15,000 (1995)*

Election

The GSD won 52 per cent of the votes for the 15-member House of Assembly in May 1996. Bossano campaigned on his platform of ever-decreasing ties with Britain. He said that a third successive victory for his party would be celebrated by the publication of a document outlining the framework for the transformation of the Rock's status from British colony free association. Bossano's insistence on self-determination for Gibraltar ruffled feathers in both Britain and Spain where this position found little sympathy – both countries wanted Gibraltar firmly under their own control. Bossano was a particular irritant to Spain; Madrid continually accused him of not doing enough to stop money laundering and contraband smuggling (mostly drugs and tax-free cigarettes via speedboats).

Caruana promised voters that negotiations on all aspects of Gibraltar's relationship with London and Madrid would be open to negotiation under the so-called Brussels process framework; this framework was implemented in the last decade. Caruana seems intent on patching up Gibraltar's relationship with both Britain and Spain but has reminded Spain that the question of sovereignty is not negotiable.

Smuggling

Spain claims that drug smuggling still operates is Gibraltar, which it says is a staging ground for hashish coming from Morocco to Spain. The April 1996 crash of a Spanish police helicopter some 40 miles off Gibraltar, resulting in the death of one of its three-person crew, again focused attention on the Rock's reputation as a haven for smugglers. The helicopter was brought down by an alleged smuggler in a fast-launch, possibly by throwing an oar at the helicopter's blades. In the aftermath, two Gibraltar-registered speedboats were captured by the Spanish police and six people were arrested, including three from Gibraltar, one from Britain, one from Spain and one Moroccan.

Shortly after taking office Caruana complained to Madrid that Spain's restrictive border controls were preventing any meaningful progress on talks over the Rock's future. These extra-strict measures, designed to increase pressure on the smuggling community, were introduced by Spain in mid-May 1996. Caruana was especially piqued by what he felt was the uneven application of the anti-smuggling operations – he alleged that there was an imbalance of attention being paid to Gibraltar in this respect and that the Spanish side's smuggling operations were not being particularly affected by the crack-down. The result was long queues at the Spain-Gibraltar border which brought irritation and inconvenience to the average citizen of Gibraltar.

Banking

At the begining of 1996, Gibraltar had 28 international banks. Of these, 21 are locally incorporated and seven are branches of banks incorporated elsewhere, but all in the European Union. Ten banks operate onshore and offshore, while 11 offer only offshore services. Gibraltar is bound to apply EU directives in banking.

Rejuvenation?

These are still early days in the life of the Caruana administration but most of the Rock's business leaders are still very hopeful that he will have a rejuvenating effect on the economy. A new passenger liner terminal is being developed; Gibraltar averages about 100 ships calls per year. The ship register was relaunched in January 1996 as a Category 1 British register and the authorities hope that this will draw ship managers and other related buinesses to Gibraltar.

Recent moves toward revitalising the Rock as a financial and business centre, have placed an emphasis on international activities. If the new government can open up a meaningful dialogue with both Spain and London on Gibraltar's role in the Mediterranean, then there may be some hope for its international business plans.

Historical profile

1704 captured by UK from Spain.
1830 Became a crown colony.
1869 Opening of Suez Canal increased Gibraltar's importance in guarding the route to India and the Far East.
1939-45 Busy naval base in Second World War. After Second World War, Spain continued to press for the return of Gibraltar, but rejected offer of UK to refer the matter to the International Court of Justice.
1967 More than 12,000 Gibraltarians voted to remain British; only 44 opted for Spanish rule. The dispute continued to disrupt friendly relations between Spain and UK; for a while Spain closed the frontier. Both countries sought a peaceful settlement, and people maintained their wish to remain British.

Political system

Gibraltar has a UK-appointed governor with executive authority, a Gibraltar Council under a chief minister, and House of Assembly comprising a speaker (appointed by the governor), two ex-officio members and 15 elected members serving a four-year term. The British Government, through the governor, remains directly responsible for security, defence and foreign affairs. The Gibraltar Socialist Labour Party (GSLP) led by Joe Bossano was returned to power in an election on 16 January 1992 with 73 per cent of the vote, on a platform calling for greater autonomy for the United Kingdom while remaining opposed to Spanish sovereignty without hostility to Spain. Peter Caruana and the Gibraltar Social Democrats (GSD) won 52 per cent of the votes in 16 May 1996 elections, voting Joe Bossano and the GSLP out after eight years in power.

Political parties

Gibraltar Social Democrats (GSD) are the party in government. Other major parties include the Gibraltar Socialist Labour Party (GSLP); Gibraltar National Party (GNP); Gibraltar Labour Party-Association for the Advancement of Civil Rights (GLP-AACR).

Media

Press: Only daily newspaper is *Gibraltar Chronicle*. Weeklies: *Panorama*, *Vox* (which publishes a Spanish section), *The Democrat* and *The People* (also carries a Spanish section).
Broadcasting: Over 7,000 combined radio and TV licences issued. Programmes broadcast by Gibraltar Broadcasting Corporation (GBC) and include advertising. GBC-Radio broadcasts in English and Spanish, the British Forces Broadcasting Service in English only, GBC-TV in English only.
Advertising: All usual media available to advertisers. Information on radio and TV advertising available from GBC.

Domestic economy

The economy is primarily dependent on service industries. Its main base is centred on providing services to tourism, the commercial port, the offshore financial services and banking. Since the full opening of the land frontier with Spain in 1985, the number of tourists visiting Gibraltar has rapidly increased to around 4m per year. The closure of the Naval Dockyard in 1985 saw the formation of a commercial ship-repair yard – Gibraltar Ship-Repair Ltd (GSL). This company ceased trading in 1991 but a Norwegian company, Kvaerner, is now operating the yard. The port provides an important source of income. The Gibraltar Government has invited the setting up of light industries there, by making available a package of incentives and other benefits to successful companies. Gibraltar's popularity as an offshore finance centre developed steadily but slowed after reports of money laundering gave the industry bad publicity; new regulations introduced in mid-1995 are designed to restore confidence. Sophisticated, confidential financial services are available with considerable tax breaks. Gibraltar became an associate member of the EC when the United Kingdom joined in 1972, and is included for all matters, except VAT, the Customs Union and the Common Agricultural Policy. Gibraltar now plans third-country or associated status with the EU.

External trade

Regular trade deficit largely offset by invisible earnings. Heavy dependence on imports of food, consumer goods, raw materials, fuels and equipment from UK. Re-exports mainly petroleum products, tobacco, manufactured goods and wine to UK, Spain and Morocco.

Legal system

Based on English law.

BUSINESS GUIDE

Time

GMT + 1 hr (GMT + 2 hrs from late Mar to late Sep).

Climate

Temperate with hot and dry summers, and fairly mild rainy winters; temperatures vary between 10–29°C.
Clothing: Lightweight for summer, medium weight and light raincoat for winter.

Entry requirements

As for United Kingdom.

Air access

Direct flights from London and Manchester operated by GB Airways and Dan Air. GB Airways also operate direct flights to Tangier, Tetuan, Jerez, Madeira, Tunis and Casablanca.
National airline: GB Airways.
International airport: Gibraltar (GIB) is served by North Front 2.5 km from town centre.

Surface access

Regular ferry services from Tangier, and road access from Málaga through La Línea frontier in Spain.

Hotels

No offical rating system. Reservations should be made in advance especially during summer. Some hotels reduce rates between Nov and Mar.

Car hire

Available through local car hire firms and travel agents. UK International driving licence and evidence of insurance required. The British Automobile clubs AA and RAC have agents in Gibraltar.

National transport

Bus and taxi services available. Total of about 45 km of roads. No railway network.

Public holidays

Fixed dates: 1 Jan (New Year's Day), 1 May (May Day), 25 Dec and 26 Dec (Christmas).
Variable dates: Commonwealth Day (Mar), Good Friday, Easter Monday, Spring Bank Holiday, Queen's Birthday (Jun), Late Summer Bank Holiday (Aug).

Working hours

Business: (Mon–Fri) 0900–1300 and 1430–1800. (Sat) 0900–1300.
Banking: (Mon–Thur) 0900–1530, (Fri) 0900–1530 and 1630–1800.
Shops: (Mon–Fri) Most shops open from 0900–1900 and some open from 0900–1300 and 1500–1900, (Sat) 0900–1300.

Business language and interpreting/translation

The official language is English but Spanish is sometimes used when dealing with Spanish business.

Telecommunications

Telephone: Rates for calls from public telephone boxes dependent on time of day. International direct dialling facilities available to over 75 countries. International dialling code: 350. There are no area codes.
Telex: Two public telex call offices. Country code 405 GK. Information from Gibraltar Telecommunications International, Main Street.
Telegram: Available 24 hours a day from Gibraltar Telecommunications International.

Banking

Domestic and offshore services available. There are some 28 banks operating in Gibraltar, and around eleven offshore banks.
Banks: See 'Business Directory, Banking'.

Electricity supply

240 V AC.

BUSINESS DIRECTORY

Hotels

Bristol, 10 Cathedral Square (tel: 76-800; fax: 77-613).

Caleta Palace, Sir Herbert Miles Road, Catalan Bay (tel: 76-501; fax: 71-050).

Continental, Engineer Lane (tel: 76-900; fax: 75-366).

Holiday Inn, 2 Governor's Parade (tel: 70-500; fax: 70-243).

Montarik, Bedlam Court, Main Street (tel: 77-065/90; tx: 2361).

Ocean Heights, Montague Place (tel: 75-548).

Queen's, Boyd Street (tel: 74-000; tx: 2269).

Rock, Europa Road (tel: 73-000; fax: 73-513).

Sunrise Motel, 60 Devil's Tower Road (tel: 41-265).

Car hire

Avis: reservations (tel: 75-552, 75-727).

Budget: Regal House, 3 Queensway (tel: 79-666; fax: 79-668).

Europcar: reservations (tel: 77-171; fax: 45-168).

Hertz: reservations (tel: 42-737; fax: 40-062).

Chambers of Commerce

The Gibraltar Chamber of Commerce, PO Box 29, Suite 11, Don House, The New Arcade, 38 Main Street (tel: 78-376; fax: 78-403).

Banking

Abbey National (Gibraltar) Ltd, 237 Main Street (tel: 76-090; fax: 72-028).

ABN Amro Bank (Gibraltar) Ltd, PO Box 100, 2-6 Main Street (tel: 79-220/79-370; fax: 78-512).

Baltica Bank (Gibraltar) Ltd, 215a Neptune House, Marina Bay (tel: 42-670; fax: 42-676

Banco Atlantico (Gibraltar) Ltd, Eurolife Building, 1 Corral Road (tel: 40-117; fax: 40-110).

Banco Bilbao Vizcaya International (Gibraltar) Ltd, 3rd Floor, Hadfield House, Library Street (tel: 79-420; fax: 73-870).

Banco Bilbao Vizcaya (Gibraltar) Ltd, 260/262 Main Street (tel: 77-797, 77-871, 77-896).

Banco Central Sa, 198/200 Main Street (tel: 73-625, 73-650, 73-675; fax: 73-707).

Banco Español de Credito, 114 Main Street (tel: 76-518; fax: 73-947).

BUSINESS DIRECTORY

Banking (contd):
Banque Indosuez, 206/210 Main Street (tel: 75-090; fax: 79-618).

Barclays Bank plc, 84/90 Main Street (tel: 78-565; fax: 79-509).

Credit Suisse (Gibraltar) Ltd, Neptune House, Marina Bay (tel: 76-606; fax: 76-027).

Gibraltar Private Bank Ltd, PO Box 407, 10th Floor, ICC, Casemates (tel: 73-350; fax: 73-475).

Hambros Bank Ltd, PO Box 375, 32 Line Wall Road (tel: 74-850; fax: 79-037).

Hispano Commerzbank (Gibraltar) Ltd, Suite 14, 30/38 Main Street (tel: 74-199; fax: 74-174).

Jyske Bank (Gibraltar) Ltd, PO Box 143, 76 Main Street (tel: 78-325, 72-782; fax: 73-732).

Lloyds Bank plc, 323 Main Street (tel: 77-373; fax: 70-023).

Midland Bank Trust Corporation (Gibraltar) Ltd, PO Box 19, Hadfield House, Library Street (tel: 79-500; fax: 72-090).

National Westminster Bank, 57 Line Wall Road (tel: 77-737; fax: 74-557).

Republic National Bank of New York (Gibraltar) Ltd, Neptune House, Marina Bay, PO Box 5578 (tel: 79-374; fax: 75-684).

Royal Bank of Scotland (Gibraltar) Ltd, 1 Corral Road (tel: 73-200; fax: 70-152).

Varde Bank International (Gibraltar) Ltd, PO Box 476, Suite E, Regal House, 3 Queensway (tel: 42-455; fax: 42-456).

Travel information

GB Airways, Iain Stewart Centre, Beehive Ring Road, Gatwick Airport, West Sussex RG6 0PB, UK (tel: (1293)664-239; fax: (1293)664-218).

Gibraltar Information Bureau, Cathedral Square (tel: 76-400; fax: 79-980).

Other useful addresses

Department of Trade & Industry, The Haven, 23 John Mackintosh Square (tel: 79-533; fax: 71-406).

Economic Planning and Statistics Office, 6 Convent Place (tel: 75-515, 70-071).

Gibraltar Hotel Association (tx: 2236).

Gibraltar Information Bureau, Arundel Great Court, 179 Strand, London WC2R 1EH (tel: 0171-836-0777; fax: 0171-240-6612).

Office of the Governor, The Convent (tel: 75-908; tx: 2223).

Internet sites

Gibraltar Tourist Office (http:\\www.gibraltar.gi).

Greece

Dan Bindman

Greece entered a new era in January 1996 when prime minister Andreas Papandreou finally resigned from politics, 15 years after he first took office at the head of the Panhellenic Socialist Movement (PASOK). His departure signalled an end to the inertia that had progressively overtaken the government since an already-frail Papandreou won a third term as prime minister in October 1993. The terminally ill 76-year-old politician, who had presided over the modernisation of Greek society, died of heart failure less than six months after turning over the reins. Notwithstanding structural obstacles to its long-term economic performance, Greece, aided by its membership of the European Union (EU), has experienced a modest recovery since the recession of 1992/93.

KEY FACTS — *Greece*

Official title: I Elliniki Dimokratia (The Hellenic Republic)

Head of state: President Constantine (Costis) Stefanopoulos (from 10 Mar 1995)

Head of government: Prime Minister Costas Simitis (leader of PASOK) (from 20 Jan 1996; sworn in Sep 1996 after PASOK won general election)

Ruling party: Panhellenic Socialist Movement (PASOK)

Capital: Athens

Official Languages: Greek

Currency: Drachma (Dr) = 100 leptae

Exchange rate: Dr247.10 per US$ (Dec 1996)

Area: 131,957 sq km

Population: 10.65m (Jul 1995)

GDP per capita: US$9,300 (1994)

GDP real growth: 1.5% (1995)

GNP per capita: US$7,710 (1994)

GNP real growth: 1.3% (1985-94)

Labour force: 4.2m (1995)

Unemployment: 8.4% (Dec 1995)

Inflation: 8.6% (Jul 1996, year-on-year, consumer prices)

Trade balance: -US$17.3bn (12 months to Feb 1996)

Foreign debt: US$36.2bn (1994)

Visitor numbers: 11m (1994)

Politics

Papandreou's replacement, the 59-year-old former industry minister Costas Simitis, immediately faced a raft of urgent problems afflicting the economy, including an inefficient state bureaucracy and the continuation of an unpopular austerity programme aimed at meeting the Maastricht economic convergence criteria for a single European currency. On taking office, Simitis, a lawyer and economist, pledged to bring the country closer to the European Union. He was narrowly elected to replace Papandreou at a caucus of PASOK MPs, in which he defeated the interior minister and acting prime minister Akis Tsohatzopoulos in a run-off by 86 votes to 75.

In choosing his government, Simitis opted for continuity by keeping in post the national economy minister Yannos Papandoniou and the finance minister Alexandros Papadopoulos, both of whom were credited with bringing inflation below double figures for the first time in more than 20 years. A new super-ministry of development was created – covering industry, commerce and tourism – under former European Commissioner Vasso Papandreou (no relation).

Simitis consolidated his grip on PASOK in June 1996, one week after Andreas Papandreou's death, when he was elected leader of the socialists at a four-day party congress. Just over half (53.5 per cent) of the party's 5,200 delegates voted for him, with the remainder backing Tsohatzopoulos. Simitis had earlier threatened to resign from the premiership if he was not elected party leader. His victory represented a triumph for the reformist wing of the party over the 'old guard' wing, which was opposed to privatisation, was intimately associated with a dubious system of political patronage, and favoured Papandreou's brand of traditional grass-roots populism. The win ensured that, barring accidents, Simitis' tenure in office would last at least until the next general election – due to be held in late 1997.

Economy

In 1995 annual growth rose by 0.5 per cent to 2 per cent of GDP, although this compared unfavourably with a European Union average of 2.7 per cent. Most of the growth was attributed to higher investment. The government reported that private investment spending rose by 6.1 per cent in 1995, compared with the 3.5 per cent envisaged by Greece's EU convergence plan. Public sector investment increased by 18.6 per cent in real terms, compared with 9.5 per cent in the plan.

This trend was expected to continue as the government's restrictive fiscal and exchange rate stance helped to keep real interest rates down. The central bank's 'hard drachma' policy – an anti-inflationary foreign exchange policy – was pledged to be continued. In late July 1996, national economy minister Yannos Papandoniou was optimistic that GDP growth for the year would reach or exceed 2.5 per cent and he forecast 'conservatively' that in 1997 it would rise to 3 per cent.

Papandoniou also predicted that the general government deficit in 1996 would fall within Greece's EU convergence target of 7.5 per cent of GDP. Of course, this would have to be cut dramatically thereafter if Greece was to have a chance of joining the first wave of currency union – an outcome that few, as of mid-1996, thought possible.

One Maastricht target that the government has all but accepted it cannot achieve is the debt to GDP ratio. Gross general government debt would have to be 60 per cent of GDP or less under the Maastricht guidelines. In 1995 Greece's debt to GDP ratio according to the Maastricht definition stood at 111.6 per cent, just 1.5 per cent lower than the 1994 figure. It was expected to fall to around 110 per cent in 1996 and to remain above 100 per cent at the end of the century.

Inflation

Greece's success in bringing consumer price inflation down from the highs of the 1980s and early 1990s – the average for the 10 years 1984-93 was 17.4 per cent – has been one of the country's proudest boasts. Headline inflation fell to 8.1 per cent in December 1995, although by April 1996 this had slipped to 9.2 per cent: roughly equal to the annual average for 1995. However, Papandoniou was confident that the rate for 1996 would fall to between 7.8 per cent and 8 per cent, a substantial revision of an earlier target of 5 per cent. Even if the government's prediction was realised, this would still leave the rate far in excess of the proposed Maastricht target of 2.6 per cent.

An ever-present threat to inflation in 1996 was a resort to inflationary tax increases to boost revenues in order to cut the budget deficit. This was particularly feared in the event of the failure of government attempts to increase revenues through reducing tax evasion, which were intended to fund spending increases contained in the 1996 budget.

Rising unemployment, which hit 10 per cent in 1995, was thought likely to have a dampening effect on wage costs, with a consequent positive effect on inflation. Encouragement was derived on this score from an agreement between trades unions and employers for wage increases of 7.5 per cent in 1996. The unemployment rate, which had averaged 7.9 per cent in the years 1984-93, was forecast to worsen gradually over the years 1996-98. However, one sector

KEY INDICATORS — Greece

	Unit	1991	1992	1993	1994	1995
Population	m	10.20	10.31	10.35	10.43	10.65
Gross domestic product (GDP)	US$bn	69.0	79.8	74.2	77.6	–
GDP per capita	US$	6,870	7,900	7,170	9,300	–
GDP real growth	%	3.2	0.8	-0.5	1.5	1.5
Inflation	%	19.5	15.9	14.4	10.8	8.4
Consumer prices	1990=100	119.5	138.4	158.4	175.7	192.0
Unemployment	%	8.6	9.1	9.8	9.6	8.4
Wages (hourly)	1990=100	116.7	132.8	146.7	165.9	–
Agricultural production	1979-81=100	111.00	106.77	103.74	111.49	110.18
Manufacturing production	1990=100	99.1	97.9	94.6	95.7	97.8
Coal production	m toe	7.2	7.6	7.7	7.8	7.9
Bauxite production	'000 tonnes	2,133	2,042	2,155	*2.400	–
Nickel production	'000 tonnes	19.3	18.7	12.6	12.5	–
Exports (FOB) (goods)	US$m	6,911	6,076	5,112	5,338	–
Imports (FOB) (goods)	US$m	16,933	17,637	15,611	16,611	–
Balance of trade	US$m	-10,112	-11,603	-10,557	-13,500	-16,000
Current account	US$m	-1,574	-2,140	-747	-146	–
Tourism receipts	US$bn	2.64	3.10	3.14	3.45	–
Total reserves minus gold	US$m	5,188.9	4,793.6	7,790.3	14,487.9	14,780.0
Foreign exchange	US$m	5,081.6	4,632.9	7,634.0	14,321.6	14,611.0
Discount rate	%	19.0	19.0	21.5	20.5	18.0
Deposit rate	%	20.67	19.92	19.33	18.92	15.75
Lending rate	%	29.45	28.71	28.56	27.44	23.04
Exchange rate	Dr per US$	182.27	190.62	229.25	242.60	231.66

* estimated figure

unlikely to produce significant job losses in advance of the general election was the over-staffed civil service. An estimated 10 per cent, or 50,000, redundancies were believed to be necessary, although the political will to bring this about had hitherto been lacking.

External trade

In 1994 Greece almost eliminated its current account deficit, yet the situation declined in 1995. While exports increased by 10.6 per cent to US$5.9 billion in 1995, imports rose by 21.9 per cent to US$20.2 billion, leaving a negative trade balance of US$14.3 billion and a current account deficit of US$3 billion, or 2.6 per cent of GDP. A central plank of Greece's foreign currency receipts is tourism. Although numbers held up in 1995, dropping just 600,000 from a record 11.3 million in 1994, per capita spending by visitors remained low.

About 10 per cent of the country's total foreign exchange earnings typically go towards interest payments on external debt, the value of which was expected to have risen by 13 per cent in 1995 to US$53 billion. However, a major source of assistance to Greece's efforts to contain the current account deficit has come from financial inflows from the EU. Total available EU structural and cohesion funds were due to amount to some US$20 billion, or 5 per cent of GDP, each year to 1999, although these have been dependent on budget targets being met and administrative efficiency being observed.

COUNTRY PROFILE — GREECE

Historical profile

In ancient times the cradle of democracy has been enjoyed only intermittently by modern Greeks. Since first independence (1928), the country has been ruled under successive systems of absolute monarchy, constitutional monarchy and republic, and suffered military coups and dictatorships. 1917 Greece entered First World War on the side of the Allies; made territorial gains.
1939 Greece rejected Italy's ultimatum seeking free passage for its troops in Second World War and repelled its attack, but was occupied by Germany. Government and king went into exile. Mass armed resistance grew out of various political groupings.
1944 Liberation from the Nazis. The returned National Unity Government under George Papandreou fought a civil war against the communists until 1949, when constitutional monarchy was re-established. Territorial gains from war.
1967 conflicts between the young King Constantine and government led military coup by a group of colonels. All political activity was barred and opposition silenced. Colonel George Papadopoulos prime minister until 1973.
1974 Civil war and Turkish invasion in Cyprus brought Greece close to war with Turkey and caused the downfall of the military junta. Referendum in favour of presidential republic; government by new Democracy Party under Constantine Karamanlis until 1980.
1979 Joined the EU.
1981-89 Government by Panhellenic Socialist Movement (PASOK) led by Andreas Papandreou, the first socialist government in Greek history.
1994 EU presidency for the first half of the year.

Political system

Under its 1975 constitution, Greece, or the Hellenic Republic, is a parliamentary democracy led by a president with largely ceremonial authority who is elected for five years by the 300-member unicameral *Vouli* (parliament). *Vouli* consists of 300 deputies elected for four years by universal adult sufferage. President appoints prime minister and, upon his recommendation, a cabinet to form the government. In 1986 the constitution was changed to limit the president's power and increase parliament's. In September 1993 Prime Minister Constantine Mitsotakis' New Democracy (ND) government was forced to resign after losing its one-seat parliamentary majority. A general election, held on 10 October 1993, saw the Panhellenic Socialist Movement (PASOK) regaining power with about 47 per cent of the vote and ND receiving about 40 Per cent. The conservative Political Spring received about 5 per cent. In the European elections in June 1994 PASOK lost some 10 per cent of its vote. Prime Minister Andreas Papandreou (PASOK's founder) resigned 15 January 1996 due to ill health and Costas Simitis became prime minister. Andreas Papandreou died in June 1996, ending the era of authoritarian control over Greek political parties, and opening the way for govenment by consensus. Next general election scheduled for October 1997.

Political parties

Party in government: Panellinion Sosialistikon Kinema (Panhellenic Socialist Movement) (PASOK). Other major parties: Communist Party, Greek Left Party, Democratic Renewal.

Main cities/towns

Athens/Piraeus (population 3.1m in 1994, Thessaloniki, Patras, Chania, Iraklion (Kriti), Volos, Larissa, Kavala.

Language

Main language Greek; English and French also spoken.

Media

Dailies: Most of the national daily newspapers are published in Athens, a few in Thessaloniki. Most popular are *Ta Nea* (circulation February 1995, 126,000), *Elefth Tipos* (108,000), *Eleftherotipia* (108,000), *Apogeymatini* (66,000), *Ethnos* (56,000), *Adesmeytos* (42,000) and *Kathimerini* (33,000). Also several regional

EU funding

Greece has sometimes been its own worst enemy in obstructing the smooth transfer of EU funds. For several months in the first half of 1996, the country single-handedly held up an ambitious EU trade and investment plan, the Mediterranean Development Aid plan (MEDA). The plan involves a five-year US$6 billion scheme to turn the region into a free trade zone. Greece objected to the inclusion in MEDA of its regional rival, Turkey, and demanded that EU foreign ministers called for MEDA nations to respect democracy and promote 'good neighbourliness'. Tension between Greece and Turkey had worsened in the first months of 1996 after a territorial dispute over an island off the Turkish coast almost led to armed conflict at the beginning of the year. Athens finally agreed to withdraw its veto on MEDA in July 1996, when a compromise was reached with the EU.

Privatisation

A key revenue-raising measure of the Simitis government has been a potentially lucrative privatisation plan. An earlier sell-off scheme was much criticised for the slow pace of its implementation. In April 1996 the government finally went ahead with a partial privatisation of the state telecommunications monopoly (OTE), although in this case the cash raised was destined for reinvestment by OTE rather than for government coffers. Also scheduled for privatisation in 1996 were three banks – the Bank of Crete, the Bank of Attica and the Bank of Central Greece – and in early 1997 a share of the Public Petroleum Company (DEP). Further privatisations could include subsidiaries of the National Bank of Greece, remaining enterprises of the Organisation of Industrial Reconstruction (IRO) and assets of the national tourist organisation (EOT).

The flotation of 8 per cent of OTE's equity was the largest ever issue on the small Athens bourse and it increased the market's total capitalisation by some 25 per cent. The share price valued the company at US$6.96 billion, a figure credible because OTE had undergone radical restructuring in preparation for the offering. Net profits in 1995 were US$585 million and annual earnings growth over the next five years was forecast to run at 15 per cent. The issue did not include an international tranche: a reaction to a disastrous attempt to sell a quarter share of OTE in 1994, which fell through at the last minute after foreign investors claimed it was over-priced. The US$377 million proceeds of the 1996 sale were due, in part, to finance the company's plans for Greece's third mobile telephone network.

Also given a comprehensive makeover before privatisation was the Bank of Crete, a private medium-sized bank that was hit by a US$200 million embezzlement scandal – involving the bribery of Socialist politicians – in the late 1980s. In January 1996 Greece's central bank, which had been charged with running the Bank of Crete after the scandal, siphoned a US$135 million package of the bank's assets and liabilities that were linked to the embezzlement, into a separate bank. It also granted the solvent Bank of Crete capital worth close to US$180 million. The bank, which has more than 80 branches across Greece, was due to be sold through a competitive bidding process.

The government's enthusiasm for raising revenues through market mechanisms has had limits, however. This became clear in mid-1996, when the Simitis government balked at a plan devised by its predecessor in 1994, to cover the country with private casinos. The minister responsible for tourism, Vasso Papandreou, had never been enthusiastic about the project and when she entered the government she took steps to regulate the operation of all casinos that were being built or were already open.

Before these measures were presented to parliament, she also revoked the licence of a casino that was scheduled to be built in the capital, Athens. In July 1996 this led to Ms Papandreou being summoned by a federal court in the United States after an American investor brought a suit for breach of contract. The minister responded that she would first implement legislation to regulate casinos and would deal with the court case later. The Greek government was perhaps justifiably confident that its defiant stand would not attract retribution from the US government on behalf of its aggrieved citizens. Within a fortnight of the law suit being brought, the US defence department announced that it had negotiated the sale of US$100 million worth of US-made tanks, artillery, trucks and other equipment to the Greek armed forces.

COUNTRY PROFILE — GREECE

Media (contd): dailies with generally low circulation although *Thessaloniki* is popular. *Athens News* is published daily in English.
Weeklies: To Vima (circulation February 1995, 186,000), *Eleftherotipia* (171,000), *Tipos Kiriakis* (123,000) and *Ethnos* (116,000).
Business: Financial and business publications include *To Vima, Naftemboriki, Kerdos, Express, Economicos Tachidromos* and *Expendytis.*
Broadcasting: State-supervised companies, Elliniki Radiophonia Tileorassi – Hellenic radio and Television operates two main television channels (ET-1 and ET-2) and a third in Thessaloniki as well as four radio channels. Local government-operated radio stations in Athens and Thessaloniki. There are more than 150 private radio stations broadcasting around the country. Most popular are: Sky 100.4 FM, 9.84 FM, Antenna 97, 1 FM. There are two private TV stations, Mega TV and Antenna TV, with nationwide coverage and 12 others in Athens and Thessaloniki.

Advertising

All usual media are used. All television broadcasts are commercial, and two of the four radio programmes accept advertising. Posters are widely used, under control of site owner. Cinema firms are also popular, and direct mail is becoming increasingly important. Newspaper and magazine advertising is constrained by relatively low circulation figures. Key categories include food, retail, cigarettes, alcohol, clothing and electrical appliances. Adspend as percentage of GDP 1.89 per cent. Total adspend US$1.4bn in 1995 (TV 63%,newspapers 12%, magazines 15%).

Domestic economy

Mixed economy with heavy dependence on tourism, agriculture and shipping. The strong service sector accounts for over 55 per cent of GDP. Economic growth has been undermined by large debt burden, high inflation and low levels of investment. Stabilisation programme introduced in January 1991. The black market economy in Greece is believed by many to account for up to 50 per cent of the total economy.

Employment

About 27 per cent of the workforce is female.

External trade

Growing current account deficit owing to increased debt payments, increasing imports and stagnating exports. Visible exports consist mainly of fruit and vegetables, live animals, textiles, petroleum products, tobacco, clothing and metals. Principal imports include raw materials, fuels and lubricants, chemicals, machinery and transport equipment, foodstuffs, basic manufactures and manufactured consumer goods. Since entry into the EU in 1981 trade with Europe has increased, particularly with Germany, Italy, France, UK and the Netherlands. Greek trade with Romania in 1994 totalled US$186m, a 40 per cent increase over 1993.
Exports: Main destinations: Germany (typically 24% of total), Italy (12%), France (6.4%), UK (5.9%), EU (54.8%).
Imports: Main sources: Germany (typically 17% of total), Italy 14%), France (7.9%), UK (6.1%), EU (60%).

Agriculture

Important sector of economy contributing 16 per cent to GDP in 1994, accounting for over 20 per cent of exports and employing 24.5 per cent of the labour force on small farms averaging less than 2 ha. Farm holdings are small and fragmented. Sector also handicapped by weak infrastructure, low levels of technology and generally poor soil. However, with the exception of meat, dairy products and animal feeds, Greece is self-sufficient in foodstuffs. Main crops include wheat, barley, maize, fruit (especially olives), vegetables, oil seeds, tobacco, cotton and sugar-beet. Forestry is being developed. Fish farms produced a record harvest of 16,000 tonnes of sea bass and gilthead bream in 1995.

Industry

Sector forms mainstay of economy accounting for 25 per cent of GDP in 1994. Manufacturing contributes about 15.6 per cent to GDP. About 26.4 per cent of the labour force is employed in industry. Small family-owned companies dominate, most of which are situated in the Athens area. The pace of mergers and acquisitions of Greek firms by foreign investors increased. Production has been sluggish and relatively few industries remain competitive on a European scale. Major manufacturing industries include textiles, clothing and footwear, chemicals, metals manufacture and cement.

Tourism

The tourism sector is Greece's biggest single source of foreign exchange earnings. The government is seeking to improve quality by developing the conference and incentives market and upgrading hotels. Investment proposals for luxury leisure complexes are being encouraged.

Mining

Relative wealth of natural resources including large deposits of bauxite (aluminium ore), marble, lignite, magnesite, ferro-chrome, ferro-nickel, lead, zinc, uranium and manganese. Mining activity is however small-scale and sector contributed only 3 per cent to GDP in 1994 and employed 1 per cent of the workforce. Greece quarried 2.6m tonnes of marble in 1994. More gold exploration was carried out in 1995; deposit of 11 tonnes of gold at Thrace but recovery costs estimated at between US$200 and US$290 an ounce; Cassandra Mines is Greece's biggest gold producer.

Hydrocarbons

Coal reserves 3bn tonnes (end-1995). Coal production 7.9m tonnes oil equivalent (1995), up 1.3 per cent on 1994 output. In January 1996 Greece invited bids from foreign companies for six concessions for onshore and offshore oil exploration in areas of western Greece. The three onshore blocks are in the north-west Pelopennese, Aetolo-Acharnania and near Ionnina. The offshore blocks are in the Ionian Sea, off Katakolo in the north-west Peloponnese, in the Patras Gulf and off the island of Paxi.

Energy

Around 55 per cent of primary energy requirements met by imported oil. Current emphasis on developing indigenous oil resources (largely from the Prinos oil field) and expanding hydroelectric and geothermal usage.

Membership of international organisations

CCC, CERN, Council of Europe, CSCE, EEA, ECAC, EIB (associate), EMA, EU, FAO, IAEA, ICAO, IDA, IFAD, IFC, IHO, ILO, IMF, IMO, INTELSAT, INTERPOL, IOOC, ITU, IWC, MIGA, NACC, NAM (guest), NATO, OECD, UN, UNESCO, UNIDO, UPU, WEU (from 6 March 1995), WHO, WIPO, WMO, World Bank, WSG, WTO.

BUSINESS GUIDE

Time

GMT + 2 hrs (GMT + 3 hrs from late Mar to late Sep).

Climate

Hot and dry summers, from Apr–Oct, with average temperatures 24–32°C. Mild winters in south but cooler in north with temperatures falling as low as 0°C.

Clothing

Lightweight for summer, medium weight with light topcoat for winter.

Entry requirements

Visas not required by nationals of most West European countries, and some others. N.B. Regulations likely to change at short notice; Greek consulate or travel agent should be consulted.
Health: Vaccination certificates may be required if travelling from infected area.
N.B. Drinking water is not always purified outside main cities.
Currency: Up to Dr100,000 in Greek currency may be taken into the country and up to Dr20,000 taken out, in denominations of up to Dr5,000 banknotes. No restrictions on movement of foreign currency.
Customs: Personal effects duty-free.

Air access

Regular direct flights by all major international airlines.
National airline: Olympic Airways.
Main international airport: Athens (ATH). The East Airport is for international and charter flights. The West Airport (Hellenikon), 15 km south of Athens, is only for the Olympic Airways flights, both domestic and international. In June 1996 a financing package was signed for construction of Athens' new international airport, due to open at the end of 2000.
International airports: Alexandroupolis (AXD), 7 km from city; Corfu (CFU), 1.6 km from city; Heraklion (HER), 5 km from city; Ioannina (IOA), 5 km from city; Kos (KGS), 27 km from city; Mykonos (JMK); Paros (PAS); Rhodes (RHO), 16 km south-west of Rhodes; Salonika (SKG), 16 km from city; Skiathos (JSI); Thira (JTR). A new airport at Spata, near Athens, is due to be completed by 1996.

Surface access

Frequent passenger ferry services from Italy to Piraeus, and car ferry service between Ancona (Italy), Brindisi, to Igoumenitsa and Patras. Road and rail routes from most parts of Europe via Italy, Yugoslavia or Bulgaria.
Main ports: Heraklion, Igoumenitsa, Patras, Piraeus, Rafina, Salonika, Volos.

Hotels

Numerous hotels in all main towns. Classified as de luxe, A,B,C,D and E. Single de luxe room without breakfast costs about Dr18,000 per night, including 15 per cent service charge but excluding tax. A small tip will also be expected. Advisable to make reservations well in advance, especially between May and Sep.

Currency

The drachma floats, with rates set by the Bank of Greece and the commercial banks. The drachma is not included in the European Monetary System, but is part of the European Currency Unit (Ecu) basket and floats against the Ecu.

Credit cards

All major credit cards are accepted.

Car hire

All major car hire companies have offices in Athens and some other main towns. Rates vary depending on size of car, length of hire and season. International driving licences recognised, but British, Belgian, Austrian and German full licences also accepted. International insurance Green Card is valid, provided Greece is mentioned. Wearing of seatbelts is compulsory.

City transport

Taxis: Taxis are plentiful in Athens but avoid rush hours. Extra charge for each piece of luggage, waiting time, journeys outside Athens/Piraeus and journeys after midnight. Yellow taxis run from Hellenikon airport to downtown Athens. Athens radio taxis (tel: 321-4058).
Buses: Run frequently throughout Athens, stopping at blue-coloured bus stop signs. Flat rate within city limits. Tickets are available at blue booths situated near the bus stops, or at many kiosks throughout the city. These tickets must be inserted into a machine inside the bus to be valid. Double decker buses run between the Hellenikon airport and downtown Athens, operating every 20 minutes from 0600 until midnight. Bus from Amalias Avenue opposite the National Gardens for East Terminal, and for West Terminal from Olympic Airways Headquarters at 96 Syngro Avenue.
Bus service (tel: 142).
Metro: From 0530 to midnight daily. Trains run approximately every four minutes during rush hour and every ten minutes at other times. Tickets must be purchased before entering the metro and must be cancelled upon entry. Only a small portion of the journey is underground. Metro (tel: 145).

National transport

Air: As well as the international airports, there are a further 25 other airports all connected by regular services operated by Olympic Airways.
Road: Approximately 40,000 km of road, of which about 9,000 km are classed as main roads. In August 1993 The EIB granted a loan for completion of the Corinth-Tripoli motorway, a two-way tunnel at Artemission and a bypass at Megalopoli south of Tripolis, as part of the planned motorway extension to Kalamata. Linked to the Athens-Thessaloniki motorway, the trans-peloponnesian section will assure the north-south transport link, creating conditions for further economic development.
Rail: Over 2,500 km of track operated by Hellenic Railways Organisation Ltd, with services to most main towns.
Water: About 80 km of navigable inland waterways, plus several regular ferry services along the coast and connecting the various islands.

Public holidays

Fixed dates: 1 Jan (New Year's Day), 6 Jan (Epiphany), 25 Mar (Independence Day), 1 May (Labour Day), 15 Aug (Assumption), 28 Oct (Oxi Day/Rejection of Mussolini's ultimatum), 25 Dec (Christmas Day), 26 Dec (St Stephen's Day).
Variable dates: First day of Lent, Greek Orthodox Good Friday, Easter Saturday and Easter Monday, Whit Monday.

Working hours

Business: (Mon–Fri) generally 0800–1400 and 1700–2000, tend to close earlier during summer and on Mon and Wed afternoons.
Government: (Mon–Fri) usually 0800–1500.
Banking: (Mon–Fri) 0800–1400.
Shops: (Mon, Wed and Sat) 0800–1500, (Tue, Thu and Fri) 0800–1400 and 1730–2030, or 0900–1730.

Business language and interpreting/translation

Can often be provided on a daily basis by hotel or travel agent. List of agencies usually available from commercial departments of embassies.

Telecommunications

Telephone and telefax: Moderately efficient, relatively cheap system, with automatic dialling throughout most of country. International dialling code: 30 followed by 1 for Athens, 31 for Thessaloniki, 81 for Heraklion and 661 for Corfu. For international dialling codes outgoing: 0044. Directory enquiries: 131.
Telex: Available at main post offices and at larger hotels. Country code 601 GR.
Telegram: Can be sent from post offices or by telephone. Services (domestic and international) operated by Greek Telecommunications Organisation (OTE).
Postal services: All overseas mail automatically

BUSINESS GUIDE

Telecommunications (contd): sent air mail. Internal service can be subject to delays.

Banking

Liberalisation of banking system was initiated in 1987. Interest rates are fully freed and commercial banks permitted to handle forward dealing in foreign exchange. In March 1993 the central bank lifted the last remaining restriction on interest rates by abolishing its 18 per cent minimum rate for deposit accounts. Central bank directives of May 1993 enable Greeks to hold foreign securities for less than one year and to invest abroad in derivatives for the first time. Companies can borrow in foreign exchange without restriction
Central bank: Bank of Greece.
Other banks: See 'Business Directory, Banking'.

Business information

Greek privatisation, beset with legal obstacles, political opposition and union resistance, is making painfully slow progress.

Trade fairs

Most important is the Salonika International Trade Fair, held annually in Sep. Other more specialised events take place in Athens and Piraeus, as well as Thessaloniki.

Electricity supply

220 V AC.

Representation in capital

Albania, Algeria, Argentina, Australia, Austria, Bangladesh, Belgium, Bolivia, Brazil, Bulgaria, Cameroon, Canada, Chile, China PR, Colombia, Costa Rica, Cuba, Cyprus, Denmark, Dominican Republic, Ecuador, Egypt, Ethiopia, Finland, France, Gabon, Germany, Ghana, Haiti, The Holy See, Honduras, Hong Kong, Hungary, Iceland, India, Indonesia, Iran, Iraq, Ireland, Israel, Italy, Japan, Jordan, Republic of Korea, Kuwait, Lebanon, Liberia, Libya, Luxembourg, Madagascar, Malaysia, Malta, Mexico, Morocco, Netherlands, New Zealand, Nicaragua, Norway, Pakistan, Panama, Paraguay, Peru, Philippines, Poland, Portugal, Romania, Russia, Saudi Arabia, South Africa, Spain, Sweden, Switzerland, Syria, Taiwan, Thailand, Togo, Tunisia, Turkey, UK, Uruguay, USA, Venezuela, Yemen, Zaïre.

BUSINESS DIRECTORY

Hotels

Athens (area code 1)
Andromeda, 22 Timoleontos Vassou Street (tel: 643-7302).

Athenaeum Inter-Continental, 89-93 Syngrou Avenue, 11745 (tel: 902-3666; fax: 924-3000).

Athens, 4-6 Rue Michail Voda et Makedonias, 10439 (tel: 825-0422; fax: 883-7816).

Golden Tulip Electra Palace, 18 Nikodimou Street, 10557 (tel: 324-1401; fax: 324-1875).

Grand Bretagne, Constitution Square, Vas Georgiou A-1, 10564 (tel: 331-5555; fax: 322-8034).

Hilton, 46 Vassilissis Sofias Avenue, 11528 (tel: 725-0201; fax: 721-3110).

Ledra Marriott, 115 Syngrou Avenue (tel: 934-7711; fax: 935-8603).

NJV Meridien, Constitution Square (tel: 325-5301; fax: 323-5856).

Stanley, 1 Odysseos Street, Karaiskaki Square, PO Box 107 (tel: 524-0142; fax: 524-4611).

Useful telephone numbers

Police: 100.

Fire: 199.

Hospitals: 106.

Car hire

Athens
Avis: Reservation Office (tel: 229-402/3; fax: 282-433).

Budget: Central Reservations (tel: 922-2442; fax: 922-4444); international airport (east) (tel: 961-3634); international airport (west) (tel: 938-3792).

Europcar: 29 Jean Moreas Str, 11741 (tel: 924-8810/8818; fax; 921-5795).

Hertz: Reservations Office (tel: 994-2850; fax: 993-3970).

Chambers of commerce

Athens Chamber of Commerce and Industry, Academias 7-9, 106-71 Athens (tel: 360-4815; fax: 361-6464).

Athens Chamber of Craft Industries, Academias 18, 106-71 Athens (tel: 363-0253; fax: 361-4726).

Athens Trades Chamber, Panepistimiou 44, 106-79 Athens (tel: 363-3080; fax: 361-9735).

Central Union of Chambers of Greece, Academias 7, 106-71 Athens (tel: 363-7184; fax: 362-2320).

Economic Chamber of Greece, Syngrou Ave 186, 176-71 Athens (tel: 952-3330; fax: 952-3339).

Geotechnical Chamber of Greece, El Venizelou 64, 546-31 Thessaloniki (tel: 0312-78817; fax: 0312-36808).

Hellenic Organisation of Small- and Medium-Size Enterprises and Handicraft Undertakings, Xenias 16, 115-28 Athens (tel: 771-5002; fax: 771-9647).

Hotel Chamber of Greece, Stadiou 24, 105-64 Athens (tel: 323-6641; fax: 323-6962).

International Chamber of Commerce, Kaningos 27, 106-82 Athens (tel: 381-0879; fax: 361-0879).

Iraklio-Kriti of Commerce and Industry, PO Box 154, Iraklio, Kriti (tel: 282-420; tx: 282-292).

Larisa Chamber of Commerce and Industry, P O Box 108, 44 Papakyriazi Street, Larissa (tel: 222-219; tx: 295-183).

Patras Chamber of Commerce and Industry, 58 Michalakopoulou Street, Patras (tel: 277-679 or 275-879; tx: 312-179).

Piraeus Chamber of Commerce and Industry, Ludovikou 1, 185-31 Piraeus (tel: 417-7241; fax: 417-8680).

Piraeus Chamber of Craft Industries, Karaiskou 111, 185-32 Piraeus (tel: 417-4152; fax: 417-9495).

Piraeus Trades Chamber, Ag Konstantinou 3, 185-31 Piraeus (tel: 417-9065; fax: 412-2790).

Technical Chamber of Greece, Kar Servias 4, 102-48 Athens (tel: 325-4591; fax: 322-1772).

Thessaloniki Chamber of Commerce and Industry, Tsimiski 29, 546-24 Thessaloniki (tel: 0312-75341; fax: 0312-30237).

Banking

ABN Amro Bank, Thiseos Ave 330, 176-75 Athens (tel: 930-4900; fax: 930-4923).

Agricultural Bank of Greece SA, Panepistimiou 23, 105-64 Athens (tel: 939-9911; fax: 323-9611).

American Express, Panepistimiou 31, 105-64 Athens (323-4781; fax: 322-4919).

Arab Bank, Stadiou 10, 105-64 Athens (tel: 325-5401; fax: 325-5519).

Aspis Bank, Othonos 4, 105-57 Athens (tel: 324-3418; fax: 322-1409).

Attica Bank, Omirou 23, 106-72 Athens (tel: 364-6910; fax: 363-4067).

Banca Commerciale Italiana, Mitropoleos 3, 105-57 Athens (tel: 324-6014; fax: 324-6017).

Bank of America, Panepistimiou 39, 105-64 Athens (tel: 325-1901; fax: 323-1376).

Bank of Athens, Santaroza 3, 105-64 Athens (tel: 321-2372; fax: 325-4069).

Bank of Central Greece, Stadiou and Emm Benaki, 105-64 Athens (tel: 325-4400; fax: 321-0310).

Bank of Cyprus, Vas Sofias 11, 106-71 Athens (tel: 361-2257; fax: 364-0327).

Bank of Greece, Panepistimiou 21, 105-64 Athens (tel: 320-1111; fax: 324-9789).

Bank of Macedonia and Thrace, I Dragoumi 5, 546-25 Thessaloniki (tel: 0315-42213; fax: 0315-43822).

Bank of Macedonia and Thrace, Syntagma Sq, 105-63 Athens (tel: 328-142; fax: 324-0005).

Bank of Nova Scotia (Scotia Bank), Panepistimiou 37, 105-64 Athens (tel: 324-3891; fax: 324-3983).

Bank of Piraeus, Kon Souri 5, 105-57 Athens (tel: 323-3311; fax: 324-6481).

Bank of Saderat Iran, Panepistimiou 25-29, 105-64 Athens (tel: 324-9531; fax: 325-1154).

Banque Nationale de Paris, Vas Sofias 94, 155-28 Athens (tel: 748-6700; fax: 748-6726).

Banque Paribas, Panepistimiou 39, 105-64 Athens (tel: 325-5021; fax: 322-8013).

Barclays Bank, Kolokotroni 1, 105-62 Athens (tel: 364-4311; fax: 324-7543).

Bayerische Vereinsbank, Heraklitou 7, 106-73 Athens (363-9315; fax: 364-0063).

Chiosbank, Vas Sofias 11, 106-71 Athens (tel: 360-9811; fax: 364-4909).

Citibank, Othonos 8, 105-57 Athens (tel: 322-7471; fax: 324-3277).

Commercial Bank, Sofokleous 11, 105-59 Athens (tel: 321-0911; fax: 323-4304).

Credit Bank, Stadiou 40, 105-64 Athens (tel: 326-0000; fax: 326-5348).

Credit Commercial de France, Amalias Ave 20, 105-57 Athens (tel: 324-1831; fax: 324-9393).

Credit Lyonnais Grece, Vas Sofias 75, 115-21 Athens (tel: 725-0323; fax: 721-0134).

Cretabank, Voukourestiou 22, 106-71 Athens (tel: 360-6511; fax: 362-2604).

Deposit and Loans Fund, Academias 4, 101-74 Athens (tel: 363-4211; fax: 360-9545).

Doric Bank, Vas Sofias 11, 106-71 Athens (tel: 334-1000; fax: 321-3119).

Dresdner Bank, Panepistimiou 43, 105-64 Athens (tel: 325-3625; fax: 323-1570).

Egnatia Bank, Omirou 22, 106-72 Athens (tel: 360-6914; fax: 362-7945).

Egnatia Bank, Komninon 1, 546-24 Thessaloniki (tel: 0315-42492; fax: 0312-86680).

Ergobank, Kolokotroni 3, 105-62 Athens (tel: 322-1345; fax: 322-2264).

Euromerchant Bank, Othonos 8, 105-57 Athens (tel: 323-0151; fax: 323-3866).

European Investment Bank, Amalias Ave 12, 105-57 Athens (tel: 322-0773; fax: 322-0776).

European Popular Bank, Panepistimiou 13, 105-64 Athens (tel: 924-1771; fax: 324-3141).

General Bank, Panepistimiou 9, 105-64 Athens (tel: 324-1289; fax: 322-2271).

Grindlays Bank, Merlin 7, 106-71 Athens (tel: 362-4601; fax: 937-1070).

Hellenic Industrial Development Bank, Syngrou 87, 117-45 Athens (tel: 924-2900; fax: 924-1513).

Instituto Bancario San Paolo Di Torino, Vas Sofias 11, 106-71 Athens (tel: 364-8106; fax: 364-8107).

Other useful addresses (contd):
Investment Bank, Korai 1, 105-64 Athens (tel: 323-0214; fax: 322-0677).

Ionian Bank, Panepistimiou 45, 105-64 Athens (tel: 322-5501; fax: 322-8273).

Interbank, Kifissias Ave 117, 151-80 Athens (tel: 805-4421; fax: 806-7500).

Midland Bank, Sekeri 1A, 106-71 Athens (tel: 364-7410; fax: 364-4301).

National Bank of Greece, Aeolou 86, 150-51 Athens (tel: 334-1000; fax: 321-3119).

National Housing Bank, Stadiou 29, 105-59 Athens (tel: 325-4984; fax: 321-0367).

National Investment Bank for Industrial Development, Amalias Ave 14, 105-57 Athens (tel: 324-2651; fax: 324-2917).

National Mortgage Bank, Panepistimiou 40, 106-79 Athens (tel: 364-8311; fax: 363-9920).

National Westminster Bank, Stadiou 24, 105-64 Athens (324-1562; fax: 322-2951).

Post-Office Savings Bank, Pesmazoglou 2-6, 105-59 Athens (tel: 323-0621; fax: 323-1055).

Societe Generale, Ippokratous 23, 106-79 Athens (tel: 364-2010; fax: 364-0047).

The Chase Manhattan Bank, Korai 3, 105-64 Athens (tel: 324-2511; fax: 323-6807).

The Royal Bank of Scotland, Akti Miaouli 61, 185-36 Piraeus (tel: 429-3210; fax: 429-3321).

Union of Greek Banks, Massalias 1, 106-80 Athens (tel: 364-6121; fax: 361-5324).

Travel information
Athens Airport (East), Helliniko, 167-00 Athens (tel: 969-9111; fax: 966-6162).

Athens Airport (West), Helliniko, 167-00 Athens (tel: 936-9111; fax: 936-3328).

Ellinikos Organismos Tourismou (tourist organisation), Odos Amerikis 2, Athens 10564 (tel: 322-3111/9; tx: 215-832).

Greek National Tourist Organisation (GNTO), Amerikis 2B, 105-64 Athens (tel: 322-3111; fax: 322-4148).

Olympic Airways, Syngrou Ave 96-100, 117-41 Athens (tel; 926-9111; fax: 926-7154).

Spata International Airport, 5th km Spata-Loutsa Rd, 190-04 Attica (tel: 663-4571; fax: 663-4709).

Other useful addresses
Agricultural Bank of Greece (Credit Division), Panepistimiou 106, 105-64 Athens (tel: 323-8169; fax: 329-8733).

Athenagence (ANA) (news agency), Odos Pindarou 5, Athens 10671 (tel: 363-9816).

Athens and Piraeus Electric Railways (ISAP), Athinas 67, 105-52 Athens (tel: 324-8311; fax: 322-3935).

Athens and Piraeus Trolleys (ILPAP), Admitou 17, 104-46 Athens (tel: 821-6305; fax: 883-7445).

Athens and Piraeus Water Company (EYDAP), Oropou 156, 111-46 Athens (tel: 253-3402; fax: 253-3124).

Athens Municipal Gas Corporation (DEFA), Orfeos 2, 118-54 Athens (tel: 346-1194; fax: 346-1400).

Athens Stock Exchange, Sofokleous 10, 105-59 Athens (tel: 321-1301; fax: 321-3938).

Centre for Planning and Economic Research (KEPE), ppokratous 22, 106-80 Athens (tel: 362-7321; fax: 361-1136).

Cotton Organisation (OBA), Syngrou Ave 150, 176-71 Athens (tel: 923-4314; fax: 924-3676).

'Democritus' Nuclear Research Centre, Ag Paraskevi, 153-10 Athens (tel: 651-8911; fax: 651-9180).

Department of Press and Information, Ministry to The Prime Minister's Office, Odos Zalokosta 10, Athens (tel: 363-0911; tx: 216-325).

Economic and Industrial Research Institute (IOBE), Tsami Karatasi 11, 117-42 Athens (tel: 924-1378; fax: 923-3977).

ETBA (Hellenic Industrial Development Bank SA), 87 Syngrou Ave, 117-45 Athens (tel: 924-2900; fax: 924-1513/16/17).

EU Press and Information Office, 2 Vassilissis Sophias Avenue, Athens 10674 (tel: 743-982/3/4).

Export Promotion Organisation (OPE), Mar Antippa 86-88, 163-46 Athens (tel: 996-1900; fax: 991-5392).

Federation of Greek Industry (SEB), Xenofontos 5, 105-57 Athens (tel: 323-7325; fax: 322-2929).

Geological and Mineral Research Institute (IGME), Mesogion Ave 70, 115-27 Athens (tel: 779-8412; fax: 775-2211).

Greek Atomic Energy Commission, Ag Paraskevi, 153-10 Athens (tel: 651-8911; fax: 651-9180).

Greek Post Offices (ELTA), Apellou 1, 101-88 Athens (tel: 324-3311; fax: 324-1228).

Greek Radio and Television (ET 1), Mesogion Ave 432, 153-42 Athens (tel: 639-0772; fax: 639-0652).

Greek Radio and Television (ET 2), Mesogion Ave 136, 115-62 Athens (tel: 770-1911; fax: 777-6239).

Greek Railways Organisation (OSE), Sina 6, 106-72 Athens (tel: 362-4402; fax: 362-8933).

Hellenic Aerospace Industry (EAB), Mesogion Ave 2-4, 115-27 Athens (tel: 779-9679; fax: 779-7670).

Hellenic Organisation for Small- and Medium-Size Enterprises and Handicraft Undertakings (EOMMEX), Xenias 16, 115-28 Athens (tel: 771-5002; fax: 771-5025).

Hellenic Organisation for the Promotion of Exports (HOPE), 1 Mitropoleos Street, 10557 Athens (tel: 324-7011/16; tx: 220-201).

Hellenic Standardisation Organisation (ELOT), Acharnon 313, 111-45 Athens (tel: 201-5025; fax: 202-0776).

Hellenic Telecommunications Organisation (OTE), Kifissias 99, 151-24 Athens (tel: 611-7466; fax: 681-0899).

Hellenic Tobacco Organisation (EOK), Kapodistriou 36, 104-32 Athens (tel: 524-7311; fax: 524-7318).

Ministry of Aegean, Syngrou Ave 49, 117-43 Athens (tel: 923-7970; fax: 923-8200) and M Asias 2, 811-00 Mytilene (tel: 0251-25200; fax: 0251-41175).

Ministry of Agriculture, Acharnon 2, 101-76 Athens (tel: 529-1111; fax: 524-0475).

Ministry of Commerce, Caningos Square, 106-77 Athens (tel: 381-6242; fax: 384-2642).

Ministry of Culture, Bouboulinas 20, 106-82 Athens (tel: 820-1100; fax: 820-1337).

Ministry of Education and Religious Affairs, Mitropoleos 15, 101-85 Athens (tel: 325-4221; fax: 324-8264).

Ministry of Environment, Town Planning and Public Works, Amaliados 17, 115-23 Athens (tel: 643-1461; fax: 644-7608).

Ministry of Finance, Karageorgi Servias 10, 101-84 Athens (tel: 331-3400; fax: 323-8657).

Ministry of Foreign Affairs, Academias 1, 106-71 Athens (tel: 361-0584; fax: 645-0028).

Ministry of Health, Welfare and Social Security, Aristotelous 17, 101-87 Athens (tel: 524-9010; fax: 522-3246).

Ministry of Industry, Energy and Technology, Michalakopoulou 80, 101-92 Athens (tel: 748-2770; fax: 770-8003).

General Secretariat for Energy and Technology, Mesogeion Ave 14-18, 115-10 Athens (tel: 775-2221; fax: 771-4153).

Ministry of Interior, Dragatsaniou 2, 105-59 Athens (tel: 322-3521; fax: 324-1180).

Ministry of Justice, Mesogeion 96, 115-27 Athens (tel: 775-7619; fax: 779-6055).

Ministry of Labour, Pireos 40, 101-82 Athens (tel: 523-3110; fax: 524-9805).

Ministry of Macedonia and Thrace, Government House, 541-23 Thessaloniki (tel: 0312-64321; fax: 0312-35109).

Ministry of Merchant Marine, G Lambraki 150, 185-35 Piraeus (tel: 412-1211; fax: 417-8101).

Ministry of National Defence, Papagou Camp, Mesogeion 227-229, 154-51 Athens (tel: 646-5201; fax: 646-5584).

Ministry of National Economy

Division for Foreign Capital and Attracting Investments, Syntagma Square, 101-80 Athens (tel: 333-2000; fax: 333-2130).

Division for Private Investment Policy, Syntagma Square, 101-80 Athens (tel: 333-2252/3; fax: 333-2326).

Regional Development Divisions of Attica, Thiras 60, 112-52 Athens (tel: 862-9810; fax: 862-9742).

Ministry of Press and Mass Media, Zalokosta 10, 101-63 Athens (tel: 363-0911; fax: 360-6969).

Ministry of - Prime Minister's Office, Vas Sofias, 106-74 Athens (tel: 339-3000; fax: 339-3020).

Ministry of Public Order, Pan Kanellopoulou 4, 101-77 Athens (tel: 692-8510; fax: 692-1675).

Ministry of Tourism, Amerikis 2B, 105-64 Athens (tel: 322-3111; fax: 322-4148).

Ministry of Transport and Communications, Xenofontos 13, 105-57 Athens (tel: 325-1211; fax: 324-7400).

National Statistical Service (ESYE), Lykourgou 14-16, 101-66 Athens (tel: 324-85118; fax: 324-1098).

Panhellenic Confederation of Farmers' Co-operatives (PASEGES), Kifissias 16, 115-26 Athens (tel: 770-4737; fax: 777-9313).

Panhellenic Exporters' Association, Kratinou 11, 105-52 Athens (tel: 522-8925; fax: 522-9403).

Piraeus Port Authority (OLP), 2as Merarchias 2, 185-35 Piraeus (tel: 452-0911; fax: 452-0852).

Piraeus Port Authority, Akti Miaouli 50, 185-35 Piraeus (tel: 451-1311; fax: 451-1121).

Prime Minister's Office, Maximos Mansion, Herod Atticus 19, 106-74 Athens (tel: 671-7071; fax: 671-5799).

Public Materials Administration Organisation (ODDY), Stadiou 60, 105-64 Athens (tel: 324-4231; fax: 324;2970).

Public Petroleum Corporation (DEP), Mesogion Ave 357-359, 152-31 Athens (tel: 650-1340; fax: 650-1383).

Public Power Corporation (PPC), Halkokondyli 30, 104-32 Athens (tel: 523-4301; fax: 523-5307).

Stock Exchange, Sophocleous 10, Athens 10559 (tel: 321-3911).

Thessaloniki International Fair, Egnatias 154, 546-26 Thessaloniki (tel: 0312-63033; fax: 0312-84732).

Union of Commercial Agents, Voulis 15, Athens (tel: 322-3148).

Urban Transport Organisation (OAS), Metsovou 15, 106-82 Athens (tel: 883-6077; fax: 821-2219).

The Holy See

Anthony Griffin

1996 saw the Holy See (since 1994 the official name adopted in preference to Vatican, although the old term is still in widespread use), and the Roman Catholic Church in general, increasingly preoccupied with the state of health of Pope John Paul II. The most anxious moment of all came in October 1996 when a team of 12 doctors attended an operation in Rome's Gemelli Hospital. Fears had been expressed that the official diagnosis – of appendicitis – was in reality a cover-up for something much more serious.

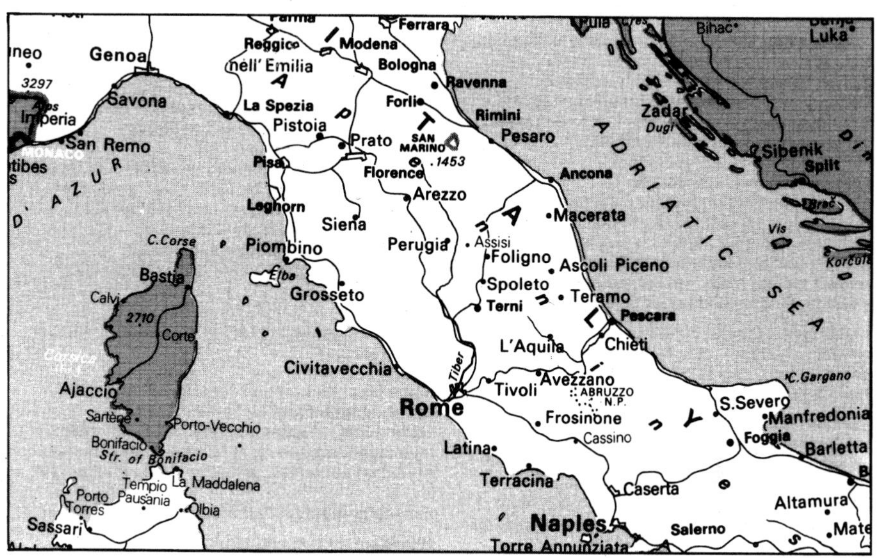

John Paul II

As things turned out, the result of the Pope's sixth operation in 15 years was encouraging. The papal appendix was removed without difficulty, as was the scar tissue that had been creating an intestinal obstruction and giving rise to fears of graver problems. Within twenty-four hours of the operation Papa Wojtyla, a hardened survivor of an assassination attempt in the early 1980s, was back on his feet.

Despite the success of the operation, John Paul II is seen to be a weakened, elderly man. The most visible, travelled and accessible Pope ever has become a shadow of his former self, uncertain in his speech, of faltering step and shaky hand. The stark contrast between the image of the once active, robust prelate and today's infirmity owes much, ironically, to the success of modern medicine. John Paul II is the first Pope willing to avail himself of modern medical facilities, to the extent of entering hospital for his now numerous operations.

John Paul II's obvious difficulty in coping with his daily duties – let alone maintain his once intensive travel programme – confronts the Holy See with an increasingly difficult dilemma. Previous popes have died in the saddle, or a secretive Vatican hierarchy has managed to prevent any intimation of Papal indisposition or incapacity from reaching the world. John Paul II is too high profile, too determined to keep going, for any possibility of secrecy to be feasible. Now the unprecedented question of resignation – strongly resisted by the Pope himself – appears on the Holy See's agenda.

Succession

Whether through resignation or death, the question of succession is already the subject of keen speculation within the Catholic Church. The front runner on the more liberal wing of the Church is the Cardinal Archbishop of Milan, Carlo Maria Martini whose star has faded latterly and whose views have not always been in sympathy with those of John Paul II. The Pope's personal preference, as his eventual successor, is the conservative Brazilian primate, Cardinal Lucas Moreira Neves. A third, and possible compromise candidate, is Cardinal Francis Arinze of Nigeria. If elected, Cardinal Arinze would be the first black Pope. Africa is the Church's fastest growing source of converts. The continent's poverty and marginalisation make it a fitting new front for the battles the Church will have to fight in the 21st century.

Legacy

John Paul II's legacy will be that of a thoroughly modern communicator, with conservative – some would say outdated – views. Having turned his back on the 'theology of liberation', John Paul II none the less often managed to hit the target on important social issues and effectively communicate the Church's concern, particularly in respect of the right to work and the need to keep the search for profit secondary to the needs of those who work. His crusade against artificial birth control has taken him on to the global stage, while distancing him from many communicants. Petitioned on all sides to soften the Church's position on divorce, homosexuality, married priests and ordination for women, John Paul II has resolutely resisted. The Pope has also alienated many neutral observers by denouncing

KEY FACTS — *The Holy See*

Official title: The Holy See (name changed from the Vatican City in 1993)

Head of state: Pope John Paul II

Head of government: Secretary of State Cardinal Angelo Sodano

Official Languages: Italian

Currency: Italian Lira

Exchange rate: Lire 1,546.55 per US$ (Jun 1996)

Area: 0.44 sq km

Population: 700 (1995)

the UN's population control policies as unacceptable and at the same time condemning the US administration's policy on abortion and homosexuality. His determination to counter the UN's population control policy has brought the Holy See into some strange, uncomfortable (some would say unholy) alliances, notably with the Islamic fundamentalists of Iran and Sudan.

Despite his weakened state, his role in governing the spiritual lives of hundreds of millions of Catholics world-wide means that the Pope is still capable of playing a weighty role in global politics. It is often difficult to distinguish between the Holy See's theological and moral positions on the one hand, and its political positions on the other. The two are often inextricably intertwined. Despite the high moral tone which often accompanies the Holy See's criticism of social ills, the Vatican remains a substantial centre of temporal and economic power. Little is known publicly of the Holy See's accounts. The Institute of Religious Works (Istituto per le Opere de Religione) is, in effect, the Holy See's bank and handles the Pope's financial affairs in spite of its disastrous association with the Banco Ambrosiano in the 1980s which culminated in Italy's largest ever banking collapse. The Holy See's investment portfolio is known to include shares in Fiat, Walt Disney and IBM. The Holy See derives its income from its investments and the Obolo de San Pietro (Peter's Pence). In recent years expenditure – on 2,000 staff, 100 Papal Nunciates throughout the world, and on maintaining a massive infrastructure which includes the Vatican Radio and the L'Osservatore Romano newspaper – have generally exceeded revenues, leading to substantial current account deficits.

COUNTRY PROFILE — THE HOLY SEE

Political system

Overall jurisdiction vested in the Pope, elected for life by conclave of members of the Sacred College of Cardinals. The Pope appoints a Pontifical Commission, headed by a president, to oversee general administration. The name of the Vatican City was changed in 1993 to The Holy See.

Media

Press: Only daily newspaper is *L'Osservatore Romano* which covers religious matters plus some general news items. Also weekly editions published in several languages. Official bulletin of The Holy See is *Acta Apostolicae Sedis*, published monthly.
Broadcasting: Vatican Radio broadcasts 40 hours a week in 35 languages, providing a link between The Holy See and Catholics throughout the world. Broadcasting centre at Santa Maria di Galeria, about 20 km from The Holy See, has diplomatic privileges similar to foreign embassies.

Domestic economy

The main sources of income are the Istituto per le Opere di Religione (Bank of The Holy See), which collects money from residents, 'Peter's pence' (voluntary contributions to the Catholic Church), sale of postage stamps, tourist mementos, fees for admission to museums, the sale of publications and interest on investments. No special agreements exist between the EU and The Holy See.

Legal system

Code of Canon Law devised 1917. New code with many revisions ratified and introduced 1983.

Membership of international organisations

FAO (observer), IAEA, INTELSAT, ITU, IWC, OAS, UN, UNESCO, UPU, WIPO, WTO.

BUSINESS GUIDE

Time

GMT + 1 hr (GMT + 2 hrs late Mar to late Sep).

Climate

Mediterranean, with hot summers and mild winters. Temperatures range from 4–30°C.

Clothing

Lightweight for summer, mediumweight and light topcoat for winter.

Entry requirements

No formal regulations.

Air access

Heliport used by The Holy See officials and visiting dignitaries.
Main international airport: Rome served by Leonardo da Vinci (Fiumicino) (FCO) 35 km from The Holy See.

Surface access

By road or rail through Rome.

National transport

Railway line covers 862 metres before leaving The Holy See.

Public holidays

Fixed dates: 6 Jan (Epiphany), 15 Aug (Ferragosto/Assumption Day), 1 Nov (All Saints'), 8 Dec (Immaculate Conception, 25 and 26 Dec (Christmas).
Variable dates: Good Friday, Easter Monday, Ascension Day.

Telecommunications

Telephone and telefax: International telephone dialling code: 3966982, followed by subscriber's number.
Telex: Telex country code 504 VA.

BUSINESS DIRECTORY

Principal newspapers

L'Osservatore Romano, Via del Pellegrino, 00120 The Holy See (tel: 698-3461; fax: 698-3675).

Other useful addresses

Agenzia Internazionale Fides (AIF), Palazzo di Propaganda Fide, Via di Propaganda 1c, 00187 Rome (tel: 679-2414).

Annuario Pontificio, Palazzo Apostolico, 00120 Città del Vaticano (tel: 698-3064); Press Room, Via della Conciciazione, 54, 00193 Roma (tel: 698-3466).

Centro Televisivo Vaticano, Palazzo Belvedere, 00120 The Holy See (tel: 698-5467).

Embassy of the United States of America, Villino Pacelli, Via Aurelia 294, 00165 Rome (tel: 639-0558; fax: 638-0159).

Istituto per le Opere di Religione (IOR) (Bank of The Holy See), 00120 The Holy See.

Radio Vaticana, Palazzo Pio, Piazza Pia 3, 00120 Roma (tel: 6988-3551; fax: 6988-3237).

The Secretariat of State, Palazzo Apostolico, 00120 The Holy See (tel: 6982).

Internet sites

Holy See http:\\www.Vatican.va

Hungary

Bob Jiggins

The harmony displayed at the congress of the ruling Magyar Szocialista Part (MSzP) (Hungarian Socialist Party) in November 1995 provided a stark contrast with the general dissension within the government. The party declared its support for the new measures and its leader, Gyula Horn, made a closing speech suggesting that discord was now an element of the past. In reality the congress was carefully stage-managed, for squabbles in the various factions within the party continued and the main fracture line between left and right was as large as ever. In the economic sphere, the finance ministry estimated in early 1996 that growth could be in the region of 3 per cent in 1996.

Politics

The government faced a number of challenges in 1995/96, including the fact that a constitutional court overturned large elements of its austerity programme. The court rulings had a direct effect on the government's attempt at tackling the budget crisis. One ruling, for example, resulted in a loss of revenue of some US$18 million, due to the court overturning the rise in mortgage rates to 25 per cent.

Various ministers had resigned during 1995, in particular the labour minister, Magda Kosa-Kovacs, who left the post over changes in sick-pay rules. Strike action by workers in a number of sectors was deflected by the promise to revise the wage cut package. The government planned to limit wage rises to an average of 19.5 per cent during 1996 compared with inflation in the third quarter of 1995 of 29.5 per cent. Horn's grip over his party held in 1995/96, and although the left was still vocal its criticisms grew increasingly mute. Even Sandor Nagy, the left-winger who resigned from his position as head of the Association of Hungarian Trade Unions in order the better to criticise government, lost much of his former influence. Mrs Kosa-Kovacs became deputy leader of the MSzP, and, surprisingly in view of her earlier resignation, publicly called for unity and co-operation with the coalition partners, the Szabad Demokratak Szovetsege (SzDSz) (Alliance of Free Democrats).

Finance Minister Peter Medgyessy enjoyed the support and confidence of his fellow ministers, and perhaps more importantly, the party. His economic programme of austerity remained on course in 1995/96, and he made much of his and Horn's belief that a return to the policies of the communist era was unacceptable. This unexpected show of unity within the ruling party, and even between the coalition partners, paid off in terms of electoral support. Previously

KEY FACTS — Hungary

Official title: Republic of Hungary

Head of state: President Arpád Göncz (since Aug 1990)

Head of government: Prime Minister Gyula Horn (since 15 Jul 1994)

Ruling party: Coalition: Magyar Szocialista Part (MSzP) (Hungarian Socialist Party) and Szabad Demokratak Szovetsege (SzDSz) (Alliance of Free Democrats)

Capital: Budapest

Official Languages: Hungarian (Magyar)

Currency: Forint (Ft) = 100 fillérs (9% devaluation Mar 1995; old 1, 2, 5, 10 and 20 forint coins went out of circulation on 30 June 1995)

Exchange rate: Ft160.96 per US$ (Dec 1996)

Area: 93,033 sq km

Population: 10.23m (1995)

GDP per capita: US$3,882 (1995)

GDP real growth: -1% (1st qtr 1996)

GNP per capita: US$3,400 (1994)

GNP real growth: 2.6% (1994)

Labour force: 2.9m (1994)

Unemployment: 9.5% (1995)

Inflation: 23% (Jul 1996) (consumer prices)

Trade balance: -US$2bn (12 months to May 1996)

Foreign debt: US$31.65bn (1995)

Aid flows: US$2.7bn (1994)

Visitor numbers: 21.43m (1994)

KEY INDICATORS — Hungary

	Unit	1991	1992	1993	1994	1995
Population	m	10.35	10.32	10.29	10.25	10.23
Gross national product (GNP)	US$bn	30.0	25.3	30.0	34.8	–
GNP per capita	US$	3,000	2,500	3,000	3,400	–
GNP real growth	%	-10.2	-5.0	-1.6	2.6	–
Inflation	%	40.1	18.5	22.7	18.8	28.2
Consumer prices	1990=100	134.2	165.0	202.1	241.7	310.1
Employment	'000	3,733	3,119	2,836	2,899	2,744
Wages (average earnings)	1990=100	124.0	150.5	180.5	226.5	–
Unemployment	%	5.4	10.7	12.8	10.9	9.5
Agricultural production	1979-81=100	113.12	85.56	79.80	82.73	80.54
Industrial employment	'000	1,129	990	882	880	833
Industrial production	1990=100	81.4	73.8	76.6	84.0	88.1
Manufacturing	1990=100	76.0	72.3	74.7	81.6	86.1
Mining	1990=100	87.2	73.6	72.5	60.9	51.7
Coal	'000 tonnes	16,974	15,836	14,122	13,451	14,469
Crude steel	'000 tonnes	1,861	1,558	1,753	1,937	1,865
Cement	'000 tonnes	2,529	2,236	2,534	2,815	2,873
Natural gas	bn cu metres	4.3	4.0	4.3	4.5	4.6
Exports	Ftbn	764.3	843.6	819.9	1,128.7	1,576.1
Imports (CIF)	Ftbn	855.6	878.6	1,158.1	1,518.3	1,894.4
Balance of trade	US$m	358	-11	-4,021	-3,600	*-2,500
Current account	US$m	403	352	-4,262	-3,900	-2,500
External debt	US$bn	22.8	21.7	24.6	28.5	31.7
Total reserves minus gold	US$m	3,936	4,428	6,771	6,810	12,052
Foreign exchange	US$m	3,935	4,348	6,691	6,727	11,968
Discount rate	%	22	21	22	25	28
Deposit rate	%	30.4	24.4	15.7	20.3	26.1
Lending rate	%	35.1	33.1	25.4	27.4	32.6
Exchange rate	Ft per US$	74.74	78.99	91.93	105.16	125.68

* estimated figure

the demagogic speeches of the populist Jozsef Torgyan of the Fuggetlen Kisgazda, Foldmunkas-es Polgari Part (FKgP) (Independent Smallholders' and Peasants' Party) had ensured that the MSzP was lagging in the opinion polls, but later figures indicated that the socialists were back in the lead. To a certain extent this reflected an increasing disunity within the ranks of the right wing – but in this context as others, success breeds success. Greater popularity and a degree of economic success yields benefits in terms of party cohesion and discipline; previously, the Horn government faced difficulties in these areas.

Foreign relations

Hungary has also been improving its foreign relations, with increased contact with its neighbours over nationality issues and the European Union (EU). The previous government had friendly relations with Croatia (it was one of the first to recognise it as independent of Yugoslavia), yet on occasions was openly hostile to the Yugoslav government in Belgrade and pursued a virulently anti-Serb line. Horn's administration, on the other hand, is mindful of the 210,000 or so ethnic Hungarians living in the Vojvodina region of Serbia, and has been conciliatory towards Belgrade. This line has been pursued with both Slovakia and Romania (both with sizable minority Hungarian populations) and resulted in a treaty with the former regarding the treatment of its Hungarian minority and their rights, especially over language. A bilateral treaty was also signed with Romania towards the end of 1996 (a prerequisite for Hugarian membership of the EU and NATO). The treaty, which guaranteed the inviolability of existing frontiers and the rights of ethnic minorities, raised protests from opposition groups in Hungary who claimed that its provisions for minority rights were insufficient.

Gaining approval

The economy performed relatively well in 1995/96, and international organisations made approving noises over the government's programme. Hungary had been seeking Organisation for Economic Co-operation and Development (OECD) membership for some time and this was finally approved in March 1996. Together with praise from the International Monetary Fund (IMF), this constituted a mark of confidence in the Hungarian economy and in the ability of the government to ensure that reforms stay on track.

The IMF approved a stand-by credit of US$387 million shortly before OECD membership, although it was thought unlikely that Hungary would actually draw on this given its record gold reserves of almost US$12 billion in the second quarter of 1996, almost double that of the previous year.

Economic reform

Privatisation accelerated in 1995; receipts rose to US$3.6 billion in that year. The current account deficit was reduced by almost a half to US$2.5 billion in 1995 and the central government budget deficit fell by an even greater amount, to US$1.1 billion. The government's setting of realistic, if tough, targets in 1996 and beyond could see an improvement on these figures.

One of the main problems facing Hungary was the size of the welfare budget which the IMF has demanded, in time-honoured fashion, be cut. In 1995 the budget deficit for social security was Ft47.2 billion and the government planned to reduce this in 1996 to Ft17.8 billion – which would be a substantial achievement. The budget should be further helped by the new determination to collect some Ft54 billion in unpaid social security contributions.

The government was well above the target for the central budget deficit in mid-1996, and this was likely to be reduced still further. The scenario for social security, however, was quite different. Projections by the finance ministry suggested that the deficit here could well be over Ft41 billion – considerably in excess of the planned Ft17.8 billion. Consequently, an overshoot in the general deficit target of 4 per cent as agreed with the IMF was likely.

Linked with the social security budget is a looming problem over pensions. Hungary is unusual in its demography compared with its neighbours, and resembles more closely the advanced industrial states of western Europe – in short it has an ageing population, as well as one that has been on the decline since 1981. A low birth rate ensures that the population comprises an ever greater share of pensioners and this demographic time-bomb needs attention if the old are not to be a severe drain on the economically active. Little can be done to alleviate demand on health care services, but in 1995/96 pensions featured prominently.

In May 1996 the government announced a through-going review of its public finances, including provision for pensions. Essentially the plan was to change the arrangements for the financing of pensions from the current system whereby employers pay a superannuation tax, to one which is effectively privatised, thus removing the burden from the state. The new system requires employers to pay 66 per cent, with employees contributing 33 per cent; both contributions will be invested in separate pension funds. This system is to commence in 1998; workers below the age of 40 will automatically move onto the new system, whilst those above will be given the choice to change or remain with the existing arrangements. A further measure to alleviate the burden was the raising of the retirement age to 62, an increase of 2 years for men and seven for women.

Export growth continues

Industrial growth fell back in the first quarter of 1996 when compared with the steady improvement throughout 1995; this was largely due to a fall in domestic demand. Prospects for growth were quite good, however, once the effects of the austerity programme have been assimilated, although it will be highly dependent on the performance of exports.

Growth will be helped by the large scale of private sector industrial investment which grew nominally by 43 per cent from 1994 to 1995; this was expected to continue through 1996. Public sector investment, however, was unsurprisingly low, reaching a proportion of only 19.8 per cent of the total in 1995, compared with 28 per cent in 1994.

The major macro-economic problem which Hungary has yet to face was the high rate of inflation. The government set targets for 1996 and 1997 of 20 per cent and 15 per cent respectively. These seemed overly optimistic as year-on-year inflation in January 1996 was 28.9 per cent, largely fuelled by the 4.4 per cent rise in consumer prices that month. Although the monthly figures fell in the few subsequent months, the year-on-year rate in April 1996 was still a high 24.4 per cent. This difficulty will be compounded by the government's intention to raise energy and fuel prices to world levels, which could involve a rise of up to 50 per cent.

Unemployment will also be difficult to bring below the current 11.6 per cent because the government planned to reduce the number of state employees from 650,000. As the actual number of jobless is 530,600, even a small reduction in the public work-

COUNTRY PROFILE HUNGARY

Historical profile

From the mid-eighteenth century, Hungary with Austria was part of the dual monarchy ruled by the Hapsburgs.
1914 Tied to Austria, entered First World War as a German ally and lost two-thirds of its lands and more than half its people. Communists seized power but were defeated by Admiral Miklos Horthy, who governed as regent until 1944.
1939-45 Hungary allied with Germany and acquired territory through the partitioning of Czechoslovakia. Having sought to break the alliance, was occupied by Germany, then by the Soviets. Lands were reduced to pre-war boundaries and severe reparations exacted.
1947 Communists largest single party in general election.
1949 People's Republic established. Under Matyas Rakosi as prime minister purges and political trials on the Stalinist model followed. Agriculture was reorganised on the Soviet pattern, and industry nationalised.
1953 The more liberal Imre Nagy became prime minister. 1956 Dissent between Rakosi and Nagy factions and general discontent led to uprising. It was put down, with the help of Soviet troops, by new Soviet-backed government of the Hungarian Socialist Workers' Party led by Janos Kadar, who dismantled collective farms, raised wages, allowed some intellectual freedom and later experimented with economic reforms.
1988 Dissatisfaction among party members with remoteness of leadership led to resignation of Kadar, and moves towards 'Socialist Pluralism'.
1990 First parliamentary elections for 45 years.
1994 The May general election resulted in a coalition led by Gyula Horn.

Political system

Republic with unicameral 386-seat National Assembly *(Orszaggyules)* which is elected by universal suffrage for a four-year term. Head of state is the president of the republic elected by the National Assembly for a five-year term.

Political parties

Coalition government: Magyar Szocialista Part (MSzP) (Hungarian Socialist Party) and Szabad Demokratak Szovetsege (SzDSz) (Alliance of Free Democrats). Other major parties include Fidesz-Hungarian Civic Party; Hungarian Justice and Life Party; Hungarian Democratic Forum; Christian Democratic People'sParty.

Population

Minor ethnic groups: German (0.3% of population), Croat (0.1%), Romanian (0.1%), Slovak (0.1%).

Main cities/towns

Budapest (population 2.4m in 1994), Debrecen (212,000), Miskolc (196,000), Szeged (189,000), Pécs (183,000), Györ (132,000), Nyiregyháza (119,000), Sopron, Székesfehérvár (114,000), Kecskemét (106,000), Tatabánya, Veszprem.

Media

Dailies: National dailies are: *Népszabadság, Nemezeti Sport, Nepszava, Blikk, Mai Nap, Kurir, Magyar Hirlap,* first colour daily), *Magyar Nemzet* and *Esti Hirlap.* The MTI Hungarian News Agency publishes *Daily News* in English – published once a week. *Uzlet* is published four times a week by Dagens Industri of Sweden.
Weeklies: Weekly newspaper with the largest circulation is *Szabad Fold.* International English language weeklies: *Budapest Week* and *The Budapest Sun; Heti Vilóggazdaság* (economics); *The Hungarian Times* launched 1993 folded/merged with *Budapest Week* in October 1993. German language weeklies: *Budapester Rundschau, Neue Zeitung.* Weekly magazines include: *TVR HIT, Kiskegyed, Tele Magazin, Reform* and *HVG.*
Periodicals: Other foreign language periodicals: *Hungarian Market Report, Hungarian Observer, Hungarian Business Herald* (quarterly) and *Hungarian Economic Review* (both published by the Hungarian Chamber of Commerce), *Hungarian Travel Magazine, Hungarian Digest, Hungarian Book Review, New Hungarian Quarterly, Hungarian Trade Journal.* Western magazines can be bought in large hotels and at some news-stalls.
Broadcasting: In January 1993 control of state TV finances were brought directly under the prime minister's office. The *Orszaggyules* (National Assembly) approved a bill on 21 December 1995, providing the legal framework for public and private broadcasting, which would enable public-service radio and television stations to operate as public foundations. In April 1996 Hungarian radio and TV were on the brink of bankruptcy and were preparing for drastic austerity measures.
Radio: Service operated by Magyar Rádió. English, German and Russian language news broadcasts during summer at 1200 hrs.
Television: Service operated by state-owned Magyar Televizió. Two channels, TV1 and TV2, broadcast around 90 hrs/week; both take advertising.
Advertising: Usually conducted through national agencies. Magyar Hirdetö, Hungexpo, Magyar Média and Interpress. Advertising space can be purchased also directly on TV and radio, in cinemas, newspapers, magazines and posters. In 1994, television accounted for 43 per cent of the total media spend; the press 49 per cent. Legislation pending on cigarette advertising (1995).
News Agency: Magyar Távirati Iroda (Hungarian news agency) (MTI).

Domestic economy

Market economy with large industrial base and heavy dependence on foreign trade. Also important agriculture and tourist sectors. Despite few natural resources high levels of economic growth achieved during 1970s. Pace of growth since slowed due to debt burden, higher inflation and reduction in industrial activity. Heavy government deficits. The new government acting since May 1994 continues to emphasise the realisation of the transition to a market economy. This process consists of speeding up privatisation, dismantling monopolies, restricting subsidies, reducing inflation, encouraging influx of foreign capital.

Employment

Approximately 37 per cent labour force employed in industry (including manufacturing and construction), 12 per cent in agriculture, 10 per cent in commerce and 8 per cent in transport and communications. Rapid growth in tertiary sector employment. Wages linked to enterprise profits. About 45 per cent of the workforce is female.

force would have serious consequences for the overall rate, especially considering any 'knock-on' effects.

External trade

The Hungarian economy has been noted for some time for its export performance; this helped reduce the trade deficit to US$827.6 million in the first quarter of 1996 from US$993 million in the same period in 1995. As in a number of former eastern bloc states, trade orientation was increasingly moving away from previous partners in the east and towards the west. In the first quarter of 1996 exports to OECD countries accounted for 75 per cent of total exports. This was a growth of 9.6 per cent over the same period a year earlier.

Exports to all eastern bloc states fell in 1995, with the exception of Poland and the Czech Republic, yielding a total of 22 per cent. Additionally, new markets now effectively exist with the removal of UN sanctions on Serbia and Montenegro and the end of the war, which was estimated to have cost Hungary some US$2.5 billion in lost trade.

Imports, on the other hand, indicated a different trend. OECD countries' representation in the figures fell by 2.4 per cent, with former Soviet states increasing by 8 per cent. Energy imports increased by 24 per cent, most of which originated from Russia. One effect of this continued export growth meant that debt-servicing ratios were reduced and thus Hungary's foreign credit rating was increased. Hungary has never rescheduled its debt which has helped to boost its credibility when issuing bonds on the international market.

Privatisation and investment

One change that marked the determination of the Horn administration was its privatisation programme. After the debacle of the proposed sale of the state music enterprise Hungarotron, where the government turned down a US$5 million offer from Polygram in favour of a US$2 million bid from a consortium of Hungarian musicians, policy was revised and privatisation became governed more by financial expediency rather than nationalism.

The Hungarian Privatisation and State Holding Company (APV) actively pursued the sale of a number of enterprises, including Budapest Bank (sold to GE Capital), the telecommunications company MATAV, the bus manufacturer Ikarus and part of the national electricity company, MVM. Foreign direct investment (FDI) in new plant is also increasing, with Suzuki increasing its presence and a number of electronics firms (Phillips, TDK, Sony and Samsung) opening new production facilities at an increasing rate. In total there were some 25,000 foreign owned enterprises in Hungary in mid-1996, generating some 70 per cent of total industrial exports. This made Hungary the main destination in the former Soviet bloc for FDI. An increasing number of the world's major companies have come to regard Hungary as the ideal springboard for central and eastern Europe.

COUNTRY PROFILE — HUNGARY

External trade

The majority of foreign trade was conducted through state monopolies, until 1990 since when there has been a considerable rise in the number of joint companies which have the right to engage in foreign trade on their own. In December 1992 Poland, Slovakia, the Czech Republic and Hungary (the Visegrad Four) established a regional trading zone designed gradually to eliminate tariff barriers. External market conditions became exceedingly difficult in 1991 due to the shrinking demand of the central and eastern European countries, in particular that of the former Soviet Union. In 1992, the value of exports settled in terms of convertible currencies and exceeded that of 1991 by 7.4 per cent, while the value of imports remained practically constant. For the first time since 1989, in 1992, even the value of exports increased, attributable to the growth of exports to the developed countries. By the end of 1992 import liberalisation affected over 90 per cent of the total imports. On 18 August 1995 Hungary signed an agreement with the other members of the Central Free Trade Agreement (CEFTA) to work towards creating a common market.
Exports: Mainly raw materials, semi-finished products, agricultural produce, machinery and other capital goods.
Main destinations: Germany (typically 29% of total), Austria (11%), Italy (10%), UK (3%), EU (42%).
Imports: Mainly raw materials, oil, basic manufactures, machinery, chemicals.
Main sources: Germany, Austria, Italy, UK, EU.
The government imposed an 8 per cent increase in import taxes in 1995.

Agriculture

Sector contributed 7 per cent to GNP in 1994 and employed 12 per cent of the workforce. High productivity. Farming is largly socialised, with co-operatives the dominant form of production in the last 40 years. Agriculture and food industry produce on average 50 per cent more food than is consumed domestically. Principal crops include wheat, maize, barley, sugar-beet and potatoes. Also important livestock sector.

Industry

Industry accounted for 25 per cent of GNP in 1994 and employed 37 per cent of the workforce. Major industries include motor vehicle components and assembly, engineering, chemicals, metallurgy, machinery and equipment, building materials, food processing and textiles. One of the fastest growing sectors in Hungary, as the country moves away from steel, machine-building and the other heavy industries, is motor vehicle components and assembly.

Tourism

The sector has traditionally played a highly important role in Hungary's foreign exchange revenues.

Mining

The mining sector accounted for 5 per cent of GNP in 1994 and employed 3 per cent of the workforce. Major European producer of bauxite. Also small-scale producer of lignite and manganese ore.

Hydrocarbons

Small-scale producer of coal, oil and natural gas. Coal production 3.9m tonnes oil equivalent in 1995, up 5.4 per cent on 1994 output. Proven reserves of natural gas 3.4 trillion cu feet (end-1995); gas production 4.1m tonnes oil equivalent, up 0.7 per cent on the 1994 figure.

Energy

Around 50 per cent dependent upon imported oil and gas from the former Soviet Union and to lesser extent Middle East. Electricity also imported via a grid from Vinnitsa in the Ukraine and exchange with Austria. Steady reduction of imported oil in energy use and increased use of domestic coal. The electricity and gas distribution sectors already being privatised.

Stock exchange

In June 1990 the Budapest Stock Exchange was established.

Membership of international organisations

Alps-Adriatic Working Community, CEFTA, CERN, Council of Europe, CSCE, Danube Commission, FAO, IAEA, IBRD, ICAC, IDA, ILO, IMF, IMO, IPU, ISO, ITC, ITU, NACC, NAM (guest), OECD (from end-March 1996), Partnership for Peace, UN, UNESCO, UNCTAD, UPU, WEU (associate partner), WFTU, WHO, WIPO, WMO, World Bank, WTO. Hungary officially applied for EU membership on 1 April 1994.

BUSINESS GUIDE

Time

GMT + 1 hr (GMT + 2 hrs from late Mar to late Sep).

Climate

Continental; average temperature between 1–3°C in winter, and around 20°C in summer. Coldest month Jan, hottest month Jul. Snow and frost in winter. Wettest month May, driest Sep.

Clothing

Medium to heavyweight and heavy topcoat for winter. Lightweight for summer. Raincoat needed in spring and autumn.

Entry requirements

Visa: Visas are no longer required for visitors holding western passports. Nationals of other countries should check with the embassy.
Currency: All foreign currency must be declared on entry if requested. No restrictions on amount of foreign currency taken in or out. Unified exchange rate in operation, which is adjusted weekly. Exchange facilities available at main banks, railway stations (24hrs), hotels and tourist offices.
Customs: Personal effects and goods bought at Intourist shops duty-free. Some restrictions on the goods that can be taken into or out of the country.

Air access

National airline: Malev Hungarian Airlines (Magyar Legikozlekedesi).

BUSINESS GUIDE

Air access (contd): *Other airlines:* Air France, Airline Lithuanie, Air Ukraine, Alitalia, Austrian Airlines, Avia Express, Balkan, British Airways, Czech Airlines (CSA), Delta, Egyptair, El Al, Eurowings, Finnair, JAT, KLM, LOT, Lufthansa, Northwest Airlines, Sabena, SAL Saxonia Airlines, SAS, Swissair, Syrian Arab Airlines, Tarom, Tunis Air, United Airlines.
International airport: Budapest (BUD), Ferihegy airport – Terminal II (MALEV and other flights), 22 km from city centre and Terminal I, 16 km from city centre.

Surface access

Good international road and rail connections; access from Vienna, Prague, Graz, Belgrade and Ljubjana. There are plans to improve the motorway from Vienna to Budapest.

Hotels

Majority of large hotels operated by the three big hotel chains, Hungar Hotels, Pannonia and Danubius. Reservations should be made in advance directly or through IBUSZ. Amex, Diners', Eurocard, Visa and Master Card credit cards accepted in larger hotels, restaurants and shops. Tipping usually 10-15 per cent. From 1 July 1994 all Budapest hotels are charging a 2 per cent tourism tax for guests staying more than one night.

Restaurants

Many types and categories. There are restaurants, inns, *csárda* and hotels. Food and drink relatively cheap. Tipping 10–15 per cent of the bill.

Credit cards

American Express is more widely accepted than other credit cards.

Car hire

Available from IBUSZ travel company, from hotels and from companies at Ferihegy airport. No international driving licence required. Speed limit in built up areas 60 kph, on main roads 100 kph and motorways 120 kph. Drinking and driving strictly prohibited. Seat belts compulsory.

City transport

Taxis: Beside the state-owned taxi services (Fotaxi, Volantaxi) there are also private taxi companies operating. Available from ranks, by telephone or can be hailed in the street. A taxi from the airport to the centre of Budapest takes about 25 minutes. Tipping usually 10-15 per cent. N.B. Tariffs are not regulated so it is advisable to agree a price with the driver in advance and avoid all unmarked cabs as they not only demand payment for mileage covered, but also for the return journey to their starting point.
For foreigners: Meters on many taxis are automatically set at the maximum tariff. There is little a visitor can do about this except complain.
Buses: Intercity service operates from Engels tér. There is a minibus service (no more than 10 minutes to wait) between the Ferihegy airport and Budapest city centre, between city centre and airport and between airport terminals; the service is available in the arrival baggage reclaim area and in the hall at the LRI Shuttle Bus Service Desk. On request individuals or groups can be transported from city centre to country areas: Airport Terminal 1 (tel: 157-6855; fax: 157-6482); Terminal 2 (tel: 157-6368; fax: 1576-2810.
Metro: The world's second-oldest undergound/metro system after London. Identified by large 'M'. Buy a day pass from stations, hotel desks or tobacconists, and have it stamped by meter on bus, tram, trolleybus or train. No tickets are sold on board and you will be fined if you do not have a meter-stamped ticket. The ticket must be stamped by the orange box before you get on the escalator to the platform. Three main lines: the Millennium (yellow line 1), East–West (red line 2), North–South (blue line 3).
Trams: Yellow tickets used.
Main railway stations: Déli Pu (Southern RW Terminal), Krisztina krt 37/a, Budapest I.
Keleti Pu (Eastern RW Terminal), Baross Tér (tel: 142-9150).
Nyugati Pu (Western RW Terminal), Teréz krt 111 (tel: 122-7860).

National transport

Road: Extensive road network. Country-wide bus service operated by Volán companies. Main terminal at Engels Tér (tel: 172-966). A ring road around Budapest and an extension of the M1 motorway to the Austrian and Slovak borders are planned.
Rail: Express service operates from Eastern (Keleti) and Western (Nyugati) railway stations. Tickets for most destinations can be booked in advance from Central office of MÁV (tel: 228-049).
Water: Around 1,700 km of navigable waterways. Hydrofoil service between Budapest and Vienna daily in summer season.

Public holidays

Fixed dates: 1 Jan (New Year's Day), 15 Mar (Anniversary of 1848 Revolution), 1 May (May Day), 20 Aug (St Stephen's Day), 23 Oct (Anniversary of 1956 Revolution), 25 & 26 Dec (Christmas).
Variable dates: Easter Monday, Whit Monday.

Working hours

Government and business: (Mon–Fri) 0800–1630.
Banking: (Mon–Fri) 0800–1630.
Shops: (Mon, Tue, Wed & Fri) 1000–1800, (Thu) 1000–2000.

Social customs

Shake hands on arriving and departing. Business cards used extensively.

Business language and interpreting/translation

Provided by hotels, travel agencies and OFFI National Translation Bureau (tel: 112-9616) and private interpreters and translators.

Telecommunications

First stage of MATAV privatisation has been completed and a further sale of the state's share in this telecom giant is likely.
Telephone and telefax: Local three minute calls can be made from public booths. For operator service dial 117-0000, 157-3333. Domestic long-distance dial 06, international automatic long-distance dial 00. For international information service dial 118-6977. Dialling code for Hungary: IDD access code + 36 followed by area code (1 for Budapest), followed by subscriber's number. Since September 1989 Budapest numbers are seven-digit, with '1' preceding the previous six-digit number.
Telex: Available from main hotels and at central post office (Városház utca 18, tel: 118-7728). Country code 61 H.
Telegram: Available at post offices and by dialling 02.

Postal service

Dial 117-2200 for information on postal matters (English, German, French, Russian language service). Budapest is divided into a number of districts (*kerulet*, abbreviated *ker*). The district number can be deduced from the middle two digits of the four-digit postal code.

Banking

Most developed system in eastern Europe, with the National Bank of Hungary playing important role in economic and financial management of economy. However, under reform of banking system in 1987, various National Bank functions devolved to commercial banks – Hungarian Credit Bank, National Commercial and Credit Bank, Budapest Bank. Foreign trade and currency transactions conducted by Hungarian Foreign Trade Bank and by some other banks; State Development Bank provides capital funds for main investment projects and also issues the majority of bonds. National Savings Bank, with extensive branch network, offers banking for the general public, and also foreigners needing foreign exchange accounts. Central-European International Bank is an internationally active offshore bank owned by the National Bank and six foreign banks. Citibank Budapest is a joint venture between Citibank and Central Bank of Exchange and Credit, a subsidiary of the National Bank. General Enterprise Bank was established in 1985 to take over enterprise fund of National Bank. A lot of small banks founded between 1988-90. The alliance of banks launched in 1990. The three big commercial banks remain structurally and financially weakened by the bad loans and low capitalisation they inherited in 1987.
Central bank: Magyar Nemzeti Bank (National Bank of Hungary).
Other banks: Agrobank, Budapest Bank, Central-European International Bank, DUNA Investment and Commercial Bank, General Bank for Venture Financing, General Banking and Trust Company, Innofinance Financial Institution, Inter-Europa Bank, Iparabank (industrial co-operative commercial bank), Ipari Fejlesztesi (industry development) Bank, Investbank (technical development), K. & H. (commercial and credit) Bank, Konzumbank (consumer co-operatives), Kultur Bank, Magyar Hitel (Hungarian credit) Bank, Magyar Kulkereskedelmi (foreign trade) Bank, Magyar Takareksovetkezeti (savings co-operative) Bank, Mezobank, Orszagos Takarekpentzar (national savings) Bank, Postabank & Takarekpenztar (post and savings), Realbank, Unicbank, YBL Epitoioari Innovacios Bank.

Business information

Privatisation cases are being processed rapidly by the State Privatisation Agency (SPA), established in March 1990.

Trade fairs

International trade fairs held in Budapest in late May (technical and capital goods) and late September (consumer goods). Each year there are also a number of specialised exhibitions. Every fifth year there is an agricultural exhibition. Information available from Hungexpo.

Electricity supply

220 V AC, 50 cycles.

Representation in capital

Afghanistan, Albania, Algeria, Argentina, Australia, Austria, Belgium, Bolivia, Brazil, Bulgaria, Cambodia, Canada, China, Colombia, Cuba, Denmark, Ecuador, Egypt, Finland, France, Germany, Greece, India, Indonesia, Iran, Iraq, Israel, Italy, Japan, Korea DPR, Republic of Korea, Kuwait, Libya, Mexico, Mongolia, Netherlands, Norway, Peru, Poland, Portugal, Romania, Russia, Spain, Sweden, Switzerland, Syria, Turkey, UK, Uruguay, USA, Venezuela, Vietnam, Yemen.

BUSINESS DIRECTORY

Hotels

Budapest (area code 1)
Agro, Normafa ut 54, 1121 (tel: 175-4011; fax: 175-6164).

Aquincum, Ardad Fejedelem utca 94, H-1036 (tel: 250-4114; fax: 250-4672).

Astoria (in city centre), Kossuth Lajos ut 19, H-1053 (tel: 117-3411; fax: 118-6798).

Hotels (contd):
Atrium Huyatt, Roosevelt tér 2, H-1051 (tel: 266-1234; fax: 118-8659).

Béke, Lenin krt 97, H-1067 (tel: 132-3300; fax: 153-3380).

Buda Penta, Kirsztina krt 41-43, H-1013 (tel: 156-6333; fax: 155-6964).

Budapest, Szilagyi Erzsebet Fasor 47, H-1026 (tel: 115-3230; fax: 115-0496).

Duna Intercontinental, Apaczai Csere Janos ut 4, H-1052 (tel: 117-5122; fax: 118-4973).

Erzsébet, Karolyi M ut 11-15, H-1053 (tel: 138-2111; fax: 118-9237).

Expo, Dobi Istvan ut 10, H-1101 (tel: 184-2130).

Expo, Dobi Istvan ut 10, H-1101 (tel: 184-2130).

Flamenco Occidental, Tas Vezér ut 7, H-1113 (tel: 161-2250; fax: 165-8007).

Forum, Apaczai Csere Janos ut 12-14, H-1052 (tel: 117-8088; fax: 117-9808).

Gellért, Szt Gellért tér 1, H-1111 (tel: 185-2200; fax: 166-6631).

Grand Corvinus Kempinski, Erzsébet tér 7-8, H-1051 (tel: 266-1000; fax: 266-2000).

Grand Hungaria, Rakoczi ut 90, H-1074 (tel: 322-9050; fax: 268-1999).

Grand Margitsziget, Margitsziget (Margaret Island) (tel: 111-1000; fax: 533-3029).

Hilton, Hess Andras tér 1-3, H-1014 (tel: 175-1000; fax: 175-1000).

Normafa, Eotvos ut 52-54, H-1121 (tel: 156-3444; fax: 175-9583).

Novotel, Alkotas ut 63-67, H-1123 (tel: 186-9588; fax: 166-5636).

Panorama, Rege ut 21, H-1121 (tel: 175-0522; fax; 175-0416).

Royal Térz krt 47-49, H-1073 (tel: 153-3133; fax: 142-1122).

Stadion, Ifjésag ut 1-3, H-1148 (tel: 163-1830; fax: 163-6894).

Thermal, Margitsziget, H-1138 (tel: 111-1000; fax: 132-1100).

Thermal Aquincum, Arpad Fejedelem ut 94, H-1033 (tel: 250-3360/4177).

Thermal Helia, Karpat ut 62-64 (tel: 129-8650).

Victoria, Bemrakpart 11, H-1011 (tel: 201-8644).

Volga, Dozsa Gyorgy ut 65, H-1134 (tel: 140-8393; fax: 140-8316).

Useful telephone numbers

Ambulance: 04.

Police: 07.

Fire department: 05.

24-hour emergency service (English-speaking): 118-8212.

Car hire

Budapest
Avis: Reservation offices, Martinelli Ter 8, H-1052 (tel: 118-4240); Ferihegy airport terminal 1 (Ibusz Desk) (tel: 147-5754); terminal 2 (tel: 157-8470).

Budget: Hotel Buda Penta I, Krisztina krt 41–43 (tel: 156-6333).

CO-OPTOURIST-Budget: IX Ferenc krt 43 (tel: 113-1466; tx: 223-242).

Europcar: Vaskapu utca 16 (tel: 133-4783; fax: 134-0999).

Hertz: Kertesz utca 24–28 (tel: 111-6116, 122-1471; tx: 226-222); downtown v, Aranykez utca 4–8 (tel: 117-7533, 117-7788; tx: 223-252); airport Ferihegy, (tel: 157-8618, 157-8629; tx: 227-868).

Hungar Motor Rent: Budapest Airport Terminal 1 (tel: 157-8280, 157-9123/78-68; fax: 157-8280).

IBUSZ-Avis: Martinelli tér, 8 (tel: 361-118-4207/4158; tx: 225-545).

VIP: Novotel, Alkotás utca 63–67, PO Box 233, H-1444 (tel: 186-9588, 166-8621; fax: 166-5636).

VOLANTOURIST-Europcar: Vaskapu utca 16 (tel: 133-4783; tx: 225-639).

Taxis

Fotaxi (tel: 222-2222).

City Taxi (tel: 211-1111).

Volantaxi (tel: 166-6666).

Chambers of Commerce

Hungarian Chamber of Commerce, PO Box 106, H-1389 Budapest (tel: 1153-3333; fax: 1153-1285).

Budapest Chamber of Commerce and Industry, Krisztina krt 99, H-1016 Budapest (tel: 1175-6764; fax: 1202-7930).

Chamber of Commerce of the Balaton Region, Budapesti ut 5, H-8200 Veszprém (tel: 8832-9008; fax: 8832-8061).

Chamber of Commerce of County Fejér, Rákóczi ut 25, H-8000 Székesfehérvár (tel: 2232-7627).

Chamber of Commerce and Industry of County Vas, Honvéd tér 2, H-9700 Szombathely (tel: 9431-6936).

Chamber of Commerce and Industry of the Tisza Region, Kis Tisza ut 4, H-6640 Csongrád (tel: 6333-1377).

Chamber of Commerce of the North-Alföld Region, Kálvin tér 6/b, H-4026 Debrecen (tel: 5231-3053; fax: 5231-9236).

Chamber of Commerce of North Hungary, Arany J ut 4, H-3540 Miskolc (tel: 4634-0492; fax: 4634-0403).

Chamber of Commerce of North Transdanubia, Alkotmány ut 20, H-9021 Gyor (tel: 9631-5775; fax: 9631-9650).

Chamber of Commerce of Pest County, Akadémia ut I IV, H-1054 Budapest (tel: 1131-4986; fax: 1131-9903).

Chamber of Commerce of Sopron, Várkerület 19, H-9400 Sopron (tel: 9931-1471; fax: 9931-2151).

Chamber of Commerce of the South-Transdanubian Region, Bem ut 24, H-7621 Pécs (tel: 7241-3040; fax: 7241-1917).

Esztergom Chamber of Commerce and Industry, Kossuth L ut 13, H-2500 Esztergom (tel: 3331-1444; fax: 3331-1186).

South Hungarian Chamber of Commerce, Tisza Lajos krt 2-4, H-6721 Szeged (tel: 6232-1512; fax: 6232-4194).

Zala Chamber of Commerce and Industry, Kosztolányi ut 10, H-8900 Zalaegerszeg (tel: 9231-1010; fax: 9231-1042).

Banking

Magyar Nemzeti Bank (National Bank of Hungary) (central bank), Szabadság tér 8–9, H-1850 Budapest (tel: 131-1723, 153-2600, 132-3320; fax: 153-1058, 131-1723, 132-4179).

ABN AMRO Bank (Magyarország) Rt (commercial bank), Nagy Jeno ut 12, H-1126 Budapest (tel: 202-2722; fax: 201-3685).

Agro Deposit and Credit Bank Co Ltd (agricultural innovation), Boszorményi ut 24, H-1126 Budapest (tel: 155-3000; fax: 155-7573).

Allami Fejlesztési Intézet (state development bank), Deák Ferenc ut 5, H-1052 Budapest (tel: 118-1200; tx: 225-672).

Banque Indosuez Magyrország Rt (commercial bank), Rákóczi ut 1-3, H-1088 Budapest (tel: 266-2713; fax: 266-5231).

BNP-KH-Dresdner Bank Rt (commercial bank), Molnár ut 19, H-1056 Budapest (tel: 266-1447; fax: 266-1321).

Budapest Bank Ltd (commercial bank), Deák Ferenc ut 5, H-1052 Budapest (tel: 269-2397; fax: 269-2400).

Commerzbank (Budapest) Rt (commercial bank), Széchenyi rkp 8, H-1054 Budapest (tel: 269-4510; fax: 269-4530).

Creditanstalt Rt (commercial bank), Akadémia ut 17, H-1054 Budapest (tel: 269-0812; fax: 153-4959).

Credit Lyonnais Bank Rt (commercial bank), József Nádor tér 7, H-1051 Budapest (tel: 266-9000; fax: 266-9950).

Dunabank Rt (commercial bank), Báthory ut 12, H-1054 Budapest (tel: 269-3377; fax: 269-3380).

Epitöipari Innovációs Bank RT (innovation bank for the building industry), Sziv ut 8–10, H-1068 Budapest (tel: 112-9010; tx: 223-743).

General Bank for Venture Financing, Stollar Bela ut 3/A, H-1055 Budapest (tel: 131-0126; fax: 111-0494).

General Banking and Trust Co Ltd (AÉB Rt) (commercial bank), Markó ut 9, H-1055 Budapest (tel: 269-1450; fax: 260-1440).

Hungarian Bank of Savings and Co-operatives (commercial bank), Pethényi koz 10, H-1122 Budapest (tel: 202-3777; fax: 156-2649).

Hungarian Commercial and Credit Bank (K&HB), Arany Janos ut 24, H-1851 Budapest (tel: 131-3570; fax: 111-1825).

Hungarian Credit Bank MBH (commerical bank), Szabadság tér 5-6, H-1054 Budapest (tel: 269-2122; fax: 269-2245).

BUSINESS DIRECTORY

Banks (contd):
Hungarian Foreign Trade Bank Ltd (MKB) (commercial bank), St István t\01er 11, H-1821 Budapest (tel: 269-0922; fax: 269-0959).

Ibusz Commercial and Retail Bank Ltd, Ajtósi Durer sor 10, H-1146 Budapest (tel: 251-1332; fax: 252-0718).

Industrial Development Bank Ltd (specialised financial institution), Hold ut 25, H-1054 Budapest (tel: 132-0320; fax: 112-9552).

Internationale Nederlanden Bank (Hungary) Ltd (commercial bank), Károly Krt 11, H-1075 Budapest (tel: 269-7800; fax: 269-6447).

Investrade and Banking Corporation Ltd, Kecskemeti ut 14, H-1053 Budapest (tel: 117-4111; fax: 117-4111/294).

Iparbankház Rt (commercial bank), Gerlóczy ut 5, H-1052 Budapest (tel: 118-5282; fax: 117-1921).

Kereskedelmi es Hitelbank RT (commercial and credit bank), Arany János ut 24, H-1051 Budapest (tel: 112-5200, 153-2022; fax: 111-3845).

Kisvállalkozási Bank/OTP Leánybank (bank for entrepreneurs–national savings bank subsidiary), Vádor ut 16, H-1054 Budapest (tel: 132-8700).

KulturBank, Dózsa György ut 150, H-1134 Budapest (tel: 120-2650, 140-2670; fax: 140-3700).

Leumi-Credit Bank Plc (commercial bank), Bárcay J ut 3-5, H-1052 Budapest (tel: 117-6904; fax: 117-7328).

Magyar Hitelbank RT (Hungarian credit bank), Szabadság tér 5–6, H-1054 Budapest (tel: 153-2600; fax: 315-901).

Magyar Külkereskedelmi Bank (foreign trade bank), Szent István tér 11, H-1821 Budapest (tel: 132-9630; fax: 132-2568).

Magyarországi Volksbank Rt (commercial bank), Rákóczi ut 7, H-1088 Budapest (tel: 266-1688; fax: 266-1680).

Mezöbank (national bank of agricultural cooperatives), Hold ut 16, H-1054 Budapest (tel: 153-1000; fax: 112-1216).

MHB-Daewoo Bank Rt (commercial bank), Rákóczi ut 1-3, H-1088 Budapest (tel: 266-0019; fax: 266-5720).

Müszaki Fejlesztési Bank Betéti Társulás (investment, technical development bank), Deák Ferenc ut 5, H-1053 Budapest (tel: 117-5833; tx: 223-250).

National Savings and Commercial Bank Ltd (OTP), Nádor ut 16, H-1876 Budapest (tel: 153-1444; fax: 112-6858).

Nomura Investment Bank Hungary Ltd, Arany János ut 19, H-1051 Budapest (tel: 112-6898; fax: 132-6631).

Polgári Bank Ltd (commercial bank), Sziv ut 53, H-1063 Budapest (tel: 132-7121; fax: 132-0567).

Portfolio Bank for Property Handling and Privatisation Ltd, Budafoki ut 79, H-1117 Budapest (tel: 161-1050).

Postabank and Savings Bank Corp (commercial bank), József Nádor tér 1, H-1052 Budapest (tel: 117-1190; fax: 117-1369).

Realbank Ltd, Andrássy ut 124, H-1052 (tel: 131-7529; fax: 132-7391).

Real Estate Bank, Bárczy I. ut 3–5, H-1052 Budapest (tel: 117-1499; fax: 117-6302).

Westdeutsche Landesbank (Hungaria) Ltd (commercial bank), Stollár B ut 3/a, H-1055 Budapest (tel: 269-1496; fax: 269-1496).

Banks with foreign participation:

Central European Credit Bank Ltd, Váci ut 16, PO 170, H-1364 Budapest (tel: 118-8377; fax: 118-9415).

Citibank Budapest Rt, Váci ut 19-21, H-1052 Budapest (tel: 138-2666; tx: 266-9129).

European Commercial Bank Ltd, Hegyalja ut 7-13, H-1016 Budapest (tel: 202-4816; fax: 202-6492).

Inter-Europa Bank Rt, Szabadság tér 15, H-1054 Budapest (tel: 269-1855; fax: 269-2526).

Unicbank Rt, Váci ut 19-21, H-1052 Budapest (tel: 266-2066; fax: 266-2846).

Principal newspapers

Budapest Week, Foul 14-18, 1016 Budapest (tel: 201-9409; fax: 202-4083).

Heti Viloggazdaseg, Kossuth Lajos ter 6-8, H-1389 Budapest (tel: 155-5411; tx: 202-550).

Hungarian Business Herald, Tanacs krt 7.1.3, H-1075 Budapest (tel: 141-7270).

Hungarian Digest, Lenin krt 9-11, H-1073 Budapest (tel: 181-1580).

Hungarian Economic Review, Herman Otto ul 41, 1026 Budapest (tel: 156-2812; fax 156-2812).

Hungarian Market Report, Naphegy ter 2, 1016 Budapest. Hungarian Observer, Rona ul 207, 1145 Budapest (tel: 251-4296).

Hungarian Trade Journal, Erssebet krt 9-11, H-1073 Budapest (tel: 1220-1285; fax 132-5335).

Hungarian Travel Magazine, Muzeum ut 11, H-1088 Budapest (tel: 136-1384).

Magyar Hirlap, Kerepesi ut 29, H-1087 Budapest (tel: 134-3330; fax: 134-0712).

Magyar Nemzet, Erzsebet krt 9-11, H-1073 Budapest (tel: 122-2400; tx: 224-269).

Nepszabadsag, Blahu Lujzater 3, H-1960 Budapest (tel: 138-2399; tx: 225-551).

Nepszava, Rakoczi ut 54, H-1964 Budapest (tel: 122-4810).

Neue Zeitung, Nagymezo ut 49, H-1391 Budapest.

New Hungarian Quarterly, Rakoczi ut 17, H-1088 Budapest (tel: 138-4214).

Travel information

Ferihegy International Airport flight enquiries (tel: 157-7155).

Hungarian Automobile Club, Francis ut 38, Budapest XIV (tel: 1691-8310).

Hungarian Tourist Board, The Office of the Ministry of Industry and Trade, 5th floor, Margit krt 85, H-1024 Budapest (tel: 1175-0419/2128; fax: 1175-2419).

IBUSZ – Hungarian Travel Agency (main Budapest office), Tanács krt 3/c, Budapest VII (tel: 142-3140; tx: 225-650).

Malev Hungarian Airlines (Magyar Legikozlekedesi), Roosevelt ter 2, Budapest H-1051 (tel: 266-9033; fax: 266-2759).

Secretariat of the Hungarian Tourist Council, 6th floor, Margit krt 85, H-1024 Budapest (tel: 1175-1682; fax: 1175-38190).

Tourinform (tourist information), Suto ut 2, H-1052 Budapest (tel: 1179-800; tx: 223-086 tinfo).

Other useful addresses

Allami Biztositó (state insurance company), Ullöi ut 1, H-1813 Budapest (tel: 117-8566; tx: 224-875)

Budapest Stock Exchange, Deak Ferenc ut 5, H-1052 Budapest (tel: 117-5226; fax: 118-1737).

Central Statistical Office, International Relations Department, Keleti Károly utca 5–7, , PO Box 51, H-1525 Budapest (tel: 212-6136; fax: 212-6378).

Federation of Scientific and Technical Societies (MTESZ), Kossuth Lajos tér 6–8, Budapest V (tel: 153-3333).

Hungária Biztositó (Hungária Insurance Company), Bánk ut 17–6, H-1115 Budapest (tel: 182-0750; tx: 223-104).

Hungarian Foundation for Enterprise Promotion, Etele ut 68, Budapest H-1115 (tel: 203-0348; fax: 161-1813).

Hungarian Investment and Trade Development Agency, ITD, POB 222, H-1364 Budapest (tel: 118-6396/0051; fax: 118-3732).

Hungarian Privatisation and State Holding Company, Pozsonyi ut 56, 1133 Budapest (tel: 129-6634, 269-8600; fax: 149-8587, 120-8850).

Hungary EU Energy Centre (Thermie), Konyves Kalman Krt 76, 1087 Budapest VIII (tel: 269-9067, 133-1304; fax: 269-9065).

Hungexpo International Fair Centre, Dobi Istvan ut 10, Budapest X.

Magyar Tavirati Iroda (Hungarian news agency) (MTI), Fem utca 507, 1016 Budapest (tel: 155-6722; tx: 224371 mtih).

Mineralimpex Hungarian Oil and Gas Co, Benczur u 13, 1068 Budapest (tel: 131-6720; fax: 153-1779, 142-3584).

Ministry of Agriculture, Kossuth L tér 11, H-1055 Budapest (tel: 302-0000; fax: 302-0402/0408).

Ministry of Culture and Education, Szalay ut 10-14, H-1055 Budapest (tel: 302-0600; fax: 302-3002).

Ministry of Defence, Balaton ut 7-11, H-1055 Budapest (tel: 332-2500; fax: 311-0242).

Ministry of Environmental Protection and Regional Policy, Fo ut 44-50, H-1011 Budapest (tel: 201-4133; fax: 201-3134).

Ministry of Finance, József Nádor tér 2-4, H-1051 Budapest (tel: 118-2066, 138-2633; fax: 118-2570).

Ministry of Foreign Affairs, Bem rkp 47, H-1027 Budapest (tel: 156-8000; fax: 155-9693).

Ministry of Home Affairs, József A ut 2-4, H-1051 Budapest (tel: 331-3700, 332-5790, 201-6288).

Ministry of Industry & Trade, Honvéd ut 13-15, H-1055 Budapest (tel: 302-2355; fax: 302-2394).

Ministry of Information, PO Box 600, H-1538 Budapest (tel: 117-1788).

Ministry of International Economic Relations, Honved 13/15, H-1055 Budapest (tel: 153-000; fax: 153-2794).

Ministry of Justice, Szalay ut 16, H-1055 Budapest (tel: 332-5330/6170).

Ministry of Labour, Roosevelt tér 7-8, H-1051 Budapest (tel: 302-2100, 311-0200; fax: 332-7379).

Ministry of Transport, Telecommunications & Water Management, Dob ut 75-81, H-1077 Budapest (tel: 322-0220, 341-4300; fax: 322-8695).

Ministry of Welfare, Arany János ut 6-8, H-1051 Budapest (tel: 332-3100; fax: 302-0925).

Pressinform (information bureau for foreign journalists), Budakeszi ut 41, H-1021 Budapest (tel: 175-1890; fax: 175-1178).

Prime Minister's Office, Kossuth L tér 1-3, H-1055 Budapest (tel: 268-3000).

Iceland

Michael Griffin

The coalition of the right-wing Independence Party (IP) and the centrist Progressive Party (PP), elected on 8 April 1995, actually increased its support rating by 10 per cent during its first year of office, buoyed by a rosy economic outlook and the charisma of Prime Minister David Oddsson. In July 1996, the left-wing former finance minister Olafur Ragnar Grimsson was elected president after the well-liked Vigdis Finnbogadtótir retired. Finnbogadtótir was head of state for 16 years.

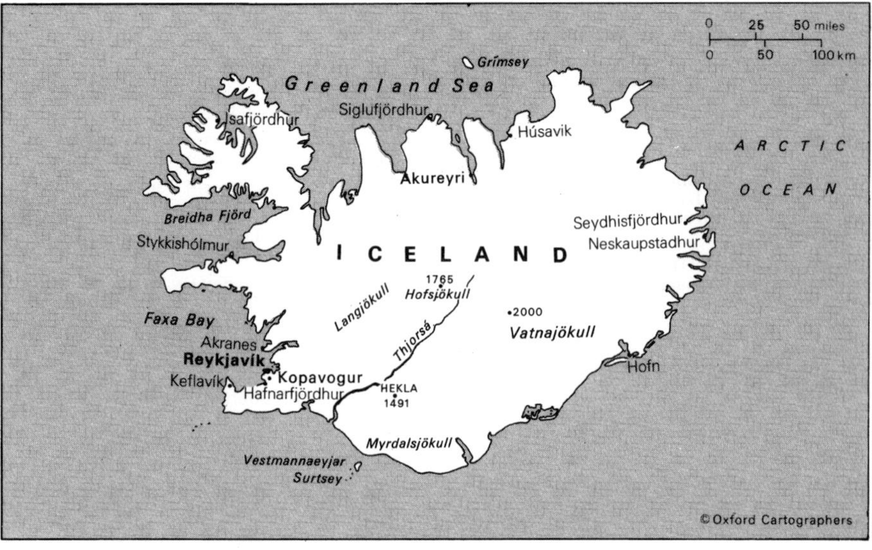

Labour grumbles

The alliance's honeymoon came to an abrupt end on 1 May 1996, however, as proposed reforms to pensions and labour rights threatened to result in labour unrest. In 1995, Iceland faced its highest rate of industrial action since the 1980s, with teachers, air staff and seamen all going out on strike. A general wage agreement of 7-15 per cent, agreed in December 1995, places serious budgetary pressure upon a government committed to reining in expenditure and attracting foreign investment.

Economy

Foreign participation in the Icelandic economy has averaged only 0.1 per cent of GDP in recent years, one tenth of neighbouring states. In mid-November 1995, Alusuisse-Lonza, the Swiss owner of Iceland's largest industrial facility, the ISAL aluminium smelter at Straumsvik, confirmed it would expand production capacity from 100,000 to 160,000 tonnes per year over the next two years through the investment of US$220 million. The expansion will also result in a 40 per cent increase in the generating capacity of the state electricity utility, Landsvirkjun. It should add an additional 0.6-0.7 per cent to the GDP growth prediction of 3 per cent in 1996, according to the National Economic Institute. Aluminium exports accounted for 10.3 per cent of total trade in 1995 and the increase could add a further US$80-90 million to annual exports.

The announcement added to the feel-good flavour of the government's first months but it remains to be seen whether Mr Oddsson will be prepared to open up the island's passionately-guarded fishing industry, the source of 73 per cent of its exports and the chief motive for Iceland's reluctance to become entwined with the European Union (EU) (no stranger to fishing controversies).

The government has ruled out applying for EU membership in its current term, preferring to bolster links through its membership of the European Economic Area (EEA). Nonetheless, the accession of Sweden and Finland in January 1995 and friction with Norway, its fellow member in the European Free Trade Association (EFTA), have strengthened fears of growing political and economic isolation. In April 1996, Iceland and Norway were both granted observer status at the Schengen Convention on border controls, another indication that the nation's direction will be increasingly subject to decisions in Brussels.

Fishing

In January 1996, the opposition Awakening of the Nation or People's Movement presented a bill before the 63-seat Althing (Parliament) proposing that non-Icelanders be allowed to control a maximum of 20 per cent in the republic's processing and vessel-operating concerns. Although

KEY FACTS — Iceland

Official title: Republic of Iceland
Head of state: President Olafur Ragnar Grimsson (from Jul 1996)
Head of government: Premier David Oddsson (leader of IP)
Ruling party: Coalition of Independence Party (IP) and Progressive Party (PP)
Capital: Reykjavík
Official Languages: Icelandic
Currency: Icelandic Krona (IKr) = 100 aurar
Exchange rate: IKr67.03 per US$ (Dec 1996)
Area: 103,100 sq km
Population: 267,809 (1 Dec 1995)
GDP per capita: US$23,037 (1994)
GDP real growth: 3% (1995)
Unemployment: 4.9% (1995)
Inflation: 1.6% (1995)
Trade balance: US$200m (1995)
Foreign debt: US$4.4bn (1995
Visitor numbers: 189,796 (1995)

fisheries minister Thorsteinn Palsson has rejected direct foreign investment in the industry, he has said he would be willing to open the sector to indirect foreign investment, although he has set no timetable. The trade and industry minister Finnur Ingolfsson, meanwhile, has lodged a bill proposing that energy and air transport should be made more accessible to foreign capital originating in the EEA.

Behind its fear of being left behind by Europe and its search for foreign capital lies the realisation that Iceland's 200-mile exclusion zone is no longer quite the guarantor of national prosperity that it once was. Economic growth in 1995 was a modest 2 per cent, but exports contracted by 2.4 per cent, largely due to conservation measures that have seen the inshore catch of cod, the backbone of the marine economy, fall from 335,000 tonnes in 1990 to just over 170,000 tonnes last year. Although Icelandic vessels landed 1.49 million tonnes between January and November, equivalent to around US$700 million, there is a growing trend to fish in the disputed 'loophole' of the Barents Sea or east of the Grand Banks. Of those species not covered in the national quota system, only one third actually came from the exclusive zone.

Iceland's strength in negotiations is increasingly overshadowed by that of its neighbours. Tempers flared in July 1995 when

KEY INDICATORS

	Unit	1991	1992	1993	1994	1995
Population	'000	256	261	265	270	268
Gross domestic product (GDP)	US$ bn	6.30	6.70	5.80	6.10	–
GDP per capita	US$	24,320	25,760	22,300	23,037	–
GDP real growth	%	1.5	-3.3	-0.4	2.8	3.0
Inflation	%	6.8	3.7	4.1	1.5	1.6
Consumer prices	1900=100	106.8	111.0	115.6	117.4	119.3
Unemployment	%	1.6	2.9	4.4	4.7	4.9
Agricultural production	1979-81=100	87.75	88.62	79.44	80.53	80.13
Total fish catch	1990=100	66.4	103.0	112.6	96.9	–
Exports (goods & services)	IKrm	124,943	121,248	134,972	136,489	159,853
Imports (goods & services)	IKrm	130,305	121,943	122,493	134,618	144,260
Balance of trade	US$m	-47.4	1.4	181.3	294.0	200.0
Current account	US$m	-311.5	-206.4	-2.0	124.8	–
Total reserves minus gold	US$m	449.5	498.3	426.4	292.9	308.1
Foreign exchange	US$m	443.6	483.9	412.0	277.5	292.5
Discount rate	%	21.0	16.0	–	4.7	5.6
Deposit rate	%	7.5	5.2	2.8	3.3	3.4
Lending rate	%	17.5	13.1	14.1	10.6	11.6
Exchange rate	IKr per US$	58.99	57.55	67.60	69.94	64.69

COUNTRY PROFILE — ICELAND

Historical profile

Under Norwegian then Danish rule from the thirteenth century; the harshness of Iceland's terrain was frequently compounded by natural disasters leading, in the nineteenth century, to large-scale emigration to the USA and Canada.
1903 Home rule.
1918 Independence under the Danish crown.
1940 German invasion of Denmark. British troops stationed in Iceland.
1944 Iceland terminated the convention linking it with Denmark and declared a republic.
1949 Membership of NATO and Council of Europe. A large US airbase was established at Keflavík.
1953 Founder member of Nordic Council.
1959-71 Coalition of Independence and Social Democratic Parties. A high-inflation economy was faced in the next two decades by a succession of three-party coalitions interspersed with more stable centre-right coalitions of the Independence and Progressive Parties.
1960s-70s Iceland's unilateral extensions of its territorial waters to protect its fishing grounds led to the 'cod wars' with the UK, and in 1976 caused a temporary break in diplomatic relations, the first such break between NATO members.
1974-78 Geir Hallgrímsson prime minister.
1980 Vigdís Finnbogadóttir elected president, the world's first popularly elected female head of state.
1985 Iceland declared a nuclear-free zone, barring entry to all nuclear weapons.
1983-87 Steingrímur Hermannsson prime minister.
1987 Thorsteinn Pálsson appointed prime minister.
1988 Hermansson prime minister again.
1991 David Oddson becomes prime minister of new coalition government.

Political system

Parliamentary republic with legislative power held jointly by the directly elected president and the *Althing* (63-member directly elected unicameral parliament). Elections every four years. Executive power vested in the government, formally appointed by the president, consisting of the prime minister and other ministers but subject to the rule of parliament. The April 1995 election returned a centre-right coalition composed of the Independence and Progressive Parties. The new coalition has a comfortable majority of 40 MPs out of 63 and continues under Prime Minister David Oddsson's leadership. Olafur Ragnar Grimsson, a left-wing former finance minister, was elected president in July 1996, replacing Vigdis Finnbogadtótir, who stepped down after 16 years in office. Next parliamentary election is scheduled to be held by April 1999.

Political parties

Independence Party (IP); Progressive Party (PP); Social Democratic Party (SDP); People's Alliance (PA); Women's Alliance (WA); Awakening of the Nation or People's Movement.

Population

Life expectancy males 75.1 years, females 80.8 years.

Main cities/towns

Reykjavík, capital area (population 156,542, 1 Dec 1994), Akureyri (14,914), Kopavogur, Hafnarfjordur and Keflavík.

Language

The Icelandic language belongs to the North Germanic branch of the Indo-European family.

Media

Dailies: There are four dailies published in Reykjavík, which generally represent the views of the main political parties. Most popular are *Morgunbladid* (Conservative), *DV* (Independent) and *Tíminn* (Progressive).
Periodicals: Several monthly and bi-monthly magazines. *Iceland Reporter* is a monthly newspaper in English. *Iceland Review* is published quarterly in English.

Norway refused to permit an Icelandic trawler fishing in the Barents Sea to dock for essential repairs, despite the fact that the 'loophole' is considered to be international waters. Successive rounds of talks between Russia, Norway and Iceland to establish catch levels broke down over cod quotas and were complicated by the EU pressing for the same amount that might be granted to Reykjavik. Similarly, in January 1996, an EU decision to declare a minimum price on salmon imported from EFTA in order to prevent dumping provoked a sharp reaction from the government. Though minor skirmishes by comparison with the 'cod wars' of 20 years ago, both incidents illustrated the vulnerability of both Iceland's stocks and markets.

Recovery continues

Despite a lacklustre growth rate, 1995's performance was a continuation of the recovery that Iceland has enjoyed since 1991, though on a more modest scale. The current account surplus fell from 2.1 per cent of GDP to 0.9 per cent but inflation remained around or below the 2 per cent mark for the third year running. Exports during the first 11 months rose by 5 per cent to US$1.64 billion, but a steep hike in imports from US$1.3 billion in 1994 to US$1.45 billion in 1995 – largely due to a 20 per cent increase in shipments to the ISAL plant – reduced the trade surplus from US$265 million in 1994 to US$187 million in 1995. Exports of ferrosilicon and aluminium were both significantly improved, at 28 and 9.6 per cent respectively, though fish exports dropped slightly to US$1.19 billion.

Budget and finance

The 1996 budget, approved in December 1995, provides for a 1.5 per cent increase in government revenues with a 2.5 cut in real expenditure, allowing for a halving of the deficit from IKr8.9 billion in 1995 to IKr4 billion – less than 1 per cent of GDP. A sharp cut in public investment and retrenchment within the health services are expected to yield the main savings, but these calculations will have been upset by the agreement with the trade unions, which included a package of benefits worth an additional US$15.5 million.

On 2 August 1995, the Central Bank of Iceland (CBI) signed a five-year multi-currency revolving credit facility worth US$200 million to provide liquidity assurance for the republic's finances and opened a new Euro-Commercial Paper Programme, raising its access to the ECU and national European currencies from US$350 to US$500 million. The agreement followed the signature in July 1995 of a Joint Growth Initiative with the European Investment Bank (EIB) for Ecu40 million, the first funds the EIB has lent to Iceland. Together with a Ecu36 million loan from the Nordic Investment Bank, the funds will finance road construction in Reykjavik and the building of a road tunnel in the Westfjiords. Both projects fall within the government's broad aim of improving infrastructure, partly to attract tourism. The number of visitors to the island rose by 10 per cent in 1995 to 190,000. Icelandair, the national carrier, made a US$10 million profit in 1995.

Currency

On September 6, the CBI announced it would change the official basket of currencies against which the rate of the krona is determined. The new basket is composed of the currencies of Iceland's 16 most important trade partners in goods and services for 1994 and replaces the previous basket of the US dollar (18 per cent) Ecu (76 percent) and the Japanese yen (6 per cent). The new basket, which will be revised annually, was introduced to reflect the floating of the sterling rate and the fact that other Nordic countries have since abandoned the Ecu peg of their own currencies.

COUNTRY PROFILE — ICELAND

Media (contd):
Radio: Over 85,000 radio sets in use. Six main radio stations broadcast nationally: Icelandic State Broadcasting Service (RUV) – Channel One and Two, plus Radio Bylgjan/Stjarnan/Adalstodin. Channel One broadcasts on medium and long wave as well as FM.
Television: Approximately 80,000 TV sets in use. Programmes broadcast by Icelandic State Broadcasting Service – Television (RUV) and Channel Two (Stod 2).
Advertising: Newspaper, radio and television advertising are the most effective. The quality of locally produced television advertising material is very high by international standards. Information can be obtained from Samband islenskra auglysingastofa (Association of Icelandic Advertising Companies), Hateigsvegur 3, 105 Reykjavík (tel: 562-9588; fax: 562-9585).

Domestic economy

Open market economy based largely on the fishing industry. Pattern of economic growth is therefore heavily determined by size of fish catch and world prices of fish products.

Employment

Around 10 per cent of the labour force is engaged in agriculture and fishing and 30 per cent in industry.

External trade

Over 60 per cent of trade turnover conducted with the EU, of which UK, Germany, France, Denmark and Netherlands are the principal traders. Other main trading partners are USA, Japan, eastern Europe and Sweden.
Exports: Main exports include fish products, aluminium products, other manfuacturing products, agricultural products. Main destinations: UK (typically 22% of total), USA (16%), Germany (11%), Japan (9%), France (8%), Denmark (5%), Spain (5%), Switzerland (4%), Norway (3%), Netherlands (2%).
Imports: Main imports include machinery and apparatus, manufactured goods, transport equipment, food and live animals.
Main sources: Norway (typically 12% of total), UK (13%), Germany (12%), Denmark (9%), USA (9%), Sweden (7%), Netherlands (6%), Japan (6%), Italy (4%), France (3%).

Agriculture

This sector contributed 16 per cent to GDP in 1994 and employed 10.3 per cent of the labour force. Scarcity of arable land, but good grazing allows for self-sufficiency in meat (mostly lamb), milk, poultry, eggs, cheese and butter. The sector is small-scale, heavily subsidised and organised into co-operatives. Fishing replaced farming early in this century as a dominant sector of economy. Fishing industry (including processing) is single most important export earner. Large modernised trawler fleet supplies over 110 freezing plants, which produce white fish fillets, frozen shrimps, capelin, scampi, scallops, fish oil and fish meal. The Icelandic Freezing Plants Corporation and Iceland Seafood Ltd are the leading fish exporters. There is rapid growth of inland and off-shore fish farming.

Industry

The industrial sector contributed 36 per cent to GDP in 1994 and employed 30.2 per cent of the workforce. It is centred on fish and food processing, aluminium smelting, ferro-silicon alloys, diatomite production and light manufacturing. A plan to build a US$1bn aluminium smelter to take advantage of Iceland's cheap hydroelectric power was shelved in the early-1990s, when aluminium prices dived to historic lows, but is being reconsidered. A decision will be made by the first quarter of 1997 by the three partners in the venture, Alumax of the USA, Granges of Sweden and Hoogovens of the Netherlands.

Energy

Rapid development of cheap hydroelectric and geothermal power has led to self-sufficiency in

COUNTRY PROFILE

Energy (contd): energy requirements. Around 81 per cent of homes have geothermal heating. Fishing industry, however, remains dependent on imported oil.

Legal system

Civil law based on Danish law.

Membership of international organisations

BIS, CCC, Council of Europe, CSCE, EEA, EBRD, ECE, EFTA, FAO, IAEA, ICAO, ICES, IDA, IFC, IHO, ILO, IMF, IMO, INTELSAT, INTERPOL, IPU, ITU, IWC, NATO, Nordic Council, OECD, UN, UNESCO, UPU, WEU (associate membership since November 1992), World Bank, WHO, WMO WSG, WTO. Iceland has a free trade agreement with the EU pending resolution of fishing limits issue.

BUSINESS GUIDE

Time

GMT.

Climate

Temperate, with mild but stormy winters and cool summers. Rainy in the south. Average temperatures vary between about -1 and 12°C.
Clothing: Medium-weight throughout year, topcoat and raincoat for winter.

Entry requirements

Visas not required by nationals of most West European countries and many others.
Health: Vaccination certificates not required.
Currency: No limits.
Customs: Personal effects duty-free, plus duty-free allowance. Tax-free shopping.

Air access

Direct flights from a number of European and US cities including Amsterdam, Baltimore, Chicago, Copenhagen, Frankfurt, Glasgow, London, Luxembourg, New York, Orlando, Oslo, Paris, Stockholm, Zurich.
National airlines: Icelandair (Flugleidir).
Airlines serving: SAS and Lufthansa.
Tax: Departure tax payable.
International airport: Keflavík (KEF) 47 km from Reykjavík, 4 km south of city, good inexpensive bus service to Reykjavík.

Surface access

Ferry services to Seydisfjóedur (in the east) from several north European ports during summer.
Main ports: Reykjavík, Akureyri, Hafnarfjördur, Seydisfjóedur and Vestmannaeyjar.

Hotels

Most towns have hotels and guest-houses available. Between June and September university hostels and boarding schools are also used as hotels. Some hostels and many farms provide bed and breakfast service. No official rating system in operation. Information on accommodation, which should always be booked in advance, available from Tourist Information Centre (see 'Business Directory, Travel information'). Tipping is not customary.

Credit cards

All major credit cards, such as American Express, Diners', Eurocard, Visa and Master Card, are accepted.

Car hire

Available in Reykjavík and several other towns. Rates vary depending on the type of car. Minimum age 20 years, and an international driving licence usually required. Advance reservations are necessary between Jun and Aug. Self-drive cars not recommended as a method of national transport as road surfaces tend to be poor.

City transport

Taxis: Used extensively. Usually summoned by telephone, but can be hailed in street. Several makes of car used, mostly displaying roof-top 'Taxi' signs.
Buses: Excellent regular services covering centre and suburbs of Reykjavík. Standard fare for any length of journey, even if it involves more than one bus route.

National transport

Air: Icelandair plus several other local services operate regular flights connecting all main towns. Light aircraft readily available for charter and sightseeing. The domestic airline market will be opened up to foreign competition by 1997.
Road: Approximately 12,000 km of roads. Main highways (approximately one quarter of total) are hard-surfaced, and the rest are gravel-surfaced. Main roads follow coastline. Regular coach services link even the remote inland areas.
Rail: No railways.
Water: Regular cargo coastal services linking all major ports. Passenger/auto ferry sails several times a day between Reykjavík and Akranes and between Thorlakshöta and Vestmannaeyian.

Public holidays

Fixed dates: 1 Jan (New Year's Day), 1 May (Labour Day), 17 Jun (National Day), 25 Dec (Christmas Day), 26 Dec (Boxing Day), (half-days on 24 and 31 Dec).
Variable dates: Maundy Thursday, Good Friday, Easter Monday, First Day of Summer, Ascension Day, Whit Monday and first Mon in Aug is Shop and Office Workers' Holiday.

Working hours

Government and business: (Mon–Fri) usually 0900–1700.
Banking: (Mon–Fri) 0915–1600 (winter), 0800–1600 (summer), plus 1700–1800 on Thu (Co-operative Bank, National Bank, Agricultural Bank (Kringlam).
Shops: (Mon–Thu) 0900–1800, (Fri) 0900–1700/1900. Most also open Sat 0900–1600 (winter only, Oct to end May). Kiosks remain open until 2330 or even later.

Social customs

Handshaking is customary on arrival and departure.

Business language and interpreting/translation

English is used in international business. List of authorised interpreters and translators available from Iceland Tourist Board.

Telecommunications

Telephone and telefax: The Icelandic P & T is 100 per cent state-owned and has a monopoly in both basic and mobile communications services. Usage of telecommunications is high, especially for business purposes. For international operator dial 09. Dialling code for Iceland, IDD access code + 354 followed by seven-digit subscriber's number (from June 1995).
Telex: Available in larger hotels and at main telephone headquarters, Austurvöll Square, Reykjavík. Country code: 501 IS.
Telegram: May be sent by phone (dial 06) or from telegraph office in Reykjavík.

Banking

In addition to the central bank there are four commercial banks operating, of which two are state-owned (Landsbanki and Bunadarbanki) and two are privately owned, Islandsbanki and Sparisjodabanki Islands, which was formed in 1994. It is owned by the 30 savings banks in Iceland and functions on their behalf. An amendment to the central Bank Act was passed in 1992 which authorised the central bank, with the consent of the government, to set the exchange rate basket, against one currency, an average of several currencies or composite currencies.
Other banks: See 'Business Directory, Banking'.

Electricity supply

220 V AC.

BUSINESS DIRECTORY

Hotels

Keflavík
Flughótelid Keflavík, Hafnarqata 57 (tel: 921-5222).

Keflavík, Vatnsnesvequr 12 (tel: 921-4377; fax: 921-5590).

Kristina, Holtsqata 47-49 (tel: 921-4444).

Reykjavík
City, Ranargata 4a (tel: 911-8650; fax: 583-0102).

Holiday Inn, Sigtuna 38 (tel: 568-9000; fax; 568-0675).

Lind, Raudararstigur 18 (tel: 562-3350; fax: 562-3150).

Car hire

Avis: reservations, Sejomubilar HF, Sigtun 5, 105 Reykjavik (tel: 562-4433; fax: 563-3590).

Budget: central reservations, Reykjavik (tel: 588-0880; fax: 588-1881).

Europcar: reservations, Tryggvabraut, 12,600 Akureyri (tel: 461-3000; fax: 462-6476).

Hertz: international reservations, Reykjavik (tel: 505-0600; fax: 505-0650).

Chambers of commerce

Iceland Chamber of Commerce (Verslunarrad Islands), Hús Verslunarinnar, Kringlan 7, 103 Reykjavík 1 (tel: 588-6666; fax: 568-6564/6511).

Banking

Sedlabanki Íslands (The Central Bank of Iceland), Kolkofnsvegur 1, 101 Reykjavík (tel: 569-9600; fax: 562-1802).

Búnadarbanki Íslands (The Agricultural Bank of Iceland), Austurstraeti 3, 101 Reykjavík (tel: 525-6000; fax: 525-6209).

Íslandsbanki (Bank of Iceland), Kringlunni, 155 Reykjavík (tel: 560-8000; fax: 560-8150).

Landsbanki Íslands (The National Bank of Iceland), Austurstraeti 11, 101 Reykjavík (tel: 560-6600; fax: 562-3071).

Principal newspapers

DV, Thverholt 11, Reykjavík (tel: 563-2700; fax: 563-2999).

Iceland reporter, Hofdabakki 9, 112 Reykjavík (tel: 567-5700; fax: 567-4066).

Iceland Review, Hofdabakki 9, 112 Reykjavík.

Morgunbladid, Adalstrtaei 6, PO Box 1555, Reykjavík (tel: 569-1100; fax: 569-1181, 568-1811).

Travel information

Airport Authority, The Leifur Eiriksson Passenger Terminal, Keflavík Airport, 235 Keflavík.

BSI Travel (buses), Umferdarmidstödin v/Hringbraut, 101 Reykjavík.

Icelandair (Flugleidir), Reykjavík Airport, Reykjavík IS-101 (tel: 505-0200; fax: 505-0300).

Icelandic Tourist Information, Ingolfsstraeti 5, 101 Reykjavík (tel: 562-3045).

Tourist Bureau of Iceland, (Ferdamalarad Islands), Gimli Laekjargotu 3, 101 Reykjavík (tel: 552-7488; fax: 562-4749).

Investment and privatisation

Invest in Iceland Bureau (privatisation and foreign investment), Hallveigarstigur 1, PO Box 1000, IS-121 Reykjavik (tel: 511-4000; fax: 511-4040).

Other useful addresses

Agricultural Production Board, Baendahollin, Hagatorg, 107 Reykjavik (tel: 19-200; fax: 562-8290).

Association of Icelandic Importers, Exporters & Wholesale Merchants, (Félag Islands St\01orkaupmanna), Húsi verslunarinnar, 103 Reykjavik (tel: 567-8910; fax: 468-8441).

British Embassy, Commercial Department, Laufasvegur 49, PO Box 460, 121 Reyjavik (tel: 551-5883; fax: 552-7940).

Confederation of Icelandic Employers (Vinnuveitendasamband Islands), Gardastraeti 41, 101 Reykjavik.

Customs Department, Tolhusid, Tryggvagata 19, 150 Reykjavik (tel: 560-0300; fax: 562-5826).

Export Council of Iceland, Lagmuli 5, Box 8796, 129 Reykjavik (tel: 568-8777; fax: 568-9197).

Federation of Icelandic Co-operative Societies (Samband of Iceland), Import Division, v/Holtavegur, 104 Reykjavik (tel: 568-1266; fax: 568-0290).

Icelandic Energy Marketing Agency, Haaleitisbraut 68, 103 Reykjavik (tel: 515-9000; fax: 515-9003).

Iceland Management Association, Ananaust 15, 121 Reykjavik (tel: 562-1066).

Ministry of Agriculture, 4th Floor, Sölvhólsgötu 7, 150 Reykjavik (tel: 560-9750; fax: 552-1160).

Ministry of Commerce and Industry, Arnarhváli, 150 Reykjavik (tel: 560-9070, 560-9420; fax: 562-1289).

Ministry of Communication, Hafnarhúsinu vio Tryggvagötu, 150 Reykjavik (tel: 560-9630; fax: 562-1702).

Ministry of Culture and Education, Sölvhólsgötu 4, 150 Reykjavik (tel: 560-9504; fax: 562-3068).

Ministry of the Environment, Vonarstraeti 4, 150 Reykjavik (tel: 560-9600; fax: 562-4566).

Ministry of Finance, Arnarhválli, 150 Reykjavik (tel: 560-9200; fax: 562-8280).

Ministry of Fisheries, Skúlagötu 4, 150 Reykjavik (tel: 560-9670; fax: 562-1853).

Ministry for Foreign Affairs, Rauoarásti\01g 25, 150 Reykjavik (tel: 560-9900; fax: 562-2373, 562-2386).

Ministry for Foreign Affairs, Trade Department, Hverfisgata 115, 105 Reykjavik (tel: 560-9930; fax: 562-4878).

Ministry of Health and Social Security, Laugavegi 116, 150 Reykjavik (tel: 560-9700; fax: 551-9165).

Ministry of Industry, Arnarhváli, 150 Reykjavik (tel: 560-9420; fax: 562-6859).

Ministry of Justice, Arnarhváli, 150 Reykjavik (tel: 560-9010; fax: 552-7340).

Ministry of Social Affairs, Hafnarhúsinu vio Tryggvagötu, 150 Reykjavik (tel: 560-9100; fax: 552-4804).

National Economic Institute (for information on economic development corporations), Thjodhagsstofnun, Kalkofnsvegi 1, Reykjavik (tel: 569-9500; fax: 562-6540).

Office of the Prime Minister (Stjórnarráoshúsinu vio Laekjargötu), 150 Reykjavik (tel: 560-9400, 560-9403; fax: 562-4014, 562-8626).

Retailers' Association of Iceland, Hus Verslunarinnar, Kringlan 7, 103 Reykjavik (tel: 568-7811; fax: 568-5569).

Society of Icelandic Advertising Agencies (Samband Islendkra Auglysingastofa (SIA), Hateigsvegur 3, 105 Reykjavik (tel: 562-9588; fax: 562-9585).

Statistical Bureau in Iceland, Hagstofa Islands, Skuggasund 3, 150 Reykjavik (tel: 560-9800; fax: 562-8865).

Trade Council of Iceland, (Utflutningsra\10d Islands), La\10gmuli 5, 108 Reykjavik (tel: 511-4000; fax: 511-4040).

Internet sites

Icelandic Energy Marketing Agency (E-mail: landsvirkjun@lv.is).

Iceland Reporter (http://www.centrum.is/icerev/).

Invest in Iceland Bureau (privatisation and foreign investment) (E-mail: Invest@icetrade.is).

Ireland

Howard Hill

Ireland is continuing its process of change. Shrugging off its reputation as a place to leave, it is becoming known as the place to be – especially if you are involved in the high-tech industries (electronics accounted for a quarter of exports in 1995). The population boom has produced a crop of younger voters less tied to tradition – as seen in the November 1995 vote to legalise divorce – and could have a strong influence on the general elections in 1997. Economically, Ireland was expected to grow at between two and three times the average for its European neighbours in 1996, making it the fastest growing economy in the European Union (EU).

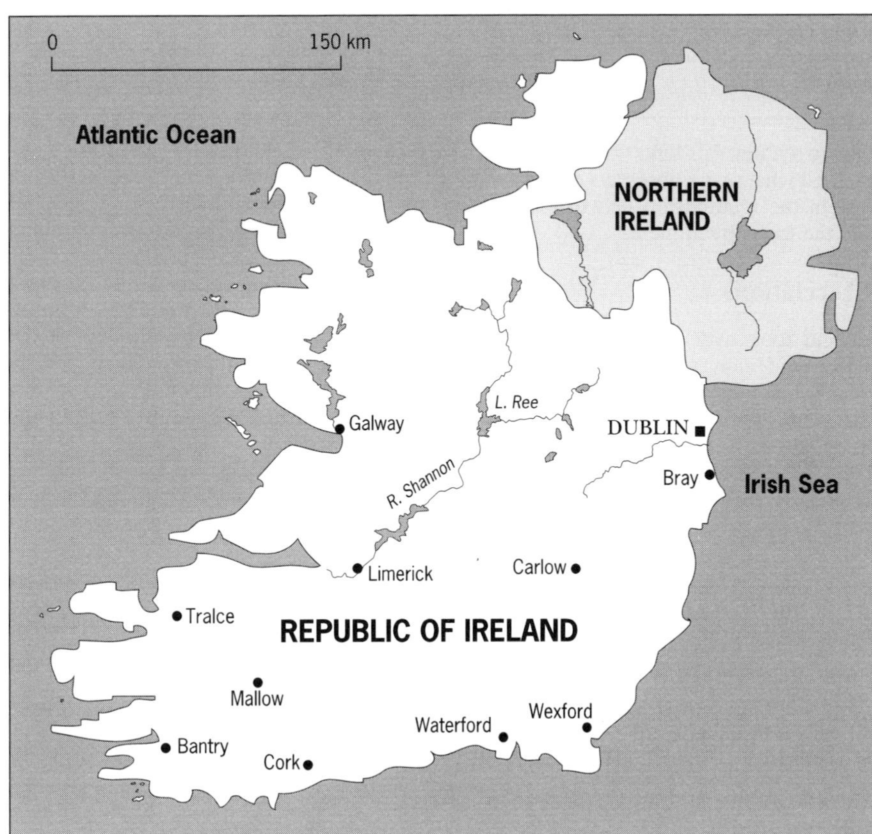

Politics

Elections must be called by the third quarter of 1997. The three ruling parties are Fine Gael (47 seats in the Dail), Labour (32) and Democratic Left (6) – this coalition has a small majority in the legislature. In 1993, the last elections, Labour gained nearly 20 per cent of the vote and a record 33 seats.

Fianna Fáil, the main opposition party with 68 seats, was stung by the collapse of its coalition with Labour in November 1994 and has yet to fully recover its composure. Some say that the party has been less able to adapt to the increasingly youthful, liberal and affluent character of the Irish electorate than its rivals.

Prime Minister John Bruton of Fine Gael, the second largest party in the Dial, has been credited with restoring a measure of public confidence in his office; this will benefit the party's performance in the next election. Labour's Dick Spring is the deputy prime minister and foreign minister. Tensions do exist within the coalition on a number of issues, such as the Northern Ireland question, but these are to be expected in such a grouping.

President Mary Robinson, the country's first female head of state, has widespread support and respect; her standing in opinion polls is consistently around the 90 per cent approval mark and at one stage she had been touted as a possible successor to UN Secretary-General Boutros Boutros-Ghali. Her term of office ends in November 1997.

Northern Ireland

The faltering peace process over the future of Northern Ireland continued in 1996. In June 1996 the multi-party talks began, but without the participation of Sinn Féin (the political arm of the Irish Republican Army [IRA]), a group which had been demanding such a forum for years. Sinn Féin was excluded from the talks because it refused to meet the condtions set by the other participants – that it declare a renewed cease-fire. The IRA had declared a cease-fire in August 1994 but this was shattered by the London Docklands bomb in February 1996.

It is widely felt that Sinn Féin-IRA lacked confidence in the talks and, in effect, chose to boycott them by refusing to give in to the cease-fire demand. Prime Minister Bruton lashed out against the IRA not long after the multi-party talks began, calling on Sinn

KEY FACTS — Ireland

Official title: Eire (Ireland)

Head of state: President Mary Robinson

Head of government: Prime Minister John Bruton (FG)

Ruling party: Fine Gael (FG)/ Labour/ Democratic Left coalition government

Capital: Dublin

Official Languages: Irish and English: Irish is first official language; official documents printed in English and Irish

Currency: Irish Punt (Pound) (Ir£) = 100 pence

Exchange rate: Ir£0.60 per US$ (Dec 1996)

Area: 70,283 sq km

Population: 3.58m (1995)

GDP per capita: US$17,000 (1995)

GDP real growth: 7.5% (1995)

GNP real growth: 8% (1995)

Unemployment: 12.7% (Jun 1996)

Inflation: 2.4% (1994)

Trade balance: US$10.9bn (1995)

Féin to renounce its links with the IRA; this marked what many observers called a new low in the relationship between the IRA and the Irish government.

EU relations

Ireland took over the presidency of the European Union from July 1996 for a period of six months. There was little doubt that the years of EU membership have been helpful to the country's industrial development and it is widely seen as being the most pro-EU country in the union. Perhaps as no coincidence, Ireland is the largest net recipient of EU fiscal transfers and some 2 per cent of the country's GNP comes from money provided by the EU.

It looks as though, paradoxically, Ireland may be becoming too prosperous for its own good as the recent economic advances risk jeopardising EU financial support. Projections show that by the turn of the century, Ireland will surpass the UK in terms of per capita income; in 1995 this figure for Ireland was 89 per cent of the EU's average.

The next five-year round of EU funding begins in 1999, and there is strong speculation that Ireland will no longer be eligible for assistance. If this were to happen, the budget-deficit-to-GNP ratio could be seriously compromised and pushed near the 3 per cent limit set by Maastricht; it was about 1 per cent in 1996. As of mid-1996 Ireland was one of only a trio of EU countries meeting the Maastricht criteria on public deficits and debt; the other two are Denmark and Luxembourg.

Ireland no longer qualifies for structural funds, because these are available only to members with per capita income less than 75 per cent of the EU average. Cohesion funds will also likely be beyond Ireland's reach under the new funding programme. The only hope is for the Commission to agree to Ireland's request to measure its economy in terms of GNP (which equals GDP plus income from abroad less income paid abroad) rather than GDP – GDP is up to 3 per cent higher than GNP.

Two decades ago, Britain received 60 per cent of Ireland's exports but this figure has now been cut in half. The Economic and Social Research Institute (ESRI) said in a report released at the end of July 1996 that Ireland's participation in the Economic and Monetary Union (EMU) will only bring small increases in output, employment and trade. This would be true whether or not the UK joined as well. Joining with the UK is expected to raise GNP by an average of 1.4 per cent, and will bring 20,000 jobs according to the ESRI. However, if the UK did not join, GNP is expected to grow by 0.4 per cent and 10,000 jobs would be gained over five years. The prospect of EMU will bring job uncertainty to many in the financial services sector and as many as 7 per cent of the sector's workforce could lose their jobs.

KEY INDICATORS — Ireland

	Unit	1991	1992	1993	1994	1995
Population	m	3.52	3.55	3.56	3.57	3.58
Gross domestic product (GDP)	US$bn	43.0	48.7	44.7	51.8	–
GDP per capita	US$	12,290	13,760	12,590	14,600	17,000
GDP real growth	%	2.5	2.7	2.7	6.5	7.5
Inflation	%	3.2	3.1	1.4	2.4	–
Consumer prices	1990=100	103.2	106.4	107.9	110.4	113.2
Unemployment	%	15.8	17.2	17.6	14.8	12.0
Agricultural production	1979-81=100	126.43	129.67	129.77	119.00	120.39
Industrial production	1990=100	102.8	112.9	119.2	134.1	–
Manufacturing	1990=100	100.5	100.2	100.0	–	–
Share prices	1990=100	92.0	85.6	106.9	121.9	133.4
Exports (FOB) (goods)	US$m	23,660	28,107	28,730	33,658	–
Imports (FOB) (goods)	US$m	19,493	21,065	20,558	24,097	–
Balance of trade	US$m	4,167	6,813	8,161	8,100	10,900
Current account	US$m	861	1,708	2,405	3,212	–
Total reserves minus gold	US$m	5,740	3,440	5,925	6,115	8,499
Foreign exchange	US$m	5,320	3,080	5,579	5,745	8,046
Discount rate	%	10.75	–	7.00	6.25	6.50
Deposit rate	%	5.21	5.42	2.27	0.33	0.44
Lending rate	%	10.63	12.66	9.93	6.13	6.56
Exchange rate	US$ per Ir£	1.62	1.71	1.47	1.50	1.60

Beef fraud

Allegations of fraud in the Irish beef industry in 1990 and 1991 landed Ireland in trouble with the European Commission. In March 1996 the Commission levied a fine of Ir£50 million for abusing the European system of intervention. This system enabled European farmers to be paid to put cattle into storage to stabilise prices. The alleged fraud was based on an abuse of the system of subsidies – yields of animals put into intervention were allegedly underestimated and the best cuts for resale on the market were skimmed off. The Irish government was successful in having the fine reduced by Ir£25 million. A further fine of Ir£18 million fine was levied in relation to alleged misuse of the tendering process for intervention beef.

1996 budget

The 1996 budget was based on the assumption that GDP growth would be at the 5 per cent rate for 1996 (GDP growth in 1995 was 7.5 per cent).

Exports were expected to grow by 9.5 per cent in 1996. Both domestic demand and consumer spending were expected to increase by 4.5 per cent in 1996 while unemployment is to fall from 280,000 at end-1995 to 270,000 at end-1996.

An increase in social welfare spending, enabled in part by an unexpectedly high amount of tax returns for 1995 and lower debt payments, is a prime feature of the budget as the government gears up for election-year 1997. Current expenditure is expected to grow by 2.5 per cent in 1996 and capital expenditure is to increase by 6 per cent.

Higher allowances will be provided for children and people living alone as part of the new provisions in the budget. The threshold at which employees begin to pay insurance has been raised to Ir£80 per week from Ir£50 per week. Recruitment subsidies will be paid to employers to take on up to 5,000 long-term unemployed people (jobless for 3 or more years). Those who accept jobs will not have to give up their right to free prescriptions and various other medical benefits for three years after finding work.

Economy

ESRI estimated that GNP grew 7.75 per cent in 1995, although other think-tanks claim that the true figure could well be 2 per cent higher. This strong level of growth was accompanied by an expansion in employment, thus bucking the European trend in the mid-1990s. However, unemployment is the second highest in the European Union. It was 12.6 per cent in 1995 and predictions at mid-1996 indicate that it could come down by 1 per cent at the end of 1996.

Inflation has been low, despite the strong level of economic growth – the average annual change was 2.5 per cent in both 1994 and 1995. Most predictions for 1996, as of the third quarter of that year, showed that inflation should not be more than 2 per cent. It is in the nature of the economy that the inflation rate is closely intertwined with the exchange rate and inflation rates of the country's trading partners.

Investment and industry

Ireland's low corporate tax rate of 10 per cent for manufacturing companies until the year 2010 is one of the big draws for multinational companies seeking to set up new operations in Europe. Over 40 per cent of factory jobs are with overseas-based companies. It is said that about 12.5 per cent of the value of total output leaves Ireland in the form of repatriated profits or interest to foreign holders of government debt.

In 1995 Ireland, with only 3.5 million people, attracted 14 per cent of all new investment in Europe. This is especially good since Ireland is the second smallest country in the EU. As a leading high-tech location, it constitutes 40 per cent of all Europe-wide US software company investment. Foreign investment accounts for 55 per cent of manufacturing output, 45 per cent of manufacturing employment and two-thirds of manufactured exports.

The service industry has been particularly targeted for growth since the early 1990s and many telephone help lines and travel-related telephone reservation centres serving Europe are located in Ireland. The Industrial Development Agency hopes to create 31,000 jobs in the four-year period starting from 1996.

Intel, the US-based computer chip manufacturer, had invested US$750 million in Ireland by 1995 and could start a US$1 billion plant before the turn of the century. Apple Computers, also of the USA, has 1,500 employees based in Ireland.

Ifox closes

Ifox, a computer-based futures exchange launched in 1989, announced that it would close at the end of August 1996 because it had a shortage of business – the volume in 1995 was only 7,000 contracts. As of August 1996 it traded three gilt futures contracts and one interest rate future. The closure is said to reflect a shift into more sophisticated dealing within the local market.

Ispat Irish link

The Irish government agreed with the Indian steel company Ispat International to inject Ir£30 million worth of re-financing into the loss-making Cork-based Irish Steel, the country's only steelworks. Irish Steel had a production rate of some 243,000 tonnes in 1994 but Ispat wants to raise production to 350,000 tonnes per year. However, this move was greeted with protest from the UK which objected on the basis that British Steel would be put at a disadvantage and that EU rules were being broken. The dispute was brought to the EU and in the third week of December 1995 the UK withdrew its objection to the support. If Irish Steel were closed, the company would have had to shed 350 jobs; local unemployment was already 16 per cent so this would have had a significant impact. But the matter was not over, and British Steel was joined by the German Steel Federation in March 1996 in objecting to the European Commission's approval of aid for Irish Steel.

COUNTRY PROFILE — IRELAND

Historical profile

Known as 'the land of saints and scholars' because Christian learning survived there during post-Roman barbarian onslaughts on the rest of Europe.
Twelfth century: British invasion, beginning centuries of influence. Irish Catholic hostility increased along with British control, following the seizure of land, the Protestant Reformation and the loss of religious and political freedoms.
1800 Act of Union: abolition of Irish parliament.
1840s Failure of potato crop. Reduction of population by one-third due to famine and emigration. Beginnings of republican movement.
1916 Suppression of republican Easter Rising and formation of Sinn Féin ('Ourselves alone').
1919-21 Ango-Irish War fought by Irish Republican Army (IRA, military arm of Sinn Féin) against British troops and police.
1920 Partition: 26 southern counties formed Irish Free State under British Crown, six north-eastern counties remained part of the United Kingdom.
1939-45 Neutral during Second World War.
1949 Republic proclaimed, but partition remained contentious and IRA mounted continuing violent campaign for reunification.
1973 Member of the European Community. Fianna Fáil, traditional party of government, lost power after 44 years in office but regained control under Jack Lynch then Charles Haughey as prime minister, apart from 1973-77 and 1982-87 when Fina Gael, Labour Party coalitions ruled under Liam Cosgrave then Garret Fitzgerald. None of a succession of elections in the 1980s produced a single-party majority government.
1985 Ango-Irish Agreement: regular participation by the Irish Government on political, legal, security and cross-border matters.
1990 Election of first left-winger and first woman, Mary Robinson, to presidency.
1995 On 25 November a referendum to change the 1937 constitution narrowly approved the lifting of the ban on divorce.

Political system

Republic, with legislative power vested in bicameral *Oireachtas* (National Parliament) consisting of the *Seanad Eireann* (Senate), which has 60 members; and the *Dáil Eireann* (House of Representatives), with 166 members elected for five years by single transferable vote system. Executive power is exercised by the cabinet, led by the *taoiseach* (prime minister) who is appointed by the *uachtarán na hEireann* (president) on the recommendation of the *Dáil*. President is directly elected for seven years. Next elections scheduled for 1997.

Political parties

Coalition government: Fine Gael (United Ireland Party); Labour Party; Democratic Left (DL). Other major parties: Fianna Fáil (Republican Party); Progressive Democrats; Comhaoltás Glas (Green Alliance); Sinn Féin.

Population

More than 50 per cent of school leavers go on to third level education. Ireland has a higher proportion of graduates with scientific skills in the 25-34 age group than any other OECD member except Japan. Emigration, which has slowed, was running at 39,500 people in 1995, compared with 70,000 in 1989, and some Irish living abroad are returning home to take advantage of the economic recovery.

COUNTRY PROFILE IRELAND

Main cities/towns

Dublin (population 920,000 in 1994), Cork, Limerick, Galway and Waterford.

Media

Dailies: Top dailies include *Irish Independent, Irish Times, Evening Herald, The Star* (all published in Dublin), *Cork Examiner* and *Cork Evening Echo* (published in Cork). All British dailies are available.
Weeklies: Sunday Independent, Sunday World and *Sunday Tribune*. British Sunday newspapers are available.
Business: Small number of business publications, mostly produced in Dublin, including *Sunday Business Post* (weekly). Most UK trade publications are available.
Broadcasting: Over 900,000 TVs in use. Radio Telefis Eireann (RTE) has responsibility for operating the national sound and television services in Ireland. RTE provides two radio channels, Radio 1 and 2FM and two television channels RTE 1 and Network 2. It also transmits Radio na Gaeltachta, a radio service in Irish, which shares a third radio network with a classical music service FM3. In 1989 RTE joined with Compagnie Luxembourgeoise de Telediffussion (CLT) to provide a long-wave radio service known as 'Atlantic 252'. Arising out of new broadcasting legislation in 1988, an independent national radio service and 20 local radio services were established during 1989-90, all of which are privately owned. Provision was also made under this legislation for the establishment of an independent television programme service. Broadcasts from the UK can also be received in many parts of the country. One-third of homes are cabled. All cable systems carry the UK channels and a number of them also carry satellite channels.

Advertising

Key categories include food, retail, beverages, motoring, financial, personal hygiene/medicinal, household equipment, theatre/culture, tourism and agriculture. Restrictions applied to advertising expenditure and form and content of advertisements. Promotion of tobacco products is banned completely, and that of alcohol strictly controlled. Commercials on TV and radio are limited to 10 per cent of transmission time. Newspapers, magazines, posters and films are also widely used. Information available from The Advertising Standards Authority in Dublin.

Domestic economy

Mixed economy with large, export-based agricultural sector and largely foreign-owned manufacturing sector. Tourism and construction also important. Ireland secured 14 per cent of all new investment in Europe in 1995, focused on electronics, pharmaceuticals, teleservices and financial services, and has the fastest-growing economy of any country within the EU.

Employment

Around half of the labour force employed in private and public services, some 16 per cent in agriculture and the rest in manufacturing and construction. Despite growth in service sector employment and rapid rise in productivity, unemployment continued to be a problem. However, in 1995 the Industrial Development Agency (IDA) reported a record 11,500 new jobs from 114 projects created from foreign investment, the best result in 21 years, and the annual increase in the total number at work totalled 43,000 in 1995. The long-term unemployed account for 30 per cent of the total. About 30 per cent of the workforce is female.

External trade

As an internationally trading economy on the periphery of Europe, with a small domestic market, Ireland is heavily dependent on foreign trade. Strong rise in exports and lower oil imports costs helped turn traditional trade deficit into a significant current account surplus in recent years. The UK remains the principal trading partner (accounting for about a third of all trade), but since accession to the EC in 1973 trade with Germany, France and Italy increased significantly.
Exports: Total exports in 1995 US$42.6bn. Exports consist mainly of live cattle, meat, dairy produce, textiles, manufactures, machinery and transport equipment and more recently chemicals and electronics. The value of Ireland's exports has shown significant growth. Most of this expansion occurred in the industrial sector. The government plans to increase exports from indigenous Irish companies by 50 per cent between 1993 and 1997, with growth coming in particular from the mainland European market. Main trading partners: UK (27.5% of 1994 total), Germany (14,1%), France (9.2%), USA (8.4%), Netherlands (5.5%), Italy (3.8%), EU (68.5%).
Imports: Total imports US$31.7bn in 1995. Imports, which have risen slower than exports, consist mainly of petroleum and petroleum products, foodstuffs, chemicals, manufactured goods and components, machinery and transport equipment. Quantitive restrictions apply to the importation of some clothing, textiles and tableware products from certain non-EU countries. Quantitive restrictions also apply to unprocessed foodstuffs. Full details may be obtained from the Revenue Commissioners, Castle House, Dublin 2. Main sources: UK (36.3% of 1994 total), USA (18.3%), Germany (7.1%), France (3.8%), Netherlands (2.8%), Italy (2.2%), EU (56%).

Agriculture

Sector accounted for 10 per cent of GDP in 1994 and around 15 per cent of export earnings, employing 15.7 per cent of the labour force. Production is centred on livestock farming, accounting for nearly 53 per cent of output, principally cattle and beef for export and other meats and dairy produce for local consumption. About 90 per cent of all land is devoted to pasture and around 10 per cent is tilled. Approximately 6 per cent of agricultural land is used for corn crops and about 3.2 per cent for fruit and vegetables. About 93 per cent of agricultural land is owner-occupied; average size of holding is 31.7 ha. Sector receives substantial development aid and price subsidy under the EU's Common Agricultural Policy. Main crops include barley, sugar-beet, potatoes, wheat and vegetables. National timber production will increase to 3m cu metres by the year 2000. Employment in the forest and wood products industry is about 13,000.

Fishing

The sea fishing industry makes a growing contribution to the economy in terms of increased output, employment and exports. Mackerel accounts for about 35 per cent of the volume of the catch, and is the most important species landed. In 1992 there were 1,400 registered fishing vessels in the Irish fleet. About 7,900 people are employed on board fishing vessels and about 3,500 people in the fish-processing industry.

Industry

This sector accounted for 24 per cent of GDP in 1994, 80 per cent of the value of exports and 27.7 per cent of employment. Indigenous manufacturing base small. Traditional industries such as food and beverages, textiles, paper, non-metallic minerals and machinery dominate, though there has been rapid growth in new export-oriented chemicals as well as the electronic engineering industries. Most of the new capital and skill-intensive industries are subsidiaries of large US and European multinationals and are heavily reliant on imported primary and intermediate inputs. The government commenced a major privatisation programme in 1991.

Tourism

Tourism is one of the fastest growing economic sectors in Ireland, accounting for an estimated 7 per cent of GNP. Ireland attracts over 3m foreign visitors each year. The sector supports an estimated 87,000 jobs. A substantial EU supported investment programme is under way to develop the range and quality of activity-based holidays throughout the country. There are more than 270 golf courses.

Mining

Mining accounts for about 1 per cent of GDP and employs 1 per cent of the workforce. Europe's largest zinc and lead deposits located at Navan, County Meath, operated by Tara Mines. Production has continued since the mid-1970s. Also reserves of gypsum, barytes, dolomite, silica sand, limestone, coal, marble and small amounts of silver. Gypsum is extracted from an open-pit at Knocknacran, Co Monaghan. Two substantial base metal deposits found in 1992 at Galmoy, Co Kilkenny, and Lisheen, Co Tipperary.

Hydrocarbons

Almost 70 per cent of Ireland's primary energy requirements are supplied by oil and coal, and about one-third of the oil requirements is imported as crude. Dependence on imported petroleum rapidly reduced due to exploitation of domestic gas and peat reserves. Natural gas represents around 16 per cent of primary energy consumption in Ireland. Identified indigenous reserves of natural gas occur in the Kinsale Head gas field and the smaller Ballycotton field in the Celtic Sea off the Cork coast. Peat continues to provide about 16 per cent of electricity generated and is also used in significant quantities as a domestic fuel.

Energy

Ireland has the only stand-alone electricity and gas grid in the EU, although new projects will increase the country's interdependence with the UK and the rest of Europe. Electricity generation and supply is the responsibility of the state-owned Electricity Supply Board. Installed generation capacity is around 4,000 MW against a peak demand of 2,600 MW. Ireland's first wind farm at Bellacorick, Co May, was completed by the end of 1992. A natural gas pipeline project linking the country to the UK will provide security of supply and meet growing demand from industry and power generation as well as enabling continued supply on depletion of the Kinsale Head field after the year 2000. The Electricity Supply Board and the National Grid of UK are planning to build a £300m high-voltage link under the Irish Sea. The cable, with a proposed capacity of 600 MW, would connect the Irish grid to the rest of Europe for the first time and would expand Ireland's generating capacity by 15 per cent.

Stock exchange

The Dublin Stock Exchange de-linked formally from London in 1995. As at June 1996, the market is narrow-based, with the top four companies accounting for more than 75 per cent of capitalisation.

Legal system

Based on English common law with substantial modifications.

Membership of international organisations

BIS, CCC, Council of Europe, CSCE, EBRD, EEA, EMS, ESA, EU, FAO, IAEA, ICAO, ICES, IDA, IEA, IFAD, IFC, ILO, IMF, IMO, INTELSAT, International Grain Council, INTERPOL, IPU, ISO, ITC, ITU, MIGA, OECD, UN, UNESCO, UNIDO, UPU, WEU (observer), WHO, WIPO, WMO, World Bank, WSG, WTO.

BUSINESS GUIDE

Time

GMT (GMT + 1 hr from late Mar to late Oct).

Climate

Temperate, with warm summers and mild winters. Rain throughout year. Average temperatures range from about 0–20°C.

Clothing

Mediumweight and raincoat throughout the year.

Entry requirements

Visas not required by EU passport holders, but may be required by others.
Health: Vaccination certificates not compulsory, but can be useful in event of temporary restrictions.
Currency: No limit on amount of currency taken in. Up to Ir£150 in Irish currency and Ir£1,200 in foreign currency may be taken out.
Customs: Personal effects duty-free, plus duty-free allowance.

Air access

Regular flights by most international airlines.
National airlines: Aer Lingus operates scheduled services to 23 destinations in the UK, Europe and North America. Aer Lingus is losing money and a restructuring plan urgently needs to be put in place. Ryanair, the country's second airline, operates scheduled services to the UK and Germany.
Main international airport: Dublin (DUB), 8 km from city centre.
International airports: Shannon (SNN), 26 km from Limerick, Cork (ORK), 5 km from city and Horan (NOC) at Knock, Co Mayo, Connaught Province.

Surface access

Several passenger and car ferry services from UK ports, such as Holyhead, Fishguard and Stranraer (via Northern Ireland); also Rosslare-Le Havre and Rosslare-Cherbourg, Cork-Le Havre and Cork-Swansea. Several road and rail crossing points from Northern Ireland.
Main ports: Dublin, Cork, Waterford, Rosslare, Dun Laoghaire, Limerick/Shannon Estuary. The seaports handle the greater part of Ireland's international trade, accounting for 78 per cent of all trade by volume and 62 per cent by value.

Hotels

Classified into three categories: Star A, Star B and Star C. Single room, including breakfast and 10 per cent VAT, in Dublin costs between about Ir£30 and Ir£95, depending on season and facilities offered. Prices are cheaper outside capital.
Tipping: 10 per cent is customary. All usual credit cards are widely accepted.

Currency

Exchange rate: Ireland is a member of the European Monetary System. The Irish pound floats within the narrow bands of the EMS grid and against other currencies.

Foreign exchange information

Account restrictions: None on non-resident accounts.
Trade policy: No import restrictions, except for armaments for which import licences are required.

Car hire

Available in all main towns, but heavy demand during tourist season. National or international driving licence required. Speed limits 30 mph (48 kph) in built-up areas and 60 mph (96 kph) on main roads. Driving is on the left.

City transport

Good bus and taxi service available in major towns. Destinations in Dublin written in Gaelic and English. Iarnród Eireann operates the Dublin Area Rapid Transit (DART) rail network. Special bus/rail tickets can be purchased for multiple journeys. Metered taxis can be hailed in the street or called by telephone.

National transport

Air: Daily services between Dublin and Shannon, and Dublin and Cork operated by Aer Lingus. Also one flight daily between Dublin and Horan Airport, Knock.
Road: Approximately 92,000 km of roads, including 16,000 km of main roads. Traffic density is low by European standards.
Buses: Bus services throughout country, including express coaches connecting main towns.
Rail: Almost 2,000 km of track operated by the Iarnród Eireann (Irish Rail) a subsidiary of the Irish Transport Company (CIE), carrying about 8m passengers per year. One express service daily between Dublin and Cork.
Water: Over 500 km of navigable inland waterways.

Public holidays

Fixed dates: 1 Jan (New Year's Day), 17 Mar (St Patrick's Day), 25 Dec (Christmas Day), 26 Dec (St Stephen's Day).
Variable dates: Good Friday, Easter Monday, June Bank Holiday (first Mon in Jun), August Bank Holiday (first Mon in Aug), October Bank Holiday (last Mon in Oct).

Working hours

Banking: (Mon–Fri) 1000–1230 and 1330–1500 (open on Thu until 1700 in Dublin and in all principal cities and towns).
Shops and business: (Mon–Fri) 0900 or 0930–1730. Supermarkets normally stay open until 2100 Thu and Fri.

Telecommunications

Telephone: Direct dialling available throughout country. International dialling code: 353 followed by 1 for Dublin, 21 for Cork, 91 for Galway, 61 for Limerick, 51 for Waterford and 53 for Wexford. For IDD access from Ireland dial 16 followed by country code etc. The percentage of households with a telephone is slightly over 70 per cent.
Telex: Public telex office at Telecom Eireann, Marlborough St, Dublin. Country code: 500 EI.
Postal services: An Post, a member of the Universal Postal Union (UPU), provides postal services through more than 2,000 local offices nationwide, handling more than 460m items of mail annually, and employing over 10,000 people. An Post provides a range of special facilities for the business and advertising sector as well as nearly Ir£3,000m worth of transactions on behalf of state agencies, and a range of general banking services.

Banking

Monetary policy and foreign exchange dealings supervised by the Central Bank of Ireland, which is independent of government. Banks operating under licence from the central bank can be classified into two main categories: the Associated Banks, four main clearing banks which dominate the payments system through 650 branches spread throughout the state; the non-Associated Banks, 28 banks with over 80 branches engage in merchant and commercial banking and in consumer finance.
Other banks: See 'Business Directory, Banking'.

Trade fairs

Several international events held in Dublin. Tend to be held at irregular times and vary from year to year. Exhibition calendar is available from Modern Display Artists Ltd (MDA), Fitzwilliam Quay, Ringsend, Dublin 4 (tel: 493-8555).

Electricity supply

220 V AC.

Representation in capital

Argentina, Australia, Austria, Belgium, Canada, China PR, Denmark, Egypt, Finland, France, Germany, Greece, The Holy See, India, Iran, Italy, Japan, Republic of Korea, Netherlands, Nigeria, Norway, Portugal, Russia, Spain, Sweden, Switzerland, Turkey, United Kingdom, USA.

BUSINESS DIRECTORY

Hotels

Dublin
Berkeley Court, Lansdowne Road, Ballsbridge, 4 (tel: 660-1711; fax: 661-7238).

Blooms, Anglesea Street, 2 (tel: 671-5622; fax: 671-5997).

Burlington, Upper Leeson Street, 4 (tel: 660-5222; fax: 660-8496, 660-5064).

Buswell's (facing Parliament), 25 Molesworth Street, 2 (tel: 676-4013; fax: 676-2090).

Clarence, Wellington Quay, 2 (tel: 677-6178, 677-6359; fax: 677-7487).

Conrad, Earlsfort Terrace, 2 (tel: 676-5555; fax: 676-5424).

Green Isle, Naas Road, Clondalkin, 22 (tel: 459-3406; fax: 459-2178).

Gresham, Upper O'Connell Street (tel: 874-6881; fax: 878-7175).

Hotels (contd):
International, Dublin Airport (tel: 844-4211; fax: 842-5874).

Jury's, Pembroke Road, Ballsbridge, 4 (tel: 660-5000; fax: 660-5540).

Marine, Sutton, 13 (tel: 839-0000; fax: 839-0442).

Mont Clare, Merrion Square (tel: 661-9355; fax: 661-5663).

Montrose, Stillorgan Road, 4 (tel: 269-3311; fax: 269-1164).

Powers (near Trinity College), 47 Kildare Street (tel: 679-4388).

Royal, 40 Upper O'Connell Street (tel: 873-3666; fax: 873-3120).

Shelbourne, 27 St Stephen's Green, 2 (tel: 676-6471; fax: 661-6006).

Tara Tower, Merrion Road, 4 (tel: 269-4666; fax: 269-1027).

Westbury, Grafton Street, 2 (tel: 679-1122; fax: 679-7078).

Car hire

Dublin
Avis: 1 Hanover Street East, 2 (tel: 605-7500).

Budget: 151 L R Drumcondra Road, Ferry Port (tel: 379-611; fax: 379-802); airport, main arrivals hall (tel: 842-0793; fax: 844-5919).

Europcar: Baggot Street Bridge, 4 (tel: 668-1777; fax: 660-2958).

Hertz: reservations office (tel: 676-7476; fax: 668-1961).

Chambers of commerce

Cork Chamber of Commerce, Fitzgerald House, Summerhill, Cork (tel: 509-044; fax: 508-568).

Dublin Chamber of Commerce, 7 Clare Street, Dublin 2 (tel: 661-4111; fax: 676-6043).

Dundalk Chamber of Commerce, Roden Place, Dundalk (tel: 34-422).

Limerick Chamber of Commerce, 96 O'Connell Street, Limerick (tel: 415-180; fax: 415-785).

Waterford Chamber of Commerce, Chamber of Commerce Buildings, Georges Street, Waterford (tel: 72-639; fax: 76-002).

Banking

Central Bank of Ireland, PO Box 559, Dame Street, Dublin 2 (tel: 671-6666; fax: 671-6561).

Allied Irish Bank Ltd, Bankcentre, PO Box 452, Ballsbridge, Dublin 4 (tel: 660-0311; fax: 668-2508).

Allied Irish Investment Bank plc, Bankcentre, Ballsbridge, Dublin 4 (tel: 660-4733).

Bank of Ireland, Lower Baggot Street, Dublin 2 (tel: 661-5933; fax: 661-5671).

The Institute of Bankers in Ireland (banking association), Nassau House, Nassau Street, Dublin 2 (tel: 679-3311).

Investment Bank of Ireland Ltd, 26 Fitzwilliam Place, Dublin 2 (tel: 661-6433; fax: 661-6433).

National Irish Bank, 7/8 Wilton Terrace, Dublin 2 (tel: 678-5066; fax: 661-3324).

Ulster Bank, 33 College Green, Dublin 2 (tel: 677-7623).

Ulster Investment Bank Ltd, 2 Hume Street, Dublin 2 (tel: 661-3444; fax: 676-3021).

Principal newspapers

Business and Finance, 50 Fitzwilliam Square, Dublin 2 (tel: 676-4587; fax: 661-9781).

Cork Evening Echo, PO Box 21, Academy Street, Cork (tel: 272-722; fax: 275-477).

Cork Examiner, PO Box 21, Academy Street, Cork (tel: 272-722; fax: 275-112).

Evening Herald, Independent Newspapers plc, 90 Middle Abbey Street, Dublin 1 (tel: 731-333; fax: 720-304, 731-787).

Evening Press, Parnell House, Parnell Square, Dublin 1 (tel: 671-3333; fax: 671-3097, 677-4148).

Irish Independent, Independent Newspapers plc, 90 Middle Abbey Street, Dublin 1 (tel: 731-666; fax: 722-657).

Irish Oifigiuil (Dublin Gazette), Stationery Office, Dublin 8 (tel: 781-666; fax: 780-645).

Irish Press Newspapers Ltd, Parnell House, 13-15 Parnell Square, Dublin 1 (tel: 671-3333; fax: 671-3097, 677-4148).

Irish Times Ltd, 13 D'Olier Street, Dublin 2 (tel: 679-2022; fax: 679-3910).

The Star, Star House, 62A Terenure Road North, Dublin 6 (atel: 901-228; fax; 902-193, 907-425).

Sunday Business Post, 27-30 Merchants Quay, Dublin 8 (tel: 679-9777; fax: 679-6496).

Sunday Independent, Independent Newspapers Ltd, 90 Middle Abbey Street, Dublin 1 (tel: 873-1333; fax: 731-787).

Sunday Press, Irish Press Newspapers Ltd, Parnell House, Parnell Square, Dublin 1 (tel: 671-3333; fax: 677-3339).

Sunday Tribune, 15 Lower Baggot Street, Dublin 2 (tel: 615-555; fax: 614-656).

Sunday World, Newspaper House, 18 Rathfarnham Road, Terenure, Dublin 6 (tel: 901-980; fax: 908-592).

Travel information

Aer Lingus, Head Office Block, Dublin Airport (tel: 705-2222; fax: 705-3832).

British Airways Office, Dublin Airport (tel: 626-747; fax: 679-0231).

Irish Tourist Board, Baggot Street Bridge, Dublin 2 (tel: 676-5871, 661-6500; fax: 676-4764, 676-4765).

Ryanair, Corporate Head Office Building, Dublin Airport (tel: 844-4489, 844-4400; fax: 844-4402).

Tourist Information Office, 14 Upper O'Connell Street, Dublin (tel: 284-4768).

Other useful addresses

Advertising Standards Authority, IPC House, Shelbourne Road, Dublin 4. (tel: 660-8766; fax: 660-8113).

British Embassy, 31-33 Merrion Road, Dublin 4 (tel: 269-5211; fax: 260-0620).

Central Statistics Office, Skehard Road, Cork (tel: 359-000; fax: 359-090).

Confederation of Irish Industry, Confederation House, Kildare Street, Dublin 2 (tel: 660-1011).

Department of Agriculture, Food and Forestry, Kildare Street, Dublin 2 (tel: 678-9011; fax: 661-6263).

Department of Defence, Colaiste Caoimhin, Mobhi Road, Glasnevin, Dublin 9 (tel: 637-9911; fax: 637-7993).

Department of Enterprise and Employment, Kildare Street, Dublin 2 (tel: 661-4444; fax: 676-2654).

Department of Finance and Department of the Public Service, Government Bldgs, Upper Merrion Street, Dublin 2 (tel: 676-7571; fax: 676-7335).

Department of Foreign Affairs, 80 St Stephen's Green, Dublin 2 (tel: 478-0822; fax: 478-1484).

Department of Taoiseach, Government Buildings, Upper Merrion Street, Dublin 2 (tel: 668-9333; fax: 678-9791).

Department of Tourism and Trade, Kildare Street, Dublin 2 (tel: 662-1444; fax: 676-6154).

Department of Transport, Energy and Communications, Clare Street, Dublin 2 (tel: 671-5233; fax: 677-3169).

IDA Ireland (Industrial Development Agency), Wilton Park House, Wilton Place, dublin 2 (tel: 668-6633; fax: 660-3703).

Irish Business and Employers' Confederation, 84 Lower Baggot Street, Dublin 2 (tel: 660-1011; fax: 660-1717).

Modern Display Artists Ltd (MDA) (for exhibition calendar), Fitzwilliam Quay, Ringsend, Dublin 4 (tel: 493-8555).

Provincial Newspapers Association of Ireland, 33 Parkgate Street, Dublin 8 (tel: 679-3679).

The Stock Exchange, 24-28 Anglesea Street, Dublin 2 (tel: 677-8808; fax: 677-6045).

Italy

Michael Griffin

On April 21 1996, Italians voted in the country's first government of the left since the end of the Second World War. The vote gave the Olive Tree alliance a slender majority in the 630-seat Chamber of Deputies and 49.8 percent of the seats in the Senate. With the support of the Reconstructed Communists (RC), who endorsed the coalition without joining its cabinet, the new prime minister Romano Prodi promised that his administration would live long enough to survive its full five-year term.

KEY FACTS — Italy

Official title: Repubblica Italiana (The Italian Republic)

Head of state: President Oscar Luigi Scalfaro (since May 1992)

Head of government: Prime Minister Romano Prodi (leader of Olive Tree Alliance) (from end-May 1996)

Ruling party: Olive Tree alliance (centre-left, elected April 1996)

Capital: Rome

Official Languages: Italian (and German in South Tyrol)

Currency: Lira (L) = 100 centesimi

Exchange rate: L1,528.15 per US$ (Dec 1996)

Area: 301,277 sq km

Population: 57.31m (1995)

GDP per capita: US$17,800 (1994)

GDP real growth: 3.4% (1995)

GNP per capita: US$19,270 (1994)

GNP real growth: 1.8% (1985-94)

Unemployment: 12.2% (Jul 1996)

Inflation: 2.6% (Nov 1996, annualised) (consumer prices)

Trade balance: US$29.7bn (12 months to Mar 1996)

Visitor numbers: 27.28m (1994)

Politics

The vote, yet again, reflected popular misgivings over the state of Italian political life. There have been three general elections in the four years that have elapsed since a wave of corruption enquiries led to the decimation of the post-war political order. The victory in March 1994 of media magnate, Silvio Berlusconi and his new movement, Forza Italia, raised hopes that Italy had finally broken with its pattern of short-lived and half-hearted coalitions. But his centre-right alliance crumbled seven months later, following the withdrawal of the Northern League (LN), headed by the erratic Umberto Bossi.

Whether the Olive Tree administration will prove any more durable is questionable. The outgoing, 'non-political' government of Lamberto Dini was formed with specific instructions to overhaul the Italian electoral system so as to produce stable majorities and more effective governments. But with the alliances of the centre-left and centre-right unable to agree on what reforms to make, the election was fought under the same rules as the 1994 poll: 75 per cent of seats were attributable under the first-past-the-post system and the remaining 25 per cent under proportional representation. Parties were, therefore, induced both to engage in unrealistic alliances for the purpose of winning elections, but to shy away from genuine consensus for fear of losing their independence.

The vote demonstrated categorically the extent of popular disenchantment with Forza Italia as a movement for change. Throughout 1995, Berlusconi had repeatedly tried to sabotage Dini's legislative programme with votes of no confidence, because of the direct threat posed by a fresh corruption enquiry and the centre-left's commitment to break up his media empire. Dini, a former minister in the Berlusconi government, only continued in office because of the unexpected support of the northern secessionists and former communists, both eager to delay fresh elections until they could mount a more effective campaign. On 31 December, however, he resigned, leaving President Oscar Scalfaro the difficult task of finding a successor to push through a package of constitutional reforms. A compromise in January 1996 between Berlusconi and Massimo D'Alema of the Party of the Democratic Left (PDS) over what kind of electoral system Italy should introduce failed, however, to deliver the kind of all-party consensus needed if Scalfaro's prime minister designate, Antonio Maccanico, were to form a durable government.

An instinctive centrist, Dini said that he had felt betrayed by Berlusconi's tactics during his one-year administration. When elections were announced for April 1996, he duly took his seat beneath the Olive Tree, along with other conservatives like Maccanico, former prime minister Carlo Azeglio Ciampi and ex-foreign minister Beniamino Andreatta. Formed only a year earlier, the alliance's composition illustrated just how much the Italian left has been forced towards the centre since 1994. Real power resides with the PDS, but its electoral success stemmed from its ability to win over the Greens, Prodi's Popular Party and the leftish splinters of the discredited Christian Democrats, without frightening voters through an accommodation with the hardline communists of the RC.

The latter's support for Dini, added to a reputation for clean local government, stood it in good stead at the polls, where it captured 35 seats in the lower house. The surprise success of the elections, however, was the separatist LN which won 59 seats in spite of Bossi's apparently unstable leadership and growing marginalisation. A thorn in the side of Berlusconi's brief administration, Bossi's credibility resides less in his championing of a federal Italy, than in the belief that he will continue his withering attacks on the murky power-broking that dominates political life in Rome, at the expense of regional interests. The new government, sworn in on 18 May 1996, will have to seek support from one of these two parties if it is to transform its 319

seats in the Chamber of Deputies into a working parliamentary majority.

The new prime minister, Romano Prodi, is a former industry minister, head of IRI, Italy's largest state-owned company and a professor of economics at Bologna University. He immediately pledged the Olive Tree to a programme of radical reform, ranging from the reduction of Italy's public debt and the return of the lira to the European Monetary Union (EMU) to the reform of the constitution and the devolution of more power to the regions. The lira rose sharply upon news of the victory and continued to strengthen as Prodi unveiled a confidence-building cabinet, which included Ciampi as treasury minister, Dini at European Union (EU) affairs and Italy's most popular man, the investigator Antonio di Pietro, as minister of public works. Prominent former communists were named as ministers of the interior, education and arts and culture. Meanwhile, a pugnacious Bossi announced on 12 May 1996 the formation of a parallel 'government' to shadow events in Rome and to 'liberate Padania', the wealthy northern region which includes the regions of Emilia Romagna, Liguria, Lombardy, Piedmont and the Veneto.

KEY INDICATORS

	Unit	1991	1992	1993	1994	1995
Population	m	56.41	56.78	57.07	57.19	57.31
Gross domestic product (GDP)	US$bn	1,134.0	1,200.0	997.0	1,020.2	–
GDP per capita	US$	19,630	21,680	17,600	17,800	–
GDP real growth	%	1.4	0.9	-0.1	2.2	3.4
Inflation	%	6.4	5.3	4.2	5.4	5.7
Consumer prices	1990=100	106.3	111.7	116.7	121.4	127.9
Unemployment	%	10.9	11.0	10.2	11.5	11.6
Wages (contractual)	1990=100	109.8	115.4	119.8	124.0	127.8
Agricultural production	1979-81=100	105.97	106.55	103.49	101.06	102.48
Coal	m toe	0.2	0.2	0.2	0.1	0.1
Exports (FOB) (goods)	US$m	169,465	178,155	169,153	189,805	–
Imports (FOB) (goods)	US$m	169,911	175,070	136,328	154,308	–
Balance of trade	US$m	-445	3,085	32,278	35,500	25,500
Current account	US$m	-24,649	-28,727	9,411	14,593	–
Total reserves minus gold	US$m	48,679	27,643	27,545	32,265	34,905
Foreign exchange	US$m	45,495	24,966	25,140	30,107	32,942
Discount rate	%	12.0	12.0	8.0	7.5	9.0
Deposit rate	%	6.64	7.11	6.12	4.78	–
Lending rate	%	13.89	15.77	13.86	11.23	–
Exchange rate	L per US$	1,241.0	1,232.4	1,573.7	1,612.4	1,629.6

Economy

The stormy political climate has tended to obscure the gains achieved elsewhere in Italian public life by the non-political administrations of Ciampi and Dini. 1995 was particularly successful for the health of the Italian economy. Strikes fell to their lowest level since the end of the war; average pay continued to rise less than price inflation; growth exceeded most of the other European economies; trade, current account and the overall balance of payments remained in clear surplus; company profitability rose to a peak; and public debt began to fall for the first time in sixty years.

The Economic and Financial Planning Document (EFPD), published in mid-1995 and covering projections for the next three years, spelled out the message that the most difficult phase in the adjustment of public finance was largely over and that less austerity will be needed to consolidate the gains in the years ahead than has hitherto been felt. According to EFPD, public debt as a percentage of GDP will decline in 1996 from 123.8 to 122.1 per cent, falling to 115.4 per cent by 1998. The annual budget deficit was projected to fall from L130 trillion (US$83.8 billion) in 1995 to L109.4 trillion in 1996 and L63.1 trillion – or 3 per cent of GDP – in 1998. The projections assume an average growth rate of 3 per cent a year and an inflation rate declining from 4.7 per cent in 1995 to 2.5 per cent by 1997-98. Although inflation rose above 5.5 per cent during 1995, the point remains that after years of failed attempts, Italy appears close to being on top of her public finance problem.

Reforms and savings

Dini's government was set up to deal with two urgent economic priorities: reforming the pensions system and curbing the 1996 budget deficit. The latter proposals, amounting to a reduction of L32.5 trillion (US$20.9 billion), were tabled in the autumn, with L15.5 trillion (US$10 billion) coming from expenditure cuts, L15.5 in net tax rises and L1.5 trillion through increases in non-tax receipts. Nearly L9 trillion (US$5.8 billion) in savings were expected from the pensions reform scheme which was proposed in May and provided for the gradual elimination of optional early retirement and changes to the way in which pensions are calculated. A further L11.5 trillion will be found by regularising the 1987-93 tax positions of Italy's notoriously reluctant tax-payers.

The balance of expenditure savings were made by reducing transfers to regional or municipal authorities, rather than attacks on the controversial sectors of health, education or social services where waste is regarded as pandemic. Such omissions, analysts claimed, were part of an attempt to retain the parliamentary support of the communists and to woo the unions in the round of wage negotiations due in January 1996. Some L6 trillion in the 1996 budget was set aside to pay for a 3 per cent rise in public sector wages to compensate for the government's erroneous inflation projections for 1994 and 1995. Parliament approved the proposals in December 1995 but, one month later, the Bank of Italy urged upon the executive the need for a supplementary budget to ensure the deficit really does fall below L110 trillion, the official target. The Prodi administration will have to raise some Lire10 trillion in its first months in office to ensure that the deficit programme remains on course.

Unlike other Organisation for Economic Co-operation and Development (OECD) countries, Italian governments are forced to meet their budgetary targets without the windfall benefits of privatisation: these are reserved for the reduction of debt which, according to Bank of Italy statistics, stood at L90 trillion at the end of 1995, down from L118 trillion in 1994 and a peak of L164 trillion in 1992. Fiscal plans for 1995 had included L10 trillion from sales of state holdings, with the same amounts in the two following years, but the privatisation schedule slowed down under Dini, due to political disagreements and delays over the creation of the regulating agencies, a precondition of the sale of ENEL, Italy's largest electric utility, and STET, the telecommunications giant. Dini had planned to place both on the market by summer 1995, along with 25 per cent of the energy and chemical company ENI and state holdings in the financial services group, IMI and the insurer INA. But after a year of debates, the government's only gains were the sale of 19 per cent of IMI – leaving the treasury with a further 6 per cent share – and parliamentary approval for the creation of an electricity regulator to grant licenses, issue regulations and set tariffs for ENEL's future owners.

Privatisation

With the transfer of power to the left-controlled Olive Tree alliance, the debate over privatisation is expected to sharpen in 1996. ENEL is the second largest generator of electricity in the world, accounting for 80 per cent of the domestic industry, with turnover of some L33 trillion in 1994. With a legal monopoly on the distribution and sale of energy – a strategic commodity in a country wholly dependent on imported hydrocarbons – it is also a source of formidable political power. The PRC, upon which the Prodi government may have to depend for a parliamentary majority, is vehemently opposed to privatisation in general, while more moderate members of the alliance doubt the wisdom of breaking up the state monopolies which have helped to mould Italian political life. Even Alberto Clo, Dini's industry minister, proposed retaining ENEL as a private monopoly after privatisation. Similar anxieties exist with regard to STET, part of Prodi's old empire at IRI and a majority shareholder in Telecom Italia. Again, the debate is over whether to privatise the parent holding or its valuable subsidiaries. STET's break-up worth has been estimated at L35 billion, nearly one third more than its value as a unified company. However, no independent regulatory authority for Italy's booming telecoms sector had been set up prior to the demise of the Dini government on 31 December 1995.

Surplus

While the government dallied over privatisation, the Italian commercial sector once again demonstrated its inherent vibrancy. For the first ten months of 1995, exports grew by 25.4 per cent and imports by 25.9 per cent with a combined trade surplus of L36.4 trillion, as against a L30 trillion surplus for the corresponding period in 1994. Italian manufacturers have revelled in their competitiveness since 1992, when the lira was pulled out of the European Monetary System, transforming the L17 trillion deficit of that year into its first surplus since 1988.

Beneficiaries include such traditionally strong sectors of the economy as machine tools, the automotive sector, fashion and textiles. Germany and France account for over half of machine tool production but, last year, domestic sales rose by a third, due to the 1994 Tremonti Law offering tax benefits for machinery supplied before the end of 1995. In November 1995, FIAT announced that it had retaken second position in the European car market, trailing Volkswagen's 17.2 per cent with 12.9 per cent. FIAT reported L1 trillion (US$644 million) in profits in 1994, expecting to double it on projected turnover of L84 trillion in 1995 as European sales jumped by 2 per cent. On 12 March 1996, FIAT's chairman for the past 30 years, Giovanni Agnelli, stepped down after handing executive control of Italy's flagship company to Cesare Romiti, its long-standing managing director.

The persistent strength of Italy's exports suggest that the lira is undervalued, in spite of its vulnerability to political strife in Rome. After a period of turbulence, it stabilised at L1,120 against the Deutsche Mark in December 1995, having fallen as low as L1,274 the previous March. Despite the resignation of the Dini government, it further appreciated by 4 percent to L1,060 in January 1996. The strength in demand for short-term government paper emboldened the Treasury to cut coupons by one hundred base points, without suffering a fall in takers.

But it is unlikely that such gains will continue uninterrupted under the Olive Tree, enabling it to keep its pledge to prepare the lira for a return to monetary union. The prospect was first raised in late 1995 by Dini, now charged with massaging Italy's often fractious relations with the Franco-German alliance. But it is political rather than economic conditions which are likely to harm the lira in the short term. The opportunities for dissension among members – both active and passive – of the Olive Tree Alliance are high; the battle against inflation is not yet won; the government has yet to hammer out a privatisation programme acceptable to its key supporters; and it may have to make even deeper cuts in social expenditure, which would alienate either the Reconstructed Communists or the currently docile unions.

Nevertheless, there is much to celebrate in Italy's demonstrable ability not just to function, but also to deal with its structural problems, in the midst of continuing political instability. Prime Minister Prodi took office with a healthy trade surplus, a deficit close to the level of other EU members and a degree of public confidence that the former communists, who have languished on the margins of political power for half a century, have a vested interest in showing they can provide the kind of responsible government that Italy has so consistently lacked.

COUNTRY PROFILE — ITALY

Historical profile

United under the Romans but not again until 1870, Italy remained poor and weak after unification.
1914–18 Fought with the allies in the First World War. Ensuing disorder and economic weakness fostered rise of Benito Mussolini and Fascist Party.
1925–26 Mussolini took dictatorial powers.
1936–39 Supported fascists in Spanish Civil War.
1940 Entered the Second World War on German side. Allied forces invaded Italy's African colonies then Italy itself, supported by anti-fascist resistance. Collapse of fascist regime.
1945 German forces surrendered; Mussolini killed.
1946 Declaration of republic.
1946–63 Relative political stability and industrial expansion under Christian Democrat governments. There then followed a succession of short-lived coalitions involving the Christian Democrats and up to four other major parties, frequently producing several regroupings and new cabinets in a year.
1983–86 Bettino Craxi first Socialist prime minister and committed to cutting budget deficit and economic reform, headed longest-running post-war government.
1989 Christian Democrat Giulio Andreotti prime minister for sixth time.
1992 Political corruption scandals broke. Government headed by Prime Minister Giuliano Amato committed to restoring country's public finances and to introducing institutional reform.
1993 In April Carlo Azeglio Ciampi became prime minister (Italy's fifty-second government since 1945).
1994 Controversial Prime Minister Silvio Berlusconi resigned in December after seven months in power, and a transitional government was formed with the mandate to tame the budget deficit and introduce electoral reform.

Political system

Democratic republic with bicameral parliament consisting of Chamber of Deputies (630 members) and Senate (315 elected members and seven life senators). Both houses elected for five years by proportional representation. President elected for a seven-year term by electoral college comprising both houses plus 58 regional representatives. Executive power exercised by Council of Ministers. The President of the Council (prime minister) is appointed by the Head of State. The 20 regions enjoy a large degree of autonomy. At the March 1994 election a new system based on the principle of majority voting but balanced by proportional representation, was introduced.

Main cities/towns

Rome (population 3m in 1994), Milan (3.7m), Naples (1.2m), Turin (992,000), Palermo (734,000), Genoa (701,000), Bologna (412,000), Florence (408,000), Catania (364,000), Bari (353,000), Venice (318,000).

Media

Press: Much of the press is controlled directly or indirectly by major industrial groups.
Dailies: Italy's top dailies are *Il Corriere della Sera* (circulation April 1995, 672,000), *La Repubblica* (531,000), *La Stampa* (417,000), *La Gazzetta Sport* (372,000), *Il Messagero* (257,000), *Corriere dello Sport) (239,000), Il Resto del*

COUNTRY PROFILE

Media (contd): Carlino (221,000), *Il Giornale* (196,000), *La Nazione* (191,000), *L'Unitá* (142,000) and *Il Gazzettino* (137,000). *Il Telegiornale* was first published in May 1995.
Weeklies: Very popular. Widest read weekly is *Sorrisi e Canzoni*. General interest weeklies include *Gente, Oggi, Panorama* and *Famiglia Cristiana* (Roman Catholic), *L'Espresso* (news). Large number of other general and special interest magazines.
Business: Many specialised trade magazines, mostly published in Milan. Major economic/business ones are *Espansione* and *Tempo Economico* both monthly, and *Il Mondo* and *Mondo Economico* both weekly, and *Il Sole 24 Ore* (circulation April 1995, 338,000) daily.
Broadcasting: Main channels controlled by Radiotelevisione Italiana (RAI-TV).
Radio: Approximately 18m receivers in use, served by three national RAI networks and over 4,000 private stations.
Television: Approximately 18.7m TV households. Three Rai channels, three Fininvest and 941 private commercial stations. Some stations from other countries can be received. Some local independents group together to form national networks. Over 94 per cent of the population watch television and 2 per cent of households subscribe to state-run teletext service. Satellite and pay-TV are growing. Reallocation of local TV licences (677 stations approved out of 1,211 applications). In June 1993 the Italian parliament approved legislation to end political control of the state-run Rai broadcasting organisation.
Advertising: Complex system of taxation in operation. Mostly conducted through agents. All usual media available. All three state-owned TV networks and two of the three radio networks carry advertising, as do all the private stations. The press, cinema, posters and direct mail are also widely used. TV main medium for advertising. Newer methods of advertising such as cinema sponsorship, packaging and phone-cards are growing slowly.

Domestic economy

Large industrial-based economy with heavy dependence on imported energy. Service sector, particularly tourism, also significant. Economic performance constrained by large and growing public sector deficit, high inflation and regional disparities in economic wealth. Standard of living considerably higher in the north than the south. The economy formally entered recession in the third quarter of 1992. There was a currency crisis in September 1992 which forced the lira to float outside the European Monetary System (EMS). Inflation during 1996 fell steadily; annualised inflation in November was 2.6 per cent, a level not touched since 1969.

Employment

Complex wage indexing system *(scala mobile)* was in operation until 1992 when there was a union-employer agreement to abolish the system. An additional accord in July 1993 created a new wage bargaining system designed to prevent the recurrence of inflationary wage settlements and to create more jobs. Unemployment is high in the depressed south – nearly three times that prevailing in the centre and the north. About 32 per cent of the workforce are female.

External trade

Improvement in balance of trade largely dependent on reduction of fuel imports; Italy imports about 85 per cent of its energy needs. Deterioration in trade balance in the late 1980s attributable to intensified foreign competition for exporters, mainly from south-east Asia.
Exports: Main destinations: Germany (typically 20% of total), France (13%), USA (8%), UK (6%), EU (53%). Main exports: machinery and transport equipment, textiles and chemicals.
Imports: Main sources: Germany (typically 19% of total), France (14%), UK (6%), USA (5%), EU (55%). Main imports: raw materials and chemicals.

Agriculture

Sector (including forestry and fishing) contributed only 3 per cent to GDP in 1994 and employed 7.5 per cent of the working population. In April 1991 a new 14-point programme was arranged to improve sector performance. Production is divided between the larger, more fertile, mechanised farms of the north (specialising in meat, dairy, cereal production and new crops like soya bean) and the smaller, labour-intensive farms of the south, which produce mainly wine, olive oil, fruit and vegetables. Italy produces crops of Mediterranean products which fail to satisfy consumers in northern EU markets and which are already in surplus. The fishing industry has a turnover of L7,000bn, but is a neglected sector of the economy.

Industry

This sector contributed 31.5 per cent to GDP in 1994 and employed 32.8 per cent of the labour force. Major industrial sectors include machinery and transport equipment, iron and steel, chemicals, food processing and textiles. The government is heavily involved in industry through three large state holding companies. The largest, IRI, controls some 500 companies across a wide range of activities. Heavy industry is found in Lombardy, Piedmont and Liguria. Problems in the sector include strong and growing competition in traditional products from developing countries, and the small share of the export market taken by high-tech products. Efforts to attract industrial investment to the south, the *Mezzogiorno*, have met with only partial success, despite large subsidies.

Tourism

The sector is Italy's third biggest source of foreign income after machinery and textiles and clothing.

Mining

The sector accounts for only 0.5 per cent of GDP and employs 0.5 per cent of the workforce. Relatively poor resources, although large quantities of iron ore and pyrites, mercury, lead, zinc, bauxite, aluminium, sulphur, gravel, alabaster and marble. Sardinia is the main mining area. Only large sulphur deposit in Europe is in Sicily but is not economically viable. Bauxite mined mainly in Abruzzi, Campania and Apulia, though output has contracted due to fall in demand from aluminium industry. However, output of lead, zinc and particularly copper have all increased. The state-controlled metals company ILVA is now the world's fifth-largest steel producer.

Hydrocarbons

Heavy reliance on energy imports (85 per cent of needs). However, plan under way to develop indigenous resources, as well as use of coal and natural gas. Coal production 0.1m tonnes oil equivalent (1995). Most oil and gas production is in and off Sicily. Gas production meets 40 per cent of demand. Natural gas production totalled 16.2m tonnes oil equivalent in 1995, a decline of 12.5 per cent on 1994 output. Natural gas reserves 13.2 trillion cu feet (end-1995). Gas is imported under long-term contracts from the former USSR and Algeria as well as the Netherlands, and a programme to convert power stations from oil to coal is under way.

Energy

Electricity needs filled by buying extra power generated by France's nuclear programme. Nuclear energy programme halted in 1987, but being reviewed.

Legal system

Based on civil law system with ecclesiastical law influence.

Membership of international organisations

ADB, Alps-Adriatic Working Community, ASSIMER, CCC, Council of Europe, DAC, EU, ECOWAS, EIB, ELDO, EMS, ESRO, FAO, IAEA, ICAC, ICAO, ICO, IDA, IDB, IEA, IFAD, IFC,IHO, ILO, International Lead and Zinc Study Group, IMF, IMO, INTELSAT, INTERPOL, IOOC, IPU, IRC, ITC,ITU, NATO, OAS (observer), OECD, UN, UNESCO, UNIDO, UPU, WEU, WHO, WIPO, WMO, World Bank, WSG, WTO.

BUSINESS GUIDE

Time

GMT + 1 hr (GMT + 2 from 27 Mar to 24 Sep).

Climate

Temperate in north, Mediterranean in south. Temperatures range from about 4–30°C. Winter is cold and dry in Alps, mild on Italian Riviera, cold and damp in Po Valley, mild in southern Italy and Sicily. Summer hot and dry along coast, pleasantly cool in Alps and Appenines. Rainfall not heavy.
Clothing: Mediumweight and light topcoat or rainwear for winter. Lightweight for summer.

Entry requirements

Visa not required by nationals of most European countries. Visitors not staying in a hotel must register with police within three days of arrival. Travel conditions liable to change at short notice due to labour disputes. Advisable to consult travel agent or Italian Consul prior to departure.
Visa: Visas are required for visitors from the following: all countries of Africa except Tunisia, Morocco and Algeria; all countries of Asia except Republic of Korea, Japan and Turkey; all countries of Middle East except Israel; Caribbean area and South/Central America – only for Venezuela, Nicaragua, Cuba and the Dominican Republic. Visas are not required for visitors from Europe, North America, New Zealand and Australia.
Health: Vaccination certificates not required. EU nationals are covered for medical treatment; an E111 form is needed, however.
Currency: No limit on amount of foreign currency brought in, but this must be declared and not exceeded by amount taken out.
Customs: Personal effects duty-free. Inspections on main international train routes.

Air access

Regular flights by all major international airlines.
National airline: Alitalia – state-owned airline (the fourth-largest in Europe).
International airports: Pisa (PSA), 2 km from Pisa, for Florence, Turin (TRN), 16 km north-west of city, Venice (VCE), 13 km north-west of city, Bologna (BLQ), 6 km from city, Naples (NAP), 6 km from city, Genoa (GOA), 6 km from city, Palermo (PMO), 20 km from city.
Main international airports: Fiumicino (FCO) 35 km south-west of Rome, Linate (LIN) 10 km east of Milan, Malpensa (MSP) 46 km north-west of Milan.

Surface access

By road from France, Switzerland, Austria and former Yugoslavia. However, several passes closed during winter. In addition to the Riviera coastal motorway, access from France and Switzerland maintained via St Bernard, Mont Blanc and Fréjus tunnels. Also several rail and sea routes.
Main ports: Genoa, Trieste, Augusta, Taranto, Leghorn, Savona, Ancona, Bari, Brindisi, Civitavecchia, Venice, La Spezia, Naples, Palermo (Sicily), and Cagliari and Porto Torres (Sardinia).

BUSINESS GUIDE — ITALY

Hotels

Classified into five star categories. Rates are fixed with Provincial Tourist Board, and vary according to class, season, services available and locality. Visitors are required by law to obtain an official receipt when staying in a hotel, and hotels are required to report the presence of all foreign guests to the authorities. All major credit cards are accepted in the large, top-category hotels in major cities but not widely elsewhere.

Restaurants

Wide range of standards and types. Service charge of 12–15 per cent usually included but customary to leave tip. Many restaurants do not accept credit cards.

Currency

Exchange rate: Italian lira floats freely against all foreign currencies, but is included in European Monetary System and floats in common with currencies in certain other West European countries. Within EMS the lira is allowed a wider band of fluctuation.

Foreign exchange information

Account restrictions: Under some conditions non-residents can have accounts in foreign currencies. Non-residents may also have 'foreign accounts' in lire.
Trade policy: Few restrictions on imports.

Car hire

Self-drive cars available; daily rate depends on the engine size, plus additional charge per kilometre. Special weekly tariffs available. VAT is charged. Official translation of driving licence required. Air and rail travellers can get special deals including car hire. Drive on the right. Maximum speed 50 kph in towns; out-of-town speed limits depend on engine capacity of car and type of road. Seat belts are obligatory by law.

City transport

Taxis: Available in all towns and tourist resorts, usually in ranks at railway stations, or can be called by phone. Fares vary considerably, and unmetered cabs should be avoided. A small tip (8–10 per cent) is usual; some drivers add this to the fare when carrying foreigners.
Buses and metro: All major cities have bus service with one standard fare. Day and monthly tickets also available. Metro *(metropolitana)* in Rome and Milan with standard single fare as for buses. In Milan tickets last for 70 minutes and can be used on both metro lines and all bus routes. A daily ticket usable for all Rome services is available.

National transport

Air: Alitalia and Aero Transporti Italiani (ATI) operate services connecting Rome to most major towns. Alisarda operate services connecting Rome, Milan and Turin with Sardinia.
Road: Total length of roads approximately 300,000 km, including a toll motorway system *(autostrade)* which connects most cities. Extensive bus services, operated by several companies, link all major towns. Fares are relatively cheap.
Rail: Efficient and fairly cheap network (over 20,000 km) operated by Italian State Railways (Ferrovie dello Stato), and several small private companies. Advisable to book 'express' tickets in advance.
Water: Ferryboat and hydrofoil services linking the mainland with Sicily, Sardinia and the smaller islands are operated by several lines including the State Railways. Ferry services connect Trieste, Ancona, Brindisi and Bari with Durres and Vlora (Albania).

Public holidays

Official list of holidays is not generally published until late in the previous year. Main holiday season is mid-July to mid-September.
Fixed dates: 1 Jan (New Year's Day), 6 Jan (Epiphany), 25 Apr (Liberation Day), 1 May (Labour Day), 15 Aug (Ferragosto/Assumption Day), 1 Nov (All Saints'), 8 Dec (Immaculate Conception), 25 and 26 Dec (Christmas). Businesses often close early on 14 Aug, Christmas Eve and New Year's Eve.
Variable dates: Good Friday, Easter Monday. Ascension Day. Local public holidays are held on the feast day of each town's patron saint.

Working hours

Business: (Mon–Fri) 0900–1300 and 1400–1800.
Government: (Mon–Sat) 0800–1400 (senior staff may return 1730–2000).
Banking: (Mon–Fri) 0830–1330 and also for one hour in afternoon.
Shops: (Mon–Sat) 0900–1300 and 1530–1930. Hours differ from town to town and in summer. All shops have one half-day closing each week.

Business language and interpreting/translation

Usually available in major towns. Can sometimes be provided at short notice by hotels or travel agents.

Telecommunications

Telephone and telefax: Efficient and cheap service. Public telephones use lire coins or token *(gettone)*, or magnetic cards, available from post offices, tobacconists and some news-stands. International dialling code: 39 followed by 6 for Rome, 2 for Milan, 11 for Turin, 81 for Naples, 41 for Venice and 55 for Florence.

For IDD access from Italy dial 00.
Telex: Available at major post offices. Country code 43.
Telegram: Can be sent from any post office or by telephone. ITALCABLE operates overseas service.

Postal service

Tends to be subject to delays. To ensure quick delivery it is best to use express and/or registered mail service. Stamps sold at post offices and tobacconists. CAI Post courier service from a few main post offices gives rapid delivery in main European cities.

Banking

There are 1,100 separate banking institutions, of which the most common are the single or two-branch rural or tradesmen's banks (more than 700). Approximately 65 per cent of banking activity is in the hands of public sector banks. In July 1990 the Amato banking reform was ratified transforming state-owned banks into joint stock companies. A minimum of 51 per cent of the banks' capital will remain under state control. Foreign banks operating include Barclays, Citibank and Deutsche Bank. In February 1993 the final piece of legislation designed to make the Bank of Italy an independent central bank was approved by the government, in line with the EU's objectives for monetary union. The legislation also allowed the central bank to decide the obligatory reserve requirements of the banking system, and ended the Treasury's ability to use the bank to fund the budget deficit. From June 1993, commercial banks are be able to own up to 15 per cent of industrial companies directly, provided the stakes do not damage their profits, the limiting criteria being set by the Bank of Italy, based on a commercial bank's size and type of business. This is a step aimed at assisting privatisation and bailing out troubled private companies.
Other banks: See 'Business Directory, Banking'.

Trade fairs

Over 300 international, national and specialist fairs held every year.

Electricity supply

220 V AC.

Representation in capital

Afghanistan, Albania, Algeria, Angola, Argentina, Australia, Austria, Bangladesh, Belgium, Bolivia, Brazil, Bulgaria, Cameroon, Canada, Chile, China PR, Colombia, Congo, Costa Rica, Côte d'Ivoire, Cuba, Cyprus, Denmark, Dominican Republic, Ecuador, Egypt, El Salvador, Ethiopia, Finland, France, Gabon, Germany, Ghana, Greece, Guatemala, Guinea, Haiti, The Holy See, Honduras, Hungary, India, Indonesia, Iran, Iraq, Ireland, Israel, Japan, Jordan, Kenya, Republic of Korea, Kuwait, Lebanon, Lesotho, Liberia, Libya, Luxembourg, Madagascar, Malaysia, Malta, Mexico, Monaco, Morocco, Myanmar, Netherlands, New Zealand, Nicaragua, Nigeria, Norway, Oman, Pakistan, Panama, Paraguay, Peru, Philippines, Poland, Portugal, Romania, Russia, San Marino, Saudi Arabia, Senegal, Somalia, South Africa, Spain, Sri Lanka, Sudan, Sweden, Switzerland, Syria, Tanzania, Thailand, Tunisia, Turkey, United Arab Emirates, UK, USA, Uruguay, Venezuela, Vietnam, Yemen, Zaïre, Zambia.

BUSINESS DIRECTORY

Hotels

Milan (area code 2)
Atlantic, Via Napo Torriani 24, 20124 (tel: 669-1941).

Excelsior Gallia, Piazza Duca d'Aosta 9, 20124 (tel: 6277; tx: 311-160).

Galileo, Corso Europa 9, 20122 (tel: 7743; fax: 656-319).

Grand, Via Washington 66, 20146 (gel: 48-521; fax: 481-8925).

BUSINES DIRECTORY

Hotels (contd):
Hilton, Via Galvani 12, 20124 (tel: 69-831; fax: 6671-0810).

Michelangelo, Via Scarlatti 33, 20124 (tel: 6755; fax: 669-4232).

Palace, Piazza della Repubblica 20, 20124 (tel: 6336; fax: 654-485).

Rome (area code 6)
Airport Palace, Viale Romagnoli 165 (tel: 569-2341; tx: 611-469).

American Palace Eur, Via Laurentina 554 (tel: 591-1551).

Bernini Bristol, Piazza Barberini 23, 00187 (tel: 488-3051; fax: 482-4266).

Bolivar, Via della Cordonata 6 (tel: 678-0123, 679-1614; fax: 679-1025).

Canada, Via Vincenza 58 (tel: 495-7385; fax: 445-0749).

Cavalieri Hilton, Via Cadlolo 101, 00136 (tel: 35-091; fax: 3509-2241).

Colosseum, Via Sforza 10 (tel: 474-3486; fax: 482-7285).

De La Ville Inter-Continental, Via Sistina 69, 00187 (tel: 67-331; fax: 678-4213).

Diplomatic, Via Vittoria Colonna 28 (tel: 654-2084, 656-1734; tx: 610-506).

Eden, Via Ludovisi 49, 00187 (tel: 474-3553; fax: 482-1584).

Esperia, Via Nazionale 22 (tel: 474-4245; tx: 614-635).

Excelsior, Via Vittorio Veneto 125, 00187 (tel: 4708; fax: 482-6205).

Giulio Cesare (near Vatican City), Via degli Scipioni 287 (tel: 310-244; fax: 321-1736).

Grand Flora, Via Vittorio Veneto 191 (tel: 497-821; tx: 680-494).

Grand Ritz, Via Chelini 41 (tel: 803-751; fax: 872-916).

Hassler, Trinita dei Monti 6, 00187 (tel: 678-2651; fax: 678-9991).

Holiday Inn Minerva, Piazza della Minerva 69 (tel: 790-650; fax: 623-7190).

Lord Byron, Via G. Notaris 5, 00197 (tel: 322-0404; fax: 322-0405).

Mediterraneo, 15 Via Cavour (tel: 464-051).

Metropole, Via Principe Amedeo 3 (tel: 4774; fax: 474-0413).

Oxford, Via Boncompagni 89 (tel: 482-8952; fax: 481-5349).

Plaza Grand, Via del Corso 126 (tel: 679-77510.

Regina Carlton, Via Veneto 72 (tel: 476-851; fax: 476-851).

Savoy, Via Ludovisi 15 (tel: 474-4141; fax: 474-6812).

Sheraton, Viale del Pattinaggio 1 (near EUR) (tel: 5453; fax: 542-0689).

Turin (area code 11)
Concord, Via Lagrange 47, 10123 (tel: 557-6756; tx: 221-323).

Grand Sitea, Via Carlo Alberto 35, 10123 (tel: 557-0171; fax: 548-090).

Holiday Inn , City Centre, Via Assietta 3, 10121 (tel: 516-7111; fax: 516-7699).

Jolly Ambasciatori, Corso Vittorio Emanuele 104, 10121 (tel: 5752; fax: 544-978).

Jolly Ligure, Piazza C. Felice 85, 10123 (tel: 55-641; fax: 535-438).

Palace, Via Sacchi 8, 10128 (tel: 515-511; fax: 561-2187).

Car hire

Rome
Avis: Via Tiburtina (tel: 413-1414).

Budget: Via Ludovisi 60 (tel: 482-0966/39; fax: 487-0010).

Europcar: Via Lombardia 7 (tel: 487-1274, 481-7162).

Hertz: Ciampino Airport (tel: 7934-0616; fax 7934-0095); FSS Railway Station (tel: 474-0389; fax: 321-6834).

Chambers of Commerce

American Chamber of Commerce in Italy, Via Agnello 12, 20121 Milan (tel: 807-955).

British Chamber of Commerce for Italy, Via Agnello 8, 20121 Milan (tel: 876-981, 877-798; fax: 2810-0262).

Camera di Commercio, Industria, Artigianato e Agricoltura, Piazza de Pietra, Palazzo Proprio, 00100 Rome (tel: 678-3280).

Unione Italiana delle Camere di Commercio Industria (Association of Chambers of Commerce in Italy), Artigianato e Agricoltura, Piazza Sallustio 21, 00187 Rome (tel: 479-961).

Banking

Banca d'Italia (central bank), Via Nazionale 91, Rome (tel: 47-921; tx: 610-021).

Banca Commerciale Italiana, Piazza della Scala 6, 20121 Milan (tel: 88-501; tx: 310-080).

Banca di Napoli, Via Toledo 177–188, 80132 Naples (tel: 791-1111; tx: 710-570).

Banca Nazionale del Lavoro, Via Veneto 119, 00187 Rome (tel: 47-021; tx: 610-116).

Banca Nazionale dell'Agricoltura SPA, Via Salaria 231, 00199 Rome (tel: 85-881; fax: 8588-3406).

Banco di Roma, Via U. Tupini 180, 00144 Rome (tel: 54-451; tx: 616-184).

Cassa di Risparmio delle Provincie Lombarde, Via Monte di Pietá 8, 20100 Milan (tel: 88-661; tx: 313-010).

Cassa di Risparmio di Roma, 320 Via del Corso, 00186 Rome (tel: 67-071; fax: 6707-3783).

Cassa di Risparmio di Torino, 31 Via XX Settembre, 10121 Torino (tel: 57-661; fax: 638-203).

Credito Italiano, Piazza Cordusio, 20123 Milan (tel: 88-621; tx: 312-401).

Istituto Bancario San Paolo di Torino, Piazza San Carlo 156, 10121 Turin (tel: 5551; tx: 212-040).

Monte dei Paschi di Siena, Piazza Salimbeni, Siena (tel: 294-111; tx: 570-080 PASDIR 1, 572-347 PASDIR 1).

Nuovo Banco Ambrosiano, Piazza Paolo Ferrari 10, 20121 Milan (tel: 85-941; tx: 335-687).

Principal newspapers

Il Corriere della Sera, Via Solferino 28, 20121 Milan (tel: 6339; tx: 31-001).

Il Giorno, Via Gaetano Negri 4, 20123 Milan (tel: 85-661; tx: 333-279).

Il Sole/24 Ore, Via Paolo Lomazzo 52, 20154 Milan (tel: 31-031; tx: 331-325).

La Repubblica, Piazza Ind Penza 11B, 00185 Rome (tel: 49-821; tx: 620-660).

La Stampa and Stampa Sera, Via Marenco 32, 10126 Turin (tel: 65-681; tx: 221-121).

Travel information

Alitalia (Linee Aeree Italiane), Centro Direzionale, Viale Alissandro Marchetti, 111, Rome 100148 (tel: 709-2780; fax: 709-3065).

Other useful addresses

Agenzia Nazionale Stampa Associata (news agency), Via della Dataria 94, 00187 Rome (tel: 678-6161).

Borsa Valori di Milano, Piazza Degli Affari, 20100 Milan (tel: 8534).

Commissione Nazionale per le Società e la Borsa (commission for companies and the stock exchange), Milan (tel: 877-841).

Confederazione Generale dell'Industria Italiana (general confederation of Italian industry), Viale dell'Astronomia 30, 00144 Rome (tel: 59-031).

Confederazione Generale Italiana del Commercio (general confederation of Italian commerce), Piazza G.C. Belli 2, Rome (tel: 588-783, 580-192).

Ente Nazionale Idrocarburi (ENI), Piazzalo E. Mattei, 00144 Rome (tel: 59-001; tx: 610-082/86).

Ente Nazionale Italiano per il Turismo (tourist board), Via Marghera 2, 00185 Rome (tel: 49-711; tx: 621-314, 612-318).

Istituto Nazionale di Statistica (ISTAT) (national statistics office), Via Cesare Balbo 16, 00100 Rome (tel: 46-731; fax: 4673-4177).

Istituto per la Ricostruzione Industriale (IRI) Via Vittorio Veneto 85, 00187 Rome (tel: 47-271).

Ente Partecipazioni e Finanziamento Industria Manifatturiera (EFIM), Via XXIV Maggio 43–45, 00187 Rome (tel: 47-101).

Istituto Nazionale per il Commercio Estero (Italian government agency for promotion of foreign trade), 21 Via Liszt, 00100 Rome (tel: 59-921).

Ministry of Agriculture and Forests, Via XX Settembre 20, 00187 Rome (tel: 4665; tx: 610-148).

Ministry of Budget and Economic Planning, Via XX Settembre 97, 00187 Rome (tel: 47-611; tx: 626-432).

Ministry of Finance, Viale America, EUR, 00144 Rome (tel: 5997; tx: 614-460).

Ministry of Foreign Trade, Viale America 341, EUR, 00144 Rome (tel: 5993; tx: 610-083).

Ministry of Industry, Via Vittorio Veneto 33, 00187 Rome (tel: 4705; tx: 622-550).

Ministry of Tourism and Performing Arts, Via della Ferratella in Laterano 51, 00184 Rome (tel: 77-321; tx: 616-400).

Office of the President, Palazzo del Quirinale, 00187 Rome (tel: 4699; tx: 611-440).

Prime Minister's Office, Palazzo Chigi, Piazza Colonna 370, 00100 Rome (tel: 6779; tx: 613-199).

Latvia

Bob Jiggins

Latvia continues to wrestle with the key issues of its relationship with Russia and the poor performance of the economy. To complicate matters further, the electorate voted almost equally for parties of the political left and right in the October 1995 election, with a marked inclination towards those groups outside the mainstream of Latvian political life. The result made the formation of a working government difficult. The only real point of agreement between the nine parties in the *Saiema* (parliament) is the desirability of both European Union (EU) and NATO membership.

Politics

As neither of the two main groupings in the *Saiema*, the rightist national Bloc and the leftist national reconciliation bloc, could agree on a choice of prime minister, President Guntis Ulmanis made the neutral selection of Andris Skele. A coalition government was subsequently created by Skele out of both left and right, largely by allocating ministries to the various parties rather than compromising on policy. However, the rightist Latvia's Way party argued that it had not received its fair share of ministries. It furthermore suggested that Prime Minister Skele was unsuitable for office as he has been connected with bankruptcy. These cabinet fractures may prove troublesome in the future.

The resurrection of the debate over the citizenship law is looking more likely. Many ethnic Lats regard this law as too generous to the sizeable 33 per cent Russian minority living in Latvia. This issue will be around for quite some time; the right-wing For Fatherland and Freedom party is already well represented in government and the even-more-rightist People's Movement for Latvia received increased support in the 1995 elections. With the EU leaning on the Latvian government to liberalise the citizenship law, splits in the coalition are all the more probable.

Guntis Ulmanis was re-elected president for a second three-year term in June 1996. Following his victory he made it clear that he would focus on foreign policy issues, particularly improving relations with Russia and working towards membership of the EU and NATO.

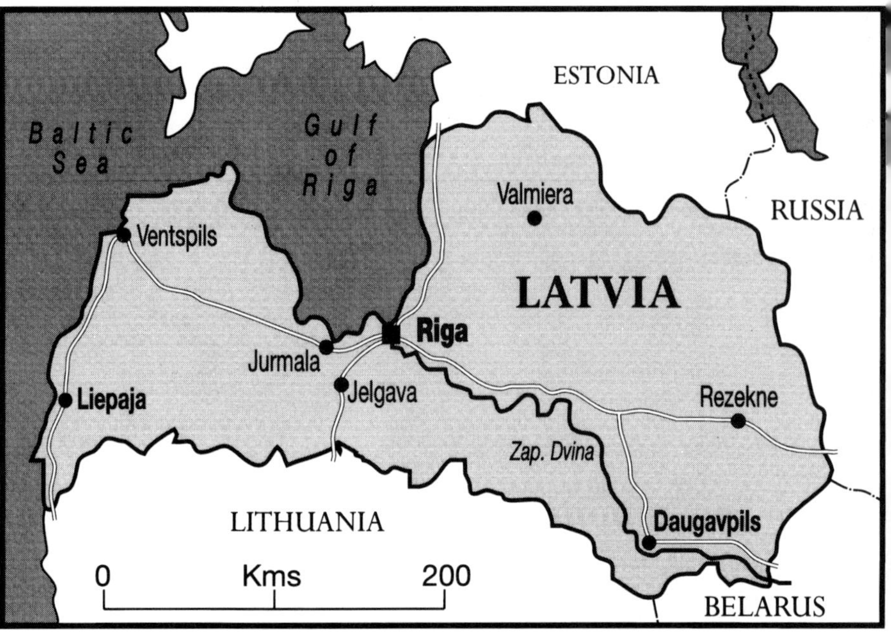

Banking

With the collapse of Baltija Bank in 1995 and it's declaration of bankruptcy in 1996, the banking system in Latvia continues to attract controversy. This affair has potential repercussions for Latvian-Russian relations, as a deal with Russia's Intertek Bank (whereby Intertek paid for part of Baltija's portfolio with apparently non-existent Russian Treasury bills) turned sour.

A number of the banks that declared insolvency in 1995 have now been liquidated or have had their licences revoked. The operations of Doma Banka and the Latvian Capital Bank have been suspended since early 1996. Only a handful of banks are considered to be well-run and free from potential collapse. Eventually, the number of institutions looks likely to be substantially reduced. Whether or not compensation will be paid to investors remains to be

KEY FACTS — Latvia

Official title: Republic of Latvia

Head of state: President Guntis Ulmanis (since 1993, re-elected 18 Jun 1996)

Head of government: Prime Minister Andris Skele (from 21 Dec 1995)

Ruling party: Coalition government

Capital: Riga

Official Languages: Lettish

Currency: Lats (Ls) (introduced March 1993; from 18 October 1993 lats became sole legal tender); Ls1 = 100 santims

Exchange rate: Ls0.55 per US$ (Dec 1996)

Area: 64,589 sq km

Population: 2.53m (1995)

GDP per capita: US$1,176 (1994)

GDP real growth: 0.35% (1995)

GNP per capita: US$2,000 (1994)

GNP real growth: 1.1% (1st qtr 1996)

Unemployment: 6.3% (1995)

Inflation: 23.2% (Jan 1996, annual) (consumer prices)

Trade balance: -US$149m (May 1996)

Foreign debt: US$513m (1995)*
* estimated figure

seen, but if the record of pay-outs for Baltija Banka is set as a precedent, the signs are not good.

The banking crisis has had a widespread effect, and it has removed any possibility of economic revival in the near future. Projections for 1995 had indicated that growth was to be in the region of 5 per cent, but in the event, the final figure was just 0.35 per cent. Data suggested that around 18,000 enterprises suffered losses on their bank deposits and this is unlikely to be fully, or even partially, compensated. In addition to these losses, rising energy prices have ensured that many firms are unable to produce at capacity and to pay their bills.

It is possible, if the budgetary crisis is brought under control and the worst of the banking crisis is over, that growth in 1996 could reach 3 per cent. But this would be from a position of weakness.

Inflation

A further aspect of Latvia's difficulties is the rise in inflation, which began to increase again from October 1995. It had fallen to an all-time year-on-year low of 22.7 per cent in the previous month. Part of this rise can be explained by the seasonal increase in agricultural products, but by far the biggest component is the increase of 43.5 per cent in electricity. Gas prices are also expected to rise, given that Latvian Gas owed US$15 million to its Russian supplier, Gazprom, in November 1995 and agreed a schedule of repayments, with the final payment in April 1996. Unemployment, however, remained relatively stable in the first part of 1996 at around 6 per cent.

Energy

One of Latvia's main problems is energy supply – the country is heavily reliant upon imports, especially from Russia. Consequently the government lays great stress upon developing domestic sources of energy, for which the discovery of oil in the Baltic has assumed great importance. Unfortunately, the area concerned is disputed with neighbouring Lithuania and both countries have adopted hard-line attitudes over exploration and extraction. The dispute is a long way from being settled and is made even more critical by the fact that neither country is well endowed with natural resources. Latvia has recently upped the ante by awarding exploration rights to two foreign firms, Amoco (USA) and OPAB (of Sweden).

The oil dispute is reaching proportions where the much vaunted Baltic unity is under threat. This, in turn, has consequences with respect to EU membership. It seems probable that the only way of resolving the dispute is by international arbitration. Despite strong domestic pressure on each government to hold out, a solution looks likely be agreed in the long run.

KEY INDICATORS

	Unit	1991	1992	1993	1994	1995
Population	m	2.69	2.63	2.59	2.55	2.53
Gross national product (GNP)	US$bn	8.3	5.6	4.6	5.0	–
GNP per capita	US$	3,100	2,000	1,800	2,000	–
GNP real growth	%	-11.1	-33.8	-14.9	2.2	–
Inflation	%	124.0	958.0	109.1	36.0	23.3
Employment	'000	1,397	1,345	1,265	1,205	1,189
Unemployment	%	–	1.1	4.7	6.3	6.3
Consumer prices	1992=100	29.1	100.0	208.8	283.8	354.6
Wages: average earnings	1992=100	–	100.0	211.7	338.6	422.1
Industrial production	1990=100	97.9	63.8	39.5	35.8	33.4
Cement	1990=100	720	340	114	244	205
Exports	Ls m	–	–	676	553	688
Imports (FOB)	Ls m	–	–	639	695	923
Balance of trade	Ls m	–	–	36.4	-141.2	-235.0
Current account	US$m	–	191	417	201	–
Discount rate	%	–	120	27	25	24
Total reserves minus gold	US$m	–	–	431.55	545.18	505.70
Foreign exchange	US$m	–	–	333.88	544.86	503.47
Interbank rate	%	–	–	–	37.18	22.39
Deposit rate	%	–	–	34.78	31.68	14.79
Lending rate	%	–	–	86.36	55.86	34.56
Exchange rate	Ls per US$	–	–	**0.60	0.55	0.54

**Ls sole leg. tender Oct 1993

Agriculture and privatisation

Privatisation in the agriculture sector is now almost complete. One result of this is the fact that numerous small agricultural units have been created which no longer have the economies of scale associated with the old state enterprises. This has caused productivity in the agriculture sector to drop. Many of the new farms cannot produce food for sale and the country is now importing food on a large scale.

Figures for 1994 suggest that food accounts for about 8 per cent of imports and this percentage is now likely to be considerably higher. The Ministry of Agriculture estimated that the country produced only 30 per cent or so of its grain requirements in 1995. This decline is set to continue with the collapse of the Baltija Bank and the lack of state investment in agriculture. It is possible, though, that the new government will pay greater attention to agriculture as both the left and right blocs in the Saiema contain agricultural parties and the leader of the Latvian Unity Party, Albert Kauls, is the new minister of Agriculture. A more interventionist policy is thus likely with the possible imposition of tariffs.

In other areas, it is expected that the new prime minister will support an extension of privatisation – Skele was head of the Latvian Privatisation Agency and a noted businessman. Foreign investors are not expected to play a major role in Latvian privatisation.

Trade and investment

Latvia's trade deficit is worsening largely because of the need to import energy supplies; this resulted in a deficit of US$580 million in 1995. Nor is the strong currency helping exports; the banking crisis is also diminishing the country's attractiveness in respect of invisible earnings. This position is mirrored by foreign investment with inflows for 1996 expected to fall.

In 1995 Latvia attracted around US$85 million of foreign capital, into 1,240 firms, compared with US$60 million in 1994. Other concerns by foreign firms, apart from the banking issue, centre on corruption, crime and bureaucracy, especially problems in acquiring land for development.

Total trade turnover increased by 29 per cent in 1995 compared to 1994, although the deficit has likewise increased as a result of the jump in imports. Exports in 1995 stood at US$688 million, while imports were higher at US$923 million. The pattern of trade is following that of other east European states with exports to and imports from the EU increasing, largely at the expense of the CIS states. Thus in the first half of 1995 exports to the EU totalled 47.2 per cent compared with 36.7 per cent a year earlier, whilst imports registered a similar increase from 36.8 per cent to 51.8 per cent. The main item of exports in 1994 was timber and associated products at 21.3 per cent of the total, while the primary import category was mineral products at 29.4 per cent of which a high proportion was fuel.

Latvia joined the European Free Trade Association (EFTA) in November 1995, along with its two Baltic neighbours.

Latvia now has a new national airline, the Air Baltic Company (ABC), formed by a merger of the passenger operations of the state airline Latavio and Baltic International, a joint enterprise with Baltic International USA. Initial destinations are the same as the two constituent companies and new routes are planned to Warsaw and Kiev. The remainder of Latavio has an uncertain future with the planned privatisation deferred owing to its insolvency.

In economic matters policy looks likely to continue much as before with perhaps an increased emphasis on protectionism over agriculture. The major problem that still needs to be dealt with is the appalling state of the banking system. If this is rectified, and the country made considerably more friendly to foreign involvement, then it is possible that investment will be forthcoming. Furthermore, if Latvia's dispute with Lithuania over the division of the oil field is resolved this will have obviously beneficial effects on the economy and future EU membership.

COUNTRY PROFILE — LATVIA

Historical profile

Elections in 1989 returned a non-communist majority to parliament. Independence from Russia declared 21 August 1991, having declared sovereignty in 4 May 1990. Latvia was admitted to the UN on 17 September 1991, regaining its independent status of November 1918 to August 1940, when it had been forcibly incorporated into the former Soviet Union under the Molotov Ribbentrop pact.

Political system

On 6 July 1993 the 1922 constitution was renewed. Legislative authority is vested in a 100-member unicameral parliament (*Saeima*) (Supreme Council), elected for a three-year term, and a president, who is indirectly elected also for a three-year term by a secret ballot of the *Saeima*. The president nominates a prime minister who nominates a 20-member Cabinet of Ministers, which is accountable to the *Saeima*. President Ulmanis was re-elected for a second term of three years on 18 June 1996.

Political parties

Elections to a new parliament in June 1993 were won by the centre-right Latvia's Way with 36 seats, more than twice as many as its nearest rival. Guntis Ulmanis, of the Latvian Peasants' Union, was elected president by the new assembly, replacing interim head of state Anatolijs Gorbunovs. Birkaus of Latvia's Way led a coalition with the Latvian Peasants' Party until July 1994, when the latter withdrew its support. A coalition comprising Latvia's Way, members of the National Economists Union and Harmony for the People was formed by Maris Gailis of the right-wing Latvia's Way, and took office on 15 September 1994. Final figures for parliamentary elections held September/October 1995 resulted in almost evenly divided support between an anti-Russian populist outsider, the People's Movement for Latvia (Siegerist's Party) (16 seats), the ruling centrist party, Latvia's Way (17 seats) and the country's main left-wing party, Democratic Party (18 seats).

Population

Mostly Latvians (52%), but includes Russians (34%), Belorussian (4.5%), Ukrainians (3.5%), Poles (2.3%). Religions: predominantly Protestant (Lutheran) with Roman Catholics in the east of the country; there is also a Russian Orthodox minority.

Main cities/towns

Riga (population 950,000 in 1994), Daugavpils (128,000), Liepaja (115,000), Jelgava (75,000), Jurmala (66,000).

Language

Latvian is the official language. It is an Indo-European, non-Slavic and non-Germanic language, and is similar only to Lithuanian. Russian, English and German are widely spoken.

Media

Dailies: Neatkariga Cina and Diena.

Weeklies: Dienas Bizness (in Russian and Latvian) is a joint-venture between Dagens Industri of Sweden and the Latvian daily *Diena*, *The Baltic Observer* (English).
Radio: On 15 April 1993 Radio SWH began broadcasting.

Domestic economy

Latvia's economic decline after the banking crisis in 1995 has been halted by the successful implementation of policies adopted by the Bank of Latvia and the government. The budget deficit in Latvia has decreased. The IMF backed a US$43m loan to Latvia at end-April 1996 to help implement the government's economic policy programme.

Employment

The workforce is highly educated and skilled. About 47 per cent is female.

External trade

Between the First and Second World Wars the bulk of Latvian trade was with other European countries. After World War Two, however, the balance of trade shifted to the east so that the majority of Latvian trade was conducted with other republics of the former Soviet Union. Since independence, Latvia's trade patterns began to shift to the west, though its largest trading partners were still Russia, which generally accounted for approximtely 50 per cent of all trade, and Ukraine accounting for approximately 10 per cent. In 1991 Latvia had a positive balance of trade with the former Soviet Union. The EU signed 10-year trade and co-operation accord with Latvia on 11 May 1992 and in April 1993 the government announced that it wished to begin negotiations on associate membership of the EU being granted to Latvia.
Exports: Exports in 1995 totalled Ls688m. Electric energy, rolled steel, mineral fertilisers, varnishes and paints, railway passenger cars, buses, wood, paper, footwear.
Imports: Imports totalled Ls923m in 1995. Electricity, gasoline, diesel fuel, fuel oil, natural gas, liquefied natural gas, coal, coke, pig iron, rolled steel, semi-finished rolled products, aluminium, rolled aluminium, zinc, rolled copper, rolled brass, rolled bronze, mineral fertilisers, synthetic resin and plastics, varnishes and paints, detergents, paper, cement.

Agriculture

The agriculture sector accounted for 25 per cent of GNP in 1994 and employed 16 per cent of the workforce. The reform and privatisation of agriculture proceeded at a much faster rate than in Lithuania and Estonia. As at 1 July 1992 there were 44,500 private farms. Many state-owned collective farms have been privatised. This sector is dominated by dairy farming, pig-breeding, grain production and potatoes. Latvia is self-sufficient in production of cattle and dairy products, pork, sugar beet, flax and potatoes and surpluses of these products are exported to Russia, other CIS republics and the west. Fishing is also important. Of total production from fisheries, 30 per cent is used domestically while 70 per cent is exported. Fish farming is practised in a small way. Forest area 2.6m ha, 41 per cent of total land area. The forestry industry has the potential to become one of the most important areas in the economy.

Industry

The industrial sector accounted for 52 per cent of GNP in 1994 and employed 30 per cent of the workforce. Latvia is one of the most heavily industrialised areas of the former Soviet Union. Well-developed infrastructure and broadly diversified industrial base which includes both light and heavy industries including 'high-tech' manufacturing. Manufacturing industry is concentrated on the production of railway carriages, buses, mopeds, washing machines and telephone systems. Mineral fertilisers and chemicals also produced.

Tourism

Tourism reached its peak in the mid-1980s with Latvia becoming a popular destination within the former Soviet market, but declined after 1988. Interest in tourism grew again after Latvia's independence in 1991 and there has been substantial investment in this sector but it is still underdeveloped. Private sector ownership began earlier in tourism, primarily because of its potential for hard currency earnings. In 1988 three private tourism firms were operating in Latvia, and by 1992, this number had grown to approximately 350. The higher level of service offered by private operators who must undergo a licensing programme, has been well received by tourists and business travellers so that private tourist firms now claim the majority of the market. Private investors have purchased several existing hotels and are refurbishing them to meet western standards.

Mining

Mineral resources include limestone, clay for cement industry, dolomite, gypsum, sand for glass, clay for pottery, sand for silicate products, sand and gravel.

Energy

Heavily dependent on coal, gas and petroleum supplies from other countries. In March 1996 the

COUNTRY PROFILE

Energy (contd): government announced that the Daugava River's hydroelectric stations will be modernised.

Stock exchange

The Riga Stock Exchange (RSE) was officially re-opened 25 July 1995.

Legal system

Comprehensive legislative framework.

Membership of international organisations

Baltic Council, Conference for Security and Co-operation in Europe (CSCE), Council of Baltic Sea States, Council of Europe (from 10 Feb 1995), CSCE, EBRD, IAEA, IDA, IFC, IMF, NACC, Partnership for Peace, WEU (associate partner), World Bank, UN. Latvia became an associate member of the EU on 12 April 1995 and officially applied for membership on 13 October 1995. EFTA signed free trade treaty with Latvia December 1995.

BUSINESS GUIDE

Time

GMT + 2 hrs (GMT + 3 hrs from late Mar to late Sep).

Climate

Temperate climate, but with considerable temperature variations. Mildest areas along the Baltic coast. Summer is warm with relatively mild weather in spring and autumn. Summer sunshine may be nine hours a day. Winter, which lasts from November to mid-March, can be very cold. Rainfall is distributed throughout the year with the heaviest rainfall in August. Snowfalls common in winter months.

Entry requirements

Visa: Visas are not required from citizens of Estonia, Lithuania, Poland, Hungary, UK, Czech Republic and Slovak Republic. It is advisable to obtain visa from embassy before travelling but can also be obtained from the customs checkpoints at Riga International Airport and at Riga passenger port. N.B. Completed application form, original passport (no copies) and one passport-sized photograph are necessary. A Latvian visa issued to the European countries (except the former Yugoslavia and Turkey), Canada, Australia and the USA is also valid for the other Baltic states. Business and tourist visas are free for USA nationals. Validity of visas: business six months; tourist three months. Specify single- or multiple-entry on application.
Currency: Carry small-denomination US dollar bills as well as local currency for tips, taxis, etc.
Customs: Small amount of personal goods duty-free. On arrival declare all foreign currency and valuable items such as jewellery, cameras, computers and musical instruments.

Health precautions

Mandatory: Vaccination certificates are required for cholera or yellow fever if travelling from an infected area.
Advisable: Water precautions recommended (water purification tablets may be useful). It is advisable to be 'in date' for the following immunisations: polio (within 10 years), tetanus (within 10 years), typhoid fever, hepatitis 'A' (moderate risk only). There has been a significant increase in the number of cases of diphtheria. While the low dose, adult booster is unavailable, travellers are advised to be boosted with a reduced dose (0.1ml) of the paediatric single antigen vaccine. If never immunised, use three dose course of the vaccine. Any medicines required by the traveller should be taken by the visitor, and it could be wise to have precautionary antibiotics if going outside major urban centres. A travel kit including a disposable syringe is a reasonable precaution.

Air access

National airlines: In July 1995 Air Baltic (ABC) took over the routes and services previously operated by Latavio. The state-owned airline, Latavio, was declared bankrupt 11 October 1995. Following reorganisation, Latavio will operate as a charter and maintenance centre. Riar (Rigas Aeronavijas) (re-named in 1995, formerly Riga Airlines) flies from Riga to Amsterdam, London Gatwick and Moscow (with the TransAero code).
Other airlines: Aeroflot, Air Express, Czech Airlines (CSA), Estonian Aviation, Finnair, Hamburg Airlines, LOT, Lufthansa, SAS, Transaero, Transeast Airlines.
Tax: International departures US$15, excluding transit passengers and children under two years (Jan 1996).
International airport: Lidosta Airport, Riga (13 km from city centre); one terminal; currency exchange; car hire; post office; business lounge; duty-free stores. A second airport in Liepaja is capable of handling international traffic.

Surface access

Main ports: Warm-water ports at Riga and Ventspils are used for commercial cargo transportation. Solid bulk and container traffic is handled primarily through Riga, while Ventspils is more specialised toward the handling of chemical cargoes and grain, though solid cargoes are also handled. Ventspils has developed into the largest export harbour for oil to western Europe, capable of handling up to 30m tonnes annually. Both ports are undergoing substantial modernisation, with further upgrading and expansion planned. The large volume of import and export activity between the CIS and the West handled by these ports is a substantial source of income, including hard currency earnings which are expected to exceed US$700m annually. Latvia's third developed warm water port, Liepaja, was converted for the use of the former Soviet Baltic fleet. Planning for development of its commercial capacity is under way and some cargo traffic is already being handled. Compared to the same time period in 1994, cargo turnover went up by 33 per cent in Latvian ports in the first half of 1995.

Hotels

Tips included in restaurant bills.

Credit cards

Eurocard, Mastercard, Visa, JCB, Diner's, American Express are accepted in Riga Commercial Bank and Deutsche-Lettische Bank.

Car hire

Hertz, Avis and Europcar have desks in the Arrivals hall of Lidosta Airport. Remember shiny western cars are a magnet for thieves. Make sure car has an alarm and steering lock.

City transport

Guests staying at the de Rome, Metropole and Eurolink hotels can pre-book a minibus transfer from Lidosta Airport or hire a private limousine.
Taxis: Riga Taxi Park desk just outside baggage hall of Lidosta Airport. Taxi fares do not include a tip, but it is usually expected.
Buses: Bus No 22 goes into town from Lidosta Airport.

National transport

Road: Latvia has a highly developed road system. Most domestic transportation needs are met by trucking. Latvia is also being developed as a transportation route for trucking between Scandinavia and Central and Southern Europe. The Via Baltica project is to serve as a transit link between Finland, parts of Scandinavia and St Petersburg in the north, and Poland, Kaliningrad and Belarus in the south. Plans also include a link up with the Trans European Motorway System now being constructed in eastern Europe.
Rail: There is an extensive rail system. To Moscow from Riga, Latvia: 1740 (arrival 1046), 1830 (arr 1200). Also Mon, Wed, Fri at 1940 (arr 1356).

Public holidays

Fixed dates: 1 Jan (New Year's Day), 1 May (Labour Day), 23 Jun (Ligo Day), 24 Jun (St John's Days\Midsummer), 18 Nov (Independence Day), 25-26 Dec (Christmas), 31 Dec (New Year's Eve).
Variable dates: Good Friday, Easter Monday, Mother's Day (second Sun in May).

Working hours

Business: (Mon–Fri) 0900–1800 (appointments best between 0900–1000).
Banking: Mainly (Mon–Fri) 0900–1600; some banks open (Sat) 0900–1230.
Shops: (Mon–Fri) 1000–1900, (Sat) 1000–1600. Grocery and department stores are usually open from 0800 until 1900. There are quite a few food stores in Riga that provide 24-hour service.

Telecommunications

Telecommunications and international access have improved substantially in the last few years. Plans for further improvements include expansion of the national and international telephone systems and the development of a modern mobile telecommunications system. A mobile cellular telephone network provides both domestic and international service.
Telephone and telefax: N.B. From August 1995 the telephone numbers of subscribers to Lattelekom digital network will contain seven digits beginning with digit 7. If in difficulty, dial 079 for information.
Countries which have not introduced the new code use code + 469, or, calling via Moscow, 7013. Calls from Latvia are booked in advance by dialling 8-194; urgent calls are booked by dialling 8-15.
Dialling code for Latvia: IDD access code + 371, followed by area code (2 for Riga (see also note above), followed by subscriber's number.
Telex: Available in the Main Post Office in Riga (open 24 hours).
Telegram: For services from public phones dial 06.

Banking

Two-tier banking system. Approximately 40 commercial banks operate. Société Générale of France, the third largest bank in Europe, started operations in Riga on 3 July 1995.
Central bank: Bank of Latvia (Latvijas Banka).
Other banks: Bank Baltija went into liquidation in April 1996. Mid-1996 the European Bank for Reconstruction and Development (EBRD) took a 23 per cent stake in Latvijas Unibanka, Latvia's largest commercial bank with an investment of about US$10m. See also 'Business Directory, Banking'.

Representation in capital

Belgium, Canada, Denmark, Estonia, Finland, France, Germany, Italy, Lithuania, Norway, Poland, Russia, Sweden, Taiwan, UK, USA. Embassies: Washington, New York, London, Paris, Bonn, Copenhagen, Brussels, Stockholm, Helsinki, Moscow, Tallinn, Vilnius. Honorary Consulates: Victoria, Ottawa, Vienna, Oslo, Edegem (Belgium), Trieste, Berlin, Zurich, Piraeus, Caracas, Tel Aviv, Seoul, Taipei, New Delhi.

BUSINESS DIRECTORY

Hotels

Riga (area code 2)
de Rome (tel: 820-050; fax: 820-058).

Eurolink (tel: 820-060; fax: 820-064).

Fremad (tel: 221-611).

Latvia (tel: 212-525, 212-503).

Hotels (contd):
Man-Tess (tel: 212-525, 212-503).

Metropole (tel: 820-065; fax: 820-074).

Ridzene (tel: 324-433).

Riga (tel: 216-107, 216-109).

Turists (tel: 615-455).

Useful telephone numbers

Fire brigade: 01.

Police: 02.

Ambulance: 03.

Road accidents: 377-000.

Accidents on railway, water, air transport: 226-343, 203-948.

Car hire

Riga
Avis: international airport (tel: 207-353; fax: 882-0441).

Europcar: 10 Basteja Boulevard, LV-1050 (tel: 222-637; fax: 782-0360, 782-0510).

Hertz: reservations office: (tel: 720-7980; fax: 720-7981).

Chambers of commerce

Chamber of Agriculture, Daugavpils iela 72, LV-1003 Riga (tel: 722-4360).

Latvian Chamber of Commerce, Brivibas bulvaris 21, LV-1849 Riga (tel: 722-5595; fax: 782-0092).

Latvian Chamber of Trade and Commerce, Brivibas bulvaris 21, LV-1849 Riga (tel: 733-3228; fax: 733-2276).

Banking

Bank of Latvia (central bank), Kr Valdemara iela 2A, Riga LV-1050 (tel: 702-2275, 702-2276; fax: 702-2300).

AKO Banka, 18 Smilsu St, LV-1050 Riga (tel: 222-3840, 222-6633; fax: 222-4019).

Association of Commercial Banks, Stabu iela 18, Riga LV-1001 (tel: 227-1640; fax: 782-8170).

Baltijas Tranzitu Banka, 3 13 Janvara St, LV-1050 Riga (tel: 222-4261, 222-5031, 222-3940; fax: 222-5031).

Banko Atmoda, 21 L Pils St, LV-1050 Riga (tel: 222-3635, 222-2562; fax: 222-2562).

Commercial Innovation Bank, 14 Basteykaina Str, LV1050 Riga.

Communication Development Commercial Bank, 1 Valnu Street, 226208 Riga (tel & fax: 226-208).

Daugavas Banka, 40/42 Maskavas St, LV-1018 Riga (tel: 221-5288, 221-5286; fax: 221-5288).

Dinastija Bank, 7 Antonijas St, LV-1239 Riga (tel: 232-3661, 232-3728; fax: 232-3851).

Latvian Land Bank, 2 Republikas Square, Riga (tel: 321-713).

Latvian Savings Bank, 58 A Caka Street, Riga (tel: 276-140).

Latvijas Biznesa Banka, 3 M Pils St, LV-1050 Riga (tel: 232-5796, 222-6486, 221-1151; fax: 222-0249).

Latvijas Ekonomiska Komercbanka, 21 Birznieka-Upisa St, LV-1011 Riga (tel: 221-0852, 221-0868, 222-1376; fax: 221-0654).

Latvijas Hipoteku un Zemes Banka, 4 Doma Sq, LV-1977 Riga (tel: 222-7600, 222-8866, 222-5462; fax: 782-0143).

Latvijas Industriala Banka (LAIN-banka), 6 Grácinieku St, LV-1587 Riga (tel: 221-6528, 221-6529; fax: 222-1135).

Latvijas Investiciju Banka, 15 Kalku St, LV-1050 Riga (tel: 222-8188, 222-7706, 221-3383, 222-9883; fax: 222-2426).

Latvijas Kapital-banka, 148a Brivibas St, LV-1012 Riga (tel: 236-4016, 236-4543, 236-4327; fax: 227-0635).

Latvijas Krájbanka, 1 Palasta St, LV-1954 Riga (tel: 222-2871, 221-2392, 221-3121; fax: 221-0807).

Latvijas Kreditbanka, 1/4 Smilsu St, LV-1920 Riga (tel: 222-6631, 221-2671; fax: 222-8813).

Latvijas Privatbanka, 11 Stabu St, LV-1001 Riga (tel: 227-5537, 227-7586, 229-3548; fax: 229-4984).

Latvijas Tirdzniecibas Banka, 4 Trijàdibas St, LV-1048 Riga (tel: 261-3608, 261-1032; fax: 261-6055).

Latvijas Unibanka, Vecriga, 23 Pils Street, Riga (tel: 220-244; fax: 323-487).

Latvijas Universala Banka, 23 L Pils St, LV-1047 Riga (tel: 221-2808; fax: 221-0775).

Latvijas Zemes Banka, 2 Republikas Sq, LV-1924 Riga (tel: 232-1713, 232-7140, 232-7647, 232-7126, 232-7431; fax: 232-7384).

Multibanka, 57 Elizabetes St, LV-1772 Riga (tel: 228-3445, 228-9546; fax: 782-8232).

Parekss Banka, 3 Smilsu St, LV-1522 Riga (tel: 221-2851, 222-1649; fax: 221-5201).

Parex-Bank, 8 Kr Valdemara Street, Riga (tel: 325-305; fax: 224-576).

Paritato Bank, 74 Dzelzavas St, LV-1080 Riga (tel: 257-4653, 222-2934, 934-3583; fax: 222-5473).

Rielumu Banka, 7 Vesetas St, LV-1013 Riga (tel: 237-1049, 237-5205, 237-6157).

Rigas Apvienota Baltijas Banka, 15 Ganibu Dambis, LV-1045 Riga (tel: 233-3803, 233-2528, 232-3281, 232-2264; fax: 733-4528).

Rigas Komercbanka, 6 Smilsu St, LV-1803 Riga (tel: 232-3967, 232-5169, 232-4568; fax: 232-3449, 232-2521).

Rigas Naftas un Kimijas Banka (Neftehimbank), 149 K Valdemara St, LV-1013 Riga (tel: 236-2638, 236-2181; fax: 237-9913).

Sakaru Banka, 3 Teára St, LV-1050 Riga (tel: 222-6208, 236-2410, 221-3788; fax: 782-8061).

Saules Banka, 16 Smilsu St, LV-1050 Riga (tel: 222-6158, 222-5369, 222-4541; fax: 222-5369).

Societa Generale, 55 Brivibas St, LV-1050 Riga (tel: 731-0051/53; fax: 731-0060).

Trasta Komercbanka, 8 Pirts St, LV-1003 Riga (tel: 714-5921, 714-5772; fax: 714-5854).

Vácijas-Latvijas Banka (Deutsch-Lettische Bank), 26 Kalku St, LV-1050 Riga (tel: 222-4514, 221-0584; fax: 882-0160).

VEF Banka, 197 Brivibas St, LV-1039 Riga (tel: 256-5202, 256-7977, 236-3261, 236-3726; fax: 782-1331).

Viktorija Bank, 19 Rurgeneva St, LV-1079 Riga (tel: 253-8203; fax: 253-8210).

Principal newspapers

Atmoda, Vecpilsetas 13–15, 226250 Riga (tel: 210-452; fax: 213-978).

The Baltic Observer, Balasta Dambis 3, 226081 Riga (tel: 462-119; fax: 463-387).

Diena, Smilsu 1–3, 226900 Riga (tel: 210-820; fax: 228-826).

Travel information

Air Baltic Corporation (ABC), Riga Airport, Riga LV-1053 (tel: 207-069; fax: 207-369, 223-659).

Latvian Association of Tourism, Bruninieku iela 48/50, LV-1001 Riga (tel: 221-3652; fax: 722-9945).

Latvian Hotel Association, Elizabetes iela 55/404, LV-1050 Riga (tel: 221-1755; fax: 782-0240).

Latvian Tourist Board, Pils Sq 4, 1050 Riga (tel & fax: 229-945).

Lidosta Airport flight enquiries (tel: 207-009; fax: 348-654).

Riar (Rigas Aeronavijas) (re-named in 1995, formerly Riga Airlines), 1 Melluzu Street, Riga LV-1067 (tel: 424-283, 424-710; fax: 860-189).

Other useful addresses

Association of Insurers, Valnu iela 1, Riga LV-1912 (tel: 722-4375, fax: 724-3286).

Baltic Data House Ltd (marketing research), Akas iela 5/7, Riga LV-1050 (tel: 227-6144; fax: 227-6246, 934-6442).

British Embassy, 5 Alunana Street, Riga LV-1010 (tel: 733-8126; fax: 733-8132).

Central Statistical Bureau of Latvia, Lacplesa Str, 1 Riga (tel: 285-929, 270-126; fax: 830-137).

Department of Citizenship and Immigration, 6 Raina Blvd, Riga LV-1181 (tel: 219-406, 219-181; fax: 332-154).

Department of Customs, 1a Valdemara Street, Riga LV-1050 (tel: 323-858; fax: 433-440).

Enterprise Support Centre, Perses iela 2-518, Riga LV-1011 (tel: 782-8250; fax: 782-8251).

Government Information Agency, 36 Brivibas Boulevard, Riga LV-1070 (tel: 282-828; fax: 281-781).

Interlatvija Foreign Trade Association, Komunaru Bulv 1, 226010 Riga (tel: 332-952, 333-597; fax 226-070).

International Advertising Association, Liela Pils iela 9, Riga LV-1755 (tel: 722-8361; fax: 722-9252).

BUSINESS DIRECTORY

Other useful addresses (contd):
Latvia Business Union (commercial information), Bundaga PO Box 475, 226001 Riga (tel: 320-888; fax: 217-633).

Latvian Association of Private Entrepreneurs, Strelnieku iela 6, LV-1010 Riga (tel: 7188-30212).

Latvian Association of Traders, Gertrudes iela 36, LV-1011 Riga (tel: 721-7372; fax: 782-1010).

Latvian Business Consultants' Association, Jauniela 24, Riga LV-1050 (tel: 722-0320, 782-0076; fax: 722-8926).

Latvian Development Agency, Business Information Centre, Perses iela 2, Riga LV-1442 (tel: 728-3425; fax: 728-2524, 782-0458).

Latvian Privatisation Agency, Kr Valdemara iela 31, Riga LV-1887 (tel: 732-1084, 732-1929; fax: 783-0363).

Latvian Retailers' Association, Kr Barona iela 48/50, Riga LV-1011 (tel: 721-7372; fax: 782-1010).

LETA News Agency, Palasta 10, 226947 Riga (tel: 223-462; fax 320-5920).

Main Post Office, Brivibas Bulvaris 21, Riga (tel: 224-155; fax: 733-1920).

Ministry of Agriculture, Republikas Lauk 2, 226168 Pdp Riga (tel: 325-107, 325-695 (External Affairs Dept); fax 320-593).

Ministry of Economic Reforms, Brivibas Bulv 36, 226169 Pdp Riga (tel: 288-446; fax 280-883).

Ministry of Economics, Brivibas Boulevard 36, LV 1519 Riga (tel: 224-444, 611-884; fax: 224-794); Department of Energy Development (tel: 728-7730, 722-0151; fax: 733-8026, 722-4794).

Ministry of Education, Culture and Science, Valnu lela 2, 507, 1098 Riga (tel: 722-3942; fax: 243-127; e-mail: vetpmu@com.latnet.lv).

Ministry of Environmental Protection and Regional Development, Peldu St, 25, 1949 Riga (tel: 226-578; fax: 782-0442; e-mail: Saule@varam.gov.lv).

Ministry of Finance, Smilsu 1-4, 5th Floor, 1050 Riga (tel: 226-672), 211-752 (External Affairs Dept); World Bank Technical Unit (tel: 722-0348; fax: 782-0168).

Ministry of Finance, Republic of Latvia (Securities Department), Smilsu iela 1, Riga LV-1932 (tel: 221-1656; fax: 782-0010).

Ministry of Foreign Affairs, 36 Brivibas Boulevard, Riga LV-1395 (tel: 222-694, 223-307; fax: 227-755).

Ministry of Foreign Trade, Kr Valdemara 26, 226329 Pdp Riga (tel: 286-489).

Ministry of Welfare of the Republic of Latvia, Skolas Str, 281331 Riga (tel: 271-173; fax; 276-115).

Ministry of Industry, Smilsu 1, 226918 Pdp Riga (tel: 227-344, 225-085 (Foreign Trade Dept; tx: 161-110 Laim Su).

Ministry of Transport, Gogola lela 3, 1743, Riga (tel: 702-8241; fax: 728-1454; External Department (tel: 285-507; fax: 211-780, 220-294 (mobile)).

Ministry of Transport, Department of Communications, Elizabetes Str 41/43, 1010 Riga (tel: 325-478; fax: 270-253).

Public Investment Unit, Brivibas Blv. 36, 1519 Riga (tel: 701-3122; fax: 782-0458).

Riga Exchange, Grecinicku Str 22-24 (tel: 224-737, 226-292; fax: 228-650).

Riga Stock Exchange, Doma Laukums 6, Riga LV-1885 (tel: 721-2431, 722-8111; fax: 782-0504).

State Property Fund (privatisation), Ministry of Economics, 36 Brivibas Boulevard, LV 1519 Riga (tel: 213-501; fax: 280-882); external department (tel: 722-5426; fax: 828-223).

US Embassy, Raina Bulvaris 7, LV-1050 Riga (tel: 210-005, 220-367; fax: 782-0047).

Ventspils Tirdznecibas Osta (Ventspils Commercial Port), Dzintaru Street 22, Ventspils LV-3602 (tel: 362-2821; fax: 362-1231).

World Trade Centre, Elizabetes iela 2, Riga LV-1340 (tel: 732-2242, 783-0034; fax: 783-0035).

Liechtenstein

Howard Hill

Liechtenstein began its second year of European Economic Area (EEA) membership in May 1996. In a ballot held in April 1995, 55.9 per cent of voters wanted this tiny nation to become the 18th member of this Europe-wide trade zone. A complicating factor inLiechtenstein's EEA membership was the fact that Switzerland, which is an integral part of Liechtenstein's economic life, remains outside the group.

Politics

With slightly over 30,000 inhabitants and an area of just 160 sq km, Liechtenstein is a delicate nation which has, in the 1990s, increasingly managed to strike a balance between protecting its prosperity and playing a wider European and international role. The country's head of state, the conservative Prince Hans Adam II, is largely responsible for this new balance.

The Prince is widely known as the last reigning European monarch who still retains significant political power. Ruling since 1989, he has orchestrated a careful re-alignment of Liechtenstein, pulling it further away from the Swiss economy's gravitational pull while avoiding any dangerous alienation of this big economic brother. During his reign Liechtenstein has become a member of the United Nations (UN), European Free Trade Association (EFTA), the General Agreement on Tariffs and Trade (GATT), and now EEA.

Economy

Liechtenstein's inflation rate was a modest 1.8 per cent in 1995, which was double the rate of just 0.9 per cent in 1994. Industrial exports amounted to Swf2.9 billion in 1995, which is higher than the 1994 figure of Swf2.6 billion and represents a not-insubstantial gain in real terms.

The April 1995 EEA vote was held to ensure that the public still supported EEA membership after a revision of the Swiss-Liechtenstein customs union. Switzerland and Liechtenstein have traditionally enjoyed a special relationship, having been bound together by a customs union, a monetary union, and an open border. But only 15 per cent of Liechtenstein's exports go to Switzerland, while 70 per cent go to the EEA countries. The EEA membership has inevitably meant closer ties to neighbouring Austria, another EEA partner.

About one third of the workforce is involved in industry and Liechtenstein has a continuous shortage of labour. The small local population is simply not able to fill all of the jobs on offer. As a result, Liechtenstein has to import a large portion of its labour force.

Tourism plays a role in the economy and employs 4 per cent of the workforce. However, there is very little room for expansion of this industry because of the strain it would put on the environment and labour force. Liechtenstein welcomes about 70,000 visitors each year but most are on very short holidays of only a day or two.

One of the main manufacturing companies in Liechtenstein is Hilti, among the world's largest providers of industrial fastener tools. Partly because of the precariousness of the domestic labour supply, Hilti has located much of its manufacturing off-shore in the US, the UK and Austria. Hilti's group turnover in fiscal 1995 was down by 11 per cent to Swf1.983 billion. The strong Swiss franc contributed to this drop. Another factor was the slow-down in the German, Austrian and Japanese construction industries. However, Hilti was able to off-set the slump in its traditional markets with increased penetration of non-traditional Asian markets such as Vietnam, China and Indonesia. Net profit increased by 15 per cent to Swf192.5 million but operating profit fell by 22 per cent to Swf171.4 million.

Financial sector

Liechtenstein is viewed by many as a favoured international haven for money, due to its banking secrecy laws and low taxes. Without question, much of the country's prosperity comes from this status in the financial world. Liechtenstein's invest-

KEY FACTS — Liechtenstein

Official title: Principality of Liechtenstein

Head of state: Prince Hans Adam II

Head of government: Prime Minister Mario Frick

Ruling party: Coalition government: Vaterlandische Union (Patriotic union) (VU) and Fortschrittliche Bürgerpartei (Progressive Citizens' Party) (FBP)

Capital: Vaduz

Official Languages: German

Currency: Swiss Franc (Swf) = 100 centimes/rappen

Exchange rate: Swf1.34 per US$ (Dec 1996)

Area: 160 sq km

Population: 30,300 (1995)

GNP per capita: US$33,000 (1995)*

Unemployment: 1.5% (1994)

Inflation: 1.8% (1995)

Visitor numbers: 70,000 (1995)*

* estimated figure

ment funds have been bolstered by the country's EEA membership, which now allows non-discriminatory access to European Union (EU) markets.

Although the secrecy aspect is widely touted, Liechtenstein does not have a reputation for being a haven for dirty money. With the entry of Liechtenstein into the EEA, a law on money laundering automatically came into effect making this activity a criminal offence if used to 'clean up' money gained from illegal drugs or insider trading.

One of the top local financial players, BIL GT Group, changed its name to Liechtenstein Global Trust (LGT) effective from 3 January 1996. This was part of the group's efforts to reorganise its private banking and assets management functions. LGT is controlled by the country's Royal Family. In mid-1996 LGT announced a US$300 acquisition of US-based Chancellor Capital Management (formerly Citicorp Investment Management). Chancellor has 300 institutional clients and manages some US$33 billion worth of funds.

By rank, the three top banks in Liechtenstein are Liechtensteinische Landesbank, LGT Bank in Liechtenstein, and Verwaltungsund& Privat-Bank. As of the end of 1995 the Liechtensteinsche Landesbank had assets worth US$8.18 million and LGT Bank in Liechtenstein had assets of US$7.64 billion.

KEY INDICATORS

	Unit	1990	1991	1992	1993	1994
Population	'000	28.9	29.4	30.0	30.0	30.0
Gross national product (GNP)	US$m	1,020	–	1,000	1,050	–
GNP per capita	US$	34,000	33,000	–	35,000	–
Inflation	%	–	5.9	4.0	3.3	0.9
Unemployment	%	–	0.2	–	1.7	1.5
Exchange rate	SwFr per US$	1.38	1.43	1.41	1.48	1.37

COUNTRY PROFILE — LIECHTENSTEIN

Historical profile

1719 Independence, followed in early nineteenth century by a period of French domination, then close connection with Austria until 1918.
1938-70 Progressive Citizens' Party (FBP) majority party in government coalition.
1970-74 Patriotic Union (VU) majority party in coalition, followed at next election by FBP.
1978 Admitted to Council of Europe. VU-led coalition, confirmed at succeeding general elections.
1984 Prince Hans Adam took over executive power from his father.

Political system

Union of hereditary monarchy and popular sovereignty. The 1921 constitution provides for a unicameral parliament (*Landtag,* 25 seats elected for a four-year term), which elects a five-member government, which is thereafter officially nominated by the head of state. Elections are held every four years on the basis of proportional representation. Voting rights for women on national issues achieved in 1984, and on local matters two years later. In the February 1993 elections voters returned to power the two parties that have ruled for over 50 years: the Progressive Citizens Party (FBP) 12 seats; the Fatherland Union (VU) 11 seats. The environmental group, Free List (FL), won two seats. Fresh elections were held in October 1993 after no-confidence vote. VU won 13 seats and FBP 11. Mario Frick became prime minister.

Population

The population included 11,579 resident aliens in 1995.

Main cities/towns

Vaduz (capital, population 5,085 in 1995), Schaan (5,106), Balzers (3,954), Triesen (3,885).

Language

German is the official language; Allemannish is spoken (dialect of German).

Media

Press: Two main dailies: *Liechtensteiner Vaterland* (Vaduz) and *Liechtensteiner Volksblatt* (Schaan).
Broadcasting: No local commercial radio, though this is now planned. Swiss, German and Austrian TV and radio broadcasts received (with commercials).

Advertising

No restrictions on newspaper advertising.

Domestic economy

Highly industrialised, export-based economy with well-developed sector. Ranks as one of the wealthiest countries in the world. Strong economic dependence on Swiss economy through customs and currency union. Tourism sector is important earner of foreign exchange. Despite being buffeted by the down-drafts of 1992, Liechtenstein's economy recovered and remained in relatively good condition. The extremely high ratio of self-financing enjoyed by domestic businesses plus their ability, if necessary, to fall back on private wealth, helped them persevere through lean periods.

Employment

About half the workforce employed in secondary sector. Extremely low levels of unemployment and heavy dependence on border-crossing workers (mostly Austrian and Swiss).

External trade

Financial services and tourism make significant contribution to balance of payments. Liechtenstein joined the EEA 1 May 1995.
Exports: Rapid growth in exports of machinery, equipment, metals, ceramics and chemicals.
Main destinations: EU (typically 45% of total), EFTA (19%).
Imports: Imports mainly from EU and EFTA countries, consist largely of raw materials and foodstuffs.

Agriculture

Small-scale, employing only about 2 per cent of workforce, compared with 40 per cent in 1930s. Activity concentrated on animal husbandry and farming of fodder cereals.

Industry

Owing to lack of raw materials and small domestic market, sector is export-based and centred on specialised and high-tech production. Manufacturing centred on machine building, precision engineering and metal working industries, employs nearly 40 per cent of the workforce. Also traditional industries such as chemicals (mainly pharmaceuticals), textiles, ceramics and food processing. The production of materials for dental medicine, of micro-sections for optics and electronics, the manufacture of preserves and deep-frozen products, upholstery, and varnishes, have all attained growing importance.

Tourism

Some 70,000 tourist arrivals each year, 33 per cent of whom come from Germany and 22 per cent from Switzerland.

Energy

Dependent on imported energy.

Legal system

Largely based on Austrian and Swiss law.

Membership of international organisations

CEPT, Council of Europe, CSCE, ECE, EEA (from 1 May 1995), EFTA, EUTELSAT, EPO, IAEA, IAEO, ICJ, INTELSAT, Interpol, ITU, UIT, UN, UNCTAD, UNICEF, UNIDO, UPU, WIPO, WTO.

BUSINESS GUIDE

Time

GMT + 1 hr (GMT + 2 from late Mar to late Sep).

BUSINESS GUIDE

LIECHTENSTEIN

Climate

Varies with altitude, generally mild and often windy. Average summer temperature 17°C. Average winter temperature 1°C.

Clothing

Mediumweight throughout year, topcoat in winter.

Entry requirements

Currency: No currency restrictions (currency union with Switzerland). N.B. Traveller's cheques must be endorsed by companies, not private persons.
Customs: Restricted amounts of alcoholic beverages, tobacco and gifts (up to value of Swf100) may be imported duty free.

Air access

Nearest international airport is Kloten, Zurich (ZRH). Approx 130 km from Vaduz.

Surface access

Good road access from Switzerland and to a lesser extent Austria; local trains (Austrian Federal Railways) do not serve Vaduz – station only at Nendeln (halts at Schaan and Schaanwald). Vaduz can be reached by bus from Buchs (Switzerland).
Motorway connections: Balzers, Vaduz, Schaan, Bendern, Ruggell.

Hotels

Around 50 hotels and inns supplying more than 1,200 beds. Tips included in hotel and restaurant bills.

Currency

Exchange rate: Responsibility of the Swiss National Bank. The Swiss franc has been floating since 1973, with occasional interventions by the central bank during unstable market conditions.

Foreign exchange information

Account restrictions: By agreement with the Swiss National Bank, accounts may be opened only when the identity of the depositor is ascertained and certain other conditions have been met.
Trade policy: There are no exchange controls over imports or exports. The only quantity restrictions on imports apply to agricultural produce.

Car hire

Service offered by Hertz AG and Beck Taxi in Vaduz. Driver must have held a valid driving licence for at least one year and be over 20 years of age. Speed limit 50 kph in city, 80 kph outside.

City transport

Regular and inexpensive post bus service. Easily obtainable taxi service. Tipping not customary.

National transport

All villages can be reached by postal bus service. Restricted rail network, with stations at Nendelny and halts at Schaan and Schaanwald. Nearest main stations at Buchs and Sargans in St Gallen, Switzerland and Feldkirch in Austria.

Public holidays

Fixed dates: 1 Jan, 6 Jan (Epiphany), 2 Feb (Candlemas), 19 Mar St Joseph), 1 May (Labour Day), 15 Aug (Assumption/National Day), 8 Sep (Nativity of Our Lady), 1 Nov (All Saints'), 8 Dec (Immaculate Conception), 25-26 Dec.
Variable dates: Shrove Tuesday, Good Friday, Easter Monday, Ascension Day, Whit Monday, Corpus Christi.

Working hours

Business: (Mon–Fri) 0800–1730.
Government: (Mon–Fri) 0800–1630.
Banking: (Mon–Fri) 0800–1200, 1330–1630.
Shops: (Mon–Fri) 0800–1200, 1330–1830, (Sat) 0800–1600.

Telecommunications

Highly efficient telex, telefax and telephone service.
Telephone: International dialling code: 4175. There are no area codes.
Telex: Telex code 45 FL.
Postal services: N.B. Swiss stamps cannot be used on letters posted in Liechtenstein.

Banking

International offshore financial centre. Largest single supplier of fiduciary funds in Europe. Three main banks in operation: Liechtensteinische Landesbank, LGT Bank in Liechtenstein, Verwaltungs und Privat-Bank AG. Close association with Swiss banking system and strict secrecy laws in operation.

BUSINESS DIRECTORY

Hotels

Vaduz
Engel, Staedtle 13 (tel: 203-1316; fax: 81-159).

Landhaus Prasch, Zollstr. 16 (tel: 24-664).

Löwen, Herrengasse 35 (tel: 20-066).

Mühle, Landstrasse 120, 9490 (tel: 24-141; fax: 21-458).

Park Sonnenhof, Mareestrasse 29 (tel: 21-192; fax: 20-053).

Real, Städtle 21, 9490 (tel: 22-222; fax: 20-891).

Schlössle, Franz Josef Strasse 60 (tel: 25-621; fax: 20-710).

Car hire

Hertz: reservation offices (Zurich, Switzerland) (tel: (41-1)730-1077; fax: (41-1)730-8050).

Taxis

Beck Taxi, Im Riet 336, FL-9495 Triesen (tel: 23-336).

Bischof Claudia, Taxi- und Pilotendienst, In der Ballota 2A, 9494 Schaan (tel: 23-597).

Piccolo Taxi Lettstrasse 4, 9490 Vaduz (22-221).

Taxi Wachter AG, Zollstrasse 82, 9494 Schaan (tel: 21-866).

Chambers of commerce

Liechtensteinische Industrie-und Handelskammer, PO Box 232, Josef Rheinberger-Strasse 11, FL-9490 Vaduz (tel:22-744; fax: 81-503).

Banking

LGT Bank in Liechtenstein AG, Herrengasse 12, FL-9490 Vaduz (tel: 51-122; fax: 51-522).

Liechtensteinische Landesbank (National Bank of Liechtenstein), Staedtle 44, FL-9490 Vaduz (tel: 68-811; fax: 68-358).

Verwaltungs-und Privat-Bank AG, Im Zentrum, FL-9490 Vaduz (tel: 56-655; fax: 56-500).

Principal newspapers

Liechtensteiner Volksblatt, Lindenplatz, TFL-9494 Schaan (tel: 24-242; fax: 22-912).

Liechtensteiner Vaterland, Fürst Franz-Josef Strasse 13, FL-9490 Vaduz (tel: 22-826; fax: 29-192).

Travel information

Liechtenstein National Tourist Office, Städtle 38, Postfach 139, FL-9490 Vaduz (tel: 21-443, 66-288; fax: 66-460); Tourist Office, FL09497 Malbun (tel: 26-577).

Reisa Reisebuero AG (travel agency), Heiligkreuz 19, FL-9490 Vaduz (tel: 23-734; fax: 22-924).

Other useful addresses

Amt fuer Volkswirtschaft (national statistics office), Kirchastrasse 7, FL-9490 Vaduz (tel: 236-6871; fax: 236-6889).

Postillion-Reisen AG, Landstrasse 9, FL-9494 Schaan (tel: 26-565; fax: 27-037).

Internet sites

Liechtenstein News (http:\\www.news.li; E-mail: news@news.li).

Lithuania

Bob Jiggins

In the October 1996 parliamentary elections the ruling Lithuanian Democratic Labour Party (LDLP) was defeated by a resurgent Homeland Union led by the hero of Lithuanian independence, Vytautas Landsbergis. A series of major scandals and the harsh economic reform programme demanded by the international financial institutes, led to widespread dissatisfaction with the LDLP during 1995 and 1996. After winning 70 of the 141 parliamentary seats the Homeland Union formed a coalition with the centre-right Christian Democratic Party and the Centre Union to gain an absolute majority.

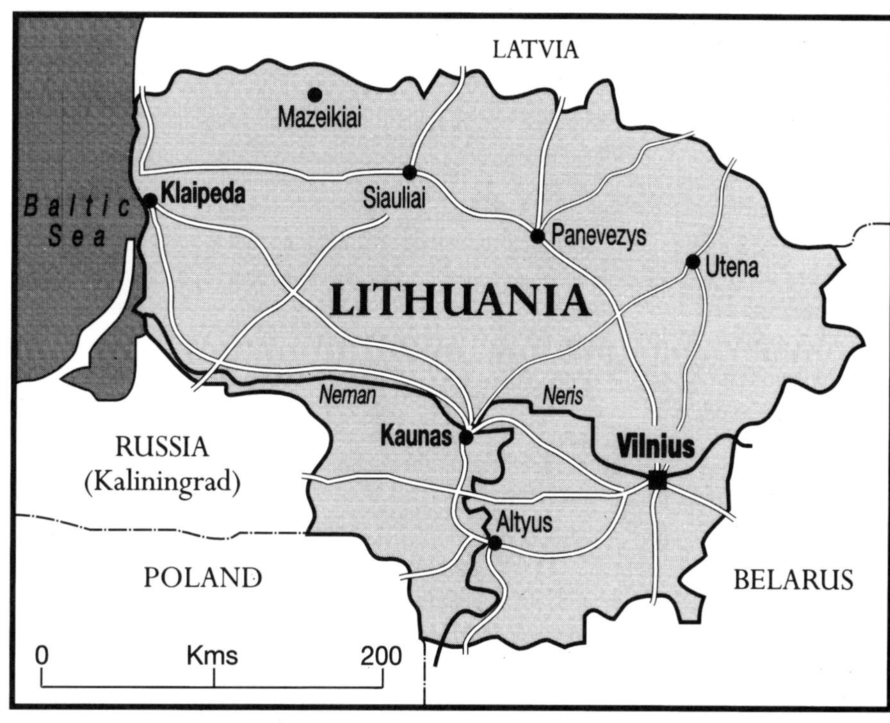

Politics

Scandals have recently emerged within this small Baltic state, which had a negative effect on the LDLP government's popularity. Some of this, to be sure, is due to the insecurity of many Lithuanians, but it is in no small measure related to the series of charges of corruption within the banking system, other financial services and the largely moribund privatisation programme.

In October 1995 the economics minister (responsible for privatisation) was sacked and replaced by Vytas Navickas, who was likewise replaced early in 1996 by Bronius Bradauskas. His task is to restart the process and persuade foreign investors that Lithuania is after all a country worth considering.

This responsibility is not an enviable one. Navickas's predecessor, Aleksandras Vasiliaukas, was largely blamed for the collapse of Aurasbankas, and this has been followed by the suspension of two of the country's largest banks, the Joint-Stock Innovation Bank and the Litimpeks bank. The suspension of the last two is interesting, in that various government ministers and highly placed officials of the ruling party – including the now ex-Prime Minister Adolfas Slezevicius – withdrew funds from the banks immediately prior to their collapse. Other investors were not so lucky, and street demonstrations occurred demanding the resignation of various perceived guilty parties, and the arrest of the directors.

President Algirdas Brazauskas criticised the ministers involved and ordered them to return their deposits but initially refused to dismiss them, arguing instead that it was purely a matter of personal ethics. Despite calls from other quarters for their resignation, they refused to do so, while Foreign Minister Povilas Gylys and Defence Minister Linas Linkevivius offered their resignations in protest. The president has also refused to accept them stating that the stability of the political system overrides their personal consciences.

Not surprisingly the conservative opposition has sought to make political capital from these and other affairs, calling for the resignation of the government and forcing no confidence votes in the Seimas (parliament). The government survived mainly because LDLP deputies originally

KEY FACTS — Lithuania

Official title: Republic of Lithuania

Head of state: President Algirdas Brazauskas (since 25 Nov 1992; elected by direct vote 15 Feb 1993)

Head of government: Prime Minister Gediminas Vagnorius (from Nov 1996)

Ruling party: Three party coalition of Homeland Union, Christian Democratic Party and Centre Union (from Dec 1996)

Capital: Vilnius

Official Languages: Lithuanian

Currency: Litas (Lt) = 100 cents (introduced 25 June 1993)

Exchange rate: Lt4.00 per US$ (Dec 1996)

Area: 65,200 sq km

Population: 3.72m (1995)

GDP per capita: US$1,078 (1995)*

GDP real growth: 2.5% (1995)

GNP per capita: US$1,500 (1994)

GNP real growth: 5% (1995)*

Labour force: 1.7m (1994)

Unemployment: 6.1% (1995)

Inflation: 35.7% (1995) (consumer prices)

Trade balance: -US$200m (1995)*

Foreign debt: US$687m (1 Jan 1996)

* estimated figure

KEY INDICATORS — Lithuania

	Unit	1991	1992	1993	1994	1995
Population	m	3.75	3.76	3.75	3.73	3.72
Gross national product (GNP)	US$bn	11.60	6.40	4.90	5.60	–
GNP per capita	US$	3,100	1,700	1,300	1,500	–
GNP real growth	%	-13.1	-56.6	-16.5	1.5	*5.0
Inflation	%	224.7	1,020.5	409.2	72.0	35.7
Consumer prices	1994=100	–	11.4	58.1	100.0	139.7
Unemployment	%	1.0	1.4	4.2	3.6	6.1
Employment	'000	1,898	1,855	1,778	1,675	–
Industrial production						
Manufacturing	Dec 1990=100	126.4	80.1	59.0	41.4	41.8
Cement	'000 tonnes	3,126	1,485	727	735	649
Mineral fertiliser	'000 tonnes	469.0	284.3	225.1	272.9	389.0
Exports	US$m	–	852.3	2,025.8	2,029.2	2,300.0
Imports	US$m	–	601.9	2,180.5	2,234.1	2,500.0
Balance of trade	US$m	–	250.4	-154.7	-204.9	*-200.0
Foreign debt	US$m	–	102	55	8	*388
Current account	US$m	–	–	-85.7	-93.8	*-50.0
Total reserves minus gold	US$m	–	45.31	350.35	525.45	761.67
Foreign exchange	US$m	–	44.00	275.20	510.30	743.50
Interbank rate	%	–	–	–	69.5	26.8
Deposit rate	%	–	–	48.7	27.4	8.4
Lending rate	%	–	–	91.9	62.3	27.1
Exchange rate	Lt per US$	–	–	**3.9	4.0	4.0

* estimated figure **Litas introduced 25 Jun 1993

abstained, although they eventually withdrew support from ex-Prime Minister Slezevicius. Ultimately the president was compelled to request parliament to dismiss the prime minister, an act which it duly performed on 8 February 1996. Slezevicius subsequently resigned as leader of the LDLP having little support within the party. A new prime minister, Mindaugas Stankevicius, was thus appointed on 15 February 1996, vacating his portfolio as local government minister. A minor reshuffle took place with Stankevicius vowing to continue policy much as before, albeit with greater attention to economic reform. As the parliamentatry elections approached, the government's lack of authority was very evident. The central bank governor, Kazys Ratkevicius, had been offering his resignation for some time (despite presidential misgivings) and was replaced by Reinoldijus Sarkinas. The banking crisis is not yet over though, as a number of other institutions have either been closed or threatened with closure. Politically the most embarrassing of these is the investigation of Tauras Bank regarding possible fraud involving a US$10 million credit which both Slezevicius and Ratkevicius approved.

The resignation of Bronislovas Genzelis, head of the parliamentary committee for education, science and culture, was the sixth such defection since the party came to power in 1993. Genzelis cited increased authoritarianism within the party, and especially from Slezevicius, as a reason for leaving.

The internal conflicts of the LDLP, coupled with considerable attacks from within the country virtually ensured the party's defeat in the October 1996 parliamentary elections. From being the largest parliamentary party, the LDLP was relegated to fourth place with just 12 seats (compared to 65 at the previous election). The Homeland Union won 70 seats and the Christian Democratic Party 16. In a suprise move the two-party coalition invited the Centre Union, who won 13 seats, to join the government in November 1996, offering them two cabinet posts. Gediminas Vagnorius was appointed prime minister (a position he held between January 1991 and July 1992) and Landsbergis became Speaker of Parliament, in preparation for a possible presidential bid in 1998.

Fallout

The collapse of three of Lithuania's largest banks, and the arrest of several figures from the Innovation Bank and Litimpeks, has had serious economic effects in addition to the political ones. Rumours of currency devaluation led to depositors withdrawing their money, despite government and central bank assurances that there was no crisis within the banking system. This created a severe shortage of foreign exchange within the entire system and a locking of corporate and personal accounts.

There have been delays in wage payments and a rise in inter-company debt, as accounts have been unpaid. At one stage an electricity blackout was feared – the Ignalina nuclear plant, which supplies 80-90 per cent of Lithuania's electricity, was a client of the Innovation Bank and could not afford to purchase fuel from Russia.

This problem continues and the plant is now operating at a reduced level, thus placing greater burdens on other energy generators. Ignalina was to have been closed entirely by 2010, with the first reactor closing in 2005 but the government announced that the first reactor is to close five years later, due to the lack of any real alternative. However, the US Plus Energy group and Lietuvos Energija are seeking to build a hydro-electric station at Kruonis, so a replacement nuclear reactor is possible in due course. Ignalina's Soviet RBMK design, despite the improvements made in respect of efficiency and safety by western firms and experts, would not be regarded as safe in the west.

Economy

The *Seimas* approved the 1996 budget, with a projected deficit of Lt655 million – equivalent to 1.8 per cent of GDP. This is below the 2 per cent limit required by the International Monetary Fund (IMF), but is based on a GDP growth rate of 5 per cent and inflation of 15 per cent. This may well be optimistic, and the deficit could exceed the IMF limits. As befits a government attempting to get re-elected, expenditure on social items increased, sometimes markedly (79 per cent on social welfare), leading to an overall increase in expenditure of some 30 per cent. Much of this deficit is to be financed through the issue of a US$60 million Eurobond, marketed by Nomura International.

Progress on privatisation has been slow, with 5,706 companies sold by the end of 1995, leaving 6,644. The pace of privatisation has slowed since the sale of 2,224 in 1992, largely because those enterprises left are harder to sell, being in industry and trade. The voucher programme has now terminated and future sales will be for cash only; the government expects to raise some Lt2 billion by 2000, leaving Lt6 billion in the hands of the state. Furthermore, agricultural land is to be brought within the programme, although certain companies considered of strategic importance to the country will not be sold.

The economy in 1995 performed rather more poorly than the government had hoped and expected, although the data for some indicators appears contradictory. Different parts of the government are issuing statistics which plainly do not add up. The Department of Statistics is suggesting that certain parts of the economy performed poorly. For example, sales of industrial goods fell slightly, while animal and poultry sales fell by 7 per cent, and large reductions were noted within transport, particularly air which fell by 40 per cent. In contrast, the Ministry of Economy has produced data which shows GDP growth in 1995 to be 3.1 per cent.

Inflation's year-on-year figures for all months in 1995 exceed the government's target of 25 per cent. The year started with figures of around 45 per cent, and finished at 35.7 per cent, with a notable rise in November 1995 of 37 per cent which ran counter to the general downward trend.

The rise in rents and energy prices accounts for a large part of the increases. Fuel rose by 40 per cent as a whole in 1995, due to the removal of state controls over pricing. It is unlikely that inflation will be brought under control in the near future as energy prices have yet to be fully liberalised, and the deal with the primary supplier, the Russian enterprise Gazprom, has resulted in higher costs than anticipated.

Other disappointing news is to be found in the unemployment statistics. It seems that the rise in the number of people out of work is inexorable, with the figure at the end of 1995 standing at 6.1 per cent, compared to 3.6 per cent at the end of 1994. The economics ministry predicts that it will rise still further to 7.9 per cent and 10 per cent in 1996 and 1997 respectively.

More ominous for Lithuania is the potential creation of a divided society, as those in work have seen their real incomes rise by over 7.3 per cent since 1994. This however masks large differences between the private and state sectors, with workers in the latter receiving the lowest increases. For those workers at the very bottom of the wage structure, the minimum wage has been increased from Lt80 to Lt180, due to be increased again in 1996 to Lt300.

External trade

Lithuania's application for membership of the European Union (EU) is progressing, at least from its own perspective, with a formal request submitted in December 1995. Although it is already an associate member

COUNTRY PROFILE — LITHUANIA

Historical profile

Lithuania was an independent state between the First and Second World Wars. Became part of the Soviet Union in 1940. Independence from USSR declared March 1990 (re-affirmed September 1991). Elections of October 1992 were won by the Lithuanian Democratic Labour Party (LDLP), with 72 of the 141 seats. On 14 February 1993, Algirdas Brazauskas, the former Lithuanian Communist Party first secretary and chair of the *Seimas* (parliament), won direct presidential elections with a 60 per cent majority.

Political system

Constitution adopted by referendum on 25 October 1992 established a legislative body, the 141-member *Seimas* (parliament) which is elected on a partly proportional, party constituency system for a four-year term. The head of state is the president, who is directly elected for a maximum of two five-year terms. Executive power is vested in a Council of Ministers, headed by a prime minister, who is appointed by the president with the approval of the *Seimas*.

Political parties

There is a three-party coalition government of Homeland Union, Christian Democratic Party and Centre Union. Other major party is the Lithuanian Democratic Labour Party (LDLP), which is the successor to the Lithuanian branch of the Soviet Communist Party and is stated to be social democratic and not communist.

Population

Lithuanian (80.6%), Russian (9.4%), Polish (7%), Belorussian (1.7%), Ukrainian (1.2%), Jewish, Latvian, German, Tatar and others. Majority Christian. About 68.8 per cent of the population live in towns. In 1992 for the first time in the last 40 years the population decreased by 22.2 thousand because of the population migration. This continued in 1993. Working population make up 56.6 per cent. Life expectancy is 76 years for women and 66 years for men.

Main cities/towns

Vilnius (population 650,000 in 1994), Kaunas (430,000), Klaipeda (206,000), Sjauliai (148,000), Panevezys (129,000), Ukmerge.

Language

On 31 January 1995 the *Seimas* passed a law establishing Lithuanian as the official state language.

Media

Dailies: Echo Litvy (Russian), *Kurier Wilenski* (Polish) (sold to employees for privatisation coupons, end-1995), Lietuvos Aidas (Lithuanian Echo), *Lietuvos Rytas Respublika, Tiesa, Vakarines Naujienos, Valstieciu Laikrastis* (Farmers' Newspaper).
Weeklies: English-language: *Baltic Independent* (published in Estonia), *Baltic Observer* (published in Latvia), *Lithuanian Weekly.*
Business: Lietuvos Ukis (economics magazine published fortnightly).
Radio: Radio Vilnius provides a daily 30 minute round-up of Lithuanian news at 0030 local time on 666 KHz.
Television: Two state-run TV channels.

Domestic economy

In October 1992 the World bank granted Lithuania its first loan to help the country maintain essential services in energy and health care and help sustain adequate agricultural production. The government reiterated its belief in moving towards a market economy but at a slower rate than the previous government, and stated it would continue to encourage foreign investment but would also strive to safeguard Lithuania's economic links with Russia.

Employment

The government controls wages in the state enterprises. Despite the collapse of output, the unemployment rate remained fairly low since various legal restrictions forced companies to retain labour for which there is no real demand. About 49 per cent of the labour force are female.

External trade

The EC signed 10-year trade and co-operation accord with Lithuania on 11 May 1992. Approximately 75 per cent of trade is conducted with the CIS and reorientation to western markets is slow. The government has created an open trade and payments system with respect to most external transactions. There are no quantitative restrictions on imports, except on goods that pose risks to national security or health. Most restrictions on exports were phased out by the end of 1992. Some 40 bilateral agreements on free trade, inward investment and economic co-operation were signed between 1991-92. The authorities are developing a rational new tariff structure, with low and relatively uniform rates, in accordance with internationally accepted principles. The involvement of the government in trade relations will be reduced.

Agriculture

The agriculture sector accounted for 28 per cent of GNP in 1994 and employed 30 per cent of the working population. Seventy per cent of total land area is cultivated. Dominated by production of meat and silk. Food produce is exported. There is some timber production. Forest area 1.8m ha, 28 per cent of total land area. The land restitution scheme went ahead quickly and created 104,000 private family farms, but many of these are too small to compete in either the domestic or foreign market and have difficulty in acquiring technology.

Industry

The industrial sector accounted for 32 per cent of GNP in 1994 and employed 40 per cent of the workforce. Main industries are shipbuilding, consumer electronics, metalworking, machine building, scientific instruments, chemicals, meat, dairy products, food processing, textiles, clothing and furniture. One of Lithuania's priorities is the development of light industry, particularly furniture using natural wood products. Industry is unable to compete when paying world market prices for oil from Russia.

Mining

Lithuania is investigating ways to exploit its amber reserves. Amber deposits have been found in the coastal region of Curonian Bay, and Juodkrante. The Juodkrante site covers 82 ha; amber deposits are estimated at 112 tonnes. Lithuania also has reserves of iron ore.

Hydrocarbons

Since only small amounts of oil and gas have been discovered, most requirements have to be imported. There are known to be reserves of very high quality oil. There is a major oil refinery in Mazheikiai that receives crude oil by pipeline from Russia. Oil production in the Genciai field started in 1993.

Energy

An ageing nuclear power plant in Ignalina, similar in construction to the Chernobyl facility and only 60 km from Vilnius, provides over half of the country's electricity-generating capacity.

this was only granted on certain conditions, such as the enshrinement of the right of foreigners to buy land. Meanwhile, an application has been made to join the World Trade Organisation (WTO), and Lithuania has already become a member of the European Free Trade Association (EFTA). This agreement took effect at the beginning of June 1996, and removes all customs and tariff duties on most manufactured and raw products. Lithuania also wants to join the Central European Free Trade Agreement (CEFTA), and has commenced negotiations with Poland for a bilateral free trade agreement (a condition of membership).

Growing trade liberalisation will inevitably increase unemployment. Some 20 per cent of the workforce are in agriculture, and this sector is expected to be hit badly by the new trading regimes. As liberalisation continues, the country's trade is shifting towards the west, with the CIS assuming less importance. Exports to the EU in 1995 increased to 37.7 per cent from 27 per cent a year earlier, while imports similarly increased from 31.3 per cent to 39.9 per cent. Exports have helped Lithuania to reduce its trade deficit, which rose by 19.7 per cent in 1995 from a year earlier.

The restriction on foreigners owning land is acting as a brake on foreign direct investment (FDI), and Lithuania is performing poorly in this respect compared with the other two Baltic states. The new law being drafted allows nationals of countries which were Organisation for Economic Co-operation and Development members before 1989 the right to buy, rather than lease, land. The government hopes that this will reverse the investment trend towards Estonia and Latvia, while dealing with the domestically-explosive problem of allowing certain foreigners (for which read Russians) to own land.

In its bid to attract foreign money, the government will be creating enterprise zones which will allow a tax break of five years, and a reduction of 50 per cent for five years thereafter. Whether these will be effective or not remains to be seen, but experience to date in other 'developing' states suggests that enterprise migration will be a problem for Lithuania.

Set against these incentives must be the fact that Lithuania is in the grip of a crime wave, with the establishment of organised syndicates in mafia-like structures. Furthermore, these syndicates appear to have good international connections, and also links into parts of the economic infrastructure and possibly government. As in Russia, terrorism linked to crime is on the increase.

COUNTRY PROFILE — LITHUANIA

Energy (contd): Although Lithuania imports the inputs for the Ignalina plant, it normally exports almost half of its domestically produced electricity.

Stock exchange

The Lithuanian Stock Exchange opened in Vilnius on 14 September 1993. Modelled on the French system, the first national stock exchange in the former Soviet Union began with 29 registered brokers and 19 listed securities, including three offering preferred and ordinary shares.

Membership of international organisations

Baltic Council, Conference for Security and Co-operation in Europe (CSCE), Council of Baltic Sea States, Council of Europe, CSCE, EBRD, EU (associate member from 12 April 1995), IAEA, IFC, IMF, MIGA, NACC, Partnerships for Peace, UN, UNESCO, WEU (associate partner), World Bank. EFTA signed free trade treaty with Lithuania December 1995. Lithuania applied for full membership of the EU on 8 December 1995.

BUSINESS GUIDE

Time

GMT + 2 hrs (GMT + 3 hrs from late Mar to late Sep).

Climate

Mildest areas along the Baltic coast. Summer sunshine may be nine hours a day, but winters can be very cold. Annual rainfall 490 mm; humidity 80 per cent.

Entry requirements

Visa: No visas required for foreign visitors.
Customs: Small amount of personal goods duty-free. On arrival declare all foreign currency and valuable items such as jewellery, cameras, computers and musical instruments.

Health precautions

Mandatory: Vaccination certificates are required for cholera or yellow fever if travelling from an infected area.
Advisable: Water precautions recommended (water purification tablets may be useful). It is advisable to be 'in date' for the following immunisations: polio (within 10 years), tetanus (within 10 years), typhoid fever, hepatitis 'A' (moderate risk only). There has been a significant increase in the number of cases of diphtheria. While the low dose, adult booster is unavailable, travellers are advised to be boosted with a reduced dose (0.1ml) of the paediatric single antigen vaccine. If never immunised, use three dose course of the vaccine. Any medicines required by the traveller should be taken by the visitor, and it could be wise to have precautionary antibiotics if going outside major urban centres. A travel kit including a disposable syringe is a reasonable precaution.

Air access

National airlines: Lithuanian Airlines, Air Lithuania.
Other airlines: Aeroflot, Austrian Airlines, Estonian Air, Finnair, Hamburg Airlines, LOT (Polish Airlines), Lufthansa, SAS.
International airport: Vilnius.

Surface access

Main port: Klaipeda is a large, ice-free port.
Water access: Two ferry lines link Klaipeda to Germany. Advisable to book at least one month in advance.
Road: The highway from Vilnius to Klaipeda and the 'M12' to Panevezys are quite good but there are potholes and open sewers on secondary roads and on some roads in town. Avoid driving at night when it is difficult to see the road.
Rail: Train connections with Poland through Grodno in Belarus (Belarus visa required). The railway line Suwalki – Sestokai reopened January 1992. Passengers to destinations outside Lithuania are asked to pay in hard currency.

Hotels

Many hotels are being restored or in the process of a takeover. Most ask for payment in hard currency. Tipping is not widely practised.

Credit cards

Only Visa, Diners' Club and American Express occasionally useful.

City transport

Taxis: Price to be negotiated. Avoid paying in hard currency. There are taxi-stands or a taxi can be booked by telephone (tel: 228-888).
Buses: Convenient and cheapest way to travel as trains do not serve every town and village. Tickets can be bought in most kiosks *(spaudos kioskas).*

National transport

Rail: Trains to Moscow from Vilnius, Lithuania: 1730 (arrival 1130), 1820 (arr 1226), 2216 (arr 1617), 2322 (arr 1810), 1540 (arr 0950), 0940 (arr 0557), 0416 (arr 2159). To St Petersburg from Vilnius, Lithuania: 0712 (arrival 2250) (Mon, Tue, Wed, Fri, Sun), 1000 (arr 0540), 1436 (arr 0848), 1520 (arr 0715), 1705 (arr 1115), 1900 (arr 1230), 2100 (arr 1240).

Public holidays

Fixed dates: 1 Jan (New Year), 16 Feb (Day of Restoration of the Lithuanian State), 6 Jul (Anniversary of Coronation of Grand Duke Mindaugas), 25 and 26 Dec (Christmas).
Variable dates: Easter, Mother's Day (first Sunday in May).

Working hours

Business: (Mon–Fri) 0900–1800 (appointments best between 0900–1000).
Shops: (Mon) 0800–1900, (Tue–Sat) 0800–2100.

Telecommunications

Telephone: Dialling code for Lithuania: IDD access code + 370 followed by area code (2 for Vilnius; 54 for Panevezys; 7 for Kaunus; 61 for Klaipeda; 14 for Siauliai; 36 for Palanga), followed by subscriber's number.
Telefax: Service available at Central Telegraph Office (Mon–Fri 10.00–1200, 1400–1600) and SIA (Sajudis Information Agency) (Mon–Fri 0900–2100).

Banking

Two-tier banking system. Foreign-owned banks may operate. Commercial banking operations removed from the central bank. The Lithuanian State Bank for Commerce commenced operations in September 1992. The commercial department of the Bank of Lithuania was reorganised in 1992. The central bank assumed the government's responsibility for setting interest policy. Bank Baltijas collapsed April 1996. Lithuania and the World Bank agreed to a corporate merger plan to be realised on 1 July 1996, under which three banks with serious financial problems (the LAIB (Lithuanian Joint-Stock Innovative Bank), Litimpeks Bank and Vakaru Bank) merge into a single Jungtinis (United) Bank. The Aurabank was declared bankrupt.
Central bank: Bank of Lithuania.
Other banks: See also 'Business Directory, Banking'.

BUSINESS GUIDE

Business information

Privatisation in process. Foreign investment law, May 1991, permitted majority holdings by non-residents and guaranteed the full transfer of profits. In June 1992 the authorities eased most restrictions on sales to foreign investors and some 35 per cent of companies had been privatised. Utilities remain state-owned but allowance has been made for investment in them.

Electricity supply

220V AC, 50 Hertz. European plugs are required.

Representation in capital

Canada, Denmark, Estonia, Finland, France, Germany, The Holy See, Latvia, Norway, Poland, Sweden, UK, USA.

BUSINESS DIRECTORY

Hotels

Vilnius (area code 2)
Astorija, Didzioji 35–2 (tel: 629-914).

Draugyste, Ciurlionio 84 (tel: 662-711; fax: 263-101).

Germa, Vilniaus 2–30 (tel: 615-460).

Lietuva, Ukmerges 20 (tel: 356-016, 356-090).

Mabre, Maironio 13 (tel: 614-162).

Neringa, Gedimino pr 23 (tel: 610-516).

Sarunas, Raitininku 4 (tel: 353-888).

Neringa (tel: 610-516).

Sarunas (tel: 353-888).

Skrydis, Airport, Rodunes Kelias 2 (tel: 669-467, 669-462).

Turistas (tel: 733-200).

Villon (tel; 505-100).

Useful telephone numbers

Directory enquiries: 09.

International operator: 8-194.

Fire: 01.

Police: 02.

Ambulance (*greitoji pagalba*): 03.

Vilnius City Road Police, Giraites 3: 631-168).

Car hire

Vilnius
Avis: reservation office, Hotel Turistas, Ukmerges St 14, 2005 (tel: 733-226; fax: 353-161); airport (tel: 291-131).

Europcar: reservation office, Vilnius Str 2/15, 2001 (tel: 222-739; fax: 220-439).

Hertz: reservations office (tel: 726-940; fax: 726-970).

Rent-a-Car Baltic Optima: PO Box 2164, 232017 (tel: 460-998; fax: 758-924).

Chambers of commerce

Association of Lithuanian Chambers of Commerce and Industry, V Kudirkos 18, 2600 Vilnius (tel: 222-630; fax: 222-621).

International Chamber of Commerce Lithuania (ICC), V Kudirkos 18, room 405, 2600 Vilnius (tel: 614-532, 222-630; fax: 222-621).

Vilnius Regional Chamber of Commerce and Industry, Algirdo 31, 2600 Vilnius (tel: 235-550; fax: 235-542).

Banking

Bank of Lithuania (central bank), Gedimino pr 6, 2600 Vilnius (tel: 224-008; fax: 221-501, 623-983).

Ancorobank (commercial bank), Raugyklos 15, 2009 Vilnius (tel: 660-311; fax: 263-314).

Hermis (commercial bank), Jogailos 9/1, 2001 Vilnius (tel: 226-165; fax: 615-634).

Lithuanian Agricultural Bank, Totoriu 4, 2600 Vilnius (628-842/927; fax: 226-047).

Lithuanian Bank for Foreign Economic Affairs, Totoriu 2-8, 232629 Vilnius (tel: 224-790).

Lithuanian Commercial Banker's Association, Vilniaus 4/35, Vilnius 2001 (tel: 227-063; fax: 227-065).

Lithuanian Development Bank, Stulginskio 4-7, 2600 Vilnius (tel: 225-259; fax: 227-360).

Lithuanian Savings Bank, Savanoriu pr 19, 2015 Vilnius (tel: 232-379; fax: 232-431).

Lithuanian State Commercial Bank, Jogailos 14, 2001 Vilnius (tel: 626-872; fax: 615-428).

Senamieschio bankas (commercial bank), Gedimino pr 37, 2600 Vilnius (tel: 220-544; fax: 220-556).

Spaudas Bankas (commercial bank), Vrublevskio 6, 232671 Vilnius (tel: 610-723).

Tauro bankas, K Kalinausko 13, 2600 Vilnius (tel: 352-466; fax: 352-213).

Ukio Bankas (commercial bank), J. Gruodis Str 9, 300 Kaunas (tel: 204-646; fax: 204-296).

Vilnius Bank (commercial bank), Gedimino pr 12, 2600 Vilnius (tel: 610-723; fax: 626-557).

Principal newspapers

Ekho Litvy, Laisvés Ave 60, 232019 Vilnius (tel: 428-463).

Kurier Wilenski, Laisvés Ave 60, 232019 Vilnius (tel: 427-901).

Lietuvos Aidas (Lithuanian Echo), Gyneju 3, 232710 Vilnius (tel: 610-475, 615-208; fax: 224-876, 226-838).

Lietuvos Rytas, Gedimino Ave 12a, 232008 Vilnius (tel: 622-680; fax: 221-571).

Lietuvos Ukis, Algirdo 31, 232600 Vilnius (tel: 662-279).

Lithuanian Weekly, PO Box 533, Vilnius (tel: 223-730).

Respublika, Sventaragio 4, 232600 Vilnius (tel: 223-112; fax: 223-538).

Tiesa, Laisvés Ave 60, 232019 Vilnius (tel: 429-788).

Travel information

Air Lithuania, 132 Veiveriu Street, Karmelava Airport, Kaunas 3010 (tel: 295-203, 291-681; fax: 226-030).

Airport (*Aerouostas*) information (tel: 630-201, 635-560); international information (tel: 669-481).

Austrian Airlines, SAS & Swissair, 2nd Floor, Vilnius Airport (tel: 662-000, 660-202; fax: 660-139).

Ferry (Klaipeda – Kiel) information (tel: 826-157-849; fax: 826-153-466); advance booking (tel: 826-155-549); (Klaipeda – Mukran) information (tel: 826-117-825); advance booking (tel: 826-199-936; fax: 826-116-681).

GT International Travel Consultants, Kalvariju 223, Vilnius (tel: 778-392; fax: 350-115).

Lithuanian Airlines, 8 Radunes, Vilnius Airport, Vilnius 232038 (tel: 630-116; fax: 266-828).

Lithuanian Tourism Association, Pylimo 6, 2001 Vilnius (tel: 750-803; fax: 227-550).

Lithuanian Tourist Board, Ukmergès 20, 2600 Vilnius (tel: 726-558; fax: 226-819).

State Tourism Department, Gedimino Ave 30/1, 2694 Vilnius (tel: 622-610; fax: 226-819).

Travel Bureau, Lietuva Hotel, Ukmerges 20, Vilnius (tel: 356-225).

Other useful addresses

Association of Light Industry Enterprises of Lithuania, Saltonishkiu 29/3, 2677 Vilnius (tel: 751-877, 738-131; fax: 721-127).

Association of Lithuanian Entrepreneurs, A Jakshto 9, 2600 Vilnius (tel: 614-963, 628-702; fax: 220-550).

BNS (English-language Baltic news service), Konarskio 49, Vilnius (tel: 660-253, 660-526).

Central Telegraph Office, Vilniaus 33-2, Vilnius (tel: 619-614).

Confederation of Lithuanian Industrialists, Saltonishkiu 19, 2600 Vilnius (tel: 751-278; fax: 723-320).

Department of Customs, A Jakshto 1/25, 2600 Vilnius (tel: 613-027, 617-310; fax: 224-948).

Department of Statistics, Gedimino pr 29, 2746 Vilnius (tel: 619-556; fax: 617-123).

Department of Standardisation and Quality, Jaksto 1-25, 232600 Vilnius (tel: 753-320).

Energy Agency, A Vienuolio 8/4, 2600 Vilnius (tel: 226-158; fax: 225-208).

Gama (import-export agency), Vilnius, Attn Mr A. Kazlauciunas, Director (tel: 60-201; fax 67-915).

Liniterp (interpreters and translators), Palace of Culture, Sporto 21, Vilnius (tel: 756-172, 357-014; fax: 623-415).

Lithuanian Construction Association, Raugyklos 15, 2600 Vilnius (tel: 622-553; fax: 226-178).

Other useful addresses (contd):
Lithuanian Economic and Foreign Investment Development Agency (FIDA), J Jasinskio 9, 4th floor, 2600 Vilnius (tel: 614-942, 618-181; fax: 618-181).

Lithuanian Information Institute, Kalvariju 3, 2659 Vilnius (tel: 753-590; fax: 723-017).

Lithuanian Investment Agency (LIA), Sv Jono 3, 2001 Vilnius (tel: 627-438; fax: 220-160).

Lithuanian Manufacturers' Confederation, Saltonishkiu 19, 2687 Vilnius (tel: 751-278; fax: 723-320).

Lithuanian-Russian Commercial Information Centre (consulting, marketing and general assistance to companies seeking to do business in Lithuania), Vilnius, (tel: 357-903, 353-010; fax 624-872).

Lithuanian State Foreign Trade Enterprise (Agrolitas), Latviu 53-54, 232600 Vilnius (tel: 352-919; fax: 352-622).

Lithuanian State Foreign Trade Enterprise (Lietuvos Prekyba), Gedimino Pr 30-1, 232600 Vilnius (tel: 618-001; fax: 612-820).

Ministry of Administration Reform and Municipal Affairs, Gedimino pr 11, 2039 Vilnius (tel: 628-518; fax: 226-935).

Ministry of Agriculture, Gedimino pr 19, 2025 Vilnius (tel: 625-438; fax: 224-440).

Ministry of Communications and Informatics, Vilniaus g 33, 2008 Vilnius (tel: 620-443; fax: 624-402, 225-070).

Ministry of Construction and Urban Development, A Jakshto 4/9, 2694 Vilnius (tel: 610-558; fax: 220-847).

Ministry of Culture, Basanavichiaus 5, 2001 Vilnius (tel: 619-486; fax 623-120).

Ministry of Defence, Totoriu 25/3, 2001 Vilnius (tel: 624-821; fax: 226-082).

Ministry of Economy, Gedimino pr 38/2, 2600 Vilnius (tel: 622-416; fax: 625-604, 623-974, 225-961). Department of Investment (tel: 622-478). Department of Privatisation (tel: 623-901).

Ministry of Education and Science, A Volano 2/7, 2691 Vilnius (tel: 622-483, 610-034; fax: 612-077, 623-120).

Ministry of Energy, Gedimino pr 12, 2600 Vilnius (tel: 615-140; fax: 626-845).

Ministry of Environmental Protection, A Juozapavichiaus 9, 2600 Vilnius (tel: 725-868; fax: 728-020).

Ministry of Finance, Shermukshniu 6, 2695 Vilnius (tel: 625-172; fax: 226-387).

Ministry of Foreign Affairs, J Tumo Vaizhganto 2, 2600 Vilnius (tel: 618-537; fax: 618-689, 620-752).

Ministry of Foreign Economic Relations, T Vaizganto 2, 232039 Vilnius (tel: 624-670; fax: 614-544).

Ministry of Forestry, Gedimino pr 56, 2685 Vilnius (tel: 626-864; fax: 622-178).

Ministry of Health, Gedimino pr 27, 2682 Vilnius (tel: 621-625; fax: 224-601).

Ministry of Industry and Trade, J Tumo-Vaizhganto 8a/2, 2739 Vilnius (tel: 628-830; fax: 225-967, 620-638); Privatisation Division, T Vaizganto 2, 232039 Vilnius (tel: 629-171; fax: 619-953); Enterprise Restructuring and Industrial Development (tel: 618-090; fax: 225-337).

Ministry of Interior, Shventaragio 2, 2754 Vilnius (tel: 626-752, 698-799; fax: 629-614).

Ministry of Justice, Gedimino pr 30/1, 2600 Vilnius (tel: 624-670; fax: 610-434).

Ministry of Social Security and Labour, A Vivulskio 11, 2693 Vilnius (tel: 651-236; fax: 652-463).

Ministry of Transport, Gedimino pr 17, 2679 Vilnius (tel: 621-445; fax: 224-335).

National Stock Exchange of Lithuania, Ukmergės 41, 2662 Vilnius (tel: 723-871; fax: 724-894).

President's Office, Gedimino pr 53, 2026 Vilnius (tel: 612-811; fax: 226-210).

Prime Minister's Office, Gedimino pr 11, 2039 Vilnius (tel: 629-038, 622-101; fax: 619-953, 221-357, 221-796).

Privatisation Agency, Gedimino Prosp 38/2, Vilnius (tel: 624-671; fax: 623-510).

SIA (Sajudis Information Agency), Gedimino pr 1, Room 104, Vilnius (tel: 224-896).

Luxembourg

Howard Hill

Prime Minister Jean-Claude Juncker, of the Christian Social Party (PCS) – in power since January 1995 – has been able to continue his country's economic diversification. The shift away from steel towards new service industries is continuing, which will likely bring long-term unemployment to many households; the unemployment rate in 1995 was a post-war high of 3 per cent. However, inflation is low, growth is respectable, and the future for key sectors such as banking looks good. With a population of less than half a million, Luxembourg is in the enviable position of qualifying for the European Union's (EU) single European currency and unique in the fact that it already fulfils all five Maastricht criteria in this regard. In May 1996 the government introduced corporate tax cuts to help ensure that the economy continues to grow.

Economy

According to the government's statistical office GDP growth was 3.7 per cent in 1995. This is a slight drop from the previous year's figure of 4 per cent but is nonetheless one of the highest growth rates in western Europe. The outlook for 1996 as a whole, as of the second quarter of 1996, was for GDP to fall to 2.8 per cent.

Annual inflation was 1.5 per cent in April 1996 (on an annualised basis). The average figure for 1995 was 1.9 per cent, putting Luxembourg virtually at the top of Europe's lowest inflationary countries. Unemployment continued to climb in the first part of 1996, reaching another record high of 3.3 per cent in March. Luxembourg's days of full employment are lost, possibly forever.

Luxembourg enjoys the distinction of being on track for the EU's economic and monetary union (EMU) – in mid-1996 it was the only EU member to meet the convergence criteria. The EMU will bring changes to Luxembourg, including the end of its bilateral union with Belgium.

Industry

The steel industry – once the pillar of the economy – continues to experience tough times in Luxembourg. Growth is expected to be flat in 1996 compared with a 1.1 per cent growth rate in industry as a whole. Some 6,000 people are currently employed in the iron and steel industry, strong evidence of the shift towards the service sector in the past decades. The fact that Arbed, the main steel producer, is setting its sights increasingly on projects outside Luxembourg will mean that within a few years, employment in the steel industry could fall to 4,000. Two decades earlier this figure was nearer 30,000.

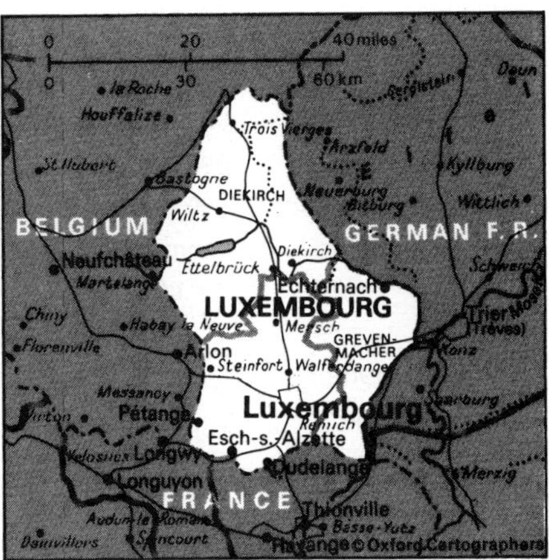

Tax cuts

Corporate tax cuts were announced by the government in May 1996. In 1997 tax revenues will be reduced by Lf4.1 billion. At present the corporate income tax rate is 33 per cent, but this will be reduced by 1 per cent a year – ending up at 30 per cent in 1999. The working capital tax, at 4 per cent, will be eliminated.

KEY FACTS — Luxembourg

Official title: The Grand Duchy of Luxembourg

Head of state: Grand Duke Jean of Luxembourg

Head of government: Prime Minister Jean-Claude Juncker (from 21 Jan 1995)

Ruling party: Coalition of Chreschtlech-Sozial Vollekspartei or Parti Chrétien Social (Christian Social Party) (CSV/PCS) and Letzeburger Sozialistesch Arbechterpartei or Parti Ouvrier Socialiste Luxembourgeois (Socialist Workers' Party) (LSAP/POSL)

Capital: Luxembourg-Ville

Official Languages: Letzebuergish, French, German

Currency: Luxembourg franc (Lf) = Belgian franc = 100 centimes (Belgian franc also legal tender)

Exchange rate: Lf32.00 per US$ (Dec 1996)

Area: 2,586 sq km

Population: 406,600 (1995)

GDP per capita: US$39,961 (1995)

GDP real growth: 3.7% (1995)

GNP per capita: US$39,850 (1994)

GNP real growth: 1.5% (1994)*

Labour force: 164,700 (1994)*

Unemployment: 2.8% (1995)

Inflation: 1.9% (1995) (consumer prices)

Trade balance: US$6.4bn (1995)

* estimated figure

KEY INDICATORS — Luxembourg

	Unit	1991	1992	1993	1994	1995
Population	'000	384	389	395	400	407
Gross domestic product (GDP)	US$bn	9.0	10.5	10.3	13.6	–
GDP per capita	US$	23,685	27,630	26,400	33,900	39,961
GDP real growth	%	3.0	2.5	1.0	3.3	3.7
Inflation	%	3.1	3.2	3.6	2.2	1.9
Consumer prices	1990=100	103.1	106.4	110.2	112.6	114.8
Unemployment rate	%	1.4	1.5	2.2	2.7	2.8
Agricultural production**	1979-81=100	130.12	139.30	144.53	137.74	137.89
Share prices	1990=100	95.5	90.7	127.5	179.7	162.7
Industrial production	1990=100	99.6	98.8	96.1	101.7	–
Steel	'000 tonnes	3,560	–	3,293	3,073	–
Exports	Lfbn	214.15	208.13	200.06	215.51	–
Imports	Lfbn	274.68	265.18	261.25	266.97	–
Balance of trade	Lfbn	–	–	-62.8	-53.5	–
Current account	Lfbn	–	–	59.2	64.0	–
Total reserves minus gold	US$m	80.42	74.13	67.38	75.73	74.98
Foreign exchange	US$m	33.40	29.48	25.40	30.73	29.79
Deposit rate	%	6.00	6.00	5.33	5.00	5.00
Lending rate	%	8.25	8.75	7.65	6.58	6.50
Exchange rate	Lf per US$	34.20	32.15	34.60	33.46	29.48

**Belgium/Lux Economic Union

Financial services

The financial sector is now responsible for one-sixth of the country's GDP. Life with the new Euro currency, which is expected to be introduced in 1999, and EMU, will mean changes for local banks, particularly their foreign exchange and Euromarket divisions. Commissions will be lost on European currency dealings and on the issuance of Lf-denominated Eurobonds. Furthermore, the Euromarkets in national European currencies will evaporate after EMU. The outlook nevertheless looks good for the sector, partly due to the soundness of the economy and to the fact that recent corporate tax cuts have been introduced as a way of enhancing competitiveness. The tax cuts intended to help the banking sector stay competitive include the reduction of the subscription tax on investment and money market funds – by 1998 this will fall to 0.01 per cent from the present 0.03 per cent.

Media

In the television field, the big players are the venerable Compagnie Luxembourgeoise de Télédiffusion (CLT) and relative newcomer Société Européene des Satéllites (SES) which is the world's biggest privately-owned TV satellite operator and owner of the Astra system. CLT has stakes in some of the most viewed television stations in Europe, including Germany's RTL, France's M6 and Netherlands' RTL4, and two stations in Belgium. A proposed merger with Germany's huge Bertelsmann group was in prospect for CLT. CLT is also a participant in the MMBG venture to bring digital television to Germany. The MMBG is led by Bertelsmann (Germany), and aside from CLT it includes Canal+ (France) and Havas (France).

COUNTRY PROFILE — LUXEMBOURG

Political system

The Grand Duchy of Luxembourg is a constitutional hereditary monarchy, with legislative power exercised by a unicameral 60-member Chamber of Deputies, which is elected for a five-year term. Executive power is vested in the Grand Duke but normally exercised by the Council of Ministers, led by the head of government, who is chosen by the Grand Duke and must have the support of the unicameral Chamber of Deputies. A 21-member Council of State chosen by the monarch acts as an advisory body and has some legislative functions. Next general election scheduled for June 1999.

Political parties

Coalition government of Chreschtlech-Sozial Vollekspartei or Parti Chrétien Social (Christian Social Party) (CSV/PCS) and Letzeburger Sozialistesch Arbechterpartei or Parti Ouvrier Socialiste Luxembourgeois (Socialist Workers' Party) (LSAP/POSL). Other major parties include the Democratic Party; Greens; Action for Democracy and Justice.

Population

Annual change in total population -0.5 per cent in 1994. Religion: Christianity.

Main cities/towns

Luxembourg-Ville (population 113,000 in 1994), Esch-sur-Alzette, Differdange, Dudelange, Pétange, Ettelbrück, Diekirch, Wiltz.

Language

French, German, Letzebuergisch.

Media

Press: *Luxemburger Wort* (*La Voix du Luxembourg*, *Tageblatt*, *Journal* and *d'Zeitung* are printed daily in German and French. The French *LeRépublicain-Lorrain* which has an extensive Luxembourg section, is widely read. Numerous journals and magazines including *Télécran*, *d'Letzebuerger Land*, *Revue*, *l'Echo de l'Industrie* and *Luxemburg News Digest*.
Broadcasting: Compagnie Luxembourgeoise de Télédiffusion, the operator of Radio-Télé Luxembourg (RTL), operates 14 television channels in six countries and 18 radio stations across eight countries. It is Europe's oldest commercial broadcasting company (set up in 1931) and has market leadership in commercial TV broadcasting in the Benelux countries, 21 per cent of the national audience in Germany, and ranks fourth in France. Its private radio stations lead the market in France, the UK and Belgium. There is also a satellite broadcasting system, Astra, which began in 1989 and is run by Société Européenne des Satellites (SES), a privately owned consortium licensed by the government. Approximately 240,000 radios and 140,000 TVs in use.
Advertising: Commercial advertising on radio and TV and posters.

Domestic economy

Luxembourg is the smallest EU member state. It has a successful economy characterised by firm growth, low inflation and low unemployment. Highly developed but small economy based on banking, other financial services, steel and chemical industries. Tourism and manufacturing also important. Heavy dependence on external trade and immigrant labour (over 50 per cent for the first time in 1995). The slowdown in the European economy caused a decline in exports, and a deep crisis in the steel sector. The service sector has been encouraged by the government. Current account surplus benefits from the surplus on services earned by the financial services, which are predominant. In 1995 Luxembourg continued to outperform its neighbours in terms of growth, inflation and public finance. There are plans for reducing the workforce once again in the steel sector, but provisional data for 1995 indicated that overall activity held up well, supported by domestic demand and, initially, exports. Luxembourg is the only EU member state which fulfils all five of the Maastricht criteria for qualifying for the single European currency.

Employment

Industry, trade and tourism remain major employers, although banking and other financial services account for a growing proportion of total employment. Relative to other western European countries the number out of

COUNTRY PROFILE

Employment (contd): work is low. Short-time work schedules are one of the reasons for the low unemployment. Nevertheless, long-term unemployment among the domestic labour force and the financial sector's dependence on non-resident employees continues to move upwards. A proportion of the workforce commute daily from France, Belgium and Germany, filling jobs for which there are no more Luxembourgers available; 50 per cent of the Luxembourg workforce are foreigners, mainly immigrants from Italy and Portugal and their children. There are around 16,000 government employees. In May 1996 the government announced a package of corporate tax cuts aimed at encouraging investment and creating jobs. There are plans for further reductions in the steel industry labour force to 4,000 by end-1997.

External trade

Regular trade deficit offset by invisible earnings from financial services and other services, e.g. transport and communications. Heavy reliance on trade with Belgium, Germany, France, Netherlands and the USA. The steel company, Arbed, played a pioneering role in winning new export markets, developing new products for the USA, and providing China with technical services.
Exports: Main merchandise exports include steel (accounting for 43 per cent), plastics, rubber, machinery and textiles. Imports dominated by energy products, machinery, metals and chemicals. Main destinations: Germany (21% of 1994 total), France (19%), Netherlands (13.2%), UK (8.5%), Italy (5.2%), USA (5%).
Imports: Imports dominated by energy products, machinery, metals and chemicals. Main sources: Germany (20.1% of 1994 total), Netherlands (17.7%), France (16.1%), UK (9.5%), USA (5.3%), Italy (4.3%).

Agriculture

Sector contributed 2.3 per cent to GDP in 1994 and employs 3.2 per cent of the labour force. Farming is concentrated on barley, oats and potatoes in the north, and fruit and grapes in the east. Food and wine account for about 1.9 per cent of exports. Beef and dairy farming has increased, with pasture accounting for 55 per cent of all cultivated farmland.

Industry

Industry accounted for 30 per cent of GDP in 1994 and employed 30.7 per cent of the workforce, the steel industry accounting for less than 8 per cent of this. Despite successful diversification programme, sector dominated by the Arbed steel company (the fifth largest steel producer in Europe), which is the country's largest single employer and exporter. The number of people employed by the steel industry had dropped to just 6,000 in 1995, from 30,000 in the seventies. After experiencing period of rapid decline, brought on partly by EU's restructuring programme, government initiated major overhaul of steel industry. Arbed diversified into service and trading activities as well as seeking foreign partners. Arbed lost Lf5.7bn in 1993 as the drop in EU steel prices took its toll on profits. However, the company recorded a consolidated profit of Lf414m in 1994. Other significant industries include chemicals, rubber, plastics, processing, glass, aluminium, metalworking and vehicle spares manufacture. Industrial production rose by only 0.1 per cent in 1995.

Tourism

Tourism is becoming a more important area of the economy and is being actively promoted by the government.

Mining

Deposits of iron ore largely depleted. As late as 1970, iron ore production amounted to 5m tonnes – production ended in Dec 1981. There are limited reserves of coal and some deposits of limestone which continue to be worked.

Energy

Heavy dependence on imported energy, mainly from Belgium and Germany. All oil and gas supplies are imported. Luxembourg has a massive hydroelectric dam at Vianden, but still imports electricity. There are no nuclear power plants.

Financial services

The principal source of growth in the domestic economy has been the financial services sector, which accounts for around 15 per cent of GDP and 10 per cent of domestic employment. The principal activities are banking and investment fund management. Luxembourg has attracted about 40 life insurance companies.

Legal system

French-based, fiscal law German-based.

Membership of international organisations

Benelux, BLEU, CCC, Council of Europe, EIB, EMS, EU, FAO, IAEA, ICC, ICAO, IDA, IEA, IFAD, IFC, ILO, IMF, INTELSAT, INTERPOL, IOOC, IPU, ITU, NACC, NATO, OECD, OSCE, UN, UNESCO, UNIDO, UPU, WEU, WHO, WIPO, WMO, World Bank, WTO.

BUSINESS GUIDE

Time

GMT + 1 hr (GMT + 2 hrs from late Mar to late Sep).

Climate

Temperate without extremes. Sea winds (south-west and north-west) shed a great part of their moisture before reaching the Luxembourg frontiers. May to mid-Oct suitable for vacations; Jul and Aug are the warmest; May and Jun the sunniest months; Sep and Oct 'Indian summer'.

Clothing

Mediumweight throughout year. Raincoat useful.

Entry requirements

Visa: Visas not required for nationals of USA, Japan, most Western European countries and many others. Luxembourg Embassy, London, UK, Schengen Visa information (tel: 0891-600-220).
Currency: No restrictions on movement of local or foreign currency. N.B. Lf not widely accepted in other countries.
Customs: Personal effects and goods up to specified value duty-free.

Air access

Regular flights by all major airlines.
National airline: Luxair.
International airport: Findel (LUX), 5 km east of capital.

Surface access

Rail connections with Brussels, Frankfurt, Amsterdam, Basle and Paris. Good road links with Brussels, Trier, Paris, Frankfurt and Saarbrücken.

Hotels

A one to five-star rating system partially in operation. Bills include service charge. Tipping optional.

Currency

Exchange rate : Value of Luxembourg Franc equals that of Belgian Franc, and is not quoted separately.

Credit cards

All main credit cards accepted.

Car hire

Readily available from airport and hotels.

City transport

Regular flat-fare bus service operates within greater Luxembourg-Ville. Metered taxi service with minimum charge. Tipping usually 15 per cent.

National transport

Around 5,140 km of roads, of which 120 km are motorways, and 280 km of railway track. State-run bus and railway services link capital with most main towns. A canal service operates on the Moselle.

Public holidays

If a holiday falls on a Sunday, the Monday following is a holiday as well (maximum two p.a.).
Fixed dates: 1 Jan, 1 May (Labour Day), 23 Jun (National Day), 15 Aug (Assumption), 1 Nov (All Saints'), 25/26 Dec. [Unofficial: 2 Nov (All Souls')].
Variable dates: Easter Monday, Ascension Day, Carnival, Whit Monday (unofficial: Shrove Monday and Luxembourg Fair Day – in Luxembourg-Ville only).

Working hours

Government and business: (Mon–Fri) 0800–1800, lunch 1200–1400.
Banking: (Mon–Fri) 0900–1630.
Shops: Large variations: typically 0900–2000, closed Mon morning.

Social customs

Polite to be punctual for appointments and to shake hands on arrival and departure.

Telecommunications

Telephone and telefax: Local and international direct dialling. International dialling code: 352 followed by subscriber's number. There are no area codes. For IDD access from Luxembourg dial 00.
Telex: Available at main hotels and Postes Luxembourg-Ville. Country code 402 LU.

Banking

Large banking sector. Activity oriented towards wholesale banking services, with a large concentration of west German and Scandinavian banks serving corporate customers in Europe, but private banking has rapidy increased. Banking secrecy covered by a 1989 law, but growing EU pressure for tighter controls. The collapse of the Bank of Credit and Commerce International (BCCI), which was legally domiciled in Luxembourg but which carried out the bulk of its activities elsewhere, has not had a lasting effect on the Grand Duchy's reputation. BCCI came to Luxembourg at the start of the banking boom in the early 1970s and the country's regulatory body, the Institut Monétaire Luxembourgeois (IML) states that a bank of this sort would not be granted a licence today. Overall, services generate 70 per cent of GDP, with banking alone accounting for 15 per cent. There are over 220 banks and investment houses.
Central bank: A monetary association with Belgium was legally established in 1979 and renewed for a further ten years in 1992. The agreement puts the National Bank of Belgium in charge of monetary policy and restricts the role of the Institut Monétaire Luxembourgeois (IML), which was created in 1983, to the issuance of notes up to one third of the total currency in circulation in the Grand Duchy. Legislation has been prepared for the IML to be transformed into a fully-fledged central bank and the Chamber of Deputies may grant its approval by end-1996.
Other banks: See 'Business Directory, Banking'.

Trade fairs

Luxembourg International Trade Fair held every spring and autumn, covering a variety of goods.

Electricity supply

220 V AC.

BUSINESS DIRECTORY

Hotels

Luxembourg-Ville
Aerogolf-Sheraton, Route de Trèves, Senningerberg L-2633 (tel: 34-571; fax: 34-217).

Arcotel, 43 Avenue de la Gare (tel: 494-001).

Carlton, 9 Rue de Strasbourg, L2561 (tel: 484-802).

Cravat, 29 Boulevard Roosevelt, L-2450 (tel: 21-975; fax: 26-711).

Dauphin, 42 Avenue de la Gare, L-1610 (tel: 488-282).

Du Chemin de Fer, 4 Rue Joseph Junck (tel: 493-528).

Europe, 1 Avenue du Bois (tel: 470-444; fax: 473-464).

Grunewald, 10-16 Route d'Echternach (tel: 431-882, 436-062; fax: 420-646).

Ibis, Route de Trèves (tel: 438-801; fax: 438-802).

Inter-Continental, 4 Rue Jean-Engling, L-1466 (tel: 43-781; fax: 436-095).

International, 20-22 Place de la Gare, L1616 (tel: 485-911; tx: 2761).

Le Royal, 12 Boulevard Royal, L-2449 (tel: 41-616; fax: 25-948).

Nobilis, 47 Avenue de la Gare (tel: 494-971; fax: 403-101).

Parc, 120 Route d'Echternach (tel: 435-643; fax: 436-903).

President, 32 Place de la Gare, L-1616 (tel: 486-161; fax: 486-180).

Pullman, Centre Européen, Luxembourg-Kirchberg (tel: 437-761; fax: 438-658).

Rix, 20 Boulevard Royal, L-2449 (tel: 471-666; fax: 27-535).

Senator, 38 Rue J. Juncker and rue Wiedal, L-1839 (tel: 492-351; fax: 485-438).

Car hire

Luxembourg-Ville
Avis: 2 Place de la Gare (tel: 489-595; fax: 404-012).

Budget: Central Reservations (tel: 441-938; fax: 443-343); airport (tel: 437-575; fax: 436-014).

Europcar: reservations (tel: 404-228; fax: 405-882, 403-344).

Hertz: reservations office: (tel: 487-777; fax: 420-351).

Chambers of Commerce

Chambre de Commerce, 7 Rue Alcide de Gasperi, L-2981 Luxembourg (tel: 435-853; fax: 438-326).

British Chamber of Commerce, BP 2740, L-1027 Luxembourg (tel: 34-239; fax: 229-867).

Banking

Institut Monétaire Luxembourgeois (IML), 63 Avenue de la Liberte, L-2983 Luxembourg (tel: 478-888; fax: 492-180).

Association des Banques et Banquiers (Banking Association), Luxembourg BP 13, L-2010 (tel: 29-501, 463-6601; fax: 460-921).

Banque Continentale du Luxembourg SA, 2 Boulevard Emmanuel Servais, L-2535 Luxembourg (tel: 474-491; fax: 477-688-333).

Banque de Luxembourg SA, 80 Place de la Gare, BP 2221, L-1022 Luxembourg (tel: 499-241; fax: 494-820).

Banque et Caisse d'Epargne de l'Etat, 1 Place de Metz, L-2954 Luxembourg (tel: 40-151).

Banque Générale du Luxembourg, Boulevard JF Kennedy, L-2951 Luxembourg (tel: 47-991, 42-421; fax: 4799-2579).

Banque Internationale à Luxembourg SA BIL), 2 Boulevard Royal, L-2953 Luxembourg (tel: 45-901; fax: 4791-2010).

Banque Nationale de Paris SA, 22-24 Boulevard Royal, L-2952 Luxembourg-Ville (tel: 47-641; fax: 26-480).

Caisse Centrale Raiffeisen SC, 28 Boulevard Royal, BP 111, L-2011 Luxembourg (tel: 462-151).

Deutsche Bank Luxembourg SA, 25 Boulevard Royal, BP 586, 2449 Luxembourg-Ville (tel: 468-181).

Fortuna, Societe Cooperative de Credit et d'Epargne, 128-132 Boulevard de la Pétrusse, BP 1203, L-1012 Luxembourg (tel: 488-888).

Kredietbank SA Luxembourgeoise, 43 Boulevard Royal, L-2953 Luxembourg (tel: 47-971; fax: 472-667).

Societe Nationale de Credit et d'Investissement, 7 Rue du St Esprit, BP 1207, L-1012 Luxembourg (tel: 461-9711).

Travel information

Luxair, Luxembourg Airport, 2987 Luxembourg-Ville (tel: 798-2311/2221; fax: 443-2482, 436-344).

Ministère des Classes Moyennes et du Tourisme, 6 Avenue Emile Reuter, L-2137 Luxembourg (tel: 4656-1406; fax: 474-011).

Office National du Tourisme, 77 Rue d'Anvers, Box 1001, L-1010 Luxembourg (tel: 400-808; fax: 404-748).

Syndicat d'Initiative et de Tourisme, Place d'Armes, L-1136 Luxembourg (tel: 222-809; fax: 474-818).

Other useful addresses

Bourse de Luxembourg SA (stock exchange), 11 Avenue de la Porte-Neuve, L-2227 Luxembourg (tel: 477-9361; fax: 22-050).

Board of Economic Development, 19-21 Boulevard Royal, L-2914 Luxembourg (tel:478-4135/4141; fax: 460-448).

Confédération du Commerce Luxembourgeois, 23 Allée Scheffer, L-2520 Luxembourg (tel: 473-125).

Fédération des Industriels Luxembourgeois, 7 Rue Alcide de Gasperi, L-1615 Luxembourg (tel: 435-366; fax: 438-326).

Groupement des Industries Sidérurgiques Luxembourgeoises (Federation of Iron and Steel Industries in Luxembourg), 3 Rue Goethe, BP 1704, 1637 Luxembourg-Ville (tel: 480-001).

Ministère de la Cuture, 20 Montée de la Pétrusse, L-2912 Luxembourg (tel: 4781; fax: 402-427).

Ministère de la Famille, 14 Avenue de la Gare, L-2929 Luxembourg (tel: 4781; fax: 478-6570).

Ministère de la Fonction Publique et de la Réforme Administrative, Plateau du St Esprit, L-2011 Luxembourg (tel: 4781; fax: 478-3122).

Ministère de la Force Publique, Plateau du St Esprit, Bâtiment Vauban, L-2915 Luxembourg (tel: 4781; fax: 462-682).

Ministère de l'Agriculture, de la Viticulture et du Développement Rural, 1 Rue de la Congrégation, L-2913 Luxembourg (tel: 4781; fax: 464-027).

Ministère de la Jeunesse, 26 Rue Zithe, L-2943 Luxembourg (tel: 4781; fax: 467-454).

Ministère de la Justice, 16 Boulevard Royal, L-2934 Luxembourg (tel: 4781; fax: 227-661).

Ministère de l'Aménagement du Territoire, 18 Montée de la Pétrusse, L-2946 Luxembourg (tel: 4781; fax: 408-970).

Département du Budget (Ministry of Finance), 3 Rue de la Congrégation, L-2931 Luxembourg (tel: 4781; fax: 475-241).

Ministère de la Promotion Féminine, 33 Boulevard Prince Henri, L-2929 Luxembourg (tel: 4781; fax: 41-886).

Département aux Relations avec le Parlement, 3 Rue de la Congrégation, L-2931 Luxembourg (tel: 4781; fax: 475-241).

Ministère de la Santé, 57 et 90 Boulevard de la Pétrusse, L-2320 Luxembourg (tel: 4781; fax: 484-903).

Ministère de la Sécurité Sociale, 26 Rue Zithe, L-2936 Luxembourg (tel: 4781; fax: 478-6328).

Ministère de l'Economie (Ministry of the Economy), 19-21 Boulevard Royal, L-2914 Luxembourg (tel: 478-4100; fax: 460-448).

Ministère de l'Education Nationale et de la Formation Professionnelle, 29 Rue Aldringen, L-2926 Luxembourg (tel: 4781; fax: 478-5113).

Ministère de l'Education Physique et des Sports, 66 Route de Trèves, L-2916 Luxembourg (tel: 4781; fax: 434-599).

Ministère de l'Energie, 19 Boulevard Royal, L-2449 Luxembourg (tel: 4781).

Ministère de l'Environnement, 18 Montée de la Pétrusse, L-2918 Luxembourg (tel: 4781; fax: 400-410).

Ministère de l'Intérieur, 19 Rue Beaumont, L-2933 Luxembourg (tel: 4781; fax: 41-846).

Ministère des Affaires Etrangères, du Commerce Extérieur et de la Coopération (Ministry of Foreign Affairs, Foreign Trade and Co-operation), 5 Rue Notre Dame L-2913 Luxembourg (tel: 4781; fax: 223-144).

Ministère des Finances, 3 Rue de la Congrégation, L-2931 Luxembourg (tel: 4781; fax: 475-241).

Ministère des Transports, 19-21 Boulevard Royal, L-2938 Luxembourg (tel: 4781; fax: 464-315).

Ministère des Travaux Publics, 4 Boulevard FD Roosevelt, L-2940 Luxembourg (tel: 4781; fax: 462-709).

Ministère d'Etat (Ministry of State), 4 Rue de la Congrégation, L-2910 Luxembourg (tel: 4781; fax: 461-720).

Ministère du Logement, 6 Avenue Emile Reuter, L-2942 Luxembourg (tel: 4781; fax: 478-4840).

Ministère du Travail et de l'Emploi, 26 Rue Zithe, L-2939 Luxembourg (tel: 4781; fax: 478-6325).

Press and Information Service of the Government, 43 Boulevard Roosevelt, L-2450 Luxembourg (tel: 478-224, 478-321; fax: 470-285, 20-090).

Radio Télé-Luxembourg (RTL), Villa Louvigny, L-2850 Luxembourg (tel: 476-6242; fax: 4766-2737).

Service Central de la Statistique et des Etudes Economiques (STATEC), 6 Boulevard Royal, L-2013 Luxembourg (tel: 4781; fax: 464-289).

Société Europienne des Satellites, PO Box 1781, L-1017 Luxembourg (tel: 499-4711; fax: 4394-71219).

Former Yugoslav Republic of Macedonia

Marko Milivojevic

Following Greece's lifting of its blockade of what the Greek government belatedly recognised as the Former Yugoslav Republic of Macedonia (FYROM), Macedonia's economic outlook significantly improved. The good news continued when the UN economic sanctions against Serbia were suspended in the following month and then abolished in October 1996. However, the attempted assassination of President Kiro Gligorov by persons unknown in October 1995 highlighted the fact that things were not well in the domestic political arena.

Politics

President Gligorov has dominated Macedonian politics since independence from the former Yugoslavia in 1991. He was last re-elected in the presidential race of October 1994, when his Social Democratic Alliance of Macedonia (SDSM) -led Alliance for Macedonia (AFM) coalition also gained a decisive parliamentary majority in concomitant elections for a new parliament. Gligorov's active political career will almost certainly end before 1998, when a new president will be elected.

As things stand, the former acting president and parliamentary speaker, Stojan Andov, who is also the Liberal Party (LP) leader, is the most likely replacement for Gligorov. The other main presidential hopeful is Vasil Tuporkovski, a former chairman of the Yugoslav State Presidency. However, both lack the popularity and undisputed authority of Gligorov. Regardless of who eventually replaces the incumbent president, the absence of his conciliatory influence in the AFM may subject the ruling coalition to increased strains.

Other than growing differences with some of its coalition partners in the AFM, the main challenge for the SDSM is that it could be electorally weakened to the advantage of the opposition Democratic Party (DPM) led by Petar Goshev. To the centre-right of Macedonian politics, the DPM is expected to gain from growing popular disenchantment with less than complete socio-economic reform, about which the neo-communist SDSM is ambivalent, and alleged government mishandling of the ethnic Albanian minority issue in Macedonia. Of the country's sensitive minority problem, which most recently exploded into serious violence in Tetovo in February 1995, the DPM has supplanted the more extreme Internal Macedonian Revolutionary Organisation-Democratic Party of Macedonian National Unity (VRMO-DPMNE) on the national question, following the collapse of the ultra-nationalist vote in the October 1994 parliamentary elections.

According to various reports, it has been alleged that the would-be assassins of Gligorov in October 1995 originated in either Bulgaria or Albania. Significantly, the Macedonian President was moving closer to both Serbia and Greece when the attempt took place. Outside the region, closer Macedonian ties with Greece and Serbia are generally welcome. Combined with increased western economic involvement in 1996, this new configuration in the region could finally put Macedonia on the road to real stability in the future.

Serbia and Montenegro (the Federal Republic of Yugoslavia), finally recognised Macedonia under its chosen official title in April 1996. This is a development that implies closer Macedonian-Serbia relations, possibly at the expense of both Albania and Bulgaria, and even Greece.

Economic performance

Freed of the considerable economic burdens

KEY FACTS — Macedonia

Official title: Former Yugoslav Republic of Macedonia (FYROM) (internationally recognised provisional official title pending final resolution of name dispute with Greece); Republic of Macedonia (local official name and generally accepted title even if unrecognised internationally)

Head of state: President Kiro Gligorov (SDSM) (re-elected Oct 1994)

Head of government: Prime Minister Branko Crvenkovski (SDSM)

Ruling party: Alliance for Macedonia (AFM) coalition government led by the Social Democratic Alliance of Macedonia (SDSM) and including the Socialist Party of Macedonia (SSM) and the Party of Democratic Prosperity of Albanians in Macedonia (PDPSM) (formerly the PDP); the Liberal Party was excluded from the government in February 1996

Capital: Skopje

Official Languages: Macedonian

Currency: Macedonian Denar (D) introduced 10 May 1993 (devalued 15 May 1995)

Exchange rate: Denar 41.18 per US$ (Dec 1996)

Area: 25,713 sq km

Population: 1.9m (1995)

GDP per capita: US$700 (1995)

GDP real growth: -4% (1995)

GNP per capita: US$730 (1994)

GNP real growth: -7% (1994)

Unemployment: 50% (1995)

Inflation: 6% (1995)

Trade balance: -US$300m (1995)

Foreign debt: US$1.3bn (1995) (not including 6 per cent share of US$4.6bn

of endless political disputes with both Greece and Serbia in 1995-96, Macedonia may finally be in a position to bring about a revival of its GDP, which is expected to grow by around 2 per cent in 1996 (compared with 1995). Expected to grow by 1 per cent in 1995 (over 1994), GDP in fact declined by 4 per cent according to official figures, mainly because of a larger-than-envisaged fall in industrial output (15 per cent in 1995 over 1994).

Although the 1995 economic performance was better than in 1994, when GDP declined by 11 per cent (over 1993), it nevertheless remained disappointing in what was then the fifth consecutive year of economic decline. Unofficially, however, 1995 was similar to 1994 in that actual GDP and GDP per capita were almost certainly far higher than official figures suggested, mainly because of the large size of the black economy.

Allowing for exchange rate fluctuations, officially recorded GDP and GDP per capita in 1995 were about the same as in 1994, US$1.5 billion and US$700 respectively. In 1995 the informal economy may have accounted for 50 per cent of officially recorded GDP. Consequently, GDP may actually have been at least 50 per cent higher than official figures suggested. For the same reason, GDP growth may have actually been slightly positive in 1995, with private-sector agriculture/food processing and services once again the major motors of real economic growth.

Previously accounting for 40 per cent of GDP and employment, industrial output continued to fall sharply in 1995, mainly because of the various effects of the Greco-Serbian economic blockade. Only in 1996, and then only very slightly, is industrial output expected to stabilise. Future industrial growth is expected to be concentrated in private-sector food processing and light manufacturing led by textiles.

Pending its financial rehabilitation and reconstruction, the traditional capital goods sector is expected to experience further decline. Unemployment, which was unofficially around 50 per cent of the employed workforce year-end in 1995, is thus expected to increase. Further major job losses took place in 1995 as part of a government restructuring plan for 25 loss-making industrial enterprises. Widespread job cuts have also taken place in a number of recently privatised enterprises. Politically controversial in Macedonia, such corporate restructuring has caused growing rifts in the AFM coalition, with the centre-left SDSM arguing for a change of industrial policy and the LS opposed to this in cabinet.

Accounting for around 25 per cent of GDP, agricultural output began to stabilise in 1995, with higher growth expected with the projected availability of new foreign markets in 1996 and 1997. Macedonia has a particular competitive advantage in agriculture-food processing.

At around 30 per cent of GDP in 1995, services of all types are increasingly important. Largely privately-owned and often in the black economy, services such as retail and wholesale trade, construction and transport are enjoying high growth. Externally, somewhere between US$750 million and US$1 billion is thought to have been generated by the private-sector by 1995 through the provision of sanctions-busting trade services for Serbia and Greece over the last five years. Another positive trend in 1995 were growing émigré hard currency remittances by the large Macedonian and ethnic Albanian diasporas elsewhere in Europe. Economically, such hidden hard currency transfers explain why real incomes in Macedonia are considerably higher than those suggested by official figures based on taxed economic activities and transfers.

KEY INDICATORS — Macedonia

	Unit	1991	1992	1993	1994	1995
Population	m	2.1	2.1	2.1	1.9	1.9
Gross national product (GNP)	US$bn	2.5	1.7	1.4	1.5	–
GNP per capita	US$	1,100	800	687	730	–
GNP real growth	%	-14	-15	-14	-7	–
Inflation	%	114.9	1,691.0	230.0	122.0	6.0
Unemployment	%	25	25	35	19	50
Exports	US$m	1,150	1,199	1,055	1,068	*1,250
Imports	US$m	1,375	1,206	1,227	1,272	*1,450
Balance of trade	US$m	-225	-7	-172	186	-300
Foreign debt	US$m	806	848	828	865	1,300
Current account	US$m	-262	-19	-88	-170	*-180
Exchange rate	D per US$	–	–	**23.2	43.3	39.30

* estimated figure **Denar introduced 10 May 1993

Financial stabilisation

Notwithstanding the growing political tensions within the ruling coalition over economic policy in 1995, the government broadly kept to the macro-economic stabilisation targets agreed with the International Monetary Fund (IMF), which agreed an US$80 million loan in November 1996 to assist in reducing inflation and the trade deficit. The government has also kept to the terms of a related US$85 million financial and enterprise sector adjustment credit (FESAC) agreed by the World Bank's soft-loan arm, the International Development Association (IDA), in March 1995. Supported by the IMF and the

World Bank in 1995/96, the government's macro-economic stabilisation programme has largely succeeded in eliminating inflation, thereby creating the conditions for sustainable and non-inflationary economic growth. Based on a restrictive central bank monetary-credit policy and strict fiscal discipline, this programme has seen inflation fall from 230 per cent in 1993 to 57 per cent in 1994. In 1995, when year-end inflation was earlier projected at 18 per cent, it actually fell to only 6 per cent.

In the fiscal sphere, the government budget deficit was 4 per cent of officially declared GDP in 1994, against a target of 5.8 per cent. In 1995, further cuts in public spending towards the end of the year resulted in a government budget deficit equal to only 2 per cent of GDP.

Denar

Three years after its introduction in May 1993, the denar (D) is now one of the more stable national currencies in the former Yugoslavia. Stabilised at parities of around D35-40 per US$ and D20-25 per DM year-end in 1995, the denar was trading at a steady D38.1 for US$ and D24.8 per DM by June 1996. In real terms, the denar has slightly appreciated against the DM and even more against the Italian lira since 1994.

According to various local exporters, the denar was over-valued in 1995/96. Despite increased calls for a competitive devaluation of the denar, the government and the central bank have so far rejected such a policy, mainly because of its possible inflationary implications and possible effect on imports. For the vitally important German and Italian markets, local exporters have also recently requested export subsidies to overcome the negative effects of an over-valued denar. Having phased out most production and other subsidies by the end of 1995 as part of its agreements with the IMF and the World Bank, the government is unlikely to meet such demands in the future. Another reason for this is that export subsidies would complicate Macedonia's relations with the European Union (EU) and its main trading partners in western Europe.

In the hitherto chaotic state commercial banking sector, lower inflation and increased denar stability of 1995/96 have slightly increased new savings, although the Macedonian economy remains largely cash-based.

The US$1 billion of private hard currency deposits expropriated by the government earlier in the 1990s remains a sore point. In 1994/95, some of this money began to be returned, but only in the form of privatised and other non-monetary assets. Also in 1994/95, the government began to recapitalise the country's commercial banking sector, where the main difficulty is very high indebtedness and non-performing loans in state industrial and other enterprises. Here the World Bank FESAC is of considerable importance. Financial sector recapitalisation and restructuring, the responsibility of the Finance Ministry's Bank Rehabilitation Agency (BRA), is currently focused on the country's top commercial bank, Stopanska Banka which accounted for 60 per cent of all bank deposits as recently as 1994. The European Bank for Reconstruction and Development (EBRD) plans to take an equity stake in Macedonia's most profitable commercial bank, Kommercijalna Banka.

In 1994/95, the EBRD became one of the largest suppliers of new loans to Macedonia, with total disbursements of over DM100 million by the end of 1995. Mainly used for infrastructure development and new fixed investment for small and medium-sized companies, EBRD loans in 1996 are expected to focus

COUNTRY PROFILE — MACEDONIA

Historical profile

Macedonia is the southernmost republic of the former Yugoslav federation. It is a small land locked country between Serbia and Greece to the north and south, and Bulgaria and Albania to the east and west. Bulgaria briefly occupied most of the area in 1878, and tried to win it back in the 1912-13 Balkan conflicts and in the two world wars. It was a constituent republic within the federation since the end of the Second World War, when Yugoslavia gained its independence and was transformed into a federation of six republics: Macedonia, Slovenia, Serbia, Croatia, Bosnia and Herzegovina since its creation in 1944. On 8 September 1991, the people of Macedonia voted overwhelmingly (95 per cent) in favour in a referendum for Macedonian sovereignty and independence. It declared its independence in December 1991. Officially Bulgaria renounced its claims and recognised the new republic as Macedonia. In March 1993 Macedonia agreed to join the United Nations with the temporary prefix of 'former Yugoslav republic', opening the way for its nomenclature dispute with Greece to be settled through international arbitration. The main obstacle to a rapprochement between the two neighbours was Greece's insistence that Macedonia should change its flag, which carries an emblem associated with Alexander the Great. An accord reached in mid-September 1995 is expected to result in the normalisation of relations between Greece and Macedonia and should ensure that Macedonians have guaranteed access to the northern Greek port of Thessaloniki, their nearest outlet to the sea. In October 1995 a new national flag replaced the Star of Vergina symbol which Greece had objected to with a sun symbol.

Political system

Under the constitution, adopted on 17 November 1991, the Former Yugoslav Republic of Macedonia is a sovereign, independent, democratic and socially responsive state with a unicameral legislature – 120-seat National Assembly *(Sobranje)*. The first multi-party assembly was officially constituted on 8 January 1991. There are 22 ministers in the Macedonian government, including the president and the prime minister. Gligorov, the former communist leader and president since January 1992, was re-elected on 14 October 1994. Next elections scheduled for 1998.

Political parties

Coalition government led by the Social Democratic Alliance of Macedonia (SDSM), (former Communist Party), and including the Party of Democratic Prosperity of Albanians in Macedonia (PDPSM) (known as the PDP until 22 April 1995) and the Socialist Party (SDM). Other major parties include the Liberal Party (excluded from the new government in February 1996); National Democratic Party; Democratic Party (DPM); the nationalist Internal Macedonian Revolutionary Organisation-Democratic Party for Macedonian National Unity (Vnatresna Makedonska Revolucionerna Organizacija-Demokratska Partija za Makedonsko Nacionalno Edinstyo) (VMRO-DPMNE).

Population

Composition of population: Macedonian (64.6%), Albanian (21.7%), Turkish (3.8%), Romanian (2.7%), others (6.9%). The Albanians are concentrated in Tetovo and Gostivar and other parts of the north-west. Life expectancy is 70 years for men and 74 for women. The official religion is Macedonian Orthodox Christian; Islam and Catholicism are practised openly.

Main cities/towns

Skopje (population 541,280 in 1994). Four major towns are over 100,000 (Tetovo, Kumanovo, Gostivar and Bitola).

Language

The official language is Macedonian which is written using the Cyrillic alphabet. Albanian, Turkish, Serbian spoken. English, French and German are often understood.

Domestic economy

Macedonia is one of the poorest republics in Europe. The country provides sanctuary to more than 30,000 Bosnians. Wild-cat strikes disrupt transport and electricity is rationed. As part of its efforts to encourage private sector growth and foreign investment, the government introduced a comprehensive stabilisation programme, which was praised by the World Bank. One of the main components of this programme was currency reform. In 1994 and 1995 604 enterprises were privatised.

Employment

Well-educated workforce – 70 per cent of the population has completed secondary or tertiary education.

External trade

The 1994 Greek trade blockade against Macedonia was finally lifted in October 1995.
Exports: Total exports in 1995 were US$1.1bn. Major exports: vegetables (during 1995, total amount in profits made from vegetable exports reached US$15m, tomatoes accounting for approximately 50 per cent), sugar beet, cheese, lamb, tobacco, footwear, textiles, metals and ores. Main destinations: Former USSR (typically 23% of total), Germany (21%), Italy (7%), : Greece (6%), Bulgaria (4%).
Imports: Total imports in 1995 were US$1.4bn. Major imports: raw materials, machinery, transportation equipment, wheat and beef. Main sources: Former USSR (typically 27% of total), Germany (17%), Greece (7%), Italy (6%), Bulgaria (5%).

mainly on financial sector rehabilitation, an area of crucial importance to the economic reform programme.

Privatisation

Although delayed until after the AFM coalition government gained a decisive parliamentary majority in October 1994, large-scale privatisation by the Privatisation Agency (PA) made relatively good progress in 1995, with the entire exercise expected to be completed by the end of 1996. In 1995, 800 of a total of 1,200 enterprises slated for privatisation by PA were disposed of, mainly through insider-orientated management-employee buyouts, with shares typically being paid for in instalments over a 5 to 10 year period in most instances. Representing around 50 per cent of the total assets of the Macedonian economy and employing over 50 per cent of its remaining employed workforce, these enterprises have so far been mainly small-to-medium-sized, and considered relatively viable by the PA.

The 25 largest loss-making enterprises, on the other hand, are being separately restructured under a government programme that may lead to their privatisation by the PA in the longer-term. In practice, some of these often-technically-insolvent enterprises may eventually have to be liquidated, although this remains politically controversial. Certain sectors of the economy are also to remain outside the remit of the PA. These include the public utilities and agricultural co-operatives. Financial sector privatisation is the separate responsibility of the BRA.

Unlike other former Yugoslav republics, such as Slovenia, Macedonia has so far gone for purely revenue-orientated privatisation and not a system of ownership transformation based on vouchers. Because of long repayment times for newly acquired equity, PA privatisation income has been relatively low to date, with only DM20 million earned from such share sales by the end of 1995. In addition, shares can also be exchanged for still-frozen hard currency deposits in local banks. Real estate assets have also been made available to private depositors by the government for such bank liabilities.

In the longer-term, investors will be able to trade shares on the Skopje Stock Exchange (SSE), which opened for business in March 1996. Co-owned by a number of commercial banks and capitalised at DM1 million, the SSE is expected to experience high growth in the future, mainly because local privatised assets are relatively cheap and the large amounts of hard currency circulating in the private-sector. If this proves to be the case, then newly privatised companies may be able to begin recapitalising themselves properly. In 1994/95, most new investment remained largely confined to the private sector.

Foreign investment

Government hopes of increased foreign direct investment (FDI) through greater foreign investor involvement in local privatisation did not materialise in 1995. Much hope was focused on the proposed sale of four major tobacco product producers, including the largest, MakTabac, for a reported US$75 million. In the event, the PA had to delay this sale, mainly because of legal disputes over the status of the company. Another complication was that the pricing of these assets may have been too high. If this and direct sales of local assets to foreign investors prove successful in 1996, then substantial FDI could begin to increase, where such foreign capital inflows have been less than US$100 million to date.

The most promising areas for FDI are

COUNTRY PROFILE — MACEDONIA

Agriculture

The agriculture sector accounted for 16 per cent of GNP in 1994 and employed 30 per cent of the workforce. Agricultural land totals 1.3m ha, of which approximately half is cultivable, and half is pasture. Macedonia has propitious conditions for agriculture and is nearly self-sufficient in food production. Main crops include wheat, rice, early market-garden vegetables, fruits, grapes and tobacco. Over 50,000 tractors are in use. The population working on the land are mostly elderly people, apart from the ethnic Albanians who specialise in sheep-breeding in the mountains of western Macedonia. Unemployed Macedonians have productive smallholdings. The private sector accounts for over 75 per cent of agricultural production. Macedonia sends agricultural products to Slovenia, including large quantities of wine. Annual tobacco output 24,000 tonnes. The relatively few state farms were responsible for development of the wine industry and early vegetable cultivation under glass in southern Macedonia. The wheat subsidy remained in place in 1995 with the aim of ensuring self-sufficiency in output, but other farm subsidies have been sharply reduced under Macedonia's economic reform programme. A ban on owning goats imposed early in the communist era in order to prevent Macedonia's forests from being eroded, has been lifted with a view to increasing milk and cheese production. Milk yields from local cows are only one-quarter of the western European average.

Industry

Industry contributed 50 per cent to GNP in 1994 and employed 46 per cent of the labour force. The industrial sector is the largest of the Macedonian economy and includes basic metal industries, metal products and chemicals, textiles and footwear, food, beverages and tobacco. Revenue from industrial production doubled between 1953 and 1988 (including tobacco and wine). The metalworking industry and production of transport facilities account for 15.8 per cent of the total industrial production, textiles for 23.1 per cent, ferrous metallurgy for 6.8 per cent and the chemical industry for 6.7 per cent. The electric power construction material and furniture industries are also important. The main exporting industries are mining and smelting, footwear, textiles and agriculture (particularly tobacco). About 10 per cent of industrial assets are privately owned. The main problems are over-employment, slow growth, a slow rate of change in the structure of production and backward technology. A project by Daewoo of South Korea started producing telecommunications equipment at a state-owned plant on Lake Ochrid at end-1992. The sector was crippled by the Greek oil embargo, shortages of energy and raw materials.

Tourism

Tourism is well developed but has been one of the hardest hit industries. Revenues, which averaged around US$50m a year during 1988-90 have declined to less than US$10m. The government plans to build three tax-free, hard currency zones along the main highways – near Skopje, near Gevgelija on the border with Greece, and a third in central Macedonia, all including hotel and leisure complexes. Summer tourism is concentrated around the lakes and the national parks. Lakes Ohrid, Prespa, Dojran and Mavrovo cover a total water surface of 679.2 sq km. Winter tourism is developing in several ski resorts; there are 14 mountain massifs with peaks over 2,000 metres and perpetual Alpine climatic conditions. Both summer and winter tourism offer good potential for development. Interesting archaeological sites exist, as well as numerous mosaics, frescoes and icons, the earliest dating from Roman times, in monasteries, churches and mosques. The old part of Ohrid town is a UNESCO-protected World Heritage Site, as is the lake itself.

Mining

The mining sector accounted for 5 per cent of GNP in 1994 and accounted for 4 per cent of the labour force. Macedonia has a complex geological structure and a large number of ore deposits, including reserves of lead-zinc, copper and nickel, also coal, decorative and architectural building stone, and non-metallic materials. Deposits of non-ferrous metals and minerals are very significant and present good opportunities for exploitation. Iron and copper are mined.

Hydrocarbons

Oil and derivatives must be imported, although there is a crude oil processing refinery. A natural gas pipeline is under construction to carry Russian gas from the Bulgarian border to Skopje. Coal is mined.

Energy

Three-fifths of energy needs are satisfied by domestic production of thermoelectric and hydroelectric power; the deficit is imported from Serbia and Bulgaria.

Stock exchange

The FYRM opened its first stock exchange in March 1996.

Legal system

Civil law system of former Yugoslavia.

Membership of international organisations

Council of Europe, CSCE (observer), EBRD, IAEA, IDA, IFC, IMF, MIGA, OSCE (from 12 October 1995), Partnership for Peace (from November 1995), UN, World Bank, WTO.

agriculture-food processing, retail and wholesale trade, textiles and tourism. Greek foreign investors are expected to provide most of the FDI in Macedonia in 1996 and this could include investment in capital goods industries, particularly non-ferrous metallurgy. Another promising area for Greco-Macedonian economic co-operation is energy, where MakPetrol is presently financing and building a new US$100 million gas import pipeline from Bulgaria.

Foreign trade

Seriously damaged by the Greek economic blockade to the south and the UN economic sanctions against Serbia to the north, Macedonia's foreign trade was expected to substantially revive in 1996. In 1995, exports slightly rose to US$1.1 billion, compared to US$1 billion in 1993 and 1994. Then equal to around two-thirds of GDP, these transfers are thought to have been mainly boosted by the revival of foreign trade with Serbia, Macedonia's single largest external market in the communist Yugoslav period.

Encouraged by a favourable denar exchange rate and private-sector growth, imports reached US$1.4 billion in 1995, compared to US$1.3 billion in 1994. In 1996, imports were expected to grow rapidly. The result of this trend will be higher foreign trade deficits. In 1994 and 1995, these were US$300 million. Because of higher foreign borrowings and increased *émigré* hard currency remittances in 1995, the year-end current account deficit remained manageable at around US$100 million, or about the same level as at the end of 1994.

Macedonia is having difficulty financing even its present balance of payments deficits. Other than higher new foreign borrowings and increased service income, only improved export performance is the solution to the balance of payments predicament in the longer term. During the 1990s, the structure of Macedonia's foreign trade changed from higher value capital goods – which were mainly sold in the protected markets of former Yugoslavia – to lower value manufactures, such as textiles, or semi-processed goods. Once mainly sourced in former Yugoslavia, Macedonia's imports have also changed, particularly as regards higher value imports from the EU and raw materials, led by oil, which now have to be paid for with hard currency.

EU markets

Previously highly dependent on former Yugoslav markets, where Serbia alone took 70 per cent of Macedonia's exports as recently as 1992, foreign trade links have moved closer to the EU and other developed markets in recent years. By 1995, these markets accounted for around 50 per cent of Macedonia's exports and imports; most of the trade deficit was with the EU. Regionally, foreign trade growth is expected to be mainly with Greece, Italy, Serbia and Bulgaria. Like other former Yugoslav republics, Macedonia aspires to closer relations with the EU, but this remains conditional on a final resolution of its outstanding political issues with Greece.

As part of its recent rapprochement with Macedonia, Greece has agreed to lift its long-standing veto against closer Macedonian economic links with the EU. Here the main economic difficulty is EU protectionism and quotas in a number of areas of vital importance to Macedonia. Foremost amongst these are foodstuffs, tobacco and textiles.

Given the EU restrictions, export growth may have to be more regionally orientated, notably in relation to the rest

BUSINESS GUIDE — MACEDONIA

Time

GMT + 1 hr (GMT + 2 hrs from late Mar to late Sep).

Climate

The river valleys of Vardar and Strumica are temperate Mediterranean, as is the eastern region. Western and northern regions are temperate continental. However, temperatures may vary from +40 degrees C in the summer to -30 degrees C in the winter. Rainfall averages 742 mm annually, but around 450 mm in Skopje which has about 100 days of rain annually.

Entry requirements

Visa: Citizens of the EU countries do not require visas. Citizens from Australia, South Korea, USA and Canada require visas which are issued free at the airport or border.

Representation overseas

Ankara, Beijing, Bern, Bonn, Brussels, Ljubljana, London, Moscow, Paris, Rome, Sofia, Stockholm, Tirana, Vienna, Washington, Zagreb,

Air access

National airlines: Palair Macedonian, Macedonian Airlines.
Other airlines: Adria Airways, Aeroflot, Avioimpex, Balkan-Bulgarian Airlines, Croatia Airlines.
Airports: Skopje (SKP), 6 km from city; Ohrid. Air traffic control system not up to European standards and therefore, the airports are by-passed by international carriers and only used by regional airlines.

Surface access

Train or bus to Skopje can be hazardous because of irregular connections and the risk of long hold-ups at the border. Many visitors take a flight to Thessaloniki in northern Greece and a taxi to the border crossing at Evzoni, then walk into Macedonia. Travel light and carry a lot of Deutsche Marks is the advice given to visitors to Macedonia. Busy border crossings with Albania and Bulgaria.
Road: Plans for construction of east-west road and rail links to run from the Albanian port of Durres, across the mountains to western Macedonia, through Skopje, and on to Bulgaria. Completion planned for turn of the century.
Rail: Construction began in 1995 of a new 55-km rail link from Kriva Palanka, east of Kumanovo, on the Serbian-Macedonian border, to the Bulgarian border. It will connect the existing Macedonian railway to a new spur of the Bulgarian railways, which will join up with the main east-west rail route to the Bulgarian Black Sea ports of Varna and Baurgas and south-east to Istanbul. The project is estimated to cost US$120m and will be partly funded by the European Bank for Reconstruction and Development (EBRD). Rail access from Greece and Belgrade.

Hotels

Some restaurants add a surcharge of 20 per cent for live music. Tipping not expected, but loose change or more is usually left depending on quality of service.

City transport

Taxis: Good service operating in all main cities. All taxis are metered, but there is no basic charge. A 10 per cent tip is usual.
Buses and trams: Most city centres are served by trams, and the suburbs by buses. The service is generally cheap and regular.

National transport

Road: There are 4,876 km of modernised roads. The main road between Ohrid and Tetovo will become a four-lane highway.
Rail: There are 922 km of railway tracks of which 231 km are electrified.

Public holidays

Fixed dates: 1-2 Jan (New Year), 8 Jan (Orthodox Christmas Day), 1-2 May (Labour Day), 2 Aug (Ilinden – Proclamation of Macedonian State, 1944; Ilinden Uprising and Creation of the Krushevo Republic, 1903), 8 Sep (Day of Independence, 1991), 11 Oct (Day of Uprising against Fascism).

Working hours

Business: (Mon–Fri) 0800–1600 or 0830–1630.
Government: (Mon–Fri) 0700–1500 or 0730–1530.
Banking: (Mon–Fri) 0730–1930; (Sat) 0800–1300.
Shops: (Mon–Fri) 0800–1200 and 1700–2000/2100, but many shops open throughout day; (Sat) 0800–1500.

Business language and interpreting/translation

No regular nationwide interpreter service, but a translation service can usually be arranged through hotels, tourist offices or local enterprises. See also 'Business Directory, Other useful addresses, and Internet sites'.

Telecommunications

Telephone and telefax: Dialling code for Macedonia: IDD access code + 389 followed by area code (91 for Skopje), followed by subscriber's number. The telephone system has 345,000 lines and is in need of a systematic overhaul. International telephone calls from Macedonia can be a major operation due to the fact that lines to Europe run through Belgrade, Sarajevo or Zagreb and are either severed or overloaded.
IDD access from Macedonia: dial 99; AT&T USA Direct: dial 99-800-4288.
Telex: Service available in most large hotels and at main post offices. Messages can be handed in at telegram counters. Country code 62YU.

Banking

The National Bank of Macedonia (NBM) is an

of the former Yugoslavia. Except Slovenia and Croatia, such transfers are likely to be on the basis of bilateral barter. Regionally, Macedonia also has considerable potential as a transportation hub in the southern Balkans. East-west, however, transportation links are poor pending the construction of a new motorway along the old Via Ignatia.

Foreign debt and payments

Macedonia's foreign debt position, poor throughout most of the 1990s, improved in 1995. Supported by the IMF, the Paris Club (PC) of official governmental creditors agreed to reschedule part of Macedonia's foreign debt. Amounting to US$218 million, this is to be repaid over 15 years, with a six-year grace period. Dating from the early 1980s, a further US$75 million is also to be repaid over the next six years. Tied to the disbursal of new IMF and World Bank loans, this key agreement with the PC also paved the way for new credits from a number of EU governments, led by Germany.

In 1995/96, official creditors are expected to provide Macedonia with US$200 million worth of new loans, with a further US$250 million likely to be pledged in due course for 1996/97. Another major creditor is the EBRD. In the longer-term, the EU's European Investment Bank is also expected to begin lending to Macedonia, notably for local infrastructure development.

In 1995, Macedonia's total allocated foreign debt increased to a post-Yugoslav high of US$1.3 billion, compared to US$1.1 billion in 1994. In the short-term, the PC rescheduling will slightly ease Macedonia's foreign debt servicing burden. Longer-term, however, this could become unmanageable based on foreign debt growth of around US$200 million per annum.

Agreement was reached in principle with the London Club (LC) of commercial bank creditors in October 1996 to repay Macedonia's share of the former Yugoslav foreign commercial debt. Under the agreement Macedonia will assume 5.4 per cent of the principle (less than initially predicted) and 3.65 per cent of the interest, which is likely to total around US$200 million. The government is set to issue bonds in exchange for the debt, and it has been granted significant debt servicing concessions by the LC. The agreement should lead some western commercial banks to resume lending to Macedonia. So far, however, only a number of Greek commercial banks have intimated that they may lend new money to Macedonia in 1996. In addition, Greece's Commercial Bank has expressed an interest in acquiring an equity stake in Stopanska Banka.

Future prospects

Following on from the signing of the November 1995 Dayton, Ohio peace accords in former Yugoslavia, Macedonia is also expected to benefit from the greater regional stability that they might create. Domestically, however, the effective end of the Gligorov era in 1995-96 has created considerable political uncertainty. Foremost amongst the challenges Macedonia faces are economic policy and the issues surrounding the country's ethnic Albanian minority population. So far, Gligorov has been the key to Macedonia's difficult post-Yugoslav political and economic transformation. Whether or not it continues successfully and peacefully will ultimately be decided by who finally replaces him, when and under what circumstances.

BUSINESS GUIDE — MACEDONIA

Banking (contd): independent central bank with the explicit objective of maintaining the stability of the denar. The republic has a tiered banking structure. The National Bank of Macedonia is responsible for the money supply, the liquidity of financial institutions and foreign currency transactions and reserves. The banking system requires a major overhaul. Competition is being introduced with the emergence of private credit institutions such as Uniprokom. To help in reconstructing the banks, the World Bank agreed in April 1995 to a US$85m financial and enterprise sector adjustment credit (Fesac).
Central bank: National Bank of Macedonia (NCM).
Other banks: See 'Business Directory, Banking'.

Trade fairs
Annual International Skopje Fair in June.

Electricity supply
220 V AC 50 Hz with two large round prongs.

Representation in capital
Albania, Bulgaria, China, Croatia, France, Germany, Italy, Japan, Romania, Russia, Slovenia, Turkey, UK, USA.

BUSINESS DIRECTORY

Hotels

Skopje (area code 91)
Bristol, Marshall Tito 1, 91000 (tel: 114-883; fax: 114-753).

Continental, Alexander Makedonski bb, 91000 (tel: 116-599; fax: 222-221).

Grand, Mosha Pijade 2, 91000 (tel: 114-466; fax: 115-503).

Jadran, 27 Mart bb, 91000 (tel: 118-427; fax: 118-334).

Turist, Marshall Tito 15, 91000 (tel: 115-774; fax: 114-753).

Useful telephone numbers
Police: 92.

Fire: 93.

Ambulance: 94.

Time: 95.

Telegrams: 96.

Telephone service: 977.

To report emergencies: 985.

Emergency road service: 987.

Telephone information: 988.

Car hire

Skopje
Avis-Autotehna: (tel: 111-692).

Dollar-Putnik Eurodollar: (tel: 114-076).

Eurcar: (tel: 116-265).

Hertz: (tel: 116-387).

Taxis

Skopje
Ekspres (tel: 9196).

Komakomerts (tel: 9193).

Kompanija S (tel: 9190).

Plava Laguna (tel: 9192).

Radio Taksi Vodno (tel: 9191).

Teniks (tel: 9194).

Vardar (tel: 9195).

BUSINESS DIRECTORY

Chambers of commerce

Chamber of Commerce and Industry of Macedonia, Dimitrie Cuposki 13, 91000 Skopje (tel: 231-460; fax: 116-210); Department of Economy and development (tel: 237-425); Department for Foreign Economic Affairs (tel: 117-101).

Chamber of Commerce of the City of Skopje, Bul Partizanski Odredi 2, PO Box 509, 91000 Skopje (tel: 112-511, 116-245; fax: 116-419).

Banking

National Bank of Macedonia (NCM) (central bank), Complex of Banks, 91000 Skopje (tel: 233-358; fax: 111-541).

Almako Banka a.d. Skopje, bil. Vasil Glavinov bb, 91000 Skopje (tel: 113-200; fax: 112-540).

Balkanska Banka, (head office), 6 Maksim Gorkl, 91000 Skopje (tel: 222-574, 233-858; fax: 237-546; International Department, bb Kej 13 Noemvrl, Skopje (tel: 231-211; fax: 233-850).

Eksport Import Banka (mixed capital: Macedonian and Austrian), Bul Partizanski Odredi 70B, PO Box 836, 91000 Skopje (tel: 364-219; fax: 364-135).

Invest Banka (domestic capital), Marshall Tito Street 9/11, 91000 Skopje (tel: 114-166, 238-965; fax: 237-349).

Izvozna i Kreditna Banka (domestic capital), 11 Oktomvri 8, 91000 Skopje (tel: 111-337; fax: 213-220).

Komercijalna Banka (domestic capital), Kej Dimitar Vlahov 4, PO Box 563, 91000 Skopje (tel: 112-077, 235-040, 229-334; fax: 111-780, 213-456, 213-456).

Kreditna Banka Skopje (mixed capital: Macedonian and Austrian), Marshall Tito 19, 91000 Skopje (tel: 116-433; fax: 116-830).

Makedonska Banka (formerly Ljubljanska Banka) (mixed capital: Macedonian and Slovenian), Bul Marks i Engels 3, Blok 12/2, 91000 Skopje (tel: 117-111; fax: 117-191).

Rado Banka (domestic capital), Dame Gruev 3, 91000 Skopje (tel: 118-500; fax: 118-160).

Sileks Banka (domestic capital), Gradski Zid, Blok 9, Lokal 5, 91000 Skopje (tel: 115-814; fax: 114-891).

Stopanska Banka (domestic capital), 11 Oktomvri 7, 91000 Skopje (tel: 115-322, 235-111; fax: 113-263, 239-321, 226-576).

Teteks Bank (domestic capital), Marshall Tito 30, PO Box 198, 91000 Skopje (tel: 119-206; fax: 119-764).

Tutunska Banka (domestic capital), 12 Udarna Brigada ;bb, PO Box 702, 91000 Skopje (tel: 112-033; fax: 231-114).

Travel information

Adria Airways (tel: 117-009; fax: 235-531).

Avioimpex (tel: 115-747; fax: 119-348).

Balkan-Bulgarian Airlines (tel: 113-022; fax: 113-022).

Croatia Airlines (tel: 115-858; fax: 114-203).

Macedonian Airlines, Bulevar Partizanski, Opodredi 17A, 91000 Skopje (tel: 116-333; fax: 229-576).

Palair Macedonian, Kuzman J Pitu bb, 91000 Skopje (tel: 162-878, 115-868; fax: 162-505, 238-238).

Tourist Union of the City of Skopje, Dame Gruev/Gradski Zid, Blok 3, PO Box 399, 91000 Skopje (tel: 118-498; fax: 230-803).

Other useful addresses

Agency for Transformation of Enterprises with Social Capital (privatisation agency), PO Box 410, Dame Gruev bb, 91000 Skopje (tel: 229-275; fax: 233-633; E-mail: agency@mpa@itl.mk).

Alumina, Ul Ivo Lola Ribar, 91000 Skopje (tel: 229-111; fax: 230-805).

Bank Rehabilitation Agency, Kompleks Banki bb, 91000 Skopje (tel: 213-490; fax: 222-427).

British Embassy, Veljko Vlahovic 26, 91000 Skopje (tel: 116-772; fax: 117-005).

Creativ Servis (interpretation, translation, meeting, research, promotion), Rajko Zhinzifov 44/1, 91000 Skopje (tel & fax: 228-959).

Customs Administration, Lazar Licenovski 13, 91000 Skopje (tel: 224-467; fax: 237-832).

Fersped International Forwarding, Str Naroden Front No 17, 91000 Skopje (tel: 234-054, 211-528, 225-511, 224-511; fax: 231-271, 213-522).

International Club (information, communications, translations), Skopje (e-mail: mils@itl.mk).

Macedonian Information Office, Kingsway House, 103 Kingsway, London WC2B 6QX (tel: 0171-404-6558; fax: 0171-404-6704).

Metalski Zavoid-Tito (tools and machinery), Ui Pero Nakov bb, Skopje (tel: 223-111, 51-151; fax: 233-252).

Ministry of Agriculture, Forestry and Water, Leninova No 2, 91000 Skopje (tel: 113-045; fax: 211-997).

Ministry of Culture, Bul Ilinden bb, 91000 Skopje (tel: 220-823; fax: 225-810).

Ministry of Defence, Orce Nikolov bb, 91000 Skopje (tel: 112-872; fax: 227-835).

Ministry of Development, Bote Bocevski 9, 91000 Skopje (tel: 111-077; fax: 112-799).

Ministry of the Economy, Bote Bocevski bb, 91000 Skopje (tel: 119-628, 112-834; fax: 111-161).

Ministry of Education and Physical Culture, Veljko Vlahovic bb, 91000 Skopje (tel: 117-277; fax: 118-414).

Ministry of Finance, Dame Gruev 14, 91000 Skopje (tel: 116-012; fax: 117-280).

Ministry of Foreign Affairs, Dame Gruev 6, 91000 Skopje (tel: 238-832; fax: 115-790).

Ministry of Health, Vodnjanska bb, 91000 Skopje (tel: 113-429; fax: 113-014).

Ministry of Internal Affairs, Dimce Mircev bb, 91000 Skopje (tel: 221-972; fax: 112-468).

Ministry of Justice and Administration, veljko Vlahovic bb, 91000 Skopje (tel: 230-732; fax: 226-975).

Ministry of Labour and Social Policy, Dame Gruev 14, 91000 Skopje (tel: 117-288).

Ministry of Science, Bul Ilinden bb, 91000 Skopje (tel: 238-610; fax: 235-573).

Ministry of Transport and Communications, Ilindenska bb, 91000 Skopje (tel: 119-378; fax: 114-258).

Ministry of Urbanism and Ecology, Dame Gruev 14, 91000 Skopje (tel: 227-204; fax: 117-163).

Office of the President, 11 Oktomvri bb, 91000 Skopje (tel: 113-318; fax: 112-147, 113-643).

Pelagonija Construction Company, V. Vlahovic 2,91000 Skopje (tel: 231-711, 231-074; fax: 226-329).

Post, Telegraph and Telephone Service (PTT), Orce Nikolov bb, 91000 Skopje (tel: 113-333; fax: 224-277).

Prime Minister's Office, Ilindenska bb, 91000 Skopje (tel: 115-389; fax: 112-561, 113-512).

Skopje Fair, ul Belasica bb, PO Box 356, 91001 Skopje (tel: 118-288; fax: 117-375).

Statistical Office, Dame Gruev 4/3/66, PO Box 506, 91000 Skopje (tel: 115-022; fax: 220-859).

Steelwork Skopje, 91000 Skopje (tel: 221-111, 221-076; fax: 221-257).

Stock Company for Insurance and Reinsurance 'Makedonija'-Skopje, 11 Oktomvri Street, No 25, 91000 Skopje (tel: 115-188; fax: 115-374).

US Embassy, 27 Mart 5, 91000 Skopje (tel: 116-180; fax: 117-103).

Internet sites

Agency for Transformation of Enterprises with Social Capital (privatisation agency), Skopje (http://www.mpa.org.mk).

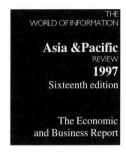

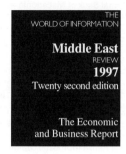

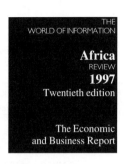

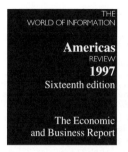

Malta

Michael Griffin

After nine years in office, Prime Minister Eddie Fenech Adami has transformed Malta from an isolated satellite of international socialism into a prosperous mixed economy knocking on the door of the European Union (EU). Negotiations for final EU membership are not due to begin until late 1997, but this will also be the deadline for fresh general elections. The Prime Minister's Nationalist Party (PN) can point to a record of solid growth and rising incomes, but the Malta Labour Party (MLP), adamantly opposed to EU membership, have in their favour public dissatisfaction with mounting taxation and the Maltese attachment to their hard-won sovereignty. Adami, moreover, has barely begun to prune the state's burgeoning payroll, accounting for 35 per cent of all jobs, or Malta's over-generous social services, both of which would seriously harm his electoral chances.

KEY FACTS — Malta

Official title: Republic of Malta

Head of state: President Ugo Mifsud-Bonnici

Head of government: Prime Minister Alfred Sant (Labour Party) (from 26 Oct 1996)

Ruling party: Labour Party (elected 26 Oct 1996,)

Capital: Valletta

Official Languages: Maltese and English

Currency: Maltese Lira (Lm) = 100 cents

Exchange rate: Lm0.36 per US$ (Dec 1996)

Area: 316 sq km

Population: 365,000 (1995)

GDP per capita: US$8,136 (1994)

GDP real growth: 4.8% (1994)

GNP per capita: US$8,000 (1994)

GNP real growth: 4.5% (1995)*

Unemployment: 3.5% (1st qtr 1995)

Inflation: 3.9% (1st half 1995)

Balance of trade: -US$560.2m (1994)

Visitor numbers: 1.176m (1994)

* estimated figure

KEY INDICATORS — Malta

	Unit	1991	1992	1993	1994	1995
Population	'000	359.5	362.9	363.0	364.0	365.0
Gross national product (GNP)	US$bn	2.57	2.90	2.72	3.00	–
GNP per capita	US$	7,500	8,000	7,500	8,000	–
GNP real growth	%	6.4	4.1	4.2	4.3	*4.5
Inflation	%	2.5	1.6	4.1	5.4	**3.9
Consumer prices	1990=100	102.5	104.2	108.5	113.0	117.5
Agricultural production	1979-81=100	127.87	126.61	131.32	152.90	160.11
Exports (FOB) (goods)	US$m	1,324.4	1,603.5	1,400.8	1,605.1	–
Imports (FOB) (goods)	US$m	1,897.3	2,104.0	1,953.8	2,165.3	–
Balance of trade	US$m	-572.9	500.5	-553.0	-560.2	–
Foreign debt	US$bn	1.27	1.27	1.40	–	–
Current account	US$m	-13.6	26.0	-86.8	-85.7	–
Tourist arrivals	'000	893	1,002	1,005	1,176	–
Total reserves minus gold	US$m	1,333.3	1,268.3	1,362.4	1,849.6	1,604.5
Foreign exchange	US$m	1,211.7	1,188.0	1,279.3	1,760.5	1,508.0
Discount rate	%	5.5	5.5	5.5	5.5	–
Deposit rate	%	4.5	4.5	4.5	4.5	–
Lending rate	%	8.5	8.5	8.5	8.5	–
Exchange rate	US$ per Lm	3.10	3.14	2.61	2.64	2.83

* estimated figure ** first half 1995

Politics

In an unguarded comment in May 1996, the Prime Minister threatened to call a snap election if the MLP and trades unions persisted with calls for strike action. Labour unrest was ultimately avoided, but the date of the elections will remain the subject of the keenest speculation. This situation raises the prospect that the longer Mr Adami delays, the more the ballot will acquire the dimension of a referendum on EU entry.

The MLP bases its opposition to EU membership on Malta's traditional non-alignment. It accepts the need for closer economic ties – the EU is the destination of two-thirds of Maltese exports – but not the transfer of sovereignty which comes with full membership. The introduction of VAT in January 1995, in line with the government's policy of harmonising its tax regime with Brussels, added the fear of rising inflation to the MLP's patriotic call for the accession process to be discontinued.

The MLP is on shifting ground, however. Though it still commands strong support in Malta's heavily unionised labour force, it is indelibly associated with the turbulent Mintoff and Bonnici governments which nationalised two thirds of all economic activity in the 1970s and aligned the former British colony with Libya and the eastern bloc. The Nationalist programme focused upon rolling back state influence in the economy, attracting investment and turning the island's strategic position between Europe and North Africa to commercial, rather than political, advantage. These are policies which have had profound impact upon the profile and loyalties of the Maltese voter. The MLP argues that the island's newfound prosperity has widened the gap between rich and poor, but it has shown little indication that it would attempt to reverse the Nationalist Party's policies.

Economy

Under Mr Adami, GDP has increased by an impressive average 6 per cent each year, providing the islanders with a standard of living comparable, if not better than, Portugal's. Real wages have risen by 38 per cent since 1987 and unemployment continues to fall, totalling just 3.5 per cent in 1995. While the state still underpins an unhealthy proportion of the total jobs in the Maltese economy, the government has generated new sources of employment in manufacturing, industry, a highly successful free port and an evolving financial services centre.

Considering the whole picture, however, Prime Minister Adami's economic record is only a qualified success. In 1995, GDP grew 6 per cent (to Lm1.187 billion), but the current account deficit soared to US$200 million, the worst since the Nationalists took office, and inflation, powered by the introduction of VAT, rose from 4.1 to 4.7 per cent, some way above the maximum allowed under the Maastricht guidelines.

Manufacturing and industry remained buoyant, with exports rising by 19 per cent from US$1.56 billion in 1994 to US$1.86 billion in 1995. But import levels surged by a massive 32 per cent from US$2.34 billion in 1994 to US$3.12 billion in 1995, partially as a result of large scale construction projects in the tourism industry and the docks. Reform of the civil service has also been slow and, since the sale of 26.2 per cent of the Bank of Valetta in March 1995, there has been little progress with the government's privatisation programme.

In his budget speech on 22 November 1995, Finance Minister John Dalli announced further modifications to the tax regime, including the raising of the income threshold to Lm3,000 (US$8,427) for single taxpayers and Lm4,000 for married couples. Total revenue in 1996 is forecast at Lm515.4 million (US$1.45 billion), of which some 80 per cent will be raised through taxation.

However, the deficit is to rise by 2.3 per cent to Lm54.1 million, on expenditure of Lm569.5 million. Social security and pensions account for 36.2 per cent of current expenditure, and the government wages bill accounts for a further 31 per cent.

Malta's visible trading performance depends heavily upon a single foreign investor,

COUNTRY PROFILE — MALTA

Historical profile

1814 Crown Colony of the UK with limited self-government.
1942 Islanders awarded the George Cross for heroism during three-year siege and severe bombing by Germans and Italians in Second World War.
1947 Self-government.
1956 Majority in referendum in favour of integration with the UK as proposed by the Malta Labour Party (MLP) under Dominic Mintoff.
1959-62 Disturbances followed rejection of British proposals by Mintoff, who resigned. British took over government.
1964 Independence within Commonwealth. Defence and aid treaties with UK.
1971 Labour government under Mintoff with nationalist and socialist aims and non-aligned foreign policy. Co-operative treaties with Eastern and Western countries, and close relations with Libya.
1974 Declaration of Republic.
1981 MLP gained more seats but fewer votes than Nationalist Party (PN) who mounted campaign of civil disobedience and boycotted the House of Representatives for over a year.
1987 PN under Dr Edward Fenech-Adami in power following constitutional amendments. Government's aim to maintain non-aligned status, while seeking closer ties with the West.
1990 EU application.

Political system

Republic with legislative power vested in unicameral House of Representatives (currently 69 members elected for five years by universal adult suffrage). Should a party polling a majority of votes fail to gain a majority of seats in the House, extra seats are allocated until a majority of one seat is achieved. The House elects the president as constitutional head of state, also for a five-year term, who then appoints the prime minister and, on the latter's advice, the cabinet, which holds executive power. Elections to be held by 1997.

Political parties

Partit Nazzionalista (Nationalist Party) (PN) is the ruling party. Other major parties: Malta Labour Party (MLP); Alternativa Demokratika (Democratic Alternative) (AD); Partit Demokratiko Malti (Democratic Party) (PDM); Partit Komunista Malti (Communist Party) (PKM).

Main cities/towns

Valletta (capital, population 210,000 in 1994), Birkirkara (21,218), Qormi (19,330) and Sliema (13,542).

Language

Maltese is the national language. Both Maltese and English are the official languages. Most business correspondence is in English. English is spoken by about 90 per cent of the population.

Media

Dailies: L-Orizzont and *In-Nazzjon Taghna* published in Maltese and *The Times* in English.
Weeklies: Most widely read are *It-Torca, Il-Mument, Il-Gens, Lehen Is-Sewwa* and *Il-Helsien* in Maltese and *The Sunday Times* in English.
Business: Few with small circulations. Include *Commercial Courier* and *Industry Today.*
Broadcasting: Supervised by Malta Broadcasting Authority. Approximately 128,000 TV licences in use. Xandir Malta (part of TeleMalta Corp) broadcasts two wireless radio services (Radio Malta) and a TV service (Television Malta). Private broadcasting services have been introduced following a liberalisation of media laws. Six private radio stations are already in operation. Over 20 Italian TV stations are clearly received in Malta, and through a cable television network so are many of the satellite stations.
Advertising: Advertisements can be placed on radio and TV through Xandir Malta in Gwardamangia. Newspapers, periodicals, cinemas and poster sites also available.

Domestic economy

International trade, and in particular export activities, represent Malta's economic lifeline. Measures designed to increase the competitiveness of Maltese exports and to widen the range of incentives available to the industrial investor are given priority. Malta's economy is closely interlinked with the European Union, with 75 per cent of its exports going to EU countries, whilst 75 per cent of its imports originate from the EU. It is the government's aim to achieve full EU membership for Malta. The economy is one of the most open in Western Europe. Emphasis in Malta's economic policy is towards the development of the manufacturing and tourism industries. Manufacturing accounts for 30 per cent of GDP and 21 per cent of employment. The government's economic strategy is to encourage the development of export-oriented high technology manufacturing industry, while upgrading the quality of tourism in Malta. A number of major projects have been completed, including the construction of the first phase of a power station to meet the island's energy demand, a state-of-the-art telecommunications system, an air terminal and a port complex which handles containers, bulk cargo, storage of mineral oils and has industrial and warehousing facilities. The government enacted legislation to transform Malta into an international business centre, and is actively promoting Malta as an offshore financial and trading centre. Transport-related services such as transshipment and ship repair are also important to the economy. Malta Freeport finalised significant transshipment agreements with a number of dominant shipping lines.

External trade

Regular trade deficit offset by invisible earnings, mainly from tourism and overseas investment. In 1988 and 1989 the government liberalised economic policies and import controls were relaxed and imports and exports surged forward. Germany, Italy and the UK account for around 60 per cent total trade turnover.
Exports: Major exports include food and beverages, clothing, footwear and accessories, furniture and fixtures, giftware and home accessories, cosmetics and toiletries, health, hygiene and cleaning products, paper and stationery products, plastic and metal products and components, building materials, electronic and electrical equipment and parts. Main destinations: EU (typically 75 per cent of total), North America (8%).
Imports: Imports consist mainly of foodstuffs, petroleum products, basic manufactures, chemicals, machinery and transport equipment. Main source: EU (typically 75 per cent of total).

the Franco-Italian electronics group SGS-Thomson, whose semi-conductors account for 60 per cent of total industrial output. Nevertheless, manufacturing – principally of electronic components, engineering products and clothing – is dwarfed in importance by the island's tourism industry, which provides one third of Maltese jobs and 40 per cent of GDP.

Tourism

After eight years of consecutive growth, demand for Maltese holidays began to flag in 1995 with the UK market, which typically supplies half of the country's peak of 1.2 million holidaymakers, falling by 10.6 per cent. The total number of arrivals was reported as 1.12 million and is predicted to slide further in 1996. Hoteliers blame the trend upon VAT, which overnight pushed up costs by 10 per cent over 1994, making a Maltese holiday comparable with the cost of a trip to Goa or Egypt.

Labour costs have also risen markedly and the phasing out of the Forward Buying Rate, which gave tour operators a modest discount on the official exchange rate of the Maltese lira, are major disincentives. To counteract the latter effect in the all-important British market, the government introduced a more generous discount of Lm0.606 to the pound sterling, provided that the operator will guarantee a certain number of bookings. Though concerns remain about the quality of the Maltese tourism 'product', confidence in the sector remains ebullient with some 3,000 new beds, largely at the upmarket end of the spectrum, due to come on stream by 1998. Hilton is also investing US$120 million in a new resort complex.

Financial services

Malta's vulnerability to fluctuations in holiday demand, as well as a domestic savings rate of 12 per cent, has lent some impetus to the government's ambition of launching the island as a financial services centre, with a particular focus on the expatriate investor. Over the past three years, the authorities have negotiated double-taxation agreements with 24 countries and are now offering incentives such as exemption from stamp duty, withholding tax and capital gains on share sales and dividends paid to non-residents.

Alongside the creation of a legal and administrative framework, there have also been efforts to deregulate Malta's financial system, ease exchange controls and set up a local capital market – the Malta Financial Services Centre (MFSC). The MFSC has received 45 applications to operate local funds but has only issued two licenses – to Hambros' Malta Development Fund and Rothschilds. After three years of operations, the Malta Stock Exchange registered total business of US$132 million last year, with the Bank of Valetta, its largest listed company, announcing record profits of Lm10.5 million, up 44 per cent on 1994. Efforts to liberalise the domestic banking scene moved a step forward when the government granted a license to Midland Bank, making it the first international bank to operate on the island.

COUNTRY PROFILE — MALTA

Agriculture

The agricultural sector accounted for 3 per cent of GNP in 1994 and employed 4 per cent of the labour force. Agriculture supplies only about 20 per cent of Malta's food needs. Limited area of land available for agriculture. Potatoes and onions are largest vegetable crops, grapes are largest fruit crop, and flower cultivation flourishing.

Industry

The industrial sector provided 31 per cent of GNP in 1994 and employed 36 per cent of the labour force. Manufactures include textiles, clothing, synthetic fibres, footwear, wines and beer, furniture, electronic goods, automobile components, measuring/controlling equipment and tobacco products. In 1988 an industrial development law was passed to stimulate private direct investment, especially foreign, in the hope of reducing dependence on clothing firms and encouraging higher technology industries. Ship repair is important.

Tourism

The tourism sector accounts for 40 per cent of Malta's GDP. By 1998 about 3,000 new four-star -category beds will be available. Malta and the neighbouring islands of Gozo and Comino have much to offer visitors.

Mining

Malta has no natural resources.

Stock exchange

The Malta Stock Exchange was set up in 1991 to encourage private investment in a range of commercial and government stock.

Legal system

Public law based on English common law.

Membership of international organisations

ACP (associate), CCC, Commonwealth, Council of Europe, CSCE, Eurocontrol, FAO, G77, ICAO, IFAD, ILO, IMF, IMO, INTERPOL, ITU, IWC, MIGA, NAM, UN, UNDP, UNESCO, UNICEF, UPU, WHO, WIPO, WMO, World Bank, WTO. Malta applied to join the EU in July 1990.

BUSINESS GUIDE

Time

GMT + 1 hr (GMT + 2 hrs from end Mar to end Sep).

Climate

Mediterranean, with hot summers and warm winters. Temperatures range from about 29°C down to about 10°C. Jan and Feb are coldest months, Jul and Aug the hottest. Best time to visit – Feb–May. Aug and Sep tend to be hot and humid, but usually sea breezes in evening.
Clothing: European clothing suitable for winter, spring and autumn; tropical weight for summer.

Entry requirements

Visa not required by nationals of Commonwealth countries, UK dependencies, Council of Europe members and some other countries including Japan, Libya, Monaco, Egypt and Kuwait. N.B. Regulations liable to change at short notice.
Health: Vaccination certificates not required unless travelling from an infected area. Water supplies are filtered, and tap water is safe to drink.
Currency: No limit on foreign currency taken in, but amount should be declared on entry, then up to this amount may be taken out.
Customs: Personal effects duty-free, plus duty-free allowance.

Air access

Regular flights from most major international airports in Europe and North Africa. In September 1993 the European Investment Bank (EIB) granted a loan to improve air traffic control facilities. Completion is scheduled for end-1997.
National airline: Air Malta.
Main international airport: Malta (MLA) at Luqa, 5 km from Valletta.

Surface access

Regular car ferry services from Sicily and Italian mainland.
Main ports: Valletta and Marsaxlokk.

Hotels

Classified from five-star to one-star. Advisable to book in advance especially during tourist season. All hotel staff English-speaking and many are multi-lingual.

Restaurants

Numerous, ranging from first- to fourth-class, to snack-bars. Cost of meals ranges from Lm1 for one-course meal with trimmings in pub atmosphere to Lm10 per head in luxury hotel restaurant, including wine. Ten per cent levy payable on meals in first-, second- and third-class restaurants only.

Currency

Exchange rate: Value of Maltese lira pegged to calculated value of a basket of three currencies, namely, the US dollar, the pound sterling and the Ecu. Composition of basket periodically reviewed, largely to reflect external trade of Malta in these currencies.

Foreign exchange information

Bank accounts: Non-resident accounts may be opened by those non-resident in Malta and also by certain residents not of Maltese origin. Permission to open such accounts can be obtained from authorised dealers, and they can be used where Exchange Control permission would otherwise be required. Foreign investors require Exchange Control permission to borrow from local sources.
Trade policy: Since 1987 more liberal import policies were introduced and import licence requirements were progressively relaxed.

Credit cards

All major credit cards are accepted.

Car hire

Self-drive cars available at daily, weekly and monthly rates (eg about Lm5 per day with unlimited mileage and fully comprehensive insurance). National or international driving licence required, which must be endorsed at Police Licensing Office, Floriana. Speed limits 40 kph in built-up areas, 64 kph elsewhere. Driving is on the left.

City transport

Metered taxis available.

National transport

Air: Recent introduction of internal flights (by helicopter) between Malta and Gozo.
Road: Regular bus services from Valletta to most towns and villages on Malta and Gozo.
Water: Gozo Channel Company operates a regular round-the-clock daily ferry service between Malta and Gozo.

Public holidays

Fixed dates: 1 Jan (New Year's Day), 10 Feb (Feast of St Paul's Shipwreck), 19 Mar (Feast of St Joseph), 31 Mar (Freedom Day), 1 May (Labour/Workers' Day), 7 Jun ('Sette Guigno'), 29 Jun (Feast of St Peter and St Paul), 15 Aug (Feast of the Assumption), 8 Sep (Victory Day), 21 Sep (Independence Day), 8 Dec (Feast of the Immaculate Conception), 13 Dec (Republic Day) and 25 Dec (Christmas Day).
Variable dates: Good Friday.

Working hours

Business: (Mon–Fri) 0830–1245 and 1430–1730.
Government: (Mon–Fri) 0745–1230 and 1315–1715; (from Jun to Sep) 0730–1330 only.
Banking: (Mon–Fri) 0830–1230, (Fri) 1700–1900, (Sat) 0830–1200.
Shops: (Mon–Sat) 0900–1300 and 1600–1900.

Telecommunications

Telephone and telefax: International dialling code: 356 followed by six-digit subscriber's number. There are no area codes. Direct dialling from Malta to most countries; others can be reached through Overseas Telephone Exchange – dial 194 (8194 from Gozo). There are around 50 telephones per 100 population.
Telex: Available at first-class hotels and at TeleMalta Corporation offices in Valletta and St Julian's. Country code 406 MW.
Telegram: Can be sent from TeleMalta in St Julian's, open 24 hours a day (tel: 224-131); and Luqa Airport open 0700–1830 (tel: 225-861).

Banking

Monetary policy and foreign exchange control exercised by Central Bank of Malta. Four major commercial banks, The Mid-Med Bank, Bank of Valletta and Lombard Bank (Malta) Ltd and APS Bank. In 1988 a law was passed to regulate and promote the establishment of offshore businesses, banks, insurances and private trusts. Two banks given licences to operate as credit institutions in 1994 – Izola Bank and First International Merchant Bank.
Central bank: Central Bank of Malta.
Commercial banks: There are four commercial banks: Mid-Med Bank Ltd (Malta's largest banking organisation), Bank of Valletta Ltd, Lombard Bank (Malta) Ltd and APS Bank Ltd.
Other banks: See 'Business Directory, Banking'.

Trade fairs

International Fair held annually during first two weeks of July at Naxxar. Permanent exhibition of Maltese manufacturers held by Malta Export Trade Corp at Trade Centre, San Gwann. Specialised fairs are also held.

Electricity supply

240 V AC.

Representation in capital

Australia, China, Egypt, France, Germany, The Holy See, India, Italy, Libya, Palestine, Russia, Spain, Tunisia, UK, USA.

BUSINESS DIRECTORY

Hotels

Floriana
Phoenicia, The Mall (tel: 225-241; tx: 1240).

Gozo
Ta'Cenc, Sannat (tel: 556-830; fax: 558-199).

Sliema
Holiday Inn, Tigne Street (tel: 341-173; fax: 311-292).

St Julian's
Dragonara Palace (tel: 336-422; fax: 336-431).

Hilton International (tel: 336-201; fax: 341-539).

Valletta
British, 267 St Ursula Street (tel: 224-730/229-711).

Cumberland, 111 St John Street (tel: 227-732).

Osborne, South Street (tel: 623-656/7; tx: 1440 OSBORN).

Car hire

Avis: reservation office (tel: 246-640; fax: 235-754).

Budget: central reservations (tel: 247-111; fax: 244-626).

Europcar: reservations office (tel: 337-361; fax: 339-627).

Hertz: reservations office, Gzira (tel: 314-637; fax: 333-153).

Chambers of commerce

Malta Chamber of Commerce, Exchange Buildings, Republic Street, Valletta VLT 05 (tel: 233-873, 247-233; fax: 245-223).

Banking

Central Bank of Malta, Castille Place, Valletta CMR 01 (tel: 247-480; fax: 243-051).

APS Bank ltd, 275 St Paul Street, Valletta VLT 07 (tel: 247-547; fax: 238-698).

Bank of Valletta Ltd, 58 Zachary Street, Valletta VLT 04 (tel: 243-261/7; fax: 230-894).

Bank of Valletta (International) Ltd, 86 South Street, Valletta VLT 11 (tel: 249-970/8; fax: 222-132).

Investment Finance Bank Ltd, 168 Strait Street, Valletta VLT 07 (tel: 232-017, 233-349; fax: 242-014).

Lohombus Corporation Ltd, Spencer Gardens, Blata il-Bajda, HMR 12 (tel: 226-030; fax: 242-660).

Lombard Bank (Malta) Ltd, Lombard House, 67 Republic Street, Valletta VLT 05 (tel: 248-411/8; fax: 246-600).

Mid-Med Bank Ltd, 233 Republic Street, Valletta VLT 05 (tel: 245-281, 235-448; fax: 230-406).

Mid-Med Bank (Overseas) Ltd, 15 Republic Street, Valletta VLT 05 (tel: 249-801/4; fax: 249-805).

Valletta Investment Bank Ltd, 144 St Christopher Street, Valletta VLT 02 (tel: 235-246; fax: 234-419).

Principal newspapers

Commercial Courier, The Malta Chamber of Commerce, Exchange Bldgs, Republic Street, Valletta (tel: 247-233).

Il-Gens, Media Centre, National Road, Blata il-Bajda (tel: 249-005, 247-460, 244-913, 224-018, 234-057, 223-047; fax: 243-508).

The Sunday Times and The Times, Allied Newspapers Ltd, 341 St Paul Street, Valletta (tel: 224-032/6, 241-464; fax: 237-150).

Travel information

Air Malta Co Ltd, Head Office, Luqa LQA 01 (tel: 824-330/9; fax: 673-241).

Malta International Airport Ltd, Luqa LQA 05 (tel: 249-600; fax: 243-042).

National Tourism Organisation, 280 Republic Street, Valletta VLT 04 (tel: 224-444/5; fax: 220-401).

Other useful addresses

Department of Industry, St George's, Canon Road, St Venera (tel: 446-259).

Department of Information, Auberge de Castille, Valletta (tel: 225-241, 224-901; fax: 237-170).

Department of Trade, Lascaris, Valletta (tel: 224-411).

Hotels and Restaurants Association, 7 Frederick Street, Valletta (tel: 336-843; fax: 237-253).

Malta Development Corporation, House of Catalunya, Marsamxetto Road, Valletta (tel: 220-516, 222-691; fax: 246-408).

Malta Drydocks, The Docks (tel: 822-451, 822-491; fax: 800-021).

Malta Export Trade Corporation, Trade Centre, PO Box 8, San Gwann SGN 01 (tel: 446-186/7/8; fax: 496-687).

Malta Federation of Industry, Development House, St Anne Street, Floriana VLT 01 (tel: 222-074, 234-428; fax: 240-702).

Malta Financial Services Centre, (formerly Malta International Business Authority – MIBA), Palazzo Spinola, St Julian's 29, STJ10 (tel: 344-230; fax: 344-334).

Malta Freeport Corporation Ltd, Freeport Centre, Port of Matrsaxlokk, Kalafrana BBG 07 (tel: 650-200; fax: 684-814).

Malta Maritime Authority, Maritime House, Lascaris Wharf, Valletta VLT 01 (tel: 250-360/4; fax: 250-365).

Malta Shipbuilding Co Ltd, Marsa (tel: 220-051, 237-297; fax: 240-930).

Malta Stock Exchange, Pope Pius V Street, Valletta VLT 11 (tel: 244-051/5; fax: 244-071).

Malta Trade Fairs Corporation, The Fair Grounds, Naxxar NXR 02 (tel: 410-371/4; fax: 414-099).

Ministry of Economic Affairs, Auberge d'Aragon, Independence Square, Valletta (tel: 239-898).

Ministry of Finance, Maison Demandols, South Street, Valletta CMR 02 (tel: 232-646; fax: 224-667).

Parliamentary Secretariat for Maritime and Offshore, House of Four Winds, Valletta (tel: 241-570).

Sea Malta Co Ltd, Sea Malta Building, Flagstone Wharf, Marsa HMR 12 (tel: 232-230/9; fax: 225-776).

Moldova

Marko Milivojevic

The presidential elections of November-December 1996 were won by Petru Lucinschi who comfortably defeated incumbent president, Mircea Snegur in the second round run-off. As in the parliamentary elections of February 1994, relations with Russia, Romania and the west, followed by the economy were the politically dominant issues. Rebels still hold Transdniestr, a strategic slither of territory bordering nearby Ukraine that has enjoyed *de facto* independence from Moldova with Russian support since a brief 1992 civil war.

Politics

Following a final split in the ruling and strongly pro-Russian Agrarian Democratic Party (ADP) in mid-1995, President Mircea Snegur once again became strongly supportive of reunification with Romania. Focused on the country's language and other contentious issues, this nationalist campaign resulted in increased political instability in Moldova, where a still weak economy continues to create social unrest. Opposed to the pro-Romanian aspirations of Snegur's Party of Revival and Reconciliation (PRCM), a breakaway faction of the ruling ADP led by Prime Minister Andrei Sangheli contested the presidential elections on a pro-Russian ticket supportive of closer relations with Russia in the Commonwealth of Independent States (CIS).

Although Sangheli was initially the favourite to win the election, his uncharismatic style and allegations of corruption worked against him. In the first round of voting he came fourth with just 9.44 per cent of the vote. Snegur won 38.75 per cent and parliamentary chairman Petru Lucinschi (standing as an independent) won 27.67 per cent. Both Sangheli and the third placed candidate, Vladimir Voronin (a communist), pledged their support for Lucinschi in the second round, which he duly won with 54 per cent against Snegur's 46 per cent.

Lucinschi's victory marks another comeback for former high-ranking Soviet officials playing on popular frustration with post-independence reforms. The new president was the last secretary of the Central Committee of the Communist Party of the Soviet Union and has retained his close links with Russia since Moldovan independence.

Political conflict

Snegur has never hesitated to play the nationalist card in 1995-96. His campaign centred on attempts to destabilise the ADP government and hence the position of his arch rival, Sangheli. The creation of the PRCM in mid-1995 reduced the parliamentary majority of the ADP, which was also weakened by the defection of another

KEY FACTS — Moldova

Official title: Republic of Moldova

Head of state: President Petru Lucinschi (elected Dec 1996)

Head of government: Prime Minister Andrei Sangheli (since Jul 1992; re-appointed 5 Apr 1994) (leader of ADP)

Ruling party: Agrarian Democratic Party (ADP)

Capital: Chisinau (Kishinev)

Official Languages: Moldavian

Currency: Moldavian Leu (L) replaced interim currency coupon 29 Nov 1993)

Exchange rate: L4.68 per US$ (Dec 1996)

Area: 33,700 sq km

Population: 4.4m (1995)

GDP per capita: US$390 (1995)

GDP real growth: -3% (1995)

GNP per capita: US$1,000 (1994)

GNP real growth: -22.1% (1994)

Labour force: 1.345m (1994)

Unemployment: 1.5% (1995)

Inflation: 25% (1995)

Trade balance: -US$10m (1995)

Foreign debt: US$1.5bn (1995)*

* estimated figure

splinter group, the Party of Social Progress of Moldova (PSPM). The splitting of the ADP reduced its parliamentary majority from 56 to 43, so making effective government more difficult. In March 1996, Snegur had attempted to dismiss the country's defence minister without consulting Sangheli in advance. Although later over-ruled by the constitutional court, this situation created conflict in the armed forces.

The power struggle between the President and the ADP government effectively paralysed all policy-making in Moldova. Economic policy-making, in particular, has been in crisis. Sangheli had forced through radical macro-economic stabilisation and structural reform, often in the face of strong opposition from hardline elements in the ADP. With rising political and economic uncertainty in 1995, these achievements could be threatened in 1996/97, mainly because of the political requirements of the forthcoming presidential elections. Any government back-tracking on economic reform would seriously harm Moldova's good relations with the International Monetary Fund (IMF) and other foreign creditors. The result of that would be less new foreign borrowing at the very time that Moldova needs it the most.

Russia, Romania, Transdniestr

Popular support for reunification with Romania is declining. Initially supportive of reunification with Romania, Sangheli's position has become more realistic and pragmatic in recent years, mainly because of the economic importance of the Russian connection for Moldova. Another key factor for this swing against reunification with Romania is that the obstacle of Transdniestr cannot be peacefully solved by alienating Russia. If Moldova were to be permanently severed from Transdniestr, the country would lose 40 per cent of its industrial capacity and 80 per cent of its power generating capacity, plus valuable agricultural farmlands. Transdniestr is also a key transportation hub for Moldova's road-rail links to Ukraine and Russia.

Parliamentary elections took place in Transdniestr in December 1995. Clearly influenced by developments in Moldova and, even more importantly, Russia, these resulted in the victory of the incumbent parties and leaders totally opposed to reunification with Moldova and supportive of union with Russia in the CIS.

Moldova moved closer to Ukraine in 1995 as Ukraine made the Transdniestr issue more of a foreign policy priority, mainly because of increased fears of a revived Russian imperialism in the region and the CIS more generally.

Outside the region, political developments in Russia have increased western support for Moldova, notably in the Organisation for Security and Co-operation in Europe (OSCE) and the Council of Europe. Combined with continued western economic support, this has enabled Moldova better to resist Russian pressure over Transdniestr and other issues. Moldova does not yet have a recognisable patron in the EU.

KEY INDICATORS — Moldova

	Unit	1991	1992	1993	1994	1995
Population	m	4.38	4.39	4.40	4.36	4.40
Gross domestic product (GDP)	US$bn	4.4	2.9	2.7	1.9	*1.7
GDP per capita	US$	1,000	850	750	500	390
GDP real growth	%	-18.0	-29.1	-8.7	-30.0	-3.0
Inflation	%	98	1,276	837	108	25
Employment	'000	2,070	2,050	1,688	1,681	1,670
Unemployment	%	–	0.1	0.6	0.9	1.5
Industrial output	%	-10	-20	-35	-35	-15
Agricultural output	%	-3	-5	-10	-22	4
Total reserves minus gold	US$m	–	2.45	76.34	179.92	239.80
Foreign exchange	US$m	–	2.44	41.92	158.57	226.69
Exports	US$m	1,000	868	451	500	660
Imports	US$m	1,200	905	905	630	670
Balance of trade	US$m	-200	-37	-454	-130	-10
Current account	US$m	-200	-100	-300	-200	-100
Foreign debt	US$bn	–	–	0.1	*1.0	*1.5
Exchange rate	Leu per US$	–	–	**3.64	4.27	4.50

* estimated figure   ** Leu introduced 29 Nov 1993

Economy

In 1995, Moldova's economy reached a major turning point. Down by a record 30 per cent in 1994, Moldovan GDP declined by only 3 per cent in 1995. In 1996, Moldova's post-Soviet economic decline is expected to end through projected GDP growth of around 5 per cent. The major causes of this economic revival are a buoyant agricultural sector, rising real wages, growing foreign trade and borrowing abroad, and a less restrictive monetary-credit policy by the government and the National Bank of Moldova (NBM). In addition, the second half of 1995 witnessed a slight revival in the industrial sector, particularly food-processing. Services are also growing rapidly.

With the completion of large-scale privatisation in 1995, the private sector accounted for around 70 per cent of GDP. Real GDP in 1995 was L7.63 billion (about US$1.7 billion); GDP per capita was around US$450. Wage arrears remain a big difficulty in Moldova. In 1996, nominal wages were set to rise by a further 25 per cent, mainly because of political factors in the run-up to the presidential elections.

Industry

Once accounting for 35 per cent of GDP, but probably no more than 25 per cent of GDP by 1995, industrial output fell by a further 15 per cent, with most of this drop taking place during the first half of the year. During the second half of 1995 industrial output began to revive. Annual growth of 8 per cent was expected in 1996.

The rate of industrial output collapse in 1995 was less than half that in 1994 (35 per cent over 1993). Sectorally, industrial output then rose the fastest in food-processing and light manufacturing. The recent large-scale privatisation of the state industrial sector is expected to lead to higher unemployment. However, the continued development of the private-sector is expected to result in higher new job creation in services, light manufacturing and industries connected to the country's strong agricultural sector.

At the end of 1995 officially recorded unemployment was still only 1.5 per cent of the employed workforce, compared to 1 per cent a year earlier. Unofficially, actual unemployment in Moldova may have been as high as 15 per cent of the employed workforce at the end of 1995, when large numbers of employees were on indefinite unpaid leave of absence.

Agriculture

Officially accounting for 40 per cent of GDP in 1995, but probably nearer 50 per cent, agricultural output increased by 4 per cent, partly reversing the 22 per cent decline of 1994, when a disastrous drought ravaged the agricultural sector. Particularly high growth was registered in the large viniculture sector. Most new investment is now going into agriculture and food processing in Moldova.

Land reform remains seriously incomplete, mainly because of opposition from the ADP élite. In this context, the ADP government has imposed a ban on the sale of farmland until 2001. Externally, exports of foodstuffs, wine and timber remain of vital economic importance for Moldova.

Services

Services accounted for around 25 per cent of GDP and an increasing proportion of employment in 1995. Services of all types continue to experience high growth. In 1995/96, rising real wages gave a major impetus to retail and wholesale trade. Although ultimately dependent on the extent of new foreign funding, local infrastructure development is expected to give a major boost to Moldovan construction companies in the future. In the longer term, Moldova may also have potential as a tourism destination, although this remains largely unrealised to date.

Monetary policy

Dating back to November 1993, when the leu was introduced at an initial parity of L3.85 per US$, the government's successful macro-economic stabilisation programme resulted in year-end inflation of 25 per cent in 1995, compared to an inflation rate of 108 per cent in 1994. Moldova has one of the best inflation records in the CIS, with consumer and other prices now expected to increase by no more than 10 per cent by year-end 1996.

Energy price rises are expected to keep inflation higher than it need be in 1996, when wages and welfare benefits are also expected to increase substantially. With monthly inflation slightly up during the last quarter of 1995 over the previous three months, the NBM revised its earlier policy of cutting local interest rates. In December 1995, the NBM base rate was increased to 21 per cent, compared to 20 per cent at the time of the last major interest rate cut by the central bank in September 1995. Over the previous three quarters, lower inflation in Moldova had enabled the NBM to cut local interest rates from a high of 400 per cent at the beginning of 1995 to 20 per cent in September of that year. This resulted in near negative interest rates for the first time since 1993.

Budget

Despite wider political uncertainties at the time, the 1996 government budget was set in December 1995. With projected revenues of L1.56 billion and expenditures of L1.9 billion, this implied a government budget deficit equal to around 3.5 per cent of projected GDP in 1996, compared to a deficit of 4.5 per cent of GDP in 1995. Well within the targets earlier agreed with the IMF, this projected L340 million deficit will again be mainly financed by NBM loans (L100 million), government bonds (L110 million) and foreign loans (L140 million). Unlike 1995, when foreign loans covered two-thirds of the government's funding short-fall, the 1996 budget deficit will be mainly financed domestically.

In 1996, tax reform became a top legislative priority for the government. In sharp contrast to the situation in Moldova, no financial stabilisation has so far been attempted in Transdniestr. The result of this has been continued hyper-inflation, the near collapse of the new rouble currency coupon introduced in August 1994 and general economic chaos. Contrary to the agreement of October 1994, the leu has not been allowed to circulate in Transdniestr.

Currency and borrowings

Trading at around L4.25/4.50 per US$ in 1994/95, the leu is one of the more stable CIS currrencies. Declining inflation, exchange rate stability and positive interest rates increased the attractiveness of leu-denominated assets in 1994/95. One result of this has been a higher level of savings in local banks.

Externally, the IMF's seal of approval has resulted in continued Moldovan access to new foreign borrowings, most notably from the European Bank for Reconstruction and Development (EBRD), which is now the country's single largest foreign creditor. By the end of 1995, the EBRD had approved a total of US$135 million for various projects. Combined with other foreign loans, this has resulted in growing hard currency reserves. These reached US$250 million in 1995, compared to US$200 million in 1994. Equal to around three months imports, local hard currency reserves were expected to increase still further in 1996. Other than general balance of payments financing, this will enable the NBM to support the leu properly and begin the recapitalisation of the country's commercial banking sector, where there is a high level of non-performing assets. Concomitantly, the NBM plans to strengthen its regulation of local banks by raising capitalisation ratios in 1996/97. In the longer term, financial services are expected to grow very fast.

Privatisation

Contrary to earlier widespread doubts about the likelihood of large-scale privatisation, the ownership transformation of the state industrial sector was largely completed in 1995. Delayed by political wrangling and the confusion surrounding the issuance of privatisation vouchers or National Patrimonal Bonds (NPB) to the public after large-scale privatisation first began in October 1993, ownership transformation was speeded up when the government imposed a final deadline for the take-up of NPBs in 1995. As a result, 90 per cent of all NPBs had been taken-up by the end of that year. Otherwise non-transferable, most NPBs were then invested in a number of privatisation investment funds.

By the end of 1995, 2,200 enterprises, two-thirds of the total, had been nominally privatised. However, the largely insider-orientated privatisation may have trouble recapitalising, especially since indebtedness and de facto insolvency are widespread. So far, the public auction of enterprise equity has been relatively limited in Moldova. There has been little direct purchase of shares, with most NPBs going through the country's powerful privatisation investment funds.

Ownership transformation may accelerate

corporate restructuring, making higher unemployment inevitable in at least the short term. Sectorally, the enterprises with the greatest potential are in food-processing, wood products, viniculture, light manufacturing and services. For the most part in Transdniestr, where privatisation is banned in law, the largest loss-makers are in traditional capital goods and primary production.

The government plans to dispose of remaining state industrial sector and other assets through auctions and cash sales and a secondary market in privatised equity is expected to emerge. Significantly, from the point of view of increased foreign direct investment (FDI), the government is to allow foreign investors to acquire up to 60 per cent of the equity in 40 key enterprises. In addition, a number of key utilities previously outside the remit of the government's privatisation programme are to be sold off in 1996. Foremost amongst these is the Fuel and Oil Association, a monopoly in the energy sector. Part of a wider energy sector development programme which is expected to cost over L3 billion over the next five years, this may lead to other sales of energy sector assets to foreign investors in the future. So far, this has mainly come from the EBRD, beginning with a US$36 million energy sector loan in 1995. In relation to Russia, with which Moldova rescheduled 260 billion rouble worth of energy supply debts in 1994, the recent Moldovan-Russian trade and economic co-operation agreements for 1996/97 call for further debt for equity swaps in local energy sector enterprises and associated oil-gas pipeline networks.

The weakest part of ownership transformation in Moldova is in the agricultural sector, where land reform remains seriously incomplete. So far, nominal decollectivisation has not resulted in the creation of a free market in farmland, so inhibiting increased new investment in agriculture and food processing. Local agricultural productivity is also low by EU standards. Other complications include low agricultural sector wages and an ageing workforce. Externally, agriculture and food processing has considerable potential for increased FDI, but only if a proper market in farmland emerges in the future. FDI in Moldova remains very low at around US$95 million at the end of 1995. Among other factors, the main reason for this is that the country has often been associated with other CIS states like Ukraine, even though economic reform is far more advanced in Moldova than in its eastern neighbour and even Romania. Another negative factor is the unresolved Transdniestr conflict.

External trade

After the disastrous foreign trade performance of 1994, Moldova's exports and imports began to revive in 1995. Heavily orientated towards foodstuffs, intermediate goods and raw materials, total exports in 1995 reached US$660 million, compared to less than US$500 million in 1994. As in 1994, 80 per cent of exports went to former Soviet and former Council for Mutual Economic Assistance (COMECON) countries, including Romania. Another continuing trend was the dominance of exports bartered for imports, notably Russian oil and gas. In 1995, around two-thirds of Moldova's foreign trade involved some form of barter. Hard currency exports, however, are growing, mainly because of increased foreign trade with the EU in 1995. In the longer term, Moldova will almost certainly have to reduce its over-dependence on CIS markets, and Russia in particular. The difficulty here is that most Moldovan exports are agricultural or related to agriculture. There is thus little economic complimentarity with Romania, where agriculture and food processing is also important. Agricultural exports to the EU are also problematical. Access to the country's largest single foreign market, Russia, could be threatened by Moldovan reluctance to enter into a full customs union with its CIS partners.

COUNTRY PROFILE — MOLDOVA

Historical profile

Moldova is one of the smallest of the former Soviet republics in terms of land area and is the most densely populated. It was created in 1940 from land annexed from Romania although further land transfers involving the Ukraine were subsequently made. The country's origins provide much of the basis for the inter-communal strife. It has close ties with Romania and the Moldovan majority consider themselves to be ethnic Romanians. Having achieved *de facto* independence from the former Soviet Union in 1989. Moldova formally declared its independence in August 1991. International recognition followed thereafter, with Moldova taking its UN seat in March 1992. Moldova has pursued a pro-western policy since then although this has had limited success to date and entered into NATO's 'Partnership for Peace' programme in 1994. Moldova's attempts to achieve real as opposed to purely nominal independence have been hindered by the country's geo-political marginality, economic weaknesses and its strained relations with Russia. Of the latter, Moscow's local ethnic Russian rebel proxies partitioned the country de facto in 1990, when a so-called 'Transdniestr Republic' was proclaimed on the left bank of the Dniestr River. On 24 December 1995 voters in the breakaway Transdniestr region approved a constitution which gave the region independence; they also voted in favour of membership of the Commonwealth of Independent States (CIS).

Political system

A new constitution to succeed that of 1977 came into force on 27 August 1994, establishing the country as a 'presidential, parliamentary republic' based on political pluralism and 'the preservation, development and expression of ethnic and linguistic identity'. The 1994 constitution further established the country's 'permanent neutrality' and barred the stationing of foreign troops on national territory. Special autonomous status was granted to the Gagauz region and the Dniestr region. In a referendum held on 6 March 1994, 95 per cent of voters favoured continued independence (from both Russia and Romania). Elections in February 1994 to the unicameral Moldovan *Parlamentul* (Parliament), which comprises 104 deputies, resulted in gains for the country's largest party, the Agrarian Democrats, which won over 43 per cent of the vote. Sangheli was reappointed as prime minister on 5 April 1994. On 8 December 1995 President Snegur stated that he would stand again in the presidential elections scheduled for 17 November 1996.

Political parties

The Agrarian Democratic Party (ADP) is the ruling party. The Party of Socialist Action was formed 17 May 1996.

Population

Moldova is the second smallest republic of the Newly Independent States (NIS) and has the biggest density of population: 129 people per one sq km. Ethnic composition: Moldovans (of Romanian descent) (64.5%), Ukrainians (13.9%), Russians (13%), Gagauzians (Christian Turks from the south of Moldova) (3.5%), Bulgarians (2%). Majority Christian. The Russian and Ukrainian minorities are predominant in the Dniester region and the Gagauzi in the south.

Main cities/towns

Chisinau (Kishinev) (capital, population 780,000 in 1994), Tiraspol (186,000), Belts (161,800), Bender (133,000), Ribnitsa (62,900), Ungeni (39,400)

Language

Moldavian or Romanian, with Russian also widely spoken.

Media

Press: East-West Observer (monthly) is the first English-language newspaper.

Employment

In July 1996 there were 26,100 unemployed persons, two-thirds of whom were women.

External trade

In February 1993 a number of trade agreements were entered into with Russia. Ukraine and Russia take the largest share in Moldova's foreign trade. Azerbaijan and Moldova signed a trade and economic co-operation agreement in September 1995. Under the terms of the accord, Azerbaijan is to export mainly oil, oil products and oil equipment in exchange for vegetables, grain, flour and consumer goods. Under a separate protocol, Moldova is to supply Azerbaijan with 200,000 tonnes of grain and 50,000 tonnes of flour in exchange for oil products. The EU ratified 10-year partnership and co-operation agreement with Moldova December 1995.
Exports: Exports totalled US$660m in 1995.
Imports: Imports totalled US$670m in 1995.

Agriculture

The agriculture sector accounted for 40 per cent of GDP in 1994 and employed 35 per cent of the working population. Major source of export revenue. Grains, meat, dairy produce, tobacco,

Payments difficulties continue to inhibit import growth. Totalling US$670 million in 1995, these were only slightly up over their 1994 level of US$630 million. As in 1994, dependency on Russian oil and gas remained high in 1995/96. The government's energy development programme aims to reduce this dependency, but it is not yet clear how this might be done. In Transdniestr, the illegal levying of taxes on goods from and to Moldova proper continues unabated. A de facto trade war that, combined with the refusal of Transdniestr to accept the leu, has severely reduced trade between Moldova and Transdniestr. Regionally, Romania continues to allow a relatively large trade deficit with Moldova for political reasons. In 1995, Moldovan trade with Ukraine began to revive for the first time in the 1990s.

Following a trade deficit of US$130 million in 1994, Moldova's foreign trade was broadly in balance in 1995, mainly because of improved export performance and stagnant imports. Higher trade deficits are expected in the future. On the current account, higher new foreign borrowings in 1995 resulted in a relatively manageable deficit of US$100 million in that year. In the longer term, higher trade deficits will also mean higher current account deficits. Foreign debt servicing is also set to rise in the future. Mainly from the EBRD and other official multilateral foreign creditors, new foreign borrowing remains uncomplicated, but relatively limited. Service income remains low. Increased FDI is also somewhat problematical. Beginning with the final stage of large-scale privatisation in 1996, FDI may increase substantially in the future. Russian investment in Moldova's energy sector is also increasing.

Foreign debt

Supported by the IMF and other multilateral creditors to the tune of around US$250 million since 1993, Moldova's successful economic reforms have enabled the country to continue increasing its new foreign borrowings in the west, where the EBRD became a sort of financing co-ordinator for Moldova in 1995. Including outstanding energy supply debts to Russia, total foreign debt at the end of 1995 was around US$1.5 billion, compared to around US$1 billion in 1994. Mainly used for budget and balance of payments financing in 1995, new foreign borrowing is expected to be more concentrated on capital projects, notably infrastructure development. A priority here for the government is the development of the energy sector.

In the longer term, Moldova is expected to enter an association agreement with the EU, thereby allowing European Investment Bank loans for local infrastructure development. Another major official creditor for such purposes is likely to be the World Bank. Regionally, Romania continues to provide concessionary financing. In relation to Russia, Moldova also benefits from the rescheduling of its energy supply debts. As things stand, Moldova would not be able to afford its current level of oil and gas imports from Russia without these special financing arrangements. Transdniestr is entirely supported by Russian economic assistance.

Outlook

As is the case in other CIS states, Moldova's political and economic prospects will be largely decided by external developments. The role of Russia in Transdniestr remains politically central. Pending a final resolution of this issue, Moldova remains partitioned and partly occupied by a foreign power. Petru Lucinschi's victory in the presidential election is likely to result in closer links with Russia. The major potential danger here is that too close an alliance with Russia could threaten Moldova's statehood and independence. Proposed reunification with Romania would have similar effects. Taken together, all these factors mean that Moldova's political and economic prospects remain uncertain, with much dependent on external factors over which this former Soviet republic has little or no control.

COUNTRY PROFILE — MOLDOVA

Agriculture (contd): grapes, vegetables, fruit and sugar beet are important. Production fell by 22 per cent in 1994 due to drought and inadequate financing.
Output increased by 4 per cent in 1995, with particularly high growth in the viniculture sector.

Industry

The industrial sector accounted for 37 per cent of GNP in 1994 and employed 28 per cent of the working population. Shortage of cash for raw materials and energy has forced 60 per cent of industrial enterprises to cut their production. The manufacturing base is relatively small; food processing, beverages and cigarettes are important; other activities include garment-making, consumer durables and farm machinery.
Industrial output fell by 15 per cent in 1995.

Energy

No fuel and energy reserves and limited electricity generating capacity. Before independence in 1991, Moldova had almost totally relied on Russia for energy supplies. Oil and gas prices rose to world levels after 1991 and Moldova has to spend approximately US$400m annually to meet domestic energy demands. The chief power supplier is Ukraine (2.5m tons of coal from 1995-2000); second is Iran (12.5m tons of oil and up to 250,000 tons of LNG between 1995-2000).

Stock exchange

In April 1991 the National Commodity Exchange of Moldova was established. The first stock exchange to trade shares in enterprises being privatised was set up in December 1993 with a founding capital of US$60,000. The exchange was formed by commercial banks and investment trust companies.

Membership of international organisations

BSECP, CIS, Council of Europe, CSCE, IMF, NACC, MIGA, OSCE, Partnership for Peace, World Bank. Moldova has requested to join the WTO.

BUSINESS GUIDE

Time

GMT + 2 hrs (GMT + 3 hrs from late Mar to late Sep).

Climate

Temperate - continental with long hot summers and cold winters; average temperature varies between -2°C and 22°C. Frosty with a good deal of ice and snow in winter.

Entry requirements

Customs: Small amount of personal goods duty-free. On arrival declare all foreign currency and valuable items such as jewellery, cameras, computers and musical instruments.

Health precautions

Mandatory: Vaccination certificates are required for cholera or yellow fever if travelling from an infected area.
Advisable: Water precautions recommended (water purification tablets may be useful). It is advisable to be 'in date' for the following immunisations: polio (within 10 years), tetanus (within 10 years), typhoid fever, cholera (within six months), hepatitis 'A' (moderate risk only). There has been a significant increase in the number of cases of diphtheria. While the low dose, adult booster is unavailable, travellers are advised to be boosted with a reduced dose (0.1ml) of the paediatric single antigen vaccine. If never immunised, use three dose course of the vaccine. Any medicines required by the traveller should be taken by the visitor, and it could be wise to have precautionary antibiotics if going outside major urban centres. A travel kit including a disposable syringe is a reasonable precaution.

Air access

National airlines: Air Moldova; Moldavian Airlines.
Other airlines: LOT.

Public holidays

Fixed dates: 1 Jan (New Year), 8 Mar (Women's Day), 1 May (May Day), 23 Jun (Sovereignty Proclamation Day), 31 Aug (Day of the Language), 25 Dec (Christmas).
Variable dates: Easter and first Mon after Easter (Remembrance Day).

Working hours

Business: (Mon–Fri) 0900–1800 (appointments best between 0900–1000).
Government: (Mon–Fri) 0900–1800.
Banking: (Mon–Sat) 0900–1500 for banking facilities; 0900–1800 for exchange of money.
Shops: (Mon) 0800–1700, (Tue–Sat) 0800–2100.

Telecommunications

Telephone and telefax: Dialling code for Moldova: IDD access code + 373 followed by area code (2 for Chisinau), followed by subscriber's number.

Banking

Central bank: National Bank of Moldova.
Other banks: Commercial (Basarabiabank), Moldovan Bank for Foreign Economic Affairs, Savings Bank of Moldova.

Business information

Privatisation Law passed July 1991. Foreign investors only permitted to participate in certain privatisations. OVA

Hotels

Chisinau (area code 2)
Codru, 127 31 August Str, 277012 (tel: 226-270; fax: 237-948).

Cosmos, 2 Piata Negruti, 277065 (tel: 261-305; fax: 264-300).

Dacia, 135 31 August Str, 277012 (tel: 232-251; fax: 237-661).

National, 4 Stefan cel Mare Blvd, 277058 (tel: 266-083; fax: 262-586).

Seabeco, 37 Ciboraru Str, 277012 (tel: 232-896; fax: 232-870).

Useful telephone numbers

Ambulance: 03

Fire: 01

Police: 02

Operator assistance for international telephone calls: 071

Chamber of Commerce

Chamber of Commerce and Industry of Moldova, Ulitsa Komsomolskaya 28, 277012 Chisinau (tel: 221-552).

Banking

National Bank of Moldova (central bank), Renashterii Avenue 7, 277006 Chisinau (tel: 221-679; fax: 229-591).

Commercial (Basarabiabank), Pushkin Street 42, 277006 Chisinau (tel: 240-757; fax: 244-754).

Moldovan Bank for Foreign Economic Affairs, Prospekt Molodiozhi 7, 277006 Chisinau (tel: 229-591).

National Association of Banks, 7 Renasterii Str, 277006 Chisinau (tel: 225-177; fax: 229-382).

Savings Bank of Moldova, Cosmonautsilor Street 9, 277006 Chisinau (tel: 225-227; fax; 244-731).

Principal newspapers

Delovaya Gazeta (business newspaper), 22 Pushkin Str, Chisinau 277012 (tel: 228-060, 229-798; fax: 228-355).

East-West Observer, M. Kogalniceanu Street 60, Room 217, Chisinau (tel: 251-285).

Kishinyovskie Novosti (Chisinau News), 22 Pushkin Str, Chisinau 277012 (tel: 229-568; fax: 237-563).

Mercuriu (Mercury), 24 Aleco Russo, Chisinau 277043 (tel: 333-656; fax: 321-817).

Other useful addresses

Department of Statistics of the Republic of Moldova, 124 Shtefan chel Mare Avenue, Chisinau 227001 (tel: 233-549; fax: 261-119).

Ministry of Economy, Department of Foreign Economic Affairs, Piata Marii Adunari Nationale 1, 277033 Chisinau (tel: 233-360; fax: 234-046).

Ministry of Finance, Cosmanavtov el 7, 277012 Chisinau (tel: 226-629, 223-439).

Ministry of Information, Chisinau (tel: 221-001).

MoldEnergo, 78 Vasile Alexandri Str, 277012 Chisinau (tel: 221-065; fax: 253-142).

Moldexpo International Exhibition Centre, 1 Ghioceilor, 277008 Chisinau (tel: 627-416; fax: 627-420).

Moldova-Gaz, 38 Albisoara Str, 277005 Chisinau (tel: 256-778; fax: 240-014).

Moldova Stock Exchange, 73 Stefan cel Mare, Chisinau 277001 (tel: 265-554; fax: 228-969).

Moldsilva (Forestry Association), 124 Stefan cel Mare Blvd, 277012 Chisinau (tel: 262-256; fax: 223-251).

National Foreign Trade Company (Moldova-EXIM), 65 Mateevici Str, 277012 Chisinau (tel: 223-226; fax: 244-436).

National Fuel Association, 90 Columna Str, 277001 Chisinau (tel: 223-078; 240-509).

State Company Teleradio Moldova National TV and Radio, 64 Hincesti Highway, 277028 Chisinau (tel: 721-077, 721-863).

Monaco

Anthony Griffin

Monaco is a hereditary monarchy, under French protection since 1861. There are no political parties, only 'organisations' commonly known as the 'lists' of those heading them. Thus in the January 1993 National Council elections, 15 of the 18 seats were won by the so-called Campora list, two by the Medicin list and one by an independent candidate.

KEY FACTS	Monaco
Official title: The Principality of Monaco	**Exchange rate:** Ff5.25 per US$ (Dec 1996)
Head of state: Prince Rainier III	**Area:** 1.8 sq km
Head of government: Minister of State Paul Dijoud	**Population:** 32,000 (1995)
Capital: Monaco-Ville	**GNP per capita:** US$25,000 (1995)*
Official Languages: French and Monégasque	**Visitor numbers:** 3m+ (1995)*
Currency: French franc (Ff) = 100 centimes	* estimated figure

Monaco's somehwat geriatric tourism industry accounts for between 20 and 25 per cent of GDP. Each year over three million visitors arrive, with Italians being the most numerous and representing almost a third of the total. But it is the financial services sector which has been receiving the greatest degree of attention recently for good and bad reasons. The head of government is Paul Dijoud, who is in the position as Minister of State.

Financial services

Monaco's economy is overhwelmingly controlled by the ubiquitous Société des Bains de Mer which, despite its innocuous name, controls all the principality's gambling activities as well as a number of the major hotels. However, as the traditional areas of real estate and tourism have declined in importance, the banking sector has been targeted for growth. Monaco's banking sector has an average annual turnover of Ff7 billion. There are some 37 banks operating and the principality's banking sector is based on portfolio management and so-called private banking. Many local financial leaders have pushed for the introduction of new products such as fiduciary services and trusts, and instruments such as holdings and reassurance infrastructures in a bid to make Monaco more of an offshore centre along the lines of Jersey or Hong Kong. A stock exchange, however, is not planned.

Anonymity is an important and, on occasion for the authorities, worrying part of the banking milieu in Monaco. The principality's secrecy is enhanced by the fact that Monaco has no fiscal conventions or agreements with other countries. The law of 7 July 1993, nevertheless, imposes an obligation upon banks to ask for information about the source of funds, and also an obligation to declare any doubts they might have concerning an account. In 1994 Monaco undertook to co-operate on a formal basis with French authorities to put an end to money laundering activities. However, fiscal agencies do not receive any financial information gathered during investigations by the French or Monegasque anti-laundering authorities.

The veil of banking secrecy can now be lifted in a number of circumstances: when customs laws are broken; when fiscal authorities prove tax evasion has taken place or a crime was committed in France; or if Interpol has proof of a criminal act. By way of contrast, in France the banks give the fiscal authorities all information regarding the opening, the modification, or the closing of a personal account.

France plays a significant role in Monaco. Monaco has a customs and currency union with its French neighbour and most of Monaco's imports come from that country. French banks are also significant players on the local financial scene. Monaco has been criticised in the past as a haven for underworld money, and a prime route for ill-gotten gains on their way to or from France, but French investors and depositors in Monaco are regulated by French legislation, and their accounts there may be investigated by the French taxation and customs authorities.

For non-French nationals there are considerable advantages in keeping their money in Monaco. No tax is payable on the interest gained on investments in Monaco, nor on the capital, and there is no stamp duty on transfers or trading of stocks or shares. For those living in the Principality there is no income tax, property tax or rates. Upon the death of a French citizen living in Monaco for more than five years, their accounts in Monegasque banks will be free of estate duty and will not be subject to wealth tax on stocks held in France.

COUNTRY PROFILE

MONACO

Historical profile

1814 Principality re-established after abolition during French Revolution.
1861 Independence under French protection.
1949 Prince Rainier III, embodying divine right, succeeded to throne.
1962 New constitution allowing for sharing of legislative powers between the prince and elected national council; principle of divine right abolished.
1983 Succeeding general elections won by National and Democratic Union.

Political system

Founded on principles of an hereditary and constitutional monarchy. Principality governed under authority of the monarch, a Minister of State and a unicameral National Council. The monarch nominates the Minister of State from a list of three French diplomats submitted by the French government. As head of the Council of Government, the Minister of State exercises executive power under the monarch, while legislative authority resides with the 18-member National Council elected every five years by universal adult suffrage.

Political parties

There are no political parties although there are various 'organisations', commonly known as the 'lists' of those heading them.

Population

The Monégasques represent nearly 5,000 of the principality's 32,000 or so inhabitants. Annual population growth 1.3 per cent.

Main cities/towns

Monaco-ville (capital); Monte Carlo.

Media

Press: Monaco editions of French newspapers *Nice-Matin* and *L'Echo de la Côte d'Azur.* Other French dailies widely read. Official weekly magazine, *Journal de Monaco,* published by Ministry of State. Two monthly magazines: *Gazette de Monaco – Côte d'Azur* and *Monaco Actualité.*
Broadcasting: About 20,000 radios and 25,000 TVs in use. Radio Monte Carlo (RMC), part-owned by French government. Broadcasts in French and Italian. Also overseas broadcasts in 12 languages. Riviera Radio, based in RMC studio complex, broadcasts in English 24 hrs/day. Evangelical programmes broadcast in numerous foreign languages by Trans World Radio. Tele Monte Carlo broadcasts 24 hrs/day, mainly pop videos.

Domestic economy

Small, open and diversified economy based on tourism, the convention business, banking and insurance but with a significant industrial sector. State income derived from taxes, postage stamps and public monopolies. Prince Rainier has endeavoured to broaden the base of the local economy, notably with the Fontvieille development of 22 ha of reclaimed land to the west of the old town, which is now a centre for light industry and low-cost housing. Monaco's total area has been increased by one-fifth by this project.

Employment

The indigenous population has guaranteed jobs in government service. All Monaco companies have to offer jobs first to the Monégasques, then to local residents, and then to the inhabitants of the four neighbouring French communes before looking further afield.

External trade

Heavily dependent upon imports from France. Member of the French Franc Zone, with customs and currency union with France. EU rules of free circulation of goods apply.

Industry

Around 200 firms employing 4,000 people, and accounting for 27 per cent of national turnover. Main products are cosmetics, healthcare, pharmaceuticals, precision instruments, glass, plastics, electrical goods, electronics, textiles and food processing. Also important are construction and public works.

Tourism

The tourism sector represents roughly 25 per cent of GDP. Tourism in Monaco was affected by the Gulf war in the early months of 1991. Most visitors are day trippers. It is now expanding its conference and exhibition activities to enhance its appeal to the business travel market. Monaco was affected by the recession and the French franc's rise after the European currency crisis, and the number of French tourists fell sharply. Italians represent almost a third of the total visitors.

Membership of international organisations

Franc zone, IAEA, ICAO, IHO, INTELSAT, Interpol, IPU, ITU, IWC, OSCE, UN (permanent observer), UNESCO, UPU, WHO, WIPO.

BUSINESS GUIDE

Time

GMT + 1 hr (GMT + 2 hrs from late Mar to late Sep).

Climate

Mediterranean with mild winters and warm summers. Hottest months Jul and Aug, with average temperatures 25°C.

Clothing

Lightweight for summer, mediumweight and light topcoat for winter.

Entry requirements

Visa not required for nationals of most West European countries. No restrictions on imports of foreign exchange.

Air access

Nearest international airport Nice (NCE), Cte d'Azur, France, 22 km from Monaco. Heliport facilities in Monte Carlo (MCM). Helicopter link with Nice Airport (journey time seven minutes). Shuttle links from the heliport to the hotels in the Principality.

Surface access

The Principality is linked to France, Italy, Germany, Switzerland, Belgium and the UK by the network of European motorways.

Hotels

Classified into one- to four-star and predominantly, four-star/luxury categories. Advisable to book in advance during summer.

Credit cards

All credit cards accepted.

National transport

Around 50 km of roads and 1.6 km of railways (operated by Société Nationale des Chemins de Fer Français).

Public holidays

Fixed dates: 1 Jan, 27 Jan (Feast of St Dévote), 1 May (Labour Day), 15 Aug (Assumption), 1 Nov, 19 Nov (National Day/ Fête du Prince), 8 Dec (Immaculate Conception), 25 Dec.
Variable dates: Easter Monday, Ascension Day, Whit Monday.

Working hours

Banking : (Mon-Sat) 0900–1200 and 1400–1630 (except Saturday afternoons preceding Bank Holidays). Banque Franco-Portugaise, Monte Carlo, is open on Saturdays.

Telecommunications

Telephone and telefax: International dialling code: 377 (from 21 June 1996), followed by eight-digit number.

Banking

There are approximately 37 banks (employing 5 per cent of local workers) in Monaco. System is controlled by French bankers' regulations. Monaco's banking sector has an average annual turnover of Ff7bn.

BUSINESS DIRECTORY

Hotels

Monte Carlo
Abela, 23 Avenue des Papalins (tel: 9205-9000; fax: 9205-9167).

Alexandra, 35 Boulevard Princesse Charlotte (tel: 9350-6313; fax: 9216-0648).

Balmoral, 12 Avenue de la Costa (tel: 9350-6237; fax: 9315-0869).

Beach Plaza, 22 Avenue Princesse Grace (tel: 9330-9880; fax: 9350-2314).

Hermitage, Square Beaumarchais (tel: 9216-4000/3636; fax: 9350-4712).

Hotel de Paris, Place du Casino (tel: 9216-3000/3636; fax: 9216-3849).

Loews, Avenue des Spélugues (ocean-front) (tel: 9350-6500; fax: 9330-0157).

Metropole Palace, 4 Avenue de la Madone (tel: 9315-1515; fax: 9325-2444).

Mirabeau, 1-3 Avenue Princesse Grace (tel: 9216-6565/3636; fax: 9350-8485).

Monte Carlo Beach, Route du Beach (tel: 9328-6666, 9216-3636; fax: 9378-1418).

Useful telephone numbers

Ambulance (emergencies): 18 (switchboard: 9330-1945).

Car pound (Parking des Ecoles car park), Av des Guelfes, Monte Carlo: 9315-3084.

Doctor or chemist on duty: 9325-3325.

Fire services (emergencies): 18 (switchboard: 9330-1945).

Police (emergencies): 17; (switchboard: 9315-3015).

Princess Grace General Hospital, Av Pasteur (emergencies): 9325-9869 (switchboard: 9325-9900).

Car hire

Avis, 9 Av d'Ostende: (tel: 9330-1753).

British Motors, 15 Bd Princesse Charlotte: (tel: 9205-8371).

Budget, 9 Av Pdt J F Kennedy: (tel: 9216-0070).

Eurodollar Mattei, 26 Quai des Sanbarbani: (tel: 9205-9009).

Europcar, 47 Av de Grande-Bretagne: (tel: 9350-7495); Héliport de Fontvieille (tel: 9350-2575).

Hertz, 27 Bd Albert 1er: (tel: 9350-7960).

Locations Carlo, 29 ter Av Hector Otto: (tel: 9350-3410).

Monaco Limousine and Car Rental, 12 Av des Spélugues: (tel: 9350-8265).

BUSINESS DIRECTORY

Car hire (contd:

Monte Carlo Limousine, Héliport de Fontvieille: (tel: 9205-6600).

Plaza International, 2a Av de Grande-Bretagne: (tel: 9330-7700).

Trans National, 25 Av de la Costa: (tel: 9350-2525).

Taxis

24-hour radio taxis (tel: 9315-0101, 9350-5628).

Chambers of commerce

Direction du Commerce, de l'Industrie et de la Propriété Industrielle, 2 Avenue du Prince Héréditaire Albert, Stade Louis II, Entrée A, MC9800 Monaco (tel: 9315-8000; fax: 9330-3974).

Jeune Chambre Economique de Monaco, 2 Avenue Prince Héréditaire Albert (tel: 9315-0422).

Banking

Banque Franco Portugaise (BFP), 5 Av Princesse Alice, MC 98000 Monaco (tel: 9350-1115; fax: 9350-1921).

Banque Générale du Commerce, 2 Av des Spélugues, Monte Carlo (tel: 9350-1762).

Banque Internationale de Monaco, Sporting d'Hiver, 2 Av Princesse Alice, Monte Carlo (tel: 9216-5757; fax: 9216-5750).

Barclays Bank plc, 31 Av de la Costa, Monte Carlo (tel: 9315-3535; fax: 9325-1568).

Crédit Foncier de Monaco, 11 Bd Albert 1er, 98000 Monaco (tel: 9310-2000; fax: 9310-2350).

Société Générale, 16 Ave de la Costa (tel: 9315-5700); also at 17 Bd Albert 1er (tel: 9350-8692).

Principal newspapers

Gazette Monaco, Côte d'Azur, 25 Boulevard Albert 1st, MC-98000 Monte Carlo.

Travel information

Automobile Club of Monaco, 23 Boulevard Albert 1er, Monte Carlo (tel: 9315-2600).

Direction du Tourisme et des Congrès, 2a Boulevard des Moulins, MC-98000 Monte Carlo (administration) (tel: 9216-6116; fax: 9216-6000); (information) (tel: 9216-6166).

Heli-Air Monaco, Av des Ligures, Monaco (tel: 9205-0050).

Monaco Bus Company, 3 Av Pdt J F Kennedy (tel: 9350-6241).

Station Master, Monaco/Monte Carlo station, Avenue Prince Pierre (rail passenger information) (tel: 9310-6015); (timetable information) (tel: 9310-6003).

Service de la Marine, Direction des Ports (information regarding yacht harbours), 7 Av du Pdt J F Kennedy, BP 468, MC 98012 Monaco Cedex (tel: 9315-8678).

Other useful addresses

Centre de Congrès, Bd Louis II, Monaco (tel: 9310-8400).

Centre d'Informations Administratives, 23 Av Prince Héréditaire Albert, Monaco (tel: 9315-4026).

Centre de Presse, 4 Rue des Iris, Monaco (tel: 9330-4227).

Centre de Rencontres Internationales, Ave d'Ostende, Monaco (tel: 9310-8600).

Comité des Fêtes, Monaco-Ville (tel: 9330-8004).

Direction de l'Expansion Economique, 2 Avenue du Prince Héréditaire Albert, BP 665, MC98014 Monaco Cedex (tel: 9315-8853; fax: 9205-7520).

Douanes, 7 Av Président J.F. Kennedy, Monaco (tel: 9330-2600).

Mairie de Monaco, Monaco-Ville (tel: 9315-2863).

Ministère d'Etat, Monaco-Ville (tel: 9315-8000).

Monte Carlo Main Post, Square Beaumarchais (Palais de la Scala) (tel: 9350-6987).

Radio Monte Carlo, 16 Bd Princesse Charlotte, Monaco (tel: 9315-1617).

Service du Contrôle Technique et de la Circulation (traffic control service), 23 Av Prince Héréditaire Albert, Monaco (tel: 9315-8000).

Service de l'Urbanisme et de la Construction, 23 Av Prince Hér\01ditaire Albert, Monaco (tel: 9315-8000).

Télé Monte Carlo, 16 Bd Princesse Charlotte, Monaco (tel: 9315-1415).

The Netherlands

Howard Hill

Job losses have been balanced by job gains in the Netherlands and hopes are high for a stronger economy in 1997, as the sluggishness of the past few years is passing. With economic and monetary union (EMU) just around the corner, the coalition government has had some success in controlling spending.

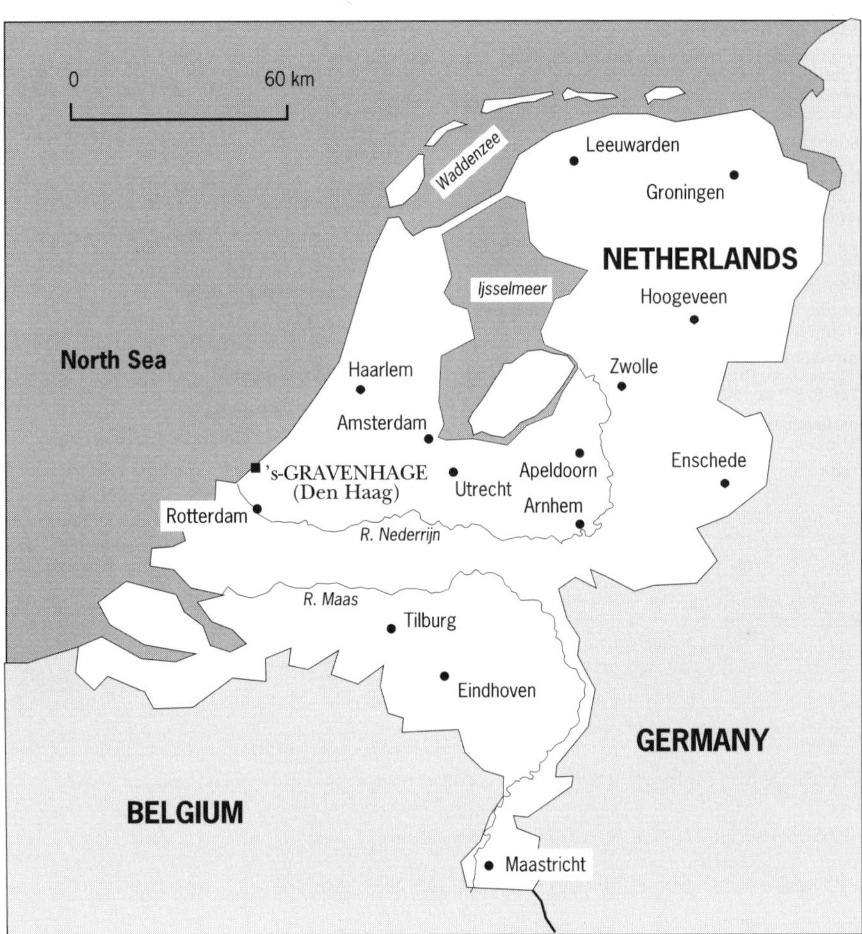

Politics

The present coalition of Social Democrats (PvdA), Liberals (VVD), and Left Liberals (D66) continue on their drive towards fiscal responsibility. They have also approved important changes to the welfare system and massive infrastructure building projects which are calculated to help the country grow into the next century.

The welfare system, which costs the country a staggering third of GDP, continues to undergo changes aimed at tightening up eligibility rules and reducing abuses. The present coalition government started this overhaul after coming to power and tough dealing had to be done between the three partners before a meaningful and workable compromise was agreed on. As of July 1996 the General Widows' and Orphans' Benefits Act was replaced by the General Surviving Dependents' Act. This change shifts the burden to the individual for insuring that dependents are provided for in case of his or her death. Another change means that bereavement benefits are now means-tested. However, the status quo is preserved for benefit recipients who were registered before the new Act went into force.

In January 1997 a new system of disability benefits was due to come into force. However, delays in getting the measure approved by parliament have resulted in a likely postponement of the change, perhaps to 1998. The changes would place a higher burden of responsibility for providing cover for employees under the system.

End of conscription

The Netherlands' last-ever army conscripts were discharged in August 1996, marking the completion of the change to a professional military in the Netherlands. Personnel levels have been dramatically reduced in the 1990s under a restructuring regime. The military consists of 85,000 personnel, about a quarter of whom are civilian support staff, and this figure will drop to 77,000 by the turn of the century. Total personnel figures were about 128,000 in the late 1980s.

Economy

GDP was f635 billion in 1995 with a growth rate of 2.1 per cent, slightly lower than the

European Union (EU) average of 2.5 per cent. This figure was revised downward by the statistics bureau in July 1996 from the previously reported 2.4 per cent. Growth in 1994 was a much higher 3.4 per cent, which was also revised, from 2.7 per cent. The government predicts that growth will settle in the 2 per cent range for two-to-three years, which would be welcome after a few years of roller-coaster-like figures. GDP swung from 4.7 per cent in 1989, to 4.1 per cent in 1990, 2.3 per cent in 1991, 2.0 per cent in 1992 and 0.2 per cent in 1993. By the third quarter of 1996 GDP growth for 1996 was on target to reach 2.5 per cent.

Prices have largely been in check since 1992. In that year the inflation rate was 3.2 per cent but this fell to 2.6 per cent in 1993, edged up to 2.7 per cent in 1994 and fell to 2.0 per cent in 1995. High wage costs are expected to pump this figure to 2.25 per cent in 1996 and 2.5 per cent in 1997.

The budget deficit was 3.7 per cent of GDP in 1995, which surprised observers who expected to see the figure at 3.4 per cent, as in 1994. The increased deficit was due in part to a decline in revenues from tax and social security levies.

The deficit figure is calculated to fall to 2.8 per cent in 1996 and to 2.3 per cent in 1997 (the critical year for EMU assessment), which would bring it well within the EMU limit of 3 per cent. However, the increase in 1995 will make these targets harder to achieve, although the finance ministry is confident. Net public sector borrowing requirements by 1997 are expected to be just under the 3 per cent EMU limit. New-found budget discipline is partially responsible for these figures, as well as low interest rates and stable GDP growth.

The Netherlands is well-known for the heavy financial burden of its social programmes. However, the trend towards ever-increasing costs is being reversed, thanks to the social security reforms of the 1990s (including the reduction of access to social security) and the falling unemployment figures in 1995 and 1996. The present coalition government, which came in during August 1994, imposed a ceiling on public expenditure for the period from 1994 to 1998. The result is that spending will not rise in real terms during this period. In addition to this overall ceiling, three others were imposed on the most draining categories of expenditure: social security, health care and central government expenditure (not including social security).

Social security expenditure has fallen from 17.9 per cent of GDP in 1993 to 17.1 per cent in 1994, 16.3 per cent in 1995 and an estimated 15.7 per cent in 1996. For 1997, social security spending should be 15 per cent.

KEY FACTS

Official title: Koninkrijk der Nederlanden (The Kingdom of the Netherlands)

Head of state: Queen Beatrix

Head of government: Prime Minister Wim Kok (PvdA)

Ruling party: Coalition of Party van de Arbeid (Labour Party) (PvdA), left-wing liberal party Democraten 66 (Democrats 1966) (D66) and right-wing liberal party Volksparty voor Vrijheid en Democratie (People's Party for Freedom and Democracy (VVD)

Capital: Amsterdam; The Hague is the seat of government

Official Languages: Dutch and Frysian

Currency: Guilder (f) = 100 cents

Exchange rate: f1.74 per US$ (Dec 1996)

Area: 41,473 sq km

Population: 15.4m (1995)

GDP per capita: US$21,300 (1994)

GDP real growth: 3% (3rd qtr 1996)

Labour force: 5m (1995)*

Unemployment: 6.6% (Aug0Oct 1996)

Inflation: 2.4% (12 months to Oct 1996) (consumer prices)

Trade balance: US$21.7bn (12 months to Aug 1996, not seasonally adjusted)

* estimated figure

External trade

The Netherlands continues to enjoy a positive balance of trade. Exports of goods and services exceeded imports in 1995 by f41.1 billion. Compared with the previous year, exports of goods and services in 1995 were up by 6.9 per cent while imports were up by 7.7 per cent. The total amount of goods exported in 1995 was f278.8 billion and exports of services (invisibles) amounted to f59.4 billion.

Unemployment

Joblessness hit a high in the later half of 1995. By mid-1996, even with the gloom of the Fokker bankruptcy, the picture looked better. The lack of upward pressure on wages appeared to have helped the situation. Inflation in general had been at a steady 2 per cent for over a year. Higher consumer spending in the first half of 1996, the highest in over 3 years, gave a clear indication that the 1995 slowdown was ending; real consumer spending was up by 3 per cent on the same period in 1995.

Anti-cartel proposal

The Netherlands has a reputation for turning a blind eye to cartels, particularly since it has no anti-trust procedure. But this might change. In May 1996 the economic affairs ministry announced that it proposed to ban cartels and review corporate mergers through a commission to operate under the ministry; after five years the government's technical veto power would be reviewed and the commission could be given greater independence.

Under the proposal to ban cartels, domestic mergers exceeding f250 million, would be subject to regulatory review. All binding vertical pricing arrangements would be outlawed, with franchises being the exception. Under the proposal, infringements would be subject to a fine of the higher of f1 million or 10 per cent of annual sales of the company.

Transportation

A new high speed rail system linking Amsterdam with Paris, and London via the Channel Tunnel, is be built. The estimated cost of the project is f7.5 billion. A second important rail project is also in the planning stage, the freight-only Betuwe line, which will connect the port of Rotterdam with Germany's heavily-industrialsed Ruhr region.

Amsterdam's Schipol airport passenger traffic rose by 7.6 per cent in 1995 compared with the previous year. Over 25 million people used the airport in 1995, representing an 8.4 per cent of total European passenger traffic. A new runway is scheduled to be completed by the year 2003 which would give the airport the biggest capacity in Europe in terms of cargo (3 million tonnes) and aircraft movements per hour (120).

After 77 years of providing aircraft to the world, Fokker's fortunes nosedived into bankruptcy in the first part of 1996 when bridging credit from the Dutch government ran out. In January 1996 Dasa, the company's controlling shareholder, cut off its financial support. Dasa is owed f1.3 billion by Fokker.

The core aircraft business of Fokker is to be wound down, resulting in redundancies for 5,664 people – the largest for a single company in Dutch history. Fokker Aviation, a newly-established holding company, will carry on with the most viable parts of the company, including defence contracts, electronics and aircraft maintenance. Various possible suitors had been in talks to save the company, including Korea's Samsung, Canada's Bombardier and China's Aviation Industries. Eleventh-

KEY INDICATORS — The Netherlands

	Unit	1991	1992	1993	1994	1995
Population	m	15.07	15.18	15.29	15.38	15.40
Gross domestic product (GDP)	US$bn	285.0	323.3	309.4	328.5	–
GDP per capita	US$	18,940	21,480	20,250	21,300	–
GDP real growth	%	2.3	2.0	0.2	3.4	2.1
Inflation	%	3.7	3.2	2.6	2.7	2.0
Consumer prices	1990=100	103.1	106.4	109.2	112.2	114.4
Share prices	1990=100	102.8	107.8	125.0	148.0	160.0
Wages (hourly earnings)	1990=100	103.7	108.2	111.7	113.8	115.0
Unemployment rate	%	7.0	6.9	8.3	8.5	8.1
Agricultural production	1979-81=100	120.36	123.31	130.14	122.32	123.98
Industrial production	1990=100	102.7	102.7	101.8	104.8	107.0
Natural gas	bn cu m	69.0	69.1	70.0	66.4	66.3
Exports	f m	249,105	246,541	258,342	286,403	313,544
Imports (CIF)	f m	236,924	236,597	231,631	256,497	280,714
Balance of trade	US$m	11,979	12,306	15,535	15,839	19,281
Current account	US$m	7,729	7,332	12,249	15,008	16,191
Total reserves minus gold	US$m	17,798	21,937	31,344	34,352	33,714
Foreign exchange	US$m	16,240	20,237	29,669	32,716	31,060
Deposit rate	%	3.18	3.20	3.11	2.95	2.63
Lending rate	%	12.40	12.75	10.40	8.29	7.21
Exchange rate	f per US$	1.87	1.76	1.86	1.82	1.60

hour talks with Samsung failed to bring any hope for the company's future.

A big shake-up at KLM was announced in November 1996. The company detailed its three-year cost saving plan which will result in the trimming of ground support staff and the chopping of uneconomical routes. The goal is to save f1 billion during the period. A new European partner was being sought.

Relations between KLM and Northwest Airlines of the USA continue to be troubled, seven years into their partnership. Reservation systems used by the airlines are still incompatible and there has been no agreement on combining their cargo operations into a single unit. Although KLM has been seeking to raise its stake in Northwest (it has 25 per cent of Northwest's ordinary equity), KLM had been unable to do so under the poison pill provisions of Northwest put in place to stop a take-over. In May 1996 KLM threatened to end their alliance altogether, although Northwest countered that it wanted it to continue and that the relationship brought additional operating profits of between US$120 and US$170 million a year to KLM. KLM agreed to sell 6,654 shares of Northwest preferred stock back to Northwest for some f650 million by July 1997.

Communications

VAT has been levied on telecommunications services since January 1996. The telecommunications market will be fully liberalised by July 1997 and KPN, the private telephone monopoly, will be facing competition in the fixed-line telecommunications sector. In October 1996 the government awarded two licences to provide new services: one to Telfort and the other to EnerTel. Telfort is a joint venture between the UK's BT and NS, the Dutch national railway company. EnerTel is a grouping of regional energy companies and cable television providers and has Canada's Northern Telecom as its international partner. Some 1,300 regional licences will be granted by the government throughout the country for voice telephony under the telecommunication liberalisation scheme.

KPN became the largest shareholder in GD Net in June 1996. GD Net is a co-owner of the TNT Express worldwide courier company with TNT of Australia. KPN's PTT Post division was to hold 54 per cent of GD Net with the remainder being held by Sweden Post. Previously, three other national postal utilities shared control of the company with Sweden Post and KPN.

Outlook

The economic recovery should continue in 1997. Household consumption is in part responsible for powering this recovery but this is expected to slow by the start of 1997 because of the lack of growth in real disposable incomes. Export growth is expected to be only moderate and should not be hampered by any erosion of market share. Falling unemployment was seen in 1996 and this trend was expected to continue into 1997, in view of the continued recovery in the economy as a whole. Inflation is expected to remain in check in 1997, with labour costs, aggravated by lowering unemployment, providing a strong upward pressure on costs.

COUNTRY PROFILE — THE NETHERLANDS

Historical profile

1579 Protestant Republic declared after uprising against domination by Catholic Habsburg Empire. A great trading nation developed with, following the French Revolution, close affinities to the French Republic. Subsequently part of the French Empire under Napoleon.
1830 Independence.
1914-18 Neutral in First World War.
1940 Occupied by Germany despite neutrality. Dutch forces fought with allies while Dutch formed resistance movement.
1945 Policy of neutrality abandoned; Netherlands became founder member of NATO and EC, and Benelux Economic Union. All post-war governments have been formed by various coalitions between several Catholic, Protestant, Socialist and Liberal parties. The formation and stability of coalitions during the 1980s were bedevilled by disagreements on economic policy and on NATO's nuclear policy of siting cruise missiles on Dutch soil (the latter problem solved by the 1987 treaty between the USA and the USSR removing intermediate range nuclear weapons from Europe).
1980 Queen Juliana abdicated in favour of her eldest daughter Princess Beatrix.
1982 Centre-right coalition of Christian Democratic Appeal (CDA) and People's Party for Freedom and Democracy (VVD) led by Ruud Lubbers.
1989 CDA-VVO government fell in its second term when VVD refused to support Lubbers' proposal for a 20-year environmental protection programme. A centre-left cabinet was formed by CDA and PvdA, with Lubbers still at the helm.
1994 May elections brought three-party coalition in August, headed by Wim Kok. CDA frozen out of power for first time since First World War.

Political system

A constitutional and hereditary monarchy with legislative power vested in the *Staten Generaal* (bicameral parliament). The *Eerste Kamer* (First Chamber) is composed of 75 members and is elected by members of the *Provinciale Staten.* The *Tweede Kamer* (Second Chamber) consists of 150 members and is elected directly on the

COUNTRY PROFILE

Political system (contd): basis of proportional representation. The Second Chamber proposes and amends bills, which can only be approved or rejected by the First Chamber. Executive power is exercised by the Council of Ministers, led by the prime minister, who is responsible to the *Staten Generaal.* Ministers may be drawn from outside parliament. MPs becoming ministers give up their seats to party colleagues on official 'list'. Both houses are elected for a four-year term. The Kingdom of the Netherlands also includes overseas territories – Netherlands Antilles and Aruba.

Main cities/towns

Amsterdam (population 1.1m in 1994), Rotterdam, The Hague (seat of government, 800,000), Eindhoven, Haarlem, Groningen, Utrecht.

Language

Dutch and Frysian official languages; English, German and French widely spoken.

Media

Press: Foreign newspapers and magazines available at kiosks, bookstalls and hotels.
Dailies: Over 50 regional daily newspapers. The top daily newspapers are *VNU Dagbladen, De Telegraaf, Wegener Dagbl, De Volkskrant, Het Algemeen Dagblad, NRC Handelsblad, Sijthoff Pers, NHD, Trouw, Rotterdams Dgbl, Leeuwarder Crt* and *Haarlems Dgbl Comb.*
Business: Major financial/business publications include *Het Financieele Dagblad* (daily), *Elseviers Weekblad* (weekly), *Bedrijfsdocumentaire* and *Management Team* (fortnightly).
Periodicals: Several weekly magazines, most of which published by United Dutch Publishers (NDU).
Broadcasting: TV and radio network co-ordinated by Nederlandse Omroep Stichting (NOS). Television programmes broadcast on three main channels by about 30 organisations, which are allotted transmission time according to the number of subscribers. TV programmes broadcast in original language – often English – with Dutch sub-titles. Overseas broadcasting in Dutch undertaken by Radio Nederland Wereldomroep. About 90 per cent of homes can receive cable TV services and the take-up rate for satellite TV is very high. Over 30 per cent of homes subscribe to teletext.
Advertising: Accepted in all forms of media, though TV and radio advertising restricted to 30 and 40 mins/day respectively. Most advertising direct, in newspapers and magazines. Main advertising subjects: cars, finance, food. Advertisements for TV and radio accepted by Stichting Ether Reclame (STER). Advice on agents from the Dutch advertising association, Nederlandse Vereniging van Erkende Reclame Adviesbureaus (VEA).

Domestic economy

Broad industrial base with heavy dependence on foreign trade. Also large service sector, with public spending accounting for around 55 per cent of GDP. Indications are that economic growth will continue. Despite recent improvements in economic performance, public sector deficit remains high. Current emphasis on export-led growth and monetary fiscal restraint. The government promised spending and tax cuts when in February 1988, it suddenly scrapped its 10-year-old tax-credit programme, designed to encourage companies to invest in fixed and capital assets. The Netherlands has been able to avoid the worst effects of recession in Germany, its biggest trading partner. Since 1993 the Dutch economy has been growing faster than Germany's.
In February 1995 the country was hit by storms which caused the worst flooding since 1954.

Employment

Around 85 per cent employed in private sector, mainly manufacturing and services. Moderate levels of unemployment. Only just over 50 per cent of women of working age are in employment. Government and union consensus over strategy for jobs involving work creation, part-time jobs, training programmes and work-sharing.
The number of jobless totalled 438,000, representing 6.6 per cent of the labour force, in the three months to October 1996, down from 6.1 per centin 1995.

External trade

Regular trade surplus since 1981 owing to increased competitiveness and relatively low levels of imports. Approximately 77 per cent of foreign trade is conducted with EU countries, particularly Germany, Belgium and France. Amsterdam is a major centre for trade in tobacco, diamonds and precious metals.
Exports: Exports were up 4 per cent year-on-year in the first four months of 1996. Major exports include gas, organic chemicals, artificial resins and plastics, agricultural products and foodstuffs, machinery and electronics.
About 30 per cent of Dutch exports go to Germany, mostly foodstuffs and gas. There is a noticeable rise in exports (most of which are aid tied) to developing countries.
Imports: Petroleum and petroleum products account for over 10 per cent of total imports. Other major imports are non-electrical machinery, raw materials and transport equipment.

Agriculture

Small-scale but highly specialised and efficient, and an important part of the economy. The Netherlands is more than self-sufficient in agricultural produce. Trend towards larger and more highly mechanised farms. Dairy farming is most important activity, involving over a third of the country's farmers. Horticulture also increasingly significant providing 60 per cent of the world trade in cut flowers.
Sector employs 4.2 per cent of the workforce, contributed 4.6 per cent to GDP in 1994 and accounts for 25 per cent of total exports. Principal products include potatoes, vegetables, flowers and plants, meat and dairy products. The fishing industry is important, and overfishing of young herring in the Skagerrak and Kattegat, Denmark, is weakening the growth of the North Sea herring population.
The agriculture sector suffered from severe floods in February 1995.

Industry

The industrial sector contributed 27 per cent to GDP in 1994, employing 22.1 per cent of the labour force. It is largely dependent on foreign markets, both for raw material imports and sales. Chemicals account for around 15 per cent of manufacturing output.
Major industries include food processing, engineering, metals, chemicals, shipbuilding, textiles, electronics, aircraft and motor vehicles.

Leading companies

Royal Dutch/Shell, Unilever, Philips, DSM and Akzo. These five companies employ nearly 1m people – almost a fifth of the workforce.

Hydrocarbons

The hydrocarbons sector accounted for 2.8 per cent of GDP in 1994 and employed 4.2 per cent of the workforce. Almost totally confined to gas and oil.
Major producer and exporter of natural gas. The Netherlands became the biggest driller for offshore natural gas in the North Sea in 1988 and can supply the country well into the next century.
Natural gas reserves 65.2 trillion cu feet (end-1995). Natural gas production 59.7m tonnes of oil equivalent in 1995, down 0.1 per cent on 1994 output.

Energy

Natural gas provides approximately 50 per cent of electric power needs. Oil production is around 28 per cent of domestic requirements. Emphasis on developing coal, gas, solar and wind power. Development of nuclear power has been slow owing to popular opposition and 94 per cent of electricity is produced by thermal rather than nuclear power stations.

Banking

System is extensive and provides a full range of services. Three main banking institutions (apart from the central bank): mortgage banks, commercial banks, savings banks and agricultural/co-operative banks. All restrictions on the import and export of capital or currencies were abolished in October 1986.

Legal system

Civil law system incorporating French penal theory.

Membership of international organisations

ADB, Benelux Economic Union, BIS, CCC, CERN, Central Commission for the Navigation of the Rhine, COCOM, Council of Europe, DAC, ECE, EEA, EIB, EMS, EPO, ESA, ESCAP, EU, Eutelsat, FAO, G-10, IAEA, ICAC, ICAO, ICES, ICO, IDA, IDB, IEA, IFAD, IFC, IHO, ILO, IMF, IMO, INRO, INTELSAT, International Lead and Zinc Study Group, International Union for Inland Navigation, INTERPOL, IOM, IPU, IRC, ITC, ITU, IWC, NACC, NAM (guest), NATO, OAS (observer), OECD, OSCE, UN, UNESCO, UPU, WEU, WHO, WIPO, WMO, World Bank, WSG, WTO.

BUSINESS GUIDE

Time

GMT + 1 hr (GMT + 2 hrs from late Mar to late Sep).

Climate

Temperate; warm summers and mild/cold winters. Temperatures range from 2–25°C. Rainfall throughout year but heaviest Nov–Jan. Coastal areas have the mildest climate and lowest rainfall.
Clothing: Mediumweight throughout year, topcoat in winter. Raincoat useful any time.

Entry requirements

Visa not required for nationals of most European countries and several others, for visits of up to three months.
Health: No vaccination certificates required. EC nationals are covered for medical treatment.
Currency: No restrictions on import or export of currency. Do check the exchange rate. Commission charges vary considerably in Amsterdam.
Customs: Personal effects duty-free.

Air access

Regular flights by all major international airlines.
National airline: KLM (Royal Dutch).
Main international airport: Schiphol (AMS), 14 km south-west of Amsterdam.
International airports: Rotterdam (RTM), 8 km north-west of city centre, Maastricht (MST), 7 km from city, Groningen (GRQ).

Surface access

Good access by road and rail from all surrounding countries, plus ferry services to all major ports. Boat trains operate to Hook of Holland from many European countries.
Main ports: Rotterdam, Hook of Holland, Scheveningen, Vlissingen, Amsterdam.

Hotels

Classified from one- to five-star by Netherlands Board of Tourism, the Royal Dutch Touring Club and the Royal Netherlands Automobile Club. Accommodation may be booked through the Netherlands Reservation Centre in Leidschendam (tel: (070)202-500). Advisable to book well in advance during spring and summer. Foreign nationals must present passports before booking in, and are automatically registered with local police.

Restaurants

Wide variety, with many specialities often available. Service charge and VAT included in prices on menus additional tips discretionary – 5-10 per cent.

Currency

Exchange rate: Netherlands is a participant in the European Monetary System. Guilder is pegged to other participants' currencies within a band of 2.25 per cent (6 per cent with respect to the Spanish peseta).

Foreign exchange information

Account restrictions: There are no restrictions on international payments of any kind.
Trade policy: Import licences not required for goods from most countries. Goods which do require an import licence or registration include some animal derivative and agricultural products, electrical equipment, raw iron and steel, some textiles, explosives and firearms. Also food products subject to quality and hygiene restrictions.

Credit cards

All major credit cards are accepted.

Car hire

Widely available. Addresses can be obtained from Tourist Information Offices (VVV). Rates vary depending on make and model. Cheaper rates for rental periods of a week or more. Drive on the right. Speed limits: urban areas 50 kph, normal roads 80 kph, motorways 120 kph. Wearing of seat belts compulsory. Information and assistance from Royal Dutch Touring Club (ANWB).
N.B. Do not ignore parking fees. Failure can result in a fine. If this is not paid within 24 hours, car will be towed away and the cost of retrieval is very expensive.

City transport

Nationwide fares zoning system also applies to cities. Buses, trams and metro charge same fare per zone. You can buy a *nationale strippenkaart* comprising 15 or 45 tickets at the Amsterdam Tourist Office (opening hours 0900–1700), Amsterdam Public Transport Office in Stationsplein, outside Central Station, transport companies, post offices and some VVV offices. Tickets for two, three or eight trips can be bought from the driver, although they work out more expensive. The number of strips needed for a journey depends on the number of zones to be crossed.
Transport from Schiphol airport presents no problem: bus, tram, metro or express tram are all quick. Most public transport (apart from the Schiphol trains) only runs from about 0600–2300, although there are some night bus services to be found. You can get information (and maps) from the public transport office in Stationsplein, outside the Central Station.
Taxis: Usually boarded at ranks, at railway stations and other parts of the city, or called by telephone. Fares vary from city to city. The meter price includes a service charge; additional tip discretionary – 5-10 per cent. In Amsterdam taxis are usually booked by phone (tel: 677-7777), although there is no shortage of ranks.
Buses: Good services throughout cities linking tram services to provincial routes.
Metro: Rapid transit systems in Amsterdam and Rotterdam. Trains are modern, frequent, punctual and inexpensive.
Trams: Good service in central regions of most large cities.
Rail: Train to the city centre from Schiphol is the best method. Train tickets can be purchased from railways stations, transport companies, post offices, tobacconists and local tourist offices.

National transport

Whole country divided into zones. Fares for bus travel depend on number of zones crossed. Tickets (covering up to 45 zones) should be obtained in advance; available from railway stations, transport companies, some VVV offices and post offices. Separate tickets are required for trains, available from railway stations. Most public transport (apart from inter-city services) only runs from about 0600–2300.
Air: Internal service linking Amsterdam with Groningen, Eindhoven, Rotterdam and Maastricht.
Road: Approximately 110,000 km of roads including 2,000 km of motorways (autowegen). Frequent bus connections between all cities. Journey times usually less than four hours.
Rail: Almost 3,000 km of track, mostly electrified. Fast regular services operated by Netherlands Railways (Nederlandse Spoorwegen).
Water: Extensive inland waterways. Scheduled boat services operate from Enkhuizen to Urk and Staveren and between the mainland and the islands in the north.

Public holidays

Fixed dates: 1 Jan (New Year's Day), 30 Apr (Queen's Day), 25-26 Dec (Christmas).
Variable dates: Good Friday, Easter Monday, Ascension Day, Whit Monday.

Working hours

Business: (Mon–Fri) 0830–1730.
Government: (Mon–Fri) 0830–1700.
Banking: (Mon–Fri) 0900–1600, some open Sat and on late shopping evenings.
Shops: 0830/0900–1730/1800, (half-day closing usually Mon or Wed). Main shops open Sat and Thu/Fri evening.

Social customs

Dutch people shake hands frequently. When invited to a meal in a Dutch home it is courteous to give flowers, chocolates or a small gift.

Business language and interpreting/translation

Available through the Association of International Conference Interpreters or the United Dutch Translation Office. Dutch is the official language, but English and German widely spoken and most business houses will correspond in English.

Telecommunications

Telephone and telefax: One of the most efficient phone systems in the world. Fully automatic inland and overseas service. Telephone information given in French, English and German. Credit facilities available. Cheap rates from 1800 to 0800 and weekends. All calls can be made from public booths and post offices. Blue phone booths require a phone card, at post offices, VVV offices and shops displaying the 'PTT-telephone card' poster.
International dialling code: 31 followed by area code, 20 for Amsterdam, 10 for Rotterdam, followed by subscriber's number. For IDD access from Netherlands dial 09.
Telex: Available in main hotels. Country code 44 NL.
Telegram: Available at all main post offices. Telegrams can also be sent direct from telephone kiosks.

Postal service

Rates vary for both land and air mail. Following items may be sent by air without extra postage: air letters, letters to all European countries, postcards and money orders.

Trade fairs

Several trade fairs and exhibitions held throughout the year. Two large exhibition centres: RAI in Amsterdam and the Jaarbeurs in Utrecht. Also smaller centres in Ahoyhal in Rotterdam, and in Maastricht.
International Hotel and Catering Industry Trade Fair, Amsterdam, Jan.

Electricity supply

220 V AC.

Representation in capital

Algeria, Argentina, Australia, Austria, Belgium, Brazil, Bulgaria, Canada, Cape Verde, Chile, China, Colombia, Costa Rica, Cuba, Denmark, Egypt, El Salvador, Finland, France, Germany, Greece, The Holy See, Honduras, Hungary, India, Indonesia, Iran, Iraq, Ireland, Israel, Italy, Japan, Kenya, Republic of Korea, Kuwait, Lebanon, Luxembourg, Malaysia, Mexico, Morocco, New Zealand, Nicaragua, Nigeria, Norway, Pakistan, Peru, Philippines, Poland, Portugal, Romania, Russia, Saudi Arabia, South Africa, Spain, Sudan, Suriname, Sweden, Switzerland, Tanzania, Thailand, Tunisia, Turkey, UK, Uruguay, USA, Venezuela, Yemen, Zaïre.

BUSINESS DIRECTORY

Hotels

Amsterdam
Alexander, Prinsengracht 444, 10017 KE (tel: 267-721; tx: 13-161).

Ambassador, Herengracht 336-353, 1016 AZ (tel: 626-2333).

American, Leidsekade 9, 1017 PN (tel: 624-5322; fax: 625-3236).

AMS Hotel Lairesse, De Lairessestraat 7, 1071 NR (tel: 683-1811).

Amstel Intercontinental, Prof. Tulpplein 1, 1018 GX (tel: 622-6060; fax: 622-5808).

Apollofirst, Apollolaan 123, 1077 AP (tel: 673-0333).

Arthur Frommer, Noorderstraat 46, 1017 TV (tel: 220-328; tx: 14-047).

Caransa Karena, Rembrandtsplein 19, 1017 CT (tel: 627-4684; fax: 222-773).

De l'Europe, Nieuwe Doelenstraat 2-4, 10122 CP (tel: 623-4836; fax: 624-2952); reservations (UK) (tel: (0)800-181-123) (Leading Hotels of the World).

Delphi, Apollolaan 101-105, 1077 AN (tel: 675-2941; tx: 16-659).

Estheria, Singel 303-309, 1012 WJ (tel: 624-5148; fax: 623-8001); reservations (UK) (tel: (0)171-413-8877) (Utell).

Forte Crest Apollo, Apollolaan 2, 1077 BA (tel: 673-5922; fax: 627-5245); reservations (UK) (tel: (0)800-404-040).

Grand, Oudezijds Voorburgwal 197, 1012 EX (tel: 555-3111).

Grand Krasnapolsky, Dam 9, 1012 JS (tel: 554-911; fax: 622-8605); reservations (UK) (tel: (0)800-898-852) (SRS).

Hans Brinker, Kerkstraat 136, 1017 GE (tel: 220-687; tx: 12-127).

Hilton, Apollolaan 138-140, 1077 BG (tel: 780-780; fax: 662-6688).

Hilton Schiphol, PO Box 7685, 1118 Schiphol Centrum (tel: 511-5911; fax: 648-0917); reservations (UK) (tel: (0)345-581-595).

Hotel de l'Europe, 2-4 Nieuwe Doelenstraat, 1012 CP (tel: 234-836; fax: 242-962).

Jan Luyken, Jan Luykenstraat 58, 1071 CS (tel: 573-0730).

Marriott, Stadhouderskade 19-21, 1054 ES (tel: 607-5555; fax: 607-551); reservations (UK) (tel: (0)171-581-9840).

Museum, PC Hoofstraat 2, 1017 (tel: 662-1402; fax: 733-918).

Novotel, Europaboulevard 10, 1083 AD (tel: 541-1123; fax: 648-2823); reservations (UK) (tel: (0)171-724-1000).

Okura, Ferdinand Bolstraat 333, 1072 LH (tel: 678-7111; fax: 671-2344); reservations (UK) (0)800-181-123 (Leading Hotels of the World).

Professor Tulpplein 1, 1018 GX Amsterdam (tel; 226-060; fax: 622-5000); reservations (UK) (tel: (0)345-581-444).

Pulitzer, Prinsengracht 315/331 1016 GZ (tel: 228-333; fax: 276-753).

Trianon, J.W. Brouwersstraat 3, 1071 LH (tel: 732-073; fax: 738-868).

Victoria, Damrak 1-6, 1012 LG (tel: 234-255; fax: 252-997).

Useful telephone numbers

Directory enquiries: 068-008 (national), 060-418 (international).

Operator: 060-410.

Police/fire: 0611.

Car hire

Amsterdam
Achilles: (tel: 381-1811).

Avis: Central Reservations (tel: 564-1611, 564-1633, 564-1641; tx: 15-669); Nassaukade 380 (tel: 683-6061; tx: 15-669); Schiphol Airport (tel: 604-1301).

Budget: Overtoom 121 (tel: 612-6066).

Diks Car Rental: (tel: 617-8505).

Euro Car: (tel: 665-4141).

Eurodollar: Overtoom 196, 2132 NA Hoofddorp (tel: 334-433; tx: 18-196).

Europcar Interrent: (tel: 590-9111).

Hertz: Overtoom 333 (tel: 370-749; tx: 15-160); Schiphol Airport (tel: 601-5416; 617-0866; tx: 11-103).

Chambers of commerce

Kamer van Koophandel en Fabrieken voor Amsterdam, Koningin Wilhelminaplein 13, 1062 HH Amsterdam (tel: 617-2882; tx: 18-888 amtra).

Kamer van Koophandel en Fabrieken voor Midden Gelderland, Nieuwe Plein 1B, 6825 KX Arnhem (tel: 516-969; tx: 45-276 kkarh).

Kamer van Koophandel en Fabrieken voor Haarlem en Omstreken, Nassauplein 4-6, 2011 PG Haarlem (tel: 319-017; tx: 41-567 kkhlm).

Kamer van Koophandel en Fabrieken voor s'Gravenhage, Alexander Gogelweg 15, 2517 JH The Hague (tel: 379-5795; tx: 33-003 kkgrh).

Kamer van Koophandel en Fabrieken voor Rotterdam, Beursgebouw, Coolsingel 58, 3011 AE Rotterdam (tel: 405-7777; tx: 23-760 kvkr).

Kamer van Koophandel en Fabrieken voor Tilburg en Omstreken, Reitseplein 1, 5037 AA Tilburg, (tel: 654-524; tx: 52-384 vaspa).

Kamer van Koophandel en Fabrieken voor Utrecht en Omstreken, Waterstraat 47, 3511 BW, Utrecht (tel: 331-412; tx: 47-730 kkutr).

Kamer van Koophandel en Fabrieken voor Noordelijk Overijssel, Weeshuisstraat 27, 8011 TZ Zwolle (tel: 218-047; tx: 42-281 kkzwl).

Banking

De Nederlandsche Bank (central bank), Westeinde 1, 1000 AB Amsterdam (tel: 524-9111; tx: 11-355).

Bank der Bondsspaarbanken, Singel 236, 1001 AR Amsterdam (tel: 550-1601; tx: 15-565).

De Nationale Investeringsbank NV (national investment bank), Carnegieplein 4, 2517 HJ The Hague (tel: 342-5425).

Ing (Internationale Nederlanden Bank) (commercial bank), De Amsterdamse Poort, 1102 MG, Amsterdam-Z.O. (tel: 563-9111).

NCB (Nederlandse Credietbank NV) (commercial bank), Herengracht 458, 1017 CA Amsterdam (tel: 655-6911; tx: 14-385).

Nederlandse Bankiersvereniging (Netherlands Association of Banks), PO Box 19870, 1000 GW Amsterdam (tel: 623-0281; tx: 16-785).

Rabobank, Croeselaan 18 (commercial bank), 3521 CB Utrecht (tel: 909-111; tx: 40-200).

Principal newspapers

The Netherlander, 85 Weesperstraat, NL-1018 VN Amsterdam (tel: 557-4511).

De Volkskrant, Wibautstraat 131, NL-1091 BA Amsterdam (tel: 562-9222; fax: 562-6289).

Travel information

Amsterdam Tourist Office (opening hours 0900 – 1700), Stationplein 10, opposite Central Station, Amsterdam (tel: 403-4066).

Netherlands Board of Tourism (NBT), Vlietweg 15, 2266 KA Leidschendam (tel: 705-705; tx: 32-588).

Schiphol Airport (tel: 503-4050).

Other useful addresses

Advertising Federation (Bond van Adverteerders), Koningslaan 34, 1007 AL Amsterdam (tel: 664-4546, 673-9551).

Algemeen Nederlands Persbureau (news agency), Eisenhowerlaan 128, 2517 KM The Hague (tel: 520-520; fax: 351-2900).

Association of International Conference Interpreters, Prinsegracht 993, 1017 KM, Amsterdam (tel: 625-2535).

Centraal Bureau voor de Statistiek (CBS), Prinses Beatrixlaan 428, Postbus 959, 2270 AZ Voorburg (tel: 373-800; fax: 877-429).

Fenedex (Federation for the Netherlands' Export), Postbus 90409, 2509 HL The Hague (tel: 305-600; fax: 305-656).

Foreign Trade Service (EVD), Bezuidenhoutseweg 151, 2594 AG, The Hague (tel: 379-8933).

Goods Inspection Service (Keuringsdienst van Waren), Prinsegracht 50, 2512 GA, The Hague. (tel: 398-8920).

Ministry of Economic Affairs, Bezuidenhoutseweg 30, PO Box 20101, 2500 EC The Hague (tel: 379-8911; tx: 31-099).

Ministry of Finance, Korte Voorhout 7, 2511 VB The Hague (tel: 376-7767; tx: 33-141).

Nederlandse Vereniging van Erkende Reclame Adviesbureaus (VEA), AJ Ernststraat 169, 1083 GT Amsterdam (tel: 642-5642).

Netherlands Association of Information Bureaux (Algemeene Nederlandse Vereniging van VVVs), Gravelandsweg 25a, 1200 AB Hilversum (tel: 48-541).

Netherlands Council for Trade Promotions (NCH), Bezuidenhoutseweg 181, The Hague (tel: 347-8234; tx: 32-306).

Netherlands Reservations Centre, POB 404,2260 AK Leidschendam (tel: 202-500; tx: 33-755).

State Printing and Publishing House (De Staatsdrukkerij en Uitgeverij), Christoffel Plantijnstraat 2, Postbus 2004, 2500 EA The Hague (tel: 378-9911; tx: 32-486).

Stichting Ether Reclame (Ster), Laapersveld 70, Postbus 344, 1200 AH Hilversum (tel: (035)11-841).

Vereniging voor de Effectenhandel (Amsterdam stock exchange), Beursplein 5, 1000 GD Amsterdam (tel: 523-4567).

World Trade Centre, Strawinskylaan 15, 1077 XW Amsterdam (tel: 575-9111).

World Trade Centre, Rotterdam, Meent 134,3011 GS Rotterdam (tel: 433-3611).

Internet sites

KLM:
http://www.ib.com.8080/business/klm/klm.html

Norway

Howard Hill

In 1996 Norway seemed intent on showing the European Union (EU) that it does not need to be a member of the Union in order to achieve economic stability and growth. Having earlier rejected EU membership in a referendum – a proposition that was supported by Brundtland and her government – Norway continued its enviable economic growth record in 1995, although the rate was lower than in the previous year. Inflation remained under control and the outlook is for continued low inflation with slowing growth rates. Oil production has propelled the economy in the last few years; output of this valuable commodity increased dramatically in 1995 and 1996. But the year was not without its surprises: Gro Harlem Brundtland resigned as prime minister in October 1996 after nine years in the job.

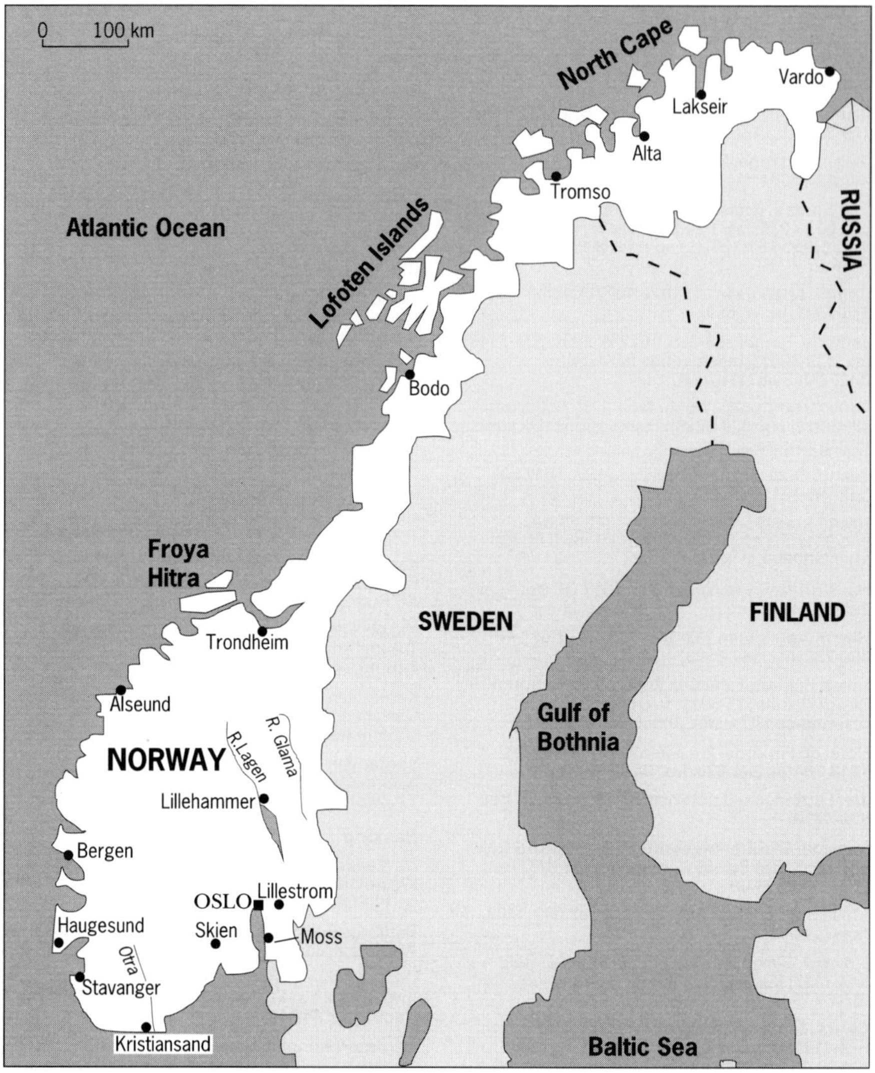

Politics

In stepping down, Mrs Brundtland wanted to give her Det Norske Arbeiderparti (Norwegian Labour Party) (DNA) enough time to groom a successor before the 1997 general election, which is due in September. Her replacement is Thorbjörn Jagland, Mrs Brundtland's clear heir apparent, and chairman of the DNA for the previous four years. He was expected to continue the policies of his predecessor. Throughout 1996 the opposition parties were beset by in-fighting and divisions, making it increasingly likely that the DNA will again be successful in the next election.

Almost immediately after coming to the prime ministership, Jagland re-shuffled his cabinet. Jens Stoltenberg, a highly regarded DNA member, was appointed as finance minister, replacing the departing Sigbjorn Johnsen. A new department of planning was also created. Terje Rod, the UN's representative to the Palestinian Authority in Gaza and the West Bank, was appointed to head this department.

In November 1995 central bank chief Thorstein Moland announced that he was stepping down temporarily from his position while he appealed against the imposition of a 45 per cent penalty tax. He formally resigned shortly thereafter. The tax penalty against Moland was applied after the tax department's claim he had been grossly negligent in a personal tax matter dating back to 1990. In February 1996 Kjell Storvik, who had been deputy governor of the central bank and the acting head in Moland's absence, was formally appointed to the governorship.

Norway has shown that it can survive, even thrive, without being an EU member. Although it currently enjoys many of the benefits of membership, and has widespread duty-free access to the EU, it need not concern itself with Brussels to the same degree as EU members. Norway has harmonised much of its laws with the EU and if voters ever have a change of heart, full EU membership could be there for the asking. Meanwhile, Norway's economic vigour, due in no small way to its oil wealth, allows it the luxury of relative independence from Brussels.

Economy

The Norwegian economy in 1995 continued to expand at an impressive rate, although slower than in 1994. Mainland GDP grew by

3.3 per cent in 1995, somewhat down from the previous year's rate of 4.8 per cent. The slowing trend was expected to continue for 1996 and 1997. The growth in 1995 was due in large part to fixed investment.

The government's budget deficit in 1995, at NKr28.4 billion, equalled 3.1 per cent of GDP. Externally, foreign debt fell by NKr45.3 billion in 1995, giving Norway a positive net foreign asset position for the first time in 50 years.

Inflation in 1995, which averaged 2.4 per cent for consumer prices, was 1.1 per cent above the 1994 figure. If the 1 per cent increase in VAT, effective from 1 January 1995, is taken into account, then the inflation rate was virtually unchanged between 1994 and 1995. This despite the fact that substantial price rises for electricity were registered. Rather unusually, high economic growth has not yet made an impact on the inflation rate.

With the VAT increase no longer affecting the year-on-year inflation rate, the average rise in January 1996 was 1.2 per cent compared with the same month in 1995, and in February 1996 it was even less at 0.9 per cent versus February 1995. The two subsequent months saw little change in the rate. The reduction in new car taxes in 1996 is expected to reflect favourably on inflation as well as boost vehicle sales.

The central bank's fear of demand-driven inflation led it to follow a fairly tight monetary policy beginning in mid-1995. The strength of the krone and relative lack of inflationary pressures gave the central bank enough confidence to keep short term interest rates at a relatively low level from the second half of 1995, but the central bank indicated that further reductions were unlikely. The three-month interest rate was just under 5 per cent.

Manufacturing production expanded at a rate of 2.5 per cent in 1995 compared with 1994; growth was 5.5 per cent in 1994 (over 1993). Retail sales rose by 3 per cent in 1995 compared with 1994 (5.3 per cent in 1994 versus 1993).

Employment

Unemployment has ceased to be a widespread problem in Norway. In the final quarter of 1995 unemployment declined by 18,000 compared with the same quarter of 1994. However, those people who have been out of work for a considerable time or are lacking in work experience were still having a difficult time finding work while manpower shortages were seen in a number of sectors.

The unemployment rate was 4.9 per cent in 1995, slightly lower than 5.4 per cent in 1994 and as low as 3.8 per cent in the final quarter of 1995. The rate had not been below 4 per cent since 1988. Wage increases, at 3.75 per cent in 1995, outstripped inflation for the year but less so than in 1994 when they were slightly over double the consumer inflation rate. By April 1996 the unemployment rate had fallen further, to 4.2 per cent of the work force.

A 1995 strike by off-shore oil workers, in support of a wage claim by 400 service workers, lasted six days. It was called off when oil workers from key projects started to withdraw their support. The service workers had already been on strike when the oil workers walked off and this earlier action did not affect output.

Labour unrest also hit industrial output in May 1996 when 37,000 mechanical engineering workers went on strike over wages. About 500 companies were directly affected by the walk-out which had a knock-on effect throughout the Norwegian economy and hurt Sweden also. The Fellesforbundet union had earlier negotiated a wage deal with the employers but this was rejected by their workers who demanded a wage increase of NKr3.00 per hour – twice the rate agreed in the offer – and more lucrative pension arrangements.

External trade

Norway's energy resources figure heavily in its export picture. For this reason,

KEY FACTS

Official title: Norge (The Kingdom of Norway)

Head of state: King Harald V

Head of government: Prime Minister Thorbjörn Jagland (from 25 Oct 1996)

Ruling party: Det Norske Arbeiderparti (Norwegian Labour Party) (DNA) minority government

Capital: Oslo

Official Languages: Norwegian

Currency: Norwegian Krone (NKr) = 100 ore

Exchange rate: NKr6.47 per US$ (Dec 1996)

Area: 323,985 sq km

Population: 4.36m (1995)

GDP per capita: US$25,268 (1994)

GDP real growth: 3.3% (1995)

Unemployment: 3.6% (Oct 1996)

Inflation: 2.4% (1995) (consumer prices)

Oil reserves: 8.4bn barrels (end-1995)

Trade balance: US$8.3bn (1994)

KEY INDICATORS — Norway

	Unit	1991	1992	1993	1994	1995
Population	m	4.24	4.29	4.31	4.35	4.36
Gross domestic product (GDP)	US$bn	107.5	112.4	103.2	108.2	–
GDP per capita	US$	23,350	26,320	24,000	25,268	–
GDP real growth	%	1.6	3.3	1.6	4.8	3.3
Inflation	%	3.4	2.3	2.3	1.3	2.4
Consumer prices	1990=100	103.4	105.8	108.2	109.8	112.5
Unemployment rate	%	5.3	6.2	6.0	5.4	4.9
Agricultural production	1979-81=100	114.29	106.33	119.97	117.30	120.70
Industrial production	1990=100	102.2	108.7	112.9	121.5	127.7
Oil	'000 bpd	1,985	2,265	2,430	2,765	2,995
Natural gas	bn cu m	27.3	29.4	28.9	30.8	31.3
Exports	NKr m	220,316	218,474	225,714	243,809	264,342
Imports (CIF)	NKr m	165,181	160,821	170,069	192,073	206,930
Balance of trade	US$m	8,696	9,303	7,995	8,321	–
Current account	US$m	5,032	2,982	2,152	3,645	–
Total reserves minus gold	US$m	13,232.0	11,940.4	19,622.4	19,025.5	22,517.8
Foreign exchange	US$m	12,209.4	11,101.0	18,641.8	17,992.4	21,109.2
Discount rate	%	10.00	11.00	7.00	6.75	6.75
Deposit rate	%	9.60	10.69	5.51	5.21	4.95
Lending rate	%	14.19	14.27	9.17	8.38	7.60
Exchange rate	NKr per US$	6.48	6.22	7.09	7.06	6.34

Norway has a substantial positive trade balance amounting to an estimated NKr55.8 billion – 6.8 per cent of GDP – in 1995. This is forecast to rise to NKr70 billion in 1996 on the back of expected higher energy exports.

Sweden, Germany and the UK are Norway's main trading partners and the economic slow-down experienced by all three of these countries has affected Norway's export growth. The value of exports rose to NKr264 billion in 1995 from NKr244 billion in 1994. Traditional merchandise exports grew by 4.4 per cent in 1995.

Imports have been rising in the past years, fuelled by consumer confidence over the economy. Overall, imports amounted to NKr207 billion in 1995, from NKr192 billion in 1994. Imports of services, however, fell by 3.6 per cent compared with 1994.

In March 1996 the Kvaerner company was successful in its UK£904 million takeover of Trafalgar House, the UK construction, shipbuilding and engineering group, in March 1996.

Energy

In 1995 Norway became the world's second biggest oil exporter although the average per day in 1995, at 2.99 million barrels, is not far from the average of the UK (the other major western European producer) at 2.75 million barrels per day (bpd). Norway's 1995 figure represents an 8.2 per cent increase in production from an average of 2.76 million barrels in 1994. Energy is a key ingredient in the country's recent growth, which has come on the coat-tails of the rebound in world prices for oil and gas.

Oil production increased in 1996 as the fruits of an expansion plan start to reveal themselves. The average for the first quarter of the year was 3.22 million bpd, climbing slightly to 3.26 million bpd in the second quarter of 1996. After a slower May 1996 averaging 3.11 million bpd due largely to the oil workers' strike, the June 1996 figures hit 3.36 million bpd.

As production increases, the end of Norway's run as a key energy producer is hastened. The BP Statistical Review of World Energy puts proved oil reserves in 1995 at 8.4 billion bpd, which is sharply down from the figure of 9.4 billion bpd in 1994. This leaves about eight years of reserves at current production rates. Any growth in reserves recently has been primarily related to improvements in drilling technology and recovery methods rather than the discovery of new fields. It is predicted that the rate of production from existing fields will drop by about a third by the turn of the century.

Natural gas reserves are also depleting. In 1995 they were 1.3 trillion cubic metres compared to 2.0 trillion cubic metres in 1994. Production in that year was 0.66 trillion cubic metres, indicating that, at this rate of production, Norway will be devoid of natural gas by 1998 unless more reserves are found.

The 16th round of oil and gas licensing took place in mid-1996. Norway planned to award new acreage in the southern region of the Barents Sea where past results have been less than inspiring. In 1994 the government's policy on licensing of acreages in this region was relaxed in order to spark interest on the part of exploration companies. However, the region's reputation as one of high risk and cost (due to its remoteness) may dampen enthusiasm despite claims by the energy ministry that the Barents Sea has about 25 per cent of the country's total petroleum resources.

Banking

The strong economic growth in 1995 benefited the commercial banks. On ordinary activities in 1995, commercial banks showed a net profit of NKr6.5 billion, which is much better than the previous year's NKr1.8 billion. Higher property

COUNTRY PROFILE — NORWAY

Historical profile

From the end of the fourteenth century Norway was joined with Sweden and Denmark. Following the lapse of Danish power, Sweden and Norway became one country though with separate laws and parliaments. 1905 Independence; union with Sweden dissolved. Norwegians elected their own monarch. 1914-18 Norway neutral in First World War. 1940 Despite neutrality, invaded by the Germans in Second World War. There was vigorous resistance to the Nazi puppet government under Vidkun Quisling. 1945 Policy of neutrality abandoned; Norway joined NATO (1949), the Nordic Council (1952) and EFTA (1960).
1935-65 Labour Party in office except for German occupation.
1955-65 Under Einar Gerhardsen as prime minister. 1957 King Olav V came to the throne. 1962, 1967 Application to join the European Community; withdrawn after defeat of minority Labour government in referendum on terms (1972). 1981-86 First Conservative government since 1928. Following labour disputes, government defeated on its austerity programme.
1986 Minority Labour government under Gro Harlem Brundtland, first woman prime minister, who had previously served for a few months in 1981.
1989 Coalition of Conservative, Christian Democrat and Centre Parties.
1991 King Olav V died on 17 January 1991. He was succeeded by his son Harald.
1993 The EU gave Norway the go-ahead for application to join the European Union. The Labour Party retained power as a minority government after increasing its vote in the September 1993 general election.

Political system

Constitutional monarch, with legislative power vested in unicameral *Storting* (parliament) used to comprise 157 members elected every four years by system of proportional representation. A change of the constitution approved in May 1988 has increased the number of representatives to 165. Executive power (nominally held by the monarch) exercised by Council of State, which is led by the prime minister and is responsible to parliament. The Labour Party retained power as a minority government after increasing its vote in the September 1993 general election.
Gro Harlem Bruntland resigned from the premiership on 22 October 1996. The cabinet was reshuffled by the new prime minister, Thorbjörn Jagland, who took over on 25 October. Next general election is scheduled for September 1997.

Main cities/towns

Oslo (population 477,781 in 1 January 1994), Bergen (219,884), Trondheim (142,188), Stavanger (102,637), Kristiansand (67,863), Drammen (52,401) and Tromso (54,164).

Media

Press: Activity concentrated in south-eastern part of country, especially around Oslo where majority of papers are published. However, local papers tend to dominate each particular region. Some 175 newspapers are printed in more than 130 different places. Newspapers receive extensive support from the state.
Dailies: VG (circulation 1995, 386,000), *Aftenposten AM* (279,000), *Dagbladet* (228,000) and *Aftenposten PM* (188,000).
Weeklies: VG Sunday (circulation 1995, 279,000), *Aftenposten Sunday* (225,000), and *Dagbladet Sunday* (162,000).
Business: Large number covering all aspects of Norwegian trade and industry, but most tend to have comparatively small, specialised readership. Includes *Økonomisk Rapport* and *Kapital* (both fortnightly).
Periodicals: Large number of general and special interest magazines. Those aimed at women and the teens/twenties market have the largest circulations.
Broadcasting: New sets purchased annually total around 500,000 radios and 180,000 TVs. All nationwide radio and TV programmes of domestic origin are broadcast by the Norwegian Broadcasting Corporation (NRK). Norway has only one nationwide television network. Nordic Channel Scansat TV-3 broadcasts Scandinavian language programmes via cable. A commercially funded second channel, TV-2, broadcasting seven hours each evening, established September 1992, and advertising will be allowed on NRK. A growing number of local FM stations have been operating since 1982, when NRK lost its monopoly. Since 1 May 1988 these stations have been allowed to broadcast advertisements, but only after securing a licence from the local authority (kommune). Many cabled foreign and satellite stations broadcast commercials. A growing number of households have their own dish antennae, enabling them to pick up satellite broadcasts directly. More than a dozen different European channels are now received via satellite-cable, including several Pan-Scandinavian channels.
Advertising: All usual media available, although NRK still carries no advertising. Cars, office equipment and travel are the 'top three' categories, as regards total expenditure. Ban on advertising for tobacco and all types of alcohol except the very weakest kind of beer.

Domestic economy

Energy apart, Norway is a small economy open to foreign trade, with exports of non-oil goods and services equivalent fo 34 per cent of GDP. North Sea oil and gas still the largest single foreign currency earner, rising sharply since Gulf crisis of August 1990. Living standards values, good profit results in commerce and industry as a whole, and fewer bad loans helped the picture.

In early June 1996 the government announced that it was re-privatising 127 million shares in Den norske Bank (DnB), amounting to 19.8 per cent of the bank. DnB is the largest bank in Norway with US$25.24 billion worth of assets in 1995. The offer of the shares is to be made to Norwegian and foreign investors and will drop the state's share in DnB to 52 per cent. Record profits in the first quarter of 1996 were announced by DnB; they reached NKr778 million compared with NKr565 million in the same period of 1995 although this was due to unusual circumstances including write-backs of previously set-aside losses.

The government has also sold off parts of its holdings in Christiana Bank (the country's second largest) and all of its shares in the Union Bank of Norway (the third largest) and Fokus Bank (sixth largest). The sale of Christiana Bank on 6 December 1995 reduced the government's stake to 51 per cent from 69 per cent. Some 18 per cent of the bank's total equity capital was on offer, corresponding to 98 million shares. The offering was a big success and was oversubscribed by almost three times. The vast majority of shares went to investors abroad, perhaps 88 per cent. In 1995 Christiana Bank recorded a healthy profit of NKr2.7 billion.

The government sold its 95.9 per cent share of Fokus Bank on 13 October 1995. Of the 63 million shares up for sale, 16 million of these were offered to Norwegian private investors and 47 million were offered to institutional investors (domestically and internationally). Those investors who had shares in the bank when the government stepped in to rescue Fokus in 1991 were allowed to buy 1.5 shares for every share they then held. The government's net profit from its involvement in Fokus was NKr530 million. However, the losers include the commercial banks' guarantee fund (NKr2.1 billion loss) and the former shareholders (who lost their entire investment).

Agriculture and fishing

A programme to eradicate a local outbreak of scrapie, announced in July 1996, required the killing of 30,000 sheep in Norway. Scrapie is particularly worrisome now as fears increase that cattle can get mad cow disease through eating fodder laced with scrapie-infected sheep or goats. Under the eradication plan, some 600 herds of sheep will be destroyed over a two-year period. Norway is still reported to be free of mad cow disease.

The herring stock in the North Sea is depleting at a significant rate and serious consequences might result if the catch is not reduced. This would be a similar situation to the 1970s when the herring stock collapsed. In mid-June 1996 the EU and Norway agreed on measures to regulate the herring catch in the North Sea. Following scientific recommendations, these measures mean that the total catch allowed will fall to 156,000 tonnes from 313,000 tonnes in the North Sea and from 120,000 tonnes to 90,000 tonnes in the Skagerrak/Kattegat.

Outlook

The result of the spring 1996 pay talks could eventually be increased pressure on the economy, through higher inflation, and will contribute to troubles ahead if the 1997 budget does not have a fairly tight fiscal outlook. Inflation may start to rise if domestic demand begins to increase substantially; higher real wages might fuel demand. The strong krone could present difficulties in that it will decrease international competitiveness and the higher wage bills will also eat into Norway's industrial strength.

COUNTRY PROFILE — NORWAY

Domestic economy (contd): remain among highest in Europe. Primary concern remains low productivity combined with level of wage costs 20-25 per cent higher than trading partners. Norway was the first Nordic country to link its currency to the European currency unit (Ecu) from 19 October 1990 but in December 1992 the krone was uncoupled from the Ecu and was floated. As a result, it suffered a 5 per cent devaluation against other European currencies.

Employment

A third of the workforce employed in the public, social and private service sector, excluding banking and financial services, and also excluding the wholesale and retail trade and hotel/restaurant business, which employs about 17 per cent. Manufacturing industry (excluding mining, and construction) also employs about 14 per cent, and agriculture, forestry and fisheries, 6.1 per cent. Unemployment remains low by OECD standards. Average wage costs are high.

External trade

Although Norway has consistently rejected EU membership, in January 1994, the European Economic Area (EEA) was established, which gives Norway access into the EU's single market.
Exports: Main destinations: UK (21.1% of 1994 total), Germany (12%), EU (64.7%), Nordic countries (17.1%).
Imports: Main sources: Germany (14% of 1994 total), UK (10.5%), EU (49.2%), Nordic countries (25.6%).

Agriculture

The agriculture sector accounted for 3 per cent of GDP in 1994 and employed 5.6 per cent of the workforce. The farming subsidy is one of the highest in the world. All farmers also benefit from protection by stringent import controls. Grain and fodder are main lowland crops; mountain farms mainly raise livestock and grow fodder. Grain production is increasing especially barley and oats. Some dairly produce is exported and there is self-sufficiency in meat, milk, cheese, butter, fish and potatoes. Forestry often combined with farming.
Fishing is a significant industry in the northern and western regions; fish, including farmed fish, is an important export. Mackerel, cod and capelin are main species caught, but catches have been falling, because of over-fishing.
Fish farms produce mainly salmon and trout, although some are experimenting with other varieties, such as halibut. Norway's salmon farmers produce about half of total Atlantic salmon supplies. A 37,500 tonne mountain of frozen salmon, representing a fifth of Norway's annual production, was sold, all but 2,000 tonnes, outside the EU at prices between NKr20 and NKr40 a kilogram. Demand for farmed salmon has increased by 20-30 per cent annually but production exceeded demand. However, with the emergence of new markets like southern Europe and with the current high level of prices, demand is set to outstrip supply. In mid-June 1996 the EU and Norway agreed on regulating the total herring catch to 156,000 tonnes in the North Sea and 90,000 tonnes in the Skagerrak/Kattegat.

Industry

The industrial sector accounted for 20 per cent of GDP in 1994 and employed 19.1 per cent of the workforce. In 1994 Norway saw the largest increase in industrial production for 20 years – up by 6 per cent. Manufacturing production rose by 2.5 per cent in 1995.

Mining

The mining and hydrocarbons sector accounted for 15 per cent of GDP in 1994 and employed 4 per cent of the workforce. Norway has a highly skilled workforce experienced in mining, quarrying and processing. Activity confined to small-scale mining of iron ore, copper, titanium, coal (on Spitsbergen), zinc, lead and pyrites. Most of these ores and concentrates are exported. Mining continues to contract, causing many problems in areas where there is no alternative employment. However, the country's mining potential has yet to be fully explored and it is believed that Norway has the capacity to develop super-quarries. On the south coast of Norway, near Lillesand, feldspars and quartz are sourced. Graphite, with differing carbon content and quality is produced on the island of Senja and research is being carried out to up-grade the quality. Large dimension stones like granite types, marbles and quartzites are available in large quantities. Larvikite is one of the most predominant types of stone and there are also exclusive types of marbles, including Norwegian Rose, to be found in the north. In northern and central Norway high-quality quartzite and phullite-slate are also processed from the quarries. Rock aggregate can be found along the coast in both large sizes and quantities, which makes transportation very easy.

Hydrocarbons

Oil reserves 8.4bn barrels (end-1995). Oil production 2.8m barrels per day (bpd) in 1995, 8.2 per cent up on 1994 output.
Natural gas reserves 1.3 cu metres (end-1995). Natural gas production 28.2m tonnes oil equivalent in 1995, up 1.6 per cent on 1994 output.

Energy

For several years Norwegian electricity output has exceeded demand (virtually all hydro), some of which is exported (to Sweden and Denmark). Plans to build gas-fired power plants. The special tax levied on electricity was dropped

Energy (contd): for energy intensive industry from 1 January 1993. A 25-year contract for Norway to supply Germany with hydroelectric power was signed in May 1993 by Statkraft, the electricity utility, and Preussen Elektra, German power company.
A new marine pipeline, the world's longest, will carry gas to France which is a major purchaser of Norway's gas. Commissioning is due on 1 October 1998.

Banking

A series of mergers has changed the face of Norwegian banking beyond recognition during the last few years as the result of deregulation and a credit boom during the 1980s which led to huge losses on lending and guarantees. Den norske Bank (DnB), comprising the former DNC and Bergen Bank, is now the nation's largest commercial bank, followed by Christiana Bank of Kreditkasse and Fokus. A number of savings banks have also merged or disappeared, several of the largest merging with ABC Bank in the new giant Sparebanken Nor from Oct 1990. Norgeskredit, the Norwegian private sector mortgage company, announced in February 1993, plans to become a commercial bank. In May 1993 the minority Labour government announced plans gradually to reprivatise the commercial banks in 1994, beginning with wholly state-owned Christiana Bank. The OECD consider that further reform of the financial system is necessary to restore a healthy and competitive domestic banking industry.

Stock exchange

The Norwegian stock exchange agreed with the stock exchanges of Sweden, Denmark and Finland in June 1993, to establish Nordquote, a common Nordic securities trading system.

Legal system

Mixture of customary law, civil law and common law traditions.

Membership of international organisations

ADB, CBS, CCC, CERN, Council of Europe, DAC, EEA, EFTA, ESA, ESRO (observer), FAO, IAEA, ICAC, ICAO, ICES, ICO, IDA, IEA (associate member), IFAD, IFC, IHO, ILO, IMF, IMO, INTELSAT, INTERPOL, International Lead and Zinc Study Group, IPU, ITU, IWC, NACC, NAM, NATO, Nordic Council, OECD (guest), OSCE, UN, UNESCO, UPU, WEU (associate member), WHO, WIPO, WMO, World Bank, WSG, WTO.

BUSINESS GUIDE

Time

GMT + 1 hr (GMT + 2 hrs from late Mar to late Sep).

Climate

Temperate in west, colder inland and in north. Average temperatures range from about 17°C down to about –10°C. Lowest recorded temperature is Karasjok with –51°C. The winters are cold and dark with snow and ice Nov–Mar. Summers warm Jun–Aug. Rain throughout year. West coast wet. Jan and Feb coldest months. North of the Arctic circle the sun shines day and night for part of the summer, with a corresponding period of total darkness in the winter.
Clothing: Mediumweight all year, heavy topcoat and overshoes for winter. Most buildings centrally heated so indoor clothing not too heavy. Some restaurants require that men wear a jacket and tie.

Entry requirements

Visas not required by nationals of most European countries and USA. Nationals from non-Nordic countries must have valid passport.
Health: Vaccination certificates not normally required.
Currency: Few restrictions.
Customs: Personal effects duty-free, plus duty-free allowance.

Air access

Regular direct flights by most major international airlines.
National airline: Scandinavian Airlines System (SAS), jointly owned with Sweden and Denmark. Private- and government-owned.
Main international airport: Oslo served by Fornebu (FBU), 8 km south-west of city and Gardermoen (GEN), 51 km from city.
International airports: Bergen (BGO), 19 km from city, and Stavanger (SVG), 14.5 km south-west of Stavanger. There are 52 airports with regular inter-continental flights to Europe and the USA.

Surface access

Frequent ferry services to Denmark, the UK and Germany. Also road and rail access from Denmark, Sweden and Finland.
Main ports: Bergen, Stavanger, Kristiansand, Oslo are all first-class sea ports.

Hotels

Wide range available in most towns, but no official rating system in operation. Advisable to book well in advance, especially during tourist season. Private accommodation can also be obtained through local tourist offices or accommodation offices in central railway stations. Service charge of 15 per cent included in bill, but tipping also expected.

Restaurants

Good selection in larger towns. Seafood is Norwegian speciality. Service charge added to bill, but 5 per cent tip is usual.

Currency

Exchange rate: Norwegian krone is pegged to a basket of currencies, including US dollar, Canadian dollar and Japanese yen. Fluctuations in rates within basket kept within certain limits.

Foreign exchange information

Account restrictions: Non-resident accounts permitted, but nature must be confirmed in writing to local bank holding the account.
Trade policy: Norway is export-oriented country, so few restrictions. Foreign currency for payment of most goods purchased abroad is subject to import licence.

Credit cards

All usual credit cards accepted.

Car hire

Available at airports and in major towns. For travel between towns public transport tends to be quicker, and much cheaper. Studded or winter tyres recommended during winter. Very strict laws against drinking and driving. 50 kph speed limit in built-up areas, 80 kph on highways. Seatbelts compulsory.

City transport

Taxis: Available in most cities. Can be obtained at ranks or by telephone (Oslo 388-090, Bergen 900-990, Stavanger 526-040). Telephone numbers of taxi stands are listed in the directory under 'Drosjer'. Meters are compulsory. It is not expected that the tip will be more than the small change.

National transport

Air: Efficient services operated by SAS, Braathens S.A.F.E. and others, linking Alta, Ålesund, Andenes, Bardufoss, Bergen, Billund, Bodø, Evenes, Farsund, Haugesund, Kirkenes, Kristiansand, Kristiansund, Lakselv, Molde, Oslo, Røros, Sandefjord, Skien, Stavanger, Svalbard, Tromsø and Trondheim. Aircraft also available for charter.
Road: The road network is extensive and is 90,500 km long. Several roads in mountainous regions are open only during summer.
Buses: Good bus service, but journeys tend to be long owing to distances between main towns.
Rail: The rail network is 4,027 km long and linked to the rest of Europe via Sweden and Denmark. Operated by Norwegian State Railways. Main lines radiate from Oslo. Good service, but advisable to make seat and sleeper reservations well in advance through State Railways Travel Bureau or other travel agencies.
Water: Regular efficient motor ship services visiting all major ports. Also numerous local ferry, hydrofoil and catamaran services.

Public holidays

Fixed dates: 1 Jan, 1 May, 17 May (National Day), 24-26 Dec.
Variable dates: Maundy Thursday, Good Friday, Easter Monday, Ascension Day and Whit Monday.

Working hours

Business: (Mon–Fri) 0830 – 1600 (1500 from 15 May to 15 Sep).
Banking: (Mon–Fri) 0815 – 1530, (Thu) 0815 – 1700.
Shops: (Mon–Fri) 0830 – 1700, except (Thu) 0830 – 1900, (Sat) 0830 – 1400.

Social customs

Punctuality is expected. Shake hands on meeting. Business lunches are rare. The main meal of the day is generally taken at home at 1700 hours, though people will expect to eat later if invited out.

BUSINESS GUIDE

Telecommunications

Telephone: Automatic system offering direct dialling to all foreign cities. Cheap off-peak rates in evening and at weekends. International dialling code: 47 followed by 2 for Oslo, 5 for Bergen, 7 for Trondheim and 4 for Stavanger. For IDD access from Norway dial 095.
Telex and telefax: Further information available from telegraph authorities in Oslo (tel: 488990) and from Telegrafbygningen near the city park in Bergen. Country code 56N.
Telegram: Available from post offices, or can be dictated over the telephone.

Trade fairs

Several international events held annually, most at Sjølyst in Oslo, Forum in Stavanger and Info-Rama in Sandvika. All major sectors of industry are covered, but emphasis is on oil, shipping and fishing. Most exhibitions are organised by Norges Varemesse (the Norwegian Trade Fair Foundation) based at Sjølyst.

Electricity supply

220 V AC.

Representation in capital

Argentina, Austria, Belgium, Brazil, Bulgaria, Canada, Chile, China, Colombia, Cuba, Czech Republic, Denmark, Ecuador, Egypt, Finland, France, Germany, Greece, Hungary, Iceland, India, Indonesia, Iran, Israel, Italy, Japan, Korea DPR, Republic of Korea, Mexico, Netherlands, Panama, Poland, Portugal, Romania, Russia, Spain, Sweden, Switzerland, Turkey, UK, USA, Venezuela.

BUSINESS DIRECTORY

Hotels

Oslo
Akershus (a ship in the harbour), Akershuskaia, N-0150 (tel: 428-660; tx: 76-858).

Ambassadeur, Camilla Colletts vei 15 (tel: 441-835).

Anker, 55 Storgate 0182 (tel: 114-005; fax: 110-136).

Bellevue, Nesbru N-1360, PO Box 10 (tel: 785-060; fax: 982-882).

Bristol, Kristian 4 gt 7 (tel: 415-840; fax: 428-651).

Continental, Stortingsgt 24-26 (tel: 419-060; fax: 429-689).

Europa, St Olavsgate 31 (tel: 209-990)

Grand, 31 Karl Johansgate N-0159 (tel: 429-390; fax: 421-225).

Helsfyr, 108 Stromsveien (tel: 654-110; tx: 76-776).

Imi, 4 Staffeldsgate, PO Box 6830 (tel: 205-330; fax: 111-749).

Munch, Munchsgate 5, N-1065 (tel: 424-275; fax: 206-469).

Oslo Plaza Hotel, Sonja Henies pl 1, N-0155, 1 (tel: 171-000; fax: 177-300).

Ritz, Fr Stangsgt 3, N-0272 Oslo 2 (tel: 443-960; tx: 19-668).

Royal Christiania, Biskop Gunnerus'gate 3, Sentrum, N-1016, 1, PO Box 768 (tel: 429-410; fax: 424-622).

SAS Park Royal, N-1324 Lysaker (tel: 120-220; fax: 120-011).

SAS Scandinavia, Holbergs Gate 30, N-0166 (tel: 113-000; fax: 113-017 EXT. 400).

Triangel, Holbergs Plass 1 (tel: 208-855; tx: 19-413).

Car hire

Oslo
Avis: Central Reservations (tel: 6677-1111; fax: 6684-7111); Munkedamsveien 27 (tel: 2283-5800; fax: 2283-1924).

Budget: Oslo Airport, 1330 (tel: 6753-7924; fax: 6753-9022); Sonja Henies Plass 4, 0185 (tel: 171-050; fax: 171-060).

Europcar: Uranienborgveien 5 (tel: 2260-7440).

Hertz: Central Reservations (tel: 6712-5555; fax: 6758-0222); Fornebu Airport (tel: 6758-3100; fax: 6712-0880).

Chambers of commerce

Bergens Handelskammer, Olav Kyrresgt 11, N-5000 Bergen (tel: 316-569).

Kristiansands Handelskammer, Østromdg 39, N-4600 Kristiansand 5 (tel: 24-370).

Oslo Handelskammer, Drammensveien 30, Oslo 2 (tel: 557-400).

Stavanger Handelskammer, Kongsgaten 10, N-4000 Stavanger (tel: 536-035).

Trondheim Handelskammer, Dronningensgt 12, N-7000 Trondheim (tel: 520-625).

Banking

Norges Bank (Bank of Norway) (central bank), Bankplassen 2, PO Box 1179, Sentrum, 0107 Oslo 1 (tel: 316-000; tx: 71-369).

Bergens Skillingsbank AS, PO Box 892/93, Rådstuplass 4, N-5001 Bergen (tel: 310-050;).

Christiania Bank og Kreditkasse, PO Box 1166 Sentrum 0107 Oslo 1 (tel: 485-000; fax: 484-749).

Den norske Bank, N-5020 Bergen (tel: 211-000; fax: 211-150).

Fokus Bank A/S, Vestre Rosten 77, PO Box 6090, N-7003 Trondheim; (tel: 882-011; fax: 888-590).

Sparebanken, Kirkegaten 18, PO Box 1172, Sentrum, N-0107 Oslo 1 (tel: 319-050; tx: 19-470).

Principal newspapers

Aftenposten, Akersgt 51, N-1080 Oslo 1 (tel: 2286-3000; fax: 2242-0893).

Dagbladet, Akersgaten 49, N-0107 Oslo 1 (tel: 0221-20209: tx: 71-020).

VG-Verdens Gang, Akersgt 55, N-0107 Oslo (tel: 2200-0000; fax: 2242-5811).

Travel information

Norwegian Tourist Board, Nortra Langkaia 1, Oslo 1 (tel: 427-044).

Other useful addresses

AS Norsk Telegrambyraø (Norwegian news agency), Holbergsgt 1, Oslo 1 (tel: 201-670; tx: 11-046).

Export Council of Norway, Drammensveien 40, N-0255 Oslo 2 (tel: 437-700; tx: 78-532).

Ministry of Finance, Akersgt 42, PO Box 8008 Dep, 0030 Oslo 1 (tel: 349-090; tx: 21-444).

Ministry of Industry, Akersgt 42, PO Box 8014 Dep, 0030 Oslo 1 (tel: 349-090).

Norges Industriforbund (federation of Norwegian industries), PO Box 5250, Majorstna, 0303 Oslo 3 (tel: 437-000).

Norges Varemesse (the Norwegian Trade Fair Foundation), Sjølystsentret, Drammensveien 154, PO Box 130, Skøyen, N-0212 Oslo 2 (tel: 438-080; tx: 78-748).

Norsk Presse Service AS (Norwegian press services), Soerkedalsveien 10B, Oslo 3 (tel: 694-495; tx: 71-019).

Norwegian Trade Council, N-0243 Oslo (tel: 926-300; fax: 926-400).

Oslo Børs (stock exchange), Tollbugt 2, Oslo (tel: 341-700).

Royal Ministry of Foreign Affairs, PO Box 8114 Dep, 0032 Oslo 1 (tel: 343-600; fax: 349-580, 349-581).

Statistics Norway, PO Box 8131 Dep, N-0033 Oslo 1 (tel: 864-500; fax: 864-973).

Utlendingsdirektoratet, PO Box 8108 Dep, Oslo (tel: 530-890).

Poland

Bob Jiggins

On 11 July 1996 Poland was granted Organisation for Economic Co-operation and Development (OECD) membership, the third ex-communist country to join the club of developed nations. Described by Warsaw International Monetary Fund (IMF) representative Markus Rodlauer as 'a further step in Poland's integration into western institutions', OECD membership provided the Polish coalition government with some welcome good news in the face of seemingly intractable macro-economic problems: a worsening trade balance and continued inflationary pressure. The tradegap for the first four months of 1996 was US$1.98 billion, dramatically up from the deficit of US$261 million recorded for the same period in 1995. While the Ministry of Finance adhered to its inflation forecast of 17 per cent for 1996, Planning Ministry officials increased their forecast by 2 per cent to 19 per cent.

None the less, Poland continues to show the signs of a boom economy, with GDP growth of 6.5 per cent for 1995 and a rate of 5.5 per cent forecast for 1996. Government sources estimate that any fall in exports (due to the continued appreciation of the zloty) will be offset by a rise in domestic demand. Real wage increases and tax reductions look like fuelling an anticipated 6 per cent rise in consumer demand.

Presidential elections

For most of 1995 events in Poland were dominated by the presidential election and the resultant political instability. Although the first round of voting gave a slight majority to the post-communist candidate, Aleksander Kwasniewski, over the incumbent president, Lech Walesa, it was wrongly assumed that Walesa would ultimately triumph.

Politics

The second round of presidential elections resulted in a surprise victory for Kwasniewski and Walesa departed from office with little in the way of benediction for his successor. Kwasniewski inherited a 'soaring eagle' of an economy and, despite being a former communist, is committed to reform.

The greatest problems which Poland faces are the burgeoning welfare state and inflation, and the new President's main task will be to preside over governmental efforts to tackle these issues – a task which he may not be suited for. Both his former party, the Democratic Left Alliance (SLD), and its coalition partner, the Polish Peasants' Party (PSL), favour policies which are opposed to this restructuring.

Presidential race

Initially it had appeared that Walesa had little chance of re-election, with opinion polls early in 1995 indicating that only 6 per cent or so of the electorate would be prepared to vote him in for another five years as president. However, Walesa managed to rebuild a high degree of support, largely by relying on his role as leader of the trade union Solidarity and the image of the working-class president.

During the election campaign, Walesa characterised his opponent as a friend of Moscow, as anti-libertarian and still very much a communist. This polarised the campaign, and ensured that it was a bitter battle, characterised by the alleged sharply-drawn distinctions between the two main opponents – at times almost a re-run of the early 1980s when Solidarity clashed with Edward Gierek's communist government.

Walesa's failed bid for re-election resulted in a number of allegations regarding the validity of the election, the honesty of Kwasniewski and the discovery that then-

KEY FACTS — Poland

Official title: Polska Rzeczpospolita; Republic of Poland

Head of state: President Aleksander Kwasniewski (SLD) (from 22 Dec 1995)

Head of government: Prime Minister Wlodzimierz Cimoszewicz (from 1 Feb 1996)

Ruling party: Two-party coalition government – Sojusz Lewicy Demokratyczyn (Democratic Left Alliance) (SLD), itself a coalition of 28 left-wing parties, groupings, trade unions, including the leading group, Social Democratic Party (SdRP), led by Józef Oleksy from February 1996, and Polski Stronnictwo Ludowe (Polish Peasants' Party) (PSL)

Capital: Warsaw

Official Languages: Polish

Currency: Zloty (Zl) = 100 groszy (Poland sliced four zeroes off its currency from 1 Jan 1995 – prices have to be displayed in the two denominations for the next two years; zloty revalued by around 6 per cent 28 Dec 1995)

Exchange rate: Zl 2.86 per US$ (Dec 1996)

Area: 312,683 sq km

Population: 38.6m (1995)

GDP per capita: US$3.050 (1995)

GDP real growth: 4% (1st half 1996); 6.5% (1995)

GNP per capita: US$2,250 (1994)

GNP real growth: 5% (1995)*

Labour force: 14.6m (end-1994)

Unemployment: 15.4% (Mar 1996)

Inflation: 19.5% (Jun 1996) (consumer prices)

Trade balance: -US$6.2bn (12 months to Sep 1996)

Foreign debt: US$44.9bn (1995)

Visitor numbers: 63m (1994)

* estimated figure

Prime Minister Józef Oleksy had apparently been a Russian agent ever since independence. Such events, and the churlish refusal of Walesa to attend the presidential swearing-in ceremony, may be best described as 'sour-grapes'. The effect of this on the population was negligible with pragmatism winning the day, although Oleksy resigned on his own volition leading to his replacement by Wlodzimierz Cimoszewicz in January 1996.

Oleksy subsequently received a vote of confidence from his own party, the Social Democratic Party (SdRP) and was appointed its leader. Furthermore, an investigation into the allegations concluded that there was no case to answer. The affair, however, raised some ugly issues from the past. The security apparatus has long kept files on prominent (and not so prominent) public figures and the release of such information is periodically threatened. Regardless of the validity of such data (which is in any case highly suspect) it would undoubtedly cause considerable harm.

The election of Kwasniewski is extremely unlikely to change the orientation of Poland's foreign policy stance. The country is now firmly locked into the western orbit, and would suffer considerably if this were changed. In any case Poland's giant neighbour appears to have little problem with such an alignment and eventual European Union (EU) membership. Difficulties do lie with eventual participation and membership of NATO as Russia is concerned about that organisation's expansion eastward, although military exercises have been held in the recent past which caused little upset. Nevertheless, Kwasniewski is expected to attempt to allay Russian fears, and is better placed to do this than Walesa would have been.

Economy

By regional standards, economically, Poland is doing well, with unemployment falling even though inflation remains high. Real wages are growing and sales in many sectors are increasing. Industrial sales have increased throughout 1995, although there has been a tendency for the rate of increase to fall off towards the end of the year. Overall, the rate for 1995 was 10.2 per cent in real terms with investment goods rising considerably faster than other areas, particularly consumer items.

Agriculture likewise did well, despite the collapse of the inefficient state sector, with output up on 1994 by 9 per cent. Construction also increased and, unlike industry, sales increased throughout 1995, to give a final figure for the year of 15 per cent.

There appears to be no sign in the much-needed revival in housing construction. Figures for 1995 show a decline of 23.3 per cent in the number of completions during the year, with most of this accounted for by the relative lack of co-operative construction when compared with the private sector. Nevertheless, it is obvious that the private sector cannot cope with the demand for housing and that unless this is reversed, the country could well have a substantial number of homeless people on its hands.

Regional disparities

One of the biggest problems that Poland has to contend with is the growing trend towards severe regional imbalance. Although a number of various urban centres are performing well in post-communist Poland, the severe regional differences within the country are clear. Under communism such differences were less noticeable, but the centralising effect of the free market has ensured that many rural areas are now experiencing a measure of underdevelopment.

Communist Poland was marked by the differences between the highly industrialised west, and the east where industry was not so prevalent and agriculture more important. These regions were known as 'Poland B' to the chattering classes of Warsaw, and included such centres as Siedla, Chelm and Lomza. Thus the creation of an economically differentiated country is not new, but has been exacerbated in the 1990s.

The east of 'Poland B' remains in difficulty, but has now been joined by the north and those centres of agriculture in the west where the state sector (always relatively small) has declined. Unemployment in some of these areas is over 25 per cent, although there are pockets of relative prosperity, especially in some border areas due to the 'suitcase' trade now developing.

Certain centres are doing well, especially Warsaw. In contrast to the rest of the country, Warsaw has the lowest unemployment (6.2 per cent in 1995), the highest income and attracts considerably higher domestic and foreign investment. Other centres identified by the Gdansk Institute for Market Economics as attracting high foreign direct investment (FDI) levels are: Katowice, Gdansk, Szczecin, Poznan and Lodz.

This highly imbalanced development is a potential problem for entry into the EU, as that organisation is already stretched in terms of regional aid. The problem will become worse as more eastern bloc states join. The Polish government has belatedly recognised the problem and is now attempting to tackle it by means of incentives, in particular economic zones and job creation. The first such trial is the town of Mielec in the south-west, which previously enjoyed a boom due to its aircraft sales to the military and which has since suffered as military expenditure has been cut back.

The Mielec Euro Park is offering some substantial incentives, specifically a 10-year holiday from business taxes and a further 50 per cent reduction over the succeeding 10 years. Other towns also are arguing for special status, particularly Gdansk which sees itself as a potential duty-free port. None of this is a new idea, and the experience of regional policy elsewhere in Europe suggests that enterprises migrate with surprising rapidity between incentives – benefiting certain regions for a while certainly, yet contributing little to overall national macro-economic development. Other measures include the direct creation of jobs, with the government allocating some US$5 million to rural areas.

External trade

Foreign trade was considerably affected by the substantial appreciation of the zloty – a full 20 per cent in real terms over the course of 1995. This is largely responsible for the considerable 40.6 per cent year-on-year rise in imports as measured in the first half of the year, although exports seem to be little affected.

Imports are also likely to grow as a result of the reduction in tariffs on EU and Central European Free Trade Agreement (CEFTA) goods. Most EU industrial trade will be reduced by 20 per cent, while CEFTA trade will be tariff-free.

Investment

Investment has taken over from exports as the engine of Polish economic growth. The performance of the Polish stock market in the first half of 1996 reflected the country's general economic prospects, with the prospect of OECD membership providing investor confidence. Foreign direct investment in 1995 was US$2.5 billion, bringing the total since 1992 to US$ 6.5 billion. Analysts estimate a further US$3 billion for 1996.

Portfolio investment is also expected to increase in 1996. The liquidity and the transparency of the Warsaw Stock Exchange (WSE) gives it an edge over its regional competitors, notably Prague and Budapest. The Polish Securities Commission is known to be very strict: 'In governance, we can be compared favourably to most western exchanges' says Jacek Socha, Chairman of the Securities Commission. 'The Polish Stock Exchange was established for local investors' observes Frances Cloud of the Nomura Research Institute in London, 'but they have realised that it will be impossible to privatise larger companies without foreign investment'.

In mid-1996 the Polish government launched its first DM bond (see below), following the success of its June 1995 Eurobond issue, upped from DM200m to DM250m in the face of high demand. These two Eurobond issues were something of a landmark for the Polish government. Failure to meet its financial obligations on both sovereign and bank debts in the 1980s had resulted in sub-investment gradings from both Moody's (which gave Poland its lowest investment grade) and Standard and Poor, which only upgraded Poland from sub-investment to investment grade in 1996. Since the 1980s Poland has been through five successive rounds of re-scheduling with commercial and official creditors. Agreement with the Paris Club Group of creditors was finally secured in April 1991, and Brady debt service reduction only in March 1994.

The DM250 million Eurobond offer was launched in July 1996 by lead managers CS First Boston and Deutsche Morgan Grenfell. Introducing the offer, Wieslaw Szczuka, director of the Polish treasury's overseas funding department explained: 'Germany is Poland's major trading partner, accounting for some 40 per cent of total Polish trade. It is a natural development of our funding policy to seek access to a market where investors are familiar with Poland's economic success story.'

Privatisation

Poland's initial privatisation drive was modelled on the British experience under Margaret Thatcher and was generally held to be less successful than hoped, particularly in the speed of its implementation. Consequently, discussions commenced in Poland in 1991 regarding a mass privatisation programme (MPP), and this was duly launched on 22 November 1995. Thus far it appears that it has been highly successful, with the public take-up of the nominally priced Zl 20 vouchers being extremely high. Such was the interest that within a few days these vouchers were being traded in the secondary market for as much as Zl 80, although the resale price has dropped in recent months. These vouchers are effectively share certificates in one of the 15 National Investment Funds (NIFs) which

KEY INDICATORS

	Unit	1991	1992	1993	1994	1995
Population	m	38.24	38.36	38.46	38.54	38.60
Gross national product (GNP)	US$bn	132.3	76.0	89.0	85.0	–
GNP per capita	US$	3,430	2,000	2,300	2,250	–
GNP real growth	%	-7.2	1.0	4.0	6.0	*5.0
Inflation	%	70.2	43.0	35.3	32.2	21.6
Employment	'000	10,406	9,575	9,163	9,106	9,353
Consumer prices	1990=100	176.7	256.8	351.5	468.4	599.8
Wages (av earnings)	1990=100	167.1	228.5	320.0	421.4	595.9
Unemployment	%	9.2	12.9	14.9	16.4	14.6
Agricultural prod	1979-81=100	114.31	101.59	108.28	92.09	101.05
Industrial emp	1990=100	91.1	87.7	83.1	81.7	82.4
Industrial prod	1990=100	84.0	87.3	97.0	108.8	120.0
Manufacturing	1990=100	87.7	91.9	103.1	117.7	132.6
Mining	1990=100	94.5	94.0	83.6	89.2	88.7
Construction	1990=100	–	119.7	132.9	129.3	144.9
Crude steel	'000 tonnes	10,439	9,867	9,937	11,055	11,886
Brown coal	'000 tonnes	69,351	66,849	68,104	66,770	63,549
Cement	'000 tonnes	12,031	11,888	12,243	13,908	13,831
Crude petrol	'000 tonnes	158	179	235	287	293
Natural gas	m cu metres	4,134	4,015	4,928	4,617	4,820
Exports (FOB) (goods)	US$m	14,393	13,929	13,582	17,100	22,900
Imports (FOB) (goods)	US$m	15,104	14,060	17,087	18,900	25,500
Balance of trade	US$m	-711	-131	-3,505	-1,800	-2,600
Current account	US$m	-2,146	-3,104	-2,300	-944	-1,100
Foreign debt	US$bn	47.8	44.3	46.5	44.0	44.9
Reserves minus gold	US$m	3,632.6	4,099.1	4,091.9	5,841.8	14,744.1
Foreign exchange	US$m	3,624.9	3,992.0	3,985.3	5,727.7	14,657.2
Deposit rate	%	53.5	37.8	34.0	30.6	24.5
Lending rate	%	54.6	39.0	35.3	32.8	26.2
Official discount rate	%	40	38	35	33	29
Exchange rate	Zl per US$	10,576	13,626	18,115	22,723	**2.4250

* estimated figure **Four zeroes sliced 1 Jan '95

are to manage and restructure over 500 state-owned firms. There have now been around five million vouchers sold, and the public enthusiasm for them remains healthy.

Despite the large takeup in shares, the privatisation issue is highly politicised. Although too few of the electorate voted to make it legally binding, the February 1996 referendum produced a resounding 'no' vote against further development of the scheme. Furthermore, trouble is occurring between the boards of the NIFs and the fund managers who appear to have widely conflicting views as to their respective roles.

The MPP looks set to increase the level of activity on the WSE. Shares of some 400 companies are held by the 15 NIFs whose units are expected to trade on the WSE. The shares of many of the individual companies held in the NIFs can also eventually be traded on the WSE.

Other privatisation measures are continuing as before, with the government searching for predominantly foreign buyers for strategic firms. The Ministry of Ownership Transformation (MOT) has decreed that only the railways, postal services and air and sea ports are exempt from privatisation, and these only until the year 2000. There has been predictably strong interest in the privatisation of the banks, especially Bank Gdanski which was sold in December 1995. Some 70 per cent of the bank was up for sale, with 33 per cent being made available on the WSE – although demand within Poland was so great that extra shares were allocated for domestic sale by reducing the number available for foreign investors. Despite these measures potential domestic shareholders received 18 per cent less than they applied for. Other bank sales are planned.

Further sales are also expected in other industries, with those tobacco plants not already transferred to British-American Tobacco (BAT) and Seita in the process of being sold. Next in line are the pharmaceutical enterprises belonging to Polfa, but the biggest sale will be one of the world's largest copper producers, KGHM Polska Miedz. This enterprise produces around 26 million tons of ore, about 4 per cent of the world's output. Also scheduled for privatisation is the national airline LOT, although in mid-1996 the airline's sale had run into difficulties following the government's refusal to accept the scale of fees proposed by the short-listed advisers on the sale. These were reported to be US$2 million, against the US$250,000 budgeted by the government.

The high profile setback of the LOT sale did little to strengthen the position of Privatisation Minister Wieslaw Kaczmarek, coinciding as it did with a vote of no confidence in the minister. In the Sejm (parliament) Kaczmarek described the unsuccessful move to topple him as 'a struggle between politicians and economists. Fortunately the latter won, and this should be seen as a good sign by foreign investors', observed Kaczmarek. Polish market specialist Pawel Tomczyk of Daiwa's London office was quoted as saying that the failure of the no confidence vote was a 'good sign for investors. It guarantees continuity in the privatisation progress'. Another analyst added that 'there are few reformists in this government, and Kaczmarek is one of them'.

COUNTRY PROFILE — POLAND

Historical profile

A separate though vulnerable and often unstable, state since the eighth century, Poland lost its independence in the eighteenth century and was partitioned three times by Austria, Russia and Prussia, in 1795 disappearing from the map altogether.
1918 Independent republic declared at the end of the First World war.
1939 Invaded by Germany and Russia, thus beginning Second World War. Occupied by Germany.
1945 after the war, former German territory along the line of the Rivers Oder and Neisse became Polish; border with USSR shifted westward.
1947 Election won by Communist-led grouping. People's Republic declared.
1948 Polish United Worker's Party (PZPR) formed. Government followed strict Stalinist line until his death (1953).
1956 Riots about food shortages resulted in the reinstatement of Wladyslaw Gomulka, party leader distrusted as too liberal in 1948. Liberalisation and some economic reform ensued.
1970 Food-price strikes brought about resignation of Gomulka. Succeeded by Edward Gierek.
1980-82 Rise of trades union Solidarity under Lech Walesa, Gdansk workers' leader, following strikes at Gdansk, Gdynia and Szczecin shipyards. Right to form unions recognised. General Wojcieck Zaruzelski became party leader. Serious unrest continued during the 1980s, including (1981-82) a period of martial law and imprisonment of Solidarity leaders, and the abolition of existing unions.
1987 Government plans for rapid economic reform, necessitating further hardship, rejected in referendum but political reform approved.
1989 Legal recognition of Solidarity in general election.
1990 Lech Walesa became first democratically elected president.
1991 First completely free parliamentary elections held in October. Resulted in election of a new centre-right government under Prime Minister Olszewski. He was succeeded by Mr Waldemar Pawlak (Peasants' Party) who was unable to form a government. 1992 In August Mrs Hanna Suchocka became prime minister (Poland's fifth prime minister since the end of the communist rule in 1989).
1993 Elections held in September under the new 5 per cent rule which reduced the number of parties in parliament. Former communists received the most votes in this election. In the September 1993 elections, voters opted for a slowdown in the pace of market-led economic reforms by bringing back the former communists – the Democratic Left Alliance (SLD) with over 20 per cent of the vote, 173 seats, and the Polish Peasants' Party (PSL) with over 15 per cent of the vote, 130 seats.

Political system

Republic in which supreme organ of power is the parliament *(Sejm)* with 460 members in lower house and 100 members in upper house (Senate) directly elected for four years. Parliament is composed of a lower and upper house and chooses the president for a six-year term. The president has power to dissolve parliament and also nominates the prime minister. Supreme executive power is vested in Council of Ministers which is responsible to the *Sejm*.
Until 1989 the leading political organisation was the Polish United Workers' Party (PZPR). After the 'Round Table' Agreement of April 1989, 299 of the *Sejm's* 460 seats were allocated to the established parties (PZPR – Polish Communist Party, Peasants' Party and Democratic Party) with the remaining 161 available to opposition parties. The June 1989 election gave the Solidarity Party all 161 available seats in the parliament, and 99 of 100 in the Senate.
In 1990 the Communist Party was reconstituted. The October 1991 elections resulted in an atomised parliament of 29 parties and a coalition government.
In August 1992 *Mala Konstytucja* (constitutional amendments) were passed enabling Mrs Hanna Suchocka's government to bypass lengthy parliamentary procedures and make economic policy decisions by decree. The government resigned in May 1993 following a vote of no confidence.
The new election law adopted by parliament introduced a 5 per cent hurdle limiting the number of parties represented in parliament. The 'constitutional majority' gives them the opportunity to govern in coalition with each other, and the power to decide the terms of the new constitution to replace the present interim *Mala Konstytucja*, or small constitution.

Population

Because of the genocide, territorial changes and population dispersal which took place during the Second World War, Poland has one of the most uniform ethnic structures in Europe. Non-Polish people, including Ukrainians, Jews, Germans, Russians and Gypsies, account for only 1.3 per cent of the total population. The remainder are all ethnically classified as Poles. Life expectancy increased during 1991-95 – for women from 75.3 to 76.4 years and for men from 66.1 to 67.6 years.
Religion: predominantly Roman Catholic.

Main cities/towns

Warsaw (population 1.7m in 1994), Lodz (851,000), Krakow (800,000), Gdansk (750,000, in Tri-City with Gdynia and Sopot)), Wroclaw (650,000), Poznan (589,000), Szczecin (412,000), Katowice (400,000), Lublin (350,000) and Bydgoszcz.

Language

Polish is the official language. English is spoken in hotels and tourist establishments. Russian and German also spoken.

Media

Press: This is beginning to flourish following the breaking up of the PSPR monopoly over the media. In May 1989 Solidarity launched *Gazetta Wyborcza*, the first daily opposition newspaper in Communist Europe for over 40 years. The Roman Catholic church has been allowed to publish for years and produces 31 weekly, monthly and quarterly titles.
Dailies: Around 100 newspapers published, mostly in Warsaw. Adam Michnik, the former civil rights activist and companion of Lech Walesa, is keeping *Gazeta Wyborcza* on a 'reform friendly' course. The *Trybuna Slaska* is

Communications

Poland's telephone network, like many others in eastern Europe, is in a poor state characterised by outdated equipment and a low subscriber base. This is set to change over the next few years, with a major emphasis on investment in both land-based and mobile technologies.

There are only around 15 telephones for 100 people, with most of these connections being in highly populated and developed urban centres. The density within rural areas is extremely low, with only around five phones per 100 people. Most of these connections are provided by the state concern Telekomunikaja Polska (TP), while the mobile market is largely catered for by Centertel.

The expansion plans for land-line connections call for a near doubling of the penetration (from 15 to 30 per 100 people) to bring Poland into line with the west European average, while within the mobile sector planned provision is even more ambitious. Currently mobile communications are provided by an analogue system which has a user base of around 75,000, although this is set to change with the allocation of two licences for a digital GSM (General Standard for Mobile Communications) network. The government hopes that the licences, given after tendering to two consortia (Polkomtel and Polska Telefon Komorkowa) will enable the subscriber base to rise to one million by the end of the century with a cumulative investment of over US$1 billion.

The development of the Polish telecommunications market is notable for the virtual invisibility of western firms, who are said to have been concerned about the near monopoly role of TP in providing connections to its backbone and the lack of information regarding regulation over pricing. The two winning consortia do have western backers, especially in the case of Polska Telefon where US West and Deutsche Telecom Mobil have a 22.5 per cent stake. Involvement by the western firms, however, is more likely in the provision of hardware rather than the service connections, with firms such as Alcatel, AT&T and Siemens likely to profit from the envisaged expansion.

Poland is benefiting from the increased FDI flows in other areas too, with western firms increasingly looking to eastern Europe, especially in the automotive market. Daewoo and General Motors (GM) are both expanding their involvement in car production, Michelin and Goodyear have purchased substantial stakes in tyre plants, and British Petroleum (BP) is extending its small chain of filling stations.

Outlook

The year ahead brings promises as well as problems for Poland. All the indications are that growth will continue throughout 1996 as exports and consumption rise and investors stream into the country. The political climate should be less fevered with the departure of Lech Walesa, yet his successor will find it hard to control some aspects of state expenditure. Undoubtedly, Poland is now on the way to becoming a middle-weight European power.

COUNTRY PROFILE — POLAND

Media (contd): the successor of the former party organ *Trybuna Ludu*. The government has 51 per cent shares in a daily newspaper, *Rzeczpospolita*. Other dailies include *Zycie Warsawy, Express Wieczomy, Super Express* and *Kurier Polski*. New daily *Zycie* (Life) published 28 September 1996.
Weeklies: Around 2,900 periodicals, of which one of the most influential is the weekly *Polityka*. Others include: *Nie* (satirical), *Przyjaciolka* (women's magazine), *Wprost* (news) and *Poradnik Domowy* (home ideas). Sports magazines, TV/radio guides and youth magazines also have sizeable readerships. The *Warsaw Voice* is published weekly in English. A new magazine *Neues Wohnen* was launched in 1993 by Gruner and Jahr, Germany. *Capital Weekly*, Warsaw's English-language weekly, closed in August 1995 after publishing 23 issues.
Business: Several commercial papers published by Polish Chamber of Foreign Trade, and Foreign Trade Publicity and Publishing Enterprise (AGPOL). Technical papers are published by Naczelna Organizacja Techniczna (NOT), Wydawnictwa Komunikacyji and Lacznosci. Most influential periodicals are *Gazeta Bankowa* (bankers' weekly), *Zycie Gospodarcze* (economic weekly), *Rynki Zagraniczne* (three per week; foreign trade) and *Handel Zagraniczny* (monthly; foreign trade).
Broadcasting: All TV and radio programmes broadcast by Polskie Radio i Telewizja (Polish Radio and Television).
Radio: Four programmes are transmitted nationally and there is a foreign service which broadcasts in most European languages.
Television: Approximately 10m TV licences issued. Polish state TV channels 1 and 2 faced their first private TV threat when the station Polonia 1 began in April 1993. This 12-station network, part controlled by Berlusconi, carries a full schedule of popular programmes.
Advertising: Two state agencies, Polish Advertising Agency (PAR) which serves domestic advertisers, and AGPOL which operates on behalf of foreign clients. Advertisements in English possible through papers such as *Warsaw Voice*.
Almost 50 per cent of advertising expenditure by foreign firms is in the form of exhibitions (organised by AGPOL), a further 30 per cent on advertising in the press, and the remainder mostly on posters. Print advertising is on the increase, due mainly to many new titles plus improved availability of raw materials. A number of privately owned or co-operative advertising and business consultancies have appeared. TV and radio are popular advertising media.

Domestic economy

A 'planned' economy, for 40 years, characterised by large industrial and agricultural sectors, but now being transformed into a western-style economy. After a decade of high import-led growth, in the 1970s, economic performance was undermined in the 1980s by high levels of inflation, heavy debt burden, labour unrest and contraction in export demand. The 1986-90 plan aimed for self-sufficiency in foodstuffs, expansion of new export industries and real growth in investment and consumption. In 1989 there were acute shortages of foodstuffs, and the west sent food to Poland and promised economic aid. The main thought of policy in 1990 was to bring hyperinflation under control. This seemed to work but at the expense of a huge drop in output and growth in unemployment. From 1989-93 Poland was transformed into the fastest-growing economy in Europe.
Until it awakened from recession in 1992, Poland was mired in hyperinflation and debt. In 1992 the painful free-market reforms finally began to bear fruit and inflation slowed to 43 per cent from 70 per cent. Production reversed a long slide and actually increased.
In August 1993 the caretaker government devalued the zloty in an attempt to boost exports. In September 1994 London Club creditors agreed to write-off 42.5 per cent (US$6.6bn) of commercial debt; US$2.4bn was then bought back by Poland for 41 per cent of its value and the remainder was exchanged for 30-year bonds for a value of US$4.6bn.
Despite initial delays, mass privatisation finally commenced in 1995. Since June 1995 the zloty has been easily convertible, helping to make unrestricted movement of capital possible.
In 1996 Poland is seen as eastern Europe's most important investment opportunity with its well-trained workforce, low wage structures, high productivity, wealth of raw material and immensely simplified requirements for the development of new businesses and companies. The private sector is producing more than half of the gross national product.

Employment

The rapidly expanding private sector accounts for 60 per cent of employment. Approximately 27 per cent of the workforce work in agriculture, 7 per cent in mining, 30 per cent in industry and 36 per cent in services. Increased productivity and rising economic activity have brought small wage increases.
There is high unemployment, particularly in the agricultural north. However, Warsaw (6.2 per cent in 1995) and Katowice have unemployment rates well below the national average.

External trade

Over the 1980s a reduction of imports helped reverse regular balance of trade deficits. Expansion of exports still constrained by lack of credit and uncompetitiveness of products. The former USSR was by far the largest trading partner, accounting on average for around 30 per cent of total trade turnover, though in 1990 this declined sharply.
Poland led the movement to the free market system in Eastern Europe. In December 1992 the EFTA countries signed free trade agreements with Poland; Hungary, Slovakia, the Czech Republic and Poland established a regional trading zone designed gradually to eliminate tariff barriers. Poland is the largest market between Germany and the former Soviet Union. It is a member of the Central European Free Trade Agreement (CEFTA) and is negotiating entry into the EU.
Exports: Traditional exports largely from agricultural and extractive industries, particularly coal, copper, foodstuffs and wood products. Exports of electrical engineering products, chemicals and motor vehicles also important.
Main destination: EU (63% of 1994 total).
Imports: Imports consist mainly of oil, gas, iron ore, zinc concentrates, cereals, industrial machinery and equipment. Import licences are

COUNTRY PROFILE

POLAND

External trade (contd): no longer required except for some goods such as petrol.
Main source: EU (57% of 1994 total).

Agriculture

The agriculture sector contributed 7 per cent to GNP in 1994 and employed 27 per cent of the workforce. Although co-operative and state farming important, just over 76 per cent of agricultural land is privately owned and farmed. Production is concentrated on livestock farming (dairy and pigs), cereals, potatoes, sugar-beet and oilseeds. Current emphasis on encouraging private sector farming, expansion of grain production and growth in meat production for export and home market. In September 1993 the European Investment Bank (EIB) announced a 20-year loan to Poland for an afforestation scheme.
The agriculture sector output increased by 9 per cent in 1995.

Industry

The industrial sector forms mainstay of economy, contributing 43 per cent to GNP in 1994 and employing 30 per cent of the workforce. Heavy export-based industries dominate, such as shipbuilding, metallurgy (particularly steel), chemicals, motor vehicles and cement. Also recent growth of electronics and light industries. Food processing, glass, beverages, textile and forestry industries are significant.
Construction of housing declined during 1995 by 23.3 per cent.
In July 1996 GKN, the UK components and engineering group, set up a company with production facilities in Poland to supply car components to the country's rapidly expanding motor industry.
The best investment opportunities are considered to be in the areas of food, textiles, timber, paper, mechanical engineering and furniture.

Mining

The mining and hydrocarbons sector accounted for 8 per cent of GNP in 1994 and employed 7 per cent of the workforce. Rich mineral resources including largest deposits of copper ore in Europe and substantial deposits of coal, zinc-lead ores, sulphur and salt. Also lesser deposits of nickel and other precious metals such as silver.
KGHM Polska Miedz is one of the world's largest copper producers – about 26m tons of ore, around 4 per cent of the world's output. It is scheduled for privatisation.

Hydrocarbons

Coal makes significant contribution to energy needs. Total coal reserves were estimated at 42.1 tonnes (end-1995); coal production 86.8m tonnes oil equivalent in 1995, up 0.2 per cent on 1994 output. In May 1996 the government approved a coal industry restructuring programme, which will cut production and close 20 pits.
Domestic supplies of oil are negligible.
Gas production currently meets around 50 per cent of local needs and reserves of natural gas are estimated at 650bn cu metres. Gas consumption is increasing due to the completion of Kobrin-Brest-Warsaw pipeline. The EIB granted a loan to assist in the production, treatment and storage of natural gas.

Energy

Imatran Voima of Finland and Vattenfall of Sweden, together with the World Bank, are backing the modernisation of the heat and power station at Leg in Cracow, southern Poland.
A seven-year plan to privatise the power sector, costing US$50bn, was announced in March 1996.

Stock exchange

The Warsaw Stock Exchange (WSE), opened in 1991.

Legal system

Mixture of continental civil law, contract law and communist legal theory.

Membership of international organisations

CBS, CEFTA, CERN, Council of Baltic Sea States, Council of Europe, CSCE, IAEA, IDA, IFC, IMF, MIGA, NACC, NAM (guest), OAS (observer), OECD (from 11 July 1996), OSCE, Partnership for Peace, Visegrad group, WEU (associate partner), WTO.
Poland has applied membership of the EU and NATO.

BUSINESS GUIDE

Time

GMT + 1 hr (GMT + 1 hr from late Mar to late Sep).

Climate

Temperate, with warm summers and cold winters. Temperature can reach 25°C from Jun–Aug, falling to an average of 10°C Sep–Oct. Most snow from Nov–Mar when temperature can fall below –10°C.
Clothing: Lightweights from Jun to Aug, medium to heavyweight for rest of year, plus heavy topcoat in winter.

Entry requirements

Passport: Required by all. Passport must be valid for at least three months after arrival.
Visa: Visa not required by UK citizens for a stay of maximum 14 days or six months, depending on endorsements in the passport. Visa not required by Irish citizens for a stay of maximum three months. Passport holders from most western countries do not need a visa. A visa is necessary for Canadian citizens who also need a letter of invitation from Poland. Anyone intending to work must have a visa which can be obtained from the embassy. Visas are easily extended by visiting the passport office (Biuro Paszportowe), 13 Okrzei Street (Mon, Tue, Thu, Fri 0830–1400, Wed 0830–1200).
Health: Reciprocal medical arrangements entitle British citizens to free basic medical care in Poland. Vaccination certificates not normally required. N.B. Avoid drinking the tap water.
Currency: No Polish currency may be taken into or out of the country. Refund possible against exchange receipt. No limit on foreign currency taken in, but this amount must be declared and not exceeded by amount taken out.
Customs: Customs and currency declaration must be completed and presented at border on entry.

Air access

National airline: Polish – LOT (Polskie Linie Lotnicze) (scheduled for privatisation).
Other airlines: Aeroflot, Air Algérie, Air France, Air Ukraine, Alitalia, Austrian Airlines, Belavia, British Airways, Delta, Czech Airlines (CSA), El Al, Eurowings, Finnair, Iberia, KLM, Latvian Airlines, Lithuanian Airlines, Lufthansa, Malev, Sabena, SAS, Swissair, Tarom, Tunis Air.
International airports: Warsaw (WAW) at Okecie (two terminals), 10 km from city centre; John Paul II (Krakow, formerly Balice international airport, re-opened on 1 December 1995 after renovations), Gdansk, Katowice, Poznan, Rzeszow and Szczecin.

Surface access

Several sea, rail and road routes from neighbouring countries. From Western Europe main road and rail routes are via Germany and there is access by ferry from Sweden, Finland and Denmark.
Main ports: Gdansk, Szczecin, Gdynia and Swinoujscie. In May 1995 the Dutch government allocated f3.4m for the second stage of the port sector survey. The projects are: renovation of the Szczecin--Swinoujscie deep water channel, the improvement of the management of the ports in Szczecin and Swinoujscie, the development of the Port Polnocny (Northern Port) in Gdansk (with special attention to the land connection of the bridge over the old Vistula river), and extending the port in Gdynia to include the area of the World Trade Centre.
In August 1996 Gdansk shipyard was declared bankrupt.
Rail: Poland is modernising its main railway line to west Europe, the 478 km stretch from Warsaw through Poznan to Kunowice on the German border. Travelling time between Warsaw and Berlin, Germany, will be reduced by 80 minutes. when the project is completed by the end of 1997 as part of the Trans-European Network.

Hotels

Classified one- to four-star and Lux. Bills include 10-15 per cent service charge; tipping around 10 per cent is customary.

Currency

US dollars, Deutsche Marks and Eurocheques accepted by a few banks in Warsaw and Katowice.

Credit cards

Accepted in most hotels, restaurants, night clubs, car rental companies and for LOT services.

Car hire

Hirer must be over 21 years and have held a full licence for a year. Available in all main towns through ORBIS. International driving licence and insurance cover required. Minimum renting period is 24 hours. Speed limits: built-up areas 60 kph, normal roads 90 kph, motorways 100 kph. Payment is by cash or credit card.

City transport

Taxis: Metered taxis available in all main towns. Customary to wait at ranks. Tipping 10 per cent is usual. Taxi drivers may insist on payment in hard currency. Radio Taxi (tel: 919). Few taxi meters have been updated in the past five years and at the end of a journey, the price on the meter will be multiplied by a ratio ranging from 1,000 upwards – normally this figure is displayed on the taxi windscreen. Agree fare in advance or insist that the meter is switched on and check with the driver what multiplier he is using. Fares are 50 per cent higher after 2200. Taxi from airport to city centre Zl 30 (June 1996).
Buses and trams: Regular public transport operates 0530–2300. Good bus services in all towns, also trams in some. Tickets can be bought at RUCH kiosks and used indiscriminately. Seven-day tram tourist tickets can be bought at 37 Senatorska Street (entrance E) (Mon-Wed) 0730–1700, (Thu-Fri) 0730–1400. Larger hotels have an airport shuttle service. Bus from Warsaw airport to city centre approximately Zl 3.50; from Katowice airport to city centre approximately Zl 60 (June 1996). There is a free Lufthansa shuttle bus upon arrival at Katowice airport; reservation 24 hours in advance necessary (by travel agent or Lufthansa).
Metro: Network of about 90 km was begun in 1983. Many delays due to lack of finance. Partially working in 1996; some still under construction.

National transport

Air: LOT operates regular services connecting Warsaw, Gdansk, Krakow, Poznan, Wroclaw, Szczecin, Rzeszow (in summer), Katowice, Koszalin, Bydgoszcz, Zielona, Gora, Slupsk and Czestochowa.
Road: Approximately 154,000 km surfaced roads of which 80 per cent are main roads.

BUSINESS GUIDE

National transport (contd): A US$6.4bn infrastructure programme was announced in January 1995 for the construction of 2,600 km of motorways by private companies, who will recover costs through tolls before handing over to the government. The motorways include a north–south expressway, the Polish section of the Henlsinki–Warsaw highway, known as the Via Baltica, and an expressway from Golonice to Opole.
Buses: Extensive bus and coach services operated by Polish Motor Communications (PKS) – state enterprise which also organises goods transport by road. Buses are best for shorter trips.
Rail: Approximately 30,000 km of track. Narrow-gauge lines operate, 33 per cent electrified, some still steam-hauled. Regular services, operated by Polish State Railways (PKP), connect major towns. Intercity express trains are inexpensive and usually very reliable. N.B. Thieves operate on trains. Keep valuables well hidden.
Water: About 4,000 km of navigable inland waterways, including about 400 km of canals. Ferries and hyrdrofoils link Baltic resorts in summer.

Public holidays

Fixed dates: 1 Jan (New Year's Day), 1 May (May Day), 3 May (Constitution/National Day), 15 Aug (Assumption Day), 1 Nov (All Saints' Day), 11 Nov (Independence Day), 25 & 26 Dec (Christmas).
Variable dates: Easter Monday, Corpus Christi.

Working hours

Business: (Mon–Sat) 0800 – 1600.
Government: (Mon–Sat) 0800/0900 – 1500/1600.
Banking: (Mon–Fri) 0800–1800. Polski Bank Kredytowy, Warsaw Okecie airport (Mon–Fri) 0730–1700, (Sat) 0730–1130. Banks at Katowice Pyrzowice airport (Mon–Fri) 0830–1500.
Shops: (Mon–Sat) usually 1100 – 1900, but food shops often 0600/0700 – 1800/1900. N.B. companies and shops, other than food shops, close on 'Free Saturdays' which vary from business to business, but usually three per month (one for shops).

Social customs

Organisations do not stop for lunch in the middle of the day. The main meal *obiad* is taken from 1500. Formal address in the Polish language is expected. Polite small talk is appreciated as a prelude to talking business. Persistence and patience required for successful conclusions to business.

Business language and interpreting/translation

Available through Polish Travel Office – ORBIS.

Telecommunications

Telecommunication facilities are substandard. Netia Telekom, Poland's sole private telephone operator, raised a US$180m loan from a foreign banking consortium led by the European Bank for Reconstruction and Development and ABN Amro of the Netherlands in June 1996 for the construction of 350,000 lines between 1996 and 1999.
There are plans for land-line connections which will nearly double the penetration (from 15 phones to 30 per 100 people), and also for expansion of mobile communications.
Telephone and telefax: Rates for calls vary with distance. Cheap rate on long-distance calls 1600–0600.
Dialling code for Poland: IDD access code + 48 followed by area code (32 for Katowice; 22 for Warsaw; from December 1995 area code for Bielsko-Biala and Zywiec changed from 30 to 33), followed by subscriber's number.
In the urban centres, there are only around 15 telephones for 100 people; around five phones per 100 people in rural areas. Most connections are provided by the state concern Telekomunikaja Polska (TP); mobile market by Centertel. Many businesses and ministries have installed international satellite telephone lines operated by Komertel.
The international code is 48 39, followed by a six-digit number which generally starts with the figure 1.
Telex: Available at main ORBIS hotels, Foreign Trade Enterprises and, 24 hours a day, at URZAD POCZTOWY in Warsaw. Country code 63 PL.
Telegram: Available in post offices and via telephone.

Banking

The central bank, Narodowy Bank Polski, is responsible for state monetary and foreign exchange policy, the balance of payments and the representation of Poland's interests in international banking circles. Specialised banks also exist.
Central bank: Narodowy Bank Polski.
Other banks: Bank Depozytowo-Kredytowy, Bank Gdanski (sold December 1995; merger with Bank Inicatyw Gospodarczych (BIG) approved February 1996), Bank Gospordarki Zywnosciowej (co-operative bank for farm food industry finance), Bank Handlowy w Warszawie (provision of credit and banking services for foreign trade), Bank PeKao SA (Bank Polska Kasa Opieki) (official savings bank), Bank Przemyslowo Bandlowy (industry & commerce), Bank Rozwoju Eksportu (responsible for export promotion), Bank Slaski (privatised January 1994), Bank Zachodni (western bank), Bydgoski Bank Komunalny Bank, Lodzki Bank Rozwoju (Lodz development bank), Pomorski Bank Kredytowy (Pomeranian credit), Powszechny Bank Gospodarczy, Powszechna Kasa Oszczednosci BP (state savings), Powszechny Bank Kreditowy (PBK) (state credit) (sale scheduled for 1996), Wielkopolski Bank Kredytowy (WBK) (privatised early-1993).

Business information

A new privatisation law was approved in June 1996 which makes electricity, gas and telecommunications top priorities.

Trade fairs

Most important is Poznan International Trade Fair, held annually in mid-June. Poznan Fairs Authority also organises specialised international fairs for goods not covered by main fair. Other international events also held regularly in various cities, including Interfashion Fair in Lodz.

Electricity supply

220 V AC, 50 cycles; adaptor need for continental-type, round two-pin sockets.

Useful tips

Do carry some form of identity at all times.

BUSINESS DIRECTORY

Hotels

Katowice (area code 32)
Aria, Kresowa 5/7, Sosnowiec (tel: 199-9426; fax: 695-353).

Warszawa Orbis, Rozdzienskiego 16 (tel: 596-010; fax: 597-088).

Warsaw (area code 22)
Bristol (Forte Hotel Orbis Bristol), ul Krakowskie Przedmiescie, 00-325 (tel: 625-2525; fax: 625-2577).

Europejski (Orbis), 13 Krakowskie Przedmiescie Street, 00-710 (tel: 265-051; fax: 261-111).

Felix, 24 Omulewska St, 04-128 (tel: 100-691, 610-2182, 109-779; fax: 130-255).

Forum (Orbis), ul Nowogrodzka 24/26, 00-511 (tel: 621-0271; fax: 625-0476).

Grand (Orbis), 28 Krucza Street, 00-522 (tel: 629-4051; fax: 621-9724/8747).

Gromada, ul 17 Stycznia 32, 02-148 (tel: 465-401; fax: 462-201, 461-580).

Holiday Inn (Orbis), 48-54 Zlota Street, 00-120 (tel: 620-0341; fax: 630-0568).

Jan III Sobieski, Plac Artura Zawisky 1, 02-025 (tel: 658-4444, 659-5501; fax: 659-8828).

Karat, 37 Stoneczna St, 00-789 (tel: 601-4411, 498-454; fax: 495-294).

Maria, Al Jana Pawla II 71, 01-038 (tel: 384-062; fax: 383-840).

Marriott, Al Jerozolimskie 65/79, 00-697 (tel: 630-6306; fax: 300-311).

MDM, Pl Konstytucji 1, 00-647 (tel: 621-6211; fax: 621-4173).

Mercure Fryderyk Chopin, Al Jana Pawla II 22, 00-133 (tel: 620-0201; fax: 620-8779).

Metropol, ul Marszalkowska 99a, 00-693 (in city centre) (tel: 629-4001; fax: 625-3014).

Novotel (Orbis), Ulica 1 Sierpnia 1, 02-134 (4km from airport) (tel: 464-051; fax: 463-686).

Polonia, Al Jerozolimskie 45, 00-692 (tel: 628-7241; fax; 628-6622).

Sheraton Hotel and Towers (opened May 1996) (close to embassies and stock exchange; 24-hour business centre gives guests access to the Internet), Three Crosses Square, Ul Prusa No 2, 00493 (tel: 657-6100; fax: 657-6200).

Solec (Orbis), 1 Zagórna Street, 00-441 (tel: 625-4400, 625-4100; fax: 621-6442).

Vera (Orbis), 16 Bitwy Warszawskiej 1920 r, 02-366 (tel: 227-421; fax: 236-256).

Hotels (contd)
Victoria Inter-Continental, ul 11 Krolewska, 00-065 (facing Victoria Square) (tel: 657-8011; fax: 657-8057).

Warszawa, Pl Powstancow Warszawy 9, 00-039 (tel and fax: 271-472).

Zajazd Napoleonski, 82 Plowiecka St, 04-501 (tel: 153-068; fax: 152-216).

Useful telephone numbers

Police emergency service: 997

Fire Brigade: 998

Emergency ambulance service: 999

Radiotaxi: 919 (complaints 224-444)

Tow-truck service: 981, 954

Customs information: 694-5596

Central Tourist Information Office: 270-000

Car hire

Katowice
Avis and Hertz: (advance reservation necessary; see Warsaw Car Hire for details).

Warsaw
Avis: Central Reservations (tel: 2650-4869); Marriott Hotel, Al Jerozolimskie 65/79, 00-697 (tel: 630-7316; fax: 630-7316); International Airport (tel: 650-4872/4870; fax: 650-4871; Sat: 3912-1516).

Budget: Central Reservations (tel: 630-7280; fax: 630-6946); Marriott Hotel, Al Jerozolimskie 65/79, 00-697 (tel: 630-7280; fax: 630-6946); Okecie Airport (tel: 467-310); 17 Stycznia St 32, pav F-4 (tel and fax: 465-986, 668-3336).

Europcar Interrent: Central Reservations, Moliera St 4/6, 00-076 (tel: 263-344; fax: 260-909); Hotel Mercure, Al Jana Pawla II/22 (tel: 248-566); Okecie Airport (tel: 650-4454).

Hertz: Central Reservations (tel: 621-0238; fax: 293-875; Parking House, Ul Nowogrodzka 27 (tel: 621-1360; fax: 293-875); Hotel Victoria, 11 Krowlewska St (tel: 274-185); International Airport (tel: 650-2896).

Intercar: 24 Powazkowska St, 01-797 (tel: 388-724; fax: 388-723).

Chambers of commerce

Foreign Investors' Chamber of Industry and Commerce, 64 Krakowskie Przedmiescie, 00-325 Warsaw (tel: 272-234, 268-593, 261-822; fax: 268-593).

Polish Chamber of Commerce, Trebacka 4 Str, 00-074 Warsaw (tel: 260-221/9; fax: 274-673/759).

Banking

Narodowy Bank Polski (central bank), ul Swietokrzyska 11–21, PO Box 1011, 00-950 Warsaw (tel: 220-0321; fax: 206-241).

AmerBank, Marszalkowska 115, 00-102 Warsaw (tel: 248-505; fax: 249-981).

Bank Gospodarki Zywnosciowej (commercial bank), ul Grzybowska 4, 00-131 Warsaw (tel: 206-606, 200-251; fax: 206-112).

Bank Handlowy w Warszawie SA, (foreign exchange bank), PO Box 129, ul Chalubinskiego 8, 00-950 Warsaw (tel: 303-000, 300-100; fax: 300-113).

Bank Polska Kasa Opieki SA (guardian bank), ul Traugutta 7–9, PO Box 1008, 00-950 Warsaw (tel: 268-832, 269-211; fax: 261-187, 273-463).

Bank Rozwoju Eksportu SA (export development bank), PO Box 728, Bankowy 2, 00-950 Warsaw (tel: 635-5926, 630-5919; fax: 635-8071, 628-7850).

Bank Zachodni we Wroclawiu (Western Bank in Wroclaw), 41–43 Ofiar Oswiecimskich St, 50-850 Wroclaw (tel: 446-621, 444-333; fax: 34-917).

Lodzi Bank Rozwoju SA, PO Box 465, ul Piotrkowska 173, 90-950 Lodz (tel: 361-716; fax: 375-893).

National Credit Bank, Nowy Swiat 6–12, 00-950 Warsaw (tel: 210-321; fax: 296-988).

Polski Bank Rozwoju SA (Polish development bank), ul Zurawia 47–49, 00-680 Warsaw (tel: 628-0490, 628-0790; fax: 628-6164; (Saturday 2120-828); satellite phone and fax: (39) 120-828, 120-844).

Powszechny Bank Gospodarczy w Lodzi, Pilsudskieo 12, 90-950 Lodz (tel: 361-470, 362-886; fax: 362-870).

Powszechna Kasa Oszczednosci Bank Panstwowy (state savings bank), ul Swietokrzyska 11–21, 00-950 Warsaw (tel: 220-0321, 226-3839; fax: 226-3863).

Travel information

Central Bus Station, Warszawa Zachodnia Aleje Jerozolimskie 144 (tel: 236-394/6).

Central Railway Station, Warszawa Centralna 54 Aleje Jerozolimskie (tel: 255-001, 255-000).

Central Tourist Information Office, Plac Zamkowy 1, Warsaw (tel: 270-000, 635-1881).

Foundation for Tourism Development, Ul Mazowiecka 7, 00059 Warsaw (tel: 269-238; fax: 269-695).

International train connections – information (tel: 204512); local train connections – information (tel: 200-361).

LOT (reservations office of the Polish Airlines), Aleje Jerozolmskie 6579, 00-697 Warsaw (tel: 306-306; tx: 816-654); airport information in Warsaw (tel: 628-1009).

ORBIS (tourist board), 16 Bracka Street, 00-028 Warsaw (tel: 260-271; tx: 814-761); tourist centre ul Krucza 16, Warsaw.

State Sports and Tourism Administration, Swietokrzyska 12, 00916 Warsaw (tel: 263-787; fax: 694-5176).

Other useful addresses

Association 'Wspolnota Polska' (previously 'Polonia'), 64 Krakowskie Przedmiescie Street, Warsaw (tel: 262-041; tx: 815-564).

British Embassy, al Roz 1, Warsaw (tel: 628-1001).

Central Customs Office, Swietokrzyska 12, 00-049 Warsaw (tel: 267-155, 265-563; fax: 273-427).

Central Statistical Office, International Co-operation Division, Al Niepodleglosci 208, 00-925 Warsaw (tel: 608-3113; fax: 608-3870; e-mail: j.szczerbinska@gus.stsp.gov.pl).

Co-operation Fund, ul Zurawia 4a, 00-503 Warsaw (tel: 693-5165/827/868; fax: 693-5815/365).

Energy Restructuring Group, Ministry of Industry and Trade, 2 Mysia St, 00926 Warsaw 63 (tel: 625-6280; fax: 625-6305, 628-0970).

Euro Information Centre Network/ Correspondence Centre, ul Zurawia 6/12, 00-503 Warsaw (tel: 625-1319; fax: 625-1290).

Foreign Exchange & International Operations Office, Wielkopolski Bank Kredytowy, pl Wolnosci 15, 60-967 Poznan (tel: 514-553; fax: 521-113).

Foreign Investment Agency, ul Chopina 1, 00-559 Warsaw (tel: 293-553; fax: 221-8427).

Foundation for Privatisation, 36 ul Krucza, 00522 Warsaw (tel: 628-2198/99; fax: 628-2290).

Industrial Development Agency, Wspolna 4, 00-926 Warsaw (tel: 628-3623, 284-114; fax: 621-1394, 282-363).

Institute of Tourism, ul Merliniego 9A, 02-511 Warsaw (tel: 488-560; fax: 488-561).

Main Post Office (open 24 hours), 31–33 Swietokrzyska Street, Warsaw.

Ministry of Agriculture and Food Economy, ul Wspolna 30, 00-519 Warsaw (tel: 221-0311, 628-5745, 623-1000; fax: 221-8987, 623-2751, 623-1140).

Ministry of Communications, Pl Malachowskiego 2, 00-066 Warsaw (tel: 226-1411, 226-1071, 227-5089; fax: 226-4840, 227-3256).

Ministry of Finance, ul Swietokrzyska 12, 00-916 Warsaw (tel: 694-5555/5974/4522, 263-370; fax: 263-110).

Ministry of Foreign Affairs, Al 1 Armii Wojska Polskiego 23, 00-580 Warsaw (tel: 628-7451, 628-8451, 628-1678; fax: 628-0906, 244-1680).

Ministry of Foreign Economic Relations, Pl Trzech Krzyzy 5, 00-507 Warsaw (tel: 628-3988; fax: 625-5159).

Ministry of Industry and Trade, ul Wspólna 4, 00-926 Warsaw (tel: 621-1482/0351; fax: 628-0970).

Ministry of Ownership Changes, Information and Negotiation Centre, ul Krucza 36, 00-525 Warsaw (tel: 628-0281; fax: 625-1114, 221-3361).

Ministry of Transport and Maritime Economy, ul Chalubinskiego 4/6, 00-928 Warsaw (tel: 300-260, 244-500, 244-509, 628-4902; fax: 621-9968).

NOT (technical interpreter service), Czackiego 3–5, Warsaw (tel: 267-461).

Polcargo (cargo experts and supervisors), Zeromskiego 32, Box 223, 81963 Gdynia (tel: 213-921/957; tx: 054-2472).

Polcomex, Marszalkowska 140, Box 478, 00-061 Warsaw (tel: 266-810; tx: 813-452).

Polish Agency for Foreign Investment (PAIZ), Aleja Roz 2, 00559 Warsaw (tel: 295-717, 621-6261, 621-0623; fax: 621-8427).

Polish Chartering Agents (Polfracht), ul Pulaskiego 8, Box 206, 81368 Gdynia (tel: 214-991; tx: 054201 and 054331).

Polish Foundation for Promotion and Development of SMEs, ul Zurawia 4a, 00-503 Warsaw (tel: 693-5868/18/27; fax: 693-5815/365).

Polish Public Roads, Ul Wspolna 1/3, Warsaw (tel: 300-885, 244-572; fax: 628-1345).

Polska Agencja Interpress (Polish information agency), ul Bagatela 12, 00-585 Warsaw (tel: 628-2221; fax: 628-4651).

Polska Agencja Prasowa (Polish press agency), Al Jerozolimskie 7, 00-950 Warsaw (tel: 628-0001; fax: 213-439).

Polskie Koleje Panstwowe (state railways), ul Chalubinskiego 4–6, 00-928 Warsaw (tel: 628-4909, 293-596; fax: 621-9557, 244-870).

Polskie Linie Oceaniczne (Polish Ocean Lines), ul 10 Lutego 24, 81364 Gdynia (tel: 201-901).

Poznan International Fairs, ul Glogowska 14, 60734 Poznan (tel: 61-221; tx: 041-5210).

Telekomunikacja Polska SA, Special Projects Department, ul Obrzezna 7, 02-691 Warsaw (tel: 275-037; fax: 276-789).

Telephony Polskie Fundacja (Polish Telephone Foundation), ul Waszyngtona, 53 A m 19, 04074 Warsaw (tel: 102-292; fax: 102-292, 120-554).

Internet sites

LOT Polish Airlines: http://www.poland.net/lot

Portugal

Howard Hill

Times are changing, literally, in Portugal. The country has switched from European time to GMT and, in an unrelated event, has switched to a socialist minority government in a swing that was more substantial than most observers had predicted. The 1 October 1995 election to the 230-member parliament gave the centre-left Socialist Party (PS) led by António Guterres more seats than the centre-right incumbent Party Social Democrata (PSD) (Social Democratic Party) and conservative Democratic Social Centre/People's P (CDS/PP)arty put together; however, they still fell four short of a majority. The socialists also won the presidency in January 1996, allowing for a period of political stability.

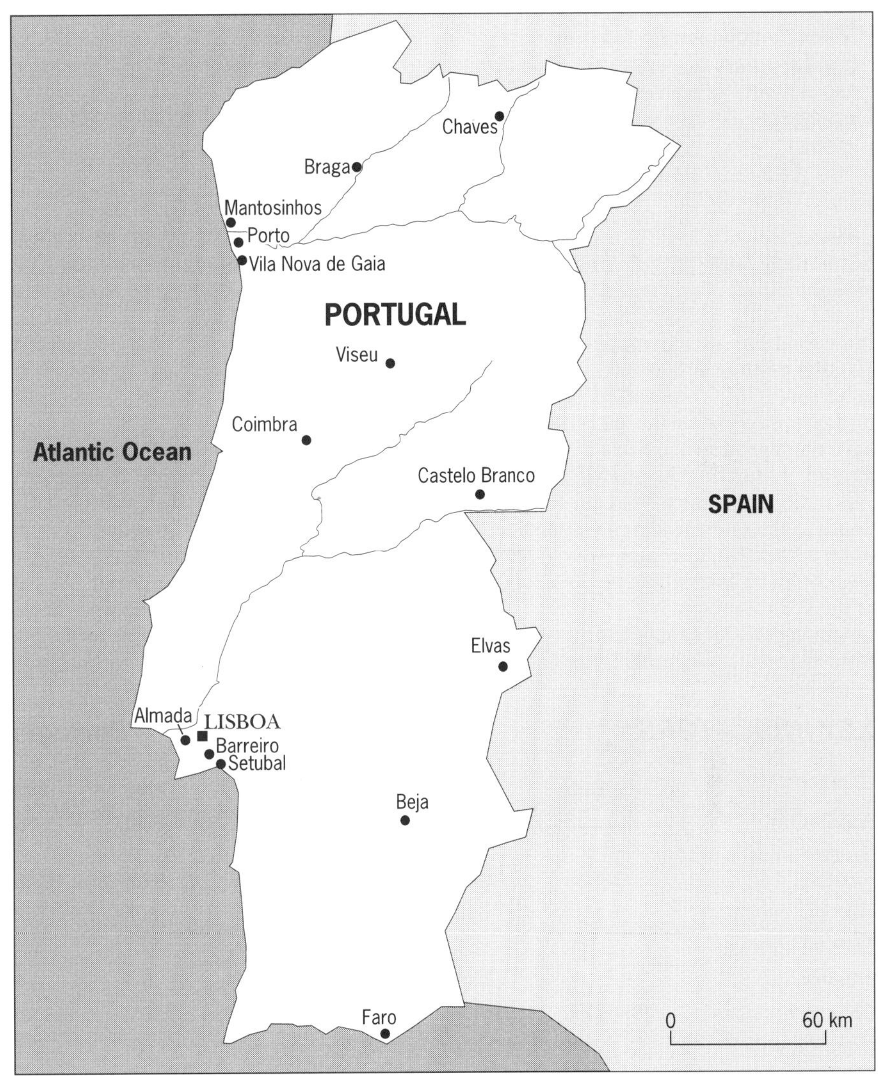

Elections

There was a very strong swing to the socialists in the October election while the PSD's share of vote fell to 34.1 per cent from 50.4 per cent. This was as much a sign of the unpopularity of the PSD in recent years as it was an indication of the support for the socialists. The size of the PS victory meant that, contrary to expectations, the hardline communists will not have to be relied upon for support.

The decisive victory came at a time when the platforms of the PS and PSD began to blur into each other. Both support the concept of a free market, favour European Union (EU) integration, a single currency and fiscal responsibility. However, the PSD's position as incumbent was a liability in the election. The economy was in a slow-down phase after years of substantial growth and corruption scandals involving the PSD seriously damaged its public credibility.

It was also clear that the public wanted a change after handing the PSD substantial victories in 1987 and 1991. The socialists' Guterres became party leader in 1992, after the party's electoral defeat, and had ample time to turn its fortunes around. He is of the younger generation of socialists responsible for injecting the party with new life.

The PSD, on the other hand, was weakened by the January 1995 decision of Anibal Cavaco Silva to step down as prime minister and party leader. In the resulting leadership race Fernando Nogueira, the longstanding deputy of Cavaco Silva, was narrowly elected in February 1995. Cavaco Silva continued in the post of prime minister until the election.

In October 1995, after the election, Cavaco Silva announced his intention to run for the presidency in the forthcoming 14 January 1996 election; most observers had anticipated that his decision to step down as prime minister was motivated by his desire to run in the presidential election. However, this presidential gamble failed to pay off. In the election to succeed socialist two-termer Mário Soares, the public clearly put their support behind Jorge Sampaio, who won 53.8 per cent of the vote to Cavaco Silva's 46.2 per cent. Sampaio, a former mayor of Lisbon and former Socialist party leader, was the clear favourite before the vote. For the first time since the return of democracy in 1974, Portugal has elected a president who is of the same party to the government.

At election time in January 1996 the socialists were still on an almost unstoppable roll after their October 1995 election victory. The public wanted to give the socialists a clear chance, and a PSD member in the presidency could have made for an uncomfortable time for both president and congress.

KEY FACTS — Portugal

Official title: República Portuguesa (The Portuguese Republic)

Head of state: President Jorge Sampaio (PS) (from Jan 1996)

Head of government: Prime Minister António Guterres (leader of PS)

Ruling party: Socialist Party (PS) (112 seats in Oct 1995 election)

Capital: Lisbon

Official Languages: Portuguese

Currency: Portuguese Escudo (Esc) = 100 centavos (devalued 6 Mar 1995)

Exchange rate: Esc156.54 per US$ (Dec 1996)

Area: 92,072 sq km

Population: 9.9m (1995)

GDP per capita: US$10,769 (1995)

GDP real growth: 1.9% (1995)

GNP per capita: US$7,770 (1994)

Labour force: 4.258m (1994)

Unemployment: 7.5% (1st quarter 1996)

Inflation: 3.5% (May 1996) (consumer prices)

Trade balance: -US$9.6bn (12 months to Mar 1996)

Foreign debt: US$17.2bn (Jun 1995)

Visitor numbers: 9.5m (1995)

The defeat of the PSD in both the parliamentary and presidential elections brought a leadership contest. Noguiera resigned as party leader in the days after the January 1996 presidential election. He avoided quitting immediately after losing in October 1995 but stayed on to avoid further weakness in the party that might have damaged Cavaco Silva's chances. At the end of March 1996 the PSD elected TV and radio personality Marcelo Rebelo de Sousa as their new leader; he is considered to be a liberal intellectual. Many feel that he may not be able to hold the rival factions of the PSD together.

Although major changes are not expected from the new government, the campaign promises of the PS will have to be heeded. These include a minimum guaranteed income, increased spending on social services, and devolving power to the mainland regions.

Economy

According to the National Statistics Institute (INE), the Portuguese economy grew by 1.9 per cent in 1995, substantially higher than 1994's GDP growth of 0.7 per cent. However, this is still less than the government's estimated figure of 2.5 per cent; the Bank of Portugal had predicted 2.25 per cent. The INE figure, according to the Bank of Portugal, failed to take into account the effect on GDP growth of the rundown of stocks held by companies; the Bank said that this figure is about 0.3 per cent. In May 1996 the Bank of Portugal estimated that growth would be between 1.75 and 2.75 per cent for 1996.

Two weeks later, the statistical division of the EU said that Portugal's economy could be about 20 per cent larger than figures currently show, due largely to the substantial size of the informal economy. Upwardly revised figures could make it easier for Portugal to meet the Maastricht criteria for economic and monetary union (EMU). However, any new method of statistical analysis will not be used until 1998 or after, which would be too late for initial entry into EMU.

Finance Minister Antonio Sousa Franco said upon taking office that the new government's plans to meet the criteria for EMU were even more stringent than the previous government's strategy. Although accused of being too ambitious in its quest to join the first group of countries to adopt a single European currency, this may be possible with considerable belt-tightening.

In February 1996 the Finance Minister said that he wants to reduce the budget deficit from 5.2 per cent of GDP in 1995 to 4.2 per cent in 1996. The EMU requirement for 1997 is 3 per cent, and this is within reach. However, the challenge will also come in keeping it at this rate or below in the following years. Cuts in 1996 are planned in the areas of defence, justice and foreign affairs while spending on social services is to rise. Tax revenue is predicted to grow by almost 8 per cent in 1996 and this will be the single most important budget reduction tool in the new, widely applauded, budget passed by parliament in March 1996. Aimed at flushing out the black economy, new decree-laws are to be enacted to force the self-employed and companies to pay tax at an average rate for their profession or trade. This is intended to single out those tax payers who end up paying unusually low taxes.

Inflation reached 4.1 per cent at the end of 1995; a year earlier it was 5.1 per cent. The outlook is for inflation to continue to fall and the government has predicted a rate of 3.5 per cent in 1996. By May 1996 things were looking fair; the annualised rate was 3.5 per cent.

In the second week of January 1996 the public sector unions agreed to a wage increase of 4.25 per cent. If the government's 1996 inflation predictions are correct, the pay rise constitutes a real increase. On the other hand, it is substantially less than the 6.5 to 8 per cent insisted on by the unions. But both the government and the unions hailed the agreement which seems to have had some affect on private sector wage negotiations.

KEY INDICATORS — Portugal

	Unit	1991	1992	1993	1994	1995
Population	m	9.85	9.85	9.85	9.90	9.90
Gross domestic product (GDP)	US$bn	69.0	83.8	75.1	87.5	100.8
GDP per capita	US$	7,030	7,880	7,600	8,894	10,769
GDP real growth	%	2.1	1.1	-1.2	0.7	1.9
Inflation	%	11.4	8.9	6.5	5.1	4.1
Consumer prices	1990=100	111.4	121.3	129.6	136.0	141.5
Unemployment	%	3.9	4.4	5.1	8.8	7.1
Agricultural production	1979-81=100	139.11	119.27	106.93	112.02	108.32
Tin production	'000 tonnes	3.1	3.0	5.3	*4.5	–
Exports	Esc bn	2,352.5	2,473.9	2,474.0	2,958.0	3,390.0
Imports	Esc bn	3,811.0	4,093.0	3,889.0	4,454.0	4,861.0
Balance of trade	US$bn	-7.8	-9.5	-6.9	-7.3	-10.3
Current account	US$m	-716	-184	233	-1,505	-229
Total reserves minus gold	US$m	20,629	19,129	15,840	15,513	15,850
Foreign exchange	US$m	20,261	18,769	15,481	15,106	15,315
Deposit rate	%	14.63	14.59	11.06	8.37	8.38
Lending rate	%	25.02	20.43	16.48	15.01	13.80
Exchange rate	Esc per US$	144.5	135.0	160.8	165.9	149.9

Two weeks after the wage deal, the government, trade unions, and employer organisations agreed on a social pact. Under its provisions, the long 44-hour working week would be reduced to 42 hours by September 1997; it would fall to 40 hours in 1998. A benchmark of 4.5 per cent for wage rises was set, and the minimum industrial wage goes up 5 per cent to Esc54,600 per month. The CGTP-Intersindical union federation, which is communist-dominated, refused to accept the pact – it particularly objected to the flexible working hours and job description provisions for workers.

The unemployment rate stayed fairly constant in 1994 and 1995. In the first quarter of 1996 the rate rose to 7.5 per cent compared with 7.3 per cent in the final quarter of 1995, but this was considered to be due to seasonal variations. In the first quarter of 1995 the rate was 7.4 per cent.

Industrial production was up by 4.6 per cent in 1995, compared with a drop of 0.2 per cent in the previous year. There were strong fluctuations seen throughout 1995 and the first quarter's growth rate by volume was 5.6 per cent compared with the previous year, which fell to 2.1 per cent in the second quarter, and to 1.2 per cent in the third quarter. By the final quarter of 1995 it had rebounded to 6.3 per cent.

Manufacturing output had a similar roller-coaster ride throughout 1995. In the first quarter the year-on-year change by volume was 6.6 per cent, falling to 2.1 per cent in the second quarter of the year, and down to -0.3 per cent in the third quarter. Output ended 1995 at 1.6 per cent.

External trade

In 1995 export volumes rose by 12.7 per cent and imports were up by 12 per cent. By value, exports totalled US$22.8 billion while imports amounted to a much higher US$33 billion. The trade deficit was US$10.3 billion in 1995, slightly less than the previous year's figure of US$7.3 billion and 1993's figure of US$6.9 billion.

In the first quarter of 1995 exports were worth Esc876 billion, and this fell to Esc840 billion in the second quarter and down to Esc797 billion in the third quarter. By the final quarter of 1995 exports rebounded to Esc877 billion.

Imports started the first quarter of 1995 at Esc1,224 billion, rose to Esc1,299 billion in the second quarter, fell to Esc1,092 billion in the third quarter, and ended 1995 at Esc1,246 billion.

In the first quarter of 1996 the trade deficit fell by 13.7 per cent to Esc302.3 billion. In this period, the trade deficit with EU members was Esc164.9 billion (a drop of 20.4 per cent compared with the first quarter of 1995) and the deficit with non-EU members amounted to Esc137.4 billion (a drop of 3.9 per cent).

Agriculture and fishing

Agriculture, forestry and fishing contributed 6.2 per cent of GDP in 1995. Portugal, with Spain, gained greater fishing access to British waters in January 1996, five years ahead of schedule; at the end of October 1996 the Iberian countries agreed on a EU plan to allow them access to the western waters of the British Isles.

Privatisation

The new government's privatisation programme is expected to raise over US$2.4

COUNTRY PROFILE — PORTUGAL

Historical profile

1143 Independence under monarchy. In following centuries development of extensive overseas empire, partially lost in sixteenth century.
1910 Declaration of republic following overthrow of monarchy.
1914-18 Fought with allies in First World War.
1926 Military coup ended instability of new republic.
1939-45 Neutral during Second World War.
1932-68 Right-wing dictatorship of Dr Antonio de Oliveira Salazar kept Portugal a poor, rural Roman Catholic society isolated from foreign influences. 1968-74 Dictatorship of slightly more liberal Marcello Caetano.
1974 Coup by group of army officers. Coalition government set up including opponents of Salazar. Political prisoners were freed and Portugal withdrew from its African territories, where wars against nationalist forces had long been a drain on the economy.
1974-86 Political instability with 17 left-wing coalition governments in power.
1982 New constitution completed transition to full civilian government.
1986 Portugal acceded to EC. The former prime minister Dr Mario Lopes Soares became first civilian president for 60 years.
1987 In general election Partido Social Democrata (Social Democratic Party) (PSD) first majority party in parliament since 1974 revolution. Prime Minister was Anibal Cavaco Silva.
1991 Mário Soares re-elected president in January and PSD won re-election in October.
1995 PSD lost to the Socialist Party (PS) in October general election. António Guterres became prime minister.

Political system

Republic with legislative power vested in the president, the Assembly of the Republic and the government. The president, who is directly elected for five years, appoints a prime minister, and, on his recommendation, the rest of the government. The principal organ of executive power within the government is the Council of Ministers which is responsible to the Assembly of the Republic. The Assembly comprises 230 members directly elected for four years. Portugal's electoral system follows the Hondt method of proportional representation. The president can dissolve the Assembly and call new elections and is Supreme Commander of the Armed Forces. The centre-left Socialist Party (PS) won the October 1995 general election ending ten years of rule by the centre-right Social Democrats. The presidential election 14 January 1996 was also won by a Socialist – Jorge Sampaio – with 63.8 per cent of the vote; Cavaco Silva (Social Democrats) (PSD) 46.2 per cent.

Political parties

Ruling party: Socialist Party (PS) (112 seats in the October 1995 parliamentary elections). Other major parties: Partido Social Democrata (PSD) (Social Democratic Party) (88 seats); Democratic Social Centre/People's Party (CDS/PP) (15 seats); United Democratic Coalition (CDU) (15 seats).

Main cities/towns

Lisbon, capital (population 2.3m in 1994), Porto, Amadora, Coimbra, Braga and Setúbal.

Language

Business languages: Portuguese, English, Spanish, French.
In July 1996 Portugal and six of its former colonies (Angola, Brazil, Cape Verde, Guinea-Bissau, Mozambique and São Tomé) launched the Community of Portuguese Speaking Countries (CPLP) to protect their common language.

Media

Dailies: A Bola, Correio da Manha, Expresso, Publico, Diario de Noticias.
Weeklies: Most popular tend to be general news magazines, such as *Expresso, Independente* and *Tal & Qual,* and women's magazines such as *Máxima, Mulher Moderna, Guia, Maria* and *Marie Claire.* Majority of weeklies are published in Lisbon.
Business: Most influential: daily *Diário Económico;* weekly *Vida Económica;* economic sections of weekly newspapers are also informative. Leading business magazines: *Valor, Expansão* and *Fortuna.* Leading expatriate paper: *Anglo-Portuguese News (APN)* has money matters economics section.
Radio: Portugal has one private national radio station, Radio Renascença, founded in 1936, which is owned by the Roman Catholic Church and has the widest audience in the country. The state-owned Radiofusão Portuguesea EP (RDP) runs three nationwide stations, Antena 1, Antena 2 (classical music) and Rádio Comercial.
Television: A nationalised company, RadiotelevisãoPortuguesa (RTP), runs the two national TV channels, RTP 1 (vhf) and RTP 2 (uhf), and the regional stations in Madeira and the Azores. SIC,headed by ex prime minister Pinto Balsemã0, and TVI, with close ties with the Roman Catholic church in Portugal, are both two relatively new private stations which ended 35 years of state monopoly.
Advertising: Television is the most popular medium of advertising, taking about 45 per cent of the total advertising, followed by radio, newspaper and magazine advertisements. Other methods used are cinema shorts, posters, direct mail and door-to-door canvassing. There are about 50 advertising agencies, mainly specialising in radio and TV work and newspapers. Market research firms also available.

Domestic economy

Small mixed economy with heavy dependence on foreign trade, less than hitherto on agriculture, and few natural resources. Tourism and export-oriented manufacturing sector also of growing importance.
Rapid industrialisation during 1970s creating a strong dependence on outside energy sources, curtailed by international recession. IMF-backed stabilisation package introduced 1983-85 in effort to reduce external debt growth, cut inflation rate and improve trade balance.
Current emphasis on modernisation, rehabilitation of public enterprises and export-led growth.

billion in 1996. Smaller privatisations include companies involved in shipbuilding, steel, oil and gas, chemicals, paper pulp, motorway construction and operation, and airport management. The biggest companies up for grabs include Portugal Telecom, Banco Fomento e Exterior, Electricidade de Portugal (EDP), the leading cement producer Cimpor and the Tabaqueira tobacco company.

EDP is the holding company for Portugal's power generating and distribution companies and the sale of 20 per cent (or more) of the company is likely to take place near the end of 1996 or early 1997; the sale would catapult it into the top of the Lisbon stock exchange in terms of capitalisation. Cimpor, the cement producer, is a healthy company with good potential for growth; 45 per cent of the government's stake will be sold, leaving it with 35 per cent. A single 60-65 per cent block of Tabaqueira will be sold through a tender offer some time in 1996.

The Portugal Telecom sale, which ended on 11 June 1996, was the Socialists' first privatisation offering and was an impressive success. This secondary global offering of 22 per cent of Portugal Telecom was a record breaker in terms of demand from both institutional shareholders and the public; over 81,000 investors applied for shares at the retail offering. The sale brought Esc147.1 billion to the government, and its share in the utility has correspondingly fallen to 51 per cent. In 1995 a 27 per cent offering of Portugal Telecom was sold by the government and raised Esc147 billion. A strategic telecommunications partner was being sought by the company in 1996, and this partner would likely buy up to 25 per cent.

Banco Portugues de Investimento (BPI), the biggest investment bank in Portugal, offered Esc 152 billion for the government-owned Banco Fomento e Exterior (BFE) but this was rejected in February 1996. The government said that it did not favour this approach to privatisation – it preferred to make the sale through competitive bidding for a controlling stake. A jury will select possible companies for the controlling stake and the highest bidder will get an indivisible block of 51 per cent of BFE. A second phase of 17.5 per cent of BFE will be offered to employees and small savers.

Derivatives market

The new Bolsa de Derivados do Porto (BDP) began trading derivatives on 20 June 1996. The Lisbon and Oporto stock exchanges had been battling for years to host derivative trading but in 1993 the government decided that Oporto should be the centre for this type of trading. At the same time, it was agreed that Lisbon should become the country's share trading centre. The BDP got underway with two futures contracts – one on the 10-year treasury bond and the other on the Portuguese Stock Index (PSI-20), an index of the Lisbon exchange's top 20 shares. The PSI-20 represents some 78 per cent of total market capitalisation and 80 per cent of total trading volume.

Industry and development

The new privately operated 12-km bridge over the river Tagus, taking commuters to and from Lisbon, is to open in spring 1998 – in time for Lisbon's Expo 98 international exhibition. The new Tagus bridge's consortium, Lusoponte, has come under pressure

COUNTRY PROFILE — PORTUGAL

Domestic economy (contd): Joining the EU brought access to funds for agriculture, industry and massive infrastructure development. Inflation and a negative trading balance are main problem areas.
In 1996 Portugal is struggling to meet the requirements for economic and monetary union (EMU), but there has been an improvement in the government deficit situation.

Employment

Around 17 per cent of labour force engaged in agriculture, 35 per cent in industry and 48 per cent in services. Portugal has a chronic shortage of skilled workers, technicians and managers. More than 60 per cent of workers have only primary education and 15 per cent of the population is illiterate.

External trade

Exports: Exports totalled US$22.8bn in 1995. Main sectors: clothing (19.6% of 1994 EU total), machinery (17%), footwear (9.5%), textiles (7.3%), paper (6.4%), transport goods (6.1%). Main destinations: Germany (19.7% of 1994 total), France (14.5%), Spain (11.4%), UK (10.8%), EU (75.6%).
Imports: Imports tottalled US$33bn in 1995. Main sectors: machinery and electrical equipment (20.7% of 1994 EU total), transport equipment (17.6%), chemicals (9.2%), agricultural equipment (9.1%), textiles (7.5%). Main sources: Spain (15% of 1994 EU total), Germany (15%), France (13%), UK (7.5%), EU (72.1%).

Agriculture

The agriculture, forestry and fishing sectors employed 11.4 per cent of the workforce in 1995 and contributed 6.2 per cent of GDP. They account for around 8 per cent of exports.
About 34 per cent of the land area is crop land, 9 per cent under pasture, 32 per cent forestry and woodland, 24 per cent for other uses.
Smallholders predominate, particularly in the north, and productivity remains low by western European standards despite mild climate and natural resources such as forests.
Recurrent droughts, fragmentation of the land, poor-quality soil and outdated methods of production continue to handicap government efforts at agrarian reform. The worst affected region is the Alentejo.
Policy is aimed at encouraging private investment, co-operatives and integration. The majority of farm produce is unable to compete effectively with other EU produce. However, although subsidies are available, technical assistance is scarce, the farmers complain, and advice on marketing is practically non-existent.
The government's five-year investment plan introduced in 1993 is to promote and improve Portuguese food products, to enable farmers to compete with their EU partners. The five-year programme includes Esc126bn of direct investment by the government.

Industry

Although contributing 38.2 per cent to GDP in 1994 and employing 32.1 per cent of the workforce, industry is underdeveloped and dependent on imported energy and materials. State-run companies predominate, particularly in the home-based sector. Production has been sluggish since the period of rapid industrialisation in the 1960s and 1970s, though there was an expansion in 1985-87 in the export-based industries such as footwear, textiles, chemicals, base metallurgical products and machine components. Portugal leads the world in ship repairs.
Other important industries include processed cork, paper, cement, fertilisers, steel, motor vehicles and glassware.
Portugal faces a difficult transition from traditional industries – clothing, textiles and footwear – afflicted by low value-added products, inefficient management and outmoded technology, to a diversified industrial base.
Industrial output increased 4.6 per cent in 1995 compared with a drop of 0.2 per cent in 1994.
The AutoEuropa mini-van joint venture between Ford and Volkswagen accounts for some 2.2 per cent of GDP.

Tourism

Net tourism revenue accounted for 2.6 per cent of GDP in 1995. The sector earns 25 per cent of total export earnings, and employs 300,000 people (6 per cent of the labour force). The Department of Tourism has encouraged investors to modernise and re-equip existing units, construct additional facilities such as golf courses and conference centres and diversify from beach holidays into sports and cultural tourism.
In 1995 a record 9.5m tourists visited Portugal, up from 9.1m in 1994. Gross tourism income in 1995 was Esc729bn, up from Esc682bn in 1994. However, the net balance rose only slightly to Esc409bn from Esc400bn, after counting spending by Portuguese travelling abroad.
The industry is largely sustained by visitors from the UK, Spain, Germany and Netherlands. Attracting more tourists from France, Italy, and eastern Europe is a priority. The Algarve continues to account for about half the country's tourism business.

Mining

The mining sector contributed 1 per cent of GDP in 1994 and employed 1 per cent of the workforce. Although there is considerable mineral wealth, deposits are scattered and not easily exploitable on a large scale. The most import mineral resources include non-metallic ores such as rock salt, pyrites (the reserves in the Alentejo region make up nearly 23 per cent of total worldwide reserves) and excellent quality marble. Large reserves of uranium are also available. Small-scale mining of tin, copper, tungsten concentrates, marble, stone and iron pyrites.

Hydrocarbons

Little on-shore or offshore natural gas or exploitable oil resources have been discovered. Coal is also scarce and of poor quality.

Energy

Portugal is heavily dependent on imported fuels, particularly oil (70 per cent). The National

for alleged environmental transgressions; activists have asked the EU to suspend its funding for 40 per cent of the construction costs. The State Attorney has begun an investigation into these charges.

The Expo 98 exhibition in Lisbon will transform 330 ha of disused riverside on the city's eastern side marking the 500th anniversary of Vasco de Gamma's discovery of the sea route to India around the Cape of Good Hope. According to the government, 27 per cent of GDP in 1998 will come directly from the fair and related activities; in the four years before the fair is set to open, Expo 98 related economic activity is expected to account for between 11 and 15 per cent of GDP.

The AutoEuropa mini-van joint venture between Ford and Volkswagen is itself responsible for some 2.2 per cent of GDP. In 1996 the slow-down in demand has kept production at 527 vans per day but this could be increased to 830 vehicles per day in 1997 if enough orders are placed. Production in 1996 was estimated to be 100,000 vehicles, with sales reaching Esc357 billion. The US$3.3 billion venture is located at Palmera near Lisbon and has received considerable financial support from the government and the EU.

Portugal and Renault have settled their differences over the fate of a Renault factory in Setubal, south of Lisbon. The outcome was hailed as a good deal for both sides and will ensure a continued presence for Renault in the country. Portugal had brought a claim for damages against Renault amounting to Esc53 billion after Renault announced that it would close the plant because it was no longer economically viable, with the loss of some 760 jobs. The government said Renault had given an undertaking to it to keep the plant open indefinitely when an investment deal was signed in 1977; in return, Portugal agreed to provide more than Esc43 billion in incentives over the years.

Under the new deal with Renault, signed in June 1996, Portugal has agreed to pay US$6.8 million to acquire Renault's 70 per cent holding in the plant. Portugal will then seek a new operator for the plant. Renault will contribute money towards reconverting the plant and will put money towards compensating workers for any job losses. Its Clio cars will be manufactured for one more year. Renault will also acquire the government's minority holdings in its other operations in Portugal.

Siemens, the German industrial giant, is to build a new high-tech semi-conductor chip plant near Porto which will result in 750 new jobs. The initial investment is Esc60 billion and the government will assist in funding the project.

Outlook

Portugal will struggle to meet the requirements for EMU but at least has a chance of meeting them in time for the first wave of unification. The government deficit situation is looking better, and the political stability provided by the combination of a strong socialist presence in parliament and a socialist president could be substantial. Social conditions are also set to improve marginally, and as the informal economy is increasingly brought into the tax system, then the extra cash will give the government room to manoeuvre. The bonanza days of massive EU-funded development may be over, but Portugal's integration with the EU is still continuing apace.

COUNTRY PROFILE — PORTUGAL

Energy (contd): Energy Plan emphasises increased conservation and shift to oil substitutes such as coal, hydroelectricity, wood, biomass, solar and wind power. Hydroelectricity contributes around 50 per cent of electricity generated.

Banking

The Bank of Portugal is the central bank of issue. The National Development Bank is responsible for medium and long-term economic development credits. State-sector mortgage-type banks harbour a larger deposit base than private and recently re-privatised banks. Few banks remain state-owned; these include Caixa Geral de Depósitos and Banco Nacional Ultramarino. Portugal is a host to a string of foreign banks. Top performing banks include: Caixa Geral de Depósitos, Banco Português do Atlântico, Banco Espirito Santo, Banco Comercial Português, Banco Totta and Açores. In 1992 the Bank of Portugal lifted restrictions on capital movements allowing foreigners to operate in Portugal's short-term money market, and enabling domestic banks to lend escudos to non-residents.

Financial services

The island of Madeira is an offshore financial centre, international services hub and international shipping register, run by Madeira Development Company (SDM). More than 1,300 companies benefit from considerable tax, duty and exchange-control advantages, including total exemption from taxes on profits and capital gains until the end of 2011. Companies in Madeira are not excluded from Portugal's double-taxation treaties and can use these to reduce withholding taxes on royalties, interest and dividends. Santa Maria, in the mid-Atlantic Azores archipelago, benefits from offshore legislation identical to that of Madeira, but companies have shown little inclination to invest.

Stock exchange

The Bosa de Derivados do Porto (BDP) began trading derivatives on 20 June 1996 and the Lisbon Stock Exchange became the country's share trading centre.

Legal system

Civil law system. Constitution adopted 1976, revised 1982 and 1989.

Membership of international organisations

ALADI (observer), CCC, CERN, Council of Europe, CSCE, EEA, EFTA, EU, FAO, IAEA, IATP, ICAC, ICAO, ICES, ICO, IDA, IDB, IEA, IFAD, IFC, IHO, ILO, IMF, IMO, INTELSAT, International Grain Council, INTERPOL, IOOC, IRC, ISO, ITU, Lusophone, MIGA, NACC, NAM (guest), NATO, OAS (observer), OECD, OSCE, UN, UNESCO, UNIDO, UPU, WEU, WHO, WIPO, WMO, World Bank, WSG, WTO.

BUSINESS GUIDE

Time

GMT (GMT + 1 hr from late Mar to late Sep).

Climate

Situated in the middle of the northern hemisphere, Portugal has a mild welcoming climate. However, the differences between the north/south and coast/inland weather is marked. Inland areas have more variable weather than coastal regions. To the south of the Tagus river the Mediterranean influences are clear. Long, hot, humid summers and dry, short, relatively mild winters. May–Oct dry and warm, Nov–Apr cool with rain in north, mild in south (though often wet and windy Jan–Mar). Temperatures vary between 8–28°C.
Clothing: Mediumweight and raincoat Nov-Feb, lightweight for summer.

Entry requirements

Visa: Visas not required by nationals of European countries, plus a few others. Portuguese consul or travel agent should be consulted prior to departure.
Health: Vaccination certificates not normally required. In main towns water is drinkable, but visitors advised to drink bottled water. Health system underdeveloped in relation to northern Europe.
Currency: No limit on import of local and foreign currency, but amount should be declared on entry.
Customs: Personal effects duty-free, plus small duty-free allowance.

Air access

Regular direct flights from most major international airports.
National airline: TAP-Air Portugal - fully professional but in economic difficulties.
Main international airport: Lisbon (LIS) a short distance (reachable in about 20 minutes) north of centre of capital.
International airports: Porto (OPO), 11 km from city, Faro (FAO), 4 km from city, Funchal (FNC) on Maderia and Santa Maria (SMA) in the Azores, 3.2 km from Vila do Porto. Lisbon, Porto and Faro airports serve the Portuguese mainland. Funchal and Porto Santo serve Madeira. San Miguel, Santa Maria and Lajes serve the Azores.

Surface access

Car and passenger ferry services from various Spanish cross-over points. Several road and rail routes through Spain, mostly via Madrid.
Main ports: The three most important ports are Lisbon, Leixes (Oporto) and Sines (south of Lisbon). Others (from north to south) are Viana do Castelo, Aveiro, Figueira da Foz, Setúbal, Portimao and Faro. There are container terminals at Lisbon and Leixes. Sines is the main oil importing terminal.

Hotels

Available to various standards throughout country, classified from one- to five-star. There is a 10 per cent service charge. A tip is also expected, usually 10 per cent. Accommodation should be booked well in advance, especially

BUSINESS GUIDE

PORTUGAL

Hotels (contd): during holiday season, when all hotels become very busy. N.B. drinking water is not purified outside main towns.

Restaurants

Numerous and varied. A 10 per cent service charge usually included in bill. Small tip usually given.

Currency

Exchange rate

Escudo is floating against basket of currencies.

Foreign exchange information

Account restrictions: No restrictions on non-resident savings deposits in foreign currency. Some accounts subject to authorisation by Bank of Portugal.

Credit cards

All usual credit cards are widely accepted.

Car hire

Self-drive and chauffeur-driven cars available throughout country. International driving licence or full national licence required, as well as international insurance Green Card. Motoring information available from 'Automovel Clube de Portugal' in Lisbon. The wearing of seat belts is compulsory outside city areas.

City transport

Taxis: Lisbon taxis are green and black. Relatively cheap but efficient service. Tip of 15 per cent expected. Taxis may be scarce during rush-hour.
Buses, trams and underground: Good services in main centres, such as Lisbon and Oporto. Lisbon also has a small but efficient métro network.
Rail: Construction of a railway line across the River Tagus at Lisbon is to commence at the beginning of April 1998.

National transport

Air: TAP and domestic charter ailrines operate scheduled flights between most major cities, Madeira and the Azores.
Road: Over 52,000 km of roads, including about 22,000 km of main or national roads. Local roads are often of poor quality and unpaved, linking rural communities with the provincial roads. Lisbon-Porto and Lisbon-Algarve roads are very good. The new privately operated 12-km Lisbon bridge over the Tagus river is due to be completed in 1998.
Buses: Regular coach services link major towns. Large variety of services between Lisbon and southern coast.
Rail: Nationalised railway company – Caminhos de Ferro Portugueses, EP (CP) – own about 3,600 km of track, of which 500 km are electrified. Services between main centres – Porto and Lisbon, Lisbon and Faro – are good and include express trains with restaurant cars; seats on these should be booked in advance, but rail services on other lines are poor. There are plans for a third major rail terminus in Lisbon due to be completed by 1997, a rail link over the Tagus River at Lisbon and high-speed links for both passenger and freight transport.
Water: About 800 km of inland waterways which are only rarely used. Some coastal shipping, including services to Madeira and the Azores.

Public holidays

Fixed dates: 1 Jan (Feast of the Circumcision), 25 Apr (Liberty Day), 1 May (Labour Day), 10 Jun (National Day), 13 Jun (Lisbon only), 24 Jun (Porto only), 15 Aug (Assumption), 5 Oct (Foundation of the Republic), 1 Nov (All Saints' Day), 1 Dec (Restoration Day), 8 Dec (Immaculate Conception), 25 Dec (Christmas Day).
Variable dates: Carnival (Feb), Good Friday, Easter Day, Corpus Christi.

Working hours

Business: (Mon–Fri) 0900 – 1300 and 1500 – 1900.
Government: (Mon–Fri) 0930 – 1200 and 1430 – 1800, closed 1730 on Mon and Tue.
Banking: (Mon–Fri) 0830 – 1500. A few banks in Lisbon open on Sat morning. Large network of automatic telling machines.
Shops: (Mon–Sun) 1000 – 2300/2359; (Sat) 0900 – 1300.

Business language and interpreting/translation

French and English fairly widely spoken in business circles, but knowledge of Portuguese useful when dealing with smaller companies. However, information on translation services for business visitors can usually be obtained from Chambers of Commerce.

Telecommunications

Telefones de Lisboa e Porto (TLP) for modernising and extending the telephone network in the Lisbon and Porto metropolitan areas.
Telephone: Government-owned system, offering direct dialling to most parts of the country and several other parts of the world. International dialling code: 351 followed by 1 for Lisbon. For IDD access from Portugal dial 00.
Telex and telefax: Available in major hotels and from main post offices in Lisbon and Porto. Facilities also available on Madeira and Azores. Telex country code 404 P.
Telegram: Can be sent from post offices or via telephone.

Banking

Central bank: Bank of Portugal (central bank) which is the bank of issue.
Commercial banks: Banco Comercial Português (acquired Banco Português do Atlantico April 1995); Banco Pinto & Sotto Mayor, Banco Espirito Santo & Comercial de Lisboa, Banco Nacional Ultramarino, Banco Borges & Irmão, Banco Totta & Açores, União de Bancos Portugueses and Banco Fonsecas & Burnay, Banco Português de Investimento, Banco de Comércio e Indústria, Banco Internacional de Crédito; Banco do Brasil.
Specialist banks: Prominent among specialist banks are Caixa Geral de Depositos (savings bank) and Banco de Fomento Nacional (medium and long-term credit for industry).
Foreign branches: Main foreign banks include Crédit Franco-Portuguais, Banco do Brasil, Chase Manhattan Bank, Citibank, Banque Nationale de Paris, Société Générale de Banque and Barclays Bank International.

Trade fairs

The main international fair (FIL) is held annually in Lisbon. Other specialist fairs are held regularly in Lisbon, Porto and several other towns. Lisbon fairs organised by Associaçao Industrial Portuguesa (AIP FIL); Porto fairs by Associacão Industrial Portuense (AIP Portuense).
Lisbon will hold the international Expo 98 exhibition to mark the 500th anniversary of Vasco de Gamma's discovery of the sea route to India around the Cape of Good Hope.

Electricity supply

220V AC.

BUSINESS DIRECTORY

Hotels

Lisbon
Altis, Rua Castilho 11, PO Box 1200 (tel: 522-496, 524-206; fax: 522-696).

Avenida Palace, Rua 1 Dezembro 123 (tel: 346-0151; fax: 346-6104).

Borges, Rue Garrett 108 (tel: 346-1951)

Continental, Tr. Marquê Sá da Bandeira, 9-13 (tel: 793-5005; fax: 773-669).

Crown Plaza (tel: 793-5222).

Diplomatico, Rua Castilho 74 (tel: 562-041; fax: 522-155).

Eduardo VII, Avenida Fontes Pereira de Melo 5 (tel: 530-141; fax: 533-879).

Fenix, Praça Marques de Pombal 8 (tel: 535-121).

Flamingo, Rua Castilho 41 (tel: 53-2191/2/3/4; fax: 532-191).

Holiday Inn, Avenida António José de Almeida 28-A (tel: 793-5222, 793-6018; fax: 736-672, 736-261, 736-572).

Lapa (tel: 395-0065).

Lisboa Penta, Avenida dos Combatentes (tel: 726-5050; fax: 726-4281).

Lisboa Sheraton e Towers, Rua Latino Coelho 1, PO Box 1097 (tel: 575-757; fax: 547-164).

Meridien, Rua Castilho 149 (tel: 690-900; fax: 693-231).

Novotel, Avenida José Malhôa, Lote 1642 (tel: 726-6022, 726-6118; fax: 726-6496).

Ritz, Rua R. da Fonseca 88 (tel: 69-2020; fax: 691-783).

Roma, Avenida da Roma 33, PO Box 1700 (tel: 767-761; tx: 16-586).

Sheraton (tel: 575-757).

Tivoli, Avenida da Liberdade 185 (tel: 530-181; fax: 579-461).

Porto
Infante de Sagres, Praça D. Filipa de Lencastre, 62 (tel: 28-101; fax: 314-937).

BUSINESS DIRECTORY

Hotels (contd):
Ipanema, Rua Campo Alegre, 156-174 (tel: 66-8061, 66-7035; fax: 63-339).

Car hire

Lisbon
Avis: Central Reservations (tel: 346-2676); Portela Airport, 1700 (tel: 849-9947/4836; Ave Praia da Victoria 12C, 1000 (tel: 356-1176); Hotel Ritz, Rua Rodrigo da Fonseca (tel: 692-020); Railway Station, St Apolonia, 1100 (tel: 887-6887).

Budget: International Airport (tel: 849-1603; fax: 849-1605); Ave Visconde Valmor 36 B/C (tel: 797-1377; fax: 793-3622).

Europcar: Central Reservations, Quinta da Francelha, Lote 7 Prior Velho 2685 (tel: 942-2306; fax: 942-5239); Ave Antonio Augusto Aguiar 24 C/D (tel: 353-5115/9); Portela Airport (tel: 801-176/63).

Hertz: Central Reservations (tel: 941-5541; fax: 941-6068); Portela Airport (tel: 849-2722; fax: 801-1496); Ave 5 de Outubro 10 (tel: 579-027/77; fax: 941-6068); Visconde de Seabra Rua Visconde de Seabra 10 (tel: 797-0458; fax: 797-0371).

Chambers of commerce

Assoc Comerical e Industrial do Funchal, Av Arriaga 41, 9000 Funchal (tel: 230-137; fax: 222-005).

Assoc Comercial de Lisboa, R das Portas de Santo Antao, 89 Lisbon Codex (tel: 342-7179; fax: 342-4304).

Assoc Comercial do Porto, R Ferreira Borges, Palacio da Bolsa, 4050 Porto (tel: 201-1448; fax: 208-4760).

Assoc dos Comerciantes de Setúbal, R Manuel Livério 20,2900 Setúbal (tel: 522-527; fax: 522-467).

Câmara de Comércio de Ponta Delgada, R Emesto do Couto 13, 9500 Ponta Delgada, Azores (tel: 25-408; fax: 24-268).

Câmara de Comércio Luso-Britânica, Rua da Estrela 8, 1200 Lisbon (tel: 396-1586, 661-586; fax: 601-513).

Câmara de Comércio e Indústria Portuguesa, Rua das Portas de Santo Antão, Lisbon 1100 (tel: 342-3277, 327-179; fax: 324-304).

Banking

Associaçao Portuguesa de Bancos (Portuguese Bankers Association), 35 Avenida da República, 1000 Lisbon (tel: 579-804; fax: 579-533).

Banco de Portugal (Bank of Portugal), Rua do Comércio 148, 1100 Lisbon (tel: 346-2931; tx: 16-554).

Banco Borges e Irmão (commercial bank), Rua Sá da Bandeira 20, 4001 Oporto (tel: 324-517; tx: 26-899).

Banco Comercial Português SA (commercial bank), Rua Augusta 62-74, 1100 Lisbon (tel: 342-7381; tx: 62-372).

Banco de Comércio e Indústria, Rua Tenente Valadim 290, 4102 Oporto (tel: 695-671; tx: 28-606).

Banco Espirito Santo, Avenida da Liberdade 195, 1200 Lisbon (tel: 578-005; tx: 12-191).

Banco Fomento e Exterior SA, Avenida Casal Ribeiro 59, 1000 Lisbon (tel: 522-279).

Banco Fonsecas & Burnay (commercial bank), Rua do Comércio 132, 1106 Lisbon (tel: 874-801; tx: 12-210).

Banco Internacional de Crédito, Avenida Fontes Pereira de Melo 27, 1000 Lisbon (tel: 527-135; tx: 62-535 banicr).

Banco Nacional Ultramarino (commercial bank), Rua Augusta 24, 1111 Lisbon (tel: 346-9981; tx: 13-305).

Banco Pinto e Sotto Mayor (commercial bank), Rua do Ouro 28, 1100 Lisbon (tel: 347-6261).

Banco Português de Investimento, Largo Jean Monnet 1-9o, 1200 Lisbon (tel: 315-3819).

Banco Português do Atlantico SA, Rua do Ouro 110, 1100 Lisbon (tel: 346-1321).

Banco Totta & Açores SA (commercial bank), Rua do Ouro 88, 1100 Lisbon (tel: 346-9421; tx: 12-266).

Caixa Geral de Depósitos (savings bank), Largo do Calhariz, 1200 Lisbon (tel: 346-1981; tx: 12-621).

Credito Predial Português, Largo do Campo Grande 81/81-E, 1000 Lisbon (tel: 793-4024).

União de Bancos Portugueses (commercial bank), Avenida José Malhoa, Lt 1682, 1000 Lisbon (tel: 726-0561).

Travel information

Direcção Geral do Turismo (tourist board), Av. António Augusto Aguiar 86, 1099 Lisbon (tel: 575-162).

Comissao Municipal de Turismo de Lisboa, Pavilhao Carlos Lopes, Parque Eduardo VII, 1000 Lisbon (tel: 315-1736, 315-1915/6/7/8; fax: 352-1472).

Comissao Municipal de Turismo do Porto, Rua Clube dos Fenianos 25, 4000 Porto (tel: 323-303, 312-543; fax: 208-4548).

Dr Francisco Sá Carneiro Airport, 4470 Maia/Porto (tel: 941-2534, 948-2141).

Faro Airport, 8000 Faro (tel: 81-8582).

Lisbon Airport, 1700 Lisbon (tel: 849-4323)

Ministry of Trade and Tourism, Av da República 79, 1000 Lisbon (tel: 793-0412).

Palácio Foz, Praça dos Restauradores, 1200 Lisbon (tel: 346-3643, 342-5231).

Praça D Joao I 43, 4000 Porto (tel: 317-514).

Vilar Formoso (Fronteira), 6355 Vilar Formoso (tel: 52-202).

Other useful addresses

Agencia de Informação LUSA (news agency), Rua Dr João Couto, Lote C, 1500 Lisbon (tel: 714-4099).

Associação Industrial Portuguesa, Praça das Indústrias, 1399 Lisbon (tel: 639-044; tx: 12-282).

Associação Industrial Portuense, Avenida da Boavista 2611, 4100 Porto (tel: 672-257).

Bolsa de Valores de Lisboa (Lisbon stock exchange), Rua dos Fanqueiros 2-10, 1100 Lisbon (tel: 879-416/7; fax: 864-231).

British Hospital, Rua Saraiva de Carvalho 49, Lisbon (tel: 603-765).

British Institute in Portugal, Rua Luis Fernandes, Lisbon (tel: 369-208).

Confederação da Indústria Portuguesa (represents employers), Avenida 5 de Outubro 35, 1000 Lisbon (tel: 547-454).

Comissao Coordenaçao Regiao Norte, Rua Rainha D Estefania 251, 4100 Porto (tel: 695-236/7/8/9/0; fax: 600-2040).

CCR Algarve, Praça da Liberdade 2, 8000 Faro (tel: 802-401; fax: 803-591).

CCR Lisboa e Vale do Tejo, Rua Artilharia Um 33, 1250 Lisbon (tel: 387-5541; fax: 691-292).

Instituto de Apoio às Pequenas e Médias Empresas Industriais (IAPMEI), Rua Rodrigo da Fonseca 73, Lisbon (tel: 562-211; tx: 15-657).

Instituto do Comércio Externo de Portugal – ICEP, Avenida 5 de Outubro 101, 1000 Lisbon (tel: 730-103; tx: 16-498).

Instituto Nacional de Estatistica (INE), Av António José de Almeida 2, P-1078 Lisbon (tel: 847-0050; fax: 848-9480).

Ministry of Agriculture, Food and Fisheries, Praça do Comércio, 1100 Lisbon (tel: 346-3151; fax: 347-7890).

Ministry of Culture, Palácio Nacional da Ajuda, 1300 Lisbon (tel: 364-9867; fax: 364-9872).

Ministry of Defence, Avenida Ilha da Madeira, 1400 Lisbon (tel: 301-0001; fax: 301-5293).

Ministry of Economy, Rua da Horta Seca 15, 1200 Lisbon (tel: 346-3091; fax: 347-5901).

Ministry of Education, Avenida 5 de Outubro 107-13o, 1050 Lisbon (tel: 795-0330; fax: 793-3618).

Ministry for Employment, Praça de Londres 2-16o, 1000 Lisbon (tel: 847-0010; fax: 840-1112).

Ministry of the Environment, Rua do Século 51, 1200 Lisbon (tel: 346-2751; fax: 346-8469).

Ministry of Finance, Avenida Infante D Henrique 5, 1100 Lisbon (tel: 888-4675; fax: 886-0032).

Ministry of Foreign Affairs, Largo do Rilvas, 1350 Lisbon (tel: 396-5041; fax: 60-9708).

Ministry of Health, Avenida João Crisóstomo 9-6o, 1000 Lisbon (tel: 354-4560; fax: 314-0196).

Ministry of Home Affairs, Praça do Comércio, 1100 Lisbon (tel: 346-4521; fax: 342-7372).

Ministry of Industry and Energy, Rua da Horta Seca 15, 1200 Lisbon (tel: 346-3091/6091; fax: 347-5901).

Ministry of Justice, Praça do Comércio, 1100 Lisbon (347-4780; fax: 346-7692).

Ministry of Planning and Territorial Administration, Praça do Comércio, 1100 Lisbon (tel: 886-8441; fax: 886-5901).

Ministry of Public Works, Transport and Communication, Praça do Comércio, 1100 Lisbon (tel: 87-9541, 886-8441; fax: 886-7622, 87-1633).

Ministry of Science and Technology, Praça do Comércio - Ala Oriental, 1100 Lisbon (tel: 886-8441; fax: 887-4197).

Ministry of Social Security, Rua Rosa Araújo 43, 1250 Lisbon (tel: 353-0049; fax: 353-0085).

Ministry of Trade and Tourism, Avenida da República 79, 1000 Lisbon (tel: 793-4049, 793-4749).

Prime Minister's Office, Rua da Imprensa a Estrela 2, 1200 Lisbon (tel: 397-4091; fax: 395-1616).

Privatisation Office, c/o Ministério das Finanças – Commissão de Acompanhamento das Privatizacões (c/o Ministry of Finance – Commission for the Accompaniment of Privatisations), Av Infante D Henrique 5, 1100 Lisbon (tel: 618-0057).

Radiotelevisão Portuguesa – RTP (Portugal's radio/television braodcasting), 197 Avenida 5 de Outubro, 1000 Lisbon (tel: 793-1774; fax: 796-6227).

Sociedade Independente de Comunicação – SIC (independent broadcasting company), 119 Estrada da Outurela, Carnaxide, 2795 Linda a Velha (tel: 417-3138; fax: 417-3118).

Televisão Independente – TVI (independent television broadcasting), Pt16-s 603-B Rua 3, Matinha, 1900 Lisbon (tel: 858-7968; fax: 858-2319).

Romania

Marko Milivojevic

The November 1996 presidential election saw the defeat of one of eastern Europe's great survivors, as Ion Iliescu was defeated by Emil Constantinescu of the reinvigorated opposition Democratic Convention (DC). Iliescu's Party of Social Democracy in Romania (PSDR) was also defeated in the parliamentary elections to complete the removal of former communists. On the economic front Romania's prospects continue to improve; high, non-inflationary economic growth the principal characteristic of 1995.

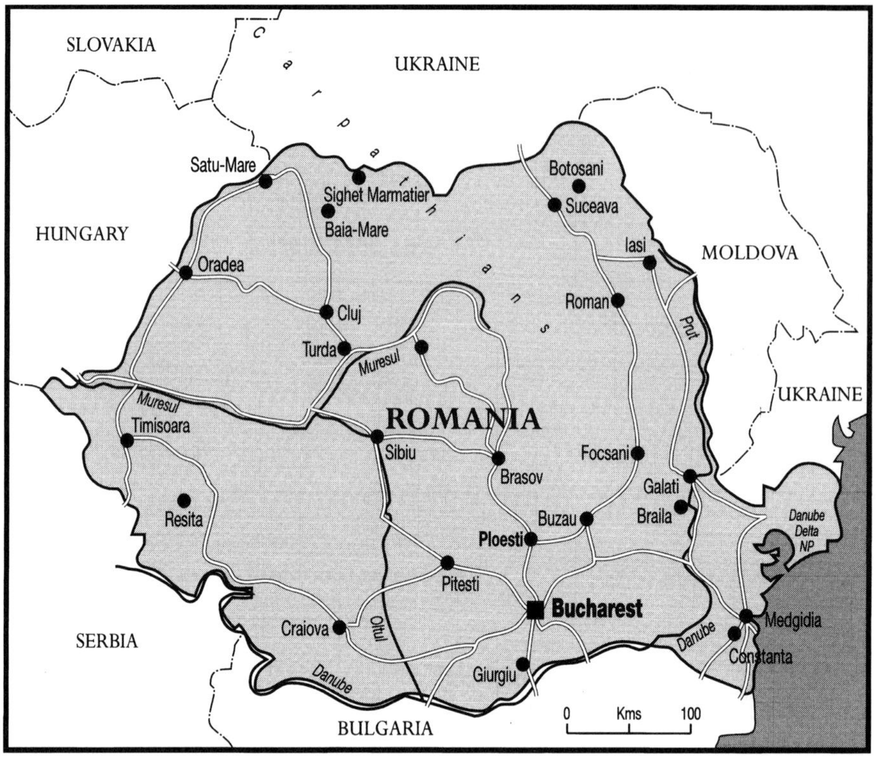

Elections

The defeat of Iliescu and the PSDR, and its peaceful acceptance, marked the end of a revolution that began seven years ago with the overthrow of Nicolae Ceausescu; it was also the first time Romanians had changed their head of state and government in free elections. The DC, a previously loose and ineffective coalition of anti-communist parties and civic groups, won 122 seats in the Chamber of Deputies compared to 91 for the PSDR. The DC formed a coalition with the Social Democratic Union (USD) and the Hungarian Democratic Union in Romania (UDMR) to gain a total of 200 seats in the 343 seat lower chamber. The three-party coalition also has a majority in the Senate. A leading figure in the DC's main party the National Peasant Christian Democratic Party (PNTCD), and the mayor of Bucharest, Victor Ciorbea, was appointed prime minister.

Even a few months before the election Iliescu and the PSDR were predicted to win the elections comfortably, but their authoritarian tendencies, resistance to reform and corruption within the party combined with a more professional and effective campaign by the DC than in 1992, all played vital roles in their downfall. The PSDR and Iliescu failed to benefit from the economic upturn of 1995 and 1996, mainly due to their failure to initiate more radical structural reforms.

Economic performance

Romania achieved high and non-inflationary economic growth in 1995, with most new demand largely domestically sourced. Although there are still some doubts about their reliability, official Romanian government figures claimed that GDP increased by nearly 7 per cent in 1995, compared to 3.5 per cent in 1994. This is almost certainly an over-estimate, with real GDP growth in 1995 probably around 5 per cent. GDP in 1995 was thus around US$27.5 billion, with a GDP per capita of around US$1,250. In 1996, GDP was expected to grow by a further 4 per cent.

On the employment front, higher job creation in the private sector resulted in another fall in unemployment in 1995; the number of people officially out of work was 9.2 per cent of the employed workforce, compared to 10 per cent in 1994. In the longer term, however, more radical structural reform of the state industrial sector will almost certainly lead to higher unemployment. Up by 15.3 per cent in 1994, new fixed investment officially increased by a record 25 per cent in 1995. Real wages increased by a record 17 per cent in 1995 compared with 1994.

An increasing proportion of this improved economic performance came from the booming private sector, accounting for about 50 per cent of GDP in 1996. Representing around 35 per cent of GDP, industrial output also increased by a record 10 per cent in 1995, compared to 3.3 per cent in 1994. As in 1994, particularly high growth took place in light manufacturing and consumer goods. In 1995, 20.1 per cent of industrial output was exported, compared to 18.6 per cent in 1994. Even more significantly, private sector industrial output increased to 16 per cent of the total in 1995, compared to 12 per cent in 1994. Concentrated in the declining state industrial sector, capital goods production continued to decline in 1995, albeit at a lesser rate than in 1994.

Energy

Domestic oil production stabilised at 6.7 million tonnes in 1995, about the same as in 1994. Gas production, at 19.3 billion cubic metres in 1995, fell slightly compared to 1994's output of 19.6 billion cubic metres. Oil and gas imports remained substantial at 8.36 million tonnes and 6.63 billion cubic metres respectively in 1995. In the longer term, dependency on expensive imported energy may be reduced by new oil-gas fields onshore and offshore in the Black Sea.

Romania's considerable oil and gas production potential is of growing interest to foreign energy companies, of which Shell alone has so far invested US$55 million, with a further US$42 million due to be provided in 1996-97. Regionally, the suspension of UN economic sanctions against Serbia in December 1995 and their final removal in October 1996 was expected to particularly benefit Romania's energy sector in 1997

Agriculture

Overwhelmingly concentrated in the private sector by 1995, when it accounted for around 25 per cent of GDP, agricultural output grew by 4 per cent in both 1994 and 1995. The 1995 cereal harvest of 19.3 million tonnes (mt) was the largest since before the Second World War. As well as providing a major boost for local food processing, this growing agricultural output is yielding a greater surplus for export. In 1996, this may reach as much as five mt of cereals. Consequently, Romania could once again become a major exporter of foodstuffs.

Structural reform of the agricultural sector remains inadequate, particularly the creation of a proper market in land. Here the major issues are lack of legal title to newly decollectivised land and, as a result, low investment in the agricultural and food

KEY FACTS

Official title: Republic of Romania

Head of state: President Emil Constantinescu (elected Nov 1996)

Head of government: Prime Minister Victor Ciorbea (from 19 Nov 1996)

Ruling party: Coalition led by Democratic Convention of Romania (CDR) (centre-right; a loose coalition; the National Peasants' Party is the mainstay of the CDR) and including Social Democratic Union (USD), a centrist group, and the ethnic Hungarian's Party (from Dec 1996)

Capital: Bucharest

Official Languages: Romanian

Currency: Leu (plural Lei) = 100 bani

Exchange rate: Lei 4,025 per US$ (Dec 1996)

Area: 237,500 sq km

Population: 23.2m (1995)

GDP per capita: US$1,250 (1995)*

GDP real growth: 5% (1995)*

GNP per capita: US$1,170 (1994)

GNP real growth: 3% (1995)*

Labour force: 6.1m (1994)

Unemployment: 9.3% (end-Feb 1996)

Inflation: 45% (Nov 1996, annual)

Oil reserves: 1.6bn barrels (end-1995)

Trade balance: -US$1.2bn (1995)

Foreign debt: US$7bn (30 Sep 1996)

* estimated figure

KEY INDICATORS — Romania

	Unit	1991	1992	1993	1994	1995
Population	m	23.19	22.79	22.76	22.71	23.20
Gross domestic product (GDP)	US$bn	40.0	35.0	27.3	26.0	*27.5
GDP per capita	US$	1,750	1,500	1,200	1,200	*1,250
GDP real growth	%	-12.9	-8.8	1.5	3.5	*5.0
Inflation	%	174.5	210.9	257.0	136.1	35.0
Employment	'000	7,574	6,888	6,672	6,133	5,884
Consumer prices	1990=100	274.4	854.0	3,033.1	7,181.2	9,496.6
Unemployment	%	3.5	6.2	9.2	10.0	9.2
Agricultural output	%	1.0	1.0	2.0	4.0	4.0
Industrial output	%	-20.0	-10.0	-10.4	3.3	10.0
Agricultural production	1979-81=100	90.62	74.53	90.04	97.90	99.12
Industrial production	1990=100	77.0	60.3	58.0	59.8	65.4
Manufacturing	1990=100	76.4	57.8	54.0	56.0	62.8
Mining	1990=100	81.7	79.8	82.0	83.4	82.9
Coal	'000 tonnes	32,414	38,316	39,696	40,533	41,128
Crude steel	'000 tonnes	7,130	5,376	5,446	5,793	6,555
Cement	'000 tonnes	7,405	6,946	6,837	6,676	7,562
Crude petroleum	'000 tonnes	6,792	6,615	6,673	6,693	6,712
Natural gas	m cu metres	24,807	22,138	21,309	19,590	19,012
Exports	US$bn	4.3	4.4	4.9	6.1	7.5
Imports	US$bn	5.4	5.8	6.0	6.6	8.7
Balance of trade	US$bn	-1.1	-1.4	-1.1	-0.4	-1.2
Current account	US$bn	-1.0	-1.5	-1.2	-0.4	-1.4
Foreign debt	US$bn	2.2	3.5	4.5	5.5	6.3
Total reserves minus gold	US$m	695	826	995	2,086	1,499
Foreign exchange	US$m	637	815	994	2,031	–
Discount rate	%	18	70	70	58	40
Exchange rate	lei per US$	76.39	307.95	760.05	1,655.09	2,044.00

* estimated figure

processing sector. Land remains politically contentious in Romania, where the PSDR government is also under intense pressure from the International Monetary Fund (IMF) and the World Bank to fully liberalise the country's agricultural sector, notably through the break-up of the Romceral grain monopoly. Given its considerable potential, Romanian agriculture and food processing is of growing interest to foreign investors.

Services

Economically dominant at around 40 per cent of GDP in 1994 and 1995, privately owned services continue to experience rapid growth. Retail and wholesale trade in particular grew by a record 25 per cent in 1995 over 1994. Largely based on increased domestic demand for consumer goods, this trend is expected to continue in 1997. By the late 1990s, services of all types are expected to account for over 50 per cent of GDP in Romania. Other fast growing service sectors include construction, boosted by large-scale infrastructure developments.

Involving projected outlays of over US$2 billion for new motorways alone over the next five to 10 years, local infrastructure development has been delayed by foreign funding difficulties, but these began to be resolved in 1995, beginning with a Ecu390 million (US$593 million) loan from the European Union's (EU) European Investment Bank for local transport and power sector development. In the longer term, Romania also has considerable potential for tourism, although its full realisation is dependent on increased investment in local facilities and related transportation infrastructure.

Financial stabilisation

Down from 257 per cent in 1993 to 136 per cent in 1994, Romania's inflation rate in 1995 was relatively low at 35 per cent. Based on a restrictive monetary-credit policy by the National Bank of Romania (NBR), this macro-economic stabilisation continued in 1996. One of a number of key targets agreed with the IMF in December 1995 – when the Fund finally authorised the disbursement of the delayed second tranche of an earlier stand-by agreement originally signed in May 1994 but suspended because of the slow pace of economic reform – lower inflation is now attainable for the first time in the 1990s. A further IMF stand-by loan worth SDR75.4 million was also released in December 1995.

The rapprochement with the IMF opened up further funding, notably US$400 million from the World Bank in 1996, beginning with the first tranche of a US$250 million Financial and Enterprise Sector Adjustment Credit (FESAC). Following these agreements with the IMF and the World Bank, which will last until April 1997 in the case of the Fund, Romania will find new foreign borrowing less difficult than in the past.

Budget deficit

The government budget deficit in 1995 was higher than expected at around 5 per cent of GDP, compared to 4.2 per cent in 1994. In September 1995, the government revised its year-end deficit target upwards from Lei1.9 trillion to Lei2.9 trillion, mainly because of expenditure over-shoots and lower than expected tax revenues. Finally agreed in February 1996, the government budget for that year envisaged expenditures of Lei20.4 trillion and revenues of Lei17 trillion, with the resultant deficit amounting to 2.9 per cent of officially projected GDP.

Under the terms of the recent agreement with the IMF, the government budget deficit for 1996 should be no more than 2.2 per cent of projected GDP for that year. If this key target is to be met, then expenditures will have to be cut in real terms, which may be politically difficult. At the same time, the government is hoping to boost tax revenues through more indirect taxation. In the longer term, government expenditures and revenues will have to be reduced as a proportion of GDP. In 1995, these amounted to 50 per cent of officially recorded GDP. Economically, this has tended to impede the development of the private sector, particularly as regards punitive levels of taxation.

Leu

Having slightly appreciated against the US dollar and the Deutsche Mark in 1994/95, the leu went into free-fall during the second half of 1995, mainly due to the uncertainty surrounding the country's worsening balance of payments, growing demand for hard currency to fund booming imports and the widening gap between the official and unofficial or market exchange rates.

In November 1995, the NBR introduced a number of emergency measures to stem the depreciation of the leu. These included a 10 per cent devaluation, tighter monetary controls, higher interest rates, stricter minimum reserve requirements for local commercial banks and restrictions on the availability of hard currency loans to non-governmental borrowers domestically.

In March 1996, by which time the exchange rate was Lei3,070 to US$ compared to Lei2,044 at year-end 1996, the NBR imposed restrictions on the country's interbank market for hard currency transactions. Formally made up of 22 commercial banks, including some foreign banks, this interbank market was also reduced to four market-makers, all of them local. This interventionism may lead to complications with the IMF, and could also result in an exchange rate fixing by the NBR.

Banking and reserves

The collapse of investor confidence in the leu was also the product of a series of serious banking scandals in 1995. Foremost among these was a run on the Cluj-based Banca Dacia Felix. Still poorly regulated by the NBR, the Romanian commercial banking sector also has other factors against it, notably a high level of non-performing assets in the financially weak state industrial sector.

So far, commercial bank recapitalisation has made little progress. In 1996/97, the World Bank's FESAC is expected to play a major role in this long-delayed process. In 1994/95, the growing strength of the leu resulted in higher savings locally but this trend was reversed in 1995/96.

The currency's obvious weaknesses, doubts about the integrity of local banks and higher demand for hard currency all resulted in lower domestic savings as investors moved out of leu-denominated assets. The major result of this was a decline in hard currency reserves. Year-end in 1995, these had fallen to below US$1.5 billion, compared to over US$2 billion at the end of 1994. By September 1995, NBR hard currency reserves fell to only US$320 million, although they later rose to US$700 million year-end, mainly due to major new foreign loans from the IMF and the World Bank. In 1996, the NBR was authorised to borrow up to US$1 billion abroad to top its reserves.

Privatisation

Although economically dominant in agriculture and food processing and services by 1995, Romania's private sector only accounted for 16 per cent of industrial production. The slowness of the government's so-called Mass Privatisation Programme (MPP) is partly to blame. By mid-1995, the State Ownership Fund (SOF) had only privatised 1,000 mainly small-to-medium-sized enterprises out of a total of 6,000 industrial and other companies slated for privatisation.

Introduced in August 1994 to give a major boost to the large-scale privatisation process, the second stage of the MPP is supposed to involve the disposal of around 3,000 enterprises (50 per cent of the total) through a voucher-based disposal programme that should have been largely completed in 1995. In the event, SOF ineptitude and popular apathy meant that less than 10 per cent of voucher holders had exchanged their Lei975,000 (US$350) coupons by the end of 1995. Exchangeable for company shares at nationwide subscription centres or investable in one of five Private Ownership Funds (POF), these coupons are widely regarded as worthless by most of the 17 million Romanian citizens they were distributed to in 1995.

As things stand, full voucher exchange looked unlikely to be completed much before the end of 1996, with most newly acquired equity likely to be placed with the POFs. Unlike other privatisation programmes in the region, the MPP disallows privatisation investment funds and hence secondary share trading, although this could change if the government allows the POFs to become investment companies.

According to its many critics, the MPP is a sham based on purely nominal ownership transformation of often technically insolvent state industrial enterprises that are in any event impossible to value. Here the major issue is the continued lack of effective bankruptcy procedures in Romania. The SOF, a body entirely controlled by PSDR nominees, has also been weakened by endless in-fighting and resignations over the modalities and pace of Romanian privatisation.

The FESAC from the World Bank has specific targets pertaining to local privatisation. In this context, the second and third tranches of the FESAC are only to be disbursed when the second stage of the MPP is completed, probably at the end of 1996 or in 1997. The SOF will still retain control over vast sections of the economy outside the present remit of the MPP.

Structurally, probably the best that can be hoped for is that the MPP will introduce more radical corporate restructuring in the run-up to full privatisation of the state industrial enterprises concerned. Also covered by the recent FESAC agreement, enterprise restructuring is focused on 151 large industrial enterprises placed under a special government rehabilitation programme in 1994. Among these companies are the country's 40 largest loss-makers. Over the next two years, 50 of these loss-makers must leave this programme fully rehabilitated or formally liquidated. Other FESAC conditions include the recapitalisation and eventual privatisation of the Romanian Development Bank, which is a major creditor of the state industrial sector.

Foreign investment

Largely confined to the booming private sector in 1995, new investment remains highly troublesome for large loss-makers in the state sector. As presently constituted, the MPP cannot in itself recapitalise the country's ageing industrial base. Here the great hope of the government is increased foreign direct investment (FDI) through foreign investor involvement in the MPP. Expected to increase substantially in 1995, total FDI by the end of that year was only between US$1.6 billion and US$1.8 billion, compared to around US$1.2 billion at the end of 1994.

At only between US$400-600 million in 1995, new FDI was below 2 per cent of GDP, compared to over 4 per cent for similar foreign capital inflows into various Visegrad Group countries in the same year. Following the IMF and World Bank agreements, and with new tax incentives and higher economic growth, FDI could substantially increase. Sectorally, automotive products, energy, agriculture and

COUNTRY PROFILE — ROMANIA

Political system

President Ion Iliescu was elected by direct vote (May 1990 and re-elected September 1992). Following the popular referendum of 8 December 1991, a new constitution was adopted, which indicates that in the event of the incompatibility of the constitution with internationally recognised principles, the internationally recognised principle is to prevail. Two-house parliament (Senate and House of Representatives) elected for two years. The country is divided into 41 counties and Bucharest municipality. Each county, town and village has its own local authority headed by an elected, executive mayor and an elected council.

Political parties

The Greater Romania Party (PRM) merged on 6 September 1996 with the small non-parliamentary Romanian Party for a New Society (PRNS).

Population

The government estimated that the population declined in 1993 by 0.3 per cent. Population growth rate 0.09 per cent (1995 estimate). Life expectancy 72.24 years (1995 estimate). Ethnic composition: Romanian (89.1%), Hungarian (8.9%), German (0.4%), Ukrainian, Serb, Croat, Russian, Turk and Gypsy (1.6%). Religions: Romanian Orthodox (70%), Roman Catholic (6%, of which 3% are Uniate), Protestant (6%), unaffiliated (18%).

Main cities/towns

Bucharest, capital (population 2.2m in 1994), Constanta (350,476), Iasi (342,994), Timisoara (334,278), Cluj-Napoca (328,008), Galati (325,788), Brasov (323,8350, Craiova (303,520).

Language

Romanian is the official language. Hungarian, German and French are the other main languages.

Media

Press: There was an explosion of publications of all political colour following the fall of the Ceausescu regime. Highly regionalised. Several publications being produced in minority languages such as Hungarian, German and Serbian. Newspapers are independent, governmental or published by a political party.
Dailies: The most important independent national dailies are *Evenimental Zitei, Adevarul, Tineretul Liber, Liberatea (Ringier)* and *Romania Libera*. The *Allgemeine Zeitung für Rumänien*, the only regional German newspaper, was launched in February 1993. It is published five times per week.
Business: Economistul is published twice-weekly, *Mesagerful Economic*, weekly, and *Romanian Insight* monthly, both published by Chamber of Commerce and Industry, *Tribuna Economica*, weekly.
Periodicals: Many special interest and business publications, mostly produced by independent companies.
Broadcasting: Radioteleviziunea Romana (Romanian Radio & Television).
Radio: Three domestic channels operated by Radiodifuziunea Romana, plus foreign broadcasts in 13 languages.
Television: Service is centred in Bucharest, with daily broadcasts operated by Televiziunea Romana. Channel 2, the first commercial television network in a former Communist state, is a joint venture between Romanian state television (RTV1) and Atlantic Television of the UK. Pro TV, the first national commercial television service in Romania, was launched by Central European Media Enterprises 1 December 1995.

Advertising

Advertisements can be placed through State Public Relations Agency (PUBLICOM), in Bucharest, on TV or radio.

Domestic economy

Formerly centralised economy with large state-owned heavy industry enterprises. Legislation in force has turned them into independent commercial companies. Reprivatisation of agricultural land carried out in spring 1991. The government's reform programme aimed at rapid transition to a market economy. However, by 1993, Romania was in severe recession. In May 1993 the final subsidies on certain essential goods and services were removed, thus completing the government's programme of price liberalisation. Romania experienced the beginnings of recovery and stabilisation in 1994. Most of the economic growth was in the growing private sector which accounted for 35 per cent of GDP in 1994.
Food supplies are adequate but expensive and there are frequent disruptions of heating and water services in the capital. The slow and painful process of conversion to a more open economy continues in 1996.

Employment

Faster new job creation in the private sector resulted in a slight fall in unemployment in 1994.

External trade

Foreign trade carried out by state enterprises, mostly through foreign trade organisations or private companies. Equipment, machinery and means of transportation included as part of the capital participation of the foreign investor, are exempt from import customs duties. All imports and exports subject to licensing. In the 1980s trade was mainly with other eastern European countries, especially the former USSR, but with the end of the Ceausescu regime, trade with the west began to open up. In December 1992 the EFTA countries signed free trade agreements with Romania. In February 1993, Romania signed its association accord with the EU. The rise in the export of industrial products helped to cut the country's trade deficit in 1994 to

food processing, consumer goods and services are of the greatest to foreign investors in Romania. Daewoo of South Korea is the largest single investor, having purchased a 51 per cent stake in Rodae Automobile for US$156 million, and a 51 per cent share of the 2 Mai shipyard for US$53 million with further investment expected. Germany, Italy and France are the next largest investors.

Foreign trade

Romania's terms of foreign trade and balance of payments deteriorated alarmingly in 1995. Although exports reached US$7.5 billion in 1995, compared to US$6.1 billion in 1994, they were far exceeded by imports of US$8.7 billion, compared to US$6.6 billion in 1994. Fuelled by the higher economic growth of 1995 and the appreciation of the leu during the first half of that year, the result of this import boom was a record US$1.2 billion trade deficit year-end. Lower than expected foreign borrowings and service income combined with increased foreign debt servicing charges to produce a record US$1.4 billion current account deficit in 1995.

Previously strongly orientated towards higher value capital goods sold or bartered in mainly non-EU markets such as the former Soviet Union, Romanian exports have become dominated by lower value goods such as textiles, which accounted for 25 per cent of all overseas sales in 1994/95. Semi-processed goods such as basic metals, minerals and base chemicals have also become more important export categories in recent years, as have foodstuffs.

Romania remains dependent on imports of higher value manufactured capital and consumer goods, many of which are essential. Import dependency on oil and gas is also high. In 1995, imports of consumer goods and even exotic foodstuffs increased rapidly. The result of this in relation to the EU was large and increasing trade deficits. In the EU, Romania only has competitive advantages in areas like textiles based on low capital inputs and labour costs.

Outside the EU, Romania continues to maintain significant levels of trade with Russia, which was the country's second largest foreign trading partner in 1995. Regionally, other important trading partners include Hungary, Serbia and Turkey. Following the removal of the UN economic sanctions against Serbia, Serbian-Romanian trade is expected to revive rapidly in 1997. During the 1990s, Romania claimed losses in excess of US$2 billion in relation to the UN trade embargoes against Iraq and then Serbia.

Regionally, Romania is anxious to develop closer economic co-operation with all its Balkan neighbours. Black Sea littoral state co-operation is another high priority area for Romania. Once a major concern for Romania, Moldova is now of less interest, mainly because of its own economic difficulties and the growing Russian influence in an area that was once part of Romania. Romania's economic relations with Ukraine are also stagnating, mainly because of payments issues and a territorial dispute over Serpent Island in the Black Sea.

Foreign debt and payments

A direct result of its difficulties with the IMF and the World Bank in 1994/95, Romania's new foreign borrowings in that year were limited. At the end of 1995, total

COUNTRY PROFILE — ROMANIA

External trade (contd): about a third of the 1993 level.
Exports: Exports totalled US$7.5bn in 1995. Main exports include metals and metal products (17.6% of 1994 total), mineral products (11.9%), textiles (18.5%), electric machines and euqipment (8.4%), transport materials (6.5%). Main destinations are EU (typically 36% of total), developing countries (27%), east and central Europe (15%), EFTA (5%), Russia (5%), Japan (1%), USA (1%).
Imports: Imports totalled US$8.7bn in 1995. Main imports include minerals (21.1% of 1994 total), machinery and equipment (19.7%), textiles (11.5%), agricultural goods (9.2%). Main sources are Germany (typically 16% of total), Russia (14%), Italy (9%), Thailand (4%), Turkey (3%), China (2%), Greece.

Agriculture

The agriculture sector accounted for about 35 per cent of GDP in 1995 and employed 21.6 per cent of the workforce.
Romania is central Europe's most important agricultural producer after Poland. Agricultural land area is 147,900 sq km, of which 94,100 sq km is arable. Approximately 72 per cent of agricultural land was socialised under the former Soviet Union, either into co-operatives or state enterprises. There is a government privatisation plan.
Large-scale irrigation programme under way and farmland is being developed in Danube delta. Important agricultural produce includes grapes (leading European producer), corn, wheat, maize, rye, sugar-beet, oilseed, potatoes, plums, apples and meat. Agriculture is severely dislocated by the transition to a market economy. As a result of an output growth of 4 per cent in 1994, Romania was able to resume grain exports for the first time in the post-communist period. Agricultural output in 1995 again grew by 4 per cent.
Total grain production was a record 19.3m tonnes in 1995 (including 7.8m tonnes of wheat). Because of a harsh winter, Romania had expected to harvest about 6m tonnes of wheat in 1996. Late spring snows followed by floods and heavy rain, however, have changed predictions to between 3m and 3.3m tonnes.

Industry

The industrial sector contributed 35 per cent of GDP in 1995. It employs 32 per cent of the workforce and accounts for 90 per cent of exports. Production is state-owned and largely export-oriented. The petro-chemical industry provides one-third of the country's total industrial resources. Main industries include metallurgy, chemicals, motor vehicles, machine building, food processing, petroleum products and timber processing.
According to the 1992-2000 strategy plan, the government will provide funds to restructure its industry.
Exports of refined oil products, mainly to neighbouring eastern European states, are a major source of Romanian hard currency earnings, accounting for over 30 per cent of exports.
Industrial output increased by 10 per cent in 1995, with high growth recorded in light manufacturing and consumer goods.

Mining

The mining and hydrocarbons sector accounted for 13 per cent of GNP in 1994 and employed 8 per cent of the workforce. Mineral deposits include salt, lignite, iron ore, bauxite, manganese and smaller quantities of gold, zinc, uranium, tin and copper. In recent years, considerable problems in mining sector as deposits declined so became increasingly difficult to provide industry with raw materials. However, Romania finds it increasingly worthwhile to exploit domestic resources instead of relying on imports, even if initial cost is high.
After the country's only zinc smelter was upgraded and restructured, the January-November 1995 zinc output increased to 26,000 tonnes; total output was 18,520 tonnes in 1994.

Hydrocarbons

Oil reserves 1.6bn barrels (end-1995). Oil production 140,000 barrels per day (bpd) in 1995, down 0.4 per cent on 1994 output.
Romania has ten oil refineries with a total capacity of 740,000 bpd, with a high conversion rate of more than 30 per cent. Crude oil imports obtained principally from OPEC countries and paid for either with hard currency or on the basis of counter-trade deals involving Romanian exports of machinery and equipment. Imports of crude from Russia are continuing, at a reduced rate (about 100,000 bpd).
Natural gas reserves 13 trillion cu feet (end-1995). Natural gas production 15.3m tonnes oil equivalent in 1995, down 2.5 per cent on 1994 output.
Coal production 7.7m tonnes oil equivalent in 1995, up 1.3 per cent on 1994 output. Shell Gas Romania venture plans to invest US$30m 1995-98 in developing the Romanian petroleum and liquefied gas market.

Energy

Significant domestic production of oil, gas and coal. Gas is the most important domestic fuel resource, though output is now declining. Also rapid development of hydroelectricity and nuclear power. Winter energy rationing in effect.
First nuclear power plant opened end-1994 near Cernavoda in northern Dobroudja; capacity 706.5 MW.
In September 1995 the World Bank approved a US$110m loan for the updating of the Romanian national electric energy supplier Renel.

Banking

Two-tier banking system. Former state-owned banks are being privatised. Commercial banks in operation in Romania are expanding to include those with private and foreign capital. There are also a number of branches of foreign banks operating.

foreign debt reached only US$6.3 billion, compared to US$5.5 billion at the end of 1994. In 1993/94, on the other hand, new foreign borrowings exceeded US$1 billion. Following the IMF and World Bank agreements, Romania's foreign debt could exceed US$8 billion by the end of 1996. In the longer term, such projected foreign debt growth may not be sustainable.

Mainly provided by official multilateral and governmental creditors in the past, future new foreign borrowings are expected to be increasingly sourced in private sector Euromarkets, where a US$150 million syndicated commercial bank loan for the NBR was over-subscribed in 1995. Romania obtained sub-investment country rating in the 'B' range from a number of foreign credit rating agencies in March 1996.

Euromarket and Eurobond capital inflows to Romania will remain confined to the NBR and other governmental entities. So far, other portfolio investments from abroad have been relatively limited, mainly because of doubts about the integrity of some of its commercial banks.

Itself a major creditor to various Middle Eastern countries during the 1980s, Romania was owed a total of US$2.6 billion at the end of 1994. Mostly tied up in Iraq, little of this money is likely to be repaid other than in the form of oil and then only after the current UN economic sanctions against Baghdad are lifted. Romania also has large outstanding claims against Russia, Moldova and Ukraine. Romania has also claimed substantial compensation from the UN for its observance of its economic sanctions against former Yugoslav. None of its claims have ever been seriously considered, let alone paid.

Outlook

Six years after the fall of its particularly damaging form of communism, Romania's political and economic prospects are significantly better than at any time during the 1990s, although a number of major issues and potential dangers remain. The election of Constantinescu and the DC should improve Romania's standing internationally, although full EU membership is unlikely until well past 2000. Part of a wider issue in the Balkans, this may reinforce a tendency already well developed in the EU to relegate countries like Romania to second division status in Europe. Macro-economic stabilisation continues to make good progress, economic growth is high and investment is also increasing. The next key step for Romania's transformation is large-scale privatisation and restructuring of the state industrial sector; whether or not the DC Government is prepared to take these painful steps which may affect its new found electoral popularity remains to be seen.

Externally, IMF and World Bank conditionality are directly connected to the all-important privatisation issue. Given Romania's continued dependence on official financing, this may force the pace of socio-economic change. Another positive trend is the growing economic integration of Romania's foreign trade with the EU.

On a more negative note, the lack of radical change in Romania means that it will continue to lag behind other central and eastern European countries. Relative to GDP, FDI also remains low. The country's foreign trade and balance of payments remain precarious. Foreign debt, however, remains relatively low. The full realisation of Romania's considerable economic potential remains some way off, with 1997 likely to prove a critical turning point for the country on this and other scores.

COUNTRY PROFILE — ROMANIA

Stock exchange

The Romanian Stock Exchange re-opened officially on 20 June 1995 after a gap of 50 years. On 8 May 1995 the Constanta Maritime and Commodities Exchange was admitted to the London Baltic Exchange as a member.

Legal system

Mixture of civil law system and legal theory.

Membership of international organisations

ALADI (observer), BSECP, CCC, Council of Europe, EBRD, EU (associate member from 1993), FAO, G77, IAEA, ICAO, ICJ, IFAD, IFC, ILO, IMF, IMO, INTERPOL, IPU, ITC, ITU, NACC, NAM (guest), OSCE, Partnership for Peace), UN, UNESCO, UPU, WEU (associate partner), WFTU, WHO, WIPO, WMO, World Bank, WTO. Free trade agreement with EFTA from 1 May 1993. Romania formally applied for EU membership on 22 June 1995; also wishes to join NATO.

BUSINESS GUIDE

Time

GMT + 2 hrs (GMT + 3 hrs from late Mar to late Sep).

Climate

Temperate – continental with long hot summers and cold winters; average temperature varies between -2°C and 22°C. Frosty with a good deal of ice and snow in winter.

Clothing

Mediumweight plus heavy topcoat and overshoes for winter. In principal hotels and most government offices heating adequate. Lightweight and light raincoat for summer.

Entry requirements

Passport: Passport required by all.
Visa: Visa is required for a stay of maximum 30 days and can be issued on arrival to passengers travelling for business purposes for a fee of US$30, and to tourists for a fee of US$15. Passengers must show tickets for onward/return journey, relevant documents for onward destinations and sufficient funds (approximately US$50 per day of stay) (June 1996).
Health: Vaccination certificates not normally required but typhoid inoculation advisable. The water is safe to drink. Emergency rooms in hospitals provide free first aid, but charge for all other medical services.
Currency: No restrictions on movement of foreign currency. Declaration required. Export of foreign currency within the limits of the declaration given, less the amounts exchanged or spent.
Import of national currency is not allowed. No refund of currency is possible. Export of up to Lei 5,000 is allowed.
Customs: Strict inspection of luggage on arrival and departure. Personal effects duty-free. No limit on amount of alcohol and tobacco taken in, provided it is for visitor's own consumption.

Air access

National airline: TAROM Romanian Air Transport.
Other airlines: Acrila Air, Aeroflot, Air France, Air Moldava, Alitalia, Austrian Airlines, British Airways, Czech Airlines (CSA), Delta, El Al, Hemus Air, Iberia, JAT, Lufthansa, Malev, Swissair, Syrian Arab Airlines, Turkish Airlines.
Main international airport: Bucharest served by Otopeni (OTP) 16 km north of capital and Baneasa (BBU) 9 km north of the centre of the capital. Otopeni airport is in the process of being modernised.

Surface access

Good rail connections with all neighbouring countries. Road links with Moldova, Ukraine, Hungary, Yugoslavia and Bulgaria, and from west Europe via Vienna and Budapest.
Main ports: Constanta, Sulina and Mangalia on the Black Sea; Tulcea, Galati, Braila, Calarasi, Giurgiu and Turnu–Drobeta–Severin on the Danube; Cernavoda, Medgidia and Basarabi on the Danube–Black Sea canal.

Hotels

Classified as de luxe, A and B. Accommodation outside Bucharest is generally cheaper. Advisable to purchase pre-paid vouchers for accommodation through travel agents, as a confirmed reservation, if not pre-paid, is not a guarantee of accommodation.

Restaurants

Main meals at hotels or at few Bucharest restaurants of similar standard. Tax on bills – sometimes called service charge – is not paid to staff; optional tip 10 per cent.

Credit cards

Credit cards not widely used but are accepted in most major hotels. American Express, Visa and Eurocard preferred.

Car hire

Self-drive and chauffeur-driven cars available through National Tourist Office (ONT). Petrol is obtained in exchange for coupons available from ONT, hotels or the Romanian Automobile Club. International or national driving licence required. Traffic drives on the right.

City transport

Bus and metro not recommended for transfer from airport to city.
Taxis: Taxis available and can be hailed in the street; a 10 per cent tip is usual. Take a metered taxi, or negotiate a price. To call for a taxi dial 953 or 941. Fare from airport to city approximately US$15 (June 1996).
Buses: Tickets may be bought in yellow-painted

City transport (contd): booths, or in some hotels. Tickets should be punched immediately upon entering a vehicle. Bus 783 from Otopeni Airport to Piata Uniriii every 30 minutes.
Metro: Limited metro service.

National transport

Air: Relatively cheap services operated by TAROM connecting Bucharest with Arad, Bacau, Baia Mare, Caransebes, Cluj–Napoca, Constanta, Craiova, Iasi, Oradea, Satu Mare, Suceava, Sibiu, Timisoara, Deva, Tirgu Mures and Tulcea. Charter service available from LAR.
Road: There are 72,816 km of public roads of various standards. Main cities connected by good roads. An US$80m loan was granted by the European Bank for Reconstruction and Development in April 1993 to improve the condition of Romania's roads. In July 1995 the government announced plans to build 3,000 km of new highways over the next 10 years, at a cost of US$10bn.
Buses: Local services to most towns and villages. Bus service not widely used.
Rail: Efficient service between principal towns operated by Caile Ferate Romane (CFR). 11,348 km of track of which 3,680 km are electrified. All long-distance trains are provided with sleeping cars. In December 1992 Romania, Hungary and Turkey signed the Trust Fund agreement for the Trans-European Railway (TER) Project.
Water: The volume of freight transported by water increased with the opening of 64.2 km canal link between Danube and Black Sea.

Public holidays

Fixed dates: 1 and 2 Jan (New Year), 1 May (May Day), 1 Dec (National Day), 25 and 26 Dec (Christmas).
Variable date: Orthodox Easter Monday.

Working hours

Government and business: (Mon–Fri) 0800 – 1700, lunch usually 1230 – 1300.
Banking: (Mon–Fri) 0900–1200 and 1300–1500. Creditbank, Bucharest Otopeni airport, open 1000–1800 daily.

Social customs

Accepting hospitality from and giving social invitations to officials is normal. Such entertainment usually takes place in restaurants and hotels. Business dress code is usually informal. Punctuality is strictly observed. Smoking is prohibited on public transport, in cinemas and theatres. However, many Romanians smoke, and gifts of cigarettes from Western Europe are appreciated.

Business language and interpreting/translation

Available from National Tourist Office.

Telecommunications

Telephone and telefax: There are public, coin-operated phones in the downtown area of Bucharest. Newer phones allowing local and inter-city calls have been installed along the main avenues. International calls can be made from main hotels, the train station, and the phone company building on Calea Victoriei. Dialling code for Romania: IDD access code + 40 followed by area code (1 for Bucharest, 21 for Brasov, 16 for Constanta, 61 for Timisoara), followed by subscriber's number. For calling from Bucharest to any destination inside Romania, dial 'O' before actual number.
For international calls from Romania dial 971; for long-distance calls 991.
Telex and telegram: Available from main hotels and post offices. Telex country code 65 R. To send telegram, dial 957.
Postal services: International deliveries should be sent by airmail to avoid delays. There are post offices in every part of Bucharest. The main post office is at 10 Matei Millo Street (near the phone company building on Calea Victoriei) and is open from 0730 – 1930.

Banking

Central bank: National Bank of Romania.
Main commercial bank: Banca Comerciala Romania.
Other banks: Anglo-Romanian Bank, Banca Agricola (agricultural bank), Banca Romana de Comert Exterior (foreign trade bank), Banca Romana de Dezvoltare (development bank), Casa de Economii si Consemnatiuni (savings bank), Cooperative Credit Bank.

Trade fairs

Important method of promotion for foreign businesses. Main international event is Bucharest International Trade Fair, organised by Bucharest International Fair Authority and held every May and October. Several small specialised fairs are also held throughout the year. Information on these available from State Public Relations Agency (PUBLICOM).

Electricity supply

220 V AC.

Representation in capital

Albania, Algeria, Argentina, Austria, Bangladesh, Belgium, Brazil, Bulgaria, Burundi, Canada, Chile, China, Colombia, Congo, Costa Rica, Cuba, Denmark, Ecuador, Egypt, Finland, France, Gabon, Germany, Greece, Guinea, The Holy See, Hungary, India, Indonesia, Iran, Iraq, Israel, Italy, Japan, Jordan, Korea DPR, Republic of Korea, Lebanon, Liberia, Libya, Malaysia, Mauritania, Mexico, Mongolia, Morocco, Netherlands, Nigeria, Pakistan, Peru, Philippines, Poland, Moldova, Russia, Somalia, Spain, Sudan, Sweden, Switzerland, Syria, Thailand, Tunisia, Turkey, UK, Ukraine, Uruguay, USA, Venezuela, Vietnam, Yemen, Zaïre, Zimbabwe.

Useful tips

Do carry some form of identity at all times. Keep your passport separate from other valuables as bogus police are known to be operating a system where they ask for identification and then steal your wallet.

BUSINESS DIRECTORY

Hotels

Bucharest
Ambassador, Blvd Magheru 10, 70156 Bucharest (tel: 615-9080, 615-9086; fax: 312-3295).

Athenee Palace, Str Episcopiei 1-3 (in city centre), 70144 Bucharest (tel: 614-0899; tx: 11-162).

Bucuresti, Blvd Victoriei 63-81, Bucharest (tel: 615-4640, 615-5850, 615-4580; fax: 312-0927).

Bulevard, Blvd Kogalniceanu 1, Bucharest (tel: 613-0310, 615-3300; fax: 312-3923).

Continental, Blvd Victoriei 56, 70104 Bucharest (tel: 638-5022, 638-2500; fax: 312-0134).

Diplomat, Str Sevastopol 13-17, Bucharest (tel: 659-2090; fax: 312-9720).

Dorobanti, Blvd Dorobantilor 1-7, Bucharest (tel: 211-5490, 211-5491; fax: 210-0150).

Flora, Blvd Poligrafiei 1, Bucharest (tel: 617-0535, 618-4640, 618-4438; Fax: 312-8344).

Hanul Manuc, Str I Maniu 30, Bucharest (tel: 613-3300).

Helvetia, Sq Aviatorilor, Bucharest (tel: 311-0567; fax: 311-0567).

Intercontinental, Blvd Balcescu 4, 79242 Bucharest (tel: 614-0400; fax: 312-1017).

Lebada, Blvd Biruintei 3, Bucharest (tel: 624-3010, 624-3000; fax: 312-8044).

Lido, Blvd Magheru 5, 70161 Bucharest (tel: 614-4930, 614-4939; fax: 312-6544).

Majestic, Str Academiei 11, Bucharest (tel: 615-5986).

Minerva, Str Gh Manu 2-4, Bucharest (tel: 650-6010; fax: 312-3963).

Modern, Blvd Republicii 44, 70334 Bucharest (tel: 616-4320; tx: 11-409).

Negoiul, Str Ion Campineanu 16, 70118 Bucharest (tel: 615-5250).

Nord Calea Grivitei 143 (near to North Station), 78102 Bucharest (tel: 650-6081; tx: 11-164).

Palas, Str C Mille 18, Bucharest (tel: 613-7969, 613-6735).

Parc, Blvd Poligrafiei 3, 71556 Bucharest (tel: 617-6577).

Sofitel, Blvd Expozitiei 2, Bucharest (tel: 618-2828; fax: 212-0646).

Triumf, Blvd Kiseleff 12, Bucharest (tel: 618-4110).

Turist, Blvd Poligrafiei 5, Bucharest (tel: 666-3020).

Union, Str Ion Campineanu 11, 70116 Bucharest (tel: 613-2640).

Useful telephone numbers

Fire brigade: 981.

Police: 955.

Ambulance: 961.

Special ambulance service (pregnant women or women with small children): 969.

Emergency hospital: 679-4310.

Special information: 951.

Time: 958.

Railway information: 952.

Weather report: 959.

Enquiries: 930, 931, 932

Car hire

Bucharest
Avis: Central Reservations (tel: 210-4344); International Airport, Otopeni (tel: 212-0011); Boulevard Expozitiei 2, World Trade Centre (tel: 223-2080); Hotel Intercontinental (tel: 312-7070/3091); Hotel Minerva (tel: 312-2738).

Europcar: Central Reservations, Blvd Magheru 7, 1 (tel: 614-4058; fax: 312-0915); Hotel Bucuresti, Calea Victoria 68/82 (tel: 614-2889); Hotel Dorobanti, Calea Dorobanti (tel: 619-2375); Hotel Intercontinental, Blvd Balescu (tel: 613-7040); Otopeni Airport (tel: 312-7078).

Hertz: (tel: 679-5284); Central Reservations (tel: 210-6555; fax: 210-6521); Otopeni Airport (tel: 212-0040; fax: 312-0434); Cihoski St 2 (tel: 611-4365).

Taxis

Taxl (tel: 953).

Taxi pick-up (tel: 952).

Chambers of commerce

Chamber of Commerce and Industry of Romania, 22 Nicolae Balcescu Blvd, 79501 Bucharest (tel: 614-0448/3965, 613-5271; fax: 312-3830).

Banking

National Bank of Romania (central bank), Floor 3/324, 8 Doamnei St, Bucharest (tel: 312-7194; fax: 312-4371).

Anglo-Romanian Bank, 1 Dimitrie Cantemir Ave, Bucharest (tel: 450-4606).

Bankco-op, 13 Ion Ghica St, Bucharest (614-3900; fax: 312-0037).

Bank of Agriculture (AGROBANK), 3 Smardan St, Bucharest 70006 (tel: 613-5520; fax: 312-0340).

BUSINESS DIRECTORY

Banking (contd):
Bank of Credit and Development Romexterra, 4300 Targu Mures 21, Trandafirilor Sq, Bucharest (tel: 965-776-047).

Bucharest Bank, 1 Dimitrie Cantemir Ave, Bucharest (tel: 321-1521; fax: 321-1520).

Casa de Economii si Consemnatiuni (Savings Bank), Calea Victorei 13, Bucharest 70411 (tel: 615-4810; tx: 11-466).

Chemicalbank, 16 Carol Ave, Bucharest (tel: 615-8414, 312-0325; fax: 312-1075).

Creditbank (Romanian-American Bank), 30 Corbeni St, Bucharest (tel: 312-1860, 211-5114; fax: 312-1860, 211-4161).

Dacia Felix Bank, 3400 Cluj-Napoca 28, Memorandumului St, Bucharest (tel: 064-116-021, 064-114-444; fax: 064-116-021).

Frankfurt-Bucharest Bank AG, 22-24 Victoriei Ave, Bucharest (tel: 613-0040, 613-1030; fax: 312-0908).

French-Romanian Bank, 11 Balcescu Ave, Bucharest (tel; 311-2812, 311-2813; fax: 312-1358).

Industrial and Commercial Credit Bank (Romanian-American Bank), 17-19 Doamnei St, Bucharest (tel: 312-3629, 615-4037; fax: 312-2345).

International Bank of Religions, 27 Unirii Ave, Bucharest (tel: 312-7441, 312-7443; fax: 312-7320).

Ion Tiriac Commercial Bank, 12 Doamnei St, Bucharest (tel: 638-7560, 613-4858; fax: 312-5878).

Mindbank, 46-48 Plevnei Ave, Bucharest (tel: 312-0034, 613-0788; fax: 312-0031).

MISR Romanian Bank (Romanian-Egyptian Bank), 4 George Enescu St, Bucharest (tel: 312-0564, 312-0893; fax: 312-0908).

Post Bank, 14 Libertatii Ave, Bucharest (tel: 312-2772; fax: 400-1362).

Romanian Bank, 35 Unirii Ave, Block A3, Bucharest (tel: 321-3624; fax: 321-3624).

Romanian Bank for Development, 4 Doamnei St, Bucharest (tel: 613-3200, 615-9600; fax: 615-7603).

Romanian Bank of Foreign Trade, 22-24 Victoriei Ave, Bucharest (tel: 614-9190, 638-4040; fax: 615-7603).

Romanian Commercial Bank, 14 Republicii Ave, Bucharest (tel: 614-5680, 615-7560; fax: 614-3213).

Romanian Eximbank, 6 Stavropoleos St, Bucharest (tel: 614-3694, 615-8200; fax: 312-1350).

Romanian-Turkish Bank, 16 Ion Campineanu St, Bucharest (tel: 311-1338, 312-6580; fax: 311-1732).

Societe Generale, 16 Balcescu Ave, Bucharest (tel: 638-2494, 638-2797; fax: 312-0060).

Transylvania Bank, 3400 Cluj-Napoca 36, Eroilor Ave, Bucharest (tel: 064-136-420, 064-193-190; fax: 064-136-602).

Principal newspapers

Adevarul, Piata Presei Libere 1, Bucharest 71341 (tel: 223-1510/1520; fax: 222-3390).

Azi, Calea Victoriei 39a, Etaj 1, Sector 1, Bucharest 70101 (tel: 614-1998/54, 613-8276; fax: 312-0128, 614-4378).

Curierul National, Ministerului Street 2-4, Bucharest (tel: 615-9512, 614-6743; fax: 613-5844).

Dreptatea, Calea Victoriei 133, Sector 1, Bucharest 70179 (tel: 650-3554; fax: 650-6444).

Economistul, Calea Grivitei 21 et VII, Bucharest 78101 (tel: 659-4834).

Mesagerful Economic, 23 Nicolae Balescu Blvd, Bucharest 79502 (tel: 613-2379; fax: 312-2091).

Romanian Insight, 22 Nicolae Balcescu Blvd, Bucharest 79502 (tel: 613-2379; fax: 613-0091).

Romnia Libera, Piata Presei Libere 1, Bucharest 71341 (tel: 222-4770/3354; fax: 223-2071).

Romaniai Magyar Szo, Piata Presei Libere 1, Sector 1, Bucharest (tel: 222-3303/5802; fax: 222-9441/3211).

Tineretul Liber, Piata Presei Libere 1, Bucharest 71341 (tel: 222-5040, 223-1510/20; fax: 222-3313/8309).

Tribuna Economica, 28-30 Gheorge Magheru Blvd, Bucharest (tel: 659-2060; fax: 659-2192).

Travel information

Baneasa, 1 Dr Minovici St, Bucharest (tel: 617-0708).

Basarab, 2 Orhideelor Ave, Bucharest (tel: 637-5705).

East Railway Station, 1 Garii Obor Ave, Bucharest (tel: 635-0702).

Domestic Railway Agencies, Str Brezoianu 10, Bucharest (tel: 613-2644/43; Calea Grivitei 139, Bucharest (tel: 650-7247).

International Railway Agency, Bd I.C. Bratianu 44 bis, Bucharest (tel: 613-4008).

Jaro International (Charter Flights) SA, 14-22 Bucuresti-Ploiesti Ave, Bucharest (tel: 212-2273, 212-2274; fax: 312-9758).

Lar-Romanian Airlines, 3-4 Stirbei-Voda Ave, Bucharest (tel: 615-3276, 615-3206; fax: 312-0148).

Lufthansa Airport Office (tel and fax: 312-7670); town office, Boulevard Magheru 18, Bucharest (tel: 650-6766; fax: 312-0211).

Mervia SA (Charter Flights), 41 Magheru Ave, Bucharest.

National Tourist Office (ONT Carpati), Blvd Magheru 7, Bucharest 1 (tel: 614-1922, 312-2598; fax: 312-2954).

North Railway Station, 6 Garii St, Bucharest (tel: 952).

Nouvelles Frontieres - Simpa Tourism, 18 Putu cu plopi St, Bucharest (tel: 615-9615; fax: 312-7485).

Otopeni Airport (tel: 633-6602).

Paralela 45 - Travel and Tours, 7-9 Kogalniceanu Ave, Bucharest (tel: 613-4450, 613-4542; fax: 312-2774).

Progresul, 319 Giurgiului Ave, Bucharest (tel: 685-6383).

Romavia SA (Charter Flights), 1 Dimitrie Cantemir Ave, Bucharest (tel: 311-1055; fax: 311-1051).

Tarom - Head Office, 16,5 km, Bucuresti-Ploiesti Ave, Bucharest (tel: 663-3137, 212-0122 information; fax: 312-9767).

Tarom Agency (Domestic Flights), 59-61 Buzesti St, Bucharest (tel: 659-4125 information, 659-2855 booking).

Tarom Agency (International Flights), 10-14 Domnita Anastasia St, Bucharest (tel: 615-0499 information, 615-2747, 613-4295 booking; fax: 614-6524).

Other useful addresses

Administration of Sulina Free Trade Zone, Dr Marcovici Str 2, Ground Floor, Bucharest (tel: 613-8733).

Agency for Restructuring, 152 Calea Victoriei, Sector 1, Bucharest (tel: 212-2424; fax: 212-1176).

Asigurara Romaneasca SA (ASIROM), Str Smirdan 5, 70406 Bucharest (tel: 312-5020; fax: 312-4819).

British Embassy, Str Jules Michelot 24, 70154 Bucharest (tel: 111-634/635, 312-0303; fax: 312-0229/9652).

Centrul Roman pentru Dezvoltarea Intreprinderilor Mici si Mijlocii (CRIMM)-PMU, 20 Ion Campineanu Str, Sector 1, 70709 Bucharest (tel: 311-1995/6/7; fax: 312-6966).

Chamber of Deputies, 1 Parlamentului Str, Bucharest (tel: 615-0200, 638-5090; fax: 312-0828).

Constantza Port Administration, Constantza (tel: 611-540; fax: 619-512).

Council for Economic Co-ordination amd Strategy, Piata Victorei 1, 71201 Bucharest (te1: 614-3400, 312-4767; fax: 222-4686).

Department for Selective Restructuring of the State Ownership Fund, 6-10, Callea Grivitei, Sector 1, Bucharest (tel: 650-4822; 659-7693).

Economic Reform and Strategy and Coordination Council, 1 Victoriei Sq, Bucharest (tel: 617-7977; fax: 312-4686).

Euro Information Network Centre/Chamber of Commerce of Romania, 22 Bd N Balcescu, Bucharest (tel: 613-5271; fax: 312-3830).

FIMAN Fund PMU, 6-8 Povernei Str, Bucharest (tel: 212-2912; fax: 211-1937).

Insurance and Reinsurance Company SA (Aatra), Str Smirdan 5, 79118 Bucharest (tel: 150-986; fax: 139-306).

Land Reclamation Agriculture Department, Sos Oltenitei 35-37, 75501 Bucharest (tel: 634-5020; fax: 312-3712).

Lignite Public Authority, Str Tudor Vladimirescu 2, 1400 Târgu-Jiu (tel: 321-2513; fax: 321-664).

Other useful addresses (contd):
Ministry of Agriculture and Food Industry, Blvd Carol I 24, 70433 Bucharest (tel: 615-4412; fax: 613-0322).

Ministry of Commerce, Str Apollodor 17, 70663 Bucharest (tel: 614-1141; fax: 312-2342). Export Promotion Division (tel: 631-4274, 312-5285; fax: 312-2342).

Ministry of Communications, Blvd Libertatii 14, 70080/5 Bucharest (tel: 400-1100, 312-0017; fax: 400-1742, 312-5642).

Ministry of Culture, Calea Presei 1, Bucharest (tel: 617-6010, 617-0906; fax: 659-4781).

Ministry of Education and Science, Str Berthelot 28-30, 70749 Bucharest (tel: 615-7430; fax: 615-7736).

Ministry of Employment and Social Protection, Str Demetru I Dodrescu 2, 70119 Bucharest (tel: 615-0200, 617-0160; fax: 613-8764).

Ministry of Finance, Str Apollodor 17, 70663 Bucharest (tel: 781-3100; fax: 781-4360).

Ministry of Foreign Affairs, Blvd Modrogan 14, 71274 Bucharest (tel: 633-4060; fax: 312-7589).

Ministry of Health, Str Ministerului 1-3, 70109 Bucharest (tel: 617-0160, 615-0200; fax: 613-6265).

Ministry of Industries, Calea Victoriei 152, 1 Bucharest (tel: 650-4190/5020/2968; fax: 650-3029, 312-0613).

Ministry of Industry, Energy Division, Calea Victorei 152, 1 Bucharest (tel: 650-2968; fax: 312-0321/0513/0613).

Ministry of the Interior, Str Mihai Voda 6, 70622 Bucharest (tel: 781-4545, 679-4545; fax: 312-1500).

Ministry of Justice, Blvd Kogalniceanu 33, 70602 Bucharest (tel: 614-8623; fax: 312-1319).

Ministry of Labour and Social Protection, Str Dem I Dobrescu 2, Bucharest (tel: 615-0200, 617-0160; fax: 613-8764).

Ministry of National Defence, Blvd Drumul Taberei 9-11, Bucharest (tel: 631-7010; fax: 614-4610).

Ministry of Public Works and Territory, Str Apollodor 15-17, Sector 6, 70663 Bucharest (tel: 312-0187, 781-3903; fax: 312-1319/1130).

Ministry of Technology and Research, Str Mendeleev 21, 70168 Bucharest (tel: 650-5095; fax: 312-1410).

Ministry of Tourism, Str Apollodor 17, 5th Floor, Room 16, Sect 5, 70663 Bucharest 5 (tel: 781-6287, 631-4455; fax: 312-2342/2345).

Ministry of Trade, Apolodor Str 17, 706663 Bucharest (tel: 781-6287; fax: 312-2342).

Ministry of Transports, Blvd Dinicu Golescu 38, 77113 Bucharest (tel: 617-1880, 617-2060).

Ministry of Waters, Forests and Environment Protection, Blvd Libertatii 12, 70500 Bucharest (tel: 631-6146/6189; fax: 312-4227, 631-6143).

Ministry of Youth and Sports, Str Vasile Conta 16, 70139 Bucharest (tel: 611-5009, 611-1005; fax: 312-0161).

Office of the Prime Minister, Piata Victoriei 1, 70210 Bucharest (tel: 143-400; fax: 592-018).

National Administration of Roads, Blvd Dinicu Golescu 38, 77113 Bucharest (tel: 312-8496).

National Agency for Privatisation, Str Ministerulei 2-4, 4th Floor, Bucharest sector 1 (tel: 615-8558, 614-9495, 312-3030, 614-7854; fax: 312-0809/3030, 613-6136).

National Committee for Statistics, 16 Libertatii Str, Sector 5, Bucharest (tel: 312-4875; fax: 312-4873).

National Council for Environmental Protection, Piata Victorei 1, Bucharest (tel: 143-400).

NAVROM (Romanian Shipping Company), 8700 Constanta (tel: 615-821; fax; 618-413).

Nord-Est Press (Independent news agency), Str Smirdan 5, 6600 Iasi (tel/fax: 144-776).

Petrotel SA, Str Mihai Bravu 235, Jud Prahova, 2000 Ploiesti (tel: 146-671; fax: 142-408).

Presidency of Republic, Cotroceni Palace, Bucharest (tel: 637-4438, 781-7502; fax: 637-4776).

Radiodifuziuna Romana, Str Gral Berthelot 61-62, PO Box 63-1200, Bucharest (tel: 633-4710; fax: 312-3640).

Radioteleviziuna Romana (Romanian Radio and Television), Calea Dorobantilor 191, PO Box 63-1200, Bucharest (tel: 334-710; fax: 337-544).

Radio Nord-Est, Str Smirdan 5, 6600 Iasi (tel: 145-530; fax: 146-363)

Research Institute for Foreign Trade, Str Apollodor 17, 5 Bucharest (tel: 312-3652, 631-1293; fax: 312-5652).

Romanian Agency for Energy Conservation, Splaiul Independentei 202A, 77208 Bucharest (tel: 650-6470; fax: 312-3197).

Romanian Commodity Exchange, 71341 Bucharest 1, Presei Libere Sq, Bucharest (tel: 01-617-2231; fax: 01-312-2167).

Romanian Development Agency (RDA), Boulevard Magheru 7, Bucharest 1 (tel: 615-6686, 312-3311; fax: 613-2415).

Romanian Electricity Authority (RENEL), Blvd Gen Magheru 33, RO-70164 Bucharest (tel: 312-3163; fax: 312-0291).

Romanian Government, 1 Victoriei Sq, Bucharest (tel: 614-3400; fax: 659-2019).

Romanian National Commission for UNESCO, Str Anton Cehov 8, 71292 Bucharest (tel: 633-3223; fax: 312-763.

Romanian State Railways (SNCFR), Blvd 38 Dinicu Golescu, Sector 1-Cod 78123 Bucharest (tel: 617-0148).

Romexpo SA (Trade fairs and exhibitions). Bd Marasti 65-67, 71331 Bucharest (tel: 618-1160; fax: 618 3725

Rompres (Romanian News Agency), Piata Presei Libere I, 71341 Bucharest (tel: 618-2878; fax: 617-0487).

Secretariat for the Privatisation and Restructuring Programmes within the Council for Co-ordination, Strategy and Economic Reform, 1 Piata Victoriei, Sector 1, Bucharest (tel: 312-8445, 222-8335; fax: 312-6932).

Senate of Romania, 1 Revolutiei Sq, Bucharest (tel: 615-0200, 617-0160; fax: 312-1752).

Societatea Nationala a Cailor Ferate, State Ownership Fund, CA Rosetti Str 21, Bucharest (tel: 611-4943).

Supreme Court of Justice, 4 Rahovei Str, Bucharest (312-0920; fax: 613-0882).

Prosecutor General's under the Supreme Court of Justice, 2-4 Unirii Ave, Bucharest (tel: 631-1750, 781-3065; fax: 781-6210).

Televiziuna Romana – Telecentrul Bucuresti, Calea Dorobantilor 191, PO Box 63-1200, Bucharest (tel: 633-4710; fax: 633-7544).

USA Embassy, Str Tudor Arghezi 7-9, Bucharest (tel: 312-4042; fax: 312-0395).

Russia

Marko Milivojevic

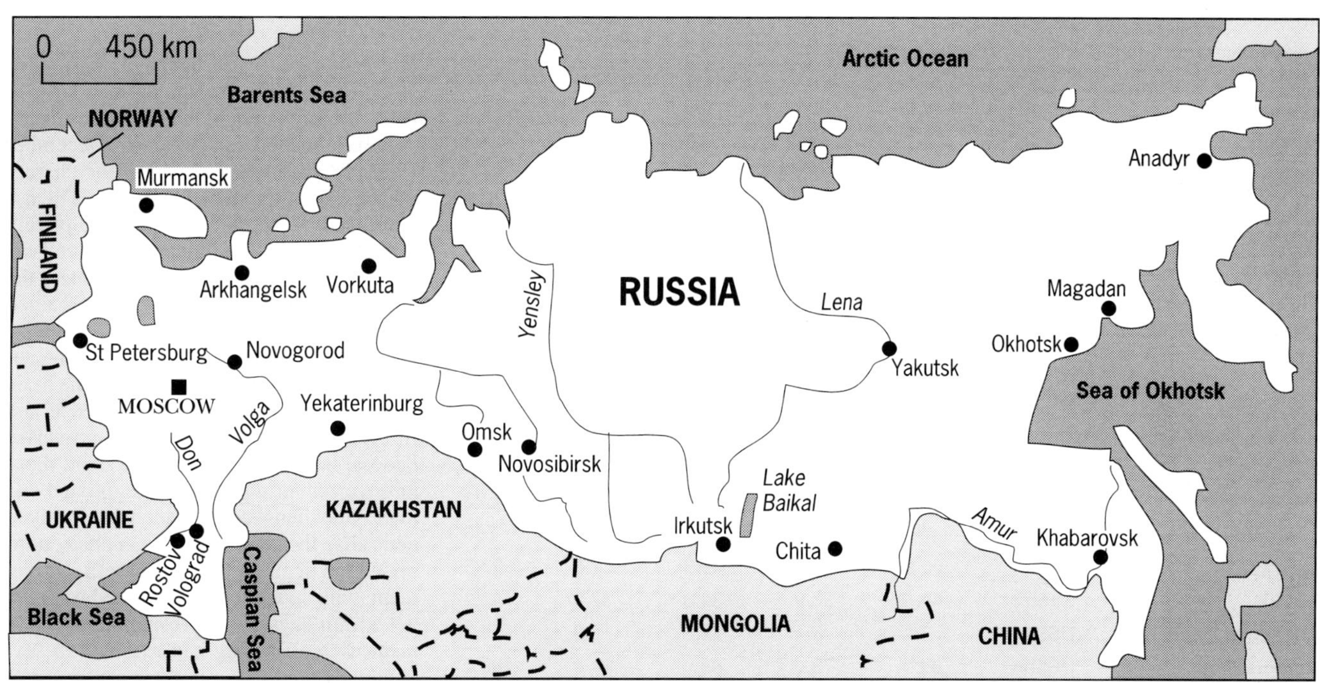

Russia reached, and successfully negotiated, a key turning point in 1995/96. In the December 1995 parliamentary elections for a new Duma, the Communist Party of the Russian Federation (CPRF) and its neo-communist ally, the Agrarian Party of Russia (APR), had gained a plurality of votes and seats. However, this was not converted into victory for the CPRF candidate, Gennady Zyuganov in the July 1996 presidential elections, as the incumbent Boris Yeltsin won what turned out to be a convincing success in a second round of voting.

Elections

After gaining a narrow lead over his CPRF rival in the first round of the presidential election, Boris Yeltsin virtually ended his opponent's hopes by immediately appointing the third placed candidate, General Alexandr Lebed, as his Security Council Secretary. Lebed had won a surprisingly high 14.52 per cent of the vote to become Russia's kingmaker. Granted widespread powers by Yeltsin, his influence was soon apparent as the unpopular Defence Minister Pavel Grachev and seven other generals were sacked. The support of Lebed and endorsements from most of the other candidates, combined with the almost unconditional support of the media all but guaranteed a Yeltsin victory in the second round against Zyuganov. Even so, the margin of victory was greater than expected, particularly with scares over Yeltsin's health and the prospect of a low turnout. Yeltsin won 53.82 per cent and Zyuganov 40.31 per cent of votes cast in the second round on 3 July 1996.

The communists (in their present unrec-

KEY FACTS — Russia

Official title: Russian Federation

Head of state: President Boris Yeltsin (from 1992; re-elected Jul 1996)

Head of government: Chairman (Prime Minister) Viktor Chernomyrdin (OHR)

Ruling party: Technocratic government nominally dominated by centrist parties in a loose coalition (Communist Party, Liberal Democratic Party, Our Home is Russia (OHR))

Capital: Moscow

Official Languages: Russian

Currency: Rouble (R) = 100 kopeks

Exchange rate: R5,552.50 (Dec 1996) (market rate)

Area: 17,075,000 sq km

Population: 149.5m (1995)

GDP per capita: US$2,393 (1995)

GDP real growth: -6% (1st half 1996)

GNP per capita: US$1,927 (1994)

GNP real growth: -6% (1995)

Labour force: 69.4m (1994)

Unemployment: 8.4% (Jan 1996)

Inflation: 15% (1st half 1996) (consumer prices)

Oil reserves: 49bn barrels (end-1995)

Trade balance: US$14.7bn (1995)

Foreign debt: US$109.2bn (1995)

Visitor numbers: 5.2m (1995)

KEY INDICATORS — Russia

	Unit	1991	1992	1993	1994	1995
Population	m	148.9	148.6	148.3	148.2	149.5
Gross domestic product (GDP)	US$bn	447	375	330	290	–
GDP per capita	US$	3,000	2,500	2,350	2,000	2,393
GDP real growth	%	-13	-18	-12	-15	-4
Inflation	%	93	1,300	940	320	150
Consumer prices	1990=100	–	–	874.62	307.38	197.41
Employment	m	73.8	72.0	70.9	68.5	67.1
Wages (average earnings)	1990=100	–	–	822.1	255.9	142.2
Unemployment	%	4.5	4.9	5.0	7.0	7.5
Agricultural output	%	-7	-11	-10	-9	-8
Industrial employment	1992=100	–	100.0	92.0	81.5	76.1
Industrial output	%	-10.0	-11.0	-16.2	-20.9	-3.0
Industrial production	1990=100	92.0	75.4	64.8	51.3	49.8
Manufacturing	1990=100	91.7	74.1	63.1	48.0	46.0
Mining	1990=100	93.4	86.7	78.5	72.7	–
Crude steel	m tonnes	76.8	66.9	58.1	48.8	51.2
Cement	m tonnes	76.3	61.2	49.9	37.2	36.4
Mineral fertiliser	m tonnes	15.0	11.0	8.6	7.5	8.8
Gold	tonnes	162	176	165	–	–
Natural gas	bn cu metre	643	639	618	607	592
Crude petroleum	m tonnes	452	384	333	316	298
Exports	US$bn	50.9	42.3	46.3	51.6	57.8
Imports	US$bn	44.4	36.9	34.3	37.7	43.1
Balance of trade	US$bn	6.4	5.4	12.0	13.8	14.7
Foreign debt	US$bn	67.0	78.0	83.0	94.3	109.2
Gross fixed investment	%	-14	-16	-10	-15	-13
Current account	US$bn	3.5	4.2	2.3	4.8	5.2
Total reserves minus gold	US$m	–	–	5,835.0	3,980.4	14,123.7
Foreign exchange	US$m	–	–	5,828.6	3,976.1	14,005.8
Foreign direct investment	US$bn	1.0	1.5	2.6	1.0	1.5
Deposit rate	%	–	–	–	–	102
Lending rate	%	–	–	–	–	319.5
Exchange rate (annual average)	R per US$	1.7	220	932	2,191	4,558

onstructed form) are unlikely ever again to achieve the same level of support as in the presidential elections and the parliamentary election of December 1995. As the old Soviet generation, those who fondly remember Stalin, dies out, and the economic benefits of the reform programme eventually make themselves felt, support for the die hard communists lools likely to wither away. Even so, if the CPRF follows the example of other former communist parties across central and eastern Europe and transforms itself into a modern social democratic party it will continue to play a major role in Russia's future.

While Yeltsin's immediate future is secure (subject to his health), a substantial minority voted against him (29 million) and the CPRF remains a powerful opposition, particularly in many of Russia's 89 regions and republics. In the December 1995 Duma elections the CPRF and its APR allies gained effective control of the new Duma. As in the December 1993 parliamentary elections, pro-government reformist parties performed very poorly and the Liberal Democratic Party (LDP) gained only half the votes it secured in the 1993 elections.

Constitutional change in December 1993 brought vast power to the Russian presidency. This has resulted in a poorly developed democracy which Yeltsin did not hesitate to exploit in order to stay in power in 1996. Against a wider background of extreme political volatility, fragmentation and uncertainty, the basic choice in the June-July 1996 presidential elections was between those who espouse continued socio-economic reform and those who want to modify, if not reverse, this policy. The presidential elections were also about which faction of the divided former Soviet *nomenklatura* will rule Russia and how.

Chechnya

The ongoing war in Chechnya, a province of the Russian Federation, loomed large in 1996. Highly unpopular since it was disastrously launched by Yeltsin in December 1994, the Chechen war has all the characteristics of a quagmire for Russia. The demoralised Russian army has completely failed to pacify Chechnya, where well-organised separatists again humiliated the army in August 1996 when they re-gained control of the capital, Grozny.

The conflict has deeply divided the so-called 'party of power' in Russia. The basic split is between the Federal Defence and Interior Ministries, plus the powerful Federal Security Service (FDS), and those in government who want a negotiated end to the Chechen war. In order temporarily to neutralise the Chechen issue, Yeltsin authorised the negotiation of a ceasefire agreement with local separatists in May 1996, yet within days of the presidential election result fierce fighting had resumed in several areas.

In September 1996 an agreement was signed between General Lebed, whom Yeltsin had charged with solving the conflict, and the Chechen Chief of Staff, Aslan Maskhadov, to bring an end to the fighting and defer a decision on Chechnya's status within the Russian Federation until 2001. Despite political manouverings within the Kremlin and occasional breaches, the ceasefire was still in force at the end of 1996, by which time the army had pulled out. Presidential elections were due in the breakaway republic in January 1997.

Within Russian politics, Chechnya undoubtedly discredited the hardline clique around Yeltsin and the ineffectual Russia army. The obvious scapegoat for the debacle, Defence Minister Pavel Grachev, was finally dismissed by Yeltsin in between the first and second round of the presidential election in a clear vote winning attempt. The prospect of army discontent spilling over to threaten Russia's fragile democracy was reduced, at least temporarily, with Lebed's appointment as Security Council Secretary and the removal of several hardline generals from the president's circle of advisors. However, the issue of massive wage arrears has yet to be solved – there were reports of soldiers suffering from malnutrition and being reduced to begging for food during 1996.

Foreign relations

Present political trends in Russia are clouding its foreign policy. Once based on a strategic rapprochement with the west, this is becoming increasingly confrontational, notably in relation to the re-creation of a Russian-dominated sphere of influence in the Commonwealth of Independent States (CIS).

A key development was a vote by the CPRF-dominated Duma in March 1996 to annul Russia's participation in the break-up of the former Soviet Union in 1991. One result of this was Yeltsin's decision to create a so-called Commonwealth of Sovereign States (SSR) in the CIS in April 1996. Possibly to include a full union between Belarus and Russia, this implicitly Greater Russian policy may well lead to increased conflict with the west, notably over the eastern expansion of NATO. Russian and western interests are also increasingly divergent in relation to Transcaucasia, Central Asia and China.

Within the west, future policy towards Russia could also turn confrontational, particularly with the USA. In the European Union (EU), there are growing doubts as to whether Russia should have been admitted to the Council of Europe in January 1996 and whether it will ever qualify for even associate membership of the EU.

Economy

After five years of consecutive economic decline following the demise of the Soviet Union in 1991, the Russian Federation was expected to experience its best economic performance, with GDP declining by about 2 per cent in 1996. Russia's first economic growth of the post-Soviet period is expected in 1997, and will mainly be generated by rising domestic demand, continued economic reform, improved foreign trade and increased new foreign borrowings and other foreign capital inflows. In 1995, officially recorded GDP declined by only 4 per cent, compared to a fall of 15 per cent in 1994.

If the large unofficial or black economy is included in the equation, however, then actual output of goods and services in 1995 almost certainly exceeded that of 1994. In 1994/95, Russia's black economy may have accounted for up to 50 per cent of officially declared GDP. Calculated on a purchasing power parity (PPP) basis, Russia's GDP in 1995 was US$626.5 billion, which gave a PPP calculated GDP per capita of US$4,200. Including the black economy, actual GDP on a PPP basis may have exceeded US$1 trillion in 1995. Official figures continue to over-state the extent of Russia's economic decline in recent years.

In September 1995, official figures on this question were in fact revised when it was announced that the cumulative fall in GDP in 1991-94 was 35 per cent, not the 50 per cent claimed earlier in the year. Although often cancelled out by large wage arrears, real disposable incomes are now rising sharply, mainly because of declining inflation and large increases in nominal wages. The major pressure for real wage rises has been increased strike activity throughout the Russian Federation.

Another positive trend for 1996 is a projected rise of 3 per cent year-end for gross fixed investment (GFI). Officially, GFI declined by 13 per cent in 1995, but this figure excludes growing new investment in the unrecorded private-sector. Local economic productivity, however, remains low by world standards, mainly because of overmanning and still-low GFI in the country's industrial sector.

Foreign debt and payments

A highly contentious issue for much of the 1990s, Russia's foreign debt position

COUNTRY PROFILE — RUSSIA

Historical profile

Following the end of the Cold War and the related collapse of communism in central and eastern Europe in 1989, the Soviet Union finally ceased to exist in December 1991. Commonwealth of Independent States (CIS) formed in December 1991 by 11 former USSR republics, including Russia. Within the Russian Federation, the former ruling Communist Party of the Soviet Union (CPSU) was banned in 1991, but relegalised as the Communist Party of Russia (CPR) in 1993. Given that the events of 1991 were more a palace rather than a popular revolution, the neo-communists remain a powerful and well-organised force in Russia, where the anti-government uprising in Moscow in October 1993 was only crushed by the President after the decisive intervention of the Russian Army. Regionally, a new Federation Treaty was agreed upon by the federal government and most of Russia's 89 ethnic republics and other regional units, and then incorporated into a new federal constitution in December 1993.

Political system

Boris Yeltsin was elected head of state in the first free parliamentary elections in June 1991. The supreme legislative body in Russia since the popular approval of a new constitution in a referendum in December 1993, is the bicameral Federal Assembly, comprising a lower house, the 450-seat state *Duma*, and an upper house, the 178-seat Federation Council. Whereas the Federal Assembly is relatively weak, the presidency is comparatively powerful, having for instance the right to veto parliamentary legislation, while issuing decrees on which the Federal Assembly may advise but which they may not cancel. The new state *Duma* and the Federation Council were elected in December 1993 after President Yeltsin dissolved the Supreme Soviet in September 1993. A new Council of Ministers, led by Viktor Chernomyrdin, was appointed from 20 January 1994. In the parliamentary elections December 1995 the Communist Party won the largest vote. Boris Yeltsin was re-elected president in 1996. In a run-off on 3 July, he won 54 per cent of the votes cast, to the Communist Gennady Zyuganov's 40 per cent.

Political parties

Major parties include: Democratic Party of Russia, Communist Party of the Russian Federation, Liberal Democratic Party, Russia's Democratic Choice, Liberal Democratic Union, Russian Social Democratic People's Party, Democratic Alternative Party, Civic Union, Party of Russian Unity and Accord.

Population

Russian (82%), Tatars (4%), Ukrainians (3%). Majority Christian.

Main cities/towns

Moscow, capital of the Russian Federation (population 12m in 1994), St Petersburg (formerly Leningrad) (5.02m), Nizhny Novgorod (formerly Gorki, 1.4m), Novosibirsk (1.4m), Ekaterinburg (formerly Sverdlovsk) (1.3m), Samara (formerly Kuybyshev) (1.2m), Omsk (1.1m).
Constituent republics: Adygheya (Republic of), capital Maikop (450,000); Altai, capital Gorno-Altaisk (203,000); Bashkortostan, capital Ufa (3.96m); Buryatia, capital Ulan-Ude (1.05m); Checheniya, capital Grozny; Chavash Respubliki (Chuvashia), capital Cheboksary (1.34m); Daghestan, capital Makhachkala (1.89m); Ingushetia, capital Nazran (246,000); Kabardino-Balkar, capital Nalchik (800,000); Kalmykia-Khalm Tangch, capital Elista (322,000); Karachaevo-Cherkess, capital Cherkessk (422,000); Karelia, capital Petrozavodsk (800,200); Khakassia, capital Abakan (590,000); Komi, capital Syktyvkar (1.27m); Mary El, capital Ioshkar-Ola (680,000); Mordovia, capital Saransk (964,000); Northern Ossetia, capital Vladikavkaz (638,000); Yakutia (Sakha), capital Yakutsk (1.08m); Tatarstan, capital Kazan (3.74m); Tyva, capital Kyzyl (314,000); Udmurtia, capital Izhevsk (1.7m).
Autonomous region: Jewish Autonomous Region, capital Birobidzhan (218,000).
Autonomous areas: Aginskoe Buryat Autonomous Area, capital Aginskoe (77,000); Chukchi, capital Anadyr (156,000); Evenk, capital Tura (25,000); Khanty-Mansi, capital Khanty-Mansiisk (1.3m); Komi-Permyak, capital Kudymkar (160,000); Koryak, capital Palana (39,000); Nenets Republic (Nenets), capital Naryan-Mar (50,000); Dolgan-Nenets (Taimyr), capital Dudinka (55,000); Ust-Ordinsky Buryat, capital Ust-Ordinsky (137,000); Yamal-Nenets, capital Salekhard (495,000).
Territories: Altai Territory, capital Barnaul (2.7m); Khabarovsk, capital Khabarovsk (2m); Krasnodar, capital Krasnodar (5m); Krasnoyarsk, capital Krasnoyarsk (4m); Maritime, capital Vladivostok (2m); Stavropol, capital Stavropol (3m).

Language

Russian is the official language although there are many local ethnic languages. English is widely read and often spoken in business circles, but not yet fluently spoken widely. Translators, of varying abilities, will be found in all sizeable organisations.

Media

In March 1993, President Yeltsin took control of the media.
Press: Approximately 8,000 dailies in some 55 languages. Most influential dailies *Izvestiya*.

considerably improved in 1995, beginning with a formal rescheduling agreement with the London Club (LC) of commercial bank creditors in October. Involving US$32.5 billion of principal repayments and consolidated interest arrears, this seminal deal with the LC covered 25 years, with a seven year grace period. Before the agreement Russia's liabilities were rescheduled through informal three month rollovers.

In April 1996, the Paris Club (PC) of mainly G7 official governmental foreign creditors agreed formally to reschedule over US$40 billion of Russian foreign debt. The fourth, and by far the most significant, Russian government understanding with the PC, this rescheduling agreement is over 25 years with a six-year grace period. It was also the largest such deal in the history of the PC, and was preceded by a key G7 meeting in Washington.

In a related series of partly politically motivated developments in 1995-96, the International Monetary Fund (IMF) agreed to increase significantly its new loan commitments to Russia, beginning with a stand-by agreement worth US$6.8 billion in April 1995 and culminating in a multi-year credit facility worth a record US$10.2 billion in April 1996. The second largest single loan to a member government in the Fund's history, the April 1996 IMF credit brought total Fund outlays to Russia since 1992 to over US$20 billion.

World Bank and other official multilateral loan exposure in Russia is also substantial and rising. Within the G7 and the PC, April 1996 also witnessed large new governmental credits from Germany (US$2.9 billion) and France (US$1.6 billion). Other major governmental creditors of Russia in 1995/96 included the USA and Japan.

In 1994/95, Russia was able to increase its total foreign debt, especially after its April 1995 agreement with the IMF. Including rolled-over principal repayments and interest arrears, Russia's foreign debt reached a record US$109.2 billion by the end of 1995, compared to US$94.3 billion at the end of 1994. By the end of 1996, Russia's total foreign debt is expected to exceed US$115 billion. Although still relatively low in relation to Russian GDP calculated on a PPP basis and the country's economic potential, this growing foreign debt is nevertheless one of the largest in the world and is increasing at the rate of around US$15 billion per annum.

Relative to exports and local hard currency reserves, Russia's foreign debt is also high. Without the rescheduling arrangements of 1995/96, Russia's foreign debt servicing ratio would have been in the region of 20 to 25 per cent. In the event, it was only 8.1 per cent in 1995.

Most of Russia's new foreign borrowings remain highly conditional particularly the April 1996 agreement with the IMF. Significantly, Russia's agreement with the IMF is one of the toughest ever entered into by a member government; loan disbursement is on a monthly basis, although some disbursements were delayed during 1996 due to low levels of tax collection. Cross conditionality means that any future difficulties with the IMF will impact immediately and negatively upon the country's present rescheduling arrangements with both the Paris and London Clubs.

Itself a major creditor to the rest of the CIS, Russia experienced serious deficiencies in this area of its foreign economic policy in 1995. Its single largest CIS debtor, Ukraine, reneged on the US$2.5 billion energy debt rescheduling agreement signed by the Russian and Ukrainian governments in March 1995. Brokered by the IMF, which also has its own difficulties with Ukraine, this agreement may have to be renegotiated.

Energy supply debts give Russia considerable political leverage in the CIS. In the case of the new SSR, Russia waived all energy supply debts repayable by Belarus in January 1996 for essentially political reasons. Beyond the CIS, Russia is owed

COUNTRY PROFILE — RUSSIA

Media (contd): Principal news agency – Russian. Information Telegraph Agency (ITAR–Tass, formerly TASS). Also more than 5,000 journals and periodicals in some 25 languages. *Pravda/}* was closed by its Greek owners August 1996.
Broadcasting: Eight main national radio stations and extensive local network. Foreign service broadcasts in 70 languages and totals over 1,000 hours daily. Six central TV stations broadcasting some 40 hours each day. Also 130 major TV centres and over 2,000 small stations. Satellite communications are used for national and international transmission of Central Television programmes. Around 100 main towns have two channels broadcasting in Russian and local language. Six channels in Moscow and three in St Petersburg. Russia's first independent TV channel, TV-6, began broadcasting in January 1993.
Advertising: Commercial advertising is expanding quickly. Limited television and radio advertising is available to Western companies; billboards and illuminated sign-space can be bought in most major cities. Most newspapers are beginning to accept Western advertising. Baltic republics are the most advanced in this area. Many co-operatives have been set up in advertising services and are expanding at a good rate, but the main foreign trade organisation dealing with advertising remains Vneshtorgreklama.

Domestic economy

The economy is in a state of reform although widespread corruption undermines this. Due to changes, industrial output is difficult to assess as indicators have changed and statistics are unreliable at present. Main emphasis is on self-financing and self-management; several sectors including food, industrial consumer goods, consumer services and the construction sector, are to be devolved to republican and local control. Continuing shortages with acute supply problems in most products, including foodstuffs, clothing and light household goods. Emphasis being placed on increased production of consumer goods for population. State intends to invest heavily in expansion and modernisation of food processing and packaging, light industry (mainly consumer goods) and modernisation including cutting energy and raw materials. The joint-venture law, liberalised in 1989 has attracted more foreign investment. Chinese labour and investment also being encouraged. Environmental issues becoming more important. Conversion of defence-related industries into civilian production continuing. Retail and wholesale price liberalisation is proceeding, along with privatisation.
In April 1995 the IMF approved a 12-month standby loan worth about US$6.8bn. The IMF delivered US$530m in November 1995, part of a US$6.4bn loan intended to help finance the 1995 budget deficit.

Employment

About 25 per cent of employment is in services not counted a part of NMP (net material product). Although some shift to employment in services, over 57 per cent of the labour force is still employed in agriculture, forestry, industry and construction. Industry is the largest employer in socialised sector, followed by agriculture and construction. Chairman of the State Commission for Economic Reform has stated that inefficient industries need to shed 12-15m workers by the end of the century. Labour productivity is increasing. Emphasis is on improving quality and skills of the labour force.

External trade

All enterprises and organisations have the right of access to foreign markets, but the right is subject to registration; imports must be financed by exports.
Export and import licensing is required for all enterprises directly involved in foreign trade. Licences are issued by relevant ministries and a fee is payable. Documents relating to licensing of foreign trade transactions are published in *Ekonomicheskaya Gazeta* (newspaper), *Vneshnyaya Torgovlya* (magazine) and the MVES (foreign trade ministry) Bulletin of Foreign Commercial Information. Special office to deal with enquiries is at MVES (tel: 244-1533 or 244-1335).
Despite reforms, ministries manage the export of fuels and raw materials and import of agricultural goods, raw materials, a good proportion of intermediate goods and equipment for new projects, accounting for 81 per cent of exports to OECD countries and around 50 per cent of Russian imports.
China, Russia, Republic of Korea, Korea DPR and Mongolia signed agreements in May 1995 aimed at revitalising a UN-sponsored scheme to develop the remote Tumen River area of north-east Asia with regard to trade and investment. The EU ratified a 10-year partnership and co-operation agreement with Russia in December 1995.
Exports: Exports totalled US$57.8bn in 1995. Main exports include fuels and raw materials.
Imports: Imports totalled US$43.1bn in 1995. In May 1996 Russia raised import tariffs by an average of 10 per cent.
Main imports include grain, machinery and transport equipment, consumer goods, agricultural goods, raw materials, intermediate goods and equipment.

Agriculture

The agriculture sector accounted for 6 per cent of GDP in 1994 and employed 13 per cent of the labour force.

somewhere between US$80 billion and US$100 billion by various Third World countries. Little of this money is likely to be repaid. In 1994/95, Russia began to provide some inter-governmental credits for the sale of armaments to Iran, India and China.

Budget

The government's target for its budget deficit was 3.9 per cent of projected GDP in 1996, although this may prove to be optimistic. In 1995, real cuts in public spending and improved revenue collection resulted in a reduced government budget deficit equal to 5.5 per cent of GDP, compared to 10.4 per cent of GDP in 1994. Even more than was the case in 1995, the 1996 government budget deficit will be mainly financed in a non-inflationary manner, notably by IMF loans and the sale of treasury bonds to domestic and foreign investors. The high T-bill yields are of vital importance for the profitability of the members of the Association of Russian Commercial Banks (ARCB).

The government agreed to borrow R9.1 trillion (just over US$2 billion) from ARCB member banks in 1995 in return for shares in those sectors of the economy still being privatised by the State Property Agency (SPA) and the Ministry of Privatisation (MOP).

Industry

Industrial sector privatisation remains largely insider-orientated, which has impeded the restructuring of many enterprises. One result is that few technically-insolvent enterprises have been made formally bankrupt, mainly because of fears of further increases in unemployment. Enterprise indebtedness also remains high, especially energy supply payment arrears.

At one time the industrial sector accounted for about 45 per cent of GDP, but this fell to around 30 per cent in 1995 when industrial output fell by 3 per cent after a fall of 20.9 per cent in 1994. In 1996 industrial output was projected to fall by a further 5 per cent, although there has been a slight revival of output in primary production, capital goods, intermediate products and construction materials. Output of light manufactures and consumer goods, on the other hand, continues to decline, mainly because of increased competition from higher quality imports. The industrial structure is skewed towards primary production and capital goods, including armaments no longer required by the Russian army.

Employment

Although rising slowly, officially recorded unemployment remains relatively low. At the end of 1995, this reached 7.5 per cent of the employed workforce, compared to 7 per cent in 1994 and 5 per cent in 1993. Politically sensitive, unemployment has been kept artificially low by the avoidance of radical restructuring of the country's industrial sector during the 1990s. Most job creation is now in the booming private sector, which exceeded 50 per cent of GDP for the first time in 1995.

Foreign trade

A depreciating rouble (R) and the declining economic importance of the rest of the CIS to Russia has resulted in growing exports of raw materials and intermediate products to the EU and other hard currency markets. In the vital oil and gas sector, energy shipments to such markets reached record levels in 1995, mainly because of lower deliveries of such products to CIS markets. One reason for this was that total CIS energy supply debts to Russia reached a record US$9 billion by the end of 1995.

Russia's total foreign trade turnover equalled only 16 per cent of GDP in 1995, when combined exports and imports came

COUNTRY PROFILE — RUSSIA

Agriculture (contd): Prior to 1990 large-scale mechanical *sovkhozy* (state farms) accounted for 53 per cent of arable land, *kolkhozy* (smaller collective farms) accounted for 44 per cent. Production is hampered by climatic problems, rural migration, inferior equipment, selection of products and pricing, and poor storage and distribution system. The special Central Committee plenum on agriculture agreed reforms in March 1989 but the major reform of agriculture only began in 1992, the aim being to transform the huge state-owned farms to a system of smaller more productive farm holdings. Land is to be leased to farmers for between five and 50 years allowing for family farms. Some of the state and collective farms are being dismantled. Some price liberalisations were agreed for potatoes, fruit and vegetables from January 1990. Hard currency to be paid for over-production should increase production, cut imports and help farmers buy western machinery. Area sown to various crops has been reduced slightly to leave more land fallow within rotation crops. Poor soil and climate means only 10 per cent of land area is suitable for cultivation.

Production declined by 9 per cent in 1994 and by a further 8 per cent in 1995. The 63.5m tonnes grain harvest in 1995 was the lowest ever, reflecting the slow pace of change in the post-Soviet farm sector.

Industry

The industrial sector accounted for 30 per cent of GDP in 1994 and employed 30 per cent of the working population.

Output indices are gross or global which means intermediate goods are counted in rather than netted out as in the west. Fuel and raw materials use is wasteful, the technology is poor, the machinery antiquated, the management poor, the workforce too large and there is very little co-ordination between production and consumer demand. No inflationary factors are shown so real output conceals hidden inflation. Official figures are also distorted by price factors. Data on capital stock tends to give clearer picture.

Heavy industry is still politically powerful. Stated intentions for new investment priorities have had little effect on capital stock. Major production bottlenecks include steel, construction outputs (like cement) and consumer and light industry products (i.e. TV sets, robots, computers).

Emphasis in 1990s is on light industry, modernisation and computerisation. More emphasis also placed on individual enterprise and factory production decisions, but no real freedom on supply, sales or pricing.

Industrial output declined by 3 per cent in 1995.

Tourism

In July 1996 Moscow's city government put 200 hotels on the market with a price tag of at least US$1bn.

Mining

The mining and hydrocarbons sector accounted for 25 per cent of GNP in 1994 and employed 7 per cent of the workforce.

World's largest producer of iron ore, asbestos, manganese ore, nickel, chromite, platinum group metals and potassium salts. Second largest producer of gold, lead and phosphate ores. Vast reserves, but extraction has been held back due to rising production costs, labour shortages and a shortage of technology.

Russia's gold reserves are estimated by the head of the Precious Metals and Stones Committee to be 320 tonnes. Estimated annual production of gold is 300 tonnes. Major foreign exchange earners include gold and diamonds. Estimated annual production of diamonds is 12,000 tonnes.

Russia is estimated to have 30 per cent of world iron ore reserves and 20 per cent of many other minerals. Most production for own use. Significant quantities of iron ore, chromium, nickel, asbestos and fertiliser materials also exported. Also large deposits of antimony, beryllium, cadmium, mercury, molybdenum, tin and vanadium plus workable deposits of all rare earth metals.

Large-scale investment in the sector is set to improve extraction and processing techniques, while reducing wastage and controlling production costs.

Russian zinc production rose 34 per cent in the first 10 months of 1995 compared to same period in 1994; lead production was down 0.9 per cent and nickel production rose 20 per cent. Nickel exports totalled 111,000 tonnes which was 22 per cent above same period of 1994. Aluminium output rose 3 per cent in Jan-Oct 1995 compared to same period in 1994 and aluminium exports rose to 1.938m tonnes, 1 per cent above 1994. Refined copper exports fell 8 per cent to 315,000 tonnes; copper production rose 14 per cent. (Source: State Statistics Committee).

Hydrocarbons

The world's largest producer of oil. Offshore oil fields have not yet been exploited. Russia has 29 oil refineries with a total capacity of more than 9m bpd. Russia exports about 2.4m bpd of crude to be fed into the refineries of the other CIS states; Khabarovsk, Sakhalin, Magadan and others are importers of crude and refined products, notably from Kazakhstan, which in turn imports Russian crude and products. With the economic chaos, recession and the increased price of petroleum products in Russia, coupled with the renovation of industries, the level of oil consumption is expected to decrease. Crude oil production fell from a peak of 570m tonnes in 1987 to 307m tonnes in 1995 (down to just under US$101 billion. The country's foreign trade growth was none the less the best yet during the 1990s. Russia has considerable scope for far higher foreign trade growth in the future. Earlier in the 1990s, lower domestic output and payments difficulties seriously damaged foreign trade. More recently, Russia's payments position has greatly improved.

Closer ties with the EU and Russia's expected admission into the World Trade Organisation (WTO) in 1996 will further integrate its foreign trade with non-CIS markets. In 1995, the EU alone accounted for 60 per cent of Russia's exports and imports. Trade with the rest of the CIS, on the other hand, reached a low of 25 per cent of the total in 1995.

At a record US$57.8 billion, Russia's 1995 exports were 12 per cent higher than in 1994 (US$51.6 billion). Unofficially, real Russian exports of fuels and raw materials in 1995 were almost certainly far higher than official figures suggested, mainly because of widespread cross-border smuggling to the EU via the Baltic states.

On the down-side, Russia's exports remain overly dependent on fuels and metals, goods where most added value takes place after they are sold abroad. In 1995, exports of fuels and metals accounted for 50 per cent of the total. Semi-processed or intermediate goods are another important export category. Timber and wood-based products enjoyed particularly high export growth in 1995. Higher added value manufactured goods, such as machinery and equipment, accounted for less than 10 per cent of total exports in 1995. Russian industry is uncompetitive internationally and this weakness is particularly acute in relation to the EU.

Russia's imports continued to grow faster than its exports in 1995. Up 15 per cent over 1994, imports reached a record US$43.1 billion in 1995, just below their 1990 level (US$44.4 billion). In 1996, imports were expected to exceed their 1990 level for the first time. Accounting for 37 per cent of total imports in 1995, higher added value machinery and equipment remain the single most important import category. As with exports, real Russian imports are almost certainly far higher than official figures suggest, mainly because of widespread cross-border smuggling in relation to the Baltic states, Poland, Turkey and China.

Protectionist pressures are growing in Russia, particularly concerning imported consumer goods and foodstuffs. This protectionist threat, however, seriously complicates Russia's relations with the IMF, the EU and the WTO that it aspires to join.

Russia registered a record trade balance surplus of US$14.7 billion in 1995, compared to US$13.8 billion in 1994. Another record trade surplus was expected in 1996. In the longer term, however, rising imports will almost certainly reduce the size of Russia's future trade surpluses. The key question then will be whether oil and gas exports in particular can keep pace with present import growth.

The current account was in surplus to the tune of US$5.2 billion in 1995, compared to a surplus of US$4.8 billion in 1994. In 1996, the current account surplus is expected to decline to US$4.4 billion. Worsening service account deficits are occurring, particularly in the tourism sector.

Services

Although relatively insignificant in the past, services of all types have become increasingly important during the 1990s. In 1995, the mainly privately owned service sector reached a record 60 per cent of GDP. By far the most dynamic and fastest growing component of the economy, services are also highly significant for job creation. In 1995, growing domestic demand and imports gave a major boost to retail and wholesale trade.

Other high growth service sectors in 1995

COUNTRY PROFILE — RUSSIA

Hydrocarbons (contd): 3.5 per cent on 1994 output). The petroleum sector is suffering from under-investment. Proven oil reserves 49bn barrels (end-1995).
Natural gas production has been declining annually since 1991. There was a drop in production in 1995 to 499.9m tonnes oil equivalent (toe) from 509.8m toe in 1994. Gazprom, the giant gas monopoly which controls about one-third of the world's proven gas reserves, is the country's biggest export earner. Proven gas reserves 48.1 trillion cu metres (end-1995).
Coal production 116.9m tonnes oil equivalent (toe) in 1995, down 3.6 per cent on 1994 output.

Energy

Second largest generator of electricity in the world with an output of about 1,705bn kW, of which about 75 per cent is produced thermally. Nuclear power is being reassessed and hydroelectric generation is being increased. Oil-fired stations are gradually being replaced by gas or coal. Wasteful energy use is a major defect of the economy. The scope for energy saving should allow current rates of output growth to take place without any increase in consumption, although this does not appear to be the case in reality.

Banking

Exceptionally underdeveloped Soviet banking system began to expand and restructure after new Banking Law from start of 1988 but modernisation only got underway in earnest after the collapse of the Soviet Union. As of mid-1995 some 2,500 banks were officially registered. Most major banks are located in Moscow. The majority of Russian banks suffer from being undercapitalised and the high rate of inflation has constantly erodes their reserves. The retail banking sector is still in its infancy and branch networking is not particularly common. The system has been criticised for having too many owner-operators and this is a situation with huge potential for abuse.

Stock exchanges

St Petersburg stock exchange has 30 listed companies and a market capitalisation of US$115m. Numerous stock exchanges have been established throughout the Russian Federation. Tradeable stocks and trading volumes remain limited although the large-scale privatisation programme should provide considerable impetus to the development of the securities market.

Legal system

Civil law system as modified by communist legal theory. Fundamental review, codification and systematisation of laws undertaken as part of legal reform. Courts should become more important and be used to bolster democracy. Also play role in contract law as self-management and financial autonomy develop (i.e. arbitration, employment, company rights).

Membership of international organisations

ALADI (observer), BSECP, CBS, CERN (observer), CIS, Council of Baltic Sea States, Council of Europe (guest), CSCE, EBRD, ECE, ESCAP, Geneva Disarmament Conference, IAEA, IBEC, ICAC, ICAO, ICCAT, ICCO, ICES, IDA, IFC, ILO, IMF, IMO, International Grain Council, International Lead and Zinc Study Group, INRO, IPU, ISO, ITC, ITU, IWC (International Whaling Commission), MIGA, NACC, OAS (observer), OSCE, Partnership for Peace, UN, UNESCO, UNIDO, UN Security Council (permanent member), UPU, WFTU, WHO, WIPO, WMO, World Bank. Russia has requested to join the WTO.

BUSINESS GUIDE

Time

Moscow and St Petersburg: GMT + 2 hrs (GMT + 3 hrs from late Mar to late Sep); Volgograd: GMT + 3 hrs; Irkutsk: GMT + 7 hrs; Tiksi, Takutsk: GMT + 8 hrs; Khabarovsk, Okhotst, Vladivostok: GMT + 9 hrs; Magadan, Sakhalin Island: GMT + 10 hrs; Anadyr, Petropavlosk: GMT + 11 hrs; Eulen: GMT + 12 hrs.

Climate

Sub-arctic to sub-tropical. Extremely cold winters (-32 degrees C). Mean daily temperatures in Moscow range from -12 degrees C in January to 18 degrees C in July.

Clothing

Take very warm outer garments and waterproof boots for winter travel. Muscovites often carry indoor shoes in plastic bags and change into them on arrival. Hats are also advised to keep out the cold.

Entry requirements

Passport: Passport required by all.
Visa: Entry and exit visas are required by all visitors and must be obtained in advance. Requirements: three passport-sized photographs, photocopy of the first five pages of old-style passports or last two pages of EU passports and copy of invitation from company or sponsor, detailing name, personal details, passport number, time and purpose of visit. Only certain institutions such as western joint ventures and Russian ministries may issues invitations. Allow at least 10 days for your invitation to come through from Moscow, and between six and ten weeks for your visa

included construction, transport, finance and telecommunications. In the telecommunications sector alone, up to US$40 billion may have to be spent upgrading inadequate capacity over the next ten years. Vast outlays are also expected in transportation and other essential infrastructure. Following on from the recent large-scale privatisation of the local economy, financial services of all types are also expected to become increasingly important.

In the longer term, Russia has considerable potential as an international tourism destination, particularly St Petersburg, Moscow and the Black Sea. In 1995, a record 5.2 million visitors came to Russia and the government is planning for up to 15 million visitors per annum by 2005. Russian tourism abroad is also increasing rapidly, creating a record tourism deficit of US$2.5 billion in 1995, mainly because of increased travel to the EU and the USA.

Inflation

Previously aborted by politically motivated monetary and fiscal expansionism on the part of government and the Russian Federation Central Bank (RFCB), long-delayed macro-economic stabilisation in Russia only began in earnest after the dramatic crash of the rouble against the US dollar in October 1994. Based on a highly restrictive monetary credit policy by the RFCB, fiscal discipline by the government and non-inflationary financing of its budget deficit, Russia's third attempt at financial stabilisation during the 1990s resulted in declining monthly inflation throughout 1995 and 1996.

Year-end inflation fell to 150 per cent in 1995, compared to 320 per cent in 1994 and 940 per cent in 1993. Supported by the US$6.8 billion and US$10.2 billion IMF loans agreed in April 1995 and April 1996 respectively, this policy was expected to result in year-end inflation of around 50 per cent in 1996. On a monthly basis, the most recent agreement with the IMF commits the government and the RFCB to an inflation rate of no more than 2 per cent per month by the end of 1996, compared to a monthly inflation rate of around 5 per cent at the end of 1995.

The October 1994 rouble crisis created a growing consensus for lower inflation and inflationary expectations in Russia. One recent result of that, in November 1995, was the appointment of a prominent reformer, Sergei Dubinin, to the key post of RFCB governor, which had been held on an interim basis by another strong supporter of financial stabilisation, Tatiana Paramonova. Significantly, these two key appointments were made by Yeltsin at a time when he was abandoning other reformers in government and the RFCB was under strong attack by the opponents of further reform in government and the Duma.

Credit

Declining inflation in 1995 enabled the RFCB to lower its key refinancing rate from a peak of 200 per cent at the beginning of the year to 160 per cent year-end. This policy would have to be changed if inflation once again becomes a serious concern, which would in turn adversely affect domestic demand and GFI. Despite increased pressure from the IMF and the World Bank, long overdue tax reform is unlikely to begin until after the presidential elections in 1996. Tax evasion is widespread, nominal taxation is high and tax laws are applied inconsistently. Tax obstacles of one sort or another are the single greatest disincentive to increased foreign direct investment (FDI) in Russia.

Foreign exchange

The rouble collapse of October 1994 prompted a major change of policy by the RFCB in 1995. Following on from increased

Entry requirements (contd): application to be processed. For a fee, travel agencies or services which specialise in obtaining visas can often secure visas much more quickly, sometimes overnight, and, at a higher price, some Russian embassies will process business visas within 48 hours. Nationals of Cyprus do not require a visa. Legislation passed in July 1996 requires foreign visitors planning to stay for more than three months to produce an HIV test certificate in order to obtain a visa, and visa applicants must prove they have enough money to fund the visit. If staying more than three days, visas must be registered through hotel or sponsor. If visiting relatives in the Russian Federation, passengers must register with local police on arrival.
Currency: No limit to amount of foreign currency taken in. Declaration required. export is allowed within the limits of the declaration given, less the amounts exchanged or spent within two months.
The national currency cannot be imported or exported. Refunds possible against exchange receipt.
Most public services can only be paid for with roubles.
Customs: Small amount of personal goods duty-free. On arrival declare all foreign currency and valuable items such as jewellery, cameras, computers and musical instruments. N.B. You will be required to fill out a customs declaration and it is vital you get this stamped and keep it in a safe place, because leaving the country without it can sometimes be very difficult.

Health precautions

US Global Health runs a clinic in Moscow. For details (tel: 00-1-914-767-7130).
Mandatory: Visitors from Asia, South America and Africa require a certificate for yellow fever inoculation; a cholera vaccination certificate is needed if coming from an area of infection; an HIV (AIDS) certificate is required for long-stay visitors only. If arriving at Moscow this is not usually demanded.
Advisable: Water precautions recommended (water purification tablets may be useful, especially in St Petersburg, where the water supply is infected by giardia). It is advisable to be 'in date' for the following immunisations: polio (within 10 years), tetanus (within 10 years), typhoid fever, cholera (within six months), hepatitis 'A' (moderate risk only). There has been a significant increase in the number of cases of diphtheria. While the low dose adult booster is unavailable, travellers are advised to avoid too close contact with people in crowded places, not to share glasses, etc, and to be boosted with a reduced dose (0.1ml) of the paediatric single antigen vaccine. If never immunised, use three dose course of the vaccine. Russian medical care is not up to western standards. Any medicines known to be required should be taken by the visitor, and it could be wise to have precautionary antibiotics if going outside major urban centres. A travel kit including a disposable syringe is a reasonable precaution.

Air access

National airline: Aeroflot-Russian International Airlines (ARIA).
Other airlines: Adria, Air Algérie, Air China, Air France, Air India, Air Koryo, Air UK, Air Ukraine, Alitalia, All Nippon Airlines, AOM French Airlines, Armenian, Austrian, Azerbaijan Hava Yollary, Balkan Bulgarian, Belavia, British Airways, Croatian, Cubana, Cyprus Airways, Czech Airlines (CSA), Damania Airways, Delta, Deutsche BA, Diamond Sakha Airlines, Egyptair, El Al, Estonian, Finnair, Iberia, Iran Air, Intourtrans, JAL, JAT, Korean Air, Korsar Krasnoyarsk Airlines, Latvian Airlines, Lithuanian, LOT, Lufthansa, KLM, MIAT-Mongolian Airlines, Malev, Moscow Airways, Northwest Airlines, Orbi Georgian Airlines, Palair Macedonian Airlines, PIA, Royal Jordanian, TAROM, SAS, Swissair, Syrian Arab Airlines, Transaero, Turkish Airlines, United Airlines, Uzbekistan Airlines, Vietnam Airlines, Yakut Aviatrans, Yemenia, Xinjiang Airlines.
International airports: Moscow-Sheremyetevo International (SVO), 29 km north-west of city centre, two terminals, duty-free, bureau de change, information desks; Moscow-Vnukovo (VKO), 29 km south-west of city; Moscow-Domodedovo (DME), 40 km south-east of city; St Petersburg-Pulkovo, 17 km from city; Irkutsk (IRK), 7 km from city.
It was announced in December 1995 that Moscow airports will undergo major reconstruction programme, completion by year 2000, together with new transport systems to and from city and between airports.

Surface access

Main ports: Arkhangelsk (White Sea), Berdyansk, Ilia, Izmail, Krasnovodsk (Caspian), Mezen, Murmansk (Barents Sea), Novorossiysk, Onega, Poti, Reni, St Petersburg* (ice-free port), Vyborg (Baltic), Ilichevsk* (near Odessa), Nakhodka*, Novorossiysk, Sevastopol, Sochi, Tuapse, Vladivostok (Pacific), Yalta, Vostochny, Zhdanov* (Sea of Azov). All ports, particularly St Petersburg, have suffered from lack of investment, resulting in serious deterioration of cargo-handling equipment. Nakhodka and Vostochnyy were privatised in 1992 and Vladivostok's trade port was privatised in April 1993..*Container facilities available.
Water access: Ferry to St Petersburg from Finland.
Overland access: Border crossings from Finland and China.
Rail: Extensive network of commuter and inter-city services, most offering first and second class seats/accomodation. Rolling stock needs modernising and trains are typically over-crowded and over-booked. Food is often

IMF support and lower inflation in 1995, rouble stabilisation was attained within a band of R4,300 to R4,900 per US$1. Subsequently widened to R4,550 to R5,150 per US$1 in January 1996, this system was replaced by a crawling corridor exchange rate system in June 1996. From July 1996 the central bank let the rouble depreciate, only intervening to stop falls of over 1.5 per cent a month. The new corridor began at between R5,000 and R5,600 against the US$, and was due to fall to between R5,500 and R6,100 by the end of 1996.

The ability of the government and the RFCB to defend the rouble has been improved by growing hard currency reserves. Totalling around US$14 billion at the end of 1995, these may reach US$15 billion year-end in 1996, especially if good relations are maintained with the IMF and other foreign creditors. The stabilisation of the rouble has also increased its attractiveness to local investors and savers, although little of the US$40 billion to US$50 billion illegally exported since 1990 has been repatriated for productive investment locally, mainly due to continued political and economic uncertainty.

RFCB and other commercial bank hard currency reserves are increasing, due to higher new foreign borrowings in 1995. In addition, the RFCB has around 350 tonnes of gold bullion. Local hard currency reserves excluding gold holdings remain low at around three months import cover at the end of 1995. In the event of a major run on the rouble, RFCB hard currency reserves would be quickly depleted. The only alternatives then would be either higher new foreign borrowings, sticking to the agreement recently signed with the IMF, or selling RFCB gold bullion holdings – a last resort option that is unlikely to be taken while domestic gold output continues to decline.

Commercial banking

In the commercial banking sector, where the ARCB is the dominant player, events in 1995 worsened the local economy. Accounting for 80 per cent of commercial bank profits, T-bill yields are declining, so reducing bank profitability.

The importance of the ARCB-dominated Moscow Interbank Currency Exchange (MICEX) has been reduced because of improved government access to IMF and other foreign loans in 1995/96. With monthly trading volumes of around US$3.8 billion in mid-1995, MICEX members were turning over only US$550 million by January 1996, the inevitable result of which will be greater commercial bank insolvency or illiquidity in 1996/97.

Another negative development for ARCB member banks was the introduction of new RFCB regulations for bank capitalisation in February 1995. Under these regulations, minimum capitalisation for existing commercial banks is to rise to Ecu5 million. If fully implemented, this measure would lead to a radical shake-out of Russia's 2,500 commercial banks. Strongly opposed by the ARCB, the RFCB policy remains largely unimplemented, but is almost certainly unavoidable in the longer-term.

Another major challenge for commercial banks is high enterprise indebtedness. Non-performing assets are being increasingly converted into bank equity holdings in technically insolvent enterprises. The result of this has been the creation of unwieldy financial-industrial conglomerates. Popular confidence in the integrity of the still poorly regulated commercial banks also remains low in what is a predominantly cash-based economy.

Privatisation

Involving the ownership transformation of over 70 per cent of the country's industrial enterprises (20,000 out of a total of 28,000)

BUSINESS GUIDE — RUSSIA

Surface access (contd): available on inter-city services but, because of the generally poor quality, most passengers bring their own. Many carriages have a samovar which produces hot water for drinks. Security can be a problem, especially on overnight services. The famous Trans-Siberian railway stretches from Moscow to Vladivostok; this 7-day journey is recommended only for hearty train lovers and adventurers.

Hotels

Moscow has an increasing number of western-run hotels. Accommodation difficult to obtain in Moscow at short notice. It is crucial to make bookings in advance as hotels refuse to check in a guest without a reservation.
First-class and tourist class available, with all prices fixed by Intourist. Main hotels have foreign currency restaurants and bars. Tipping increasingly common, typically 10 per cent.

Restaurants

Difficult to find top-class restaurants. Selection of food is limited to one or two main dishes. Foreign currency readily accepted.
Co-operatives now opening throughout country. Bookings recommended; prices vary but food and service usually better than state sector.

Currency

It is possible to withdraw money from automated teller machines in Moscow and St Petersburg using cards belonging to the leading western networks. Bring unmarked US dollar bills (printed after 1991) for travel to more obscure regions.

Credit cards

Diners', American Express, Bank of America, Carte Blanche, Eurocard and AIT credit cards are accepted at main hotels. (Eurocard at Beriozka Stores). Credit cards are not widely accepted outside Moscow and St Petersburg.

Car hire

Available in major towns. International driving licence required with Russian translation of details. Notification of route to be taken should be given if travelling outside main cities.

City transport

Taxis: May be identified by checkerboard on side of car. Green light at top righthand corner of windscreen indicates availability. Can be hired at taxi ranks or by telephoning – all regions (927-0000, 457-9005); for Kutuzovsky, Gruzinsky, Sadovaya and centre (137-0040); Izmailovo (167-9011). Charges for foreigners are often subject to negotiation and only acceptable in hard currency. Also possible to hail private (unofficial) cars by raising arm in street. Prices negotiable and usually higher than taxis, but availability plentiful although service patchy. On arrival you can now approach a reliable taxi firm in the airport arrivals section after clearing customs. Payment is by credit card. Fares can be negotiated with the driver. The fare shown on the meter may not correspond with the fare asked. Alternatively you may arrange in advance through Intourist to be met at the airport.
The journey by taxi from Sheremetyevo 2 airport to the centre of Moscow takes 40 minutes to one hour and costs approximately US$60; from Pulkovo airport to the centre of St Petersburg approximately US$30 (June 1996).
N.B. Beware of illegal taxi touts operating both in the airport area and in the city centre.
Buses: Cheap and reliable, though often crowded, available from 0600 to 0100. Standard flat fare of five kopeks. The cheapest way to and from Sheremetyevo Airport is by bus (payment by rouble only) but the service is not reliable.
Metro: Flat fare service in Moscow connecting some 120 stations. Excellent service.
N.B. Avoid travelling on the metro at night.

National transport

Air: Extensive internal service operated by Aeroflot and Transaero (due to small fleet, flights more often delayed than those of Aeroflot).
Road: Major highways connecting Moscow with Kiev (Ukraine), St Petersburg, Minsk (Belarus), Riga (Latvia) and Warsaw (Poland). Secondary roads often untarred. Roughly 60 per cent of the road network needs to be rehabilitated or upgraded.
Rail: The railways are wide-gauge. Almost all the rail network is electrified. Major means of transport. Cheap and efficient service to all major towns. Sleepers should be booked well in advance.
Water: The largest inland waterway is the River Volga. Number of inland ports and canals.

Public holidays

Fixed dates: 1-2 Jan (New Year Holiday), 7 Jan (Russian Orthodox Christmas), 23 Feb (Defenders of the Fatherland Day), 8 Mar (International Women's Day), 1-2 May (May Day Holiday), 9 May (Victory Day), 12 June (Independence Day), 22 Aug (National Flag Day), 7 Nov (Anniversary of the October Revolution), 31 Dec (New Year's Eve). N.B. If holiday falls on a Saturday or Sunday the following Monday is treated as a holiday.
Variable dates: Orthodox Easter.

Working hours

Business: (Mon–Fri) 0900 – 1730/1800 (appointments best between 0900 – 1000).
Banking: (Mon–Fri) 1000–2000. Moscow Sheremetyevo 2 airport 0800–2030 daily. Open 24 hours at St Petersburg Pulkovo airport.
Shops: (Mon) 0800 – 1900, (Tue–Sat) 0800 – 2100.

by mid-1995, large-scale privatisation of the Russian economy by the SPA and the MOP has become effectively irreversible. Including the large black economy, Russia's private sector accounted for over 70 per cent of GDP by the beginning of 1996. By that time, over 90 per cent of Russia's employed workforce was working in newly privatised enterprises of one sort or another. Continued IMF and World Bank support for Russia remains conditional on further large-scale privatisation and related enterprise restructuring, particularly in areas such as bankruptcy procedures and auditing standards.

Structurally, the greatest weakness of the large-scale privatisation programme is that it has been overwhelmingly insider-orientated and motivated by wider political considerations in the run-up to the 1996 presidential election. At the end of 1995, outside shareholders controlled only 21 per cent of newly privatised equity. The result of this has been slow progress on questions such as enterprise restructuring, over-manning, low productivity and declining profitability.

Stock market

Russia's securities market remained undeveloped in 1995. Year-end company valuations on the Moscow and other stock exchanges remained at just US$19 billion in 1995. Relative to GDP and Russia's economic potential, this is a derisory figure raising major doubts about valuation procedures. Newly privatised companies remain reluctant to use local stock exchanges to raise capital because of a widespread fear of hostile takeovers by outside investors.

The recently created Commission on Securities and Capital Markets (CSCM) has only made limited progress in regulating the often chaotic securities markets; scandals continue to surround the country's privatisation investment funds. Worryingly, the powerful Russian mafia is particularly well entrenched in financial services and privatisation. The CSCM has done little to encourage local investors to provide capital investments for newly privatised companies listed on local stock exchanges.

Thought to control over US$20 billion in cash alone, many investors and savers have illegally exported large amounts of money abroad; little of their cash is being invested locally. Where it does take place, domestic investment tends to concentrate on safe and highly profitable T-bill and bond markets, where turnover reached a record US$16 billion year-end in 1995.

Foreign investment

Continued political and economic uncertainties have had the effect of keeping FDI relatively low throughout the 1990s. At the end of 1995, total FDI was only US$5.3 billion, compared to US$3.8 billion at the end of 1994. However, FDI inflows are increasing, with a record US$1.5 billion committed in 1995. In 1996, FDI inflows were expected to exceed US$2 billion by the end of the year.

Another positive trend that became particularly noticeable in 1994/95 was increased portfolio capital inflows. By the end of 1995, these exceeded cumulative FDI. Including these portfolio and other short-term foreign capital inflows, total foreign investment in Russia at the end of 1995 was estimated at around US$12 billion. From the point of view of foreign investors, the attractions of Russia as an emerging market are relatively cheap securities and other assets, a rich resource base, a large domestic market and the possibility of significantly higher economic growth in the longer term. Local interest rates and T-bill and bond yields all also remain high. Another attraction is that the top Russian commercial banks are now fully connected to the international SWIFT clearing and payments system.

BUSINESS GUIDE — RUSSIA

Social customs

Customary to take a small gift on business/social visit. Offering basic food is considered insulting. Offer little luxuries. Many Russians take certain of their superstitions somewhat seriously. Do not give an even number of flowers, for example, as this is for funerals only; do not greet people in a doorway - considered unlucky. Strict punctuality is of no great importance and you may be kept waiting for appointments. On the other hand a certain amount of attention is paid to niceties such as seeing someone off at a train station.

Business language and interpreting/translation

Available from Intourist and Sovincentr.

Telecommunications

The telephone network remains underdeveloped. Foreign assistance in modernising the communications network in the form of joint ventures, is under way.
Telephone: Local calls may be made free of charge from hotels. Telephone directories rarely available. Numbers of official organisations and enterprises can be obtained at hotels or street information kiosks (spravochnoe).
Direct dialling available, but service is slow. Best conducted through hotel or central post office. Dialling code for Russia: IDD access code + 7 followed by area code (3432 for Ekaterinburg, 095 for Moscow, 8312 for Nizhny Novgorod, 3832 for Novosibirsk, 812 for St Petersburg, 8462 for Samara), followed by subscriber's number. International, direct dial phone boxes now in operation in Moscow, use western credit cards or phone cards purchased for hard currency. Telephone lines are, however, unreliable.
To make an international call dial 8, wait for a tone, then dial 10 followed by the country code, city code and then the phone number. For calls within the former Soviet Union, dial 8, wait for a tone, then dial the city code and local number.
Telex and telefax: Efficient and relatively cheap service. Codes and ciphers must not be used. Country code: 64 SU. Also available through joint venture with Rank Xerox are photocopying and facsimile services – only in Moscow at present.
Telegram: Available at most major hotels and post offices.

Postal service

Air mail facilities available. Surface mail often slow.

Banking

Foreign banks represented in Moscow include: American Express, ABN-AMRO Bank, Banca Commerciale Italiana, Banca Nationale del Lavoro, Banco Central Madrid, Banco di Napoli, Banco di Roma, Banco Exterior de Espana, Banco Hispano Americano, BFG (Bank für Gemeinwirtschaft), Bank-Melli-Iran, Bank of America, Bank of Scotland, Banque Paribas, Banque Nationale de Paris, Barclays Bank, Bergen Bank, Chase Manhattan Bank, Cic-Union Europêene, International et Cie, Commerzbank Aktiengesellschaft, Creditanstalt, Credit Lyonnais, Credito Italiano, Deutsche Bank, Donau-Bank, Dresdner Bank, Garanti Bank, Generale Bank (Brussels), Gotabanken, Kansallis-Osake-Pankki, Lloyds Bank, Midland Bank, Monte dei Paschi di Siena, Morgan Grenfell and Co, Moscow Narodny Bank, National Westminster Bank, Okobank, Ost-West Handels Bank, Postipankki, Pk Banken, Privatbanken, San Paolo (Instituto Bancario San Paolo di Torino), Skandinaviska Enskilda Banken, Skopbank, Société Générale, Société Générale de Banque, State Bank of India, Svenska Handelsbanken, Swedbank, Union Bank of Finland, Union Bank of Switzerland, Westdeutsche Landesbank Girozentrale, Yapi ve Kredi Bankasi. The Russian central bank took over the administration of the Tveruniversalbank, ranked 17th in the country, in July 1996. The bank's assets are estimated at R6.1bn. Some 2,500 banks have been inaugurated since the beginning of market reforms.
Central bank: Russian Federation Central Bank.
Other banks: Agricultural Bank, Bank for Foreign Trade, East–West Investment Bank, Russian Exchange Bank.

Business information

Privatisation legislation was introduced in July 1991. There were 112,000 firms privatised in 1994, compared with 89,000 in 1993.

Trade fairs

Numerous international trade fairs and exhibitions held by Foreign Trade Corporation, Expocentre, Moscow. Other trade fairs organised from time to time by non-Soviet exhibition specialists. Moscow Consumexpo, Jan.

Electricity supply

220 V AC.

Representation in capital

Afghanistan, Algeria, Angola, Argentina, Australia, Austria, Bangladesh, Belgium, Benin, Bolivia, Brazil, Bulgaria, Burkina, Burundi, Cambodia, Cameroon, Canada, Cape Verde, Chad, China, Colombia, Congo, Costa Rica, Côte d'Ivoire, Cuba, Cyprus, Denmark, Ecuador, Egypt, Equatorial Guinea, Ethiopia, Finland, France, Gabon, Germany, Ghana, Greece, Guinea, Guinea-Bissau, Guyana, Hungary, Iceland, India, Indonesia, Iran, Iraq, Ireland, Israel, Italy, Jamaica, Japan, Jordan, Kenya,

Political uncertainty, a chaotic tax system and a far from optimal legal regime for property are the principle deterrents for potential investors in Russia.

Energy

Low levels of GFI in the energy sector meant that oil and gas output continued to fall in 1995. Russian oil and gas output in 1995 was thus 307 million tonnes (mt) and 555 billion cubic metres (bcm) respectively, compared to 318 mt and 566 bcm respectively in 1994, a downward trend that was expected to continue.

Agriculture

Once accounting for around 15 per cent of GDP, but probably no more than 6 per cent by 1995, agricultural output continues to decline sharply in Russia, falling by 8 per cent in 1995 after a fall of 9 per cent in 1994. Output is expected to grow by no more than 1 per cent year-end in 1996. Timber output continues to decline although exports of timber and wood-based products began to revive in 1995 for the first time in the 1990s.

The all-important grain harvest fell to below 80 million tonnes in 1995 for the first time ever. Structurally, the major causes of this negative trend is low GFI in agriculture and food processing and incomplete land reforms. The powerful APR, in particular, is strongly opposed to the decollectivisation of farmlands and land reform remains a highly contentious issue in Russia.

As in the Soviet period, an incredible 25 to 30 per cent of all agricultural output is lost due to poor storage and distribution infrastructure. Despite its immense potential, food processing is also poorly developed. One result of this has been growing foodstuff imports to compensate for declining agricultural output and productivity. In the longer term, Russia has the potential to become a major exporter of foodstuffs, but only after its decaying agricultural sector is radically restructured and reformed.

Outlook

The December 1995 parliamentary elections represented the resurgence and resilience of communism in Russia. The result of that was growing political polarisation and uncertainty, culminating in the 1996 presidential elections. However, Boris Yeltsin's convincing victory – and the communists' peaceful acceptance of defeat – removed the prospect of serious civil unrest. Yet with the war in Chechnya escalating in mid-1996 and questions over President Yeltsin's state of health, hopes for post-election period of calm and consolidation were quickly dashed. Within weeks of the election, presidential hopefuls were vying with each, using the Chechen conflict to increase their power and discredit their opponents.

Yeltsin's victory, followed by the replacement of most of his hardline advisors with recognised reformers, should ensure that Russia's economic progress continues its steady, if erratic progress. Any major change in Russia's economic policy would lead to a run in with the IMF, which has already delayed several tranches of its April 1996 credit, and with its other foreign creditors. Without foreign financial assistance, Russia can only experience further economic decline. If such a scenario unfolds, then Russia's immense economic potential will continue to remain unrealised, with political factors once again responsible for this state of affairs.

Externally, the present political uncertainties in Russia represent a major challenge for the west. There could thus be more, rather than less, conflict between the two in the future, although Zyuganov's defeat was warmly welcomed by the EU and the USA.

BUSINES GUIDE — RUSSIA

Representation in capital (contd): Korea DPR, Republic of Korea, Kuwait, Laos, Lebanon, Libya, Luxembourg, Madagascar, Malaysia, Mali, Malta, Mauritania, Mexico, Mongolia, Morocco, Mozambique, Myanmar, Namibia, Nepal, Netherlands, New Zealand, Nicaragua, Niger, Nigeria, Norway, Oman, Pakistan, Palestine, Papua New Guinea, Peru, Philippines, Poland, Portugal, Romania, Rwanda, Saudi Arabia, Senegal, Sierra Leone, Singapore, Somalia, Spain, Sri Lanka, Sudan, Sweden, Switzerland, Syria, Tanzania, Thailand, Togo, Tunisia, Turkey, Uganda, United Arab Emirates, United Kingdom, Uruguay, USA, Venezuela, Vietnam, Yemen, Zaïre, Zambia, Zimbabwe.

Useful tips

Dress well as business people are judged by their attire. A firm handshake is important. Negotiating an agenda at the beginning of the meeting is very important. Smoking in meetings is very common. Ask permission before lighting a cigarette and offer cigarettes generously. Written communications are particularly important with large bureaucracies. Address the recipient formally and keep a copy of everything. To use modems, pack an adaptor for the five-pronged telephone jacks.
Do carry some form of identity at all times.

BUSINESS DIRECTORY

Hotels

Moscow (area code 095)
Aerostar, 37 Leningradsky Prosp, Korpus 9, 125167 (tel: 213-9000).

Baltschug Kempinski, ul Baltschug, dom 1, 113035 (tel: 230-6500; fax: (501)230-9503).

Belgrade 2, 5 Smolenskaya Street (tel: 248-7848).

Berlin, 3 Zhdanov Street (tel: 225-6901).

Bukharest, 1 Ylitsa Balchag (32 km from Vnukovo airport) (tel: 233-1005).

Cosmos, 150 Prospect Mira, 129366 (tel: 217-0785).

International, Krasnopresnenskaya Nab 12 (tel: 253-7729).

Intourist, 3/5 Tverskaya St or 3/5 Gorky Street, 103600 (tel: 203-4007/8).

Kempinski (tel: 230-6500).

Leningradskaya, 21/40 Kalanchevskaya Ulitsa (36 km from Vnukovo airport) (tel: 225-5730).

Marco Polo Presnja (tel: 202-0381).

Metropol, 1 Marksa Prospekt, 103012 (tel: 927-6000).

Mezhdunarodnaya (tel: 253-1391).

Minsk, 22 Ulitsa Gorkovo (33 km from Vnukovo airport) (tel: 299-1448).

Moskva, 1 Prospekt Marksa (tel: 292-2121).

Mozhaisky, 165 Mozhaisky Hwy (tel: 447-3434).

National (re-opened May 1995 after four-year restoration), 1/14 Marksa Prospekt (tel: 203-6539).

Novotel Sheremetyevo, Airport Sheremetyevo 2, 103339 (tel: 578-9407/8).

Olympic Penta Renaissance, Olympiskij Prosp 18/1, 129110 (tel: 971-6301).

Ostankino, 29 Botanicheskaya Ulitsa (opposite Botanical Gardens) (tel: 219-5411).

Palace, Tverskaya St 48, 125047 (tel: 447-3434, 956-3010).

Peking, 1/7 Bolshaya Sadovaya Ulitsa (tel: 253-8347).

President (tel: 239-3800).

Pullman Iris, 59A Beskudnikovsky Bulvar, 127486 (tel: 488-8000, 220-8000).

Radisson Slavjanskaya, Berezhovskaya Nab 2, 21059 (tel: 941-8020).

Rossiya, 6 Razin Street (opposite the Kremlin) (tel: 298-1442).

Savoy, Ul Rozhdestvenka 3, 103012 (tel: 929-8500, 929-8555).

Soyuz, 12 Levoberezhnaya Ulitsa (tel: 458-3240).

Ukraina, 2/1 Kutuzovsky Prospekt (tel: 243-2596, 243-3020/21).

St Petersburg
Astoria, Ul Gertsena 39, (tel: 311-4206).

Helen, 43/1 Lermontovsky Prosp, 198016 (tel: 259-2084).

Moscow, 2 Alexander Nevsky Square (tel: 274-9505, 274-2051).

Nevskij Palace, Nevskij Prosp 57, 191025 (tel: 113-1470).

Okhtinskaya (tel: 227-4438).

Pribaltiyskaya, 14 Ul Koroblestroiteley (tel: 356-5112/0263).

Pulkovskaya, Ploschad Pobedy 1, 196240 (tel: 264-5135/52, 264-5122; tx: 121477).

Reso Grand Hotel Europe, Nevski Prosp/Mikhailovskaya Ul 1/7, 191073 (tel: 312-0072).

Rossiya, 11 Chernyshevskogo Sq (tel: 987-649).

Sovetskaya, Lermontovsky Prosp 49 (tel: 259-2546).

St Petersburg, 5/2 Vyborgskaya Embankment, 194300 (tel: 542-9411).

BUSINESS DIRECTORY

Hotels (contd):

St Petersburg (area code 812)
Astoria (offers limousine service), Ul Gertsena 39, (tel: 311-4206).

Grand Europe Kempinski (centrally located), Mikhailovskaya 1-7 (tel: 329-6000; fax: 329-6001).

Helen, 43/1 Lermontovsky Prosp, 198016 (tel: 259-2084).

Moscow, 2 Alexander Nevsky Square (tel: 274-9505, 274-2051).

Nevskij Palace (offers limousine service), Nevskij Prosp 57, 191025 (tel: 113-1470).

Okhtinskaya (tel: 227-4438).

Pribaltiyskaya, 14 Ul Koroblestroiteley (tel: 356-5112/0263).

Pulkovskaya, Ploschad Pobedy 1, 196240 (tel: 264-5135/52, 264-5122; tx: 121477).

Reso Grand Hotel Europe, Nevski Prosp/Mikhailovskaya Ul 1/7, 191073 (tel: 312-0072).

Rossiya, 11 Chernyshevskogo Sq (tel: 987-649).

Sovetskaya, Lermontovsky Prosp 49 (tel: 259-2546).

St Petersburg, 5/2 Vyborgskaya Embankment, 194300 (tel: 542-9411).

Useful telephone numbers

Operator numbers: international calls (English-speaking operator) 8196.

General enquiries (Moscow area) 09, police 02.

Car hire

Moscow
Avis: Central Reservations (tel: 240-9863/2307, 241-3816; fax: 240-9932); International Airport, Sheremetevo (tel: 578-5646; fax: 240-9932); Entree 15/1, Berejkovskaya Naberejnaya 12, 121059 (tel: 240-9932; fax: 240-9932).

Budget: Central Reservations (tel: 254-4125; fax: 254-7030); Bolshaya Gruzinskaya ul 57 (tel: 254-4125; fax: 254-7030).

Europcar: Central Reservations, Leningradsky Prospect 64, 125829 (tel: 155-0170; fax: 151-6326); International Airport, Sheremetevo 2 (tel: 578-3878); Hotel Mezdunarodnaya 1, Krasnopresnenskaya Nab 12 (tel: 253-1369); Hotel Pullman, Iris, Korovinskoye, Chausse 10 (tel: 488-8000).

Hertz: Central Reservations (tel: 284-3741; fax: 284-4391); International Terminal, Sheremetevo 2 (tel: 578-7532); MTDS, Suite 11, Prospect Mira 49 (tel: 284-4391; fax: 284-3741).

St Petersburg
No international representations; local companies only.

Chambers of commerce

Chamber of Commerce and Industry, Ul Llinka 6, 103684 Moscow (tel: 929-0003/0009; fax: 206-7779).

Chamber of Commerce Consultancy Centre, same as above (tel: 925-3529; tx: 411431).

Banking

Russian Federation Central Bank (central bank). ul Zhitnaya 12, 117049 Moscow (tel: 237-5145; fax: 237-5165).

Agroprombank, Neglinnaga 12, 103016 Moscow (tel: 921-7747/5119; fax: 921-7646).

Association of Russian Banks, 4-2 Pushkinskaya Str, Moscow (tel: 292-0244; fax: 292-0448).

Commercial Bank St Petersburg, 70-72 Fontanka Embankment, 91038 St Petersburg (tel: 219-8037; fax: 315-8327).

East-West Investment Bank, 56 Nova Arbat, 121205 Moscow (tel: 290-7667; fax: 203-2804).

Foreign Trade Bank of the RSFSR, Kouznetskiy Most 16, 103031 Moscow (tel: 925-5231; fax: 412-362).

Promstroibank (All-Union capital investment bank), Tverskoybul 13, Moscow (tel: 229-2292; fax: 200-7151).

Sberbank (savings bank), ul Seleznevskaya 40, 103473 Moscow (tel: 281-8467; fax: 224-1041).

Principal newspapers

Biznes Dlya Vsekh, Volgogradsky Prospekt 26, Moscow 109316 (tel: 270-6984).

Delovoi Mir, 4th Floor, Delovoi Mir 1-5, Karopanskiy Pereulok, Moscow 103012 (tel: 928-4110/2020; fax: 928-9707, 525-7382).

Ekspress Gazeta, 15th Floor, Vadkovsky Pereulok 18A, Moscow 103055 (tel: 257-5030, 206-8306; fax: 973-3920).

Moscow Times, Room 570, Ulitsa Pravdy 24, Moscow 125866 (tel: 257-3201; fax: 257-3621).

Travel information

Aeroflot, Moscow (flight enquiries) (tel: 156-8002 [international]; 155-0922 [domestic]; St Petersburg (tel: 293-9031).

American Express Travel Service (tel: 956-9000/4).

British Airways (tel: 578-2736).

Central Hotels Information Centre, Kompositorskaya ul 25-5, Moscow.

Intourservice (trade and travel association), ul Mokhovaya 16, 103009 Moscow (tel: 203-3191/6780).

Lufthansa Sheremetyevo 2 Airport Office (tel: 578-3151, 578-2752; fax: 578-2771); town office, c/o Hotel Olimpic Penta, Prospettiva Olimpiskij 18/1, Moscow (tel: 975-2501; fax: 975-6784).

Lufthansa Pulkovo Airport Office (tel: 104-3432). town office, Uosnessenskis Pr 7, St Petrsburg (tel: 314-4979, 314-5917; fax: 312-3129).

Railway Enquiries (Moscow) (tel: 266-9000/333).

Thomas Cook Russia (tel: 244-2754).

Other useful addresses

Agentstvo Pechati Novosti (news agency), Moscow, Zubovsky bul 4 (tel: 201-2424; tx: 411323).

All-Union Central Council of Trades Unions, Leninsky Prospekt 42, 117119 Moscow.

Autoexport (vehicles, spares and garage equipment), Volkhonka Ulitsa 14, Moscow 119902 (tel: 202-8535; tx: 411125).

British Embassy, Sofiskaya Embankment, (Nabreznaya) 14, Moscow (tel: 230-6333, 230-6555; fax: 956-7420).

BSCC British-Russian Business Centre, 42 Southwark Street, London SE1 1UN (tel: (0)171-403-1706; fax: (0)171-403-1245); 22/25 Bolshoi Strochenovskiy Pereulok, Moscow 113054 (tel: 230-6120; fax: 230-6124).

Chief State Sanitary Inspector, Vodkovskiy Pereulok 18-20, Moscow.

Customs House, Komsomolskaya Ploshchad la, Moscow (tel: 208-4584).

Expocentr, 1a Sokolnicheskiy val, Moscow 107113 (tel: 268-7083; tx: 411185) (responsibility for organising, on a commercial basis, international and foreign exhibitions and symposia).

Exportkhleb (agriculture and most foreign trade corporations), 32-34 Smolenskaya Sennaya Ploshchad, Moscow 121200 (tel: 244-4701, 244-1247; tx: 411145/7).

Exportles (timber and timber products), 32-34 Smolenskaya Sennaya Ploshchad, Moscow 121200 (tel: 244-7432, 244-7440; tx: 411229).

Foreign Trade Arbitration Commission, Moscow (tel: 205-6855).

Ingosstrakh (insurance organisation), ul Pyatnitskaya 12, Moscow (tel: 233-2070; tx: 411144).

Institut Mirovoj Ekonomiki i Mezhdunarodnigh Oatnoshenij (national statistics), Jaroslavskaja 3, Moscow.

Interstate Statistical Committee of the Commonwealth of Independent States, 39 Myasnitskaya Str, Moscow 103450 (tel: 207-4237/4802/4567; fax: 207-4592; E-mail: Statpro @ Sovam.com).

Litsenzintorg (licensing), Minskaya ul 11, Moscow 121108 (tel: 145-1111; tx: 411246).

Maritime Arbitration Commission, Moscow (tel: 205-2953).

Metallurgimport (mining), ul Arkhitektora Vlasova 33, Moscow 117393 (tel: 128-0775, 128-3720; tx: 411388/9).

Ministry of Agriculture and Food, 1-11 Orlikov Lane, Moscow 107139 (tel: 207-8000; fax: 207-8362, 288-9580).

Ministry of Atomic Energy, 24-26 Bolshaya Ordynka Str, Moscow 101100 (tel: 239-4753; fax: 233-4679).

Ministry for Civil Defence, Emergencies and Disaster Resources, 3 Teatralniy Pr-D, Moscow 103012 (tel: 926-3901; fax: 924-5683).

Ministry for Communications, 7 Tverskaya Str, Moscow 119332 (tel: 229-6966, 292-7070; fax: 292-7128).

Ministry of Construction, Comp 2, 8 Stroitelei Str, Moscow 117987 (tel: 930-1755; fax: 938-2202).

Other usedul addresses (contd):

Ministry for Cooperation Between CIS Member Countries, 7 Varvarka Str, Moscow 103073 (tel: 206-1365; fax: 206-1084).

Ministry of Culture, 7 Kitaiskiy Pr-D, Moscow 103693 (tel: 925-1195; fax: 928-1791).

Ministry of Economics, 19 Noviy Arbat Str, Moscow 103025 (tel: 203-7534; fax: 203-7482).

Ministry of Education, 6 Chistoprudniy B-R, Moscow 101856 (tel: 927-0568; fax: 924-6989).

Ministry for Environmental Protection and Natural Resources, 4-6 B Gruzinskaya Str, Moscow 123812 (tel: 254-7683; fax: 254-8283).

Ministry of Finance, 9 Ilyinka str, Moscow 103097 (tel: 298-9101, 923-0967; fax: 925-0889).

Ministry of Foreign Affairs, 32-34 Smolenskaya-Sennaya Sq, Moscow 121200 (tel: 244-1606; fax: 230-2130).

Ministry for Foreign Economic Relations, 32-34 Smolenskaya-Sennaya Sq, Moscow 121200 (tel: 244-2450; fax: 244-3068/3981).

Ministry for Fuel and Power Development, 7 Kitaiskiy Pr, Moscow 103074 (tel: 220-5500; fax: 220-4818).

Ministry of the Interior, 16 Zhitnaya Str, Moscow 117049 (tel: 237-7585, 924-6572, 222-6669; fax: 925-2098).

Ministry of Justice, 4 Vorontsovo Pole Str, Moscow 109830 (tel: 209-6009/98; fax: 916-2903).

Ministry of Labour, 1 Birzhevaya Sq, Moscow 103706 (tel: 261-2030, 928-8208; fax: 230-2407).

Ministry for Nationalities and Regional Policy, 19 Trubnikovskiy Lane, Moscow 121819 (tel: 248-8635; fax: 202-4490).

Ministry of Public Health, 3 Rakhmanovskiy Lane, Moscow 103051 (tel: 928-4478; fax: 921-0128).

Ministry for Railways, 2 Novo-Basmannaya Str, Moscow 107174 (tel: 262-9901; fax: 262-9095).

Ministry for Science and Technology, 11 Tverskaya Str, Moscow 103905 (tel: 229-1192; fax: 230-2823).

Ministry for Social Protection, Bld 1, 4 Slavianskaya Sq, Moscow 103715 (tel: 220-9511/9384; fax: 924-3690).

Ministry of Transport, 10 Sadovo-Samotyochnaya Str, Moscow 101433 (tel: 200-0809; fax: 200-3356).

Ostankino Hotel (post office inside for parcel collection), Botanicheskaya ul 29, Moscow (tel: 218-1365).

Promsyrioimport (metal products), ul Chaikovskovo 13, Moscow 121814 (tel: 203-0577, 203-0646, 203-0595; tx: 411151/2, 411112).

Russian Commodity Exchange, Moscow (tel: 272-4901, 262-8080).

Russian Federation Foreign Trade Organisation, Barrikabnaya Str Bld 8-5, 123242 Moscow (tel: 254-8090; fax: 253-9675).

Russian Information Telegraph Agency (ITAR-TASS) (news agency), Tverskoy bul 10, Moscow (tel: 3229-8053; tx: 411186).

Russian Railways, ul Novobasmannaya 2, 107174 Moscow (tel: 262-1628; fax: 262-6561).

Russian Television and Radio, Corolov St 12, Moscow (tel: 217-7898; fax: 288-9508).

Sovicentr, Krasnopresnenskaya Nab 12, Moscow 123610 (tel: 256-6303; tx: 411486).

Soyuzchimexport (chemicals), 32-34 Smolenskaya Sennaya Ploshchad, Moscow 121200 (tel: 244-2284, 244-2181; tx: 411295, 411296, 411297).

Soyuzkoopvneshtorg (trade with foreign co-operative organisations), Bolshoi Cherkasskiv Perevlok 15, Moscow 103626 (tel: 923-7930; tx: 411127/9).

State Committee for Science and Technology, ul Gorkovo 11, Moscow (tel: 229-2236, 229-2039; tx: 411241).

State Committee for Standards, Leninsky Prospekt 9, Moscow (tel: 236-0300).

State Committee for the Control of State Property, Dom Pravitelstva, Moscow (tel: 291-9198).

State Committee for Statistics, 39 Myasnitskaya Street, Moscow 103450 (tel: 207-4902; fax: 207-4640).

Vneshtorgreklama (All-union advertising agency), ul Kakhovka 31 Korpus 2, Moscow 113461 (tel: 331-8311, 121-4190; tx: 411265).

Internet sites

Aeroflot:
http://www.seanet.com/Bazar/Aeroflot/Aerflot.ht

San Marino

Anthony Griffin

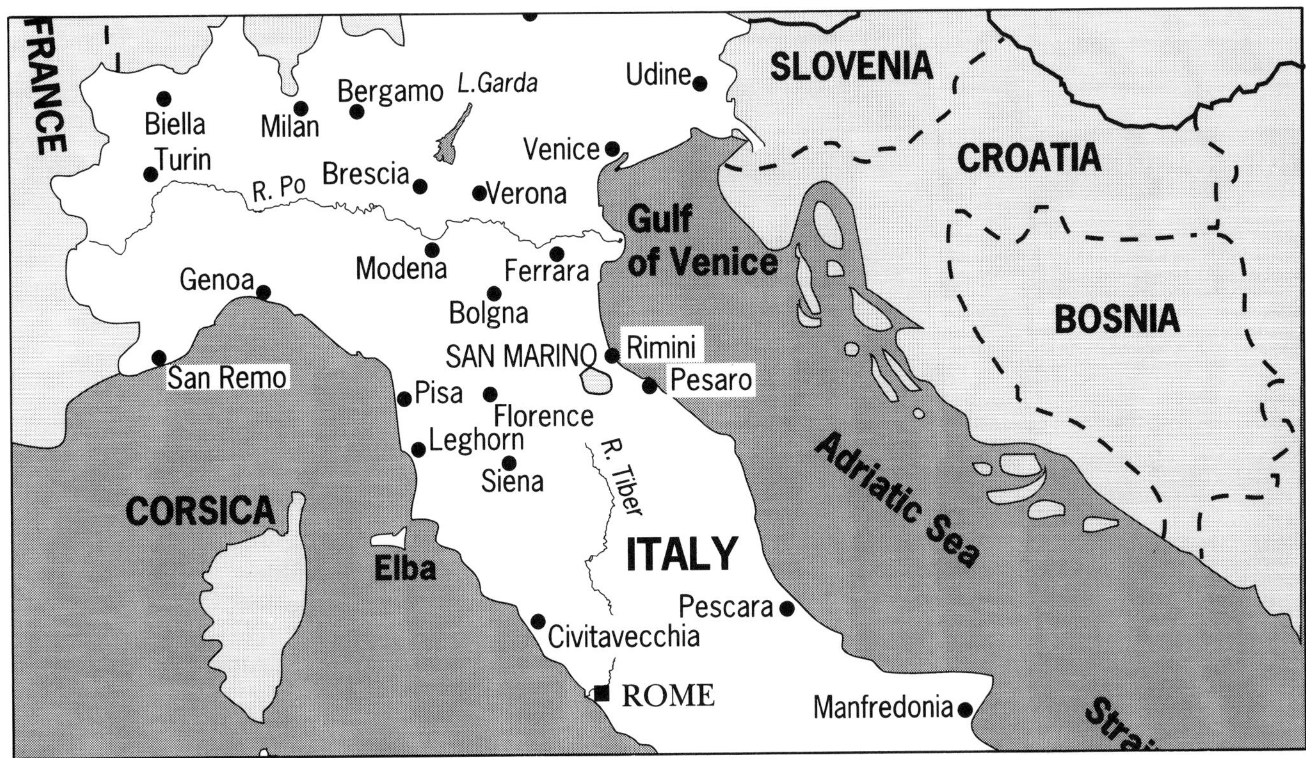

Formerly dependent on agriculture, forestry and quarrying, the 25,000 residents of San Marino, (the San Marino diaspora amounts to 13,000, 7,000 of whom are in Italy, with a further 3,000 in the USA) situated in north-central Italy near the Adriatic Sea, now rely heavily on tourism as their main source of revenue. Some three million souvenir-buying visitors each year flock to the tiny republic which has been called too touristy for its own good. Tourism accounts for 60 per cent of the government's income.

History

As the oldest surviving republic in the world, San Marino is proud of its history. A republic since the year 301, in 1996 San Marino celebrated 1695 years of independence. Located just down the road from Rimini in Italy, the country is set in a very advantageous position with superb views, from Monte Titano, of surrounding mountains and coastal areas.

Even though its population is small and the country is just over 60 square kilomeyres in size, San Marino has many of the trappings of a fully-fledged nation – it mints its own coins, issues its own stamps, and has its own army. Membership of the United Nations and the International Monetary Fund came in 1992 (February and September respectively) as a way of further asserting the country's nationhood and coming out from under the umbrella of big-brother Italy, although Italy accounts for 85 per cent of all external trade.

Elections

The May 1993 general elections – the last to be held in San Marino – showed a swing to the right, with the Partito Democratico

KEY FACTS — San Marino

Official title: The Republic of San Marino

Head of state: two Captains-Regent elected for six months at a time

Ruling party: Coalition: Partito Democratico Cristiano Sammarinese (PDCS) (San Marino Christian Democratic Party) and Partito Socialista Sammarinese (PS) (San Marino Socialist Party)

Capital: San Marino

Official Languages: Italian

Currency: San Marino Lira and Italian Lira (L) = 100 centesimi

Exchange rate: L1,528.15 per US$ (Dec 1996)

Area: 60.5 sq km

Population: 24,927 (1995)

GNP per capita: US$30,000 (1995)*

Labour force: 16,026 (1995)

Unemployment: 3.9% (1995)

Inflation: 5.4% (1995)

Visitor numbers: 3m (1995)*

* estimated figure

Cristiano Sammarinese (PDCS) (San Marino Christian Democratic Party winning 26 of the 60 seats, followed by the Socialist Party in second place with 14 seats and the Progressive Democratic Party (PDP) (the former Communist Party) gaining 11 seats. A coalition of the PDCS and the PS was formed, holding a majority of 40 seats in the Council.

In a unique system, San Marino has two heads of state known as the *Capitani Reggenti* (Captains Regent), appointed for a six-month term of office from among the 60 members of San Marino's Great and General Council. Executive power is retained by the 10 member Congress of State. Additionally, a Council of Twelve, also presided over by the *Capitani Reggenti*, is appointed by the Great and General Council to perform administrative functions and as a court of third instance.

Economy

Reliable economic figures are still hard to come by for San Marino, primarily because economic data is intermingled with figures from Italy as a result of the customs union which the countries share. Some estimates in the early 1990s put the GNP per capita at over US$20,000 per year and the World Bank calls it a high income nation. The 1995 budget reportedly balanced at L521 million. Tourism is the main source of foreign exchange, but an expansion in the capacity of its hotels and restaurants is necessary before tourism can grow beyond its day-tourist image. However, many residents are opposed to this since any expansion could irreparably spoil San Marino's unique small-country atmosphere.

Agriculture is based on livestock, wheat and grapes. The main export is wine; sales of postage stamps provide 10 per cent of the exchequer's revenues. San Marino also receives annual subsidies from the Italian government.

COUNTRY PROFILE — SAN MARINO

Political system

San Marino is the oldest surviving republic in the world. A republic since the year 301, with legislative power vested in unicameral Great and General Council, with 60 members elected every five years. Council elects two members every six months to act as *Capitani Reggenti* (Captains-Regent) who function jointly as head of state and who, with a 10-member Congress of State, exercise executive power. Country divided into nine 'Castles', each governed by a Castle-Captain.

Political parties

The Partito Democratico Cristiano Sammarinese (PDCS) (San Marino Christian Democratic Party) won the May 1993 election and formed a coalition government witht the Partido Socialista Sammarinese (PS) (San Marino Socialist Party).
The former communist Partito Democratico Progressista (PDP) (Progressive Democratic Party) has not had a share of power since it was ousted from the governing coalition in March 1992. Other major parties include the Rifondazione Comunista (RC) (Communist Refoundation); Movimento Democratico (MD) (Democratic Movement); Alleanza Democratica Popolare (ADP) (Popular Democratic Alliance).

Population

As at 1995, annual population growth was 1.55 per cent; births 10.83 per 1,000 persons; deaths 7.38 per 1,000. The population includes Sammarinese and Italians. Approximately 15 per cent of the population under 14 years of age; 68 per cent 15-64 years; 16 per cent over 65 years. Life expectancy 81 years.
Religion: Christianity (Roman Catholic).

Main city

San Marino (population 4,178).

Media

Press: Several periodicals, mostly organs of the political parties, including *Quotidano Sammarinese* and *Tribuna Sammarinese* and the *Quotidiano Si Fax* (distributed to subscribers by facsimile). Daily insert in Italian newspapers.
Broadcasting: San Marino RTV is the state broadcasting company. Broadcasts from Radiotelevisione Italiana are also received. Daily local information bulletins from private TV and radio stations in Italy.

Domestic economy

San Marino's main source of revenue is tourism. Formerly, the republic was dependent on agriculture and forestry.
San Marino mints its own coins and postage stamps. Sales of postage stamps to foreign collectors provide 10 per cent of the government's income.
The traditional industry of quarrying for building stone is also important. Emphasis is being placed on light manufacturing industries.

External trade

Customs and currency union with Italy. Import dependence on Italy. Customs union with EU. Italy accounts for 87 per cent of all external trade.
Exports: Major export is wine. Other important exports include textiles, furniture, stone, stamps, coins and ceramics.

Agriculture

The republic was formerly dependent on agriculture and forestry. The sector employed only 1.6 per cent of the workforce in 1995. Livestock is reared and wheat and grapes are important crops.

Industry

Quarrying for building stone is a traditional industry.
The industrial sector as a whole employed 16.5 per cent of the workforce in 1995.

Tourism

Tourism accounts for 60 per cent of the government's income with some 3m visitors annually.

BUSINESS GUIDE

Time

GMT + 1 hr (GMT + 2 from late Mar to late Sep).

Climate

Mediterranean, with warm summers and dry, cold winters. Temperatures can range from below 0–30˚C.

Clothing

Lightweight for summer, mediumweight and topcoat for winter.

Entry requirements

No regulations in operation.

Air access

Main international airport: Rimini (RMI) 27 km from San Marino, or Bologna (BLQ) 135 km from San Marino.

Surface access

Regular bus service along highway between Rimini and capital. Funicular operates between Borgo Maggiore and capital.

Hotels

Approximately 30 hotels, of various standards.

National transport

No railways. Limited bus service operating from Italy. Good internal services. 104 km of good roads.

Public holidays

Fixed dates: 1 Jan (New Year's Day), 6 Jan (Epiphany), 5 Feb (Liberation Day), 19 Mar (St Joseph's Day), 25 Mar, 1 Apr, 1 May (Labour Day), 29 Jun, 28 Jul, 15 Aug, 3 Sep (Republic Day), 1 Oct, 1 Nov, 2 Nov, 8 Dec (Immaculate Conception), 24 and 26 Dec (Christmas) and 31 Dec.
Variable dates: Good Friday, Easter Monday, Ascension Day, Corpus Christi.

Telecommunications

Telephone and telefax: International dialling code: 378. There are no area codes.
Telex: Telex country code: 505 1, SO.

BUSINESS DIRECTORY

Hotels

San Marino
Grand, Via Antonio Onofri 31, 47031 (tel: 992-400; fax: 992-274).

Titano, Contrada del Collegio 21, 47031 (tel: 991-007; fax: 991-375)

Business advice and information

There is no chamber of commerce in San Marino. The following government offices are useful sources of information:

Office for Industry, Handicrafts and Trade, Palazzo Mercuri (tel: 992-745, 991-385).

Secretariat of State for Finance and the Budget, Palazzo Begni (tel: 992-345; tx: 330).

Travel information

Ufficio di Stato per il Turismo (tourist board), Contrada Omagnano 20, 47031, San Marino (tel: 882-998).

Other useful addresses

Azienda Autonoma di Stato Filatelica e Numismatica (AASFN) (postage stamps and coins), Piazza Garibaldi 5, 47031 San Marino (tel: 882-370; fax: 882-363).

British Consulate, Lungarno Corsini 2, 1-50123 Florence (tel: 212-594; fax: 219-112).

Direzione Generale PPTT (post and telecommunications), Contrada Omerelli, 17 (tel: 882-555; fax: 992-760).

Notizie de San Marino, Radiotelevisione Italiana, Viale Mazzini 14, 1-00195 Rome (fax: 372-5680).

Slovakia

Marko Milivojevic

Prime Minister Vladimir Meciar and his ruling party, the Movement for a Democratic Slovakia (HZDS), have been criticised for turning Slovakia into a *de facto* one-party state reminiscent of the communist past and far removed from the democratic norms and human rights standards of the European Union (EU) and the Council of Europe. Strongly supported by the opposition Christian Democratic Movement (KDH), President Michal Kovac now sees himself as the leader of the democratic resistance. Slovakia's high GDP growth in 1995 increased the popularity of Meciar and the HZDS.

Politics

Prime Minister Meciar's HZDS government continued to be embroiled in a bitter conflict with President Michal Kovac. In August 1995, in a bizarre move, the HZDS-controlled Slovak Intelligence Service (SIS) allegedly went so far as to kidnap Kovac's son for the purposes of handing him over to the Austrian police for alleged crimes committed in that country. Other alleged SIS dirty tricks aimed at discrediting Kovac have included the publication of forged documents purporting to show that the Slovak President had stolen and illegally exported large sums of money.

Meciar's basic objective is to impeach and remove Kovac from office even though various public opinion surveys show that most Slovaks oppose such an impeachment. So far, the HZDS has attempted to secure the two-thirds parliamentary majority needed to do this by claiming that many opposition MPs were elected to parliament with falsified ballot papers in 1994. This tactic has mainly been directed at weaker opposition parties, such as the Democratic Union of Slovakia (DE).

At the same time, Meciar has skilfully played upon divisions within a divided opposition, particularly the right-left conflicts between the KDH and the Party of the Democratic Left (SDL) – a neo-communist grouping that is itself expected to split into pro-HZDS and anti-HZDS factions. If this happens, then a direct and possibly politically fatal attack against Kovac is almost certain.

Regional relations

Thought to have been resolved when Slovakia and Hungary signed a state treaty in March 1995, the sensitive issue of Slovak-Hungarian relations has in fact continued to worsen. Vocally supported by the virulently anti-Hungarian Slovak National Party (SNS), the HZDS has yet to ratify this treaty in the Slovak parliament. Further, an implicitly anti-Hungarian language law in November 1995 virtually guarantees future conflict with the country's large ethnic Hungarian minority. Strongly opposed by Kovac and the main opposition parties on the grounds that it would needlessly provoke Hungary and the EU, this controversial legislation had to be signed into law by Kovac, thereby politically humiliating himself.

Although all this effectively precludes the possibility of a genuine Slovak-Hungarian rapprochement in 1996, it is unlikely to damage Meciar and the HZDS domestically.

KEY FACTS — *Slovakia*

Official title: Slovak Republic

Head of state: President Michal Kovac

Head of government: Prime Minister Vladimir Meciar (HZDS) (since Dec 1994)

Ruling party: Three-party coalition government led by Hnutie za Demkratiche Slovensko (HZDS) (Movement for a Democratic Slovakia) and also including extreme right-wing Slovenska Narodna Strana (SNS) (Slovak National Party) and radical left-wing Association of Slovak Workers (ZRS)

Capital: Bratislava

Official Languages: Slovak

Currency: Slovak koruna (Sk introduced 6 February 1993)

Exchange rate: Sk32.06 per US$ (Dec 1996)

Area: 49,035 sq km

Population: 5.4m (1995)

GDP per capita: US$3,244 (1995)

GDP real growth: 6.4% (1995)

GNP per capita: US$2,150 (1994)

GNP real growth: 3.4% (1995)

Labour force: 1.96m (1994)

Unemployment: 11.9% (May 1996)

Inflation: 6.1% (May 1996)

Trade balance: US$59m (1995)

Foreign debt: US$5.8bn (1995)

KEY INDICATORS — Slovakia

	Unit	1991	1992	1993	1994	1995
Population	m	5.33	5.34	5.34	5.40	5.40
Gross domestic product (GDP)	US$bn	9.6	10.9	11.3	12.4	15.7
GDP per capita	US$	1,900	2,100	2,200	2,500	3,244
GDP real growth	%	-14.5	-1.6	-4.1	4.8	6.4
Inflation	%	-57.8	10.0	23.2	13.4	10.6
Unemployment	%	7.0	11.3	15.0	13.0	12.0
Employment	'000	2,008	1,995	2,012	1,977	2,020
Agricultural output	%	-6.0	-8.0	-4.0	0.0	3.0
Consumer prices	1990=100	–	–	218.5	247.7	272.3
Industrial output	1990=100	–	–	62.2	69.3	80.2
Industrial production	%	-15.0	-11.0	-10.6	6.0	10.0
Brown coal	m toe	1.2	1.0	1.0	1.0	0.9
Natural gas	m cu metres	313.4	277.3	263.6	287.8	348.8
Crude petroleum	'000 tonnes	72	62	67	67	74
Services output	%	0.0	1.0	2.0	3.5	5.0
Exports	US$bn	**8.3	**7.1	3.1	4.2	8.5
Imports	US$bn	**8.8	**7.5	4.0	4.6	8.5
Balance of trade	US$m	**-500	**-400	-900	-200	59
Foreign debt	US$bn	**2.7	**2.6	2.9	4.3	5.6
Current account	US$m	**300	**300	-700	650	450
Foreign investment	US$m	**320	**360	400	540	700
Total reserves minus gold	US$m	–	–	416	1,691	3,364
Foreign exchange	US$m	–	–	415	1,605	3,360
Discount rate	%	9.5	9.5	12.0	12.0	9.75
Deposit rate	%	–	–	8.02	9.32	8.34
Lending rate	%	–	–	14.41	14.56	15.64
Exchange rate	Sk per US$	***29.6	***28.3	30.8	32.0	29.7

**former Czechoslovakia

***former Czechoslovak Koruna

Other than widespread anti-Hungarian xenophobia, the main reason for this is the provocative posturings of the country's ethnic Hungarian parties and the implicit irredentism that they seem to espouse.

Slovakia's improved economic prospects have allowed Meciar to pursue an active economic and political engagement with Russia. This controversial policy culminated in a major Slovak-Russian summit in November 1995. Among other things, it was agreed that Russia would help rehabilitate the controversial nuclear power plant at Mochovce, which the EU would like to see closed. At that time, there were also rumours of a possible customs union between Slovakia and Russia. However, this is a risky politico-economic strategy that could leave Slovakia more isolated than ever in relation to both the EU and the USA.

A strongly nationalist party, the HZDS may benefit from Slovakia's growing international difficulties. US, EU and other foreign criticisms of Meciar and the HZDS have been branded as evidence of alleged anti-Slovak plots abroad and denounced as unacceptable foreign meddling in the country's internal affairs. As in the Czech Republic, local nationalist sentiments are also strongly anti-German.

On the other hand, Meciar has been careful not to allow his present complications with the west to escalate out of control. The hardline communist Association of Slovak Workers (ZRS) has thus not been allowed any real say over economic policy made by HZDS technocrats and the National Bank of Slovakia (NBS). This economic policy has been largely successful, which in turn has reduced external leverage over Slovakia in recent years.

Economy

Up from a negative 4.1 per cent in 1993 to a positive 4.8 per cent in 1994, Slovakia's GDP grew by a record 6.4 per cent in 1995. This gave Slovakia a GDP and GDP per capita of US$15.7 billion and US$3,000 respectively in 1995. Relative to the Czech Republic, Slovak GDP in 1995 was around a third of that of its former Czechoslovak partner (US$45.5 billion in 1995). Slovak GDP per capita in 1995 remained at just below two-thirds of its level in the Czech Republic (US$4,300 in 1995).

Year-end inflation fell to 10.6 per cent in 1995 compared to 13.4 per cent in 1994. Based on lower and declining monthly inflation during the last quarter of 1995, single figure inflation is possible in 1996.

Unlike the Czech Republic, Slovakia has been able to increase its exports faster than its imports, mainly because of a controversial import surcharge in 1995. Accounting for a record 65 per cent of GDP by 1995, the booming private sector was expected to generate higher domestic demand in 1996/97. Assuming export growth continues, then year-end GDP growth in 1996 could be higher than the 4.8 per cent projected at the end of 1995.

Following on from rapid export growth, increased domestic demand and full currency stability in 1995, fixed capital formation increased by 2.4 per cent, with even higher levels of new investment expected by year-end 1996. Although not yet as significant as in the Czech Republic, increased levels of investment represent an important trend in Slovakia, particularly with regard to the ongoing recapitalisation of its private sector.

Year-end unemployment in 1995 was 12 per cent of the employed workforce, compared to 13 per cent a year earlier. Particularly high job creation was experienced in private sector services and light manufacturing.

Even more so than in 1994, real wages rose rapidly in 1995. Year-end real wage growth was 10 per cent, compared to 5 per cent in 1994. In April 1996, the country's minimum wage was also increased by 10 per cent, mainly at the urging of the ZRS. In the longer term, this may not be sustainable, especially if local productivity continues to lag behind that of the Czech Republic and other Visegrad Group (VG) states.

Budget and IMF

Despite wider political uncertainties, the government and the NBS continued with macro-economic stabilisation in 1995. The 1996 government budget was passed without delays in December 1995. With projected expenditures of Sk189.4 billion and revenues of Sk162.4 billion, this envisages a deficit of Sk27 billion, or well below 3 per cent of projected GDP in 1996. In 1995, the government budget deficit was equal to a higher 4 per cent of GDP.

This situation led to some difficulties with the International Monetary Fund (IMF), with whom the government had earlier agreed an economic policy memorandum. At the time that this memorandum was signed in June 1995, it was thought that Slovakia would draw its third and final tranche of its 1994 stand-by loan from the IMF. In the event, Slovakia's improved economic prospects in 1995 resulted in growing government ambivalence about accepting any further IMF conditionality. Among other things, the disbursement of existing IMF loans worth US$100 million and the provision of new credits for 1996 would be conditional on a number of key policy changes that the HZDS government opposes. These include the lifting of all import surcharges, energy price liberalisation and the removal of all remaining price controls. On the macro-economic stabilisation front, however, Slovakia has already fulfilled most of its commitments to the IMF. For this reason, some sort of new agreement with the IMF is possible.

External trade

Accounting for nearly 50 per cent of GDP in 1995, Slovakia's exports reached a record US$8.53 billion in that year, a rise of 26.2 per cent over their 1994 level. Over the same period, imports rose by a similar amount to a record US$8.48 billion. As in 1994, this resulted in a small trade surplus, or US$59 million in 1995. In 1996, Slovakia's foreign trade was expected to continue growing rapidly, albeit at a lesser rate than in 1995.

Foreign demand for Slovak base chemicals, machinery, equipment and consumer goods remains buoyant. Import growth in 1995 would have been even higher but for the government's import surcharge policy. Demand for imported energy resources remains high, as does demand for consumer goods, particularly automotive products.

Although not yet as economically integrated with the EU as the Czech Republic, Slovakia's foreign trade is increasingly orientated towards the west. In 1995, the EU accounted for 35 per cent of the country's exports and imports. Almost uniquely in the Visegrad Group, Slovakia continues to run a trade surplus with the EU. As of 1 January 1996, Slovak steel exports to the EU were no longer subject to quotas; this measure will have greatly benefited Slovakia in 1996. In 1995, the Czech Republic accounted for a third of Slovak foreign trade. Following the end of the special clearing account between the two sides in October 1995, bilateral Slovak-Czech trade was expected to decline, but this did not happen in 1996. Only with Russia, from where Slovakia imports most of its oil and gas, is Slovak foreign trade in deficit. Following the signing of trade agreements, Slovak exports to Russia are expected to grow rapidly.

Slovakia's better than expected foreign trade performance in 1995 meant that its current account remained in surplus to the tune of US$450 million. This surplus was mainly generated by increased oil-gas transit fee income from Russia, a positive tourism account balance and greater construction services income abroad.

Foreign debt and funding

Slovakia continues to have the lowest foreign debt in the VG. Following the signing of stand-by credit agreements with the IMF in 1993/94, this increased from US$2.9 billion to US$4.3 billion in that one year. At the end of 1995, Slovakia's foreign debt reached US$5.6 billion. Almost uniquely in the VG, Slovakia's foreign debt management strategy is highly conservative and prudent, with nearly all new foreign borrowing set aside for the NBS or productive investment in infrastructure development.

Unlike the Czech Republic, Slovakia does not use new foreign borrowings for general balance of payments financing. One result of this in 1995, was the attainment of the second-best country debt rating in central and eastern Europe. At the end of 1995, the NBS was not planning to increase substantially its new foreign borrowings.

Notwithstanding its political difficulties with the EU, Slovakia has been able to continue profiting from EU economic assistance. Signed in December 1995, Slovakia's latest loan from the EU involves Sk220 million (US$280 million) over the next five years under the Phare programme. Mainly to be used for infrastructure development, this money may also be supplemented from new loans from the European Investment Bank. Also in 1996, a joint European Bank for Reconstruction and Development-European Union (EBRD-EU) funding project may provide up to US$85 million for new motorway construction. Previously costed at US$220 million, these new road links to Vienna and Prague are part of a wider US$3.8 billion 10-year infrastructure development programme in Slovakia.

Politically, some of these projects are controversial, notably the Mochovce nuclear power plant. Here, Russia is now playing a major role, beginning with a US$25 million rehabilitation loan in 1996. Over the next five years, Russia is also to provide US$240 million worth of goods and services for the modernisation and expansion of nuclear power generation in Slovakia. An earlier EBRD offer to fund the reconstruction of Mochovce was turned down by the government in 1995.

Slovakia has significant debt claims against Russia, which has agreed to pay them off by reconstructing Mochovce and through the supply of armaments to the Slovak armed forces.

The Czech Republic's termination of the special clearing account in October 1995 resulted in the payment of Ecu98.9 million (US$126.6 million) to the NBS by the Czech central bank in December 1995. Representing 76 per cent of Czech debt to Slovakia of Ecu130 million, this payment was to be followed by the supply of goods to the value of Ecu31.1 million to Slovakia in 1996. After the imposition of UN economic sanctions against Iraq and the Federal Republic of Yugoslavia during the 1990s, Slovakia asked for international compensation for its trade and other losses in these two countries.

Foreign investment

Foreign direct investment (FDI) in Slovakia is relatively limited to date. At the end of 1995, total FDI amounted to only US$700 million, less than 15 per cent of the level in the Czech Republic (US$5.5 billion in 1995). Although double its level in 1994, 1995 FDI in Slovakia remains way below the country's economic potential.

Slovakia's strong economic performance since 1993 has enabled Meciar and the HZDS to be extremely selective about allowing FDI into the local economy. FDI is low and looked unlikely to increase substantially in 1996, mainly because the proposed large-scale privatisation of the state industrial sector implicitly favours local and insider-orientated methods of ownership transformation.

Under different circumstances and upon attainment of the sort of investment grade country rating recently given to the Czech Republic, FDI in Slovakia could rise substantially, especially from nearby Austria, which accounted for 21 per cent of all foreign investment in the country in 1995. Unlike the Czech Republic, Slovakia is not yet seen as a major emerging market by foreign portfolio investors. Some of the largest foreign investors in Slovakia have been from the USA.

Foreign exchange

With declining inflation, exchange rate stability and then full external convertibility in 1995, the koruna remains one of the stronger national currencies of the VG. Since its introduction in February 1993, when the currency union with the Czech Republic ended, the koruna has been relatively stable, based on a semi-fixed exchange rate of Sk30 per US$ and Sk20 per DM1. As of 1 January 1996, the NBS widened the band within which it fixes the exchange rate against a 60 per cent DM and 40 per cent US dollar basket from plus or minus 1.5 per cent to plus or minus 3 per cent. In practice, this represented a slight *de facto* devaluation of the koruna, given that the NBS will almost certainly fix the exchange rate daily at the upper end of the wider 3 per cent band.

In 1995 there were increased calls locally for a more significant competitive devaluation of the koruna, but these were resisted by the government and the NBS on the grounds that such a policy would fuel inflation through higher import costs. With higher than expected export growth in 1995 there was also less reason for such a devaluation by the end of that year.

Following the end of the special clearing account with the Czech Republic in October 1995, the koruna was given added credibility when the government and the NBS decided to make it fully externally convertible for all current account transactions. This move was prompted by a similar move by the Czech Republic. Although this could lead to greater exchange rate volatility, it is unlikely to do so in practice, not least because NBS hard currency reserves for intervention and other purposes reached record levels in 1995.

Following on from the improved economic prospects of 1995, when koruna-denominated assets became increasingly attractive to local investors and savers, total hard currency reserves as of January 1996 reached a record US$5 billion, of which the NBS held US$3.4 billion. Over 1994, when year-end hard currency reserves were US$3 billion, this represented a rise of 90 per cent in one year. Externally, this positive trend gave the government greater leeway in relation to the IMF and other foreign creditors in 1995/96.

Within the former Czechoslovakia, the greater availability of hard currency in Slovakia meant that the end of the special clearing account with the Czech Republic in October 1995 proved to be far more manageable than originally envisaged. Domestically, the move into koruna-denominated assets in 1995 has increased local savings substantially, so increasing the resources available for new investment.

In the longer term, the NBS may reduce the price of money through a lowering of still highly positive interest rates, but only when inflation and all inflationary expectations are completely eliminated in Slovakia. This could make Slovakia theoretically eligible for full membership of the OECD.

COUNTRY PROFILE — SLOVAKIA

Historical profile

The Czech Republic and Slovakia previously formed a federation, Czechoslovakia. However, on 1 January 1993 it divided into two independent countries, the Czech Republic (comprising the regions of Bohemia and Moravia) and the Slovak Republic.

Political system

Legislative authority is vested in a 150-member National Council of the Slovak Republic which is directly elected for a four-year term. The National Council elects the president, who is head of state, for a five-year term by a secret ballot. Michal Kovac was elected president by the National Council on 15 February 1993.
In elections held in September/October 1994, the populist Movement for a Democratic Slovakia (HZDS), under the leadership of Vladimir Meciar, won the largest number of seats and a coalition government was formed in December 1994 with the Slovak National Party (SNS) and the Worker's Union (ZRS).

Political parties

Coalition government comprising Hnutie za Demkraticke Slovensko (HZDS) (Movement for a Democratic Slovakia); Farmers' Party of Slovakia (RSS); extreme right-wing Slovenska Narodna Strana (SNS) (Slovak National Party) and radical left-wing Association of Slovak Workers (ZRS).
Other major parties: Democratic Union of Slovakia (DE), breakaway from HZDS, led by Jozef Moravcik; Strana Demokratickej l'Avice (SDL) (Party of the Democratic Left), former communist party; Socialne Demokraticka Strana na Slovensku (SDSS) (Social Democratic Party in Slovakia); Farmers' Movement; Green Party; Krestanskodemokraticke Hnutie (KDH) (Christian Democratic Movement); Hungarian minority coalition comprising the Madarske Krestanskodemokraticke Hnutie (MKDH) (Hungarian Christian Democratic Movement), Egyutteles, Spoluzitie, Wspolnota, Suzitie and Magyar Neppart (Hungarian People's Party).

Population

The chief minorities are Hungarians (10.8% of the population), Czechs (3%) and Ruthenians, Ukrainians, Germans and Poles.

Main cities/towns

Bratislava (capital, estimated population 460,000 in 1995), Kosice (238,000).

Language

Slovak is the only official language. Czech and Slovak languages are mutually comprehensible. Russian was the official language under the previous regime but is not widely spoken. A large proportion of the population, particularly those engaged in industry and foreign trade, speaks German. English is not so widely known but knowledge of it is increasing, especially among the younger generation. In academic and cultural circles, especially among the older generation and in the ministries, a knowledge of French is usual, but this is declining. Hungarian is widely spoken, especially in the south and east.

Media

Press: The newspaper and periodicals scene is changing constantly, with new titles appearing and unsuccessful ones disappearing virtually all the time. *The Slovak Spectator*, an English-language newspaper, was launched on 1 March 1995. It is published every second Wednesday.
Dailies: The main daily newspapers include *Novy Cas, Pravda, Praca, Sport Nike, Narodna Obrada, Slovenska Republica, Smena, Slovensky Vychod* and *Ujazo* (Hungarian).
Weeklies: The main weekly magazines include *Eurotelevizia, Zivot, Slovenka* and *Express.*
Radio: Slovenska Radio broadcasts nationally. Since the 1989 overthrow of the communist regime radio underwent major changes and was divided strictly along the republican lines. A new law on broadcasting came into effect in 1991. From 1992 foreign radio stations were allowed to broadcast – Europe 2 (French), Radio Free Europe and BBC World Service (English, Czech and Slovak).
Television: State-owned Slovenska Televizia (STV), broadcasts nationally on channels STV1 and STV2. A third channel (OK3) broadcasts a mixture of CNN, BBC, Sky and other international stations. TV Markiza, Slovakia's first private terrestrial station, began broadcasting 31 August 1996.

Domestic economy

The republic is moving more slowly on free-market reforms than the Czech Republic. Currency union with the Czech Republic dissolved 8 February 1993. The Slovak economy has been stabilised and is growing. The second phase of privatisation, which began in September 1994, although temporarily suspended by the Meciar government in December 1994, is slowly proceeding.

Employment

The calibre of the workforce is high; a large percentage is well educated, and some skilled labour is available. The economic growth of 1994 resulted in a higher level of new job creation in the private sector. Real wages are also rising.

External trade

Slovakia's foreign trade is increasingly orientated towards the west. From January 1996 Slovak steel exports to the EU are no longer subject to quotas.
In 1995 the Czech Republic accounted for a third of Slovak foreign trade.
Exports: Exports totalled US$8.53bn in 1995, a rise of 26.2 per cent over the 1994 total. Main exports include semi-manufactured goods, notably petro-chemicals, steel and textiles.
Main destinations: CEFTA (44.3% of 1995 total, of which Czech Republic 35.2%), EU (37.4%), former Soviet Union (7.1%).
Imports: Imports totalled US$8.48bn in 1995.
Main sources: EU (34.7% of 1995 total), CEFTA (32.9%, of which Czech Republic 27.5%), former Soviet Union (19.5%).

Agriculture

The agriculture sector accounted for 5 per cent of GDP in 1995. The sector employs 10 per cent of the labour force. This is still the most heavily

Banking

First introduced before parliament in 1995, a new banking law was due to be promulgated in 1996. Among other things, this would strengthen the regulatory powers of the NBS, particularly as regards capitalisation ratios, bad debt provisions and the monitoring of new loans by commercial banks.

More controversially, the HZDS government plans to privatise most of the country's top commercial banks. Suddenly announced by the government without consultation with the NBS and the National Property Fund (NPF) in January 1996, this radical change of policy was immediately denounced by the opposition as yet another example of insider-orientated privatisation designed to aid the ruling party and its supporters.

Political factors aside, this rushed privatisation plan will have adverse economic consequences, particularly as regards greater enterprise ownership of creditor commercial banks and all that this would inevitably entail. As expected, foreign commercial banks are to be excluded from the proposed privatisation of the Slovak banking system.

Privatisation

Cancelled by the incoming HZDS government in December 1994, the second and most crucial stage of large-scale privatisation in Slovakia continues to generate intense political controversy. Drafted by the KDH government before it lost power in October 1994, this privatisation plan was to have involved ownership transformation based on vouchers distributed to 3.5 million Slovak citizens. Involving 600 large state companies with a nominal book value of US$6 billion, voucher-based privatisation may have created the sort of share-owning democracy that already exists in the Czech Republic.

In the event, this radical form of ownership transformation was abandoned by the HZDS government in favour of insider-orientated privatisation. HZDS privatisation is also generally hostile to foreign investors. According to the HZDS government, its amended privatisation policy is proper and legal and this view was upheld by the constitutional court in a controversial ruling in December 1995. Politically, the HZDS-controlled NPF has also generated controversy by publicly supporting Meciar in his feud with Kovac.

At the popular level, the abandonment of voucher-based privatisation has been less controversial than expected. The main reason for this is that the government decided to compensate voucher holders with five-year bonds worth Sk10,000 (US$330) each, with an annual interest rate of 19.5 per cent. Issued on 1 January 1996, these transferable bonds can now be used to purchase NPF shares or be used in lieu of money payable for retirement and health contributions.

There is some indication that the government's emphasis on insider-orientated privatisation has a degree of popular support, not least because it stresses job retention and excludes outside investors from newly privatised enterprises. Economically, however, this approach to privatisation will do little to recapitalise and

COUNTRY PROFILE — SLOVAKIA

Agriculture (contd): subsidised sector of the economy and is relatively labour intensive. The most common forms are the agricultural co-operative and the state farm. Cultivation of private plots is minimal, accounting for approximately 4 per cent of agricultural land and output. The main crops are sugar beet, wheat, maize and potatoes. In May 1991 the Federal Assembly passed a law on land restitution under which all agricultural land taken by the state after February 1948 is to be returned to its original owners, or if such a return is not possible, for the owners to be compensated. The take up for private ownership is low although many collective farms are being broken up into smaller units. The forestry sector has suffered serious environmental damage caused by toxic emissions from industry and power stations. Official statistics show that 14 per cent of forests have been damaged or destroyed.

Industry

The industrial sector accounted for 50 per cent of GDP in 1995. The sector employs 35 per cent of the labour force. Particularly strong growth took place in the metal-working and petro-chemical sectors. The extent of industry ranks the Slovak Republic among the most industrialised countries of the world. The principal industries are the manufacture of machinery, chemicals and rubber, food and beverages, and iron metallurgy. Much of its military-related heavy industry is slowing down. Slovakian industry is much more vulnerable to the instability of eastern European markets than its Czech neighbour. As an example, the Slovakian Steel Works (VSZ) is the main employer in Kosice, the main city of the eastern region. The long-term prospects for Slovakian industry depend on how successfully the country can recover from the dislocation of its traditional markets and find new ones for such key industries as steel. The Slovakian government puts much faith in winning markets in the European Community (EU).

Mining

Slovakia has workable deposits of antimony, mercury, lead, zinc, precious metals, magnesite, limestone, dolomites, gravel, brick loam, ceramic materials and salt. In each case except iron ores, only small quantities are actually mined. Argosy Mining Corporation started exploration programme in December 1995 on the Pukanec epithermal gold project in central Slovakia.

Hydrocarbons

Coal is mined on a large scale. Reserves could last more than 40 years. Coal production 0.9m tonnes oil equivalent in 1995, down 10 per cent on 1994 output. Most is low quality brown coal (lignite) which causes pollution.
Oil and natural gas resources are very limited, providing only 1 per cent and less than 5 per cent, respectively, of the country's requirements.

Energy

Most of the electrical capacity is from thermal sources, the rest comes from hydroelectric and nuclear stations. Emphasis is placed on the commission of new nuclear power stations and the upgrading of Chernobyl-style reactors. Hydroelectrical generation was to be boosted by the building of a large-scale dam project on the river Danube to be built with the close collaboration of the Hungarian government. Pressures from environmental lobbies led to the withdrawal of Hungarian involvement in 1992. New nuclear capacity is due to come on stream from the station at Mochovce; there are plans for another reactor at Jaslovske Bohunice and a completely new station at Kacerovce, where work was scheduled to begin in 1995.

Banking

Two-tier banking system introduced.

Stock exchange

The Bratislava Stock Exchange began trading in April 1993 and trades one day each fortnight. It is financed by four Slovak banks and insurance companies.

Legal system

The state adopted all federal laws (except those which would be unconstitutional).

Membership of international organisations

Bank for International Settlements, CEFTA, CERN, Council of Europe, CSCE, EBRD, EU (associate member), IAEA, IDA, IFC, IMF, MIGA, NACC, Partnership for Peace, WEU (associate partner), World Bank, WTO. Slovakia has applied for full EU membership.

BUSINESS GUIDE

Time

GMT + 1 hr (GMT + 2 hrs from late Mar to late Sep).

Climate

A continental climate (warm summers and cold winters). Maximum temperatures are 32 degrees C to 35 degrees C; July is the hottest month (average 29.9 degrees C). Minimum temperatures are -12 degrees c to -20 degrees C. January is the coldest month (average -8 degrees C). Long-term average rainfall is approximately 490 mm.

Entry requirements

Visa: No visa is needed for UK citizens visiting for periods of up to six months. No visa is required for citizens of most European countries for visits of up to three months but for stays for longer than 30 days, they are required to register with the immigration services. People staying in hotels are automatically registered with the authorities. Holders of Canadian passports require a visa. If you plan to obtain visa in Prague, please note that the embassy only accepts US dollars cash and the only place to get US dollars is the Amex office in Wenceslas Square.
Health: Citizens of European states entering Slovakia from Europe are not required to show a certificate of inoculations. An inoculation certificate is required only from citizens of, or visitors arriving from, states outside Europe.

restructure the enterprises concerned. Slovak privatisation, as it is presently being implemented, leaves little room for the development of privatisation investment funds or the Bratislava Stock Exchange. Furthermore, the government banned all informal over-the-counter share trading in 1995, thereby precluding the possibility of more widespread share ownership. Even where the NPF has privatised enterprises by selling stock at a discount to managers and employees, the government has nearly always retained a controlling interest.

In 1995, the NPF agreed to dispose of Sk50 billion worth of shares in around 500 enterprises. So far, most of the enterprises so privatised have been small-to-medium sized. More important state industrial enterprises – those deemed to be strategic to the national economy – have been handled differently by the government and its NPF nominees.

In the case of Slovnaft, the highly profitable oil and gas monopoly and the largest industrial company in Slovakia, the NPF held a 75 per cent stake in 1994. This NPF stake was to be reduced to just 35 per cent, with the balance to be offered to domestic and foreign investors at Sk1,000 per share. In early 1995 this attracted considerable foreign investor interest, notably from Austria's OMV-AG and the EBRD, which bought a 10.5 per cent stake in the company. In June 1995, the government announced it intended to retain a controlling interest in Slovnaft and 29 other strategic companies. In August 1995, the NPF sold 39 per cent of Slovnaft stock to its managers and employees at a discounted Sk156 per share, harming the interests of outside shareholders, including the EBRD.

It is clear that privatisation is now too far advanced to be reversible in Slovakia and the HZDS government has disregarded the views of its junior coalition partner, the ZRS, which would like to stop it altogether. Privatisation of the state industrial sector is expected to be completed in 1996/97, but on terms that mainly benefit insiders and the ruling party.

Industry and agriculture

Accounting for 50 per cent of GDP, industrial output increased by 10 per cent in 1995, compared to 6 per cent in 1994. Particularly high growth was registered during the second half of 1995, with the best results recorded for base chemicals, steel and machine-building.

Relatively marginal at 5 per cent of GDP in 1995, agricultural output began to stabilise; higher output was expected in 1996. In 1995/96, the government decided to maintain the 6 per cent VAT rate for foodstuffs, so boosting demand for cheaper locally-produced agricultural products as opposed to imports of similar commodities.

In addition, the reduction of VAT more generally on 1 January 1996 from 25 per cent to 23 per cent was accompanied by an extension of the 6 per cent tax band for foodstuffs to other consumer goods, which further strengthened local demand, and hence industrial output including processed agricultural products.

In September 1995, in a related measure, tariffs on imported passenger vehicles were also reduced so as to stimulate demand for automotive products. The main aim of these measures is to ensure that more econ-

BUSINESS GUIDE — SLOVAKIA

Entry requirements (contd): There are no health hazards for foreign visitors in Slovakia and if needed, medical aid is provided free of charge within the range stipulated by the appropriate international agreements. First-aid services operate round the clock in all regional and district towns as well as in some smaller towns. Visitors may be asked to pay (in hard currency) for dental treatment.
Currency: Traveller's cheques can be changed at official bureaux.

Weights and measures

Metric system. In addition, the following measures are used: quintal or metric hundredweight = 100 kg. Food is usually purchased by the decagramme and kilogram.

Air access

It is easier to reach Bratislava from Vienna than to fly direct. Vienna and Bratislava are only 50 km apart - the train takes an hour and a half, while a taxi takes one and three quarter hours. CSA operates flights from Prague to Bratislava and Kosice.
Airlines serving: Aeroflot, Air Saravi, Czech Airlines (CSA), Donavia, Hemus Air, Tatra Air.
Tax: International departures US$7.40, except transit passengers and children under two years (Jan 1996).
International airport: Bratislava - Ivanka Airport, 8 km from city centre.
Airport: Kosice - Barca Airport, 3.2 km from city centre.

Credit cards

Credit cards are generally accepted by the major hotels and restaurants.

City transport

Taxis: Good service operating in all main towns - cheap and plentiful. Most taxi drivers produce a receipt on request. Surcharges for journeys between 2200 and 0600.
Buses: The journey from Prague to Bratislava takes about four hours by bus. Bratislava is well served by trams and buses.

Public holidays

Fixed dates: 1 Jan (Establishment of the Slovak Republic), 6 Jan (Epiphany and Orthodox Christmas), 1 May (Labour Day), 5 Jul (St Cyril and St Methodius Day), 29 Aug (Anniversary of the Slovak National Uprising), 1 Sep (Constitution Day), 15 Sep (Our Lady of Sorrows Day), 1 Nov (All Saints' Day), 24 Dec (Christmas Eve), 25 Dec (Christmas Day), 26 Dec (Boxing Day).
Variable dates: Good Friday, Easter Monday.

Working hours

Business: (Mon-Fri) 0600 - 0830 and 1400 - 1800.
Banking: (Mon-Fri) 0800 - 1400. There are also exchange offices in the main city centres, which operate seven days a week until 1900.
Shops: (Mon-Fri) 0900 - 1200 and 1400 - 1800; (Sat) 0900 - 1200; some shops remain open late on Thursday evenings.

Social customs

Shaking hands is customary when meeting people and on parting. When drinks are served, it is customary to wait for everyone to be served and then wish each person *Na zdravi*. When eating, it is usual to wait for everyone to be served before eating and to wish everyone *bon appetit* or *dobrou chut* just before eating. The terms Pan (Mr.), Pani (Mrs.) and Slecna (Miss) are used. Slecna is used for single women under 30 only; single women over 30 will usually be addressed as Pani.

Telecommunications

The government is seeking to double the number of telephone lines in Slovakia by the year 2000 through digitalisation of the public network. Tariffs were set to increase from 1 April 1993. A comprehensive privatisation project for the telecommunications system was expected to be completed by June 1993 although it seemed likely that part will remain under state control.
Telephone and telefax: Direct dialling available from major towns. International dialling code: 421 (from 1 March 1997) followed by 7 for Bratislava.

Banking

Banks: In January 1993 there were four state-owned banks and 11 private banks. A joint venture between the French state-owned bank Crédit Lyonnais and the Vseobecna Uverova Banka, the largest Slovak bank, created a new bank 90 per cent controlled by Crédit Lyonnais. The new bank is in Bratislava and is called Crédit Lyonnais Bank Slovakia. It offers a complete range of services and financing for state companies, joint ventures with foreign businesses and units of foreign companies.

Trade fairs

For information regarding trade fairs in Bratislava and Kosice, contact INCHEBA, Drienova ul. 24-826 17 Bratislava (tel: 801-111; fax: 848881).

Electricity supply

Domestic: 220 V, 50 cycles AC is almost universal. Most of the better hotels have standard international two-pin plugs. Where these are not fitted, standard Czechoslovak sockets are used; ordinary plugs will not fit, as they have an arrangement of two sockets and a grounding pin. Lamp fittings are screw-type. Industrial: 360 V, 50 cycles.

BUSINESS DIRECTORY

Hotels

Bratislava
Devine, Riecna 4, 89721 (tel: 3300851/4).

Forum, Mierove Namesti 2, 81625 (tel: 3480115).

Interhotel, Urxova 9, 82900 (tel: 2380920).

Interhotel Carlton, Hviezdoslavovo Namesti 5, 89828 (tel: 231-851).

Interhotel Kiev, Rajska ul 2, 89516 (tel: 52-041).

Interhotel Zlate Piesky, Senecka cesta 12, 81800 (tel: 65-170).

Tatra, Nam 1 Maje 5, 81106 (tel: 52-100).

omic demand is domestically sourced, even if this implies higher import growth in the future.

Services

The service sector continued to experience rapid growth in 1995, particularly retail and wholesale trade, construction and transport. Services account for around 45 per cent of GDP. Significantly aided by major infrastructure development in 1995, Slovak construction companies substantially increased their overseas service earnings, notably in the Czech Republic and Russia.

Although not as significant as in the Czech Republic, tourism services are growing rapidly. In 1995, Slovakia registered a large surplus on its tourism services account. Another positive development on the services front in 1995 was increased transit fees from Russian oil and gas transfers over Slovakia's pipeline network.

Previously relatively insignificant, financial services are expected to grow rapidly throughout the rest of the 1990s. Ideally situated close to Vienna, Slovakia has considerable potential as a regional transportation hub, particularly with regard to the EU, the VG and Russia.

Outlook

The re-election and subsequent policies of the HZDS government have caused considerable concern abroad, particularly in the EU, where Slovakia is clearly at a growing disadvantage in relation to the Czech Republic on the key issue of securing full EU membership. Full Slovak membership of NATO is equally questionable.

Slovakia could become increasingly isolated in the west due to a number of factors. These include the HZDS government's less than complete commitment to democratic politics, the country's poor human and minority rights record, the unsettled internal political struggle, worsening relations with Hungary and a drift towards Russia. This isolation would virtually guarantee Slovakia's exclusion from the EU and NATO well into the future.

Economically, however, Slovakia is now one of the strongest members of the VG. Macro-economic stabilisation has been largely achieved, resulting in high and non-inflationary economic growth, a stable and fully convertible currency, large hard currency reserves, a favourable foreign trade structure and balance of payments, and a relatively low foreign debt.

Large-scale privatisation has so far been largely motivated by political rather than longer term economic considerations, although the trend towards an economically dominant private sector is now effectively irreversible. Related to this, FDI remains relatively low, with political factors once again largely responsible for this state of affairs.

Externally, Slovakia's growing economic strength largely precludes major IMF influence over domestic economic policy. Domestically, this trend is also strengthening the dominance of Meciar and the HZDS, virtually guaranteeing that they will remain in power until 1998 at least, and possibly well into the next century.

BUSINESS DIRECTORY — SLOVAKIA

Car hire

Bratislava

Europcar: Hotel Dunube, Rybne Namestie 1 (tel: 534-0841/7); Letisko Ivanka Airport (tel: 522-0285).

Hertz: Airport (tel: 291-482); Hotel Forum, Mierove Namestie 2 (tel: 334-441; fax: 334-441).

Kosice

Europcar: Tovarenska 1 (tel: 622-4066).

Hertz: Central Reservations (tel: 633-0656; fax: 633-0444); Kosice Airport (tel: 622-2570; fax: 30-444); Watsonova 5 (tel: 30-656).

Chambers of commerce

Slovak Chamber of Commerce and Industry, Gorkého 9, 816093 Bratislava (tel: 490-596; fax: 330-754).

Banking

National Bank of Slovakia, Stúrova 2, 81854 Bratislava (tel: 319-1111/2440; fax: 319-2271, 210-3412).

Consolidation Bank SFI, Cintori\01nska 21, 81499 Bratislava (tel: 321-087; fax: 321-353).

Czechoslovak Commercial Bank, Michalská 18, 81563 Bratislava (tel: 534-5230; fax: 533-2775).

Devi\01n Banka as, Frantiskánske nám 8, 81310 Bratislava (tel: 333-376; fax: 330-376).

General Credit Bank, Námestie SNP 19, 81856 Bratislava (tel: 531-7283; fax: 531-7020/05).

Investment and Development Bank, Stúrova 5, 81855 Bratislava (tel: 326-121; fax: 321-433).

Istrobanka as, Laurinská 1, 81101 Bratislava (tel: 539-7524; fax: 533-1744).

Polnobanka as, Vajnorská 21, 83265 Bratislava (tel: 273-964; fax: 259-024).

Post Bank, PO Box 149, Gorkého 3, 81499 Bratislava (tel: 329-253; fax: 211-204).

Slovak Credit Bank, Námestie SNP 13, 81499 Bratislava (tel: 306-5409; fax: 362-691).

Slovak Savings Bank, Námestie SNP 18, 81607 Bratislava (tel: 560-6580; fax: 560-6220).

TATRA Bank, Vajanského nábrezie 5, 81006 Bratislava (tel: 210-3519; fax: 324-760).

Volksbank, Námestie SNP 15, 81000 Bratislava (tel: 381-1140; fax: 364-847).

Travel information

Ministry of Economy, Section of Tourism, Mierova 19, 82715 Bratislava (tel: 230-066; fax: 299-8306).

Slov-Air (domestic flights), Ivanka Airport, Bratislava.

Tatravour, Alzbetina 6, 04001 Kosice (tel: 24-872).

Other useful addresses

Amex Representative Offices, Tatratour, Frantiskanske nam 3, 81509 Bratislava (tel: 335-852).

Bratislava International Commodity Exchange, Ruzinovská 1, 82102 Bratislava (tel: 522-6311; fax: 522-6318).

Bratislava Options Exchange, Dunajská 4, 81481 Bratislava (tel: 362-127; fax: 362-134).

Bratislava Stock Exchange, Vysoká 17, 81499 Bratislava (tel: 386-121; fax: 386-103).

Federation of Employers' Unions and Associations of Slovak Republic, Information and Consulting Centre, Drienová 24, 82603 Bratislava (tel: 235-024; fax: 233-542).

Government Public Relations and Media Office, Levstikova 10, 61000 Ljubljana (tel: 125-0111; fax: 212-312).

Ministry of Agriculture, Forestry and Food of the Slovak Republic, Dobrovicova 12, 81266 Bratislava (tel: 306-6339, 363-7235; fax: 306-6338, 332-150).

Ministry of Culture of the Slovak Republic, Dobrovicova 12, 81331 Bratislava (tel: 367-7813, 325-551; fax: 323-484).

Ministry of Defence of the Slovak Republic, Kutuzovova 7, 83103 Bratislava (tel: 279-9111, 25-400; fax: 258-8710).

Ministry of Economy of the Slovak Republic, Mierova 19, 82715 Bratislava (tel: 299-8111; fax: 237-827).

Ministry of Education and Science of the Slovak Republic, Hlboká 2, 81330 Bratislava (tel: 491-811; fax: 497-098).

Ministry of the Environment of the Slovak Republic, Hlboka 2, 81235 Bratislava (tel: 492-451, 492-002; fax: 311-368).

Ministry of Finance of the Slovak Republic, Stefanovicova 5, 81308 Bratislava (tel: 431-111; fax: 498-042).

Ministry of Foreign Affairs, Gregorciceva Ulica 25, 61000 Ljubljana (tel: 178-2000; fax: 178-2341).

Ministry of Foreign Affairs of the Slovak Republic, Stromova 1, 83336 Bratislava (tel: 370-4111; fax: 376-364).

Ministry of Healthcare of the Slovak Republic, Limbova 2, 83341 Bratislava (tel: 376-036/38; fax: 377-934).

Ministry of Interior, Stefanova 2, 61000 Ljubljana

Ministry of Interior of the Slovak Republic, Pribinova 2, 81272 Bratislava (tel: 206-1111; fax: 364-095).

Ministry of Justice of the Slovak Republic, Zupné námestie,13, 81311 Bratislava (tel: 353-1111; fax: 315-952).

Ministry of Labour, Social Issues and Family of the Slovak Republic, Spitálska 4, 81643 Bratislava (tel: 441-111; fax: 325-381).

Ministry of Transportation, Communications and Public Works of the Slovak Republic, Mileticova 19, 82006 Bratislava (tel: 67-236/44; fax: 254-800).

National Agency for Development of Small and Medium Enterprises, Nevdzov 5, 82101 Bratislava (tel: 237-472/563, 231-873; fax: 522-2434); External Advisors (tel: 237-472; fax: 522-2434); BIC (Business Innovation Centre) (tel: 290-7417; fax: 522-2434, 290-7217).

National Council, Subiceva 4, 61000 Ljubljana (tel: 126-1222; fax: 212-251).

National Property Fund PARP PMU, Drienova 27, 82656 Bratislava (tel: 561-1258, 561-1230, 561-1447, 235-280, 231-300, 231-531; fax: 561-1446, 235-280); external department (tel: 250-248; fax: 259-208).

President's Office (tel: (61) 125-7311).

Prime Minister's Office, Gregorciceva 20, 61000 Ljubljana (tel: 125-9148; fax: 224-240).

Slovak National Agency for Foreign Investment and Development (SNAFID), Sládkovicova 7, 81106 Bratislava (tel: 533-5175; fax: 533-5022);

Slovenska polnohospodarska a potravinarska komora, Krizna 52, 82108 Bratislava (tel: 566-2657, 526-1778; fax: 526-7336, 211-251).

Statistical Office of the Slovak Republic, Mileticova 3, 82467 Bratislava (tel: 215-802; fax: 214-587).

Transport Department, Dept of European Integration, Namestie Slobody 6, 81370 Bratislava (tel: 499-766, 498-156 Ext. 331, 498-841, 495-251; fax: 499-761).

Slovenia

Marko Milivojevic

Following the departure of the neo-communist United List (ZL) from the coalition government in January 1996, the parliamentary elections due in December 1996 were brought forward to 10 November. Although the Liberal Democracy of Slovenia (LDS) of Prime Minister Janez Drnovsek won the largest number of seats in the election, it was not immediately able to form a new government.

Politics

Despite managing a successful economic policy and recovery in 1995/96, the LDS proved unable to translate this into continued popular support, winning 25 seats in the November 1996 election compared to 30 in the 1992 election. Following the local elections of December 1994, the Slovene People's Party (SLS) and Social Democratic Party of Slovenia (SDSS) gained greater political credibility which led to both parties increasing their share of the vote at the parliamentary election. The SLS won 19 seats and the SDSS 16. The Slovene Christian Democratic Party (SKD), on the other hand, lost six seats and may be in terminal political decline in the longer term.

Despite winning the largest number of seats in the 90 member parliament, it took two months and the defection of an opposition deputy before Drnovsek was able to win re-election as prime minister, and then only by the narrowest of margins, 46-44. The deadlock arose following the creation of two blocks, both with 45 deputies. The SDSS, SLS and SKD formed a centre-right alliance, the so-called 'Slovenian Spring', while the LDS led a grouping of smaller parties. Although the defection of Ciril Pucko, who remained an independent but supported Drnovsek's candidacy, led to the prime minister's re-election without support from any of the main opposition parties, Drnovsek immediately said that he would approach the SLS to join a coalition government.

Whichever group of parties forms the next government, it is likely to be more inclined to nationalist positions externally and populist economic policies domestically.

Economic performance

Following an increase of 5 per cent in 1994,

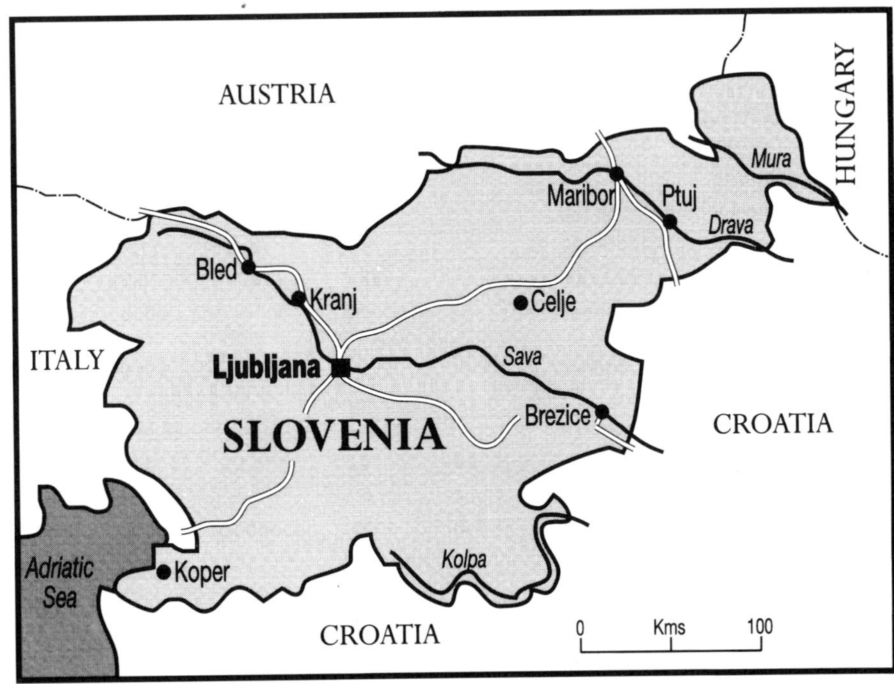

Slovene GDP increased by a further 4.8 per cent in 1995, when GDP and GDP per capita reached US$18 billion and US$9,100, respectively. This was by far the best economic performance in former Yugoslavia and highly respectable even in relation to the European Union (EU) and certainly the Visegrad Group (VG) countries of Central Europe, where Slovenia had the highest GDP per capita in 1994/95. Such strong economic growth was expected to continue in 1996, when year-end GDP was expected to be 2.5 per cent higher than at the end of 1995.

KEY FACTS — Slovenia

Official title: Republic of Slovenia

Head of state: President of the Presidency Milan Kucan (re-elected Dec 1992) (election Dec 1997)

Head of government: Prime Minister Janez Drnovsek (LDS) (re-elected 9 Jan 1996)

Ruling party: Liberal Democracy of Slovenia (LDS) (25 seats in Nov 1996 election); Slovene Pepole's Party (SLS) (19 seats); Social Democratic Party of Slovenia (SDSS) (16 seats)

Capital: Ljubljana

Official Languages: Slovene

Currency: Tolar (T)=100 Stotin (replaced Yugoslav Dinar 8 Oct 1991)

Exchange rate: T139.99 per US$ (Dec 1996)

Area: 20,251 sq km

Population: 1.99m (1995)

GDP per capita: US$9,100 (1995)

GDP real growth: 4.8% (1995)

GNP real growth: 5% (1995)*

Labour force: 843,000 (end-1994)

Unemployment: 13% (1995)

Inflation: 10.7% (Apr 1996) (annual)

Trade balance: -US$800m (1995)

Foreign debt: US$2.5bn (1995) (excluding 18 per cent of US$4.6bn unallocated former Yugoslav foreign debt)

* estimated figure

KEY INDICATORS Slovenia

	Unit	1991	1992	1993	1994	1995
Population	m	1.994	1.994	1.992	1.990	1.990
Gross domestic product (GDP)	US$bn	12.6	12.3	12.6	14.4	18.0
GDP per capita	US$	6,000	6,195	6,366	7,267	9,100
GDP real growth	%	-8.1	-5.4	1.3	5.0	4.8
Inflation	%	117.7	201.3	32.3	19.8	9.0
Consumer prices	1990=100	–	658.5	868.6	1,040.4	1,171.8
Employment	1990=100	–	86.1	84.2	82.7	82.5
Wages	1990=100	–	545.586	825.784	1,058.5	1,256.4
Unemployment	%	8.2	12.0	15.0	14.2	13.0
Agricultural output	%	-10.0	-5.9	-3.7	6.6	2.0
Industrial output	%	-15.0	-13.2	-2.8	6.4	5.0
Industrial production	1990=100	–	74.7	73.1	78.9	80.5
Manufacturing	1990=100	–	74.3	72.4	77.2	79.3
Mining	1990=100	–	88.2	79.1	75.0	75.7
Coal production	'000 tonnes	–	5,558	5,121	4,853	4,883
Crude petroleum production	tonnes	–	2,079	1,925	1,716	1,858
Natural gas production	'000 cu m	–	16,518	13,392	12,595	18,220
Exports	US$bn	**3.8	6.6	6.0	6.0	8.5
Imports	US$bn	**4.1	6.1	6.5	7.2	9.3
Balance of trade	US$m	**-300	500	-500	-400	-800
Current account	US$m	**190	900	150	500	150
Foreign debt**	US$bn	1.5	1.7	1.8	2.2	2.5
Debt service ratio	%	5.2	5.4	5.5	5.5	5.5
Hard currency reserves	US$bn	1.0	1.1	1.5	2.7	4.0
Import cover	months	2.2	2.3	2.9	4.5	6.5
Total reserves minus gold	US$m	112.14	715.54	787.80	1,498.98	1,820.79
Foreign exchange	US$m	112.14	715.54	770.07	1,480.12	1,801.59
Discount rate	%	–	25	18	16	10
Deposit rate	%	673.60	151.53	32.66	27.89	15.32
Lending rate	%	853.50	203.82	49.61	39.41	24.84
Exchange rate (annual average)	T per US$	27.6	81.2	113.2	128.8	118.5

**excl former Yugoslav debt

As in 1994, this economic growth was due primarily to foreign trade turnover, which reached a record 120 per cent of GDP in 1995. New investment grew rapidly in 1995, increasing by 16 per cent in real terms over its level in 1994. Delayed by continued uncertainties in the industrial sector, new fixed investment accounted for 25 per cent of GDP in 1995, compared to 20 per cent in 1994. Among other things, this resulted in higher job creation and lower unemployment in 1995.

Accounting for 34.2 per cent of GDP in 1995, industrial output increased by 5 per cent, compared to 6.4 per cent in 1994. Most of the growth in industrial output in 1995 was during the first half of the year. Beginning in the second quarter of 1995, industrial output continued to decline during the third quarter compared with the same period of 1994. Caused by the adverse impact on exports of an over-valued exchange rate and continued increases in production costs, this was a worrying development, particularly as regards lower output of consumer goods aimed at the EU.

Resisted by the government and the National Bank of Slovenia (NBS), a revision of the strong tolar policy became inevitable during the second half of 1995, making improved export performance more probable in 1996/97. This *de facto* devaluation of the tolar may help to curb import growth in the future. Structurally, the other major impediment to improved export performance – ever higher real wages often unrelated to issues of productivity – has only been partly corrected to date, notably through the incomes policy agreed between the government and the trade unions in April 1995. Following a spate of major strikes in 1995/96, this policy basically collapsed in 1996, with the government caving in to trade union demands in what was an election year.

Although economically marginal at only 5 per cent of GDP in 1994/95, agriculture remains politically sensitive; the SLS in particular has made much of its alleged decline and the loss of self-sufficiency in foodstuffs. In 1995, agricultural output increased by only 2 per cent, compared to 6.6 per cent in 1994. Over the same year, foodstuff imports increased dramatically.

Agricultural and other lands are sensitive for other reasons, notably the controversy over the proposed restitution of large forested areas to the Roman Catholic Church, and the EU's demand that its nationals be allowed to own real estate. Of these two issues, the one with the EU is the most serious, given that public opinion polls reveal widespread ambivalence about the desirability of EU membership if this means possible foreign ownership of any local land. These strongly nationalist sentiments could also have other adverse economic consequences, notably renewed agricultural protectionism.

Services

Collectively accounting for around 25 per cent of GDP in 1994/95, services of all types continue to experience high growth. In 1995, the output of services increased by 4.6 per cent, compared to 3.6 per cent in 1994. Dominated by tourism, total non-factor services earned a record US$1 billion in 1995, compared to US$600 million in 1994. Combined with higher new foreign borrowings and foreign direct investment (FDI) in 1995, this service income enabled Slovenia to run a record trade deficit.

Tourism services income is weakening, mainly because more Slovenes are taking their holidays abroad. Traditional tourism infrastructure also remains inferior to that of nearby Austria and Italy. In 1995, new tourism services such as gambling facilities grew rapidly. Boosted by a multi-year US$2.5 billion infrastructure development programme, construction services are expected to peak in 1996/97. Further strengthened by the import boom of 1995, wholesale and retail trade continues to have high growth potential. By the end of the 1990s, the booming financial services sector is expected to become as dominant in Slovenia as it is in the EU. Earlier relatively limited, secondary share trading will give local financial services a major boost upon the completion of large-scale privatisation of the state industrial sector in 1996/97. Another high growth area in financial services is insurance.

Financial stabilisation

Down from 19.8 per cent in 1994 to 9 per cent in 1995, Slovene inflation and inflationary expectations are very low and declining. The main precondition for high and sustainable non-inflationary economic growth has thus been achieved locally. 1996 year-end inflation was expected to be around 10 per cent, with annual price rises of below 5 per cent possible by the end of the 1990s.

What made this ongoing financial stabilisation all the more significant was that it was achieved despite high wage inflation. As in 1994, this issue continued unabated in 1995/96. Social benefits also remain very generous and fully index linked. Structurally, the main effect of this has been faltering export performance, most notably during the second half of 1995. In the longer term, escalating production costs pose the major threat to Slovene export competitiveness. At around US$750, average monthly incomes in Slovenia in 1995 were by far the highest in the VG and way ahead of the rest of former Yugoslavia.

In the fiscal sphere, government expenditures and revenues remained high at around 45 per cent of GDP in 1995. In relation to growing GDP, however, the government's share of total economic resources in any one year is slightly declining. The government had intended to reduce this to 43 per cent of GDP by 1995, but this will not be possible until towards the end of the 1990s.

Broadly in balance in 1994, when the budget deficit equalled only 0.2 per cent of GDP, expenditures grew faster than revenues in 1995, when the government budget deficit increased to 0.9 per cent of GDP. This was due a greater emphasis on social welfare spending in 1995, a trend that was expected to continue in 1996, for which a government budget was set in October 1995. As in 1994/95, this should broadly balance expenditures and revenues at around T570 billion (around US$4.4 billion) each, with a projected government budget deficit equal to 0.4 per cent of projected GDP year-end in 1996.

Slovenia may experience greater fiscal expansionism in the longer term. According to the centre-left political parties in particular, Slovenia's recent economic performance is such that this can be done without stoking up inflation.

With lower inflation in 1994 and 1995, the government and the NBS were able to reduce interest rates in April 1995. Even more significantly, the country's strong tolar policy was amended later the same year when an appreciating exchange rate against the DM in particular began to affect adversely Slovenia's all-important export performance. The NBS intervened to reverse this trend through a de facto devaluation of the tolar during the third quarter of 1995. As a result, the tolar depreciated against the DM from T81.7 per DM in August to T89.5 per DM in December 1995.

In September 1995, the NBS made the tolar fully convertible for all international transactions for the first time. Internally convertible since its introduction in October 1991, the tolar is now one of the most stable currencies in former Yugoslavia and even the VG. Domestically, the

COUNTRY PROFILE — SLOVENIA

Historical profile

After a 10-day war in June 1991, the republic won independence from Yugoslavia - independence declared 25 June 1991. Recognised as an independent state by the EC on 15 January 1992.

Political system

Republic with multi-party parliamentary democracy. The State Chamber (three houses until end-1992, then two houses) is the highest legislative power and is composed of ninety representatives elected every five years. The Italian and Hungarian minorities each elect one representative. The State Council fulfills an advisory function and is composed of 40 counsellors with a five-year mandate. The president heads the five-member Presidency and is elected in general elections for a period of five years. The prime minister, nominated by the president, leads the government which is responsible to the State Chamber. In early December 1992 Slovenia held its first national elections. Mr Milan Kucan, the incumbent, won re-election as president, with 64 per cent of the ballot. The centrist Liberal Democrats (LDS) led the vote for a new 130-seat bicameral parliament, with 23 per cent. The Christian Democrats, received 14.9 per cent and the United List, including the former communists, 13.26 per cent. A coalition government was formed under the leadership of the Liberal Democrats in January 1993. The next general election is scheduled for 10 November 1996; referendum on reforming the electoral system will be held after election. Next presidental election December 1997.

Political parties

Liberal Democracy of Slovenia (LDS), formerly the Socialist Youth Organisation-Liberal Party (25 seats in 10 November 1996 election); Slovene People's Party (SLS) (19 seats); Social Democratic Party of Slovenia (SDSS) (16 seats). Other major parties include Slovene Christian Democratic Party (SKD); and the neo-communist United List (ZLSD).

Population

In mid-1994 there were 1.97m Slovene citizens in the republic. The ethnic structure of the population is Slovenes (90 per cent), with some Italians, Albanians, Hungarians, Serbs and Croats. Only the Italian and Hungarian communities are officially recognised minorities. As of mid-1994 there were also 20,000 to 30,000 Bosnian Muslim refugees in Slovenia. Main religion Roman Catholicism (75 per cent). Other religions include Serbian Orthodox, Protestant and Muslim.

Main cities/towns

Ljubljana (population 269,972, mid-1994), Maribor (108,000), Celje (41,000), Kranj (37,000), Velenje (28,000), Koper, Novo Mesto.

Language

The official language is Slovene. Business people are fluent in English and/or German, Italian, French. Serbo-Croat is widely understood, but no longer widely used. The main minority languages are Serbo-Croat, Albanian, Hungarian and Italian. Only Hungarian and Italian are officially recognised as minority languages.

Media

The *Uradni list (Official Gazette of the Republic of Slovenia)* is published according to need.
Dailies: There are several daily newspapers including *Delo, Dnevnik, Republika, Slovenec, Vecer* and *Slovenske Novice.*
Weeklies: Druzina (religious topics), *Antena* (target group young people), *Doleniski* (general information and local news), *Goreniski Glas, Jana, Kmecki Glas, Mladina, Nedeliski Dnevnik, Primorske Novice, 7D, Vestnik Murska Sobota* (general information) and *Stop* (media information) all have circulations of over 20,000. *In* is published Friday in Slovenian and English by the Ljubljana International Press Centre.
Business: Several English-language publications, including *Slovenian Business Report*; also *Flaneur* (bi-monthly, politics, economy) and *MM Slovenia* (marketing).
Broadcasting: In 1990 there were 22 radio stations and one television station, run by Radio Slovenija and TV Slovenija. During the tourist season, there are reports and news in German, English and Italian each day: news, traffic news, weather, tourist directions 0930; weather report for the Adriatic 0630 (except Sundays); traffic information every hour from Friday to Sunday from 1430 to 2200 (July, August).

Domestic economy

Slovenia has a strong industrial base and a well-established trading culture. Its economic indicators show an end to the recession, growing consumer confidence, and drastically reduced inflation. It reduced its 1991 retail price inflation index of 247 to 22 per cent in 1993. Recovery in the economy has been rapid; inflation has fallen significantly. In an attempt to encourage domestic rather than foreign borrowing, interest rates were cut significantly in April 1995.

Employment

High living standards; Slovenians are the best paid east Europeans. The average monthly wage was about US$750 in 1995. Approximately 42 per cent are employed in manufacturing, mining and energy, 2 per cent in agriculture and fishing, 1 per cent in forestry, 5 per cent in construction and 50 per cent in services.

External trade

Some 70 per cent of Slovenia's foreign trade was conducted with the EU in 1994/95, while trade with the former Yugoslavia countries totalled just 11 per cent. The EU initialled an association agreeement in June 1995 with Slovenia, which now hopes to submit a formal application for full EU membership.

increased attractiveness of tolar-denominated assets in 1994/95 resulted in ever higher levels of savings, thereby providing the resources for increased new investment in 1995/96.

Another outcome of tolar stability has been further rapid growth in hard currency reserves, which were a record US$4 billion in 1995, compared to US$2.7 billion in 1994. Externally, speculative foreign capital inflows became a major issue for the first time in 1995, when the NBS had to take action to stem them by lowering interest rates in April of that year.

The government announced in 1995 that Slovenia had already met three of the five Maastricht convergence criteria for EU membership, with the other two expected to be attained in 1996 or 1997. Slovenia's complications with Italy and the EU are thus purely political and not economic. In April 1996, Slovenia's attainment of an 'A' country rating gave it added international credibility.

Ongoing privatisation

Although preceded by extensive corporate restructuring, large-scale privatisation of the still dominant state industrial sector did not begin in earnest until 1995, when the Slovene Privatisation Agency (SPA) provisionally approved the privatisation plans submitted to it in 1994 by around 1,000 socially-owned enterprises. A further 500 companies had received the SPA's final approval for registration as privately-owned entities by February 1996. Of this figure, around 80 companies had completed public share issues by the end of 1995, with another 40 on the verge of doing so in early 1996. So far, most ownership transformation has been heavily insider-orientated, with management-employee buy-outs the favoured disposal option by the SPA. In such companies job retention is the basic priority for existing share-holders. Foreign investor participation in local privatisation remained relatively minimal in 1994/95.

Pending the completion and full institutionalisation of large-scale privatisation, the recapitalisation of local enterprises will remain the responsibility of the country's commercial banks. Here the growth in savings and increasingly negative interest rates has already led to increased investment. The restructuring of the industrial sector and its privatisation has also improved company finances, allowing more new borrowing to take place. On the credit supply side, the government's ambitious bank rehabilitation programme finally began in earnest in 1995, when bank balance sheets began to improve for the first time in the 1990s. The responsibility of the Bank Rehabilitation Agency (BRA), this programme began nominally in 1992, when non-performing bank assets began to be recapitalised with 30-year government bonds. Focused on the country's largest commercial bank, Nova Ljubljanska Banka (NLB) and Kreditna Banka Maribor (KBM), BRA recapitalisation and related restructuring has been generally successful, with NLB returning to profitability (for the first time in over five years in 1995). Now in its final and decisive stage, bank rehabilitation will culminate in the privatisation of NLB, KBM and other commercial banks, although this proposed ownership transformation in financial services is unlikely to begin until after the November 1996 parliamentary elections.

The earlier break-up of the former Ljubljanska Banka has created far too many commercial banks – over 30 in 1995 – for what remains a relatively small economy. So far, the NBS has attempted to encourage bank consolidation

COUNTRY PROFILE — SLOVENIA

External trade (contd): *Exports:* Exports totalled US$8.5bn in 1995.
Imports: Imports totalled US$9.3bn in 1995.

Agriculture

The agriculture sector contributed 5 per cent to GDP in 1994/95 and employed 8.4 per cent of the workforce. The agricultural area is approximately 863,000 ha; area under cultivation 650,000 ha. Livestock is reared (cattle, pigs and poultry) and wheat, potatoes, fruit and grapes are grown. There is some fishing.
Forests cover almost half of the country.
Agricultural output only increased by 2 per cent in 1995 compared to 6.6 per cent in 1994.

Industry

The industrial sector accounted for some 34.2 per cent of GDP in 1994 and employed 42 per cent of the labour force. Hit by the loss of the exports to the former Yugoslav republics, industrial output dropped by 10 per cent in 1991 and output in the manufacturing and mining sectors in 1992 was down by 13.2 per cent.
Electronics, electrical machinery, transport equipment, vehicles and spare parts account for the main part of Slovenia's export.
Other important sectors are metal processing, ferrous metallurgy, food processing, chemicals, furniture manufacture, wood, paper, footwear, sports equipment and textiles.
Slovene enterprises, particularly those in the furniture, electronics, paper and white goods sectors, are exporting to EU countries.
Renault, French car manufacturer, which assembles cars in Slovenia, and Siemens, German-based mechanical and electrical goods maker, which has a joint venture with Iskra, Slovenia's electronic and telecommunications giant, have used Slovenia as a base for exporting to former Yugoslavia as well as to western Europe.
Principal manufactured products are automobiles, electric appliances, chemicals, textiles, food products and printing.
Industrial production increased by 5 per cent in 1995 compared to 6.4 per cent in 1994.

Tourism

Improvements in hotels and infrastructure are needed. Slovenia can provide 75,000 beds in various accommodation facilities (hotels, motels, tourist villages, health-resorts, boarding-houses) all over the country. Slovenia also hosts many international congresses in its congress centres in Ljubljana, Portoroz, Radenci and Rogaska Slatina. In 1995 gambling facilities grew rapidly.

Hydrocarbons

There are significant coal deposits.

Energy

Oil requirements are imported. About 16 per cent of the country's power supply needs are imported.

Banking

In February 1993 the government and the central bank, Banka Slovenije, introduced a set of measures in order to facilitate the strengthening of the banking system in Slovenia. New banking system legislation and a restructuring of the banking system are two of the most essential needs for the future development of Slovenia.
The biggest commercial bank is Nova Ljubljanska Banka (NLB). SKB Banka DD is the second largest commercial bank.

Stock exchange

The Yugoslav Stock Exchange Inc was founded in December 1989 and renamed Ljubljanska Borza after Slovenia declared its independence and is legally a Slovenian institution.

Legal system

Slovenia has replaced most federal legislation with its own.

Membership of international organisations

CEFTA (from 1 Jan 1996), Council of Europe, CSE, IAEA, IDA, IFC, IMF, MIGA, NAM (guest), Partnership for Peace, World Bank, WTO.

BUSINESS GUIDE

Time

GMT + 1 hr (GMT + 2 hrs from late Mar to late Sep).

Climate

Slovenia has three different climates: Middle-European, Alpine, Mediterranean.
Average summer temperature: 21 degrees C.
Average winter temperature: 0 degrees C.

Entry requirements

Passport: EU nationals do not require a passport.
Visa: Australian and New Zealand nationals do not require a visa.
Currency: Traveller's cheques widely accepted.

Representation overseas

Bonn, Brussels, Budapest, London, Paris, Rome, Vienna, Washington, Zagreb.

Air access

National airline: Adria Airways.
Other airlines: Aeroflot, Air France, Austrian Airlines, Interimpex-Avioimpex, Lufthansa, Swissair.
International airports: Ljubljana–Brnik (LJU), 27 km from city centre; Maribor; Portoroz (POW), 10 km from city.

Surface access

Main ports: Izola, Koper and Piran. Koper is a modern-equipped port with several container terminals.

by raising minimum capitalisation requirements to DM60 million, but few mergers have taken place to date. This reluctance to merge has caused particular difficulties for Slovenia's largest and most ambitious private bank, SKB Banka, which has thus been rebuffed a number of times by smaller commercial banks hostile to takeovers.

It is not clear how bank consolidation can proceed. Externally, there has also been increased competition from a number of mainly Austrian banks in recent years, but their local operations so far remain relatively insignificant. According to the government and the NBS, at least one of the commercial banks due to be privatised by the BRA in due course should go to a strategic foreign investor. Although this would be economically beneficial, such a foreign takeover of a major commercial bank is likely to prove highly controversial. The current management of NLB in particular strongly opposes the NBS on this key question. So far, the only Slovene commercial bank with significant foreign investor participation is SKB Banka, where the European Bank for Reconstruction and Development (EBRD) holds a 15 per cent equity stake.

Foreign trade

Exports increased by 24 per cent to US$8.5 billion in 1995. However, imports increased by a record 33 per cent to US$9.3 billion in 1995. The result of this was a record trade deficit of US$800 million in 1995, double its 1994 level. In 1996, exports were expected to be in the region of US$9.2 billion, with imports rising to US$10.6 billion, creating a projected trade deficit of US$1.4 billion. On the current account, the trade deficit of 1995 meant the surplus recorded for the year was just US$150 million, compared to US$500 million in 1994. In 1996, the current account is expected to go into deficit for the first time. In the longer term, Slovenia may not be able to sustain its growing trade and current account deficits.

In 1994/95, the EU accounted for a record 70 per cent of Slovenia's foreign trade, and in 1995/96 Organisation for Economic Co-operation and Development countries will account for well over 80 per cent of Slovenia's foreign trade. Slovene trade with the EU remains in large and growing deficit. Elsewhere in Europe, Slovenia has traditionally run trade surpluses, most notably in central and eastern Europe, but these have not been large enough to compensate for its excessive trade deficit with the EU.

At the beginning of 1996, Slovenia became a full member of the Central European Free Trade Area (CEFTA). Although relatively insignificant by 1995, Slovenia's foreign trade with the rest of the former Yugoslavia remained in surplus. Following the stabilisation of the situation in the former Yugoslavia in 1995/96, Slovene foreign trade with Serbia in particular is expected to grow rapidly in the future.

Foreign debt and payments

Up from US$2.2 billion in 1994 to US$2.5 billion in 1995, Slovenia's foreign debt continues to grow. Mainly provided by official multilateral and governmental creditors, the country's new foreign borrowings are expected to grow rapidly in the future. Economically, Slovenia's growing hard currency reserves and low debt service ratio – 5.5 per cent in 1995 – means that it can easily double or even treble its foreign debt over the next five years. Earlier in the 1990s, its only real obstacle on the foreign debt front was a dispute with the London

BUSINESS GUIDE — SLOVENIA

Surface access (contd): *Road:* Slovenia borders on Austria, Italy, Hungary and Croatia.

Credit cards

Most supermarkets and car hire firms will accept credit cards. The most commonly accepted are American Express, Eurocard (Mastercard), Visa and Diners.

City transport

Taxis: Good service operating in all main cities. All taxis are metered, but there is no basic charge. A 10 per cent tip is usual.
Buses and trams: Most city centres are served by trams, and the suburbs by buses. The service is generally cheap and regular. Tokens for buses can be purchased on newspaper stands, at post offices and on newspaper stands in supermarkets. Fares can be paid in cash but tokens are cheaper.
Rail: Reservations are recommended.

National transport

Road: The following are toll motorways: Ljubljana-Razdrto, Arja vas-Hoce and Ljubljana-Kranj. About two-thirds of the roads are inadequate and the few short expressways are not properly maintained. Upgrading the roads and building new ones is a priority.

Public holidays

Fixed dates: 1-2 Jan (New Year), 8 Feb (Preseren/Culture Day), 27 Apr (Uprising against Occupation), 1-2 May (Labour Day), 25 Jun (National Day), 15 Aug (Feast of the Assumption), 31 Oct (Reformation Day), 1 Nov (All Souls' Day), 25 Dec (Christmas Day), 26 Dec (Independence Day).
Variable dates: Easter, Whit Sunday.

Working hours

Business: 0700 – 1500 (Mon–Fri). Some firms have adapted to European working hours: 0800 – 1600/0900 – 1700 (Mon–Fri).
Government: 0800 – 1600 (Mon–Fri).
Banking: 0800 – 1800 (Mon–Fri), 0800 – 1100 (Sat).
Shops: 0700 – 1900 or 0800 – 2000 (Mon–Fri); some shops also open 0800 – 1300/1400 (Sat), 0800 – 1200 (Sun).

Social customs

Business visitors should be smartly dressed. It is not unusual for Slovenians to prefer to hold business discussions over lunch.

Business language and interpreting/translation

No regular nationwide interpreter service, but a translation service can usually be arranged through hotels, tourist offices or local enterprises.

Telecommunications

Telephone: Dialling code for Slovenia: IDD access code + 386 (used to be 38) followed by area code (64 for Kranj, 61 for Ljubljana, 62 for Maribor, 66 for Portoroz, 67 for Postojna). Calls can be made with either tokens or magnetic cards (only available at post offices that have magnetic card public telephones). Tokens are available at post offices and newspaper stands: 'A' tokens for local calls and 'B' tokens for long-distance calls. For IDD access from Slovenia dial 99. Operator assistance in Ljubljana: dial 901. There were 4,000 cellular telephone subscribers in January 1993. Ljubljana numbers starting with 1 now have seven digits. After the first digit you have to dial number 2,3,4,5 or 6 according to the following system:

Telephone number	New second digit
from 110-000 to 133-999	3
from 150-000 to 161-999	2
from 181-000 to 188-999	6
from 101-000 to 109-999	4
from 171-000 to 172-999	2
from 191-000 to 198-999	5

Telex and telefax: Services available in most large hotels and at main post offices. Messages can be handed in at telegram counters. Telex country code 62YU.
Postal services: There is a 24-hour service at the post office on Cigaletova 5 in Ljubljana. Postal facilities and services are of a European standard.

Banking

Central bank: Bank of Slovenia.
Commercial banks: Ljubljanska Bank, SKB Banka DD; some smaller commercial banks have been established, including three Austrian banks.
Other banks: Ljubljanska Banka-Zdruzena Banka, UBK Banka.

Business information

By March 1994 six Slovenian companies had completed their privatisation out of the 223 who submitted programmes to the Slovenian Agency for Privatisation. The six offered 60 per cent of shares to management and employees, and 40 per cent were allotted to state funds.

Trade fairs

For information regarding trade fairs, contact Ljubljanski Sejem, d.d., 61116 Ljubljana, Dunajska 10 (tel: 117-200; fax: 117-101). The World Trade Centre combines a congress hall, parking for 1,000 cars, a five-star hotel and shopping mall.

Electricity supply

220 V AC. Round two-pin plugs are used.

Weights and measures

Metric system.

Representation in capital

Austria, Belgium, Central African Republic, Finland, Germany, Italy, Netherlands, Norway, Thailand,

Club (LC) of commercial bank creditors. Focused on Slovenia's disputed share of unallocated former Yugoslav foreign debt, which totals US$4.6 billion, this issue was finally settled in 1995, when the government agreed to take an 18 per cent share of these liabilities, with repayment to be in the form of government bonds worth US$822 million and maturing in 2006.

Formally approved by the Slovene parliament in February 1996, this debt deal will increase Slovenia's allocated foreign debt to US$3.3 billion. The following month, however, Slovenia's full international financial rehabilitation was implicitly called into question when the central bank of rump Yugoslavia launched legal proceedings in London to abort this deal, claiming that it violated the terms of the last formal rescheduling of all-Yugoslav foreign debt in 1988, when Slovenia and its then partners in Yugoslavia agreed that they were liable jointly and severally for the external liabilities of the federation.

Pending a final resolution of this court case, which focuses on the legality or otherwise of bilateral approaches to the issue of unallocated former Yugoslav foreign debt, Slovenia may not be able to extricate itself once and for all from the financial chaos of the rest of former Yugoslavia.

Slovenia's 'A' country rating and cooperation with the LC led to the success of a US$812.5 million NBS Eurobond issue in June 1996. A number of Slovene commercial banks have also been able to tap the Euromarkets for new syndicated loans, beginning with SKB Banka as far back as 1994. Short-term foreign capital inflows have also increased in recent years. In 1996, foreign portfolio and FDI capital inflows were expected to increase substantially.

Relatively limited at below US$300 million in 1993, FDI grew by a further US$100 million in 1994, and a record US$150 million in 1995. Excluding foreign portfolio capital inflows, FDI in Slovenia by the end of 1995 was around US$500 million. Mainly from Germany, Austria and Italy, FDI is expected to grow substantially in the future. Sectorally, automotive products, paper and pulp, electrical goods and cigarette manufacturing have been of the greatest interest to foreign investors to date. Other sectors with high potential in the longer term are food processing, pharmaceuticals and tourism. So far, the government has not provided any special incentives for attracting FDI, but this policy may have to be changed in due course. By 1995, a number of Free Trade Zones (FTZ) were operating in Slovenia, which is well positioned regionally for increased FTZ-related FDI, notably at Koper and Ljubljana. In the longer-term, Slovene FDI is also expected to increase substantially in former Yugoslavia, the VG and Germany in the EU.

Prospects

Economically comparable to the VG countries and even the less developed members of the EU, Slovenia is far ahead of the rest of former Yugoslavia in every respect. Politically, Slovenia remains stable, although the parliamentary elections created some uncertainty over future economic and foreign policy. Another important imponderable politically is the enigmatic figure of President Kucan.

As in the rest of central and eastern Europe, Slovene politics may move further to the left in the longer term. Nationalist sentiments are also growing in relation to Italy and hence the EU. In practice, the attainment of associate and then full membership of the EU is likely to prove more difficult and protracted than originally envisaged. Full international financial rehabilitation is now assured. All in all, the country's political and economic prospects are very good.

BUSINESS GUIDE — SLOVENIA

Useful tips

Do carry some form of identity at all times.

BUSINESS DIRECTORY

Hotels

Austrotel Ljubljana, Miklosiceva 9, 61000 (tel: 132-6133; fax: 301-181).

GH Union, Miklosiceva 1, 61000 (tel: 125-4133; fax: 217-910).

Holiday Inn, Miklosiceva 3, 61000 (tel: 125-5051; fax: 125-0323).

Kompas Motel Medno, Medno 54, 61212 (tel: 611-200/1).

Lev. Vosnjakova 1, 61000 (tel: 132-155; fax: 321-994).

Slon, Slovenska 34, 61000 (tel: 151-232).

Union, Miklosiceva 1, 61000 (tel: 143-133; fax: 217-910).

Useful telephone numbers

Police 92.
Fire brigade 93.
First aid, ambulance 94.
Telegrams 96.
Road assistance (AMZS automobile association) 987.
General information 981.
Telephone information 988.

Car hire

Ljubljana
Avis: Central Reservations, Dunajska 389, 61231 (tel: 374-497/398; fax: 374-151); International Airport 64210 Brnik (tel: 223-311, 261-685); Ljubljana Downtown, World Trade Centre, Dunajska 160 (tel: 168-7204; fax: 168-7204).

Budget: Central Reservations (tel: 211-781; fax: 213-947); Ljubljana Airport, Brink (tel: 642-2340); Stefanova 13A (tel: 126-3118).

Europcar: Central Reservations, Letaliska 16, 61000 (tel: 132-2238/1307; fax: 132-2058); Brnik International Airport.

Hertz: Central Reservations (tel: 571-987; fax: 572-088); International Airport (tel: 6422-3366); Kompas, Miklosiceva 11 (tel: 311-241); Celovska 206 (tel: 575-004).

Taxis

Hlt Taxi (tel: 9701).

Radio Taxi (tel: 9700).

Taxi service, Bezenskova 26 (tel: 325-393).

Chambers of commerce

Chamber of Craft of Slovenia, Celovska 71, pp 50, 61000 Ljubljana (tel: 159-3241/3312/4143; fax: 559-279, 554-373).

Chamber of Economy of Slovenia, Slovenska Cesta 41, 61000 Ljubljana (tel: 125-0122; fax: 219-536, 218-242).

Regional Chambers:
Celje Regional Chamber, Ljubljanska Cesta 14/II (tel: 6344-3450).

Dravograd Regional Chamber, Mariborska 64/II (tel: 6028-3080).

Koper Regional Chamber, Ferrarska 2 (tel: 663-2721).

Kranj Regional Chamber, Bleiweisova 16 (tel: 6422-2584).

Krsko Regional Chamber, Bohoriceva 9 (tel: 6082-2387).

Ljubljana Regional Chamber, Igriska 5 (tel: 6122-4739).

Maribor Regional Chamber, Ul Talcev 24/II (tel: 6222-7371).

Murska Sobota Regional Chamber, Kocljeva 10/III (tel: 693-2728).

Nova Gorica Regional Chamber, Trg Edvarda Kardelja 3 (tel: 652-7175).

Novo Mesto Regional Chamber, Novi Trg 5 (tel: 6832-2182).

Postojna Regional Chamber, Cankarjeva 6 (tel: 672-4059).

Trbovlje Regional Chamber, C Oktobrske Revolucije 14 (tel: 6012-1780).

Velenje Regional Chamber, Trg Mladosti 2 (tel: 6385-6920).

Chamber of Small Businesses of Slovenia, Celovska 71, 61000 Ljubljana (tel: 159-3241; fax: 559-270).

Banking

Bank of Slovenia (central bank), Slovenska 35, Ljubljana (tel: 125-7333; fax: 215-516).

Bank Association of Slovenia, Subiceva 2, 61000 Ljubljana (tel: 215-076; fax: 125-2106).

Members of the Bank Association:

Abanka dd, Slovenska 58, 61000 Ljubljana (tel: 133-7260; fax: 302-445).

Bank Austria dd, Wolfova 1, 61000 Ljubljana (tel: 125-9350; fax: 211-217, 212-977).

Banka Creditanstalt dd, Kotnikova 5, 61100 Ljubljana (tel: 132-0070; fax: 132-5295).

Banka Noricum dd, Trdinova 4, 61000 Ljubljana (tel: 133-4030; fax: 133-7125).

Factor Banka dd, Zelezna 16, pp 126, 61109 Ljubljana (tel: 131-1136; fax: 132-8066).

Komercialna Banka Triglav dd, Kotnikova 28, 61000 Ljubljana (tel: 132-4323; fax: 132-4221).

Ljudska Banka dd, Miklosiceva 30, 61001 Ljubljana (tel: 131-1009; fax: 131-2180).

M Banka dd, Dunajska c 107, 61000 Ljubljana (tel: 168-1255; fax: 168-1077).

BUSINESS DIRECTORY

Banking (contd):

Nova Ljubljanska Banka dd, Trg Republike 2, 61000 Ljubljana (tel: 212-255; fax: 222-655).

Postna Banka Slovenije dd, Copova 11a, 61000 Ljubljana (tel: 125-3050; fax: 125-3202).

SKB Banka dd, Ajdovscina 4, 61000 Ljubljana (tel: 131-5072; fax: 132-9122).

Slovenska Investicijska Banka dd, Copova 38, 61000 Ljubljana (tel: 125-0102; fax: 125-8200).

Slovenska Zadruzna Kmetijska Banka dd, Miklosiceva 4, 61000 Ljubljana (tel: 126-4240; fax: 126-3261).

UBK Univerzalna Banka dd, Trzaska 116, 61000 Ljubljana (tel: 268-141; fax; 273-082).

Zveza HKS, Miklosiceva 4, 61000 Ljubljana (tel: 219-404; fax: 224-203).

Banka Societe Generale Ljubljana dd, Trg Republike 3, 61000 Ljubljana (tel: 126-2214; fax: 126-2158/3283).

Bank Rehabilitation Agency of the Republic of Slovenia, Trg Republike 3, 61000 Ljubljana (tel: 125-7350; fax: 125-6070).

Komercialna in Hipotekarna Banka, Titova 38, 61000 Ljubljana (tel: 319-166; fax: 328-256).

Ljubljanska Banka-Zdruzena Banka, Trg Revoluci je 2, PO Box 534, 61001 Ljubljana (tel: 125-0155; fax: 222-422).

Travel information

Adria Airways (domestic and European International flights), Kuzmiceva 7, 61000 Ljubljana (tel: 133-4336 (reservations: 131-8155); fax: 323-356).

Brnik international airport flight information (tel: 212-844; fax: 212-474).

Bus information (tel: 325-885).

Centre for the Promotion of Tourism, Dunajska Cesta 156, 1000 Ljubljana (tel: 188-1165; fax: 188-1164).

Ljubljana Airport (tel: 222-700; fax: 221-220).

Ljubljana City Secretariat for Tourism, Trubarjeva 5, 61000 Ljubljana (tel: 133-3155; fax: 133-2007).

Ljubljana Station (railway), Trg Of 6, 61000 Ljubljana (tel: 131-5167).

Maribor Airport (tel: 691-541; fax: 691-253).

Matic (tourist information centre), Grajski Trg 1, 62000 Maribor (tel: 211-262; fax: 25-271).

Ministry of Economic Activities, Tourism Section, Kotnikova 5, 61000 Ljubljana (tel: 171-3311; fax: 132-2266).

National Tourist Office, Miklosiceva Cesta 38, 61000 Ljubljana (tel: 132-0141; fax: 133-2338).

Novo Mesto (tourist information centre), Novi Trg 6, 68000 Novo Mesto (tel: 322-512; fax: 322-512).

Port of Koper, Vojkovo Nabrezje 38, 66000 Koper (tel: 456-100; fax: 34-418).

Portoroz Arport (tel: 79-001; fax: 79-215).

Public Transport (Potniski promet), Vilharjeva 24 (tel: 323-062, 323-094).

Slovenska Zeleznice (railway), Kolodvorska 11, 61000 Ljubljana (tel: 325-989).

Tourist Information Bureau, Cesta Svobode 15, 64260 Bled (tel: 741-122; fax: 741-555).

Tourist Information Centre, Slovenska 35, 61000 Ljubljana (tel: 224-222; fax: 222-115).

Other useful addresses

Agency for Reconstruction and Privatisation, Kotnikova 28, 61000 Ljubljana (tel: 131-2122; fax: 131-2061).

Agency of the Republic of Slovenia for Payments, Supervision and Information, Trzaska Cesta 16, Ljubljana (tel: 123-1171; fax: 263-984).

Agency of the Republic of Slovenia for Restructuring and Privatisation, Kotnikova 28, 61101 Ljubljana (tel: 131-2122, 131-6030; fax: 131-6011).

Association of Employers of Slovenia, Slovenska Cesta 41, 61000 Ljubljana (tel: 126-2293, 125-0122).

Association of Entrepreneurs of Slovenia, Slovenska Cesta 41, 61000 Ljubljana (tel: 215-583, 125-0122).

Centre for International Co-operation and Development (CICD), Kardeljeva Ploscad 1, PO Box 97, 61109 Ljubljana (tel: 168-3597; fax: 343-696).

Channel A, Tivolska 50, 61000 Ljubljana (tel: 133-4133; fax: 133-4222).

Development Fund of the Republic of Slovenia, Kotnikova 28, 61000 Ljubljana (tel: 131-2122; fax: 131-6011).

Government Public Relations and Media Office, Levstikova 10, 61000 Ljubljana (tel: 125-0111; fax: 212-312).

Institute for Macroeconomic Analysis and Development, Gregorciceva 25, 61000 Ljubljana (tel: 126-4283; fax: 224-318).

Ljubjanska Borza, Kraigherjev Trg 1, 61000 Ljubljana (tel: 216-644; fax: 314-459).

Ljubljana Stock Exchange Inc, Slovenska 56, 61000 Ljubljana (tel: 171-0211; fax: 171-0213).

Mednarodno tiskovno sredisce Ljubljana (International Press Centre), Dunajska 107, 61113 Ljublijana, p.p. 49 (tel: 372-302; fax: 349-560).

Ministry of Agriculture and Forestry, Parmova 33, 61000 Ljubljana (tel: 323-643; fax: 313-631).

Ministry of Culture, Cankarjeva 5, 61000 Ljubljana (tel: 125-9122; fax: 210-814).

Ministry of Defence, Kardeljeva Ploscad 24-26, 61000 Ljubljana (tel: 133-1111; fax: 131-9145).

Ministry of Economic Affairs, Kotnikova 5, 61000 Ljubljana (tel: 171-3230; fax: 132-4210).

Ministry of Economic Relations and Development, Trade and Investment Promotion Office, Kotnikova 5, 61000 Ljubljana (tel: 171-3527/21; fax: 171-3611).

Ministry of Education and Sport, Zupanciceva Ulica 6, 61000 Ljubljana (tel: 178-5443; fax: 214-820).

Ministry of Energy, Hajdrihova 2, 61000 Ljubljana (tel: 213-669; fax: 213-804).

Ministry of Environment and Physical Planning, Zupanciceva Ulica 6, 61000 Ljubljana (tel: 125-4208; fax: 224-548).

Ministry of Finance, Beethovenova 12, 61000 Ljubljana (tel: 125-2193; fax: 125-2067); external department (tel: 176-5211; fax: 125-1190).

Ministry of Finance, Zupanciceva 3, 61000 Ljubljana (tel: 178-5211; fax: 214-640).

Ministry of Foreign Affairs, Gregorciceva Ulica 25, 61000 Ljubljana (tel: 178-2000; fax: 178-2341).

Ministry of Health, Stefanova 5, 61000 Ljubljana (tel: 125-1028; fax: 217-752).

Ministry of Industry and Building, Gregorciceva 25, 61000 Ljubljana (tel: 150-300; fax: 224-362).

Ministry of Information, Levstikova 10, 61000 Ljubljana (tel: 150-111; fax: 212-312).

Ministry of the Interior, Stefanova 2, 61000 Ljubljana (tel: 1251-400; fax: 214-330).

Ministry of Justice, Zupanciceva 3, 61000 Ljubljana (tel: 178-5211; fax: 210-200).

Ministry of Labour, Family and Social Affairs, Kotnikova 5, 61000 Ljubljana (tel: 178-3311; fax: 178-3456).

Ministry of Science and Technology, Slovenska Cesta 50, 61000 Ljubljana (tel: 131-1107; fax: 132-4140).

Ministry of Tourism and Catering, Cankarjeva 5, 61000 Ljubljana (tel: 216-177; fax: 210-940).

Ministry of Trade, Trg republike 3, 61000 Ljubljana (tel: 224-313; fax: 222-011).

Ministry of Transport and Communications, Presernova 23, 61000 Ljubljana (tel: 125-6256; fax: 218-707).

National Council, Subiceva 4, 61000 Ljubljana (tel: 126-1222; fax: 212-251).

National Customs Administration, Smartinska 130, 61000 Ljubljana (tel: 140-1044; fax: 140-2155).

Office of the Republic of Slovenia for Protection of Industrial Property, Kotnikova 6, 61000 Ljubljana (tel: 131-2322; fax: 314-133).

President's Office (tel: 125-7311).

Prime Minister's Office, Gregorciceva 20, 61000 Ljubljana (tel: 125-9148; fax: 224-240).

Privatisation Agency, Kotnikova 28, 61000, Ljubljana (tel: 131-9030/6030/2122; fax: 131-6011).

Radio Koper Capodistria, Ul Of 15, 66000 Koper (tel: 22-457; fax: 21-011).

Radio Maribor, Ilichova 33, 62000 Maribor (tel: 101-333; fax: 103-555).

Radio Murskival, Slovenska 14, 69000 Murska Sobota (tel: 33-019; fax: 22-419).

Radio Slovenia, Tavcarjeva 17, 61000 Ljubljana (tel: 131-1333; fax: 133-4007).

Slovenian Export Corporation, Ul Josipine Turnograjske 6, 61000 Ljubljana (tel: 126-2238; fax: 125-3015).

Slovenian Press Agency, Cankarjeva 5, 61001 Ljubljana (tel: 126-2222; fax: 301-321).

Slovenian Statistics Office, Vozarski Pot 12, 61000 Ljubljana (tel: 125-5322; fax: 216-932).

Slovenska tiskovna agencija (Slovenian Press Agency), Cankarjeva 5, 61000 Ljubljana (tel: 224-505; fax: 301-321).

Small Business Development Centre, c/o Ministry of Economic Affairs, Kotnikova 5, 61000 Ljubljana (tel: 171-3232; fax: 132-4210).

Standards and Metrology Institute, Kotnikova 6, 61000 Ljubljana (tel: 131-2322; fax: 314-882).

TV Slovenia, Kolodvorska 2-4, 61000 Ljubljana (tel: 131-1333; fax: 133-5079).

World Trade Centre Ljubljana, Dunajska 156, 61000 Ljubljana (tel: 344-666; fax: 168-3480).

Internet sites

Chamber of Economy of Slovenia, Ljubljana (http://www.gzs.si, e-mail: infolink@hq.gzs.si; BBS: +386 61 12 57 140).

Spain

William Chislett

After 13 years of Socialist rule, one of Spain's very few freely elected conservative governments this century took power in May 1996, headed by José María Aznar of the Popular Party (PP). Only once in the past 60 years has power been transferred from one elected party to another and that was when Felipe González won his first landslide victory in 1982. The PP's victory marked a turning point in the European Union's (EU) most recent democracy, establishing the principle of alternating governments, but it was far from the absolute majority predicted by all opinion polls and opened up an uncertain period at a crucial stage in Spain's arduous march towards economic and monetary union (EMU). The country still meets none of the EMU criteria.

KEY FACTS — Spain

Official title: The Kingdom of Spain

Head of state: King Juan Carlos I

Head of government: Prime Minister José María Aznar (leader of the PP) (from 5 May 1996)

Ruling party: Centre-right Popular Party (PP) (narrow victory in 3 Mar 1996 election, 20 seats short of a working majority; first general election win)

Capital: Madrid

Official Languages: Spanish (Castilian, Catalán, Gallego – Galician, Basque)

Currency: Peseta (Pta) = 100 centimos

Exchange rate: Pta130.85 per US$ (Dec 1996)

Area: 504,782 sq km

Population: 39.2m (1995)

GDP per capita: US$12,335 (1994)

GDP real growth: 1.9% 2nd qtr (1996)

Unemployment: 21.9% (3rd qtr 1996)

Inflation: 3.5% (Sep 1996, year-on-year) (consumer prices)

Trade balance: -US$21.6bn (12 months to Sep 1996)

Foreign debt: US$277.5bn (1995)

Elections

The centre-right PP, founded after General Franco's death in 1975, was, to its astonishment, left 20 seats short of a parliamentary majority. The PP's hunger for power was brilliantly pinpointed in a cartoon in El País by El Roto which showed Franco and above him the words, 'If the right does not win this time, I will no longer believe in democracy.' Aznar's PP is a medley of consensus-seeking centre-rightists, the residue of the old Francoist right and economic liberals.

The PP increased its number of seats to 156 from 141, while the Socialists dropped to 141 from 159. The 3 March 1996 election produced a situation similar to that of the last parliament except that the positions of the PP and the Socialists were reversed and the distance between them – 15 seats – was narrower. Once again the powerbroker was Jordi Pujol, for the past 16 years president of the Catalan regional government and leader of Convergència i Unió (CiU), which won 16 seats.

After 57 days of horse trading, during which the PP was made to sweat and grovel, the CiU and the Basque Nationalist Party (5 seats) agreed to support the PP but not to enter a coalition government. There was considerable bad blood between the regional parties, particularly the Catalans, and the PP, epitomised by the slogan chanted by PP supporters on polling day: 'Pujol, enano, habla castellano' ('Pujol, little man, speak Spanish if you can'). The price was the devolution of more powers and an increase in the share of income tax earmarked for spending by the regions. The deal risked upsetting the delicately forged balance between the 17 regions and the varying degrees of autonomy they enjoy.

The election was a personal triumph for González for whom the polls were a kind of referendum on his period in office. Although rocked by corruption scandals and the judicial investigation into the government-funded GAL death squads which conducted a dirty war against the Basque terrorist organisation ETA, the Socialists were only beaten by 300,000 PP votes. The formidable González headed a strong opposition. No one would be surprised if he returned to power before the PP's term of office is up in the year 2000.

The election showed Spain to be almost equally divided into right and left-wing camps: almost 12.5 million people voted for 'left-wing' parties and 11.5 million for 'right-wing' ones. The peculiarities of the Spanish electoral system and changes in political culture make it virtually impossible for any party to win an absolute majority. This raises the spectre of an 'Italianisation' of the political scene and, in turn, makes it more difficult for a government to implement the structural reform that Spain needs.

Economy

Average 12-month inflation, the EMU yardstick, (as opposed to year-end), was running at 4.6 per cent in early 1996 (against a maximum limit of 2.9 per cent), long-term interest rates were 11 per cent (9.6 per cent requirement), the general government budget deficit was 5.8 per cent of GDP in 1995 (3 per cent limit) and public debt was 64.8 per cent of GDP (60 per cent). The budget deficit is the Gordian knot which Spain has to unravel if it wants to be included among the core group of countries that will launch the third phase of EMU in 1999 at the earliest.

Interest payments on the public debt, which has ballooned in the last eight years, (in 1988 it was just over 40 per cent of GDP) represented 90 per cent of the budget deficit in 1995 and 5.4 per cent of GDP. However, the primary deficit (which excludes interest payments) was reduced to 0.4 per cent of GDP from 1.1 per cent in 1994 and in 1996 there was expected to be a primary surplus. Stablisation of the level of public debt and reduced spending were expected to cut the budget deficit to 4.4 per cent in 1996, but this still means that it has to be halved in 1997 if Spain wants to be in the running for EMU.

The economy expanded by 3 per cent in 1995, largely fuelled by investment, but the pace of growth was on a downward trend; most private economists believed GDP would grow by no more than 2.25 per cent in 1996. Private consumption remained

LAND OF VALENCIA

land of opportunities

DELEGATIONS

Canada
USA-New York
USA-Los Angeles
USA-Miami
Japan
Germany
Mexico
Costa Rica
Bolivia
Peru
Chile
Argentina
Dubai
Morocco
Algeria
Poland
Taiwan
Korea
Hong Kong
China

Comunidad Valenciana

- Located at the centre of the Mediterranean Arch.
- Excellent platform for European, African and Latin American Markets.
- Gateway to 320,000,000 potential consumers.
- Regional leader in exports.
- Highly diversified industrial base with unlimited subcontracting opportunities.
- Extensive availability of industrial land with direct access to ports, railroads and highways.
- Skilled and highly productive labour force.
- An incentive package and tax advantages for investment.
- Preferred place of residence for 25% of the foreigners living in Spain.
- Excellent quality of life, making the Land of Valencia a favoured place to live and to work.

This is a great opportunity for you!

I·V·E·X
Instituto Valenciano de la Exportación

GENERALITAT VALENCIANA

Plaza de América, 2
46004 Valencia (SPAIN)
Tf. (34.6) 395 20 01
Fx. (34.6) 395 42 74

IVEX TOKYO
Tf.(81.3) 5561 98 31
Fx.(81.3) 5561 98 30

IVEX DUSSELDORF
Tf.(49.211) 17 34 20
Fx.(49.211) 17 34 210

IVEX NEW YORK
Tf.(1.212) 922 90 00
Fx.(1.212) 922 90 12

IVEX is the Worldwide Investment and Foreign Trade Agency of the Valencian Government

sluggish, reflecting the cautious stance of households towards spending because of the increased precariousness of jobs. Fixed-term jobs accounted for 35 per cent of total employment in 1995, the highest proportion in the EU. Registered unemployment was down to 15.3 per cent of the labour force in March 1996 from 16.7 per cent at the end of 1994, but the stated jobless rate (measured by a quarterly survey) was still close to 23 per cent, twice the EU average. Taking into account fraud in unemployment benefits and the underground economy, the true figure probably lies between the two. The outgoing Socialist government believed there were at least 13.2 million jobholders, one million more than that revealed by the regular labour force survey.

Reforms

The landmark 1994 reforms which injected greater flexibility into the labour market have quickened the pace of job creation, but the decline in unemployment is slow because of growth in the labour force, particularly female workers. High unemployment has made unions take a much more pragmatic line in wage negotiations, accepting very low or zero wage rises in ailing companies in return for job preservation. The average increase agreed in collective wage bargaining was 3.6 per cent in 1995, lower than inflation for the second year running, and it was about the same in 1996.

Economic growth well below Spain's potential was one factor which enabled the Bank of Spain to quicken its pace of interest rate cuts. Its key intervention rate stood at 7.75 per cent in April 1996, compared with 9.25 per cent in June 1995. A strong peseta, annual inflation running at a 26-year low of around 3.5 per cent and the need to spur consumption were the other factors. The 10-year yield gap with Germany, a key yardstick of Spain's risk premium, was below 300 basis points (bp) at one time in April, down from around 500 bp in June 1995.

There has been a major improvement in the current account balance of payments. Spain's merchandise exports grew 12 per cent in real terms in 1995, lower than 1994's 21 per cent, as the impact of devaluations wore off, but the performance was still impressive. The external sector's contribution to GDP growth was 0.4 points negative in 1995 against 1.2 points positive in 1994. Spain was ranked the world's 15th largest exporter in 1995 by the World Trade Organisation (WTO), with a 1.8 per cent market share, but its position just behind Taiwan, with a much smaller economy, shows how much further it can go if it gets the fundamentals right. The trade balance, however, was still heavily in deficit, reflecting the country's high import dependence, but another bumper tourism year, a

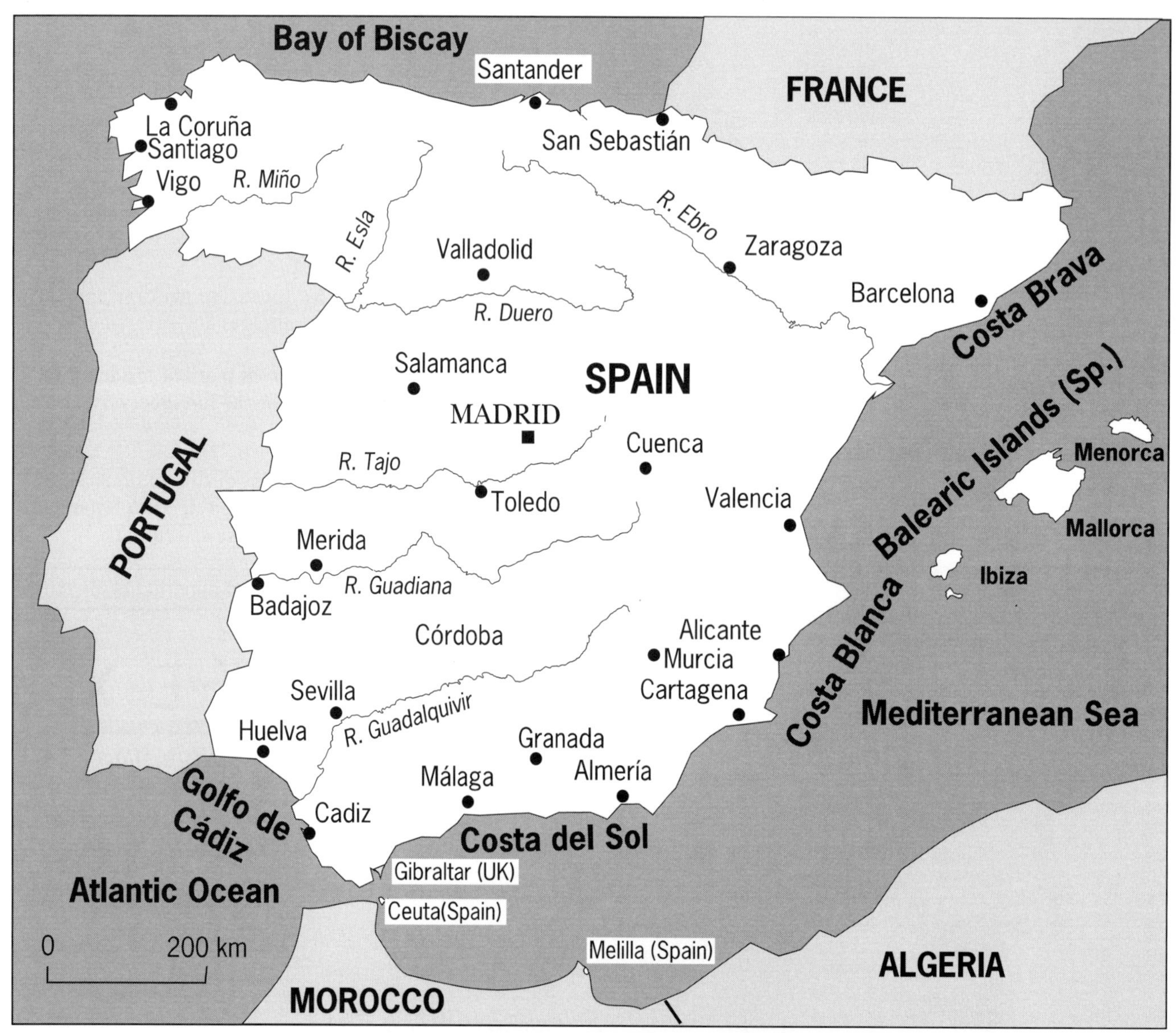

reduced investment income deficit and EU transfers produced a current account surplus of 1.3 per cent of GDP, the first since 1986.

More dramatic was the ending of Spain's five-year drought. Heavy rain at the end of 1995 was greeted with national rejoicing. Spain has always been prone to droughts, which occur in cycles every seven to 10 years, but the last one was the severest in 120 years. Total output of cereals (primarily wheat and corn) plummeted to 11 million tonnes in 1995, from 15.3 million in 1994 and a record 23.8 million in 1988. The 1996 harvest was estimated at 16 million tonnes. Some basic products, such as olive oil, increased by more than 50 per cent in 1995 because of the devastated crop. Water restrictions which affected nearly one-quarter of Spain's population of 39 million in the summer of 1995 were lifted in early 1996.

Profits

Corporate results have greatly improved. The combined pre-tax profits of the 380 most traded companies on the Madrid Stock Exchange increased 23.8 per cent in 1995. Commercial banks emerged from one of their most trying period of their recent history with higher profits, enhanced solvency and healthier balance sheets. The total pre-tax profits of banks rose 3.2 per cent, after falling 20.6 per cent in 1994. The star was Banco Bilbao Vizcaya (BBV) whose net attributable profit rose 16.2 per cent to Pta84 billion, while Santander is absorbing the cost of Banesto, which it acquired in 1994 after the Bank of Spain intervened to stave off a near collapse, more quickly than expected. Santander lifted its net consolidated attributable profit 8.2 per cent to Pta75.3 billion.

A Madrid judge completed a 17-month inquiry in April 1996 into Banesto which paved the way for the trial of Mario Conde, Banesto's former chairman, and nine other directors on charges including embezzlement. Conde, once the role model for Spanish yuppies, ran the bank like a private fiefdom.

More rigorous lending policies and the economy's upturn helped to reduce the non-performing loans of banks to 4.9 per cent of total lending in February 1996 from a peak of 9.2 per cent in 1993.

Among the most significant purchases in the financial sector was Merrill Lynch's acquisition in February 1996 of FG, Spain's largest independent brokerage business. The Pta3.7 billion deal, by far the biggest of its kind by an international institution in Spain, followed Merrill Lynch's takeover of Smith New Court in the UK and introduced strong competition to the big Spanish banks which dominate the domestic broking business.

Iberia, the national airline, was saved from collapse, at the end of 1995 when the European Commission approved an injection by the Spanish government of up to Pta87 billion in new capital. This fell short of the demand for Pta130 billion, but the Commission was prepared to consider a request for a further Pta20 billion in 1997. Thanks to the capital increase and long-overdue cost-cutting measures, Iberia was expected to make a profit in 1996 after losses of Pta45 billion in 1995.

Iberia was the only part of Teneo, the state holding company whose other interests include energy and aerospace, which did not show an improvement in 1995. Overall, the Teneo group more than doubled net earnings from Pta30 billion to Pta71 billion. Teneo was formed in 1992 to group together the more viable parts of the former Instituto Nacional de Industria (INI) which was wound down in 1995 in a reorganisation of the state sector.

Seat, the subsidiary of Volkswagen acquired from the Spanish state in 1986, also received a controversial injection of aid, and was on course to break even in 1997 after reducing losses by 62 per cent to Pta11.3 billion. It last made a profit in 1991.

Telefónica, where the government's stake was reduced to 20 per cent in 1995 from 32 per cent, continued to forge ahead, increasing its net profit 18 per cent to Pta133 billion. Tisa, its international unit, which is becoming an aggressive multinational, particularly in Latin America, generated 16 per cent of the group's revenue.

Telefónica was scheduled to reduce its charges for calls to the US and the EU by 23 per cent and 13 per cent respectively in 1996, in preparation for the full liberalisation of the domestic telecoms sector in 1998. The only dark cloud on the considerably brighter horizon of this former dinosaur was how the new government would cope with the European Commission's order to repay Pta85 billion to the Airtel consortium, which operates Spain's second mobile phone network, because Telefónica was not charged a similar fee when it set up its mobile system. The government must either repay the money, charge a similar fee to Telefónica or adequately compensate Airtel.

Although support for EU membership has waned over the 10 years since Spain joined, the country remains broadly enthusiastic. The González government acted as midwife to the birth of the Euro, the single currency, at the December 1995 EU summit in Madrid. Cracks, however, have opened up in the seemingly united front in favour of Spain forming part of the core group of EMU countries. Foremost among the critics is Miguel Boyer, the economic supremo in the Socialists' first government

KEY INDICATORS

	Unit	1991	1992	1993	1994	1995
Population	m	38.92	39.01	39.08	39.14	39.20
Gross domestic product (GDP)	US$bn	526.0	585.3	482.8	480.3	–
GDP per capita	US$	13,480	14,850	12,330	12,335	–
GDP real growth	%	2.3	1.0	-1.0	2.1	2.9
Inflation	%	5.9	5.9	4.6	4.7	4.4
Consumer prices	1990=100	105.9	112.2	117.3	122.9	128.6
Unemployment	%	15.9	18.0	22.7	23.9	22.7
Share prices	1990=100	102.6	89.1	104.6	121.6	114.4
Agricultural production	1979-81=100	119.07	122.15	115.16	109.55	99.63
Industrial production	1990=100	99.2	96.4	91.8	98.8	103.3
Coal	m toe	15.4	15.4	14.5	13.5	13.0
Silver production	tonnes	180	160	180	181	–
Exports (FOB) (goods)	US$bn	60.2	65.8	62.0	73.9	92.6
Imports (FOB) (goods)	US$bn	90.5	96.2	77.0	88.8	110.4
Balance of trade	US$bn	-30.3	-30.4	-15.0	-14.8	-17.7
Current account	US$bn	-19.79	-21.3	-5.8	-6.8	1.3
Total reserves minus gold	US$m	65,822	45,504	41,045	41,546	34,485
Foreign exchange	US$m	64,295	44,176	39,798	40,182	32,491
Deposit rate	%	10.47	10.43	9.63	6.70	7.68
Lending rate	%	14.38	14.23	12.78	8.95	10.05
Exchange rate	Pta per US$	103.9	102.4	127.3	133.9	124.6

BASQUE COUNTRY

A PARTNER OF PROMISE

10 TEN REASONS WHY THE BASQUE COUNTRY IS TODAY AN ATTRACTIVE, UP-TO-DATE PROPOSITION:

A STRATEGIC GEOGRAPHICAL SETTING

A vital link in the communications axis between Lisbon and Stockholm, the Basque Country has one of Spain's leading merchant shipping port and Europe's deepest docking facilities (32 metres). The region also has three airports, motorways and a direct Spanish connection with Europe's high-speed rail network.

A NETWORK OF INTELLIGENT HIGHWAYS

The Basque Country has a latest -generation micro-wave network and a broad-band optical fibre trunk network covering 85% of the Basque population and all university campuses and industrial centres.

BROAD-BASED, DIVERSIFIED POWER INFRASTRUCTURE

Efficiency and savings programmes have enabled the Basque Country as a whole to reduce energy consumption by 14% since 1980. The area currently depends on oil for 36.7% of the energy it needs. Power sources have been diversified in recent years, with particular attention being paid to natural gas, which has its own gas field and modern distribution network.

SPAIN'S INDUSTRIAL POWER HOUSE

Much of Spain's production in a number of strategic sectors comes from the Basque Country: machine-tools, the automotive ancillary industry, capital goods and the iron and steel industry. The Basque Country is also home to the Mondragón Corporación Cooperativa (MCC), the world's largest industrial cooperative group, and Iberdrola, Europe's fifth largest power generating company.

INVESTMENT INCENTIVES AND GUARANTEES

Treasury bonds issued by the Basque Government have been given an Aa2 rating by American ratings agency Moody's and AA by Standard & Poor's. Among the most noteworthy tax incentives for the year are the general rate of company tax of 32.5% and an outright grant of up to 25% for new investments.

TECHNOLOGY RESEARCH APPLIED TO INDUSTRY

The Basque Country has seven Research Centres employing more than 900 professionals; the largest science and technology park in northeastern Spain; engineering firms and other companies involved in international research projects.

ONE OF EUROPE'S LEADING FINANCIAL CENTRES

The Banco Bilbao Vizcaya, Spain's leading bank in terms of the volume of savings managed, the Bolsa de Bilbao, the country's second busiest Stock Exchange, Elkargi, the first mutual guarantee company in Spain.

HUMAN RESOURCES, THE BASQUE COUNTRY'S MOST IMPORTANT RAW MATERIAL

There are two universities in the Basque Country, one of which, Deusto, is Spain's most famous seat of learning. Students can choose from 22 faculties, 8 technical and 3 Higher colleges and schools. The Basque Country also has 172 vocational training centres.

A UNIQUE, AGE-OLD CULTURE

Euskera, the Basque language. Part of mankind's linguistic heritage, Euskera is the oldest language in Europe, a survival from the pre-Indo-European era.

AN UNRIVALIED NATURAL SETTING

The UNESCO recently declared the Gernika estuary a "Biosphere Reserve". According to the 1992 Economic Report on the Spanish Autonomous Communities, the Basque Country has the most complete environmental protection infrastructure in all Spain.

BASQUE COUNTRY

For further information:

GOBIERNO VASCO
VITORIA-GASTEIZ / BASQUE COUNTRY, SPAIN
TLF: 34.45.18 80 92 • FAX: 34.45.18 80 81

Visit us at:
Http: //www.euskadi.net

SPRI-SOCIEDAD PARA LA PROMOCION INDUSTRIAL
BILBAO / BASQUE COUNTRY, SPAIN
TLF: 34.4.479 70 12 • FAX: 34.4.479 70 23

(1982–85) and one of the experts who helped draw up the report on the single-currency project with Jacques Delors, the last European Commission president. Boyer does not question the wisdom of meeting the four criteria but he believes the merits of a single currency would be far outweighed by the 'enormous economic and social cost' of getting rid of flexible exchange rates. He handed in his party card in early 1996 and now openly supports the Popular Party.

The PP said it would not ease up the efforts to meet the EMU criteria, though it was vague about the structural reforms that all parties except the United Left agree that Spain needs, and the urgency of which the Bank of Spain never ceases to highlight and which the Socialists failed to deliver. The PP had intended to cut the highest personal income tax rate from 56 per cent to 40 per cent, but it was difficult to see how it could achieve anything more than a token cut without jeopardising the budget deficit reduction unless it really does get to grips with spending.

Outlook

Several reports have sounded alarm bells about the viability of the state pension and unemployment benefits systems unless cutbacks are made. A report sponsored by BBV said the social security deficit could reach 2 per cent of GDP in the year 2000. Spain's predicament is that its population is rapidly greying and an increasingly smaller proportion of the labour force is supporting the growing number of pensioners and the unemployed. Sixty-two out of every 100 Spaniards over the age of 14 are 'inactive', compared with a EU average of fifty-one. While the number of pensioners increased 56 per cent between 1980 and 1995 to 6.4 million, the number of Social Security contributors only rose 13 per cent to 12.4 million.

Reforms generally considered insufficient were approved in 1995 by an all-party parliamentary commission, including increasing the number of years for calculating pensions from eight years prior to retirement to 15.

After so many years of telling the Socialists how to put Spain's house in order it remained to be seen whether the PP would take the bull by the horns and implement unpopular measures.

COUNTRY PROFILE — SPAIN

Political system

Parliamentary monarchy, with legislative power vested in the Cortes Generales (divided into the Congress of Deputies and a Senate). Congress has 350 deputies elected every four years by a proportional system and 208 of the 252 senators are chosen in direct elections. The remaining senators are designated by the autonomous regions. Mr Felipe González, whose Socialist Workers' Party (PSOE) was short of an overall majority in the June 1993 general elections, was returned to power for a fourth term with the support in a congress investiture vote on 9 July 1993 of the Catalan and Basque nationalist parties.

Main cities/towns

Madrid (population 4.6m in 1994), Barcelona (4m), Valencia, Seville, Zaragoza, Bilbao, Málaga.

Language

Most Spaniards understand 'standard' Castilian but a third of the population speaks one of the other three official tongues: Catalán (which became an EU language in 1990), Gallego (Galician) and Basque. Some English and French is also spoken.

Media

Press: Only 34 per cent of the adult population reads a newspaper every day.
Dailies: Published regionally, though those published in Madrid are available in most parts of the country. The top dailies are *Marca, El País, ABC, El Mundo del Siglo XXI, La Vanguardia, El Periódico de Cataluña* (Barcelona) and *El Correo Español.*
Weeklies: El País, ABC, Marca and *El Mundo.* Several general and special interest magazines, plus news magazines such as *Cambio 16* and *Tiempo.*
Business: Major business magazines *Actualidad Económica, Dinero* and *Mercado.*
Broadcasting: Co-ordinated by Radiotelevisión Española (RTVE). Radio programmes are broadcast by Radio Nacional de España (RNE) and several commercial and independent stations. All TV programmes are broadcast by Television Española (two channels). Various private TV channels available.
Advertising: All usual media are available. TV and hoardings tend to be most popular method, though radio, newspaper and cinema advertising is also widespread. Information, including current rates, appears in quarterly magazine *Guía de los Medios.* Major advertising products: food, automotives. Newspapers and TV are the major advertising media.

Domestic economy

Mixed economy with large agricultural and industrial sectors. Also important: tourism and banking industries. By 1989 the Spanish economy was growing faster than anywhere else in Europe; foreign investment was pouring in; jobs were being created at the rate of 400,000 a year and welfare spending was generous.
The economy has been considerably restructured and rationalised between 1986 and 1996. The government is trying to achieve the financial targets laid down at Maastricht in 1991 in order that Spain may be among the first participants in the European single currency scheduled for January 1999.

Employment

Spain's unemployment rate is one of the highest in Europe but is falling. A major factor behind higher unemployment is insufficient wage moderation.

External trade

Exports: Spain was ranked the world's 15th largest exporter in 1995 by the World Trade Organisation (WTO). Major exports include wine, fruit and vegetables, metals, motor vehicles, machinery and transport equipment.
Main destinations: France (20.5% of 1995 total) Germany (15.4%), Italy (9.2%), Portugal (8.3%), UK (8%), USA (4.1%), Netherlands (3.7%), Belgium-Luxembourg (3.1%), Japan (1.4%), Switzerland (1.1%).
Imports: Main imports include foodstuffs, energy products, raw materials, basic manufactures and machinery.
Main sources: France (17.1% of 1995 total), Germany (15.3%), Italy (9.2%), UK (7.8%), USA (6.4%), Netherlands (4.3%), Belgium-Luxembourg (3.4%), Japan (3.3%), Portugal (2.9%), China (2%).

Agriculture

Formerly mainstay of the economy, contributed 4.8 per cent to GDP in 1994 and employed about 10.1 per cent of the labour force. Near self-sufficiency in wheat, barley, sugar and poultry. Major exporter of wine, fruit and vegetables. Spain hopes to increasingly supply Europe with early harvested, and sub-tropical, fruits and vegetables, thereby replacing Florida and California as the major supplier. Largest fishing fleet in EU.
Heavy rain ended Spain's five-year drought in December 1995. Total cereals output had dropped to 11m tonnes in 1995, from 15.3m tonnes in 1994, after a previous record 23.8m tonnes in 1988.

Industry

This sector contributed 33.6 per cent to GDP in 1994 and employed 29.7 per cent of the labour force. Emphasis on restructuring industry and promoting hi-tech industries – most important are steel, shipbuilding, textiles, footwear, automobile parts and home appliances.

Tourism

Spain pioneered mass tourism in the early 1960s. Income from tourism grew by 9 per cent in 1995; most tourists came from France (22.3%); Portugal (16.7%), Germany (15.8%), UK (14.9%), Italy (4.6%), Netherlands (3.7%). The leisure industry as a whole accounts for about 9 per cent of GDP and for about one out of every 10 jobs.

Mining

The mining sector accounted for 1 per cent of GDP in 1994 and employed 1 per cent of the workforce. Extensive mineral deposits including iron pyrites, copper, mercury, uranium, wolfram, lead and zinc. A large mercury deposit has been found in Almaden in southern Spain which will raise Spain's mercury levels to nearly a quarter of proven world reserves. Also large reserves of coal and lignite, production of which has risen due to increased domestic demand. World's second-largest producer of natural stone. The Huelva copper smelter capacity expanded by 20 per cent from 150,000 tonnes to 180,000.
Work began in October 1996 on the US$45m El Valle project, the first modern gold mine in the Asturias region (gold mines 2,000 years ago provided the Roman Empire with much of its wealth), which is scheduled to produce about 100,000 troy ounces a year.

Hydrocarbons

Repsol, the state oil company, is looking for a long-term arrangement with an oil-producing country. Spain is heavily dependent on imported oil, with Mexico its largest supplier. Repsol is being prepared for further partial privatisation.
Spain is also very dependent on imported gas, although the government is trying to increase consumption. On 1 November 1996 Spain opened the US$2.3bn Algerian gas link, the Maghreb-Europe pipeline, which will supply Spain with 6.2bn cu metres of gas by year 2000. Coal production 13m tonnes oil equivalent in 1995, down 3.7 per cent on 1994 output.

Energy

Nuclear and hydroelectric power stations provided just over half its electricity in 1990.

COUNTRY PROFILE SPAIN

Energy (contd): There are eight nuclear power plants on stream.

Legal system

Civil law system with regional applications.

Membership of international organisations

Advisory Committee for the International Protection of Nature, ADB, ADF, Andean Pact (observer), Antartic Treaty, ASSIMER, CCC, CERN, Council of Europe, EBRD, EMS, ESA, ESO, ESRO, EU, FAO, IADF, IAEA, IAEO, ICAC, ICAO, ICES, ICO, IDA, IDB, IEA, IFAD, IFC, IHO, ILO, IMF, IMO, INTELSAT, International Lead and Zinc Study Group, International Grain Council, INTERPOL, IOOC, IPU, ITC, ITU, NATO, OAS (observer), OECD, UN, UNESCO, UNICEF, UPU, WHO, WIPO, WMO, World Bank, WSG, WTO.

BUSINESS GUIDE

Time

GMT + 1 hr (GMT + 2 from late Mar to late Sep); then Canaries GMT (GMT + 1 hr during summer).

Climate

Very varied. Mainland is temperate in the north, hot, dry summers in central and southern regions. On central plateau weather very cold Dec–Mar. Northern coastal region has mild winters and warm summers with slightly less sunshine than the rest of Spain. Rainfall Jan–Apr. Summer storms can be violent. Temperatures range from 1–35°C.
Clothing: Mediumweight for winter, plus topcoat in central and northern areas. Lightweight for summer.

Entry requirements

Visa not required by nationals of EU and American countries, and several others, for visits up to three months. N.B. regulations liable to change at short notice. Travel agent or Spanish consulate should be consulted prior to departure.
Health: Vaccination certificates not normally required. Tap water not always safe to drink outside cities, so bottled water advisable.
Currency: No restriction on amount of Spanish or foreign currency that may be taken into the country. Up to Pta100,000 in Spanish banknotes and the equivalent of Pta350,000 in foreign currency may be exported. (Greater amounts may be re-exported provided such amounts were declared on entry to the country.)
Customs: Personal effects duty-free. Duty-free goods facilities at main international airports.

Air access

Regular flights by all major international airlines. Very busy during holiday season.
National airline: Iberia – government-owned – is continuing to make heavy losses despite a capital injection from public funds.
Main international airport: Barajas (MAD) 16 km north-east of Madrid, Barcelona (BCN) 10 km south-west of city and Málaga (AGP) 8 km south-west of city.
International airports: Alicante (ALC), 12 km south-west of city, Bilbao (BIO), 9 km from city, Almeria (LEI), 9 km from city, Valencia (VLC), 10 km west of city, Santiago (SCQ), 10 km north-east of city. Also on Balearic and Canary Islands. In July 1995 the Spanish airport authority, Aeropuertos Espanoles y Navegacion Aerea (AENA), announced a US$3bn programme for the renovation and expansion of its airports at Madrid Barajas and Bilbao.

Surface access

Good road and rail access from France. Regular ferry and shipping services from several countries, including Plymouth–Santander.
Main ports: Barcelona, Valencia, Alicante, Málaga, Algeciras, Cádiz, La Coruña, Bilbao.

Hotels

Classified from one- to five-star, plus a 'Grand De Luxe' category (pensions/hostels classified from one- to three-star). Also paradores (national tourist inns) increasingly popular. Accommodation should be booked well in advance, especially during holiday season. N.B. term 'Residencia' denotes establishments without dining-room facilities.

Restaurants

Numerous and varied. Even modest restaurants offer very substantial meals. Service charge usually included in bill, but small tips customary.

Currency

Exchange rate: Peseta floats freely against all foreign currencies. Spain is a member of the EMS.

Foreign exchange information

Account restrictions: Non-resident accounts may be convertible or non-convertible.

Trade policy

Tariff reductions associated with membership of EU. Quotas imposed on some goods. Spanish import duties being replaced by EU Common External Tariff. Proceeds of exports must be surrendered in return for local currency. Credit may be obtained to finance exports at favourable rates of interest.

Credit cards

All major credit cards are accepted.

Car hire

Available in most large towns. International driving licence, or foreign licence translated into Spanish and authorised by Spanish consulate, required. Third-party insurance compulsory, and a Green Card is advisable, also Bail Bond. Details of hire from local tourist offices. Drive on the right. Speed limits: towns 60kph, national highways 110kph, motorways 120kph, others 90kph. Traffic coming from right generally has priority. Seat belts must be worn in front seats.

City transport

Taxis: Available in most major cities; all metered. Tend to have a distinct colour in each city. Tipping between 5–10 per cent.

National transport

Based on radial routes centred on Madrid. Often very busy during holiday season.
Air: Frequent services from Madrid to all major centres operated by Iberia and Aviación y Comercio (Aviaco).
Road: Good roads connecting all main towns. Network of over 150,000 km, including 2,000 km of motorways (usually toll) mostly confined to coastal regions.
Buses: Regular bus and coach services between main towns.
Rail: Approximately 14,408 km of track, of which about 11,500 km is operated by Red Nacional de los Ferrocarriles Españoles (RENFE), and the rest (narrow gauge) by Ferrocarriles Españoles de Vía Estrecha (FEVE). The EIB granted loans in 1993 to improve the Madrid-Seville rail link and the public railway network in Santander and Bilbao.
Water: Regular steamer and hydrofoil services operated by Compañía Transmediterránea connect Balearic Islands with Barcelona, Valencia and Alicante. Also weekly ferry service to Las Palmas (Canary Islands) from Barcelona.

Public holidays

Fixed dates: 1 Jan, 6 Jan (Reyes), 1 May (St Joseph), 15 Aug (Assumption), 12 Oct (National Day), 1 Nov (All Saints'), 6 Dec (Constitution Day), 8 Dec (Immaculate Conception), 25 Dec.
Variable dates: Holy Thursday, Good Friday, Corpus Christi. Each town and region also has its own fiesta, e.g. Madrid in May and Nov, Barcelona in Jun and Sep, and Valencia in Jan. Dates of these also vary.

Working hours

Business: Usually open (Mon–Fri) 0900 – 1400 and 1630 – 1930.
Government: Vary considerably from region to region and according to time of year. In Madrid: (Mon–Fri) generally 0900 – 1330 and 1500 – 1800; except Jul and Aug, 0830 – 1430 (1400 on Fri) with only skeleton staff remaining during afternoon.
Banking: (Mon–Fri) 0900 – 1400, (Sat) 0900 – 1300.
Shops: (Mon–Sat) 0900 – 1300, 1500 – 1930.

Social customs

Lunch 1430, dinner 2130. Spaniards hospitable towards business visitors but do not usually invite them to their homes.

Business language and interpreting/translation

Available in all major towns. Working knowledge of Spanish great advantage to business visitor.

Telecommunications

Telefónica, which is mostly in private hands, plans to improve international connections. The EIB granted a loan in 1993 to extend the telecommunications network.
Telephone: Automatic system in operation throughout most of country. Rates vary from province to province. International dialling code: 34 followed by area code (3 for Barcelona, 1 for Madrid, 5 for Sevilla), followed by subscriber's number. N.B. Area code plus customer's number should consist of eight digits.

BUSINESS GUIDE

Telecommunications (contd): For IDD access from Spain dial 07.
Telex and telefax: Services available in main post offices and larger hotels. Telex country code 52E.
Telegram: Available in post offices and by telephone.

Postal service

Letters may be sent *poste restante* care of main post offices. These should be addressed: Addressee, Lista de Correos, Name of village etc.

Trade fairs

Many specialised fairs and exhibitions held in various parts of the country. Important method of promotion. Goods may be imported temporarily, with an ATA carnet, then later either fully imported or returned to country of origin. Most important place is 'IFEMA' the Madrid Trade Fair Institution which hosts, among other things, the international fashion week. Information regarding fairs in Barcelona is available from Fira de Barcelona, Avenida Reina Maria Cristina s/n, 08004 Barcelona (tel: 423-3101; fax: 423-8651).

Electricity supply

220 V AC (occasionally 110–125V AC in older buildings).

BUSINESS DIRECTORY

Hotels

Barcelona
Avenida Palace, Gran Via 605, 08007 (tel: 301-9600; fax: 318-1234).

Victoria, Avenida Pedralbes 16, 0803 (tel: 204-2754; fax: 204-2766).

Diplomatic, Pau Claris 122 (tel: 317-3100).

Gran Sarria Sol, Avenida de Sarria 50, 08029 (tel: 239-1109; tx: 51-638).

Presidente, Diagonal 570, 08021 (tel: 200-2111; fax: 209-5106).

Ritz, Gran Via 668, 08010 (tel: 318-5200; fax: 318-0148).

Bilbao
Aranzazu, Rodrigues Arias 66 (tel: 441-3100; tx: 32-164).

Carlton, Plaza Federico Mayua 2, 48009 (tel: 416-2200; fax: 416-4628).

Gran Ercilla, Ercilla 37/39, 11 (tel: 443-8800; fax: 443-9395).

Villa de Bilbao, Gran Via López de Haro 87, 11 (tel: 441-6000; tx: 32-164).

Madrid
Alameda (airport), Avenida de Logroño 100, Barajas-Madrid 28042 (tel: 747-4800, 223-9868; fax: 747-8928).

Arosa, Gran Via 29 (tel: 532-1600; fax: 531-3127).

Carlton, Paseo Delicias 28 (tel: 239-7100; tx: 44-571).

Castellana, Paseo de la Castellana (tel: 410-0200; fax: 319-5853, 308-6035).

Cuzco, Paseo de la Castellana 133, PO Box 16 (tel: 456-0600; tx: 22-464).

Emperador Plaza (reservations office), Princesa 40, PO Box 8 (tel: 247-2800; fax: 247-2817).

Eurobuilding, Padre Damián 23 (tel: 457-7800; tx: 22-548; fax: 457-9729).

Florida Norte, Paseo de la Florida 5 (tel: 542-8300; fax: 247-7833).

Gran Colon, 119 Avenida Doctor Esquerdo (tel: 273-5900; fax: 273-0809).

Los Galgos Sol, Claudio Coello 139 (tel: 262-6600; fax: 261-7662).

Meliá, Calle Princesa 27 (tel: 541-8200; fax: 541-1988).

Meliá Castilla, Capitan Haya 43 (tel: 571-2211; fax: 571-2210).

Miguel Angel, Miguel Angel 29/31 (tel: 442-0022; fax: 442-5320).

Palace, Plaza de la Cortes 7 (tel: 429-7551; fax: 429-8266).

The Ritz, Plaza de la Lealtad 5 (tel: 521-2857; fax: 532-8776).

Villa Magna, Paseo de la Castellana 22 (tel: 564-1236; fax: 275-3158).

Wellington, Velazquez 8 (tel: 275-5200; tx: 22-700).

Car hire

Madrid
Avis: Central Reservations (tel: 348-0348; fax: 22-410); Plaza Colón-Terminal, Bus Airport, 28001 (tel: 576-2862, 577-9695); Holiday Inn, Orense 22/24, 28020 (tel: 556-7492).

Budget: Central Reservations (tel: 402-1034; fax: 402-6637); Hotel Diana, Centro Comercial, Calle Galeón 27, 28042 (tel: 329-5048; fax: 329-5049); Calle Alcantará 59, 28006 (tel: 401-2460; 402-6637).

Europcar: Central Reservations, General Yagüe, Nr 6 Bis, 28020 (tel: 556-1500; fax: 556-9935); Airport, Barajas (tel: 305-5325/163).

Hertz: Central Reservations (tel: 542-1000; fax: 559-8060); Airport (tel: 305-8452; fax: 305-5092).

Chambers of commerce

The British Chamber of Commerce in Spain, Plaza Santa Barbara 10, 28004 Madrid (tel: 308-3081; fax: 302-4896).

Cámara Oficial de Comercio, Industria y Navegación de Barcelona, Avenida Diagonal 45, 08006 Barcelona (tel: 219-1300; tx: 54-713).

Cámara Oficial de Comercio, Industria y Navegación de Bilbao, Alameda Recalde 50, 48008 Bilbao (tel: 444-4054; tx: 444-5891, 32-182).

Cámara Oficial de Comercio, Industria y Navegación de Cádiz, Ahumada 2, 11004 Cádiz (tel: 323-050; tx: 76-013).

Cámara Oficial de Comercio, Industria y Navegación de Ibiza, Historiador J. Clatés 4, Ibiza, Balearic Islands (tel: 301-492; tx: 69-679).

Cámara Oficial de Comercio, Industria y Navegación de Las Palmas de Gran Canaria, León y Castillo 24, Las Palmas, Canary Islands (tel: 371-000, 361-130; tx: 95-317).

Cámara Oficial de Comercio e Industria de Madrid, Huertas 13, 28012 Madrid 12 (tel: 429-3193; tx: 27-307, 23-261).

Cámara Oficial de Comercio, Industria y Navegación de Málaga, Bolsa 1, Málaga (tel: 211-673; tx: 77-368).

Cámara Oficial de Comercio e Industria de Zaragoza, Don Jaime 1 18, Zaragoza (tel: 295-900; tx: 58-702).

Cámara Oficial de Comercio, Industria y Navegación de Sevilla, Plaza de la Contratación 8, 41004 Sevilla (tel: 211-204; tx: 72-407).

Cámara Oficial de Comercio, Industria y Navegación de Valencia, Poeta Querol 15, 46002 Valencia (tel: 351-1301; tx: 62-518).

Banking

Argentaria (Banco Exterior de España), Carrera de San Jerónimo 36, Madrid (tel: 537-7000)

Banco de España (central bank). Alcalá 50, 28014 Madrid (tel: 446-9055; tx: 49-461).

Banco Atlántico SA, Diagonal 407 bis, Barcelona (tel: 237-1240; tx: 52-267).

Banco Central, Calle de Alcalá, 28014 Madrid (tel: 222-2991; tx: 42-003).

Banco Bilbao Vizcaya, Vizcaya Plaza de San Nicolas 4, 48005 Bilbao (tel: 424-4620).

Banco de la Exportación SA, Barcas 10, Valencia 2 (tel: 351-7862; tx: 62-676).

Banco de Sabadell, Plaza Sant Roc 20, 08201 Sabadell (tel: 726-2100; tx: 52-847).

Banco Español de Crédito (Banesto), Paseo de la Castellana 7, Madrid (tel: 338-1000; tx: 27-410).

Banco Hispano Americano, Plaza de Canalejas 1, Madrid (tel: 522-4660).

Banco Internacional de Comercio, José Ortega y Gasset 56, 28006 Madrid (tel: 402-8362; tx: 23-914).

Banco Popular Español, Velázquez 34, 28001 Madrid (tel: 435-3620; tx: 44-351).

Banco Santander, Apartado de Correos 00045, Santander (tel: 221-200; tx: 35-833).

Caja de Pensiones para la Vejez y de Ahorros de Cataluña y Baleares, Avenida Diagonal 621-629, 08028 Barcelona (tel: 330-3000; fax; 330-0480).

Confederación Española de Cajas de Ahorros (confederation of Spanish savings banks), Alcalá 27 Madrid 14 (tel: 232-7810).

Consejo Superior Bancario (central committee of Spanish banking), José Abascal 57, Madrid 9 (tel: 441-0611).

La Caixa de Barcelona (savings bank), Avenida Diagonal 530, 08006 Barcelona (tel: 201-6666).

Travel information

Turespaña, Secretaria Gral de Turismo, Castello 115-117 Maria de Molina 50, 28001 Madrid (tel: 411-4014, 411-6011).

Other useful addresses

Agencia EFE, SA (news agency), Espronceda 32, Apartado 1112, 28003 Madrid (tel: 441-5599).

Bolsa de Comercio de Valencia (stock exchange), Pascual y Genis 19, 46001 Valencia (tel: 352-1487; tx: 62-880).

Bolsa de Madrid (stock exchange), Palacio de la Bolsa, Plaza de la Lealtad 1 (tel: 232-8484).

Central de Reservas de los Paradores de España, Calle Velázquez 25, 28001 Madrid (tel: 435-9700/9744/9768/9814; tx: 46-865 RRPPE).

Confederación Española de Organizaciones Empresariales (Spanish confederation of employers' organisations), Diego de León 50, 28006 Madrid (tel: 262-4410; tx: 46-527).

Instituto Nacional de Estadistica (INE), Paseo de la Castellana 183, E-28071 Madrid (tel: 583-9100; fax: 573-2713).

Instituto Nacional de la Seguridad Social, Subdirección General de Relaciones Internacionales, Padre Damián 4, 28036 Madrid (tel: 450-1900).

Ministry of Economy, Finance and Trade, Alcalá 9, Madrid 14 (tel: 232-6124; tx: 48-387).

Ministry of Industry and Energy, Paseo de la Castellana 160, Madrid 16 (tel: 458-8010; tx: 42-112).

Internet sites

Iberia Airlines:
http://www.civeng.carleton.ca/SiSpain/travelli/iberia/menu.html

Sweden

Michael Griffin

The appointment of former finance minister Göran Persson to replace Ingvar Carlsson, who stepped down as premier in March 1996, ended an extended period of instability in the ruling Sveriges Socialdemokratiska Arbetarepartiet (SAP) (Swedish Social Democratic Labour Party, elected with 45.4 per cent of the vote in September 1994. Mr Carlsson explained his decision, announced in August 1995, by saying he had achieved his three main political goals: to return the SAP to power, bring Sweden into the European Union (EU) and to 'sanitise' an economy with the highest rate of public expenditure in the industrialised world. The elevation of Mr Persson, chief architect of Carlsson's pledge to balance public finances, reassured the international markets but the Swedes' opinion of the EU has soured since the SAP narrowly swung the referendum in favour of membership in November 1994.

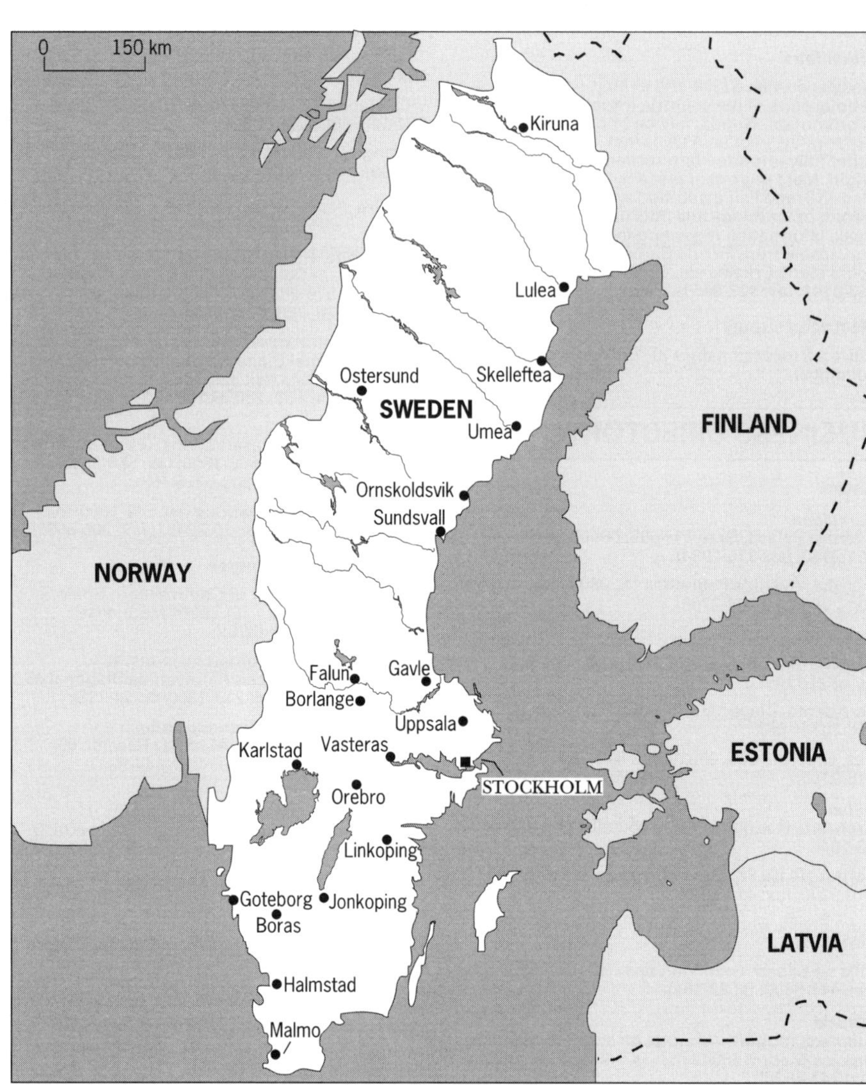

Politics

The favourite for Carlsson's succession was 38-year-old Mona Sahlin, the deputy vice premier, but she was knocked out of the running following revelations that she had used an official credit card for private transactions. The extended hiatus at the summit of power was only resolved in December 1996 when Mr Persson, an intensely private man, finally bowed to pressure by accepting the unanimous nomination for the leadership. In his inaugural speech to the Riksdag on 22 March 1996, he reiterated his commitment to reducing unemployment to 4 per cent by the end of the decade, achieving a balanced state budget by 1998, introducing a contract to keep wage increases within acceptable limits and to meet the convergence criteria of economic and monetary union (EMU) by 1997.

To execute these objectives, Mr Persson made sweeping changes to the cabinet. For the important post of finance minister, he chose the technocrat Erik Asbrink, an indication to many that he intends to retain a firm hold on the workings of his former portfolio. His closest aide, Leif Pagrotsky, is also an economist. But it is the anti-EU campaigner, Margareta Winberg, who has the hottest seat. Replacing Annika Ahnberg as labour minister, she will be responsible for creating 150,000 new jobs in a bid to rein in Sweden's unprecedented 13 per cent unemployment rate. Mr Persson has also maintained a conciliatory tone towards the Centrepartiet Riksorganization (Cp) Centre Party which, under a pact reached after the 1994 elections, guarantees it a voting majority in exchange for concrete progress towards the reform of public finances.

Identity crisis

Fresh elections are not expected until late 1998 when the results of Mr Persson's deficit and debt reduction programmes should also become apparent. The fiscal crisis which precipitated these reforms has also triggered a debate within the SAP between the 'renewers' and the 'traditionalists'. The former, who include the premier and many in the cabinet, believe that Sweden's notorious cradle-to-grave welfare system is no longer sustainable and must be radically trimmed if it is to survive into the twenty-first century in anything approaching its current form. The traditionalists, who represent the views of the SAP's power-base in the unions and the public sector, want to see benefit payments fully restored once the immediate crisis in public finances is overcome.

The disagreement is not only about welfare; it is also about Swedish identity. After more than half a century of egalitarian socialism, there is a growing awareness that Sweden must adjust its priorities if it is to compete with the more market-oriented economies of Europe. But those adjustments entail a break with the past that large numbers of Swedes – and 30 per cent work in the public sector alone – find unacceptable. Unemployment is at its highest levels since the Second World War and there is much more in the pipeline, as Mr Persson pursues an austerity programme which, in bringing Sweden into linc with Europe, appears to be losing sight of its own firmly held humanitarian values.

Carlsson's legacy has been blemished recently. The popularity of the SAP fell from 45 per cent in the general elections to just 28.1 per cent in the European elections in September 1995 when over half the delegates sent to Strasbourg were anti-EU candidates from the Left and Environment Parties. Voters were disappointed that membership has not delivered new jobs or reduced food prices, as the government campaign had implied, while simultaneously depriving Sweden of its cherished neutrality. For a country with a long-standing tradition of non-alliance and a highly sophisticated defence industry to enforce such a policy, the prospect of sacrificing its independence to the Western European Union, the EU's security forum, is profoundly unsettling.

KEY FACTS

Official title: Kungriket Sverige (The Kingdom of Sweden)

Head of state: King Carl XVI Gustaf

Head of government: Prime Minister Göran Persson (from 14 Mar 1996)

Ruling party: Sveriges Socialdemokratiska Arbetarepartiet (SAP) (Swedish Social Democratic Party) (from Sep 1994)

Capital: Stockholm

Official Languages: Swedish

Currency: Swedish Krona (SKr) = 100 ore

Exchange rate: SKr6.83 per US$ (Dec 1996)

Area: 448,964 sq km

Population: 8.85m (1995)

GDP per capita: US$22,300 (1994)

GDP real growth: 1.4% (first qtr 1996)

GNP per capita: US$23,630 (1994)

GNP real growth: 3% (1995)

Labour force: 4.3m (1995)*

Unemployment: 7.1% (May 1996) (not seasonally adjusted)

Inflation: 1.7% (Feb 1996, year-on-year) (consumer prices)

Trade balance: US$19.5bn (12 months to Oct 1996)

Foreign debt: US$115bn (1994)

* estimated figure

Economy

Swedish industry, which has a higher proportion of multinationals to its size than any other country in Europe, remains strongly pro-Europe. In 1995, foreign direct investment in Sweden soared to a record level of SKr100 billion (US$14 billion), due to

KEY INDICATORS — Sweden

	Unit	1991	1992	1993	1994	1995
Population	m	8.64	8.69	8.75	8.80	8.85
Gross domestic product (GDP)	US$bn	250.0	250.0	185.3	194.7	-
GDP per capita	US$	27,700	29,200	21,200	22,300	-
GDP real growth	%	0.77	-1.8	-2.6	2.3	3.5
Consumer prices	1990=100	109	112	117	120	123
Inflation	%	9.3	2.3	4.6	2.2	2.7
Unemployment	%	2.7	5.3	8.2	7.9	7.8
Wages (hourly earnings)	1990=100	105	110	113	118	123
Agricultural production	1979-81=100	92.96	85.89	97.04	87.61	92.32
Share prices	1979-81=100	94	80	106	133	149
Industrial employment	1990=100	92	84	77	76	80
Industrial production	1990=100	95	93	94	104	114
Silver	tonnes	253	282	277	252	-
Iron	'000 tonnes	1,200	12,100	11,800	12,400	-
Zinc	'000 tonnes	158	172	169	*130	-
Exports (FOB) (goods)	US$bn	54.5	55.4	49.4	60.2	79.2
Imports (FOB) (goods)	US$bn	48.2	48.6	41.8	50.6	63.2
Balance of trade	US$m	6,357	6,720	7,548	9,561	15,973
Current account	US$m	-4,652	-8,829	-4,161	807	4,633
Foreign debt	SKr bn	121.56	135.99	309.41	513.41	552.48
Total reserves minus gold	US$m	18,331	22,624	19,050	23,254	22,273
Foreign exchange	US$m	17,476	21,959	18,372	22,527	21,161
Discount rate	%	8	10	5	7	7
Deposit rate	%	7.96	7.80	5.10	4.91	6.16
Lending rate	%	16.05	15.20	11.40	10.64	11.11
Exchange rate	SKr per US$	6.05	5.82	7.78	7.72	7.13

* estimated figure

internal deregulation and improved access to the European market. However, the majority of Swedes are against joining EMU. The krona has been floated against a basket of currencies since November 1992, when an 18-month linkage to the Ecu collapsed amid speculation and a massive outflow of capital. A subsequent devaluation of 20 per cent provided the platform for Sweden's astonishing export performance.

Sweden has enjoyed a sustained recovery since 1993, though a slowdown was evident in 1995 when a 4 per cent rise in GDP early in the year fell back to a year-on average of 3.5 per cent. The government has predicted 2 per cent growth in 1996, in view of a widening slowdown in Europe, with averages of between 2.5–3.5 per cent until the end of the decade. But this recovery has been generated largely by exports, which have risen by a third in two years and in 1995 accounted for around 40 per cent of total GDP. Aided by the krona depreciation, Swedish exporters raked in a trade surplus of US$15.9 billion in 1995, as sales surged by 12.6 per cent, against a 10 per cent increase in imports.

The current account has also improved since 1991, though not as spectacularly as the trade balance. For only the second time in a decade, the 1995 account was in surplus to the extent of US$4.6 billion, equivalent to 2 per cent of GDP. Domestic demand, by contrast, has been hard hit by job insecurity, higher taxation and government cuts – leading to a rise in consumer spending of less than 1 per cent in 1995.

Public finances

Sweden's public finances are among the most distorted in Europe, with some 70 per cent of GDP devoted to paying the welfare bill and a government debt, equivalent to 80 per cent of GDP, that until 1991 was growing faster than anywhere else in the industrialised world. Since 1994, Mr Persson has introduced a succession of budgetary measures aimed at reducing the deficit by SKr117 billion, or 7.5 per cent of GDP, over a three-year period. Family subsidy, children's allowance, sickness benefit, pensions and unemployment eligibility have all been affected and additional revenue is to be levied through increased national insurance and energy taxes in the 1997/98 budget. Although this will not be presented until September 1996, bringing the Swedish fiscal time-table into line with Brussels, the government said in November 1995's 'Agenda for Growth', that it would impose a ceiling for welfare expenditure in the coming budget.

The measures worked faster than had been expected. Backed by the strong recovery, the fiscal deficit of 10.8 per cent of GDP in 1994 fell to an estimated 8.1 per cent in 1995, with a forecast of 4.9 per cent for 1996 and a balanced budget thereafter. The strengthening of the krona against the Deutsche Mark and US dollar, meanwhile, helped ease the burden of the government's foreign debt from December 1995 onwards. Gross government debt doubled from 40 per cent of GDP in 1990 but recent indications suggest that the ratio may have levelled out from its 1995 peak. Mr Persson's target was for gross debt to fall to 69 per cent of GDP by 2000, though this will still be in excess of the 60 per cent ratio required under the Maastricht guidelines.

Fragile recovery

The recovery remains fragile, however, and the government's optimistic expectations could yet be undermined if the slowdown deepens in Europe and the United States. Analysts are concerned, moreover, that Mr Persson may be pressured into blunting his programme of cuts, particularly if new jobs fail to materialise. His stated ambition is to halve the 300,000 'open' unemployed, but a further 150,000 people are in retraining or job creation schemes. His pledge, however, comes at a time when budget constraints preclude any expansion of the public sector, when employment in industry is in decline and union demands for reduced hours and higher wages are raising real barriers to fresh recruitment.

An additional threat to the budgetary position is the government's commitment to phase out Sweden's 12 nuclear power plants. Nuclear power accounts for half the national electricity supply but, under a pledge extracted by referendum 16 years ago, they are to be replaced by gas-fired technology before 2010, at an estimated cost of some SKr350 billion (US$49 billion). Mr Persson said he intends to begin the wind-down by 1998, adding a potentially serious distortion to the state of public finances.

Investment and industry

Sweden's recent export boom has more to do with the krona than its membership of the EU, although the latter has considerably enhanced its investment appeal. This is particularly true for Japanese companies which poured some SKr630 million into new ventures in 1994. In previous decades, outward investment had always exceeded inward, as a result of restrictions on capital flow into the country. The phasing out of these laws in 1992 led to a spate of foreign acquisitions or mergers, culminating in the

COUNTRY PROFILE — SWEDEN

Political system

Constitutional monarchy, with legislative power vested in unicameral *Riksdag* (parliament) (349 members directly elected for three years).
Executive power exercised by the *Regeringen* (cabinet) which is led by the prime minister and is responsible to parliament. The Swedish constitution consists of four separate documents: the *Regerinhsformen* (Instrument of Government) passed in 1974, *Successionsordningen* (Act of Succession) dating from 1810, the *Tryckfrihetsforordninhen* (Freedom of the Press Act) of 1949 (originating from 1766), and the *Yttrandefrihetsgrundlagen* (Freedom of Expression Act) of 1991.
Last election: 18 September 1994; next election September 1998.

Political parties

Ruling party: Sveriges Socialdemokratiska Arbetarepartiet (Swedish Social Democratic Labour Party) (SAP). Other major parties: Moderata Samlingspartiet (M) (Moderate Unity Party); Folkpartiet Liberalerna (Fp) (People's Party, also known as the Liberal Party); Centerpartiet Riksorganization (Cp) (Centre Party).

Population

Religion: Christianity (89% Lutheran, 8% other Protestants, 1.7% Roman Catholic).

Main cities/towns

Stockholm (population 1.06m in 1994), Gothenburg, Malmö and Uppsala.

Media

Dailies: Major medium for political discussion as many are owned or run by political parties or trades unions.
Most influential include *Expressen* (Liberal, circulation September 1995, 418,000), *Dagens Nyheter* (liberal, independent, 382,000), *Aftonbladet* (Social Democratic, 353,000), *Svenska Dagbladet* (Conservative), Gothenburg-based *Göteborgs-Posten* (Liberal, 274,000), *Svenska Dagbladet* (Conservative, 200,000) and *GT/Kvällsposten* (137,000).
Weeklies: Main Sunday newspapers include: *Expressen* (circulation September 1995, 520,000), *Aftonbladet* (470,000), *Dagens Nyheter* (435,000) and *Goteborgs Posten* (307,000).
Business: Main publications: *Affärsvärlden* and *Veckans Affärer* (both weekly) and the daily *Dagens Industri*. Some business publications are in English.
Radio: Approximately 3.3m receivers in use. Sveriges Radio broadcasts three national channels and there is also a network of 24 independent local stations. Also overseas service, Radio Sweden, broadcasts in six languages, including English. Private local radio stations financed by advertising permitted in Sweden as from 1 January 1993.
Television: A great variety of satellite channels is available throughout the country. There are two commercial Swedish-language satellite channels, TV3 and TV4, with more than half the nation's households receiving them. Over 1m households receive cable television.
Advertising: Modern and of a high standard, but tends to be expensive. All media available except radio and state TV. Key categories include automotive, food, financial, fuel and household appliances. Promotion of alcohol is not allowed (except for light beers), while tobacco advertising is restricted to the press only. The classified advertising market is dwindling fast. Advertisements for alcohol or cigarettes are not allowed on TV or radio and in print they are restricted.

1995 union between the pharmaceutical giant Pharmacia and Upjohn of the US. The value of foreign holdings in the Swedish economy has been estimated at SKr300 billion, or around one third of the total, and foreigners were net buyers of SKr28.1 billion of Swedish shares in the first 10 months of 1995.

In the all-important automotive trade, by contrast, EU membership has actually had distinct drawbacks with Volvo and Saab facing increased foreign competition in a domestic market already reeling from low consumer confidence. Engineering, in one form or another, accounts for 53 per cent of Sweden's exports and the pronounced appreciation of the krona, as well as signs of slackening global demand, has led government analysts to predict export growth slowing from 12.6 per cent to 8.2 per cent in 1996. Sweden's 'Big Three' – Volvo, Saab and Scania – all posted poor domestic sales. Volvo said its car unit had been caught in a currency squeeze – sales in weak currency countries, sourcing in hard currency ones.

Volvo is currently expanding production capacity from 360,000 cars a year to 500,000 and in 1995 formed a joint venture in the Netherlands with Mitsubishi to build its smaller models. Saab, half-owned by General Motors since 1989, failed to meet its 100,000 sales target for 1995, but it remained in the black for the second year running, with a modest profit of SKr148 million. Both manufacturers, renowned for safety and reliability, are in the midst of developing new models to expand their market appeal.

If car sales were disappointing in 1995, Volvo and Scania, 100 per cent owned by Investor, the Wallenberg family's holding company, roared ahead on the surge in demand for heavy trucks. Scania, detached from its longstanding association with Saab earlier in 1995, pushed up pre-tax profits from SKr2.6 billion to SKr3.8 billion in the first nine months and. in October, unveiled the 4 Series, its first new range in 15 years. Volvo, the world's second largest heavy truck manufacturer after Mercedes, reported a 55 per cent increase in operating profits over the same period to SKr4 billion. In addition to the 30,000 vehicles manufactured in North America, Volvo is expanding capacity elsewhere from 42,000 to 60,000 trucks per year and developing its first light truck model.

Ericsson, which single-handedly produces 10 per cent of Sweden's total exports, also had a good year, with a 50 per cent sales rise in the mobile phone business and a 75 per cent increase in orders. The company is the world's leading supplier of mobile phone infrastructure with 40 per cent of the market, and its third largest producer of handsets, after Motorola and Nokia. Chief executive Lars Ramqvist predicts that the market for mobiles will rise from its current level of 70 million to 350 million by the end of the century and, in 1995, it launched a corporate reorganisation so as to face the expected sharp competition. In October 1995 the group raised a war-chest of SKr7.8 billion in what was Sweden's largest rights issue. But it too has qualms about the strengthening krona which, it warns, could cost the company 'hundreds of millions'.

The worst performer on Sweden's stock market was pulp and paper which, despite record profits from the country's big forestry groups, fell by 14 per cent over the year amid signs that the feast was over. Sweden, the world's second largest exporter of sawn conifer after Canada, has watched pulp prices leap from US$350 per tonne in the early 1990s to over US$1,000 at the peak of the curve, boosting forestry's share of exports to 18 per cent. The first signs of slackening demand for pulp, newsprint, packaging board and kraftliner emerged in June 1995 and, by November 1995, the US giant, Weyerhaeuser, lowered its listed price to US$950 per tonne, forcing Swedish manufacturers, such as Sodra Skogsagarna, to cease production for 8 weeks so as to avoid saturating the market. Amid fears of overcapacity and an imminent downturn, analysts have predicted an average price of US$850 in 1996 and US$700 in 1997. SCA overtook the Wallenberg's Stora group, as Sweden's largest forest company in 1995, through its acquisition of 75 per cent of the shares in Germany's PWA, Europe's third largest manufacturer of paper tissue. Their combined turnover in the first nine months of 1995 was SKr50.2 billion.

After a prolonged period of turbulence in the early 1990s, the airline SAS is once more flying into calmer skies again, returning to profit for the first time in five years in 1994. In 1995 it placed an order for 35 Boeing 737-600s, worth SKr8.5 billion, with options for 35 more over the next decade. In May 1996 it announced a far-reaching co-operation agreement with Lufthansa which, Brussels permitting, will combine the two airlines flight networks, as well as co-ordinate ticketing, marketing and frequent flier programmes. On the ground, meanwhile, the government is pressing ahead with the Hoga Kusten project in northern Sweden, the country's largest infrastructure programme. The scheme, which is valued at SKr2.1 billion and due to be completed by 1997, comprises 30 new bridges and 32km of highway. The centrepiece of the project will be the 1,800-metre-long Hoga Kusten bridge, the fourth largest suspension bridge in the world.

COUNTRY PROFILE — SWEDEN

Domestic economy

Well developed mixed economy strongly dependent on international trade. Stable socio-political environment combined with effective utilisation of local resources has helped maintain high living standards despite effects of recession. Major constraints to growth include heavy dependence on imported oil, large budget deficit and relatively high rates of inflation.
The uncoupling of the UK pound and the Italian lira in September 1992 from the Exchange rate mechanism (ERM) which resulted in a *de facto* devaluation of the two currencies, put unprecedented pressure on the Swedish krona. The Bank of Sweden responded by raising the marginal interest rate – the interest rate that banks pay on loans from the Bank of Sweden – to an unprecedented 500 per cent. In November 1992 Sweden abandoned efforts to peg the Krona to the European currency unit.
During 1994 and 1995 there has been an improvement in the economy. Unemployment is high which the government is attempting to rectify, but employment in industry is in decline, and union demands for reduced hours and higher wages are barriers to this.

Employment

The standard working week is 40 hours by law, although in practice it averages about 38 hours. About 30 per cent of the labour force work in the public sector.

External trade

In January 1995 Sweden became member of EU.
Exports: Export earnings account for about 30 per cent of GDP, and over 50 per cent of industrial sales.
Major exports include engineering products, (typically 48.8 per cent of total), forest products (18.2 per cent), minerals (10.1 per cent), chemicals (9.2 per cent), oil and petroleum products (2.9 per cent), foodstuffs (2.1 per cent), textiles and footwear (2 per cent), other products (6.7 per cent).
Main destinations: Germany (11.1% of 1995 total), UK (8.5%), Norway (6.8%), USA (6.7%), Denmark (5.8%), Finland (4%), EU (49.6%).
Imports: Main imports include engineering products (typically 43.8 per cent of total), chemicals (11.6 per cent), minerals (8.3 per cent), textiles and footwear (8.7 per cent), oil and petroleum products (7.8 per cent), foodstuffs (7 per cent), forest products (3.2 per cent), other products (9.6 per cent).
Main sources: Germany (16.1% of 1995 total), UK (8.4%), USA (7.5%), Denmark (5.9%), Finland (5.5%), Norway (5.3%), EU (54.7%).

Agriculture

This highly subsidised sector is very efficient although it contributed only 2 per cent to GDP in 1994 and employed 3.5 per cent of the workforce. Farming concentrated in southern regions, where livestock farming predominates. Large forestry sector supplying raw materials to industry and for export. With 57 per cent of the land area covered in forest, Sweden has the largest timber reserves in west Europe. During the post-war boom years, Swedish forests were often referred to as 'green gold'. Out of Sweden's over 80,000 farms with more than 5 ha of arable land, about 76,000 are cultivated by individual farmers. Sweden won an Ecu3.6bn concession from the European Parliament for compensation to farmers in the first four years of membership of the EU.

COUNTRY PROFILE

SWEDEN

Industry

Sector contributed 31.5 per cent to GDP in 1994 and employed 24.9 per cent of the labour force. It is based largely on indigenous resources (iron ore, timber and water-power). About 90 per cent of Swedish industry in private hands. Major industries include motor vehicles, food processing, chemicals, iron and steel, transportation equipment, electrical and electronic equipment and forestry products. Production is export-based and import-dependent. Investment in the transport equipment sector will remain weak until the auto industry generates a satisfactory level of profitability. Steel accounts for about 4 per cent of the total value added of Swedish industry.

Tourism

The sector is an important part of the growing service sector in Sweden. The tourist industry accounts for 3-4 per cent of Sweden's GDP. Foreign tourism in Sweden accounts for more than 4 per cent of the country's total export of goods and services and is an industry of vital importance to the economy and employment in many parts of the country. The floating of the krona in November 1992 made Sweden more attractive for tourists.

Mining

The mining sector accounted for 0.5 per cent of GDP in 1994 and employed 0.5 per cent of the workforce. Rich in mineral deposits, the most important of which are iron ore, zinc, lead, copper, silver and pyrites. Also large deposits of uranium, exploitation of which has been held back by environmental and political objections. Sweden's share of total world iron ore output comes to around 2 per cent and is a major iron ore exporter – the largest in Europe. Sweden's shares of the western world's production of copper, lead and zinc concentrates amount to 1 per cent, 3.7 per cent and 3.3 per cent, respectively. In 1993 the mining industry accounted for 1.4 per cent of the market value of Sweden's total industrial production and employed 1.2 per cent of the total industrial labour force.

Energy

High levels of energy consumption. Sweden is dependent on imports. Expanding hydroelectric power and other indigenous energy resources. Nuclear power accounts for half Sweden's energy needs, hydroelectricity supplying the rest. The start of decommissioning the country's nuclear power industry is proposed for 1998. Gas is imported from Denmark.

Stock exchange

The Swedish stock exchange agreed with the stock exchanges of Denmark, Norway and Finland in June 1993, to establish Nordquote, a common Nordic securities trading system.

Legal system

Swedish legislation is based on a strong domestic tradition of Germanic law, but it has also been influenced by foreign law. Swedish law as it exists today is the result of a long historical development marked by continuity rather than abrupt changes. Thus until 1974 the most important source of constitutional law was the Instrument of Government dating from 1809. It has been superseded, however, by a new Instrument of Government which came into force in 1975. As far as civil law and criminal law are concerned, the National Law Code of 1734 is still in force, at least officially. However, little of the Code's original contents remains. The majority of the *balkar* or books into which the National Law Code of 1734 is divided have gradually been replaced during the present century. Thus there have come into existence completely new books for marriage, parents, wills, and successions, real estate, criminal offences, judicial procedure, and enforcement of judgements. In modern times, moreover, a mass of special legislation has grown outside the Code in such fields as company law, copyright, protection of industrial property and labour relations. In the case of public law, too, important legislation has been passed in recent times, not least in the fields of local and national physical planning, environmental protection and nature conservation.

Membership of international organisations

ADB, AG (observer), CCC, CERN, Council of Baltic Sea States, Council of Europe, CSCE, DAC, EEA, ESA, ESRO, EU (from 1 January 1995), FAO, G-10, IAEA, ICAC, ICAO, ICES, ICO, IDA, IDB, IEA, IFAD, IFC, IHO, ILO, IMF, IMO, INTELSAT, International Grain Council, INTERPOL, International Lead and Zinc Study Group, IPU, ISO, ITU, MIGA, NAM (guest), Nordic Council, OECD, Partnerships for Peace, UN, UNESCO, UNIDO, UPU, WHO, WIPO, World Bank, WTO.

BUSINESS GUIDE

Time

GMT + 1 hr (GMT + 2 hrs from late Mar to late Sep).

Climate

Mild summers, cold winters. Large north–south variations with north colder and drier. Very cold from Nov–Apr.

Clothing

Mediumweight throughout year, heavy topcoat for winter and preferably snowboots.

Entry requirements

Visa not required by nationals of most European countries and several others. Passports not required by Scandinavian nationals.

N.B. Regulations liable to change at short notice. Travel agent or Swedish Embassy should be consulted prior to departure.
Health: Vaccination certificates not required unless travelling from an infected area.
Currency: There are no limits on the amounts of Swedish or foreign currency which can be imported into Sweden.
Customs: Personal effects duty-free.

Air access

Regular flights by all major international airlines. Swedish airport tax included in cost of ticket.
National airline: Scandinavian Airlines System (SAS) which serves all of Scandinavia (nearly half owned by AB Aero transport).
Main international airport: Stockholm (STO) served by Arlanda (ARN) 40 km north of capital.
International airports: Gothenburg (GOT), 25 km east of Gothenburg, and Malmö (MMA), 31 km east of Malmö.

Surface access

Several ferry links with northern Europe. Rail and road links with Norway and Finland.
Main ports: Gothenburg, Norrköping, Hëlsingborg, Malmö.

Hotels

No official rating system in operation. Shortage of accommodation in major cities so reservations should be made well in advance. Booking agencies available in Stockholm and Malmö.

Currency

Exchange rate: The Swedish krona is related to a trade-weighted basket of 15 major currencies. Only minor fluctuations around a base are allowed, with the central bank intervening to counteract larger imbalances.

Foreign exchange information

Account restrictions: Non-residents may hold accounts in krona for payments to or from residents. Foreign currency non-resident accounts are credited or debited for payments made under an exchange control permit.
Trade policy: Certain iron and steel products, textiles and certain goods from eastern Europe have import restrictions.

Car hire

Available at all airports and stations in main towns. Speed limits: urban areas 50 kph, normal roads 70 or 90 kph, motorways 90 or 110 kph. Strict enforcement of drink-driving, speeding and other laws. Information and assistance from automobile club – Motormannens Riksforbund/Kungliga Automobile Klubben (M/KAK).

City transport

Taxis: Available in all major towns. If you order the taxi in advance there is an extra charge. Taxi telephone numbers are listed in telephone directories.
N.B. Do not take the first available taxi from Arlanda Airport to the city. It is advisable to see the cab controller and check that you will only pay the officially approved fixed price for the journey to the city as some drivers will try to leave the meter running, which could result in paying for a round-trip.
Buses, trams and underground: Books of 20 travel coupons available for purchase at Press Agency news-stands.

National transport

Network of over 100,000 km of roads, including about 1,000 km of motorways. Efficient bus service, mainly controlled by the State Railways (Statens Jarnvagar). Services integrated with rail service. The controversial US$6bn Oresund road-rail bridge-tunnel is being built between Malmo and Copenhagen, Denmark, on the Danish island of Fyn. The bridge-tunnel is designed to stretch for 17 km and carry vehicles and trains. The project will help boost Swedish trade to Europe by improving delivery times, and with another bridge in lower Denmark, due to open in 1995, it will provide an important commercial transport link between northern and southern Europe. Infrastructural investments totalling US$13bn will be made in Sweden 1993-2003 including national trunk roads, railway trunk lines, country roads and road improvements. High-speed trains, now in regular service on the Stockholm-Gothenburg and Stockholm-Karistad lines, will be introduced between Stockholm and Malmo, Malmo and Gothenburg, from Stockholm to Oslo in Norway via Orebro and Karlstad, from northwards to Sundsvall.
Air: Scandinavian Air Systems (SAS) operates daily flights connecting all main towns.
Rail: Network of over 11,000 km, about 60 per cent electrified, operated by State Railways. Generally efficient service. Seats on express services must be booked in advance.
Water: Over 2,000 km of navigable inland waterways. Ferry service operated by State Railways.

Public holidays

Fixed dates: Day preceding holiday often taken as half-day holiday. 1 Jan (New Year's Day), 6 Jan (Epiphany),1 May (Labour Day), 25 Dec (Christmas Day), 26 Dec (Boxing Day).
Variable dates: Good Friday, Easter Monday, Ascension Day, Pingst (Whit Monday), Midsummer's Day, All Saints' Day.

Working hours

Business: (Mon–Fri) 0830 – 1700 (often closed one hour earlier in summer).
Banking: (Mon–Fri) 0930 – 1500 (larger branches open longer).
Shops: (Mon–Fri) 0900 – 1800 (closed 1400 or 1600 on Sat).

BUSINESS GUIDE

Social customs

It is usual to take flowers when being entertained in a Swedish home for the first time. Punctuality is important.

Business language and interpreting/translation

Available through major Chambers of Commerce.

Telecommunications

Telephone: In mid-1995 there were one million mobile telephones. Telephone service is widely used, especially long-distance. Direct dialling throughout country and to most parts of the world. Shops displaying 'TELE' or 'TELEBUTIK' sign offer cheap international phone services (also telex and telefax). During 1992 Swedish Telecom made major improvements to national network. International dialling code: 46 followed by area code (8 for Stockholm, 31 for Gothenburg) followed by subscriber's number. For IDD access from Sweden dial 009.
Telex: Available in some major hotels and at telegraph offices. Country code 54 S.
Telefax: Available throughout Sweden.
Telegram: Can be sent by telephone or from telegraph offices (telexpedition). Also accepted by a few post offices.

Postal service

Good service. Stamps available at most newspaper kiosks and tobacconists. Main post office in Stockholm opens daily from 0800 – 1800.

Banking

The four main commercial banks are Skandinaviska Enskilda Banken (SE Banken), Svenska Handelsbanken, Nordbanken and Sparbankernas Bank. There are 14 domestic commercial banks, 109 savings banks and 389 co-operative banks. Foreign banks were allowed to open branch offices in 1990.

Trade fairs

Several international events, mostly held in Stockholm, Gothenburg and Malmö. Wide range of products covered, but heavy emphasis on boats (Gothenburg late Jan/early Feb, Stockholm late Feb/Mar). International Fashion Fair (Feb and Sep, Stockholm).

Electricity supply

Electricity supply 220 V AC.

Representation in capital

Albania, Algeria, Angola, Argentina, Australia, Austria, Bangladesh, Belgium, Bolivia, Botswana, Brazil, Bulgaria, Canada, Chile, China, Colombia, Cuba, Denmark, Ecuador, Egypt, Ethiopia, Finland, France, Germany, Greece, Guatemala, Guinea Bissau, Hungary, Iceland, India, Indonesia, Iran, Iraq, Ireland, Israel, Italy, Japan, Kenya, Korea DPR, Republic of Korea, Laos, Lebanon, Libya, Malaysia, Mexico, Morocco, Mozambique, Netherlands, Nicaragua, Nigeria, Norway, Pakistan, Panama, Peru, Philippines, Poland, Portugal, Romania, Russia, Saudi Arabia, Senegal, Somalia, South Africa, Spain, Sri Lanka, Switzerland, Tanzania, Thailand, Tunisia, Turkey, UK, Uruguay, USA, Venezuela, Vietnam, Zambia, Zimbabwe.

BUSINESS DIRECTORY

Hotels

Stockholm
Anglais, Humlegardsgatan 23 (tel: 249-900; fax: 211-629).

City, Slojdgatan 7, Hoetorget (tel: 222-240; fax: 208-224).

Eden, Sturegatan 10 (tel: 223-160; fax: 660-8067).

Fars Hatt, Kungalv, S-442 23 (tel: 030-310-970; fax: 19-637).

Flamingo, Hotellgatan 11, S-17125 Soina (tel: 830-800; fax: 839-814).

Flyghotellet Arlanda (near Airport), Brommaplan, S-161-47 Bromma (tel: 262-620; fax: 261-946).

Grand, Sodra Blasieholmshammen 8, PO Box 16424, S-103 27 (tel: 679-3500; fax: 611-8686).

Malmen, Gotgatan 49-51 (tel: 226-080; fax: 411-148).

Oden, Karlbergensvagen 24, S-102 34 (tel: 349-340; fax: 322-299).

Palace, St Erikgatan 115 (tel: 241-220; fax: 302-329).

Sara Amaranten, PO Box 8054, Kungsholmsgatan 31, S-104 20 (tel: 541-060; fax: 526-248).

Scandic Hotel Slussen, Guldgrand 8, PO Box 15270, S-104 65 (tel: 702-2500; fax: 642-8358).

Sergel Plaza, Brunkebergstorg 9, PO Box 16411, S-103 27 (tel: 226-600; fax: 215-070).

Sheraton Hotel and Towers, Tegelbacken 6, PO Box 195, S-101 23 (tel: 142-600, fax: 217-026).

Strand, Nybrokajen 9, PO Box 16396, S-103 27 (tel: 678-7800; fax: 611-2436).

Terminus, Vasagatan 20, S-101 23 (tel: 222-640; fax: 248-295).

Car hire

Stockholm
Avis: Central Reservations (tel: 46910-26460); Stockholm Airport, Arlanda (tel: 5951-1500; fax: 5951-0198).

Budget: Central Reservations (tel: 5936-2100; fax: 5936-0068); Bromma Airport (tel: 828-366; fax: 836-802); Arlanda Airport (tel: 797-8470; fax: 5936-2349); Sveavagen 155 (tel: 334-383; fax: 376-284); Katarinavagen 16 (tel: 714-8245; fax: 702-0432).

Europcar: Central Reservations, Medborgarplatsen 25, 11826 (tel: 642-0720); Arlanda Airport (tel: 5936-0940); Hotel Sheraton, Tegelbacken 6 (tel: 210-650, 211-199); Ostermaim, Fiskartorpsvagen 22 (tel: 204-463); Bromma, Ulvsundavagen (tel: 800-807); Hammarby Fabriksvag 45 (tel: 640-0485, 723-5770); Taby, Stockholmsvagen 101 (tel: 473-0870); Kista, Malaxgatan 2 (tel: 751-4949).

Hertz: Arlanda Airport (tel: 797-9900; fax: 5936-0081); Vasagatan 26 (tel: 240-720; fax: 107-621).

Chambers of commerce

East Sweden Chamber of Commerce, Box 1343, S-60043 Norrköping (tel: 129-100; fax: 137-719).

Federation of Swedish Commerce and Trade, Box 5512, S-11485 Stockholm (tel: 666-1100; fax: 662-7457).

Federation of Swedish Industries, Box 5501, S-11485 Stockholm (tel: 783-8000; fax: 662-3595).

Handelskammaren for Gavleborgs, Kopparbergs och Uppsala lan, Drottninggatan 25, 0311 Gavle (tel: 105-430).

International Chamber of Commerce, PO Box 16050, S-10322 Stockholm (tel: 243-810; fax: 411-3115).

Southern Sweden Chamber of Commerce, Skeppsbron 2, S-21120 Malmö (tel: 73-550; fax: 118-609).

Stockholm Chamber of Commerce, Box 16050, S-10321 Stockholm (tel: 613-1800; fax: 411-7570).

Western Sweden Chamber of Commerce, Box 5253, S-40225 Göteborg (tel: 835-900; fax: 835-936)

Banking

Sveriges Riksbank (central bank), Box 16283, 10325 Stockholm (tel: 787-0000; fax: 210-531).

Götabanken, Sveavägen 14, 10377 Stockholm (tel: 7904000; tx: 19420) and Hamngatan 16, 40509 Gothenburg (tel: 625-000; tx: 21-750).

Handelsbanken, S-20540 Malmö (tel: 245-000; fax: 236-134).

Nordbanken, Hamngatan 12, S-10571 Stockholm (tel: 614-7000; fax: 200-846).

Nordbanken, S-40509 Göteborg (tel: 625-000; fax: 159-662).

Skandinaviska Enskilda Banken, Kungsträdgårdsgatan 8, S-10640 Stockholm (tel: 763-5000; fax: 242-394).

Svenska Bankforeningen (Swedish bankers' association), Regeringsgatan 42, Box 7603, 10394 Stockholm (tel: 243-300; tx: 10-427).

Svenska Handelsbanken (commercial bank), Kungsträdgårdog 2, S-10670 Stockholm (tel: 701-1000; fax: 611-5071).

Svenska Sparbanksforeningen (Swedish savings banks association), Drottninggatan 29, Box 16426, 10327 Stockholm (tel: 572-000).

SwedBank (commercial bank), Brunkebergstorg 8, 10534 Stockholm (tel: 790-1000; tx: 19-505).

Principal newspapers

Aftonbladet, Vattugatan 12, 10518 Stockholm (tel: 788-0000; fax: 245-555).

Dagens Nyheter, Ralambsvägen 17, 10515 Stockholm (tel: 738-1000; fax: 545-790).

Expressen, Gjorwellsgatan 30, 10516 Stockholm (tel: 738-300).

Principal newspapers (contd):
Göteborgs-Posten, Polhemsplatsen 5, 40502 Göteborg (tel: 624-000; fax: 159-963).

Svenska Dagbladet, Gjorwellsgatan 28, 10517 Stockholm (tel: 135-000; fax: 511-524).

Travel information

Sveriges Turistrad (Swedish tourist board), Hamngatan 27, Box 7473, 10392 Stockholm (tel: 789-200; fax: 213-555).

Sveriges Rese- och Turistrad AB (Swedish travel and tourism council), Box 3030, S-10361 Stockholm (tel: 725-5500; fax: 725-5531).

Other useful addresses

British Embassy, Skarpögatan 6-8, Box 27819, 11593 Stockholm (tel: 671-9000; fax: 662-9989).

Federation of Commercial Agents of Sweden, Hantverkargatan 46, 11221 Stockholm (tel: 540-975).

Federation of Commercial Agents of Sweden, Western Division, Box 36059, 40013 Gothenburg (tel: 192-045; tx: 27-080).

Federation of Swedish Industries, Storgatan 19, 11485 Stockholm (tel: 783-8000; fax: 662-3595).

Federation of Swedish Wholesalers and Importers, Grevgatan 34, Box 5512, 11485 Stockholm (tel: 635-280).

Handels Arbetsgivareorg (HAO) (commercial employers' confederation), Box 1720, 11187 Stockholm (tel: 762-7700).

Invest in Sweden Agency, S-10338 Stockholm (tel: 676-8876/0; fax: 676-8888).

Handelsdepartementet (Ministry of Trade), 10333 Stockholm (tel: 763-1000).

Landsorganisationen (LO) (Swedish trades union), 10553 Stockholm (tel: 796-2500).

All ministries in Sweden have the same address: S-10333 Stockholm (tel: 405-1000; fax: 723-1171).

National Board of Forestry, S-55183 Jönköping (tel: 155-600; fax: 190-740).

National Board of Housing, Building and Planning, Box 534, S-37123 Karlskrona (tel: 53-000; fax: 53-100).

National Board of Trade, Box 1209, S-11182 Stockholm (tel: 791-0500; fax: 200-324).

National Electrical Safety Board, Box 1371, S-11193 Stockholm (tel: 453-9700; fax: 453-9710).

National Maritime Administration, S-60178 Norrköping (tel: 191-000; fax: 101-949).

National Post and Telecom Agency, Box 5398, S-10249 Stockholm (tel: 678-5500; fax: 678-5505).

SACO/SR (confederation of professional associations), Box 2206, 10315 Stockholm (tel: 225-200).

Sollentunamassan (organisers of trade fairs), Box 174, 19123 Sollentuna (tel: 925-900; fax: 929-774).

Statistics Sweden, Karlavägen 100, S-11581 Stockholm (tel: 783-4000; fax: 661-5261).

Stockholm International Fairs, S-12580 Stockholm (tel: 749-4100; fax: 992-044).

Stockholm Stock Exchange, Kallargrand 2, Box 1256, 11182 Stockholm (tel: 613-8800; fax: 610-8110).

Stockholm Technical Fair (Stockholmsmassan AB), Alvsjo, 12580 Stockholm (tel: 749-4100; fax: 992-044).

Svenska Arbetsgivareforeningen (employers' confederation), Sodra Blasieholmshammen 4A, 10-330 Stockholm (tel: 762-6000; fax: 762-6290).

Sveriges Exportrad (Swedish Trade Council), PO Box 5513, 11485 Stockholm (tel: 783-8500; fax: 663-6706).

Swedish Automobile Association (Motormannens Riksforbund), Sturegatan 32, PO Box 5855, 10248 Stockholm 5 (tel: 782-3800; fax: 666-0371).

Swedish Board for Investment and Technical Support, BITS, Box 7837, S-10398 Stockholm (tel: 678-5000; fax: 678-5050).

Swedish Board of Agriculture, S-55182 Jönköping (tel: 155-000; fax: 190-546).

Swedish Board of Customs, Box 2267, S-10317 Stockholm (tel: 789-7300; fax: 208-012).

Swedish Civil Aviation Administration, S-60179 Norrköping (tel: 192-000; fax: 192-575).

The Swedish Institute, Box 7434, 10391 Stockholm (tel: 789-2000; tx: 10-025).

Swedish National Board of Fisheries, Lilla Bommen 6, S-40126 Göteborg (tel: 630-300; fax: 156-577).

Swedish National Board for Industrial and Technical Development (NUTEK), S-11786 Stockholm (tel: 681-9100; fax: 196-826).

Swedish National Road Administration, S-78187 Borlänge (tel: 75-000; fax: 84-640).

Swedish Nuclear Power Inspectorate, S-10658 Stockholm (tel: 698-8400; fax: 661-9086).

Swedish Patent Office, Box 5055, S-10242 Stockholm (tel: 782-2500; fax: 666-0286).

Swedish Standards Institution, Box 3295, S-10366 Stockholm (tel: 613-5200; fax: 411-7035).

Swedish Trade Council, PO Box 5513, S-11485 Stockholm (tel: 783-8500; fax: 662-9093).

Swedish Trade Fair Foundation (Svenska Massan), Skanegatan 26, Box 5222, 40224 Gothenburg (tel: 109-100; fax: 160-330).

TCO (central organisation of salaried employees), Box 5252, 10245 Stockholm (tel: 782-9100).

Tidningarnas Telegrambyra (news agency), Kungsholmstorg 5, 10512 Stockholm (tel: 132-600; fax: 515-377).

Trafik Sakerhetsverket (National Swedish Safety Office) (tel: 024-378-000).

Switzerland

Bob Jiggins

The next few years will see an interesting debate within Switzerland, which has been moving towards a greater degree of integration with both the European Union (EU) and the wider political world. Results of the October 1995 election indicate a shift away from the centre towards both the left and right – the left is in favour of greater co-operation with the EU and the right is opposed. Due to the complex nature of Swiss federalism, these elections mean less in terms of future developments than is the case in other European states although an interesting development in the debate is the differences between the broadly pro-EU French speakers and their more conservative German-speaking compatriots.

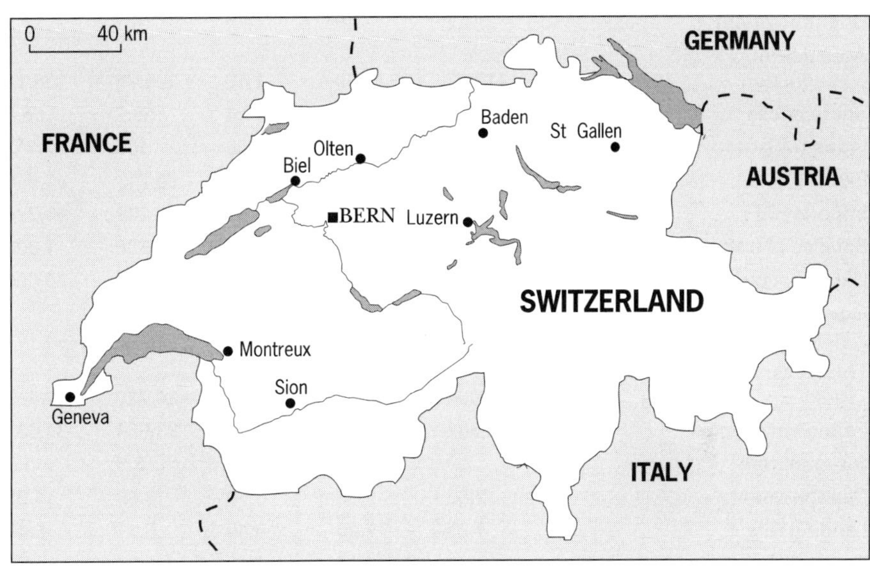

Politics

The elections held on October 1995 returned the four-party coalition which has governed Switzerland since 1959. This coalition comprises the Social Democratic Party (SSP), the Radical Democratic Party (FDP), the Christian Democratic Party (CVP) and the Swiss People's Party (SVP). Some commentators predicted that a shift towards the right would occur but both the Liberty Party and the Swiss Democrats lost the degree of electoral support that they had in the last federal elections in 1991. The coalition in fact gained more support than in 1991 (73.90 per cent compared with 69.50 per cent).

In terms of seats on the Federal Assembly the coalition now has 162 compared with 147 in 1991. The changes in terms of the political balance have, however, occurred within the coalition rather than without. Formerly, the largest number of seats was held by the right, in the shape of the FDP, but as of these elections, the more left-inclined SPS now has a majority of nine, gaining 12 from 1991. Similarly the SVP gained four seats to bring it to a total of 29, only five less than the CVP, which had previously eclipsed its more right-wing rival.

These changes in the composition of the assembly thus a sea-change in Swiss politics, with the parties of left and right gaining ground at the expense of the centre. Such a change, small in comparison with other European states, is in Swiss terms something of a landslide, promising more acrimonious debates over the future of the country within a Europe which is rapidly integrating and widening in the form of the EU. The upper house Council of States (whose members represent the cantons) remains firmly in the hands of the right, with the FDP, CVP and the SVP together possessing 38 out of the 46 seats.

In December 1995 the Federal Council (which is the state's executive or cabinet) was elected by the new Federal Assembly. Of the total of seven members, the composition of the council has not changed since 1959, with 2 members each from the SPS,

KEY FACTS — Switzerland

Official title: Schweizerische Genossenschaft (German); Conféderation Suisse (French); Confederazione Svizzera (Italian) (The Swiss Confederation)

Head of state: President Jean-Pascal Delamuraz (FDP) (1996) (rotated annually among ministers)

Head of government: President Jean-Pascal Delamuraz (FDP) (1996)

Ruling party: Four-party coalition of Social Democratic Party (SPS) (54 seats in 22 October 1995 parliamentary elections), Radical Democratic Party (FDP) (45 seats), Christian Democratic Party (CVP) (34 seats), Swiss People's Party (Agrarians) (SVP) (29 seats)

Capital: Bern

Official Languages: German, French and Italian

Currency: Swiss franc (Swf) = 100 centimes; the Swiss franc is the world's strongest currency

Exchange rate: Swf1.34 per US$ (Dec 1996)

Area: 41,293 sq km

Population: 7.2m (1995)

GDP per capita: US$42,518 (1995)

GDP real growth: -0.5% (2nd qtr 1996)

GNP per capita: US$35,750 (1994)

Unemployment: 4.8% (Oct 1996) (not seasonally adjusted)

Inflation: 0.7% (12 months to Dec 1996) (consumer prices)

Trade balance: US$1.2bn (12 months to Sep 1996)

Visitor numbers: 32.6m (1995) (overnight)

KEY INDICATORS — Switzerland

	Unit	1991	1992	1993	1994	1995
Population	m	6.79	6.90	6.94	6.99	7.20
Gross domestic product (GDP)	US$bn	230.0	244.5	232.8	259.6	306.1
GDP per capita	US$	33,480	35,650	33,400	36,400	42,518
GDP real growth	%	-0.1	-0.6	-0.8	1.2	1.1
Inflation	%	5.8	4.0	3.3	0.8	1.8
Consumer prices	1990=100	105.8	110.1	113.8	114.7	116.8
Unemployment	%	1.2	3.0	4.5	4.5	4.2
Agricultural production	1979-81=100	112.67	112.70	111.13	105.78	106.26
Share prices	1990=100	101.0	107.8	137.4	159.2	166.0
Industrial production	1990=100	101	100	100	108	111
Exports	Swf m	87,947	86,148	86,659	90,213	91,555
Imports (CIF)	Swf m	95,032	86,739	83,767	87,279	90,775
Balance of trade	US$m	-3,806	490	2,237	5,500	1,000
Current account	US$bn	10.34	14.24	17.85	18.50	20,000
Government budget deficit	Swf m	-3,297	-2,437	-8,351	-4,443	-5,141
Total reserves minus gold	US$m	29,004	33,255	32,635	34,729	36,413
Foreign exchange	US$m	29,002	32,440	31,650	33,554	34,685
Discount rate	%	7.0	6.0	4.0	3.5	1.5
Deposit rate	%	7.63	5.50	3.50	3.63	1.28
Lending rate	%	7.83	7.80	6.40	5.51	5.48
Exchange rate	Swf per US$	1.43	1.41	1.48	1.37	1.1

FDP and CVP, and one from the SVP. Although the FDP attempted to nominate its own member when the SPS finance minister Otto Stich retired in August 1995, the SPS's strong performance in the federal elections has effectively destroyed the FDP's move to break the traditional 'magic formula'. Although the Swiss constitution defines the Federal Council as collective head of state, in practice this role is filled by the president of the council, who is selected under a rotating system. The new president is the FDP's economy minister, Jean-Pascal Delamuraz, and he should be succeeded by the Christian Democrat justice minister, Arnold Koller, in 1997.

EU debate

The Swiss government has been in bi-lateral talks with Brussels since December 1994 covering seven areas. Three of these areas are especially contentious: the movement of persons, air and land transport.

After the referendum which resulted in a negative vote for Swiss membership of the European Economic Area (EEA) – a free trade zone comprising EU and European Free Trade Association (EFTA) members – the federal government has been keen to see some progress in the relationship with Europe. The Swiss government is unwilling to allow total freedom of access for EU nationals to work in Switzerland, and the EU's proposal to allow 40 tonne lorries (the current Swiss limit is 28 tonnes) from EU states to traverse the country has been an explosive public issue.

With respect to the freedom to work of EU nationals, almost all the parties and other organisations are in favour of allowing this, although there is concern that a nationalistically-inclined electorate may well vote against the proposal in a referendum. Similarly the 28 tonne limit, which has been in place since 1971, has been regarded for many years as sacrosanct. There are however indications that the electorate are becoming more inclined to compromise with the EU's proposals, with a recent opinion poll showing that 70 per cent were in favour of allowing EU nationals to work in Switzerland.

Elsewhere, there are other signs that the much-vaunted Swiss autonomy may be drawing to a close. The federal government agreed to allow NATO personnel and equipment the right to transit the country en route to the Implementation Force (Ifor) peacekeeping duties in Bosnia-Herzegovina. So far it appears that NATO has preferred to use other routes and thus there is little debate about this within Switzerland. The government has indicated that this decision is consistent with the new notion of Swiss neutrality, as promulgated in 1993, and that moreover global public opinion demands such an act of fellowship. Whatever the merits of this, this decision is very much a first in Switzerland.

Furthermore, as Switzerland is the president of the Organisation for Security and Co-operation in Europe (OSCE) in 1996, it is sending unarmed volunteers to Bosnia-Herzegovina to assist in political and economic reconstruction. Although this is technically a neutral area, the Dayton peace accords having been finalised, it is far from clear whether or not the different groups in that conflict will see this decision as being consistent with neutrality. Switzerland refrained from sending troops to assist with IFOR. In a similar vein the country has abided with UN resolutions regarding sanctions against certain countries including Yugoslavia. It has also stated that it will observe the war crimes tribunal currently taking place in the Hague.

Recovery postponed

The slow recovery that Switzerland was showing throughout most of 1995 came to an abrupt halt as the country fell into recession in the final quarter of 1995 – growth fell by 0.3 per cent in that period compared with one year before. Switzerland started 1996 inauspiciously as GDP fell by 0.7 per cent compared with the same period in 1995.

In the third quarter of 1995, the year-on-year figures indicate an overall growth rate of only 0.7 per cent, compared with 1.4 per cent the previous quarter. In terms of sectors, private consumption grew by only 0.8 per cent in the final quarter, while in the public sector it fell by 0.3 per cent. Much of the rise in private spending can be attributed to the extra amounts spent on fuels. Other items of consumer spending fell, however, with one prime indicator, new car registrations, falling compared with a year earlier. Public expenditure has fallen largely because of public spending cuts – even though some 60 per cent of public expenditure is required by various legal and constitutional obligations. Investment has also been falling, with the construction sector experiencing a year-on-year rate of -1.9 per cent and spending on plant falling to 12.4 per cent from 25.2 per cent at the beginning of 1995.

Export growth declined and imports rose, albeit slowly. In real terms exports increased between the third quarters of 1994 and 1995, although this was largely corroded by the rise in the value of the franc. Within this figure performance by sector was patchy, with chemicals, electronics and machinery performing well, while jewellery, watches and textile exports decreased. Exports of services also fell, largely as a result of the fall in the number of foreign tourists caused by the high franc.

By region, exports to the EU improved only slightly, but within this exports to Germany declined. Imports in the third quarter of 1995 rose only slightly by 3.1 per cent over the previous 12 months, and this is considerably lower than has been the case for some time.

Production has been falling with a drop in domestic orders experienced by all industries; only within the machine-building industry was there an increase of foreign orders. This is reflected in the employment situation with an increase in the number of jobless. In January 1996 the total out of work increased to 4.5 per cent of the workforce, an increase of 0.2 per cent over the previous month.

While these unemployment figures are low compared with some other European states, what is more worrying for Switzerland is the distribution of this unemployment. Long-term joblessness (defined as those out of work for more than a year) has now reached 25 per cent, and there are problems as regards other spatial measurements. Women are more likely to be out of work, as are non-German speaking Swiss nationals. It is the number of long-term unemployed as well as the ethnic distribution of unemployment which suggests that all is not well within the Swiss federation.

The good news in all of this is that inflation has continued to fall, although this is more a measure of the slow-down than a general structural strength in the economy. In January 1996, the annual inflation average was just 1.5 per cent, a fall of 0.4 per cent from the previous month; in 1995 the average was 1.8 per cent. Over the next few months inflation is expected to fall as the effect of the imposition of VAT in January 1995 works itself through.

Trade declines

Merchandise exports, having increased throughout 1994, have been steadily falling in 1995 and fell back further in the third quarter to Swf22.9 billion. Imports similarly dropped to Swf22.4 billion from Swf24 billion in the second quarter, and in both cases this was measured across almost all categories of goods. This drop in value belies the increase in volume over the same period and reflects both the desire of exporters to cut prices and hence profit margins to maintain market share, and the strong franc. Overall, the trade surplus has increased to Swf0.5 billion from a balanced position in the previous quarter.

The current account is still in surplus; data for the third quarter puts this at Swf5.5 billion, a small increase from the previous one. Swiss government estimates for 1995 indicate an increase of Swf1.50 billion over the Swf25.1 billion for 1994. This current account surplus translates into large investment abroad,

COUNTRY PROFILE — SWITZERLAND

Political system

Federal state composed of 26 cantons and half-cantons, with bicameral parliament (federal assembly) consisting of a Council of States or upper house (46 members – two from each canton, one from each half-canton) and a National Council or lower house (200 members elected for four years). Executive power exercised by seven-member Federal Council, elected by the federal assembly, representing the four government parties, and headed by an annually elected president. Major issues frequently decided by referendum. In the parliamentary elections of October 1995 the ruling four-party coalition won a combined 163 of the 200 lower house seats, compared with 147 seats in 1991.

Political parties

The composition of the National Council for the 1995-99 term is Social Democratic Party (SPS) (54 seats), Radical Democratic Party (FDP) (centrist) (45), Christian Democratic Party (CVP) (conservative) (34), Swiss People's Party (Agrarians) (SVP) (ultra-conservative) (30), Environmentalists (GPS) (9), Liberal Democrats (LPS) (7), Auto/Freedom Party (FP) (7), Independent Landesring (LDU) (3), Swiss Democrats (SD) (3), Ticino League (Lega) (1), Workers' Party (PdA) (2), Evangelical Party (EVP) (2), others (3).

Population

Religion: Roman Catholic (48%), Protestant (44%).

Main cities/towns

Berne (population 300,000 in 1994), Zürich (850,000), Geneva (400,000), Basle, Lausanne.

Language

Switzerland is a multi-language country. Most Swiss are able to speak several languages, usually including English. The national languages are German (65%) in north, central and east, French (18%) in west, Italian (12%) in south and Romansch (1%) in south-east.

Media

Press: Decentralised press owing to regional variations in language and culture. Large number of publications with relatively small circulations.
Dailies: About 120 regional newspapers (75 per cent printed in German, 20 per cent in French). Most popular are *Blick* and *Tages Anzeiger*, both published in Zürich. Other dailies include *AG Kombi*, *Berner Zeitung* and *Basler Zeitung*.
Weeklies: Sonntags Blick (circulation 1995, 356,000), *Le Matin Dimanche* (202,000), *Sonntags Zeitung* (181,000) and *Weltwoche* (110,000).
Business: The daily *Neue Zürcher Zeitung* (circulation 154,000 in 1995) is published daily in Zürich and is of international repute. There are also *Finanz und Wirtschaft* (twice weekly) and *Schweizer Handelszeitung* (weekly). Two major business magazines *Bilanz* and *Politik und Wirtschaft* (both monthly).
Periodicals: Several general and special interest magazines, including large number imported from Germany, France and Italy.
Broadcasting: Controlled by Swiss Broadcasting Corporation (SBC), under licence from the Federal Government. Actual transmission is controlled by Swiss postal and telecommunications service.
Radio: Approximately 2.6m receivers in use. There are three SBC programmes broadcast in French and German, two in Italian and also some broadcasts in Romansch as well as some private stations. Swiss Radio International broadcasts in nine languages.
Television: Over 2.3m receivers in use. Each linguistic region has its own TV channel, and also receives other regions' broadcasts. Satellite, cable and TV and teletext available.
Advertising: Expensive due to language variations. TV advertising restricted to specific times, and there is no advertising on Swiss state radio. Newspapers, cinemas and direct mail are widely used, but poster advertising is confined to selected sites. Information from Union Suisse d'Agences-Conseils en Publicité, in Zurich. Major subjects cars, banks and tobacco; main advertising media newspapers and magazines.

Domestic economy

Switzerland is one of the richest countries in the world, with a well developed manufacturing sector as well as a highly skilled labour force, an important tourist industry and leading banking and insurance sectors. However, Switzerland is almost completely dependent on imported raw materials and is vulnerable to world economic developments. The recession gripped Switzerland since mid-1991. The unemployment figures indicate the most serious economic conditions since the 1930s.
In 1995 the recovery from recession proved weak. Although Switzerland rejected membership of the European Union (EU) and the European Economic Area (EEA), it is in the process of introducing similar market reforms and business practices in order to minimise the effects of being outside the single market.

Employment

Heavy reliance on foreign labour.
Unemployment rate is lowest of any OECD country.

External trade

Switzerland still tends to run a trade deficit counterbalanced by net earnings from tourism and service sector. In the December 1992 referendum the Swiss people voted against joining the European Economic Area (EEA), the enlarged free trade area being created between the EU and the member-countries of the European Free Trade Association (EFTA).
Exports: Principal exports include electrical/non-electrical machinery, chemical/pharmaceutical products, clocks and watches, textiles and clothing, metals, jewellery and foodstuffs.
Main destinations: Germany (23.4% of 1994 total), France (9.2%), Italy (7.5%), UK (6.6%), USA (9.1%), Japan (3.9%), EFTA (0.5%).
Imports: Imports consist mainly of fuels and lubricants, industrial machinery, metals, motor vehicles, chemicals, jewellery, foodstuffs and clothing.
Main sources: Germany (32.8% of 1994 total), France (11%), Italy (9.9%), UK (6.6%) USA (6.2%), Japan (3.4%), EFTA (0.3%).

Agriculture

State-subsidised sector contributed 2.9 per cent to GDP in 1994 and employed 5.6 per cent of the workforce, with activity concentrated on dairy farming. Production sufficient to satisfy around 50 per cent of domestic food requirements. Major crops include wheat, barley, maize, potatoes, sugar-beet, grapes and apples. One of the largest tractor densities in the world. Farmers have use of large and expensive equipment through machinery syndicates.

which increased in 1995, with Swiss assets rising to Swf370 billion from Swf361 billion in 1994.

The franc has been rising steadily since 1992 and has appreciated in value by some 15 per cent in real terms, although there were signs that this trend is coming to an end, with a clear weakening in the early part of 1996.

Swissair, which has been making some large losses for some time, is set to make an alliance with the Belgian carrier, Sabena. In September 1995 Swissair released its half-year figures which showed a doubling of its losses. In dealing with this, which the company is largely blaming on the high value of the franc, it aims to shed some 1,600 jobs by 1997. It further hopes to benefit from its proposed alliance with Sabena, which will further enable it to cut costs (perhaps Swf100 million per year), and from a proposed 'open-sky' agreement with the US. The partnership of the US airline Delta, Swissair, Sabena and Austrian Airlines would enable them to augment code-sharing agreements. Swissair has also signed an agreement with Transwede, a small Scandinavian airline, following the end of its agreement with Scandinavian Airlines System (SAS).

Elsewhere in the transport system, part of the Swiss Asea Brown Boveri (ABB) is scheduled to merge with Daimler-Benz, to create the largest railway systems company in Europe. This new group concluded a deal with General Electric of the US to develop a new diesel-electric locomotive, which it expects to sell in large numbers with revenue totalling US$1 billion to the year 2001. ABB has also created three new joint ventures in eastern Europe to manufacture power-distribution equipment. This deal is in addition to some 50 or so other ventures throughout the former Soviet bloc that ABB is involved in. The new Russian ventures alone are expected to net some US$500 million per year.

Electrowatt, Switzerland's largest generator of electricity, has recently bought out Landis & Gyr for Swf1.8 billion, for which it already held 42 per cent of the shares. Landis and Gyr are world leaders in power control systems and payphones and rank third in building control systems – the main interest of Electrowatt. This takeover gives the company a status as joint world leader with Honeywell and should have annual sales in the region of Swf2.1 billion. The purchase is to be funded by the sale of other assets, mainly within electronics. International food giant Nestlé likewise has been concentrating on building up its core business, with the purchase of several small ice-cream producers across much of Europe, the US and the far east.

The new electronic system for the Swiss bourse (EBS), which has so far cost Swf115 million, has had to be delayed, as test runs highlighted problems. Eventually, when the system is fully operational, it will combine several operations into one system, and should therefore reduce costs which

COUNTRY PROFILE — SWITZERLAND

Agriculture (contd): Productive land area 1m ha (less than a quarter of the total land area). Swiss farmers were among the most protected in the industrialised world. The comprehensive system of subsidies, price guarantees and import controls enabled Switzerland, a traditional dairy exporter to become self-sufficient in wheat and meat. Heavy use of chemicals and intensive farming methods were encouraged by generous guaranteed prices for production. The system had few supporters among consumers, as butter, meat, sugar, fruit and vegetables were often two or three times as expensive in Switzerland as in France, Italy or Germany, and reform was called for. The first focus of reform of the agriculture sector was in dairy products.

Industry

This sector contributed 32.2 per cent to GDP in 1994 and employed 33.2 per cent of the labour force. Developed export-based manufacturing sector with emphasis on production of finished goods. Traditional industries include machines, tools, chemicals and pharmaceuticals, textiles, watch-making, food processing, chemicals and engineering. Emphasis on increased specialisation and development of high-technology products. Swiss companies spend 2.9 per cent of GDP on research and development, one of the highest figures in the world.

Leading companies

Nestlé, Ciba-Geigy, Sandoz and Jacobs Suchard.

Energy

Hydroelectricity is the only natural energy resource and supplies 12 per cent of the country's total energy requirements. Declining dependence on imported oil and gas. Switzerland is one of Europe's largest per capita users of nuclear fuel. However, in 1990, following a referendum, a 10-year moratorium on building new nuclear power plants means that Switzerland could experience a shortfall of electricity by the turn of the century.

Banking

Zürich ranks as one of the leading international banking centres. Five main commercial banks – Union Bank of Switzerland, Swiss Bank Corporation, Crédit Suisse, Swiss Volksbank and Zurcher Kantonalbank (SwFr35,460m); 29 cantonal banks and numerous foreign banks operating. Banking system characterised by strict secrecy laws, though these will be reformed because of evidence that the private banks are being used for the laundering of illegal money, especially from drug rackets.

Legal system

Civil law system marginally influenced by customary law. Constitution adopted 1874, has been amended several times.

Membership of international organisations

ADB, BIS, CCC, Council of Europe, DAC, EFTA, ESA, ESRO, FAO, IAEA, IBRD, ICAC, ICAO, ICC, ICO, IDA, IDB, IEA, IFAD, IFC, ILO, IMF, IMO, INTELSAT, INTERPOL, IPU, ITU, IWC, MIGA, OECD, UN (permanent observer), UNESCO, UNIDO, UPU, World Confederation of Labour, WFTU, WHO, WIPO, WMO, World Bank, WSG, WTO. Nato's Partnership for Peace programme (11 December 1996).

BUSINESS GUIDE

Time

GMT + 1 hr (GMT + 2 hrs from late Mar to late Sep).

Climate

Temperate; large variations with altitude. Temperatures range from about –1°C to 18°C. Generally warm summers and cold winters.

Clothing

Mediumweight throughout year. Topcoat and lined boots for winter.

Entry requirements

Visa not required by nationals of Germany, Austria, Belgium, France, Luxembourg, Netherlands, Portugal, Italy, Spain, UK and Greece and several others. N.B. Strict laws apply to business visits. Advisable to check with Swiss embassy regarding regulations.
Health: Vaccination certificates not usually required. Medical insurance advisable as treatment is expensive.
Currency: No restrictions on Swiss and other currencies. Importation of coins of gold and platinum are liable to turnover-tax.
Customs: Personal effects, and gifts up to value of SwFr100, duty-free.

Air access

Regular flights by all major international airlines. Reservations should be made in advance during holiday season.
National airline: Swissair. The merger of Swissair with Sabena, Belgium's state-owned airline, was approved in July 1995. Under the deal Swissair acquires a 49.5 per cent stake in Sabena which will remain in Belgian control.
International airports: Zürich (ZRH), 13 km north of city; Geneva (GVA), 16 km north of city, Berne (BRN), 9 km from city, Basle (BSL), 12 km from city, and Lugano (LUG), 7 km from city. Zürich and Geneva airports directly linked to national rail system. A new terminal for Zürich Airport will get under way by 1997.

Surface access

Good road and rail links with all surrounding countries. Advisable to book for rail travel beforehand.

Hotels

High standard throughout country. Classified by Swiss Hotel Association from one- to five-star. A 15 per cent service is included on bill.

Restaurants

Fairly expensive but usually good quality. Service charge included in bill.

Currency

Exchange rate: Swiss franc has been floating since 1973. Switzerland does not officially try to maintain exchange rates for Swiss franc within margins, but sometimes does intervene.

Foreign exchange information

Account restrictions: Non-resident accounts allowed, but certain criteria must be met.
Trade policy: No exchange controls over imports or exports. Apart from agricultural produce and some chemicals, there are few restrictions on imports. There are some 22 free ports or zones, where goods may be stored for an unlimited period duty-free.

the banks are hoping will boost Switzerland's competitiveness on the world trading market.

In a June 1996 referendum, voters in Geneva rejected a proposal to build a new link across Lake Geneva; the only existing central fixed link is the Mont Blanc bridge, built in the last century, which is suffering from overuse. Some 70 per cent of voters rejected the tunnel proposition and 68 per cent were against a bridge. The cost of a new crossing would be in the region of Swf700 million.

Banking

The banking sector looks set for further rationalisation in the wake of the takeover in 1995 of the cantonal bank of Solothurn by the Union Bank of Switzerland (UBS). A number of cantonal banks are in financial trouble, as they tend to be small and thus exposed to the difficulties experienced by the sector in recent times. These banks operate only within the cantons they serve, and are effectively controlled by their respective cantonal governments. The latest acquisition by UBS is of Appenzell Outer-Rhoden, for which it paid Swf180 million; it is expected that this will not be the last transfer from the public to the private sector.

Elsewhere one of the periodic probes that the banking authorities make for Jewish funds hidden from the Nazis prior to 1945 has revealed another Swf38.7 million hidden in 775 accounts. In total since 1945, Swf64.2 million has been found, although Jewish organisations allege that as much as US$7 billion exist which the banks are holding on to.

A recent trend noted in Switzerland is towards the provision of joint insurance and financial products, with CS Holding and Winterthur establishing joint ventures. Similarly SBC and Zurich Insurance, and UBS and Swiss Life have also announced similar deals which are also spreading to smaller organisations.

Outlook

It is likely that 1997 will witness a small resurgence in growth, as consumer spending rises as a result of lower interest rates and export demand rises from the important German market. However, the predominance of the political right in the upper house (Council of States) is likely to result in public expenditure cuts which will not be necessarily helpful in this process.

If this recovery happens it will not be of any magnitude, and it is unlikely that unemployment, already at record levels in Swiss experience, will be much reduced. In the longer term, much depends upon Switzerland's relationship with the EU. It would appear that Swiss neutrality and independence in political and economic matters is coming to an end, and the country's future growth will be intimately bound with European monetary and political union.

BUSINESS GUIDE — SWITZERLAND

Credit cards

All major credit cards are accepted.

Car hire

Self-drive and chauffeur-driven cars available in all main towns. Valid national or international driving licence required, and insurance is compulsory. Speed limits, built-up areas 50kph, normal roads 80kph and motorways 120kph. Information from The Touring Club Suisse or the Automobile Club Suisse. For road information tel: 163.

City transport

Taxis: Widely available but do not ply for hire. Fare usually includes tip (check notice in cab), otherwise 15 per cent. N.B. It is wise to avoid taking a taxi in Zürich which is one of the most expensive towns in Europe for taxi rides.
Buses and trams: Good services in major towns. Tickets should be bought in advance from vending machines. Multi-journey tickets also available. Flat fare up to five stops.

National transport

Air: Crossair (Swissair subsidiary), Switzerland's regional airline, is set to double in size to be world's largest regional airline by 1997. Several daily flights linking Zurich, Geneva, Basle, Lugano and Berne, but only Zurich-Geneva route is widely used.
Road: Network of about 70,000 km, including 1,000 km of motorways. Good quality but tend to be slow due to terrain and volume of traffic.
Rail: Over 5,000 km of track, practically all electrified, of which about 60 per cent is operated by Swiss Federal Railways (Schweizerische Bundesbahnen), and the rest by about 120 small private companies. Good services with journeys between major towns rarely exceeding two or three hours.

Public holidays

Fixed dates: 1 Jan (New Year's Day), 2 Jan (2nd New Year's Day), 1 May (Labour Day), 1 Aug (Swiss National Day, entire day in Fribourg, Geneva, Schaffhausen, Ticino, Thurgau, Vaud, Zürich, rest of Switzerland afternoon only), 24 Dec (Christmas Eve, afternoon only), 25 Dec (Christmas Day), 26 Dec (St Stephen's Day, not observed in Geneva, Neuchatel and Valais), 31 Dec (New Year's Eve, Geneva entire day, rest of Switzerland afternoon only).
Variable dates: Good Friday, Easter Monday, Ascension Day and Whit Monday. There are other local holidays in specific cantons depending on the main religion.

Working hours

Business: (Mon–Fri) 0800 – 1200, 1330 – 1700.
Government: (Mon–Fri) 0730 – 1145, 1330 – 1800, or 0800 – 1230, 1315 – 1730.
Banking: Regional variations but generally (Mon–Fri) 0830 – 1630. Money exchange at any airport and larger railway stations daily until 2200.
Shops: (Mon–Fri) 0800 – 1215, 1330 – 1830 (in larger cities also during lunch hours but Mon morning often closed); (Sat) 0830 – 1600.

Social customs

If being entertained at someone's home give the hostess flowers or chocolates.

Business language and interpreting/translation

Available from the Internationale Vereinigung dipl. Dolmetscher and various associations. Can be difficult to obtain at short notice. Rates fixed by International Association of Interpreters. Though English often spoken by business people, a knowledge of French and German is advantageous.

Telecommunications

Telephone and telefax: Excellent service. Subscriber trunk dialling in operation throughout country. International dialling code: 41 followed by 31 for Bern, and 1 for Zürich. Cheap rate at certain times for internal calls over 20 km. International directory enquiries: 191 (for specific number in Germany call 192, for France, call 193). For IDD access from Switzerland dial 00.
Telex: Available at main post offices in larger towns and at hotels. Country code 45 CH.
Telegram: Efficient service, but seldom used within country.

Postal service

Reliable. Use of four-figure postal code obligatory. Post offices open (Mon–Fri) 0730 – 1200, 1345 – 1830, (Sat) until 1100.

Trade fairs

Several fairs of international significance held throughout the country. Also three official national fairs.

Electricity supply

220V AC.

Turn to page 106 to order your copy now!

Representation in capital

Algeria, Argentina, Australia, Austria, Belgium, Brazil, Bulgaria, Burundi, Canada, Chile, China PR, Colombia, Costa Rica, Côte d'Ivoire, Cuba, Denmark, Ecuador, Egypt, Finland, France, Germany, Ghana, Greece, Guinea, The Holy See, Hungary, India, Indonesia, Iran, Iraq, Ireland, Israel, Italy, Japan, Jordan, Korea DPR, Republic of Korea, Lebanon, Libya, Liechtenstein, Luxembourg, Malaysia, Mexico, Monaco, Morocco, Netherlands, Nigeria, Norway, Pakistan, Peru, Philippines, Poland, Portugal, Romania, Russia, Rwanda, Saudi Arabia, Senegal, South Africa, Spain, Sweden, Thailand, Tunisia, Turkey, UK, Uruguay, USA, Venezuela, Yemen, Zaïre.

BUSINESS DIRECTORY

Hotels

Bern
Bellevue Palace, Kochergasse 3-5 (tel: 224-581; fax: 224-743).

Bern, Zeughausgasse 9 (tel: 211-021; fax: 211-147).

Kreuz, Zeughausgasse 41 (tel: 221-162; fax: 223-747).

Metropole, Zeughausgasse 26-28 (tel: 225-021; fax: 211-153).

Savoy, Neuengasse 26 (tel: 224-405; fax: 211-978).

Schweizerhof, Schweizerhoflaube 11 (tel: 224-501; fax: 222-179).

Touring (near railway), Zieglestrasse 66 (tel: 458-666; fax: 462-680).

Geneva
Beau Rivage, Quai du Mont Blanc 13 (tel: 310-221; fax: 738-9847).

Metropole, Général-Guisan 34 (tel: 211-344; fax: 211-350).

Président, Quai Wilson 47 (tel: 731-1000; fax: 738-4750).

Zürich
Baur an Lac, Talstrasse 1 (tel: 221-1650; fax: 211-8139).

Dolder Grand, Kurhausstrasse 65 (tel: 251-6231; fax: 251-8829).

Zürich, Neumühlequai 42 (tel: 363-6363; fax: 363-6015).

Useful telephone numbers

Police: 117

Fire brigade: 118

Ambulance: 144 (not yet valid countrywide)

Motor breakdown service: 140

Swiss Air Rescue: 47-47-47

Emergency service of Touring Club of Switzerland: 35-80-00

Currency information: 160

Car hire

Zürich
Avis: Central Reservations (tel: 298-3333; fax: 242-8831); Kloten Airport, 8058 (tel: 813-0084; fax: 814-0545); Gartenhofstrasse 17, 8004 (tel: 242-2040; fax: 809-1991).

Budget: Central Reservations, Industriestrasse 14, 8302 Kloten (tel: 813-5797; fax: 813-4900); Zurich Airport, 8058 (tel: 813-3131; fax: 813-3472); Lindenstrasse 33, 8008 (tel: 383-1747; fax: 383-1749).

Europcar: Central Reservations, Badenerstrasse 812 8048 (tel: 432-2424; fax: 433-0177); Zurich Airport, Kloten (tel: 813-2044); Josefstrasse 53 (tel: 271-5656); Thurgauerstr 100 (tel: 302-7522).

Hertz: Central Reservations (tel: 730-1077; fax: 730-8050); Zurich Airport (tel: 814-0511; fax: 814-1282); Hertz Autovermietung, Morgartenstrasse 5 (tel: 242-8484; fax: 242-2586); Hardturstrasse 319 8005 (tel: 272-5050; fax: 272-5420).

Chambers of commerce

Basler Handelskammer, St Albangraben 8, CH-4051 Basel (tel: 231-888).

Berner Handelskammer, Gutenbergstrasse 1, CH-3001 Bern (tel: 261-711).

British-Swiss Chamber of Commerce, Freiestr 155, CH-8032, Zrich (tel: 422-3131; fax: 422-3244).

Chambre de Commerce et d'Industrie de Genéve, PO Box 65, Boulevard du Théâtre 4, CH-1211 Geneva 11 (tel: 215-333; fax: 200-363).

Chambre Fribourgeoise du Commerce et de l'Industrie, Rue de la Banque 1, CH-1700 Fribourg (tel: 225-655).

Chambre Vaudoise du Commerce et de l'Industrie, Avenue d'Ouchy 47, CH-1000 Lausanne 13 (tel: 277-291; tx: 25-405).

Handelskammer-Kaufmännisches Directorium, Gallusstrasse 16, CH-9001 St Gallen (tel: 231-515).

Zürcher Handelskammer, Bleicherweg 5, CH-8001 Zürich (tel: 221-0742, 221-0742).

Banking

Banque Nationale Suisse (central bank), Börsenstrasse 15, CH-8022 Zürich (tel: 221-3750; tx: 812-400).

Banca della Svizzera Italiana, 2 Via Magatti, 6901 Lugano (tel: 587-111; tx: 841-020).

Bank Leu, Bahnhofstrasse 32, CH-8001 Zürich (tel: 219-1111; tx: 812-174).

Crédit Suisse, Paradeplatz 8, CH-8021 Zürich (tel: 215-1111; tx: 812-412).

Swiss Bank Corporation, Aeschenvorstadt 1/Gartenstrasse 9, Basel (tel: 202-020; tx: 962-334 BVB CH).

Swiss Bankers' Association, Aeschenplatz 4, Postfach 4182, CH-4002 Basel (tel: 235-888; tx: 963-248).

Swiss Volksbank, Weltpoststrasse 5, 3015 Bern (tel: 328-111; tx: 912-486).

Union Bank of Switzerland, Bahnhofstrasse 45, CH-8000 Zürich (tel; 234-1111; tx: 822-802).

Zürcher Kantonalbank, Bahnhofstrasse, PO Box 4039, 8022 Zürich (tel: 41-1220; fx: 411-211-1525).

Principal newspapers

Basler Zeitung, Hochbergerstr 15, CH-4002 Basle (tel: 639-1111; fax: 631-1959).

Bilanz, Edenstrasse 20, 8021 Zürich (tel: 207-7221; tx: 816-765).

Blick, Dufourstrasse 23, 8021 Zürich (tel: 259-6262; tx: 817-300).

Der Bund, Effingerstrasse 1, CH-3001 Berne (tel: 385-1111, 641-111; fax: 385-1112, 253-207).

Finanz und Wirtschaft, Bäckerstrasse 7, Postfach, 8021 Zürich (tx: 812-577).

Journal de Geneve, Gazette de Lausanne, 12 rue de Hesse, CH-1211 Geneva 11 (tel: 819-8888; fax: 819-8989).

Neue Zürcher Zeitung, Falkenstrasse 11, Postfach, 8021, Zürich (tel: 258-1111; tx: 817-099).

Tages Anzeiger Zürich, Werdstrasse 21, 8021 Zürich (tel: 248-4411; tx: 812-236).

Weltwoche, Edenstrasse 20, 8021 Zürich (tel: 207-7311; tx: 815-503).

Travel information

Swiss National Tourist Office, Bellariastrasse 38, 8038 Zürich (tel: 202-3737; tx: 815-391).

Other useful addresses

Basel Stock Exchange, Aeschenplatz 7, 4002 Basel (tel: 230-666; tx: 962-524).

British Embassy, Thunstrasse 50, CH-3005 Berne 15 (tel: 445-021; fax: 440-583).

Bundesamt für Statistik (BFS) (central statistics office), Schwarzftorstrasse 96, CH-3003 Bern (tel: 323-6011; fax: 323-6061).

Embassy of the United States of America, Jubilumstrasse 93, CH-3005 Berne (tel: 357-7011; fax: 357-7344).

Federal Department of Finance, Bundesgasse 3, 3003 Bern (tel: 66-111; tx: 912-868).

Federal Department of Public Economy, Bundeshaus-Ost, 3003 Bern (tel: 612-111; tx: 912-889).

Federal Office for Industry, Crafts and Labour, Bundesgasse 8, CH-3003 Bern (tel: 612-944).

Fédération Suisse des Agences de Voyages, Postfach, Hardstrasse 316, CH-8027 Zürich (tel: 426-442).

Federation of Swiss Employers' Organisations, Florastrasse 44, CH-8034 Zürich (tel: 363-5285).

Swiss Federal Tax Administration, Eidgenössische Steuerverwaltung, Eigerstrasse 65, CH-3003 Bern (tel: 617-112).

Swiss Federation of Commerce and Industry, Börsenstrasse 26, CH-8022 Zürich (tel: 221-2707; tx: 813-294).

Swiss Lawyers' Federation, Lavaterstrasse 83, CH-8027 Zürich (tel: 202-5650).

Swiss News Agency, Langgasstrasse 7, CH-3012 Bern (tel: 244-461; tx: 33-733).

Union Suisse d'Agences-Conseils en Publicité (advertising), Kurfürstenstr 80, CH-8002 Zürich (tel: 202-6540).

Zürich Stock Exchange, Bleicherweg 5, CH-8021 Zürich (tel: 229-2111; tx: 813-065).

Turkey

Howard Hill

In 1995 Turkey's political change and constitutional reform were accompanied by an economic crisis worse than anything seen since the 1920s. The first half of 1996 was not any better. Elections were held in December 1995 but little was resolved by the vote. After months of post-election political indecision, and aborted attempts at forming a lasting government, Turkey's first Islamist prime minister was confirmed by a parliamentary vote of confidence on 8 July 1996. The political debate embraced the customs union with the European Union (EU), a public sector strike, and opposition to the country's treatment of dissent, particularly Kurdish separatism. An attempt was made on the life of President Demirel in May 1996 by a gunman but only a bodyguard of the President was hurt in the incident. The assassin had a history of mental illness and had been disturbed over a military co-operation agreement signed between Turkey and Israel.

Politics

The 73-year-old secular Turkish republic got its first Islamist prime minister after the Refah-True Path Party coalition was approved by the 550-seat parliament in June 1996. The margin of victory in the vote was 13. The coalition came about after Necmettin Erbakan's Refah (Welfare) Party and former prime minister Tansu Ciller's True Path finally buried their differences; Ciller had strongly opposed any alliance with the Islamists for months after the December 1995 election. Whether the coalition will remain in power for long is open to speculation but some pundits are anticipating that elections will be called before the end of 1997.

The turbulence begins

Deniz Baykal, a lawyer, was elected to lead the centre-left Republican People's Party (CHP) in September 1995. Upon his election, Baykal said that he would continue the coalition with the right-wing True Path but would consider a separation if the True Path was not accommodating enough to the CHP's platform. This happened sooner than most people had anticipated – within a few days the CHP had resigned from the government, forcing Ciller to step down as prime minister and attempt to find a new

KEY FACTS — Turkey

Official title: Turkiye Cumhuriyeti (The Republic of Turkey)

Head of state: President Suleyman Demirel

Head of government: Prime Minister Necmettin Erbakan (leader of the Welfare Party) (from Jul 1996) (Turkey's first Islamist prime minister)

Ruling party: Coalition of Welfare Party & True Path Party (from Jul 1996)

Capital: Ankara

Official Languages: Turkish

Currency: Turkish Lira (L)

Exchange rate: L106,645 per US$ (Dec 1996)

Area: 779,452 sq km

Population: 62.3m (1995)

GDP per capita: US$2,733 (1995)

GDP real growth: 7.1% (1995)

GNP per capita: US$2,193 (1994)

GNP real growth: 7.1% (1995)

Labour force: 22.14m (Oct 1994)

Unemployment: 10.24% (1995)

Inflation: 82.9% (Jun 1996) (consumer prices)

Trade balance: -US$8.96bn (1995)

Foreign debt: US$73.61bn (1995)

Visitor numbers: 6.5m (1994)

coalition partner. Baykal announced his support for early elections but the economic crisis and the electorate's widespread dissatisfaction with the government made this an unsatisfactory option to the True Path.

The opposition centre-right Motherland Party (ANAP) was initially the most likely True Path partner to replace the CHP in a coalition. However, an agreement could not be struck. After two weeks of negotiations, a minority government was formed comprising the True Path with support from two small parties, the right-wing Nationalist Action Party (MHP) and the moderate Democratic Left Party (DSP). This arrangement required a further six votes in parliament to form a majority, but Ciller clearly thought the situation was worth the risk.

The True Path's proposed minority government lost the vote of confidence when only 191 members voted for it – the DSP suddenly withdrew its backing an hour before the vote because of the government's refusal to budge substantially on its pay offer to the public sector workers. The Confederation of Turkish Trade Unions (Turk-Is) had been intensely lobbying parliament in the run-up to the confidence vote.

Ciller immediately turned to the CHP and revived the coalition before early elections were held. As a gesture, Ciller finally capitulated to CHP demands to sack the hard-line head of police in Istanbul, Colonel Necdet Menzir. Menzir had attracted the CHP's ire by being a harsh critic of CHP's human rights minister. By the end of October 1995 the renewed True Path-CHP arrangement had been given the approval of President Suleyman Demirel, elections had been called for 24 December 1995, and a cabinet had been announced.

KEY INDICATORS — Turkey

	Unit	1991	1992	1993	1994	1995
Population	m	57.31	58.40	59.49	60.58	62.3
Gross domestic product (GDP)	US$bn	112.0	115.5	138.4	134.5	–
GDP per capita	US$	1,940	1,975	2,300	2,159	2,733
GDP real growth	%	2.0	5.9	7.0	-5.4	7.1
Inflation	%	66.0	70.1	66.1	125.5	64.9
Consumer prices	1990=100	166.0	282.3	468.8	967.0	1,872.5
Unemployment	%	7.7	7.9	8.6	10.85	10.24
Agricultural production	1979-81=100	134.10	133.81	134.80	133.13	139.04
Industrial production	1990=100	105.6	111.1	120.1	112.6	–
Coal	m toe	20.2	22.3	20.8	19.1	18.0
Exports (FOB) (goods)	US$m	13,594	14,716	15,343	18,106	–
Imports (FOB) (goods)	US$m	21,047	22,872	29,174	23,270	–
Balance of trade	US$m	-7,326	-8,190	-14,162	-4,270	-8,960
Foreign debt	L bn	104,809	177,697	311,299	903,477	73,610
Current account	US$m	250	-974	-6,433	2,631	–
Total reserves minus gold	US$m	5,144	6,159	6,272	7,169	12,442
Foreign exchange	US$m	5,098	6,115	6,227	7,121	12,391
Interbank money market rate	%	72.7	65.3	62.8	136.4	72.3
Deposit rate	%	62.93	68.74	64.58	87.89	76.13
Exchange rate	L per US$	4,171.8	6,872.4	10,984.6	29,608.7	45,845.1

December election

The opposition led a court challenge to postpone the date of the election; this was not allowed but the court insisted on two alterations to the election law. The Constitutional Court ruled that the minimum regional vote threshold for each party before they can represent in parliament had to be lowered. The new plan to allocate 100 newly-created seats on a national basis was also changed to allocate seats to constituencies throughout Turkey.

In the event, to the dismay of the True Path, the Prime Minister's gamble to hold an election backfired – Refah won the largest percentage of the vote – and the results meant more uncertainty. Refah's 21.4 per cent of the vote (16.9 per cent in 1991) translated into first place in the seat race at 158 (62 in 1991). The True Path managed second place with 135 (178 in 1991) and ANAP was third with 132 seats (115 in 1991).

Despite Refah's electoral success – and noises from the party that it was not bent on doing away with the modern Turkish state founded by Kemal Ataturk – it was the odd man out during talks to form a new government. For months, no party wanted to join them in a coalition, although the ANAP had seemed interested for a time.

It was not until early March 1996 that an agreement in principle was made between the True Path and the ANAP to form a government dubbed MotherPath. This centre-right pairing had been widely anticipated since the election. The combined strength of the two parties, at 261 in March 1996, was 15 members short of the 276 required to win a vote of no confidence, necessitating the co-operation of the DSP. The prime ministership was to be shared between bitter rivals Ciller and Mesut Yilmaz, with Yilmaz starting in this role in March 1996. Ciller would then take over in 1997/98 and then hand back to Yilmaz for one year. In the fifth year a True Path member would head the government.

The True Path and ANAP may share similar pro-western free-market philosophies but are otherwise antipathetic towards each other, with each party claiming the crown of Turkish conservatism. The initial weeks of the coalition were marked by mistrust and in-fighting between the True Path and ANAP. Further complications arose when parliament decided to pursue corruption charges against Ciller, who was especially angry over the lack of solid ANAP support for her during the vote on this issue. The allegations implied that Ciller could be linked to contract irregularities at TEDAS, the state-run electricity distribution company. Shortly thereafter another committee was set up to investigate corruption allegations against Ciller, this time in relation to the privatisation of automobile manufacturer Tofas. The ANAP overwhelmingly supported the Refah-led vote.

In the first week of June 1996 the Mother-Path coalition was in ruins. Yilmaz resigned as prime minister upon the release of the full text of the constitutional court's ruling that the March 1996 vote of confidence in his government was invalid. The decision was handed down three weeks earlier in May 1996.

In the June 1996 local elections, held before the negotiations on a new government began, Refah won 33.5 per cent of the vote in 41 local polls. The ANAP emerged in second place with 20.9 per cent while the True Path was in a distant third place with 12 per cent. The poor showing for the True Path at the local level may have shaken it into accepting an alliance with Refah at the national level, especially because both the ANAP and the DSP refused to work with Ciller. Upon agreeing the controversial pact with Refah, only a handful of True Path members quit the party but this brought the True Path's strength in parliament down to 128, dropping it to third place behind the ANAP.

Foreign relations

The airforce military training exercises carried out by Israel using Turkish bases has raised hackles in the Islamic countries of the middle east. But the as yet unresolved question of Kurdish separatism is a much bigger issue in local politics and regional relations. For instance, Syria has been accused by the Turkish government of giving a home to rebel PKK Kurdish fighters and Ankara has issued threats that PKK bases in Syria will be bombed. As if this was not enough to send bilateral relations on a steep decline, Syria is angry over Turkey's alleged pollution of the Euphrates river; the river rises in Turkey flowing to Syria and beyond.

Relations with Russia are also fragile. Of particular concern to the Russians is Turkey's desire to strengthen its relations with the regional Turkic-Islamic countries of the former Soviet Union; Moscow still enjoys considerable influence in the region and wants to keep these countries tightly under its wing. Russia particularly opposes the routing of a new oil pipeline from central Asia through Turkey.

Greece, the ancient enemy, almost came to blows with Turkey in January 1996 over the sovereignty of the Imia islets, which are close to the Turkish border. Both Turkey and Greece are NATO members, which complicates their roles in this international defence alliance. Unless and until the divided Cyprus issue is resolved, and other age-old simmering differences are settled, Greece and Turkey will be very uneasy neighbours.

Public strike

From 20 September 1995, the date the CHP resigned from government, public sector workers went on strike, organised by the Confederation of Turkish Trade Unions (Turk-Is). The government's offer of a 5.4 per cent pay rise sparked the action, which

COUNTRY PROFILE — TURKEY

Historical profile

The republic of Turkey was established in 1923 as the successor to the multinational Ottoman empire, which dated back to the thirteenth century. Ataturk led the country in the war of national liberation (1920-22), following the dismemberment of the empire by the entente powers at the end of the First World War. The independence of the Turkish state was recognised by the Treaty of Lausanne on 24 July 1923. Elected as the Republic's first president, Ataturk held power until his death in 1938. He introduced a programme of reforms seeking to esablish a secular political system and to develop the necessary basis for the new Republic to set off on a path of western-style industrialisation. Sweeping changes were made in all areas – legal, political, social and economic. The Islamic legal codes were replaced by western ones. Turkey is the only Muslim country in the world where the principle of secularism is written into the constitution. The economy, which was in a poor state, was brought under government control.

Political parties

Coalition government: Refah (Welfare) Party and True Path Party. Other main political parties: Motherland Party, Democratic Left Party (DSP), Democracy Party (DEP), Nationalist Action (MHP); the Social Democratic Populist Party (SHP) merged in May 1995 with the Republican People's Party (CHP).

Population

More than half the population is under 25. In 1945 only 18 per cent of the population lived in towns; the figure is over 75 per cent in 1996.

Main cities/towns

Ankara (population estimated at 2.9m in 1994, capital), Istanbul (12m), Izmir (2.8m), Adana (1.1m), Bursa (1.02m), Gazientep (730,435), Konya (584,785), Mersin (422,357), Kayseri (421,362), Eskiserhir (413,082).

Language

The official language is Turkish. Almost all educated Turks have command of a foreign language and English is the dominant language for international business. German and French also spoken.

Media

Dailies: The seven most influential include *Sabah, Hürriyet, Milliyet, Turkiye, Zaman, Meydan* and *Bugun*. Also several hundred regional papers. The *Turkish Daily News* is the main English-language publication.
Weeklies: Nokta and *Tempo* are the most significant.
Business: Monthly magazine *Capital*; weekly *Ekonomik Panorama, Ekonomist* and *EP*.
Periodicals: English-language bi-monthly Istanbul Guide.
Broadcasting: In April 1994 the government ended the state monopoly on broadcasting and established a radio and television council whose nine members regulate the stations.
Radio: There are 35 national radio stations, 109 regional and almost 1,000 local ones.
Television: Cable and satellite television are rapidly growing. There were 297 television sets per 1,000 persons in 1994. Sixteen national TV and 15 regional stations, as well as about 300 local ones.
Advertising: Local code of practice/ethics in operation. Adspend as percentage of GDP 1.6 per cent. Adspend per capita US$14 (1993). Total adspend US$700m in 1995 (TV 74%, press 25%).

Domestic economy

High levels of economic growth during 1970s based on well-developed agricultural sector and rapidly expanding manufacturing sector. Stabilisation programme introduced 1980 owing to rising imported energy costs, hyperinflation and growing debt burden. Gulf crisis would probably keep inflation above 60 per cent. Underlying structural problems remain, despite relative success of massive sales drive abroad and domestic monetary austerity. Tourism expanding fast, but was hit late in 1990 season by Gulf crisis.

Employment

Agricultural sector employs about 50 per cent of the workforce, industry over 14 per cent, public and personal services 30 per cent.
Approximately 1.6m nationals working abroad, mainly in Germany. Workers' remittances important source of foreign exchange.
Real earnings falling because of inflation. In 1995 average incomes were a mere US$2,200 a year (average incomes in EU countries US$15,835 a year).
Prime Minister Necmettin Erbakan announced a 50 per cent pay rise for the country's 1.8m state employees in July 1996. This will increase the lowest grade of civil service salary to US$231 a month (industrial workers are paid around US$200 a month); top civil servants will receive just under US$2,000. The pay increase will compensate for inflation of nearly 40 per cent in the first half of 1996.

External trade

Rapid growth in exports since 1980, particularly textiles, metals, foodstuffs and agricultural products but exports to Middle East have fallen sharply since drop in oil prices in 1986. However, export growth has slowed with phasing out of tax incentives to comply with GATT, while imports surged in 1990 through customs liberalisation and demand boom.

was well below inflation, anticipated at the time to be some 70 per cent in 1995. On 9 October 1995 the new minority government revised its offer to 11.6 per cent for six months and 8.5 per cent thereafter.

Turk-Is is against binding arbitration for public sector workers because it considers that the government has an unfair advantage through a minority representation on the arbitration board. Some 260,000 workers were on general strike in early October 1995; the number rose to 335,000 by the middle of the month. This was another unwanted headache for then-caretaker prime minister Ciller as she tried to form a new government. After mid-October 1995, as talks were held between the True Path and CHP regarding the finer points of their coalition, Ciller ordered one-third of the striking workers back to the job. The government has the power to suspend public sector strikes for 60 days at a time on the basis that they were jeopardising health and national security. The government and Turk-Is finally reached agreement at the beginning of November 1995, which provided a total pay rise of US$1.3 billion in 1995 alone. A 53 per cent public sector pay rise was agreed, effective from 15 November 1995; in April 1995 their pay was raised by 35 per cent.

Anti-terrorism pact

The anti-terrorism act, which effectively gives the government widespread powers in dealing with Kurdish dissent, caused considerable trouble for the government's reputation internationally. The European Parliament said that unless the law was relaxed or scrapped, it would reject the proposed EU-Turkey customs union. Article 8 of the act has drawn international scorn for the fact that it has been used to justify the imprisonment of various writers and speakers over their commentary on the Kurdish separatism issue.

Customs deal with EU

The European Parliament voted in mid-December 1995 to go ahead with the proposed Turkey-EU customs union with 343 votes for and 149 against, much to the relief of Prime Minister Ciller. In the months before the vote, many European Members of Parliament threatened to reject the pact based on Turkey's human rights record. Ciller had been a tireless campaigner for the customs union, both within and without Turkey; this agreement was a rallying-point for opposition groups, especially Refah.

Key provisions of the deal include Turkey's immediate removal of customs tariffs on imports of industrial goods from the European Union once the agreement comes into effect. The EU had already eliminated a majority of customs duties and quotas on imports of industrial goods from Turkey, with the exception of textiles. Turkey has given its assurances that it will update its laws on intellectual property protection, especially with regard to patents on pharmaceuticals. Free trade in agricultural products is expected by the year 2005. Talks on issues concerning workers rights and free movement of workers were postponed to a later date. Estimates suggest that the loss of revenue from tariffs in 1996 for Turkey as a result of the customs union will be between US$2 billion and US$3 billion.

Economy

According to the State Institute of Statistics, Turkey's 1995 GDP grew by 7.3 per cent and the GNP was up by 8.1 per cent. In 1994 these figures had contracted by 5.5 per cent and 6.1 per cent respectively. However, experts agree that these figures only tell part of the story and that Turkey's unrecorded unofficial economy – pushed off the books in an attempt to avoid taxes and regulations – is substantial. At the beginning of April 1996 the government was predicting growth to reach 4.5 per cent for the year. Provisional figures for the first quarter

COUNTRY PROFILE — TURKEY

External trade (contd): Turkey has seven free trade zones. All are in the areas of the major ports on the Black Sea, Aegean and Mediterranean.
Customs union between the EU and Turkey came into force 1 January 1996.
Exports: Textiles and clothing (37% of 1994 total), agricultural products (20%), iron and steel (11%), machinery (including electrical machinery), fruits, chemical industrial products, hides and skins, and motor vehicles.
Main destinations: Germany (21.7% of 1994 total), USA (8.4%), Italy (5.7%), UK (4.9%), France (4.7%), Russia (4.5%), EU (45.7%).
Imports: Major imports in 1994 included machinery (including electrical machinery), fuels, coals etc, chemical industrial products, iron and steel products, motor vehicles and processed petroleum products.
Main sources: Germany (15.7% of 1994 total), USA (10%), Italy (8.6%), France (6.3%), Saudi Arabia (5.3%), UK (5%), EU (44.2%).

Agriculture

Mainstay of economy accounting for 15 per cent of GDP in 1994 and over 20 per cent of exports, and employing about 45 per cent of the labour force. Declining in relative importance, but with strong growth potential. Country runs steady food balance of payments surplus despite liberalisation of food imports since 1984.
Self-sufficiency in basic foodstuffs although only a third of arable land under cultivation. Sector continues to suffer from lack of irrigation and low levels of productivity. A vast area irrigated when the Ataturk hydroelectric dam in south-east Turkey was completed in 1994. Food processing growing rapidly and agricultural products continue to provide bulk of export revenue.
Principal crops include wheat, cotton, fruit and nuts, tobacco and sugar-beet.
The agricultural sector grew by 2.6 per cent in 1994. Exports of agricultural produce were worth US$2.314bn in 1995, compared to US$2.47bn in 1994. Total cereal production in 1995 was 27.955m tonnes, almost 1,000 tonnes more than in 1994. Total pulse production rose in 1995 to 1.829m tonnes from 1.679m tonnes in 1994. Turkey's cotton crop of 836,655 tons in 1995 made the country the biggest cotton grower in Europe, and one of the top five producers in the world.

Industry

Industry accounted for 28 per cent of GDP in 1994 and employed 17.9 per cent of the labour force. Dominated by large state-owned industries, State Economic Enterprises (SEEs), mainly engaged in textiles, food processing, chemicals, metals and motor vehicles. The privatisation programme has been slow. High levels of industrial growth since mid-1970s despite low levels of capital investment and plant utilisation. Rapid development of light industry and growth in exports of manufactured goods.
The private industry sector grew by almost 21 per cent in 1995, having contracted by 11.8 per cent in 1994.

Tourism

Turkey is one of the fastest growing tourism markets. Its share of the world tourism market grew from 0.3 per cent in the early 1980s to 1.2 per cent in the early 1990s. Tourism accounts for 26 per cent of export revenues and 3.3 per cent of GNP.
Arrivals were up by 15.8 per cent to 7.726m in 1995 compared to 6.67m in 1994. Revenue to Turkey totalled US$5bn in 1995, up from US$4.2bn in 1994. The number of visitors from the UK more than doubled in four years from 314,000 in 1992 to an estimated 800,000 in 1996.

Main holding companies

Sabanci, Koc, Cukurova, Enka, Dogus, Kutlutas, Tekfen, Anadolu, Transturk.

Mining

The sector contributed 2 per cent to GDP and employed 2 per cent of the working population in 1994. Substantial mineral reserves, including copper, zinc, lead, iron ore, coal and lignite. Deposits of borax, wolfram and chromite are internationally significant. Turkey is the world's second largest producer of boron and a leading exporter of chrome. Etibank controls 60 per cent of all mining activity.

Hydrocarbons

Turkey has five oil refineries with a total capacity of 710,000 bpd. Modernisation is needed. Most of the country's crude needs are imported, notably from OPEC countries. In December 1996 Turkey signed an agreement with Iraq to import 75,000 barrels of oil a day. Coal reserves 7.2bn tonnes (end-1995); coal production 18m tonnes oil equivalent, down 5.8 per cent on 1994 output.

Energy

Heavy dependence on oil and gas imports despite efforts to develop local energy resources and stepping up of energy conservation programme. Extensive oil exploration under way to bolster falling indigenous oil production. Rapid expansion of hydroelectricity capacity, including development of the Ataturk dam. Also plans to develop nuclear energy as prime source of electricity. There is a major project under way to introduce natural gas from Siberia into the energy system, and to use 54 per cent of this gas for electricity production.

of 1996 show that GDP was up by 8.1 per cent compared with the same period a year earlier.

Private industry helped fuel the growth in 1995 when this sector grew by almost 21 per cent. In contrast, private industry actually contracted by 11.8 per cent in 1994. In the first quarter of 1996 industrial production was up 8.5 per cent compared with a drop of 4.2 per cent in the same quarter of the previous year. The manufacturing industry grew 7.9 per cent in the first quarter of 1995 compared with a contraction of 5.8 per cent in the same period of 1995.

Inflation in 1995, although high, was much less than in 1994. Consumer prices went up 78.9 per cent in 1995 compared with 125.5 per cent in 1994, while wholesale price inflation was 64.9 per cent in 1995, less than half the 149.6 per cent increase recorded in 1994. The official inflation target for 1996 was 65 per cent.

The unemployment rate, measured semi-annually by the State Institute of Statistics, was 6.6 per cent in October 1995, down from 7.2 per cent in the previous six months. However, unofficial estimates of unemployment put the figure at 15 per cent.

Budget

The budget deficit target in 1996 was US$10.5 billion; some US$5 billion is due to be raised internationally in order to cope with this shortfall. Although the government had been attempting to reduce its foreign debt, the budget deficits have made this aspiration very difficult to achieve. At the end of 1995 the total amount of external debt was US$73.28 billion, or 44 per cent of GNP. Some 31 per cent of this debt was in the public sector.

In the January to May 1996 period the fiscal budget deficit was three times higher than in the same period in 1995. The main reason for the increase was a sharp rise in interest payments on domestic debt and public sector salary increases. The consolidated budget deficit was L378 trillion in the first five months of 1996.

External trade

Since the end of 1994, the Turkish lira's depreciation has been kept on a par with inflation, under the guidance of the central bank. Exports from the manufacturing sector amounted to US$18.9 billion in 1995 compared with US$15.36 billion in 1994 – the increase in value terms was more a reflection of higher prices that the goods were fetching than an increase in quantity sold. By volume, the export growth of goods in 1995 was marginal at best.

A total of US$21.975 billion worth of exports were sent abroad (FOB) in 1995 compared with US$18.390 billion in 1994. The biggest export in 1995 was apparel. Exports of cotton t-shirts alone were worth US$575 million and exports of women and girls' cotton wear were worth US$442 million. Iron and steel rods accounted for US$398 million in exports and sales of other pressed steel abroad totalled US$284 million.

Imports were substantially higher in 1995 than in the previous year, by about 54 per cent, partially because the inauguration of the gold bourse in July 1995 meant that the central bank no longer had a monopoly on the import of gold; gold imports were up by 175 per cent. Total value of imports (CIF) reached US$35.7 billion in 1995 compared with US$23.27 billion in 1994.

The higher level of imports in 1995 wreaked havoc on Turkey's trade balance. In 1994 the trade deficit was declared to be US$4.216 billion but a year later this figure climbed to US$13.212 billion. The new EU customs pact was expected to put further pressure on the situation with cheaper imports becoming available from the EU states.

Privatisation

Turkey's Privatisation Administration (OIB) has state shares in 59 companies. The

COUNTRY PROFILE — TURKEY

Legal system

In 1926 Ataturk used the laws of certain countries as a basis for other elements of law. In the main Switzerland's civil law code replaced the Holy Law; the administrative law was taken from France and the penal code from Italy. The commercial law was prepared in Turkey and put into effect in 1957.

Membership of international organisations

ACP (associate), ASSIMER, BIS, BSEC (Black Sea Economic Co-operation), CCC, Council of Europe, CERN (observer), EBU, ECO, EU (associate member), Economic Co-operation Organisation (ECO), ECOSOC, FAO, GATT, IAEA, ICAC, ICAO, IDA, IATA, IEA, IFAD, IFC, IHO, ILO, IMF, IMO, INTELSAT, INTERPOL, IOOC, IPU, Islamic Development Bank (IsDB), ITC, ITU, NACC, NATO, OECD, OIC, UN, UNESCO, UNIDO, UPU, WEU (associate member), WHO, WIPO, WMO, World Bank, WSG, WTO. Free trade agreement with EFTA from 1 April 1992.

BUSINESS GUIDE

Time

GMT +2 hrs (GMT +3 hrs from late Mar to late Sep).

Climate

Coastal regions have a Mediterranean climate, with mild, moist winters and hot, dry summers. The interior plateau has low and irregular rainfall, cold and snowy winters and hot, almost rainless summers. Ankara: (Jan) 0.3 degrees C; (Jul) 23 degrees C; annual rainfall 367 mm. Istanbul: (Jan) 5 degrees C; (Jul) 23 degrees C; annual rainfall 723 mm. Ismir: (Jan) 8 degrees C; (Jul) 27 degrees C; annual rainfall 700 mm.

Clothing

Lightweight May-Sep, tropical in southern areas. Mediumweight and light topcoat Sep-Nov and Mar-Apr. Warm clothing for Nov-Feb.

Entry requirements

Passport: Full passport required for entry.
Visa: Visas required by all except nationals of Albania (from 1 January 1996), some European countries and a few others. Citizens of the UK and Ireland require visas; available only at the port of entry (June 1995).
Health: Cholera certificate required if travelling from an infected area. Anti-malaria and anti-cholera precautions advisable. Not usual to drink tap water, but hotels and restaurants supply spring water which is safe to drink, except at times of epidemic when all water and milk should be boiled.
Currency: No restrictions on amounts of foreign currency taken in; amounts exceeding US$5,000 must be declared and endorsed by authorities. Not more than US$5,000 worth of Turkish currency may be brought in or taken out; must be declared. Money can be changed at post offices. Exchange slips for conversion of foreign currency into Turkish lira should be retained, to be shown when reconverting lira and as proof of legally exchanged currency when taking souvenirs out of Turkey.
Customs: Personal effects allowed in duty-free and gifts up to the value of DM500 may be brought in duty-free. Purchases over US$50 are subject to VAT refund. Advisable to produce invoices and foreign currency exchange slips to cover value of purchases. Export of antiquities and some antiques prohibited.

Air access

National airline: Turk Hava Yollari (THY Turkish Airlines).
Other airlines: Adria Airways, Aeroflot, Air Algérie, Air France, Air Malta, Air Ukraine, Alitalia, Austrian Airlines, Azerbaijan Hava Yollari, Balkan, British Airways, Croatia Airlines, Cyprus Turkish Airlines, Czech Airlines, Delta Airlines, Egypt Air, El Al, Emirates, Finnair, Gulf Air, Iberia, Iran Air, Istanbul Airlines, KLM, Kuwait Airways, Latvian Airlines, Lithuanian Airlines, LOT, Lufthansa, Malev, Malaysian Airlines, MEA, Moscow Airways, Olympic Airways, Orbi Georgian Airways, Palair Macedonian Airlines, PIA, Royal Jordanian, Sabena, SAS, Saudia, Singapore Airlines, Swiss Air, Syrian Arab Airlines, Tarom, Thai Airways International, Tunisair.
International airports: Istanbul-Atatürk (IST), 24 km south-west of city; Ankara Esenboga (ESB), 35 km north of city; Izmir-Adnan Menderes (IZM), 16 km south of city.
A new airport at Kartal will be built and there are plans to extend Ataturk airport.

Surface access

Express rail services from Munich, Vienna, Venice, Belgrade, Baghdad and Tehran. Coach services from Austria, France, Germany and Switzerland, as well as a number of countries in the Middle East.
Main ports: Mersin, Iskenderun, Istanbul, Izmir, Samsun, Trabzon.

Hotels

Classified into five categories – de luxe and first- to fourth-class. Prices vary and many hotels reduce their rates between mid-Oct and mid-Apr. Service charge of 15 per cent usually added and tipping is extra. 12 per cent VAT is also added. Advance reservations are advisable. Tap water is drinkable in major hotels.

Restaurants

Both in hotels and outside as going to restaurants is a national pastime. Bill usually

OIB's priorities include the selling of Petrol Ofisi, the petroleum distributor, Tupras, the petrochemical company, Rergi, the steel producer, a minority stake in Turkish Airlines, and Turk Telecom.

Although the recent governments have been pro-privatisation, their plans were constantly being delayed by constitutional challenges. Refah, for instance, is particularly opposed to privatisation and many of the anti-privatisation measures have come from their camp.

In 1995 the government had planned to raise as much as US$3 billion through the partial sale of Turk Telecom. Other sales in 1995 were expected to yield another US$2.5 billion. However, the final figure amounted to about US$600 million due in part to a ruling of the constitutional court in March 1996; the court annulled key provisions of the privatisation law, and this effectively stopped the sale of part of Turk Telecom. Some 34 per cent of Turk Telecom had been sold to investors and 5 per cent to employees.

The Petkim petrochemicals group is to be disposed of either as a trade sale or as part of an international share offer; the government holds 96 per cent of the company's capital. Petkim, the top tax paying company in Turkey in 1995, is generously valued at around US$2 billion. Reports in June 1996 indicate that the favoured option is to dispose of the company piece by piece. Its large size and complexity means that it would be difficult to find a buyer for the entire package, especially since some parts are not performing as well as others and modernisation is needed.

Petrol Ofisi AS, the country's leading petroleum products distributor and marketer, is due to be sold at the end of 1996 or early in 1997. The company has a 50 to 60 per cent share of the market.

Development

The Birecik hydroelectric power plant and irrigation dam was given the go-ahead in November 1995. It will produce 2.5 billion kilowatt-hours per year worth of electricity and will take over five years to construct. In December 1995 a turnkey contract and financial agreement was signed to build the 189 MW Karagamis dam on the Euphrates near the border with Syria. Work is expected to take four years.

The Istanbul underground railway system is progressing. The tunnels have been completed since 1991 and the construction of platforms is nearing the final stages. A Siemens-led consortium won the contract to lay tracks for the 7.8 km line which runs between the Taksim and Fourth Levent districts in Istanbul. The work, including the provision of railway cars and electrification, is due to be completed by the end of 1997.

The US$35 million Ovacik gold mine, Turkey's first, is expected to start up in the later part of 1997. Problems had beset the joint venture for years while its owners struggled to get the necessary permits. There is a minimum of four years worth of reserves in the mine and production will be at an initial rate of 110,000 troy ounces per year.

Agriculture

The agriculture sector grew by 2.6 per cent in 1995 compared with the previous year. Exports of agricultural produce were worth US$2.314 billion in 1995 compared with US$2.47 billion in 1994. Cotton is a key raw ingredient in Turkey's primarily cotton-based textile and apparel industry. Production of this crop in 1995 reached 836,655 tons, making Turkey the biggest cotton grower in Europe and putting it in the top five producers in the world. In 1994 628,000 tons of cotton was harvested.

Total cereal production in 1995 was 27.955 million tonnes which is almost 1,000 tonnes more than in the previous year. Total pulse production also rose in 1995, to 1.829 million tonnes from 1.679 million tonnes in 1994.

BUSINESS GUIDE — TURKEY

Restaurants (contd): includes service charge, but optional extra tip for good service of up to 10 per cent.

Currency

Exchange rate: Turkish lira floats via rates determined daily by central bank of Turkey dealing room based on value of US dollar. All banks free to establish own rates within margins set by central bank.

Foreign exchange information

Account restrictions: Blocked accounts in operation. Non-residents and residents can maintain accounts in Turkey and use these accounts freely.
Trade policy: Recent liberalisation of import controls. Around 95 per cent of imported goods are now allowed free entry (subject to duties).

Credit cards

Access, Diners Club, VISA, American Express and Eurocard credit cards accepted in most hotels, restaurants and shops, and can be used to withdraw money from automatic cash dispensers at banks.

Car hire

Available at main hotels, airports and travel agents but expensive. International driving licence preferred, but most foreign licences accepted. Roads are generally good but local driving erratic.

City transport

Taxis Metered taxis available in major towns and cities. Also available are the much cheaper 'Dolmus' taxis, which have fixed routes and carry 8-12 passengers. Tipping not customary. Drivers rarely speak much English and may be new to the city, so advisable to buy a road map.

National transport

Air: Turkish Airlines operate regular services between Istanbul, Izmir, Ankara and other major towns. Travelling by air within Turkey is relatively inexpensive.
Water: Steamship service between Istanbul and most major coastal towns.
Road and rail: In 1994 there were 59,832 km of roads; 8,452 km of rail track. Most major cities and towns are linked by regular rail and coach services. In December 1992 Turkey, Hungary and Romania signed the Trust Fund agreement for the Trans-European Railway (TER) Project. In September 1995 the Islamic Investment Company of the Gulf (Bahrain) E C (IICG) completed a facility supporting the US$1.30bn Tarsus–Pozanti–Ayrimi–Gaziantep (Tag) motorway project. Tag connects the southern Antolian region with the rest of Turkey, providing a vital link for the future growth of the region.

Public holidays

Fixed dates: 1 Jan (New Year's Day), 23 Apr (National Sovereignty and Children's Day), 19 May (Commemoration of Atatürk and Youth and Sports Day), 30 Aug (Victory Day), 28-29 Oct (Republic Day).
Variable dates: Ramadan (three days), Seker Bayrami and Kurban Bayrami (four days) (Muslim holidays). Dates are fixed by position of the moon.

Working hours

Business: (Mon–Fri) 0900 – 1230 and 1330 – 1800.
Government: (Mon–Fri) 0830 – 1230 and 1330 – 1730.
Banking: (Mon–Fri) 0830 – 1200 and 1330 – 1700.
Shops: (Mon–Sat) 0900 – 1300 and 1400 – 1900. Large shopping centre (Atakoy Galleria) on the coast road to Istanbul Airport, opens until 2200 every day. Many flower shops open late. Pharmacies display the location of one opening late. Many food shops open on Sun.

Social customs

Hospitality very important. Turkey is a Muslim country and religion plays an important part in Turkish life. Practically all business entertaining conducted in restaurants and clubs.

Business language and interpreting/translation

Available from Turk Argus Ajans, Istanbul (tel: 244-16-34, 249-84-66); Universal, Istanbul (tel: 267-24-88); Modern Tercume Burosu, Ankara (tel: 417-81-22, 418-14-70) and many other sources.

Telecommunications

Alcatel of France took control of Telekomunikasyon Endustri Ticaret (Teletas) of Turkey by buying the government's 18 per cent shareholding for US$20m in August 1993.
Telephone and telefax: Approximately 5.5m phones, around half of which are in Istanbul or Ankara. In 1994 there were 203 telephones per 1,000 persons. International dialling code: 90 followed by 2 for Istanbul, 4 for Ankara. Public phones operated by discs. Direct dialling available. For long distance calls first dial 9, and for overseas calls 99. N.B. Telephone and fax numbers for Istanbul starting with '1' are changed to '2' and those for Ankara starting with '1' changed to '4'.
Telex: Available in major hotels and certain main post offices in Ankara and Istanbul. Country code: 607TR.

Postal service

Main post offices in major cities are open 24 hours a day. Money exchange rates better than at banks. Open only for telephone and post at night.

Energy

Total crude oil imports accounted for a substantial US$2.49 billion in 1995. Oil consumption in 1995, at 28.4 million tonnes, was 10 per cent higher than in the previous year. Natural gas consumption rocketed by 32.3 per cent in 1995 compared with the previous year to 7.7 million barrels of oil equivalent – about on par with Spain which has about two-thirds the population of Turkey. By comparison, the UK, which has roughly the same number of people as Turkey, consumed 65.8 million tonnes of oil equivalent in 1995.

In June 1996 Iraqi oil was flowing through Turkey at a rate of 350,000 barrels per day. The crude is transported westward to Ceyhan and had not flowed through the pipeline in six years. In the days before Iraq invaded Kuwait some 1.5 million barrels per day of crude were exported from Iraq via Turkey.

Investment

The climate for foreign investor confidence has been shaken by the recent political uncertainty in Turkey. In 1995 Dutch companies were the single largest investors in terms of foreign direct investment (FDI); in 1995 their investment stood at US$559 million, which represents 19.4 per cent of the total FDI. France is a close second with 17.8 per cent of FDI while Germany is 11.2 per cent and the USA is 11.1 per cent.

Before the December 1995 election two major build operate transfer (BOT) projects were agreed by the government. The first is a 672 MW hydroelectric plant and dam located on the Euphrates at Birecik. The project had been under negotiation for a decade and is worth US$1.6 billion. The other BOT project calls for the completion of a dam – which is already under construction near Istanbul at Yuvacik – and the building of a water treatment plant and a 146-km-long water pipeline. Under the terms of these BOT deals, the company constructing the plant is responsible for operating it for a period of 15 years from the time construction is complete. The government guarantees the company's financial obligations and the price of the plant's produce.

Tourism

Tourism is on an upward swing again in Turkey. The terrorism-related drop in tourist numbers seen in 1993 and 1994 had seemed to be a thing of the past in 1995 when arrivals were up by 15.8 per cent to 7.726 million compared with 6.67 million. In 1995 the industry brought US$5 billion to Turkey, up from the US$4.2 billion registered in 1994. The number of German tourists almost doubled between 1994 and 1995 because of the perception that the country had become much safer; in 1995 there were 1.856 million tourists versus 994,301 million in 1994. The Commonwealth of Independent States provided the second largest group of tourists at 1.356 million.

One of the first acts of Yilmaz upon taking power was to abolish the US$100 Mass Housing Fund levy. This amount was payable by all Turks leaving the country. However, the system was structured in such a way that only one person in five ended up paying the levy.

Outlook

While it is still early days for the new Refah-True Path coalition, it appears that the hard-core Islamic faction of Refah have been kept in check. Economically, in the coalition's early stages it was business as usual, especially since the True Path have strong control over the economic side of government – the pro-western, free-market policies of the True Path will likely continue in the short term until a radical shake-up occurs.

BUSINESS GUIDE — TURKEY

Banking

The state-owned central bank is Türkiye Cumhuriyet Merkez Bankasi, which has its head office in Ankara and sub-offices in a few major cities. The state-owned TC Ziraat Bankasi acts as agent for the central bank in places where the central bank does not have an office. There are 32 domestic commercial banks, six investment banks and 21 foreign banks in Turkey. Ziraat Bankasi, the completely state-owned commercial bank, and Türkiye Is Bankasi, in which the state has major holding, are the two largest banks. The largest banks in the private sector are Akbank and Yapi ve Kredi Bankasi. There are close links between banks and industry – several banks are owned by industrial holdings or specialise in particular sectors. However, the specialisation of such banks as Sekerbank (sugar), Etibank (minerals), Pamukbank (cotton) is steadily declining as they go more and more into general commercial banking. The government is seeking to privatise several of the smaller state banks.

Trade fairs

International trade fairs held in Izmir and Istanbul. Annual Fair (Aug-Sep), Izmir. The Istanbul World Trade Centre is the biggest in Turkey and the Middle East.

Electricity supply

220 V AC (110 V in parts of Istanbul).

Representation in capital

Afghanistan, Albania, Algeria, Argentina, Australia, Austria, Bangladesh, Belgium, Brazil, Bulgaria, Canada, Chile, China, Denmark, Egypt, Ethiopia, Finland, France, Germany, Greece, The Holy See, Hungary, India, Indonesia, Iran, Iraq, Israel, Italy, Japan, Jordan, Republic of Korea, Kuwait, Lebanon, Libya, Malaysia, Mexico, Morocco, Netherlands, Norway, Pakistan, Poland, Portugal, Romania, Russia, Saudi Arabia, Somalia, Spain, Sweden, Switzerland, Syria, Thailand, Tunisia, Turkish Republic of Northern Cyprus, UK, USA, Venezuela.

BUSINESS DIRECTORY

Hotels

Ankara

Bulvar Palas, Ataturk Bulvari 141 (tel: 417-5020; tx: 42-613).

Büyük Ankara, Ataturk Bulvari 183-06680 (tel: 425-6655; fax: 425-5070).

Dedeman, Buklum Sok No 1 06660 (tel: 417-6200; fax: 417-6214).

Etap Mola, Ataturk Bulvari 80 (tel: 417-8585; fax: 417-85-92).

Kent, Mithatpasa Caddesi 4 (tel: 435-5050; fax: 434-4657).

Stad, Istiklal Caddesi 20, Ulus (tel: 310-4848; fax: 310-8969).

Istanbul

Aden, Rihtim Caddesi Yogurtcu, Sukru, Sok. 2 Kadikoy (tel: 345-1000; fax: 346-2567).

Akgun, Vatan Caddesi (tel: 534-4879; fax: 524-9969).

Berr, Akdeniz Caddesi 78, 34250 Fatih (tel: 534-2070; fax: 531-9975, 531-1924).

Buyu-k Surmeli, Saatci Bayiri Sok. 3 80310 Gayrettepe (tel: 272-1160; fax: 266-3669).

Carlton, Fevziye Caddesi 22, Sehzadebasi 34470 (tel: 511-4224; fax: 519-3507).

Cinar (near Ataturk Airport), Fener Mevkii, 34800 Yesilkoy (tel: 573-3500, 573-2910; fax: 573-5701).

Ciragan Palace, Kempinski Istanbul, Ciragan Caddesi 84 (tel: 258-3377; fax: 259-6687, 159-8974).

Dedeman, Yildiz Posta Caddesi 50, 80800 Esentepe (tel: 274-8800; fax: 275-1100).

Dilson, Siraselviler Caddesi 49, 80090 Taksim (tel: 252-9600; fax: 249-7077).

Divan, Cumhuriyet Caddesi 2, 80200 Taksim (tel: 231-4100; fax: 248-8527).

Eysan, Rihtim Caddesi Kadikoy (tel: 346-2440; fax: 347-2329).

Grand Tarabya, Kefelikoy Caddesi, Tarabya (tel: 262-1000, 162-0710; fax: 262-2260).

Hilton, Cumhuriyet Caddesi, Harbiye (tel: 231-4650; fax: 240-4165).

Holiday Inn, Sahilyolu 34710, Atakoy (tel: 560-4110; fax: 559-4905).

Kalyon, Sahilyolu, Sultanahmet (tel: 517-4400; fax: 517-6770).

Macka, Eytam Caddesi 35, 80200 Tesvikiye (tel: 234-3200; fax: 240-7694).

Marmara (The), Taksim Square, 80090 Taksim (tel: 251-4696; fax: 244-0509).

Mim (Inter Hotels), Ihlamur Yolu, Nisantasi (tel: 230-7994; fax: 230-7999).

Movenpick, Buyukdere Caddesi Ucyol Mevkii, 49 Maslak 80670 (tel: 276-4000; fax: 276-8731).

Nippon, Topcu Caddesi 10 Taksim (tel: 254-9900; fax: 250-4553).

Parksa Hilton, Bayildim Caddesi 12, Macka 80680 (tel: 258-5674; fax: 258-5695).

Pera Palas, Mesrutiyet Caddesi 98–100, Tapebasi (tel: 251-4560; fax: 251-4089).

Hotels (contd):
President (The), Tiyatro Caddesi 25, Beyazit (tel: 516-6980; fax: 516-6999).

Prestige, Koska Caddesi 8 Laleli (tel: 526-1371, 528-0294; fax: 512-5759).

Pulman Etap, Mesrutiyet Caddesi Tepebasi (tel: 251-4646; fax: 249-8033).

Ramada, Ordu Caddesi 226, 34470 laleli (tel: 513-9300; fax: 512-6390).

Resteria, Laleli Caddesi 43 Laleli (tel; 512-0435; fax: 511-6463).

Sheraton, 80174 Taksim Parki (tel: 231-2121; fax: 231-2180).

Swissotel (The) Bosphorus, Taslik, Macka (tel: 259-0101; fax: 259-0105).

Car hire

Istanbul
Avis: Central Reservations (tel: 257-7670/10; fax: 263-3918, 257-5632); Istanbul Ataturk Airport (tel: 663-0646/7; fax: 663-0648); Beyazit Ordu Cad 159 (tel: 516-6109/8; Elmadag Hotel Hilton/Arcade (tel: 241-7896/2917, 246-5256; fax: 231-6244); Kadikoy, Selamicesme (tel: 355-3665, 350-4878; fax: 369-9421).

Budget: Central Reservations (tel: 253-9200; fax: 256-2611); Istanbul International Airport (tel: 663-0858; fax: 663-0724); Cumhuriyet Cad Gezi Airport (tel: 253-9200; fax: 237-2919).

Europcar: Central Reservations, Cumhuriyet Cad 47/2, 80090 Taksim-Istanbul (tel: 254-7788; fax: 250-7649); Istanbul Airport, Ataturk International Terminal (tel: 663-0746/7); Kadikoy Bagdat Cad 222, Ciftehavuzlar (tel: 360-3333/4); Talimhane Topcu Cad 1, Taksim (tel: 254-7799, 253-3927).

Hertz: Ataturk Airport (tel: 0663-0807, 574-6948; fax: 232-9260); Cumhuriyet Cad, 295 Harbiye (tel: 246-2794; 247-2284; fax: 232-9260).

Chambers of commerce

Adana Chamber of Commerce, Abidinpasa Caddesi 42/4, Adana (tel: 12-404; tx: 62-492 ADTO).

Ankara Chamber of Commerce, Sehit Tegmen Kalmaz Caddesi 30, Ankara (tel: 310-4810; fax: 310-8436).

Istanbul Chamber of Commerce, PO Box 377, Eminonu, Istanbul (tel: 511-4150; fax: 526-2197).

Istanbul Chamber of Industry, Mesrutiyet Cadessi 116, Beyoglu, Istanbul (tel: 252-2900; fax: 249-3963).

Istanbul and Marmara, Aegean, Mediterranean Chambers of Shipping, Meclisi Mebusan Cadessi 22, 80054 Salipazari, Istanbul (tel: 252-0130; fax: 293-7935).

Istanbul and Marmara Region Maritime Chamber of Commerce, Istiklal Caddesi, 286 Odakule, KAT 10, 80050 Beyoglu, Istanbul (tel: 243-5495; fax: 243-7935).

Izmir Chamber of Commerce, Ataturk Cadessi 126, Izmir (tel: 441-7777; fax: 483-7853).

Izmir Chamber of Industry, Cumhuriyet Bulvari 63, Izmir (tel: 484-4330; fax: 483-9937).

The Union of Chambers of Commerce, Industry, Maritime and Commodity Exchanges, Ataturk Bulvari 149, Bakanlilar, Ankara (tel: 418-4290; fax: 418-3268).

The Unions of Chambers of Agriculture, Izmir Cadessi 24, K 5/6, Kizilay, Ankara (tel: 225-2313).

Izmir Chamber of Commerce, Atatürk Caddesi 126, Izmir (tel: 144-355 or 134-119; tx: 52-331 IODA).

Banking

Türkiye Cumhuriyet Merkez Bankasi (central bank), Istiklal Cadessi 10, 06100 Ulus, Ankara (tel: 310-3646; fax: 310-7434/9118).

ABN Amro Bank, Inönü Cadessi 15, 80090 Gümüssuyu/Taksim, Istanbul (tel: 293-8802; fax: 249-2008).

Adabank, Büyükdere Cadessi 40, 80290 Mecidiyeköy, Istanbul (tel: 272-6420; fax: 272-6446).

Akbank, Sabanci Center, 80745 4.Levent, Istanbul (tel: 270-2666/0044; fax: 269-7383/8081).

Alternatif Bank, Inönü Cadessi 76-78, 80090 Taksim, Istanbul (tel: 252-6920; fax: 252-2307).

Arap Türk Bankasi, Valikonagi Cadessi 10, 80200 Nisantasi, Istanbul (tel: 225-0500; fax: 225-0526, 224-9992).

Avrupa Türk Yatirim Bankasi, Yapi Kredi Plaza, C Blok, Kat 15, 80620 Levent, Istanbul (tel: 279-7070; fax: 282-6301).

Banca Di Roma, Tünel Cadessi 18, 80000 Karaköy, Istanbul (tel: 251-0917; fax: 249-6289).

Bank Ekspres, Kore Sehitleri Cadessi 43, 80300 Zincirlikuyu, Istanbul (tel: 288-3838; fax: 288-3867).

Bank Mellat, Büyükdere Cadessi Binbirçiçek Sok 1, 80620 1 Levent, Istanbul (tel: 269-5820; fax: 264-2895).

Birlesik Türk Körfez Bankasi, Büyükdere Cadessi 42, 80290 Mecidiyeköy, Istanbul (tel: 288-2000; fax: 288-1217/8).

Birlesik Yatirim Bankasi, Cumhuriyet Cadessi 16/3, 80200 Elmadag, Istanbul (tel: 231-6666; fax: 232-1866).

BNP - AK Dresdner Bank, Tak'i Zafer Cadessi Vakif Is Hani, 80090 Taksim, Istanbul (tel: 293-8780; fax: 243-6742).

Chemical Bank, Abdi Ipekçi Cadessi 63, 80200 Maçka, Istanbul (tel: 231-4010; fax: 248-3791).

Citibank, Büyükdere Cadessi 100, 80280 Esentepe, Istanbul (tel: 288-7700; fax: 288-7760).

Credit Lyonnais, Setüstü Haktan Ishani 45/4, 80040 Kabatas, Istanbul (tel: 251-6300; fax: 251-7724).

Demirbank, Büyükdere Cadessi 122, 80280 Esentepe, Istanbul (tel: 275-1900; fax: 267-4794/2786).

Derbank, Abide-i Hürriyet Cadessi 125, 80220 Sisli, Istanbul (tel: 224-9494; fax: 231-4759).

Development Bank of Turkey, Kizilay, Ankara (tel: 417-9200; fax: 418-3967).

Disbank, Türk Dis Ticaret Bankasi, Yildiz Posta Cadessi 54, 80280 Gayrettepe, Istanbul (tel: 274-4280; fax: 272-5278/9).

Egebank, Büyükdere Cadessi 106, 80280 Esentepe, Istanbul (tel: 288-7400; fax: 288-7316).

Esbank, Eskisehir Bankasi, Mesrutiyet Cadessi 141, 80050 Tepebasi, Istanbul (tel: 251-7270; fax: 243-2396).

Etibank Bankacilik, Tunus Caddesi 33, 06680 Kavaklidere, Ankara (tel: 417-6230, 425-0277; fax: 418-2938, 419-4576).

Finansbank, Büyükdere Cadessi 123, 80300 Gayrettepe, Istanbul (tel: 275-2450; fax: 275-2496).

Garanti Yatirim Ve Ticaret Bankasi, Mete Cadessi 40 Park Han, 80060 Taksim, Istanbul (tel: 251-0880/3622; fax: 251-1278/3103).

Habib Bank Limited, Abide-i Hürriyet Cadessi Geçit Sok 12, 80222 Sisli, Istanbul (tel: 246-0220/3; fax: 234-0807).

Iktisat Bankasi, Büyükdere Caddesi 165, 80304 Esentepe, Istanbul (tel: 274-1111; fax: 274-7028).

Iller Bankasi, Atatürk Bulvari 21, 06053 Opera, Ankara (tel: 311-2672, 310-3141; fax: 310-7459, 312-2989).

Interbank, Büyükdere Cadessi 108/C, 80496 Esentepe, Istanbul (tel: 274-2000; fax: 272-1622/1623).

Kapital Bank Türk, Yapi Kredi Plaza, C Blok, Kat 14, 80620 Levent, Istanbul (tel: 279-7311/7070; fax: 282-6301).

Kentbank, Tevfik Erdönmez Sokak 18, 80280 Esentepe, Istanbul (tel: 274-8900; fax: 274-8920).

Kibris Kredi Bankasi, Büyükdere Cadessi 118, 80280 Zincirlikuyu, Istanbul (tel: 274-4788; fax: 274-6059).

Koçbank, Barbaros Bulvari, Morbasan Sokak, Koza Is Merkezi C Blok, 80692 Besiktas, Istanbul (tel: 274-7777; fax: 267-2987).

Midland Bank, Cumhuriyet Cadessi 8, 80200 Elmadag, Istanbul (tel: 231-5560; fax: 230-5300, 231-4400).

Osmanli Bankasi, Voyvoda Cadessi 35-37, 80000 Karaköy, Istanbul (tel: 252-3000; fax: 244-6571, 252-6138).

Pamukbank, Büyükdere Cadessi 82, 80450 Gayrettepe, Istanbul (tel: 275-2424; fax: 266-6224).

Parkbank, Park Yatirim Bankasi, Büyükdere Cadessi Meseli Sok 9, 80620 4 Levent, Istanbul (tel: 281-4820; fax: 278-0445).

Saudi American Bank, Cumhuriyet Cadessi 233, 80230 Harbiye, Istanbul (tel: 230-0284/6; fax: 233-0201).

Sekerbank, Atatürk Bulvari 171, 06680 Kavaklidere, Ankara (tel: 417-9120/7500; fax: 425-4919, 417-8017).

Sinai Yatirim ve Kredi Bankasi, Akdogan Sokak 41-43, 80690 Besiktas, Istanbul (tel: 259-7414; fax: 258-7154).

Societe Generale, Yapi Kredi Plaza, B Blok, Kat 12, 80260 Levent, Istanbul (tel: 279-7051; fax: 282-6988).

In a fabulous city of timeless treasures, a premier meeting place

Introducing the Istanbul Convention and Exhibition Centre

The newest jewel on the fabled Istanbul horizon – the Istanbul Convention and Exhibition Centre (ICEC) – first opened its doors in June 1996 with the United Nations HABITAT II Conference. The UN organisers who literally 'took over' the entire ICEC for two weeks were delighted with what the new centre had to offer. Ideally located in the heart of the city's business, cultural and shopping areas, the ICEC is in walking distance of 16 hotels containing 3,400 guestrooms.

Whether it's a meeting for ten or a conference with 2,000 delegates, ICEC has the facilities, professional management and highly trained staff to make a meeting successful and enjoyable.

The Auditorium and other meeting rooms are fully equipped to serve total convention and production requirements. Acoustics are rated as absolutely excellent in the versatile 2,000-armchair auditorium where it is possible to stage a multi-faceted dream event with the use of the world's third largest moveable screen, an expandable stage, extensive lighting capabilities, electronic voting system, 12-language simultaneous translation system and state-of-the-art audio-visual equipment. All equipment usage is supported by a professional technical team.

A 1,500 square-metre foyer space for product and service exhibitions complements the meeting facilities, as does the fully-equipped business centre.

ICEC has facilities for the handicapped, and the most modern 24-hour security system and trained staff are in place.

The top-quality five star in-house food service is equipped to cater to every type of event, from a proper business lunch to an elegant cocktail reception or buffet dinner. The Bogazici Borsa Restaurant, specialising in international and Turkish cuisines, seats up to 400 persons. Banquet seating for up to 1,500 persons may be reserved on the adjoining summer terrace.

ICEC truly offers spaces for every occasion. Istanbul as a city naturally draws incentives and meetings groups, and at ICEC they are delighted to find flexible facilities and professional, co-operative personnel, coupled with prices 15-20% under hotel prices for meeting space and catering.

Among the fine rooms for smaller meetings are the Dolmabahçe and the Marmara rooms where up to 400 people can gather in a comfortable environment with a wonderful view of the Bosphorus while having every technical and service requirement met.

Ultra-modern amenities, experienced destination management companies, the splendours of the Ottoman past and the honoured traditions of Turkish hospitality combine to make Istanbul the perfect meeting city, one that will impress treasured and lasting memories.

What more could a meeting organiser wish for?

Let us know!

Istanbul Convention and Exhibition Centre

Harbiye 802 Istanbul - Turkey
Tel: (90-212) 296 30 55 pbx: Fax: (90-212) 224 08 78
General Manager: Sinan Bilsel
Sales & Marketing Director: Orhan Sanus
North American Representative: International Destinations Inc
1700 Connecticut Ave., N>W. Suite 401, Washington, D.C. 20009 USa
Tel: (1-212) 797 12 22; Fax: (1-212) 265 59 30
President: Ms Patricia W Fisch

Banking (contd):

Tatbank, Kemeralti Cadessi 24, Kat 2-3, 80030 Karaköy, Istanbul (tel: 249-5040/60; fax: 249-4685).

Tekfenbank, Tekfen Yatirim ve Finansman Bankasi, Büyükdere Cadessi 103/7, 80300 Mecidiyeköy, Istanbul (tel: 275-2013; fax: 272-8356).

Tekstil Bankasi, Tekstilbank, Abide-i Hürriyet Cadessi, Geçit Sok 10, 80270 Sisli, Istanbul (tel: 224-1313; fax: 232-8313).

The Chase Manhattan Bank, Yildiz Posta Cadessi 52, Kat 11, 80700 Esentepe, Istanbul (tel: 275-1280; fax: 275-9932).

Toprakbank, Büyükdere Cadessi Nilüfer Han, 103/1, 80300 Mecidiyeköy, Istanbul (tel: 288-4120; fax: 272-5619).

Türk Boston Bank, Yildiz Posta Cadessi 17, 80280 Esentepe, Istanbul (tel: 274-5222; fax: 272-3348).

Türk Ekonomi Bankasi, Meclis-i Mebusan Cadessi 35, 80040 Findikli, Istanbul (tel: 251-2121; fax: 249-6568).

Türk Merchant Bank, Cevdet Pasa Cadessi 288, 80810 Bebek, Istanbul (tel: 257-7684; fax: 257-7327).

Türk Sakura Bank, Büyükdere Cadessi 108/A, 80280 Esentepe, Istanbul (tel: 275-2930; fax: 272-4270).

Türk Ticaret Bankasi, Yildiz Posta Cadessi 2, 80280 Gayrettepe, Istanbul (tel: 288-5900; fax: 288-6113).

Turkish Bank, Vali Konagi Cadessi 7, 80200 Nisantasi, Istanbul (tel: 225-0330; fax: 225-0353/5).

Türkiye Bankalar Birligi (bankers' association), Nispetiye Caddesi Ak Merkez, B3 Blok, Kat: 12-13, Etiler 80630, Istanbul (tel: 282-0973; fax: 282-0946).

Türkiye Emlak Bankasi (Konutbank), Büyükdere Caddesi No 43, Maslak 80650, Istanbul (tel: 276-1620; fax: 276-1659).

Türkiye Garanti Bankasi, Büyükdere Cadessi 63, 80670 Maslak, Istanbul (tel: 285-4000; fax: 285-4040).

Türkiye Ihracat Kredi Bankasi, Türk Eximbank, Milli Müdafaa Cadessi 20, 06100 Bakanliklar, Ankara (tel: 417-1300; fax: 425-7896).

Türkiye Imar Bankasi, Büyükdere Cadessi 42-46, Mecidiyeköy 80290, Istanbul (tel: 275-1190; fax: 266-5514).

Türkiye Is Bankasi, Atatürk Bulvari 191, 06684 Kavaklidere, Ankara (tel: 428-1140; fax: 425-0750/2).

Türkiye Kalkinma Bankasi, Necatibey Cadessi 98, 06570 Bakanliklar, Ankara (tel: 231-8400; fax: 231-3125, 418-3967).

Türkiye Sinai Kalkinma Bankasi, Meclis-i Mebusan Cadessi 137, 80040 Findikli, Istanbul (tel: 251-2800; fax: 243-2975).

Türkiye Tütüncüler Bankasi, Tütünbank, Barbaros Bulvari 121, 80700 Balmumcu, Istanbul (tel: 275-8400; fax: 272-8314).

Westdeutsche Landesbank (Europa), Nisbetiye Cadessi 38, Kat 1-2, 80630 1 Levent, Istanbul (tel: 279-2537; fax: 280-2941).

Yapi ve Kredi Bankasi, Büyükdere Cadessi Yapi Kredi Plaza, A Blok, 80620 Levent, Istanbul (tel: 280-1111; fax: 280-1670/1).

Yatirim Bank, Dr Sevket Bey Sok 5, 80220 Sisli, Istanbul (tel: 225-7090; fax: 231-9599).

Yurtbank, Yurt Ticaret ve Kredi Bankasi, Cumhuriyet Cadessi 16, Kat 5-6, 80200 Elmadag, Istanbul (tel: 225-8779/80, 6855/6; fax: 224-5861).

Principal newspapers

Cumhuriyet, Trkocagu Cad 39, Cagaloglu, TR-34334 Istanbul (tel: 512-0505; fax: 512-8595).

Hürriyet, Babiali Cad 15-17, Cagaloglu, Istanbul (tel: 512-0000; fax: 512-0026).

Milliyet, Nuruosmaniye Cad 65, Cagaloglu, Istanbul (tel: 511-4410; fax: 528-3018).

Sabah, Medya Plaza Basin Ekspres Yolu, Ikitell, Istanbul (tel: 550-4900; fax: 502-8200).

Tercuman, Davutpasa Cad 115, Topkapi, Istanbul (tel: 612-9717; fax: 612-9719).

Turkish Daily News, Tunus Cad 50-A/7, Kavaklidere, Ankara (tel: 428-2956; fax: 427-8890).

Travel information

Tourism Information Office, Gazi Mustafa Kemal Bul 121, Demirtepe, Ankara (tel: 229-3661, 488-7007; tx: 42-448 iib).

Turban Travel Avency, Atatürk Bulvari 169, Atayurt Han, Bakanliklar, Ankara (tel: 418-2919; tx: 42-614).

Turk Hava Yollari (THY Turkish Airlines), General Administration Building, Ataturk Airport Yesilk-y, Istanbul (tel: 574-7402, 663-6300; fax: 574-7444, 663-4744); Cumhuriyet Cad No 199-201, Sisli, Istanbul (tel: 248-2631; fax: 240-2984).

Other useful addresses

Borsa Komiserligi (stock exchange), Menkul Kiymetler ve Kambiyo Borsasi, Rihtim Caddesi 245, 80030 Karakoy, Istanbul (tel: 252-4800; fax: 243-7243).

British Embassy, Sehit Ersan Caddesi 46/a, Cankaya, Ankara (tel: 468-6230/42; fax: 468-3214, 0113-6643).

Export Promotion Centre (IGEME), Mithatpasa Cad No 60, Kisilay, Ankara (tel: 417-2223; fax: 417-2223).

Foundation for Privatisation, 36 ul Krucza, 00525 Warsaw (tel: 628-2198/99; fax: 625-1114); external department (tel: 693-5419/5818; fax: 693-5300).

General Directorate of Foreign Investment, Inönü Bulvari, 06510 Emek, Ankara (tel: 212-8914/5; fax: 212-8916).

Industrial Development Agency, ul Wspolna 4, 00930 Warsaw (tel: 628-7954, 628-0934; fax: 628-2363).

Istanbul Convention and Exhibition Centre, Lütfi Kirdar Uluslararasi, 80230 harbiye, Istanbul (tel: 296 3055; fax: 224 0878).

Ministry of Communications, 91 Sok No 5, Emek, Ankara (tel: 212-6730).

Ministry of Finance and Customs, Maliye ve Gümrük Bakanligi, Dikmen Cadessi, Ankara (tel: 419-1200; tx: 42-285).

Ministry of Foreign Affairs, Sisisleri Bakanligi, Yeni Hizmet Binasi, 06520 Balgat, Ankara (tel: 287-2555).

Ministry of Tourism, Ismet Inönü Bul, 5 Balgat, Ankara (tel: 212-8300).

Ministry of Trade and Industry, Sanayi ve Ticaret Bakanligi, Tandogan, Ankara (tel: 231-7280).

Modern Tercume Burosu (translation service), Karanfil Sokak 21/4, Yenisehir, Ankara (tel: 417-8122).

Prime Minister's Office, Basbakanlik, Ankara (tel: 230-8720).

Prime Ministry, Under-Secretariat for Treasury and Foreign Trade, Eskisehir Yolu Inönü Bul Emek, Ankara (tel: 212-8800; fax: 212-8778).

State Institute of Statistics, Necatibey Caddesi 114, Ankara (tel: 417-6440).

State Planning Organisation, Necatibey Cadessi 108, Ankara (tel: 417-6440).

Turk Argus Ajansi (translation service), Lamartin Caddesi 32/4 Taksim, Istanbul (tel: 250-5200).

Turk Haberler Ajansi (news agency), Turkocagi Caddesi 1/4, Cagaloglu, Istanbul (tel: 511-4200).

Turkish International Co-operation Agency, Kizilirmak Cadessi 31, Kocatepe, Ankara (tel: 417-2790).

Turkiye Isveren Sendikalari Konfederasyonu (Turkish confederation of employers' unions), Mesrutiyet Caddesi 1/4-5, Bakanlikar, Ankara (tel: 418-3217).

Turkiye Radyo Televizyon Kurumu, Nevzat Tandogan Caddesi 2, Kavaklidere, Ankara (tel: 428-2230; fax: 414-2767).

Turk Snayicileri ve Isadamlari Dernegi (Turkish industrialists' and businessmen's association), Cumhuriyet Caddesi, 233/9-10 Harbiye, Istanbul (tel: 246-2412, 240-1205).

Embassy of the United States of America, 110 Ataturk Blvd, Ankara (tel: 426-5470, 468-6110; fax: 467-0057/19).

Ukraine

Marko Milivojevic

Five years after declaring an often nominal independence from the former Soviet Union in 1991, Ukraine's political and economic prospects remain uncertain. The conflict between parliament – dominated by left-wing parties opposed to socio-economic reform – and President Leonid Kuchma continued unabated in 1995/96. To further complicate matters, Kuchma was in worsening conflict with his prime minister, Yevenhii Marchuk ending in the Prime Minister's sacking in May 1996. On the economic front, Ukrainian GDP continued to decline in 1995, albeit at a lesser rate than in 1994. No real GDP growth is expected until 1997.

Political challenges

Elected to power on a reformist ticket in 1994, President Kuchma is confronted with the sort of political deadlock that destroyed his precursor, Leonid Kravchuk. This political instability has gravely weakened economic policy-making and other vitally important issues – particularly the final status of the disputed Crimea. In 1995, parliament failed to promulgate a new constitution for the Crimea.

Parliamentary obstruction delayed the promulgation of a new constitution based on strong presidential powers until June 1996. The final version gave new powers to the president, including the right to appoint cabinet members and the prime minister without parliamentary approval.

Kuchma vs Marchuk

President Kuchma's relations with Prime Minister Marchuk collapsed in 1995. Originally appointed to advance local economic reform, Marchuk later turned against Kuchma, his mentor, mainly by building himself an independent political base in parliament for the purpose of challenging Kuchma for the presidency in 1998. During the course of 1995, it emerged that Marchuk, and not Kuchma, was the most popular politician in Ukraine. At that time, Marchuk repeatedly charged that Kuchma had an inconsistent and ineffective approach to the key issue of economic reform. Within cabinet, two major reshuffles worsened the political confusion, with Kuchma alternately promoting and demoting reformers.

In May 1996, this culminated in the sacking of Marchuk. His replacement as prime minister, Pavlo Lazarenko, a former deputy premier, is a close associate of Kuchma and is not regarded as any sort of economic reformer. Kuchma's flagging popularity in 1995/96 then led him to promote anti-reform industrial and agricultural lobbies in government. The main adverse effect of this erosion of government credibility and authority was a major wave of strikes over unpaid wages in 1995/96 – thus raising the possibility of a general strike in Ukraine.

The independence question

Russian influence over Ukraine remains strong, notably in the area of energy supplies. Ukraine may not be able to avoid closer ties with Russia in the Commonwealth of Independent States (CIS), where a new Commonwealth of Sovereign States (SSR) was created in April 1996. One of its founding members was Belarus but Ukraine has so-far refused to join. The final division of the Black Sea Fleet (BSF) was agreed in 1995, but disputes still continue over the status of the Sevastapol naval base.

Although still relatively strong, western support for Ukrainian independence is by no means unconditional. The continued absence of real economic reform is a factor in this. Continued International Monetary Fund (IMF) and other foreign economic support is thus uncertain, with ominous implications for the country's balance of payments. The US is now the strongest supporter of Ukrainian independence and wider political considerations could bring about a more accommodating stance by the IMF and the European Union (EU).

In the eastern region of Ukraine, declining popular support for Ukrainian independence has been caused primarily by the country's economic decline. The growing political deadlock in Kiev has also revived latent secessionist sentiments in pro-Russian Crimea. Once partly checked by Kuchma's rapprochement with Russia in 1995, this trend could become more pronounced and further political instability in the Crimea cannot be discounted entirely. In the nationalist western

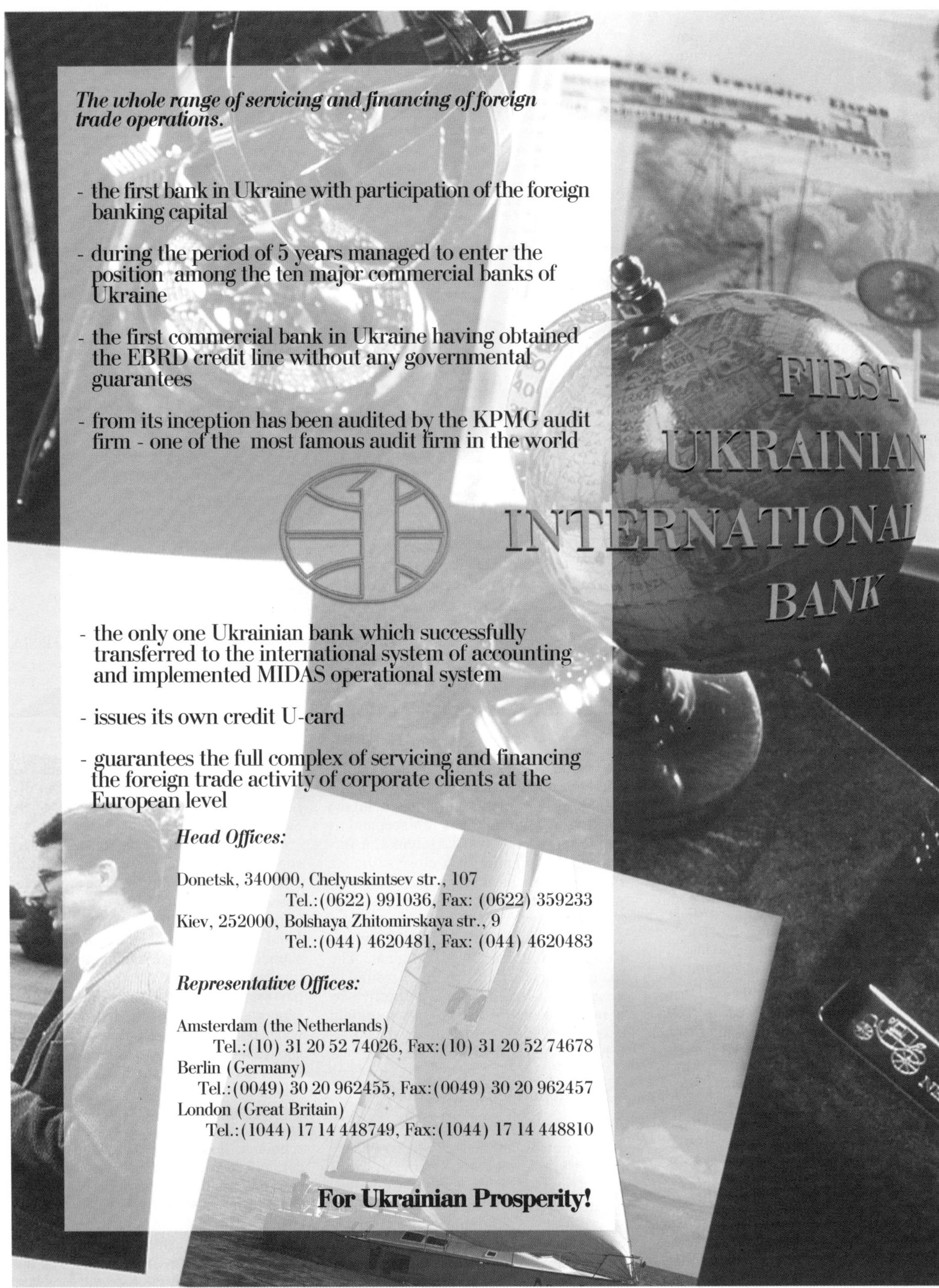

The whole range of servicing and financing of foreign trade operations.
- the first bank in Ukraine with participation of the foreign banking capital
- during the period of 5 years managed to enter the position among the ten major commercial banks of Ukraine
- the first commercial bank in Ukraine having obtained the EBRD credit line without any governmental guarantees
- from its inception has been audited by the KPMG audit firm - one of the most famous audit firm in the world
FIRST UKRAINIAN INTERNATIONAL BANK
- the only one Ukrainian bank which successfully transferred to the international system of accounting and implemented MIDAS operational system
- issues its own credit U-card
- guarantees the full complex of servicing and financing the foreign trade activity of corporate clients at the European level
Head Offices:
Donetsk, 340000, Chelyuskintsev str., 107
Tel.:(0622) 991036, Fax: (0622) 359233
Kiev, 252000, Bolshaya Zhitomirskaya str., 9
Tel.:(044) 4620481, Fax: (044) 4620483
Representative Offices:
Amsterdam (the Netherlands)
Tel.:(10) 31 20 52 74026, Fax:(10) 31 20 52 74678
Berlin (Germany)
Tel.:(0049) 30 20 962455, Fax:(0049) 30 20 962457
London (Great Britain)
Tel.:(1044) 17 14 448749, Fax:(1044) 17 14 448810
For Ukrainian Prosperity!

Ukraine, adverse political developments are also probable. At worst, these mutually contradictory centrifugal tendencies could split Ukraine in two.

After improving slightly in 1995, Ukrainian-Russian relations became more uncertain in 1996, mainly because of the presidential election campaign in Russia. This was mainly because President Boris Yeltsin could not be seen conceding anything of substance to Ukraine or any other CIS republic at a time when his communist opponents were demanding the restoration of another Russian empire in the former Soviet Union.

Russia is also actively discriminating against Ukrainian goods, thereby further aggravating Ukraine's foreign trade difficulties. Despite closer ties with the EU in 1995/96, Ukraine's dependence on Russia for most of its foreign trade is expected to continue well past 2000.

In 1995, a major territorial dispute broke out with Romania over Serpent Island in the Black Sea, a development that could abort an earlier Ukrainian-Romanian rapprochement over other issues in the region.

KEY FACTS

Official title: Republic of Ukraine

Head of state: President Leonid Kuchma (from 10 Jul 1994)

Head of government: Prime Minister Pavlo Lazarenko (from 28 May 1996)

Capital: Kiev

Official Languages: Ukrainian (Russian also widely spoken)

Currency: Hryvnia (H) introduced 2 Sep 1996; Karbovanets (Krb) (interim currency coupon) (plural Karbovantsi) introduced 16 Nov 1992 to be exchanged for hryvna at 16,023 special kiosks)

Exchange rate: H1.77 per US$ (Dec 1996)

Area: 603,700 sq km

Population: 51.44m (1995)

GDP per capita: US$600 (1995)

GDP real growth: -8.7% (1st half 1996); -11.8% (1995)

GNP per capita: U$1,570 (1994)

GNP real growth: -19% (1994)

Labour force: 26.6m (1994)

Unemployment: 1% (end1995)

Inflation: 7%+ (Feb 1996, monthly); 380% (1995)

Trade balance: US$400m (1995)

Foreign debt: US$9bn (1995)

Economy

Down by 23 per cent in 1994 (over 1993), Ukrainian GDP declined by less than half that, 11.8 per cent, in 1995. In 1996, GDP is expected to fall by only 2 per cent, followed by the first economic growth of the post-Soviet period in 1997. In 1995, nominal GDP and GDP per capita were US$30 billion and US$600 respectively. In 1995 real wages also rose for the first time since independence.

Because of the large size of the unofficial or black economy in Ukraine, actual GDP and GDP per capita were almost certainly larger than official figures suggested in 1995. The black economy may have accounted for anywhere between 30 per cent and 40 per cent of officially declared GDP. Local living standards remain relatively low even when compared to the rest of the CIS, let alone Europe more generally. Real incomes remain way below those of Russia. As in Russia, wage arrears remain high.

Industry

Accounting for 40 per cent of GDP in 1995 and still highly dependent on foreign trade with Russia, the Ukrainian industrial sector continues to decline, with total output down by a further 11.5 per cent in that year. As in 1994, particularly heavy output falls were registered in light manufacturing (34 per cent) and engineering (28 per cent), relatively higher added value sectors. Primary production and semi-manufactured goods registered lower output falls in 1995. One result of this has been a shift towards primary production in the Ukrainian industrial sector in recent years. Consisting of electricity, oil, gas, coal and steel, primary production accounted for 53 per cent of total industrial output in 1995, compared to 38 per cent in 1990.

Ukrainian manufactured goods have suffered greatly through the loss of former Soviet markets. At home, their generally low quality has made them vulnerable to imports from the EU, where such goods are also uncompetitive. Structurally, the Ukrainian industrial sector is in urgent need of radical reform if it is to move away from primary production towards more modern light manufacturing, food processing and consumer goods.

The industrial sector suffers from chronic energy shortages and energy supply payment arrears totalling Krb144 trillion (US$792 million) at the end of 1995. Formally rescheduled in March 1995, Ukrainian energy supply debts to Russia are in serious and growing arrears. Totalling over US$3 billion at the end of 1995, these may have to be renegotiated.

KEY INDICATORS — Ukraine

	Unit	1991	1992	1993	1994	1995
Population	m	51.94	52.15	52.18	52.91	51.44
Gross domestic product (GDP)	US$bn	–	20.0	15.0	26.5	30.0
GDP per capita	US$	–	400	300	550	600
GDP real growth	%	-11.9	-17.0	-14.2	-23.0	-11.8
Inflation	%	91	1,310	4,735	891	380
Employment	m	25.0	24.5	23.9	22.2	–
Agricultural output	%	–	-5	-10	-17	-30
Industrial output	%	–	-10	-15	-30	-11.5
Coal	m tonnes	135.6	133.7	115.7	94.6	83.6
Crude steel	'000 tonnes	44,995	41,759	32,347	24,081	22,309
Cement	'000 tonnes	21,745	20,121	14,991	11,435	7,621
Natural gas output	m cu metres	24,362	20,882	19,221	18,316	18,121
Crude petroleum output	'000 tonnes	4,993	4,474	4,248	4,198	4,010
Imports	US$bn	–	–	15.3	10.1	9.8
Exports	US$bn	–	–	12.8	10.2	10.2
Balance of trade	US$bn	–	–	-2.5	0.1	0.4
Current account	US$bn	–	–	-0.8	-1.4	-1.7
Hard currency reserves**	US$bn	–	–	0.5	0.7	1.0
Exchange rate	Krb per US$	–	241	12,610	108,855	179,497

** incl gold bullion holdings

Energy

In January 1996, Ukraine and Russia came to terms for the transit of Russian gas through local pipelines in 1996. Under the terms of this deal, Russia will supply US$800 million worth of gas to Ukraine and pay up to US$2 billion in transit fees for its own gas exports bound for western Europe, but this will not be enough to cover even half the US$6 billion worth of Russian oil and gas that Ukraine will require in 1996 alone. Domestically, the government increased the price of gas to 60 per cent of its cost price in January 1996, with further price hikes expected. Given the extent of outstanding energy payment arrears, it is unclear how these increased prices will be met by domestic customers.

While Ukraine hopes to renegotiate its outstanding energy supply debts to Russia, it is not at all clear whether the Russian government will agree to this without major concessions from the Ukrainian government in other areas of mutual interest. Foremost amonge these are debt for equity swaps, gas transit charges and possibly even Ukrainian membership of the new SSR grouping in the CIS. The Crimea is another area where Russia is now looking for further concessions from Ukraine.

The government remains committed to doubling the country's nuclear power generation capacity by 2000 as a way of overcoming difficulties with Russia over oil and gas supplies. In 1995, five nuclear power stations produced 36 per cent of the country's electricity output. Western governments are opposed to the expansion of nuclear power in Ukraine and, so far, the EU and G7 governments have only been willing to finance its replacement by safer electricity generation methods, beginning with Chernobyl.

Services

Accounting for around 30 per cent of GDP in 1995, mainly privately owned services remain the most dynamic component of the Ukrainian economy. Virtually all new job creation is now in private sector services, where retail and wholesale trade registered particularly high growth in 1995, mainly due to rising real wages. Because of the very slow pace of economic restructuring, Ukrainian unemployment remains very low at 1 per cent of the employed workforce at the end of 1995. Politically, fears of increased unemployment continue to inhibit real economic reform in Ukraine.

Financial stabilisation

In relation to the hyper-inflation of 1993, Ukrainian inflation continues to fall substantially, although it still remains high in absolute terms. In 1995, inflation was 380 per cent, compared to 891 per cent in 1994. Based on a restrictive monetary-credit policy by the National Bank of the Ukraine (NBU) dating back to September 1994, when a financial stabilisation programme was first agreed with the IMF, this declining inflation may fall to below 100 per cent year-end for the first time since 1991 in 1996.

Continued NBU off-budget outlays, fiscal imbalances and energy price rises meant that inflation did not fall as much as was expected in 1995. The year-end monthly inflation target of 2 per cent was not achieved by the end of 1995, when monthly inflation was just under 5 per cent. Continued wage growth in the state sector looked like producing a similar result in 1996.

The threat of a general strike in 1996 made it difficult for a weak government to resist inflationary pay awards, notably in the uneconomic coal mining sector. Following the increase of January 1996, pensions and other welfare payments are also rising in real terms, where any cuts in public spending have proved very difficult politically in recent years.

Budget deficit

In 1995, the government budget deficit reached Krb331 trillion (US$2.1 billion), or 8.1 per cent of GDP. Continued fiscal expansionism and lower than expected tax revenues meant that the budget deficit target of 7.3 per cent agreed with the IMF was exceeded. Overall, government expenditures (Krb1,772 trillion) and revenues (Krb1,441 trillion) remained at a very high 50 per cent of GDP in 1995.

Much of the government budget deficit in 1995 was covered by non-inflationary financing, notably foreign loans and treasury bonds. During the first half of 1995, the government budget deficit was only 6.4 per cent of GDP. The main positive outcome of this was a new US$1.5 billion stand-by loan facility with the IMF in June 1995. Disbursable in five tranches, this was indefinitely suspended by the IMF in January 1996, when three tranches of US$350 million each remained unpaid. The main reason for this was a higher than expected government budget deficit during the second half of 1995. Another issue at that time was the government's failure to set a credible budget for 1996.

With projected expenditures of Krb3,916 trillion and revenues of Krb2,558 trillion, this envisages a deficit of Krb427 trillion, or 6 per cent of expected GDP in 1996. Preceded by intense political wrangling, the budget's targets may not be achievable in 1996, mainly because of escalating wage and welfare costs in the state sector.

Even more than was the case in 1994/95, the 1996 budget deficit is to be financed by new foreign loans (US$1 billion), followed by government bonds (US$800 million) and NBU credits (US$600 million). The main difficulty here is that continued foreign borrowing for 1996 is now conditional on a new agreement worth around US$900 million in undisbursed credits. Without such an agreement, greater NBU monetary emission is inevitable, thereby making higher inflation almost certain in the future.

Another bout of local inflation further weakened the already precarious exchange rate of the karbovanets in 1995/96. Only partly stabilised at around Krb130,000-140,000 per US$ by late 1994, this exchange rate continued to slightly depreciate in 1995, when its annual average was around Krb160,000 per US$.

Ukraine finally replaced the 'temporary' karbovanets with a new national currency, the hyrvania, in September 1996. The hyrvania traded simultaneously with the karbovanets for two weeks, with citizens free to change any amount of the old currency for the new during that period. During its first two months the hyrvania remained steady at about 1.7 to the US$. However its value fell by 3.5 per cent in October and by 15 November 1996 was trading at 1.87 per US$. The depreciation was caused by the printing of money to pay for energy imports.

Banking

Following increased instability in the commercial banking sector in 1995, the NBU strengthened its regulatory activities in 1996. At the end of 1995, only 50 per cent of the country's 200 or so commercial banks had raised their capitalisation ratios to the minimum level set by the NBU in that year (US$1.3 million). Other troublesome areas include the high levels of non-performing assets in the indebted state industrial sector, bank illiquidity and a reluctance on the part of smaller banks to consolidate into larger and more viable units. Popular confidence in the integrity of local banks remains very low.

The state savings bank, Oshchadbank, which dominates the market, agreed to begin compensating depositors previously deprived of rouble accounts in 1992. Compensation is to be in the form of bonds denominated in karbovantsi and exchangeable for newly privatised shares. Following increased pressure from the IMF, restricted hard currency trading and foreign trade regulations were partly liberalised in 1995. This could bring with it the repatriation of illegally exported capital from foreign banks. Although up on 1994, local hard currency reserves remained relatively precarious at around US$1 billion at the end of 1995. Low NBU hard currency reserves are another major reason why Ukraine still lacks a proper national currency.

Privatisation

Originally envisaged to run in tandem with macro-economic stabilisation, more radical structural reform of the local economy continued to be avoided for essentially political reasons in 1995. Imposed by parliament and then rescinded by the Kuchma government in late 1994, a wholesale moratorium on any sort of large-scale privatisation remained in practice in 1995. During 1995, the government and the State Property Fund (SPF) agreed the disposal of 8,000 enterprises, but in the event only 2,700 were nominally privatised through insider-orientated manager-employee buyouts at a discount. Strong opposition in the Council of Peoples' Deputies (CPD) and the left-wing parties in the national parliament helped to slash these privatisation plans.

In November 1995, parliament voted to shift control of privatisation from the SPF to the CPD, although this contradicted earlier presidential decrees on the subject and the 1992 Privatisation Law. Concomitantly, parliament also voted against any further privatisation of the energy sector, where the state oil company, Ukrnafta, had been partly privatised earlier in 1995. However, it was announced in September 1996 that Ukraine plans to transform the oil and gas sectors into privatised, vertically integrated companies.

By the end of 1995 the SPF had privatised a record 13,000 enterprises. Totalling around 60,000 businesses and mainly located in the service sector, Ukraine's small enterprises should have been privatised by the end of 1994. In 1995, the SPT envisaged the disposal of 23,000 such enterprises, but only managed to sell off 58 per cent of this target figure. Among other things, this has limited the extent of the official private sector in Ukraine.

Political factors aside, Ukrainian privatisation has also been hindered by an inadequate legal framework. Popular apathy is also another major obstacle. As in other CIS republics, the lack of proper privatisation has created endless opportunities for insider corruption, discrediting the whole notion of privatisation among a jaded and indifferent populace.

Ukraine's poor privatisation record has been a major cause of concern for the IMF and the World Bank. In December 1995, when the government announced its economic programme for 1996, accelerated privatisation was said to be a key priority, but this claim had little credibility externally.

To complicate matters further, SPF privatisation is intimately bound up with relations with Russia. Agreed under IMF auspices in March 1995, when Ukraine rescheduled US$2.5 billion worth of energy supply debts to Russia, Russian debt for equity swaps have proved to be politically controversial in practice. One reason for this is that Russian interest in Ukrainian assets has been focused on the country's valuable energy sector. A casualty of this could be the Ukrainian-Russian joint venture, Gaztranzit, created in

COUNTRY PROFILE — UKRAINE

Historical profile

Eastern Ukraine was under the control of Moscow from 1918 to the country's independence from Russia in 1991. Parts of western Ukraine belonged to Poland during the inter-war years and the city of L'vov near the Slovak border formed part of the old Austro-Hungarian empire. Political power was transferred from the government of the former Soviet Union to Kiev after the failed coup of August 1991. As a result of a referendum in December 1991, this was followed by full independence and the recognition of Ukraine as an independent state by the international community.

Political system

A nationally elected presidency was instituted 1 December 1991. The 450-seat Supreme Council is the highest legislative body. Communists and allied parties were the main victors in legislative elections in March and April 1994, although nominally independent candidates performed extremely well. A former prime minister, Kuchma, was elected president on 10 July 1994. Kuchma had campaigned on a platform of gradual economic reform and closer links with Russia.
New constitution adopted 28 June 1996 by the *Verkhovna Rada* (Supreme Council) gives new power to the president including the right to nominate the prime minister.

Political parties

The following parties won seats in the 1994 elections: Communist Party, Peasants' Party (left-wing), Socialist Party of Ukraine, Inter-Regional Bloc for Reform (pro-reform, led by Leonid Kuchma), Party of the Democratic Rebirth of Ukraine, Civic Congress, Social Democracy Party of Ukraine, Labour Party, Christian Democratic Party, Rukh, Ukrainian Republican Party, Congress of Ukrainian Nationalists, Democratic Party of Ukraine, Ukrainian Self-Defence Organisation, Ukrainian Conservative Republican Party.

Population

Ukrainian (73%), Russian (22%), Belarus, Moldovan and Polish. Religion: Christianity (Ukrainian Orthodox, Autocephalous Orthodox, and Uniate (Eastern rite Catholic)).

Main cities/towns

Kiev (population 3.13m in 1994), Kharkov (1.6m), Odessa (1.2m), Kharkov, Dnepropetrovsk (1.2m), L'vov (790,000).

Language

Few Ukrainians speak German, English or French. The further east you go, the more likely it is that people will speak Russian. Ukrainian, Polish and German are spoken more widely in western Ukraine.

Media

Dailies: Main dailies include *Golos Ukraine, Kievski Vedomosti, Pravda Ukraini, Vseukrainskie Ved* and *Vecerni Kiev.*
Weeklies: Main weekly is *Kievski Novosti.*
Radio: BBC World Service launched its first Ukrainian radio service in June 1992, with daily half-hour bulletins, featuring news and current affairs. The programmes are broadcast on short-wave radio at 2100 local time (1800 GMT). The broadcasts will increase to one hour a day.
Advertising: The total Ukraine advertising market is expected to grow to US$35m in 1996 from US$15m in 1995, with television advertising rising to US$20m by end-1996, from US$9m in 1995.

Domestic economy

Ukraine suffered a severe economic crisis between 1990 and 1994. The outlook improved in 1995, with the rate of decline slowing, and the unofficial economy thriving.
Initially Ukraine gave priority to protecting industry and jobs at the expense of economic reform. However, President Kuchma provided a new direction to economic policy-making and reform is under way although there has been limited progress on privatisation, which has been a major cause of concern for the IMF and the World Bank.
The government has greatly increased most energy and agricultural prices, communal tariffs and rents in real terms, and is pushing ahead with further price liberalisation.
In 1995, real wages rose for the first time since independence was declared, but remain way below those of Russia, with high wage arrears. The black economy in Ukraine may have accounted for between 30 and 40 per cent of officially declared GDP in 1995.

External trade

Barter trade is permitted where a licence has been obtained. A decree published on 18 May 1993 removes quotas and licences for all exports except agricultural products, chemicals and coal. The government considers restoring trade links with former Soviet republics is a priority. The EU ratified 10-year partnership and co-operation agreement with Ukraine December 1995.
Ukraine's foreign trade performance remains in difficulty. Total nominal foreign trade turnover in 1995 was about US$20bn, or around two-thirds of officially declared GDP, with exports stagnant, amounting to around US$10.2bn in 1994 and 1995.
Exports: Main destinations: Germany, Italy, USA, France, UK, Canada, EU.
Main exports include coal, iron ore, machinery and manganese ore.
Imports: Imports totalled US$9.8 billion in 1995. Main sources: Italy, Germany, USA, France, UK, Canada, EU.
Main imports include oil, timber, machinery and laboratory/scientific equipment.

Agriculture

The agricultural sector accounted for 30 per cent of GDP in 1995 and employed 19 per cent of the workforce. The agricultural sector, despite Ukraine's rich land resources, has been in decline for several years as a result of general inefficiency, late payments and a lack of finance for fuel, fertilisers and machinery.
Historically known as the bread basket of the former USSR, Ukraine produced 18 per cent of the total Soviet agricultural output including 33

1995 using privatised local assets as part of its start-up capital. Politically, any reimposition of direct Russian control over Ukrainian pipeline networks, gas reserves and other valuable assets is strongly opposed by nationalists in western Ukraine.

Agriculture

Agriculture accounted for 30 per cent of GDP in 1995, and remains of vital economic importance in Ukraine. However, agricultural output continues to decline, with 1995 the worst year on record since independence. Output fell by 30 per cent in 1995, compared to a 17 per cent fall in 1994. One result of this has been a rapid rise in imports of foodstuffs. Apart from the adverse weather conditions of 1995, the major structural causes of this decline are slow land reform, low investment and energy shortages. Externally, continued state subsidies to the agricultural and industrial sectors are one of the major causes of Ukraine's difficulties with the IMF.

Land reform remains seriously incomplete in Ukraine. Introduced in 1995, a new government land code designed to speed up rural privatisation was finally rejected in a key parliamentary vote in November 1995.

The government is trying increasingly to keep the favour of the country's powerful agricultural lobby, particularly by waiving all tax on rural incomes paid in kind in 1995. Direct and indirect state subsidies for the agricultural sector are substantial and the government may reimpose tariffs on foodstuff imports. In January 1996, administrative controls for certain foodstuffs were reimposed. The government plans to create a new State Committee for Land Resources, but it remains unclear how this will help matters locally.

Foreign trade

Although official figures continue to be contradictory on this question, Ukraine's foreign trade performance seems set to remain in difficulties for many years to come. In 1995 total nominal foreign trade turnover was around US$20 billion, around two-thirds of officially declared GDP. At around US$10.2 billion in both 1994 and 1995, exports are stagnant.

However, more exports were sold for hard currency outside the CIS in 1995 than in 1994. Exports to Russia in particular continue to decline, falling to 45 per cent of the total in 1995 from 55 per cent in 1994. Barter trade with the rest of the CIS remained substantial at around 35 per cent of the total value of goods exported. Unofficially, large-scale cross-border barter trade is almost certainly far higher than suggested by official figures, particularly in relation to imports from Russia.

On the imports side, payments difficulties led imports to fall to around US$9.8 billion in 1995 from US$10.1 billion in 1994. Even more than was the case in 1994, Ukrainian imports of energy supplies from Russia continued to decline in 1995. In 1995, imports from Russia and the rest of the CIS accounted for 52 per cent of the total, compared to around two-thirds of the total in 1994. Imports from the EU continued to rise.

Exports continue to shift from higher added value manufactured goods in favour of lower value primary production, semi-manufactures and raw materials, notably in relation to

COUNTRY PROFILE — UKRAINE

Agriculture (contd): per cent of the vegetables, 20 per cent of the grain and 60 per cent of the sugar beet. Livestock is reared. The main agricultural products are wheat, barley, potatoes, sugar beet and flax.
Agriculture food processing is of vital economic importance. However, agricultural output continued to decline by 30 per cent in 1995, compared to a fall of 17 per cent in 1994.

Industry

The industrial sector accounted for 40 per cent of GDP in 1995 and employed 37 per cent of the workforce. Having been heavily industrialised while part of the former Soviet Union, Ukraine inherited a decaying and outdated capital stock in desperate need of restructuring.
The industrial sector continued to decline in 1995 by a further 11.5 per cent. Ukrainian manufactured goods were previously exported mainly to Russia, and as a consequence of losing this market, have suffered greatly. Ukrainian industry is in urgent need of reform and needs to move away from primary production towards modern light manufacturing, food processing and consumer goods. The local industrial sector suffers from chronic energy shortages.

Mining

The mining and hydrocarbons sector accounted for 10 per cent of GNP in 1993 and employed 3 per cent of the workforce. Rich in mineral deposits, including iron ore, manganese ore, mercury, titanium and nickel. Ukraine produced 50 per cent of the iron ore of the former USSR and 40 per cent of world manganese ore.

Hydrocarbons

Ukraine, the second-largest oil refining republic in the region after Russia, has seven refineries with a total capacity of 1.24m bpd – Lischansk, Kremenchug, Kherson, Odessa, Drogobych, Nadvornaya, and L'viv. Lischansk refinery is fed by west Siberian crude arriving from Kuybyshev by pipeline. The Ukrainian refineries refine all crude from the western and eastern Ukraine, plus Volga-Ural crudes, west Siberian, and some Mangysshlak and Turkmen crudes. Ukrainian refineries have the highest percentage capacity utilisation in the region (at 98 per cent), and products are consumed mostly by the domestic market.
In February 1993 Iran signed a deal with Ukraine to supply four million tonnes of oil a year and jointly build a gas pipeline between the two countries.
The price of Russian oil increased by 3,000 per cent over 1992 and Russia announced in February 1993 that Ukraine would get only 15m tonnes of oil in 1993, less than half that of 1992.
A joint stock Hermes-Dnieper oil company was set up in February 1993 to provide for oil purchase and delivery from Russia to Ukraine.
Russia reduced its gas supplies to Ukraine by more than a half in August 1993 because the republic had failed to pay for previous deliveries.
Natural gas production 15.2m tonnes of oil equivalent in 1995, down 0.5 per cent on 1994 output. Natural gas reserves 1.1 trillion cu metres (end-1995). Gas deposits were discovered in the Lugansk region of eastern Ukraine in December 1995.
Coal production 42.8m tonnes of oil equivalent in 1995, down by 11.9 per cent on 1994 production.
Oil reserves 1.05bn tonnes in 1996, with domestic annual crude demand standing at between 15 and 20m tonnes; Ukraine expected to import 12m tonnes of oil in 1996.
The state oil company, Ikrnafta, was partly privatised in 1995. It was announced in September 1996 that Ukraine has plans to transform its state-run oil and gas sectors into privatised, vertically integrated companies.

Energy

Ukraine was heavily dependent on imports of Russian oil and gas to meet its energy needs. As Russia began to phase out its subsidies on energy supplies, Ukraine suffered a considerable deterioration in its terms of trade and built up large debts with Russia.
Ukraine's energy sector is going bankrupt as a result of a large number of defaulting customers. The country's coal stocks are dangerously low. A total of 50 loss-making coal mines are to close.
In September 1995 the Ukrainian government set up a body within the Ministry of Environment and Nuclear Safety to monitor safety precautions at nuclear power plants, nuclear waste storage sites, and nuclear fuel production facilities. The government is committed to doubling the country's nuclear power generating capacity by 2000 to overcome difficulties with Russia over oil and gas supplies.
In 1995, Ukraine's five nuclear power stations produced 36 per cent of the electricity output.
State-owned company, Enerhoatom, was established in September 1996 to oversee all five nuclear power plants and to manage foreign aid for shutting down Chernobyl nuclear power station.

Banking

A two-tier banking system is being established. There are 114 banks, 25 licensed to deal in foreign currency.

Financial markets

Although the Ukraine Stock Exchange, founded in 1991, is the most regulated and centralised trading system in Ukraine, no independent and transparent share registration and share custody exists and the rights of minority shareholders are not protected. The creation of a state committee to regulate the securities market was decreed in June 1995. The stock exchange also trades investment certificates of investment funds. The average daily trading volume in mid-1995 was US$3,000.
At the beginning of 1995 there were 91 exchanges operating in Ukraine, 14 trading in stocks, four in real estate and the remainder in commodities, with trading concentrated in Kiev. The majority of trade took place through an unregulated over-the-counter market.

Membership of international organisations

Council of Europe, CSCE, IAEA, IFC, IMF, NACC, Partnerships for Peace, World Bank. Ukraine has requested to join the WTO.

the EU. Non-energy imports, on the other hand, continue to be dominated by higher value manufactures from the EU. Another negative trend is higher foodstuff and consumer goods imports in recent years.

After lower imports in 1995, Ukraine's foreign trade balance in that year was officially US$400 million. Unofficially it may have been in growing deficit. In relation to the rest of the CIS, the total trade deficit was US$1.1 billion in 1995. Although an improvement over 1994, when the deficit with the rest of the CIS was US$1.7 billion, this large foreign trade imbalance with Russia in particular is Ukraine's main foreign trade difficulty.

Mainly covered by barter transfers, more of this deficit has had to be financed with hard currency in recent years. Payment difficulties and mutually non-convertible national currencies have hurt Ukrainian trade with the rest of the CIS.

Outside the CIS, where Ukraine now runs a trade surplus with the EU, the country's terms of trade continued to improve in 1995, mainly because of lower imports. So far, however, Ukraine has made relatively little progress in decisively shifting its foreign trade away from the CIS and towards the EU.

On the current account, high foreign debt servicing outlays, including those payable to Russia for past energy supplies, resulted in a record deficit of US$1.7 billion in 1995. In 1995, service income was also less than expected, notably for gas transit fees from Russia. Ukraine has demanded higher gas transit fees, but may not get them due to continued Russian leverage over energy supplies and debts.

Ukraine's difficulties with the IMF led to lower than expected capital inflows from abroad in 1995/96. Foreign direct investment (FDI) also remained relatively low at around US$600 million at the end of 1995. On a more positive note, the US$2.7 billion pledged by the EU and the G7 for the replacement of the nuclear power facilities at Chernobyl will help to strengthen Ukraine's capital account over the next five years.

Foreign debt and payments

Including outstanding and more recent energy supply debts to Russia, Ukraine's total foreign debt at the end of 1995 was around US$9 billion, 50 per cent higher than the US$6 billion at the end of 1994. Totalling US$3.5 billion at the end of 1994, energy supply debts to Russia and other CIS states reached nearly US$5 billion by the end of 1995. Despite rescheduling US$2.5 billion worth of energy supply debts to Russia under IMF auspices in March 1995, Ukraine has been unable to meet many of its debt servicing obligations to Russia.

Because of its difficulties with the IMF in 1995/96, Ukraine's new foreign borrowings outside the CIS have been less than expected over the last year or so. As of January 1996, less than half of the US$1.5 billion provided by the IMF in June 1995 had actually been disbursed. Similar difficulties attended the disbursement of a related US$500 million loan package from the World Bank. Worth up to US$2 billion in total, the complete disbursement of these loans is dependent on another agreement with the IMF.

Other than the IMF and the World Bank,

BUSINESS GUIDE — UKRAINE

Time

GMT + 2 hrs (GMT + 3 hrs from late Mar to late Sep).

Climate

Average temperature in Kiev: 20 degrees C (July), -7 degrees C (January). Average temperature in L'vov: 16 degrees C (July), -5 degrees C (January).

Entry requirements

Passport: Passport required by all.
Visa: Visas valid for one month. Tourists must obtain visas from embassies in advance. Visas will only be issued on arrival to passengers travelling for business purposes for a fee of US$150 on presentation of a letter of invitation from an organisation in Ukraine. Although business visas are available at Borispol airport (Kiev), long queues are generally encountered. Visas are required for visitors holding passports from the following countries: USA, Canada, UK, Germany, France, Italy, Austria, Switzerland, Sweden, Norway, Finland. If child's name appears on passport of parent, it must also appear on the visa of that parent. If visiting relatives in Ukraine, passengers must register with local police on arrival.
Customs: Small amount of personal goods duty-free. On arrival declare all foreign currency and valuable items such as jewellery, cameras, computers and musical instruments.

Health precautions

Mandatory: Vaccination certificates are required for cholera or yellow fever if travelling from an infected area. An HIV (AIDS) test is required for long-stay visitors only. A UK-issued certificate is usually accepted.
Advisable: Water precautions recommended (water purification tablets may be useful). It is advisable to be 'in date' for the following immunisations: polio (within 10 years), tetanus (within 10 years), typhoid fever, cholera (within six months), hepatitis 'A' (moderate risk only). There has been a significant increase in the number of cases of diphtheria. While the low dose, adult booster is unavailable, travellers are advised to be boosted with a reduced dose (0.1ml) of the paediatric single antigen vaccine. If never immunised, use three dose course of the vaccine. Any medicines required by the traveller should be taken by the visitor, and it could be wise to have precautionary antibiotics if going outside major urban centres. A travel kit including a disposable syringe is a reasonable precaution.

Air access

National airlines: Air Ukraine; Ukraine International – a joint-venture airline between Guinness Peat Aviation (GPA), the Irish aircraft leasing company, and Air Ukraine, Ukraine's national carrier, formed in September 1992.
Other airlines: Aeroflot, Air France, Austrian Airlines, Balkan Bulgarian Airlines, Belavia, Czecho Airlines (CSA), Egyptair, Estonian Air, Finnair, KLM, Lithuanian Airlines, LOT, Lufthansa, Malev, SAS, Swissair, Transaero, Turkish Airlines.
International airport: Kiev (KBP (Borispol), 27 km from city centre, duty-free and tax-free shops. There are plans to renovate the airport. It is highly advisable to be met at the airport, because few taxis wait there and hardly any drivers understand German or English.
Airports: Zhulhany Airport (domestic flights), 11 km from Kiev; L'vov Airport, 7 km from city centre.

Surface access

Main ports: The Ukraine has developed sea and river transportation systems, with the largest ports located on the Black Sea (Odessa, Ilyichovsk and Nikolaev) which handle bulk cargo and container traffic. Ukraine is planning to establish a 40-vessel oil tanker fleet with a terminal near Odessa as a long-term means to meet its energy needs.

Hotels

Hotels: Kiev has a shortage of hotels. Western-standard hotels do not exist. It is worth booking rooms several weeks in advance through Intourist.

Currency

It is possible to withdraw money from automated teller machines in Kiev, using cards belonging to the leading western networks. Bring unmarked US dollar bills (printed after 1991) for travel to more obscure regions.

Credit cards

Credit cards are accepted in a few hotels.

City transport

Taxis: Borispol Airport downtown approximately US$30; Odessa Airport downtown approximately US$15-20 (June 1996).

National transport

Road and rail: Extensive road and rail network with major centres at L'viv, Kiev and Kharkov.

Public holidays

Fixed dates: 1 Jan (New Year's Day), 7 Jan (Orthodox Christmas), 8 Mar (International Women's Day), 1 & 2 May (International Workers' Solidarity Day), 9 May (Victory Day), 24 Aug (Independence Day), 7 & 8 Nov (former Anniversary of the October Revolution).
Variable dates: Orthodox Easter (Sun & Mon), Orthodox Holy Trinity (Sun & Mon).

Working hours

Business: (Mon–Fri) 0900 – 1800.
Banking: Open 24 hours at Kiev Borispol airport. (Mon-Fri) 1000–1700, service sometimes only until noon, at Odessa airport.
Shops: (Mon) 0800 – 1900, (Tue–Sat) 0800 – 2100.

Telecommunications

Telephone and telefax: Dialling code for the Ukraine: IDD access code + 380 followed by area code (44 for Kiev, 57 for Kharkov, 48 for Odessa), followed by subscriber's number. N.B. It is difficult to get through to Kiev in business hours and it is advisable to book a call through the operator.

a number of other official creditors have also recently agreed to increase their lending to Ukraine. These include a US$130 million loan from the European Bank for Reconstruction and Development (EBRD); a US$230 million trade credit from Japan's Export-Import Bank; and US$225 million worth of foreign aid credits from the US government.

The political importance of Ukraine to the US is reflected in the fact that it is now the largest single recipient of US foreign aid in the CIS. Having recently entered into closer relations with the EU, Ukraine may also be eligible for increased loans from the European Investment Bank in due course. Of the US$2.3 billion provided for the replacement of the Chernobyl nuclear facilities over the next five years, the EU is by far the largest contributor in the G7. Within the EU, the largest single official creditor of the EU is Germany, followed by France and the UK.

FDI

Foreign direct investment in Ukraine remains relatively limited. However, 1995 was the best year yet for new FDI. Totalling US$350 million at the end of 1994, FDI increased by US$250 million to a total of US$600 million by the end of 1995.

In 1996, the government was hoping to see new FDI of up to US$350 million, mainly through more generous tax incentives for foreign investors. In order to better co-ordinate future FDI inflows, the government has created a new Ukrainian Credit and Investment Company. By countries of origin, most FDI in Ukraine has been from the US, followed by Germany and France. Sectorally, FDI has so far been concentrated in food-processing, services and light manufacturing. Other promising areas for increased FDI include energy, notably offshore in the Black Sea. The Ukrainian energy sector is also of interest to Russian investors.

Outlook

Despite increased hopes of more radical political and economic reform, this did not happen in practice. As a result, considerable uncertainty surrounds the political and economic future of Ukraine.

The conflict between parliament and Kuchma continues, with matters further complicated by a divided cabinet. The result of this has been inconsistent and ineffective policy making. At worst, all this could lead Ukraine back to the political paralysis of the early 1990s.

Regionally, the Crimean issue and the east-west division of Ukraine remain unresolved and the future course of Ukrainian-Russian relations is becoming more uncertain. Closer Ukrainian relations with Russia may be unavoidable in the longer-term.

Beyond the CIS, western support for Ukraine is not unconditional and is being compromised by its economic failings; the IMF will want to see some substantial improvements before it continues to support the country. In the longer term, radical economic reform is as unavoidable in Ukraine as in the rest of the CIS, but it remains unclear and uncertain as to how this will be done, when and with what consequences.

BUSINESS GUIDE — UKRAINE

Banking

Central bank: National Bank of the Ukraine.

Useful tips

Knowing both Russian and Ukrainian and when to use the language is vital. Small efforts to speak Ukrainian in the west of the country will be appreciated. In the east, Russian is used. Extreme deference is shown to those in authority by people in junior positions.
Do carry some form of identity at all times.

BUSINESS DIRECTORY

Hotels

Kiev

Dnipro, Leninsky Komsomol 1 (tel: 229-8287; fax: 229-8213).

Hreshchatik, Hreshchatik 14 (tel: 229-7339).

Intourist, 12 Gospitalnaya (tel: 220-4144).

Kijewskaja, Ul Gospitalnaja 12 (tel: 220-4624; fax: 220-4568).

Lybid, Victory Sq, 252163 (tel: 272-0063, 274-4261).

Moskva, 4 October Revolution St (tel: 229-2804).

National, Vul Rozi Luxembourg 5 (tel: 291-8888; fax: 291-5468).

Russ, 4 Gospitalnaya, 252023 (tel: 220-5122; fax: 220-4396).

Salyut, Vul Sichnevogo, Povstannya 11a (tel 290-2044).

Ukraina, 5 Shevchenko Blvd (tel: 229-8464).

Odessa

Krasnaya, Pushkinskaia Ulitsa 15 (tel: 227-220; tx: 232132).

Londonskaya, Primorski Bulvar 11 (tel: 225-019; fax: 255-370).

Ship 'Shevshenko', Port Ul Suvorova 2 (tel: 245-112; fax: 223-360).

Car hire

Kiev

No international car rental representations, local companies only.

Academic/research institutes

The Ukraine has large scientific and educational centres in Kiev, Odessa, Lvov, Kharkov and Donetzk with more than 200 higher educational institutes. There are ten full university campuses.

Chambers of commerce

Kiev Chamber of Commerce and Industry (Kievvneshservice), Velyka Zhytomyrska, 254601 Kiev (tel: 212-2958; fax: 228-2477).

Ukrainian Chamber of Commerce and Industry, 33 Bolshaya Zhitomirskaya St, 254601 Kiev (tel: 212-2911/2804; fax: 212-3353).

Banking

Aggio Joint Stock Bank, Leskova Str 9, 252011 Kiev (tel: 295-0305; fax 295-3164).

Commercial Bank (Ekspobank), Volodarskogo Street 2-4, 254025 Kiev (tel: 216-1676; fax: 216-6073).

First Ukrainian International Bank, Lipskaya St 3, Suite 3, 25202 Kiev (tel: 291-8741; fax: 293-2064).

Gradobank, 1 Dimitrova Str, 252650 Kiev (tel: 261-9191; fax: 268-1530).

Inki Bank, 10/2 Mechnikova ul, 252023 Kiev (tel: 294-9219; fax: 290-6292).

National Bank of the Ukraine (central bank), Institutskaya ul 9 (formerly Zhovtnevoji Revolyutsiji), 252007 Kiev (tel: 293-4264, 226-2914; fax: 293-1698).

Ukreximbank, 8 Kreshchatik Str, Kiev (tel: 226-33 63; fax: 229-8082).

Ukrainian Bank for Foreign Economic Affairs, Kreshchatik ul 8, 252001 Kiev (tel: 293-1698).

Ukrainian Financial Group Joint Stock Commercial Bank, 7 Vokzalnaya St, 252032 Kiev (tel: 245-4560; fax: 245-4587).

Travel information

Borispol Airport, Kiev (tel: 296-7454, 212-2592).

International Touristic Corporation, Golden Shore, Nahimov Prospekt 4, 335000 Sevastopol, Crimea (tel: 524-114, 523-001; fax: 523-213).

Intourist, 5 Druzhba Narodov Blvd, Kiev (tel: 268-9096).

Ukrintour (tourism association), Yaroslaviv Val ul 36, 252034 Kiev (tel: 212-5570; fax: 212-4524).

Other useful addresses

British Embassy, 9 Desyatinna, 252025 Kiev (tel: 229-1287, 228-0504; fax: 228-3972).

Foreign Trade Organisation (UKRIMPEX), ul Vorovskogo 22, 252054 Kiev (tel: 216-4296; fax: 216-1926).

Ministry of Finance, Hrushevski ul 12-2, 252008 Kiev (tel: 226-2062).

Ministry of Foreign Affairs, Karla Libknekhta ul 15-1, 252024 Kiev (tel: 226-3379; fax: 293-6950).

Ministry of Foreign Economic Relations, 8 Lvivska Sg, GSP 655, 254655 Kiev (tel: 226-2733; fax: 212-5202).

Ministry of Information, Prorizna ul 2, 252601 Kiev (tel: 226-2871).

Ministry of Statistics, 3 Shota Rustaveli Avenue, Kiev 23 252601 (tel: 226-2021; fax: 227-6611).

Ministry of Telecommunications, Kreshchatik ul 26, 252001 Kiev (tel: 226-3144, 221-1898).

Ukrainian Exchange (commodities and stock exchange), Proreznaya ul 15, 252601 Kiev (tel: 228-6481; fax: 229-6376).

Ukrainian League of Industrialists and Entrepreneurs, 34 Kreshchatik str, 252001 Kiev (tel: 229-7480; fax: 226-3152).

Ukrainian National News Agency (UKRINFORM), 8-16b Khemlnitski St, 252601 Kiev (tel: 226-2469, 229-0143; fax: 229-2439/8007, 228-1659).

UKRINTERENERGO State Foreign Trade Company, Komintern st 27, 252032 Kiev (tel: 291-7296; fax: 220-1885).

United Kingdom

Bob Jiggins

Late 1996 saw Britain in the grip of pre-election fever, with less than six months left before the government has to call a general election. The 20 per cent or so lead that the Labour Party has established in the opinion polls looks unlikely to be much reduced and a victory by that party is probable. Events in 1996 have done much to reduce John Major's Conservative Party's credibility, particularly the Scott Report into arms sales to Iraq and the mismanaged scare over BSE. Resignations over the sexual antics of some Conservative ministers and the 'cash for questions' affair have also caused controversy, but despite the damage done by the so-called 'sleaze factor' it is unlikely to remain at the forefront of the minds of the electorate.

KEY FACTS — United Kingdom

Official title: The United Kingdom of Great Britain and Northern Ireland (UK)

Head of state: Queen Elizabeth II

Head of government: Prime Minister John Major

Ruling party: Conservative Party

Capital: London

Official Languages: English (English and Welsh in Wales)

Currency: UK Pound (£) = 100 pence

Exchange rate: £0.65 per US$ (Dec 1996)

Area: 244,103 sq km

Population: 58.4m (1995)

GDP per capita: US$16,304 (1995)

GDP real growth: 2.3% (3rd qtr 1996)

Unemployment: 7.2% (Oct 1996)

Inflation: 2.7% (Oct 1996) (annual headline rate)

Oil reserves: 4.3bn barrels (end-1995)

Trade balance: US$20.3m (12 months to Sep 1996)

Visitor numbers: 11.6m (1st half 1996); 24m (1995)

Politics

The release of the Scott Report into the 'arms for Iraq' scandal caused much political controversy; as no minister resigned over the affair, the Conservative government's already tarnished reputation for honesty in public affairs appeared further damaged. The government seemed to have escaped too much approbation, however, as the report was, in certain parts, ambiguous. It was clear, however, that individual ministers were guilty of misleading parliament in relation to the covert changing of the guidelines-interpretation relating to arms sales abroad.

More importantly perhaps for the government's chances of re-election is the scandal over the BSE crisis. The government admitted in March 1996, after much prevarication, that Creutzfeldt-Jakob Disease (CJD) in humans may be caused by the consumption of beef cattle infected with Bovine Spongiform Encephalopathy (BSE) – otherwise known as 'mad cow disease'. The problem stems from the agricultural policies pursued after the Second World War, where government policy was to produce as much food as possible at the least cost. This industrialisation of farming has led to the situation where sterilisation of animal feed in the early 1980s was changed to a cheaper system. By 1986 the first case of BSE was identified with the suspicion that feed made from sheep infected with scrapie (a disease common in sheep) was the cause. Although it was thought that scrapie could not pass between species, it appears that BSE is very similar to it, and this has given rise to the fear that BSE in turn can be passed onto humans in the form of CJD.

The government reacted with tardiness to the scientific evidence, and only after 18 months did it offer limited compensation to farmers which did little to encourage them to declare infected cattle; the feed was not banned until 1988. It took until early 1996 for the government to admit that BSE could be passed to humans, and take preventative action. The widespread quotation of the government's own Chief Scientific Advisor that he would not feed any beef to his children further embarrassed the government. The result was a near-total collapse of the domestic beef market, and the global banning of beef exports from the UK by the European Union (EU). As a result of pressure from both the EU and domestic consumers, the government introduced new measures, including the progressive slaughter of beef cattle. As of June 1996, these were not rigorous enough for the EU, and it is likely that further measures would have to be taken – perhaps the slaughter of the entire UK herd.

Whatever is done, reduced confidence both in the UK and abroad is unlikely to return demand to its previous level, which was anyway reducing as consumers have been switching towards perceived healthier food options. The government's response to pressure from the EU was a policy of 'non-co-operation' with the EU, in an attempt to reverse the world-wide ban. This involved the use of the veto at EU meetings, and was widely regarded by business organisations as damaging the interests of both the UK and the EU. The Confederation of British Industry (CBI), and some government ministers, were particularly critical of this approach.

These factors bade ill for the Conservative government in the run-up to the election as it

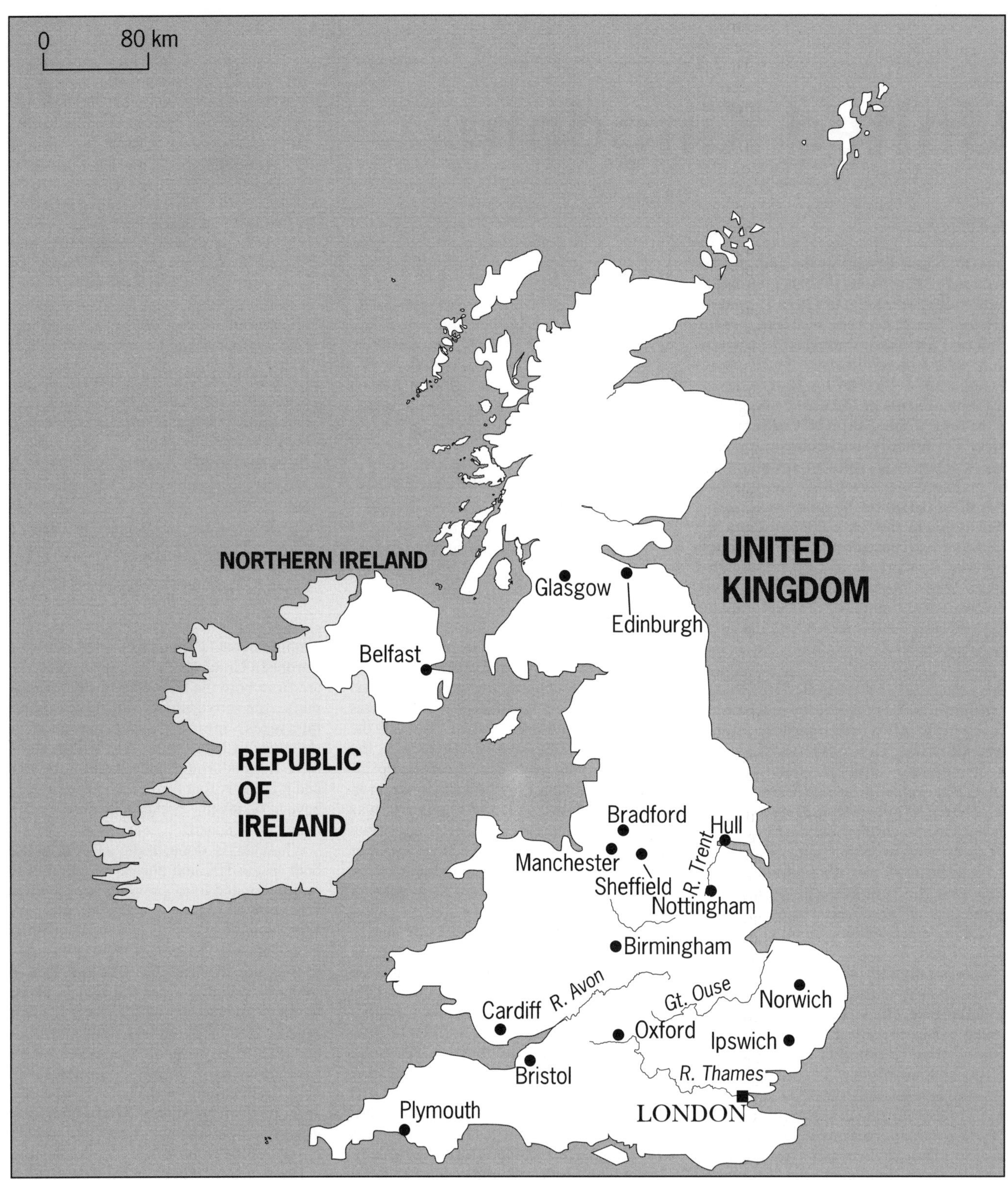

lagged 20 per cent behind Tony Blair's Labour Party. The 1997 election however will see little of substance between the major parties – especially the two main contenders. The Labour Party has to date said little regarding its future policy in any field, especially taxation.

Certainly there are differences between the two main contenders, but the Labour Party (in its bid to become more electable) is jettisoning large parts of its socialist ideology in favour of the more elusive concepts of 'stake-holding' and communitarianism. It remains more interventionist and publicly orientated than the Conservatives, and is certainly better disposed towards the EU, but these are hardly differences of which electoral choice is made. In many respects, British politics is rapidly becoming a mirror image of politics in the USA, both in terms of style and content.

Moderate recovery

In general terms the economy is performing well, although still characterised by the fundamental weakness of low investment in manufacturing industry. This is one area which the Labour Party has indicated it will tackle, although whether this will become policy (and more to the point, effective policy) is open to question.

Growth bumped along at a steady 0.4 per cent per quarter for most of 1995; the cause of this has largely been domestic consumption within the private, rather than public sector. However, even private consumption has remained somewhat subdued largely as a result of increased disposable income being placed into savings, rather than consumption; the general depression in the housing market; and changes in the nature of employment. For the whole of 1995, GDP growth was at a moderate 2.4 per cent, with private and public consumption rising by 2.3 per cent and 0.9 per cent respectively.

Investment, a long standing problem of the UK economy, was at a very low level in 1995. Real industrial investment grew by a mere 0.2 per cent, although manufacturing accounted for 7.6 per cent. Other sectors though account for very low levels – especially housing, capital investment by the government is falling. This lack of investment is something which has characterised the UK economy for many years. Manufacturing (rather than trade) has always been a secondary concern for government, and as an institution the City of London is considerably more influential than the CBI. As a result, the UK's industrial base is considerably more outdated than most of its competitors, a fact reflected in poor productivity growth rates.

The problem lies in the fact that the rates of return demanded by investors are high in comparison with similar economies, and opportunities for higher rates are often to be found abroad in the Newly Industrialising Countries (NIC's). Furthermore, the 'short-termism' of British financial institutions compares badly with the more long-term infra-structural approach of similar bodies in Germany and Japan.

With little investment in industry, services are the main growth sector, with the 1995 annual output figure some 3 per cent higher than for the preceding year. Industrial output has been erratic, but slowed somewhat over the course of 1995.

Unemployment is still falling and has done so for two years, albeit at a slower rate than previously. Figures for October 1996 indicate that some 7.2 per cent of the workforce are registered as unemployed. Numerous changes have been made to the way in which the figures are compiled and benefit eligibility established since 1979. If unemployment was still measured as it was when the current government came to power in that year, then various estimates would put the final figure between 9 and 14 per cent. Using International Labour Office (ILO) criteria (which produces internationally comparable data) the figure would have been perhaps 8.4 per cent.

Inflation, as measured by the rate of annual increase in the Retail Price Index (RPI), has declined steadily since its peak of 3.7 per cent in the third quarter of 1995 to 2.8 per cent in the first two months of 1996. Other measurements of inflation, however, show increases. The index excluding mortgage interest payments (RPIX) has been steady at 2.9 per cent since the third quarter of 1995, having risen from a low of 2.2 per cent in the final quarter of 1994. However, both year-on-year producer prices and wage inflation have fallen in 1996. By January 1996, wages had risen by only 3 per cent, a rate of increase lower than for most of 1995. Differences have, however, emerged across sectors, with manufacturing showing the highest increases of 3.8 per cent in January 1996, whereas services only displayed a rate of 2.5 per cent. The lowest increase has been in the public sector as this is where the government has more or less direct control over the level of wages, and has actively sought over the last few years to use this as the main means for wage control. Pay increases for most of the sector since 1994 have had to be financed from cost savings. Overall, inflation as measured by UK government figures is reasonably good, although data from the EU's Eurostat indicates otherwise. Eurostat is now in a position to calculate inflation using a harmonised index across all EU countries, and these figures show that UK inflation is higher by some 0.3 per cent than the government's own data. This has implications for full membership of Economic and Monetary Union (EMU), as the criterion used for this suggests that the UK's inflation rate for January 1996 should have been 0.6 per cent lower than Eurostat's estimate.

KEY INDICATORS

	Unit	1991	1992	1993	1994	1995
Population	m	57.80	57.85	57.92	58.10	58.40
Gross domestic product (GDP)	US$bn	1,006.0	1,060.3	927.4	1,013.6	–
GDP per capita	US$	17,470	18,400	15,980	17,400	16,304
GDP real growth	%	-1.9	-1.0	2.0	3.8	2.4
Inflation	%	5.9	3.7	1.6	2.0	2.9
Consumer prices	1990=100	105.9	109.8	111.5	114.3	118.2
Unemployment	%	8.7	10.1	10.0	9.4	8.7
Agricultural production	1979-81=100	114.18	111.33	105.74	104.73	106.11
Share prices	1990=100	109.8	114.7	131.7	141.5	147.3
Wages (monthly earnings)	1990=100	108.0	114.6	118.5	123.3	–
Industrial production	1990=100	96.3	96.2	98.1	103.1	105.4
Oil production	'000 bpd	1,915	1,915	1,975	2,115	2,680
Natural gas production	bn cu m	50.7	51.6	60.7	65.4	71.5
Coal production	m toe	57.3	51.4	41.5	29.8	32.0
Total reserves minus gold	US$bn	41.89	36.64	36.78	41.01	42.02
Foreign exchange	US$bn	38.73	34.09	34.63	38.53	39.18
Exports (FOB) (goods)	US$m	182,579	188,451	182,064	206,456	240,383
Imports (FOB) (goods)	US$m	200,853	211,879	202,305	222,943	258,768
Balance of trade	US$m	-18,274	-23,428	-20,240	-16,488	-18,385
Current account	US$m	-14,260	-18,349	-16,210	-3,498	-4,632
Lending rate	%	11.54	9.41	5.92	5.48	6.69
Deposit rate	%	10.07	7.30	3.76	3.44	4.14
Exchange rate	£ per US$	0.565	0.566	0.666	0.650	0.634

Trade

Overall, the UK's overseas trade position is good, with the balance of payments deficit having been reduced from £2.1 billion in the third quarter of 1995 to £1.8 billion in the last. Within this, the visible trade deficit fell back last year to £11.6 billion, largely offset by income from overseas investment, as the invisible balance has been reduced from the £2.3 billion high in the third quarter of 1994 to a low £0.9 billion.

Trade with other EU states has improved recently as exports have continued to rise and the deficit reduced. In the last quarter of 1995 this was reduced to £573 million, down from a high point of £1.6 billion a year earlier. The situation with the rest of the world, however, is not so good. The deficit with non-EU states stood at £2.2 billion in the last quarter of 1995, down from the previous quarter's high of £2.5 billion, but not encouraging.

Merger and reconstruction in the privatised utilities has continued, with the electricity boards the primary targets for acquisition. In November 1995, Norweb, the electricity supplier for the north-west was acquired by North West Water, and South Wales Electricity was purchased by Welsh Water. Interest has also been shown in these and other regional electricity supply companies by US firms seeking to expand their operations into the European area. The former water boards are in the news also because they are themselves in many cases the subject of takeovers. Lyonnaise des Eaux has been allowed to bid for Northumbrian Water and others will undoubtedly follow, as many of these now-privatised firms have made good profits. However the drought of summer 1995 saw a good deal of criticism of the water companies, especially Yorkshire Water. This firm hit the headlines when it had to bring water into the worst affected areas of Yorkshire by tanker. The fact that the area of Yorkshire most affected by the lack of water supplies has one of the highest rainfall figures in the UK, and the 50 per cent increase in profits declared by the firm for its half-year profits to November 1995 attracted a great deal of media criticism. Had the crisis affected the London area, rather than a province, it is possible that a state of emergency would have been declared such was the scale of the problem. Yorkshire Water later declared its profits for 1995/96, 14 per cent above the figures for the previous year. Other water companies are also under investigation by the industry regulator, Ofwat for their shortcomings and lack of investment.

British Gas also faces serious problems with competition from newer gas supply companies, who are able to supply gas at cheaper prices. The problem stems from the contracts that British Gas has with producers in the North Sea, struck at a time when gas production prices were at a high. Since then the world price of gas has fallen, although British Gas is not able to benefit from this, as it is impotent to escape from its old contracts. Newer firms are not affected and can make contracts at the current, lower, price – and hence pass these (lower) input costs onto consumers.

Rail privatisation has also hit problems since the government announced its intention to sell off the network to the private sector. British Rail has been prepared for sale by the hiving off of different parts of its operations, with the separation of passenger and freight services on a largely

COUNTRY PROFILE — UNITED KINGDOM

Political system

Monarchy, with sovereign as head of state. Legislative power vested in bicameral parliament consisting of House of Commons (650 members directly elected by universal adult suffrage for up to five years) and House of Lords (composed of hereditary and life peers). Executive power is vested in the cabinet, led by the prime minister, which is responsible to the House of Commons. In March 1993 the European parliament approved proposals for a uniform electoral system.
General election due before 1 May 1997.

Political parties

Ruling party: Conservative Party. Other major parties: Labour Party, Liberal Democrats, Scottish National Party (SNP), Plaid Cymru (Party of Wales), (Official) Ulster Unionist Party (OUP), Democratic Unionist Party (DUP), Ulster Popular Unionist Party (UPUP), Social Democratic and Labour Party (SDLP), Sinn Féinn, Green Party.

Main cities/towns

London (population 7.7m), Birmingham, Glasgow, Leeds, Sheffield, Liverpool, Bradford, Manchester, Edinburgh, Bristol, Belfast, Cardiff and Newcastle.

Media

Press: National and regional press, dominated by seven dailies with combined circulation of over 10m. The Press Council (a voluntary body under an independent chairman) responsible for maintaining general standards and dealing with complaints.
Dailies: Most influential broadsheets: *The Times, Financial Times, The Guardian, Daily Telegraph* and *The Independent.* The top five sellers are *Daily Mirror/Record, The Sun, Daily Mail, Daily Express* and *Daily Telegraph.* The London evening newspaper is the *Evening Standard. Today* closed in November 1995.
Weeklies: Several Sunday newspapers – most influential: *The Sunday Times, The Observer, Sunday Telegraph* and *The Independent on Sunday.* Most popular: *News of the World, Sunday Mirror* and *The People.* Most widely read weekly magazines include *Radio Times* (radio and TV programme listings), *TV Times* (radio and TV programme listings), *Woman's Weekly, Woman* and *Woman's Own.* Also vast number of general and special interest magazines.
Business: Large number covering all aspects of business, often with international circulation including *Financial Times* (daily), *The Economist* (weekly, worldwide) and *Investors Chronicle* (weekly).
Broadcasting: Public broadcasting is controlled by the British Broadcasting Corporation (BBC), which is financed by TV licence fees and does not carry advertising. The Independent Television Commission (ITC) has authority over Independent Television (ITV) and the Channel Four Television Company – both commercial stations. The Radio Authority has authority over Independent Local Radio (ILR), which are financed primarily by sale of advertising time.
Radio: BBC operates five national networks and 32 local radio stations. Increasing number of privately operated commercial radio stations.
Television: Four national terrestial TV networks in operation – BBC1 and BBC2 controlled by BBC; and ITV and Channel Four (in Wales *Awdurdod Sianel Pedwar Cymrw* – S4C). ITV and Channel Four programmes are produced by 15 regional TV companies. Wideband cable and satellite systems are growing, especially the Sky network which includes news and sports channels.
Advertising: Highly developed industry covering all usual media. Television advertising is particularly important, with both ITV and Channel Four accepting advertisements (limited to a daily average of six minutes per hour). Radio advertising also effective (limited to nine minutes per hour). Practically all newspapers and magazines carry advertising in some form, and high circulation figures make this a particularly useful form of promotion. Newspapers take around 30 per cent share of the media market compared to 40 per cent for television. Cinemas carry short advertisements and posters – on billboards and public transport – are also widely used. The Advertising Standards Authority acts as an independent watchdog, maintaining general standards. Key categories include food, household equipment, financial, leisure and automotive.

Domestic economy

Large and open mixed economy characterised by export-oriented manufacturing sector, successful financial centre, energy self-sufficiency and growing service industry. Mining and highly mechanised agriculture also important. Economic growth has been sluggish despite increased offshore oil and gas earning and reductions in inflation. Government policy remains essentially monetaristic with particular emphasis on increased liberalisation, cuts in public sector spending, reduction in labour costs, and a competitive market economy.

Employment

Around 20 per cent of the workforce is employed in industry, just over 2 per cent in agriculture, 60 per cent in services and 17 per cent self-employed.

External trade

Traditional deficit on non-oil visible trade offset by invisible earnings (which account for 30 per cent of total export earnings). However, recent rise in imported manufactured goods, capital outflows and slump in non-oil exports significantly reduced current account surplus. Major European exporter of manufactured goods, oil, aerospace products, chemicals, motor vehicles, metals, finished textiles and machinery. Also major importer of agricultural products, raw materials, semi-manufactures and most recently finished manufactures. In 1993 the Ministry of Trade agreed to extend by at least three years, the 'transitional' reinsurance support provided to export insurers by the government's Export Credits Guarantee Department. The facility – introduced when the ECGD's short-term export credit insurance business was privatised in 1991 – was to be phased out at the end of 1994, threatening more than UK£1bn in exports annually.
Major trading partners include the EU (typically 52 per cent of total) (especially Germany, France and the Netherlands, also the USA.
Exports: Exports totalled US$238.2bn in 1995.
Imports: Imports totalled US$26.3bn in 1995.

Agriculture

An efficient sector which contributes about 2 per cent to GDP, but meets over two-thirds of national food requirements. Also an important European exporter of agricultural produce, fertilisers and foodstuffs. The sector employs about 2 per cent of the labour force. Farm

regional basis in an attempt to recreate the romanticism of the 'golden age' of steam. Similarly the infrastructure, as opposed to the services, has been privatised in the shape of Railtrack, which controls the permanent way, stations and signalling. Numerous problems have arisen with the sales, including the outdated state of the rail network, inadequate signalling and safety, alleged managerial fraud, inadequate minimum service provisions and lack of through ticketing. There is a possibility that if the Labour Party wins the election, Railtrack shares may be repurchased, although less radical measures are more probable.

Elsewhere on the rail network, the contract to build the high speed link between London and the Channel Tunnel was finally awarded in February 1996 to the London and Continental Railways Consortium (LCR), a group comprised of seven members, including Virgin, Bechtel, SG Warburg and the coach operator, National Express. Construction will however not start until 1997, and the link will not be ready until 2003. The Belgian link will be completed in 1998 – all a long way behind the completion of the French link in 1993. Financing will come partly from the state in the form of a £1.4 billion contribution. The company which built the tunnel, Eurotunnel, remains in trouble with an £8 billion debt which it is not able to service. Eurotunnel received a severe setback in November 1996 when, following a fire on a freight train, the tunnel was forced to close for several weeks.

Outlook

In the run-up to the election, the government will be caught in a dilemma; whether to introduce tax cuts for electoral purposes or to improve public finances. As the Public Sector Borrowing Requirement (PSBR) is expected to reach 4.5 per cent of GDP in 1995/96 (on the government's definition, which is below the EU estimate of 6 per cent), and hence well below the 3 per cent target set by the Maastrict conference for entry into EMU, effective rises in overall government spending are unlikely. Likely control measures, as in the past, will probably involve further restrictions on public expenditure.

If Labour wins the election, it seems likely that much of this policy will continue as before. Incoming Labour governments always face problems of confidence from the City of London and thus have to be fiscally stricter than a Conservative administration. In any case, the Labour Party under Tony Blair now seems to have finally accepted the logic of a market economy and is unlikely to invoke radical changes. Both parties seem to be bereft of adequate theories of political economy, and thus the choice before the UK electorate is essentially the same as is as faced by citizens in the US – that of reactive marginal policy differences rather than proactive change.

COUNTRY PROFILE — UNITED KINGDOM

Agriculture (contd): holdings are largely owner-occupied and production is concentrated on livestock rearing and growing of wheat, barley, oats, potatoes, oilseed and sugar-beet. Because of feeding methods, there have been major diseases reported in both chickens and cows. Horticulture and trawler fishing also important.

Industry

Sector forms mainstay of economy contributing 30 per cent to GDP and accounting for around 65 per cent of visible exports. It employs about 20 per cent of the labour force. There has been a gradual decline in international competitiveness. Principal industries include metal manufacturing, chemicals, engineering, motor vehicles, aircraft, textiles, telecommunications, shipbuilding, electronics, food processing and other agro-business. Emphasis on privatisation, rehabilitation and development of high-tech industries. The UK is attractive to Japanese and other foreign firms looking for a manufacturing base with cheap labour costs inside Europe. The manufacturing output is growing at a faster rate than other areas of the economy. Electronics, with electrical engineering, is the UK's second largest manufacturing industry.

Tourism

Tourism is firmly established as one of the UK's top industries, worth in excess of UK£25bn a year, employing 1.5m people in the UK. The number of visitors in the first six months of 1996 totalled 11.6m, a 12 per cent rise on the same period of 1995.

Mining

Significant producer of zinc, lead, limestone, sand and tin. Other minerals include small-scale deposits of silver, copper, gold, iron ore and potash. Cornwall's sole surviving working tin mine has 20 years of reserves. MIM, the Australian mining and metals group bought the UK's only zinc smelter - the Avonmouth plant - in 1993. It has an annual capacity of 105,000 tonnes of zinc and 45,000 tonnes of lead, and is the largest in the world using the Imperial Smelting Process. A production improvement programme is expected to lift capacity to 120,000 tonnes of zinc and 55,000 tonnes of lead.

Hydrocarbons

Exploitation of oil and gas from continental shelf under North Sea enabled self-sufficiency in energy and made the UK one of the most energy-rich EU nations. Around 25 offshore fields producing crude oil including Brent and Forties. Shell UK announced in 1993, a £1.3bn project to extend the life of the Brent field, the biggest combined oil and gas field in the UK North Sea. British Petroleum (BP) announced in 1993 the biggest UK oil discovery for five years – 250m to 500m barrels of oil, west of the Shetland Isles, and BP told of its £400m development of the Forth oilfield in the North Sea, to come on stream in early-1996.
Oil production totalled 2.8m barrels per day (bpd) in 1995, up 2.6 per cent on 1994 output; proven oil reserves 4.3bn barrels (end-1995). An estimated 530m to 3.3bn tonnes of oil are left to be discovered.
Output and reserves of natural gas, which are playing a fast-growing role in the country's energy balance, are both rising. Proved natural gas reserves at end-1995 were 23.3 trillion cu feet. Production of natural gas totalled 64.4 tonnes oil equivalent in 1995, up 9.3 per cent on 1994 production. Natural gas trapped in coal seams could give Britain a vast new source of usable energy.
UK reserves of coalbed methane may exceed 1,000bn cu metres, comparable with the total volume in conventional North Sea gas fields. Major European coal producer with estimated proved reserves 2.5bn tonnes at end-1995. Coal production 32m tonnes oil equivalent in 1995, up 7.4 per cent on 1994 output.

Energy

Nuclear power accounts for 18 per cent of electricity generated. The Dounreay nuclear reactor was closed in July 1994 in spite of a plea to save the research project there. British Gas was privatised in 1986 and British Petroleum (BP) in 1987. In 1990 the government split the Central Electricity Board into two distribution companies, National Power and PowerGen, and privatised these and 12 regional electricity companies in England and Wales. The sell-off of Scottish Power and Scottish Hydroelectric took place in 1991. The Central Area Transmission System pipeline, the backbone of an important new natural gas transmission system in the North Sea, was completed in August 1992. Up to 1.4bn cu feet of gas a day is carried from the central North Sea to north-east England. A new gas-fired power station at Spodon, Derby commissioned mid-1995, is being financed by the European Investment Bank (EIB).
Construction of a 290m gas pipeline linking the UK to Belgium is planned to be completed by 1997. The 215 km pipe would carry 15bn cu metres of gas a year to Zeebrugge in Belgium. It could then be distributed on the European gas grid. The pipeline could also be used for importing gas into the UK from Europe.
Department of Trade and Industry report in 1993 stated that tidemills to harness fast-flowing sea currents around the coast could supply almost one-fifth of the UK's electricity needs.

Banking

Highly developed system with the City of London acting as major international financial centre. Monetary policy and Exchange Equalisation Account managed by Bank of England (central bank). Also four main clearing banks (Lloyds, National Westminster, Barclays and Midland), Girobank, Trustee Savings Bank, numerous merchant banks and over 500 overseas banks and financial institutions.

Legal system

Common law tradition with early Roman and modern continental influences. No written constitution.

Membership of international organisations

The UK is a member of over 130 international organisations. The principal ones include: ADB, AG (observer), BIS, CCC, CENTO, CERN, Colombo Plan, Commonwealth, Council of Europe, CSCE, DAC, EEA, ESA, ESCAP, ESRO, EU, FAO, G-5, G-7, G-10, IAEA, ICAC, ICAO, ICC, ICES, ICO, IDA, IDB, IEA, IFAD, IFC, IHO, ILO, International Grain Council, International Lead and Zinc Study Group, IMF, IMO, INTELSAT, INTERPOL, IOOC, IPU, IRC, ISO, ITC, ITU, MIGA, NACC, NATO, OECD, SPC, UN, UNIDO, UN Security Council (permanent member), UPU, WEU, WHO, WIPO, WMO, World Bank, WSG, WTO.

Time

GMT (GMT + 1 hr from late Mar to late Oct).

Climate

Temperate, with warm summers and cold winters. Rainfall throughout year, heaviest Oct–Mar. Average temperatures range from about 5–15°C.

Clothing

Mediumweight and raincoat throughout year, topcoat for winter.

Entry requirements

Passport: Passport (valid until at least two months after intended departure date) required by all visitors.
Visa: Required by nationals of Saudi Arabia; East European countries except Poland; all Asian countries except Japan and Republic of Korea; all African countries except Côte d'Ivoire, Morocco, Niger, Tunisia and South Africa; Cuba and Argentina.
Health: Vaccination certificates not normally required.
Currency: No restrictions on movement of UK or foreign currencies.
Customs: Personal effects duty-free (other than alcoholic drink, tobacco products, perfume), plus small duty-free allowance. EU regulations apply.

Air access

Regular direct flights operated by all major international airlines.
National airline: British Airways.
Tax: Airport tax £5 for departures to Europe; £10 for departures to the rest of the world.
N.B. From 1 November 1997 the tax will go up to £10 for European departures, and to £20 for rest of the world.
International airports: London Heathrow (LHR), 24 km west of capital; London Gatwick (LGW), 46 km south of London; London Stansted (STN), 55 km north-east of London; London Luton International (LTN), 51.2 km north-west of London; Manchester International (MAN) - Terminal 2 opened March 1993; Birmingham International (BHX), 13 km east of city and Prestwick (PIK), 14 km west of Glasgow; Newcastle (NCL).

Surface access

Regular ferry and hovercraft connections from the continent. Eurotunnel shunts automobiles, freight and foot passengers under the English channel to France.
Main ports: London, Liverpool, Grimsby, Southampton, Milford Haven, Tees and Hartlepool, Dover and Felixstowe. Tees and Hartlepool, Clyde, Forth, Medway and Tilbury were all privatised in 1992.
The UK's ports had a record-breaking year in 1995 with a 2 per cent rise in total import and export traffic to 548m tonnes: London was busiest with 51m tonnes followed by the Forth ports with 47m tonnes; Felixstowe was largest container port handling 1.7m containers and truck trailers.

Hotels

Classified from one- to five-star by AA and RAC (automobile clubs). Rating system in Northern Ireland – A star, A, B star, B, C and D. Single room (five-star) generally costs £60-75 per night. Prices usually include 10-15 per cent service charge, but tipping also expected.

Currency

Exchange rate: The UK pound floats, with intervention by the Bank of England during unstable market conditions.

Foreign exchange information

Account restrictions: There are no blocked or non-resident accounts.
Trade policy: There are no exchange controls over imports or exports. Imports of certain items such as food products, livestock and textiles are subject to quota or other restrictions.

Credit cards

Major credit cards widely accepted.

Car hire

Widely available at airports and in main towns, with all major international hire firms represented. International driving licence or full national licence required. Drive on left. Speed limits: motorways/dual carriageways 70 mph (113 kph), normal roads 60 mph (97 kph) and built-up areas 30 or 40 mph (48 or 64 kph).

City transport

Taxis: Available in all major cities, and can be hailed in the street, at ranks, or be called by telephone. Taxis may charge extra – over and above metered charge – for number of passengers, large items of luggage, journeys at night, at weekends and journeys over 8 km. Tipping (about 10 per cent) expected. For black cab in London, tel: 071-253-5000 or 071-272-0272.
Buses and underground: Operated in London by London Regional Transport (LRT). Extensive network linking all parts of the capital. Good bus services also available in all other major towns. Reliable metro services in Glasgow, Liverpool, Manchester (metrolink train system) and Newcastle.

National transport

Air: Most major cities linked by regular flights to 21 main commercial airports provided by seven domestic operators. Not widely used, with exception of London-Scotland services, due to expense and relatively short distances between principal commercial centres.
Road: Extensive network of about 370,000 km including 2,800 km of motorway. A second road bridge across the Firth of Forth, Scotland is being considered and may be open by year 2000.
Buses: Regular bus and coach services, mainly operated by National Express and Scottish Bus Group, and various municipal and private companies.
Rail: Relatively expensive first and second-class service. Network of about 18,400 km. All principal towns are connected by regular inter-city services. The 1993 budget gave the go-ahead to plans for the UK£300m Heathrow Express, a joint venture between British Rail and BAA, the private-sector airports operator. Passengers will be able to travel from London Paddington station to Heathrow airport in 16 minutes when the line opens in 1997.
Water: Over 3,000 km of navigable inland waterways, under control of the British Waterways Board.

Public holidays

Fixed dates: 1 Jan, 25 and 26 Dec.
Variable dates: Good Friday, Easter Monday, May Day (first Mon in May), Spring Bank Holiday (last Mon in May) and Summer Bank Holiday (last Mon in Aug). N.B. Some variations in Scotland and Northern Ireland.

Working hours

Government and business: (Mon–Fri) usually 0900 – 1700.
Banking: (Mon–Fri) 0930 – 1530 or 1630, some banks open Sat morning and there are variations in hours in Scotland and Northern Ireland. Trend towards longer opening hours.
Shops: (Mon–Sat) generally 0900 – 1730, usually early closing one day per week.

Business language and interpreting/translation

Available from The Institute of Linguists (tel: (0)171-359-7445), the Guild of Guide Lecturers (tel: (0)171-839-7438); or see 'Translators and Interpreters' section of 'Yellow Pages' telephone directory.

Telecommunications

British Telecom, although no longer having statutory monopoly to provide telecommunications, continues to operate vast majority of services. Mercury Communications is the second-largest telecom provider.
Telephone: Direct dialling available on all local and overseas calls. Calls to emergency services are free (dial 999 and ask for police, fire brigade or ambulance). Operator service dial 100. Public phones are found at railway stations, in the streets and in hotels and restaurants. A growing number are operated by telephone cards, which can be purchased at post offices and many shops. For international telephone enquiries dial 153; for international operator assistance 155. International dialling code: 44 followed by 171 for inner London or 181 for outer London.
For IDD access from UK dial 00 (from 16 April 1995).
Telex: Full automatic service with direct dialling available to most countries. Available in all major hotels and there is a public telex facility at Electra House, Victoria Embankment, London.
Telefax: Public service available in some post offices and shops.
Telegram: Can be sent via telephone or from any post office. Telegrams are transmitted through computer-controlled Telegram Retransmission Centre in London to 81 other countries.

Postal service

The Post Office has a monopoly on the collection and delivery of letters, and provides specialist high-speed delivery services. There are also a number of other privately owned courier companies. Stamps can be purchased at supermarkets, tobacconists and newsagents as well as post offices.

Trade fairs

Several annual events of international significance such as the Motor Show, the Boat Show, the Ideal Home Exhibition and many others covering all aspects of trade and industry. Principal exhibition venues are Earls Court, Olympia and Wembley in London, the National Exhibition Centre (NEC) in Birmingham, and the G-Mex Centre in Manchester. Further information available from UK Trade Fairs Department of the Department of Trade and Industry in London.

Electricity supply

230 V AC. The electricity supply voltage throughout the EU was standardised from 1 January 1995.

Representation in capital

Afghanistan, Algeria, Antigua and Barbuda, Argentina, Australia, Austria, Bahamas, Bahrain, Bangladesh, Barbados, Belgium, Belize, Bolivia, Botswana, Brazil, Brunei, Bulgaria, Cameroon, Canada, Chile, China, Colombia, Costa Rica, Côte d'Ivoire, Cuba, Cyprus, Denmark, Ecuador, Egypt, El Salvador, Ethiopia, Fiji, Finland, France, Gabon, Gambia, Germany, Ghana, Greece, Grenada, Guatemala, Guyana, The Holy See, Honduras, Hungary, Iceland, India, Indonesia, Iran, Ireland, Israel, Italy, Jamaica, Japan, Jordan, Kenya, Republic of Korea, Kuwait, Lebanon, Lesotho, Liberia, Libya, Luxembourg, Malawi, Malaysia, Malta, Mauritius, Mexico, Mongolia, Morocco, Mozambique, Myanmar, Nepal, Netherlands, New Zealand, Nicaragua, Nigeria, Norway, Oman, Pakistan, Panama, Papua New Guinea, Paraguay, Peru, Philippines, Poland, Portugal, Qatar, Romania, Russia, St Kitts & Nevis, St Lucia, St Vincent and the Grenadines, Saudi Arabia, Senegal, Seychelles, Sierra Leone, Singapore, Somalia, South Africa, Spain, Sri Lanka, Sudan, Swaziland, Sweden, Switzerland, Syria, Tanzania, Thailand, Togo, Tonga, Trinidad and Tobago, Tunisia, Turkey, Uganda, United Arab Emirates, Uruguay, USA, Venezuela, Vietnam, Yemen, Zaïre, Zambia, Zimbabwe.

BUSINESS DIRECTORY

Hotels

Birmingham (area code (0)121)
Midland, New Street, B24JT (tel: 643-2601; fax: 643 5075).

Plough & Harrow, Hagley Road, Edgbaston, B168IS (tel: 454-4111; fax: 454-1868).

Royal Angus Thistle, St Chads, Queensway, B46HY (tel: 236-4211; fax: 233-2195).

Strathallan Thistle, Hagley Road, Edgbaston, B169RY (tel: 455-9777; fax: 454-9432).

Glasgow (area code (0)141)
Albany (The), Bothwell street, G27EN (tel: 248-2656; fax: 221-8986).

Holiday Inn, Anderston Cross, Argyle Street, G38RR (tel: 226-5577; fax: 221-9202).

MacDonald Thistle (The), Eastwood Toll, Giffnock, G46 6RA (tel: 638-2225; fax: 638-6231).

Stakis Grosvenor, Grosvenor Terrace, Great Western Road, G120TA (tel: 339-8811; fax: 334-0710).

Tinto Firs Thistle, Kilmarnock Road, G432BB (tel: 637-2353; fax: 633-1340).

London
Belgravia-Sheraton, 20 Chesham Place, SW1X 8HQ (tel: (0)171-235-6040; fax: (0)171-259-6243).

Britannia Inter-Continental, Grosvenor Square, W1A 3AN (tel: (0)171-629-9400; fax: (0)171-629-7736).

Brown's, Albemarle Street, W1A 4SW (tel: (0)171-493-6020; fax: (0)171-493-9381).

Cavendish, Jermyn Street, SW1Y 6JF (tel: (0)171-930-2111; fax: (0)171-839-2125).

Charing Cross, Strand, WC2N 5HX (tel: (0)171-839-7282; fax: (0)171-839-3933).

Chesterfield, 35 Charles Street, W1X 8LX (tel: (0)171-491-2622).

Churchill, Portman Square, W1A 4ZX (tel: (0)171-486-5800; fax: (0)171-935-0431).

Claridge's, Brook Street, W1A 2JQ (tel: (0)171-629-8860; fax: (0)171-499-2210).

Cumberland, Marble Arch, W1A 4RF (tel: (0)171-262-1234; fax: (0)171-724-4621).

Dorchester, Park Lane, W1A 2HJ (tel: (0)171-629-8888; fax: (0)171-409-0114).

Dukes, 35 St James's Place, SW1A 1NY (tel: (0)171-491-4840; fax: (0)171-493-1264).

Gloucester, 4-18 Harrington Gardens, SW7 4LH (tel: (0)171-373-6030; fax: (0)171-373-0409).

Grosvenor, 101 Buckingham Palace Road, SW1W 0SJ (tel: (0)171-834-9494; fax: (0)171-630-1978).

Grosvenor House, Park Lane, W1A 3AA (tel: (0)171-499-6363; fax: (0)171-493-3341).

Hilton-London-Kensington, 179-199 Holland Park Avenue, W11 4UL (tel: (0)171-603-3355; fax: (0)171-602-9397).

Hilton-London on Park Lane, 22 Park Lane, W1A 2HH (tel: (0)171-493-8000; fax: (0)171-493-4957).

Holiday Inn Marble Arch, 134 George Street, W1H 6DN (tel: (0)171-723-1277; fax: (0)171-402-0666).

Hyatt Carlton Tower, 2 Cadogan Place, SW1X 9PY (tel: (0)171-235-5411; fax: (0)171-235-9129).

Inn on the Park, Hamilton Place, Park Lane, W1A 1AZ (tel: (0)171-499-0888; fax: (0)171-493-1895).

Inter-Continental, 1 Hamilton Place, Hyde Park Corner, W1V 0QY (tel: (0)171-409-3131; fax: (0)171-409-7460/1).

London Marriott, Grosvenor Square, W1A 4AW (tel: (0)171-493-1232; fax: (0)171-491-3201).

Mayfair Inter-Continental, Stratton Street, W1A 2AN (tel: (0)171-629-7777; fax: (0)171-629-1459).

Park Lane, Piccadilly, W1Y 8BX (tel: (0)171-499-6321; fax: (0)171-499-1965).

Portman Inter-Continental (The), 22 Portman Square, W1H 9FL (tel: (0)171-486-5844; fax: (0)171-935-0537).

Ritz, Piccadilly, W1V 9DG (tel: (0)171-493-8181; fax: (0)171-493-2687).

Royal Garden, Kensington High Street, W8 4PT (tel: (0)171-937-8000; fax: (0)171-938-4532).

Russell, Russell Square, WC1B 5BE (tel: (0)171-837-6470; fax: (0)171-837-2857).

Savoy (The), The Strand, WC2R 0EU (tel: (0)171-836-4343; fax: (0)171-240-6040).

Waldorf, Aldwych, WC2B 4DD (tel: (0)171-836-2400; fax: (0)171-836-7244).

Westbury, New Bond Street at Conduit Street, W1A 4UH (tel: (0)171-629-7755).

Manchester (area code (0)161)
Embassy Piccadilly, Piccadilly Plaza, PO Box 107, M60 1QR (tel: 236-8414; fax: 228-1568).

Post House, Palatine Road, Northenden, M22 4FH (tel: 998-7090; fax: 946-0139).

The Grand, Aytoun Street, M1 3DR (tel: 236-9559; fax: 436-2340).

The Portland Thistle, 3 Portland Street, Piccadilly Gardens, M1 6DP (tel: 228-3400; fax: 228-6347).

Car hire

Head offices
Avis: Trident House, Hayes, Middlesex (tel: (0)181-848-8733; tx: 945670).

Budget: 41 Marlowes, Hemel Hempstead, Herts (tel: 0800-181-181).

Eurodollar: Swan National House, 3 Warwick Place, Uxbridge, Middlesex (tel: (0)1895-233-300; fax: (0)1895-256-050).).

Europcar: 2nd Floor, Bank House, Park Place, Leeds (tel: 422-233; fax: 429-495).

Hertz: Radnor House, 1272 London Road, London SW16 (tel: (0)181-679-1799).

Chambers of commerce

Association of British Chambers of Commerce, Sovereign House, 212 Shaftesbury Avenue, London WC2H 8EW (tel: (0)171-240-5831).

Birmingham Chamber of Industry and Commerce, 75 Harborne Road, Birmingham B15 3DH (tel: 454-6171; tx: 338024 BIRCOM G).

Cardiff Chamber of Commerce and Industry, 101-108 The Exchange, Mount Stuart Square, Cardiff CF1 6RD (tel: 481-648; tx: 497492).

Edinburgh Chamber of Commerce and Manufacturers, 3 Randolph Crescent, Edinburgh EH3 7UD (tel: 225-5851; tx: 72465 CHAMCO G).

Glasgow Chamber of Commerce, 30 George Square, Glasgow G2 1EQ (tel: 204-2121; tx: 777967 CHAMCOM G).

International Chamber of Commerce (UK), Centre Point, 103 New Oxford Street, London WC1A 1DU (tel: (0)171-240-5558).

Leeds Chamber of Commerce and Industry, Commerce House, 2 St Alban's Place, Leeds LS2 8HZ (tel: 430-491; tx: 55293 CHACOM G).

London Chamber of Commerce and Industry, 69 Cannon Street, London EC4N 5AB (tel: (0)171-248-4444; tx: 888941 LCCI G).

Manchester Chamber of Commerce and Industry, 56 Oxford Street, Manchester M60 7HJ (tel: 236-3210; tx: 667822 CHACOM G).

Sheffield Chamber of Commerce and Manufacturers (Incorporated), Commerce House, 33 Earl Street, Sheffield S1 3FX (tel: 730-114; tx: 547676 CHAMCO g).

Banking

Bank of England (central bank), Threadneedle Street, London EC2R 8AH (tel: (0)171-601-4444; tx: 885-001).

Bank of Scotland, The Mound, Edinburgh EH1 1YZ (tel: 442-7777; tx: 72-275).

Barclays Bank, 54 Lombard Street, London EC3P 3AH (tel: (0)171-626-1567; tx: 887-591).

British Bankers' Association, 10 Lombard Street, London EC3V 9EL (tel: (0)171-623-4001)

British Overseas and Commonwealth Banks Association, 99 Bishopsgate, London EC2P 2LA (tel: (0)171-636-2366).

Institute of Bankers, 10 Lombard Street, London EC3V 9AP (tel: (0)171-623-3531).

Institute of Bankers in Scotland, 20 Rutland Square, Edinburgh EH1 2BB (tel: 229-9869).

Lloyds Bank, 71 Lombard Street, London EC3P 3BS (tel:( )1071-626-1500; tx: 888-301).

Midland Bank, Poultry, London EC2P 2BX (tel: (0)171-260-8000; tx: 881-1822).

National Westminster Bank, 41 Lothbury, London EC2P 2BP (tel: (0)171-726-1000; tx: 888-388).

Royal Bank of Scotland, 42 St Andrew Square, Edinburgh EH2 2YB (tel: 556-8555; tx: 72-230).

Standard Chartered Bank, 38 Bishopsgate, London EC2N 4DE (tel: (0)171-280-7500; tx: 885-951).

Trustee Savings Bank, 25 Milk Street, London EC2V 8LU (tel: (0)171-606-7070; tx: 881-2487).

Principal newspapers

Daily Express, Ludgate House, 245 Blackfriars Road, London SE1 9UX (tel: (0)171-928-8000).

Principal newspapers (contd):
Daily Mail, 2 Derry Street, Kensington, London W8 5EE (tel: (0)171-938-6000; tx; 28-301).

Daily Mirror, 1 Canada Square, Canary Wharf, London E14 5QP (tel: (0)171-510-3000).

Daily Telegraph, Peterborough Court, South Quay, 181 Marsh Wall, London E14 9SR (tel: (0)171-353-4242; tx: 22-874).

Financial Times, No 1 Southwark Bridge, London SE1 9HL (tel: (0)171-873-3000; tx: 922-186).

The Guardian, 119 Farringdon Road, London EC1R 3ER (tel: (0)171-278-2332; tx: 881-1746); and 164 Deansgate, Manchester M60 2RR (tel: 832-7200).

The Independent, 1, Canada Square, Canary Wharf, London E14 5DL (tel: (0)171-510-3000; tx: 941-9611).

Morning Star, 1-3 Ardleigh Road, London N1 4HS (tel: (0)171-254-0033; fax: (0)171-254-5950).

News of the World, 1 Virginia Street, Wapping, London E1 9DD (tel: (0)171-782-4000; tx: 262-135).

The Sun, 1 Pennington Street, Wapping, London E1 9BD (tel: (0)171-782-5000; tx: 925-088).

Sunday Mirror, 1 Canada Square, Canary Wharf, London E14 5QP (tel: (0)171-510-3000).

The Sunday People, 33 Holborn, London EC1P 1DG (tel: (0)171-353-0246; tx: 27-286).

Sunday Telegraph, Peterborough Court, South Quay, 181 Marsh Wall, London E14 9SR (tel: (0)171-353-4242; tx: 22-874).

Sunday Times, 1 Pennington Street, Wapping, London E1 9BD (tel: (0)171-782-5000; tx: 262-139).

The Times, 1 Pennington Street, Wapping, London E1 9BD (tel: (0)171-782-5000; tx: 925-088).

Travel information

Aberdeen Airport (tel: (0)1224-722-331).

Automobile Association, Fanum House, Basingstoke, Hampshire RG21 2EA (tel: (0)1256-20-123).

Belfast Airport (tel: (0)1849-422-888).

Birmingham Airport (tel: (0)121-767-5511).

British Airways, PO Box 115, West London Terminal, Cromwell Road, London SW7 4ED (tel: (0)171-370-8466).

British Tourist Authority, Queen's House, 64 St James' Street, London SW1A 1NF (tel: (0)181-846-9000).

Cardiff Airport (tel: (0)1446-711-111).

Edinburgh Airport (tel: (0)131-333-1000).

Folkestone Ferry Port (Le Shuttle) (tel: (0)1303-271-100).

English Tourist Board (tel: (0)181-846-9000).

Gatwick Airport (tel: (0)1293-535-353).

Glasgow Airport (tel: (0)141-887-1111).

Heathrow Airport (tel: (0)181-759-4321).

Manchester Airport (tel: (0)161-489-3000).

National motorways (motoring information) (tel: (0)836-401-110).

Northern Ireland Tourist Board (tel: (0)1232-246-609).

Passport Office, Clive House, 70-78 Petty France, London SW1 (tel: (0)171-213-3434).

Prestwick Airport (tel: (0)1292-79-822).

Royal Automobile Club (RAC), PO Box 700, Spectrum, Bond Street, Bristol BS99 1RB (tel: (0)345-331-133).

Scottish Tourist Board (tel: (0)131-332-2433).

Stansted Airport (tel: (0)1279-680-500).

Wales Tourist Board (tel: (0)1222-499-909).

Weather information (national) (tel: (0)891-500-400).

Other useful addresses

Advertising Standards Authority, Brook House, Torrington Place, London WC1E 7HN (tel: (0)171-580-5555).

Association of Independent Businesses, Trowbray House, 108 Weston Street, London SE1 3QB (tel: (0)171-403-4066).

Banking Information Service, 10 Lombard Street, London EC3V 9AR (tel: (0)171-930-8466).

BBC External Service, Bush House, Strand, London WC2B 4PM (tel: (0)171-204-3456; tx: 265-781).

British Council, 10 Spring Gardens, London SW1A 2BN (tel: (0)171-930-8466).

British Export Houses Association, 69-75 Cannon Street, London EC4N 5AB (tel: (0)171-248-4444).

British Overseas Trade Board, 1 Victoria Street, London SW1H OET (tel: (0)171-215-7877).

British Railways Board, 222 Marylebone Road, London NW1 (tel: (0)171-262-3232).

British Waterways Board, Melbury House, Melbury Terrace, London NW1 6JX (tel: (0)171-262-6711).

Central Government Office of Information, Hercules Road, Westminster Bridge Road, London SE1 7DU (tel: (0)171-928-2345; tx: 915-444).

Central Statistical Office (CSO), Great George Street, London SW1P 3AQ (tel: 270-6357; fax: 270-6019).

Confederation of British Industry (CBI), Centre Point, 103 New Oxford Street, London WC1A 1DU (tel: (0)171-379-7400).

Department of Trade and Industry, 1 Victoria Street, London SW1H OET (tel: (0)171-215-5000; tx: 881-1074); UK trade fairs (tel: (0)171-212-0405).

Institute of Export, 64 Clifton Street, London EC2A 4HB (tel: (0)171-488-4766).

Institute of Marketing, Moor Hall, Cookham, Maidenhead, Berkshire SL6 9QH (tel: 524-922).

National Exhibition Centre Limited, Birmingham B40 1NT (tel: 780-414; fax: 780-2517).

Press Council, 1 Salisbury Square, London EC4Y 8AE (tel: (0)171-353-1248).

The Guild of Guide Lecturers, 2 Bridge Street, London SW1A 2JR (tel: (0)171-839-7438).

The Institute of Linguists, 24a Highbury Grove, London N5 2EA (tel: (0)171-359-7445).

The Stock Exchange, London EC2 (tel: (0)171-588-2355).

Trades Union Congress (TUC), Congress House, 23-28 Great Russell Street, London WC1B 3LS (tel: (0)171-636-4030).

Treasury, Parliament Street, London SW1P 3AG (tel: (0)171-270-3000; tx: 941-3704).

Internet sites

Air UK: http://www.airuk.co.uk/

British Airways: http://www.british-airways.com/bans/checkin.html

British Midland Airways: http://www.iflybritishmidland.com

Eurodollar (UK): http://www.eurodollar.co.uk/

Eurostar: http://oworld.avonibp.co.uk/eurostar/eurostar.html

London Hotels Discount Reservations: http://www.demon.co.uk/hotel-net/lhdr.from.html

Virgin Atlantic Airways: http://www.fly.virgin.com

Federal Republic of Yugoslavia (Serbia, Montenegro)

Marko Milivojevic

The signing of the Dayton, Ohio peace accords by the Bosnian, Croatian and Serbian Presidents in November 1995, and the subsequent suspension and removal of the United Nations (UN) economic sanctions imposed on the Federal Republic of Yugoslavia (FRY) have revitalised the country's economic and political prospects. But five years of war, international isolation, chronic socio-economic decline and weeks of popular protests against the Serbian Government of Slobodan Milosevic following his rejection of opposition victories in the November 1996 municipal elections have taken their toll. Following the beginnings of a post-Yugoslav economic recovery in 1994, when the combined GDP of Serbia and Montenegro increased by 6.5 per cent, virtually all major economic indices changed for the worse in 1995, mainly because of the collapse of macro-economic stabilisation and the avoidance of any real economic reform in Serbia.

Politics

Serbian President Slobodan Milosevic's peace policy, the suspension of the UN economic sanctions and their final removal on 1 October 1996 won him respect at home and abroad. However, this honeymoon period did not last for long. Although parties loyal to Milosevic and his Serbian Socialist Party (SSS) easily won elections at the federal level in November 1996, the Zajedno opposition coalition made significant inroads at the local level, winning majorities in Serbia's 12 largest urban areas. The nullification of these results by the authorities sparked off a wave of massive protests as crowds of up to 250,000 protested peacefully against the regime of Milosevic – Europe's largest such demonstrations since 1989.

Not only did the rejection of the municipal election results lead to condemnation at home, many western leaders denounced the government's actions, urging it to refrain from violence against the protestors and reinstate the original results. The USA has been particularly critical, maintaining that an outer wall of sanctions will be maintained against Serbia and that membership of the international financial institutions will be blocked while the govenment ignores its electoral defeats. Even so, the opposition parties have not gained unqualified support from the west, as several have ties with Bosnian Serb nationalists and paramilitaries. In addition, the parties which make up the Zajedno coalition range from democrats to arch-Serbian nationalists who are against Milosevic's 'sell-out' of the Krajina and Bosnian Serbs in 1995 and it is therefore unclear whether they could retain their present cohesion if their common enemy were to be defeated. Milosevic's isolation increased when the normally supportive Serbian Orthodox Church condemned his actions. The army also made it clear that it would not be used to suppress protestors, leaving the Serbian president to rely entirely on the support of the well armed and loyal police force.

KEY FACTS — Federal Republic of Yugoslavia

Official title: Federal Republic of Yugoslavia (FRY) (Republic of Serbia (ROS) and Republic of Montenegro (ROM)

Head of state: President Zoran Lilic (FRY); President Slobodan Milosevic (ROS); President Momir Bulatovic (ROM)

Head of government: Prime Minister Radoje Kontic (FRY); Prime Minister Mirko Marjanovic (ROS); Prime Minister Mile Djukanovic (ROM)

Ruling party: Serbian Socialist Party (SSS) (FRY and ROS); Democratic Socialist Party of Montenegro (DSS) (ROM)

Capital: Belgrade (FRY and ROS); Podgorica (ROM) (formerly Titograd)

Official Languages: Serbian

Currency: New Yugoslav Dinar (D) (replaced old Yugoslav Dinar 24 Jan 1994)

Exchange rate: D5.09 per US$ (Dec 1996)

Area: 102,173 sq km

Population: 10m (1995)

GDP per capita: US$1,550 (1995)

GDP real growth: 6% (1995)

GNP per capita: US$1,000 (1994)

GNP real growth: 6.5% (1994)

Unemployment: 50% (end-1995)

Inflation: 100% (1996)*

Trade balance: -US$1bn (end-Jul1996)

Foreign debt: US$6bn (1995) (excluding 36.5 per cent share of US$4.6bn unallocated former Yugoslav foreign debt)

* estimated figure

In an attempt to calm the situation, Milosevic called in the Organisation for Security and Co-operation in Europe (OSCE) to assess the fairness of the elections. Yet when the OSCE ruled that the poll had been fair and that opposition victories should be recognised, it was ignored. By early January 1997 the demonstrations continued, as did the authorities's refusal to compromise.

The SSS seems to be in a leftward drift into a sort of rehabilitated Titoism based, above all, on the continuation of state controls over the economy. In 1995–96, this political trend became more pronounced, particularly through the growing influence in Serbia of the so-called United Yugoslav Left (JUL), a neo-communist grouping opposed to economic reform and co-founded by Milosevic's powerful wife, Mirjana Markovic.

Politically motivated fiscal expansionism almost certainly helped to gain the SSS government votes in the contentious November 1996 parliamentary elections. Milosevic seemed prepared to take the risk of this leading to another bout of hyper-inflation in the longer term, a more or less inevitable scenario, with political considerations once again overriding economics in Serbia at least.

In Montenegro, on the other hand, President Momir Bulatovic's Democratic Socialist Party of Montenegro (DSS) government saw radical socio-economic reform as the best way to boost its faltering popularity in the run-up to the parliamentary elections. At the federal level, Serbia's opposition to this and other Montenegrin policies has further worsened relations between Belgrade and Podgorica, thereby giving a further impetus to pro-independence parties. However, the DPS was comfortably re-elected ahead of pro-independence parties in November 1996, gaining an absolute majority in the 71 seat parliament.

Elsewhere in the FRY, pro-autonomy sentiments have also gathered pace in Vojvodina. Separatist passions in the Sandzak and, even more so, Kosovo remained high. Should Kosovo, the Sandzak or Montenegro explode into violent conflict in the future, Milosevic's new domestic and international standing would be seriously compromised.

KEY INDICATORS — Federal Republic of Yugoslavia

	Unit	1991	1992	1993	1994	1995
Population	m	–	–	–	9.5	10.0
Real GDP growth	%	–	–	–	6.5	6.0
Inflation	%	–	–	–	72	79
Unemployment	'000	–	–	–	–745	785
Industrial production	%	–	–	–	1.3	3.8
Exports	US$bn	–	–	–	1.5	1.4
Imports	US$bn	–	–	–	1.9	2.4
Gross debt	US$bn	–	–	–	10.8	11.2

Economic performance

Year-end GDP growth in the FRY was 6 per cent in 1995 compared to 6.5 per cent in 1994. The majority of the growth was once again in agriculture and private-sector services. In 1995 these two sectors reportedly accounted for between 70 and 80 per cent of Yugoslav GDP. Industrial output, which accounted for 40 per cent of GDP and employment in the late communist Yugoslav period was probably for no more than half that figure by 1994, increased by 3.8 per cent in 1995. Among other things, this meant that actual unemployment in the FRY at the end of 1995 remained at about the same level as at the end of 1994, 50 per cent of the country's employed workforce. Following a major improvement in 1994, real wages in the state sector declined during 1995, mainly due to higher inflation. Pending a revival of industrial output and lower inflation, real living standards in Serbia and Montenegro will continue to decline.

Over the period 1990–94, the GDP and GDP per capita of the FRY declined from US$26 billion and US$2,500 to US$15.4 billion and US$1,500. GDP and GDP per capita in Serbia and Montenegro in 1995 were estimated at around US$16 billion and US$1,550 respectively. Overall, economic activity in 1994/95 was only 60 per cent of its 1990 level, the last year of comparative economic normality in the former Yugoslavia. In the industrial sector, or what remains of it, 1995 output was probably less than 20 per cent of its level five years earlier.

Over the past five years, total economic losses from lost output, the costs of the Yugoslav wars and the international isolation of the FRY have been estimated at between US$50 and US$60 billion. Some recent estimates have even placed these cumulative losses in the region of US$100 billion. During the 1990s, one particularly negative trend has been a collapse in new investment. Reversing this chronic economic decline, or at least returning to the situation that existed in 1990, is expected to take at least 10 to 15 years. The living standards of 1990 will not be attained until 2005 at the earliest.

The critically important agricultural and food processing sector has performed more or less normally during the 1990s, with another record grain harvest recorded in 1995. This means that Serbia can once again become a major exporter of foodstuffs and wood-based products. Also in the private sector, services of all types are a high growth area. Unlike other former Yugoslav republics, Serbia and Montenegro have not experienced any great damage to local infrastructure during the 1990s. Infrastructure only needs to be modernised and not replaced. In certain areas of primary production, such as electricity generation, capacity is far in excess of local consumption. The FRY is also on strategic transportation routes between the European Union (EU), Greece and Turkey. Relatively well-developed by the end of the 1980s, a number of local industrial sectors also have considerable potential, but only if they are restructured and recapitalised. These include automotive products, petro-chemicals, paper, pulp and other wood-based products, certain categories of machine-building and consumer durables.

The key challenge in the post-sanctions period revolves around realising this potential, particularly concerning recapitalisation, increasing output and boosting foreign trade. In practice, this can only be done through renewed macro-economic stabilisation, radical economic reform based on privatisation and increased foreign borrowing externally. Foreign direct investment (FDI) will also have to be increased substantially.

Macro-economic stabilisation remains seriously incomplete in the FRY. More radical socio-economic reform has begun in Montenegro but not in Serbia. Both republics are struggling with shortages of hard currency to pay for higher import growth and the absence of capital for the revival of industrial output and exports.

Without increased foreign borrowing and FDI, import growth can only be financed through higher exports and increased service income. As things stand, the latter is more likely than the former, at least in the short-term future. Emigré remittances, transport and tourism are likely to be the principal sources of such hard currency. Still frozen overseas financial assets will only become available once these former Yugoslav resources are equitably divided between the successor states of the former Yugoslav federation.

Financial failings

Inflation reached 79 per cent year-end in 1995, wiping out all the gains made since the federal government and the National Bank of Yugoslavia (NBJ) introduced the new dinar (D) as part of a macro-economic stabilisation plan begun in January 1994. Structurally, the major cause of this inflation is essentially political – the impossibility of maintaining a restrictive monetary-credit policy at a time of rising fiscal expansionism at all levels of government. This was particularly acute in Serbia in 1995, when the SSS government reduced the power and influence of the then NBJ Governor, Dragoslav Avramovic. More generally, 1995 also witnessed increased confusion in economic policy making, with the NBJ and Montenegro opposed to the policies being persued by the Serbian government.

Increased inflation led to the rapid depreciation of the dinar in 1994/95. Initially pegged at a one-to-one parity against the German DM in January 1994, the dinar weakened throughout 1995 on the black or free currency market, creating a widening disparity between the official and unofficial exchange rates in Serbia and Montenegro. In November 1995, the NBJ was forced to devalue officially the dinar from D1 per DM1 to D3.3 per DM1. At the same time, in a move clearly motivated by the signing of the Dayton peace accords and the suspension of the UN economic sanctions against the FRY, Avramovic announced the second stage of the macro-economic stabilisation programme introduced, but not completed, in 1994/95.

Other than the maintenance of the new dinar to DM exchange rate, the key features of this policy initiative were the linking of primary emission to local hard currency reserves; positive interest rates to reflect market demand and hence a limited supply of money; the removal of export and import quotas; and, related to this, sharply reduced import tariffs and liberalised hard currency export earning retention regulations. If ever fully implemented, this package of measures would reduce inflation and reintroduce market mechanisms, most notably in the area of foreign trade. The main aim is to revive local output for export in conditions of low inflation and exchange rate stability.

The key question at the beginning of 1996 was whether Avramovic could prevail upon Milosevic to implement such policies. However, the dismissal of Avramovic in May 1996 provided an emphatic answer, with the SSS and the JUL moving in exactly the opposite direction for political reasons bound up with the impending

COUNTRY PROFILE — FEDERAL REPUBLIC OF YUGOSLAVIA

Historical profile

Federal Republic of Yugoslavia (FRY) declared in April 1992 as the sole successor state to the former Yugoslav federation, but not formally internationally recognised as such. FRY thereafter deprived of UN seat, although most major foreign governments still maintain *de facto* diplomatic relations at below ambassadorial level. On 24 August 1996, FRY and Croatia signed an agreement on mutual recognition, formally ending five years of hostility.

Political system

Federative republic with multi-party parliamentary democracy based on new federal constitution of April 1992, plus Serbian and Montenegrin constitutions of 1989. Bicameral federal parliament elected every four years, plus Serbian and Montenegrin parliaments elected every four years, together constitute the highest legislative power, although the Serbian parliament is the key legislative body in practice. Federal president and government also largely symbolic. Effective executive power with Serbian president, who nominates Serbian premier and government, which is confirmed by the Serbian parliament. Elections to a new bicameral Federal Assembly, comprising a 138-seat Chamber of Citizens (108 members from Serbia and 30 from Montenegro) and a 40-seat Chamber of the Republics (in which the seats were divided equally between Serbia and Montenegro), took place on 31 May 1992. Lilic was elected federal president by the Federal Assembly in June 1993, replacing Dobrica Cosic, who had criticised Milosevic. In elections to the Serbian parliament held on 20 December 1993, the ruling Socialist Party again emerged as the largest single party. Mirko Marjanovic was appointed Serbian Prime Minister in February 1994.

Population

Serbia is a mixture of many peoples: Serbian (66%), Albanian (20%), Hungarian (10%), Croatian (2%). Ethnic minorities in Montenegro: Muslim (13%), Albanian (6.5%). Religions: Christianity (Serbian Orthodox and Roman Catholic), Islamic minority. Only one tenth of the population is living above the poverty line.

Main cities/towns

Belgrade (population 1.47m in 1995), capital of Serbia; Podgorica (formerly Titograd) (population 130,290), capital of Montenegro.

Language

Serbian, Macedonian, Slovenian. Others include German, English and Italian. English is the most common business language.

Media

Weeklies: Most significant weeklies are *Nin* (Belgrade) and *International Weekly* (Belgrade, published in English).
Business: Main business papers are *Privredni pregled* (Belgrade/daily) and *Ekonomska politika* (Belgrade/weekly).
Broadcasting: Two main radio and TV networks, one in Serbia (based in Belgrade, Novi Sad and Pristina) and one in Montenegro (based in Podgorica). Radio Yugoslavia broadcasts daily in six foreign languages on short wave.
Advertising: All principal media available through advertising agencies or directly.

Domestic economy

Market economy based on various types of ownership; socialist-style ownership still predominates, but private enterprise is encouraged. Sanctions imposed on Serbia by the UN Security Council in an attempt to stop aggression in Bosnia, which included trade, financial and travel embargoes were suspended November 1995. The USA suspended sanctions 29 December 1995. It is estimated it will take six to seven years to get production up to the 1990 levels, but 1990 living standards will not be attained until 2005 at the earliest.
Overall economic activity in 1994-95 was only 60 per cent of its level in 1990. However, after four years of economic decline, gross domestic product in Serbia-Montenegro showed a positive development in 1994, a rise of 6.5 per cent, and again in 1995, a rise of 6 per cent. From 1990-95 total economic losses from lost output, costs of wars and international isolation, were estimated at between US$50bn and US$100bn.

Employment

Real incomes continue to lag behind inflation.

External trade

Trade badly disrupted since August 1991 when violence first flared between Serbia and Croatia.

parliamentary elections in Serbia. In the longer term, though, such economic reform is probably unavoidable if hyper-inflation is not to reappear.

Externally, any resumption of normal foreign borrowing by the FRY will clearly be conditional on the implementation of such economic reform. A key post-sanctions aim for Milosevic is to see the FRY readmitted to the International Monetary Fund (IMF) and the World Bank. However, the removal of Avramovic is likely to hinder this process, as he is a former World Bank official who is well regarded internationally.

More than anything else, it will be this external dimension that will eventually force the FRY to adopt genuine macro-economic stabilisation and economic reform based on privatisation, although this will probably be in the long rather than the short-term future.

Another key aim of the NBJ is to rehabilitate the state banking sector and, related to this, the finances of highly indebted and often technically insolvent industrial enterprises that are presently unable to revive output and exports because of chronic shortages of working capital. Most of the state industrial sector is bankrupt or not functioning at all. The country's top five commercial banks hold largely worthless assets and as such are themselves technically insolvent. Largely cash-based, the economies of Serbia and Montenegro consequently do not have any proper financial intermediaries between savers and borrowers. It is not at all clear how this state of affairs might be improved, not least because of the vast costs of recapitalising the state banking system and hence the rest of the economy. In practice, such financial rehabilitation remains dependent on radical socio-economic reform and the creation of the necessary preconditions for both renewed foreign borrowing and the channelling of privately held hard currency into productive investments locally.

Privatisation

Although explicitly provided for in both the first and second stages of the federal government's macro-economic stabilisation programme, large-scale privatisation of the state industrial sector and its implementation remains the responsibility of the Serbian and Montenegrin governments. Undoubtedly the key to the FRY's economic future, such ownership transformation and associated corporate restructuring has yet to begin in Serbia, where the SSS and the JUL regard it as a threat to their power. Even worse, the neo-communist JUL has actually introduced and helped to pass legislation in the federal assembly that aims to reverse what little privatisation has taken place in the FRY to date. Inter alia, this has further worsened already tense relations between Serbia and Montenegro, where large-scale privatisation of the state sector finally began in 1995. More generally, the recent left-ward drift of the SSS, under the growing influence of the JUL, has resulted in ever more intrusive state intervention in the Serbian economy, particularly as regards the use of questionable administrative measures to curb price increases in both the public and private-sectors. Although relatively ineffective, such measures cause concern in that they seek to eliminate market mechanisms from the Serbian economy.

SSS government policy has also, for the most part, impeded rather than advanced the development of the private sector in Serbia. Other than attempted price regulation, this has mainly been through punitive taxation and the crowding-out of private sector borrowers by high government spending and borrowing. This has had the effect of driving much of the private sector into the underground or black economy, which may have accounted for as much as 50 per cent of GDP in 1995. Concentrated in agriculture, services and light manufacturing, the private sector is also increasingly dominant in exports and imports and is without doubt the most dynamic component of the economies of Serbia and Montenegro.

In 1995, the Yugoslav Chamber of Commerce (YCC) reported that the private sector in the FRY accounted for over 30 per cent of its officially recorded GDP and over 50 per cent of its foreign trade. Nearly all job creation in the FRY is now in the private sector, particularly as regards services. In 1995, YCC data also revealed that more private sector producers were moving into industrial production and consumer goods.

COUNTRY PROFILE — FEDERAL REPUBLIC OF YUGOSLAVIA

External trade (contd): The Federal Republic of Yugoslavia and China signed a trade accord in September 1995. UN trade sanctions imposed in 1992 suspended November 1995; Hungary lifted sanctions against Yugoslavia November 1995, but not against the Serbian territories of Bosnia-Herzegovina; the USA and Albania suspended sanctions December 1995. However, during the course of 1995 the economic sanctions against Serbia and Montenegro had fallen apart mainly due to record levels of sanctions-busting in the Balkan region.
Over the period 1990-94, total foreign trade turnover of the FRY fell from US$12.5bn, just under 50 per cent of GDP in 1990, to around US$2bn to US$3bn, or around 25 per cent of its 1990 level, by 1994. In 1995, technically illegal sanctions-busting foreign trade by the FRY reached around US$3bn to US$4bn, or over 30 per cent of GDP.
Exports: Major exports include textile manufactures, non-ferrous metals and agricultural produce. Main destinations: Germany, CIS, Italy, USA.
Imports: Major imports include mineral fuels, chemicals, transport equipment, machinery. Main sources: Germany, CIS.

Agriculture

The agriculture sector accounts officially for more than 50 per cent of GDP. Main crops: wheat, maize and sugar beet. Extensive orchards, livestock and fresh water fisheries. Tobacco was among Serbia's main farm exports. Shortage of artificial fertiliser.
Record grain harvest was recorded in 1995. The maize crop in 1995 totalled 5.7m tonnes from 1.36m ha of land. About 20 per cent of the 1996 maize crop was severely hit by drought. Sugar beet production reached 1.7m tonnes in 1995.

Industry

Manufacturing and mining accounted for about 40 per cent of GDP before 1991. Diversified industrial base. Major industries include: metal processing, electricity, food production, textile and other manufacturing. Textile and clothing industry, and vehicle manufacturing disrupted. In 1990 it accounted for almost US$1bn of former Yugoslavia's exports. All energy-dependent industry, including chemicals and iron and steel, is collapsing because of shortages of energy and raw materials.
The industrial sector accounted for around 20 per cent of GDP in 1994, with production increasing 3.8 per cent in 1995 over 1994. Output in 1995 was estimated to be less than 20 per cent of its level in 1990.

Tourism

Excellent opportunities for further development of summer tourism at Montenegrin coast (Adriatic), and for winter sports in Serbian mountains (especially Mt Kopaonik and Mt Sara). There are numerous health resorts (with mineral water springs) in Serbia. After industry, tourism is the second most important branch of the economy. Belgrade, situated on the River Danube, is a popular city with tourists.

Mining

Diverse resources, such as coal (lignite), non-ferrous metal ores (including copper, lead and zinc) and bauxite.

Hydrocarbons

Small reserves of oil and gas. Coal reserves in Kosovo stand at 13bn tonnes (end-1995) and will last for 13 centuries; annual coal extraction in Kosovo is 16m tonnes.

Energy

Serbia depends on imports of oil and gas for about 40 per cent of its energy despite increased utilisation of local resources (large deposits of coal, and water power). Hydroelectric power accounts for nearly 60 per cent of electricity generation, and thermal, 40 per cent.

Banking

A two-tiered banking structure with the National Bank of Yugoslavia (Narodna Banka Jugoslavije) (the National Bank of the republic having responsibility for the money supply, the liquidity of financial institutions and foreign currency transactions and reserves) on one tier, and the commercial banks (independent profit-making companies) on the other.

Stock exchange

A small stock exchange in Belgrade.

Legal system

Civil law system.

Membership of international organisations

AG (observer), CERN (observer), CSCE suspended, G-24, IAEA, NAM. The government

Reviving foreign trade

Eased in September 1994, suspended in November 1995 and abolished in October 1996, the UN economic sanctions against Serbia and Montenegro essentially fell apart during the course of 1995, mainly due to record levels of sanctions-busting in the Balkan region. Total foreign trade turnover fell from US$12.5 billion, or just under 50 per cent of GDP in 1990, to around US$2-US$3 billion, or around 25 per cent of its 1990 level by 1994.

In 1995, sanctions-busting foreign trade by the FRY reportedly reached around US$3-US$4 billion, over 30 per cent of officially recorded GDP. Although not enough to revive the economy, which had been highly dependent on foreign trade, these sanctions-busting transfers were adequate for economic survival, particularly as regards oil imports.

By 1995 the only significant impediment to even higher foreign trade was a shortage of hard currency to pay for imports. Post sanctions, these have become cheaper and more easily available. Resulting improved energy supplies are expected to have a positive impact on industrial and agricultural output in 1996/97.

Foreign debt and payments

In de facto default on its large foreign debt during the period of the UN sanctions, the FRY is anxious to normalise the servicing of its outstanding external liabilities. At around US$6 billion, 30 per cent of the total foreign debt of the former Yugoslav federation, these are already substantial. In addition, the FRY is expected to be liable for about 36.5 per cent of the US$4.6 billion of still unallocated former Yugoslav foreign debt.

At one stage, the FRY was intent on assuming full responsibility for this unallocated former Yugoslav foreign debt, which would have strengthened its contested claim to be the sole legal successor of the former Yugoslav federation. Had this been accepted by its foreign creditors, the total foreign debt of the FRY would have been over US$10 billion, two-thirds of its GDP in 1994/95.

Following the recent Slovene and Croatian government agreements with the London Club (LC) of commercial bank creditors, which the NBJ is legally contesting, the FRY will probably only be liable for 36.5 per cent of unallocated former Yugoslav foreign debt. This will give Serbia and Montenegro a combined foreign debt of around US$7.6 billion in 1996.

Given the highly precarious finances of the FRY, its foreign debt will almost certainly have to be formally rescheduled by the Paris and London Clubs. In practice, this will have to be done in tandem with renewed IMF membership and an agreement with the Fund on economic reform. To complicate matters further, renewed IMF membership and hence renewed foreign borrowing is conditional on an equitable division of former Yugoslav financial and other assets.

Outlook

Although unlikely in the short term, the Yugoslav wars could restart, most notably in Bosnia, where the Bosnian Serbs retain the sympathy of many influential political figures in Serbia. In the longer term, all of this could cause considerable grief for Milosevic, whose abandonment of a 'Greater Serbia' in former Yugoslavia is clearly a high risk strategy. Within the FRY, the Serbian nationalism question is by no means fully resolved, especially in the context of renewed conflict in Bosnia in the future.

Externally, the FRY also remains in a somewhat uncertain position. Any renewal of conflict in Bosnia could result in the reimposition of UN economic sanctions against Serbia and Montenegro. Serious conflict in Kosovo could have similar effects, as could a violent clampdown on protestors in Serbia itself. President Milosevic and the Serbian government have been thrown on the defensive by the scale and commitment of the opposition protests, and the authorities refusal to adhere to democratic norms is further complicating the FRY's already precarious return to international acceptance. Economically, a sustainable economic recovery remains dependent on radical economic reform and foreign aid and investment – none of which have been forthcoming to date.

COUNTRY PROFILE — FEDERAL REPUBLIC OF YUGOSLAVIA

Membership (contd): is a member of all UN organisations and agencies. Various professional and technical associations are members of most relevant international non-governmental organisations.

BUSINESS GUIDE

Time

GMT + 1 hr (GMT + 2 hrs from late Mar to late Sep).

Climate

Mediterranean on Montenegrin coast with warm summers and mild winters. Inland areas have cold winters with heavy snow. Average summer temperature in Belgrade 22°C, in winter at freezing point.
Clothing: Inland – lightweight for summer, mediumweight and raincoat for spring and autumn, topcoat and hat for winter.

Entry requirements

Passport: Passport required by all. Must be valid for at least six months after journey.
Visa: Visa required for British and Irish citizens. No visa required for nationals of countries which had diplomatic or consular relationship with Yugoslavia. Australians and Canadians require visas. If child's name appears on passport of parent, it must also appear on the visa of that parent. Visitors must possess a return or onward ticket, sufficient funds and all relevant documents for onward destinations.
Health: Vaccination certificates not required.
Currency: Amounts up to D15,000 may be taken freely in and out of the country (in units of D1,000). No limit on amount of foreign currency brought into and taken out of country. Only a verbal declaration is necessary.
Customs: Various personal articles and goods allowed duty-free.

Air access

National airline: JAT (Yugoslav Airlines). Montenegro has its own airline, Oki Airways, which was founded in Podgorica in November 1995.
Other airlines: Aeroflot, Air France, Alitalia, Balkan, CSA, Cyprus Airways, Lufthansa, Swissair, Tarom.
Tax: International departures D50; domestic departures D10.
Main international airport: Belgrade (BEG) – 19 km west of city centre.
Airports: Nis (INI), 4 km from city; Tivat (TIV), 4 km from city; Podgorica and Pristina.

Surface access

Border crossings from: Hungary, Romania, Bulgaria, and Albania, as well as from the former Yugoslav republics of Croatia, Bosnia and Herzegovina, and Macedonia. Serbia and Bosnia agreed to restore transport links July 1996.
Main port: Bar.

Hotels

Hotels are classified into five categories: L (extra), A, B, C and D; boarding houses into three, I, II and III. There is a 10-20 per cent service charge. Visitors must also pay a residential tax, which varies between regions.

Restaurants

A wide variety with most serving regional food. Service charge generally not included on bills and tip of up to 10 per cent should be added.

Currency

Eurocheques should be issued in foreign currency.

Credit cards

International credit cards are accepted in large hotels and businesses.

Car hire

Cars can be hired in most main towns through travel agencies. There is a speed limit of 120 kph on motorways, and 60 kph in built-up areas. Drive on the right and give way to traffic from the right unless clearly marked otherwise. Seat belts are compulsory in front seats.

City transport

Taxis: Good service operating in most large cities/towns. All taxis are metered. Extra charge for baggage. Transfer by taxi from Belgrade airport D100 (June 1996).
Buses and trams: All cities/towns are served by buses; trams only in the centre of Belgrade and in Subotica. The service is generally regular. Transfer from Belgrade Airport by JAT airport bus D7, by minibus D25 (June 1996).

National transport

Air: Regular air services by JAT linking the five airports. Advance reservation is advisable in summer months.
Road: There are some 46,000 km of roads, including 374 km of motorways. The main route links Belgrade with Subotica (via Novi Sad), Kragujevac and Nis. An extensive network of express buses links all Yugoslav towns. The Zagreb–Belgrade motorway reopened 7 May 1996.
Buses: Cheap and efficient coach services to most towns.
Rail: There are some 4,000 km of track, of which over a fourth is electrified. International express and fast trains link Belgrade with Subotica, Novi Sad, Kragujevac, Nis, Pristina and Titograd, as well as the port of Bar.
Water: Well established inland waterways system, based on the Danube, Sava, Tisa and Begej.

Public holidays

Fixed dates: 1 & 2 Jan (New Year), 27 Apr (Constitution Day), 1 May (Labour Day), 4 Jul (Veterans' Day (joint)), 7 Jul (Veterans' Day for Serbia), 13 Jul (Veterans' Day for Montenegro).

Working hours

Business: (Mon–Fri) 0800 – 1500.
Government: (Mon–Fri) 0730 – 1530.
Banking: (Mon–Fri) Belgrade airport 0800–2000.
Shops: (Mon–Fri) generally in larger towns: 0800 – 2000 (some shops closing between 1200 and 1500); (Sat) 0800 – 1500.

Social customs

The approach to business is quite casual. It is traditional for the chairman of negotiations to welcome his guests formally with drinks before commencing a meeting.

Business language and interpreting/translation

No regular nationwide interpreter service, but a translation service can usually be arranged through hotels, tourist offices or local enterprises.

Telecommunications

Telephone and telefax: Dialling code for Serbia, Montenegro: IDD access code + 381 followed by area code (11 for Belgrade, 81 for Podgorica (formerly Titograd)), followed by subscriber's number. Operator numbers: international calls 901, internal long-distance 900, telegrams 96. For IDD access from Serbia, Montenegro dial 99.

Serbia and Bosnia agreed to restore telephone links July 1996. The number of telephone lines will increase by one-third after 700,000 have been installed during 1996.
Telex and telefax: Service available in all hotels and main post offices.
Telegram: Post offices operate ordinary and express rates.

Banking

Commercial banks (head offices): Beogradska Banka, Beobanka, Investbanka, JIK Banka, Jugobanka, Kreditna Banka Beograd, Montenegrobanka, Panonska Banka, PKB Banka, Privredna Banka, Vojvodjanska.

Trade fairs

International trade fairs in Belgrade (Motor Show, Clothing, Leather and Footwear, Engineering, Book Fair), Leskovac (Textiles), Novi Sad (Agricultural, Hunting) and Budva (Tourism).

Electricity supply

220 V AC.

Useful tips

Do carry some form of identity at all times.

BUSINESS DIRECTORY

Hotels

Belgrade (area code 11)
Balkan, Prizenska 2, 11000 (tel: 687-466; tx: 72224).

Excelsior, Kneza Milosa 5, 11000 (tel: 331-381; fax: 335-916).

Hyatt Regency, Vladimira Popovica (tel: 222-1234; fax: 222-2234).

Inter-Continental, Vladimira Popovica 10, 11070 (15 minutes from airport) (tel: 222-3333; fax: 222-1402).

Majestic, Obilicev Venac 28, 11000 (tel: 636-022; fax: 630-793).

Metropol, Bulevar Revolucije 69, 11000 (tel: 330-911; fax: 332-991).

Moskva, Balkanska 1, 11000 (tel: 686-255; fax: 688-389).

Park, Njegoseva 2, 11000 (tel: 334-722; fax: 33-029).

Prag, Narodnog Fronta 27, 11000 (tel: 687-355; tx: 12494).

Slavija, Svetog Save 1, 11000 (business centre) (tel: 450-842; fax: 444-9455).

Union, Kosovska 11, 11000 (tel: 187-036; tx: 12955).

Car hire

Belgrade
Avis: Central Reservations (tel: 433-314); Belgrade Airport, 11000 (tel: 605-488/690); Obilicev Venac 25 (tel: 620-362, 629-423); Congress Centre Sava-Hotel, Milentija Popouica 9 (tel: 222-2910); Railway Station, Trg Bratstva 1 (tel: 683-007); Maksima Gorkog 30 (tel: 444-5366, 457-677; fax: 444-5366).

Chambers of commerce

Chamber of Economy of Belgrade, Belgrade, Terazije 23, 11000 Belgrade (tel: 324-8247; fax: 324-8754, 322-5903).

Chamber of Economy of Montenegro, Novaka Miloseva 29, 81000 Titograd (tel: 31-067; fax: 34-926).

Chamber of Economy of Serbia, Generala Zdanova 13-15, 11000 Belgrade (tel: 340-611; fax:330-949).

Banking

National Bank of Yugoslavia (Narodna Banka Jugoslavije) (central bank), 11000 Belgrade, Bulevar Revolucije 15, Box 1010 (tel: 332-001; fax: 341-927).

Association of Yugoslav Banks (Udruzenje Banaka Jugoslavije), Belgrade, Masarikova 5 (tel: 683-412; fax: 684-974).

Beogradska Banka, Belgrade, Knez Mihailova 2–4 (tel: 624-455; fax: 627-007).

Beobanka, Belgrade, Zeleni Venac 16 (tel: 630-566; fax: 632-829).

Investbanka, Belgrade, Terazije 7–9 (tel: 321-161; fax: 320-617).

JIK Banka, Belgrade, Knez Mihailova 42 (tel: 632-822; fax: 183-198).

Jugobanka, 11000 Belgrade, 7 Jula 19–21 (tel: 636-281; fax: 636-910).

Kreditna Banka Beograd, Belgrade, Lenjinov Bulevar 111 (tel: 222-4428; fax: 144-923).

Montenegrobanka, 81000 Podgorica, Bulevar Revolucije 1 (tel: 0814-4344; fax: 0815-1199).

Panonska Banka, 21000 Novi Sad, Bulevar 23 Oktobra 76 (tel: 021-612-444; fax: 021-613-939).

PKB Banka, Belgrade, 29 Novembra 68/a (tel: 753-366; fax: 750-932).

Privredna Banka, Belgrade, Brace Jugovica 17 (tel: 623-272; fax: 627-247).

Privredna Banka, 21000 Novi Sad, Grckoskolska 2 (tel: 0212-6333; fax: 021-623-025).

Vojvodjanska Banka, 21000 Novi Sad, Trg Slobode 7 (tel: 021-621-277; fax: 021-624-940).

Yugoslav Bank for International Economic Cooperation (JUBMES), 11070 Belgrade, Bulevar Avnoj-a 121, PO Box 219 (tel: 215-7222; fax: 131-457).

Travel information

Automobile Association of Yugoslavia (AMSJ), Information Centre, Belgrade, Ruzveltova 16 (tel: 980-419-555; fax: 419-888).

Lufthansa Belgrade Airport Office, Terazije 3/VII, 11000 Belgrade (tel: 227-529); reservation service (tel: 224-974/75/76; fax: 225-009).

Tourist Association of Montenegro, 81000 Podgorica, Bulevar Lenjina 2 (tel: 0814-1591).

Tourist Association of Serbia, Belgrade, Dobrinjska 11 (tel: 645-166; tx: 72-689).

Yugoslav Airlines (JAT), Belgrade, Ho Si Minova 16 (tel: 224-222; tx: 11-401).

Yugoslav Association of Travel Agents (YUTA), Belgrade, Kondina 14 (tel: 328-686; tx: 12-662).

Other useful addresses

British Embassy, Generala Zdanova 46, 11000 Belgrade (tel: 645-055/34; fax: 659-651).

Embassy of the United States of America, BP 5070, 11000 Belgrade (tel: 645-655; fax: 645-221).

Federal Ministry of Trade, Kneza Milosa 26, 11000 Belgrade (tel: 683-266; fax: 684-569).

Jugoslovenska Radio-Televizija, Generala Zdanova 28, 11000 Belgrade (tel: 330-194; fax: 434-023).

Medjunarodni Pres Centar, Trg Republike 5, 11000 Belgrade (tel: 637-722; fax: 184-576).

Ministry of Finance, Belgrade, Palata Federacije (tel: 222-4240; fax: 646-775).

Ministry for Foreign Affairs, 11000 Belgrade, Kneza Milosa 24 (tel: 682-555; tx: 11-173).

Ministries for Information, International Economic Relations, Economy, Trade, Agriculture, Transport and Communications, Belgrade, Omladinskih Brigada 1 (tel: 602-555; fax: 195-244).

Ministry of Transport, Belgrade (fax: 113-512).

Standardisation Office (Savezni zavod za standardizaciju), Belgrade, Slobodana Penezica Krcuna 35 (tel: 644-066; fax: 235-1036).

Statistical Office, 11000 Belgrade, Kneza Milosa 20, Box 203 (tel: 685-572; fax: 681-995).

Jugoslovenska Pomorska Agencija (shipping agency), Belgrade, Bulevar Lenjina 165A, Box 210 (tel: 130-004).

Novinska Agencija Tanjug (news agency), 11001 Belgrade, Obilicev Venac 2, Box 439 (tel: 332-231).

Uoruzenje strucnik prevodilaca SR SRBIJE (translation agency), 11000 Belgrade, Kic\06evska 9 (tel: 444-2997).

Vece saveza sindikata Jugoslavije (confederation of trades unions), 11000 Belgrade, trg Marksa i Engelsa 5 (tel: 330-481; tx: 11-121).

Zajednica jugoslovenskih zeleznica (railways), 11001 Belgrade, Nemanjina 6, Box 563 (tel: 688-722; tx: 12-495).